To Ryan & Mar[...]
From Dad.

CHRISTIAN LIGHT PUBLICATIONS INC.
P.O. BOX 1212
Harrisonburg, Virginia 22803-1212
(540) 434-0768

BOOKS BY THE SAME AUTHOR.

Freedom of the Will. 12mo. $1 20

WORKS IN TWO VOLUMES:

Vol. I. Essays, Reviews, and Discourses. 12mo. . . . 1 25
Vol. II. Statements, Theological and Critical. 12mo. . . . 1 25

OLD AND NEW TESTAMENT COMMENTARY.

INTENDED FOR POPULAR USE.

THE NEW TESTAMENT.

BY D. D. WHEDON, LL.D.

FIVE VOLUMES. 12mo.

Per Volume, Cloth, $1.50; Morocco, Extra, $4.50; Half Morocco or Half Calf, $2.50.

Vol. I. **Matthew and Mark.**
Vol. II. **Luke and John.**
Vol. III. **Acts and Romans.**
Vol. IV. **Corinthians to Second Timothy.**
Vol. V. **Titus and Revelation.**

THE OLD TESTAMENT.

Edited by D. D. WHEDON, LL.D.

EIGHT VOLUMES. 12mo.

Per Volume, Cloth, - - - - - - $2.

Vol. I. **Genesis and Exodus.** By Milton S. Terry, D.D., and Fales H. Newhall, D.D.
Vol. II. **Leviticus and Numbers.** By D. Steele, D.D. **Deuteronomy.** By John W. Lindsay, D.D.
Vol. III. **Joshua.** By D. Steele, D.D. **Judges to Second Samuel.** By Milton S. Terry, D.D.
Vol. IV. **Kings to Esther.** By Milton S. Terry, D.D.
Vol. V. **Psalms.** By F. G. Hibbard, D.D.
Vol. VI. **Job.** By J. K. Burr, D.D. **Proverbs.** By W. Hunter, D.D. **Ecclesiastes and Solomon's Song.** By A. B. Hyde, D.D.
Vol. VII. **Isaiah.** By H. Bannister, D.D. **Jeremiah, and the Lamentations of Jeremiah.** By F. D. Hemenway, D.D.
Vol. VIII. **Ezekiel and Daniel.** By Camden M. Cobern.

COMMENTARY

ON

THE OLD TESTAMENT.

VOL. I.—GENESIS AND EXODUS.

BY

MILTON S. TERRY, D.D.,

AND

FALES H. NEWHALL, D.D.

ISBN 0-88019-216-X

Copyright, 1889, by
PHILLIPS & HUNT,
NEW YORK.

PREFACE.

THE great favour with which the successive volumes of Whedon's *Commentary on the New Testament* were received encouraged the publishers to project a *Commentary on the Old Testament* in uniform size and style, under the editorial supervision of the late Dr. Daniel D. Whedon. The entire series was to comprise thirteen volumes: eight on the Old Testament and five on the New. Twelve different writers were engaged, and the work has gone steadily forward until the entire New Testament and five volumes on the Old have been published. Meantime five of the twelve persons originally selected to prepare the Old Testament Commentary, and the General Editor himself, have been called away from their labours on earth.

The Commentary on Genesis and Exodus was undertaken by the late Professor F. H. Newhall, D.D., but his death left this portion of the work for several years unprovided for. Among the latest official acts of the General Editor was a request that these books and an Introduction to the Pentateuch be prepared by Dr. M. S. Terry, who had already furnished the Commentary on Judges, Ruth, Samuel, Kings, Chronicles, Ezra, Nehemiah, and Esther. The manuscript of Dr. Newhall was found to be nearly complete on Genesis v to xii, and is here published substantially as he left it. The rest of his notes on Genesis consisted of a number of fragments, most of which had been published in *Zion's*

Herald in connexion with the International Sunday-School Lessons of 1873. As far as possible these notes have been gathered up, and treated as a sacred trust. On chapters xxxvii, xxxix, xlv–xlviii, and l they appear in fullest form. Outside of chapters v–xii all of Dr. Newhall's comments which could be utilized are marked as quotations, and his name appended to each separate note. The commentary on the first seventeen chapters of Exodus is also the work of Dr. Newhall, and was published in pamphlet form as a help to the Sunday-school lessons of 1874.

But two more volumes remain to complete the series— one on the remaining books of the Pentateuch, and one on Ezekiel, Daniel, and the Minor Prophets. These are in able hands, and may be expected at no distant day.

INTRODUCTION TO THE PENTATEUCH.

THE word Pentateuch means fivefold book, and has become the most common title of the first five books of the Old Testament. By many writers these ancient volumes are called the Five Books of Moses, and in the later portions of the Old Testament they are spoken of as "The Book of the Law of the Lord by the hand of Moses," (2 Chron. xxxiv, 14,) "The Book of the Law of Moses," (Neh. viii, 1,) "The Book of Moses," (Neh. xiii, 1,) and "The Law of Moses," (Ezra vii, 6.) In later times they were frequently designated by the simple name Torah, (תּוֹרָה,) *the Law.* The Mosaic origin of these sacred books is thus apparently assumed as an unquestioned belief in the later books of the Bible, was accepted by the New Testament writers, and is indicated by such passages in the Pentateuch itself as the following: "The Lord said unto Moses, Write this for a memorial in a [Heb. the] book," (Exod. xvii, 14;) "Moses wrote all the words of the Lord," (Exod. xxiv, 4;) "And the Lord said unto Moses, Write thou these words," etc., (Exod. xxxiv, 27;) "Moses wrote their goings out, according to their journeys by the commandment of the Lord," (Num. xxxiii, 2;) "Moses wrote this law, and delivered it unto the priests the sons of Levi," (Deut. xxxi, 9.)

Unity.

The five books are now commonly known as Genesis, Exodus, Leviticus, Numbers, and Deuteronomy; but these names, like the word Pentateuch, are of Greek origin, and the division of the Book of the Law into these five parts is believed by many to have been made by the Septuagint translators. In the Hebrew text these parts form so many intimately connected sections of one whole, and are designated by the first words of each section. In Hebrew manuscripts the entire law is divided into fifty-four sections, called *Parshiyoth,* thus providing a distinct reading lesson for each Sabbath of the year : for according to Jewish modes of reckoning, some years had fifty-four Sabbaths, and care was accordingly taken that in these longer years no Sabbath should be unprovided with its separate lesson. Some of the ancient Jews divided the law into one hundred and fifty-five sections, called *Sedarim*, thus providing a series of Sabbath lessons to continue through three consecutive years. But all these divisions of the Pentateuch recognise the unity of the entire work, and this unity becomes more apparent by a careful study of its contents.

Whatever one's views of the origin, number, and variety of documents used in the composition of the Pentateuch, it is scarcely possible fairly to deny that it presents in its present form an orderly and well related whole. The Book of Genesis is an appropriate and necessary introduction to the history of the covenant people. It opens with the creation of man, and traces his history in narrowing circles down to the divine call of Abraham, and thence onward to the burial of Jacob, when the twelve tribe-fathers of Israel had become clearly set in personal and historical outline before us. The Book of Exodus opens with the names of those great tribe-fathers of the nation, and furnishes a vivid history of the exodus from the land of Egypt, the journey to Sinai, and the legislation and worship ordained at that holy mount. The Book of Leviticus follows, in natural order, furnishing an additional record of the Sinaitic legislation, especially as it related to the Levitical priesthood, and the sacrifices, offerings, and ceremonial rites of the chosen people. The Book of Numbers appropriately follows, and records the numbering and journeys of Israel in the wilderness, from their departure from Sinai until they became established on the east of the Jordan. Deuteronomy is professedly a recapitulation of the wilderness journeys of Israel and of the legislation mediated through Moses, and, with the exception of the last chapter, (Deut. xxxiv,) might well have been prepared under the personal oversight and dictation of Moses himself.

Traditional Belief.

That these five books, in substantially their present form, originated with Moses, or under his immediate supervision, was the common belief of all Jewish and Christian antiquity. The great body of evangelical Christians still regard these sacred records as embodying the most ancient monuments of history, biography, laws, poetry, and prophecy. Whatever their date or origin, they are of incalculable worth. They shed invaluable light on ancient customs and important epochs in the history of ancient nations. As literary documents they are vastly more valuable than all that has been or is likely to be deciphered from the monuments of Egypt, Assyria, Babylon, and Persia. As records of divine revelation, they constitute the historical and legislative groundwork of the Jewish and the Christian faith. By them we are made acquainted with the creation and fall of man, with the repeated appliances of divine grace and judgment to restrain him from sin and lead him in the ways of righteousness, with successive and gradually fuller disclosures of God's word and will, and with the methods and purposes of redemption. It is in fact difficult to overrate the value of these first books of the Bible as embodying the substantial elements of all subsequent divine revelation.

That this ancient tradition is well grounded appears from a variety of considerations. The last four books of the Pentateuch claim over and over again, in the plainest and most positive manner, to be a record of what the Lord communicated to Moses and commanded him to set before the Israelitish people. The three middle books are filled with details of what "Jehovah spake unto Moses." We find no law or statement thus introduced which contains any thing inconsistent with such claims. No character depicted in the Old Testament has such a unique grandeur as that of Moses; and there is none besides to whom such a body of laws as those of the Pentateuch can be so fittingly attributed. The subsequent history of Israel is full of incidental allusions to laws, customs, and institutions of which the Pentateuch makes him, under God, the author. The ark and tabernacle appear as the central seat of worship at Shiloh until the ark was captured by the Philistines and God forsook the tabernacle. 1 Sam. iv, 22; Psa. lxxviii, 60. The irregularities of worship between that time and the building of the temple at Jerusalem were owing to the fact that during this dark period there was no central sanctuary, and the people were greatly demoralized. 1 Kings iii, 2. The Prophets and the Psalms abound in allusions to the exodus from Egypt and the ministry of Moses in such ways as to recognise that period as the greatest epoch of the national history. Finally, our Lord himself accepted this tradition, and expressed himself in language which cannot be naturally explained without admitting that he corroborated the common belief of his nation. John v, 46, 47 ; vii, 19, 22.

This ancient and uniform tradition must, according to all legitimate principles of criticism, be accepted as *prima facie* evidence in favour of the Mosaic authorship of the Pentateuch. It is indeed only *presumptive proof* of such authorship, and so has the right to stand, until its incorrectness has been shown. The burden of proof falls, therefore, rightly upon those who doubt the ancient tradition. When evidence adverse to the Mosaic authorship is brought forward, it becomes the student of history and all lovers of the truth to weigh such evidence, and to see if it be of a nature to set aside the ancient view. We should allow no love of ancient opinions, no prejudice of any kind, to hinder our careful examination of facts, or to bias our judgment; but we are not called upon to give up our opinions, though based on incomplete evidence, until other and better evidence shall be brought against them. The truth, the whole truth, so far as it may be ascertained, and nothing but the truth, will satisfy the honest Christian scholar.

The Higher Criticism of the Pentateuch.

That the Pentateuch, but especially the Book of Genesis, is of composite origin, and embodies a variety of ancient documents, is obvious to every critical student. Ancient as well as modern readers have observed in the "Book of the Law of Moses" passages which could not well have been written by the great lawgiver himself. The tradition of some revision or reproduction by the hand of Ezra is almost as uniform as that of the Mosaic authorship. It appears in the apocryphal Revelation of Ezra, in the Clementine Homilies, and in many of the Christian Fathers. Aben Ezra in the twelfth century, and Carlstadt and Masius in the sixteenth, maintained that the so-called Books of Moses were not composed by him in their present form, but by Ezra or some other inspired man, who substituted new names of places for old and obsolete ones, by which the memory of events could be best apprehended and preserved. In the seventeenth century we find Hobbes arguing, that we should no more suppose these writings to have been composed by Moses, because they are commonly called Books of Moses, than we should believe the Books of Joshua, Ruth, and Samuel to have been written by the individuals whose names they bear; "for in titles of books the subject is marked as often as the writer." Similar views were advanced by Isaac Peyrère, a French Protestant who went over to Romanism, and also by Spinoza, who held that all the books from Genesis to Kings form one great historical work, composed of many documents of diverse authorship, not always in harmony with each other, but arranged and edited in their present form after the Babylonian exile, and probably by Ezra. In the year 1678 Richard Simon's Critical History of the Old Testament appeared, and gave a new turn to Pentateuchal criticism by calling attention to the varieties of composition and style apparent even in closely connected narratives, (as in the account of the flood, especially in Gen. vii, 17-24.) Simon's work was sharply criticised by Le Clerc, who, however, put forth the singular theory that the Pentateuch, though containing documents both older and later than Moses, was probably compiled by the exiled priest whom the king of Assyria sent to instruct the Samaritan colonists. 2 Kings xvii, 27. These various criticisms made little impression at the time of their appearance, but they opened the way for the more thorough study of the Pentateuch, which began about the middle of the eighteenth century, and continues with growing interest to the present hour. Modern criticism, so far as it has opposed the Mosaic authorship of the Pentateuch, or attempted to explain its origin, exhibits a series of theories; and no intelligent discussion of the latest phases of Old Testament criticism is possible without some acquaintance with the history of these successive theories. There are four theories which have obtained notable currency, and will be briefly described in the following pages.

Theory of Documents.

Biblical scholars like Vitringa and Calmet, who believed in the Mosaic authorship of the Pentateuch, admitted that the great lawgiver made free use of ancient traditions, genealogies, and annals of the patriarchs, arranging, revising, and supplementing them to suit his purpose. But the first attempt to indicate the number and distinctive character of these documents was made by Jean Astruc, professor of medicine in the College of France, who published at Brussels and Paris, in 1753, a work entitled "Conjectures upon the Original Memoirs which Moses appears to have used in Composing the Book of Genesis." This writer detected a noticeable use of the divine names ELOHIM and JEHOVAH, by means of which different chapters and sections of Genesis were distinguishable, and he conjectured that Moses had for the most part made use of two original memoirs, each of which was still traceable by the occurrence of one or the other of these names. He also held, that, besides these principal sources, some nine or ten other documents might still be traced by the notable absence of any divine name, or by the use of another name than Elohim or Jehovah, (for example, Gen. xix, 30–38; xxii, 20–24; xxv, 12–18.) Astruc supposed that these different documents were at first arranged by Moses in separate columns, but were afterward copied into one continuous narrative, by which process some of them came to be misplaced.

Astruc's views do not appear to have commanded much attention until about 1762, when J. F. W. Jerusalem gave them a favourable notice in his Letters on the Mosaic Writings, and soon afterward Eichhorn, profiting by the work of all his predecessors in this field of criticism, gave them great notoriety, and presented them in more complete and scholarly form, first in his Repertorium for Biblical and Oriental Literature, (1779,) and subsequently in the successive editions of his Introduction to the Old Testament, (1780–1823.) Eichhorn's brilliant essays in this department of biblical study opened the way for a host of similar attempts to ascertain the age and authorship of the constituent parts of the Pentateuch. John G. Hasse maintained that it was compiled at the time of the Babylonian exile, from writings which belonged in part to Moses, but which had become greatly enlarged and altered by later hands. F. C. Fulda also argued that portions of the Pentateuch are of Mosaic authorship, such as the decalogue, most of the songs contained in the last four books, and the list of encampments in Numbers xxxiii. He supposed that a collection of laws was made in the time of David, but that our Pentateuch in its present form was composed by some unknown redactor after the exile. Similar views were put forward by H. Corrodi, G. L. Bauer, and K. D. Ilgen. This last named writer attempted a more minute analysis of Genesis than that of Eichhorn, and maintained the theory of a second Elohist. Eichhorn himself modified some of his earlier views in the fourth edition of his *Einleitung*, (1824.)

Theory of Fragments.

Near the close of the last and in the earlier part of the present century, several rationalistic critics endeavoured to show that the Pentateuch was of a more fragmentary character than the current theory of documents allowed. Some of the advocates of that hypothesis, however, had given utterance to opinions which led very naturally to the conclusion that these books were but a loose compilation of heterogeneous fragments. This theory was put forward by Dr. Alexander Geddes, a Roman Catholic divine, in his annotated new translation of the Bible, the first volume of which appeared in London in 1792. He held that the Pentateuch and the Book of Joshua were compiled by the same author, and consisted of a great variety of composite elements, some coeval with Moses, some older, and some later, and some of them probably oral traditions. He argued that it could not have been written before the time of David, nor after that of Hezekiah, and probably belonged to the period of Solomon's long and peaceful reign. J. G. Nachtigal (under the name of Otmar) published a similar view in Henke's *Magazin für Religionsphilosophie, Exegese und Kirchengeschichte*, and at first (vol. ii, 1794) maintained that much of the Pentateuch might have originated with Moses, and all of it might have been collected and arranged in its present form before the division of the kingdom; but the next year (vol. iv, 1795) he attributed to Moses little else than the decalogue, the list of encampments in the desert, a few genealogical tables, and a few songs. He aimed to show that, besides some documents of that kind, there were probably very few, if any, literary monuments among the Hebrews before the time of Samuel, but that in the schools of the prophets and among wise men numerous histories and songs were composed. These were afterward collected into books, and thus originated the so-called Books of Moses, which were brought to their present form about the time of the Babylonian exile, and perhaps under the supervision of Jeremiah. Substantially the same hypothesis was advocated in Vater's Commentary on the Pentateuch, (three parts, Halle, 1802–5.) This writer argued, from the non-observance of many important Mosaic laws, that they could not have been in existence before the reign of David or Solomon. A. T. Hartmann subsequently repeated these arguments, and maintained that the art of writing was unknown among the Israelites until the age of the Judges, and was not used in the composition of books until Samuel's time. Von Böhlen took the position that Deuteronomy is the oldest portion of the Pentateuch, and first appeared in the time of Josiah. The other books were subsequently added, but the entire work could not have been completed until after the exile. In substantial accord with Von Böhlen were the conclusions of W. Vatke and J. F. L. George; but these last two writers anticipated in some important points the theory of the gradual development of the religion of Israel, which has become so prominent in recent critical discussions. De Wette also for a long time held to the theory of fragments, but his work may be better treated in another connection.

Theory of Supplements.

The Fragment Hypothesis soon became unsatisfactory to some of its ablest advocates. It was mainly held by extreme Rationalists, who treated the Mosaic narratives as altogether mythical or legendary. But the unity of the Pentateuch was too apparent, and the evidences of plan and purpose running through the whole were too many, for the most arbitrary critics to set aside. One of Ewald's earliest publications contributed largely to establishing the unity of the Book of Genesis. The way for what is commonly known as the Hypothesis of Supplements was prepared by such writers as Bertholdt, Herbst, and Volney, men not readily classed with any special school, but who maintained that the Pentateuch was in great part the work of Moses, but much revised and supplemented by later hands. According to Bertholdt, the work was brought to its present form sometime between the beginning of Saul's and the end of Solomon's reign. According to Herbst, the final redaction was probably made after Ezra's time by the college of Elders. Volney allowed less to Moses, and supposed that the Pentateuch in its present form was the product of the combined labours of Hilkiah, Shaphan, Achbor, (2 Kings xxii, 8–12,) and other scribes and prophets of the age of Josiah.

De Wette made use of all the suggestions of his predecessors, and in his earlier publications on this subject adopted in the main the Hypothesis of Fragments. Many single fragments of the Pentateuch could not, in his opinion, have originated earlier than the times of David. The different narratives were written independently of one another, and afterward put together by different collectors. The compilation of Leviticus was probably by another hand, and certainly later than that of Exodus. Numbers was a supplement to the earlier collections, and Deuteronomy was composed in the time of Josiah. He subsequently modified his views, and in the fifth and sixth editions of his Introduction to the Old Testament (1840, 1845) he maintained that the Pentateuch and Joshua bore evidences of a threefold redaction, showing traces, first, of the Elohist, second, of the Jehovist, and third, of the Deuteronomist. The earliest of these must have lived after the Israelites were ruled by kings, and the latest belongs to the time of Josiah. He also allowed that among the sources employed by the first redactor were many ancient and genuine monuments of the Mosaic age.

The views of Friedrich Bleek were, like those of De Wette, gradually developed. As early as 1822 he maintained that there are many parts of the Pentateuch which cannot be later than the age of Moses, and nothing which requires us to believe that the last revision was made as late as the time of the Babylonian exile. His more mature views appear in his Lectures on Old Testament Introduction, according to which the most ancient and original documents now contained in the Pentateuch and Joshua were worked over into one continuous narrative by a first writer, commonly called the Elohist. This was the *Grundschrift*, or fundamental writing, and contained an account of the creation, the flood, and the lives of Abraham, Jacob, Joseph, Moses, and Joshua, and was probably composed in the time of Saul. It embraced documents older than the time of Moses, and a large portion of the laws which were enacted by Moses himself. The writer employed the name Elohim until he came to the narrative of Moses's life, after which the name of Jehovah appears. This fundamental history was made the basis of a larger work, namely, that of the Jehovist, who lived in the time of David, and supplemented the Elohistic writing with numerous additions. This Jehovist produced the first four books of the Pentateuch and the Book of Joshua in substantially the form in which we find them now, (excepting particularly Lev. xxvi, 3-45.) The final redaction was made by the author of Deuteronomy sometime during the reign of Manasseh.

This Theory of Supplements received the support of J. J. Stähelin, who, however, would not allow that any part of our Pentateuch was composed by Moses. He held it to be a work of Samuel, or of one of his scholars, based upon an older history which extended from the creation of the world to the conquest of Canaan, and contained a large part of Genesis, nearly all the three middle books of the Pentateuch, and the geographical portions of the Book of Joshua. Friedrich Tuch also adopted this theory, but supposed the Elohist to have written in the time of Saul, and the Jehovist in the time of Solomon. Ewald is noted for propounding an analysis of the Pentateuch and Joshua so minute as to detect therein the work of eight different writers, whose several parts, with the dates of composition, his critical instinct assumed to determine with remarkable nicety. He recognised a fundamental Elohistic document, which extended from the creation to the time of Solomon, and embraced three older writings, namely, the Book of Jehovah's Wars, a life of Moses, and the Book of the Covenants. This ancient history he named the Great Book of Origins, and attributed it to a contemporary of Solomon. To this work subsequent writers made numerous additions, and the Hexateuch received its present form from the Deuteronomist, who wrote in Egypt during the latter part of Manasseh's reign. Cæsar Von Lengerke also placed the composition of the Elohistic document in the time of Solomon, and supposed it to have been enlarged by the Jehovist in the time of Hezekiah, and further worked over and supplemented by the Deuteronomist, who brought it to its present form (excepting, perhaps, Deut. xxxiii) during the reign of Josiah. Vaihinger makes the three different writers to be a Pre-Elohist, (of whose work only a few fragments remain,) the Elohist, and the Jehovist. Hupfeld made out four writers, the Elohist, a second Elohist, a Jehovist, and a Redactor, who gave the entire work its final unity and finish. Böhmer adopted Hupfeld's theory in the main, but attempted to ascertain more definitely the extent of the Redactor's work. Riehm laboured to show that Deuteronomy is a literary fiction, but in no way a dishonest or blameworthy performance; from the mention of ships in chap. xxviii, 68, he concluded that it was written in the time of Manasseh. Knobel produced one of the most minute and elaborate works on the Pentateuch extant, and distributed its several component parts among five different writers, namely, the authors of the fundamental document, (*Grundschrift*,) the Law-Book, (*Rechtsbuch*,) the War-book, (*Kriegsbuch*,) the Jehovist, and the Deuteronomist. The first of these lived probably in the time of Saul, the last under Josiah. Nöldeke apportioned the work among at least four writers, the Elohist, the Jehovist, a Redactor, and the Deuteronomist, the first of whom was a priest living at Jerusalem in the time of David or Solomon, the last in the reign of Josiah.

Other writers, less distinguished, contributed to the elaboration of this Theory of Supplements, each one producing some new discovery touching the relationship of the different parts of the Pentateuch. Among the more recent and thorough discussions of this hypothesis is that of Schrader, as given in the eighth edition of De Wette's *Einleitung*, (Berlin, 1869.) He supposes four successive writers, and points out their characteristic differences of language, style, and religious conceptions. The first he calls the Annalist, who belonged to the earlier part of David's reign; the second wrote soon after the division of the kingdom, and is named the Theocratic Narrator. These two writers composed separate and independent works, which were combined a generation later and supplemented by a third writer, who is called the Prophetic Narrator. The final Redactor of the Pentateuch was the Deuteronomist, who composed his book and revised the whole before the eighteenth year of Josiah's reign.

Delitzsch and Kurtz, while holding to the Mosaic origin of the main parts of the Pentateuch, adopt the essential elements of the Supplementary Hypothesis. In the Introduction of his Commentary on Genesis Delitzsch makes Exod. xix–xxiv the kernel of the Pentateuch, and supposes it to have been written by Moses. The other laws were given orally by Moses and written down by the priests. Deuteronomy must be accepted as in substance the work of Moses. After the conquest and occupation of Canaan, some man like Eleazar (Num. xxvi, 1, xxxi, 21) compiled the main (Elohistic) work, incorporating in it the roll of the covenant, and, perhaps, the last words of Moses. This was supplemented by Joshua (Deut. xxxii, 44, Josh. xxiv, 26) or one of the elders, (Num. xi, 25,) who added Deuteronomy in its present form, and the Jehovistic sections. (*Commentar über die Genesis*, p. 31. Leipzig, 1872.) Much has been said of the recent change in Delitzsch's views, which appear in a series of twelve articles in Luthardt's *Zeitschrift für kirchliche Wissenschaft* for 1880. He now admits the use of parallel documents running through much of the Pentateuch, the priority of the Jehovistic portions, and that Deuteronomy comes between the two. Excepting the priority of the Jehovist these latter views are not materially different from those advanced in his Commentary on Genesis. He still maintains the Mosaic origin of much of the Pentateuch, but concedes that many of the laws originated with the needs of the people at a later day, and maintains that the legislation

INTRODUCTION TO THE PENTATEUCH. 17

begun by Moses was doubtless continued by the priests, to whom such matters were intrusted after Moses's death. He believes that Deuteronomy is in substance Mosaic, but in form has been modified by the subjectivity and style of the writer, (the *Deuteronomiker,*) who nevertheless was in fullest spiritual accord with Moses, and has reproduced his last traditional discourses in an authentic form. He rejects the main positions of the theories of the school of Wellhausen, and strenuously opposes the notion that Deuteronomy originated at the time of Josiah. He admits that Ezra may have participated in the codification of the Mosaic laws, but he stoutly controverts the idea that the Levitical legislation was a post-exilian fiction. According to Kurtz, the Pentateuch is of Mosaic origin in that it was, in the main, prepared under Moses's direct supervision, and completed by his assistants and contemporaries. Probably Moses himself composed with his own hand only those portions which are expressly attributed to him. In the historical parts he admits two distinct sources, a fundamental and a supplementary writing. The last revision of the entire work as we possess it was probably made near the close of Joshua's life, or, perhaps, soon after his death.

Theory of Ethnic Development.

We thus designate the latest phase of Old Testament criticism, which is particularly noted for the stress it lays upon the national religious development of the Israelitish people, and the dates and order of what it affirms to be distinct and successive legal codes. We have noticed above that Von Böhlen, Vatke, and George, as early as 1835, maintained that Deuteronomy is the oldest book of the Pentateuch. But the monograph of K. H. Graf on the Historical Books of the Old Testament (Leipzig, 1866) marked an epoch in the criticism of the Pentateuch. This writer was a pupil of Prof. Edward Reuss, who had long previously argued for the priority of Deuteronomy, but whose more fully developed views were published at a later date. Graf's theory supposes an ancient Elohistic work which has been subjected to three great revisions and enlargements. The first was done by the Jehovist in the time of the earlier kings, and contained the legislation recorded in

Exod. xiii, xx–xxiii, and xxxiv. The second was made by the Deuteronomist, who was the author of the book found by Hilkiah. 2 Kings xxii, 8. This book is supposed to have been that portion of our Deuteronomy which extends from chap. iv, 45, to chap. xxix, 1, excepting chap. xxvii. Its author made free use of the older work of the Jehovist, and afterward combined that work with his own and added Deut. i–iv, 44, as a new preface. The third revision was made during and after the Babylonian exile, and is notable for having added, in the body of the work, the Levitical legislation, which now appears in Exod. xii, xxv–xxxi, xxxv–xl, most of Leviticus, and the greater part of Numbers. These Levitical laws are held to exhibit numerous evidences of a later origin and a more elaborate ritual than those of Deuteronomy.

This theory of the origin of the law-books of Israel was taken up and presented in a still more radical form by A. Kuenen, first in his Historico-Critical Inquiry into the Origin of the Books of the Old Testament, (Leyden, 1861–65,) and later in his Religion of Israel, (1869–70,) his Five Books of Moses, (1872,) and his Prophets and Prophecy in Israel, (1875.) According to Kuenen, the religion of Israel is nothing more nor less than one of the principal religions of the world, and must be explained in its genesis and development like all other religions. The Israelites in Egypt were probably polytheists; by and by they came to consider their national deity as distinct from other gods, and called him El Shaddai; afterward they were taught by Moses, who gave them the decalogue, to call this god Jehovah. The stories of the patriarchs are ancient myths, and have been wrought over by various writers. The first written documents of note are those of the prophets of the eighth century before Christ, such as Amos, Hosea, and Isaiah, and the historical books of the Kings. Under the ministry of the prophets the worship of Jehovah became purer, and during the reign of Hezekiah the Book of Deuteronomy was written and made to serve the purpose described in 2 Kings xxii and xxiii. A programme of national worship was outlined by Ezekiel, and became the basis of the subsequent Levitical legislation, which first came into use after the return from exile, and was formulated by Ezra.

INTRODUCTION TO THE PENTATEUCH. 19

This distinguished scribe compiled the voluminous Book of the Law in the shape in which we now possess it.

This theory, strange as it may seem, has captivated many modern critics, and is maintained in substance by Kalisch in his Commentary on Leviticus, by Aug. Kayser, by Bishop Colenso, and by Smend in his recent Commentary on Ezekiel. But among all its advocates, the most famous at the present time are probably Profs. Wellhausen and Reuss in Germany, and W. Robertson Smith in Scotland. According to Wellhausen, the Pentateuch is composed of three separate and independent works, which were wrought over, and, with additions from other sources, fashioned into a connected whole by Ezra or one of his contemporaries. The oldest document is the work of the Jehovist, compiled from previously existing Jehovistic and Elohistic records, and therefore by this critic designated by the letters J. E. This ancient composition was mainly historical, but contained the laws of Exod. xx–xxv. The second in order of the great documents was Deuteronomy, composed in the reign of Josiah, (designated D.) The third, called the Priest-Codex, (P. C.,) contained the laws of Exod. xxvi–xl, Leviticus, and Numbers i–x, and was accompanied by an historical introduction reflecting the spirit and opinions of the time of the exile when it was produced. This Priest-Codex is also called the Book of the Four Covenants, (designated Q., from the Latin *Quatuor*.) After the exile, Ezra or one of his generation constructed our present Pentateuch by a free use of all these documents, and also of other materials at his command.

Edward Reuss, of Strasburg, claims to have advanced this theory as early as the year 1834, and says that in many respects it was with him "a product of intuition." After slowly elaborating it in his university lectures for nearly half a century, he has recently published his matured critical analysis and arrangement of the whole body of Old Testament literature in a large octavo, entitled "The History of the Holy Scriptures of the Old Testament." He traces the composition of the Pentateuch through four distinct stages, the oldest portion of which was first compiled in the time of Jehoshaphat. This was subsequently revised and supplemented with important additions by the Jehovist. The third great contribution was made by the Deuteronomist in the time of Josiah, and the fourth, containing the Levitical legislation, was incorporated with the whole after the exile. W. R. Smith's position is not materially different from that of the school of Reuss, though he presents his views with greater moderation and caution. He distinguishes three separate groups of laws, which he calls the First Legislation, (Exod. xxi–xxiii,) the Deuteronomic Code, (especially Deut. xii–xxvi,) and the Levitical Legislation, which is scattered through Exodus, Leviticus, and Numbers. The exact date of Deuteronomy is not determined, but "the book became the programme of Josiah's reformation, because it gathered up in practical form the results of the great movement under Hezekiah and Isaiah, and the new divine teaching then given to Israel." The distinctive features of the Levitical legislation were first sketched by Ezekiel, afterward developed in numerous details, incorporated with many ancient laws and traditions, and adapted "to the circumstances of the second temple, when Jerusalem was no longer a free State, but only the center of a religious community possessing certain municipal privileges of self-government." (*The Old Test. in the Jewish Church*, pp. 363, 382. Edinb., 1881.) So far as these laws or writings are ascribed to Moses, they are to be understood merely as a legitimate continuation of a cultus which began with Moses. They were, by conventional usage or legal fiction, called ordinances of Moses, but every one would understand that they were not of Mosaic authorship.

The adverse criticism of the Pentateuch has called out numerous replies from scholars who have steadfastly defended the traditional belief. Among the most eminent of these we may name, of the older writers, Carpzov, Witsius, Vitringa, and Calmet; and, in later times, Hengstenberg, Hävernick, Keil, M'Donald, and Green. Not a few of the ablest and most satisfactory answers to the several theories above detailed are to be found in the higher periodicals of Germany, England, and America. These vary in their methods of defense, some admitting numerous documents and interpolations, while others are slow to concede that any thing save the account of Moses's death is inconsistent with Mosaic authorship.

Results of Criticism.

What now, we may ask, are the results of all this critical study of the Pentateuch? It will be conceded, by every one competent to judge, that the researches and discussions of the Higher Criticism have developed a more thorough and scientific study of the Old Testament. Philological, archæological, and historical questions connected with Hebrew literature have been investigated with rich results to the cause of sacred learning. As to the origin and authorship of the Pentateuch, we regard the following propositions as fairly settled :

1. The Pentateuch contains a number of passages which cannot, without doing violence to sound critical principles, be attributed to Moses as their author.

2. The Pentateuch, especially the Book of Genesis, contains documents of various dates and authorship, which have been worked over into an orderly and homogeneous whole.

3. The laws of the Pentateuch were either unknown or else very largely neglected and violated during most of the period between the conquest of Canaan and the Babylonian captivity.

4. The Books of Exodus, Leviticus, and Numbers show different stages of legislation, and Leviticus contains a noticeably fuller and more elaborate priestly code and ritual than appear in Deuteronomy.

We are frank to say that we regard the above propositions as simple statements of fact. But the divergent and conflicting opinions detailed in the foregoing pages admonish us that many unsound and illogical conclusions may be drawn from well-established facts. It is one thing to recognise positive results of criticism; quite another to accept theories which the critics build, or assume to build, upon such results. Let us now inquire if these four propositions are inconsistent with the Mosaic origin of the Pentateuch.

I. Passages not Written by Moses.

Our space will not allow a full discussion of all the passages in the Pentateuch which have been thought to be inconsistent with Mosaic authorship; nor need we, for our purpose, more than mention some of the more prominent examples. Those most frequently cited are Gen. xii, 6, xiii, 7, where the observation is made that "the Canaanite was then in the land;" the mention of Dan in Gen. xiv, 14, and Deut. xxxiv, 1, (a name not given to the place until the times of the Judges, Judg. xviii, 29;) Gen. xxxvi, 31, where a list of Edomite kings is given who reigned "before there reigned any king over the children of Israel." Exod. xvi, 35, contains a statement which seems inappropriate at that place, breaks the otherwise natural connexion of verses 34 and 36, and may not unreasonably be believed to be an interpolation. The laudatory remark touching Moses in Num. xii, 3, is hardly such as a meek man would write about himself, and no one believes that Moses wrote the account of his own death in Deut. xxxiv. The words in Deut. ii, 12, have been thought to point to a time when Israel had taken possession of the promised land, and the whole context (verses 10–12, and also verses 20–23 of the same chapter, and verses 9–11 of chap. iii) may easily have been an editorial addition. So, too, the words, "unto this day," in Deut. iii, 14, most naturally imply a time subsequent to the days of Moses.

Some of the above passages, we doubt not, may be legitimately explained so as to harmonize with the idea that Moses wrote them. Thus the statements made in Gen. xii, 6, and xiii, 7, do not necessarily imply that the Canaanite was not in the land at the time of the writer, for his purpose may have been to show that Abraham was not the first dweller in that land; the Canaanites and the Perizzites had already settled there. So, too, Deut. ii, 12, is most accurately translated: "Even as Israel has done to the land of his possession, which Jehovah has given to them;" and this might well have been written by Moses after the Israelites had taken possession of the land east of the Jordan. But granting that all these, and probably other passages also, are of later date than the time of Moses, what must be our conclusion? Two methods of accounting for such facts at once suggest themselves: (1) The books of which these passages form a part were not composed until some time after the Mosaic age, or (2) these passages are additions made by a later hand. Either of these suppositions is sufficient to account for the facts; but these facts alone are not sufficient to determine the date or authorship of the Pentateuch, taken as a whole. If we have other reasons sufficient to convince us that these books are in substance the work of Moses, or originated in his day, the class of passages cited above present no considerable difficulty, for it is perfectly reasonable that such additions may have been inserted by the hands of editors and transcribers.

II. Documents Incorporated in the Pentateuch.

That the Pentateuch contains ancient documents of various dates and authorship is readily conceded. The wonder is, that any one should ever have disputed this proposition, especially in regard to Genesis. This ancient narrative recounts numerous events which, as the writer's own chronology shows, occurred centuries and millenniums before Moses's day. The only rational supposition is, that written documents and oral traditions were employed in its composition; and this hypothesis holds equally well whether we attribute the work to Moses or to some other writer. But sober students will be slow to commend, much less to follow, the attempts of critics to detect and dissect the particular sources, and determine the work of each writer even to the divisions of single verses! This microscopic refinement of criticism will be likely to refute itself. There is not an ancient work extant which, if subjected to such a process, could not be shown to have come from a variety of authors; and not a few learned treatises of modern times might be greatly improved, in the judgment of wearied readers, if only shorn of much that exact criticism might justly pronounce redundant, obscure, or slovenly.

A great deal has been said about the substantial agreement of critics concerning the ancient sources, and Prof. Ladd exhibits, in eight pages of his recent work, (*The Doctrine of Sacred Scripture*, vol. i, pp. 517–525, New York, 1883,) the comparative harmony of Knobel, Schrader, Dillmann, and Wellhausen, in their analysis of the Hexateuch. But those same tables also serve admirably to show, by their numerous minute variations, the purely subjective principles of this species of criticism. There need be little, if any, dispute about the facts detailed; the controversy must turn upon the use made of the facts. Let it be assumed that the use of Elohim, or Jehovah, or some other divine name, must always indicate diverse authorship; let it be admitted that all differences of style and redundancy and repetition are proof of so many different "sources," and the work of analytical criticism is very simple. The harmony of critics adopting these principles is very much of the nature of a mechanical necessity. It scarcely needs the learning of a Knobel or a Dillmann to perform such labour. An ordinary schoolboy, with a few pedagogical directions, might go through the Bible and pick out and classify such distinctions as Elohistic and Jehovistic chapters and verses. Repetitions and marked differences of style are recognised by every careful reader; and few, if any, will dispute that many of these differences, and the peculiar use of the names Elohim and Jehovah in some parts of Genesis, are most naturally explained by the hypothesis of different documents appropriated by the author of the book, and by him wrought over into one continuous narrative. The real question of criticism, we repeat, is not about the facts, but about theories assuming to rest upon these facts. The critics of one school affirm the existence of an original Elohistic document running through the entire Hexateuch; and they are positive that the Jehovistic and other portions are later supplements. But the most recent school has changed to the very reverse of this, and conclude that the Elohist was the final redactor of the whole. Why should we follow either of these schools? Why may not Moses himself have gathered up the different traditions and documents, and compiled the Book of Genesis, and, in the course of forty years, have added the other books which from time immemorial have been ascribed to him? Later editors have added here and there a sentence, and Eleazar or Joshua (comp. Josh. xiv, 1, xxiv, 26) might very appropriately have appended the account of the great lawgiver's death, and, indeed, have compiled the whole of Deuteronomy, using in the main the last sayings of Moses; but such admissions furnish no valid argument against the Mosaic authorship of the great body of the work.

III. Ignorance and Neglect of the Law after the Age of Moses.

It appears from the extant records of Israelitish history that the laws of the Pentateuch were either unknown or else very generally neglected and violated during most of the period between the conquest of Canaan and the Babylonian exile. In proof of this we may cite the story of Micah and the Levite, (Judg. xvii, xviii,) the sacrilege of Eli's sons, (1 Sam. ii,) the offering of Jephthah's daughter as a human sacrifice, (Judg. xi,) the rash vows and illegal acts of Saul, and the widespread habit of worship at high places, the idolatry of Solomon, the calf worship at Bethel and Dan, the Baal worship under Ahab and his heathen wife, and the multiplied idolatries of later kings. Facts of this character may be adduced in abundance, and critics of the school of Kuenen and Wellhausen appeal to them as evidence that the Mosaic laws and ritual were at the time unknown. Amos's mention of "the high places of Isaac" and the "sanctuaries of Israel" (chap. vii, 9) is cited to show that worship at high places was the ancient and hereditary practice of the nation, against which they knew no law. The facts cited certainly show either great ignorance or great neglect and violation of the laws of Moses; but do they warrant the inference that those laws were not then in existence? We answer, No; and for the following reasons:

1. Neglect, violation, or ignorance of sacred laws is no proof of their non-existence. According to Hosea iv, 2, swearing, falsehood, theft, adultery, and murder abounded in his day; but is this any evidence that the commandments of the decalogue prohibiting those crimes were then non-existent or unknown? Saul's fell purpose to murder David might be as fairly cited to prove that no law against homicide was then extant. The whole drift and implication of the history of those times show that it was a period of violence and neglect of God's laws. How far those laws were known we cannot now determine; but there is much reason to suppose, that from Joshua to Josiah the great mass of the Israelites knew very little of the sacred books of their nation. Almost universal ignorance of the Holy Scriptures prevailed in Europe for more than six hundred years before the Lutheran Reformation; more easily, we believe, might a similar ignorance of the Book of the Law have prevailed for as many centuries in Israel before the reign of Josiah.

2. We have no need to assume that even great prophets, like

Samuel and Elijah, must have been familiar with the Books of Moses. They may have known much of the sacred laws and customs, as such, without any particular acquaintance with the books in which they were written. Neither they nor the later prophets were representatives of the sanctuary or ritual, but they were sent forth with the fresh, living oracle of God, which everywhere extols the spirit rather than the letter. The keynote of Old Testament prophetism was sounded by Samuel himself, who, though reared at the house of Jehovah in Shiloh, (1 Sam. i, 9, 24, iii, 3,) and after its desolation offering burnt offerings at other places, (1 Sam. vii, 9, 10,) said to Saul: "Hath Jehovah as great delight in burnt offerings and sacrifices, as in obeying the voice of Jehovah? Behold, to obey is better than sacrifice, and to hearken than the fat of rams." 1 Sam. xv, 22. But how much Samuel, or Elijah, or Amos, or Hosea knew, or did not know, about the written laws, or any literary documents of their nation, must be matter of conjecture, and cannot be made the basis of an argument. The import and value of any allusion they make must be determined by valid exegesis; but it always awakens suspicion to find a modern writer assuming to say what Elijah or Amos *did not know*, and then proceeding to rest an argument or build a theory upon such supposed ignorance. Suppose Elijah had never seen or read or heard of the Books of Moses; does it follow that no such books existed? According to 1 Kings xix, 10, he did not know that there were seven thousand in Israel who refused to worship Baal. Hundreds of our most excellent citizens have never read the Constitution of the United States, and an immense portion of our national literature reveals no hint of its existence. Multitudes among us who have been made familiar from childhood with the great names and facts of sacred history never read any considerable portion of the Bible, and some such often betray lamentable ignorance. There might have been seven thousand copies of the Pentateuch in existence at Elijah's time, and all of them unknown to him, and out of the way of the most conspicuous persons of that period.

3. There is evidence, however, in the Historical Books, the Prophets, and the Psalms, to indicate the priority of the legis-

INTRODUCTION TO THE PENTATEUCH. 27

lation recorded in the Pentateuch. We meet with numerous allusions, which are best explained by accepting the traditional belief of the antiquity of the Books of Moses. The tabernacle and central place of worship was at first established at Shiloh. Josh. xviii, 1, 10; xix, 51. This fact is again recognised in Judges xviii, 31. In 1 Sam. i, 3, 9, 24, the house of God is still at Shiloh, and thither all Israel bring their offerings. 1 Sam. ii, 22, 29. The ministering priests are descendants of Aaron. 1 Sam. ii, 27, 28. The ark is known as "the ark of the covenant of Jehovah;" (iv, 3; comp. Exod. xxv, 21; Num. x, 33; xiv, 44;) but when captured by the Philistines, and while separated from the tabernacle, the glory departed from Israel. 1 Sam. iv, 21, 22; vii, 2. This fact largely explains the irregularities of worship and the demoralization that prevailed thereafter. Comp. 1 Kings iii, 2. The tabernacle, with its priestly service, was removed to Nob, (1 Sam. xxi, 1-7,) and afterward to Gibeon. 1 Kings iii, 4; 1 Chron. xvi, 39. David brought the ark to Jerusalem, and instituted a provisional worship there, (2 Sam. vi,) and under Solomon the temple became the great national sanctuary, which all Israel recognised as the place where Jehovah recorded his name. 1 Kings viii, 29; comp. Deut. xii, 11. The prominence of the priests and the ark at the dedication, and the numerous allusions in 1 Kings viii to the exodus, the ministry of Moses, and the language of our present Pentateuch, imply the previous existence both of the Levitical and the Deuteronomic code. The disruption of the kingdom under Rehoboam, and Jeroboam's shrewd policy of turning the national heart away from Jerusalem, (1 Kings xii,) abundantly explain the disorder and idolatry that followed. In the light of this history, the notion that the worship at Bethel and Dan and other local sanctuaries represents the ancient ante-Mosaic cultus, against which there was as yet no law, appears in the highest degree absurd. The prophets thenceforward address the nation as rebellious and backslidden children. Hosea proclaims that Israel has apostatized from Jehovah, until the many precepts of his written law have become a strange thing. Hosea viii, 12. Amos declares that Judah also has despised the law of Jehovah, and has not kept his commandments. Amos ii, 4. Isaiah complains that the entire nation had become utterly corrupt. Isa. i, 4-6. The older Psalms recognise Zion as the holy hill, (Psa. ii, 6, iii, 4,) Jehovah as dwelling in his holy temple, (xi, 4,) and the duty of observing his statutes, (xviii, 22.) These and other similar facts imply the previous existence of the substance of the Mosaic history and legislation, and utterly nullify all *e silentio* arguments against the traditional opinion of the Mosaic books.

IV. Relation of the Levitical and Deuteronomic Codes.

Until the rise of the new critical school, represented by Reuss, Graf, Kuenen, and Wellhausen, Deuteronomy was believed to be of later origin than the other books of the Pentateuch. The contrary theory, propounded in 1835 by Von Böhlen, Vatke, and George, obtained little currency, and such German critics as Schrader and Dillmann still maintain that Deuteronomy is the later work. But the critics of both these schools agree that the Book of Deuteronomy originated in the latter period of the Jewish monarchy, and its main portions constituted "the Book of the Law" which was discovered by Hilkiah. Three questions accordingly present themselves for our consideration: 1. What evidence exists to show that the book discovered by Hilkiah consisted solely of Deuteronomy? 2. Where is the proof that Deuteronomy, or any considerable portion of it, was first written in the times of Manasseh or Josiah? 3. What is the real relation of Deuteronomy to the three middle books of the Pentateuch?

1. What evidence exists to show that the book discovered by Hilkiah consisted of Deuteronomy only? It is called "the Book of the Law," and "the Book of the Covenant." 2 Kings xxii, 8, 11; xxiii, 2, 21; comp. 2 Chron. xxxiv, 14, 15, 30; xxxv, 12. The reforms instituted by Josiah were warranted by laws found in Exodus, Leviticus, and Numbers, as well as in Deuteronomy. Did the king destroy idolatrous images? This was enjoined in Exod. xxiii, 24, 33; xxxiv, 12-17, and Num. xxxiii, 51, 52. Did he put down the cruel worship of Molech? The only places in the Pentateuch where this god is mentioned by name are Lev. xviii, 21, and xx, 2-5. Did he abolish witchcraft? That also is condemned in the law of

Leviticus, (xix, 31; xx, 27.) And the law of the Passover appears in Exodus, (xii, xxiii, 15, xxxiv, 18,) Leviticus, (xxiii, 5-8,) and Numbers, (ix, 2, 3.) Why then assume that Josiah's "law-book" consisted solely of Deuteronomy? That it contained Deuteronomy is not disputed; but when we are told that there is no evidence that Josiah had any thing more than Deut. xii–xxvi on which to base his reforms, it is an ample and complete reply to say, that there is also no evidence that this "Deuteronomic Code" was all his book contained. The plea that he did not observe some commandments which are found in other parts of the Pentateuch is nullified by the fact that he did not, so far as appears from the history, observe numerous things which are enjoined in Deuteronomy. There exists, therefore, no valid evidence that the Book of the Law, or Book of the Covenant mentioned in 2 Kings xxii, 8, and xxiii, 2, contained Deuteronomy only.

2. What evidence exists to show that the Book of Deuteronomy was first written at or near the time of Josiah's reign?

It is alleged that the style of composition is notably different from that of the other books of the Pentateuch. This is admitted by all, but is sufficiently accounted for by the nature of its subject matter. It professes to be in substance a series of discourses delivered by Moses at the conclusion of his long life and ministry. Years probably intervened between the composition of these discourses and most of his other writings; and the time, the occasion, and the purpose of Deuteronomy, according to the traditional belief, would warrant the expectation of finding in such a repetition of history and laws a different style from that of previous books. "The fervor and warmth," says Eichhorn, "which breathe in every line, make it apparent that countless emotions in the soul of the great man crowded themselves into his writing, and set on every page the seal of a work composed on the verge of the grave." — *Einleitung in das A. T.*, vol. ii, p. 405. Leipzig, 1803. As for the character of the Hebrew employed in Deuteronomy, Kleinert has adduced controlling evidence to show that it savours of an older time than the later period of the Jewish monarchy. He shows by the citation of numerous examples that it resembles the previous Books of Moses more than it does the Books of Jeremiah and Kings. (*Das Deuteronomium und der Deuteronomiker*, p. 235. Leipzig, 1872.)

It is argued that the new order of things introduced by Josiah, and based upon this book, is evidence that the book itself could not have been in existence before. This argument, however, rests upon the assumption, already shown to be unsound, that national ignorance and non-observance of laws are proof of their non-existence. But, on the other hand, if Deuteronomy, or any considerable portion of the "Law of Moses," originated in the days of Josiah, and was first made public as narrated in 2 Kings xxii, it was manifestly a forgery. The more radical critics do not hesitate to acknowledge this, and treat it as a pious fraud. Others endeavour to explain it as a literary fiction or a legal fiction, not intended to deceive, but merely to put in practical shape the doctrines of the prophets. But the subject matter and historical position of the work are incompatible with any such hypothesis. We cannot conceive how a code of laws originating under such circumstances, could have become the basis and rule of a national religion so pure and lofty. A writer of Josiah's time might, indeed, have published a book in the name of Moses. Poems, proverbs, philosophical disquisitions, and prophetical books have often been put forth under assumed names. Perhaps the Book of Ecclesiastes is a work of this kind, put forth, for obvious reasons, in the name of Solomon. We have numerous apocryphal and pseudepigraphal works of this character. But such books never had any notable influence on the national government and worship. Such a production, which every body knew to be a fiction, could have had no authority to warrant the innovations undertaken by Josiah. Why should a book written in the reign of Manasseh or Josiah contain commandments to exterminate Canaanites and Amalekites, (Deut. xx, 16–18, xxv, 17–19,) tribes which were not then in existence? Was it done to give the work the tone of an ancient writing? Such a supposition would only make the fraudulent character of the book more glaring. It is for us easier a thousand times to believe the traditional authorship of the Pentateuch than to accept the hypothesis of such a forgery and fraud, in which Hilkiah the priest, and Huldah the prophetess, joined together to deceive the king and the whole Jewish nation, and succeeded so completely as to make a fictitious book the legal and constitutional basis of the national religion. Nay, this surreptitious introduction of the Book of the Law was so deftly done that it raised no suspicion or outcry at the time, and for more than two thousand years has been stupidly supposed to be a genuine work of Moses!

3. But what is the real relation of Deuteronomy to the three middle books of the Pentateuch? It is claimed by the Wellhausen school that there are three different codes or groups of laws traceable in the books of Moses, of which the most ancient is the Book of the Covenant, embracing Exodus xx-xxiii, adapted to an early period of the national life, and recognising a plurality of altars or local sanctuaries. Next in order is the Deuteronomic Code, which aimed to abolish the local sanctuaries and centralize the national worship at Jerusalem. The Levitical legislation followed at a later date, was first planned during the exile, and appears in outline in Ezekiel's writings, but was worked over and incorporated in the three middle books of our Pentateuch by Ezra, or one of his contemporaries. Deuteronomy, accordingly, becomes the oldest book of the Pentateuch, and the other books, in their principal contents and present form, are postexilian.

That different stages of legislation are traceable in the Pentateuch, and that the Book of Leviticus contains a more elaborate priestly code than appears in Deuteronomy, may be readily admitted. Our present concern, is to know whether these codes are inconsistent with each other, or of such a nature that they might not all have originated in the times of Moses. The main arguments against the traditional belief rest upon an alleged inconsistency in the different codes touching (1) places of sacrificial worship, (2) the offerings required, (3) the number of feasts, and (4) the distinction between priests and Levites.

1. *Places of Sacrificial Worship.*—In Exod. xx, 24, provision is made for building an altar "in all places (בְּל־הַמָּקוֹם) where I record my name," but according to Deut. xii, 5, *ff.*, all the offerings of Israel must be presented at a central sanctuary,

"which Jehovah your God shall choose out of all your tribes to put his name there." The Levitical legislation recognises a central altar, (Exod. xxix, 18, 38 ; Lev. i, 3, 5 ; iv, 4 ; vi, 14,) but its provisions are applicable both to the tabernacle in the wilderness and to the temple at Jerusalem.

There is no inconsistency between these different legal regulations. The first legislation, made at Sinai, provides for an unsettled people, contemplates future journeyings, and the probable need of successive altars at different places. It does not allow the erection of altars on every high hill, or wherever the people or their leaders choose to place them, but only at such places as Jehovah should designate. This is perfectly compatible with the Deuteronomic order for a central sanctuary, made nearly forty years later, when Israel was about to enter the land of promise. The Deuteronomic law itself explains that this regulation would be in place only after Jehovah had given them full possession of the land. Deut. xii, 9–11. Moreover, there is nothing in Deuteronomy inconsistent with the supposition, that after the central sanctuary had been divinely chosen, Jehovah himself might, under exceptional circumstances, authorize sacrifice in other places. The critics urge that the sacrifices at Bochim (Judg. ii, 5) and at Ophra, (Judg. vi, 26,) the offerings of Manoah (Judg. xiii, 19, 20) and Samuel (1 Sam. vii, 9, 17) and David, (2 Sam. xxiv, 25,) and the prevalence of local sanctuaries of later times, are evidence that the Deuteronomic law was unknown to the holiest men of Israel. But the history shows that these exceptional altars were authorized by special theophanies, or justified by peculiar circumstances. Those occurring under the ministry of Samuel are explained by the fact that the sanctuary at Shiloh was then desolate, and Jehovah had forsaken the place where he first recorded his name. Psa. lxviii, 60, 68 ; Jer. vii, 12, 14. All other worship at high places was idolatrous, and, in part, a natural result of the demoralized state of the nation, when there were numerous violations of the Mosaic laws, and great ignorance and superstition prevailed among the people. Prof. W. H. Green goes through the whole list of so-called "local sanctuaries," and very clearly shows, "that apart from idolatrous perversions, there was not a single sanctuary for permanent worship among them. Deduct the two or three instances, in the period of the Judges, in which Jehovah or the Angel of Jehovah appeared to men, and sacrifices were offered on the spot; deduct further the sacrifices offered when Israel had no sanctuary, after God had withdrawn from Shiloh and before the temple was built, or in the peculiar circumstances of the Ten Tribes in the lifetime of Elijah—deduct these sacrifices, which were due to special causes and were strictly limited to the occasion that called them forth, and there is not a particle of evidence that any one of these places was a sanctuary for the worship of Jehovah." — *Moses and the Prophets*, p. 167. New York, 1882.

2. *The Offerings Required.*—Exodus xx, 24, mentions only burnt offerings and peace offerings; Deut. xii, 6, 11, speaks of burnt offerings, heave offerings, freewill offerings, tithes, and vows; Leviticus provides for all these, and also for the meat offerings, (ii, 1,) and the sin and trespass offerings. Chaps. iv, v. Peace offerings are not mentioned in Deuteronomy, except incidentally at chap. xxvii, 7, and the meat offerings not at all. Leviticus enjoins a great number and variety of ceremonies and purifications, which are held to indicate a later period, when the priesthood had control of the nation and had instituted an elaborate ritual. But every careful reader must see that the differences here pointed out are in no sense contradictory. There is nothing connected with any of these offerings that is inconsistent with a Mosaic origin. The hortatory style and purpose of Deuteronomy did not require a minute repetition of all the details of ritual, which were elsewhere sufficiently recorded; and will any one contend that, when one book does not specify all the items of another bearing on the same subject, its author must have been ignorant of such omitted items? Is no other explanation possible? Surely a theory based upon such variations as these will not be likely to command the confidence of a logical mind.

3. *The Number of Sacred Feasts.*—The same kind of disparity is urged respecting the Feasts. Exodus (xxiii, 10–17) specifies the three feasts of unleavened bread, harvest, and ingatherings, and the observance of the seventh day and the seventh year. Deuteronomy, chaps. xv, xvi, mentions all these,

except the Sabbath law, (which, however, is mentioned in chap. v, 12–15,) and the feasts of harvest and ingatherings are here called the feast of weeks and the feast of tabernacles. Leviticus mentions all these, together with the feasts of pentecost, (xxiii, 15–21,) and of trumpets, (xxiii, 24,) and the day of atonement, (xvi,) and the year of jubilee, (xxv, 8–13.) These are simply facts of the record, but how any one can derive from them a valid argument against the Mosaic origin of any or all the accounts is more than we are yet able to comprehend. That one code, or, as we may better say, one section of the great law-book of Israel, should contain a fuller and more minute description of details than another, is certainly no strange thing. The ingenuity of a theory which traces in these various sections different and successive stages of legislation may be admired; its validity as an argument against the Mosaic authorship of the Pentateuch is not commendable.

4. *The Priests and the Levites.*—It is claimed that the first legislation (Exod. xx–xxiii) knows no special order of priests or an Aaronic priesthood; in Deuteronomy there is no distinction between priests and Levites, the constantly recurring expression being " the priests, the Levites," or " the priests, the sons of Levi ; " but in Leviticus (viii–x) the sons of Aaron are formally set apart to the special work of the priesthood, and the other Levites appear as subordinate ministers. Here again are simple facts as recorded, but they do not warrant the conclusions which the new school critics presume to draw from them. There was no occasion in Exod. xx–xxiii to refer to the distinction named, for Aaron and his sons had not yet been set apart. According to the history itself, their separate consecration followed much other legislation. Then, further, there was no occasion or necessity for Moses, in the circumstances under which Deuteronomy claims to have been issued, to recapitulate the details of priestly office and ritual, or do more than make such general references to the ministers of the sanctuary. The language employed in Deuteronomy assumes Israel's knowledge of numerous laws already established, and if we adopt the view (which the book itself abundantly warrants) that Deuteronomy is especially " the people's book "—a more simple, practical, and hortatory repetition of the principal facts and

laws of the Mosaic legislation—the mention of details of priestly office and ritual would have been manifestly out of place. What avails it to repeat over and over: "Deuteronomy knows no Levites who cannot be priests, and no priests who are not Levites."—SMITH, *Old Testament in Jewish Church*, p. 360. Why not candidly face the question: Why should Moses, under the circumstances assumed in Deuteronomy, be expected to do more than allude as he does to the whole tribe of Levi as the chosen ministers of religion? He does NOT say that any Levite may be a priest. This is a notion foisted in by the critic. Why, moreover, should the school of Graf and Wellhausen try to force the proposition that from the exodus to the exile there was no high priest as distinguished from ordinary priests and Levites? To affirm this in the face of the express mention of "Eleazar the priest," (Josh. xix, 51, xxi, 2,) and "Eli the priest," (1 Sam. i, 9, comp. ii, 27, 28,) and "the great priest" in the reign of Joash, (2 Kings xii, 10,) and of Josiah, (2 Kings xxii, 4, 8, xxiii, 4,) and of "the head priest" in the reign of Zedekiah, (2 Kings xxv, 18,) looks like a desperate purpose to carry out a theory at all hazards. "What shall we say," writes Prof. S. I. Curtiss, "of a development which in the time from Moses (1320 B. C.) to Josiah (625 B. C.) only gets as far as Levitical priests, and in a single generation can develop the Aaronic priesthood and the high priest with all his glory?"—*The Levitical Priests*, p. 163. Edinb., 1877.

What, now, may we conclude as to the relation of Deuteronomy to the three middle books of the Pentateuch? We find no evidence of the priority of Deuteronomy. We find nothing to warrant the opinion that any one of the first four books, or any considerable portion of any one of them, was composed after the death of the great lawgiver. The different legislation recorded in the several books was probably enacted at different times during the forty years of Moses's ministry, but we have no means of determining the particular date or occasion of each section of the Torah. Whatever the particular dates and sources of the various documents and laws, no sufficient reason has yet been given why the Pentateuch might not have received substantially its present form under the immediate supervision of Moses.

A formal attempt to refute theories like those above described would be idle unless some agreement could first be made upon fundamental principles and methods of procedure. The difficulty, if not the impossibility, of such agreement will be apparent from the following considerations:

1. Most of these critics enter upon the study of the Bible under a prejudice hostile to any supposable manifestation of the Supernatural in human history. Many of them confess this at the outset. With such writers all miracles are myths or legends, and he is the ablest critic who devises the most plausible theory of their origin.

2. A dispassionate study of the works of these critics begets a conviction that the detailed arguments by which they endeavour to support their theories, are not the real steps of the process by which their conclusions were reached. The entire history of critical assaults upon the Mosaic authorship of the Pentateuch has been notably a succession of adjustments. One theory has given place to another, and the methods by which they have been put forward and urged are largely of the nature of special pleading to maintain a position already definitely taken.

3. The critical methods of Reuss, Kuenen, and their school, are not so much based on a candid examination of all the contents of the sacred books of Israel as they are deduced from the application of a speculative philosophy of human history to these books, and an ingenious attempt to make the philosophy account for the history. Reuss tells us in the Preface of his work that his point of view is not that of the biblical history but of the legal codes, and, beginning with an intuition, he has aimed and hoped " to find the Ariadne thread which would lead out of the labyrinth of current hypotheses of the origin of the Mosaic and other Old Testament books, into the light of a psychologically intelligible course of development for the Israelitish people."—*Die Geschichte der heiligen Schriften des A. T.*, p. 8. This is reversing the true logical method which should rather formulate a philosophy of history upon an induction of facts, and not first construct the philosophy and then force the history into accord with it.

4. The arbitrary exegetical principles of these critics are not

INTRODUCTION TO THE PENTATEUCH. 37

of a nature to carry conviction to the minds of candid readers. Such an analysis of books and chapters as assumes with an air of dogmatic confidence to point out a variety of authors in a single paragraph, and to furnish a detailed account of all the sources from which an historian of two thousand years ago derived his knowledge, is too wonderful for us. It borders hard on the supernatural. It seems also at times to have positive acquaintance, not only with all the ancient author knew, but even with all that he did not know! Certainly, more use is often made of what the writer does not say than of what he does say. Discrepancies also are needlessly magnified, and any passage or event, however important, that stands in the way of the critic's theory, is arbitrarily set aside as the addition of a different writer, or the product of a later age. The Books of Hosea, Amos, and Ezekiel are accepted as genuine, but Deuteronomy, which claims to be a record of the words of Moses, is set aside as a fiction.

5. The notion that Ezekiel's highly wrought vision of the temple and cultus was the outline of a priestly Torah to be observed by the exiles at their restoration to Jerusalem, is beset with insuperable difficulties. Ezekiel's language cannot without violence be interpreted literally. The details were never observed by the returning exiles, and the idea that Ezekiel's prophecy, issued in his own name, became the basis of an elaborate code of laws issued in the name of Moses is really too great a tax upon the credulity of earnest seekers after truth. Add to this the assumption that Ezra and Nehemiah, who wrote so much of their own work in their own name, were parties to this fictitious legislation! Why should critics make no difficulty of conceiving Ezekiel, more than forty years before the restoration, planning an imposing ritual for his nation, and yet imagine it impossible for Moses to do it less than forty years before the conquest of Canaan?

6. The idea that the prophets of Israel set themselves against the ancestral faith and worship of the people, and aimed to overthrow a system which had been sanctioned by the "First Legislation" at Sinai, is contrary to the entire contents and scope of their prophecies. Their constant testimony is, that Israel had apostatized from God. The chosen nation had be

come like an unfaithful wife, who had violated her marriage covenant, and the worship in high places is characterized as a shameful prostitution. Hosea ii, 13; v, 7; vi, 7; Amos ii, 4; Isaiah i, 2-4. Can an unbiased reader of these prophets believe that they contemplated the prevailing idolatry of Israel and Judah,—especially the worship of high places,—as the ancient and hereditary practice of the nation?

7. Finally, the assumption that an elaborate ritual and ranks of priesthood come in the natural order of development after the more spiritual word of prophecy may be boldly challenged. History shows the reverse to be true. Forms of worship, especially sacrifices and oblations, belong rather to undeveloped and imperfect periods of religious life. The Mosaic tabernacle, with its elaborate cultus, was admirably adapted to serve as an "object lesson" to instruct Israel when a child. But a theory which makes the tabernacle a fiction, the priestly code an invention of Ezekiel, and the minute account of boards, and sockets, and bars, and hooks, and pillars, and curtains, and loops, and taches, and pots, and basins, and bowls, and spoons, and shovels, and plates, and pans, the conception of Jewish priests at the time of the exile, ought to tell us how such "bondage of the letter" fits in a theory of religious development. Is not the survival of the fittest a fundamental law of such development? But behold! the lofty lessons of Amos, Isaiah, and Micah, who, according to these critics, denounced sacrifices as a vain thing, without divine authority, and hateful to Jehovah, are superseded and overgrown by a ceremonial of outward service, concocted by designing priests, and foisted upon the chosen people in the name of Moses!

Positive Evidences of Mosaic Origin.

Having now cleared the way of objections, and seen the inconclusiveness of the critical arguments against the Mosaic origin of the Pentateuch, we add in brief outline the positive argument in favor of the ancient traditional belief. We have discovered no valid evidence sufficient to discredit this belief; we do find many things, within and without the work, which go directly to confirm it.

Internal Evidence.

1. The several passages which speak of Moses as writing a book, or writing in the book, are at least so many direct claims of Mosaic origin. In Exod. xvii, 14, Moses is commanded to write "in the book" (בַּסֵּפֶר) an account of the victory over the Amalekites. In Exod. xxiv, 4, 7, it is said that "Moses wrote all the words of Jehovah," that is, the divine communications, judgments, and commandments which he had received in the mount, " and he took the Book of the Covenant, and read in the audience of the people." Here is witness of a book of divine laws, written by Moses and read by him to the people. Compare also Exod. xxxiv, 27. These passages, it will be said, refer only to these particular portions of the Pentateuch, and not to the work as a whole; and this is readily granted. For according to the manifest tenor of the record, the entire law was not communicated at one time. It was given in many parts and modes, (comp. Heb. i, 1,) and the various wars, (like this with Amalek,) and marches, and murmurings, and judgments, would naturally have been recorded as they occurred. It is not claimed that such texts as those just cited prove the Mosaic authorship of the entire Pentateuch. But this is the argument: If Moses wrote down such an event as the war with Amalek, and the words of Jehovah at Sinai, is it not probable that he also from time to time wrote other important events and other laws? In Num. xxxiii, 2, we are told that "Moses wrote their goings out, according to their journeys, by the commandment of Jehovah," and in Deut. xxxi, 24, that he "made an end of writing the words of this law in a book," and gave orders to have a copy of the same deposited in the side of the ark. Ver. 26. Let it be granted that "the Book of this Torah" here (as in Deut. xxviii, 61, xxix, 20, xxx, 10, comp. xvii, 18) refers only to the "Deuteronomic Code," we have this much, then, which claims to have been written by Moses himself. Nor are we careful to know whether Moses wrote even this much with his own hand, so long as it is clear that he was, under God, the responsible author. Paul wrote by an amanuensis, and so might Moses. Here, then, according to the most direct claims, Moses is said to have written down events

40   INTRODUCTION TO THE PENTATEUCH.

and laws with which he was immediately concerned. But if he was careful to have the war of Amalek and the Sinaitic and the Deuteronomic legislation carefully recorded, is it likely he would have had no similar care for the plagues of Egypt, the events of the exodus, and the soul stirring incidents of the journeys through the desert, and the conquest of the east-Jordanic territory?

2. The Levitical legislation of the third book of the Pentateuch is explicitly asserted to have been given through Moses. Almost every chapter begins with the words: "Jehovah spake unto Moses, saying," and the book concludes (Lev. xxvii, 34) with the statement: "These are the commandments which Jehovah commanded Moses for the children of Israel in Mount Sinai." It does not follow from these statements that Moses himself wrote down these laws, but the language used most clearly teaches that the laws were communicated through Moses to the people. Others may have done the writing, but Moses was, under God, the great legislator. The other legislative portions of the Pentateuch are largely given in the same way. Num. vi, vii, etc.

3. The numerous traces of familiarity with Egypt favour the traditional belief. Such are the making of bricks by slaves, portrayed on the monuments of the eighteenth dynasty; the ark of papyrus, indicating familiarity with the Nile; the plagues of Egypt, which have been shown to be, in the main, but an intensifying of troubles which often afflict that country, and which were so manifestly directed against Egyptian superstitions. The Levitical regulations of the priesthood and other ceremonies are in striking analogy with corresponding Egyptian customs. Under this head, see especially Hengstenberg's *Egypt and the Books of Moses*, Eng. trans., (Edinb., 1843.)

4. There are also traces of the desert journey, which naturally indicate a writer contemporary with the events described, and an eye-witness of the same. The manner in which Marah (Exod. xv, 23) and Elim (27) and the desert of Sin (xvi, 1) and Mount Sinai are mentioned, and the accuracy of the descriptions as confirmed by the most careful researches, favour the opinion that the record of all this was made by one who was a part of the Israelitish camp. The itinerary given in Numbers xxxiii is

INTRODUCTION TO THE PENTATEUCH.

additional evidence of the same thing. The mention of the camp and the tents, the minute description of the tabernacle and its various parts and vessels, the shittim or acacia wood, (a product of the Sinaitic peninsula,) the manna and quails, all tell the same way.

5. Those passages which refer to the land of Canaan as a future possession necessarily imply the Mosaic age. Such are found in Exod. xii, 25 ; xiii, 5, 11 ; xxiii, 23, 24; xxxiv, 11–13; Lev. xiv, 34 ; xviii, 3 ; xix, 23 ; xx, 22 ; xxiii, 10 ; xxv, 2; Num. xv, 2, 18 ; xxxiv, 2; xxxv, 10; Deut. vi, 10 ; vii, 1; xii, 10 ; xix, 1 ; xxvi, 1. Unless these texts be sheer forgeries, they show that, at the time of writing, the Israelites had not yet entered into the possession of Canaan.

6. A number of notable archaisms in the Pentateuch favour the belief of the Mosaic origin. The forms especially remarkable are הוא, used for both *he* and *she;* נַעַר, used in the same way for either a *boy* or a *girl;* and אֵל, *these*, instead of the later אֵלֶּה. The plural ending ן, instead of י, is a constantly recurring feature. Numerous other peculiar words and forms have been pointed out as evidences of the earlier period of the language; but the Hebrew language is especially noted for suffering comparatively few changes from the time of the exodus to that of the exile.

Evidence from the Subsequent History.

The other books of the Old Testament, and the subsequent history of Israel as traceable therein, abound in references and allusions which imply the Mosaic legislation and the great events of the exodus as recorded in the Pentateuch. Those very narratives which show the apostasy of later times, and prove that the Mosaic laws were largely neglected and violated, contain indications of the existence of Mosaic institutions.

1. The Book of Joshua is so full of references to Moses and his work, and such specific mention is made therein of "the Book of the Law of Moses," (viii, 31–35,) that writers who deny the Mosaic authorship of the Pentateuch affirm that the Book of Joshua was written by the same author. Plainly its whole subject matter and scope imply the existence of the Pentateuch. Eleazar, the son of Aaron, has succeeded his father in the priesthood, (xiv, 1,) and the tabernacle is set up

at Shiloh, (xviii, 1.) To deny the substantial truthfulness of the history recorded in Joshua is most uncritical and arbitrary; but if Joshua be true the Pentateuch must be genuine.

2. The Book of Judges abounds in allusions to Mosaic history and institutions. In chap. i, 1, we are told that after Joshua's death Israel "inquired of Jehovah," manifestly alluding to the use of the urim worn by the high priest. Num. xxvii, 21; Exod. xxviii, 30. The same custom is mentioned again at Judges xx, 18. Phinehas, the son of Eleazar, the son of Aaron, bears the urim, and officiated before the ark in those days, (xx, 27, 28.) The notable irregularities, and the idolatrous regard for ephod, and teraphim, and other images, (viii, 27, xvii, 5, xviii, 14-20,) are incidental evidences of the preexistence of the Mosaic laws. For why should a Levite be sought as a priest, (xvii, 10, 13, xviii, 19,) and how came Levites to be scattered among the other tribes, (xix, 1,) and why should they be "going to the house of Jehovah," (xix, 18, comp. xviii, 31,) unless the Levitical laws were already in existence? These allusions may not be proof that the Pentateuch was then known as a written code, or that Moses wrote any thing, but they are capable of natural explanation only by recognizing that Levitical and sanctuary regulations, as provided for in the Pentateuch, were already well known customs, and, as further appears at 1 Samuel i, had their centre of interest at the house of Jehovah at Shiloh. Whatever deviations from the law, or neglect and violation of law, are noticeable, are accounted for by the writer himself in his oft-repeated statement that there was no king in Israel and every man acted his own pleasure, (xvii, 6, xviii, 1, comp. Deut. xii, 8.) There are also numerous manifest allusions to the language of the Pentateuch, as in the covenant and promise, (ii, 1, comp. Gen. xvii, 7, 8, xxviii, 13, xxxv, 12,) in warnings against affiliation with the Canaanites, (ii, 2, 3, comp. Exod. xxiii, 33, xxxiv, 12, Deut. vii, 2, xii, 3,) and in the mention of the Sinaitic theophanies in Deborah's song, (v, 4, 5.) Gideon exhibits the old theocratic spirit in refusing to be king, (viii, 23,) and Manoah and Samson recognise the covenant relations of Israel in their language concerning the "uncircumcised Philistines," (xiv, 3, xv, 18.) Jephthah's message to the Ammon-

ites (xi, 14-27) is full of minute references to the events of the later years of Moses's life. Comp. especially Num. xx-xxii. The express reference to what "Moses said" in chap. i, 20, and the law of the Nazarite recognised in the narrative of Samson, (xiii, 5, comp. Num. vi, 2-5,) are conspicuous witnesses of pre-existent Mosaic legislature. The Book of Ruth, belonging as it does to the times of the Judges, may here be cited for its specific references to pentateuchal facts and laws. The mention of Leah and Rachel and Pharez and Tamar (iv, 11, 12) shows an acquaintance with facts recorded in Genesis. Ruth's gleaning in the harvest-field accords with the law given in Lev. xix, 9, 10, xxiii, 22, Deut. xxiv, 19, and the entire narrative of chapter iv, 1-10, is based upon the levirate law as recorded in Deut. xxv, 5-10.

3. Probably no more controlling evidence of the antiquity of the Levitical legislation and ritual can anywhere be found than the facts which are recorded at the beginning of the First Book of Samuel, and which show the state of Israelitish worship at the close of the period of the Judges. The tabernacle is still at Shiloh, and is known as the house of Jehovah, (i, 3, 24,) to which the pious Israelites go up yearly to worship and to sacrifice. Eli, who was a descendant of Aaron, chosen out of all the tribes of Israel to offer sacrifice, to burn incense, and to wear the ephod, is the priest, (ii, 28.) His sons abused their holy office and were slain for their sins, and with such a priesthood we need not wonder that there were many violations of law and irregularities in the sanctuary service. But the lamp was kept burning (iii, 3) according to the law, (Exod. xxvii, 21; Lev. xxiv, 3;) the ark of God was the holiest of symbols, and Jehovah was thought of as dwelling between the cherubim, (iv, 4; comp. Exod. xxv, 22.) After the capture and disgrace of the ark, Shiloh was forsaken, and the glory departed from Israel, (iv, 21, 22;) and we need not greatly wonder that the people soon lost the old theocratic spirit, and fell to worshipping in high places, because, until the erection of the temple at Jerusalem, more than a century later, "there was no house built unto the name of Jehovah." 1 Kings iii, 2.

4. The erection of the temple and the centralization of the national worship there were in manifest accord with the spirit

and purpose of the Mosaic law. The temple was in all its main outlines a reproduction of the pattern of the tabernacle, only enlarged and built of enduring material, as was manifestly fitting, now that Israel had become established in the land, and would provide a settled place for Jehovah's special abode. 1 Kings viii, 13. From all that can be gathered, the ritual of the temple service was in accord with the Levitical regulations of the Pentateuch, and the prayer of Solomon, offered at the dedication, (1 Kings viii,) is notably full of allusions to the very language found in various parts of the books of Moses. The sins of Solomon's later life, and his building high places to other gods, (xi, 1–13,) could have had no other effect than a most demoralizing one on all Israel. The division of the kingdom, which occurred soon after his death, (chap. xii,) and the far-sighted but wicked policy of Jeroboam to prevent his people from "going up to do sacrifice in the house of Jehovah at Jerusalem," (xii, 27,) abundantly account for the neglect and violation of the Book of the Law which followed. That book, however, was not lost. It is referred to as influencing the action of Amaziah in not putting to death children for their fathers' crimes, (2 Kings xiv, 6; comp. Deut. xxiv, 16;) and Hezekiah is expressly said to have "kept the commandments which the Lord commanded Moses." 2 Kings xviii, 6. This king sought also to destroy the worship of the high places, and all idolatry, and broke in pieces the brazen serpent made by Moses (Num. xxi, 9) because it had become an object of idolatrous worship. Num. xviii, 4. The Book of the Law of Moses, discovered in the days of Josiah, was evidently recognised as genuine, and its commandments and statutes were followed by that king and his princes in their efforts at national reformation. The idea that this book was a literary forgery, or a legal fiction, or that it consisted solely of the Deuteronomic Code, we have seen to be untenable.

5. The prophets, moreover, make repeated allusions to the Mosaic history and law. Amos refers to the exodus and the wilderness journey, (ii, 10; iii, 1;) to the law of the Nazarites, (ii, 11, 12;) and to the tithes after three years, (iv, 4; comp. Deut. xiv, 28,) Hosea alludes to Adam's transgression of the covenant, (vi, 6;) to the exodus from Egypt, (ii, 15; xi, 1;) to

INTRODUCTION TO THE PENTATEUCH.

Jacob's taking his brother by the heel in the womb; and to the events of Peniel and Bethel, (xii, 3, 4.) He also clearly alludes to the many things of Jehovah's law which have been written, (viii, 12.) Isaiah speaks of the law of Jehovah which the people will not hear, (xxx, 9;) Micah mentions the exodus, the ministry of Moses, Aaron, and Miriam, the counsels of Balak and Balaam, (vi, 4, 5,) and the promises of Jacob and Abraham, (vii, 20.) Joel speaks of the meat and drink offerings, the priests and assemblies at the house of Jehovah, (i, 9, 13, 14.) He speaks of Zion as the holy mountain, and is familiar with the use of the trumpet to sound an alarm and convene an assembly, (ii, 1, 15; comp. Num. x, 1-10.)

It would be superfluous to add other references, which appear in later books, and such as are scattered through the Psalms. The above are allusions which so manifestly imply the antiquity of the Mosaic legislation that, taken in connexion with the internal evidence already adduced, they may be confidently cited as corroborative evidence of the early existence of the Mosaic writings.

III. Collateral Evidence.

Under this head we may appropriately add a number of considerations which serve to show that Moses might have written the books which are ascribed to him. The following facts make it evident that it was not only possible, but altogether probable, that Moses put on record the great facts of his life and ministry and the laws which were given through him at Sinai and during the journeys of the desert.

1. The art of writing was known before the age of Moses, and was extensively used by the Egyptians. We suppose it to be now generally conceded that inscriptions on Egyptian, Phœnician, Assyrian, and Babylonian monuments put this fact beyond all question. It is now commonly believed that the most ancient Vedas of India were committed to writing as early as the age of Moses. Mommsen testifies to the high antiquity of writing even in Rome. (*History of Rome*, vol. i, p. 15.) The tradition of Cadmus shows that alphabetic writing in Greece was older than the beginning of the historic period. "The use of letters," says Pliny, "would seem to have been

eternal." That Moses, brought up at the court of Egypt, was ignorant of the art of writing, is not supposable. According to Wilkinson, "We meet with papyri of the most remote Pharaonic periods; and the same mode of writing on them is shown, from the sculptures, to have been common in the age of Suphis or Cheops, the builder of the great pyramid, more than 2,000 years before our era." (*Manners and Customs of the Ancient Egyptians*, vol. ii, p. 98.) The remarkable papyrus, written in hieratic characters, which was discovered by Brisse, and translated by Chabas, is of very remote antiquity. (See Rougé, *Recueil de Rapports*, p. 55, Paris, 1867; Brugsch, *Hist. d'Egypte*, p. 63.)

2. Great epochs in human history develop great writers. Influences are then brought to bear on men of intellectual vigour which serve as an unusual stimulus to mental effort. We need not wonder that the exodus and the desert journey furnished occasion for the composition of poems and books of history. National odes and records of war and victory would meet a popular demand. We find, also, that the great rulers of Egypt, Assyria, and other ancient nations were in the habit of putting on record the great events of their times. David and later kings of Israel had official scribes and recorders. 2 Sam. viii, 16, 17. Mesha, king of Moab, had an outline of his conquests inscribed on a monumental stone. Why should it be doubted or denied that Moses also made a record of the great events of his last forty years? That he did so is clearly indicated in such passages as Exodus xvii, 14; and, aside from such testimony, is every way probable in the nature of things.

3. The versatility of the Israelitish mind, as seen in all times, and wherever they have been scattered by persecution, affords a presumption that they would not have been without any literature, and ignorant of the art of writing, when the leading nations about them had made great progress in such things. The arts of Egypt had furnished Hebrews like Bezaleel and Aholiab (Exod. xxxvi, 1, 2) an opportunity to become skilled workmen in cutting and engraving. Such fragments of song as that of Num. xxi, 17, 18, imply poetic genius at work in Israel during the journey of the wilderness. Deborah's song

witnesses the same in the age of the Judges. The incidental reference to writers in the tribe of Zebulun (Judg. v, 14) suggests that contact with the Phœnicians, in the times of the Judges, might have served to develop in Israel the skilful use of the pen or pencil.

Having seen that the current objections to the Mosaic authorship of the Pentateuch are insufficient to set aside the traditional belief, and that internal, external, and collateral evidences combine to strengthen and confirm the opinion that these ancient books are a product of the Mosaic age, we may, in concluding this discussion, appropriately add a word touching the supposable revision of the work by later hands. Accepting every essential element of the traditional belief, we may at the same time admit the three following suppositions, which are plausible in themselves, analogous with what we know of other ancient writings, and suggested by a careful study of all the facts involved in the critical treatment of the question.

1. Moses may have employed amanuenses to write down his own words, and to arrange, compile, and transcribe various documents according to his dictation and desire. It might even be admitted that he himself wrote not a line of the Pentateuch in its present form, and yet the work be as truly and genuinely his as the Epistle to the Romans is a genuine work of Paul. No one questions Paul's authorship of Romans, although it is expressly asserted that it was written by Tertius. Rom. xvi, 22. Moses might have employed Aaron for a scribe as well as a spokesman, (comp. Exod. iv, 10–16; vii, 1,) and other chosen men might have been called to a similar service.

2. It is supposable that the discourses of Moses, as recorded in Deuteronomy, were edited and furnished with their introductory and supplementary narratives by Eleazar or Joshua. It is every way reasonable to believe that the three great historical and legislative discourses, and the two songs of Moses, were carefully written out by himself or one of his assistants before the day on which they were spoken to Israel, and were intrusted to the priests and elders for preservation. Comp. Deut. xxxi, 9, 26. It is equally supposable, and indeed, prob-

able, that after the settlement in the land of Canaan some such man as Eleazar or Joshua arranged these discourses and songs in their present form, and supplied such passages as Deut. i, 1–5, iv, 41–49, xxix, 1, and most of chap. xxxi and chap. xxxiv. This hypothesis helps to explain some forms of expression as used in this book, (as, for example, the mention of Moses in the third person, and the phrase "beyond Jordan" in i, 1, 5, as compared with iii, 25,) and at the same time allows all that is essential to the claims of Mosaic authorship as put forth in the book itself.

3. It is also probable, and in accordance with the ancient tradition, that Ezra, the "ready scribe in the Torah of Moses, which Jehovah, the God of Israel, gave," (Ezra vii, 6,) transcribed the entire Pentateuch, and added in the margin or inserted in the work itself most of those words and passages which are generally believed to have been added long after the age of Moses.

INTRODUCTION TO THE BOOK OF GENESIS.

Contents and Plan.

THE Book of Genesis lies at the basis of the Old Testament revelation, and assumes to be a record of the beginnings of human history. It consists of a series of records, arranged in a well-defined order, and exhibiting a unity and finish which prove it to have proceeded from one constructive mind. In chapter i, 1–ii, 3, we have an account of the creative BEGINNING—the formation of the heavens and land, the seas, and the various classes of living creatures. This introductory narrative is followed by ten sections of varying length, each beginning with the heading, "These are the generations," (תּוֹלְדוֹת.) The plan of the writer appears to have been, first, to describe the miraculous preparation of the sky, soil, animal tribes, and visible environments of the first man, Adam, and then to trace, from that beginning, his outgrowth and development through ten notable evolutions. The outline is as follows:

1. THE CREATIVE BEGINNING .... Chap. i, 1–ii, 3.
2. THE GENERATIONS OF THE HEAVENS AND THE LAND .... ii, 4–iv, 26.
3. BOOK OF THE GENERATIONS OF ADAM...... v, 1–vi, 8.
4. THE GENERATIONS OF NOAH .... vi, 9–ix, 29.
5. THE GENERATIONS OF SHEM, HAM, AND JAPHETH............................... x, 1–xi, 9.
6. THE GENERATIONS OF SHEM .... xi, 10–26.
7. THE GENERATIONS OF TERAH.............. xi, 27–xxv, 11.
8. THE GENERATIONS OF ISHMAEL............. xxv, 12–18.
9. THE GENERATIONS OF ISAAC .... xxv, 19–xxxv, 29.
10. THE GENERATIONS OF ESAU............... xxxvi, 1–xxxvii, 1.
11. THE GENERATIONS OF JACOB.............. xxxvii, 2–l, 26.

1. Here is a well defined plan, which shows that the book is no patchwork of fragments, but a carefully digested whole. The narrative of creation is so symmetrical in its construction as to be conspicuously artificial. The work of the six days is divisible into two corresponding orders:

1. Light.
2. Expanse of heaven.
3. Dry land.

4. Luminaries.
5. Fowls of heaven, and living things of the waters.
6. Living creatures of the land, and man.

2. We notice, next, that the first outgrowths or developments of this creation are called "generations of the heavens and of the earth," (ii, 4.) The starting point, or conceptual position of the writer, is, "a day of Jehovah-God's making land and heavens," when as yet no plant or herb of the new creation had begun to grow; no rain had yet fallen on that new soil, and no man to till it had yet appeared. It appears, therefore, that, at the beginning of this new section, the writer goes back in thought to the morning of the sixth day of the creative week already described. The *day* of chap. ii, 4, is not the whole creative week, as many suppose, for the writer is not thus careless in his use of words. It is the *terminus a quo* of the "generations" about to be described, the day on which, according to verse 5, the Edenic growths began, and the first human pair were brought together. Man was formed of the dust of the soil, and became (וַיְהִי) a living soul by the breath of Jehovah-God. His formation, be it observed, is thus conceived as a generation, or birth, produced from the heavens and the land by the breath of God. A garden was planted in the eastern part of Eden to receive the man, and then the woman was formed from the man—another step in the process of these generations. Then follows the narrative of the fall, showing how primeval man was of the earth and earthy, (1 Cor. xv, 47,) and by disobedience lost his original relation to God. The first generations ran to violence and crime, and became more and more degenerate until Seth was born, and with him the history takes a new departure.

3. "The book of the generations of Adam" (v, 1) is not a record of Adam's origin, for his birth and earliest progeny have already been conceived and treated as a generation out of the heavens and the earth by the breath of Jehovah-God. This next book of generations takes up the line of Seth, who was introduced in the previous section, (iv, 25,) and looked upon as a substitute for the pious Abel. But the race again deteriorates, and the land is filled with violence.

4. "The generations of Noah" (vi, 9) is the title of the section which narrates the great event of the latter part of Noah's life, the judgment of the Deluge, in which he and his family were preserved, and the rest of mankind were wiped off from the face of the earth.

5. "The generations of Noah's sons" (x, 1) is a table of the families and nations by whom the earth was peopled after the flood—a most ancient and venerable document, worth more for historical purposes than any oriental inscription yet deciphered.

6. Next follows the table of the generations of Shem, a succinct genealogy, (xi, 10-26,) which serves to introduce us to the great ancestor of the chosen people by tracing the line of Shem down to Terah, the father of Abraham.

7. "The generations of Terah" extend to those of Ishmael, and comprise the great events of the life of Abraham.

8. The generations of Ishmael are briefly sketched, (xxv, 12–18,) as having no considerable importance in the author's plan.

9. The generations of Isaac (xxv, 19) extend to the death of that patriarch, and include the history of Jacob and Esau to the time when the former had returned from Mesopotamia to the land of Canaan, and the latter had fixed his abode in Mount Seir.

10. The generations of Esau are next given, including his wives, his sons, and the dukes and kings who traced their lineage to him.

11. "The generations of Jacob" is the title of the last great section of the book, (beginning at chap. xxxii, 2,) giving in much detail the events of Jacob's later life, the history of Joseph, the conduct and character of the fathers of the twelve tribes, and their settlement in Egypt. The patriarch's dying prophecy (chap. xlix) reveals to his sons a vivid picture of what shall befall them in after times.

It will be noticed that the length of these several sections is in proportion to their relative importance in a history which lies at the basis of God's self-revelation to his chosen people. After the opening narrative of the creation, each series of generations goes back and attaches itself to a name or character introduced to us in the preceding section. Again and again the history, darkened by the growth and power of human wickedness, fastens upon a divinely chosen name, and from it takes a new departure. With each new departure some fresh hope or promise is given, or some great purpose of God is brought to light. While the tendency of the race is to grow worse and worse, there appears also the unwavering purpose of the Almighty to choose out and maintain a holy seed, and thus the Book of Genesis presents itself to us as an essential part of the history of redemption.

Use of the Names Elohim and Jehovah.

Of the authorship of Genesis, and the probable use of various documents and traditions in its composition, we have already sufficiently treated in discussing the Higher Criticism of the Pentateuch. But the peculiar use of the two divine names, ELOHIM and JEHOVAH, deserves some further notice. In the first section of the book, (i, 1–ii, 3,) which treats of the creative beginning, the name Elohim alone occurs; in the next (ii, 4–iv, 26) the double name Jehovah-Elohim is principally used; but Elohim occurs in the conversation between Eve and the serpent, (iii, 1–5,) and in Eve's words at the birth of Seth, (iv, 25;) and Jehovah alone is used elsewhere in chap. iv. In the "book of the generations of Adam" (v, 1–vi, 8) the use of Elohim prevails, but Jehovah occurs at v, 29, and at vi, 3, 6–8. In the section devoted to the generations of Noah, (vi, 9–ix, 29,) which contains the account of the flood, Elohim prevails almost exclusively, but Jehovah occurs seven times, namely, at vii, 1, 5, 16; viii, 20, 21, (*bis;*) ix, 26. In the generations of Noah's sons (x, 1–xi, 9) Jehovah is used exclusively, but the name occurs only in connexion with Nimrod (x, 9) and the tower of Babel, (xi, 5–9.) In the generations of Shem, (xi, 10–26,) Ishmael, (xxv, 12–18,) and Esau (xxxvi) no divine name occurs, but the history of Abraham, which is given under the generations of Terah, (xi, 27–xxv, 11,) is mainly Jehovistic, although Elohim and other divine names repeatedly appear, (Elohim especially in chaps. xvii, xx, xxi, and xxii,) and the histories of Isaac and Jacob, which take up the latter half of the Book of Genesis, are mainly Elohistic. After the beginning of Abraham's history, however, the interchange of names frequently appears, and the exclusive use of either Elohim or Jehovah in any given section is not particularly noticeable.

The critics have essayed to make a great deal more out of these names than a careful examination of their usage warrants. Outside of the first two sections, the numerous variations and the frequent interchange of one for the other are such as to cast doubt upon the current theories of Elohistic and Jehovistic *sources*. But the uniform use of Elohim in chaps. i–ii, 3, and of Jehovah-Elohim in chap. ii, is certainly notable. When, however, we observe that the symmetrical form of statements in narrating the successive works of the six days in chap. i required the use of the same name, it is evident that any change would have been more remarkable than the uniformity, and no reason would appear to account for it. On this view the change of divine names in the first and second sections becomes of less note.

Two methods of solution have been put forward. One maintains that this diversity of names is due to the use of different written documents in the compilation of the Book of Genesis. The Elohist sections are assumed to have been written by one who never used the name Jehovah, and was, indeed, ignorant of it. This view has in itself much plausibility, and receives strength from Exodus vi, 3, compared with Exod. iii, 13–15. But a strict exegesis of the passages in Exodus will not sustain the position that the name Jehovah was unknown as a divine title, or a designation of God, before the time of Moses. The thought is, rather, that the *significance* of the name Jehovah had not been revealed before. Moreover, it is not said or implied that even Elohim had been known before, but Jehovah is represented as saying to Moses that he had appeared to the patriarchs בְּאֵל שַׁדָּי, *in El-Shaddai*, that is, in the character of El-Shaddai, or God Almighty. What titles or designations and names of Deity had been in use before the time of Moses is not the point in question, and for aught that appears

INTRODUCTION TO THE BOOK OF GENESIS. 53

Jehovah is as ancient a name as Elohim. Fair criticism also requires us to allow a writer the benefit of his own explanations, and nothing is more apparent than that the writer of the Pentateuch, whoever he was and whenever he lived, understood that the name Jehovah was in use long before the time of Moses. Abraham called the place where he was about to offer Isaac Jehovah-jireh, (Gen. xxii, 14,) and, as far back as the birth of Seth, men called on the name of Jehovah. Gen. iv, 26. It is therefore both unnecessary and unfair to force upon Exod. vi, 3, a meaning which is inconsistent with other parts of the patriarchal history, and which the writer himself evidently did not understand as involving such inconsistency. Another and all-sufficient explanation can be given.

The opinion that these names denote the different sources from which the author of Genesis compiled his work, has against it the fact that the Elohistic and Jehovistic sections do not correspond with the eleven parts into which the book is divided. Whatever explanation we give to his use of the divine names, it is evident that the author constructed the plan of his work without any special deference to them. If his sources were characterized by the use of particular designations of the Deity, he himself so interchanged these terms in his own book as to make it impossible for any of his critics or readers to determine with certainty the limits of the original documents. The interchange of Jehovah, Elohim, El, and Shaddai in the other historical books, in the prophets, and in the Psalms, serves also to show that no valid conclusions can be drawn from such premises to determine the sources or the authorship of any of these books.

Others find the solution in the different meanings of the divine names. Elohim is a title rather than a name, denoting Deity in general, and is often used of false gods; Jehovah, on the other hand, is a proper name. Elohim designates God as the supreme power, the creator and general ruler. The plural form of the name denotes the majesty and manifold power of the God of creation and providence. Elohim, therefore, is used exclusively in the first section of Genesis, (i, 1–ii, 3,) where the account of creation is given. Jehovah, on the other hand, is the name of the covenant God, and designates the Deity in those more special aspects of his character in which he reveals himself as the source of law, of grace, and of condescending relationship to his chosen people. This opinion also has its plausibility, and is not without support in the noted passage Exod. vi, 3. No doubt all the divine names are capable of separate and distinct significance, just as the names Jesus and Christ in the New Testament have each a clearly distinguishable import; and there are passages and formulas in which one name is more suitable than the other. This peculiarity of meaning may largely explain the usage of Elohim and Jehovah in the first two sections of Genesis, but in other parts of the book it fails to account for the occurrence of one name rather than another. The elaborate and minute essays of Hengstenberg and others to carry out this theory are far from convincing, and many of their explanations of particular texts are manifestly farfetched and fanciful. We may say of these two methods of solution that they both contain some elements of truth, and yet as theories they both fail to account for all the facts apparent in the use of the names. The author of Genesis was thoroughly master of his sources of information; wrought out his work upon a well defined plan and with conspicuous unity; and was farthest possible from patching together a mass of ill adjusted documents, the origin and meaning of which he himself imperfectly comprehended. Such repetitions as appear in Gen. vii, 17–24, are not satisfactorily explained by supposing a conglomeration of written sources used by the compiler. If the repetition of statements be explained as a slovenly amalgamation of different documents, it involves the writer, whoever he was, in a charge of confusion and carelessness which itself, on such grounds, would sufficiently account for the repetitions in question. Surely the hypothesis of different documentary sources is not the only or the most satisfactory way of accounting for such repetition. In this passage, moreover, there is no mention of Elohim or Jehovah, or any other divine name.

While, therefore, we acknowledge in portions of the Book of Genesis a peculiar use of the names Elohim and Jehovah, we believe the methods of explanation described above fail to account for all the facts involved. They may each be allowed some measure of value in the interpretation of particular passages; but there are many more passages where the occurrence of one or the other of the names is more naturally explained as having no special significance, but as arising from a familiar use of both names, just as we say Jesus, or Christ, or Jesus Christ, without being conscious of any intent to use one title rather than another. Sometimes the interchange is probably designed for the sake of variety of expression.

Genuineness and Value of the Book of Genesis.

The genuineness and credibility of this book are evinced by its minute and lifelike portraiture of persons, places, and events, and by its fundamental historical relation to the entire development of the plan of human redemption. If God has revealed himself in the history, prophecy, and symbolism of the other Old Testament books, and in the Gospel of Jesus Christ, it is manifest that the Book of Genesis supplies an indispensable link in this chain of revelation. The simple, straightforward, and artless manner in which the narrative portions are written,

INTRODUCTION TO THE BOOK OF GENESIS. 55

the accuracy of topographical and geographical descriptions, the incidental allusions, the genealogies and vivid outlines of personal character, are so many internal proofs of the trustworthiness of the book. These facts, taken in connexion with the other, namely, that the whole subsequent divine revelation looks back to this early history and recognises it as "the beginning," stand opposed to all theories which would make the contents of Genesis a tissue of myths or legends.

The contents of this ancient book, whether considered as throwing invaluable light on the beginnings of human history or as revealing the preparatory steps and sublime displays of the redemption of Christ, are of unspeakable importance. We admire the lofty monotheism apparent from the beginning; the unique grandeur of the account of creation; the orderly progress and commanding wisdom which stand out so prominently in the details of the first historic week, opening with the light of God and ending with the holy Sabbath rest. The narrative of man in the garden of Eden is too simple and artless to be considered as a myth, an allegory, or a fiction. The sin and punishment of the first pair, taken in connexion with the promise of the redeeming Seed, and the symbols of final glorification and of flaming justice placed at the gate of Eden to watch the way of the tree of life, are too profound and apocalyptic to be conceptions of human origin. The same may be said of the continued contrasts between the degenerate heathen world and the chosen seed, which constitute so prominent a feature of the history.

The line of Cain stands opposed, first, to Abel, and then to Seth, who was appointed in his stead. Again the whole race run to evil and perish by the flood, but Noah and his household escape the ruin—another striking contrast. The descendants of Shem, blessed of Jehovah, rise in moral power above those of Ham and Japheth; and again of the race of Shem, Terah has preeminence. As the families and tribes multiply and become scattered abroad, Abraham is chosen out of country, kindred, and even his father's house, to be the great father of a holy seed, and obtains the covenant and promise of redemption. The same great plan and purpose appear in the history of Isaac and Jacob; and, unless we keep this theocratic conception in mind, we lose much of the power and significance of the relations of these patriarchs to the nations and individuals with whom they come in contact. And with this series of contrasts and revelations how much true light is shed upon the beginnings of history! Where can be found a tablet, inscription, or record comparable for antiquarian and ethnological value with the generations of Noah's sons in chapter x? How remarkable, that recently deciphered inscriptions from the stones of the Euphrates valley and vicinity confirm and illustrate the account of the battle of the kings narrated in chapter xiv! How the judgments of the flood and of Sodom and Gomorrah are typical of the various penal judgments of all after time! How the dreams of the patriarchs, and their migrations and sacrifices, are prophetic of the richest experiences and holiest hopes of men! Surely, he must be perversely blind who fails to see, in these and other facts of Genesis, both records and revelations of incalculable value.

The Narrative of the Creation.

The exposition of the first chapter of Genesis has occupied so large a place in modern biblical and apologetical literature as to require a fuller treatment than our notes on that chapter will allow. In order, therefore, to furnish the reader with some account of the various views which have been propounded, and at the same time not to disturb the unity of our comments on the text itself, we introduce at this place a special section on the so called "biblical cosmogony."

That this ancient document presents grave difficulties to the exegete no thoughtful reader questions. Long before scientific research had made evident the great age of our planet, and the order and magnitude of the solar system, discerning minds had recognised such difficulties as that of light appearing three days before the sun, and the production of dry land and vegetation before the creation of sun, moon, and stars. Augustine spoke in wonder of days without luminaries, and called them unutterable days, (*dies ineffabiles.*) But when the study of geology and astronomy became more fully developed, there began to be heard whisperings of an irreconcilable conflict between science and revelation, and thereupon followed a great variety of explanations and attempts to harmonize the biblical record with the testimony of the rocks and the stars. Some were bold to affirm that the fossiliferous rocks were originally created, with all their imbedded skeletons, just as they now appear. Others suggested that the fossil deposits were made during the period between the creation and the deluge; while others argued that they were caused by the deluge itself. All these notions have been effectually exploded, and are now unworthy of attention, except as indicating the history of opinion and controversy.

The more recent treatment of these questions may be classified under four heads, representing so many different hypotheses or methods of explanation. We designate them, respectively, as geological, cosmological, idealistic, and grammatico-historical interpretations.

1. The first named theory has for its principal distinctive feature the idea that the days of Genesis correspond with so many long periods of geological development traceable in the crust of the earth. Some tell us that the word *day* is used in Scripture in a figurative way to denote an indefinite period of time, and such passages as John viii, 56,

INTRODUCTION TO THE BOOK OF GENESIS. 57

and 2 Peter iii, 8, are cited as examples: "Abraham rejoiced to see my day;" "One day is with the Lord as a thousand years." Hugh Miller advanced the theory that the sacred writer saw the works of the successive days of creation pass in vision as so many pictures before his eye, and he undertook to show how the creations of the third, fifth, and sixth days of Genesis harmonized with so many periods of geological development. Of the works of the first, second, and fourth days he claimed that we should not expect to find any trace or record in the rocks. (*Testimony of the Rocks*, p. 159.) Prof. C. H. Hitchcock argues in favour of what he calls the symbolical theory of the six days, and regards the days not as denoting primarily long periods, but as symbolical of previous periods of unknown length. The word day is, accordingly, not taken in its literal sense, but interpreted as a time-symbol of a past æon. (*Bibliotheca Sacra*, vol. xxiv, 1867, pp. 433, 434; compare also *Bibliotheca Sacra*, vol. xiv, p. 81, and vol. xvii, p. 689.) We observe, in reference to these various forms of presenting the geological theory, that, with all their laboured essays to make a day mean an æon or long period, its advocates have not been able to adduce a single parallel Scripture in which the term "day" is thus employed. The indefinite and metaphorical use of the word in such isolated texts as those above cited cannot be fairly quoted as illustrating its meaning in a straightforward narrative of the work of six successive days, which have each an evening and a morning. Moreover, this theory confessedly fails to find exact or even substantial agreement between the days of Genesis and the eras of geology. Hugh Miller's evasion of responsibility for finding a solution of the work of three of the days is any thing but satisfactory, and shows that in practical application his theory breaks down. There is also a glaring incongruity in identifying the vegetation of the third day with the coal beds of our mountains, and the animal races of waters, sky, and land over which man was to have dominion with the monster tribes which had become largely, if not altogether, extinct before man appeared. It scarcely relieves this difficulty to say that the biblical record refers only to the periods when these several forms of vegetable and animal life first appeared, for the common understanding will still insist that the fruit tree yielding fruit for man cannot well mean the coal beds which supply his fuel, nor can the animal tribes subject to his sway be the extinct specimens found only in the fossiliferous rocks. Of what possible use could it be in the volume of divine inspiration to reveal the origin of extinct plants and animals whose existence was never recognised by man until thousands of years after his creation? The average skeptical mind will not feel much force in Professor Hitchcock's supposition, that "the creative chapter was designed at the outset to confirm the truth of the sacred

58 INTRODUCTION TO THE BOOK OF GENESIS.

narrative in a remote skeptical age." (*Bibliotheca Sacra*, vol. xxiv, 1867, p. 436.)

2. A more fascinating and impressive method of harmonizing Genesis and science is that which employs the nebular hypothesis of the solar system as a means of solution, and identifies the days with vast cosmogonic ages of development. This theory we may appropriately designate the cosmological. It supposes that the primordial creation first brought into existence the material or substance of the universe. This was a vast nebulous mass, without form and void, inert and dark. Then motion was imparted by the divine word, and, as the necessary result of molecular action, there was cosmical light through the whole vast nebula. The systems and planets were flung off one by one, each separate mass becoming in time a sphere, and thus our planetary system was first one vast nebulous substance, from which the outer planets and their satellites were the first to become detached, and so the process continued until the sun, the remaining central mass, became too much solidified to fling off any more planets. Our earth having been, like the other planets, detached, in due time cooled until it became opaque, after which time its axial revolution would cause day and night. So the first day of creation commenced with the earliest movement of the cosmical nebula, which then included the sun and all the planets, and closed when light and darkness were divided on the earth by its diurnal rotation. The second period was one of combined igneous and aqueous action, which resulted in depositing waters on the earth's surface, clearing a transparent space or expanse above them, and causing the exhalations to rise in clouds to the upper atmosphere, thus forming the waters below and the waters above the firmament. According to Prof. Warring, (*The Mosaic Account of Creation the Miracle of To-Day*, New York, 1875,) the fourth day was the epoch when the present inclination of the earth's axis took place, resulting in a change of seasons, and unequal days and nights. Then and thus the sun and moon were appointed to measure seasons, and to rule the day and the night. This inclination he supposes to have been caused by the attraction of the sun and moon on polar upheavals during the glacial period. In treating the fifth and sixth days this theory follows essentially that of Hugh Miller and his school. This theory is ably set forth and advocated by Prof. Guyot in various essays, and in his volume on *Creation; or, The Biblical Cosmogony in the Light of Modern Science*, (New York, 1884.) He regards the days as vast cosmogonic ages, and calls them "organic phases of creation." He treats the word earth as "equivalent to matter in general," and affirms that in Genesis i, 2, it means "the primordial cosmic material out of which God was going to organize the heavens and the earth." Other distinguished scientists of recent times (Win-

chell, Dana, Dawson) have favoured this cosmological method of explaining Genesis, and while each has his own way of stating his views, they agree in the main outlines given above. The chief thought with all is, cosmical and geological development.

The nebular hypothesis of the origin of the universe appears to have very much in its favour, and we see no good reason why God might not have produced the world in that way, as well as in any other imaginable. Atheistic evolution is conspicuously inconsistent not only with the beginning of Genesis, but with the entire biblical revelation; but theistic evolution is not to be condemned without a patient hearing. Our objection to this cosmical exposition of Genesis arises from no feeling that the nebular hypothesis is unsound or untenable. We believe it is not yet proven, but its main points may be true, and the theory itself may yet prove itself to be of the highest scientific value. Our conviction is, that it furnishes no sound or satisfactory explanation of the first chapter of Genesis. So far as it coincides with the geological exposition already noticed, we urge against it the same objections. It is ever twisting words out of their natural and established usage, and importing into them the conceptions of modern science. It violates one of the first principles of sound interpretation, which requires us to place ourselves in the position of the writer and his first readers; and we are not aware that any one seriously believes that the ancients entertained such conceptions as this theory attaches to the biblical record, or reads between its lines.

Taking up the different views of particular writers, we find varying individual opinions, which are often difficult to accept. Prof. Warring, for example, makes the work of the first day extend from the first flash of cosmical light in the vast nebula to the time when our planet became opaque, after which the days were measured by the axial revolution of the earth. The days, he holds, are literal days, but vast cosmogonic periods are to be understood as preceding them, and terminating in them. Prof. Guyot affirms that in the first two chapters of Genesis the word "day" is used in five different senses! But not to lay stress on individual notions, we may say in general that all these writers ignore in the main the miraculous element so noticeable in the biblical narrative. Admitting that God is to be recognised as the great Cause back of all these evolutions, they nevertheless proceed to treat the creation throughout as a development from natural causes. There is such a lugging in of what may be called naturalism that we become suspicious of the whole procedure as a legitimate exposition of Scripture. We notice this tendency also in writers who do not commit themselves to any scientific theory. A leading doctrine of Tayler Lewis, in his work on the *Six Days of Creation*, (Schenectady, 1855,) is that these days are long, indefinite periods with supernatural beginnings, followed by natural growths. "From a higher world than the natural there was an occasional sudden flashing in of the extraordinary, of the supernatural, of a new morning after the long night of nature," but each of these divine interpositions was "followed again by a long rest, sleep, or night, as we may call it, of nature's tardy growth," (page 98.) Also in an article in the *Methodist Quarterly Review*, (for 1865, page 207,) he calls the events of creation "a series of supernatural growths," but explains them as natural processes. All this may not be in itself objectionable, and is as harmless as all other poetical fancies which recognise the supernatural above and beyond all natural phenomena; but when applied to the exposition of Genesis, it seems to us to make the whole record a riddle, and to resolve the interpretation into a series of transcendental fancies. We hesitate at such methods, and feel that if these modern theorists are correct the ancient writer made a great mistake in his style of recording facts. We turn away and ask, Is there not some other and better way of explaining this unique but simple narrative ?

3. Another class of interpreters, not satisfied with the methods and dubious results of the theories above described, have adopted what we call the idealistic method of exposition. They lay stress upon the correspondencies of the double triad of creative days, claim a measured poetic rhythm in the construction, and conclude that the successive days of creation furnish us with an order of thought rather than of actual or accurate chronology. This view is set forth by Mr. Rorison in an essay on the "Creative Week," (in *Replies to Essays and Reviews*,) and by Prof. B. F. Cocker, in his volume on *The Theistic Conception of the World*, (New York, 1875.) It is favoured by the manifest symmetry of the works of the several days, and a structure which conforms to some of the usual features of Hebrew parallelism. The first chapter of Genesis may, perhaps, be appropriately called the "Inspired Psalm of Creation," and be treated as a most ancient poem, peculiarly adapted for transmission by oral tradition through many generations. But such admissions do not affect the question of the author's meaning. The artificial form and symmetrical structure of a narrative do not change the import of a writer's words. Mr. Rorison's exposition transfigures the days "from registers of time into definitives of strophes or stanzas—lamps and landmarks of a creative sequence—a mystic drapery, a parabolic setting—shadowing by the sacred cycle of seven the truths of an ordered progress, a foreknown finality, an achieved perfection, and a divine repose." (*Replies*, etc., p. 290.) This style of interpretation carries its followers out of the region of fact into a realm of fancy. It opens a field for all manner of dreamy speculations, but as a fair interpretation of the language employed in Genesis i, it is utterly

INTRODUCTION TO THE BOOK OF GENESIS.

unsatisfactory. Our writer's statements are too specific, and his narrative altogether too prosaic to allow an interpreter the license of "transfiguring" and "draping" his words in idealistic fancies so far removed from the range of Hebrew thought and feeling.

4. The grammatico-historical interpretation insists upon the literal and most obvious import of the words of the sacred writer. It maintains that the language employed to describe the firmament or expanse in verses 6–8, and the sun and moon in verses 16–18, is not scientific but popular, and the interpreter should not exercise his ingenuity to discover reconciliations between these phenomenal descriptions and the results of learned research, but transfer himself to the standpoint of the ancient Hebrew writer, attend to the exact meaning of his words, and obtain as far as possible the ideas he intended to express.

This method of interpretation is followed in the main by those who adopt what is commonly known as the Chalmerian hypothesis, or renovation theory of expounding Genesis and geology. This hypothesis supposes the first verse of Genesis to state the primordial creation of the universe; but between the first and the second verse it allows indefinite ages for the geological development of the earth. It maintains that between these verses, or between the first and third, we may admit the existence of as many ages and successive races or creations as the results of scientific research require, but with all this the biblical writer was not concerned. It is believed that immediately before the introduction of man upon the earth there was a period of geological catastrophe, attended by the general, if not universal, destruction of then existing vegetable and animal life. Geological science recognises several such catastrophes in long past ages, and it is assumed that the creation described in Genesis was the renovation and reconstruction of things at the beginning of the present human period. This view was set forth by Chalmers in 1804; it was ably advocated by Buckland in his Bridgewater Treatise; and is adopted by many exegetes of Germany, Great Britain, and America. We believe that no valid argument can be brought against it on the ground of grammatical exegesis, for it violates no usage of words, and conforms to established principles of interpretation. Tayler Lewis, indeed, has made the charge that such a separation between the first and second verses "violates the principles of a rational and grammatical exegesis," (Lange's Genesis, Am. ed., p. 168,) but the passage he cites (Job i, 1) does not fairly confirm his position, for it is perfectly supposable that many years might have elapsed between the time when Job first appeared in the land of Uz and the time when he became perfect and upright. But this question is not to be settled solely by the usage of the verb הָיָה. We are rather to inquire if anywhere in Hebrew usage two closely connected verbs relating to one general subject allow an indefinite period of time, and other events than those predicated, to be supposed between them. A pertinent example is Exod. ii, 1, 2, where it is said in the first verse that Moses's father "went and took a daughter of Levi," and, in the next sentence, "and the woman conceived and bare a son." The context shows that this son was Moses, and that many years elapsed between the two events, during which time Miriam and Aaron were born to these same parents; but who would have imagined it, from the language used in these two verses? So it is idle for any one to say that the Chalmerian hypothesis would never have been seriously maintained but for the difficulties of geology. The statement is true, but it is no valid objection; for it may as truly be said that it would never have been seriously supposed, solely from Exod. ii, 1, 2, that twelve or fifteen years and the birth of two other children are to be understood as coming between these two closely connected verses.

Weightier objections are urged against this renovation theory on other grounds. It is affirmed by the highest authorities that there is no evidence of such a universal catastrophe as this exposition supposes immediately before the appearance of man on earth. If this be so, it must be seen to lie heavily against an interpretation which requires such a state of things at the beginning of the present period. It may also be urged against this theory that it imposes upon our faith a dubious strain. We are required to believe that, as preparatory to the formation of man, all the continents, islands, and oceans of our globe were at once upheaved and divided off, and all living species of fish, bird, beast, and cattle, together with all vegetable creations, in all zones and climates, were produced in two or three ordinary days. We are ever ready to accept the record of the miraculous, and can admit without scruple that, with omnipotence, all this was possible; but we frankly confess that this range and extent of miracle are out of all proportion to the conditions under which the first man appears to have been formed.

These difficulties connected with the universal renovation theory of creation led John Pye Smith to suggest a more natural explanation of the biblical narrative. In his work on the *Relation Between the Holy Scriptures and Some Parts of Geological Science*, (4th ed., Lond., 1848,) he showed, by a variety of evidence, "that there must have been separate original creations, perhaps at different and respectively distant epochs," (p. 49.) He also maintained that a strict interpretation of the language of Genesis required no wider application of its terms than to "the part of our world which God was adapting for the dwelling of man and the animals connected with him. Of the spheroidal figure of the earth, it is evident that the Hebrews had not the most distant conception." He understood the *land* or *earth* of Gen. i to be only "a portion of the surface of the earth, adjusted and furnished for most glorious purposes, in which a newly formed creation should be the object of those manifestations of the authority and grace of the Most High which shall, to eternity, show forth his perfections above all other methods of their display," (pp. 189, 190.) This view of the biblical creation has not obtained general favour, but we have searched in vain to find a single valid argument against it. The only objections we have seen are, first, the *a priori* assumption that it belittles the idea of divine creation to limit this grand picture to a limited portion of the earth, and, second, that it is inconsistent with the words of the fourth commandment. To which it may be most effectually replied, that no interpreter has a right to come to the exposition of the first of Genesis with any *a priori* assumptions of what ought to be found there. Prof. Barrows says, that "it is hard to bring it into harmony with the spirit of the narrative, which almost irresistibly inclines one, in the words of Hugh Miller, 'to look for a broader and more general meaning . . . than I could recognise it as forming, were I assured it referred to but one of many existing creations—a creation restricted to, mayhap, a few hundred square miles of country, and to, mayhap, a few scores of animals and plants.'" We submit that what is here called "the spirit of the narrative" is rather the spirit of the interpreter himself, who is so freighted with cosmical and geological ideas of the magnitude of the universe that he reads them into the language of the old Hebrew writer. Nothing, in fact, is more conspicuous in the treatment of this subject by modern Christian scientists than their persistent *a priori* assumptions that the biblical creation must needs be identical with the primordial universal cosmogony. We hope to show, in our notes on Gen. i and ii, that the language of the sacred writer does not warrant such assumptions.

The other objection is, that this limited conception is inconsistent with the words of the fourth commandment, which declares that "in six days Jehovah made heaven and earth, the sea, and all that in them is," (Exod. xx, 11.) It might be replied that this objection comes with an ill grace from those who make the six days mean six cosmogonic æons. They are the last exegetes who should venture to press the literal import of these words, for the obvious meaning is utterly inconsistent with their hypothesis. For if the "six days" of Exod. xx, 11, mean six indefinitely long ages, the "third day" of Exod. xix, 15, 16, ought to have like meaning, and untold generations should be included in the period referred to in Matt. xvii, 1: "After six days Jesus taketh," etc. But when we observe the stress placed on the words "all that in them *is*," we note the worthlessness of the objection.

Does this mean "all that in them *is*," or "all that in them" *was?* The Hebrew is כָּל־אֲשֶׁר־בָּם, *all which—in them.* There is no connecting verb expressed, and why supply *is* rather than *was?* If Jehovah, speaking at Sinai to Moses and the thousands of Israel there assembled, must be understood as affirming that in six days he made all that *is* in heaven and earth and sea, he must have included those Israelites, and all their cattle and effects.

Here, then, is a new revelation. We must henceforth understand between the lines of Genesis i, 24–27, not Adam and his wife only, and the cattle, etc., by which they were surrounded, and to which Adam gave names (ii, 20,) but the Israelites, Egyptians, and all other things in existence at the time this commandment was uttered at Sinai! Plainly, the "all in them" of Exodus xx, 11, refers to all which the creative narrative in Genesis describes, nothing more, nothing less. The words simply mean that in six days God did what he is said to have done in Gen. i, 1–ii, 3, and the heavens, land, sea, and all in them, mean in the one passage precisely what they do in the other. It is, therefore, begging the whole question, and carrying all the *a priori* assumptions named above into it, when this objection is offered. We appeal from all such assumptions and prejudgments to the strict meaning of the language of the sacred writer, and insist that before any conclusion is formed we first ascertain the *usus loquendi* of the Hebrew words for *heavens* and *earth*, and, as far as possible, the ancient Hebrew conceptions of the world. Nothing, in our view, seems so improper and misleading as to come to the interpretation of such an ancient writing loaded with the discoveries of modern science, and seeking to find them outlined by a writer who could have had no such knowledge. The idea that, because this record was given by inspiration of God, we may expect to find superhuman wisdom in it, is pressed altogether too far when we assume that its language is not to be interpreted in accordance with the *usus loquendi* of an age and people who knew little or nothing about modern science.

In the following notes on the narrative of creation, we adopt no hypothesis, and commit the exposition to no theory. We follow the grammatico-historical sense of the language, and where this involves difficulties, we make no effort to conceal them. We show that the words שָׁמַיִם and אֶרֶץ, *heavens* and *earth*, into which we have become so accustomed to read the stupendous results of scientific research, mean, according to the *usus loquendi* of the writer of Genesis, what we would now more naturally express by the terms *sky* and *land*, or climate and soil. Having once transferred ourself to the age and conceptions of the early world, there seems to us a monstrous incongruity in the interpretation which supposes the land, visible sky, surrounding waters, and vegetable and animal species by which the first man was encompassed, to mean all the continents and islands of the globe, the astronomic universe, with its cosmical history, and all the oceans, and plants, and living organisms (even of the fossiliferous rocks) which modern science has brought to our knowledge. A portion of land no larger than the Malay peninsula or the island of Ceylon would have been sufficient for the entire human race before the Noachic deluge. Why, then, load down this simple narrative by lugging into it all our modern ideas of the cosmos? The language of the writer and the very conditions of the case are against the assumption of a universal cosmogony. Far more natural is it to think here of the sky, climate, and soil where the first human pair were created. The most natural import of the narrative is, that God miraculously prepared the Edenic region for the residence of man, and that such scenery and surroundings as are described by the sacred writer were the primeval conditions under which he was placed. Subsequently, when mankind became corrupt, and that land was filled with violence, (vi, 11,) the fountains of the great deep were broken up, and that land was submerged with all its tribes except what Noah's ark preserved. At the subsidence of the deluge, the ark rested, not again in Eden, but on the mountain of Ararat, probably far remote, perhaps thousands of miles from the place where it was builded. The original Eden was probably obliterated by the flood, but the names of its countries and rivers would have been preserved in tradition, and naturally transferred to the new land and rivers discovered and occupied by the sons of Noah.

This interpretation, as Hugh Miller observes, "virtually removes Scripture altogether out of the field of geology;" and it does so, not by erecting a hypothesis to meet supposed exigencies, but by following the strict meaning of the language. It maintains that the biblical creation is only that which attended the introduction of man upon the earth, and, therefore, essentially of limited extent. What had taken place on other portions of the globe, or what classes of living creatures existed before or at the time of this beginning of human life, are questions remote from the purpose of the biblical narrative. How and when God created matter, and what were the first forms and modes of life—whether vegetable, animal, or angelic—it appears not the purpose of revelation to inform us ; but this beginning of the Bible does inform us of the miraculous creation of man in the image of God, and the conditions and environments of his first estate. As a more careful attention to the usage of Hebrew terms and the nature of things has led nearly all modern exegetes to abandon the notion that the Noachic deluge was universal, so we believe a closer study of the Hebrew text of the first and second chapters of Genesis will set aside the idea that those chapters were designed to describe a universal cosmogony.

This interpretation, recognising the specific reality of all that is here recorded, maintains all the great doctrines of God the Creator as clearly as any of the more pretentious expositions, and by a more valid implication. (See concluding notes at end of chapter ii.) The entire conception is taken, not from the position of a modern scientist, nor from a heavenly point of vision as of one who observed the construction and movements of the sidereal universe, but from the position of the first man, who looked above and around him, and might well have asked the origin of the things which he beheld. Nothing in this picture of creation necessarily goes beyond what was visible from the garden of Eden. So far as the terms used indicate universality they must be understood of the whole creation as known to the first man. Tayler Lewis admits "that the author of the account in Genesis probably regarded himself as describing the creation of *the all*, since to his knowledge our immediate earth and heaven, with the phenomenal luminaries appearing as fixed in it and belonging to it were the all; but that he meant to tell us of the first matter even of this, or of its coming out of nothing, cannot be certainly determined by any etymology of words, or by any infallible exegesis of the passage. There are certainly some things that look the other way."—(*Lange's Commentary on Genesis*, Am. ed., p. 128.) Further on he adds: "The argument or implication is: He who made light to be at one place or time made it to be at all times, even at that time which was the absolute beginning of its existence; He who made the human spirit must have made all spirits, whether coeval with or immeasurably more ancient than man."

As to the origin of the biblical narrative of creation, and the manner in which the details were made known to man, we have no knowledge, and any reasonable hypothesis is admissible. We dismiss as unsatisfactory and inconsistent with the implication of divine revelation the theory of many modern writers, (Tuch, Dillmann, Lenormant, Ladd,) that this narrative is merely a monotheistic improvement upon the traditional cosmogonies current among the ancient nations. We may properly ask: Is this account of creation true or false? Is it a revelation of what God did, or merely the dream, the ideal conjecture, of some ancient Leibnitz or Pythagoras? Prof. Ladd, in his *Doctrine of Sacred Scripture*, (vol. i, p. 272,) informs us, with the air of one who seems to know all about it, that "the traditional cosmogony of the Hebrews preceding this account, probably told of eight or more separate works of creation. But this author has fused and moulded the ideas of the traditional cosmogony according to the idea of God which entered into his own exalted monotheism, and as well according

INTRODUCTION TO THE BOOK OF GENESIS.

to the Sabbath idea." That is, as appears from the scope of his argument, the Hebrew writer picked up the floating heathen traditions of the East, and shaped them into what he considered a becoming form. It is, therefore, essentially a human invention, and at best only an improvement of "the cosmogonies of the other nations, which originated in their observations of nature as interpreted by philosophic and religious conceptions." And yet the writer of the above considers the theory of Chalmers, especially as modified by Pye Smith, "dangerous to the very life of religious doctrine"(!) and suggests (p. 267) that he must be a notorious errorist who conceives "the *Tohu va-bhohu* of the Mosaic cosmogony" in any other light than as "representing the universal star dust from which all worlds came!" We venture to suggest that such a theory as that of Pye Smith, which makes no "attempt at *reconciliation*," because it finds no "universal star dust" in the narrative or conceptions of the sacred writer, conserves "the very life of religious doctrine" far more nobly than the theory which insists on seeing "universal star dust" there, and, of course, as a necessary consequence, finds "the Mosaic cosmogony at variance with several valid conclusions of modern astronomy and geology," and containing "many errors of fact and faults of conception,"(p. 284.) Is it not the great trouble of all this class of writers that their eyes are too full of "star dust?"

We adopt as a more reasonable hypothesis—one more in keeping with the idea of divine revelation, and far less dangerous to the life of religious doctrine—that this biblical narrative is no imitation of heathen cosmogonies, and no attempt to revise or improve them, but rather the original picture from which they were traditionally derived, and were afterward mixed with legendary and incongruous accretions. Until some valid reason to the contrary be shown, we shall accept the doctrine that man was originally created upright, in the image of God, and that this account of his creation was probably communicated to him in the same way as that by which he received the law recorded in Gen. ii, 16, 17. This hypothesis, in its full analysis, logically and necessarily begins and ends in supernaturalism ; the other hypothesis, described above, as logically and necessarily begins and ends in naturalism.

OUTLINE OF CONTENTS.

I. The Creative Beginning, i-ii, 3.
1) Light. 2) Heavens. 3) Land, Seas, and Vegetation. 4) Luminaries. 5) Fish and Fowls. 6) Animals and Man. 7) Sabbath.

II. The Generations of the Heavens and the Land, ii, 4-iv, 26.
Man in the Garden of Eden, ii, 1-25. First Sin, iii, 1-24. Cain and Abel, iv, 1-15. Cainites, iv, 16-24. Seth and Enos, iv, 25, 26.

III. Book of the Generations of Adam, v, 1-vi, 8.
Sethite Genealogy from Adam to Noah, v, 1-32. Antediluvian Wickedness, vi, 1-8.

IV. The Generations of Noah, vi, 9-ix, 29.
History of the Deluge, vi, 9-viii, 22. Covenant with Noah, ix, 1-17. Prophecy of Noah, ix, 18-29.

V. The Generations of Shem, Ham, and Japheth, x, 1-xi, 9.
Genealogy of Nations, x, 1-32. Confusion of Tongues, xi, 1-9.

VI. The Generations of Shem, xi, 10-26.

VII. The Generations of Terah, xi, 27-xxv, 11.
Migration from Ur, xi, 28-32. Call of Abram, xii, 1-3. Abram in Canaan, xii, 4-9. Abram in Egypt, xii, 10-20. Return from Egypt, xiii, 1-4. Separation of Abram and Lot, xiii, 5-13. Promise Renewed to Abram, xiii, 14-18. Invasion of the Eastern Kings, xiv, 1-12. Abram's Military Victory, xiv, 13-16. Abram and Melchizedek, xiv, 17-20. Abram and the King of Sodom, xiv, 21-24. God's fuller Revelation to Abram, xv, 1-21. Hagar and Ishmael, xvi, 1-16. The Covenant of Circumcision, xvii, 1-27. Entertaining Angels, xviii, 1-15. Abraham's Intercession for Sodom, xviii, 16-33. Lot Rescued by Angels, xix, 1-23. Destruction of Sodom and Gomorrah, xix, 24-28. Lot's Infamous Daughters, xix, 29-38. Abraham and Abimelech, xx, 1-18. Birth of Isaac, xxi, 1-8. Expulsion of Hagar and Ishmael, xxi, 9-21. Covenant between Abraham and Abimelech, xxi, 22-34. Offering of Isaac, xxii, 1-19. Nahor's Children, xxii, 20-24. Death and Burial of Sarah, xxiii, 1-20. Isaac's Marriage, xxiv, 1-67. Abraham's Sons by Keturah, xxv, 1-6. Death and Burial of Abraham, xxv, 7-11.

VIII. The Generations of Ishmael, xxv, 12-18.

IX. The Generations of Isaac, xxv, 19-xxxv, 29.
Birth of Esau and Jacob, xxv, 19-26. Sale of Esau's Birthright, xxv, 27-34. Isaac and Abimelech, xxvi, 1-33. Esau's Marriage, xxvi, 34, 35. Isaac Blessing his Sons, xxvii, 1-40. Jacob's Departure to Haran, xxvii, 41-xxviii, 5. Esau Marries Mahalath, xxviii, 6-9. Jacob at Bethel, xxviii, 10-22. Jacob's Arrival at Haran, xxix, 1-14. Jacob's Double Marriage, xxix, 15-30. Leah's First Four Sons, xxix, 31-35. Sons of Bilhah and Zilpah, xxx, 1-13. Other Children of Leah, xxx, 14-21. Birth of Joseph, xxx, 22-24. Jacob's Artifice, xxx, 37-43. Jacob's New Bargain with Laban, xxx, 25-36. Jacob's Flight from Padan-Aram, xxxi, 1-21. Laban's Pursuit, and Covenant with Jacob, xxxi, 22-55. Jacob at Mahanaim and Peniel, xxxii, 1-32. Meeting of Jacob and Esau, xxxiii, 1-16. Jacob at Shechem, xxxiii, 17-20. Troubles with Hamor and Shechem, xxxiv, 1-31. Jacob again at Bethel, xxxv, 1-15. Death of Rachel, xxxv, 16-20. Reuben's Incest, xxxv, 21, 22. List of Jacob's Sons, xxxv, 23-26. Isaac's Death and Burial, xxxv, 27-29.

X. The Generations of Esau, xxxvi, 1-43.
Esau's Wives and Children, and their Removal to Mount Seir, xxxvi, 1-8. Sons and Grandsons of Esau as Heads of Tribes, xxxvi, 9-14. Dukes of Esau, xxxvi, 15-19. Sons of Seir the Horite, xxxvi, 20-30. Kings of Edom, xxxvi, 31-39. Dukes of Esau, after their Places, xxxvi, 40-43.

XI. The Generations of Jacob, xxxvii-l.
Joseph and his Dreams, xxxvii, 1-11. Joseph Sold into Egypt, xxxvii, 12-36. Family of Judah, xxxviii. 1-30. Joseph in Slavery and in Prison, xxxix, 1-23. Dreams of the Butler and of the Baker, xl, 1-23. Dreams of Pharaoh, xli, 1-8. Joseph Interprets Pharaoh's Dreams, xli, 9-36. Joseph Made Overseer of Egypt, xli, 35-57. Joseph's First Meeting with his Brethren, xlii, 1-38. Second Journey to Egypt for Food, xliii, 1-15. Reception and Feast at Joseph's House, xliii, 16-34. Further Troubles, and Judah's Appeal, xliv, 1-34. Recognition and the Message to Jacob, xlv, 1-28. Journey to Egypt, xlvi, 1-7. Muster-Roll of Israel, xlvi, 8-27. Israel in Egypt, xlvi, 28-34. Introduction to Pharaoh and Settlement in Egypt, xlvii, 1-12. Joseph's Administration during the Years of Famine, xlvii, 13-26. Jacob's Desire to be Buried with his Fathers, xlvii, 27-31. Adoption and Blessing of Joseph's Sons, xlviii, 1-22. Jacob's Prophetic Blessing on his Sons, xlix, 1-27. Death of Jacob, xlix, 28-33. Funeral of Jacob, l, 1-14. Fears of Joseph's Brethren, l, 15-21. Death of Joseph, l, 22-26.

THE BOOK OF GENESIS.

CHAPTER I.

IN the ᵃbeginning ᵇGod created the heaven and the earth. 2 And the earth was without form, and void; and dark-

---
a John 1. 1, 2; Heb. 1. 10.——b Psa. 8. 3; 33. 6; 89. 11, 12; 102. 25; 136. 5; 146. 6; Isa. 44. 24; Jer. 10. 12; 51. 15; Zech. 12. 1; Acts 14. 15; 17. 24; Col. 1. 16, 17; Heb. 11. 3; Rev. 4. 11; 10. 6.

CHAPTER I.
The Creative Beginning, i–ii.

Verse 1 is to be taken as a heading to the present section, (i, 1–ii, 3,) corresponding to the headings of the other sections. Comp. chap. ii, 4; v, 1; vi, 9; x, 1; xi, 10, etc. This first section has not the common formula, "These are the generations," etc.: for this first chapter is a history of *creations*, not of *generations*. This is a distinction to be kept constantly in mind. See below, on verse 2, and notes on chap. ii, 4.

In the following notes an effort is made to indicate as fully as practicable the grammatico-historical meaning of the language of this most ancient Scripture. The world is full of attempts to "reconcile Genesis and geology:" we assume no such task, but endeavour to keep prominent the query, whether the vast amount of learned labour bestowed upon such attempted reconciliation has not been wasted over a false issue. Our exposition does not essay to solve the mysteries of creation, but merely to determine, as far as the original meaning and usage of his words admit, the most obvious import of the Hebrew writer's language. See Introduction, pp. 56–67.

1. **In the beginning**—At the commencement of that series of events with which the creation and history of the human race are associated. Here is no necessary reference to the origin of matter, but simply to the opening of an epoch. **God created**—בָּרָא אֱלֹהִים; a plural noun with a singular verb. Some have supposed this plural form of the name of God to be a relic of primitive polytheism, but its construc- tion here with a verb in the singular, and its frequent use in the Hebrew Scriptures as the name of the One only God, forbids such a conclusion. The plural form of the name denotes rather the manifold fulness of power and excellency that exists in God. Not without reason have many Christian divines suggested that in this plural of majesty may also be an intimation of the plurality of persons in the Godhead. No sound logician, however, would cite this as a *proof* of the doctrine of the Trinity. It is to be mentioned only as a suggestion—a profound intimation—of the plurality of Eternal Powers in the Creator. It will be noticed that the writer does not here formally state the existence of God; much less does he attempt to prove his existence; but he simply assumes it as a fact. The word בָּרָא, which means, primarily, to *cut*, to *cut down*, (a meaning preserved in the Piel form of the verb, Josh. xvii, 15, 18,) and thence by a natural and easy process, to *construct*, to *fashion*, to *produce*, is in the Kal and Niphal always used to denote divine creations. It is never used to denote human productions. In verse 21 it denotes the creation of "great sea-monsters;" in verse 27, the creation of man; (comp. also chap. v, 1, 2; vi, 7; Deut. iv, 32; Psa. lxxxix, 47;) in Psa. lxxxix, 12, the establishing of the north and the south; in Isa. iv, 5, the creation of "a cloud and smoke by day, and the shining of a flaming fire by night;" in Isa. xlv, 7, the creation of darkness and evil, and in lvii, 19, the creation of "the fruit of the lips"—praise to God, or prophecy. This varied usage of the word shows, that to create out of

nothing is not its legitimate meaning, for pre-existing material is commonly supposed. Hence the meaning to *found*, to *produce*, to *cause to arise*. Applied thus uniformly to divine creations, בָּרָא is a more elevated word, and also more specific, than עָשָׂה, to *make*, which occurs much more frequently. This latter word is also used of divine creations, and so far may be said to be interchangeable with בָּרָא. Thus in verse 7, "God *made* the firmament"— verse 16, "God *made* two great lights"— verse 25, "God *made* the beast of the earth"—verse 26, "Let us *make* man" —verse 31, "Every thing that he had *made*"—chap. ii, 2, "His work which he had *made*"—chap. v, 1, "In the likeness of God *made* he him"—ix, 6, "In the image of God *made* he man"—Exod. xx, 11, "In six days the Lord *made* heaven and earth." But though applied to every thing to which we find בָּרָא applied, the word עָשָׂה has a much wider and more general application, referring to any work of man, as to *make* a feast, (chap. xix, 3, xxi, 8, xxvi, 30;) to *make* a heap of stones, (xxxi, 46;) to *do* wickedness, (xxxix, 9;) to *do* or *show* mercy, (Exod. xx, 6;) to accomplish a desire, (1 Kings v, 8;) and so in a great variety of ways. Another word of kindred meaning is יָצַר, to *form*, to *fashion*. This is used in chap. ii, 7, 8, "The Lord God *formed* man of the dust;" and "the man whom he had *formed;*" and also in verse 19: "Out of the ground the Lord God *formed* every beast of the field, and every fowl of the air." It is used of the forming of the dry land, (Psa. xcv, 5;) and of leviathan to play in the broad sea, (Psa. civ, 26;) of the fashioning of a graven image, (Isa. xliv, 12;) and of clay by the hand of a potter. Isa. xxix, 16; lxiv, 8. These three synonyme words are used together in Isaiah xliii, 7, and xlv, 18: "I have *created* him for my glory; I have *formed* him; yea, I have *made* him." The distinction to be drawn between these words seems to be this: בָּרָא denotes especially the bringing something

into being; causing something to arise which had not appeared before; עָשָׂה is a less dignified expression, indicating in general the same idea, but often applied to things and predicated of subjects which are never construed with בָּרָא. The word יָצַר, on the other hand, conveys the idea of giving particular *form* or *shape* to something. In this narrative of creation the three words are all alike applied to the divine production of man and beast upon earth. Comp. verses 21, 25-27, and chap. ii, 7, 8, 19. **The heaven and the earth**—Rather, *the heavens and the land*. What mean these words? It has been the prevailing assumption that in this first verse of the Bible they must stand for the entire universe. They have been explained as equivalent to the primordial matter of the universe; the original substance out of which the universe was subsequently formed. But why not allow the sacred writer to explain his own words? In verse 8, we are told that God called the firmament (or expanse above the land) *Heaven*, and in verse 10, the dry ground is called אֶרֶץ, *Land*. According to the constant *usus loquendi* of the Hebrew language, שָׁמַיִם, *heavens*, denotes the ethereal expanse above us, in which the luminaries appear to be set, and the birds fly, and from which the rain falls. Comp. verses 14, 15, 17, 20, 26, 28, 30; ii, 19, 20; vi, 7, 17; vii, 3, 11; viii, 2, etc. This may be safely said to be the common and almost universal sense of the word. When occasionally used of the abode of God, it is from the natural conception of him as the Most High, who is exalted above the heavens. Psa. lvii, 5, 11; cxiii, 4. The word is dual in form, perhaps from some notion of the expanse as a divider of the waters above and below it, as described in verse 7. Tayler Lewis regards the word as more probably a plural which originated in the effort of the early world to penetrate in thought beyond the visible heaven, and conceive of a heaven beyond that, and a heaven of heavens higher still, from which God looks down to "behold the

ness *was* upon the face of the deep. ^cAnd the Spirit of God moved upon the

c Psa. 33. 6; Isa. 40. 13, 14.

things that are in heaven (that is, the nearer heavens) and the earth." Psa. cxiii, 6. It is equally plain that the word אֶרֶץ, *land*, denotes (not the cubic or solid contents of the earth, considered as a globe; such a conception seems never to have entered the Hebrew mind) an area of territory, a country, a region. The word occurs over three hundred times in this Book of Genesis alone, and in most of those places it can have no other meaning than that which we give above, and in no place does it require any other word to represent it than our word *land*. The word *earth*, in our modern usage, is so commonly applied to the matter of the earth, or to the world considered as a planet, or solid sphere, that it misleads us when used as a translation of the Hebrew אֶרֶץ.

2. And the earth was without form and void—Having stated in the first verse the great fact of the creation, the writer now proceeds to unfold the manner and order of that creation. Here we must differ from those critics who understand verse 1 of the primordial matter of the universe, and the following verses of a subsequent series of growths. The analogy of the entire Book of Genesis confirms the view of those who regard verse 1 as a heading or general statement of the substance of the whole following section, which the succeeding verses go on to elaborate in detail. So chap. ii, 4; v, 1; x, 1; xi, 10, 27, etc., are respectively the headings of so many sections of this ancient Book of the Beginning and Generations of human history. In every instance, after first positing a general statement of his subject, the writer proceeds to narrate the details which his statement involves. The words used in the first verse needed an explanation, which the rest of the chapter at once supplies. The statement, so often made, that the conjunction *and* (וְ) at the beginning of verse 2 forbids the supposition that verse 1 is a face of the waters. 3 ^dAnd God said, ^e Let there be light: and there was light.

d Psa. 33. 9.——*e* 2 Cor. 4. 6.

summary of the whole chapter, is seen to be futile by a comparison of the immediate sequence of other headings of sections named above. The words תֹהוּ וָבֹהוּ are rendered by Onkelos *waste and empty;* by Aquila, *emptiness and nothing;* by Vulgate, *empty and void;* and by the Sept., *invisible and unformed.* The words appear in the same form again in Jer. iv, 23. They here describe the land as waste and empty, and the context shows that it was as yet covered with waters, so as to form a part and condition of the **deep,** over the surface or **face** of which there was **darkness.** Whether light had ever beamed upon that deep, or how the land and the waters came to be so intermixed, are questions on which the writer utters no sentiment. **The Spirit of God moved** (מְרַחֶפֶת, *brooding,* comp. Deut. xxxii, 11) **upon the face of the waters**—The Divine Spirit hovered down upon the deep, as the mighty Agent by whose power the darkness will be made to vanish, and beauty and order arise out of desolation and emptiness. Observe, here is no broad statement that darkness prevailed through the entire universe of God; nor is the **deep** or the **waters** to be identified with the entire surface of the globe.

FIRST DAY—LIGHT, 3-5.

3. **And God said**—Or, *Then says God.* Having stated the condition of things at the time and place of the fiat of the " omnific word," the writer now denotes a sequence by introducing the future or imperfect tense-form of the verb. The perfect tense of the preceding verbs, בָּרָא (verse 1) and הָיְתָה, (verse 2,) puts the reader back to an ideal standpoint—the beginning; the future tense of וַיֹּאמֶר denotes a point of time future from that standpoint, though really in the past. Every creation of this chapter is preceded by these words, **God said,** from which doubtless arose

72 GENESIS. B. C. 4004.

4 And God saw the light, that *it was* good: and God divided ¹ the light from the darkness. **5** And God called the light ᶠ Day, and the darkness he called the darkness.—ƒ Psa. 74. 16; 104. 20.

1 Heb. *between the light and between*

the sublime New Testament conception that the worlds (*ages*) were made by the WORD of God. Heb. xi, 3. Hence, too, the doctrine of the *Logos* in John i, 1-3. **Let there be light: and there was light**—Well might Longinus and others call attention to the sublimity of this passage. The natural meaning is, that at the fiat of the Almighty light supernaturally broke in upon the confused deep, and revealed its desolate and empty condition. Whence the light proceeded, by what means it was produced, and how large an area it illumined, are questions as idle to essay to answer as, Of what did God create the great sea monsters, (of ver. 21,) and how many of them did he make? We are told in the verses next following that "God divided the light from the darkness, and called the light *Day* and the darkness *Night*." The old question, Why this production of light on the first day, when the luminaries first appear on the fourth day? may be anticipated here. The making of an expanse to divide the waters above and the waters below, (verses 6, 7,) and the chaotic condition of the land and waters as previously described, warrant the conclusion that the atmosphere far into the upper heavens was filled with impenetrable mist, utterly shutting out the light of the sun and moon and stars. These luminaries were, of course, in existence, but at the time of this "beginning," and from that portion of the earth's surface here described, they were concealed. We know what it is now to have an impenetrable fog settle upon a region and abide for days. Comp. Acts xxvii, 20. The plague of darkness which covered Egypt for three days was such as could be felt, and prevented any one from moving from place to place. Exod. x, 21-23. Is it, then, difficult to conceive a darkness covering all that region where God planted the garden of Eden, so dense as utterly to shut the celestial luminaries from view? We may, indeed, suppose that the light produced by this word of God was the light of the sun, forced through the intervening clouds and mist without dispelling them for three days. The sun would, in such a case, have been invisible. But as the earth continued its axial revolution, day and night were alternately produced, and thus God divided between the light and the darkness. Nothing hinders our supposing such a mode of producing the light, and dividing the light from the darkness.

5. God called the light Day—By whatever means or method God caused "the light to shine out of darkness," (2 Cor. iv, 6,) it is important to observe that *he called that light* **Day**. Why now should we take it on ourselves to say, as so many expositors have ventured to do, that "day" in the first chapter of Genesis means a vast cosmogonic period or age? Shall we permit the sacred historian to define his own terms, as he most certainly assumes to do, or foist into his words the speculative theories of modern times? "The Hebrew word *yom*, (day,)" says Professor Guyot, "is used in this chapter in five different senses, just as we use the word *day* in common language: 1. The day, meaning light, without reference to time or succession. 2. The cosmogonic day, the nature of which is to be determined. 3. The day of twenty-four hours, in the fourth cosmogonic day, where it is said of the sun and moon, 'Let them be for days, and for seasons, and for years.' 4. The light part of the same day of twenty-four hours, as opposed to the night. 5. In Gen. ii, 4, the week of creation, or an indefinite period of time."—*Creation, or the Biblical Cosmogony*, pp. 50, 51.

Could any thing be more uncritical, arbitrary, and dogmatic than this deliverance of a Christian scientist? If we may put five different meanings upon one simple word, when the writer himself so definitely gives his own meaning, what may we not make the Bible say? The definition No. 4 above is the one which we adopt, (not, however,

B. C. 4004. CHAPTER I. 73

Night. ²And the evening and the morning were the first day.
6 And God said, ᶠ Let there be a ³ firmament in the midst of the waters, and let it divide the waters from the waters.

7 And God made the firmament, ʰ and divided the waters which *were* under the firmament from the waters which *were* ¹ above the firmament: and it was so. 8 And God called the firmament

2 Hebrew, *And the evening was, and the morning was.*— *g* Job 37. 18; Psalm 136. 5; Jeremiah 10. 12; 51. 15.—— 3 Hebrew, *expansion.*—*h* Proverbs 8. 28.—*i* Psalm 148. 4.

limiting it to twenty-four hours,) as being that of the sacred writer himself, and this, we believe, will be sufficient to meet the demands of this entire narrative of creation. The length of this day is not told. It was the period of light, whether twelve hours or a much greater length of time. So far as mere length of time is here denoted, there may have been but one day and one night in a year of our time. This would accord with Professor Warren's hypothesis of the beginning of human life within the Arctic circle. (See his *Paradise Found ; the Cradle of the Human Race at the North Pole.* Boston, 1885.) **And the evening and the morning were the first day**—Better, *And there was evening and there was morning, one day.* That is, the first day had its evening and its morning. We are not to understand the morning as equivalent to the day, and the evening to the night, nor are we to construe one **day** as grammatically in apposition with **evening** and **morning.** The simplest meaning is, that this first day, like all other days, had an evening and a morning. Evening was probably mentioned before morning in accordance with the ancient custom of reckoning days from evening to evening ; not to indicate that the primeval darkness constituted the first evening.

SECOND DAY—HEAVENS, 6–8.

6. **Let there be a firmament**— Heb., רָקִיעַ; Sept., στερέωμα; Vulg., *firmamentum.* The Hebrew word properly means *something spread out ;* margin, *expansion.* It means the expanse, the open space above the surface of the land through which an observer looks away to what appears a vast concave surface above him. This open sky is metaphorically called the " firmament ;" but we are not to suppose that the ancients, any more than the moderns, believed in a solid metallic firmament. The poetical language of Job xxxvii, 18, Isa. xl, 22, Psa. lxxviii, 23, etc., no more implies such a belief than similar metaphors in the poetry of the present day. **In the midst of the waters**—Between the waters below and the waters above, as is immediately explained. **Let it divide**—Let it serve as a divider of the waters below, (namely, the deep,) and the waters that float in cloudy masses above the face of the deep. Psa. cxlviii, 4.

7. **God made the firmament**—By his almighty fiat the dense mist that hung over the face of the deep, and was itself a vast expanse of waters, was lifted up to find a local habitation on high. Thus was formed the vast reservoir of the heavens, from which the rains descend to fertilize and refresh the land. " Next to the light," says Jacobus, " is the law of the atmosphere, so essential to life in the vegetable and animal world. Here it is set forth as supporting the floating vapour, and keeping in suspense a fluid of greater specific gravity than itself. The formation of clouds is referred to by Job in language which reveals an acquaintance with the laws here established by the Creator : ' He maketh small the drops of water : they pour down rain according to the vapour thereof ; which the clouds do drop and distil upon man abundantly. . . . Dost thou know the balancings of the clouds ? ' " Job xxxvi, 27, 28 ; xxxvii, 16 ; compare also chap. ii, 6. " But why, it may be asked, did he not speak of this storehouse of waters as diffused *through* the firmament, instead of placing it *above* it ? We answer : This would have been to convert the *firmament* of sense into the atmosphere of science, and phenomena into natural philosophy, which doubtless God could have done, but did not see fit to do."—*Barrows.*

8. **God called the firmament**

GENESIS. B. C. 4004.

Heaven. And the evening and the morning were the second day.

9 And God said, ᵏ Let the waters under the heaven be gathered together unto one place, and let the dry *land* appear: and it was so. **10** And God called the dry *land* Earth; and the gathering together of the waters called he Seas: and God saw that *it was* good. **11** And God said, Let the earth ¹ bring forth ⁴ grass, the herb yielding seed, *and* the fruit tree yielding ᵐ fruit after his

---

k Job 26. 10; 38. 8; Psalm 33. 7; 95. 5; 104. 9; 136. 6; Proverbs 8. 29; Jeremiah 5. 22; 2 Peter 3. 5. —— *l* Hebrews 6. 7. —— 4 Hebrew, *tender grass.*—— *m* Luke 6. 44.

Heaven — Rather, *called the expanse Heavens.* Here the writer defines the meaning of the word "heavens," which he had used in the first verse. And he further represents the luminaries as set in *the expanse of the heavens,* (verses 14–17,) and the winged fowls as flying upon its face, (verse 20,) and hence called the *fowl of the heavens.* Verses 26, 28, 30. By a most natural process the word would become associated with things above, and be used to denote the dwellingplace of God. Hence, too, the notion of many heavens. Compare 2 Cor. xii, 3.

THIRD DAY — LAND, SEAS, AND VEGETATION, 9–13.

9. Let the waters...be gathered ...the dry land appear—The import of these words is, that the land was partially, if not wholly, hidden by the waters; thus further explaining the statement of verse 2, that it was desolate and empty, and made so by the dark overflowing deep. Now, by the divine fiat, the land is supernaturally elevated above "the face of the deep," and the waters are made to flow off together into surrounding seas. How large a portion of land was thus made to appear is nowhere intimated. A very natural supposition is, that a large island was suddenly heaved up in the midst of the deep. And this was "the land" of the antediluvian world. On this land, thus raised in the midst of the seas, the garden of Eden was planted, and here man was first introduced. This miraculous elevation of the land from the waters we understand to be the true conception of 2 Pet. iii, 5, which literally and accurately translated, is, "For it is hidden from them who will it, that the heavens were from of old, and the land (γῆ) from water and by means of water, consisting by the word of God." Thus Fronmüller, *in loc.:* "The earth originated out of water—out of the dark matter in which it was comprehended —and through water, that is, through the agency of water, which partly descended into the lower parts of the earth and partly formed the clouds in the sky." But all was effected by God's word.

10. God called the dry land Earth—Or, *called the dry* (substance) *land.* The name "land" was given to the dry ground, as distinguished from the surrounding **waters,** which were named **Seas.** Here every thing is simple and plain, and as verses 6–8 explained how "God created the *heavens,*" (verse 1,) so verses 9 and 10 show how he created the *land.*

11. Let...earth bring forth grass —In explaining this entire narrative as a supernatural preparation of the soil, climate, and vegetation of the region where the first man appeared, we do not go about seeking the secondary causes by which any of the divine fiats were brought to pass. The divine power by which the **grass, herb,** and **fruit tree** of one particular region was brought into existence is doubtless competent to originate all forms of matter and of life. But we have no good reason to expect in this Scripture an answer to the many mysterious questions of biology Here we have revealed to us the Almighty personal God, infinite in ability and wisdom to originate all things; but how he brought into being the numberless things which now arrest the observation or attract the inquiry of men, we do not believe it is the purpose of this Scripture to explain. It is certainly supposable that he produced the vegetation of Eden miraculously, as Jesus made the water wine, and multiplied the loaves and fishes; but it does not follow that he produced all other vegetation in the same way. We

B. C. 4004.   CHAPTER I.   75

kind, whose seed *is* in itself, upon the earth: and it was so. 12 And the earth brought forth grass, *and* herb yielding seed after his kind, and the tree yielding fruit, whose seed *was* in itself, after his kind: and God saw that *it was* good. 13 And the evening and the morning were the third day.

14 And God said, Let there be ⁿ lights in the firmament of the heaven to divide ⁵ the day from the night; and let them be ᶠor signs, and ᵒ for seasons, and for days, and years: 15 And let them be for lights in the firmament of the heaven to give light upon the earth: and it was so. 16 And God ᵖ made two great lights; the greater light ⁶ to rule the day, and ᑫthe lesser light to rule the night: *he made* ʳ the stars also. 17 And God set them in the firmament of the heaven to give light upon the earth, 18 And to ˢ rule over the day and over the night, and to divide the light from the darkness: and God saw that *it was* good. 19 And the evening and the morning were the fourth day. 20 And God said, Let the waters bring forth abundantly the ⁷ moving creature that hath ⁸ life,

---

n Deut. 4. 19; Psa. 74. 16; 136. 7.——5 Heb. *between the day and between the night.*——*o* Psa. 74. 17; 104. 19.——*p* Psa. 136. 7, 8, 9; 148. 3, 5.   6 Heb. *for the rule of the day.*——*q* Psa. 8. 3.——*r* Job 38. 7.——*s* Jer. 31. 35.——7 Or, *creeping.*——8 Heb. *soul.*

---

note here three classes, or perhaps three stages, of vegetable life: **grass, herb yielding seed,** and **fruit tree bearing fruit.** In the first the seed is not taken into account; in the second it is the principal consideration; while in the third the fruit which envelops the seed is made most prominent.

FOURTH DAY—LUMINARIES, 14–19.

14. **Lights**—מְאֹרֹת, *luminaries,* or *lightbearers,* thus differing from אוֹר, *light,* in verse 3. Light was made to shine out of the darkness upon the deep three days before these lightholders were made to appear in the expanse above the Eden land. Every interpreter has felt the difficulty of explaining this. For our hypothesis, see note on verse 3. The sacred writer speaks of these luminaries merely in their phenomenal relation to the land of Eden, and not as an astronomer of the nineteenth century A. D. He therefore fittingly assigns them to that day of the creative week when they first became visible from the land already described. **Let them be for signs, and for seasons**—That is, let them serve this purpose to the earth. Some suppose here a *hendiadys, signs of seasons.* This, however, is not necessary. There is also no sufficient reason for abandoning the natural meaning of the word **signs,** (אֹתֹת,) as indicating remarkable phenomena in the heavens which, according to the Scriptures, sometimes indicate great events of judgment or of blessing. Comp. Jer. x, 2; Joel ii, 30; Matt. ii, 2; xxiv, 29; Luke xxi, 25. The luminaries also serve as signs to indicate different points of the compass—signals to direct the path of the traveller on the land and on the deep. מוֹעֲדִים, *seasons,* or *appointed times;* from יָעַד, *to fix, to appoint.* The heavenly bodies serve to regulate and measure off these weekly, monthly, or yearly recurring seasons.

16. **Two great lights**—This designation of the sun and moon is of itself sufficient to show that the work of the fourth day is phenomenal and popular, not scientific. We know that the moon is but the small satellite of a relatively small planet, and a mere atom as compared with the magnitude of some of the stars. But to man it is one of the two great lightbearers. **He made the stars also**—The Hebrew is simply, *and the stars.* That is, they, too, were made and placed in the heavenly expanse. They now first appeared above the newly elevated land where man was about to be created.

FIFTH DAY—FISH AND FOWLS, 20–23.

20. **Bring forth abundantly**— Heb., *Let the waters teem with creeping things, living beings.* נֶפֶשׁ חַיָּה, *soul of life,* or *living soul,* is in apposition with שֶׁרֶץ, *creeping thing.* These *crawlers,* or creeping things, are meant to include "whatsoever passeth through the paths of the seas." עוֹף יְעוֹפֵף, *and let fowls fly.* In chapter ii, 19, the fowls are said to be formed out of the ground.

GENESIS.

and ⁹ fowl *that* may fly above the earth in the ¹⁰ open firmament of heaven. **21** And ᵗ God created great whales, and every living creature that moveth, which the waters brought forth abundantly, after their kind, and every winged fowl after his kind: and God saw that *it was* good. **22** And God blessed them, saying, ᵘ Be fruitful, and multiply, and fill the waters in the seas, and let fowl multiply in the earth. **23** And the evening and the morning were the fifth day.

24 And God said, Let the earth bring forth the living creature after his kind, cattle, and creeping thing, and beast of the earth after his kind: and it was so. **25** And God made the beast of the earth after his kind, and cattle after their kind, and every thing that creepeth upon the earth after his kind: and God saw that *it was* good.

26 And God said, ᵛ Let us make man in our image, after our likeness: and ʷ let them have dominion over the fish of the sea, and over the fowl of the air,

---

9 Heb. *let fowl fly.*—10 Heb. *face of the firmament of heaven.*—*t* Chap. 6. 20; 7. 14; 8. 19; Psa. 104. 26.—*u* Chap. 8. 17.

v Chap. 5. 1; 9. 6; Psa. 100. 3; Eccles. 7. 29; Acts 17. 26, 28, 29; 1 Cor. 11. 7; Eph. 4. 24; Col. 3. 10; James 3. 9.—*w* Chap. 9. 2; Psa. 8. 6.

All these creatures were first introduced by God's word. They were *creations*, not *evolutions*. But their subsequent multiplication is conceived of as *generations*.

21. Great whales—תַּנִּינִם, *dragons*, *sea-serpents*, or some other of the great monsters of the deep. The Septuagint has τὰ κήτη; the Revised Version, *great sea monsters*.

SIXTH DAY—ANIMALS AND MAN, 24–31.

24. Cattle ... creeping thing ... beast—As the sacred writer distributes the growth of the vegetable kingdom into three classes, (see verses 11, 12,) so also he presents three classes of land animals: בְּהֵמָה, *cattle*, that is, the domestic animals; רֶמֶשׂ, *creepers*, that is, reptiles and insects of the land, corresponding to the creeping things (שֶׁרֶץ) of the waters; and חַיְתוֹ־אֶרֶץ, *beasts of the land*, that is, wild animals as distinguished from domestic cattle.

26. Let us make man in our image—This form of speaking in the first person plural is explained by some as conformity to the usage of human dignitaries, who are accustomed to speak of themselves in this way; while others suppose that God here addresses the angels of his presence. Others, again, find in these words a reference to the plurality of persons in the divine nature, but the ancient readers of the record would not be likely to comprehend this meaning. Nevertheless, here may be the germ which, by successive revelations, was at last developed into the Christian doctrine of the Trinity. All things conceptual or phenomenal *originate* in the great, uncreated, self-existent Essence, the fountain of Deity, the Father. These things become *thought* and *form* by and through the Divine Word, by whom all things exist. These existences are objects of approval to the Spirit, the Sensibility, so to speak, of God. As God looks over the objects of creation, it is the divine feeling that pronounces them "very good." Accordingly, man bears the triune image of his God in having will, thought, and feeling, which correspond with our highest conceptions of Father, Word, and Spirit. *Will*, by which we mean the whole self-acting, conscious *Ego; Thought*, the only begotten and always begotten offspring of the self-acting, conscious Ego; and *Feeling*, or Sensibility, by which we appreciate and love; these are the personalities of man's immortal nature. God is a spirit, and man's immortal nature is a spirit also, bearing the divine triune impress of the Godhead. We should accordingly understand the "righteousness," "true holiness," and "knowledge" of Eph. iv, 24, Col. iii, 10, as qualities or attributes of the divine image in which man was created, but not as constituting the image itself. The likeness was rather in the spiritual personality which made him Godlike as distinguished from all the rest of the animate creation. **Likeness** is not to be understood as something different from **image**, but rather as explanatory of it. **And let them have dominion**—This dominion is the natural

and over the cattle, and over all the earth, and over every creeping thing that creepeth upon the earth. **27** So God created man in his *own* image, 'in the image of God created he him; "male and female created he them. **28** And God blessed them, and God said unto them, ᵛ Be fruitful, and multiply, and replenish the earth, and subdue it: and have dominion over the fish of the sea, and over the fowl of the air, and over every living thing that ¹¹ moveth upon the earth.

29 And God said, Behold, I have given you every herb ¹² bearing seed, which *is* upon the face of all the earth, and every tree, in the which *is* the fruit of a tree yielding seed; ʷ to you it shall be for meat. **30** And to ˣ every beast

of the earth, and to every ʸ fowl of the air, and to every thing that creepeth upon the earth, wherein *there is* ¹³ life, *I have given* every green herb for meat: and it was so. **31** And ᶻ God saw every thing that he had made, and, behold, *it was* very good. And the evening and the morning were the sixth day.

CHAPTER II.

THUS the heavens and the earth were finished, and ᵃ all the host of them. **2** ᵇ And on the seventh day God ended his work which he had made; and he rested on the seventh day from all his work which he had made. **3** And God ᶜ blessed the seventh day, and sanctified it: because that in it he had rested from all his work which God¹ created and made.

---

t 1 Cor. 11. 7.——*u* Chap. 5. 2; Mal. 2. 15; Matt. 19. 4; Mark 10. 6.——*v* Chap. 9. 1, 7; Lev. 26. 9; Psa. 127. 3; 128. 3, 4.——11 Heb. *creepeth.*——12 Heb. *seeding seed.*——*w* Chap. 9. 3; Job 36. 31; Psa. 104. 14, 15; 136. 25; 146. 7; Acts 14. 17.

x Psa. 145. 15, 16; 147. 9.——*y* Job 38. 41.——13 Heb. *a living soul.*——*z* Psa. 104. 24; 1 Tim. 4. 4.——*a* Psa. 33. 6.——*b* Exod. 20. 11; 31. 17; Deut. 5. 14; Heb. 4. 4.——*c* Neh. 9. 14; Isa. 58. 13.——1 Heb. *created to make.*

---

superiority and headship which man holds over all the inferior orders of creation. Compare Psalm viii, 5-8. Verses 29 and 30, taken in connexion with chapter ix, 3, have been supposed to show that previous to the flood man's food was restricted to substances in the vegetable kingdom. This was probably the case; but, after all, these passages do not prove that animal food was *prohibited* before the flood; and possibly the skins mentioned chap. iii, 21, were those of animals slain, not for sacrifices only, but for food.

CHAPTER II.

SEVENTH DAY—SABBATH, 1-3.

1. **All the host of them**—That is, all the things, animate and inanimate, which made up the several works of creation.

2. **On the seventh day God ended his work**—"The completion or finishing (כִּלָּה) of the work of creation on the seventh day (not on the sixth, as Sept., Sam., Syr., erroneously render it) can only be understood by regarding the clauses which are connected with וַיְכַל by *Vav consec.* as containing the actual completion, that is, by supposing the completion to consist, negatively, in the cessation of the work of creation, and positively, in the blessing

and sanctifying of the seventh day. The *cessation* itself formed a part of the completion of the work. For this meaning of שָׁבַת, see chapter viii, 22,

Job xxxii, 1. As a human artificer completes his work just when he has brought it to his ideal and ceases to work upon it, so, in an infinitely higher sense, God completed the creation of the world with all its inhabitants by ceasing to create any thing new, and entering into the rest of his all-sufficient eternal Being, from which he had come forth, as it were, at and in the creation of a world distinct from his own essence."—*Keil.* ¶ God did not rest because he was weary, but because he had finished his work; and his rest was the divine refreshment of holy contemplation. Exod. xxxi, 17. The fact that there is no mention of the morning and evening of the seventh day is no evidence that that day, as here intended, continues still.

3. **Created and made**—Heb., *created to make.* That is, created for the purpose of moulding into such forms and putting to such uses as are here described.

The Generations of the Heavens and the Land, ii, 4-iv, 26.

In chapters i, and ii, 1-3, the sacred writer gives us his account of the *crea-*

GENESIS.

4 ^d These *are* the generations of the heavens and of the earth when they were created, in the day that the LORD God made the earth and the heavens,

d Chap. 1. 1; Psa. 90. 1, 2.

tion of the heavens and the land; he now proceeds to give us their *generations*, תּוֹלְדוֹת. His historical standpoint is the day from which these generations start; the day when man was formed of the dust of the ground, and of the breath of life from the heavens. So the first man is conceived of as the product of the heavens and the land by the word of God. Hence, Adam was the son of God, (Luke iii, 38,) and the day of his creation was the point of time when *Jehovah-God* first revealed himself in history as one with the Creator. In chapter i, which narrates the *beginning* of the heavens and the land, we find mention of *Elohim* only, the God in whom (as the plural form of the name intimates) centres all fulness and manifoldness of Divine Powers. At the beginning of this section stands the name יְהֹוָה, *Jehovah*, the personal Revealer and Redeemer, who enters into covenant with his creatures, and places man under moral law.

The information supplied in this chapter is fundamental to the history of redemption. Here we learn of man's original estate; the conditions of the first covenant of works; the sanctity of the family relation; and the innocency of the first human pair. Without the information here supplied the subsequent history of man and of redemption would be an insoluble enigma.

4. **These are the generations**— This verse is the heading to chapters ii, 4–iv, 26, and, of course, refers to what follows, not to what precedes. In every other passage of the Pentateuch where this formula occurs, it serves as a heading to what follows, and never as a summary of what precedes. Compare v, 1; vi, 9; x, 1; xi, 10, 27; xxv, 12, 19; xxxvi, 1, 9; xxxvii, 2; Num. iii, 1. "This would never have been disputed," says Keil, "had not preconceived opinions as to the composition of Genesis obscured the vision of commentators.... Just as the generations of Noah, (chap. vi, 9,) for example, do not mention his birth, but contain his history and the birth of his sons; so the generations of the heavens and the land do not describe the origin of the universe, but what happened to the heavens and the land after their creation." He further observes, that "the word תּוֹלְדוֹת, *generations*, which is used only in the plural, and never occurs except in the construct state, or with suffixes, is a Hiphil noun, (from הוֹלִיד, Hiphil of יָלַד,) and signifies, literally, the generation or posterity of any one, then the development of these generations or of his descendants; in other words, the history of those who are begotten, or the account of what happened to them and what they performed. In no instance whatever is it the history of the birth or origin of the person named in the genitive, but always the account of his family and life."

Accordingly, it should be particularly noted that what follows is not *the generations of Adam*, though Adam and his immediate progeny are the subject of this section. The generations of Adam are given at chap. v, 1, *ff.*, and consist of his outgrowth and development through Seth; but vegetable growths, and the forming of Adam and Eve and paradise, and the narrative of the temptation and fall and expulsion from the garden, and of Cain and Abel and the progeny of Cain, are all treated as *generations of the heavens and the land.*

When they were created — Heb., בְּהִבָּרְאָם, *in their being created*. That is, in their condition as having been created; or, *upon their being created*. To define this more fully we have the following immediately added: **In the day that the Lord God made the earth and the heavens**—That is, the historical *terminus a quo* of the following **generations** is the day in which JEHOVAH-GOD made land and heavens. The word **day** is not to be taken here as denoting the whole period of the creative week, as most commentators

5 And every ᵉ plant of the field before it was in the earth, and every herb of the field before it grew: for the LORD God had not ᶠcaused it to rain upon

ᵉ Chap. 1. 12; Psa. 104. 14.   ᶠ Job 38. 26, 27, 28.

have supposed. Such a construction of the word misses the great controlling idea of this whole section. It grows out of the notion that the word **generations** refers back to what precedes, and so controls the exegesis of some writers who deny such reference of the word. We understand the word **day** here to denote the day in which God *completed the land and the heavens*, planted the garden of Eden, and formed Adam and Eve. The land and the heavens were not fully *made* until that day—the sixth day of the preceding narrative. Here comes out the great distinction between בָּרָא and עָשָׂה. This *making* (עֲשׂוֹת) *of the land and the heavens* by *Jehovah-Elohim* is a different conception from the *creation* (בָּרָא) *of the heavens and the land* by *Elohim* in chapter i, 1. It points rather to a purpose for which the land and heavens were made. It denotes not so much their origin as their subsequent moulding into definite forms, and putting to definite uses. Compare note on ver. 3 above, where both words occur together. Then note that the word *land* here precedes *heavens*, and, having the more emphatic position in the sentence, denotes that it now becomes the prominent scene of events. We are now to be told of *generations*, processes of birth, growth, and development, and the word בָּרָא does not occur in this whole section. Accordingly, the *terminus a quo* of this section is the sixth day of the creative week, and so, according to the uniform usage of the Book of Genesis, the narrative here laps back upon the preceding section, and takes its start from the day in which God is conceived of as having made (completed) the land and heavens. We must notice, too, that land and heavens are here mentioned without the article, as being in themselves less definite than the idea of their *being made by Jehovah-Elohim*. Creation, so to speak, began with the Almighty and Pluripotent God, *Elohim;* its comple-

tion was wrought by *Jehovah*, the Personal God of revelation, of moral law, and of love. But these are not two different Beings. "In this section the combination *Jehovah-Elohim* is expressive of the fact that Jehovah is God, or one with Elohim. Hence, Elohim is placed after Jehovah. For the constant use of the double name is not intended to teach that Elohim who created the world was Jehovah, but that Jehovah who visited man in paradise, who punished him for the transgression of his command, but gave him a promise of victory over the tempter, was Elohim, the same God who created the heavens and the earth."
—*Keil.*

5. **And every plant . . . before it was in the earth**—The common version is utterly wrong in connecting this verse with what precedes, and so punctuating it as to make **plant** and **herb** grammatically the objects of **made** in ver. 4, the same as **earth** and **heavens** of that verse. Literally this verse reads: *And every shrub of the field not yet was* (יִהְיֶה, future form, involving the idea of *becoming, arising, growing*) *in the land, and every herb of the field not yet was sprouting, for Jehovah-God had not caused it to rain upon the land; and no man to work the ground.* This exhibits the Hebrew idiom, but a more proper translation would be: *And no shrub of the field was yet arising in the land, and no herb of the field was yet sprouting.* The future form יִהְיֶה, *will be*, taken in connexion with the future יִצְמָח, *will sprout*, shows that *a process of growth* is contemplated; not the simple fact of existence. Hence the meaning is, (not that there was yet no plant or herb existing in the land, but,) none of the plants or herbs of the fields of Eden had as yet entered upon the processes of growth. A reason for this is given in the statement that rain had not yet fallen. The dry ground had been made to appear, (chap. i, 9,) and grass and

80　　　　　　　　GENESIS.　　　　　　B. C. 4004.

the earth, and *there was* not a man [g] to till the ground. **6** But [2] there went up a mist from the earth, and watered the whole face of the ground. **7** And the LORD God formed man [3] *of* the [h] dust of the ground, and [i] breathed into his [k] nostrils the breath of life; and [l] man became a living soul.

g Chapter 3. 23.——2 Or, *a mist which went up from*, etc.——3 Heb. *dust of the ground*.——*h* Chapter 3. 19, 23; Psalm 103. 14; Ecclesiastes 12. 7; Isaiah 64. 8; 1 Corinthians 15. 47.——*i* Job 33. 4; Acts 17. 25.——*k* Chapter 7. 22; Isaiah 2. 22.——*l* 1 Corinthians 15. 45.

herb had been produced by the Almighty fiat, (i, 11, 12,) but the ground was not yet watered with rain, and the processes of vegetation were not yet in progress. **Not a man to till the ground**—Here note that the conceptual standpoint is previous to the formation of man; and the whole narrative naturally reverts to what we may suppose to have been the condition of things on the morning of the sixth day. Nevertheless the exact order of events in this chapter is not definitely stated, as in chapter i.

6. A mist—אֵד, a *mist*, a *vapour*. This first watering of **the whole face of the ground** was accomplished by an ascending vapour. Here is no mention of *rain falling;* but rather of *mist going up.* Perhaps, however, the one thought is designed to imply the other. The sacred writer thus also intimates how the vast reservoir of "waters above the firmament" (i, 7) were thenceforth to be supplied.

7. Formed man—Here occurs for the first time the word יָצַר, to *form.*

The production of man is here viewed not so much as a *creation*, but rather as a *formation.* Comp. note on chap. i, 1. It is viewed from the standpoint of the generation of the heavens and the land, and conceived as a process: **dust . . . breath of life . . . living soul.** Having passed from the narrative of *creation* to a narrative of *generations,* the sacred writer would have us think of man as not merely created by miracle, but also as *brought forth into form and activity* by a gradational process of creation. First, God "formed man of dust from the ground." עָפָר, *dust*, is here grammatically the "accusative of the material," and denotes **the ground** as the source of the primeval generation of man's body. Hence mortal man is from the earth, (Psa. x, 18,) and we speak of "mother earth." **Breathed into his nostrils the breath of life**—So man is not only earthborn, but heavenborn. As to his body, he is from the dust; but as to his soul he is, as the Greek poet and Paul affirm, the offspring of God. Acts xvii, 28, 29. God breathed out of himself into the body of the first man the **breath of life,** נִשְׁמַת חַיִּים, *breath of lives.* Some have held that the plural, *lives,* in this Hebrew expression, was designed to denote the twofold life of man—animal and spiritual; or perhaps the various powers and operations of the human soul. But the frequent use of the same plural form in other connexions (*as tree of life,* verse 9; *ways of life,* Prov. ii, 19) is against such an interpretation. In chapter vii, 22, we have the expression *breath of the spirit of life* applied to the whole living animal creation. **And** (the) **man became a living soul**—This is the third stage, and the outcome of the creative process. Man thus *became* a self-conscious, living creature. The expression נֶפֶשׁ חַיָּה, *soul of life,* or *living soul,* is used also in chap. i, 20, 21, 24, 30, of fishes, birds, and other animals. But the divine process by which man comes to be such a living creature is what we are to note. His soul-endowed nature is the result of an extraordinary divine inbreathing; an "inspiration from the Almighty." Job xxxii, 8; xxxiii, 4. Hence we incline, with Delitzsch, to regard the **breath of life** in this verse (and which occurs nowhere else in this section) as denoting the spirit as distinguished from the soul of man. Accordingly, while discarding the low mechanical anthropomorphic conception of God as a workman, fashioning a clod of earth with his hands, and then standing near it to breathe into it a breath from without, we nevertheless

B. C. 4004. CHAPTER II. 81

8 And the LORD God planted ᵐ a garden ⁿ eastward in ᵒ Eden; and there ᵖ he put the man whom he had formed. 9 And out of the ground made the LORD

---

m Chap. 13. 10; Isa. 51. 3; Ezek. 28. 13; Joel 2. 3.—*n* Chap. 3. 24.

o Chap. 4. 16; 2 Kings 19. 12; Ezek. 27. 23.—*p* Verse 15.

---

discern in this narrative a divine process in the creation of man. "It begins," says Delitzsch, "with the constitution of the body, as the regeneration (*palingenesia*) of man shall one day end with the reconstitution of the body. God first formed the human body, introducing the formative powers of entire nature into the moist earth taken from the soil of Eden, and placing them in co-operation; whereon he then breathed into this form the creative spirit, which, because it originated after the manner of breathing, may just as well be called his spirit as man's spirit, because it is his breath made into the spirit of man. This spirit, entering into the form of the body, did not remain hidden in itself, but revealed itself, by virtue of its likeness to God, as soul, which corresponds to the *doxa* (glory) of the Godhead, and by means of the soul subjected to itself the corporeity, by combining within the unity of its own intrinsic vitality the energies of the bodily material, as they reciprocally act on one another in accordance with the life of nature. . . . For the soul, as Tertullian says, is the body of the spirit, and the flesh is the body of the soul."—*Biblical Psychology*, p. 102.

8. **Planted a garden eastward in Eden**—The word **Eden** is here first introduced, and without any explanation. It seems most natural to understand it as the proper name of the *land* (אֶרֶץ) of the preceding narrative. The word signifies *pleasure, delight,* and thus corresponds with the Greek ἡδονή. The Septuagint and Vulgate translate פן, *garden*, by the word *paradise*, (a park,) and the word came at length to be used as a proper name for the garden of Eden, and also for the abode of disembodied spirits. Compare Luke xxiii, 43; 2 Cor. xii, 4. The Vulgate never renders Eden as a proper name; and the Septuagint only here, in verse 10, and in chap. iv, 16. Accordingly some translate: *God planted a garden in a delightful region.* But the word **eastward** (מִקֶּדֶם, *from the east,* or, *on the east,* that is, in the eastern part) serves to put on **Eden** the character of a proper name. And a most suitable name it was for the land where man first appeared, created in the image of God. That land, from the dust of which Adam was formed, in which every tree and shrub and herb was very good, being supernaturally produced by the power of God, might well be called **Eden**. The garden was planted in the eastern section of this Eden-land. **There he put the man whom he had formed**—These words, taken in connexion with verse 15, are supposed to imply that Adam was created outside of paradise, and afterward transported thither. But the word שׂוּם, here used, and נוּח, in verse 15, both convey the idea of establishment in some place without any necessary allusion to a previous state. We might say of Eve, as well as of Adam, that God took her and placed her in paradise, without necessarily implying that she was created outside of the garden. The order of the narrative would indicate that man was formed before the garden was prepared for him. But the order of the narrative by no means implies, or requires us to assume, a corresponding chronological sequence of the things narrated.

It would require volumes to chronicle all the opinions and discussions relative to the location of the garden of Eden, and the four rivers mentioned verses 11-14. Three theories have been particularly urged—one which locates the garden near the junction of the Tigris and Euphrates, or somewhere between that junction and the Persian Gulf; another which locates it in the highlands of Armenia, near the sources of these rivers; and a third which places it in the far East, in the mountainous highlands of Central Asia, near the sources of the Indus, the Helmend, the

God to grow *q every tree that is pleasant to the sight, and good for food; *r the tree of life also in the midst of the garden, *s and the tree of knowledge of good and evil. **10** And a river went out of Eden to water the garden ; and from thence it was parted, and became into four heads. **11** The name of the first *is*

q Ezek. 31. 8.——*r* Chap. 3. 22; Prov. 3. 18; 11. 30; Rev. 2. 7; 22. 2, 14.——*s* Verse 17.

Oxus, and the Jaxartes rivers. All these theories become worthless the moment we allow that the deluge may have borne the family of Noah far away from the primeval home of man. The notion that the rivers and countries subsequently known as Hiddekel, Euphrates, Havilah, Cush, etc., are identical with the lands and rivers of Eden is also destitute of any sure foundation. For we must remember the universal habit of migratory tribes and new colonies to give old and familiar names to the new rivers, mountains, and countries which they discover and occupy. Nothing could have been more natural than for the sons of Noah to give to new objects names from the old fatherland. Prof. W. F. Warren, in his *Paradise Found, the Cradle of the Human Race at the North Pole*, Boston, 1885, adduces a variety of arguments to prove that the primitive Eden was at the Arctic pole. Nothing in the legitimate interpretation of this Scripture is inconsistent with such an hypothesis; but we make no attempt to determine the site of paradise, inasmuch as we find nothing in this narrative that appears sufficient to solve that problem. It is, however, very probable that the original Eden of the human race was submerged and obliterated by the deluge.

9. **Out of the ground . . . every tree**—These growths of the garden may be regarded as special creations; a part of the special work of fitting up the garden for man: or they may be understood as a general statement made without reference to time. The context makes the former supposition the more probable one. **The tree of life** — A tree of special value and significance, the eating of whose fruit perpetuated life forever. Chap. iii, 22. Prof. Warren cites the singular agreement of many ancient religions in associating their paradise-tree with the axis of the world, and observes: "If the garden of Eden was precisely at the North Pole, it is plain that a goodly tree standing in the centre of that garden would have had a visible and obvious cosmical significance, which could by no possibility belong to any other.—*Paradise Found*, p. 263. **In the midst of the garden** — As if it were to be the most conspicuous object there, and a constant prophecy to man that he was made for immortality. Comp. Rev. ii, 7 ; xxii, 2. **And the tree of knowledge of good and evil**—The notion that the tree of life and the tree of knowledge were identical is not the most natural meaning of this language. This tree, says Jacobus, " was so-called not merely as a test for proving man, and showing whether he would choose the good or the evil; nor merely because by eating it he would come to know both good and evil, and the evil so that he would know the good in the new light of contrast with the evil. Both these are involved. But it was set also as a symbol of the divine knowledge to which man should not aspire, but to which he should submit his own judgment and knowledge. The positive prohibition was to be a standing discipline of the human reason, and a standing symbol of the limitation of religious thought." These two trees being named in immediate connexion with the other trees of the garden, are to be understood literally of two particular trees, and not allegorically, as if they were merely symbols. See more on verse 17, and iii, 7.

10. **A river went out of Eden**—This river, like the trees just named, constituted a part of the perfection of the earthly paradise. Comp. Rev. xxii, 1, 2. **From thence**—From the garden. The verse clearly implies that the river had its source in the garden, and from that place, as a centre, divided itself off, **was parted** so as to become the fountain **heads** of four different streams. Hence by **river** we may un-

B. C. 4004.   CHAPTER II.   83

Pison: that is it which compasseth ᵗthe whole land of Havilah, where there is gold; 12 And the gold of that land is good: ᵘthere is bdellium and the onyx stone. 13 And the name of the second river is Gihon: the same is it that compasseth the whole land of ⁴ Ethiopia.

14 And the name of the third river is ᵛHiddekel: that is it which goeth ⁵toward the east of Assyria. And the fourth river is Euphrates. 15 And the LORD God took ⁶the man, and ʷput him into the garden of Eden to dress it and to keep it. 16 And the LORD God com-

---

t Chap. 25. 18.——*u* Num. 11. 7.——4 Heb. *Cush*. ——*v* Dan. 10. 4.

5 Or, *eastward to Assyria*.——6 Or, *Adam*. ——*w* Verse 8.

---

derstand *river system*, set of rivers, all identified as to their origin, but whether flowing from four neighboring fountains or from one may be left undecided. Some suppose the river flowed as one stream through the garden, and after leaving it became divided into four **heads** or beginnings of rivers.

11. **Pison . . . Havilah**—After the views above given as to the site of paradise and the land of Eden, it would be idle to enumerate the diverse speculations and conjectures touching the rivers and lands designated in this and the following verses. The name **Pison** occurs nowhere else; but **Havilah** appears in chapter x, 7, as the name of a son of Ham, and in verse 29 as that of a son of Shem. Nothing would have been more natural than for the sons of Noah to transfer antediluvian names to their children. In chap. xxv, 18, and 1 Sam. xv, 7, the name appears as that of a country south-east of Palestine—probably because settled by the descendants of a patriarch of this name. **Where there is gold**—The land of Eden was rich in precious metals and other costly substances.

12. **Bdellium**—The word הַבְּדֹלַח occurs only here and in Num. xi, 7. The Septuagint renders it by ἄνθραξ in this passage, and by κρύσταλλος in Numbers. Gesenius, following Bochart and the rabbins, takes the word collectively in the sense of *pearls*. The English version, *bdellium*, follows Josephus, the Vulgate, and the Greek versions of Aquila, Theodotion, and Symmachus, and is as probably correct as any. Bdellium is a transparent, waxlike resin, now found on the trunks of trees in India. **Onyx stone**—Some render *beryl*; others, *sardonyx*. Some precious **stone** is meant, but it is impossible to determine its identity.

13. **Gihon**—This name occurs again only as denoting a fountain near Jerusalem. 1 Kings i, 33, 38, 45; 2 Chron. xxxii, 30. **Compasseth the whole land of Ethiopia**—The attempt to explain this as referring to any of the lands subsequently known as **Ethiopia**, or *Cush*, are, perhaps, the best possible refutation of the notion that the rivers of Eden are identical with any rivers now known. *Cush* was evidently the name of a region or country in the land of Eden, and it was very natural for Ham, the son of Noah, after the flood to name one of his sons in memory of this ancient country. Chap. x, 6. The same considerations apply to the names *Hiddekel*, *Assyria*, (or *Asshur;* compare chap. x, 11, 22,) and *Euphrates*, or *Phrath*, in the following verse. There is no sufficient reason for the belief that the original rivers and countries of Eden remained traceable after the flood.

15. **Took the man**—See note on verse 8. **To dress it and to keep it**—The world was made for man, and it became his noble intellect and skilful hand to give direction to its growths. Man was made for work, and labour was honourable in the primitive Eden. God himself is revealed as working, and furnishing a divine example. Hence the commandment: "Six days shalt thou labour,...for in six days the Lord made heaven and earth." Exod. xx, 9, 11. **To dress**, that is, to work and cultivate the garden, was one means of *keeping* it, for its vegetation might grow wild, and suffer also from the beasts of the field. The man was placed in paradise **to keep it**, (שָׁמַר, *guard, preserve,*) not to lose it. Perhaps the word may indicate that an evil enemy was lurking near.

16. **The Lord God commanded**

manded the man, saying, Of every tree of the garden ⁷thou mayest freely eat:

---
7 Heb. *eating thou shalt eat.*

---

the man—The Hebrew form of expression, וַיְצַו עַל־הָאָדָם, *and put a commandment upon the man*, suggests the thought of an authoritative law coming down upon him from above. The word **man** is to be understood here as in chap. v 2, of the man and his wife, and not as excluding the woman from the obligation of the law. The woman herself acknowledges this in chap. iii, 2, 3. The commandment might, indeed, have been given first to the man, and afterward repeated to the man and his wife together, thus intensifying in them both a sense of its importance. An exact chronological order of particular events is evidently not exhibited in this chapter. Here is the first revelation of moral law. The divine commandment appeals to man's intellectual and moral nature, recognising him as a thinking religious being. The commandment is simple, specific, positive, and so adapted to test the free and responsible nature of the being to whom it was addressed. Observe that the first great commandment, which served to test man's moral life, was of a negative form—a prohibition. See next verse. **Freely eat** —The intensified form of expression (Heb., *eating thou mayest eat*) confers the most unrestricted enjoyment of all the fruitage of the garden. Many understand from this reference to the fruit of trees, as also from chap. i, 29, that man at first subsisted on the fruit of trees alone. This, taken in connexion with the absence of any allusion to the use of animal food in these first records of the race, may be a legitimate inference, but is nowhere clearly asserted.

17. Of the tree of the knowledge of good and evil—It is idle to speculate on the physical nature of this mysterious tree; and the supposition that its fruit contained a natural poison, which must sooner or later have resulted in the death of the eater, is without warrant in the Scripture. Nor

17 ˣBut of the tree of the knowledge of good and evil, ʸthou shalt not eat of

---
x Verse 9.——*y* Chap. 3. 1, 3, 11, 17.

---

do we see sound reason in classing this account of the tree of knowledge with the myths and traditions of prophetic trees, or in seeking to identify it (or the tree of life) with the sacred plant or branch which appears so noticeably on Chaldean, Assyrian, and Persian monuments. All that clearly appears in this narrative is, that the fruit of a particular tree (or, perhaps, class of trees) was designated as not to be eaten, and the name seems to have been given in anticipation of what would result from eating the forbidden fruit. Its name, therefore, indicated the moral purpose which it served rather than any natural or physical character of the tree itself. The design of the prohibition of this particular fruit was to test man's moral nature, to develop his love for his Maker by deliberate choice of the good and deliberate rejection of the evil. Thus would he come to distinguish clearly between good and evil by acquiring a godlike permanence in the good, and like steadfast opposition to all evil. By disobedience he came to know good and evil in the Satanic way, becoming experimentally identified with the evil, and thus opposed to God.

The disposition which some have shown to ridicule the literal interpretation of this narrative, and to assume that it was unworthy of God and incompatible with the dignity of man's original state to make his and his posterity's happiness depend upon the non-eating of a certain tree, springs from notions of God and of man which are unscriptural. The simplicity, clearness, and positive character of the prohibition are conspicuous marks of its fitness as a moral test. The newly created Adam, with great possibilities, was yet undeveloped and undisciplined. His mental and religious nature, like that of a child, would be best trained by a positive commandment, which rested in the authority of the Creator rather than in the reason of the creature whose love and loyalty

B. C. 4004.   CHAPTER II.   85

it: for in the day that thou eatest thereof ᶻ ⁸ thou shalt surely die.

18 And the LORD God said, *It is* not good that the man should be alone ; ᵃ I will make him a help ⁹ meet for him.

19 ᵇ And out of the ground the LORD God formed every beast of the field, and every fowl of the air; and ᶜ brought *them* unto ¹⁰ Adam to see what he would call them: and whatsoever Adam called every living creature, that *was* the name thereof.   **20** And Adam ¹¹ gave names to all cattle, and to the fowl of the air, and to every beast of the field ; but for

---

z Chap. 3. 3, 19; Rom. 6. 23; 1 Cor. 15. 56; James 1. 15; 1 John 5. 16. —— 8 Heb. *dying thou shalt die.* —— *a* Chap. 3. 12; 1 Cor. 11. 9;

1 Tim. 2. 13.——9 Heb. *as before him.*——*b* Chap. 1, 20, 24.—— *c* Psa. 8. 6; see chap. 6. 20.——10 Or, *The man.*——11 Heb. *called.*

---

were to be tested. Moreover, as food was a natural want of man, the most convenient and suitable form of the first law given for his moral guidance was one in which a broad permission and a single prohibition related to the matter of eating. **In the day that thou eatest thereof thou shalt surely die**—Solemn and startling words to be uttered in the bowers of paradise ! What all this terrible penalty involved was doubtless a mystery to the man, and no subsequent revelation has fully cleared the awful mystery. The comments of Müller (*Christian Doctrine of Sin*, vol. ii, page 291, Edinburgh, 1868) furnish an excellent statement of the doctrine of the ancient Scripture: "If we compare the penalty of death threatened Gen. ii, 17, with the fulfilment of the sentence after the first transgression, (Gen. iii, 16–22,) two things are manifest. On the one hand we find that the death which was to follow the commission of sin included not only physical death, but the various ills that flesh is heir to—the manifold pains and miseries of our earthly lot; and these are represented as resulting from sin, which ends in death. Thus the well known difficulty involved in the word בְּיוֹם, *in the day*, is at once obviated. In the very day of disobedience a life begins which is at the same time a death. It thus appears, too, that when the serpent in his subtlety said to Eve, 'Ye shall not surely die,' this was not a bare lie, but a half truth, and therefore a double deception. But, on the other hand, we find by comparing the two passages that physical death is the real kernel and gist of the punishment. For the sentence pronounced concludes with the prophecy of death, making this the most important element, by emphatic repetition; (Gen. iii, 19;) and the account of the execution of the sentence lays stress chiefly upon the fact of man's exclusion from the means of imperishable life." See chap. iii, 22, 24.

18. Not good that the man should be alone—He was designed to be a social being, capable of holding intercourse with other beings like himself, as well as with God and angels. **Help meet** — Heb., *I will make for him a helper as over against him*, כְּנֶגְדּוֹ, *corresponding to him*—that is, a suitable companion; one who can assist him in his labours, share his counsels, and reciprocate his feelings.

19. Every beast of the field—That is, representative animals of the garden; not, as some would understand, (and thence erect a skeptical objection to the history,) all the genera, species, and individuals of the animal creation of all climates throughout the world. The apparent design of the writer in introducing here this statement of the animals of Paradise was to show that among all these lower orders of animal life there was no proper companion for the man. He gave these several creatures names according to their natures; but *for Adam was not found a helper corresponding to him* (verse 20) among them all. It required no very long time for God to cause the animals of Paradise to pass before Adam and receive their names from him. This was a very proper prelude to the formation of the woman, for it served to awaken in the man a consciousness of his need of a companion.

20. Adam gave names to all cattle—Adam was the first great scientist. For what is all natural science but a discovery of the objects of nature, observing, discriminating, and giving them names ? Adam, by a lofty

Adam there was not found a help meet for him. **21** And the Lord God caused a ᵈ deep sleep to fall upon Adam, and he slept; and he took one of his ribs, and closed up the flesh instead thereof. **22** And the rib, which the Lord God had taken from man, ¹²made he a woman, and ᵉbrought her unto the man. **23** And Adam said, This *is* now ᶠbone of my bones, and flesh of my flesh: she shall be called ¹³Woman, because she was ᵍtaken out of ¹⁴man. **24** ʰTherefore shall a man leave his father and his mother, and shall cleave

d. Chapter 15. 12; 1 Sam. 26. 12. —— 12 Heb. *builded.*——*e* Prov. 18. 22; Heb. 13. 4.——*f* Chap. 29. 14; Judg. 9. 2; 2 Sam. 5. 1; 19. 13; Eph. 5. 30.

13 Heb. *Isha.*——*g* 1 Cor. 11. 8.——14 Heb. *Ish.* ——*h* Chap. 31. 15; Psa. 45. 10; Matt. 19. 5; Mark 10. 7; 1 Cor. 6. 16; Eph. 5. 31.

intuition, and a judgment and inspiration unrivaled by any of his sons, first gave facile expression in names to the qualities of the creatures he observed. "Still we are not to suppose that Adam's insight into the character of the animals was a perfect comprehension of the secrets of nature; it is rather to be regarded as the pure, simple, lively view of an innocent child full of undeveloped depth of mind."—*Gerlach.* And yet we may suppose that he uttered the names by means of a divine impulse acting vigorously on his human powers, and giving them a normal development. "The man sees the animals, and thinks of what they are and how they look; and these thoughts, in themselves already inward words, take the form involuntarily of audible names, which he utters to the beasts." —*Delitzsch.* And to this we may add the words of Keil: "The thoughts of Adam with regard to the animals, we are not to regard as the mere results of reflection; but as a deep and direct mental insight into the nature of the animals."

21. Caused a deep sleep to fall— תַּרְדֵּמָה, *deep sleep,* not an ordinary slumber, but a profound sleep in which all self-consciousness was suspended. **One of his ribs** — Hence the force of the old proverb: The part of which woman was made was not taken from his head, as if she were to be a lord over him, nor from his feet, as if he might tread upon her; but from his side, to show that she was to be his companion and equal.

22. Made he a woman — Heb., *Built . . . the rib which he had taken from the man into a woman.* This is a simple statement of fact, and skeptical speculation and jest respecting it are idle and absurd. "The woman was created, not of the dust of the earth, but from a rib of Adam, because she was formed for an inseparable unity and fellowship of life with the man, and the mode of her creation was to lay the actual foundation for the moral ordinance of marriage."—*Keil.* **Brought her** — Not that she was formed at a great distance from him, but as soon as he awoke from his deep sleep, she was brought to his notice, that is, stood before him.

23. This is now bone—Heb., *This* —*the time*—**bone of my bones,** *etc.* הַפַּעַם, *the time,* is here equivalent to the adverb *now.* Comp. chap. xxx, 20. The words are an exclamation, and indicate the joyful surprise with which he recognises *this time,* after having looked hitherto repeatedly among the lower animals in vain, a suitable companion for himself. **Shall be called Woman** —He gives her at once her proper name, and he does it by means of the same deep insight into her nature as that by which he named the living creatures of Paradise. Thus now has the sacred writer completed a fuller description of the creation of man, male and female, than it was his design to give in the previous section, chap. i, 27. That was *creation,* this *formation.* See above on verse 7. On the proper name of the woman, see chap. iii, 20.

24. Therefore shall a man leave his father and his mother, and shall cleave unto his wife: and they shall be one flesh—Some interpreters (Delitzsch, Lange) regard these as the words of Adam, spoken as by a prophetic impulse from God; while others (Keil, Gerlach, Turner) regard them as the words of the inspired historian. The latter is the more probable view. In Matt. xix, 3-6, Jesus showed from this passage that the marriage tie is most

unto his wife: and they shall be one flesh. ⸱**25** ¹ And they were both naked,

the man and his wife, and were not ᵏ ashamed.

---

i Chap. 3. 7, 10, 11. | *k* Exod. 32. 25 ; Isa. 47. 3.

---

holy and inviolable. Says Otto von Gerlach : "There will be times and circumstances when a man is permitted, nay, is commanded, to leave his father and his mother, but his wife he is never permitted to leave—they both shall be one. This is not said of the woman, because she already, by her marriage, has left father and mother, and become subject to her husband. Here it is not spoken of leaving father and mother for the sake of marrying, but of a leaving after marriage."

25. **Not ashamed**—For where there is no sin, but a heavenly consciousness of perfect innocence, there can be no sense of shame.

EXCURSUS ON PRIMEVAL MAN.

The foregoing narrative of the beginning of human history is singularly simple and free from numerous characteristics of the myths and legends of other nations, as well as from their pantheistic and polytheistic conceptions. "According to the ideas commonly prevailing among the peoples of antiquity," says Lenormant, "man is regarded as autochthonous, or issued from the earth which bears him. Rarely, in the accounts which treat of his first appearance, do we discover a trace of the notion which supposes him to be created by the omnipotent operation of a deity, who is personal and distinct from primordial matter. The fundamental concepts of pantheism and emanatism, upon which were based the learned and proud religions of the ancient world, made it possible to leave in a state of vague uncertainty the origin and production of men. They were looked upon, in common with all things, as having sprung from the very substance of the divinity, which was confounded with the world; this coming forth had been a spontaneous action, through the development of the chain of emanations, and not the result of a free and determinate act of creative will, and there was very little anxiety shown to define, otherwise than under a symbolical and mythological form, the manner of that emanation which took place by a veritable act of spontaneous generation."—*Beginnings of History*, p. 47.

Which, now, is the more reasonable and probable hypothesis, that this biblical account of man's origin is the true and genuine tradition of the most ancient times—of which the legends of other nations are the degenerate outgrowths, mixed with various pantheistic and polytheistic notions—or, that the ethnic myths are the source of this unique theistic record, which was compiled by some ancient sage who aimed to purge the floating traditions of their heathenish features, and to express them in consistency with the doctrine of a personal God ? In other words, is this narrative a development out of pantheistic myths, or are the myths and legends a perversion of the true account of man's origin, of which this biblical record is the most ancient historic monument ?

The answer to this question will be mainly governed by the belief or non-belief in the existence of a personal God, who is concerned with man and with all things of this world. The doctrine of the Omnipotent and Omniscient Deity is the logical basis of all belief in the supernatural creation of man, and that belief is of the nature of an intuition rather than the result of any process of reason.

Accepting, therefore, as we do, the Scripture doctrine of the personal God and Father of us all, we also believe that these Scriptures contain his own revelation of the beginning of human history. Portions of the record may be regarded as symbolical or parabolic in form, from the necessity of thus accommodating the record to the capacity of man's understanding. The anthropomorphism of these ancient narratives, far from being a ground for discrediting them, is rather a mark of their genuineness. The concept of creation must be given, if given at all, in harmony with human modes of thought and feeling. The central fact revealed is, that God produced man partly from the earth and partly from himself—his body from the dust, his soul from the divine breath. All we can comprehend is, the idea that he was formed by Him who had all power in heaven and earth. As no man can tell *how* Jesus made the water wine, so can no man tell *how* God made dust and breath into a living soul, or *how* he builded the man's rib into a woman. The great fact revealed is, that "Adam was first formed, then Eve," and " the man is not of (or from) the woman, but the woman of the man." 1 Tim. ii, 13; 1 Cor. xi, 8.

Accepting this great fact as matter of divine revelation, we of course reject the evolution hypothesis of a naturalistic development of man from some extinct race of pithecoids, like the gorilla or the orang-outang. We reject this hypothesis, not only because it seems in conflict with the biblical narrative, but also because its main positions do not commend themselves. In such a struggle for existence as the current doctrines of evolution assume, we would naturally suppose that the terrible gorilla, according to all known analogy, would develop into a still more ferocious animal. The struggle with a cold climate after the glacial era, and with the mighty animals of that period, would certainly seem to have produced something very diverse from the tender skin and comparatively frail mechanism which the *genus homo* every-where presents to our observation. By what process of "natural selection" a ferocious orang-outang, fighting for existence, would come to lose his thick hairy hide, strong jaws, and sharp claws, is more than we can rationally conceive. But it appears, rather, that the apes are man's contemporaries, not his predecessors. If allied at all by flesh and blood they are man's cousins, or brothers, not his ancestors.

The Darwinian theory of evolution must fill up many wide gaps before it can be accepted as accounting for the origin of man. The distance between man and the most highly developed monkey yet discovered is immensely great. "Zoologically," says Dawson, "apes are not varieties of the same species with man; they are not species of the same genus, nor do they belong to genera of the same family, or even to families of the same order." Nor should we forget that the regions most favourable for apes are least favourable for human life. A great gulf lies between the low animal nature of the ape, or of any other beast, and the reasoning moral nature of man. Another gap which Darwinians have not been able to bridge is, that between any two species of animals. Great varieties of species appear, but no real transmutation of species has yet been shown. Another gap back of these is, that which separates vegetable and animal life; and even if this were covered, there would be another, still broader, between any living thing and inert matter.

The notion that man was originally a savage, and elevated himself into civilization by the pressure of his own necessities, is also destitute of any evidence that commends it to the thoughtful mind. The most ancient nations of which we have any trustworthy history were highly civilized. Witness the monuments along the Euphrates and the Nile. There is no shadow of proof that these nations raised themselves out of a previous barbarism. On the other hand, it is well known that tribes and colonies, once separated from a civilized state, have deteriorated, and become savage and barbarous. Indo-European philology enables us to trace many a rude western people to an oriental source. "Within a century or two," writes Whedon, "a large number of Caucasians excluded by slavery from a suitable place in the social system, have, even within hailing distance of what claimed to be a high civilization, changed in color, diminished in size, and forgotten letters, mechanic arts, and religion." But no one can point as a matter of fact to a single savage tribe which became civilized and enlightened otherwise than by coming in contact with other and higher forms of civil life. Only moral forces, connected with an elevating form of religion, have lifted savage men up to higher modes of life. Left to themselves they sink lower and lower. Geology, also, sustains the doctrine of degeneracy in types of life. According to Dawson, the laws of creation, as illustrated by the record of the rocks, are these: "First, that there has been a progress in creation from few, low, and generalized types of life to more numerous, higher, and more specialized types; and, secondly, that every type, low or high, was introduced at first in its best and highest form, and was, as a type, subject to degeneracy, and to partial or total replacement by higher types subsequently introduced. In geological times," he adds, " the tendency seems to be ever to disintegration and decay. This we see everywhere, and find that elevation occurs only by the introduction of new species in a way which is not obvious, and which may rather imply the intervention of a cause from without."—*Story of the Earth and Man*, p. 235.

Some modern writers have fallen into the habit of using the terms "stone age," "bronze age," and "iron age," as if the entire human race had developed in civilization according as they had used implements of these various qualities. Rude tribes, indeed, naturally make use of stone from ignorance of the manufacture of better material. But to assume that nations, or races, or mankind generally, have passed by regular gradations from a stone age to a bronze age, and from a bronze age to an iron age, is utterly fallacious and misleading. Other circumstances than those of savagery and ignorance may oblige a people to use stone or wooden implements. Compare Judges v, 8, and 1 Sam. xiii, 19-22. Nothing is better known than that some tribes have employed stone utensils at the same time that others have used brass and iron. In the old Chaldean tombs flint, bronze, and iron implements are found mingled together. In Xerxes's great army were found all sorts of weapons made of wood, bone, flint, bronze, and iron. In the trenches of Alesia, where Cæsar fought his last battle with the Gauls, stone, bronze, and iron weapons were mixed together in one promiscuous bed. Schliemann's excavations on the site of ancient Troy discovered stone and bronze in the lowest relic bed, representing, as he thinks, an age anterior to the Homeric Troy. Above this was another bed in which the relics were stone and bronze; and in another, still higher and more modern, he found no traces of metal at all. But in a fourth and later bed, stone and bronze again appeared. Here, it would seem, two bronze ages preceded a stone age, and then followed another age of bronze. While, therefore, the use of stone, bronze, or iron may serve to indicate the degree of civilization to which a people has attained, it can furnish no evidence of the age of man on earth, or of his primitive condition.

From all the confusing speculations of those who, from most meagre data, rush to the conclusion that primeval man was a rude savage, self-evolved from a still more savage brute, we turn with inexpressible satisfaction to the ancient Scripture doctrine that "God created man in his own image." He did not first involve him in savagery in order that he might evolve himself into a higher life, but he made him upright, and gave him "dominion over the fish of the sea, and over the fowl of the air, and over every living thing that moveth upon the earth." That first period was his golden age, and afterward he "corrupted his way" upon the earth. This biblical account of man's primitive condition and subsequent degeneracy is confirmed by the traditions of many nations, and is entirely compatible with reason and all the well-established facts of human history. This unique account we do well to accept until it is clearly shown to be false, and something better and more rational is given us in its stead.

As to the perfection, mental capacity, and knowledge of the first man, speculation is idle, and extreme views are to be avoided. While we may well hesitate to believe, with Knapp, that at the time of his first consciousness he was as destitute of ideas as a new born child, we should also repudiate such extravagant assumptions as those of Dr. South, who says of Adam, that "he came into the world a philosopher; he could perceive the essences of things in themselves, and read forms without the comment of their respective properties; he could see consequences yet dormant in their principles, and effects yet unborn, and in the womb of their causes; his understanding could almost pierce into future contingents; his conjecture improving even to prophecy, or the certainties of prediction. Could any difficulty have been proposed, the resolution would have been as early as the proposal; it could not have had time to settle into doubt."—*Sermons*, vol. i, pp. 24, 25. This is being "wise above what is written." It is sufficient to know that man's original estate was one which his divine Creator pronounced VERY GOOD.

In marked contrast with all the cosmogonies and traditions of other nations are the doctrines of these first two chapters of Genesis. Aside from any special significance in the names Elohim and Jehovah, we legitimately deduce from this record of creation the doctrine of an infinite God, a personal Creator, an all-sufficient First Cause, almighty, wise, good, condescending to the tenderest care for his creatures; a God of order, of law, of righteousness and holiness. He is a self-revealing Spirit and communicates instruction to his created intelligences. Here, also, is the doctrine of man created in the image of God, good, upright, in a state of perfect innocence, with unspeakable possibilities before him. He is the lord of the lower creations, but is himself under law. The woman is his fitting companion, and the marriage relation is to be regarded as sacred, and even more binding than other ties of human kinship. The spiritual nature of man is emphasized; he is a moral being, capable of acquiring great wisdom, and also capable of sin. The animate and inanimate creation, the land, the heavens, the sun and moon and stars are all God's work. To sum all up in a word, here we read the doctrines of a lofty Theism and a rational and ennobling Anthropology.

CHAPTER III.

THE FIRST SIN, 1-24.

Having given a picture of the original uprightness and blessedness of the first human pair, the writer hastens on to delineate their first transgression. How long man continued in his primeval estate of holiness we are not informed, and suppositions are here worthless. We accept the statements of this Scripture as a narrative of facts. The representation of man's original transgression, as here given, may, indeed, be admitted to have elements of a symbolical drapery, but there is no part of the narrative which may not be explained literally, and accepted as a truthful description of the most important events in the history of our race. We accordingly reject the rationalistic hypothesis, which treats this momentous event as a mythical representation of man's breaking loose from the purity and innocence of childhood, and his attaining the conscious use of his reason and of moral freedom. A sound and self-consistent interpretation, according to grammatico-historical principles, requires us also to reject the allegorical explanation, which denies that any real serpent was associated with the original transgression, and maintains that the temptation was entirely subjective or internal.

That Satan was the tempter is evidently the import of such Scripture passages as John viii, 44, where our Lord calls him the father of lies in allusion to the record of the original temptation, and Rev. xii, 9, where he is called "that old serpent,...the Devil, and Satan, which deceiveth the whole world." That this invisible tempter employed the serpent as his agent in deceiving the woman appears from the obvious import of the language which records the transaction, and also from the consideration that one of the creatures pronounced "very good," had not in itself alone the lying nature disclosed in the seductive words which this serpent uttered.

CHAPTER III.

NOW [a] the serpent was [b] more subtile than any beast of the field which the LORD God had made. And he said unto

a Rev. 12. 9; 20. 2.   *b* Matt. 10. 16; 2 Cor. 11. 3.

The fact that the serpent figures so prominently in the religious symbolism of ancient heathen nations is no good reason for disputing the credibility of this biblical narrative of the fall. Whence arose those ethnic myths of the serpent which seem to personify the evil principle? Is it not more rational to maintain that they sprung from such a momentous fact in human history as this third chapter of Genesis records, than to suppose that they originated in human speculations and fancies touching the conflict of good and evil in the world? As we hold the biblical account of creation to be the true original from which the various ethnic cosmogonies were derived, (see Introd., p. 67,) so we also hold, as the most reasonable hypothesis, that those heathen myths which represent the evil principle in creation under the form of a serpent, had a traditional origin in the fact that the father of lies made use of a serpent in deceiving the mother of mankind.

1. **The serpent** is here represented as a **beast of the field which the Lord God had made,** and, therefore, must have been good, as all the rest of the creation. Chap. i, 25. Hence we should not understand the word עֲרוּם, **subtile,** in a bad sense, implying malignant craftiness, as some expositors have done. This term is frequently employed in the Old Testament in a good sense, as meaning *prudent*, or sagacious. Such is the import of the Septuagint, φρόνιμος. Our Lord enjoined upon his disciples to be "wise as serpents." Matt. x. 16. The serpent's sagacity is seen in its keen eye, its power to charm birds and men, its prudence in avoiding danger, its skill in shielding the head, its most vulnerable part, from the attack of man. The words **more subtile** do not imply that all other beasts of the field were also subtile, but rather that this feature separated or distinguished the serpent *from* them. As to the prominence which the serpent holds in the religious symbolism of ancient peoples, Lenormant observes: "These creatures are there used with the most opposite meanings, and it would be contrary to all the rules of criticism to group together and in confusion, as has been done by scholars of former times, the very contradictory notions attached in this way to the different serpents in the ancient myths, in such wise as to create a vast ophiolatric system, derived from a single source, and made to harmonize with the narration of Genesis. But side by side with divine serpents of an essentially favourable and protective character, oracular, or allied with the gods of health, of life, or of healing, we find in all mythologies a gigantic serpent, personifying the nocturnal, hostile power, the evil principle, material darkness, and moral wickedness." — *Beginnings of History,* pp. 107, 108. **He said unto the woman**—The serpent spoke in an intelligible way. Le Clerc (after some of the rabbies) supposes that the serpent tempted Eve, not by language audibly spoken, but by significant signs, and by repeatedly eating the fruit in her sight. Others imagine she was charmed into a visionary or ecstatic condition in which the movements of the serpent seemed to her like words. Some, as we have seen, deny that any real serpent was connected with the event, and hold that the temptation was purely spiritual; while others have denied the agency of Satan in this temptation, and affirmed that the tempter of Eve was nothing but a serpent, which, by repeatedly using the forbidden fruit before her eyes, at length induced her to follow its example. Less strained, and far more compatible with the general doctrine of the Scriptures, is that ancient interpretation which has been commonly received by Christian scholars, namely, that Satan made use of a serpent in his work of falsehood and ruin. There is no sufficient ground for denying the possibility of Satan speaking through the organs of a serpent.

GENESIS. B. C. 4004.

the woman, ¹Yea, hath God said, Ye shall not eat of every tree of the garden? **2** And the woman said unto the serpent, We may eat of the fruit of the trees of the garden: **3** ᶜ But of the fruit of the tree which *is* in the midst of the garden, God hath said, Ye shall not eat of it, neither shall ye touch it, lest ye die. **4** ᵈAnd the serpent said unto the woman, Ye shall not surely die: **5** For

---

1 Heb. *Yea, because,* etc.——c Chap. 2. 17.   d Verse 13; 2 Cor. 11. 3; 1 Tim. 2. 14.

Mind and spirit are superior to matter, and control it. A fallen spirit is, in intellect, untold degrees above a brute. The mystery of demoniacal possession is too great for us to allow any *a priori* assumptions to govern our interpretation. According to the New Testament records, evil spirits usurped the powers of human speech, and entered also into swine. Mark v, 1–17. ¶ Why the Almighty should have permitted Satan to make such an approach to the first woman is as idle as to ask why he permits any sin or sinners to exist in his universe. We regard this first temptation and transgression as a great mystery, and a momentous event, but not a myth nor a fable. The mystery of God in Christ, by which God himself becomes flesh and redeems sinful man, implies other mysteries that may well surpass our knowledge. The incarnation, temptation, righteousness, death, and resurrection of the One who accomplishes the work of redemption, furnish to our thought a series of stupendous events; if we believe them, why do we stagger over that which appears startling and wonderful in the offence of the one by whom "judgment came upon all men to condemnation?" Rom. v, 18. **Yea, hath God said**—Or, as the Hebrew strictly implies: *Really, is it true that God has said,* **Ye shall not eat of every tree of the garden?** The language seems like the continuation of a conversation, the previous part of which is not given. The question was adapted to awaken doubt in the woman's mind, and the tempter shrewdly addressed himself to the woman first, as the one more easily to be deceived than the man. Chrysostom thus expands the thought in the serpent's words: "What good is life in Paradise if we may not enjoy the things which are found therein, but must feel the pain of seeing before our eyes what we are forbidden to take and eat?" Critics have raised a needless and profitless question over the serpent's use of the name *Elohim,* rather than *Jehovah.* Keil thinks, that the tempter felt it necessary to ignore the personality of God by this omission of his covenant name in order to work distrust in the woman's mind. Lange says, that the demon could not utter the name of the covenant-God Jehovah, not knowing him in that relationship. According to Knobel, the writer omitted the name of Jehovah from fear of profaning it in such a connexion. All which seems far-fetched and worthless. See Introd., pp. 51–54.

2. **The woman said**—Her pausing to parley with so serious a temptation was a fearful mistake. To entertain the thoughts of an evil spirit is the sure way to become partaker of some measure of his nature.

3. **Neither shall ye touch it**—This is the woman's own addition to the commandment as given in chap. ii, 17, and is thought by many to imply that in her own mind the commandment was too severe. The tempter started a thought which she develops, as if soliloquizing: "Yes, it is even so. We may eat of all other fruit, but this particular tree we must not even **touch,** lest we die!" And thus the way is prepared for bolder words from the deceiver.

4. **Ye shall not surely die**—A direct and malicious contradiction of God's word as given in chap. ii, 17. Here the devil is revealed as Satan, *the adversary,* "a liar, and the father of it." John viii, 44. This daring advance in the temptation is commonly supposed to imply a noticeable wavering on the part of the woman.

5. **For God doth know**—The Satanic utterance here recorded is a specimen of blasphemously changing God's truth into a lie. The deceiver would make the woman believe that God was

B. C. 4004.   CHAPTER III.   93

God doth know that in the day ye eat thereof, then ᵉ your eyes shall be opened, and ye shall be as gods, knowing good and evil. **6** And when the woman saw that the tree *was* good for food, and that it *was* ² pleasant to the eyes, and a tree to be desired to make *one* wise, she took of the fruit thereof, ᶠ and did eat, and gave also unto her husband with her; ᵍ and he did eat. **7** And ʰ the eyes of them both were opened, ⁱ and they knew that they *were* naked; and they sewed fig leaves together, and made themselves ³ aprons. **8** And they heard ᵏ the

---

e Verse 7; Acts 26. 18.——2 Heb. *a desire.*——
f 1 Tim. 2. 14.——*g* Verses 12, 17.

h Verse 5.——*i* Chap. 2. 25.——3 Or, *things to gird about.*——*k* Job 38. 1.

---

keeping her in ignorance of some great good. **Your eyes shall be opened**—"'Your eyes,'" says the voice of the tempter, 'instead of closing in death, will be for the first time truly opened.' Here it is to be remarked that the hour when unbelief is born is immediately the birth hour of superstition. . . . And so, in like manner, is every sin a senseless and superstitious belief in the salutary effects of sin."—*Lange.* **Ye shall be as gods**—Rather, *as God.* The tempter would pervert the image of God in man by inducing a false aspiration. Elohim has made you in his own image, and yet withholds from you the honour and glory of **knowing good and evil.** Break this bond, eat this forbidden fruit, and you will at once become like Elohim, your Maker.

6. Good for food . . . pleasant to the eyes . . . to be desired to make one wise—Observe the threefold form of this first temptation. First, appeal is made to the animal appetite; next, to the longing eye; and then to an ambition to become wise and godlike. Thus, too, the apostle comprehends all generic forms of human temptation under "the lust of the flesh, and the lust of the eyes, and the pride of life." 1 John ii, 16. It is notable that when this same old serpent attempted the ruin of the Second Adam he employed the same threefold method of assault. The first, was based upon his sense of hunger; the second, was a suggestion to exhibit a vain display at the temple of God; and the third, to make himself a hero-god of the world. Comp. Matt. iv, 1–11. After the failure of the first Adam and the triumph of the Second in conflict with the devil, we may not plead that we are ignorant of Satan's devices. **She took of the fruit thereof, and did eat**—So it is that "when lust hath conceived it bringeth forth sin," (James i, 15,) and the heart walks after the eyes. Job xxxi, 7. **Her husband with her**—This is understood by some to imply that Adam was present with the woman during her temptation; but such a supposition seems inconsistent with the narrative, which exhibits Satan and the woman so prominently, and makes no allusion to the man. Better, therefore, to understand the עִמָּהּ, *with her*, of his subsequent partnership with her in transgression. Manifestly we have here a very concise record of a most important event. The great facts are stated, the guile of the tempter is exposed, and the sad result is chronicled. Other details are not attempted.

7. Knew that they were naked—Here is a stinging irony. Literally, *Opened were the eyes of both of them, and they knew that—naked were they!* Their eyes were opened, indeed, as the serpent had predicted, but his word was like the lying oracles of the heathen world, which contained a delusive double sense. What were their eyes opened to *know?* That they were like God? No; but that they were naked! Here is a standing type of the vanity, vexation, shame, and confusion of face into which the glowing assurances of the old serpent always lead. **Aprons** — Or *girdles*, of **fig leaves**, fastened about the hips.

8. Heard the voice of the Lord — Some interpreters understand this voice to have been the *sound* or *noise* made by the approach of Jehovah. Comp. "sound of a going" in 2 Sam. v, 24. But the two following verses imply that it was the voice of Jehovah *calling*, rather than the noise of his movement, that is here intended. Both ideas, however, may be combined, for the anthropomorphism here is a notable

Vol. I.—7

O. T.

94　　　　　　　　GENESIS.　　　　　　　B. C. 4004.

voice of the LORD God walking in the garden in the [4] cool of the day: and Adam and his wife [l] hid themselves from the presence of the LORD God amongst the trees of the garden. **9** And the LORD God called unto Adam, and said unto him, Where *art* thou? **10** And he said, I heard thy voice in the garden, [m] and I was afraid, because I *was* naked; and I hid myself. **11** And he said, Who told thee that thou *wast* naked?

Hast thou eaten of the tree, whereof I commanded thee that thou shouldest not eat? **12** And the man said, [n] The woman whom thou gavest *to be* with me, she gave me of the tree, and I did eat. **13** And the LORD God said unto the woman, What *is* this *that* thou hast done? And the woman said, [o] The serpent beguiled me, and I did eat. **14** And the LORD God said [p] unto the serpent, Because thou hast done this, thou *art*

---

[4] Heb. *wind.*——[l] Job 31. 33; Jeremiah 23. 24; Amos 9. 3.——[m] Chapter 2. 25; Exodus 3. 6; 1 John 3. 20.

[n] Chapter 2. 18; Job 31. 33; Prov. 28. 13.——[o] Verse 4; 2 Cor. 11. 3; 1 Tim. 2. 14.——[p] Exod. 21. 29, 32.

---

feature of the description. The voice that called was the well-known voice of One who had spoken to them before, and who now came **walking** to and fro **in the garden** as aforetime, but his **voice** now inspired fear rather than delight. **In the cool of the day**—Literally, *at the wind of the day*. That is, at the time of the evening breeze. It was the closing day of Adam's Eden life, and, as Delitzsch has observed, that hour is adapted to weaken the dissipating impressions and excitements of the day, and beget a stillness in the soul. Then arise in man's heart the sentiments of sadness and loneliness, of longing, and of the love of home. " Thus with our first parents: when evening comes, the first intoxication of the Satanic delusion subsides, stillness reigns within; they feel themselves isolated from the communion of God, parted from their original home, while the darkness, as it comes rushing in upon them, makes them feel that their inner light has gone out." **Hid themselves**—This action was on their part a confession of conscious guilt and shame.

9. **Where art thou**—אַיֶּכָּה, *where—thou?* or, *where* (shall I find) *thee?* How is it that I must now search for thee, who hast been wont to watch for my coming, and hail it with delight? The entire passage is in condescension to human conceptions. Not that Jehovah was unable to find the guilty one, but to intensify the picture of the sinner attempting to hide himself from Omniscience. Here, truly, is revealed the Good Shepherd seeking after the lost sheep.

10. **I was afraid, because I was naked**—Adam's self-defence was a self-betrayal. Fear, consequent upon a sense of guilt, distracts the reason, demoralizes the judgment, and exposes the transgressor to certain condemnation. His nakedness was, for the moment, more prominent in his thought than a proper sense of his guilt.

11. **Who told thee**—A question adapted to suggest to him the cause of his sense of nakedness. How is it that thou wast never conscious of thy nakedness before? This plea of nakedness was itself a confession of guilt.

12. **The woman whom thou gavest to be with me**—Observe the natural effort of a fallen nature to excuse its own guilt by casting the blame on another. And not only is **the woman** blamed, but a sinister reflection on Jehovah himself appears in the words **whom thou gavest to be with me**. This woman by my side, whom thou gavest to be my companion and helper, she has been the occasion of my eating the forbidden fruit.

13. **The serpent beguiled me**—The woman also, in her turn, throws the blame of her offence upon another. The serpent, she pleads, had imposed upon her by deception.

14. **The Lord God said**—Now follows the threefold judgment, pronounced first upon the serpent, next upon the woman, (verse 16,) and finally upon man, (17-19.) The malediction against the serpent (verses 14, 15) is itself threefold. The prime tempter is not asked, What is this thou hast done? for "the trial had now reached the fountain-head of sin, the purely evil purpose, the demoniacal, having no deeper ground, and requiring no fur-

cursed above all cattle, and above every beast of the field; upon thy belly shalt thou go, and ᑫ dust shalt thou eat all the days of thy life: **15** And I will put enmity between thee and the woman, and between ʳ thy seed and ˢ her seed; ᵗ it shall bruise thy head, and thou shalt bruise his heel. **16** Unto the woman

q Isaiah 65. 25; Micah 7. 17. —— *r* Matthew 3. 7; 13. 38; 23. 33; John 8. 44; Acts 13. 10; 1 John 3. 8. —— *s* Psalm 132. 11; Isaiah 7. 14; Micah 5. 3; Matthew 1. 23, 25; Luke 1. 31, 34, 35; Galatians 4. 4. —— *t* Romans 16. 20; Colossians 2. 15; Heb. 2. 14; 1 John 5. 5; Rev. 12. 7, 17.

ther investigation."—*Lange.* **Cursed above all cattle** — Not that other cattle or beasts were in their measure cursed, any more than in verse 1 is implied that they were subtile. Nor is the meaning *cursed by all cattle*, (as Gesenius, Lex., under מִן;) but, cursed *from 'all;* that is, thou only out of all. As the serpent was distinguished from all the beasts on account of his subtilty, (verse 1,) so is he doomed to a like distinction in this condemnation. "The ground was cursed for man's sake," says Keil, "but not the animal world for the serpent's sake, nor even along with the serpent." **Upon thy belly shalt thou go** — Thou shalt ever be thought of as an abominable crawler. Comp. Lev. xi, 42. This has been supposed by many to imply that the shape and movements of the serpent were miraculously changed by this curse. Thus Delitzsch: "As its speaking was the first demoniacal miracle, so is this transformation the first divine." Some have supposed that originally the serpent walked erect; others, that it had wings like a cherub, and could fly. All this, however, is in the realm of conjecture, and not necessarily implied in the words. The serpent may have crawled and eaten dust before as well as after the curse, but as all was then very good, no sense of shame, or curse, or humiliation, attached to these conditions. As the nakedness of the man and the woman excited no thoughts of shame or improper exposure, so the creeping things of the earth, and the serpent among them, had no unfavourable associations attached to their bestial shape or habits. But the serpent's connexion with man's sin caused him, as apart from all other beasts, to have his natural form and locomotion cursed into that which ever suggests disgust, meanness, and enmity. **Dust shalt thou eat**—For being a crawler on the ground and eating its food in the dirt, the serpent must needs devour much dust along with his food. Hence to "lick the dust like a serpent" is a proverbial expression. Micah vii, 17. "And while all other creatures shall escape from the doom which has come upon them in consequence of the fall of man, (Isa. lxv, 25,) the serpent, the instrument used in the temptation, shall, agreeably to the words in the sentence, **all the days of thy life,** remain condemned to a perpetual abasement, thus prefiguring the fate of the real tempter, for whom there is no share in the redemption."—*Hengstenberg.*

15. **Enmity between thee and the woman**—That a sense of enmity exists between the entire serpent race and mankind is a conspicuous fact, account for it as we may. But no better reason for it can be given than that presented in this Scripture, namely, because it was basely associated with man's original sin. **It shall bruise thy head, and thou shalt bruise his heel.**—It is difficult to ascertain the precise meaning of the word שׁוּף, here rendered *bruise.* It occurs but three times, namely, here, Job ix, 17, and Psa. cxxxix, 11. The Septuagint renders it here by τηρέω, to *watch for ;* in Job by ἐκτρίβω, to *rub ;* in the Psalm by καταπατέω, to *tread upon.* The Vulgate translates it by two different words in this passage, *contero,* to *bruise,* in the first sentence, and *insidior,* to *lie in wait for,* in the second, but in Psa. cxxxix it has *conculco,* to *tread upon.* The word evidently denotes some sort of deadly stroke or wound, and the universal habit of man to seek to wound the serpent's head, while the serpent is apt to wound the heel, (comp. chap. xlix, 17,) confirms the realistic character of this narrative.

But while this Scripture is capable of such a simple and literal interpretation, it has also its profounder allusions. As the serpent was but the instrument of the devil, the father of lies, (see note on verse 1,) so the curse pronounced against the crooked, crawling beast has a deeper application to Satan and his seed. The base crawling, the dust-eating, and the heel-biting of serpents symbolize the habits of the old serpent, the devil. He evermore moves about his demoniacal work in conscious condemnation, as if in trembling (James ii, 19) and in torment. Matt. viii, 29. Like unto the natural enmity existing between the serpent-race and man is that irrepressible conflict between Satan and the redeemed man. Tayler Lewis suggests that **head** and **heel** in this Scripture may denote the strong contrast between the methods of contest of these two eternal foes. The seed of the woman fights in a bold and manly way, and strikes openly at the head. Biting or striking at the heel, on the contrary, "denotes the mean, insidious character of the devil's warfare, not only as carried on by the equivocating appetites, but also as waged by infidels and self-styled rationalists in all ages, who never meet Christianity in a frank and manly way."

But who, in this deeper sense, is that "seed" who shall bruise the serpent's head? The masculine pronoun HE (הוא) is not without significance. The reading is not *ipsa, she herself*, as the Vulgate has it, and which some Romanists understand of the Virgin Mary; nor **it**, of the English version, which fails to convey the force of the Hebrew, הוא. We fully accord with the great body of Christian interpreters who recognise here the first Messianic prophecy, the *protevangelium*. But this prophecy, given in Paradise before the expulsion of the transgressors, should not be explained exclusively of the personal Messiah. That promised seed comprehends also the redeemed humanity of which he is Head—that great company who both suffer with him and with him shall also be glorified. Rom. viii, 17. The final triumph will not be won without much bloodshedding and many wounds. The old serpent has more than once bruised the great Conqueror's heel, and many of the faithful "have resisted unto blood, striving against sin." Heb. xii, 4. So only those who belong to Christ as their great head and leader, are the seed of promise; all others, though born of woman, by espousing the serpent's cause and doing the lusts of the devil (John viii, 44) are of the seed of the serpent, a "generation of vipers," (Matt. xxiii, 33,) whose end is perdition. "Against the natural serpent," says Keil, "the conflict may be carried on by the whole human race—by all who are born of woman—but not against Satan. As he is a foe who can only be met with spiritual weapons, none can encounter him successfully but such as possess and make use of spiritual arms. Hence the idea of the seed is modified by the nature of the foe. If we look at the natural development of the human race, Eve bore three sons, but only one of them, namely, *Seth*, was really the seed by which the human family was preserved through the flood, and perpetuated in Noah. So, again, of the three sons of Noah, *Shem*, the blessed of Jehovah, from whom Abraham descended, was the only one in whose seed all nations were to be blessed; and that not through Ishmael, but through Isaac alone. Through these constantly repeated acts of divine selection, which were not arbitrary exclusions, but were rendered necessary by differences in the spiritual condition of the individuals concerned, the seed to which the victory over Satan was promised was determined, and ceased to be co-extensive with physical descent. This spiritual seed culminated in Christ, in whom the Adamitic family terminated, henceforward to be renewed by Christ as the Second Adam, and to be restored by him to its original exaltation and likeness to God. . . . On the other hand, all who have not regarded and preserved the promise, have fallen into the power of the old serpent, and are to be regarded as the seed of the serpent, whose head will be trodden under foot." Matt. xxiii, 33; John viii, 44; 1 John iii, 8. Comp. the conflict between Michael and his angels, and the dragon and his angels in Rev. xii, 7-9.

CHAPTER III.

he said, I will greatly multiply thy sorrow and thy conception; ^u in sorrow thou shalt bring forth children; ^v and thy desire *shall be* ⁵ to thy husband, and he shall ^w rule over thee. **17** And unto Adam he said, ^x Because thou hast hear-

---
u Psalm 48. 6; Isaiah 13. 8; 21. 3; John 16. 21; 1 Timothy 2. 15.——*v* Chapter 4. 7.——5 Or, *subject to thy husband.*——*w* 1 Corinthians 11. 3; 14. 34; Ephesians 5. 22, 23, 24; 1 Timothy 2. 11.

---

16. Unto the woman he said— A fourfold sentence: 1) multiplied pains of conception and pregnancy; 2) the pangs of childbirth; 3) the desire of the husband; and 4) the subjection to the authority of the man. Or the sentence may be treated as twofold by connecting the first and second together, the pains of pregnancy and childbirth being naturally associated; and the third and fourth are, in like manner, closely related in thought. The words **thy sorrow and thy conception** are properly regarded by most commentators as a hendiadys, meaning the *sorrow of thy conception*. The anxiety and pains of woman in conception, pregnancy, and childbirth are a most impressive commentary on this Scripture. The travail of childbirth is frequently alluded to as the image of deepest distress. Isa. xiii, 8; Jer. xxx, 6; Micah iv, 9. **Thy desire shall be to thy husband**—Not sensual desire, though that may be remotely implied, but that instinctive inclination and tendency of heart which the female sex has ever shown toward man. The woman seems to have aspired to headship and leadership, but, being first in transgression, is doomed to be the "weaker vessel," instinctively clinging to the man who has lordship over her.

17. Unto Adam he said—The examination began with Adam, (verse 9,) and the offence was traced to the serpent, (verse 13;) the condemnation was pronounced first upon the serpent (verse 14) and last upon the man. The curse pronounced against the man seems manifold. It contains, at least, five elements of woe: 1) On account of him the very soil is cursed, and, as a penal result of that curse, 2) the ground he tills will produce thorns and thistles along with the herb which is

kened unto the voice of thy wife, ^y and hast eaten of the tree, ^z of which I commanded thee, saying, Thou shalt not eat of it: ^a cursed *is* the ground for thy sake; ^b in sorrow shalt thou eat *of* it all the days of thy life; **18** ^c Thorns also

---
12; Titus 2. 5; 1 Peter 3. 1, 5, 6.——*x* 1 Samuel 15. 23.——*y* Verse 6.——*z* Chapter 2. 17.——*a* Ecclesiastes 1. 2, 3; Isaiah 24. 5, 6; Romans 8. 20. ——*b* Job 5. 7; Ecclesiastes 2. 23.——*c* Job 31. 40.

---

to be his food. Verse 18. Moreover, 3) the cultivation of the grain which is to be his food, will involve toilsome and tiring labour, causing the sweat to stand upon his face, (verse 19,) and consequently, 4) his very eating will be **in sorrow.** 5) At last he himself must die and return to the dust from which he was taken. **Because thou hast hearkened...and hast eaten** — To *listen* was a culpable weakness, to *eat* the forbidden fruit a crime. The plea of Adam (in verse 12) is of no avail. For the weakness of hearkening to his transgressing wife he must expend his manly strength in life-long painful struggle with a cursed soil, and for his own transgression of the commandment he must return to dust. **Cursed is the ground**—Instead of a delightful Paradise, he shall find the ground becoming barren and unfruitful. Often since this general curse was uttered has God, by special judgments, cursed the land for the sins of the people. See Isa. xxiv, 1 – 6; Jer. xxiii, 10.

In sorrow shalt thou eat — עִצָּבוֹן, *labour, distress.* The same word employed in verse 16 to denote the woman's sorrow. Her perpetual reminder of the original sin is to be the pain of childbearing; his, the corresponding sorrow of oppressive labour for food in the midst of manifold vocations.

18. Thorns also and thistles— Not that these had never yet grown, though they may not have existed in the garden. They become a curse and a plague by often outstripping the better herbs. They become luxuriant in spite of human effort to root them up and destroy them, while the much desired edible products of the soil demand great labour, sweat, and care. This fact should also remind fallen

and thistles shall it ᵉ bring forth to thee; and ᵈ thou shalt eat the herb of the field: **19** ᵉ In the sweat of thy face shalt thou eat bread, till thou return unto the ground; for out of it wast thou taken: ᶠfor dust thou *art*, and ᵍ unto dust shalt thou return. **20** And Adam called his wife's name ⁷ Eve ;⁸ because she was the mother of all living. **21** Unto Adam also and to his wife did the LORD God make coats of skins, and clothed them. **22** And the LORD God said, ʰ Behold,

---

6 Hebrew, *cause to bud.* —— *d* Psalm 104. 14. —— *e* Eccles. 1. 13; 2 Thess. 3. 10. —— *f* Chapter 2. 7. —— *g* Job 21. 26; 34. 15; Psalm 104. 29;

Eccles. 3. 20; 12. 7; Romans 5. 12; Heb. 9. 27. —— 7 Heb. *Chavah.* —— 8 That is, *Living.* —— *h* Verse 5; like Isa. 19. 12; 47. 12, 13; Jer. 22. 23.

---

man that evil will grow in his heart more readily than good, and the "fruits of the Spirit" are not obtained and kept except by constant watching and working. The wild olive grows untilled, but not the good olive-tree; if that receive not cultivation, it will also run wild. Romans xi, 24. **Thou shalt eat the herb of the field**—These words may be understood as enhancing the idea of the curse and vexation of thorns and thistles just mentioned. Thus taking **herb**, in the broad sense of vegetable products necessary to man's subsistence, the thought would be: The herb of the field will be necessary for thy subsistence; but not as heretofore will it grow without the troublesome admixture of thorns and thistles. These ugly growths will furnish an element of vexation in procuring thy daily bread. But a better view is, that which takes the **herb of the field** as a sad contrast of the fruit of the trees of the garden. Chap. ii, 16; compare iii, 2. The fruits of Eden, furnished in profusion and without laborious toil, shall be thine no longer, but in their stead thou shalt be compelled to eat the herbs of the field.

19. **In the sweat of thy face shalt thou eat bread**—Not only shall the sweat oppress thee in thy toil, but even when thou sittest to eat bread, it shall appear on thy face. "This sentence includes all the sorrows, pains, and sweating toils to which men are subject in gaining a livelihood." — *Jacobus.* "No man eats bread but by the sweat of some man's face."—*Conant.* **Dust thou art,** (chap. ii, 7) **and unto dust shalt thou return**—Excluded from the garden and the tree of life, man must, sooner or later, suffer bodily dissolution. He may live nine hundred and thirty years, (chap. v, 5,) but the death will surely come. The perfection and vigour of the first man may reasonably be believed to have been the cause of patriarchal longevity. The vigour of the race gradually deteriorated until human life rarely continued beyond a hundred years. See note introductory to chapter v.

20. **Eve . . . the mother of all living**—The account of man's original sin concludes with four statements too important and suggestive to have been accidental. The new naming of the woman, (comp. chap. ii, 23,) the first clothing, the expulsion from the garden of Eden, and the two sacred symbols placed at the gate, are full of significance. The name **Eve,** חַוָּה, *Hhavvah*, from the intensive stem חָיָה, signifies *life-spring,* or *quickener of life.* Given in the very face of the death foreshadowed by the penal sentence, it seems to have arisen from Adam's faith in the promise that the woman's Seed should wound the serpent's head. In chap. ii, 23 he named her *Woman,* in view of her origin; here he names her *Eve,* in view of her hopeful destiny.

21. **Coats of skins** — To procure these, animals must have been slain, and this was probably done by the man in accordance with a divine commandment. With much reason, therefore, have Christian divines believed that this was the origin of sacrifices, the offering of blood as an atonement for the soul. Comp. Lev. xvii, 11. Possibly these animals were slain for food, but chap. ix, 3, taken in connexion with chap. i, 29, 30, has been thought to imply that animal food was not used by man before the flood. The covering of skins might have been an appropriate object-lesson to enforce the deeper lesson of the covering of guilt by the shedding of vicarious blood. Only by symbol could this deep lesson be then set forth.

CHAPTER III.

the man is become as one of us, to know good and evil: and now, lest he put forth his hand, ⁱ and take also of the tree of life, and eat, and live for ever: 23 Therefore the LORD God sent him forth from the garden of Eden, ᵏ to till

i Chap. 2. 9.——*k* Chap. 4. 2; 9. 20.

the ground from whence he was taken. 24 So he drove out the man: and he placed ¹ at the east of the garden of Eden ᵐ cherubim, and a flaming sword which turned every way, to keep the way of the tree of life.

l Chap. 2. 8.——*m* Psa. 104. 4; Heb. 1. 7.

22. **As one of us, to know good and evil**—The plural form of expression is the so-called *plural of majesty*, as in chapter i, 26. Some, however, imagine that the angels are here addressed. The likeness is defined and limited by the words, **to know good and evil**, and this entire utterance of Jehovah Elohim is a solemn declaration of judgment. The allusion to the serpent's words, in verse 5, is too marked to be denied, and hence we may allow that this word of the Lord contains an element of irony. This opinion is not to be set aside by the assertion that irony, at the expense of a fallen soul, would befit Satan rather than Jehovah. The irony is an element of the penal judgment, and as Gœschell (quoted in Lange) well observes, "a divine irony is everywhere the second stage in all divine acts of punishment." Lange himself thus paraphrases: "He is become like God; true, alas! God pity him! He knows now, in his guilty consciousness, the difference between good and evil." God, in his infinite holiness and wisdom, possesses absolute knowledge of good and evil, but not by participation in the evil. By a perfect knowledge and possession of good, sinning is with him immutably impossible. Heb. vi, 18. Man should have attained like knowledge in a normal way, not by an opening of his eyes through disobedience. Compare note on chap. ii, 17. **Take also of the tree of life**—The word **also** does not necessarily imply "that the man had not yet eaten of the tree of life," (*Keil*,) nor are we to suppose that once eating of the fruit of that tree would secure exemption from death. Often, during his sojourn in Eden, might he have eaten of that tree. But now, lest by continuing to eat he maintain himself in immortal vigour, he must be excluded from the garden, and allowed no access to the tree of life.

23. **Therefore the Lord God sent him forth**—The divine utterance in the previous verse was impressively left unfinished, a notable example of aposiopesis. The writer here passes abruptly to state what immediately followed the penal sentence, as if unwilling to express the awful words of the Judge. **To till the ground from whence he was taken**—His toilsome labour in the dust is to be a constant reminder both of his bodily origin and of his future dissolution. Compare verse 19.

24. **Cherubim, and a flaming sword**—More accurately the Revised Version: *the cherubim, and the flame of a sword.* There is nothing in this narrative to assure us that these cherubim were "real creatures, and not mere symbols." (*Murphy.*) Their introduction into a history of what was real does not prove that they, any more than the flaming sword, were real creatures. Rather, both cherubim and sword were significant symbols **placed at the east of the garden of Eden**, in sight of our first parents, (as Moses lifted up a brazen serpent in view of penitent Israel, Num. xxi, 9,) and adapted to inculcate some important fact or lesson of divine revelation. The flame of the sword—probably a flame of fire in the form of a sword—would have served as a symbol of divine justice to intensify the certainty of retributive judgment on every transgressor. Such a spectacle, turning to and fro before the eyes of the first man, was a significant "object lesson" to inspire holy fear of God, the righteous Judge. In connexion with the words of promise (verse 15) and the doctrine of sacrifice and atonement, (verse 21, note,) it was necessary to impress the lesson that the Justifier must himself be just. See Rom. iii, 26. But what was the appearance of the cherubim, and what

did they signify? In Ezek. i, 5-14, they are represented as "living creatures," combining the four highest types of animal life, namely, man, lion, ox, and eagle, and moving in closest connexion with the mystic wheels of divine providence and judgment. Ezek. i, 15-21. Over their heads was enthroned the appearance of the likeness of the glory of Jehovah. Ezek. i, 26-28. In Rev. iv, 6-8, they appear also as living creatures "in the midst of the throne, and round about the throne," and the New Testament seer combines with them some features peculiar to the seraphim of Isaiah vi, 2, 3. These latter seem to have been the same in the heavenly temple as the cherubim were in the temple and tabernacle. Moses was commanded to make two cherubim of gold, and place them in the holy of holies, one at each end of the mercy-seat, with their faces toward each other, and their wings spread out over the mercy-seat. Exod. xxv, 18-20. Hence Jehovah was thought of as dwelling with, or sitting upon, the cherubim. 1 Sam. iv, 4; 2 Sam. vi, 2; Psa. lxxx, 1; xcix, 1; Isa. xxxvii, 16. Whatever the various import of these composite figures, we should observe that they everywhere appear in most intimate relation to the glory of God, and to be filled with intensity of life. As now the flaming sword symbolized the righteous judgment of God and proclaimed his fearful justice, so, on the other hand, the cherubim were suggestive symbols of the eternal life and heavenly glory to be secured to man through the mystery of redemption. Their composite form would serve to illustrate the immanence and intense activity of God in all created life—an incarnation or embodiment of divine life in earthly form, by which all that was lost in Eden might be restored to heavenly places in Christ. Thus the Edenic symbols were a grand apocalypse, revealing the glorious truth that man, redeemed and filled with the Spirit, shall again have power over the tree of life which is in the midst of the Paradise of God. Comp. Rev. ii, 7, and xxii, 14. Though of composite form, and representing the highest kinds of creature-life on earth, those symbols had pre-eminently the likeness of a man. Ezekiel i, 5. Jehovah is the God of the living, and has about the throne of his glory the highest symbols of life. So at the gate of Eden and in the holy of holies, the cherubim were signs and pledges that in the ages to come, having made peace through the blood of the cross, God would "reconcile all things unto himself," whether things upon the earth or things in the heavens, (Col. i, 20,) and sanctify them in his glory. Exod. xxix, 43. The redeemed are to "reign in life" through Jesus Christ. Rom. v, 17. It is significant, therefore, that these prophetic symbols were set to **keep the way of the tree of life.** That way was not to be closed up forever. It was guarded both by justice and love, and will be until the work of redemption becomes complete, and "there shall be no more curse." Rev. xxii, 3. Then the redeemed of Adam's race, having washed their robes, shall have the right to come to the tree of life, and shall "enter through the gates into the city." Rev. xxii, 14. The New Testament vision of new heavens and new earth, and New Jerusalem, are but a fuller revelation of what was shown in symbol at the east of the garden of Eden. The whole earth shall become a blessed Eden, (comp. Micah iv, 1-5,) the holy city shall, like the happy garden, become its holy of holies, into which fallen man, having washed his robes, shall freely enter, for then, in the highest reality, "the tabernacle of God" shall be "with men, and he will dwell with them, and they shall be his people, and God himself shall be with them, and be their God. And God shall wipe away all tears from their eyes; and there shall be no more death, neither sorrow, nor crying, neither shall there be any more pain: for the former things are passed away." Rev. xxi, 3, 4.

It is significant, that in the New Testament Apocalypse no cherubim appear about the throne of God and the Lamb. For the mere symbols of redeemed humanity are supplanted by the innumerable multitude in blood-washed robes, (comp. Rev. vii, 9-17,) from whom the curse has been removed, and who take the places of the cherubim and seraphim about the throne, behold the glory of Christ, (comp. John xvii, 24,) look upon the face of God and the Lamb, act as his servants, and have his name upon their foreheads. Rev. xxii, 3, 4. So the New Testament Apocalypse completes what the one at the garden of Eden but dimly foreshadowed.

CONCLUDING NOTE ON GENESIS iii.

This third chapter of Genesis presents a number of the most mysterious questions occurring to the mind of man, but it does not solve the mysteries. We recognise in it four elements of symbolic revelation. We may well hesitate to interpret all its statements in their extreme realistic and literal sense, but we may at the same time perceive that this unique narrative deals with momentous facts, not with fancies. "It is just as little a mere allegory," says Lange, "as the human race itself is a mere allegory." In its descriptions and manifold suggestions it is in harmony with the deepest experiences of the human heart, and with all other lessons of divine revelation. Among its lessons we note the following:

1. The problem of moral evil is connected with a spiritual world, and with a demoniacal being, who had become sinful and malicious before man appeared. Already God's universe was somewhere dark with hell. How evil entered—when and where the tempter first appeared—are questions which this Scripture suggests but does not answer. That sin originated in an abuse of moral freedom is implied in this account of man's first sin. That the tempter was in fact a personal evil nature, acting in the guise of a serpent, appears from later revelations of Scripture. See especially John viii, 44, and Rev. xii, 9. That the old serpent, the devil, is chief of legions of like demoniac beings appears from the New Testament, and there is no good reason for believing that this doctrine of evil spirits was first learned by the Jews in the land of their exile.

2. The wiles of the devil notably appear in the craft with which he tempted Eve; and his threefold appeal to the lust of the flesh, the lust of the eye, and the lust of power, (see note on verse 6,) are strikingly analogous to the three temptations of our Lord. The credibility of this ancient narrative is confirmed by this fidelity of its description to the manifold experiences of men in the midst of foul temptation. As human nature is ever the same in its weakness and exposure, so the wiles of the old adversary continue the same from age to age.

3. But whilst Satan has mysteriously obtruded himself into the realm of human life and experience, so, on the other hand, a merciful but righteous God has, by many supernatural theophanies, revealed himself to man. His interposition is for the purpose of crushing the old serpent's head. The enmity will be exhibited through ages of conflict. Satan will be permitted to reveal himself with all variety of power and signs, and lying wonders, and with all deceit of unrighteousness, (2 Thess. ii, 9, 10;) but, on the other hand, the mystery of God in Christ will also be revealed by many miraculous signs, and by symbolic revelations adapted to cheer and strengthen those who look for redemption. The benevolent Creator adapts himself to the wants of his creatures, and gradually unfolds a revelation of infinite wisdom and worth. So far from acceding to the rationalistic assumption that the miraculous in human history is impossible and incredible, we rather assume the opposite, suggested by this narrative of man's original estate and first sin—that, to overcome the evil one, miraculous interposition of a stronger than Satan is to be expected. And so all the theophanies and all the miracles recorded in the ancient Scriptures are but a fitting preparation for the incarnation and redeeming work of the Son of God. In keeping with this it is notable that the two impressive symbols revealed at the gate of Paradise embody the substance of all subsequent Scripture revelation.

4. How far man's original sin affected

the physical creation may be left an open question. The ground was cursed for man's sake, (verses 17, 18,) and some have thought that all suffering of animals is a consequence of human sin. Here, however, we should proceed with great caution. Decay and death in the vegetable and animal world appeared long before the creation of man, as the fossil rocks abundantly declare. The passage in Rom. viii, 19-21, even if understood of the animal creation, does not affirm that the subjection to suffering was a penalty or consequence of man's sin. Many things have been made a curse to man; thorns and thistles, cold and heat, pestilence and famine, ravenous beasts and destructive insects, have scourged the sons of Adam. But while these facts abundantly confirm the word spoken in verses 17 and 18, there is no proof that any part of the physical or animal world suffered change on account of man's sin. So the serpent's form and man's nakedness were made a curse, but not by undergoing any natural or physical change.

But while we may deny that suffering and death in the animal creation are a consequence of man's sin, we may well hesitate to affirm that they are in no way whatever a consequence of sin. The existence of the Satanic tempter suggests that sin was in the world before God planted the garden of Eden. We may even venture the statement that before a serpent appeared among "the beasts of the field," "that old serpent, called the Devil and Satan," was abroad in the world. But whether the first sin known in the universe of God originated with Satan we may not affirm. As little do we know what havoc and disorder had been previously introduced into creation by wicked "principalities and powers." Eph. vi, 12. This we do know, that sin spreads ruin and death in the moral world, and, reigning in the spirit of man, it affects his body also, and subjects him to manifold miseries. Who can say how far sin and rebellion in mighty spirits of wickedness in the heavenly regions (Eph. vi, 12) may have had to do in subjecting the creation of God to suffering and death? We know also that, in the gracious economy of our heavenly Father, suffering and tribulation are made to serve a wise disciplinary purpose, and to work for us an eternal glory. 2 Cor. iv, 17. The rich depths of divine wisdom and knowledge are too great for our understanding, (Rom. xi, 33;) and, for aught we know, the power of Christ's mediation may so extend to "things in the heavens" (Col. i, 20) as to reconcile disorders and mischiefs introduced by sin before the foundation of this earth.

CHAPTER IV.
CAIN AND ABEL, 1-15.

"The consequences of the fall now appear in the history of the first family. By careful attention to the record, we may learn the true nature of the primitive religion, its rites, its hopes, and faith. We may also see here most instructive traces of the primeval civilization. While fearful sin stains the firstborn of man, sadly crushing the joyful hopes of the first mother, a pious son also appears, setting forth thus early the contrast and conflict between good and evil, which is to run through human history. The good at first is overcome by the evil; Abel is slain by Cain; but another son (Seth, *set* or *placed*) is set in his place at the head of the godly line."—*Newhall*.

In the following chapter the careful reader will note, 1) in the two types of men the first outward development of the two seeds—that of the serpent and that of the woman, (chap. iii, 15;) 2) agriculture and the keeping of flocks as the earliest employments of men; 3) the doctrine of sacrifices established at the very gate of Paradise; 4) God's earliest manifestations of favour to the righteous and of displeasure towards the sinner; 5) the beginnings of polygamy; 6) art, culture, and human depravity and sinfulness keeping pace with one another; so that an advanced civilization, in spite of all the refining and ennobling tendencies of art and culture, may, without the divine favour, only serve to intensify the corruption and violence of men; 7) the Cainites, in founding the first

CHAPTER IV.

AND Adam knew Eve his wife; and she conceived, and bare [1] Cain, and said, I have gotten a man from the LORD. 2 And she again bare his brother [2]Abel.

[1] That is, *Gotten,* or, *Acquired.*
[2] Heb. *Hebel.*

city, and by worldly inventions and arts, lead the way in building up the godless kingdom of the beast, the world-power of Antichrist; the godly seed, by faith and piety begin to build the kingdom of heaven.

1. **Adam knew Eve** — A euphemism, based upon a profound conception of the marital relation. "Generation in man is an act of personal free-will, not a blind impulse of nature. It flows from the divine institution of marriage, and is, therefore, *knowing* the wife."—*Keil.* **Bare Cain**—In the Hebrew the word **Cain** has the emphatic particle את before it, *the Cain.* In these most ancient narratives names have special significance, and the name **Cain** is most naturally derived from the Hebrew קן, *kun,* or קָנָה, *kana,* the word immediately used by Eve, and translated in our text, **I have gotten.** A better translation would be, *I have begotten.* The name **Cain**, then, would signify *offspring,* or *one begotten,* rather than *possession,* as held by many writers. See Fürst's *Heb. Lex.* and T. Lewis's note in Lange *in loc.* **A man from the Lord**—Literally, *a man, the Jehovah.* This exact rendering appears to us better than our common version, which follows the Targum of Onkelos; better than the Sept. and Vulg. *by the Lord;* better than any attempt to paraphrase the passage, or construe the את as a preposition. With MacWhorter (see *Bib. Sacra* for January, 1857, and the volume entitled "*Yahveh Christ,* or, *the Memorial Name*") and Jacobus, we understand Eve's exclamation as a kind of joyful *eureka* over the firstborn of the race, as if in this seed of the woman was to be realized the promise of the *protevangelium* recorded in chap. iii, 15. Keil's objection to this view, on the ground that Eve knew nothing of the divine nature of the promised seed, and could not have uttered the name Jehovah, because it was not revealed until a later period, is unwarrantable assumption. The statement of Exodus vi, 3, (where see note,) that the name Jehovah was not known to the patriarchs, does not mean that the name was never used before the days of Moses; and if these are not the very words of Eve, or their exact equivalent, why should we believe that she said any thing of the kind? If the name JEHOVAH was used at all by Eve, it is likely that something of its profound significance had been revealed in connexion with the first promise of the coming One. And it would have been very natural for the first mother, in her enthusiasm over the birth of her first child, to imagine him the promised Conqueror. But, as T. Lewis observes, "The greatness of Eve's mistake in applying the expression to one who was the type of Antichrist rather than of the Redeemer, should not so shock us as to affect the interpretation of the passage, now that the covenant God is revealed to us as a being so transcendently different. The limitation of Eve's knowledge, and perhaps her want of due distinction between the divine and the human, only sets in a stronger light the intensity of her hope, and the subjective truthfulness of her language. Had her reported words, at such a time, contained no reference to the promised seed of the woman, the Rationalist would doubtless have used it as a proof that she could have known nothing of any such prediction, and that therefore Gen. iii, 15, and Gen. iv, 1, must have been written by different authors, ignoring or contradicting each other." Eve's hasty and mistaken expectation of the coming Deliverer is a fitting type of the periodic but mistaken premillennialism of New Testament times, which has, with almost every generation, disturbed the Church with excitement over the expected immediate coming of Christ.

2. **She again bare**—Literally, *she added to bear;* which expression has usually been construed to mean that

GENESIS. About B. C. 3875.

And Abel was [3] a keeper of sheep, but Cain was [a] a tiller of the ground. 3 And [4] in process of time it came to pass, that Cain brought [b] of the fruit of the ground an offering unto the LORD. 4 And Abel, he also brought of [c] the firstlings of his [5] flock and of the fat thereof. And the LORD had [d] respect unto Abel and to his offering: 5 But unto Cain and to his offering he had not respect. And Cain

---

[3] Heb. *a feeder.* — [a] Chap. 3. 23; 9. 20. — [4] Heb. *at the end of days.* — [b] Num. 18. 12.

[c] Num. 18. 17; Prov. 3. 9. — [5] Heb. *sheep,* or, *goats.* — [d] Heb. 11. 4.

Cain and Abel were twins; but such meaning is not necessarily in the words. They simply mean that Eve bore another son. Nor is it necessary to suppose that Abel was born next after Cain; between the two, Adam and Eve may have begotten many sons and daughters. Chap. v, 4. The name **Abel,** (which means *a breath, a vapour, vanity,* or *nothingness,*) suggests that the mother, so joyful and hopeful over her firstborn, had now perceived her error, and the vanity of hopes of human birth. Or, perhaps, the name **Abel** was given with a fearful presentiment of his lamentable death. **A keeper of sheep . . . a tiller of the ground** — Thus the occupations of shepherding and agriculture appear side by side in this most ancient history. The notion that man's primitive condition was that of savagery, in which he lived by hunting, and from which he subsequently advanced into nomadic pursuits, and later still into the pursuits of agriculture, has no support here. Adam was put in the garden to dress and keep it, (ii, 15,) and on his expulsion thence he was probably instructed to keep sheep for sacrifice and clothing, (iii, 21.) But there is no evidence that the first generation of men were endued with any superior gifts or with a high civilization. The conditions of such a civilization were, from the nature of the case, wanting. The first men were neither savages nor barbarians; but their numbers were limited, and their habits and pursuits of the most simple kind.

3. **In process of time**—Heb. *at the end of days.* Of how many days is not specified, and some understand at the end of the year, or at the time of the gathering of fruits; others explain the phrase indefinitely, as our version, or as Keil: "After a considerable lapse of time." It seems better, however, to understand it of the days of the week — that is, at the end of the ordinary and well-known week of seven days. In this sense we have here another trace of the original institution of the Sabbath as a day of worship. **Cain brought of the fruit**—A most natural offering for a tiller of the ground to bring, and a gift sufficiently proper in itself. But his failure to bring also a bleeding sacrifice may well be looked upon as evidence of a want of faith in the doctrine of sacrifices, and a disposition to substitute what was most convenient to him for all that the law of sacrifice required.

4. **Abel . . . brought of the firstlings of his flock and of the fat thereof**—The best and most complete offering which he could make, not the most convenient, or the ones that came first to hand. He seems to have apprehended something of the profound doctrine, afterward made so prominent, that without shedding of blood there is no remission, and hence especially the reason why **the Lord had respect unto Abel and to his offering.** In what way this **respect,** or favourable *look,* was shown is not recorded, but the ancient and prevailing opinion is, that God sent down fire from heaven to consume the sacrifice. Comp. Lev. ix, 24; Judg. vi, 21; 1 Kings xviii, 38. Jehovah's look was thus a fire-glance from heaven that set the offering aflame. The word translated **offering** (מִנְחָה) is always used in the Mosaic laws of a "meat offering," or bloodless sacrifice; but here it is applied to Abel's gift as well as to Cain's.

5. **But unto Cain . . . not respect** —Why? From Hebrews xi, 4, we infer that it was because of some lack of faith, for "by faith Abel offered unto God a more excellent sacrifice than Cain." Cain's, then, was not the blossomings or the fruit of faith in Jehovah. It sprung from no profound con-

About B. C. 3875.　　CHAPTER IV.　　105

was very wroth, *e* and his countenance fell. **6** And the LORD said unto Cain, Why art thou wroth? and why is thy countenance fallen? **7** If thou doest well, shalt thou not *e* be accepted? and if thou doest not well, sin lieth at the door: and *ⁿ* unto thee *shall be* his desire, and thou shalt rule over him. **8** And

Cain talked with Abel his brother: and it came to pass, when they were in the field, that Cain rose up against Abel his brother, and *f* slew him.
  9 And the LORD said unto Cain, *g* Where *is* Abel thy brother? And he said, *h* I know not: *Am* I my brother's keeper? **10** And he said, What hast

---

e Chap. 31. 2.——6 Or, *have the excellency?* Heb. 11. 4.——7 Or, *subject unto thee,* chap.　　3. 16.——*f* Matt. 23. 35; 1 John 3. 12; Jude 11.——*g* Psa. 9. 12.——*h* John 8. 44.

---

ception of the grounds or need of sacrifice. And, perhaps, as suggested above, Cain's lack of faith was evinced by his neglect to bring a bleeding victim. If animal sacrifices were of divine institution, (see note on iii, 21,) Cain must have known the fact and the mode; but so far from regarding it, he seems not to have been even careful to bring the *firstfruits* of the ground. Hence his offering was not a *doing well.*
Verse 7. **Cain was very wroth**—Manifestly yielding to passions of jealousy and anger. **His countenance fell**—Like a sullen, spoiled child, pouting with bad passion, and waiting for an opportunity of revenge.
  6. **The Lord said unto Cain**—By an angel or by the lips of Adam, or by one of Cain's brothers or sisters. **Why . . . wroth**—A question and an appeal that might well have wrought in Cain a conviction of his wrong.
  7. **Shalt thou not be accepted**—Rather, *is there not an uplifting,* that is, of the countenance. The downcast, sullen look is not a mark of him that doeth well. **Sin lieth at the door**—In the Hebrew **sin** is a feminine noun, and **lieth** is a masculine participal, because, says Keil, with evident allusion to the serpent, "sin is personified as a wild beast, lurking at the door of the human heart, and eagerly desiring to devour his soul." 1 Pet. v, 8. But we cannot, with Keil and others, understand that which follows, **unto thee shall be his desire,** as referring also to sin personified, for the words as used can scarcely justify the paraphrase: sin, lying at the door of thy heart, has strong desire to enter in and control thee; nevertheless, if thou do well, thou shalt obtain the mastery, and rule over sin. The better interpretation is that which refers the pronouns **his** and **him** to Abel. The Lord thus assures Cain that he has nothing to fear from Abel, whose תְּשׁוּקָה, *desire,* (tender and loyal devotion,) is strong and fervent towards him as his elder brother, and, therefore, certain to attempt no interference with Cain's right of primogeniture to **rule over him,** and thus enjoy all the privileges of his natural pre-eminence.
  8. **Talked with Abel**—Rather, *said to Abel.* The Septuagint, Samaritan, Syriac, and Vulgate supply: *Let us go into the field;* but the Hebrew text does not relate what he said, but, as in chap. iii, 22, 23, hastens to the sequel, the bloody action **in the field.** The repetition of the words, **his brother,** seems designed to impress the awful wickedness of the deed. **Slew him**—The first death was by violence; the first murder a fratricide. "And wherefore slew he him?" inquires the apostle. 1 John iii, 12. "Because his own works were evil, and his brother's righteous." "Cain was of that wicked one," whom the Lord declares (John viii, 44) to have been "a murderer from the beginning," "a liar, and the father of it." By his lying he deceiveth the whole world and makes himself the murderer of man. Cain identified himself with that wicked one, became a child of the devil, and representative of the seed of the serpent. The first murder sprung from jealousy; jealousy begat hatred, and hatred begat murder. Hence the apostle says: "Whosoever hateth his brother is a murderer." 1 John iii, 15.
  9. **Where is Abel**—God's judgment with Cain, as with Adam, begins with the searching WHERE? Comp. chap. iii, 9. **I know not**—It is easy for a murderer to lie. **I my brother's**

thou done? the voice of thy brother's ᵃblood ⁱ crieth unto me from the ground. 11 And now *art* thou cursed from the earth, which hath opened her mouth to receive thy brother's blood from thy hand. 12 When thou tillest the ground, it shall not henceforth yield unto thee her strength; a fugitive and a vagabond shalt thou be in the earth. 13 And Cain said unto the LORD, ᵍMy punishment *is* greater than I can bear. 14ᵏ Behold, thou hast driven me out this day from the face of the earth; and ˡ from thy face shall I be hid; and I shall be a

---

8 Hebrew, *bloods.*——*i* Hebrews 12, 24; Revelation 6. 10.——9 Or, *Mine iniquity* is *greater than* that it may *be forgiven.* —— *k* Job 15. 20-24.——*l* Psalm 51. 11.

---

keeper—Am I his shepherd, to watch over him? A word of daring impudence and defiance; a sort of retort on the Lord's care of Abel. "How is it that thou, who hadst delight in him, and didst show him such favouritism, hast not watched over him!"

10. **What hast thou done**—In this verse it is well to emphasize and compare together the words **thou, thy brother, me.** The guilt of the bloody deed rests upon Cain's dark soul; the brother's blood cries to heaven; God hears, and will not ignore the cry. "The pious Abel had pleaded with his fierce brother in vain, but the great God hears the cry of injured innocence. He is the God of those whom men forget and scorn. Every groan and cry that tyranny and persecution crush from broken hearts are gathered up in the all-embracing heaven, and poured into that ever-listening ear."—*Newhall.* The Hebrew words for **blood** and **crieth** are in the plural, as if to suggest that *all the drops* or *streams* of blood thus violently shed took on so many imploring tongues. "The blood, as the living flow of the life, and the phenomenal basis of the soul, has a voice which is as the living echo of the blood-clad soul itself. It is the symbol of the soul crying for its right to live."—*Lange.*

11. **Cursed from the earth**—The curse shall seem to come forth out of the earth, **which hath opened her mouth to receive thy brother's blood.** As the next verse further explains, the ground, which so readily drank the innocent blood, will not be fruitful to the murderer's tilling. The earth, cursed by reason of Adam's sin, (iii, 17,) will seem to pour forth special judgments upon Cain. Others explain, less in keeping with the natural meaning of the words and the context: Thou art cursed *away from* the land; that is, banished out of this land, or district, where thy father and brothers dwell.

12. **Not henceforth yield**—Not add, or continue to yield, so abundantly as in the past. How much has righteousness in man to do in securing bountiful harvests, and averting pestilence and famine! **Her strength**—Her full fruitage, as the forceful and legitimate outcome of her fertility. In Job xxxi, 39, the word (כֹּחַ) is translated *fruits.* **A fugitive and a vagabond**—The Hebrew words here form a paranomasia, נָע וָנָד, *naʻ wa-nadh,* something like *plodding and nodding.* The first word means a restless wanderer, the second a roving fugitive.

13. **My punishment is greater than I can bear**—The words thus rendered will bear two interpretations, that given in the text, and that of the margin: *My sin is greater than can be forgiven.* Both interpretations are very ancient, and both yield a pertinent sense; but the next verse, in which Cain goes on to bewail the greatness of his curse, sustains the view that Cain deplored his punishment more than his sin. Both views, however, may be so far united as to show that in the murderer's soul there was a mingling of guilt, sorrow, and dismay.

14. **Thou hast driven**—Cain seems to charge all his curse on God, as if ignoring that he himself was the guilty cause. **From the face of the earth** —Special reference to the district of Eden. Compare verse 16. His sentence to be a vagabond and a fugitive involved this separation from Eden. **From thy face**—From that hallowed spot on the east of the garden of Eden where the symbols of the divine Presence were set, (chap. iii, 24,) and where,

About B. C. 3875. CHAPTER IV. 107

fugitive and a vagabond in the earth; and it shall come to pass, ᵐ *that* every one that findeth me shall slay me. 15 And the LORD said unto him, Therefore whosoever slayeth Cain, vengeance shall be taken on him ⁿ sevenfold. And the LORD ᵒ set a mark upon Cain, lest any finding him should kill him.

16 And Cain ᵖ went out from the presence of the LORD, and dwelt in the land of Nod, on the east of Eden. 17 And Cain knew his wife; and she conceived, and bare ¹⁰ Enoch: and he builded a city, ᑫ and called the name of the city, after the name of his son, Enoch. 18 And unto Enoch was born

---

m Chap. 9. 6; Num. 35. 19, 21, 27. —— *n* Psa. 79. 12.—*o* Ezek. 9. 4, 6.

p 2 Kings 13. 23; 24. 20; Jer. 23. 39; 52. 3.—10 Heb. *Chanoch.*—*q* Psa. 49. 11.

---

probably, all sacrifices to Jehovah had hitherto been offered. Comp. verse 16. **Every one . . . shall slay me**—Thus in that first age we note how the guilty conscience fears the avenger of blood. It has been plausibly supposed that the murder of Abel occurred not long before the birth of Seth, (see verse 25,) when Adam was one hundred and thirty years old, (chap. v, 3;) at which time there was probably a considerable population in man's primeval seat. "By **every one** we are not to understand *every creature*, as though Cain had excited the hostility of all creatures, but every man. Cain is evidently afraid of revenge on the part of relatives of the slain, who were either already in existence or yet to be born."—*Keil.*

15. **Therefore**—Because there was just reason for such fear of the blood-avenger, and in order to save Cain from such death, the Lord uttered what follows in the text. **Vengeance . . . sevenfold**—Judgment and penalty of the most extreme character, passing down, perhaps, to children's children through many generations. God takes the punishment of Cain into his own hands, not because he was not deserving of death, but because in that early time it were better to preserve Cain a living monument of the curse of blood-guiltiness. **Set a mark upon Cain**—Some sign by which he would be everywhere known as the cursed man, and which also might serve as a token to him that he should not fall by the avenger of blood. But the exact nature of the **mark** no one now knows, and conjectures are worthless.

THE CAINITES, 16–24.

16. **Cain went out from the presence of the Lord**—From that sacred spot on the east of the garden, where Jehovah had revealed his presence and glory to Adam and his sons. Comp. verse 14. **Land of Nod**—The word **Nod** means *wandering*, and is from the same root as that translated *vagabond* in verses 12 and 14. It probably took this name from Cain's fleeing and dwelling there, and the writer uses it here proleptically. Its location, **on the east of Eden,** may serve to suggest the contrast between **Nod** (*flight, banishment, wandering*) and **Eden,** (*delight, pleasure.*) Arabia, Susiana, India, and other countries have been fixed upon as the land of Nod, but these are mere conjectures.

17. **Cain knew his wife**—See on verse 1. "The text assumes it as self-evident that she accompanied him in his exile; also that she was a daughter of Adam, and, consequently a sister of Cain. The marriage of brothers and sisters was inevitable in the case of the children of the first men, if the human race was actually to descend from a single pair, and may, therefore, be justified in the face of the Mosaic prohibition of such marriages, on the ground that the sons and daughters of Adam represented not merely the family, but the race, (*genus,*) and that it was not till after the rise of several families that the bonds of fraternal and conjugal love became distinct from one another, and assumed fixed and mutually exclusive forms, the violation of which is sin."—*Keil.* **Enoch**—Meaning *initiated,* as if with this son, and the city called after his name, Cain was instituting a new order of things. **He builded**—Literally, *he was building.* He began to build the city, perhaps before Enoch was born, and he continued building it long after. "The word **city** is, of course, not to be interpreted by modern

GENESIS.

Irad: and Irad begat Mehujael: and Mehujael begat Methusael: and Methusael begat [11] Lamech.

19 And Lamech took unto him two wives: the name of the one *was* Adah, and the name of the other Zillah. **20** And Adah bare Jabal: he was the father of such as dwell in tents, and *of* such as have cattle. **21** And his brother's name *was* Jubal: he was the [r] father of all such as handle the harp and organ. **22** And Zillah, she also bare Tubal-cain, an [12] instructor of every artificer in brass and iron: and the sister of Tubal-cain *was* Naamah. **23** And Lamech said unto his wives, Adah and Zillah,

---

[11] Hebrew, *Lemech.*

[r] Rom. 4. 11, 12.——[12] Heb. *whetter.*

---

ideas; a village of rude huts, which was distinguished from the booths or tents of the nomads, would satisfy all the conditions of the text."—*Speaker's Com.* And yet something more pretentious than mere huts may well be understood. Nor is it far-fetched and irrelevant to trace in this first city-building the earliest attempt to centralize worldly forces, and construct something like world-empire, one of the outward forms of the later Antichrist. For the "mystery of iniquity" was already working in this very line of Cain, "who was of that wicked one." 1 John iii, 12. The location of this city named Enoch is, like the land of Nod, unknown.

18. Irad ... Mehujael ... Methusael—Compare the similar names in the Sethite genealogy recorded in the next chapter, *Jared, Mahalaleel,* and *Methuselah.* Hence some have supposed a confusion growing out of two forms of one and the same old legend. But why may not different families have adopted similar or identical names in that as in later ages? **Enoch** and **Lamech** are names that occur in both genealogies, but the piety of the sons of Seth, bearing these names, is in notable contrast with the worldliness of Cain's Enoch and the polygamy of Cain's Lamech. This contrast seems to have been drawn out, as if to prevent the possibility of confounding the two genealogies.

19. Lamech took ... two wives —Here is the first recorded instance of bigamy, and it is here noted as originating in the race of Cain. "The names of the women," says Keil, "are indicative of sensual attractions, **Adah**, the adorned; and **Zillah**, the shady, or the tinkling."

20. Jabal ... father of ... tents ... cattle—Though descended from a city-builder, he adopted the nomadic life; but, unlike Abel, who probably held to a settled habitation and kept only sheep or small cattle, Jabal led a wandering life, living in tents, which were easily pitched and easily removed from place to place. Thus he was the originator of genuine nomadic life.

21. Harp and organ—Here used as general names of stringed and wind instruments of music. "That the inventor of musical instruments should be the brother of him who introduced the nomad life is strictly in accordance with the experience of the world. The connexion between music and the pastoral life is indicated in the traditions of the Greeks, which ascribed the invention of the pipe to Pan and of the lyre to Apollo, each of them also being devoted to pastoral pursuits."—SMITH'S *Dictionary of the Bible.*

22. Tubal-cain—It is quite natural to compare this name and character with the *Vulcan* of Roman mythology, but the names have no necessary connexion. **Instructor of every artificer**—Rather, *a forger of all that cuts brass and iron.* The invention of metal instruments marks an advancing civilization, but is no evidence in itself that the previous times were barbarous or savage. Their wants were fewer, but increasing population, pursuing new arts and enterprises, furnishes the conditions of many inventions. **Naamah**—This name of Tubal-cain's sister, which means *the lovely,* or *the beautiful,* is apparently introduced as further showing the worldly spirit and tastes of the Cainites. According to the Targum of Jonathan, she was the mistress of sounds and songs—a poetess.

23. Lamech said—This father of skilful inventors was himself a genius, and the author of this oldest fragment

About B.C. 3874–3769. CHAPTER IV.

hear my voice; ye wives of Lamech, hearken unto my speech: for [13] I have slain a man to my wounding, and a young man [14] to my hurt. **24** ⁸ If Cain shall be avenged sevenfold, truly Lamech seventy and sevenfold. **25** And Adam knew his wife again; and she bare a son, and ᵗ called his name [15] Seth: [16] For God, *said she*, hath appointed me another seed instead of Abel, whom Cain slew. **26** And to Seth, ᵘ to him also there was born a son: and he called his name [17] Enos: then began men [18] to call ᵛ upon the name of the LORD.

---

13 Or, *I would slay a man in my wound*, etc. —— 14 Or, *in my hurt*. —— ⁸ Verse 15. —— *t* Chap. 5. 3. —— 15 Heb. *Sheth*. —— 16 That is, *Appointed*, or, *Put*.

u Chap. 5. 6. —— 17 Heb. *Enosh*. —— 18 Or, *to call* themselves *by the name of the* LORD.—— *v* 1 Kings 18. 24; Psa. 116. 17; Joel 2. 32; Zeph. 3. 9; 1 Cor. 1. 2.

---

of poetical composition, of which the following is a literal translation:

Adah and Zillah, hear my voice;
O wives of Lamech, listen to my saying;
For a man have I slain for my wound,
And a child for my bruise.
For sevenfold avenged should Cain be,
And Lamech seventy and seven.

It is not strange that this mere fragment of antediluvian song is obscure and difficult of explanation. The common version conveys the idea that Lamech was smitten with remorse over the murder of a young man, and this is the explanation of some of the older expositors. But the language of verse 24 illy accords with such a view, and the entire passage breathes the spirit of violence and confident boasting rather than of remorse.

A better interpretation is, that which supposes Lamech to have slain a man in self-defence. The words "for my wound" and "for my bruise" would then be equivalent to "for wounding me," "for bruising me," and the song is Lamech's attempt to comfort his wives in view of the manslaughter, and assure them that no one would dare avenge the deed.

Others make the poem a sort of triumphant exultation over Tubal-cain's invention of brass and iron weapons, and translate the past tense of the verb *slay* as future, or else as present, expressing confident assurance: "I will slay the man who wounds me, and the youth who presumes to harm me." Verse 24 is understood to express the boast that he could now avenge his own wrongs ten times more completely than God would avenge the slaying of Cain. This interpretation accords with the context, and brings out the spirit of the passage, but has against it the perfect tense of the verb **I have slain**, הֲרַגְתִּי.

May we not blend the two last mentioned views, and, retaining the strict sense of the words, as translated above, explain that Lamech, by the use of weapons of his son's invention, had in some duel or personal conflict slain a young man, possibly one of his own children, יֶלֶד; and yet, so far from feeling remorse or penitence over the deed, exultingly sang to his wives this song of his prowess, and boastingly declared that any one who should attempt to take vengeance on him for the deed would suffer more than ten times the vengeance pronounced against the murderer of Cain. "By the citation of the case of his ancestor Cain he shows," says Lange, "that the dark history of the bad man had become transformed into a proud remembrance for his race." According to this view, we discern in this old Cainite song that spirit of violence and lust which waxed worse and worse until it brought upon the wicked world the judgment of the flood. For a full synopsis of the various expositions of this passage, see M'CLINTOCK and STRONG, *Cyclopedia*, art. *Lamech*.

SETH AND ENOS, 25, 26.

Having traced the development of the race of Cain, the sacred writer now turns to record the origin of that godly line whose genealogy appears at greater extent in the following chapter.

25. Seth—The name means *placed*, or *appointed*, as Eve explains in the words: **For God...hath appointed me another seed**, etc. The mother of this divinely chosen seed speaks by a divine inspiration.

26. Enos—Or *Enosh*. This name, according to most critics, means *weakness*, *frailty*, and according to Keil, "designates man from his frail and mortal condition. Psa. viii, 4; xc, 3. In this name, therefore, the feeling and knowledge of human weakness and frailty were expressed—the opposite of the pride and arrogance displayed by the Cainite family." **Then began men to call**—Literally, *Then it was begun to call in the name of Jehovah.* That is, with the line of Seth began a more open and established mode of worship by calling directly upon God in prayer, and using the hallowed name *Jehovah.* Thus the Sethites came in time to be known as "the sons of God." Chap. vi, 2. These devout worshippers had probably now come to believe that the promised Deliverer, whom Eve had hoped to see in her first-born, was to be God himself, and to him they now transfer the name Jehovah. "With a new divine race, and a new believing generation, there ever presents itself the name Jehovah, and even with a higher glory. Now it is for the first time after Eve's first theocratic jubilee-cry of hope."—*Lange.*

CHAPTER V.

The Book of the Generations of Adam, v, 1–vi, 8.

Here begins another of the main divisions of our volume. As observed in the Introduction, (p. 50,) it is not an account of the origin or creation of Adam, nor even of his oldest progeny, but of his posterity through the line of Seth, who is treated as having taken the place of Abel. Chap. iv, 25. It is our author's habit to unfold a series of events connected as in a chain of causes and effects, and then to return and take up one or another for further development and detail. So in the following genealogy, the age, offspring, and death of each patriarch are given, and then the record returns in every case to narrate events in the lives of his descendants which transpired before his death.

THE SETHITE GENEALOGY FROM ADAM TO NOAH, 1–32.

Having now recorded the main features in the development of the race of Cain, and having also informed us of the birth of Seth and his appointment to pious Abel's place, the sacred writer proceeds in the present chapter to record a more detailed and complete genealogy of this child of hope and of prophecy. Names, dates, and ages are carefully given, for this is the record of a chosen seed, through which, in an age long subsequent, the evangelist will trace the human lineage of man's adorable Redeemer. Comp. Luke iii, 36–38. Cain's race had no such future, but all perished by the flood. They were, therefore, more rapidly passed over by the sacred historian, as calling for no such details as the permanent historic line of the godly race.

There are strong resemblances and contrasts between the Sethitic and Cainitic lines. There is an obvious similarity and sometimes identity of names. The names **Enoch,** or Henoch, and **Lamech** occur in both; **Adam** and **Enos** both signify *man;* and the resemblance between **Cain** and **Cainan, Irad** and **Jared, Methuselah** and **Methusael,** and **Mehujael** and **Mahalaleel** is striking. But there is a marked contrast when we consider the signification of the names. The etymology of some of them is obscure, but we give the two lines in contrast, with the most probable meanings attached to the names:

Cainitic line, chap. iv.

1. Adam, (man of the earth.)
2. Cain, (begotten.)
3. Henoch, (initiating, or initiated.)
4. Irad, (city dweller.)
5. Mehujael, (smitten of God.)
6. Methusael, (man of God.)
7. Lamech, (the strong.)
   Adah, (ornament;) Zillah, (song;) Naamah, (loveliness.)
8. Jabal, (wanderer;) Jubal, (player;) Tubal-cain, (lance-forger.)

Sethitic line, chap. v.

1. Adam, (man of the earth.)
2. Seth, (appointed.)
3. Enos, (weak man.)
4. Cainan, (possession.)
5. Mahalaleel, (praise of God.)
6. Jared, (condescension.)
7. Henoch, (initiated.)
8. Methuselah, (man of the dart, or man of growth.)
9. Lamech, (the strong.)
10. Noah, (rest.)

CHAPTER V.

The names which are identical probably have different meanings in the two lists. Henoch the son of Cain is so named (chap. iv, 17) from the *initiation* of city life, his birth co-existing with the foundation of the first city; Henoch the Sethite is "initiated" in the ways of God. Lamech the Cainite is a "strong" warrior, Lamech the Sethite is "strong" in faith, as we see from his prophecy (verse 29) at the birth of Noah. Methusael may mean "man of might," as "cedars of *El*" is equivalent to lofty cedars. A glance down these lists of names will show the strong contrast in character. The Sethitic names breathe godly faith, fears, and aspirations; they tell of a primitive religion; while the Cainitic names tell of primitive art and industry, of warlike prowess, of luxury, and the lust of the eye. Yet two of the Cainitic names show that God was not yet forgotten in that family, and "Methuselah" shows that the Sethites had their heroes of war as well as of faith. But see on verse 27 for another etymology of this name; it may be prophetic of the deluge. The antediluvian piety comes to its "bright consummate flower" in Henoch, the seventh of the Sethites, the man "initiated" into secret sacred communion with God; while the fierce passions, the warlike violence —a lust of that long age—culminate in Lamech, the seventh of the Cainites. No ages and dates are given in the Cainitic line; the general features of the family are described for a few generations and there the record closes.

Two objections have been urged against the contents of this chapter: 1) That the age of the antediluvian patriarchs is too great, and 2) that the time from the creation to the deluge is too short. These ten antediluvian patriarchs reach an age which stretches over ten times the present period of human life, a longevity declared by many objectors to be incredible. But man was not created subject to death. The vigour of the paradisaical state, wherein man had free access to the tree of life, although impaired by sin, was yet in some degree transmitted to the first generations. While the primeval men were simple in their tastes and habits, the increase of luxury and the transmission and multiplication of the weaknesses which are the results of sin, through successive generations, gradually shortened human life. God's wise purposes can be seen in this longevity. While literature did not yet exist the individual observation and experience of centuries supplied the place of historic learning, and oral communication transmitted and preserved great historic facts as well as it can be done now by books or monuments. The great longevity of the primeval man is the almost universal tradition of antiquity. See note on verse 5. While the science of physiology can authoritatively pronounce upon the probabilities of life with regard to a constitution enervated and impaired by many successive ages of sin, it can know nothing of the vigour of man fresh from the creative hand, or drawing his life directly from those who were endowed with eternal youth.

The second objection is drawn from the supposed proofs of human antiquity in heathen history and in geological science. But in regard to both classes of objections it is for the present enough to say, that it will be ample time to reply to them when eminent antiquaries on the one hand, and eminent scientists on the other, agree among themselves as to the real state of the facts. Scripture exegesis is not to be changed or modified by any questionable hypothesis. The immense antiquity which has been claimed for the early Egyptian dynasties rests upon a single author, Manetho, whose work exists only in fragments, the genuineness of many of which is yet under discussion, and which, if genuine and authentic, can thus far be only hypothetically interpreted. Moreover, eminent Egyptologists claim that Manetho's statements are contradicted by the monuments. Bunsen and Lepsius differ by many thousand years while reasoning from the same data, and Rougé states that Manetho's text has been so tampered with, and the monumental series is so

CHAPTER V.

THIS is the [a] book of the generations of Adam. In the day that God created man, in [b] the likeness of God made he him; 2 [c] Male and female created he them; and blessed them, and called their name Adam, in the day when they were created.

---

a 1 Chron. 1. 1; Luke 3. 38.——*b* Chap. 1. 26; Eph. 4. 24; Col. 3. 10.——*c* Chap. 1. 27.

---

incomplete, as to render all chronological deductions from them uncertain. Concerning the geological evidences of man's antiquity see the Excursus at the end of chap. ii.

The numbers, and consequently the chronology, of this chapter, as given in the Samaritan and Septuagint, differ much from those of the Hebrew. The Septuagint makes six of the patriarchs older at the birth of the first son mentioned—the first five, a hundred years older—and the ninth, Lamech, six years older. This, it will be seen, adds six hundred and six years to the chronology given in the Hebrew text. It also makes Lamech's age twenty-four years less. On the other hand, the Samaritan makes three of the patriarchs much younger at the birth of the first-mentioned son, (thus diminishing the chronology by two hundred and forty-nine years,) and, besides, diminishes the age of Jared, Methuselah, and Lamech. Thus the Hebrew text gives one thousand six hundred and fifty-six years from the Creation to the Deluge, while the Samaritan gives one thousand three hundred and seven, and the Septuagint two thousand two hundred and forty-two. Careful examination and comparison will show that the balance of probability is decidedly in favour of the Hebrew text. The Septuagint shows the marks of a systematic and designed variation.

The following table gives the figures of the Hebrew, Samaritan, and Septuagint in parallel columns. The numbers in parentheses are the readings of the Codex Alexandrinus of the Septuagint.

NAMES.	Hebrew Text.			Samaritan Text.			Septuagint.		
	Age at birth of firstborn.	Rest of life.	Whole life.	Age at birth of firstborn.	Rest of life.	Whole life.	Age at birth of firstborn.	Rest of life.	Whole life.
Adam............	130	800	930	130	800	930	230	700	930
Seth.............	105	807	912	105	807	912	205	707	912
Enos.............	90	815	905	90	815	905	190	715	905
Cainan...........	70	840	910	70	840	910	170	740	910
Mahalaleel.......	65	830	895	65	830	895	165	730	895
Jared.............	162	800	962	62	785	847	162	800	962
Enoch............	65	300	365	65	300	365	165	200	365
Methuselah	187	782	969	67	653	720	167 (187)	802 (782)	969
Lamech...........	182	595	777	53	600	653	188	565	753
Noah.............	500	450	950	500	450	950	500	450	950
To the flood......	100			100			100		
Total...........	1,656			1,307			2,242		

1. **This is the book**—סֵפֶר, translated *book*, is not necessarily an extended treatise; it is simply a writing complete in itself, long or short. The "bill of divorcement" (Deut. xxiv, 1, 3) is סֵפֶר. In this passage the word is applied to an ancient genealogical register, perhaps of the age of Noah, which the inspired author incorporates in his work. **In the likeness of God**—Repeated from chapter i, 26, setting forth, in a single phrase, man's original nature and character.

2. **Called their name Adam** — Adam, אָדָם, is the Hebrew word for *man*, and the reference is to Gen. i, 26, Let us make אָדָם. Adam means *man of the soil:* our word man, (Sanscrit, *ma-*

B. C. 3874–3317. CHAPTER V. 113

3 And Adam lived a hundred and thirty years, and begat *a son* in his own likeness, after his image; and ᵈ called his name Seth: **4** ᵉAnd the days of Adam after he had begotten Seth were eight hundred years: ᶠand he begat sons and daughters: **5** And all the days that Adam lived were nine hundred and thirty years: ᵍand he died. **6** And Seth lived a hundred and five years, and ʰ begat Enos: **7** And Seth lived after he begat Enos eight hundred and seven years, and begat sons and daughters: **8** And all the days of Seth were nine hundred and twelve years: and he died.
9 And Enos lived ninety years, and begat ⁱ Cainan: **10** And Enos lived after he begat Cainan eight hundred and fifteen years, and begat sons and daughters: **11** And all the days of Enos were nine hundred and five years: and he died.
12 And Cainan lived seventy years, and begat ʲ Mahalaleel: **13** And Cainan lived after he begat Mahalaleel eight hundred and forty years, and begat sons and daughters: **14** And all the days of Cainan were nine hundred and ten years: and he died.
15 And Mahalaleel lived sixty and five years, and begat ³ Jared: **16** And Mahalaleel lived after he begat Jared eight hundred and thirty years, and begat sons and daughters: **17** And all the days of Mahalaleel were eight hundred ninety and five years: and he died.
18 And Jared lived a hundred sixty and two years, and he begat ⁱ Enoch: **19** And Jared lived after he begat Enoch eight hundred years, and begat sons and daughters: **20** And all the days of Jared were nine hundred sixty and two years: and he died.
21 And Enoch lived sixty and five years, and begat ⁴ Methuselah: **22** And Enoch ᵏ walked with God after he begat

---

ᵈ Chap. 4. 25.——ᵉ 1 Chron. 1. 1, etc.——ᶠ Chap. 1. 28.——ᵍ Chap. 3. 19; Heb. 9. 27.——ʰ Chap. 4. 26.——1 Heb. *Kenan*.——2 Gr. *Maleleel*.

3 Heb. *Jered*.——ⁱ Jude 14, 15.——4 Gr. *Mathusala*.——ᵏ Chap. 6. 9; 17. 1; 24. 40; 2 Kings 20. 3; Psa. 16. 8; 116. 9; 128. 1; Micah 6. 8; Mal 2. 6.

---

nuscha, Latin, *mens*, Saxon, *gemynd*,) signifies thinking being. Man and woman were one at creation; their name was Adam.

3. In his own likeness, after his image—Not God's image and likeness, in which man had been created. The contrast is designed and striking. God's image and likeness could not be transmitted in their purity through the fallen Adam. **Seth**—See chap. iv, 25. Seth only is here named of Adam's sons, because he was the one divinely *appointed* to take Abel's place as the heir of the great primeval promise. This is not a history of the antediluvian world, but of the gradually unfolding plan of salvation. They only are chronicled who transmitted God's torch from age to age.

5. Nine hundred and thirty years—Widespread heathen traditions preserve the memory of the antediluvian longevity. Persian annals relate that the first Persian kings reigned from five hundred to one thousand years. The Arcadians had traditions that their first kings lived three hundred years. Berosus, the Chaldean historian, states that there were ten antediluvian patriarchs, and preserves the tradition of their great longevity. Josephus states (*Antiq.*, i. 3, 9) that "all who have written antiquities, both among the Greeks and barbarians," are witnesses of this fact; and he mentions, among others, Manetho, Hieronymus the Egyptian, Berosus the Chaldean, Hesiod the Greek poet, and Hecatæus and Hellanicus, the earliest Greek historians. The works that he mentions exist now only in fragments, so that most of his statements cannot be verified; but it is not likely that he would thus have appealed to these authorities when extant unless they had corroborated the Scripture narrative.

6. Enos—This word signifies man, and may denote that the race begins anew from Seth. For the meaning of the other names in the list, see above, page 110.

22. And Enoch walked with God — וַיִּתְהַלֵּךְ חֲנוֹךְ אֶת־הָאֱלֹהִים

Not *before* God, as a messenger, or a workman beneath his eye; nor *after* him, as a servant; but *with* him, as a friend. A remarkable expression, occurring but twice in Scripture: in the text as applied to Enoch, and in chap. vi, 9, to Noah. In Mal. ii, 6, it is, in our translation, applied to the faithful priest, but the Hebrew verb in this

Methuselah three hundred years, and begat sons and daughters: **23** And all the days of Enoch were three hundred sixty and five years: **24** And ¹Enoch walked with God: and he *was* not; for God took him. **25** And Methuselah lived a hundred eighty and seven years, and begat ⁵Lamech: **26** And Methuselah lived after he begat Lamech seven hundred eighty and two years, and begat sons and daughters: **27** And all the days of Methuselah were nine hundred sixty and nine years: and he died. **28** And Lamech lived a hundred eighty and two years, and begat a son: **29** And he called his name ⁶Noah,⁷

l 2 Kings 2. 11; Hebrews 11. 5. —— 5 Hebrew, *Lemech*.

6 Gr. *Noe*, Luke 3. 36; Heb. 11. 7; 1 Pet. 3. 20. ——7 That is, *Rest*, or, *Comfort*.

passage is in *Kal*, not reaching the high spiritual idea of the text. The verb as applied to Enoch and Noah is in *Hithpael* implying a *voluntary* and *delightful* walk. The passages which speak of *walking before God* (Gen. xxiv, 40, etc.,) and *walking after him* do not rise to the high conception of this text. The article is here, for the first time, used with Elohim, *the* one only God. The LXX translates Καὶ εὐηρέστησεν Ἐνὼχ τῷ Θεῷ, *and Enoch pleased God*, which version Paul uses in Heb. xi, 5: "He had this testimony, that he pleased God." Intimate and confidential communication, such as exists between the nearest friends, is suggested by this peculiar language. This single example of eminent piety stands forth sublimely solitary in the antediluvian waste. While the patriarchs from Seth to Enoch, and from Enoch to Lamech, are but a series of Hebrew names, we see Enoch's face as it shines in his godly walk, and hear him, as a prophet, testify against the sin of his age, and proclaim a coming judgment. Jude 14, 15. The Jews have manifold traditions concerning Enoch, most of which are gathered in the apocryphal Book of Enoch, written, probably, in the last century B. C. There is a heathen tradition of the same wonderful history in the Phrygian legend of *Annacus*, a pious king, who lived and prophesied three hundred years, predicting the deluge of Deucalion.

24. The testimony to the exalted piety of Enoch is emphatically repeated; and where we might expect to read again the solemn phrase, "and he died," we find instead the mysterious words, **and he was not; for God took him.** The expression, **and he was not**, has frequent parallels in the Hebrew Scriptures, denoting any sudden and mysterious departure. Thus, Jacob says of his lost sons, (Gen. xlii, 13, 36,) "Joseph is not, and Simeon is not." The LXX translates, "And he was not found," quoted in Hebrews xi, 5. He was suddenly withdrawn from sight, for God took him. If the expression, "and he was not," does not teach annihilation, much less, as Murphy remarks, does the phrase, "and he died." Enoch's life, by its brevity, strongly contrasts with that of the other patriarchs. His earthly existence was a year of years, symbolic thus of an ideal human life in its perfect cycle. Thus, perhaps, would man have lived and been "taken" had he never fallen. The apocryphal Book of Wisdom says happily of him, (chap. iv, 13, 14,) "He being made perfect in a short time fulfilled a long time." The Targums show that the story of Enoch was regarded by the Jews as a revelation of human immortality. It was also proof of the great doctrine afterwards intimated by the translation of Elijah, and fully revealed by the transfiguration and resurrection of Christ, that the human body will share in the bliss and glory of immortality.

27. Methuselah—The etymology of this word is uncertain. Gesenius gives it *man of the dart;* it may also mean, *he dieth, and sendeth forth,* (that is, the deluge,) a prophetic name, given by his father, Enoch, when prophesying of God's judgments, indicating that the deluge would take place at his death. He died in the year of the flood, having reached the greatest age recorded, nine hundred and sixty-nine years.

29. Noah—This name signifies *rest* or *comfort*. The godly hope and prophetic aspiration of the Sethite, Lamech, as expressed in this name, con-

saying, This *same* shall comfort us concerning our work and toil of our hands, because of the ground ᵐ which the LORD hath cursed. **30** And Lamech lived after he begat Noah five hundred ninety and five years, and begat sons and daughters: **31** And all the days of Lamech were seven hundred seventy and seven years: and he died. **32** And

Noah was five hundred years old: and Noah begat ⁿ Shem, Ham, ᵒ and Japheth.

CHAPTER VI.

A ND it came to pass, ᵃ when men began to multiply on the face of the earth, and daughters were born unto them, **2** That the sons of God saw the daughters of men that they *were* fair;

---

m Chap. 3. 17; 4. 11.—*n* Chap. 6. 10.   *o* Chap. 10. 21.—*a* Chap. 1. 28.

---

trast strongly with the fierce and defiant ssog of the warrior and polygamist of the same name, who was descended from Cain. Lamech groans under the curse of severe bodily toil, the consequence of sin. In this son he expects deliverance, and, therefore, names him *Rest.* Rest and deliverance came to man through Noah, but in a way that Lamech had not thought. Exactly what Lamech expected is not clear; perhaps, like Eve, he looked upon his firstborn son as the great promised Deliverer.

32. **Noah was five hundred years old**—It is not meant that Noah had no children born to him for five centuries. Only those sons are mentioned with whom the narrative is specially concerned. Each patriarch had sons and daughters whose descendants multiplied through these centuries, but their names are lost to history. The order of age in Noah's family is a matter of discussion. Shem is mentioned first, but it may be because he was the heir in the line of promise. Japheth, in chap. x, 21, seems to be called the elder, but the meaning may be, " Shem, the elder brother of Japheth," that is, older than Ham, though not older than Japheth. Ham is called the youngest in chap. ix, 24, yet the Hebrew may also be rendered *younger.* See Gesen. *Heb. Gram.*, § 119. From chapter xi, 10, it seems that Shem was a hundred years old two years after the flood, that is, in Noah's six hundred and third year. He must, then, have been born in Noah's five hundred and third year, and, as Ham was younger than he, it follows that Japheth only could have been born in Noah's five hundredth year. Yet some understand that in chapter x, 21, Shem is declared to be " elder " than Japheth, but this view cannot be harmonized with chap. xi, 10.

Japheth is not called the eldest of the three in chapter x, 21, but is conclusively shown to be so by the above comparison of passages. The Arabic writers represent Japheth as the eldest. **Shem** means *name, fame;* **Ham** means *burnt,* and **Japheth** means *enlargement.* Shem, the heir of Messianic hopes, the man of *name,* is placed first because Christ and salvation are ever first in revelation.

CHAPTER VI.

ANTEDILUVIAN WICKEDNESS, 1–8.

After finishing the genealogical records of the Cainites and Sethites, the narrative now, in the short section, verses 1–8, returns to a general description of the antediluvian race. Having distinctly traced each family down to the time of Noah, the writer now describes the mingling of the two which resulted in the widespread corruption that immediately preceded the deluge. So this introduction to the history of the Deluge is properly connected with the " generations of Adam," (v. 1,) rather than with the " generations of Noah." Comp. Introd., p. 50.

2. **Sons of God**—There has been much dispute as to the nature and character of the " sons of God " mentioned in this section Three different theories have been maintained in the Jewish and Christian Churches. The first, arising apparently from the Samaritan, which translates the phrase *sons of mighty men,* is found in the Targums of Jonathan and Onkelos, and was maintained by eminent Jewish commentators, like Aben Ezra and Rashi, but is now abandoned. A second view, which seems to have some countenance from the LXX, some copies of which read ἄγγελοι τοῦ Θεοῦ, instead of υἱοὶ τοῦ Θεοῦ, makes the sons of God angels, as

116   GENESIS.   B. C. 2448.

and they ᵇ took them wives of all which they chose. **3** And the Lᴏʀᴅ said, ᶜ My

ᵇ Deut. 7. 3, 4.   ᶜ Gal. 5. 16, 17; 1 Pet. 3. 19, 20.

in Job i, 6; ii, 1. The Alexandrian commentators, and Jews who fell under strong Greek influences, as Philo and Josephus, in their anxiety to bridge over the chasm between Judaism and heathenism, and many of the Rabbins and oldest Church Fathers, (Justin., Clem. Alex., Tertul., Cyp., etc.,) adopted this view; while others of the Rabbins, and Chrysostom and Augustine, vehemently opposed it. Modern commentators who regard the early history of Genesis as mythical, as well as some orthodox commentators, from Luther to Stier and Delitzsch, embrace this view. The third view, that of Chrysostom, Cyril, etc., and now generally held, is, that the "sons of God" were the children of the godly Sethite line. Against the second view it may be conclusively urged 1) that we have had thus far no account of the creation of the angels, and the author would not for the first time mention them thus incidentally. 2) Our Lord expressly says (Matt. xxii, 30) that angels "neither marry nor are given in marriage." 3) Although in poetical pieces (as in Job i, 6, ii, 1, xxxviii, 7, Psalm xxix, 1, lxxxix, 6) angels are styled *sons of God*, in pure historical composition this never occurs. On the other hand, godly men and the chosen race are expressly said to stand in this filial relation to God. Exod. iv, 22, 23, "Israel is my son;" Deut. xiv, 1, "Ye are the children of the Lord your God;" also, Hos. xi, 1. 4) It is not the corruption of angels but of men that forms the subject of the narrative. No judgment is pronounced upon angels, but a flood destroys the race of men. If the sin of angels is here recorded, it is inappropriate to follow it with an account of the punishment of men. 5) "Sons of God," is a Hebrew idiom for "men in the likeness of God." Noah (v, 32) is called the "son of five hundred years;" Abraham calls Eliezer (chap. xv, 3) "son of my house;" Rachel named her son Ben-oni, "son of my sorrow," but Jacob called him *Benjamin*, "son of the right hand;" "sons of the prophets" (1 Kings xx, 35, etc.) are the *disciples* or *followers* of the prophets. "Son" thus has a latitude of meaning in the Hebrew idiom that specially fits it to convey the idea of the text, as is also seen in the New Testament phraseology, wherein "sons of God" and "born of God" are applied to true Christians. John i, 12, 13. **Took them wives of all which they chose**—Sensuality, polygamy, and the intermarriage of the Sethite and Cainite families were the great causes of the "corruption" and "violence" that now filled the earth. These causes may have been centuries in operation, even from the time of Seth and of Cain. The author has separately described the fleshly and the godly race; and now, after his manner, he returns to take up events which were transpiring contemporaneously. From the time that "men began to multiply" the godly race did not keep itself wholly distinct, but the "sons of God" *looked on the beauty* of the "daughters of men," rather than on their moral character, and took them wives of all which they chose, that is, took such and as many as carnal choice might prompt. The personal charms of the daughters of the Cainites are commemorated in the names of Lamech's wives, (iv, 19,) yet we are not to suppose that it was these women only that are intended by **the daughters of men.** The phrase is general, and means simply *womankind*. The word מִכֹּל, *from all*, is noteworthy and emphatic. The choice was indiscriminate among those that were *fair*, selecting one or many, according to a carnal desire. Not the amours of angels, but family degradation, does the historian assign as the great cause of the antediluvian corruption. This is written for our instruction. It is a solemn warning against poisoning with sin the family fountain. See the Mosaic law, Deut. vii, 3, 4, repeated by Joshua. Josh. xxiii, 12. Thus Israel was led into apostasy in the desert, (Num. xxv,) and in the time of the judges. Judges iii, 6. Thus Solomon fell, and Ezra

Spirit shall not always strive with man, and Nehemiah could not deliver the restored nation from idolatry till the people had put away their "strange wives." The anxiety of Abraham concerning the marriage of Isaac, and of Isaac and Rebekah for their sons Jacob and Esau, (Gen. xxiv, 3, xxvi, 34, 35, xxvii, 46,) will illustrate the text.

3. **My Spirit shall not always strive with man**—דּוּן, here rendered *strive*, occurs nowhere else, and its meaning is doubtful. Our translation assumes that it is the same as דִּין, following in this respect Symmachus (οὐ κρίνει) and Kimchi. This is not impossible, as the verbs עוּ and עִי often interchange their middle radical. Gesenius renders the word *to be made low, depressed;* (so Vatablus and Ewald;) and, if this be the meaning, the sense of the text would seem to be, *my Spirit shall not be trampled on, despised by man forever;* language of weariness after long forbearance. Some (as Grotius) have favoured the translation *ensheathed,* and understand that Jehovah here threatens that his spirit (the soul breathed into man by God) shall not forever be sheathed in the human body, as a sword in the scabbard; that is, the human race shall be cut off. But most of the ancient versions, as well as the Targums, render, *my spirit shall not abide,* or *dwell among men;* and understand the words to threaten that the spirit breathed into man at his creation shall no more dwell on the earth, now that man has become brutalized with fleshly lusts. T. Lewis somewhat modifies this view, understanding by **my spirit** not simply the life principle, but the spiritual or rational in man, as distinguished from the carnal — (the πνεῦμα, as distinguished from the ψυχή,)—and, moreover, considers it a sorrowing prediction rather than a threat. The meaning *shall dwell* or *abide,* is more in harmony with the context than **strive**. The reason of the threat, or prediction, is *because he is flesh*. This would seem to be a reason why the Spirit should continue

ᵈ for that he also *is* flesh: yet his days

d Psa. 78. 39.

to *strive*, unless, indeed, we understand it as the language of weariness and hopelessness in view of man's degradation. But this expression furnishes a reason, most forcible and appropriate, why God should refuse to allow his image to be longer defiled upon the earth. Man's kinship with God, his sonship, (comp. verse 2,) gives special flagrancy to his guilt. Man has dishonoured the divine image; it is the "Spirit of God that giveth him understanding;" that he has defiled, and, therefore, that "Spirit shall return unto God who gave it." Eccl. xii, 7. It was a resolution made in divine justice and mercy. It was a fearful sin for a son of God to prostitute his highest powers in the service of the flesh, a sin that called for the divine wrath. But the very enormity of the sin leads a merciful God to resolve on blotting out the race, to stop the ever-increasing flood of wretchedness that flows from increasing wickedness. So he drove man away from the tree of life, lest he should secure an immortality of sin. **For that he also is flesh**—Or, *because of their transgression, he is flesh,* (Ewald, Nordh., Fürst, Gesen.,) that is, *he is all flesh.* The **flesh**—the body, with its appetites and passions, has risen above the spirit. The divine has become quenched in the carnal. Jehovah describes the being whose nobler part was made an image of himself, as now *wholly* **flesh.** Flesh and spirit were originally made in happy, harmonious adjustment; but now all is flesh. From this text arose the Pauline phraseology *carnal* and *spiritual, flesh* and *spirit,* so common in the epistle to the Romans. The difficult word בְּשַׁגַּם may also be construed with what precedes, thus disregarding the Masoretic punctuation and reading: *My spirit shall not dwell with men forever in their errors. He is flesh, and his days,* etc. In this case, the word is composed of the preposition בְּ, and pronominal suffix ם, connected with the construct infinitive of the verb שָׁגַג. **His days** — His allotted time

GENESIS.

shall be a hundred and twenty years. 4 There were giants in the earth in those days; and also after that, when the sons of God came in unto the daughters of men, and they bare children to them, the same *became* mighty men which *were* of old, men of renown. 5 And GOD saw that the wickedness of man *was* great in the earth, and *that* [1] every *e* imagination of the thoughts of his heart *was* only evil [2] continually.

1 Or, *the whole imagination:* The Hebrew word signifieth not only *the imagination,* but also *the purposes and desires.*

e Chapter 8. 21; Deuteronomy 29. 19; Proverbs 6. 18; Matthew 15. 19.——2 Hebrew, *every day.*

on the earth. **Hundred and twenty years**—This language is used of *man,* the race with whom God's Spirit dwelt, not of individual men. It refers, then, to the duration of the then existing race, and not, as some have supposed, to the length of human life. It was then in the four hundred and eightieth year of Noah's life that the antediluvian world received its sentence; but it was allowed a respite of one hundred and twenty years, during which, according to 2 Pet. ii, 8, Noah was a "preacher of righteousness," "when once the longsuffering of God waited" for the world's repentance, "while the ark was a preparing." 1 Pet. iii, 20.

4. **Giants in the earth**—Literally, *The Nephilim were in the land in those days, and also after that,* (or specially *after that,) when the sons of God came in unto the daughters of man, and they bare children to them, these are the heroes (Gibborim) who from the olden time were the men of name*—renowned, notorious men. There is no authority in the Hebrew for the translation **giants.** The word comes from the Sept., which renders *Nephilim,* γίγαντες, *earth born,* from which it has been supposed that the *Nephilim* were men of immense size and stature. *Nephilim* is derived from נָפַל, *to fall,* (fallo, σφάλλω,) and this *fall* may be understood physically or morally. Some (Kimchi) understand it to mean those who *caused men to fall,* (through fear;) others, (Aq., Symm., Ges., Keil,) understand *those who fell upon men,* (ἐπιπίπτοντες,) fierce and violent men. The word occurs in but one other passage, (Num. xiii, 33,) where it is applied by the terrified spies to the sons of Anak. The word vividly pictures scenes of violence and bloodshed in the antediluvian world. Lewis supposes another derivation, making it mean *famous* men, corresponding to the *Gibborim,* who afterward arose from the marriage of the "sons of God" and the "daughters of men," and who, in the last clause of the verse, are called *men of name.* **Of old**—That is, in the old or ancient time; applied to the warlike heroes of the antediluvian epoch.

It is noteworthy that no mention is made of kings, rulers, or civil government of any kind in this antediluvian era. In this respect the record presents a remarkable contrast to all profane histories. The eye of the author was upon the moral rather than upon the political condition of man; he surveys the world not from a political or scientific, but from a spiritual, point of view.

5. **God saw . . . only evil**—A fearful picture of human depravity, in its thoroughness and universality. The genealogy of the lust and violence that now raged through the world is powerfully traced in a few pregnant words. First, the foul *heart,* then the *thinking,* (process,) then the *thought,* (product,) the imaged sin, (יֵצֶר,) then the foul *deed.* From the corrupt heart swarm the carnal thoughts; in these are bred the sinful imageries and purposes, whence are spawned the abominable crimes which break upon the world. How philosophically is this deluge of universal evil traced by secret channels to the parent fountains in the human heart. Comp. Matt. xv, 19. **Continually**—Heb. *only evil all the day.* There is terrible emphasis in the few Hebrew monosyllables here employed, which express the idea of sin in every thought and deed, at every time and place.

B. C. 2448. CHAPTER VI. 119

6 And ᶠ it repented the LORD that he had made man on the earth, and it ᵍ grieved him at his heart. 7 And the LORD said, I will destroy man whom I have created from the face of the earth; ³ both man, and beast, and the creeping thing, and the fowls of the air; for it repenteth me that I have made them. 8 But Noah ʰ found grace in the eyes of the LORD.

ᶠ See Num. 23. 19; 1 Sam. 15. 11, 29; 2 Sam. 24. 16; Mal. 3. 6; James 1. 17.——ᵍ Isa. 63. 10; Eph. 4. 30.

3 Heb. *from man unto beast.*——ʰ Chap. 19. 19; Exod. 33. 12, 13, 16, 17; Luke 1. 30; Acts 7. 46.

6. **It repented the Lord**—The pain of the divine love at man's sin is thus tenderly and forcibly set forth; explained more fully by the following words: **It grieved him at his heart** —Or rather, *He grieved himself to the heart.* A beautiful picture of God's tenderness, yearning over the sinful child who had so fearfully corrupted his way and befouled the earth (made "very good" for him) by abominable wickedness. God's acts and purposes are here, as everywhere, necessarily described in human words, which can only in a figurative sense be applied to Him whose ways are not our ways, nor his thoughts our thoughts. *Repentance* appears no more at variance with immutability, when we look closely into the matter, than any divine act, purpose, or resolve that is revealed. As in man all such mental acts and states involve the idea of change, it is impossible for us to reconcile them with immutability. But all revelation is a condescension to human weakness, a clothing of divine thoughts in human draperies, for thus only could it be of any value to man. So God, the Infinite, imprisons himself in time and space that he may talk with the child who dwells there. It is the condescension of all instruction, wherein the teacher must come down to the plane of the pupil, and adapt himself to his thoughts and feelings in order to convey the lessons of wisdom. In fact, absolute truth in regard to supernatural things can be conveyed to man only in negations; that is, it can only be said that the supernatural facts are not like the natural. But absolute truths like these are pointless, soulless, and spiritually profitless, and, therefore, God gives us relative truths that are positive to meet the deep religious wants of the soul. But he gives us the negative absolute truths also, in order that we may see that the affirmative truths are only relative. Thus of the spirits of the just made perfect it is said "they neither marry nor are given in marriage," and, "a spirit hath not flesh and bones," while yet these saints hold harps, sing songs, wear robes and crowns, and dwell in a city made of precious metals and precious stones. God is described, in this relative language of imagery, as having a human form, yea, even human eyes, and hands, and feet, and, as in this passage, human voice and thoughts; yet the absolute truth is also revealed to correct and modify the relative. "Ye saw no manner of form;" "God is a spirit;" "the ETERNAL ONE of Israel . . . . is not a man that he should repent." 1 Sam. xv, 29. This is a paradox, but it is the paradox of revelation. He who understands its spirit can believe that *they saw the God of Israel,* (Exod. xxiv, 10,) while yet *no man hath seen God at any time,* and feel that there is no contradiction.

7. **I will destroy**—Literally, *I will wipe out man.* When God destroys his own creature, the creature must have made itself fearfully guilty and corrupt. **Both man, and beast**—Heb. *from man unto beast;* that is, beginning at man, the destruction shall descend to beasts, man's subjects and servants. It is one of the deep mysteries of this life that the lower orders of animate beings rejoice and suffer in sympathy with man, and are, therefore, involved in the calamities which result from human sin. But they are also a part of the whole creation, (πᾶσα ἡ κτίσις,) which groans and travails together with sinning and suffering man, waiting "for the manifestation of the sons of God." Rom. viii, 19–21. What and how much the apostle means by these wondrous words we cannot conceive, but it is something ineffably glorious.

8. **Noah found grace**—Because of his godly filial fear and faith, (Hebrews xi, 7,) which wonderfully showed itself

in preaching righteousness to that corrupt generation, and especially by working through more than a century in the construction of the vast ark for the saving of his house.

Generations of Noah,
vi, 9–ix, 29.

Note here, again, how the history doubles back upon itself. Noah has been already introduced, (chap. v, 29, 32,) but now the divine record of *beginnings* and *developments* takes a new departure. Compare note at beginning of chap. v, and Introd., pp. 49, 50.

HISTORY OF THE DELUGE, vi, 9–viii, 22.

The traditions of a deluge which at one time covered the whole inhabited earth and swept away the whole human race except a single family, or very few persons, who were saved in an ark, (ship, boat, or raft,) is almost, if not quite, as widely spread as the human race itself. Some terrible event of this character; some dreadful catastrophe that overwhelmed the race in destruction by water, is deeply impressed on the memory of mankind. Among the nations of Western Asia, the Chaldeans, Phrygians, and Phenicians remarkably reproduce the biblical account. Noah is the Xisuthrus of the Chaldee Berosus, while the Sibylline books mention that the earth was peopled by his three sons, one of whom was named Japetus. The traditions of Eastern Asia, as the Persian, Indian, and Chinese, though more or less mixed up with their peculiar mythologies and cosmogonies, are yet unmistakable. The Noah of the Chinese is Fahhe, who escaped from the deluge with his wife, three sons, and three daughters, and was the second father of the human race. In a Chinese Buddhist temple is a beautiful stucco picture of Noah floating in his ark amid the watery deluge, while a dove flies toward the vessel with an olive branch in her beak. (*Journal of the Royal Asiatic Society*, xvi, 79.) The Noah of the East Indians is Manu, to whom Bramah announced the approach of the deluge, and bade him build a ship, store it with all kinds of seeds, and then enter into it with seven holy beings. When the flood covered the earth Bramah, in the form of a horned fish, drew the ship through the waters and landed it finally on the loftiest summit of the Himalaya. Manu was the father of a new race. The Koran relates the story with peculiar amplifications and embellishments, describing, at great length, Noah's faithful preaching, and picturing its rejection by the scoffing world, stating that one of his sons was among the scoffers, who attempted to escape to a mountain and was drowned before his father's eyes. In the well-known Greek traditions Noah appears as Ogyges or Deucalion. The story is found in various forms in Pindar and Apollodorus, and is related with graphic power and poetic embellishment by Ovid and Lucian. Lucian describes Deucalion, the single righteous man, putting his family and many kinds of animals into a *chest*, when a heavy rain fell, and the earth opened, sending forth floods of water by which the greater part of Hellas was submerged, while Deucalion's chest floated to the top of Parnassus. The traditions of the deluge among the various aboriginal American nations are interesting and remarkable. The Noah of the Aztecs is Coxcox, who saved himself, with his wife, on a raft. Humboldt describes Mexican pictures of this deluge and of the confusion of tongues; the race being represented as dumb after the catastrophe, and a *dove* being pictured distributing among them tongues from the top of a tree. He also relates that the Noah of another Mexican nation was called Tezpi, who was saved in a spacious bark with his wife, children, some animals and food. "When the Great Spirit ordered the waters to withdraw Tezpi sent out from his bark a vulture. The bird did not return on account of the carcases with which the earth was strewn. Tezpi sent out other birds, one of which, the humming-bird, alone returned, holding in its beak a branch clad with leaves." In the Chaldee tradition, Xisuthrus sends out the birds three times, the second time they returned with mud on their feet, and the third time they return no more. Many of the American traditions blend the history of Noah with that of Adam, while the Chaldee and Phrygian stories confuse Enoch and Noah. Thus Xisuthrus is taken to heaven after the ark is stranded, while the Phrygian Annakos, or Nannakos, (Enoch,) foretells the flood and weeps and prays for the people. In the reign of Septimus Severus, (A.D. 193-211,) a coin was struck in Apamea of Phrygia, which commemorates this local tradition, though by that time it may have been modified by the Bible history. This city was anciently called *Kibotos*, or the "Ark," and the medal represents a square vessel, floating in the water, containing two persons, while on its top is perched a bird, another flying toward it bearing a branch. Before the ark are represented the two inmates stepping on the dry land. Some specimens have the name NΩ, or NΩE, on the vessel.

COIN OF APAMEA IN PHRYGIA, REPRESENTING THE DELUGE.

Was the deluge universal? The universality of this tradition certainly points to a deluge that was universal as far as mankind is concerned. The Scripture language demands, Delitzsch remarks, that the flood be considered as universal for the earth as *inhabited*, but not for the earth *as such*; Scripture has no interest in the universality of the flood in itself, but only in the universality of the judgment of which it was the execution. Our exposition of the whole narrative is determined in the settlement of the primary question,

Was this a miraculous or simply a providential judgment? Did God in this catastrophe destroy the human race through natural or supernatural causes? For if it were a miracle, it is perfectly idle, because utterly unphilosophical, to speculate as to its causes and effects. Miraculous events are entirely beyond the province of reasoning; and if the deluge belongs to this class we can no more tell how the waters were made to cover the earth, and how Noah could gather and preserve the animals in the ark, than we can tell how Christ turned water into wine, or rose from the dead. No Christian doubts that God's power is adequate to the production of even such a series of stupendous miracles as are involved in the hypothesis of a universal deluge; but the simple question is, Does the text, on fair interpretation, teach that such a vast array of miracles were concentrated in this event, or does it describe the destruction of a wicked race by natural causes? We think that all the circumstances of the event, abounding as they do in allusions to natural causes and effects, show that the sacred historian did not intend to describe a miracle, but a natural catastrophe, by which God destroyed the "world of the ungodly," and which is, therefore, as to all its phenomena, a legitimate subject for speculation. Commentators are now agreed, that if it were universal it must have been a miracle, yet few realize the stupendousness of the miracle supposed. Unless there were a new creation after the flood, which some gratuitously imagine without the least authority from the sacred narrative, and which, if assumed, renders any preservation of animals in the ark unnecessary, all existing species of land-animals, including mammals, birds, and insects, must have been saved in the ark. In former times, when the extent of the animal kingdom was imperfectly known, commentators (as Clarke) were able to show, with great plausibility, that the ark furnished ample accommodations. But several important items have always been omitted; the insects, of which there are probably half a million of species, and which would have been as surely destroyed by a universal deluge as cattle or fowls; marine animals, which have their habitat on the shores between the tide-marks, and cannot live under fifty fathoms of water; the coral animals, which would all have been destroyed by water standing at the depth supposed; and the fresh water fishes, if the waters of the deluge be supposed to have been salt, or the salt water fishes, if they be supposed to have been fresh. Also, it is not generally considered that, miracle apart, it was necessary to preserve the vegetable as well as the animal kingdom in the ark, since many terrestrial plants and seeds would have been destroyed by such a deluge. But Noah was not commanded to gather marine animals nor seeds. Each continent and zone has now its zoölogical provinces, determined by climate, elevation, soil, etc. The polar bear cannot live in the torrid zone; the *carnivora* of the tropics cannot live within the Arctic circle. The animals of America are wholly different from those of the old continent in the corresponding zones. The South American jaguar must have travelled through several zones and the greater part of two continents, to have reached the ark. If, after a cursory study of the zoölogical provinces of the earth, we endeavour to imagine a procession of animals from the uttermost parts of both continents and from the isles of the sea, towards Western Asia, one thousand six hundred pairs of mammals, six thousand pairs of birds, insects more numerous than all other animals together, gathering about the ark, it is only by supposing a series of miracles that the picture can be made possible to thought. These miracles multiply in number and magnitude as we try to think of this vast menagerie dwelling together in harmony, fed and kept clean for a year by Noah and his sons, and finally departing in safety from Ararat, and thence diffusing themselves through the world. All this, we most freely admit, is possible to God. If it were a miracle, all these questions and objections are idle; but in that case it is also idle to attempt to reason on the matter at all. All miracles are alike easy to God. He could have gathered these animals to Noah and afterwards have dispersed them, as easily as he created them in their various provinces at first, but the text says, that *Noah was commanded to bring them into the ark*. Chap. vi, 19. God could have fed them as he fed Israel with manna, as he fed Elijah by ravens, and if the text stated that they were thus miraculously fed we should believe it, but it states (vi, 21) that Noah was commanded to *gather of all food that is eaten* for the sustenance of all the population of the ark. There is no indication of miraculous help in this work; all is described as a natural transaction.

Some (Prichard, Kurtz, Jacobus) suppose that new species were created after the flood, but if this be so there was obviously no need of making any provision for animals in the ark; besides, there is not a word in the text on which to base such a supposition, while the whole narrative clearly implies that the work of creation ceased at the end of the creative week. Others (Wordsworth, Lange) strongly favour the Darwinian theory of the origin of species, and suppose, or hint, that new species were brought into being, naturally or supernaturally, after the deluge. This is not the place to discuss Darwinism, but it is certainly premature for the Scripture commentator to call in its aid before it has been made to appear as even a plausible hypothesis. It would be more consistent for those who regard the transaction as miraculous not to attempt to explain it in any way.

Many eminent biblical scholars (for example, Stillingfleet, Poole, Le Clerc, Dothe, Pye Smith, Murphy, Lewis) interpret the text as teaching that the deluge was, as Delitzsch expressed it, universal for mankind, but not for the earth. This is simply a question of exegesis, and as such should be settled. The first impression naturally received by the English reader from the narrative is certainly that the waters covered the whole geographical earth, rose above the highest mountains, and destroyed every living terrestrial thing except the dwellers in the ark. " Behold, I, even

CHAPTER VI.

9 These *are* the generations of Noah:

i Chap. 7. 1; Ezek. 14. 14, 20; Rom. 1. 17;

I, do bring a flood of waters upon the earth, to destroy all flesh wherein is the breath of life, from under heaven." Chap. vi, 17. "And all flesh died that moved upon the earth. . . . All in whose nostrils was the breath of life, of all that was in the dry land, died." Chap. vii, 21, 22, etc. "And all the high hills, that were under the whole heaven, were covered." Chap. vii, 19. But the change of a single word in these passages would greatly modify this impression, and yet this is a change which parallel passages fully warrant us in making. The word אֶרֶץ, here translated *earth*, is quite as often rendered *land* throughout the Old Testament. In the Pentateuch it is applied in a multitude of instances to the land of Egypt and of Canaan. Comp. Exod. i, 7, 10; iii, 8, 17, etc. Thus in Gen. xliii, 1: "And the famine was sore in *the land*," that is, of Canaan. Gen. xli, 56. "And the famine was over all the face of the *earth*," (certainly not the geographical earth, but Egypt and the adjacent countries.) Exod. x, 15, "Locusts . . . covered the face of the whole *earth*," that is, land of Egypt. The Concordance will show a multitude of such passages. Hence Murphy renders the word *land*, throughout the description of the deluge. In the mind of the inspired writer this word meant simply that portion of the earth where man dwelt— and which was the *inhabited land*. Of the vast geographical *earth* he had no idea, and so to him the word could not have had the meaning that it now conveys. See Introd., pp. 64, 65, and notes on chap. i, 1.

Again, the word כֹּל, rendered *all* or *every* in this description, in common with other Hebrew words and phrases of a similar character, often has a partial signification. Until accustomed to this idiom the text sometimes appears even to contradict itself. For example, in Exod. ix, 25, we read, "And the hail smote throughout all the land of Egypt, *all* that was in the field, both man and

¹ Noah was a just man *and* ⁴ perfect in

Heb. 11. 7; 2 Pet. 2. 5.——4 Or, *upright*.

beast; and the hail smote *every* herb of the field, and brake *every* tree of the field." Yet that the word "all," or "every," is not to be understood literally, in a universal sense, appears from Exod. x, 15, wherein it is said that the locusts "did eat *every* herb of the land, and *all* the fruit of the trees *which the hail had left*." So also in Exod. ix, 6, in describing the plague of the murrain, it is said "*all* the cattle of Egypt died;" yet the next two plagues—that of the boils and that of the hail—are said to have fallen upon the cattle that *were in the field*. King Nebuchadnezzar (Dan. iv, 1) and Darius (Dan. vi, 25) make their proclamations "unto *all* people, nations, and languages that dwell in all the *earth*;" language that would seem to be emphatically and laboriously universal; yet in Dan. vi, 26, we find it explained by "every dominion of my kingdom." The New Testament Greek shows the same idiom. Thus in Acts ii, 5, we read, "There were dwelling at Jerusalem Jews, devout men, out of *every nation under heaven*." Yet in verses 9–11 we have a list of these nations given, which by no means embraces the whole human race. So Paul speaks of the Gospel which he declares was then "in *all* the world;" and "preached to *every creature which is under heaven*." Col. i. 6, 23. Thus we see that the expression, "all the high hills which were under the whole heaven" may, without the least exegetical strain upon the language, be understood to describe a deluge that, with reference to the earth, geographically considered, was local and partial.

9. **These are the generations of Noah**—First came the history (generation) of the heavens and earth; then that of man, and now that of the just and perfect man, who was a second father of the race. In a few strong words Noah's high religious character is sharply contrasted with the surrounding moral corruption which his godly walk and wonderful faith condemned. The ark, during one hundred and twen-

his generations, *and* Noah ᵏ walked with God. **10** And Noah begat three sons, ˡShem, Ham, and Japheth. **11** The earth also was corrupt ᵐ before God; and the earth was ⁿ filled with violence. **12** And God ᵒlooked upon the earth, and, behold, it was corrupt; for all flesh had corrupted his way upon the earth.

13 And God said unto Noah, ᵖ The end of all flesh is come before me; for the earth is filled with violence through them; ᵠand, behold, I will destroy them ⁵with the earth.

14 Make thee an ark of gopher wood; ⁶rooms shalt thou make in the ark, and shalt pitch it within and without with

---
k Chap. 5. 22. — *l* Chap. 5. 32. — *m* Chap. 7. 1; 10. 9; 13. 13; 2 Chron. 34. 27; Luke 1. 6; Rom. 2. 13; 3. 19. — *n* Ezek. 8. 17; 28. 16; Hab. 2. 8, 17.

o Chap. 18. 21; Psa. 14. 2; 33. 13, 14; 53. 2, 3. — *p* Jer. 51. 13; Ezek. 7. 2, 3, 6; Amos 8. 2; 1 Pet. 4. 7.—— *q* Verse 17.——5 Or, *from the earth*. —6 Heb. *nests*.

---

ty years slowly rising under the hands of its builders and steadily prophesying God's judgment, was a manifestation of faith unique and perhaps unparalleled in sublimity. **Just man**—Justified by faith. Heb. xi, 7. **Perfect**—תָּמִים, literally, *whole;* for holiness is wholeness. So integrity, from *integer*. He who walks with God in the faith of Noah is whole-minded toward God. Christian perfection is essentially the same as that righteousness, which some of the patriarchs are said to have attained through faith. It is Christian holiness, integrity, *entirety*. **Walked with God**—This touch completes the picture. It is a trait assigned only to Noah and Enoch. Comp. note on chap. v, 22.

10. Three sons—In this and in the three following verses the narrator, after his manner, goes back again over the ground already traversed.

11-13. The earth also was corrupt—This verb, in the same form, is used in Exod. viii, 24, to describe the land of Egypt *corrupted by the swarms of flies*, the black, blood-sucking multitudes that made the land uninhabitable. It is also used in Jeremiah xiii, 7, of a girdle rotted in the ground, which symbolized to the prophet the awful sin of idolatrous Israel. **Earth**, or rather the *land*, is used by metonymy for the inhabitants of the land, as in the last clause of verse 13. The expression is repeated and thus explained in the following verse. **Before God**—In the three successive verses this sinful corruption and violence is described in words of increasing vigour and vividness, as going on before the very eyes of God. **Violence**—A chaos of sinful destructive passion raged through the inhabited world. **God looked upon the earth, and, behold**—A sublime and solemn anthropomorphism. The universal destruction of the sinful race rises before God's eye as a vivid fearful vision, and he describes what he sees to the solitary righteous man who "walked with him" in confidential communion. **Through them** —Heb., *from before their face*. Violence heralded their steps wherever they trod. **I will destroy them**—Heb. *I am destroying them, even* (the inhabitants of) *the earth*. The determination to destroy having been formed, the event is spoken of as already in process of execution.

14. **Make thee an ark**—תֵּבָה, a word applied only to the structure built by Noah and to the little papyrus vessel made by the mother of Moses, (Exod. ii, 3,) and like this, "daubed with slime and with pitch," to make it water-tight, in which she put her child, (afterwards the Noah of Israel,) and laid it in the flags of the Nile. It was a *chest*, or oblong box, and in no sense a ship. It was flat-bottomed, not boat-shaped, as often pictured, was without spars or sails, oars or rudder, built simply for floating and carrying a precious freight, not for sailing. **Gopher wood** — Or pitch wood; a general name for resinous timber, and especially cypress, which the Phenicians used for ship-building on account of its lightness and durability. **Rooms**—Literally, *nests;* little compartments arranged for the accommodation of Noah's family and of the various animals which were to dwell for a year in the ark, as well as for the provisions that were to sustain their lives through this long period. **Pitch**—Heb. כֹּפֶר, *kopher*, cognate with *gopher*. Mineral

B. C. 2448.   CHAPTER VI.   125

pitch. **15** And this *is the fashion* which thou shalt make it *of:* The length of the ark *shall be* three hundred cubits, the breadth of it fifty cubits, and the height of it thirty cubits. **16** A window shalt thou make to the ark, and in a cubit shalt thou finish it above; and the door of the ark shalt thou set in the side thereof; *with* lower, second, and third *stories* shalt thou make it. **17** *r* And, behold, I, even I, do bring a flood of waters upon the earth, to destroy all flesh, wherein *is* the breath of life, from under heaven; *and* every thing that *is* in the earth shall die. **18** But with thee will I establish my covenant; and

---

r Verse 13; chap. 7. 4, | 21, 22, 23; 2 Pet. 2. 5.

---

pitch or asphalt; an opaque, inflammable, very tenacious substance, used, according to Josephus and Strabo, for mortar and for the calking of ships, (chap. xi, 3, where it is called *slime*,) and, according to Wilkinson, used by the Egyptians to make their papyrus boats water-tight.

15. Three hundred cubits — The cubit being at first a natural measure, like the foot and the hand, denoted the distance from the elbow to the end of the middle finger, and varied from 18 to 21.888 inches. It was generally reckoned (Ges., Jahn., Smith's Dict.) at 21 inches, or 1.75 feet. This would make the ark 525 feet long, 87½ feet wide, and 52½ feet high. Experiments made in Holland and Denmark show that vessels built on this model are admirably adapted to freightage, though, of course, unfit for rapid progress through the water.

16. A window—צֹהַר. The Hebrew word here employed occurs nowhere else in the singular, but is frequently found in the dual, denoting the noontide. A different word is used in chap. viii, 6, to describe the window which Noah opened to send forth the raven. The making of *that* window is nowhere described. **In a cubit... finish it above** — Or, *unto a cubit* (within a cubit of the ridge) *shalt thou finish it* (the ark) *from above,* (on the roof, measuring from the eaves upward.) Leave an aperture the whole length of the roof and a cubit wide, on each side of the ridge. This seems to be the best interpretation of this concise and obscure passage. This aperture, two cubits wide and running through the middle of the roof, was at once a sky-light and a ventilator, being wholly or partially closed by some sort of a covering, perhaps a semi-transparent awning, (chap. viii, 13,) during the rain, and which Noah lifted up to get a wide view of the face of the earth. Directly beneath the ridge there was probably a wide space, or hall, the whole length and depth of the ark, into which the rooms or stalls opened on the right and left. It was thus a vast three-story building, with a hall through the middle from floor to ridge. **The door**—One large door for entrance and exit in the side.

17. Behold, I, even I, do bring a flood—Language setting forth a special and awful providence. The word מַבּוּל, *flood,* here used, is applied only to the deluge of Noah; Psa. xxix, 10, is no exception; and every-where except in Gen. ix, 15, where it is promised that a similar judgment shall never recur, it invariably has the article, pointing out *the* great inundation that once washed out the world's sin in judgment. **To destroy all flesh**—This language is absolute and unqualified, as in verse 13, yet afterward the exceptions are introduced. Such rhetorical peculiarities mark the extreme antique simplicity of the style. These simple, absolute assertions, pictorially describing facts when seen, as it were, on successive sides, would have been interwoven into balanced periods in a more modern historical production.

18. With thee will I establish my covenant—בְּרִית, *covenant;* Septuagint and New Testament, διαθήκη. For the origin of the word, see notes on chap. xv. This word and act contain the weightiest and most vital truths. God's personal condescension and love, man's dignity and sonship, with all the duties and obligation involved in these exalted relations, are contained in this word. It is a rich, strong, elevating,

Vol. I.—9   O. T.

thou shalt come into the ark, thou, and thy sons, and thy wife, and thy sons' wives with thee. **19** And of every living thing of all flesh, 'two of every *sort* shalt thou bring into the ark, to keep *them* alive with thee; they shall be male and female. **20** Of fowls after their kind, and of cattle after their kind, of every creeping thing of the earth after his kind; two of every *sort* ᵘ shall come unto thee, to keep *them* alive. **21** And take thou unto thee of all food that is eaten, and thou shalt gather *it* to thee; and it shall be for food for thee, and for them. **22** ᵛ Thus did Noah; ʷ according to all that God commanded him, so did he.

CHAPTER VII.

AND the LORD said unto Noah, ᵃ Come thou and all thy house into the

s Chap. 7. 1, 7, 13; 1 Pet. 3. 20; 2 Pet. 2. 5.——
t Chap. 7. 8, 9, 15, 16. —— *u* Chap. 7. 9, 15; see chap. 2. 19.

v Heb. 11. 7; see Exod. 40. 16.——*w* Chap. 7. 5, 9, 16.——*a* Verses 7, 13; Matt. 24. 38; Luke 17. 26; Heb. 11. 7; 1 Pet. 3. 20; 2 Pet. 2. 5.

and consoling word. Man, God's image, God's son, is accepted by him as a partner in promises and obligations. There is something indescribably ennobling and inspiring in the thought. God's fatherly nearness and man's immortal nature and destiny are implied in the word. 1) It was solemnly repeated to Abraham, the father of the covenant people; revealed to Isaac and Jacob; enlarged, explained, and more formally ratified with Moses; and all of these covenants were but typical of that sublimest and most mysterious transaction, "the new testament," (διαθήχη,) revealing that infinite condescension and love which "the angels desire to look into," ratified by the blood of the Son of God. A covenant of works was made with Adam at his creation, wherein man, as his part, was to furnish legal obedience, and God, as his part, eternal life; but when the promise came to sinful man, "faith was counted for righteousness" in the covenant of mercy. How empty, belittling, and cold are those systems of religion that would substitute obedience to the laws of nature for worship in faith and love, which takes hold on a personal, covenant-keeping Father! A covenant with man was implied in his moral nature; it was first expressed in the promise of the woman's seed, but now, for the first time, appears under the covenant name.

19. **Two of every sort**—From this statement, repeated in the next verse, as well as from that made in chap. vii, 15, 16, it would be understood that only a pair of the animals were to be preserved; but from chap. vii, 2, 3, we see that the clean beasts and fowls went into the ark by seven pairs. Animals instinctively foresee great natural convulsions or earthquakes, volcanic eruptions and tornadoes, and often, on such occasions, quite subdued by fear, seek human protection. It is natural to suppose that there would have been in the earth, atmosphere, and clouds fearful premonitions of this unparalleled convulsion, which lasted through forty days, and which is described as opening the windows of heaven and breaking up "the fountains of the great deep." Beasts and birds of all kinds, that is, of all the species in that region, affrighted by these signs of the coming tempest, and tamed by their fears, may be reasonably believed to have gathered around or settled on the vast ark, during the few days before the deluge actually began. From *these* Noah selected twos or sevens of each kind. Instinct was thus providentially (we need not say miraculously) made the means of their preservation. **Shalt thou bring** — They *came* unto Noah, (v, 20,) and he *caused them to come* (for this is the true idea of the word rendered **bring**) into the ark.

21. **All food**—Noah had had abundant opportunity to lay in provisions for the animals before the signs of the catastrophe appeared. It was not till the last seven days that they began to enter the ark. Chap. vii, 4, 10.

22. **Thus did Noah**—And thus he showed his faith (Heb. xi, 7) by ready and long-continued obedience **to all that God commanded him**, "by the which he condemned the world, and became heir of the righteousness which is by faith."

CHAPTER VII.

1. **Come thou and all thy house into the ark**—"The long period of

B. C. 2349.   CHAPTER VII.   127

ark; for ᵇ thee have I seen righteous before me in this generation. **2** Of every ᶜ clean beast thou shalt take to thee by ¹ sevens, the male and his female: ᵈ and of beasts that *are* not clean by two, the male and his female. **3** Of fowls also of the air by sevens, the male and the female; to keep seed alive upon the face of all the earth. **4** For yet seven days, and I will cause it to rain upon the earth ᵉ forty days and forty nights; and every living substance that I have made will I

b Chap. 6. 9; Psa. 33. 18, 19; Prov. 10. 9; 2 Pet. 2. 9.——*c* Verse 8; Lev. chap. 11.   1 Heb. *seven seven*.——*d* Lev. 10. 10; Ezek. 44. 23.——*e* Verses 12, 17.

warning and preparation had now nearly passed. The one hundred and twenty years had rolled on, and were now within a week of their termination. The ark itself was at length completed and ready for occupancy. Against all the reviling of men and the temptations of Satan Noah's faith had triumphed. Now it remained to introduce to the majestic structure its tenants, and God's time has come for them to enter. The command to enter is a gracious command. The plan of God from the beginning has been to dispense his grace by a household covenant. He has been pleased to propagate his Church by means of a pious posterity. Hence we have the household baptisms in the Christian Church."—*Jacobus.*

2. Every clean beast—"The objection that this was an anticipation of the Levitical distinction of beasts into clean and unclean, is wholly groundless. The boundary line between clean and unclean animals is marked by nature. Every tribe of mankind would distinguish between the sheep and the hyena, between the dove and the vulture. Whether animal food was eaten before the deluge or not, it is certain that flocks and herds were fed for the sake of their milk and wool, and that of them victims were offered in sacrifice. This alone would separate between the clean and the unclean. It is not improbable, that the distinction even of the names *clean and unclean* had been fully established by custom long before it was recognised and ratified by the law."—*Speaker's Com.* **By sevens**—Heb. *seven seven.* Seven pairs of every clean beast is, doubtless, the meaning of the writer, as implied by the additional words, **the male and his female.** This statement Kalisch declares to be totally "irreconcilable with the preceding narrative," and imagines that the discrepancy may be easily explained by the hypothesis of Elohistic and Jehovistic documents. He supposes that the Jehovist "prudently introduced the significant number of seven pairs" in order to provide for Noah's offering of clean beasts and fowls after the flood. Chap. viii, 20. And yet he admits that the Jehovist "neither thought, nor did he in any way intend, to be in opposition to the statement of the Elohist. He understood the two animals which Noah was to bring, as merely signifying that always male and female were to be chosen, that they were to be *pairs,* without the *number* of these pairs being stated; for he writes: 'Two and two went in to Noah into the ark, male and female, as Elohim had commanded Noah.'" Verse 9. Is it not strange that a writer who can so readily understand that this "Jehovist" (who wrote the narrative as it now stands, and "designed full harmony with the Elohist") saw no discrepancy here, but "understood that they were to be pairs without the number of these pairs being stated," will insist that the two statements are utterly irreconcilable with each other? If the "Jehovist" had no trouble in reconciling these statements, probably Moses had none; nor need we. "The command here is but an amplification of the former injunction, which had probably been given one hundred and twenty years before. In the first instance it was said that Noah's family should be preserved, together with a pair of every kind of beast. In the second, that, while the general rule should be the saving of a single pair, yet, in the case of the clean beasts there should be preserved not one pair only, but seven."—*Speaker's Com.*

4. Yet seven days—One full week yet remained for gathering all into the ark. **Seven . . . forty . . . forty**—We naturally note here the occurrence

128　　　　　　　　GENESIS.　　　　　　B. C. 2349

destroy² from off the face of the earth. 5 ʳAnd Noah did according unto all that the LORD commanded him. 6 And Noah *was* six hundred years old when the flood of waters was upon the earth.

7 ᵍAnd Noah went in, and his sons, and his wife, and his sons' wives with him, into the ark, because of the waters of the flood. 8 Of clean beasts, and of beasts that *are* not clean, and of fowls, and of every thing that creepeth upon the earth, 9 There went in two and two unto Noah into the ark, the male and the female, as God had commanded Noah. 10 And it came to pass ³after seven days, that the waters of the flood were upon the earth.

11 In the six hundredth year of Noah's life, in the second month, the seventeenth day of the month, the same day were all ʰ the fountains of the great deep broken up, and the ⁴ windows ⁱ of heaven were opened. 12 ᵏAnd the rain was upon the earth forty days and forty nights. 13 In the selfsame day ˡ entered Noah, and Shem, and Ham, and Japheth, the sons of Noah, and Noah's wife, and the three wives of his sons with them, into the ark; 14 ᵐ They, and every beast after his kind, and all the cattle after their kind, and every creeping thing that creepeth upon the earth after his kind, and every fowl after his kind, every bird of every ⁵ sort. 15 And they ⁿ went in unto Noah into the ark, two and two of all flesh, wherein *is* the breath of life. 16 And they that went in, went in male and female of all flesh, ᵒ as God had commanded him: and the LORD shut him in. 17 ᵖAnd the flood

---

2 Heb. *blot out.*—ƒ Chap. 6. 22.—*g* Verse 1.
—3 Or, *on the seventh day.*—*h* Chap. 8. 2;
Prov. 8. 28; Ezek. 26. 19.—4 Or, *floodgates.*
—*i* Chap. 1. 7; 8. 2; Psa. 78. 23.

k Verses 4, 17.—*l* Verses 1, 7; chap. 6. 18;
Heb. 11. 7; 1 Pet. 3. 20; 2 Pet. 2. 5.—*m* Verses
2, 3, 8, 9.—5 Heb. *wing.*—*n* Chap. 6. 20.—
o Verses 2, 3.—*p* Verses 4, 12.

---

of these significant numbers. Comp. also chap. viii, 4, 10, 12 (notes); and Moses forty days on the mount; Israel forty years in the desert; the spies forty days in searching Canaan. But in these historical narratives there is no reason to question the literal significance of the numbers. Their prominence in history made them specially significant in prophecy.

11. Six hundredth year . . . second month . . . seventeenth day— Dates and measures throughout the narrative are given with an arithmetical minuteness which removes it entirely out of the region of poetry. In fact, there is no poetic colouring, no vividly emotional expression, such as might naturally be expected in the description of such an awfully impressive judgment. It reads like a simple diary of events from an eye-witness who is profoundly impressed with their divine origin and purpose, but who makes no attempt at rhetorical embellishment. See further on viii, 4. **Fountains of the great deep**—The fathomless ocean. **Broken up**—Rent, or cloven asunder. **The windows**—Lattices, sluices; margin, *floodgates.* The waters came from the **great deep** and from the skies. Two natural causes of the deluge are here, then, clearly assigned—the overflowing ocean and the descending rains. The word *deep* (תְּהוֹם) primarily signifies the original watery abyss (chap. i, 2) out of which the "dry land" was elevated, and would here, therefore, be naturally applied to the ocean returning over the sinking land. This unique event is described in wholly unique phraseology. The water rushes upon the earth from the ocean as if from a multitude of suddenly opened fountains. Bursting fountains from the deep and opened lattices in the skies are pictorial conceptions of one who saw and felt the awful judgment; yet, as said above, there is no attempt at an elaborate description of scenes which have furnished poetry and painting an exhaustless field.

13. The selfsame day entered— בָּא, might here be rendered in the pluperfect, *had entered;* that is, on that day the embarkation had ended. There may have been fearful portends of the approaching convulsion of nature while Noah was making his final preparations; but when the great rain actually began and the great deep burst over the barriers of the shore, Noah and his family, and the animals that were to be preserved, were safe in the ark.

16. The Lord shut him in—Noah in the ark was encompassed by the

B. C. 2349. CHAPTER VII. 129

was forty days upon the earth; and the waters increased, and bare up the ark, and it was lifted up above the earth. **18** And the waters prevailed, and were increased greatly upon the earth; ᑫand the ark went upon the face of the waters. **19** And the waters prevailed exceedingly upon the earth; ʳand all the high hills, that were under the whole heaven, were covered. **20** Fifteen cubits upward did the waters prevail; and the mountains were covered. **21** ˢAnd all flesh died that moved upon the earth, both of fowl, and of cattle, and of beast, and of every creeping thing that creepeth upon the earth, and every man: **22** All in ᵗwhose nostrils *was* ⁶the breath of life, of all that *was* in the dry *land*, died. **23** And every living substance was destroyed which was upon the face of the ground, both man, and cattle, and the creeping things, and the fowl of the heaven; and they were destroyed from the earth: and ᵘNoah only remained *alive*, and they that *were* with him in the ark. **24** ᵛAnd the waters

---

q Psa. 104. 26. —— *r* Psa. 104. 6; Jer. 3. 23.——
s Chap. 6. 13, 17; verse 4; Job 22. 16; Matt. 24. 39; Luke 17. 27; 2 Pet. 3. 6.——*t* Chap. 2. 7.

6 Heb. *the breath of the spirit of life.* —— *u* 1 Pet. 3. 20; 2 Pet. 2. 5; 3. 6.——*v* Chap. 8. 3, 4, compared with verse 11 of this chapter.

---

arms of the covenant-keeping God. While the elemental war raged so fiercely above and beneath, he was shut in with Jehovah. The use of the two divine names is here most suggestive and impressive. It was *Elohim*, the mighty God, the Creator, who brought the flood of waters upon the earth; but it was *Jehovah*, the God of the promise and of the covenant, the Unchanging One, (ὁ ὢν καὶ ὁ ἦν καὶ ὁ ἐρχόμενος,) who now covered him with his wings. Thus will God close the door of the Church when the final storm of judgment shall fall upon the world. They "went in unto the marriage and the door was shut." Matt. xxv, 10. This verse, blending, as it does, the two divine names in one sentence, conclusively demonstrates the unity of the narrative, showing that in its present form it proceeded from a single mind.

17, 18. **Forty days**—That is, as we understand it, for forty days the rain burst from the "lattices of heaven," and the waters rushed from the great deep upon the subsiding land. At last they lifted up the ark from off the earth, so that it **went upon the face of the waters.** Repetitions like those in verses 17-19 (comp. also verse 12, and verses 20-23) favour the theory that the narrative is a compilation from different documents; but the compiler may as well have been Moses or one of his contemporaries as any writer living a thousand years later.

19. **High hills . . . covered**—Waters rose above the summits of the high hills, or rather, they gradually settled beneath the inundating flood, until, to the observer in the floating ark, the world was a monotonous waste of waters, vast and mighty, (Heb., *mighty exceedingly*,) and as far as the eye could see, **all the high hills, that were under the whole heaven, were covered.** On the usage of such universal terms, see above, note introductory to chap. vi, 9.

20. **Fifteen cubits upward**—The arithmetical exactness here is noteworthy. Here, as in the minute specifications of time, which are given as carefully as if they had been set down in a logbook, we have the language of one who was in the midst of the scene—a spectator who was profoundly impressed by the rushing floods, the rising and slowly moving ark, the sinking hills, the drowning men and beasts, yet was not confused or bewildered amid the awful scene. He notes and records the precise date of each critical event, and coolly fathoms the deluge itself. Probably the ark drew fifteen cubits of water, and as it did not ground upon the hills, the spectator saw that they were covered to this depth. Shut in with Jehovah, though in the unwieldy ark, floating he knew not whither, faith gave Noah a confidence more calm and grand than skill and science can ever give the navigator, though in a seaworthy ship traversing familiar waters.

21. **And all flesh died**—In the land inhabited by man. Far as the narrator could see the mountains were covered, and all living things were swept away. See the introductory note on the extent of the deluge.

prevailed upon the earth a hundred and fifty days.

CHAPTER VIII.

AND God ª remembered Noah, and every living thing, and all the cattle that *was* with him in the ark: ᵇ and God made a wind to pass over the earth, and the waters assuaged. **2** ᶜ The fountains also of the deep and the windows of heaven were stopped, and ᵈ the rain from heaven was restrained. **3** And the waters returned from off the earth ¹ continually: and after the end ᵉ of the hundred and fifty days the waters were abated. **4** And the ark rested in the seventh month, on the seventeenth day of the month, upon the mountains of Ararat. **5** And the waters ² decreased

---

a Chap. 19. 29; Exod. 2. 24; 1 Sam. 1. 19.—
b Exod. 14. 21.——*c* Chap. 7. 11.——*d* Job 38. 37.

1 Heb. *in going and returning.*——*e* Chap. 7. 24.——2 Heb. *were in going and decreasing.*

---

24. A hundred and fifty days—Five months elapsed from the time Noah entered the ark until it rested on the mountains of Ararat. He entered in on the seventeenth day of the second month, (chap. vii, 11,) and the ark rested on the seventeenth day of the seventh month. Chap. viii, 4.

CHAPTER VIII.

1–3. God remembered Noah—The ark, containing the seed of the Church and of the human race, a solitary speck in the watery wilderness, was **remembered** by God. The tokens of that remembrance followed. The providential means by which the land was dried and made once more a habitation for man are now related. Three causes are mentioned: a wind *passing* **over the earth,** (toward the sea,) which dispelled the clouds and laid open the earth to the sun, (a land breeze, which carried the clouds seaward;) as a consequence of this, the shutting of **the windows of heaven;** and, thirdly, the stopping of the **fountains** of the great **deep,** which was probably effected by the gradual re-elevation of the land which had been gradually subsiding during the increase of the deluge. As the sun broke through the clouds the waters were thus seen to follow the wind. As the result of these causes *the waters subsided.* And the waters turned from off the earth, continually turning, and diminished at the end of the **hundred and fifty days.**

4. The ark rested—Here is the reason of the statement made in the previous verse; at the end of five months, or one hundred and fifty days, it is known that the waters had begun to diminish, because the ark, which had hitherto floated freely, now caught ground, and finally rested.

It is not likely that the year of the flood was reckoned from Abib, the beginning of the sacred year as established at the Exodus; but, as the *Speaker's Commentary* observes, about the autumnal equinox. "If so, the seventeenth day of the second month (vii, 11) would bring us to the middle of November, the beginning of the wintry or rainy season. . . . With regard to the forty days' rain, it seems pretty certain that these were not additional to, but part of, the one hundred and fifty days of the prevalence of the flood. Supposing the above calculation to be correct, we have the very remarkable coincidences that on the seventeenth day of Abib (five months later than November) the ark rested on Ararat; on the seventeenth of Abib the Israelites passed the Red Sea, and on the seventeenth of Abib our Lord rose from the dead." **Upon the mountains of Ararat**—Not the mount or double peak now called Ararat, which from its height, steepness, ruggedness, and cold (the summit is higher than Mont Blanc) would have been totally unsuited for the ark's resting-place; but the highlands of the country or district of Ararat, probably the central province of Armenia. Von Raumer has shown that this was the most suitable spot in the world for the cradle of the human race. "A cool, airy, well-watered mountain-island in the midst of the old continent," whence the waters descend toward the Black, Caspian, and Mediterranean Seas and the Persian Gulf. At the center of the longest land-line of the ancient world from Behring Straits to the Cape of Good Hope, it stood in the great highways of colonization, near the seats of the greatest nations of antiquity.

5. Waters decreased—Heb., *the*

B. C. 2349.   CHAPTER VIII.   131

continually until the tenth month: in the tenth *month,* on the first *day* of the month, were the tops of the mountains seen.

6 And it came to pass at the end of forty days, that Noah opened ᶠ the window of the ark which he had made:
7 And he sent forth a raven, which went forth ³ to and fro, until the waters were dried up from off the earth. **8** Also

---

ƒ Chap. 6. 16.——3 Heb. *in going forth and*

---

waters were going and decreasing (steadily decreasing) **until the tenth month.** The waters slowly settled for two months and thirteen days after the ark rested, until, on the first day of the tenth month, (of the six hundredth year of Noah's life,) the mountain tops were seen. The various epochs of the narrative are given in the years, months, and days of the life of Noah. It commenced (chap. vii, 11) in his six hundredth year, second month, and seventeenth day, and ended (chap. viii, 13) in his six hundred and first year, first month, and first day.

6. Forty days—It is a question whether these forty days are to be reckoned from the landing of the ark on Ararat, (as Calvin,) or from the time that the mountain summits became visible. If the first view be taken, then the raven and the dove were sent forth after the ark grounded and before any land was seen. This seems to be the most reasonable view, for it does not appear likely that Noah would send forth the raven and the dove "to see whether the waters had abated" after the mountain tops had become visible. We understand, then, that verses 6–12 detail events which transpired while the waters were decreasing, and before the mountain tops were seen, as described in verse 5. **The window**—Not the window mentioned in chap. vi, 16, which was an aperture for light. See the note at that place.

7. A raven—Heb., *the raven;* the well known: historic from this event. **To and fro**—Heb., *it went going and returning;* that is, going away from the ark and returning to it, settling upon but not entering into it. The raven may have found abundant sustenance from the floating carcases, so that it needed not to return to the ark

he sent forth a dove from him, to see if the waters were abated from off the face of the ground. **9** But the dove found no rest for the sole of her foot, and she returned unto him into the ark; for the waters *were* on the face of the whole earth. Then he put forth his hand, and took her, and ⁴ pulled her in unto him into the ark. **10** And he stayed yet other seven days; and again he sent

---

returning.——4 Heb. *caused her to come.*

---

for food. This black bird of death, finding a congenial home in the watery sepulchre of the antediluvian world, is a symbol of judgment and wrath.

8. Also he sent forth a dove—Rather, *the dove;* so well known from this event. Probably seven days after the raven had been sent forth, (Aben Ezra, Kimchi, Knobel,) for verse 10 states, that he waited yet *other* seven days. The dove, unlike the raven, alights only where it is clean and dry; and so the fact of her not returning would give more certain information in regard to the state of the earth.

9. No rest for the sole of her foot —The state of the earth is thus graphically and beautifully described. The delicate dove, the bird of the plains, finding no clean dry place on which to alight, and nothing fit for her food, instinctively returned to the window from which she was sent forth. The mountain summits were bare, but the desolate scene was as yet only a fit abode for the raven. May we not find here the origin of the heathen practice of bird divination?

10. Yet other seven days—Here and in verse 12 is a clear allusion to the sevenfold division of time, the week, a period which was adopted by all the Shemitic races, by the Egyptians, by the Chinese and Hindus as far back as authentic history extends, and which was even found among the ancient Peruvians. Unlike the year, the month, the day, this division does not correspond with any natural phenomena, and can only be reasonably accounted for by supposing it to be a traditional remembrance of the creative week. It is probable that Noah, on the Sabbath, sent forth the raven and the dove, in earnest prayer seeking providential aid

forth the dove out of the ark. **11** And the dove came in to him in the evening, and, lo, in her mouth *was* an olive leaf plucked off: so Noah knew that the waters were abated from off the earth. **12** And he stayed yet other seven days, and sent forth the dove, which returned not again unto him any more. **13** And it came to pass in the six hundredth and first year, in the first *month*, the first *day* of the month, the waters were dried up from off the earth: and Noah removed the covering of the ark, and looked, and, behold, the face of the ground was dry. **14** And in the second month, on the seven and twentieth day of the month, was the earth dried. **15** And God spake unto Noah, say-

and guidance. These weekly waitings from Sabbath to Sabbath were additional trials to his faith.

11. Olive leaf plucked off — Not picked up. The freshly torn leaf or twig showed that the bird had plucked it from the tree. The olive tree puts out its leaves even if covered with water; and Noah saw by this freshly plucked leaf that the waters had subsided to the plains or slopes where the olive trees grew, and that their tops at least now rose above the surface. This fresh leaf was the first sign of the earth's resurrection to life. The dove, with the olive branch in her mouth, has thus become the herald of peace and salvation.

13. First month—Noah waits another month before removing the covering of the ark, and nearly two months more before he went forth. The successive epochs are given with the minutest accuracy, removing the narrative entirely from the region of the poetical or mythical, as will be seen by the following comparison of texts which form the Noachian calendar:

Year.	Month.	Day.	Text.	EVENT.
600	2	17	Chap. vii, 11	Flood commences.
600	3	27	Chap. vii, 17	The ark floats.
600	7	17	Chap. viii, 4	Ark rests.
600	10	1	Chap. viii, 5	The mountain tops are seen.
600	11	11	Chap. viii, 6	The raven is sent out.
600	11	18	Chap. viii, 8*	The dove is sent out, and returns.
600	11	25	Chap. viii, 10	The dove is again sent out, and returns with the olive leaf.
600	12	2	Chap. viii, 12	The dove is again sent out, but does not return.
601	1	1	Chap. viii, 13	Face of the ground dry.
601	2	27	Chap. viii, 14	Ground fully dry.

* Comp. verse 10.

The whole time that Noah remained in the ark was, then, one year (probably a lunar year is meant) and ten days, making, as nearly as is possible to be expressed in days, a solar year of three hundred and sixty-five days. What kind of a year and month is here intended is a question yet discussed among chronologists; from comparing chap. vii, 11, and viii, 3, 4, we find that five months were reckoned as one hundred and fifty days, and this points to months of thirty days each, and a year of twelve such months, or three hundred and sixty, or by the addition of the five intercalary days, three hundred and sixty-five days, that is, the solar year. The Hebrew year at the time of the Exodus was evidently lunar; but the Egyptians, as appears from their monuments, were before this time acquainted with the year of three hundred and sixty-five days. The Jewish lunar year consisted of three hundred and fifty-four days, and if this be intended, Noah remained in the ark just a solar year. **Noah removed the covering of the ark**—מִכְסֵה. This word is elsewhere used only of the badger-skin and ram-skin coverings spread upon the holy vessels in the tabernacle, the ark of the testimony, etc., and this usage would seem to imply that in the present case some such covering was spread on the top of the ark. We suppose that it was some kind of flexible, and probably semi-transparent, covering thrown over the windows which ran the whole length on both sides of the ridge, and which would shed the rain, while it could be

B. C. 2348. CHAPTER VIII. 133

ing, **16** Go forth of the ark, *g* thou, and thy wife, and thy sons, and thy sons' wives with thee. **17** Bring forth with thee *h* every living thing that is with thee, of all flesh, *both* of fowl, and of cattle, and of every creeping thing that creepeth upon the earth; that they may breed abundantly in the earth, and *i* be fruitful, and multiply upon the earth. **18** And Noah went forth, and his sons, and his wife, and his sons' wives with him: **19** Every beast, every creeping thing, and every fowl, *and* whatsoever creepeth upon the earth, after their *5* kinds, went forth out of the ark. **20** And Noah builded an altar unto the LORD; and took of *k* every clean beast, and of every clean fowl, and offered burnt offerings on the altar. **21** And the LORD smelled *6* a *1* sweet savour; and

---

g Chap. 7. 13.——*h* Chap. 7. 15.——*i* Chap. 1. 22. ——*5* Heb. *families.*——*k* Lev. chap. 11.

6 Heb. *a savour of rest.*——*l* Lev. 1. 9; Ezek. 20. 41; 2 Cor. 2. 15; Eph. 5. 2.

---

easily removed in fair weather. See note on chap. vi, 16.

16. Go forth—Noah patiently waited for the divine word, and did not hasten to leave the ark, although it was now about two months since he lifted the cover and saw that the earth was dry. Although, probably, he could see no reason for delay, and the narrative does not enable us to assign any reason for it, yet walking by faith, as one does who " walks with God," he waited for Jehovah, who " shut him in," to lead him forth. They who dwell most closely with God are often thus mysteriously bidden to stand and wait when every thing seems to call for action.

20. Noah builded an altar—This is the first **altar** mentioned in history, although it is generally supposed that Abel built one for his acceptable offering. It is possible that the antediluvian saints brought their gifts to the gate of Eden, where God had "tabernacled the cherubim." Chap. iii, 24. Whether this were so or not, all traces of that paradise were obliterated by the deluge, so that even the geographical marks of the antediluvian record cannot now be identified. מִזְבֵּחַ, the Hebrew for *altar*, is from זָבַח, *to slay*, a place where victims were slain in confession of the desert of sin. Noah, the priest of the human race, type of the Great High Priest who offered himself without spot unto God, comes forth upon the baptized earth, and his first act is to make this solemn confession of sin in behalf of the rescued remnant of humanity. This man, who alone was perfect in his generations, and who walked with God, built the first altar, and sprinkled it with the blood of every clean bird and beast as a confession of sin. Sacrifice is symbolic in its very essence. The slain victim represents the worshipper, its death being typical of the desert of sin; the consumed offering going up from the earth in smoke typifies the prayer in which the man sends his inmost being up to God; while at the same time all these sacrifices, divinely appointed, prepared man to understand God's great Sacrifice, wherein Christ offered himself up unto God, that He might be just and the justifier of all that come unto him by faith. Noah did not see Calvary, but God saw it; and we now see the smoke from this first historic altar, together with that from the tabernacle and the temple, blending in the cloud on the gospel mercy-seat.

21. A sweet savour—Or, *an odour of rest.* Septuagint, ὀσμὴν εὐωδίας, the Levitical phrase often used of acceptable sacrifices, (comp. Lev. i, 9, xiii, 17, ii, 9, etc.,) and is quoted by Paul (Eph. v, 2) in reference to the great Antitype, who was at once Priest and Victim: " as Christ also hath loved us, and hath given himself for us an offering and a sacrifice to God, for a sweet-smelling savour." Noah, as the priest of the new humanity, offers every clean bird and beast on his solitary altar, and consecrates the renewed earth to God. The whole earth is the altar on which the Infinite Victim is offered up as a spotless offering in behalf of all mankind; and in his dying cry are gathered the prayers of universal humanity, which come up before God as a savour of sweet smell. No other figure of speech could so perfectly and beautifully express God's delight in genuine prayer—that offering in which the soul's

the LORD said in his heart, I will not again ᵐ curse the ground any more for man's sake: ⁷ for the ⁿ imagination of man's heart *is* evil from his youth : ᵒ neither will I again smite any more every thing living, as I have done. **22** ᵖ ˢ While the earth remaineth, seed-time and harvest, and cold and heat, and summer and winter, and ᵠ day and night shall not cease.

CHAPTER IX.

AND God blessed Noah and his sons, and said unto them, ᵃ Be fruitful,

---

m Chap. 3. 17; 6. 17. —— 7 Or, *though*. —— *n* Chap. 6. 5; Job 14. 4; 15. 14; Psa. 51. 5; Jer. 17. 9; Matt. 15. 19; Rom. 1. 21; 3. 23.

o Chap. 9. 11, 15.——*p* Isa. 54. 9.——8 Heb. *As yet all the days of the earth.*——*q* Jer. 33. 20, 25.——*a* Chap. 1. 28; verses 7, 19; chap. 10. 32.

---

very essence ascends to him. **The Lord said in his heart**—A divine soliloquy inspired by infinite tenderness and mercy. God smells the sweet savour of prayer that rises, and is to rise, from earth, especially that of the Great High Priest, and covenants with man not to smite the earth again. **Imagination of man's heart** — The things imaged in his heart. **Evil from his youth** — From the very dawn of his consciousness. The reason here given for the divine promise seems strange at first, as if the magnitude and hopelessness of man's sins were grounds of mercy, yet this is in perfect harmony with the whole plan of salvation. Man's innate sinfulness is to the merciful God a reason why he is not to be treated as a being under law, and hence in fatherly mercy he makes with him a covenant of grace. This is the rich and tender purpose of the divine heart in regard to the child that is lost, and *because* he is so hopelessly lost. Interpretation should not strive to soften away the bold, strong language of texts like this. Let it be noted, that it is while Jehovah smells the sweet odour of sacrifice—it is while man's confession, consecration, and prayer rise before him—that this soliloquy of mercy is spoken to his heart.

22. **While the earth remaineth**— Some (as Delitzsch) understand this promise to teach that the present alternation of the seasons did not take place in the antediluvian world ; •but the language does not warrant such an inference. A great convulsion had interrupted the regular order of nature, so that there had been no seedtime nor harvest through the whole inhabited world. Here it is promised that the great natural changes shall be orderly and uniform *all the days of the earth.*

(Heb.) The six agricultural seasons, as known among the Hebrews and the Arabs, are here mentioned. Yet we are not to think of them as dividing up the year among themselves after the manner of our four seasons. The words rendered **seedtime and harvest** have reference to the sowing and the reaping of grains, while the words rendered **summer and winter** have reference primarily to the cutting and gathering of fruits, and more exactly correspond to our summer and autumn. Of course the times of sowing, reaping, and gathering vary according to latitude and zone. The year is also divided, with regard to temperature, into **cold and heat**. The promise, then, is universal for mankind, and declares that the earth's annual changes, with regard both to productions and temperature, shall be regular and perpetual. There are included, also, in this promise, the regular alternations of light and darkness, although these were not interrupted by the flood. Man craves these changes in his present state, for they are essential to his happiness and development, but will not be so with man renewed and restored, who " needs no candle, neither light of the sun," and John says of the New Jerusalem, " there shall be no night there." Rev. xxi, 25.

CHAPTER IX.

THE COVENANT WITH NOAH, 1–17.

1. **God blessed Noah**—Noah, as the second founder of the race, receives a renewal of the blessing and the promise given to Adam, (Gen. i, 28, 29,) but modified by the altered relations which had been introduced by sin. Had man never fallen, the beasts of the field would willingly and naturally have owned his dominion ; but the fallen

and multiply, and replenish the earth. 2 ᵇAnd the fear of you and the dread of you shall be upon every beast of the earth, and upon every fowl of the air, upon all that moveth *upon* the earth, and upon all the fishes of the sea; into your hand are they delivered. 3 ᶜEvery moving thing that liveth shall be meat for you; even as the ᵈgreen herb have I given you ᵉall things. 4 ᶠBut flesh with the life thereof, *which is* the blood thereof, shall ye not eat. 5 And surely your blood of your lives will I require: ᵍat the hand of every beast will I require it, and ʰat the hand of man; at the hand of every ⁱman's brother will I require the life of man. 6 ᵏWhoso sheddeth man's blood, by man shall his blood be

---

b Chap. 1. 28; Hosea 2. 18. —— *c* Deut. 12. 15; 14. 3, 9, 11; Acts 10. 12, 13. —— *d* Chap. 1. 29. —— *e* Rom. 14. 14, 20; 1 Cor. 10. 23, 26; Col. 2. 16; 1 Tim. 4. 3, 4. —— *f* Lev. 17. 10, 11, 14; 19. 26;

Deut. 12. 23; 1 Sam. 14. 33, 34; Acts 15. 20, 29. —— *g* Exod. 21. 28. —— *h* Chap. 4. 9, 10; Psa. 9. 12. —— *i* Acts 17. 26. —— *k* Exod. 21. 12, 14; Lev. 24. 17; Matt. 26. 52; Rev. 13. 10.

---

king must struggle for his sceptre, and can govern only by **fear** and **dread.** Verse 2.

3. **Meat for you**—Animal food is here granted to man. It may have been used before, but is now for the first time expressly permitted. Man is permitted freely to eat whatever he desires in the vegetable and animal creation.

4. **Flesh with the life thereof**—Literally, *Only flesh in its life, its blood, ye shall not eat*—a humane restriction, the necessity of which is seen in the barbarous and gluttonous cruelty of some heathen nations. The animal is not to be used for food until life has become wholly extinct. The restriction forbidding the eating or cooking of an animal while capable of suffering pain is in that benevolent spirit which pervades all the Bible, and has a care for the sparrow that falls. Another reason for this prohibition is, that blood is considered as typical of expiation and atonement. This is assigned in the Mosaic law, (Lev. xvii, 10, 11,) "for the life of the flesh is in the blood; and I have given it to you upon the altar to make an atonement for your souls." By this legislation the way was prepared for the reception of the great gospel doctrine that without the shedding of blood there is no remission of sins, and that Christ is the propitiation for our sins.

5. **And surely**—In the original, verses 4 and 5 both commence with the particle, אַךְ, *except*, or *but*, which introduces two stringent prohibitions supplementary to the liberty granted in verses 2 and 3. 1) The life, or blood of the animal, is never to be used as food. 2) The life of man is to be held sacred. **Blood of your lives**—Rather, *Your blood, for your lives*, (in requital for them,) *will I require*, (seek for, demand.) A command sternly guarding the life of man. **At the hand of every beast**—Beasts should be killed that endanger the life of man, (Exod. xxi, 28,) for the animal creation exists for man. By this precept the sacredness of human life is impressively declared. **At the hand of every man's brother**—The brotherhood of man is the foundation of this precept. The beast is man's servant—made for him—but man, wherever met, of whatever race or condition, is his **brother.** How completely this strikes at the root of national pride, at the aristocracy of family or race! Man's life is to be sacred simply because he is a *man*, a brother, God's image. The Noachian precept is the germ of the Pauline declaration uttered in the ears of the proud Athenians, amid the very glories of Greek civilization, God "hath made of one blood all nations of men." Acts xvii, 26.

6. **Whoso sheddeth**—The command is here repeated and enforced more explicitly. The beast that endangered human life should be slain, (verse 5;) so it shall be man's duty to take the life of the murderer, for murder is a crime against the divine majesty, which is imaged in man. These words are the divinely granted charter of civil government. The means by which this precept is to be carried out in the details of human government are left to human wisdom and experience, but man is here authorized and commanded to form institutions for the protection and welfare of society, and to defend them, if need be, at the sacrifice of life. Civil government is of God; "The powers that be are or-

shed: ¹ for in the image of God made he man. 7 And you, ᵐ be ye fruitful, and multiply; bring forth abundantly in the earth, and multiply therein.

8 And God spake unto Noah, and to

his sons with him, saying, 9 And I, ⁿ behold, I establish ᵒ my covenant with you, and with your seed after you: 10 ᵖ And with every living creature that is with you, of the fowl, of the cattle,

l Chap. 1. 27.——*m* Verses 1, 19; chap. 1. 28.   *n* Chap. 6. 18.——*o* Isa. 54. 9.——*p* Psa. 145. 9.

dained of God." Rom. xiii, 1. So the heathens regarded the magistrate as God's vicegerent. (*Iliad*, i, 239.) Luther remarks: "If God here grants to man the power over life and death, much more does he also grant him power over inferior things, such as fortune, family, wife, children, servants, lands. God intends that all these should be placed under the authority of certain men, whose duty is to punish the guilty." The rulers, as God's representatives, were designated Elohim among the Hebrews. Psa. lxxxii, 1. "He judgeth among the Elohim"—magistrates. From these commands the Jewish synagogue drew what they styled the seven Noachic precepts, which were obligatory upon all proselytes. These are seven prohibitions forbidding, 1) idolatry, 2) blasphemy, 3) murder, 4) incest, 5) theft, 6) eating blood, 7) disobedience to magistrates. Civil government has its authority, not from expediency, not from any primeval social compact, but from the ordinance of God. It is not founded on the shifting sands of popular opinion, but on the eternal rock of the divine justice. Obedience to magistrates is enjoined, not because of its expediency, not because of a social covenant, but because "whosoever resisteth the power, (of the magistrate,) resisteth the ordinance of God." Rom. xiii, 2. **For in the image of God made he man**—This is the reason for the stern and stringent command. He who slays a man slays God's image, and God demands blood for blood. The murderer's life is forfeited, and it is not only the right, but the duty, of the magistrate, who "bears the sword," to fulfil the ordinance of God. This was the universal sentiment, or rather instinct, of antiquity, as shown in heathen poetry and law. This, let it be noted, is not a Mosaic precept given to the Hebrew people, but one enjoined upon the race as it goes forth from its cradle upon the renewed earth. Hence in the infancy of society, before judicial processes became regular and methodical, those nearest the scene of a murder felt called upon to avenge it. This is the origin of the institution of Goëlism, which, in the patriarchal times, provided for the punishment of the murderer. By the Goël (גֹּאֵל) is to be understood the nearest relative of the murdered man, whose duty it was to avenge his death, and who is, therefore, called "the avenger," or rather, the "redeemer, of blood;" that is, one who pays for blood with blood. Goël thus came to mean simply the *nearest blood relative*. Ruth iv, 1, 6, 8, etc. Hence the word is transferred, with great tenderness and power, to the divine Redeemer, the Goël of the race. Christ is our nearest kinsman, our elder brother, who redeems us by giving blood for blood, and who will avenge our spiritual murder upon Satan, that archetypal murderer in the spiritual world. Heb. ii, 14.

8. **God spake unto Noah**—The Elohistic narrative here describes more fully the covenant with Noah, briefly mentioned before in the Jehovistic narrative. Chap. viii, 20–22. The covenant promised (chap. vi, 18) is now consummated. But there is no inconsistency, as Knobel and others have alleged, between the two narratives. They may have been appropriated by the author of Genesis from different ancient documents, but, if so, the compiler saw, as every candid reader must now see, that these verses (8–17) are supplementary, and supply most interesting information not previously given.

10. **With every living creature**—The covenant is made, first, with all creatures which went forth from the ark, and then, with all flesh; "*with* every living creature . . . *from* all that go out of the ark, *to* every beast of the earth." In the words which relate the

B. C. 2348. CHAPTER IX. 137

and of every beast of the earth with you; from all that go out of the ark, to every beast of the earth. 11 And ᑫI will establish my covenant with you; neither shall all flesh be cut off any more by the waters of a flood; neither shall there any more be a flood to destroy the earth. 12 And God said, ʳ This *is* the token of the covenant which I make between me and you, and every living creature that *is* with you, for perpetual generations: 13 I do set ˢ my bow in the cloud, and

q Isa. 54. 9.   *r* Chap. 17. 11.——*s* Rev. 4. 3.

establishment of the covenant with the animal creation, Keil remarks, "The prepositions are accumulated, first, בְּ, embracing the whole, then the partitive, מִן, restricting the enumeration to those which went out of the ark, and, lastly, לְ, *with regard to* extending it again to every individual."

13. **Do set my bow**—נָתַתִּי, *I have set*. The verb is in the perfect tense, but the perfect is often used with reference to future events in promises and assurances, where the speaker wishes to represent the event as so absolutely certain that it may be regarded as having already taken place. Especially is this the case in prophecies. Comp. Gen. xv, 18, and vii, 16, the promises to Abraham; Jer. xxxi, 33: "I will put my law in their inward parts," (lit., *I have put*.) Kimchi remarks of this usage in the prophecies: "The thing is as certain as though already performed, it having been long determined on." (Comp. Ges., *Heb. Gr.*, 126, 4.) Some (Knobel, Del., Keil, Bush, Jac.) understand the text as teaching that there had been no rainbow before the flood, perhaps from the lack of the atmospheric conditions which the phenomenon is now observed to follow. Others, following Maimonides and the most celebrated Jewish scholars, as well as Chrysostom, understand that a phenomenon which had existed from the beginning, was now made a sign of this covenant. They accordingly render נתן, " appoint, constitute," as in 1 Kings ii, 35. But if the rainbow were familiar to the antediluvians, in what sense could it be a token to Noah and his family that the human race should not again be destroyed by a deluge of water? This is the question that has always perplexed expositors, especially since the natural causes of the rainbow were un- folded by the discoveries of Newton. Of course there is no difficulty to the Christian expositor in assuming, with Bush and Delitzsch, that the peculiar atmospheric conditions which now precede the rainbow did not exist before the deluge, being providentially prevented, from a foresight of the moral uses to which it was hereafter to be applied. Yet assumptions of this character are obviously to be avoided. We are decidedly of the opinion that science has increased rather than diminished the lustre of this promise, and that no unwarrantable assumption or meddlesome softening away of the express statements of the text is required by modern discoveries. After the terrible deluge storm, the sun bursts through the retiring clouds, and the glorious arch appears. It is a sign that the storm is vanquished by the sun, a beautiful trophy woven by the sunbeams and water-drops on the skirts of the retreating tempest. God points it out to Noah as a symbol of peace restored after the fierce elemental war, and science now shows us how completely it is such a symbol, it being the first flashing glance of the victorious sun through the discomfited clouds as they discharge their last shower upon the air. And Jehovah says, "I *have set* my bow in the cloud;" "*set*" is the emphatic word. He has bound the bow, wherein is the essence of the promise, to the stormy heavens; that is, the bow, or in other words, by immutable laws, the causes that produce the bow, shall never fail. The sun shall always burst through the clouds. There was a storm which, to the antediluvian world, had no end; to that doomed race no bow appeared; but man hereafter shall always see the bow in the heavens. God has *set*, established, it there by an immutable decree. Nature is so constituted, its forces so adjusted, that another similar convul-

it shall be for a token of a covenant between me and the earth. **14** And it shall come to pass, when I bring a cloud over the earth, that the bow shall be seen in the cloud: **15** And ᵗI will remember my covenant, which *is* between me and you and every living creature of all flesh; and the waters shall no more become a flood to destroy all flesh. **16** And the bow shall be in the cloud; and I will look upon it, that I may remember ᵘthe everlasting covenant between God and every living creature of all flesh that *is* upon the earth. **17** And

God said unto Noah, This *is* the token of the covenant, which I have established between me and all flesh that *is* upon the earth. **18** And the sons of Noah, that went forth of the ark, were Shem, and Ham, and Japheth: ᵛand Ham *is* the father of ¹Canaan. **19** ʷThese *are* the three sons of Noah: ˣand of them was the whole earth overspread. **20** And Noah began *to be* ʸa husbandman, and he planted a vineyard: **21** And he drank of the wine, ᶻand was drunken; and he was uncovered within his tent. **22** And

---

t Exod. 28. 12; Lev. 26. 42, 45; Ezek. 16. 60.—
u Chap. 17. 13, 19.—*v* Chap. 10. 6.—1 Heb. *Chenaan*.

w Chap. 5. 32.—*x* Chap. 10. 32; 1 Chron. 1. 4, etc.—*y* Chap. 3. 19, 23; 4. 2; Prov. 12. 11.—*z* Prov. 20. 1; 1 Cor. 10. 12.

---

sion can never occur. Thus is the bow *set* in the heavens.

16. **And I will look upon it**—A tender and beautiful anthropomorphism. God remembers us in every earthly storm. The bow is a symbol of his tender look upon frail, sinning man. The fragment of a vast and glorious circle, formed from the sunshine and storm, it typifies eternal mercy blended with justice, as seen from earth; binding earth to heaven, it typifies God's perpetual covenant. We hear scattered echoes of this promise from the heathen poetry and mythology. Homer calls the rainbow a *sign*, (τέρας.) *Iliad*, ii, 324. The Latin poets make *Iris*, or the rainbow, the messenger of the gods. Virgil, *Æn.*, iv, 694; Ovid, *Met.*, 1,270. The ancient Germans considered the bow as the *bridge of the demigods*, by which they went to and fro between heaven and earth; and the Indians, according to Kuhn, had a similar tradition. Compare Delitzsch.

PROPHECY OF NOAH, 18–29.

The historical occasion of the remarkable prophecy uttered by Noah in regard to his sons is now given. The sin or error of Noah brings out the character of his sons, and gives rise to predictions which concern the whole family of mankind. This prediction, in style and occasion, is a fair sample of some Scripture prophecies. It has an historic cause, and relates first to immediate events. Compare, in these respects, the remarkable Messianic prophesies in Isaiah vii and ix. The immediate events, which concern the individuals involved in the transaction, are there regarded as typical of far more momentous events, involving their descendants in distant ages. The material and transitory are regarded as typical of the spiritual and eternal. The deep and wide spread correspondencies between the natural and supernatural, between the near and the distant, are so clear to the prophetic insight that the present and the future, the seen and unseen, seemed blended into a single picture. The prophet ever sees in the earthly, patterns of the heavenly.

18. **Sons of Noah**—Japheth was the eldest and Ham the youngest. See note on chap. v, 32. **Father of Canaan**—This clause is added in this place, and in verse 22, because Noah's prophetic curse lighted on the Canaanites, with whom the Hebrews were so familiar as a people accursed of God. It is, perhaps, a Mosaic addition to the original document.

20. **Began to be a husbandman** —Or, *Noah began to be a man of the soil, and he planted a vineyard.* That is, began to cultivate the vine, which probably had grown only spontaneously hitherto, and perhaps its intoxicating properties had not yet been discovered.

21. **Was drunken**—Here is the first recorded instance of drunkenness, and its revolting consequences. It is probable that in this case it was a sin of ignorance, for Noah's character as a "perfect" man, who "walked with God," seems to warrant this assumption.

B. C. 2347.   CHAPTER IX.   139

Ham, the father of Canaan, saw the nakedness of his father, and told his two brethren without. **23** ᵃAnd Shem and Japheth took a garment, and laid *it* upon both their shoulders, and went backward, and covered the na- kedness of their father; and their faces *were* backward, and they saw not their father's nakedness. **24** And Noah awoke from his wine, and knew what his younger son had done un- to him. **25** And he said, ᵇ Cursed be

---
a Exod. 20. 12; Gal. 6. 1.   *b* Deut. 27. 16.

22. Saw the nakedness of his fa- ther, and told his two brethren without — Ham displays immodesty and sensuality, as well as an unfilial glorying in his father's shame.

23. Took a garment — Heb., *the garment;* that is, the loose mantle with which he would naturally have covered himself on going to sleep. The Mosaic law was specially stringent in enjoining filial reverence, and in prohibiting such moral uncleanness as seems to have given pleasure to Ham. Compare Lev. xviii, 7, etc. Sensuality, with its attendant abomina- tions, were the great sins which brought such terrible judgment upon the Ca- naanites, so that the land "vomited them out." Comp. Lev. xviii, 24–28.

24. Awoke . . . and knew—His stupor was not so deep as to prevent his being conscious of Ham's shameful conduct.

25. And he said—Render the whole prophecy thus:

Cursed be Canaan,
A servant of servants let him be unto his brethren.
And he said:
Blessed be Jehovah, God of Shem;
And let Canaan be a servant unto them.
Let God enlarge Japheth,
And let him dwell in the tents of Shem,
And let Canaan be a servant unto them.

The futures in this passage have an imperative sense, the prediction taking the form of blessing and imprecation. It will be noted, that in reference to both Shem and Japheth the plural pro- noun *them* is used, showing that each patriarch's name is used in a collective sense, embracing his posterity. The preposition and suffix לָמוֹ is incorrect- ly rendered *his* in our version, although the margin gives the real meaning. Comp. Ges., *Gr.*, § 103, 2, note. There is a play upon words, after the favourite method of the Old Testament writers and speakers, which cannot be well shown in translation. Japheth signifies *enlarge- ment*, and Noah uses, in the blessing, the verb from which the name is derived. The predictions touched the individ- uals addressed only as they were inter- ested in their posterity. The sin of Ham and the etymology of the names, furnish starting points for prophecies of world-wide interest. Noah is now, for the first time, made to understand the prophetic significance of the names which, under divine guidance, he had given his children, as Lamech, his fa- ther, saw that Noah would be *Noah*, or *Rest*, to mankind. The filial piéty of Shem and Japheth was the means by which the revealing Spirit lifted the curtain of the future, and showed Noah how the knowledge of Jehovah should make the children of Shem illustrious (שֵׁם, *name*, a *great name*), how the de- scendants of Japheth should be spread over vast continents yet unknown, while the sensual impiety of Ham typified the degradation of the children of Canaan, his son, who should be enslaved or ex- terminated by the Shemites, as the re- ward of their dreadful iniquities. But this foresight had no causative power, and in no sense necessitated the sin or holiness of those far-off generations; for necessary sin or holiness is an im- possibility. Their actions were fore- seen, not foreordained. **Cursed be Canaan**—Not Ham, as might be ex- pected. The prediction begins with the youngest, as his sin was its im- mediate cause, (compare the order in Gen. iii, 14–16,) and as certainly would have been the case had Noah been left to vent a natural ebullition of wrath upon his unnatural son. The curse lights only upon the descendants of Canaan, the youngest son of Ham, and father of the nations who dwelt in Canaan in the time of Abraham, and down to the era of its conquest by Joshua. It is, then, pure assumption

Canaan; *a servant of servants shall he be unto his brethren. **26** And he said, *d* Blessed *be* the LORD God of Shem; and Canaan shall be ²his servant. **27** God shall ³enlarge Japheth, *and he shall dwell in the tents of Shem; and Canaan shall be his servant. **28** And Noah lived after the flood three hundred and fifty years. **29** And all the days of Noah were nine hundred and fifty years: and he died.

c Josh. 9. 23; 1 Kings 9. 20, 21. —— *d* Psa. 144. 15; Heb. 11. 16.

2 Or, *servant to them.* —— 3 Or, *persuade.* —— *e* Eph. 2. 13, 14; 3. 6.

to apply the prediction to the African families who descended from the other children of Ham. Shem and Japheth are mentioned by name, but the curse of Ham is expressly limited to Canaan. It is true that in modern times slavery has mostly fallen to the African race, but it is only in extremely modern times; and this slavery is not to be compared in universality or in severity to that which prevailed in ancient times and involved the children of Shem and Japheth as much as those of Ham. Slavery was the normal condition of the masses in the Greek and Roman world. It was a fundamental characteristic of all ancient society. Aristotle, the greatest political philosopher of antiquity, lays it down as an indispensable condition of civilization. (*Polit.*, i, cap. 3, 6.) Greeks enslaved Greeks, and Roman fathers, at the time of Christ, enslaved their own children.

26. Blessed—The blessing of Shem is an ejaculation of praise, as the patriarch sees that *Jehovah*, the one only God, will be the God of his children, the Hebrew people. This made them a nation, and gave them an historic position grander than was ever occupied by any other people, making the Hebrew character, ritual, and literature the channels of the sublimest moral and religious truths to the world. Thus has the world learned, or rather remembered, the momentous truths of the unity, spirituality, and holiness of God, and the unity, spirituality, and depravity of man.

27. God — Elohim, the generic, not the covenant name, as used with Shem. **Shall**—Rather, *let*. **Enlarge Japheth**—Japheth goes forth to conquer worlds of matter and worlds of thought. The Shemitic nations are spiritual and contemplative, preferring a pastoral or agricultural life; the Japhetic nations are intellectual, enterprising, nomadic. Intellectual activity characterizes them, as spiritual insight characterizes the descendants of Shem. The conquests of Xerxes, Alexander, the Cesars, and Napoleon—the logic and philosophy of the Sanscrit, the Greek, the German, the English—the vast migrations of the Tartars and Goths—the colonies and the commerce of the Greeks, the Romans, and the English, show how deeply prophetic is the name of Japheth. **He shall dwell in the tents of Shem**—*Let him dwell in the tents of Shem.* Many commentators, following the Targum of Onkelos, make Elohim the subject here, but most follow the Targum of Jonathan, and consider Japheth the subject. The first interpretation destroys the unity of the prophecy, and is harsh and forced. As Japheth and Shem had united in this work of filial piety, so should their children be united in participating in world-wide blessings. The aggressive, intellectual Japheth shall dwell in the tents of the quiet, spiritual Shem, and share in the wondrous promises which he inherits. Each shall share the strength and glory of the other. The Hebrew religion was poured upon the world through the languages, the logic, and rhetoric of the Greek and Roman. The words of Jesus (who bore the "NAME above every name," typified by Shem) come to us in a language of Japheth. Paul, a Hebrew of the Hebrews, preached and wrote in Greek, yet was protected in his work as a Roman citizen, and carried the glad tidings over Roman roads and in Roman ships.

28. Noah lived after the flood— The narrative up to this verse may have been composed during the life of Noah, and in all probability the details of the deluge, the covenant, and these wondrous predictions, minute and graphic as they are, were written by Noah or by Shem, not in the present form, for the Hebrew did not then exist, but in a more primitive tongue, from which they were afterward translated by some one of their descendants, probably before the time of Moses.

CHAPTER X.
Generations of Shem, Ham, and Japheth, x–xi, 9.

Under this head our author records, first, the genealogy of nations which sprang from Noah as a second root of the human race, (verses 1–32,) and next, the confusion of their languages, (xi, 1–9.)

GENEALOGY OF NATIONS, 1–32.

This chapter furnishes the most ancient and most valuable ethnological document in the world. Knobel says, "Progressive investigation will ever more and more confirm the credibility of this, our oldest description of the races of men. It is a priceless fragment of ancient history." It is the great purpose of the inspired author to trace the history of redemption, which he knew, from the promise given to Abraham, would embrace all nations. While, therefore, his chief attention is given to the chosen family, as the channel of this salvation, he here points out their relationship to all the known nations of the earth, representing humanity as a trunk dividing into three great branches, and sprouting into the manifold peoples existing at the time. The great truth proclaimed by Paul to the haughty Athenians, that God hath made of one blood all nations of men, and that all men are essentially equal before him — a truth very unpalatable to the most advanced heathen nations, and unimagined by the most profound heathen thinkers, like Plato and Aristotle, yet a truth which lies at the roots of all true education, civilization, and religion — this truth was firmly grasped as fundamental by the writer of this chapter. See here the marvellous guidance of inspiration! No Hebrew prejudice, deep as we know it to have been, was allowed to tinge this ancient page. The children of Eber are but a twig on the mighty tree.

This description of the nations bears the clear marks of an antiquity far higher than Moses. Probably he received it from a writer of the time of Abraham. Tyre, which was a "strong city" at the time of the conquest of Canaan, was not yet founded, or it would certainly have been mentioned with Sidon. Sodom and Gomorrah were yet standing, (verse 19,) but they were destroyed in the time of Abraham. The whole style of the document indicates that at the time of its original composition the Hebrew people had as yet no distinct existence. (Fürst.) The original authorship of this venerable chapter was not only pre-Mosaic, but pre-Hebraic; but, under inspired guidance, it is interwoven by Moses into his work to map out the dispersion of the nations, as described in the next chapter. Probably the original author obtained his knowledge of these nations from the Phenicians, who, even in the age of Abraham, had extended their commerce down the Red Sea, and along the coasts and through the islands of the Mediterranean, probably to the Atlantic.

Japheth, Shem, and Ham correspond, in a general way, to Europe, Asia, and Africa, respectively; to the white, brown, and black races of men, which are here all traced to a common ancestor, that they may hereafter be shown to be subjects of the same salvation. But it is only in a rough and general way that this distinction can be maintained, especially as the Hamitic Babylonians are found in Asia, and the Sidonians in Asia and Europe. The Japhetic family stretched from Armenia, east and south-east, into Media and Persia, west and north-west around the Black Sea, and along the northern shores of the Mediterranean; the Hamitic family skirted the south-eastern shore of the Mediterranean, and extended southward over the African peninsula; while the Shemitic occupied the intermediate territory — the irregular parallelogram stretching south-east through Arabia, having the Tigris Valley and the Persian Gulf on the east, and the Red and Mediterranean Seas on the west.

In this very ancient record the words "father" and "son" are used not in a genealogical, but in an ethnic, sense, as (verse 4) Chittim and Dodanim, plural national names, as shown by the ending *im*, are called "sons;" that is, nations sprung from Javan, who (see note) represents a national Japhetic family. So Mizraim (a plural national name) is said to have begotten the Ludim, the Anamim, etc., (verses 13, 14;) and in verses 16, 17, etc., the Jebusite, Amorite, etc., are represented as begotten by Canaan. The greater part of the names were regarded by the writer as national and geographical, not as individual.

The identification of these nations and tribes with those known to us through ancient profane history is beset with many difficulties, on account of the extreme antiquity of the record; for we are to remember that Moses wrote his work about one thousand years before Herodotus, the "father of history," was born. Bochart, Michaelis, and Rosenmüller have given the subject exhaustive study, but the monogram of Knobel, (*Die Völkertafel der Genesis*, Giessen, 1850,) although damaged by rationalistic assumptions, is, on the whole, the most reliable authority upon the subject. We herewith present the facts in a concise tabular form, for the sake of perspicuity.

I. JAPHETH.
1. Gomer. (Kymri, Kelts.)
   (1.) Ashkenaz. (Asen, Asiatic.)
   (2.) Riphath. (Ripaeans.)
   (3.) Togarmah. (Armenians.)
2. Magog. (Scythians.)
3. Madai. (Medes.)
4. Javan. (Ionians or, Greeks.)
   (1.) Elishah. (Æolians.)
   (2.) Tarshish. (Tartessus.)
   (3.) Kittim. (Cyprians.)
   (4.) Dodanim. (Dardanians, or Trojans.)
5. Tubal. (Tibareni Iberians.)
6. Meschech. (Moschi, Muscovites.)
7. Tiras. (Thracians.)

II. HAM.
1. Cush. (Ethiopians.)
   (1.) Sebah. (Meroe.)
   (2.) Havilah. (Macrobi.)
   (3.) Sabtah. (Sabotha.)
   (4.) Raamah. } *a*. Sheba. (Sabaean and Dedanic (Rhegma.) } *b*. Dedan. Cushites.)
   (5.) Sabtechah. (Carmanian Ethiopians.)
   (6.) Nimrod. (Nineveh, etc., Asiatic Cushites.)
2. Mizraim. (Egyptians.)
   (1.) Ludim. (In Mauritania.)
   (2.) Anamim. (In Nile Delta.)
   (3.) Lehabim. (Egyptian Lybians.)
   (4.) Naphtuhim. (Middle Egyptians.)
   (5.) Pathrusim. (Upper Egyptians, Pathros.)
   (6.) Casluhim. (North-east Egyptians.) Philistines.
   (7.) Caphtorim. (Coptic, Crete.)
3. Phut. (Lybians of North Africa.)
4. Canaan, or Kenaan. (Canaanites.)
   (1.) Sidon. (Sidonians of Phenicia.)
   (2.) Heth. (Hittites, or Chittim.)
   (3.) Jebusite. (In Jebus, Jerusalem.)
   (4.) Amorite. (The chief Canaanitish tribe.
   (5.) Girgashite. (Gergesenes.) (?)
   (6.) Hivite. (North-west Palestine, about Hermon and Lebanon.)
   (7.) Arkite. (Arka, north of Sidon.)
   (8.) Sinite. (Sinna, north of Arka.)
   (9.) Arvadite. (Arvad, or Arad, north of Sidon.)
   (10.) Zemarite. (Phenician Simyra, or Sumra.)
   (11.) Hamathite. (Hamath, on the Orontes.)

III. SHEM.
1. Elam. (Elymais, Persia.)
2. Asshur. (Assyria.)
3. Arphaxad. (Arrapachitis, North Assyria.) Shelah. { Heber. (Hebrew.) { Peleg, (ancestor of Abraham.) Jok- { Thirteen tribes of the tan. } Joktanite Arabs.
4. Lud. (Lydians of Asia Minor.) (?)
   Amalekites. (?)
   Primitive Amorites. (?)
   Philistines. (?)
5. Aram. (Syria.)
   (1.) Uz. (North of Arabia, Ausitus?)
   (2.) Hul. (Coelo-Syria.) (?)
   (3.) Gether. (Unknown.)
   (4.) Mash. (Masius?)

CHAPTER X.

N OW these *are* the generations of the sons of Noah; Shem, Ham,

a Chap. 9. 1, 7, 19.

and Japheth: ᵃ and unto them were sons born after the flood. **2** ᵇ The sons of Japheth; Gomer, and Magog, and Madai, and Javan, and Tubal, and Me-

b 1 Chron. 1. 5, etc.

SONS OF JAPHETH, 2–5.

2. **Gomer**—The word occurs elsewhere in the Scriptures only in Ezek. xxxviii, 6, where it is, as here, associated with Togarmah. The name is undoubtedly preserved in the Homeric name Κιμμέριοι, the Gimiri in the cuneiform inscriptions of Darius Hystaspes, Cimmerians, Kymri or Kymbri, the original Kelts, (Celts,) and Gauls, who were found in possession of all northern and western Europe at the dawn of western civilization. This race settled first on the north of the Black Sea, where they have left traces of their name, as *Crimea, Crim*-Tartary; driven thence by the Scythians before the time of Herodotus, (*Her.*, 4, 11,) they moved west and south-west to the sea. Traces of the original Celtic language are still preserved in Ireland, the Isle of Man, Wales, and the Scotch Highlands. The Galatians of Asia Minor, the Celtic people to whom Paul wrote his famous epistle, were called *Gomerites* by Josephus. The Celts call themselves *Kymr*, and by orthoepic changes between the liquids L, M, R, as well as the palatals K and G, changes such as are constantly taking place in spoken languages, the names *Gomer, Kymr, Gaul, Kelt, Galatae, Kimmeri, Crimea, Cambria, Cumberland*, all come from the same root. Linguistic affinities show that these people, the earliest inhabitants of Europe of whom we definitely know, were Asiatic in origin, for the Keltic is an Indo-European language.

Magog—The name probably means "the place," (or region,) of Gog, and appears in Ezekiel xxxviii, 2, and xxxix, 6, as the name of a people dwelling "in the sides of the north," over whom Gog is king, identified by Josephus, Jerome, and most moderns with the Scythians, who in the time of Herodotus had their home north of the range of Caucasus, in what is now Russia. Fürst interprets Magog as *Great*

Mount, that is, Caucasus. The region between the Black and Caspian Seas was called Magog by the Arabians. They came into Europe after the Kelts, a fierce, formidable, nomadic race, who poured down upon Asia Minor and Egypt in the seventh century B. C. (*Herod.*, iv.)

Madai—This word is nowhere else in the Bible rendered as the name of a person, but, whenever it occurs, it is translated *Media*, or *the Medes*, (see 2 Kings xvii, 6, Esther i, 3, 18, 19,) a powerful nation who once dwelt south and south-west of the Caspian, east of Armenia and Assyria. The Medes are here represented in close affinity with the Kelts (Gomer) and the Greeks, (Javan,) confirming Schlegel's theory, now deemed established by linguistic researches, that the principal European and East Indian nations are of the same Aryan stock, having in a prehistoric period migrated westward and eastward from the high land of Ivan. This theory is embodied in the word Indo-European.

Javan—יָוָן, *Yavan*, translated *Greece* in Zech. ix, 13, Dan. viii, 21, etc.; and its plural is rendered *Grecians* in Joel iv, 6. *Ionia*, the name of a western province of Asia Minor, colonized at an early period by the Greeks, and applied by the Orientals to the Greeks in general. The Rosetta Stone shows that the Egyptians called the Greeks by the same name. The word occurs with the same meaning in Sanskrit and old Persian, showing that the name existed before the rise of the Aryan, Hamitic, and Shemitic families of speech. (Knobel.) The famous Greco-Italian races, which did not arise till many centuries after the composition of this narrative, inhabiting Macedonia, Thessaly, the Greek and Italian peninsulas, and west Asia Minor, are foreshadowed in this name.

Tubal, and Meschech—These peoples are constantly associated together

144 GENESIS. B. C. 1998.

shech, and Tiras. 3 And the sons of Gomer; Ashkenaz, and Riphath, and Togarmah. 4 And the sons of Javan; Elishah, and Tarshish, Kittim, and ¹ Do-

---

1 Or, as some read it, *Rodanim*.

---

by Ezekiel, (chapters xxvii, 13, xxxii, 26, xxxviii, 1, 2, etc.,) and by Herodotus, (*Herod.*, iii, 94, vii, 78.) They are likewise, according to Rawlinson, associated in the Assyrian inscriptions. Josephus identifies Tubal with the Iberians, who once dwelt between the Caspian and Euxine Seas. Knobel considers the Tibareni to have been only a branch of the wide-spread Iberians, some of whom settled in the east, some in the west. The Moschi were the ancestors of the Muscovites, builders of Moskwa, or Moscow, and still give Russia its name throughout the East. Ezekiel says that they came down from the "sides of the north," and traded in copper and slaves in the markets of Tyre. Ezek. xxvii, 13.

Tiras — Thracians, who dwelt between Mt. Hæmus and the Ægean, on the south-west shore of the Black Sea. They are associated with Meshech (Meshnash) on the old Egyptian monuments. (Rawlinson.)

3. **Sons of Gomer**—Sub-families of the Gomeridæ, or Cimmerians, Kimbri.

Ashkenaz — Or Askenaz. Kenaz means *family, family of the Asi*, who lived in the north-west of Asia Minor, and from whom *Asia* derives its name. (Knobel.) By metathesis the name becomes *Aksenaz*, possibly the old name of the Black Sea, which the Greeks called ἄξενος, *Euxine*. (Lewis.) The Greek name is usually understood, however, to mean *inhospitable*.

Riphath—The portion of the Kelts who, according to Plutarch, crossed the *Rhipœn* (Carpathian) mountains, and poured over northern Europe, seem to have preserved this name.

Togarmah — The Armenians, who, according to their own historians, had *Thorgon* for their founder, and call themselves *the house* (family) *of Thorgon*. (Fürst, Knobel.) They originally dwelt in Armenia and Asia Minor, but poured across the Hellespont into Europe before the dawn of history, and, according to Sallust, (*Jugurtha*, 18,) spread over the Mediterranean peninsulas even to Spain. They are mentioned by Ezekiel (chap. xxvii, 14) as trading at the Tyrian markets in horses, horsemen, and mules, which they brought down from the Armenian highlands to the sea.

4. **Sons of Javan**—Rather, *Yavan*, the Ionian families.

Elishah—The Æolians, (Elis,) who occupied three fourths of Greece, and spread to the coasts and isles of Asia Minor. (Josephus, Knobel.)

Tarshish — A famous commercial people well known to the sacred and classic writers, (Isaiah, Ezekiel, Strabo, Herodotus,) whence the Greek Tartessus and Tartessis, a town and region in southern Spain at the mouth of the Guadalquivir. According to Herodotus, Tartessus was settled by a colony of Phocæan Greeks, (i, 163,) the word signifying in Phenician, *younger brother*, (Rawl.,) a very suitable name for a colony. Their ships were so celebrated for size and fleetness as to give the name "ships of Tarshish" to all large merchant vessels wherever sailing. The ships of Tarshish (Ezek. xxvii, 12, etc.) brought gold and silver, iron, tin, and lead to Tyre, and these are precisely the articles which the classic writers, Strabo, etc., make the staple products of Spain. Knobel and Fürst understand the word to refer to that Pelasgic-Hellenic race called *Etruscans, Tuscans, Tyrsenians*, who before the Roman dominion peopled Italy and the Sicilies, and thus carried the name to Spain. (Knobel, p. 86.) Hence, perhaps,*Tarsus* in Cilicia. (Josephus.)

Kittim — Cyprians, who still preserve the name in the term *Kitti*. Josephus says (*Ant.* i, 6) that the Helvens transferred the name *Kittim* to all the Mediterranean isles and coasts. The Cyprian Kittim is shown by its monuments to have been a Phenician colony, or at least to have had Phenician or Hamitic settlers. But there were also Hamitic Chittim, (Hittites, sons of Heth or *Cheth*,) see verse 15, a wide-spread people in the age of Solomon;

danim. **5** By these were ᶜ the isles of the Gentiles divided in their lands; every one after his tongue, after their families, in their nations.

ᶜ Psa. 72. 10; Jer. 2. 10; 25. 22; Zeph. 2. 11.

---

and the Japhetic *Kittim* seem to have mingled at Cyprus with the Hamitic *Chittim.* (Knobel.)

D o d a n i m—Dardanians, Trojans, or perhaps it should be *Rodanim,* (interchange of ר and ד, in the first syllable,) as it is given in 1 Chron. i, 7, and in some copies by the Septuagint and Samaritan. The *Rodani,* or Rhodians.

5. By these were the isles of the Gentiles divided—Rather, *from these* [Japhethites] *have the* [dwellers on the] *islands of the* [Gentile] *nations divided themselves in their lands.* "Islands," in the Old Testament, means the isles, coasts, and peninsulas of the Mediterranean. The writer knew only of the "enlargement" of Japheth over the Mediterranean coasts and isles, but modern linguistic and monumental research shows that these ancient Hebrew names outline those vast pre-historic migrations of the Japhetic race from the great plateau of Iran eastward into Asia, westward and northwestward into Asia Minor and Europe, the traces of which may be found today from the Indian peninsulas to the Atlantic, and from the Mediterranean to the frozen ocean. **After his tongue ... their families ... nations** — The peoples called Turanian (a linguistic, rather than an ethnic, name) were on the ground at the dawn of tradition itself, and their origin is yet obscure; successive families of the Indo-European (Aryan) race swept eastward and westward, wave after wave, each to a great degree obliterating the traces of its predecessor, yet, as Rawlinson expresses it, leaving detached fragments of the superseded race in holes and corners, as the Turanian Laps and Fins are left in their remote peninsulas—as the Keltic Welsh and Scotch are left in their highlands, mountains, and islands—scattered patches of peoples who once thinly covered the continent.

SONS OF HAM, 6-20.

The three first sons of Ham settled in Northern Africa. 1) The Ethiopians (Cushites) of the Upper Nile. 2) The Egyptians (Mizraim) of the Lower Nile. 3) The Libyans (the Phutites) west of the Egyptians, in the east of Northern Africa. The Cushites appear to have removed from the high North-east, (of Central Asia,) passing over India, Babylonia, and Arabia, in their course towards the south. The Canaanites settled between the Mediterranean Sea and the Jordan, and gave their name to the country. The name Pœni (Φοινός) blood-red, denotes the original Hamitic colour of the Phenicians. Eastward from these the various families of the Hamites occupied the whole country of Arabia to the Persian Gulf; and under Nimrod they became the people of the first great empire, Babylonia. See Lange.

6. Ham—Or rather *Cham,* is from a root signifying to be *hot,* and hence *burnt, black.* The Hamites are dark-skinned peoples, dwelling mainly in the torrid zone. Ham is used frequently in Scripture for Egypt and the Egyptians, an Hamitic country and people. It, or its Egyptian equivalent, was also the common name for that land and people among the Egyptians themselves. It is written with two letters in the hieroglyphic language, K M, and occurs in the form Ch M E more than ten times on the Rosetta Stone. The Hamites are presented here, 1) as Cushite Ethiopians, Assyrians, Babylonians; 2) Egyptians; 3) Lybyans; 4) and Canaanites.

Cush — *Ethiopia* in the Sept. and Vulg., and so often rendered in our version. Isaiah xliii, 3; xlv, 14, etc. Monumental and linguistic research has now established the long-disputed theory that there was an Asiatic as well as an African Cush. Lepsius finds the name in Egypt on monuments of the sixth dynasty, and Rawlinson proves an ethnic connexion between the Ethiopians and the primitive Babylonians. The later Babylonians were Shemitic in origin, but Knobel shows (*Völk.,* p. 246) that the Cushites primarily peopled

6 ᵈ And the sons of Ham; Cush, and Mizraim, and Phut, and Canaan. **7** And the sons of Cush; Seba, and Havilah, and Sabtah, and Raamah, and Sabtecha:

---

d 1 Chron. 1. 8, etc.

Babylonia and spread eastward to India. Thus has it been shown by the research of our own day that the Asiatic kingdoms of Nineveh and Babylon are Hamitic in origin. The African and the Asiatic Cush freely communicated with each other through Meroe, on the upper Nile, and the Red Sea, by caravans and ships.

Mizraim — This is the Hebrew name for Egypt and the Egyptians. It is primarily a geographical word, in the dual number, well rendered by Lewis *the Narrows*, a designation singularly descriptive of Egypt, which is a narrow strip of verdure threaded by the Nile, hundreds of miles in length and only a dozen or so in breadth, stretching from Ethiopia to the Mediterranean, and separating the deserts of Africa and Asia. The name was naturally imposed by the first Hamite settlers, and afterwards transferred from the country to its inhabitants.

Phut — Lybyans, in the wide sense of the word inhabitants of the North African coast west of Egypt. Ptolemy and Pliny mention a river *Phtuth*, (φθουθ,) in north-western Africa. The Egyptian designation of Lybya is *Phet*, from *Pet*, Coptic *Phit*, *a bow*, by which symbol it is represented in the hieroglyphics. (Knobel, p. 296.) Jeremiah (xlvi, 9) associates Phut (Lybyans) with Cush, (Ethiopians,) as rising up against Pharaoh-necho; and Nahum (iii, 9) makes Phut an ally with Nineveh in connexion with Ethiopia and Egypt.

Canaan — Rather, Kenaan, from a root signifying *to be low*. Hengstenberg supposes that Ham thus named his son in a tyrannical spirit, to denote the obedience which he exacted from him, though so irreverent himself, while God's secret providence had a national humiliation in view in permitting the child to receive this name. Comp. chap. ix, 25, and the note. Some understand Kenaan as geographical, signifying *Lowland*, but this is not in harmony with Noah's prophecy in chap. ix, 25, etc. Herodian states that the ancient name of Phenicia (Palm-land) was Χνά, or Kenaan.

7. Sons of Cush—The Cushite Ethiopians and Arabians.

Seba — Inhabitants of Meroe of the Upper Nile, situated on the peninsula (called an island by Herodotus) formed by the Astaboras and the Nile, about eight hundred miles south of Syene. It is often mentioned by the classic writers, and by the Hebrew poets and prophets, as a land of precious woods and metals, the thoroughfare of caravans that traded between Egypt and Ethiopia, and between both of these countries and India. Queen Candace, mentioned in Acts viii, 27, seems to have reigned here. Heeren and others consider Meroe the mother of Egyptian civilization, but Rawlinson considers it the daughter. (*Herod.*, ii, 46.)

Havilah — The Macrobian Ethiopians, who dwelt in what is now Abyssinia. There was also a Shemitic Havilah (verse 29) in Arabia. The two families probably intermingled, and thus bore a common name. See note on *Cush*.

Sabtah — Ethiopians of Hadramont, in South Arabia, whose chief city was *Sabta*, *Sabota*, or *Sabotha*. Arrian mentions inhabitants of South Arabia, distinguished from true Arabs by stature, darker skin, and habits of life, such as eating fish, (ichthyophagi.) Niebuhr and other travellers and missionaries confirm these differences, and also declare that the language of this people differs wholly from the Arabic. (Knobel.)

Raamah — This name still remains in South-eastern Arabia, the Rhegma of the old geographers, where, according to Pliny and Ptolemy, dwelt a fish-eating people, (ichthyophagi.) We learn from travellers that they still exist in Omaun, distinguished from the Arabs by colour, language, and habits. (Ritter.) The merchants of Raamah and Sheba are mentioned by Ezekiel (xxvii, 22) as trading at Tyre in spices, precious stones, and gold. **Sheba**

and the sons of Raamah; Sheba, and Dedan. **8** And Cush begat Nimrod: he began to be a mighty one in the earth. **9** He was a mighty *e* hunter *f* be-

e Jer. 16. 16; Micah 7. 2.——*f* Chap. 6. 11.

fore the LORD: wherefore it is said, Even as Nimrod the mighty hunter before the LORD. **10** *g* And the beginning of his kingdom was *²* Babel, and Erech,

g Micah 5. 6.——2 Gr. *Babylon.*

is to be distinguished from the Shemitic Sheba, (verse 28.) The Cushite Sheba was on the Persian Gulf, traces of which may, perhaps, be found in the modern *Saba*, the thoroughfare of the Hebrew commerce with India. The Shemitic Sheba was an Arabic town in South Arabia, and appears as a kingdom in the days of Solomon, when the "queen of Sheba" came, with a caravan laden with gold and precious stones and "great store of spices," to test the wisdom of the Hebrew king. **Dedan** is probably still to be traced in *Dodan*, on the east coast of Arabia. Sheba and Dedan are also given (chap. xxv, 3) as descendants of Abraham by Keturah. This also seems to point to an early intermingling of the Shemitic and Hamitic families.

Sabtecha—The dark-skinned Carmanians. (They were a fish-eating people,) described by the old settlers as dwelling on the coast east of the Persian Gulf. They had a river and a city *Sabis*.

8. Nimrod—If this is a Hebrew or Shemitic word, it is probably related to the verb מָרַד, *to rebel,* and means, *let us rebel;* but it may be an Hamitic name. The author here naturally turns aside to notice the foundation of the first great monarchies of the earth, Babylon and Nineveh. Brief digressions of this kind are not uncommon with the Hebrew chroniclers. Comp. 1 Chron. ii, iv. Nimrod is clearly a person, and appears to be separately introduced as such, but he may have been removed several generations from Cush; for the Hebrew usage allows the dropping out of intermediate names in order to introduce an important personage. **A mighty one**—Mighty in personal prowess; warlike.

9. A mighty hunter—Or, *a hero of hunting;* a powerful man in the chase. Such a hero would also be likely to become a mighty warrior.

Bold and expert hunters have usually been the great pioneers of civilization, and their prowess became developed by fierce conflicts both with savage beasts and savage men. The Assyrian monuments, covered with scenes of hunting and of war, commemorate the daring and the prowess of ancient Ninevite kings. Accordingly some of the best interpreters (as Delitzsch and Lange) regard this description of Nimrod as a praiseworthy account of his work as a pioneer of culture and civilization; and the proverb recorded in this verse, instead of being a stigma on his name, was rather intended to commemorate him as a benefactor of the race. Others, however, understand the words **before the Lord** to imply some hostility towards Jehovah; like the phrase *before God* (Elohim) in chap. vi, 11, which seems to enhance the wickedness of the antediluvians. So the Septuagint (ἐναντίον) and the Jerusalem Targum. These regard him as notoriously violent; *so bad that God could not take his eyes from him.* (Lewis.) Nimrod was the first of the long line of bloody conquerors whose cruel ambition has cursed the earth.

10. **The beginning of his kingdom**—He was the first to build great cities, the seats of luxury and idolatry, which have crushed the masses of mankind by bloody despotisms, whereas the primary design of God seems to have been for mankind to scatter themselves in smaller masses under a patriarchal government. The four places here mentioned may not have been founded by Nimrod personally; they are mentioned as the germs of the great Babylonian empire. **Babel**—Babylon, whose origin is more fully described in the next chapter, identified with the modern *Babil*. **Erech**—The great necropolis of Babylonia, situated on the Euphrates. **Accad**—A name often found by Rawlinson in the Babylonian inscriptions, the native name of the primitive

and Accad, and Calneh, in the land of Shinar. **11** Out of that land [3] went forth Asshur, and builded Nin-

eveh, and [4] the city Rehoboth, and Calah, **12** And Resen between Nineveh and Calah: the same *is* a great city.

---

3 Or, *he went out* into *Assyria.*

4 Or, *the streets of the city.*

---

inhabitants (and language) of Babylonia, (Rawl. *Her.*, i, 319,) situated on the Tigris. This was the beginning of the famous empire of Babylon. **Calneh** — Ctesiphon, Sept., χαλ-άννη, a compound of Kal or Khal, the almost universal Babylonian and Assyrian prefix denoting place, as Khal-asar, *fort of Asshur*, Khal-nevo, *temple of Nebo*, etc. (Rawl., *Her.*, i, 480.) Anna is a Babylonian name for the first god in the Chaldean triad, corresponding to the Greek Pluto, and so Kal-neh, or χαλ-άννη, probably means *temple of Anna.* **Shinar** is the early Hebrew name for the great plain afterward known as Babylonia or Chaldea, through which flow the lower Euphrates and the Tigris; perhaps derived from *sh'ne* and *ar*, signifying "two rivers." The monuments and the cuneiform inscriptions of this region, now being deciphered, show the Hamitic origin of this kingdom, and its intimate relationship with Egypt. The Babylonian and Assyrian languages contain strong Shemitic elements, as well as Aryan traces, which have been very baffling to scholars; but Renan, a high authority on such a subject, concludes, from purely philological reasons, that the basis of the Assyro-Babylonian nationality was an Hamitic race, resembling the Egyptians; that this was succeeded by a large Shemitic population; and that this, in turn, was dominated over by Aryan (Japhetic) warriors. G. Rawlinson proves at length the Hamitic origin of the Chaldees (*Ancient Mon.*, I, iii) from tradition, language, and physical characteristics. Thus was there a primeval fusion, as well as separation, of races on the plain of Shinar.

Babylon is often made in Scripture the type of unholy ambition, despotism, and idolatry. It is noteworthy that the covenant people founded no vast cities or military monarchies. *Cain* builds the first city; *Nimrod* founds Babylon and Nineveh; the descendants of *Ishmael* and *Esau* dwelt in cities, while the sons of Isaac and Jacob yet dwelt in tents, confessing "that they were strangers and pilgrims on the earth."

11, 12. **Went forth Asshur**—Rather, [Nimrod] *went forth to Asshur* [Assyria.] So reads the margin, after the Targums of Onkelos and Jonathan; (so Baumgarten, De Wette, A. Clarke, Delitzsch, and Knobel.) This is certainly the meaning of the text, for the author would not here describe the *person* Asshur, who is not introduced till verse 22; and besides, if Asshur be not here a place, the locality of these four cities would not be designated in the text at all. Nimrod first founded Babylon, (verse 10,) and then he (or his descendants) ascended the Tigris valley and founded the Assyrian kingdom, (Asshur,) whose capital city was Nineveh, identified of late years with the mass of ruins on the east bank of the Tigris, opposite Mosul. **And the city Rehoboth**—This should be rendered either *Rehoboth, a city*, or as a compound name, *Rehoboth-Ir*, so called, perhaps, from being the *market places* of the city Nineveh. Verses 11 and 12 should accordingly be translated: "From that land he went forth unto Assyria, and builded Nineveh, and Rehoboth-Ir, and Calah, and Resen between Nineveh and Calah. This was the great city." As **Rehoboth, Calah,** and **Resen** have not been identified, it is very possible that they became a part of Nineveh, and the pronoun הוא, *this*, (common version, **the same,**) is to be understood not of **Calah**, the last named city, but **Nineveh,** called **great,** because thus composed of four cities, the name Nineveh being in the first instance applied in a restricted sense to the city whose ruins lie opposite Mosul, and then being extended to other cities along the east bank of the Tigris, so as to embrace the whole region where are now found the ruins called *Nimroud*, south of Mosul, *Konyunjik* and *Nebbi Yunus*, opposite Mosul, and Khorsabad, to the

About B. C. 2218. CHAPTER X. 149

13 And Mizraim begat Ludim, and Anamim, and Lehabim, and Naphtuhim, **14** And Pathrusim, and Casluhim, (ʰ out of whom came Philistim,) and Caphtorim. **15** And Canaan begat ⁵ Sidon his first-

h 1 Chron. 1. 12.   5 Heb. *Tzidon.*

north. This is the opinion of those most eminent Assyrian scholars, Rawlinson, Layard, and Grote, and also of Delitzsch, Knobel, and Ewald.

13. **Mizraim**— The descendants of Mizraim formed the Egyptian nations. Comp. note on verse 6. The names of these seven Egyptian peoples cannot all be with certainty identified. All these words are plurals in *im*.

Ludim— Must be distinguished from the Shemitic Lud. Verse 22. A warlike people of Northern Africa, associated by the prophets with the Lybyans and Ethiopians as those who handle the bow and shield. Isa. lxvi, 19; Jer. xlvi, 9; Ezek. xxvii, 10, etc. It is possible, but not probable, that the prophets in the above passages may refer to the Shemitic Lud. Some (Movers) make this a Mauritanian race; others (Knobel) assign them to North-east Egypt.

Anamim— Inhabitants of the Nile Delta.

Lehabim—Elsewhere called Lubim, *Lybyans*, yet not the Lybyans proper, who descended from *Phut*, but the Egyptian Lybyans, dwelling west of the Nile Delta. Shishak, king of Egypt, had them in the army which he led against Jerusalem in the days of Rehoboam, (2 Chron. xii, 3,) and Nahum and Daniel associate them with the Ethiopians.

Naphtuhim—Middle Egyptians, people of *Phtah*, which is the name of an Egyptian god. *Memphis* means the *dwelling of Phtah*. (Gesen., Champol.)

14. **Pathrusim**—Inhabitants of Pathros, an Egyptian word meaning *southern region*, (Gesenius,) Upper Egypt, Thebais.

Casluhim— Or better, *Kasluchim*. The word is, according to Knobel, Egyptian,meaning *dwellers in the dry* (or desolate) *mountain;* probably Mount Casius and the region about it. Casiotis, (the modern Cape El-Cos preserves the name,) the sandy region of North-east Egypt towards Philistia.

From this people sprang the Colchians, who dwelt on the east shore of the Black Sea. (*Herod.*, ii, 104.)

Out of whom came Philistim— The Philistines, so often mentioned in the Old Testament; the Palestinians, as Philistia was the original Palestine, a name which afterwards came to mean the same as Canaan. Amos (chap. ix, 7) and Jeremiah (chap. xlvii, 4) describe the Philistines as coming from Caphtor, (Crete;) but this was also colonized from Egypt, so that there is no discrepancy. The primitive Philistine colony, probably, came from Casiotis, in Egypt, and was afterward re-enforced from Crete. Knobel (p. 215) understands this phrase to describe the place whence the Philistines came, that is, from Casiotis, and not to set forth their origin, translating מִשָּׁם, *whence*, and the word may certainly apply to the country or people. Knobel believes the Philistines to have been descendants of Shem through Lud.

Caphtorim—This name is preserved in the ancient Egyptian *Coptos*, whence *Copt* and *Coptic*, the names applied to the modern Egyptians. Probably it here refers to the island of Crete, which was colonized from Egypt. The Greek myths of Cecrops and Danaus point to an early colonization of the Greek coasts and cities from Egypt.

15-18. Eleven Canaanitish nations are here enumerated. The first two names are probably personal, the last nine are certainly national. The descendants of Canaan, it is observable, are given with unusual fulness, they being the foreign tribes with whom the Hebrews came into most immediate contact, and, therefore, the sources of information were in this case unusually complete. The descendants of Canaan were, first, the Phenicians; second, the Canaanites proper.

Sidon—Sidonians, Phenicians. Recent studies of Phenician monuments establish the view, long since on other

born, and Heth, **16** And the Jebusite, and the Amorite, and the Girgasite,

grounds entertained, that the Phenicians spoke a Shemitish language, very closely allied to the Hebrew, if not identical with it. Thus *Carthage* (the name of a Phenician colony) signifies *New-Town*; *Barcas*, Carthagenian for *Hamilcar*, is the Hebrew *Barak*, signifying *thunderbolt*, a name appropriate to a military hero. The *bal* of *Hannibal* and *Hasdrubal* is the Phenician and Hebrew *Baal*, signifying *Lord*. These facts accord well with the Scripture record of Canaanitish proper names, and of the free intercourse between the Hebrew patriarchs and the Canaanitish aborigines. Some have insisted that the Phenicians must have been of Shemitic origin, but they show no Shemitic peculiarities, except in language. There is much obscurity yet to be cleared up in the early Phenician history; but the facts seem best explained by supposing a very early mingling of Hamites and Shemites in what is now Palestine, whereby the Hamites acquired a Shemitic language, yet retained, in a most marked manner, the leading Hamitic peculiarities, such as sensuality and idolatry, and, as contrasted with the Shemites, commercial enterprise. The ancient myths and the Assyrian monuments show a similar mingling of the two races, in prehistoric times, in Mesopotamia. Rawlinson, however, supposes that Sidon and Tyre were originally Canaanitic, but afterwards Shemitic, the Phenicians being a Shemitic race, who immigrated into Palestine from the shores of the Persian Gulf in about the 13th century B. C. The free and friendly intercourse maintained between the Hebrews and the Phenicians in the days of David and Solomon, certainly seems to separate them, in a marked manner, from the Canaanitish tribes who were devoted so solemnly to destruction, and with whom the Hebrews were forbidden to form any alliances. The subject can by no means be regarded as settled. (RAWL., *Her.*, book vii, Essay ii; Knobel, p. 305.) **Sidon**, or *Zidon*, or *Tsidon*, signifies *hunter*, or *fisher*. This was the chief city of the Phenicians, from which Tyre was colonized. It was situated on the Mediterranean shore, where its ruins may now be seen. The Sidonians were the first navigators, being the first to steer by the stars; they had colonies in Africa, Spain, and even in Britain. Tyre surpassed Sidon in power and commercial splendor. The great variety and richness of the Tyrian commerce is described by Ezekiel in lofty strains, chapters xxvi, xxvii. The name Sidon is used by the Greeks and on the Tyrian coins, as equivalent to Phenician. There are Phenician names along the Persian Gulf, which attest the westward movement of this people in very ancient times. (RAWL., *Her.*, i, 1.)

Heth — Or *Cheth*, ancestor of the Hittites or Chittites, who are also called *sons of Heth*, chap. xxiii, 3, etc. They were a Canaanitish tribe, who, in the time of Abraham, occupied the hill country about Hebron, (then called Kirjath-Arba,) and who treated the patriarch with much kindness and hospitality, chap. xxiii. They afterwards spread northward, and the name Hittite becomes synonymous with Canaanite. In the time of Solomon and of Elisha we read of their "kings." 1 Kings x, 29 ; 2 Kings vii, 6.

Jebusite—A mountain tribe who dwelt in Jebus, afterwards Mount Zion, and who held that strong fortress for centuries after the conquest of Canaan, being only finally subdued by David. 2 Sam. v. 7.

Amorite — The most powerful and widespread of the Canaanitish tribes, and hence their name is often equivalent to *Canaanite*, as in chap. xv, 16, and xlviii, 22. They founded powerful kingdoms on both banks of the Jordan, the eastern Amorites being conquered by Moses and the western by Joshua. Yet a remnant of this, as of other Canaanitish tribes, survived, even in the days of Solomon. 1 Kings ix, 20. It is made quite probable by Knobel that the word Amorite is used not only of an Hamitic tribe, but also in a larger sense of a widespread people who dwelt in Canaan before the Ca-

17 And the Hivite, and the Arkite, and the Sinite, **18** And the Arvadite, and the Zemarite, and the Hamathite: and afterward were the families of the Canaanites spread abroad. **19** ⁱAnd the border of the Canaanites was from Sidon, as thou comest to Gerar, unto ⁶ Gaza; as thou goest unto Sodom, and Gomorrah, and Admah, and Zeboim, even unto Lasha. **20** These *are* the sons of Ham, after their families, after their tongues, in their countries, *and* in their nations. **21** Unto Shem also, the father of all the children of Eber, the brother of Japheth the elder, even to him were *children* born. **22** The ᵏ children of

---

i Chap. 13. 12, 14, 15, 17; 15. 18-21; Num. 34. 2-12; Josh. 12. 7, 8.

6 Hebrew, *Azzah*. — *k* 1 Chronicles 1. 17, etc.

---

naanitish occupation, and were descended from the Shemitic Lud. The gigantic Amorites, of whom Og and Sihon were kings, he believes to have been Shemites. (So FÜRST, *Gesch. Bib. Lit.*, pp. 19, 127, etc.)

Girgasite—A tribe of whom, as Josephus says, there is left only the name.

Hivite—Or *Chivite;* a people who, in the time of Jacob, lived in Shechem, (Gen. xxxiv, 2,) who were also found by Joshua in Gibeon, (Josh. xi, 19,) but whose chief seat at the time of the conquest of Canaan seems to have been in North-west Palestine, about Hermon and Lebanon. Josh. xi, 3.

Arkite—This people dwelt on the Mediterranean shore north of Sidon. Their name is still preserved in the modern *Arka*, famous as being the birthplace of the Emperor Alexander Severus. Its ruins, including great columns of granite and of syenite, are scattered about a lofty mound twelve miles north of Tripoli.

Sinite—This people seem to have left their relics in the mountain fortress of *Sinna*, mentioned by Strabo, and the town of *Sini*, or *Syn*, north of *Arka*.

Arvadite—Inhabitants of the island *Arvad* or *Arad*, and the adjacent shore. Arvad was a rocky island fortress, two miles from the shore, north of Arka and Sini. It was colonized from Sidon, and was the mother of Tarsus, ranking at one time next to Tyre. It is ranked with these renowned Phenician cities by Herodotus, (vii, 98,) by Ezekiel, (chap. xxvii, 8, 11,) and by the historian of the Maccabees. 1 Mac. xv, 23. It is still inhabited by a maritime population bearing the name of *Ruad*, and retains some well-preserved remnants of heavy, bevelled Phenician walls.

Zemarite — This people has not, as yet, been with certainty, identified by any historical or geographical traces. Perhaps the town of *Sumra* or *Shoumra*, at the foot of Lebanon, between Arka and the sea, is one of the memorials of this tribe, (so Knobel,) but there is no other proof than its vicinity to the other identified Phenician remains.

Hamathite — Or *Chamathite;* inhabitants of Hamath or *Chamath Rabba*, that is, *Chamath the Great*, (Amos vi, 2,) a city on the Orontes, now known by the same name, in the great valley between Lebanon and Anti-Lebanon. This valley is known in the Old Testament as "the entering in of Hamath," and formed the northern boundary of the promised land. See Num. xiii, 21; 1 Kings viii, 65.

19. The territory of the Canaanites is now described, in general terms, as commencing at the Phenician city of Sidon and running southward to **Gerer** and **Gaza**, cities of the Philistines, then spreading eastward to the great plain of Siddim, which is now covered by the southern portion of the Dead Sea, but which, at the time this narrative was written, was occupied by the cities of Sodom, Gomorrah, Admah, and Zeboim. This statement shows that this chapter must have been written at least as early as the time of Abraham. The location of **Lasha** is unknown, although Jerome, and others following him, identify it with Callirhoe, north-east of the Dead Sea. But there are no remains there, and the identification is doubtful.

THE SHEMITIC FAMILY, 21–31.

21. Unto Shem also, the father of all the children of Eber, the brother of Japheth the elder, even to him were children born—That is, older than Ham, though younger

152 GENESIS. About B. C. 2218.

Shem; Elam, and Asshur, and [7]Arphaxad, and Lud, and Aram. **23** And the children of Aram; Uz, and Hul, and Gether, and Mash. **24** And Arphaxad

---

[7] Hebrew, *Arpachshad.*

than Japheth. Comp. note on chap. v, 32. This expression, "elder brother," seems to be inserted here to remind the reader that, although Shem was mentioned after Ham, he was really older than he. Shem's posterity is mentioned last, to form a more immediate and natural connexion with the following history, which pertains to them exclusively. **Shem** signifies *name,* that is, great or distinguished name; made illustrious as the line through which God shines on the world—the line in which arose the "NAME that is above every name." Shem was the ancestor of the Persians, Assyrians, Arabians, and Lydians, (perhaps also of the Phenicians, see verse 15,) all great nations of western Asia; but he is especially conspicuous in this history as father of the "children of Eber," the Hebrew people, through whom came revelation and the Messiah. For the meaning of "Hebrew," see verse 24 and note. The names of most of these sons of Shem became early transferred to the countries they occupied.

22. **Elam**—The Elymæans who originally peopled the country west of Persia, between it and Mesopotamia, *Elymais,* stretching from the Caspian to the Persian Gulf; called Susiana by the old geographers, the Cissia of Herodotus. It had become important and powerful in the time of Abraham, (chap. xiv, 1, etc.,) although before that time, having been overrun by a Cushite race, it had lost its Shemitish language.

Asshur—Assyria; probably the word signifies *plain,* originally applied to the plain along the east bank of the Tigris, north of Susiana, (Elam,) which was the original seat of the great Assyrian empire. The recently discovered Assyrian monuments show that the people originally spoke a Shemitic language, although Aryan and Hamitic elements were afterwards mingled with it. (Fürst, *Gesch. Bib. Lit.,* p. 9.)

Arphaxad — Ewald interprets this word *fortress of the Chaldees;* Fürst, *country of the Chaldees,* but the etymology is doubtful. Following Bochart, scholars have usually identified this name with *Arrapachitis,* a region on the east bank of the Tigris, north of the primitive Assyria and joining Armenia.

L u d—Supposed by eminent ethnologists to be the Lydians, a warlike race who spread westward into Asia Minor, and there founded a powerful kingdom, which was conquered by Cyrus, and swallowed up in the Medo-Persian empire. But the undoubted Aryan (Sanskrit) derivation of certain Lydian proper names (for example, *Sardis, Candaules*) makes the conclusion at least doubtful. The matter must be regarded as yet unsettled. (Comp. Rawl., *Her.,* i, *Essay* ii; Fürst, *Gesch., Bib. Lit.,* p. 19.) The Arabic historians assign to Lud the Amalekites and the primitive Arabs, the Joktanite (verse 26) and Ishmaelite (chap. xxv, 13) Arabs being younger branches of the nation. With this Knobel coincides, and also makes it probable that the *primitive* Amorites and the Philistines were Shemitic peoples of the stock of Lud. (*Volktfl.,* p. 198, etc.)

A r a m — *High land,* Aramea, or Syria, especially that part north of Palestine. Mesopotamia is the *Aram of the two rivers,* that is, Euphrates and Tigris—that part of Aram which falls between these streams; so there is an Aram of Damascus—Aram Zoba, north of Damascus, etc. It probably receives its name from Lebanon, the conspicuous mountain chain of the region. The Shemitic languages, Syriac and Chaldee, originated in Aram.

23. **Uz**—Who gave name to the country of Job, in the north of Arabia Deserta. The manners and habits of this people may, to a considerable extent, be learned from this ancient poem.

Hul, Gether, and **Mash** are not identified to any degree of certainty, although some think that the last may be traced in Mysia of Asia Minor, and the Mount Masius, or Masion, and the Masei Arabs of Mesopotamia. The Arabic geographers call two districts of

B. C. 2247.   CHAPTER X.   153

begat ⁸ Salah;¹ and Salah begat Eber. 25 ᵐ And unto Eber were born two sons: the name of one was ⁹ Peleg; for

8 Heb. *Shelah*.——*l* Chap. 11. 12.

Syria by the name of *Hul*, (*Chul*,) and also trace to **Gether** the Themudites of Hedjaz and the Djasites of Jemama. (Knobel.)

24. The line of **Arphaxad** is now specially taken up, as that with which the narrative is mainly concerned. **Salah,** or *Shelah*, from שָׁלַח, *to send forth*, one sent; hence *Shiloah*, or *Siloah, sent.* John ix, 7. **Eber,** or *Heber*, from עֵבֶר, *beyond*, that is, beyond the river, (Euphrates,) an *emigrant.* Both of these names seem to point to the migration of the Hebrew people from Aram westward. The name *Hebrew*, עִבְרִי, first occurs in Gen. xiv, 13, in the phrase *Abram the Hebrew*, and seems to be derived from the same root, meaning " one coming from beyond," (the river Euphrates,) that is, *immigrant, pilgrim.* So the Seventy understood the word, and, therefore, translated it ὁ περάτης, *one from beyond.* (So Jerome, Theodotion, Chrysostom, Origen, Rosenmüller, Gesenius, Fürst, Knobel.) In later years the term became narrowed to those who came from beyond the Jordan, that is, the Israelites proper, who dwelt west of the Jordan. (Fürst.) The sacred historian is supposed by many to have traced the word *Hebrew* to the person Eber, making it a patronymic, in styling Shem the " father of all the children of Eber." Verse 21. (So Gesenius.) But he calls the Hebrew people *sons of Eber* simply because the name Eber expresses their character ; they were a *pilgrim* people, going forth by faith to a land that was not their own ; wandering there for generations before they obtained possession, yet believing it theirs, (Heb. xi, 8, 9,) and conquering it at last by divine help. They were owners of the land where they dwelt, not by original possession or conquest, but by faith. The word *Eber* expresses this distinguishing trait of the Hebrew people. Comp. chap. xii, 1, 2. Thus were they typical of the spiritual

in his days was the earth divided ; and his brother's name *was* Joktan. 26 And Joktan begat Almodad, and Sheleph, and

m 1 Chron. 1. 19.——9 That is, *Division.*

Israel, who are *pilgrims* and *strangers* here, but seek a heavenly country. Heb. xi, 13, 14. This is the name by which the chosen people were designated by foreigners (see Gen. xxxix, 14, 17, etc.) and by the Greek and Roman writers until the term *Jew* (from Judah) came into use. They called themselves *Israelites*, except when speaking of themselves to foreigners, or in contrast with foreigners. Chap. xl, 15 ; Exod. i. 19 ; ii, 11, 13. This trait made them a *peculiar* people.

25. **Peleg**—*Division*, relating, it is generally thought, to the division of tongues which the narrator immediately proceeds to describe in the next chapter, but Knobel makes it refer to the division in the family of Eber between the brothers Peleg and Joktan. He presents reasons for the view which seem to have weight. It is doubtful if the matter can be decisively settled, but we follow the current opinion. Smith's Dictionary follows Knobel. **His brother's name was Joktan**.— Called in the Arabian genealogies *Kahtan*, the ancestor of thirteen tribes in South Arabia. The name signifies *Little.* Niebuhr mentions a town and province *Kahtan.* Some of these thirteen names following are still found in Arabia, others have become extinct, and others are not as yet identified.

26. **Almodad**—This name seems to be preserved in the Arabic El-Mudad, or Al-Modhadh, a famous Arab prince. The name was borne by several Arab chiefs in a tribe that lived first in Yemen, (South-west Arabia,) and then in Hedjaz, (along the upper Red Sea.)

Sheleph—Probably *Salif*, or *Sulaf*, the *Salapani* of Ptolemy, an Arab people of Yemen.

Hazarmaveth — *Court of death.* The modern Hadhramant, or Hadramant, east of Yemen, in south Arabia, on the Indian Ocean ; so named for its unhealthy climate. The modern name has the same meaning. This identification is undisputed.

Hazarmaveth, and Jerah, **27** And Hadoram, and Uzal, and Diklah, **28** And Obal, and Abimael, and Sheba, **29** And Ophir, and Havilah, and Jobab: all these *were* the sons of Joktan. **30** And their dwelling was from Mesha, as thou goest unto Sephar, a mount of the east.

31 These *are* the sons of Shem, after their families, after their tongues, in their lands, after their nations. **32** ⁿ These *are* the families of the sons of Noah, after their generations, in their nations: ᵒ and by these were the nations divided in the earth after the flood.

---

n Verse 1.   *o* Chap. 9. 19.

Jerah — *The moon.* Michaelis and Gesenius understand this to designate what are now called the Moon Coast and the Moon Mountain, near Hadhramant.

27. Hadoram — The *Adramites* of Pliny and Ptolemy, in the eastern part of Hadhramant.

Uzal—The modern *Sanaa*, the chief city of Yemen, a walled town; said to be the finest in Arabia.

Diklah—*Palm-tree.* Probably some place abounding in palms, but not identified.

28. Obal—Not identified.

Abimael—*Father of Mael.* An Arabic style of naming. Among the Arabs a man is sometimes named from his son, as among the Hebrews from his father.

Sheba — A kingdom in Yemen, or Arabia Felix, often mentioned by the classic and Arabic writers. Its chief cities were Uzal and Sepher. It was the queen of this country who visited Solomon. There are ancient buildings in this region, evidently of Cushite origin, showing a very ancient connexion between this and the Cushite Sheba of verse 7.

29. Ophir — A land celebrated in Solomon's time for its trade in gold, gems, apes, and peacocks. Probably it was a port in Arabia on the Red Sea, although some assign it to India. There is an El-Ophir in the modern Oman or Omaun, east Arabia.

Havilah — A district of north Yemen. There was also a Cushite Havilah. See verse 7, and note on *Cush.*

Jobab—Not identified, but supposed by Bochart and others to be in Arabia Deserta.

30. Their dwelling was from Mesha — In this verse are given the boundaries of the Joktanite Arabs, probably as they existed in the time of Abraham. But it is now impossible to follow them with any degree of certainty. Yet, in the language and monuments of South Arabia there are, as shown above, abundant traces of these thirteen Joktanite tribes. The position of **Mesha** is uncertain, but it was probably located in North-west Yemen, and the seaport *Mousa,* on the Red Sea, may be its modern representative. **Sepher** is undoubtedly the modern *Zafar, Dafar, Dhafari,* a seaport beneath a lofty mountain on the shore of the Indian Ocean, in Hadhramant, an ancient mart of the Indian trade. These boundaries would fix the primitive seat of the Joktanite Arabs in Yemen and Hadhramant, mostly in Arabia Felix — a district stretching from the Nikkum mountains to the Red and Arabian Seas.

CHAPTER XI.

THE CONFUSION OF TONGUES, 1–9.

The narrative here again doubles back upon itself to give the cause of the national divisions described in chap. 10. It reverts to an event which took place in the days of Peleg, (chap. x, 25,) the fourth in descent from Shem. As the unity of the human race, in the strictest sense of the word, is declared by the account of the deluge, which reduced all mankind to a single family from which the whole world was repeopled, so in this chapter the unity of language is declared, and the primal cause of all the lingual-diversities is set forth. The diversity of languages is a divine judgment upon human selfishness and pride, leading to manifold national misunderstandings and bloody conflicts, thus sorely hindering intellectual and moral progress, yet also serving as a providential hinderance to sin. Pride had already broken the bond of brotherly unity, and hence

CHAPTER XI.

A ND the whole earth was of one ¹ language, and of one ² speech. 2 And it came to pass, as they journeyed ³ from

1 Heb. *lip*.——2 Heb. *words*.——3 Or, *eastward*, as chap. 13. 11; 2 Sam. 6. 2, with 1 Chron. 13. 6.

the human family, feeling the lack of that inward attraction, sought an outward unity. Thus ever in history is man drawn to his brother by his instincts, yet perpetually repelled from him by selfishness. Hence the vast monarchies which in all ages have striven to consolidate the race, yet have ever been distinguished by luxury, or have exploded in revolution. Hence the hierarchies, which, through bloody centuries, have blindly striven to make good the lack of love's fusing flame by chaining men in the unity of ecclesiastical despotism. As sin vanishes, and the brotherhood of charity is restored, these differences of language will vanish also, for in the Messianic reign all "people, nations and *languages* shall serve Him," (Dan. vii, 14,) an epoch foreshadowed by the Pentecostal miracle, which made every man to hear the truth in his own language.

1. Whole earth ... one language ... one speech — Hebrew, as margin, one *lip* and one *words*. The whole population of the earth was one lip, and one kind of words. They were one in the manner (lip) and the matter (words) of language, that is, they had the same words for things, and the same modes of expression. There is no tautology, as in the common translation, but there are here two distinct ideas, 1) the same stock of words, and 2) the same inflexions and pronunciation. The Noachian language was probably the immediate parent of the Hebrew, Arabic, and Syriac. This primitive language has long ago vanished, but its ruins or *debris* are scattered everywhere, and can, with more or less certainty, be traced toward a parent formation. There are known at present, according to Kaulen, 860 languages, divided into three great families: 1) *isolating*, 2) *agglutinative*, and 3) *inflective*, each of the last two being regarded as derived from the next preceding; and the science of philology, by studying their manifold analogies and differences, is steadily reducing them to species and genera, all leading up to ultimate unity. The lines of variation all converge toward a distant centre, which, though it may never be scientifically reached, yet is seen by scientific faith. While languages are structurally divided, as above, they are also genealogically divided into Shemitic, Hamitic, and Aryan. This last is a provisional division, having a great number as yet unclassified. We give on pp. 156, 157, Schleicher's genealogical tree of the Shemitic and Aryan families, the dotted lines representing the dead languages. Of course this represents the present phase of philological knowledge and opinion, and is subject to revision by the advance of science. The Hamitic family has not yet been satisfactorily analysed.

SCHLEICHER'S GENEALOGY OF LANGUAGES. DIAGRAM I. GENERAL DIVISION.

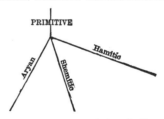

It may be mentioned that the Egyptian is considered by Max Müller as an offshoot of the original Asiatic tongue, before it was broken up into Turanian, Semitic, and Aryan.

One or two illustrations of the unity in this vast variety may suffice. The consonant *t*, interchanged with its cognates *d* and *th*, is the essential element of the second personal pronoun (English *thou*) in the principal languages of the Shemitic and Aryan families, both as a separate pronoun and as a personal termination. The Hebrew for *thou* is *attah* (masc.) and *at*, (fem.,) *thou killest* is Kata*lta* (masc.) and

156   GENESIS.

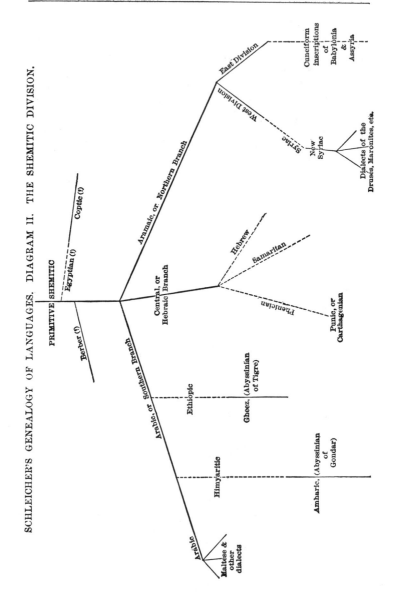

CHAPTER XI.

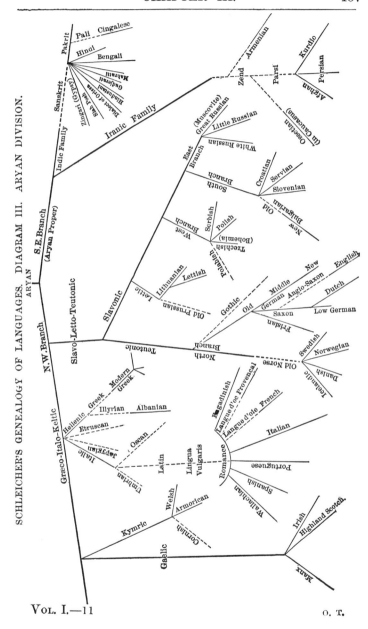

158　　　　　　　　　GENESIS.　　　　About B. C. 2247.

the east, that they found a plain in the land of Shinar; and they dwelt there. **3** And ⁴ they said one to another, Go to, let us make brick, and ⁵ burn them thoroughly. And they had brick for stone, and slime had they for mortar.

4 Heb. *a man said to his neighbour.*

5 Heb. *burn them to a burning.*

Katal*t*, (fem.) This consonant conveys the idea of the second person through all the conjugations, or species. The same law is seen in Arabic, Syriac, Ethiopic, and Coptic of the Shemitic family. Look now into the Aryan or Indo-European family, and we find in Sanscrit, *tua ;* in Beng., *tui ;* Russ., *tü ;* Greek, συ; Latin and its descendants, *tu ;* German, Dutch, and Danish, *du ;* Gothic and Saxon, *thu ;* English, *thou*. As a personal ending it is replaced by or used in connexion with its cognate *s ;* thus, for *thou art*, we have Sanscrit, *asi ;* Russ., *gesi ;* Greek, εἷς; Latin, *es ;* German, *bist*, etc. All languages, as far as analyzed, may, according to Max Müller, be reduced to four or five hundred roots, or phonetic types, which form their constituent elements. These sounds are not interjections, nor imitations, but are produced by a power inherent in human nature when the appropriate occasions arise. Man instinctively uses these sounds to express certain conceptions, and they become modified by composition, inflexion, etc., so as to finally produce the infinite varieties of language. Thus the two consonants B (with its cognates P and F) and R, taken together, are instinctively used to express the idea of *bearing*, or *sustaining ;* take as examples, פָּרָה, φέρω, *fero*, *bhri, bairan, bären,* βάρος, *bairn, bear, burden, pario, fructus, fruit*, etc.

2. As they journeyed—Literally, *in their breaking up* (their encampments;) as they struck their tents and slowly moved with flocks and herds from day to day. The word sets forth the leisurely movements of a nomadic company. It is not necessary to suppose that the whole human race were in this movement. Noah and Shem, who were probably living at the time, would hardly sympathize in the godless enterprise about to be described. **From the east**—Or better, as the margin, *eastward*. Comp. Josh. vii, 2 ; Judges viii, 11. They slowly moved from the table-land of Armenia, eastwardly and southerly, along the Euphrates valley to the rich alluvial **plain . . . of Shinar,** the region afterwards known as Chaldea and Babylonia. Here was a fertile country in a genial climate, offering a delightful place for permanent residence.

3. Said one to another—Heb., *each man to his neighbour*. **Go to**—An obsolete English expression, equivalent to *come on*. **Burn them thoroughly**—In distinction from the sun-dried bricks, so common in Babylonia, which yet are very hard and durable **They had brick for stone**—Stone being the building material with which the Hebrews were chiefly familiar in Egypt. **Slime** — *Bitumen ;* mineral pitch or asphalt. Although the Babylonian plain has no quarries in or near it, yet, being largely composed of fine sand and clay, it furnishes ample material for the most beautiful and durable bricks. All the splendid edifices of Babylon were built of burnt or sun-dried brick. The plain also abounds in *bitumen ;* called *naphtha,* when it appears as a thin yellow fluid ; *petroleum,* when thicker and darker ; and *asphaltum* when solid. This substance furnishes an imperishable cement. It was used by Noah in the construction of the ark; by the mother of Moses in the manufacture of her little papyrus boat; by the Egyptians in fastening the cerements of mummies ; and is now used by the natives of ancient Shinar in making the ferry boats of the Tigris, which are simply round baskets, daubed with bitumen. The asphalt springs of Is, or Hit, a small stream flowing into the Euphrates, are mentioned by Herodotus, and are thus quaintly described by an old traveller: "Near unto which town (Hit on the river Hit) is a valley of pitch, very marvellous to behold, and a thing almost incredible, wherein are many springs throwing out

About B. C. 2247.   CHAPTER XI.   159

4 And they said, Go to, let us build us a city, and a tower, [a] whose top *may reach* unto heaven; and let us make us a name, lest we be scattered abroad upon the face of the whole earth. **5** [b] And the LORD came down to see the city and the tower, which the children of men builded.

6 And the LORD said, Behold, [c] the people *is* one, and they have all [d] one language; and this they begin to do: and now nothing will be restrained from them, which they have [e] imagined to do. **7** Go to, [f] let us go down, and there confound their language, that they may

---

a Deut. 1. 28.——*b* Chap. 18. 21.——*c* Chap. 9. 19; Acts 17. 26.   *d* Verse 1.——*e* Psa. 2. 1.——*f* Chap. 1. 26; Psa. 2. 4; Acts 2. 4, 5, 6.

---

abundantly a kind of black substance like unto tar, or pitch, which serveth all the countries thereabouts to make staunch their barks and boats, every one of which springs maketh a noise like a smith's forge, in puffing and blowing out the matter, which never ceaseth, night or day, and the noise is heard a mile off, swallowing up all weighty things that come upon it. The Moors call it the mouth of hell."— Quoted in Rawlinson's *Herodotus*, i, 316.

4. A city, and a tower—Nimrod, the beginning of whose kingdom was Babel, (chap. x, 10,) is recognized by almost universal tradition as the leader in this movement. His name, which signifies "Let us rebel," concisely expresses the sentiment of this verse. It was not to escape another deluge, as Josephus imagines, that a lofty tower was to be built, for, had this been the object, a mountain would certainly have been selected for its site rather than a plain; but to establish a conspicuous rallying point, and to erect a strong citadel, whereby the despotic unity at which they aimed could be enforced. They proposed to build a city and a very lofty tower, with its summit in the sky. So the Israelites spoke of the Canaanitish cities as *walled up to heaven.* Deut. i, 28; ix, 1. This hyperbolical expression, passing to the heathen nations, perhaps gave rise to the fable concerning the giants who piled up mountains to scale the heavens and dethrone Jupiter. (Homer, *Odys.*, xi, 311, etc.) **Let us make us a name**—Hebrew, a *Shem*, perhaps in allusion to Shem who sought renown from God, and refused to engage in their impious schemes. God had promised enduring fame to him, (chap. ix, 26;) they would seek it for themselves. Despotic unity, military power and fame, with the attendant conse-

quences of war, luxury, and slavery, these were the ends of their heaven-defying pride.

5. The Lord came down—God had familiarly dwelt with man before his fall, but he is here represented as living above and afar, visiting the earth only on occasions of special judgment and mercy. The language here employed is "after the manner of men;" and it is to be noted that it is not only after the manner of men of a simple and primitive age, but of a modern and cultured age as well. All our language concerning God's actions is, and must be, tropical or figurative. To say that in this case God *perceived* and *judged* man's sin, would sound more appropriate to those who do not think precisely and profoundly; but those who do thus think see that *perceive* and *judge* are just as tropical, when applied to God, as *come down, see,* and *say.* The tropes are more remote, but equally real. The inspired author would teach that God does not punish without examination.

6. This they begin to do—This is only the beginning of their deeds, and if this daring act of impiety be not rebuked, and their far-reaching plans of centralized human power be not frustrated, **nothing will be restrained from them,** (Heb., *cut off from them;*) that is, there will be no bound or limit to their purposes.

7. Let us ... confound their language—The solemn deliberation and decision of the Triune God is mysteriously intimated in this language. See note on chap. i, 1, 26. So in the miracle of the Pentecost, which foreshadowed the restoration of the unity shattered at Babel, CHRIST, at the right hand of the FATHER exalted, shed forth the SPIRIT upon the multitude from "every nation under heaven,"

160 GENESIS. About B. C. 2247.

not ^g understand one another's speech.
8 So ^h the LORD scattered them abroad from thence ⁱ upon the face of all the earth: and they left off to build the city.
9 Therefore is the name of it called

^g Chap. 42, 23; Deut. 28, 49; Jer. 5, 15; 1 Cor. 14, 2, 11.—*h* Luke 1, 51.

that is, representatives of the whole race.

The language of this verse certainly implies a sudden and miraculous, rather than a gradual and providential, action in the modification of human speech. The mode of such a miracle, as of all miracles, is, of course, inexplicable, for explanation is simply reference to some natural law, and where a miracle is concerned, causes above nature come into action. But the probable character of the miracle may be seen from considering the nature of language. All language, as shown above, can be reduced to some four or five hundred verbal roots, or consonantal combinations—for in the power to produce consonants man's vocal organs differ essentially from those of brutes—and it was made natural, or instinctive, at creation, for man to produce these sounds to express the elementary ideas, (for example, to produce the sound *st* to denote fixedness, firmness, etc., as in *stand, sto*, ἵστημι, see also on verse 1,) just as the dove instinctively coos and the cock crows to express certain emotions. These roots furnished man's primary outfit, from which, by manifold modifications, he has developed language. Originally these modifications, to express action, passion, time, manner of action, (voice, mood, tense, etc.,) were the same for all men; but now each family of languages has its own peculiar way of expressing them. The Shemitic family conveys these ideas mainly by internal modifications, interposing sounds between the root letters, the Aryan by external modifications, prefixes, and affixes. This may help us understand where the miraculous stroke fell on human nature at the Babel catastrophe, and thus was the "*lip*," the manner of expression, not the essential matter, changed. Historical and geographical philology furnish a most remarkable confirmation of the

⁶ Babel; ^k because the LORD did there confound the language of all the earth: and from thence did the LORD scatter them abroad upon the face of all the earth.

ⁱ Chap. 10, 25, 32.——6 That is, *Confusion.*——*k* 1 Cor. 14, 23.

miracle of Babel. The fixedness and generic persistency of the great linguistic types point to a violent cleavage and projection asunder in the remotest past. The Finnish was in Northern Europe before the Celts arrived, and there it still is. It may perish, but it will never change to Slavonic. The Gaelic survives in a few patches of the British Islands, dwindling slowly away, but while it lives it will ever be Gaelic, it cannot develop into English. It is many centuries since the Shemitic, stretching through the Euphrates valley and the Arabian peninsula, clove the Aryan district asunder. But, as in the days of Solomon, the Sanscrit lay on the east and the Pelasgic on the west of the Hebrew, so to-day the same Sanscrit and its children live in the Indian peninsula, and the children of the Greek and Latin and Teutonic flourish in Europe, while the Arabic, in all its Shemitic integrity, lies between, neither family mingling with the other. (See Lewis, *Excursus on Gen. xi*.)

8. Scattered them — Thus, in the days of Peleg, (chap. x, 25,) was effected the division of the nations. It is possible, however, that the Shemites were not involved in this judgment, and that the primitive Shemitic tongue, from which have descended the Hebrew, Arabic, and Syriac, was the language that came out of the ark. Jewish and Gentile traditions relate that lightning split the tower to its foundations; such embellishments of the history would, however, naturally arise from imagination. The present appearance of the Borsippa tower (see on verse 9) may have given rise to this tradition.

9. Babel — *Confusion;* בָּבֶל, contracted from בַּלְבֵּל, derived from the verb בָּלַל, *to pour together*, to confound. (Gesenius.) So the Septuagint. But the local tradition concerning the modern *Babil*, so generally identified with Babel, is, that it signifies the *Gate of Il*, that is, *Gate of God*. Perhaps this name was originally imposed by Nimrod in defiance, and after the judgment described in the text, it changed its meaning, since originally the tower was a symbol of human pride and subsequently of the divine wrath. This would be entirely natural, and both etymologies are equally admissible. What Nimrod meant as a monument of despotic power became a memorial of his discomfiture and shame. It would hardly seem possible that any relics of this ancient structure could now be discovered; but the researches of modern travelers render it highly probable that this edifice was afterwards completed by the kings

BIRS-NIMRUD.

of Babylon, who have left in the cuneiform inscriptions a record of their work. Oppert, the eminent orientalist, is confident that the modern Birs-Nimrud, at Borsippa, on the west bank of the Euphrates, about six miles from Hillah, is the ruin of this ancient tower, which, he thinks was finished by Nebuchadnezzar, whose name is found stamped upon its bricks, and upon the clay cylinders buried at its angles. It was a temple to *Nebo*, or *Nabu*, a deity of the Babylonian kings, whose names are often compounded from *Nabu*, as Nebuchadnezzar, which was in their orthography *Nabu-kuduri-uzur*.

Oppert, in his restoration of Babylon, locates this tower near the southwest corner, between the inner and outer walls. At present Birs-Nimrud is a huge pyramidal mound, 153 feet high, rising in solitary grandeur from a vast plain, appearing like a natural hill crowned with a ruin of solid brickwork which rises 37 feet from the summit. This tower-like ruin is rent about half-way down, and vitrified, as if by lightning. Immense masses of fine brickwork, which seem to have been molten, strew the mound, which is wholly composed of the *débris* of the temple. Its form—an oblong square, the angles facing the four cardinal points—seems to indicate an astronomical or astrological purpose. Aside from what seems to have been the vestibule, the main ruin is about 400 feet square at the base. It was, according to Oppert, the temple of Belus, described by Herodotus (i, 181) as a square pyramid in seven receding stages, coloured so as to represent the seven planetary spheres, each stage 25 feet in height, the whole resting on a vast substructure 75 feet in height, and a stadium, or over 600 feet, square.

Nebuchadnezzar named it the Temple of the Seven Lights of the Earth, that is, the sun, moon, and planets. Herodotus says that the basement stage was coloured black with bitumen, to give it the hue of Saturn, the most distant planet known to the ancients; the next stage orange, or raw sienna, the hue of Jupiter, which was the natural colour of the burnt brick; the third was colored bright red, by the use of half-burnt bricks of a peculiar red clay, the bloody hue of Mars; the fourth was cased with golden plates, to represent the sun; the fifth stage was built of pale yellow bricks, to represent Venus; the sixth was tinted blue, the colour of Mercury, by vitrifying the bricks to a slag; and the seventh was cased in silver, to give it the colour of the moon. (RAWLINSON, *Her.*, *App.*, book iii.)

Oppert agrees with the Talmudists in making Borsippa the true site of the tower of Babel, and explains the word as meaning, in Babylonian, *Tower of Tongues*. But the most remarkable thing of all is the cuneiform inscription here found, as by him deciphered. We extract from Oppert's note, in Smith's *Dictionary*, giving a few lines of the inscription to show its character.

"Nabuchodonosor, king of Babylon, shepherd of peoples, who attests the immutable affection of Merodach, the mighty ruler-exalting Nebo; the saviour, the wise man who lends his ears to the orders of the highest god, the lieutenant without reproach, the repairer of the Pyramid and the Tower, eldest son of Nabopolassar, king of Babylon.

"We say: Merodach, the great master, has created me; he has imposed on me to reconstruct his building. Nebo, the guardian over the legions of the heaven and the earth, has charged my hands with the sceptre of justice."

Then follows a description of a pyramid that he had built, and then we have this account of the Borsippa edifice: "We say for the other, that is this edifice, the house of the Seven Lights of the Earth, the most ancient monument of Borsippa. A former king built it, (they reckon 42 ages,) *but he did not complete its head. Since a remote time people had abandoned it, without order expressing their words.* Since that time the earthquake and the thunder had dispersed its sun-dried clay, the bricks of the casing had been split, and the earth of the interior had been scattered in heaps. Merodach, the great lord, excited my mind to repair this building. I did not change the site, nor did I take away the foundation stone," etc.

The allusion to the Babel catastrophe in the lines italicised is too plain to be mistaken. It is proper to say, in further explanation of this wonderful monument, that this famous King Nebuchadnezzar came to the throne of Babylon in B. C. 604, and built or rebuilt cities, temples, and all manner of public works, on a scale of magnificence unsurpassed in all history.

The Generations of Shem, xi, 10-26.

The narrative here again doubles back upon itself, returning over a century to take a new departure from the birth of Shem's eldest son, two years after the flood. Having described the judgment that scattered the nations, the historian now returns to give at one

10 ¹ These *are* the generations of Shem: Shem *was* a hundred years old, and begat Arphaxad two years after the flood: **11** And Shem lived after he begat Arphaxad five hundred years, and begat sons and daughters. **12** And Arphaxad lived five and thirty years, ᵐ and begat Salah: **13** And Arphaxad lived after he begat Salah four hundred and three years, and begat sons and daughters. **14** And Salah lived thirty years, and begat Eber: **15** And Salah lived after he begat Eber four hundred and three years, and begat sons and daughters. **16** ⁿ And Eber lived four and thirty years, and begat ᵒ Peleg: **17** And Eber lived after he begat Peleg four hundred and thirty years, and begat sons and daughters. **18** And Peleg lived thirty years, and begat Reu:

---

l Chap. 10. 22; 1 Chron. 1. 17.——*m* See Luke 3. 36.   *n* 1 Chron. 1. 19.——*o* Called, Luke 3. 35, *Phalec.*

---

view the pedigree of Abraham, the heir of the promises made successively to Adam, Seth, Noah, and Shem, and the father of the covenant people. The great post-diluvian rebellion, which gave rise to all the manifold idolatries of the Gentile nations, has been described, to set forth the need of the Abrahamic call and the Israelitish election; in other words, the dark background of the picture has been painted to set forth more vividly the forms of Abraham, Isaac, Jacob and Judah, to whom the divine artist now turns all his attention. Abraham was the tenth, inclusive, from Shem, and the twentieth from Adam.

Important variations from the Hebrew text are here found in the Samaritan and Septuagint, similar to those described in the notes on chap. v, giving rise to two different systems of chronology, the *long*, or Septuagint, that of Jackson, Hales, etc.; and the *short*, or Hebrew Masoretic chronology, that of Usher, adopted in our English Bibles. There is also a third system, the Rabbinic, which follows the Hebrew with certain variations. These chronological discrepancies seem, on the whole, to have arisen from arbitrary changes made by the Septuagint translators, although the question will long remain an open one among the most judicious scholars. The Samaritan, also, adds 650 years to the period between the flood and Abraham's call, by making six of the patriarchs 100 years older, and one of them, Nahor, 50 years older, at the time of begetting the firstborn son. But the Septuagint, in addition to this, interposes another name, *Cainan*, (comp. Luke iii, 36,) between Arphaxad and Shelah, making him 130 years old at the birth of Shelah, and also adds 100 years more to the age of Nahor at the time of the birth of Terah, thus increasing the Samaritan period by 230 years and the Hebrew period by 880 years. By the Hebrew chronology, followed in our English Bibles, it is, then, 422 years from the flood to the time when Abraham entered Canaan, while by the Samaritan it is 1072 years, and by the Septuagint it is 1302 years. Josephus gives minute chronological data, but he cannot be fully harmonized with either of the above systems, or with himself, although it is evident that the Hebrew numbers are the basis of his calculations.

Now since we find by the Peshito and the Targum of Onkelos that the Hebrew text was the same as now up to the time of the Christian era, and since most of the variations above recounted can be accounted for by the supposition of arbitrary changes on the part of translators and transcribers, it seems wise, with our present light, to adhere to the Hebrew chronology. The reasons for so doing may be found well set forth by Murphy in his Commentary, and are also fully given in M'Clintock & Strong's Cyclopedia, (Art., Chronology.) It is, meanwhile, to be remembered that these chronological facts, although scientifically most important, yet form no essential part of divine revelation.

10. **Shem was a hundred years old, and begat Arphaxad two years after the flood**—Hence he was ninety-eight years old when he came out of the ark. Comp. chap. v, 32; vii, 11, and notes. The generations to Peleg are repeated from chap. x, 21-25.

18. **Peleg** — *Division;* that is, of the peoples at Babel. At the flood the

19 And Peleg lived after he begat Reu two hundred and nine years, and begat sons and daughters. **20** And Reu lived two and thirty years, and begat ᵖ Serug: **21** And Reu lived after he begat Serug two hundred and seven years, and begat sons and daughters. **22** And Serug lived thirty years, and begat Nahor: **23** And Serug lived after he begat Nahor two hundred years, and begat sons and daughters. **24** And Nahor lived nine and twenty years, and begat ᵍ Terah: **25** And Nahor lived after he begat Terah a hundred and nineteen years, and begat sons and daughters. **26** And Terah lived seventy years, and ʳ begat Abram, Nahor, and Haran.

27 Now these *are* the generations of Terah: Terah begat Abram, Nahor, and Haran; and Haran begat Lot. **28** And

---

p Luke 3. 35, *Saruch.* — q Luke 3. 34, *Thara.*   r Josh. 24. 2; 1 Chron. 1. 26.

---

average duration of human life was shortened nearly one half : Noah, 950 ; Shem, 600 ; Arphaxad, 438 ; Salah, 433 ; etc. And now, after the Babel catastrophe, it is shortened about one half again : Peleg, 239 ; Reu, 239 ; Serug, 230. After the call of Abraham it was shortened again about one fourth : Abraham, 175 ; Isaac, 180 ; Jacob, 147. There are, then, three distinct epochs in human longevity, marked by three divine judgments : the deluge, the Babel judgment, and the call of Abram, which left the idolatrous nations to their own ways.

26. And Terah lived seventy years, and begat (began at that time to beget) **Abram, Nahor, and Haran**— Although Abram is mentioned first, as father of the covenant people, as Shem is mentioned first among the sons of Noah, yet Haran was probably the oldest son, begotten when his father was 70 years old. Abram was 75 years old when he left Haran, (chap. xii, 4,) which, according to St. Stephen, (Acts vii, 4,) was after Terah's death. But Terah died in Haran at the age of 205, (verse 32.) Hence Terah must have been at least 130 years old at the time of Abram's birth. But see note on verse 32. Nahor is here mentioned because he was the ancestor of Rebekah, Leah, and Rachel; and Haran as the father of Lot and Iscah, (Sarah,) all of whom were blended with the covenant people.

Shem was ninety-eight years contemporary with Methuselah, who was two hundred and forty-three years contemporary with Adam; so that, if we assume that the genealogy is here completely given, no generations being omitted, there was but one link of tradition through which the story of the creation and of the fall passed over the flood. Shem was, also, one hundred and fifty years contemporary with Abraham, so that the father of the faithful received from an eye-witness the narrative of the flood, and was removed but two generations from the creation; that is, he received that history of events that Adam witnessed and experienced as if from his great-grandfather. The successive links were Adam, Methuselah, Shem, Abraham, thus :

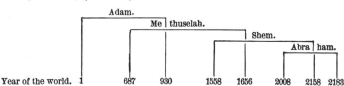

Year of the world.   1   687   930   1558   1656   2008   2158 2183

From this plan it is clearly seen that Methuselah was contemporary with Adam from A. M. 687 to 930, and with Shem from 1558 to 1656 ; and that Abraham was also contemporary with Shem from 2008 to 2158. Thus there was little chance for false tradition.

Generations of Terah, xi, 27–xxv, 11.

27. This heading is properly the beginning of the history of Abraham, which gives account also of the peoples most intimately related to the covenant people. The following plan shows the genealogy of the fathers and mothers of these patriarchal nations, or tribes, as far as it is given in the sacred record:

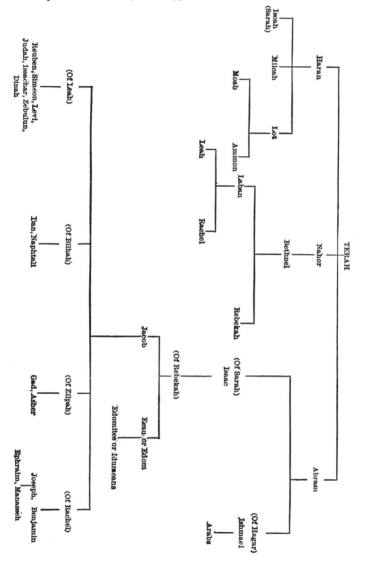

Haran died before his father Terah in the land of his nativity, in Ur of the Chaldees. 29 And Abram and Nahor took them wives: the name of Abram's wife was *Sarai; and the name of Nahor's wife, † Milcah, the daughter of

s Chap. 17. 15; 20. 12.　　　　*t* Chap. 22. 20.

Thus from Terah sprang not only the Israelitish nation, but also the peoples with whom their history is most intimately blended in the patriarchal times: the Moabites, Ammonites, Edomites, and Ishmaelitish Arabs.

MIGRATION FROM UR, 28–32.

28. **And Haran died before his father Terah**—That is, in the presence of Terah, or it may mean *before*, as a designation of time, (see Gesenius,) since the phrase refers to both place and time. If Haran were, as we suppose, the eldest son, there is a special reason why his death should here be mentioned. Terah, as the head of the family tribe, adopts Lot, his grandson, in the place of Haran, his son, as heir to the chieftainship, and then, perhaps, saddened at his loss, under a providential leading, resolves to emigrate from his native land. Abram, as we learn from Acts vii, 2, had already heard a divine call to break loose from the idolatries that surrounded him, and in which it seems that Terah's family were involved, for Joshua says to the Israelites: "Your fathers dwelt on the other side of the flood [Euphrates] in old time . . . and they served other gods." Joshua xxiv, 2, note. **Ur of the Chaldees**—Ur was a city, or district, of the כַּשְׂדִּים, *Kasdim*, Kardi, Kurds, or *Kaldees*, a people not mentioned in the table of nations, Gen. x, under this name, but whose native name, *Accad*, as it appears in the Babylonian inscriptions, is mentioned in Gen. x, 10, as designating a city in the land of Shinar, the beginning of the (Hamite) kingdom of Nimrod. The primitive Chaldees were an Hamitic people, descendants of Cush, famous as the builders of the first cities, inventors of alphabetic writing, and discoverers in science, especially in astronomy. The name was afterward applied (as in Daniel) to a sect of astrologers and philosophers, who inherited the science and astrologic arts of the ancient Chaldees, and transmitted them in the Cushite language, although dwelling among Shemitic peoples. These Chaldeans of the time of Daniel were thus a learned aristocracy, who had their schools, corresponding to modern universities, (Strabo, xvi, 1, 6,) at Orchoe and Borsippa, and also (Pliny, *H. N.*, xi, 26) at Babylon and Sippara. Chaldea is the great alluvial plain of the Euphrates and Tigris, stretching from the mountains of Kurdistan to the Persian Gulf, about 400 miles in length, and about 100 in breadth, ascending on the east to the chalky limestone wall of the great table-land of Iran, and descending on the west to the Arabian desert. Covered for many centuries with the mighty cities, and teeming with the vast populations, of the Assyrian and Babylonian empires, the whole plain fertilized through a network of canals branching from the two great arterial rivers, it is now a desert, with swamps and marshes and pools, the dwelling-place of lions and jackals and wolves, although in early spring it seems a wilderness of flowers. The great plain is ridged here and there along the courses of ancient canals, and dotted with mounds of earth-covered ruins, from which now and then a solitary mass of ragged brickwork rises into the malarious air. **Ur** is supposed by Rawlinson to be the *Hur* of the Babylonian inscriptions, the modern *Mugheir*, in lower Chaldea, about six miles west of the Euphrates. Orfa, in upper Chaldea, is a rival site, but this place is too near Haran, being only a day's journey distant. On the rude bricks of Mugheir are found legends of *Urukh, king of Hur*, the most ancient inscriptions known, unless it be those of a king called *Kadur-mapula*, found in the same region, who is likely to have been the Elamite Chedorlaomer of Gen. xiv. The ruins of a Chaldean temple dedicated to the moon, built in stages like the Tower of Babel, (see above, p. 162,) and composed of sun-dried and

CHAPTER XI.

Haran, the father of Milcah, the father of Iscah. **30** But ⁿSarai was barren; she *had* no child. **31** And Terah ᵛ took Abram his son, and Lot the son of Haran his son's son, and Sarai his daughter in law, his son Abram's wife; and they went forth with them from ʷUr of the Chaldees, to go into ˣthe land of Canaan; and they came unto Haran, and dwelt there. **32** And

u Chap. 16. 1, 2; 18. 11, 12.——*v* Chap. 12. 1. | *w* Neh. 9. 7; Acts 7. 4.——*x* Chap. 10. 19.

kiln-burnt bricks cemented with bitumen, are yet found at Mugheir, whose inscriptions are deemed by Assyrian scholars to show an antiquity higher than Abram's call. This venerable temple, now nearly 4,000 years old, when it stood in massive magnificence, a monument of Chaldean idolatry, we may probably regard as the very shrine where the family of Terah worshipped; and they turned away from its splendours at the divine call to wander to a far land, there to dwell in tents for centuries, that they might learn to teach mankind the lessons of the ONE only GOD. Whether Terah himself had these higher motives is doubtful. See on verse 31.

29. Iscah is, by Josephus, (*Ant.*, i, 6,) and by the Jewish writers generally, identified with Sarai or Sarah. If so, Abram married his niece, and Lot was his brother-in-law as well as his nephew. See the plan under verse 27. That Sarah was in some way descended from Terah appears from Abram's statement to Abimelech, chap. xx, 12, "She is the daughter of my father, but not the daughter of my mother."

31. Terah took—Terah, the patriarch of the tribe, here appears as the leader of this movement. In this memorable emigration the divine and the human are seen to co-operate and interact, as in the case of all the great movements of Providence. Natural causes, and even selfish human motives, are taken up into the divine plan. So God uses the avarice of Laban (chap. xxxi) to bring Jacob back again into Canaan; the envy of Joseph's brethren to plant Israel in Egypt, (chap. xlv, 8;) and the tyrannical cruelty of Pharaoh to transfer them to their final home. In this history, and in the heathen traditions, we see other traces of westward movements from the Mesopotamian plain and the Asiatic table-land around the desert, and down the Jordan valley to the Mediterranean shore. Warlike expeditions from beyond the Tigris, as we see from chapter xiv, had already brought the kings of the vale of Siddim under tribute to the king of Elam. Shemitic tribes were at this same time pressing westward and southward into the Arabian peninsula, and the Aramæans were ascending the Euphrates and settling in Eastern Syria. The migration of Terah and his tribe was thus a part of a general movement of the Shemitic people, settling towards the Mediterranean from the east, divinely guided so as to rescue a branch of that people from the prevailing idolatry, and bless, in their old age, the nations of the earth. **They went forth with them**—That is, Lot and Sarai, the two just previously mentioned, went forth with Terah and Abram. **To go into the land of Canaan**—There is no indication that Terah had any other than secular motives, but St. Stephen tells us in Acts vii, 2, that Abram had already received a divine call. The tribe, with their dependents and cattle, moved slowly up the Mesopotamian plain, intending to advance northward, around the desert, and then south-westerly into the land of Canaan, but arriving in the vicinity of Haran, (*Charran* of the New Testament, the *Carrhae* of the Greeks and Romans,) and encamping there, perhaps the advancing infirmities of the aged Terah prevented his moving farther, and so **they...dwelt there** till Terah was dead. Acts vii, 4. Then the migration continued, under the leadership of Abram. But more probably we are to understand the text to state that Terah *started on the expedition which terminated in Canaan*, that is, which Abram continued to Canaan, although Terah himself had not this issue in mind when he left Ur of the Chaldees. This harmonizes better with chap. xii, 1, "Unto the land that I will show thee," implying that the particular land was not then made known

the days of Terah were two hundred and five years: and Terah died in Haran.

to Abram, and also with Paul's language, in Heb. xi, 8, "and he went out, not knowing whither he went." Haran, or *Charran*, in north-west Mesopotamia, on the stream Belilk, a little affluent of the Euphrates, situated in a large plain surrounded by mountains, was a natural halting-place for caravans, being but a very little out of the direct route to Canaan, and the point whence diverged the great caravan routes to the fords of the Euphrates and Tigris. There was once here a temple of the moon goddess, as in Ur. The city is remarkable in Roman history as the scene of the defeat of Crassus. It had quite a population under the caliphs, but is now a ruined village, inhabited by a few Arabs.

32. Two hundred and five years —We see, from chap. xii, 4, that Abram was seventy-five years old when he left Haran. If now he remained in Haran till Terah's death, then Terah must have been at least one hundred and thirty years old at the time of Abram's birth, since 205—75=130. But this does not seem likely, since Abram regards it a miraculous thing that he should be a father at one hundred, (chap. xvii, 17,) and this surprise at the divine promise is unaccountable if he were himself born when his father was one hundred and thirty. But the narrative allows us to suppose that Abram left Haran some years before Terah's death, the history of Terah being finished up in this chapter, and the narrative then doubling back upon itself to resume the history of Abram. The only difficulty in this interpretation is, that we find St. Stephen, in his discourse, (Acts vii, 4,) assuming that Abram remained in Haran till the death of Terah. In this, however, Stephen, as we see from Philo, followed a Jewish tradition, which was probably erroneous. We do not certainly know in what year of Terah's life Abram was born.

CHAPTER XII.

THE CALL OF ABRAM, 1-3.

The history now narrows again to a single branch of the family of Terah— Abram and his descendants. The other branches, which are only incidentally alluded to hereafter as they are connected with the fortunes of the covenant people, remained in Chaldea at least for generations, and a large portion of them settled around the wells of Haran, where, in the days of Isaac and Jacob, we find them forming a community which furnished these patriarchs wives of their kinsfolks, Rebekah, Rachel, and Leah, while the sons of Abram were still sojourners among the children of Ham. It was now more than four centuries since God's last revelation to Noah, and the blessing of Shem. The scattered nations were fast sinking into idolatry; but that the knowledge of God was yet in the earth, incidental notices, as that of "Melchizedek, king of Salem and priest of the most high God," sufficiently declare. Where there was such a priest, and a royal priest, there must have been established worship and a number of worshippers. Probably the history of Job, the patriarch of Uz, wherein, as Ewald says, the manners, customs, style of thought and expression are all of the pre-Mosaic age, furnishes another example of genuine faith in the true God among a people who had never heard of the Abrahamic covenant. But Abram was now called from the family of Terah to be a blessing to the whole earth; the father of a missionary nation, who should preserve and disseminate the knowledge of the true God through all nations and ages. His whole life was to be an education in faith, which is the root of true religion. "Every movement in the physical and ethical history of Abraham is fraught with instruction of the deepest interest for the heirs of immortality. The leading points in spiritual experience are here laid before us. The susceptibilites and activities of a soul born of the Spirit are unfolded to our view. These are lessons for eternity." — *Murphy*. It is in this way that the biblical history is so profitable for doctrine, counsel, and instruction in righteousness.

CHAPTER XII.

NOW the ᵃ Lord had said unto Abram, Get thee out of thy country, and from thy kindred, and from thy father's house, unto a land that I will show thee: 2 ᵇAnd I will make of thee a great nation, ᶜand I will bless thee, and make thy name great; ᵈand thou shalt be a blessing: 3 ᵉAnd I will bless them that bless thee, and curse

---

a Chap. 15. 7; Neh. 9. 7; Isa. 41. 2; Acts 7. 3; Heb. 11. 8.——*b* Chap. 17. 6; 18. 18; Deut. 26. 5; 1 Kings 3. 8.——*c* Chap. 24. 35.——*d* Chap. 28. 4; Gal. 3. 14.——*e* Chap. 27. 29; Ex. 23. 22; Num. 24. 9.

---

1. **The Lord had said**—Rather, *the Lord said*. The pluperfect rendering was adopted by our translators from a supposed necessity of harmonizing this verse with Acts vii, 2. But it is not necessary to suppose the writer here refers to a second call, which Abram received in Haran. According to a usage often noticed in these pages, the writer goes back and takes up his narrative at a point previously recorded —so we may believe, with Stephen, that this call of Abram occurred "before he dwelt in Haran." The history of Terah was in the last chapter finished, and now begins the continuous history of the chosen seed from the great event in which it had its birth. It was a Jewish tradition, as we see from the book of Judith, that the descendants of Terah were driven out from Chaldea because they refused to follow the prevalent idolatry: "For they left the way of their ancestors, and worshipped the God of heaven, the God whom they knew: so they [the Chaldeans] cast them out from the face of their gods, and they fled into Mesopotamia, and sojourned there many days. Then their God commanded them to depart from the place where they sojourned, and to go into the land of Canaan." Judith v, 8, 9. **Get thee out**—*Go for thyself;* a special command. Note four particulars in this divine call. 1) Abram was to leave his native **country**, the fertile land where his fathers had dwelt for centuries, with its cities and its civilization, the mountains and noble rivers of his childhood. 2) His **kindred**, the stock of Eber, whom he left in Chaldea. 3) His **father's house**, the family of Terah, whom he left in Haran. The closest earthly ties were to be broken. 4) He was to go forth, he knew not whither, **unto a land** that God should show him. Heb. xi, 8. He was to exchange the town and the pastoral life for that of the nomad; to leave the massive temples of Chaldea to build altars here and there in the wilderness. But by faith he saw his father-land, his home, in the promise of God. Heb. xi, 14.

2. **I will make of thee a great nation**—Great promises correspond with the great sacrifices commanded. 1) He left his ᴀation, but should himself be the founder of a **great nation**. 2) He sacrificed kindred, but should be blessed with a spiritual kinship, as yet by him unimagined and inconceivable, but hailed afar off by faith. Hebrews xi, 13. 3) He broke away from ancestral ties, but his own **name** should be illustrious as father of the faithful, ancestor of the Hebrew people, and of the world's Messiah. 4) Most glorious of all, **Thou shalt be a blessing**—Heb., *Be thou a blessing*. "It is more blessed to give than to receive;" and, like the great Antitype, Abram's highest glory was in being a fount of blessing to all mankind. He should be famous, not for what he took from men, but for what he gave to men; not like Sesostris, Cæsar, Alexander, for the victories of the sword, but for the grander victories of truth and love. Abram signifies "the lofty Father," and to-day Christians, Mohammedans, and Jews contend with each other in the veneration which they show for Abram as a father. Alexander Severus, the Roman emperor, built a chapel in his palace in which all the great religions of the earth were honored; and it is related that the statues of Abram and Zoroaster stood there with those of Orpheus and of Christ. Probably no human name is to-day so widely honored as that of the "father of the faithful."

3. **I will bless . . . curse**—The promise is here expanded—Abram, as the man of faith, is to be identified with the divine plan for human redemption; his friends are, therefore,

him that curseth thee: *f* and in thee shall all families of the earth be blessed. 4 So Abram departed, as the LORD had spoken unto him; and Lot went with him: and Abram *was* seventy and five years old when he departed out of Haran. 5 And Abram took Sarai his wife, and Lot his brother's son, and all their substance that they had gathered, and *g* the souls that they had gotten *h* in Haran; and they went forth to go into the land of Canaan; and into the land of Canaan they came. 6 And Abram *i* passed through the land unto the place of Sichem, *k* unto the plain of Moreh. *l* And the Canaanite

f Chap. 18. 18; 22. 18; 26. 4; Psa. 72. 17; Acts 3. 25; Gal. 3. 8.——*g* Chap. 14. 14.   *h* Chap. 11. 31.——*i* Heb. 11. 9.——*k* Deut. 11. 30; Judg. 7. 1.——*l* Chap. 10. 18, 19; 13. 7.

God's friends, his enemies God's enemies. Faith makes man one with God; takes up his plans into the divine plan. Thus "all things work together for good to them that love God, to them who are the called [as was Abram] according to his purpose," who elects, as sons of God, those in whom this faith is foreknown. Rom. viii, 28, 29. The foreknowledge of Abram's faith was the basis of the great promise, **in thee shall all families of the earth be blessed.** This promise was conspicuously fulfilled in three modes by Abram. Abram became a channel of the divine law to all mankind. 1) From him came the Hebrew people, who for fifteen centuries preserved the knowledge of the unity, spirit, and holiness of God amidst manifold and abominable idolatries, which saturated all the ancient ceremonies. 2) From him thus came the *Bible,* God's book, to the world. 3) And from him came the Messiah, the Incarnate God and Redeemer. This promise is as broad as mankind, as deep and high as human wants and aspirations, as far reaching as immortality itself. Abram believed it, though imperfectly comprehending it; not receiving in his earthly lifetime the thing promised, yet having God's testimony of acceptance through faith, (Heb. xi, 39,) God having, in all this preparatory dispensation, *provided,* (Heb. xi, 40,) foreseen, and arranged for better things concerning us who enjoy the revelations in full sunshine, whose twilight gleam patriarchs saw afar off. Yet they were *made perfect* in their love by this distant view; what then must be our responsibility, who have come unto Mount Zion?

ABRAM IN CANAAN, 4–9.

4. Departed — Abram obeys, and goes forth from Haran, westward, over the river, as it was ever called by the Hebrews, the great Euphrates, afterwards the boundary of the kingdom of David and Solomon, separating Aram from Padan-Aram, the fertile Mesopotamian plain from the Syrian desert, and henceforth he was Abram, the *Hebrew,* the man who *had crossed* the border from *beyond* the great river, (ὁ περάτης, LXX of chap. xiv, 13,) the *emigrant,* the *pilgrim,* (*peregrinus, per-ager,*) a typical name of spiritual depth and beauty. See note on x, 24. He crossed the high chalk cliffs which wall the plain on the west, and forded the broad strong stream with wife and nephew and dependants, his flocks and his asses and camels, and entered the Syrian desert, a pilgrim, henceforth a type of all who set out on the heavenly pilgrimage. The manners and habits of the East are to day so nearly what they were in Abram's day that we can easily picture the scene.

5. **Substance**—Literally, *possessions which they had gained possession of*— flocks and herds. **Souls** —Persons, *which they had acquired,* the dependent followers of the household establishment. We find afterwards that Abram has three hundred and eighteen *trained servants* whom he leads forth in a warlike expedition, to rescue Lot. Chap. xiv, 14.

6. **Passed through the land** — Descending, probably, by way of Damascus—as we find afterwards that the steward of his house is a native of that city— thence southward and along the valley of the Jabbok by the route afterwards followed by Jacob, and across the Jordan **unto the place of Sichem,** or Shechem, the region in which afterwards, and in the writer's time, the town of Shechem was situated. (Neapolis and Nablus in subsequent time.) Yet the name, meaning *shoulder,* was prob-

was then in the land. 7 ᵐAnd the LORD appeared unto Abram, and said, ⁿ Unto thy seed will I give this land: and there builded he an ᵒ altar unto the LORD, who appeared unto him. 8 And he removed

m Chap. 17. 1.——*n* Chap. 13. 15: 17. 8; Psa.

ably given the locality from its being the water shed between the Jordan and the Mediterranean, and from the place passed to the *man* Shechem, son of Hamor. The particular spot of Abram's halt was the *oak* or *oak grove* (not **plain**) of **Moreh,** the name of its owner or planter. The town of Shechem, which we find here in the time of Jacob, lay in a beautiful sequestered valley between Mount Ebal on the north and Gerizim on the south. These mountains are in the narrowest place only sixty rods apart, and rise in bold bluffs to the height of about one thousand feet. Groves of evergreen oak and terebinth, as well as luxuriant orchards of orange and citron, vocal with birds and running waters, are a delightful feature of the valley of Nablus to-day. In this lovely valley, beneath and between these bold crags, which more than four centuries afterwards echoed with the solemn blessings and cursings of his descendants as they covenanted with God at their entrance into the land of promise—here, near the spot where, more than nineteen centuries afterwards, Jesus sat on the well of Jacob and made "this mountain" a stepping-stone to the spiritual kingdom in which men shall worship the Father in spirit and in truth—it was fit that here the father of the chosen people should first pitch his tent and build his altar. But the oak grove under which he encamped belonged to Moreh the Canaanite. The land whose very earth and air were to be saturated with his name was the possession of idolatrous strangers, **the Canaanite was** (even) **then in the land,** as he was when this narrative was written. This remark seems to have been added to show why it was impossible at that time for Abram to take possession. This handful of pilgrims, when they arrived in the vale of Shechem, found a widely-spread nation already in possession of the land of promise.

from thence unto a mountain on the east of Beth-el, and pitched his tent, *having* Beth-el on the west, and Hai on the east: and there he builded an altar unto the LORD, and ᵖ called upon the name of the

105. 9, 11.——*o* Chap. 13. 4.——*p* Chap. 13. 4.

7. **The Lord appeared unto Abram** —This is the first time that *Jehovah* is said to have *appeared* to man; and here, at Shechem, Christ revealed himself as the Messiah to a woman of Samaria. *How* Jehovah appeared at this time to Abram no man is now competent to say, and speculation and theories seem idle. Here was the first altar built to Jehovah as the covenant God; but we may be sure that " Melchizedek, king of Salem, and priest of the Most High God," was also at this time offering acceptable worship in this land of idolatry. Now for the first time Abram is told what is the land promised him, and yet it is not to be an inheritance for him, but only for his children. **Unto thy seed will I give this land**—There was now no established priesthood; the head of the family was priest in his own household. Abram builds an altar of earth and rough stones, and in the midst of his assembled household calls upon God by the mysterious covenant Name. He thus enters the land of promise with the solemn worship of Jehovah.

8. **Removed from thence**—Abram moved southward from Shechem and pitched his tent on the little round mount now seen strewn with stones, as if for the building of an altar, south-east of Bethel—now called Beitin by the Arabs—a little spot covered with foundation stones and half-standing walls, while east of this mount, and at about the same distance, may be seen a hill covered with the gray ruins of Ai, the modern *Et-Tel.* See Josh vii, 2, note. The name Beth-el (house of God) is said to have been given to this spot by Jacob on two different occasions, (chap. xxviii, 19, xxxv, 15,) so that here the historian may mean that Abram pitched his tent at the place *afterwards* called Beth-el ; or it may have borne this name already in Abram's day, an interesting relic of ancient piety, such as we meet with in the name Melchizedek, and the

LORD. **9** And Abram journeyed, ¹ ᑫ going on still toward the south.

10 And there was ʳ a famine in the land: and Abram ˢ went down into Egypt to sojourn there; for the famine was ᵗ grievous in the land. **11** And it came to pass, when he was come near to enter into Egypt, that he said unto Sarai his wife, Behold now, I know that thou *art* ᵘ a fair woman to look upon:

---

1 Heb. *in going and journeying.*—q Chap. 13. 3.—r Chap. 26. 1.

s Psa. 105. 13.—t Chap. 43. 1.—u Verse 14; chap. 26. 7.

---

name may have again been applied to it *in a new sense* by Jacob after his wondrous vision there.

9. Abram journeyed — Literally, and *Abram pulled up*, (his tent-pins,) *going and pulling up*, (encamping and striking his tents.) **Toward the south** —Hebrew, *towards the Negeb*, that is, the country south of Palestine; probably encamping in the vale of Hebron, where we afterwards find him. Thus he dwelt in tabernacles (tents) with Isaac and Jacob, heirs with him of the promise, a stranger in the land which yet he called his own. Heb. xi, 9.

ABRAM IN EGYPT, 10–20.

10. Famine in the land—Famine comes on him in the land of promise, and thus his faith is sorely tried. Not only were idolaters in possession of the ground on which he pitched his tents, but famine comes also. Canaan is watered by periodic rains; when they fail the ground dries up, and scarcity becomes no uncommon event. But Egypt, being watered by the regular overflow of the Nile, which was utilized by artificial irrigation, was rarely afflicted with famine, although when it did occur it was terribly destructive. Egypt was the granary of the adjacent nations in times of want. But Abram went there only **to sojourn** (גּוּר) till the famine was passed, not to dwell there. Abram passes down through the desert, as Jacob and his sons did afterwards for a similar cause to go down into Egypt. Abram, Israel, and the promised Seed fled before calamity through the same desert into the same land of refuge, sojourned there awhile amid its idolatrous civilization, its massive gods and temples, and then returned to Canaan—three advancing dispensations and divine manifestations which broke upon the world from this mysterious land, that it might be fulfilled that was spoken by the prophet, "I . . .

called my son out of Egypt." Hosea xi, 1.

11. Thou art a fair woman—Sarai was sixty-five years of age when Abram left Haran, being ten years younger than he, but, considering the longevity of the patriarchs, we may assume that at that period of life she would retain much of her youthful beauty, appearing much as a woman of thirty in our time. To the more dusky Egyptians an Asiatic woman would appear especially beautiful. The Egyptians were not Negroes, as is shown by the monuments; they were tawny in color, with straight hair, and features more Asiatic than African, (Rawl. *Herod.*, ii, 104;) but there was still a strong contrast between them and the true Asiatics, whose women might, therefore, appear to them very fair. Abram's fear was by no means groundless, for the Egyptian monarchs were unscrupulous in exercising their despotic power for the gratification of their desires. But we here meet with a manifestation of unbelief and of a lack of sensitiveness in regard to the marriage tie on the part of the father of the faithful, which, to a Christian, is startling. But we must, as Kurtz observes, "Consider what Abram could gain by pretending that Sarai was merely his sister. If she had been introduced as his wife, any one who wished to possess her could only attain this by violence, which would have greatly endangered Abram's life. But if she passed for his sister, it seemed probable that overtures would be made, and thus time, in this case the one thing requisite, be gained. Besides, he probably hoped that Jehovah, who had destined his wife to be the mother of the promised seed, would vindicate the honour of his promise." But while the narrative furnishes a faithful picture of Abram's struggle into true faith through the heathen cor-

About B. C. 1920. CHAPTER XII. 173

12 Therefore it shall come to pass, when the Egyptians shall see thee, that they shall say, This *is* his wife: and they ᵛ will kill me, but they will save thee alive. **13** ʷ Say, I pray thee, thou *art* my sister: that it may be well with me for thy sake; and my soul shall live because of thee.

14 And it came to pass, that, when Abram was come into Egypt, the Egyptians ˣ beheld the woman that she *was* very fair. **15** The princes also of Pharaoh saw her, and commended her before Pharaoh: and the woman was ʸ taken into Pharaoh's house. **16** And he ᶻ entreated Abram well for her sake: and

v Chap. 20. 11; 26. 7.——*w* Chap. 20. 5, 13; see chap. 26. 7.

x Chap. 39. 7; Matt. 5. 28.——*y* Chap. 20. 2.——*z* Chap. 20. 14.

ruptions which surrounded him, it teaches us also lessons of the divine discipline, and at the same time furnishes valuable incidental evidence of the impartial truthfulness of a history that so frankly sets down most humiliating truths concerning the father of the chosen people. Overawed by the splendours of the Egyptian civilization and by the absolute power of the Pharaohs, his faith in God's power wavers, and he resorts to a prevarication for the preservation of his life, which it seems he had preconcerted with Sarai at the commencement of his wanderings. Chap. xx, 13. Sarai was, it seems by chap. xx, 12, his half sister, daughter of his father by another mother, and he tells a half truth by calling her simply his sister, thus weakly exposing her to save himself. Of course, the sin was not so great as it would be under the Gospel or even the Mosaic law, but the course of Providence by which its weakness and wickedness was revealed to Abram is detailed for our instruction, while God's forgiving tenderness is also set forth in his remarkable interposition to rescue Sarai from her peril. Abram—reproved and punished, yet spared and forgiven, as one who yet walked in the twilight of revelation—is thus trained for fuller manifestations of the divine will, and thus in his weakness as well as his strength—in his sin as well as virtue—becomes an encouragement and warning to his children, the heirs of faith. In judging of the magnitude of this sin we are to remember that Abram was everywhere encompassed by idolatry, and where there is idolatry there is always sensuality and falsehood. Such a lapse is not to be wondered at in one who breathed such a tainted air, although privileged to receive direct revelations from God. In fact, how truthful to human nature is this incident! how unlike the artificial virtue of legendary saints and heroes!

14. Beheld—The Egyptian women were not veiled, like the Orientals. The pictorial representations in Egypt show the women unveiled, associating with men in all the freedom of modern civilization.

15. Commended her before Pharaoh—The result is as Abram anticipated. He sins to help Providence, and Providence abandons him. This was also the sin of Jacob in stealing Esau's blessing, and is no uncommon sin in God's Church to-day. **Pharaoh**—This is the same as the PI-Ra and PHRAH of the hieroglyphics, meaning "The Sun," and applied as a title to the Egyptian kings. P-RE is written as a hieroglyphic symbol over the titles of the Egyptian kings. In the monuments the sun is treated as the visible representation of the generative principle of nature, and sun worship may have been a primitive idolatry brought into Egypt from the East. The colossal Theban statues, representing kings as brothers of the gods, show how they assumed divine dignities, and furnish a comment on the name Pharaoh. **Taken into Pharaoh's house**—An Egyptian harem. Herodotus mentions that the Egyptians had but one wife; but Diodorus says that this restriction was confined to the priests, while other men took as many wives as they pleased. Polygamy seems to have been allowed, while monogamy was deemed more reputable. Wilkinson states that the monuments show evidence that the kings had many foreign wives or concubines, captives taken in war.

16. He entreated Abram well—Observe that the presents which Pha-

Vol. I.—12

O. T.

he had sheep, and oxen, and he asses, and menservants, and maidservants, and she asses, and camels. **17** And the LORD ⁿplagued Pharaoh and his house with great plagues, because of Sarai, Abram's wife. **18** And Pharaoh called Abram, and said, ᵒWhat *is* this *that* thou hast done unto me? why didst thou not tell me that she *was* thy wife? **19** Why saidst thou, She *is* my sister? so I might have taken her to me to wife: now therefore behold thy wife, take *her*, and go thy way. **20** ᵖAnd Pharaoh commanded *his* men concerning him: and they sent him away, and his wife, and all that he had.

CHAPTER XIII.

AND Abram went up out of Egypt, he, and his wife, and all that he had, and Lot with him, ᵃ into the south. **2** ᵇAnd Abram *was* very rich in cattle, in silver, and in gold. **3** And he went on his journeys ᶜ from the south even to Beth-el, unto the place where his tent had been at the beginning, between Beth-el and Hai; **4** Unto the ᵈplace of the altar, which he had made there at the first: and there Abram ᵉ called on the name of the LORD.

---

n Chap. 20. 18; 1 Chron. 16. 21; Psa. 105. 14; Heb. 13. 4.—*o* Chap. 20. 9; 26. 10.—*p* Prov. 21. 1.

a Chap. 12. 9.—*b* Chap. 24. 35; Psa. 112. 3; Prov. 10. 22.—*c* Chap. 12. 8, 9.—*d* Chap. 12. 7,.8.—*e* Psa. 116. 17.

---

raoh makes Abram are such as were suited to his nomad life. It is noticeable that nothing is here said of *horses*, which, as shown by the monuments, were introduced at a later period of Egyptian civilization. We find them there in the time of Moses.

17. The Lord plagued Pharaoh—As another Pharaoh and his people were afterwards smitten for their cruel oppression of Abram's seed. What these **plagues** were we are not told, but they seem to have fallen upon all who were engaged in this despotic proceeding, and probably were of such a nature as to prevent Pharaoh from consummating his marriage with Sarai, and led him to see that his design ran counter to the purposes of Abram's God. According to Josephus, the priests told Pharaoh the cause of the plagues; but Patrick suggests, that Sarai confessed the truth to Pharaoh.

18. What is this—The heathen despot reproves the sin of the God-fearing Abram! What a humiliation!

20. Sent him away—The language implies an honourable escort, and a safe conduct out of Egypt. " It deserves to be noticed that throughout the history of the chosen race, Egypt was to them the scene of spiritual danger, of covetousness and love of riches, of worldly security, of temptation to rest on man's arm and understanding, and not on God only. All this appears from the very first, in Abram's sojourn there, Sarai's danger, and their departure full of wealth and prosperity."—*Speaker's Commentary.*

CHAPTER XIII.

RETURN FROM EGYPT, 1–4.

1. Abram went up out of Egypt—An exodus typical of that later one of Israel, when another Pharaoh was plagued, and Abram's sons and daughters went forth with much Egyptian spoil. Exod. xii, 36. **Lot with him**—Hitherto Lot had accompanied his uncle in all his wanderings to the west and to the south; but the time of separation draws near. **Into the south**—The *Negeb*, or *south country*, (xx, 1,) a name constantly used to designate the district immediately south of Palestine. So, whether Abram journeys *southward*, as in chap. xii, 9, or northward, as here, he *goes into the Negeb ;* that is, enters the South Country bordering on Canaan. See note on Josh. x, 40.

2. Very rich in cattle—Largely acquired in Egypt. Comp. chap. xii, 16. **In silver, and in gold**—" This species of wealth is intended to describe a higher social scale to which the patriarch had risen, and which significantly points to a future more settled state, when the bare necessities of life would be adorned by comforts, and cheered by embellishments."—*Kalisch.*

3. On his journeys—An expression peculiar to the nomadic life—a pulling up of tent-pins, breaking up of camp, and moving onward. Comp. xii, 9, note. **Even to Beth-el**—See on chap. xii, 8. **At the beginning**— *Formerly.* His first stop was then at Sichem. xii, 6.

4. There Abram called on the name

About B. C. 1918.   CHAPTER XIII.   175

5 And Lot also, which went with Abram, had flocks, and herds, and tents. **6** And ᶠthe land was not able to bear them, that they might dwell together: for their substance was great, so that they could not dwell together. **7** And there was ᵍa strife between the herdmen of Abram's cattle and the herdmen of Lot's cattle: ʰand the Canaanite and the Perizzite dwelt then in the land.

8 And Abram said unto Lot, ⁱLet thei be no strife, I pray thee, between me and thee, and between my herdmen and thy herdmen; for we be ¹ brethren. **9** ᵏ*Is not the whole land before thee?* separate thyself, I pray thee, from me: ¹if *thou wilt take* the left hand, then I will go to the right; or if *thou depart* to the right hand, then I will go to the left. **10** And Lot lifted up his eyes, and be-

f Chapter 36. 7. — *g* Chapter 26. 20. — *h* Chapter 12. 6. — *i* 1 Corinthians 6. 7. — 1 Hebrew, *men brethren:* see chapter 11. 27;

31; Exodus 2. 13; Psalm 133. 1; Acts 7. 26.— *k* Chapter 20. 15; 34. 10. — *l* Romans 12. 18; Hebrews 12. 14; James 3. 17.

of the Lord—At the old altar, where he had once faithfully worshipped the holy Name, he offers sacrifice again, and calls aloud in praise and prayer to Him who has saved him from famine and from the power of Pharaoh. Blessed worship after long and hazardous exile!

SEPARATION OF ABRAM AND LOT, 5–13.

The time has come to separate Abram and his household more fully from kindred and connexions which he cannot "command." Chap. xviii, 19. His father's house in far-off Chaldea was tainted with idolatry, and he was to be removed from its power, and so Jehovah ordered him thence. But the love of kindred is strong, and Terah, his father, accompanied him as far as Haran. There he dwelt and died, and Abram resumed his journey westward. Lot, his brother's son, still clings to him, but his earthly love and selfishness, as now to be exhibited, made him an unfit companion for the father of the chosen seed, and in the providence of God a peaceable separation is effected.

5. Lot also . . . had flocks—His associations with Abram had been to him a source of temporal prosperity, as well as a means of grace.

6. Land was not able to bear them—Having been impoverished by the recent great famine, and being already occupied, as the next verse states, by other dwellers, they were cramped for pasturage for their immense flocks and herds.

7. A strife between the herdmen— "Such disputes were unavoidable in the circumstances. Neither party had any title to the land. Everybody availed himself of the best spot for grazing he could find unoccupied.

We can easily understand what facilities and temptations this would offer for the strong to overbear the weak. We meet with many incidental notices of such oppression: Gen. xxi, 25; xxvi, 15–22; Exod. ii, 16–19." — *Murphy.* "The germinal divisions of masters ofttimes reveal themselves clearly in the strifes of their servants and dependents. Even the wives are often in open hostility while their husbands are still at peace. Abram teaches us how to observe these symptoms in the right way." — *Lange.* **The Canaanite**—Comp. chap. xii, 6. **Perizzite** —This name, not appearing among the descendants of Canaan in chap. x, 15–17, is supposed to designate some tribe not of Hamite origin. The Hebrew word, which means *rustics,* or *countrymen,* may designate them as nomads, or dwellers in the country as distinguished from dwellers in towns and cities. See note on Josh. iii, 10. They probably occupied the best pastures, and so partly occasioned the strife between Abram and Lot's herdmen.

8. Abram said—Abram's words and proposition on the occasion are most magnanimous, and every way worthy of the father of the faithful. "He walks," says Murphy, "in the moral atmosphere of the Sermon on the Mount. Matt. v, 38–42." **We be brethren**—Heb., *Men brethren are we.* Compare Acts xv, 13; xxiii, 1. Their kinship and religious affinity would authorize this warm expression.

10. Lot . . . beheld all the plain of Jordan—כִּכַּר, here rendered **plain,** means *the region around,* or *circuit;* ἡ περίχωρος, Matt. iii, 5. "At the time when Abram and Lot looked

held all ᵐ the plain of Jordan, that it was well watered everywhere, before the LORD ⁿ destroyed Sodom and Gomorrah, ᵒ *even* as the garden of the LORD, like the land of Egypt, as thou comest unto ᵖ Zoar. **11** Then Lot chose him all the plain of Jordan; and Lot journeyed east: and they separated themselves the one from the other. **12** Abram dwelt in the land of Canaan, and Lot ᵠ dwelt in the cities of the plain, and ʳ pitched *his* tent toward Sodom. **13** But the men of Sodom *were* wicked and ᵗ sinners before the LORD exceedingly.

14 And the LORD said unto Abram, after that Lot ᵘ was separated from him,

m Chap. 19. 17; Deut. 34. 3; Psa. 107. 34.—*n* Chap. 19. 24, 25.—*o* Chap. 2. 10; Isa. 51. 3.—*p* Chap. 14. 2, 8; 19. 22.

q Chap. 19. 29.—*r* Chap. 14. 12; 19. 1; 2 Pet. 2. 7, 8.—*s* Chap. 18. 20; Ezek. 16. 49; 2 Pet. 2. 7, 8.—*t* Chap. 6. 11.—*u* Verse 11.

down from the mountain of Beth-el on the deep descent beneath them, and Lot chose for himself the *circle* of the Jordan, that circle was different from any thing that we now see. **It was well watered everywhere . . . as the garden of the Lord, like the land of Egypt**—And this description is filled out in detail by subsequent allusions. It is described as a deep valley, distinguished from the surrounding desert by its fertile fields. If any credence is to be attached to the geological conclusions of the last fifty years, there must have been already a lake at its extremity, such as that which terminates the course of the Barada at Damascus, or of the Kouik at Aleppo. Then, as now, it must have received in some form or other the fresh streams of the Jordan, of the Arnon, of En-gedi, of Callirrhoe, and at the southern end, as Dr. Robinson has observed, more living brooks than are to be found in all the rest of Palestine. On the banks of one or some of these streams there seems to have been an oasis, or collection of oases, like that which is still, from the same causes, to be found on a smaller scale in the groves of En-gedi and of Jericho, and in the plain of Gennesareth, or, on a larger scale, in the paradise of Damascus. Along the edge of this lake or valley Gentile and Jewish records combine in placing the earliest seat of Phœnician civilization. Sodom, Gomorrah, Admah, Zeboim, are (with Lasha [probably Laish] by the sources of the Jordan, and Sidon on the seashore) mentioned as the first settlements of the Canaanites. Gen. x, 19. When Lot descended from Beth-el, 'the cities of the round' of the Jordan formed a nucleus of civilized life before any city, except Hebron, had sprung up in Central Palestine."—STANLEY: *Sinai and Palestine, p.* 281. The mention of **the garden of the Lord** shows how the traditions of Eden still lingered in the thoughts of men, and Lot's recent sojourn in the valley of the Nile would naturally prompt the comparison of the well-watered Jordan valley to **the land of Egypt.** The words, **as thou comest unto Zoar,** are not to be connected, grammatically, with **land of Egypt,** but with **plain of Jordan,** from which they are separated by the intervening description of the Jordan plain.

12. **Lot dwelt in the cities . . . and pitched his tent**—He seems to have divided his interests between city and country. Having **pitched his tent toward Sodom,** (עַד־סְדֹם, *unto Sodom,* or *at Sodom,*) and leaving his flocks and herds in charge of herdmen, he himself "dwelt in Sodom." Chap. xiv, 12. It is thought that he was not married until after his separation from Abram, and that then he took a woman of Sodom for his wife, thus mingling himself with the ungodly.

13. **Wicked and sinners**—As more fully exhibited in chap. xix. The fairest and most inviting regions of the earth,

"Where every prospect pleases,
And only man is vile,"

may furnish the conditions of excessive licentiousness and crime. Sadly did Lot mistake in looking more on outward and temporal beauty than on moral and religious worth.

THE PROMISE RENEWED TO ABRAM, 14–18.

14. **After that Lot was separated from him**—Now, in the gracious prov-

About B. C. 1917. CHAPTER XIII. 177

Lift up now thine eyes, and look from the place were thou art ᵛnorthward, and southward, and eastward, and westward: 15 For all the land which thou seest, ʷto thee will I give it, and ˣto thy seed for ever. 16 And ʸI will make thy seed as the dust of the earth: so that if a man can number the dust of the earth, then shall thy seed also be numbered. 17 Arise, walk through the land in the length of it and in the breadth of it; for I will give it unto thee. 18 Then Abram removed *his* tent, and came ᶻand dwelt in the ²plain of Mamre, ᵃwhich *is* in Hebron, and built there an altar unto the LORD.

---

v Chap. 28. 14.——*w* Chap. 12. 7; 15. 18; 17. 8; 24. 7; 26. 4; Num. 34. 12; Deut. 34. 4; Acts 7. 5. ——*x* 2 Chron. 20. 7; Psa. 37. 22, 29; 112. 2.—— *y* Chap. 15. 5; 22. 17; 26. 4; 28. 14; 32. 12; Exod. | 32. 13; Num. 23. 10; Deut. 1. 10; 1 Kings 4. 20; 1 Chron. 27. 23; Isa. 48. 19; Jer. 33. 22; Rom. 4. 16, 17, 18; Heb. 11. 12. —— *z* Chap. 14. 13. —— 2 Heb. *plains.*——*a* Chap. 35. 27; 37. 14.

---

idence of Jehovah, the father of the faithful is cut loose from all his kindred according to the flesh. Thoroughly separated from home, country, and kin, (comp. chap. xii, 1,) he is free to move in the line of the divine call and purpose.

In this renewal of the promise to Abram, (verses 14–17,) we notice the following: 1.) **Look** — Feast thine eyes on it in all directions. 2.) It is thine **for ever,** and will be known through the centuries as the Land of Promise. 3.) **Thy seed** shall be as the multitudinous particles of **the dust of the earth,** innumerable by man. 4.) **Walk through the land** — At pleasure; survey it as thine own, although thou, in thy lifetime, dost not possess it. 5.) Know and remember it as a GIFT. אֶתְּנֶנָּה, **I will give it,** is twice repeated. Verses 15 and 17.

18. **Plain of Mamre** — Rather, *oaks of Mamre.* Abram now pitches his tent among the oaks (or in the oak-grove) of Mamre, as formerly at the oak of Moreh. Chap. xii, 6, note. About a mile from Hebron is one of the largest oaks of Palestine, and bears the name of "Abram's Oak." **Mamre** is not to be identified with **Hebron,** but seems to have been the name of the oak-grove or plain **in Hebron,** that is, *at* or *near* Hebron; perhaps so called from Mamre the Amorite, the friend and confederate of Abram. Chap. xiv, 13. **Hebron** is celebrated as the most ancient city of Canaan, "built seven years before Zoan in Egypt." Num. xiii, 22. Its more ancient name was *Kirjath-arba.* Chap. xxiii, 2; Josh. xiv, 15. Abraham, Isaac, and Jacob spent much of their lives in the vicinity of this city, and here was Machpelah, the tomb of these patriarchs. Chap. xxiii. Hebron is now called *El-khalil,* "the friend." **Built there an altar**—The third altar he had built in Canaan, (comp. chap. xii, 7, 8,) and thus is he careful to "keep the way of the Lord." Chap. xviii, 19. "This remarkable narrative," says Bunsen, "bears upon its face every evidence of historic truth, and is most fitly assigned to a time soon after 2900 years before Christ." Notable concession from such a source.

CHAPTER XIV.

INVASION OF THE EASTERN KINGS, 1–12.

Considered merely as an historical document, the following chapter is invaluable. Its antiquity is greater than that of any of the records of the past as yet deciphered, and the internal marks of its genuineness are beyond dispute. This is acknowledged by many of the ablest rationalistic critics, who regard this part of the narrative as a most ancient historic document, inserted here by the compiler of the Book of Genesis.

Here we find the earliest record of those hostile invasions from the East which in later times so repeatedly troubled the nations of western Asia, Egypt, and Greece. The narrative here serves a twofold purpose, namely, 1) to show the mistaken policy of Lot's choice, in selecting for residence the cities of the plain, and 2) to exhibit Abram's generous heart and military sagacity and prowess. In this first conflict between the world-powers and the chosen seed we also note the arbitrary and rapacious spirit of the former and the righteous principle and honour of the latter. The heir of the Land of Promise appears as the protector and

CHAPTER XIV.

AND it came to pass in the days of Amraphel king *a* of Shinar, Arioch king of Ellasar, Chedorlaomer king of *b* Elam, and Tidal king of nations; 2 *That these* made war with Bera king of Sodom, and with Birsha king of Gomorrah, Shinab king of *c* Admah, and Shemeber king of Zeboiim, and the king of Bela, which is *d* Zoar. 3 All these were joined together in the vale of Siddim, *e* which is the salt sea. 4 Twelve years *f* they served Chedorlaomer, and in the thirteenth year they rebelled. 5 And in the fourteenth year came Chedorlaomer, and the kings that were with him, and smote *g* the Rephaim *h* in Ashteroth Karnaim, and *i* the Zuzim in

a Chapter 10. 10; 11. 2.——*b* Isaiah 11. 11.——*c* Deuteronomy 29. 23.—— *d* Chapter 19. 22.——*e* Numbers 34. 12; Deuteronomy 3. 17; Joshua 3. 16; Psalm 107. 34.——*f* Chapter 9. 26.——*g* Chapter 15. 20; Deuteronomy 3. 11.——*h* Joshua 12. 4; 13. 12.——*i* Deuteronomy 2. 20.

defender of his own. God honours him, and he maintains righteousness and honours God.

1. **Amraphel king of Shinar**—Successor of Nimrod, and perhaps mentioned first because of his location in this most ancient seat of empire. Comp. chap. x, 10. The derivation of the name is uncertain, though some have sought to trace it in the Sanscrit *Amarapala*, "guardian of the immortals." No other record of this king is known besides what is contained in this chapter. The same is the case with **Arioch king of Ellasar**. The modern town *Senkerah*, between Ur and Ereck, is supposed by many to be the site of the ancient **Ellasar** here mentioned. It was known to the Greeks as *Larissa*, and appears from the inscriptions to have been one of the primitive capitals of this region. **Chedorlaomer**, though mentioned third in order here, appears from verses 4, 5, and 17 to have been the chief king, and the leader of the expedition. **Elam**, the province which he ruled, is doubtless the same as the vast district known as Elymais, east of the lower Tigris, and first settled by the children of Shem. Chap. x, 22. The name *Kadur Mapula* has been found on Chaldean bricks, and he is called "Ravager of the West." **Tidal**—Sept., *Thargal*. This name, according to Rawlinson, is found in the early Hamitic dialect of the lower Tigris and Euphrates country, and means "the Great Chief." The title **king of nations** may denote that Tidal was chief of a number of nomadic tribes, without settled dominion. Some render גּוֹיִם, *nations*, as a proper name, *Goyim*. But we have no knowledge of any nation or district of that name.

2. **Bera . . . Birsha**—The names of the kings of the pentapolis of this Jordan plain live only in this record. **Sodom, Gomorrah, Admah,** and **Zeboiim** are said in chapter x, 19, to have been settled by the sons of Ham. **Bela,** more commonly known as **Zoar,** is generally supposed to have been situated at the southern end of the Dead Sea. But Grove, in Smith's *Bib. Dict.*, places it at the northern, as also Sodom and Gomorrah. This new theory of Grove is controverted, and the older view ably defended by Wolcott in *Bib. Sacra*, for 1868, vol. xxv, p. 112, ff.

3. **These were joined together** —They were allies and confederates. **The vale of Siddim** is, according to the obvious import of the words here used, the name of the ancient plain or valley in which the five kings joined together, but which, at the time of our writer, was covered by the waters of **the salt sea**. But these waters may cover a larger extent of surface than was included in the vale of Siddim. The word **Siddim** (שִׂדִּים) itself means *fields* or *plains*. The sea here called **the salt sea** is called in Deut. iv, 49, "the sea of the plain;" in 2 Esdras v, 7, "the Sodomitish sea;" in Josephus, "the Asphaltic lake;" by the Arabs, *Bahr Lut*, "Sea of Lot;" and by the Greek writers and most moderns, "the Dead Sea."

4. **Twelve years they served**—During these years they were probably required to pay annual tribute to the king of Elam, the leader and most powerful of the eastern kings. **Rebelled** —Threw off this yoke and refused to pay homage to eastern sovereignty.

5. **Smote the Rephaim in Ashteroth Karnaim**—The word *Rephaim*

CHAPTER XIV.

Ham,[k] and the Emim in [1]Shaveh Kiriathaim, **6** [l]And the Horites in their mount Seir, unto [2]El-paran, which is

[k] Deut. 2. 10, 11.——1 Or, *The plain of Kiriathaim.*——[l] Deut. 2. 12, 22.

is in the Hebrew plural, and designates an ancient people of gigantic stature, of whom Og, king of Bashan, is spoken of as the last remnant. Deut. iii, 11. Of their origin the Bible is silent. Their chief seat was at **Ashteroth Karnaim,** or Ashteroth of *the two horns,* so called, probably, from the worship of the two-horned Astarte, the Syrian Venus and moon-goddess. See note and cuts on Judges ii, 13. Some identify this place with the Ashtaroth near Edrei, where Og dwelt, (Deut. i, 4,) which is generally identified with the modern Tell-Ashtereh, some 25 miles east of the Sea of Galilee. Others locate it at the modern Es-Sanamein, about half way between Tell-Ashtereh and Damascus. After this defeat these Rephaim seem to have settled in other parts of Canaan, and the "valley of Rephaim" south-west of Jerusalem probably derived its name from them. We find traces of them in the time of David. 2 Sam. xxi, 18, 20, 22. The **Zuzim** were probably the same as the *Zamzummim* of Deut. ii, 20, a people akin to the Rephaim, and described as "great, and many, and tall." **Ham,** where they dwelt, is probably represented in the modern Amman, east of the Jordan, better known as *Rabbath-Ammon,* the capital city of the Ammonites. **The Emim** are represented in Deut. ii, 10, 11, as the ancient occupants of the land of Moab, and also "a people great, and many, and tall, as the Anakim." **Shaveh Kiriathaim,** or the "plain of the two cities," is probably the same as *Kirjathaim,* allotted to the Reubenites. Num. xxxii, 37; Josh. xiii, 19. The name still lingers in the extensive ruins of Kureiyat, east of the Dead Sea, and about three miles southeast of Mt. Attarus.

6. The Horites in their mount Seir were the original settlers of the wild and mountainous country south of the Dead Sea, and were, as the name denotes, "cave dwellers." Mt. Hor perhaps derived its name from these an-

by the wilderness. **7** And they returned, and came to En-mishpat, which is Kadesh, and smote all the country of the

[2] Or, *The plain of Paran;* chap. 21. 21; Num. 12. 16; 13. 3.

cient people, whose excavated dwellings in the rocks abound in all that region, especially in Petra. They were succeeded in later times by the descendants of Esau. Deut. ii, 12. **El-paran,** or the *oak of Paran,* was probably some notable landmark (an ancient oak) on the border of the great **wilderness** of Paran, the modern desert et-Tih. This wilderness embraced the great central region of the Sinaitic peninsula north of the Sinai mountains.

It appears from this account, that the whole country east of the Jordan from Damascus on the north to the Paran wilderness on the south was, in Abram's time, occupied by a gigantic race all belonging to the same stock, and distributed in the order here indicated: The Rephaim on the north in the region afterward known as Bashan; the Zuzim next, centring at or near the modern Amman; the Emim next, south of these and directly east of the Dead Sea; and the Horites in the mountains of Seir.

7. They returned, and came to En-mishpat—Having pursued their victorious march southward through all the regions named as far as the wilderness of Paran, they turned northward, fetching a compass to **En-mishpat,** which seems to have been the ancient name of **Kadesh.** The site of Kadesh was for a long time an unsettled question. Stanley identified it with Petra; Robinson with Ain-el-Weibeh, some twenty miles northwest of Mt. Hor; Rowlands with Ain Gades, forty miles west of Mt. Hor. But it was reserved for an American traveller, H. C. Trumbull, to confirm the opinion of Rowlands, and put beyond reasonable doubt the locality of this ancient and long lost fountain. Some eighty miles southwest of Hebron he discovered several large springs issuing from underneath a ragged spur of a range of limestone hills, and still bearing the name *Qadees.* The abundant waters fill several wells or pools, are remark-

180   GENESIS.   About B. C. 1913.

Amalekites, and also the Amorites, that dwelt [m] in Hazezon-tamar. **8** And there went out the king of Sodom, and the king of Gomorrah, and the king of Admah, and the king of Zeboiim, and the king of Bela, (the same is Zoar;) and they joined battle with them in the vale of Siddim; **9** With Chedorlaomer the king of Elam, and with Tidal king of nations, and Amraphel king of Shinar, and Arioch king of Ellasar; four kings with five. **10** And the vale of Siddim was full of [n] slimepits; and the kings of Sodom and Gomorrah fled, and fell there; and they that remained fled [o] to the mountain. **11** And they took [p] all the goods of Sodom and Gomorrah, and all their victuals, and went their way. **12** And they took Lot, Abram's [q] brother's son, [r] who dwelt in Sodom, and his goods, and departed. **13** And there came one that had es-

[m] 2 Chron. 20. 2.——[n] Chap. 11. 3.——[o] Chap. 19. 17, 30.   [p] Verses 16, 21.——[q] Chap. 12. 5.——[r] Chap. 13. 12.

ably pure and sweet, and flow off under the waving grass. The fountain creates an oasis of verdure and beauty in the midst of the great desert et-Tih. "A carpet of grass covered the ground. Fig trees laden with fruit nearly ripe enough for eating, were along the shelter of the southern hillside. Shrubs and flowers showed themselves in variety and profusion."—TRUMBULL'S *Kadesh-Barnea*, pp. 272, 273. New York, 1883. Returning from the great wilderness of Paran, the victorious kings would have passed through the region afterward known as **the country of the Amalekites,** which bordered on the south of Palestine. The Amalekites were a branch of the Edomites, (chap. xxxvi, 12,) and are mentioned here proleptically. It is not said they smote the Amalekites, but **the country** (Heb. *the whole field*) of the Amalekites. **Also the Amorites . . . in Hazezon-tamar** — Hazezon-tamar is said to be the same as En-gedi, (2 Chron. xx, ii,) and the latter name lingers in the modern Ain-Jidy, on the western shore of the Dead Sea. **The Amorites,** descendants of Canaan, (chap. x, 16,) early settled in the palm groves of this region. The conquerors, returning from the south by way of Kadesh, would naturally enter the vale of Siddim from the west, and smite these Amorites on their way.

9. Four kings with five—And the four, flushed with many victories and grown fierce by war, conquered the five. What were the weapons and what the modes of warfare used by these ancient kings we have no means of knowing. Their principal arms were probably the sword, the bow, and the spear.

10. Full of slimepits — Sept., φρέατα ἀσφάλτου, *pits of asphaltum;* Vulg., *puteos multos bituminis,* many *pits of bitumen.* The Hebrew may be rendered: *The vale of Siddim was pits, pits of mineral pitch;* that is, such bituminous pits abounded there; and this abundance of asphalt has given the Dead Sea the name *Asphaltic Lake.* These pits served as so many snares to **the kings of Sodom and Gomorrah,** who, with their forces, were defeated, **and fled, and fell there.** These two kings seem to have taken the lead in the battle, and so are mentioned as representing all the rest. From verses 17 and 21 we infer that the king of Sodom himself escaped capture, probably by fleeing to the mountains. **They that remained**—That is, those who were neither killed in battle nor taken prisoners.

11. All the goods—All property of the Sodomites that they could lay hands on and remove.

12. Took Lot—This fact our writer is careful to note. Lot and all his family and possessions (comp. verse 16) were taken, and it is also stated that Lot now **dwelt in Sodom.** He had first "pitched his tent toward Sodom," (chap. xiii, 12,) but now has come to dwell in the city. "It does not seem that Lot had taken part in the revolt, or in the war; but as a prominent man his capture may have been deemed the more important."—*Jacobus.*

ABRAM'S MILITARY VICTORY, 13–16.

13. One that had escaped—Heb. *the fugitive,* emphatic as representing a class, or company. **The Hebrew**— Or *the Eberite,* a patronymic of Eber, (chap. x, 21,) the ancestor of Abram.

caped, and told Abram the Hebrew; for he *dwelt in the plain of Mamre the Amorite, brother of Eshcol, and brother of Aner: *t* and these *were* confederate with Abram. **14** And when Abram heard that *u* his brother was taken captive, he armed *3* his trained *4* servants,*v* born in his own house, three hundred and eighteen, and pursued them unto *w* Dan. **15** And he divided himself against them, he and his servants, by night, and *x* smote them, and pursued them unto Hobah, which *is* on the left hand of Damascus. **16** And he brought back *y* all the goods, and also

s Chap. 13, 18.——*t* Verse 24.——*u* Chap. 13. 8.——3 Or, *led forth.*——4 Or, *instructed.*

v Chap. 15. 3; 17. 12, 27; Eccl. 2. 7.——*w* Deut. 34.1; Judg.18.29.——*x* Isa.41.2,3.——*y* Vers.11,12.

Abram is called the Eberite in distinction from **Mamre the Amorite** with whom he held friendly alliance. What gave Eber such prominence in connexion with Abram's descendants we do not know, but the language of chap. x, 21, assigns him a notable prominence among the sons of Shem. Others derive the name **Hebrew** from עֵבֶר, *the region beyond,* and understand it of Abram because he was an immigrant *from beyond* the great river Euphrates. This latter view appears in the Septuagint and Vulgate, and is held by most ancient interpreters. **Confederate with Abram**—Heb. *lords of a covenant with Abram.* They had joined an alliance, and, as appears from verse 24, they went with Abram to the war.

14. When Abram heard—He had no pleasure in the misfortune of his more worldly kinsman, who had taken advantage of his offer (chap. xiii, 9) and chosen the fertile plain, but moved immediately for his rescue. The word **brother** is here used in the wider sense of *kinsman,* a usage not unfrequent. Exod. ii, 11; Num. viii, 26. **Armed his trained servants**—Rather, *led forth his trained ones.* The word rendered **trained** is of the same root as that rendered *train* in Prov. xxii, 6: "Train up a child in the way he should go." These were drilled and practiced in the use of weapons, as well as to (xviii, 19) "keep the way of the Lord." Chaps. xxxiv, 25, xlix, 5, further show that the pastoral patriarchs were skilful in the use of arms. This was probably often necessary for purposes of self-defence. These trained and skilful adherents of Abram are further described as **born in his own house,** a regular part of the patriarchal family; not bought, nor taken in war. Comp. chap. xvii, 12. And the number, **three hundred and eighteen,** shows what a powerful community one patriarchal family might be. To these were added the forces of Mamre, Eshcol, and Aner. Verse 24. **Pursued them unto Dan**—From which it appears that the victorious kings made no hurried march homeward, but took a northerly route. There is no reason to suppose the Dan here mentioned as any other than the well known city of this name near the source of the Jordan. It is doubtless the same as the Dan-jaan of 2 Sam. xxiv, 6, and the Dan mentioned in Deut. xxxiv, 1; for the language of the latter passage does not necessarily imply that the Dan there mentioned was in the land of Gilead. The ancient name of the place was Laish or Leshem, (Josh. xix, 47, Judges xviii, 29,) but Dan is here used either proleptically, or else was substituted by a later editor as being the more common name of the place.

15. Divided himself against them —Abram was the leader and commander in the war, and the forces of his confederates, as well as **his** own **servants,** were at his disposal. This dividing up into several squads and attacking the enemy from different quarters, and **by night,** explains how Abram's company might, without any miraculous help from God, put to flight the combined armies of four Asiatic kings. Compare the similar strategy of Gideon. Judges vii, 15–23. **Hobah** — Perhaps at the modern Burzeh, three miles north of Damascus, where there is a tomb called the "praying place of Abraham," and marking, according to local tradition, the place where Abram gave thanks to God after this victory over the kings. It was **on the left hand of Damascus,** that is, to one facing the east.

brought again his brother Lot, and his goods, and the women also, and the people.

17 And the king of Sodom [a] went out to meet him, [a] after his return from the slaughter of Chedorlaomer and of the kings that *were* with him, at the valley of Shaveh, which *is* the [b] king's dale. **18** And [c] Melchizedek king of Salem brought forth bread and wine: and he *was* [d] the priest of [e] the most high God.

[a] Judg. 11. 34; 1 Sam. 18. 6. — *a* Heb. 7. 1. — [b] 2 Sam. 18. 18.
[c] Heb. 7. 1. — *d* Psa. 110. 4; Heb. 5. 6. — [e] Micah 6. 6; Acts 16. 17.

16. Brought back ... Lot, ... goods ... women ... people—The victory of Abram was complete, and resulted in recovering **all** that had been taken, both persons and property. So that while the broken remnant of the eastern armies fled homeward, panic stricken and without any spoil, of all their conquests, Abram led back in triumph all that had been taken away.

ABRAM AND MELCHIZEDEK, 17–20.

17. The king of Sodom—Hence it appears that this king survived the defeat, probably by flight to the hills. Verse 10 does not necessarily mean that the kings there named were killed. Some expositors, however, so understand it, and suppose that the king here mentioned was successor to the one who fell in battle. **Valley of Shaveh**—According to Gesenius and Fürst, *Shaveh* means *plain* or *valley*. This valley was afterwards known as **the king's dale**, probably from the occurrences here recorded. We find the name again in 2 Sam. xviii, 18, and old tradition identifies it with the valley of the Kedron. In the absence of any thing more definitely known, and in view of the probability that Salem was the ancient name of Jerusalem, we do well to adhere to the traditional location of Shaveh. Abram returning southward from the source of the Jordan may well have passed through the Kedron valley; and there would have been a suitable place both for the king of Sodom to meet him, and for the king of Salem to bring forth refreshments.

18. Melchizedek king of Salem—This mysterious stranger here suddenly emerges from the dim background of the old Canaanitish heathenism, "without father, without mother, without descent, having neither beginning of days nor end of life," (Heb. vii, 3,) that is, without any recorded genealogy, (a matter of prime importance with a Hebrew,) or mention of birth, age, or death. His name and title are significant, "first being, by interpretation, *king of righteousness*, and after that also king of Salem, which is, *king of peace*." Heb. vii, 2. His bringing forth **bread and wine** suggests to the Christian the symbols of the holy Eucharist, and his benediction on Abram, his receiving tithes of him, and his position and title as **priest of the most high God,** (a title never used of Abraham,) place him above the father of the faithful. No wonder the psalmist, a thousand years later, caught inspiration from the name, and, in prophetic vision, used this sacred character as a type of the Messiah. Psa. cx, 4.

From the earliest times there have been strange speculations and various conjectures as to this mysterious person. Some have identified him with the patriarch Shem, supposing that survivor of the flood to have lingered until Abram's time. But if so, why should his name have been changed to Melchizedek, and how could it be said of Shem, with Gen. xi, 10–27, before us, that he was without pedigree? Heb. vii, 3. Others have maintained that Melchizedek was the Son of God himself, appearing in human form. But such a Christophany, without a word of explanation, is scarcely supposable, and the sublime comparisons drawn in Psa. cx, 4, and Heb. vi, 20, vii, 3, are reduced to the empty platitude of making Christ *like himself.* A sect called Melchizedekians arose in the third century, and were so named because of their strange doctrine that Melchizedek was not a man, but some heavenly power, an intercessor for the angels, and so superior even to Jesus Christ. For other notions, unnecessary to record here, see the Bible Dictionaries.

Doubtless the proper view to take of

About B. C. 1913.   CHAPTER XIV.   183

19 And he blessed him, and said, *f* Blessed be Abram of the most high God, ^g possessor of heaven and earth: **20** And ^h blessed be the most high God,

---
f Ruth 3. 10; 2 Sam. 2. 5.—*g* Verse 22; Matt. 11. 25.

---

this mysterious character is to regard him as an exceptional instance in that early time of a venerable Hamite, or perhaps, like Abram, a Shemite, who had been kept pure from the prevailing idolatry of the world, and like Job and Jethro was a worshipper of the one true God. Nor need we deem it strange that such an example of righteousness should have been living in that place and time. God has had, in all ages and nations, men eminent for uprightness and even sanctity of life. The Noachic covenant, of which the rainbow is the gracious sign, embraces " in every nation him that feareth God and worketh righteousness." Acts x, 35. The mystery which invests Melchizedek is chiefly owing to our utter lack of knowledge of his pedigree, his subsequent life, and his death. His name breathes a strange charm, and may have indicated his far-famed eminence for righteousness. Some take the words **king of Salem** as a title, *melek-shalem*, (king of peace,) and urge that Heb. vii, 2, favours this view. But such suppositions are not to be pressed, for the writer to the Hebrews evidently uses the meaning, both of his name and residence, homiletically. **Salem** is undoubtedly the name of a place, the residence of this saintly king, and is probably the archaic name of Jerusalem, as used also in Psa. lxxvi, 2. Identification with *Shalem*, of chap. xxxiii, 18, or *Salim*, of John iii, 23, is far less satisfactory. See notes on Heb. vii.

Melchizedek came forth from his royal city, and was, like the king of Sodom, grateful to Abram for ridding the land of its invaders and oppressors. He also **brought forth bread and wine**, general terms for food and refreshments, in token of his gratitude, and of his appreciation of the services of the noble Hebrew. On the use of divine names in this passage, see on verses 19, 22.

which hath delivered thine enemies into thy hand. And he gave him tithes ⁱ of all. **21** And the king of Sodom said unto Abram, Give me the ⁵ persons, and

---
h Chapter 24. 27.—*i* Heb. 7. 4.—5 Heb. *souls.*

---

19. **He blessed him**—And to enhance the greatness and grandeur of Melchizedek, the writer of Hebrews (vii, 7) argues: "Without contradiction the less is blessed of the better." This blessing pronounced on Abram rises to a poetic strain:

Blessed be Abram of God most high,
Possessor of heaven and earth.
And blessed be God most high,
Who has delivered thine enemies into thy hand.

The divine names here used are אֵל עֶלְיוֹן, *El Elion*, God, the Highest; the Supreme God; that is, the one God over all. Note how Abram, in verse 22, uses the same words but prefixes the name Jehovah. **Possessor**—The Hebrew word קֹנֵה may be rendered *maker* or *founder*, (Sept. and Vulg. *creator*,) as well as *possessor*. The word really involves both these meanings. **Hath delivered** — Here the providential interposition of God in the affairs of man is recognised. Accordingly, in the words of Melchizedek, we find the doctrines, 1) of God's unity and supremacy; 2) of his dominion of heaven and earth; 3) of the duty of praise and thanksgiving to him; 4) of divine Providence. **He gave him tithes of all**—That is, Abram gave Melchizedek tithes of all the booty he had taken. Thus early do we find the mention of the tenth, as a suitable portion of things acquired to be devoted to religious purposes.

ABRAM AND THE KING OF SODOM, 21–24.

21. **King of Sodom said** — His northward journey to meet Abram is mentioned in verse 17, but his action was anticipated by that of Melchizedek. **Give me the persons**—Heb., *the soul,* the singular used collectively for all the rescued life of those taken captive.

take the goods to thyself. **22** And Abram said to the king of Sodom, I ᵏ have lifted up mine hand unto the LORD, the most high God, ¹the possessor of heaven and earth, **23** That ᵐ I will not *take* from a thread even to a shoelatchet, and that I will not take any thing that *is* thine, lest thou shouldest say, 1 have made Abram rich: **24** Save only that which the young men have eaten, and the portion of the men ⁿ which went with me, Aner, Eshcol, and Mamre; let them take their portion.

k Exodus 6. 8; Daniel 12. 7; Revelation 10. 5, 6.

l Verse 19; chap. 21. 33.——*m* So Esther 9. 15, 16.——*n* Verse 13.

22. I have lifted up mine hand—A solemn form of making oath before God. **Unto the Lord, the most high God**—Unto *Jehovah El Elion.* The God of Melchizedek was *El Elion,* (verse 19,) a name that first appears in this connexion; not *Elohim,* nor yet *Eloah.* Elion is mentioned by Sanchoniathon as the name of the Phenician deity, and was probably common among the early Semitic nations as the name of the Supreme God. But Abram knows God under another name, *Jehovah,* the God of gracious revelation and promise. Although as king and priest of the most high God, blessing Abram and receiving tithes from him, Melchizedek appears as one superior to "the friend of God," yet, as Kalisch well observes, "the religious enlightenment of the king of Salem was but a ray of the sun of Abram's faith, and scarcely sufficient as it was, in itself, entirely to dispel the darkness, it could not be intended to spread a light to distant regions." Abram can appropriately use the name *El Elion,* **possessor of heaven and earth,** thus repeating, with thankful recognition, the name of the God of Melchizedek, but he puts before it the NAME to him more sacred, the name of the God who had appeared to him in this land of promise, and to whom he had erected altars. Chap. xii, 7, 8; xiii, 18.

23. That I will not take—Literally, *If from a thread even to a shoelatchet, and if 1 take from all that is thine; and thou shalt not say—I have enriched Abram.* Observe the emotionality of Abram's language. In the face of temptation, and in possible danger of being misunderstood by those who could scarcely appreciate his lofty standpoint, he declares his holy vow not to take to himself any of the spoils. The particle *if* appears prominently in the ancient formulas of swearing. The full form appears in 1 Sam iii, 17: "God do so to thee, and more also, if, etc." "There is a marked difference between Abram's conduct to Melchizedek and his conduct to the king of Sodom. From Melchizedek he receives refreshment and treats him with honour and respect. Toward the king of Sodom he is distant and reserved. Probably the vicious lives of the inhabitants of Sodom made him careful not to lay himself under any obligation to the king, lest he should become too much associated with him and them."—*Speaker's Commentary.*

24. The young men—The trained ones of his own household. Comp. verse 14. **The men which went with me**—His allies in the war. Abram keeps himself from all entanglement or occasion of reproach; but he allows his warriors their natural and obvious right, and his allies to act their own pleasure.

CHAPTER XV.

GOD'S FULLER REVELATION TO ABRAM, 1-21.

The narrative of this chapter is remarkable for its visional symbolism and far-reaching lessons of divine revelation. Here, for the first time, occurs that profound expression, "the Word of Jehovah," significant of the self-revealing of God through Him who "was in the beginning with God." John i, 2. This "Word" is the more impressive here as coming to Abram in "a vision." Possibly Abram lay down to sleep under the open sky, heavy and despondent over the uncertainty of the divine promises touching his seed. In his dreams the Lord speaks loudly to him, and impresses the spoken word by a soul-stirring vision of his power. Comp. Num. xii, 6. He arouses from his

CHAPTER XV.

AFTER these things the word of the *a* Lord came unto Abram *b* in a vision, saying, Fear not, Abram: I am thy

a Dan. 10. 1; Acts 10. 10, 11.

b Chap. 26. 24; Dan. 10. 12; Luke 1. 13, 30.

sleep with the profound spell of the vision still upon him and gives utterance to the words of verses 2 and 3. Then "behold," (verse 4,) the WORD again speaks, and pledges him an heir, and under the power and leading of this Word, he cannot sleep, but rises and walks abroad under the night sky; and again the WORD tells him to look on high and number the stars, if he would know the number of his posterity. Verse 5. The fulness and force of the revelation dispel all doubt, and he passes from the gloomy state of dubious "fear" (verse 1) to the righteousness of faith. Verse 6. All the rest of the night he seems to have communed with God, and with the break of the morning asked to have his faith deepened and intensified into knowledge, (verse 8,) and in answer to that yearning, the covenant, by means of five representative sacrificial offerings, (verse 9,) is visibly established between Jehovah and Abram. Verses 10-18. Here we note the symbolism of *cutting* a covenant. All day long the "Friend of God" is busy in preparing the victims, and keeping off the birds of prey, (verse 11,) and the shadows of another evening begin to gather round him, when he falls into a deep, prophetic, trance-sleep, (verse 12,) in which his soul is made to feel the terror of some of the dark aspects of his vision. Along with that sense of horror comes the verbal prediction of Israel's bondage and exodus, together with the doctrine that God is the great ruler and judge of nations. Verses 13-16. The whole vision closes with the movement of smoke and fire symbols of God's presence between the pieces, (verse 17,) thus sealing the covenant, and giving Abram to "know of a surety" (comp. verses 8, 13) the promise of his great inheritance, and ten Canaanitish nations are mentioned as types of world-powers to be destroyed before the ultimate triumph of the chosen seed.

1. **After these things**—After the exciting events of the last chapter Abram returned to the oak grove of Mamre, and seems to have grown despondent. He had implicitly confided in Jehovah, and would not entangle himself with the nations around him beyond the simple alliances of mutual friendship. But where was his reward? The years passed on and he remained childless, and yet Jehovah had promised to make his seed as the dust of the earth. Chap. xiii, 16. It would have been only human, under such circumstances, to yield to doubts and fears, and the recent invasion of the Eastern kings may well have impressed him with a feeling of insecurity and danger. Under such circumstances a fresh revelation from Jehovah was especially opportune. **The word of the Lord came**—"This is the first time in which the **word** of the Lord is said to 'come'" (Heb., to *be*) unto man. The ancient Jews regarded all the manifestations of Jehovah as made through his Word, or through the Shechinah, and hence the Targums often translate *Lord* by *Word of the Lord* where there is such manifestation. God is also often said to reveal himself by his angel, or messenger; and yet this angel is identified with him, as Jacob wrestled with an angel in the form of man, (xxxii, 24,) who yet is called God. Chap. xxxii, 28-30. Hagar receives a communication from an angel whom yet she names God. Chap. xvi, 7, 13. The promised Messiah was to be the 'angel of mighty counsel,' (Isa. ix, 5, in LXX,) the 'angel of the covenant,' (Mal. iii. 1,) and when at last the 'Word was made flesh' these Old Testament adumbrations of the Incarnation were understood as they could not have been by patriarchs and prophets. The God revealed was ever the Word, afterwards Incarnate, although they knew it not."—HENGST. *Christol.*, iii, 2. **Vision**—All the incidents of this chapter may have passed before Abram in vision, that is, "in a state of ecstasy by an inward spiritual intuition, and that not in a nocturnal vision, as

e shield, *and* thy exceeding d great reward. **2** And Abram said, Lord God, what wilt thou give me, e seeing I go childless, and the steward of my house is this Eliezer of Damascus? **3** And Abram said, Behold, to me thou hast given no seed: and, lo, f one born in my house is mine heir. **4** And, behold, the

c Psalm 3. 3 ; 5. 12; 84. 11 ; 91. 4 ; 119. 114.—— e Acts 7. 5.——
d Psalm 16. 5 ; 59. 11 ; Proverbs 11. 18. —— f Chap. 14. 14.

in chap. xlvi, 2, but in the daytime."—*Keil*. But more likely it continued through one day and parts of two nights. See note at the beginning of the chapter. **Fear not.**—Why this admonition? 1) The flesh shrinks when the purest are brought face to face with God. So Daniel, (Dan x. 19,) Mary, (Luke i, 30,) and John, (Rev. i, 17,) shrank before their wondrous revelations, and heard the strengthening words, "Fear not." 2) Abram had just fought and vanquished the confederate kings of the East (chap. xiv,) in order to rescue Lot, his "brother," and would naturally fear a rally and return of these powerful chiefs. **I am thy shield** — A mighty defence against all earthly foes. With such a cover, why **fear? Exceeding great reward**—Or, *thy reward shall be great exceedingly ;* grow greater and greater with the coming years. "There is here a double promise, 1) of protection from evil, and 2) bestowal of good. God would be a **shield** between him and all his foes, and would be himself a reward 'great exceedingly' (not simply bestow rewards) for his obedience and trust. He was childless and landless, but Jehovah himself, the Self-existent, would be his inheritance."—*Newhall*.

2. Abram said — Abram's words here betray a sort of doubt and some trouble. **Lord God** — Heb., *Adonai Jehovah*, words occurring in this connexion here for the first time. The same combination of the words occur elsewhere in the Pentateuch only at verse 8, Deut. iii, 24, and ix, 26 ; and in all these instances the words are a direct address to God. **What wilt thou give me**—What is that "great reward" to be? All the riches of the earth are worthless to me without an heir. **I go childless**—The expression may mean either, I *continue* childless, that is, go on in life without issue ; or, I *go forth* childless ; that is, as one of the Targums has it, *go forth out of the world* without an heir. **The steward of my house**—Heb., *A son of possession of my house*. The one who would have the possessions of my house, on my decease, would be my principal servant, and overseer of my entire household. **This Eliezer of Damascus**—Heb., *this Damascus Eliezer ;* or, *he of Damascus, Eliezer*. This Eliezer is commonly supposed to be the eldest servant of Abram's house mentioned in chap. xxiv, 2, and the supposition is every way probable. When Abram departed from Haran and came into the land of Canaan he would naturally have passed through Damascus. An old tradition related by Nicolaus of Damascus, (see Josephus, *Ant.* i, 7,) associates the Hebrew patriarch with that city, and this Eliezer may have been born in Abram's household while he tarried in or near Damascus, and thence have been known afterward as *the Damascene*. Kitto's notion, (see Kitto's *Cyc.*,) that he was a relative of Abram nearer than Lot, and therefore first heir to his possessions, seems farfetched, and altogether unnecessary. The patriarchal law of inheritance seems to have preferred the members of the household before any other relations. The Mosaic law of inheritance (Num. xxvii, 8–11) was a later institution ; but even if prevalent in Abram's time, it applied to landed estates rather than moveable possessions. Abram was now utterly cut off from native land and kindred, and not yet owning a foot of land, he would not contemplate the passing over of his flocks and herds and other riches to any but his own dependents.

3. One born in my house — Heb., *a son of my house*. Abram here refers again to Eliezer, whom he has just called *a son of possession of my house ;* and this confirms our view stated above, that the oldest servant of a childless patriarch was regarded as the principal heir.

About B. C. 1913.   CHAPTER XV.   187

word of the LORD *came* unto him, saying, This shall not be thine heir; but he that ᵍ shall come forth out of thine own bowels shall be thine heir. 5 And he brought him forth abroad, and said, Look now toward heaven, and ʰ tell the ⁱ stars, if thou be able to number them : and he said unto him, ᵏ So shall thy seed be.

6 And he ˡ believed in the LORD ; and he ᵐ counted it to him for righteousness. 7 And he said unto him, I *am* the LORD that ⁿ brought thee out of ᵒ Ur of the Chaldees, ᵖ to give thee this land to inherit it. 8 And he said, Lord GOD, ᑫ whereby shall I know that I shall inherit it? 9 And he said unto him, Take

---

g 2 Sam. 7. 12; 16. 11; 2 Chron. 32. 21.— *h* Psa. 147. 4.—*i* Jer. 33. 22.—*k* Chap. 22. 17; Exod. 32. 13; Deut. 1. 10; 10. 22; 1 Chron. 27. 23; Rom. 4. 18; Heb. 11. 12; see chap. 13. 16.— *l* Rom. 4. 3, 9, 22; Gal. 3. 6; James 2. 23.

m Psalm 106. 31.——*n* Chapter 12. 1.——*o* Chapter 11. 28, 31. —— *p* Psalm 105. 42, 44; Romans 4. 13. —— *q* See chapter 24. 13, 14; Judges 6. 17, 37; 1 Samuel 14. 9. 10; 2 Kings 20. 8; Luke 1. 18.

---

4. **Behold**—How vivid the revelation! **This shall not be thine heir** —Such an express answer touching his **heir** was potent to quell all further doubt and fear.

5. **Brought him forth abroad**— Whether in vision, or on the night following the day of the vision of verse 1, has been disputed. Either supposition is allowable, and some think the whole transaction occupied two nights and one day. Another view is, to regard the whole transaction up to verse 12 as a vision of the daytime. See note at the beginning of the chapter. **Tell the stars**—Rather, *number the stars.* The Lord had promised him posterity numberless as the grains of dust, (xiii, 16;) now he compares their number to the stars. "God does not tell him how, but a third time, more emphatically and sublimely than ever, the great promise is repeated, and Abram is led forth, 'whether in the body or out of the body' it matters not, to look into the deep Asiatic heavens, and the stars are pointed out to him as emblems of his seed. **So shall thy seed be**—In numbers, in heavenly splendor. No proof or evidence whatever is offered him, nothing but the naked word of God."—*Newhall.*

6. **He believed**—"Heb., *and he trusted in Jehovah, and he counted it to him righteousness,*" or *it was counted,* (one counted,) so Sept., followed by Paul in Rom. iv, 3. A weighty comment of the inspired historian, which unifies the patriarchal, Mosaic, and Christian dispensations, as shown by Paul in the Epistle to the Romans. He is landless and childless, yet in the word of JEHOVAH, the SELF-EXISTENT, he has land and seed. This special act of trust in God, this signal instance of naked faith, (not Abram's general or habitual faith,) was reckoned as righteous : not only by God, but in all generations of the faithful it stands forth as a monument of Abram's righteousness. There is a parallel passage in Psa. cvi, 30, where the deed of Phinehas, in executing God's judgment, is commended, 'and that was counted to him for righteousness,' that is, this single act called for God's special approval. So here, Abram's trust in God's simple word is stamped as righteousness, because such faith is the root of all virtues, it is the central scource of the godly life, without which all outward works are as plants having no root. As Abram, in darkness and discouragement trusted God for the blessings promised him, and thus received God's approval and this monumental position among believers, so, as Paul shows us, shall we be reckoned righteous if, in our darkness, we believe on Him who raised up Jesus our Lord from the dead, Rom. iv, 24."—*Newhall.*

7. **I . . . brought thee out of Ur** —Jehovah now reminds Abram of the past, and assures him of the former pledge to give him that land for an inheritance. As if to say : "I have had a purpose with thee from the beginning of thy wanderings, and will I be likely to let it fail?"

8. **Whereby shall I know**—Abram would pass from belief to knowledge. He would have some visible token or sign. "Even where there is much faith, a man may distrust himself ; may feel that, though now the belief is strong, yet ere long the first impression, and so the firm conviction, may fade away. Thus Gideon, (Judges vi, 17,)

me a heifer of three years old, and a she goat of three years old, and a ram of three years old, and a turtle-dove, and a young pigeon. **10** And he took unto him all these, and ʳ divided them in the midst, and laid each piece one against another: but ˢ the birds divided he not. **11** And when the fowls came down upon the carcasses, Abram drove them away. **12** And when the sun was going down, ᵗ a deep sleep fell upon Abram; and, lo, a horror of great darkness fell upon him. **13** And he said unto Abram, Know of a surety ᵘ that thy seed shall be a stranger in a land *that is* not theirs, and shall serve them; and ᵛ they shall afflict them four hundred years; **14** And also that nation, whom they shall serve,

---

r Jer. 34. 18, 19.——*s* Lev. 1. 17.——*t* Chap. 2. 21; Job 4. 13.

u Exod. 12. 40; Psa. 105. 23; Acts 7. 6.—— *v* Exod. 1. 11; Psa. 105. 25.

Hezekiah, (2 Kings xx, 8,) the blessed Virgin, (Luke i, 34,) asked a sign in confirmation of their faith, and, as here to Abram, it was graciously given them."—*Speaker's Commentary.*

9. Take me—Select for me. Not any of the animals taken at random is a suitable victim for sacrifice, or for symbolic revelations. **Heifer . . . goat . . . ram . . .** — Three separate animals representing the three classes of animals suitable for sacrificial offering, and each to be **three years old**, the age of full maturity and vigour. The fowls suitable for sacrifice were to be represented by **a turtle-dove and a young pigeon.** These two kinds of fowls were also adopted among the Mosaic offerings. Comp. Lev. i, 14; v, 7; xii, 8.

10. Divided them in the midst— Cut them into two halves, and placed the portions opposite to each other, with space enough for one to walk between. This explains the Hebrew expression בָּרַת בְּרִית, *to cut a covenant.* See verse 18. The two parts of the victim seem to have represented the two parties to the covenant; and when the two parties thus covenanting passed between the pieces, their union was represented as sealed by the blood of life. Comp. Jer. xxxiv, 18, and see further on verse 17. **Birds divided he not**—So also the Mosaic law, Lev. i, 17. Probably Abram laid the dove on one side and the pigeon on the other, as if they were two pieces.

11. Fowls came down—Birds of prey, seeking to devour **the carcasses.** These unclean birds may be regarded as types of the enemies of the chosen seed, and Abram's driving them away until the darkness of evening came on, was a sign that the covenant people would be delivered from the destruction threatened by their foes. Some see in these birds of prey a type of the Egyptians.

12. When the sun was going down—Heb., *was about to go down.* All day long had Abram been busy selecting the victims, slaying them, and placing them in order. See introductory note to the chapter. Now night comes on again, and **a deep sleep fell upon Abram**—A profound slumber, like that which fell on Adam when Jehovah God would take one of his ribs. Gen. ii, 21. This sleep was superinduced by divine agency, and is called in the Sept. *an ecstasy.* It doubtless served a special purpose in conveying or impressing the word of God upon his soul. **And, lo, a horror of great darkness fell upon him**—Both the **horror** and the **darkness** seem to have been a deepening effect of the manner of the vision. The language used cannot legitimately mean that "when he awoke he was terrified by the dense darkness which surrounded him."—*Kalisch.* The horror and darkness were rather a part of the vision of his sleep.

13. Thy seed shall be a stranger —The Egyptian bondage is here foretold. That oppressive, but important, period in the history of the chosen seed, and its duration, is stated in round numbers as **four hundred years.** In Exod. xii, 40, it is said that "the sojourning of the children of Israel, who dwelt in Egypt, was four hundred and thirty years." There we have the exact statement of history; here the more general one of prophecy. For the question of chronology here involved, see note on Exod. xii, 40.

14. That nation . . . will I judge

About B. C. 1913.   CHAPTER XV.   189

ʷ will I judge: and afterward ˣ shall they come out with great substance. 15 And ʸ thou shalt go ᶻ to thy fathers in peace; ᵃ thou shalt be buried in a good old age. 16 But ᵇ in the fourth generation they shall come hither again: for the iniquity ᶜ of the Amorites ᵈ is not yet full. 17 And it came to pass, that, when the sun went down, and it was dark, behold a smoking furnace, and ¹ a burning lamp

w Exod. 6. 6; Deut. 6. 22. —— x Exod. 12. 36; Psa. 105. 37. —— y Job 5. 26. —— z Acts 13. 36. —— a Chap. 25. 8.

b Exod. 12. 40. —— c 1 Kings 21. 26. —— d Dan. 8. 23; Matt. 23. 32; 1 Thess. 2. 16. —— 1 Heb. a lamp of fire.

—As seen in the history of the plagues of Egypt. **Come out with great substance**—See Exod. xii, 31-36.

15. **Go to thy fathers**—A profound expression, suggestive of reunion in another and immortal life. Comp. chaps. xxv, 8; xxxix, 29; xlix, 33. To go to one's father or people implies that they were somewhere living still. That the words do not here mean being buried in the ancestral tomb is evident from the fact that Abram was not buried with his father; and then, in all the passages cited above, the *burial* is mentioned as subsequent and distinct. **A good old age**—One hundred and seventy-five years old; chap. xxv, 7, 8.

16. **In the fourth generation** — Evidently reckoning one hundred years as an average generation among these patriarchs. **For the iniquity of the Amorites is not yet full** — Another sentence of profound significance. **The Amorites** were the most powerful and widespread of all the inhabitants of Canaan, and are here named as representing all the Canaanitish tribes. Their origin is noted in chap. x, 16, where see note. Those who "dwelt in Hazezontamar" had been recently smitten by the eastern invaders. Chapter xiv, 7. But Abram was at this time confederate with one of their princes, (xiv, 13,) and the presence of such saintly characters as Melchizedek preserved the many from utter moral degeneracy and ruin. But Melchizedek would depart, and Abram's seed be removed from the land, and the nations would fill up the cup of their iniquity and become ripe for destruction. In this verse Murphy notes the following lessons: "1) The Lord foreknows the moral character of men. 2) In his providence he administers the affairs of nations on the principles of moral rectitude. 3) Nations are spared until their iniquity is full. 4) They are then cut off in retributive justice."

17. **When the sun went down, and it was dark**—The progress of time is marked; in verse 12, when the sun was going down; here when it **went down**, and darkness was on all things. The Hebrew word for *darkness* in this verse is different from that so rendered in verse 12. There it means soul darkness; here night's darkness. **A smoking furnace**—Heb., *an oven of smoke.* According to Jahn, the *tannur*, here rendered fur-

ANCIENT EGYPTIAN OVEN AND BAKERS.

nace, was a moveable oven, constructed of brick, and plastered within and without with clay. The **burning lamp** is not to be regarded as another and distinct object, separate from the furnace. A better version is, *flames of fire.* The thing seen was a moving oven, from the top of which issued a flame of fire in the midst of a cloud of smoke. Like the pillar of cloud and fire, (Exod. xiii, 21,) this smoke and flame were symbols of the presence and power of Jehovah; not solely "symbols of the wrath of God," (Keil,) nor yet to be construed as "the smoke of destruc-

that ᵉpassed between those pieces. **18** In that same day the LORD ʳmade a covenant with Abram, saying, ᵍUnto thy seed have I given this land, from the river of Egypt unto the great river, the river Euphrates: **19** The Kenites, and the Kenizzites, and the Kadmoites, **20** And the Hittites, and the Perizzites,

e Jer. 34. 18, 19.——*f* Chap. 24. 7.——*g* Chap. 12. 7; 13. 15; 26. 4; Exod. 23. 31; Num. 34. 3; Deut. 1. 7; 11. 24; 34. 4; Josh. 1. 4; 1 Kings 4. 21; 2 Chron. 9. 26; Neh. 9. 8; Psa. 105. 11; Isa. 27. 12.

tion, and the light of salvation."—*Murphy.* All these thoughts lie in the background, but the great thought is, that Jehovah himself, by these symbols of his personal presence and manifestation, condescends to covenant with Abram, and **passed between those pieces.** God's penal judgments may well be symbolized by a smoking furnace, (comp. chap. xix, 28, Mal. iv, 1,) and flaming fire may denote either the consuming wrath (Psa. lxxxix, 46, Lam. ii, 3) or the salvation of God, (Isa. lxii, 1:) and Jehovah's presence and power among his covenant people would be displayed in both these ways—avenging them on their enemies when they were injured, and chastening and smiting them when they sinned.

18. Made a covenant—Heb., *cut a covenant,* in allusion to the cutting of the victims into pieces and passing between them. Abram had passed between the pieces before the sun went down, and now Jehovah completes the cutting of the covenant by causing the burning symbols of his presence to pass between the pieces and repeating, for the fourth time, **Unto thy seed have I given this land.** Comp. verses 7, 12, and chap. vii, 13, 15. The utmost boundaries of the land are here given as **the river of Egypt** on the southwest, **unto the great river, the river Euphrates,** on the north-east. The designation of the Euphrates as **the great river** favours the opinion that **the river of Egypt** is not the Nile, which was also great, but the wady-el-Arish, called the river (or *brook* נחל) of Egypt, in Josh. xv, 4. This view is further confirmed by the fact that the dominion of Israel did actually extend, in Solomon's time, between these borders, (see 1 Kings iv, 24,) but never extended to the Nile. Most commentators, however, understand the Nile here, and think these two great rivers are mentioned in a general way, as representing the two great nations or world-powers on the east and west of Canaan.

19. **Kenites** . . . **Kenizzites** . . . **Kadmonites**—Ten nations are now mentioned as occupying this vast territory, seven of whom (those mentioned verses 20 and 21) have been previously noticed. The number ten, occurring in such a prophecy as this, may well be understood to have some symbolistic significance. It seems to be the symbolic number of completed development in godless worldly empire and rule, as the toes of the image in Nebuchadnezzar's dream, (Dan. ii, 42,) and the ten horns of the fourth beast. Dan. vii, 7, 20, 24. Comp. Rev. xiii, 1, xvii, 3, 12. These ten heathen nations rise in prophetic vision before Abram, as representing all that long line of opposing world-forces which shall make war upon the godly seed, but in the end of the ages be overcome, so that "the kingdom and dominion, and the greatness of the kingdom under the whole heaven, shall be given to the people of the saints of the Most High." Dan. vii, 27. "**The Kenites** inhabited rocky and mountainous tracts in the south and south-west of Palestine, near the territory of the Amalekites. Num. xxiv, 21. They may have spread, in a western direction, to the land of Egypt; so that by their expulsion the frontiers of the promised land would have nearly touched the valley of the Nile."—*Kalisch.* Moses's father-in-law was of this tribe, and some of his descendants journeyed with the children of Israel, (Judg. i, 16, see note,) and settled in the north of Palestine. Judg. iv, 11; v, 24. In Saul's time a friendly feeling was still shown toward them on account of ancient kindness, 1 Sam. xv, 6; comp. 1 Sam. xxvii, 11, xxx, 29. Of **the Kenizzites** we have no other mention, and they were probably destroyed at an early date. The name of **the Kadmonites** would seem to designate them as *eastern,* and it is plaus-

and the Rephaim. **21** And the Amorites, and the Canaanites, and the Girgashites, and the Jebusites.

CHAPTER XVI.

NOW Sarai, Abram's wife, ^a bare him no children: and she had a handmaid, ^b an Egyptian, whose name was ^c Hagar. **2** ^dAnd Sarai said unto Abram, Behold now, the LORD ^e hath

---

a Chap. 15. 2, 3.——*b* Chap. 21. 9.——*c* Gal. 4. 24.——*d* Chap. 30. 3.——*e* Chap. 20. 18; 30. 2; 1 Sam.

---

ibly conjectured that they occupied the eastern part of the territory here given to Abram's seed. No other mention of their name occurs.

20. **Hittites**—Descendants of Heth. See on chap. x, 15. **Perizzites**—See on chap. xiii, 7. **Rephaim**—See on chap. xiv, 5. For an account of the tribes mentioned in verse 21, see on chap. x, 16, 19.

CHAPTER XVI.
HAGAR AND ISHMAEL, 1–16.

It is sad to pass from such a sublime elevation as that into which we have seen Abram lifted in the last chapter, to the low moral plain in which he next appears before us. It would seem that the presence and force of the divine revelation and promise begat a burning expectation, which grew impatient at the long delay. This impatience shows itself in Sarai, and prompts her to resort to an unhallowed expedient in order to build her house. The polygamous conduct here recorded is not to be defended or even apologized for. It had its reason and occasion, but, like other immoralities in Abram's life, is to be condemned as contrary to God's order. Comp. chap. ii, 24, and Mark x, 2–12. The history of polygamy every-where shows how the unholy practice breeds mischief, strife, bitterness, and sorrow. In this short chapter all these evils are seen to flow from a single instance of bigamy in one of its mildest forms. Polygamy has ever been practiced among the descendants of Ishmael, and has been to them a moral and physical curse, never more manifest than at the present time.

1. **Handmaid**—A family servant, restrained me from bearing: I pray thee, ^f go in unto my maid; it may be that I may ¹ obtain children by her. And Abram ^g hearkened to the voice of Sarai. **3** And Sarai, Abram's wife, took Hagar her maid the Egyptian, after Abram ^h had dwelt ten years in the land of Canaan, and gave her to her husband Abram to be his wife.

4 And he went in unto Hagar, and

---

1. 5, 6.——*f* So chap. 30. 3, 9.——1 Heb. *be builded by her*.——*g* Chap. 3. 17.——*h* Chap. 12. 5.

---

whose special duty it was to wait upon the mistress of the household. The Sept. has παιδίσκη, *a young girl*, or a young female slave. From her being here called **an Egyptian**, we infer that Abram obtained her during his sojourn in Egypt, when he received from Pharaoh "menservants and maidservants." Chap. xii, 16. The name **Hagar** means flight. So, also, the well-known Arabic word *hezrah* or *hegira*, used so commonly in the flight of Mohammed from Mecca. It may have been given to Sarai's handmaid after her flight from her mistress, and used here proleptically; or it may have been given her on account of her departure out of Egypt.

2. **It may be that I may obtain children by her**—Heb., *Perhaps I shall be builded from her*. The word rendered **obtain children** is בנה, *to build*, from which comes the Hebrew word בן, *ben, son*. Hence *to be builded* means, to become a house; to beget a family. See Ruth iv, 11, note. Sarai's expedient to obtain offspring was according to an ancient custom still prevalent in the East. Comp. chap. xxx, 3. The child of her waiting-maid, thus given to her husband, she might call her own, and her impatient haste to see the word of God fulfilled urges Abram into this unholy measure. Sarai's zeal, like Eve's hasty and mistaken expectation of the promised seed, (chap. iv, 1, note,) is a fitting type of the impatience and feverish excitement of New Testament times touching the promised millennial kingdom.

3. **Ten years in . . . Canaan**—Abram was now eighty-five years old, (compare verse 16, chap. xii, 4,) and Sarai seventy-five. Chap. xvii, 17.

she conceived: and when she saw that she had conceived, her mistress was ¹ despised in her eyes. **5** And Sarai said unto Abram, My wrong *be* upon thee: I have given my maid into thy bosom; and when she saw that she had conceived, I was despised in her eyes:

ᵏ the LORD judge between me and thee. **6** ¹ But Abram said unto Sarai, ᵐ Behold, thy maid *is* in thy hand; do to her ² as it pleaseth thee. And when Sarai ³ dealt hardly with her, ⁿ she fled from her face.

7 And the angel of the LORD found

---

i 2 Samuel 6. 16; Proverbs 30. 21, 23. — *k* Chapter 31. 53; 1 Samuel 24. 12.—*l* Proverbs 15. 1; 1 Peter 3. 7.

m Job 2. 6; Psa. 106. 41, 42; Jer. 38. 5.— 2 Heb. that which is *good in thine eyes.*— 3 Heb. *afflicted her.*—*n* Exod. 2. 15.

---

4. Her mistress was despised— Sarai is thus the first to feel the natural curse of the adulterous union. "Among the Hebrews barrenness was esteemed a reproach, (see chap. xix, 31, xxx, 1, 23, Lev. xx, 20,) and fecundity a special honour and blessing of God, (chapter xxi, 6, xxiv, 60, Exod. xxiii, 26, Deut. vii, 14 ;) and such is still the feeling in the East. But very probably Hagar may have thought that now Abram would love and honour her more than he did her mistress. Comp. chap. xxix, 33."—*Speaker's Com.*

5. My wrong be upon thee— Sarai, stung by feelings of jealousy, and suspecting that Abram's affections were turned from herself to her handmaid, complains to him of the wrong she suffers. She assumes that it is his place to redress the wrong, and in passionate haste implies that he has failed to do so because of his devotion to Hagar. **The Lord judge** — "She would leave his conduct to the judgment of Jehovah, more as an appeal to his conscience than as a decided condemnation."—*Lange.*

6. Thy maid is in thy hand—By this he repudiates the implication of having wronged his wife by exalting another to her place in his affections, or in his household. Sarai's maid is still her own. At her proposal he had treated her as a wife, and now she has her at disposal to treat her as she pleased. **Dealt hardly with her**— Treated her with such oppressive rigour and humiliation that she **fled from her face,** resolved not to submit to such affliction. "The proud, unyielding passion of the Ishmaelite for freedom shows its characteristic feature in their ancestress."—*Lange.*

7. The angel of the Lord—Here we meet, for the first time, with this much-debated expression—מַלְאַךְ יְהֹוָה, *angel of Jehovah ;* but we are not to assume that this was the first appearance of this angel. Comp. chap. xii, 7, note. There have been two different opinions of this mysterious angel: one that he was a created angel, a ministering spirit, (Heb. i, 14,) sent forth to speak the message of Jehovah, and to act in his name; the other that he was a manifestation of God in human form, and accordingly Jehovah himself, speaking in his own divine name. Each of these opinions has been maintained under two forms. Of those who hold that he was a created or ordinary angel, 1) some regard him as an angel specially commissioned at each different appearance; not necessarily the same angel every time: 2) another class regard him as the same individual angel, here appearing as Jehovah's angel; again, as Captain of the Lord's host, (Josh. v, 14,) and in Dan. xii, 1, as the great Prince of the covenant people. Of those, again, who hold him to be Jehovah himself, in human form, 1) one class of interpreters understand the word *Jehovah,* in the term *angel of Jehovah,* as a genitive of apposition; that is, *angel-Jehovah,* or *Jehovah-angel ;* a mysterious and miraculous manifestation of the God of Abram. This would be a sort of Sabellian exposition. 2) Others distinguish between Jehovah and his angel as between sender and sent, and see in the latter the Old Testament administration of the second Person of the Trinity, the Logos or Word of God. The main question to determine is, whether this was a created angel or Jehovah himself,—a question on which devout and eminent divines have divided. On the principle that "what one does through another, he himself does," many exegetes, with much show of reason, hold that the angel of Jehovah was a created spirit, capable of assuming human form and modes of life, (comp. chap. xviii, 2, 8,) sent forth as the representative of Jehovah and authorized to speak in his name. Accordingly such language as that of verses 10 and 13, and chap. xviii, 13, 14, and many similar passages, is to be understood as Jehovah speaking by his angel. In chap. xxi, 17, where the *angel of God* (*Elohim*) again addresses Hagar, there is nothing to indicate that the speaker was other than an ordinary angel. And the expression *angel of Jehovah* occurs in many other places where there is no necessity of understanding that the angel is Jehovah, but quite the contrary. See Num. xxii, 22; 1 Kings i, 3, 15; Zech. i, 11, 12, 13; iii, 5, 6. Further, the angel of the Lord, in the New Testament, (ἄγγελος κυρίου,) is an ordinary angel, (Luke i, 11; ii, 9, etc.;) and Kurtz asks, "Why should the 'angel of the Lord' who announces the birth of John the Baptist be different in nature from him who announces that of Samson? Why should the 'angel of the Lord' who smites Herod Agrippa, so that he dies, be different in nature from him who, in one night, destroyed the host of Sennacherib? Why should the 'angel of the Lord' who encourages Paul in his bonds be different in nature from him who comforts Hagar when she is driven forth?" If this view be adopted, it matters little whether we regard the angel as one chosen messenger for every occasion, or different angels of heaven, each selected for his separate and special mission.

But while some passages readily admit and favour the view that Jehovah's angel is only an ordinary angel, there are passages in which the language is not fully met by such an exposition. The other and profounder view, according to which the angel of Jehovah is the revealing Word of God,—the Old Testament gracious manifestation of Him who in the fulness of time became flesh in the person of Jesus Christ,—is maintained by the following considerations: 1) The sacred writer uses the terms Jehovah and angel of Jehovah interchangeably. Compare verses 9, 10, 11, 13; chap. xviii, 13, 16, 17, 22, 33; xlviii, 15, 16. 2) While other angels are careful not to identify themselves with God, (see chap. xix, 13, Rev. xix, 10, xxii, 8, 9,) this angel speaks so absolutely in God's name and person as to exclude the idea that he is an ordinary messenger. See verse 10; xviii, 17, 20, 21; xxii, 12, etc. 3) The solemn and explicit language of Exod. xxiii, 20–23, is utterly inappropriate to any created angel, —especially the language of verse 21, "Beware of him, and obey his voice, provoke him not; for he will not pardon your transgressions: for my name is in him." Comp. Exod. xxxii, 34; xxxiii, 14; Isa. lxiii, 9. 4) He allows prayers and sacrifices to be offered unto him, as if he were Jehovah himself. Chap. xviii, 22–32; Judges vi, 11–22; xiii, 19, 20.

This view of the angel of Jehovah is very ancient. It was a part of the theology of the ancient synagogue, according to which this angel was the *Shekinah*—the manifested power and mediation of God in the world. This was the doctrine of the *Metatron*, who was regarded as an emanation from God, equal with him, and in whom he revealed himself to man. This doctrine, divested of some of its later foreign elements, was adopted by most of the Fathers of the early Christian Church, and is held by the majority of evangelical divines of the present day.

We should not deem it strange that thus early in the history of the covenant there should have been such a mysterious revelation of God by the divine angel of his presence. The doctrine is not contrary to the idea of a progressive revelation, for these ancient administrations of the Word of God evidence no higher a consciousness of God and his self-manifestation than the deep symbolism of sacrifice and covenanting. Nor are we to suppose that the mediation of this angel would supersede the necessity of the ministry of other angels. Many of

her by a fountain of water in the wilderness, ° by the fountain in the way to ᵖ Shur. **8** And he said, Hagar, Sarai's maid, whence camest thou? and whither wilt thou go? And she said, I flee from the face of my mistress Sarai. **9** And the angel of the LORD said unto her, Return to thy mistress, and ᵠ submit thyself under her hands. **10** And the angel of the LORD said unto her, ʳ I will multiply thy seed exceedingly, that it shall not be numbered for multitude. **11** And the angel of the LORD said unto her, Behold, thou *art* with child, and shalt bear a son, ˢ and shalt call his name ⁴ Ishmael; because the LORD hath

o Chap. 25. 18.——*p* Exod. 15. 22.——*q* Titus 2. 9; 1 Pet. 2. 18.——*r* Chap. 17. 20; 21. 18; 25. 12.

s Chap. 17. 19; Matt. 1. 21; Luke 1. 13, 31.—— 4 That is, *God shall hear*.

these latter accompanied him in his ways, and who the particular angel was, in any instance, must be determined from the context. Even the title *angel of Jehovah* may, in some passages, be used of any ministering angel, and, as Keil observes, "where the context furnishes no criterion, it must remain undecided." Such passages as Psalms xxxiv. 7, xxxv. 5, 6, where the angel of Jehovah is not more particularly described, or Num. xx, 16, where the words are general and indefinite, furnish no evidence that *the* angel of Jehovah, who proclaimed himself on his appearance as one with God, was not in reality equal with God; unless we are to adopt as the rule for interpretation of Scripture the inverted principle, that clear and definite statements are to be explained by those that are indefinite and obscure.

As to the less-important question, whether in *angel of Jehovah* we are to understand the latter word as a genitive of apposition, or as defining more fully the word angel, we believe the latter to be the true construction. We naturally distinguish between the angel and Jehovah, although this distinction is one of the profoundest mysteries of Deity. Like the Word of God in John i, 1, this Angel was with God and was God. So in the expressions "servant of Jehovah," and "messenger of Jehovah," there is the same obvious distinction as between sender and sent.

The angel . . . found her—It has been often asked why the angel of Jehovah should have appeared first to an Egyptian bondmaid. But that this was the first appearance of this angel is a pure assumption. See note on chap. xii, 7. Nevertheless, would it not be just as well to ask, Why should Jesus, after the resurrection, have appeared first to Mary Magdalene? Why not rather to his mother, or else to that disciple whom he loved? The redeeming angel, (chap. xlviii, 16,) whose great work is to seek and to save the lost, **found** this lost child **by the fountain in the way to Shur.** The wilderness of Shur extended between Beer-sheba on the north-east, and Egypt on the south-west. Into this wilderness the Israelites entered after they had passed the Red Sea. Exod. xv, 22, note. Hagar, the Egyptian, would naturally have fled by the most direct route to Egypt, which lay through this desert.

8 **Sarai's maid**—The words were calculated to remind her that she was not her own, nor yet Abram's wife. **Whence . . . whither**—These questions were adapted to arouse her conscience and her fears.

9. **Return . . . submit** — The only way to attain the true freedom and independence. The word rendered **submit thyself** is the Hithpael form of the verb rendered *dealt hardly* in verse 6. עֲנִי, rendered *affliction* in verse 11, is from the same root. The sense is: Go back, and allow thyself to be afflicted under the hands of thy mistress. Her reward for such self-humiliation is announced in the next three verses.

11. **Ishmael** — The name means *God will hear*, and would ever remind Hagar how Jehovah heard her affliction. Compare 1 Sam. i, 20, note. "Misery sighs; the sighs ascend to God; hence misery itself, if not sent as a curse, is a voiceless prayer to God. But this is true especially of the misery of Hagar, who had learned to pray in the house of Abram."—*Lange.*

CHAPTER XVI.

heard thy affliction. **12** 'And he will be a wild man; his hand *will be* against every man, and every man's hand against him: ᵘ and he shall dwell in the presence of all his brethren. **13** And she called the name of the LORD that spake unto her, Thou God seest me: for she said, Have I also here looked after him ᵛ that seeth me? **14** Wherefore the well was called ʷ ᵇ Beer-lahai-roi: behold, *it is* ˣ between Kadesh and Bered. **15** And ʸ Hagar bare Abram a son: and Abram called his son's name, which Hagar bare, ᶻ Ishmael. **16** And Abram *was* fourscore and six years old, when Hagar bare Ishmael to Abram.

---

t Chap. 21. 20. —— *u* Chap. 25. 18. —— *v* Chap. 31. 42. —— *w* Chap. 24. 62; 25. 11. —— 5 That is, *The well of him that liveth* and *seeth me*. —— *x* Num. 13. 26.—— *y* Gal. 4. 22.——*z* Verse 11.

---

12. He will be a wild man—Heb., *a wild ass man*, that is, a man like the wild, free, untamable creature described in Job xxxix, 5–8, that makes the wilderness his dwelling, and "scorneth the multitude of the city, neither regardeth he the crying of the driver." Hagar is to be the mother of a numerous and mighty race, but not of the chosen seed. Her progeny were to become the lawless rovers of the desert. "The character of the Ishmaelites, or the Bedouins," observes Kalisch, "could not be described more aptly or more powerfully. They have preserved it almost unaltered during three or four thousand years. Against them alone time seems to have no sickle, and the conqueror's sword no edge. They have defied the softening influences of civilization, and mocked the attacks of the invader. Ungovernable and roaming, obeying no law but their spirit of adventure, regarding all mankind as their enemies, whom they must either attack with their spears or elude with their faithful steeds, and cherishing their deserts as heartily as they despise the constraint of towns and communities; the Bedouins are the outlaws among the nations." **His hand... against every man**—Such a wild and lawless race could never be at peace with a civilized community, and hence, whenever there is any contact with other peoples, there is continual discord. They are also known to have constant feuds among themselves. **In the presence of all his brethren** — The **brethren** here are doubtless to be understood of other descendants of Abram, especially those by Keturah, (see chap. xxv, 1–4,) and the fact that the descendants of Ishmael have ever occupied the deserts south and east of Palestine is to serve in interpreting these words. Many critics understand the phrase **in the presence of** as equivalent to *east of*, a meaning which the words will bear. The persons of whom the words are thus used are supposed to be looking toward the sunrise. But the expression may with equal propriety be used in the sense of contiguity. The Ishmaelites occupied the country in front of the Hebrews,—bordering on the south and east, and especially dwelt in immediate proximity to the Midianites, Edomites, and other descendants of Abram.

13. **Thou God seest me**—Translate, *And she called the name of Jehovah, who spoke unto her, Thou art a God of sight*, (that is, capable of being seen,) *for she said, "Have I also hither seen after sight?"* The words of Hagar here are emotional and broken, and, therefore, obscure. The meaning seems to be: "Jehovah is truly a God that may be seen, for I also have seen him, and yet here I am seeing still after having seen God!" She is astonished that she has had this vision of God and yet lives. Compare chap. xxxii, 30; Exod. xxxiii, 20; Judges xiii, 21. The common version follows the Sept. and Vulg., and mistakes the noun רֳאִי for a participle. But if it were designed for a participle, we should have the form רֹאֲנִי.

14. **Beer-lahai-roi** — בְּאֵר לַחַי רֹאִי, *well of life of sight*, or, *well of living vision;* that is: well where one saw God and remained alive after the vision. This well is mentioned again in chaps. xxiv, 62; xxv, 11. Its location, **between Kadesh and Bered**, is now unknown. On the identification of **Kadesh** with *Ain Qadees*, see note on chap. xiv, 7. The spring *el Muweileh*, far to the

196   GENESIS.   B. C. 1898.

CHAPTER XVII.

AND when Abram was ninety years old and nine, the LORD ª appeared to Abram, and said unto him, ᵇ I *am* the Almighty God; ᶜ walk before me, and be thou ¹ ᵈ perfect. **2** And I will make my covenant between me and thee, and ᵉ will multiply thee exceedingly. **3** And Abram ᶠ fell on his face: and God talked with him, saying, **4** As for me, behold, my covenant *is* with thee, and thou shalt be ᵍ a father of ² many nations. **5** Neither shall thy name any more be called Abram, but ʰ thy name shall be ³ Abraham; ⁱ for a father of many nations have I made thee. **6** And I will

a Chap. 12.1.——*b* Chap. 28. 3; 35.11; Exod. 6. 3; Deut. 10. 17.——*c* Chap. 5. 22; 48. 15; 1 Kings 2. 4; 8. 25; 2 Kings 20. 3.——1 Or, *upright*, or, *sincere*.——*d* Chap. 6. 9; Deut. 18. 13; Job 1.1; Matt. 5. 48.
e Chap. 12. 2; 13. 16; 22. 17.——*f* Verse 17.——*g* Rom. 4. 11, 12, 16; Gal. 3. 29.——2 Heb. *multitude of nations*.——*h* Neh. 9. 7.——3 That is, *Father of a great multitude*.——*i* Rom. 4. 17.

south of Beer-sheba, has been suggested as Hagar's well, but this suggestion has not been sufficiently confirmed.

CHAPTER XVII.

THE COVENANT OF CIRCUMCISION, 1-27.

1. **Ninety years old and nine**— Thirteen years after the birth of Ishmael. Comp. chap. xvi, 16; xviii, 25. Slowly the years roll on, and God keeps promising, but not fulfilling. **The Lord appeared**—The words imply some visible theophany. Probably the appearance of Jehovah's Angel, as in chapter xvi, 7. Comp. verse 22. **I am the Almighty God**—Heb., I *am El-Shaddai*. Compare the use of this word in xxviii, 3; xxxv, 11; xliii, 14; xlviii, 3; xlix, 25; and in Exod. vi, 3; where see note. We have met with the name *El - Elion* in chapter xiv, 18, 19, 20, 22, which designates the Supreme God, or God Most High. *El-Shaddai* denotes the Powerful or Omnipotent God. This name is appropriately introduced here as designating the Almighty Power which can override all opposing forces, and work miracles in order to fulfil the divine promises and plans. The deadness of Abram's body, and also that of Sarai's womb, (Rom. iv, 19,) shall not hinder the accomplishment of what El-Shaddai pledges. **Walk before me**—Let thy heart, thy life, thy character be such as one should be on whom El-Shaddai gazes. The long deferring of the promised seed was, that Abram might acquire a permanence of faith in God: something like Enoch, who walked three hundred years with Elohim. Chap. v, 22. El-Shaddai would lift Abram from a passive to an active faith. **Be thou perfect**—Complete, finished,

blameless. The conscientious walking as in the sight of the Almighty leadeth on to perfection.

2. **I will make my covenant**— The formal and symbolical *cutting* of the covenant was described in chap. xv; here Jehovah *gives* Abram the sign and seal of the covenant. Accordingly we note that in chap. xv, 18, the Hebrew expression is *cut* (כרת) a covenant; here it is *give* (נתן) a covenant. "The freedom of the covenant of promise is expressed in this latter phrase. It was a gift from a superior, rather than a bargain between equals; and as it was accompanied by the rite of circumcision, it was typical of the freedom of that covenant made afterwards to Christians, and sealed to them in the sacred rite of baptism."—*Speaker's Commentary.*

3. **Abram fell on his face**—Overwhelmed by the fulness and majesty of the revelation. **God talked with him** — Here the word for God is *Elohim*; and so in the space of these three verses we have the three divine names, Jehovah, El-Shaddai, and Elohim —a strange anomaly in the Jehovistic and Elohistic document hypothesis. Compare Introd., pp. 51-54.

4. **As for me**—Contrast the *thou* in verse 9. Here God declares what he will do for his part; there he directs what Abram must do. **A father of many nations**—Or, *of a noise of nations*; a tumultuous mass of nations. The Ishmaelites, the Edomites, and the descendants of Keturah, (xxv, 1,) as well as the twelve tribes of Israel, sprang from Abram. So that Abram was literally the father of a great multitude of nations, and no name is more honoured in the East to day.

5. **Abram . . . Abraham** — With

CHAPTER XVII.

make thee exceeding fruitful, and I will make ᵏ nations of thee, and ˡ kings shall come out of thee. 7 And I will ᵐ establish my covenant between me and thee and thy seed after thee in their generations, for an everlasting covenant, ⁿ to be a God unto thee and to ᵒ thy seed after thee. 8 And ᵖ I will give unto thee, and to thy seed after thee, the land

⁴ᑫ wherein thou art a stranger, all the land of Canaan, for an everlasting possession; and ʳ I will be their God.
9 And God said unto Abraham, Thou shalt keep my covenant therefore, thou, and thy seed after thee in their generations. 10 This is my covenant, which ye shall keep, between me and you and thy seed after thee; ˢ Every man child

---

k Chapter 35. 11. —— *l* Verse 16; chapter 35. 11; Matthew 1. 6, etc.—*m* Galatians 3. 17.—— *n* Chapter 26. 24; 28. 13; Hebrews 11. 16. —— *o* Romans 9. 8.

p Chap. 12. 7; 13. 15; Psa. 105. 9, 11.——4 Heb. *of thy sojournings.*——*q* Chap. 23. 4; 28. 4.—— *r* Exod. 6. 7; Lev. 26. 12; Deut. 4. 37; 14. 2; 26. 18; 29. 13.——*s* Acts 7. 8.

---

the giving of the covenant of circumcision is given also a new name. Hence the custom of giving names at the time of circumcision. **Abrám** signifies *high father;* **Abraham,** *father of a multitude,* (by the addition of הם apparently shortened form of המון, translated *many,* or *multitude,* in this same verse and in verse 4. This seems a simpler derivation than to assume, as Gesenius and others, a lost root, רהם.) Compare verse 15, where Sarai's name is changed to Sarah. Thus the letter H, (ה,) which occurs twice in the memorial name *Jehovah,* is incorporated in the new names of both the father and mother of the chosen seed. Comp. the " new name" of Rev. ii, 17; iii, 12. By these new names Abraham and Sarah become divinely consecrated, as they had not so fully been before.

6. **Exceeding fruitful . . . nations . . . kings**—A threefold promise, enhanced in the two following verses by the mention of "an everlasting covenant" and "an everlasting possession." Mark the gradation. 1) A numerous posterity, in itself an enviable blessing, and the glory of a Hebrew. 2) That posterity would branch out into nations; a higher honour still than merely that of a numerous family. 3) These nations should rise to the dignity of mighty civil powers, and be represented and ruled by mighty kings. 4) God's covenant with Abraham would abide through all the ages, an everlasting covenant, by which all the families of the earth should be blessed. 5) The land of Canaan for an everlasting possession. The whole is crowned by the closing words of verse 8.

8. **And I will be their God**—Here,

observes Murphy, "the temporal and the spiritual are brought together. The land of promise is made sure to the heirs of promise *for a perpetual possession,* and God engages to **be their God.** The phrase perpetual possession has here two elements of meaning: first, that the possession, in its coming form of a certain land, shall last as long as the co-existing relations of things are continued; and, secondly, that the said possession, in all the variety of its ever grander phases, will last absolutely forever. Each form will be perfectly adequate to each stage of a progressive humanity. But in all its forms, and at every stage, it will be their chief glory that God is **their God.**"

9. **Thou shalt keep**—God has now said what he for his part will do; here he directs Abraham's part of observing the covenant. Comp. verse 4, note.

10. **This is my covenant, which ye shall keep**—That is, this is the sign or seal of the covenant which it will be your place to observe. Hence Stephen said: "He gave him the covenant of circumcision." Acts vii, 8. **Every man child among you shall be circumcised**—Here was a positive commandment, as direct and uncompromising as the absolute prohibition of the fruit of the tree of knowledge. Chap. ii, 17. Obedience must now supplement faith. "Circumcision was confined to the male sex. This was neither owing to the physical nor to the ethical state of woman, but to the dependent position which she occupied in antiquity. Circumcision implies as much the humiliation as the exaltation of man, expressing as it did both his natural incapacity for being a member of the covenant, and his special

among you shall be circumcised. **11** And ye shall circumcise the flesh of your foreskin; and it shall be ᵗa token of the covenant betwixt me and you. **12** And ⁵he that is eight days old ᵘshall be circumcised among you, every man child in your generations, he that is born in the house, or bought with money of any stranger, which *is* not of thy seed. **13** He that is born in thy house, and he that is bought with thy money, must needs be circumcised: and my covenant shall be in your flesh for an everlasting covenant. **14** And the uncircumcised man child whose flesh of his foreskin is not circumcised, that soul ᵛshall be cut off from his people; he hath broken my covenant.

---

t Acts 7. 8; Rom. 4. 11. —— 5 Heb. *a son of eight days.*

u Lev. 12. 3; Luke 2. 21; John 7. 22; Phil 3. 5. —*v* Exod. 4. 24.

---

divine calling in that direction. The absence of circumcision does not convey that these lessons and privileges applied not to woman also, but that she was dependent, and that her position in the natural and covenant life was not *without* the husband, but *in* and *with* him, not in her capacity as *woman*, but as wife and mother."—*Kurtz.*

11. **Circumcise the flesh of your foreskin**—The act of circumcision consisted in cutting off the prepuce, or **foreskin**, which covers the glans of the penis in males. Whether this custom originated with this covenant with Abraham, or whether it was in use among ancient peoples before this time, is a disputed question. It appears probable, on the whole, that the practice was older than Abraham, and the language here used seems to favour this view. Were this the origin of circumcision, we should naturally have expected particular directions as to the mode of performing it, but the absence of such directions rather implies that the custom was not new, or strange. As the rainbow appeared in the sky before it was made the token of God's covenant with Noah, and as divers baptisms were in use before the baptism of water was made a sacrament of the Christian Church, so circumcision may have been practised before Abram's time, but was consecrated into a new meaning by the Abrahamic covenant. Abraham "received the sign of circumcision," says the apostle, "a seal of the righteousness of the faith which he had yet being uncircumcised." Rom. iv, 11. The typical significance of circumcision arises from the consideration that, as the depravity and corruption of human nature are transmitted by generation, and the promise is to the seed of Abraham, so the organs of generation receive the symbol of "putting off the body of the sins of the flesh," (Col. ii, 11,) and the chosen *seed* are thereby set apart and consecrated as holy unto the Lord. The spiritual significance of the rite is recognised in such texts as Lev. xxvi, 41; Deut. x, 16; xxx, 6; Ezek. xliv, 7; Rom. ii, 28, 29. For more on the subject of circumcision, see note at the end of this chapter.

12. **Eight days old**—A whole seven days must pass, and on the eighth day the ceremony. Comp. chap. xxi, 4; Lev. xii, 3; Luke i, 59; ii, 21; Phil. iii, 5. For this, perhaps, a twofold reason may be assigned: the symbolism of the sacred number seven, and the necessity that the child should have sufficient age to endure the operation.

13. **He that is born in thy house** —The bond slave of a patriarchal family as distinguished from one bought or taken in war. Comp. chap. xiv, 14.

14. **Shall be cut off from his people**—This may mean either excommunication, or, as these words seem to signify in Exod. xxxi, 14, the penalty of death. The neglect of such a sign and ordinance would be an open breach of the covenant, and demand a severe penalty. **He hath broken my covenant**—To neglect this sign was looked upon as open and defiant disobedience. It was equivalent to a violation of the covenant itself.

Note now the five points of circumcision: 1) It was an outward ceremony of the flesh. 2) It was the token of the covenant. 3) It was to be performed on the eighth day. 4) It was to be applied to all the regular household. 5) It was imperative and inviolable under penalty of death.

CHAPTER XVII.

15 And God said unto Abraham, As for Sarai thy wife, thou shalt not call her name Sarai, but ⁶ Sarah *shall* her name *be*. **16** And I will bless her, ʷ and give thee a son also of her: yea, I will bless her, and ⁷ she shall be *a mother* ˣ of nations; kings of people shall be of her. **17** Then Abraham fell upon his face, ʸ and laughed, and said in his heart, Shall *a child* be born unto him that is a hundred years old? and shall Sarah, that is ninety years old, bear? **18** And Abraham said unto God, O that Ishmael might live before thee! **19** And God said, ᶻ Sarah thy wife shall bear thee a son indeed; and thou shalt call his name Isaac: and I will establish my covenant with him for an everlasting covenant, *and* with his seed after him. **20** And as for Ishmael, I have heard thee: Behold, I have blessed him, and will make him fruitful, and ᵃ will multiply him exceedingly; ᵇ twelve princes shall he beget, ᶜ and I will make him a great nation. **21** But my covenant will I establish with Isaac, ᵈ which Sarah shall bear unto thee at this set time in the next year. **22** And he left off talking with him, and God went up from Abraham. **23** And Abraham took Ishmael his son, and all that were born in his house, and all that were bought with his money, every male among the men of Abraham's house; and circumcised the flesh of their foreskin in the selfsame day, as God had said unto him. **24** And Abraham *was* ninety years old and nine, when he was circumcised in the flesh of his foreskin. **25** And Ishmael his son *was* thirteen years old, when he was circumcised in the flesh of his foreskin. **26** In the selfsame day was Abraham circumcised, and Ishmael his son. **27** And ᵉ all the men of his house, born in the house, and bought with money of the stranger, were circumcised with him.

---

6 That is, *Princess*. —— *w* Chap. 18. 10. —— 7 Heb. *she shall become nations.*—*x* Chap. 35. 11; Gal. 4. 31; 1 Pet. 3. 6.——*y* Chap. 18. 12; 21. 6. —— *z* Chap. 18. 10; 21. 2; Gal. 4. 28. —— *a* Chap. 16. 10.——*b* Chap. 25. 12, 16.——*c* Chap. 21. 18. ——*d* Chap. 21. 2.——*e* Chap. 18. 19.

---

15. Sarai . . . Sarah—The precise meaning of the name **Sarai** (שָׂרַי) is not easy to decide, but the sense of *my princess*, generally adopted by the older interpreters, appears the most simple. In this sense she is *heroine, princely, noble,* in a more special idea of being the princess of a single race; or *high princess,* as Abram was high father. **Sarah** means *princess,* and "aptly is she so named, for she is to bear the child of promise, to become nations, and be the mother of kings."—*Murphy.* Compare note on change of Abram's name, verse 5. Though Sarah and her female descendants receive not the sign of the covenant, they nevertheless are divinely recognised as identified with the chosen people, and heirs of the promise.

16. She shall be a mother of nations—Heb., *she shall become nations.* Hence appropriately named Sarah, the princess.

17. Laughed — Abraham's prostration, and the whole tenor of this history, forbid the supposition that this was the laughter of incredulity. It was the excessive outburst of joyful emotion over these precious promises. By faith Abraham now saw the day of redemption and was *glad.* John viii, 56.

Said in his heart — The questions which follow are not to be understood as the expressions of doubt, but as exclamations of exultant wonder.

18. O that Ishmael might live before thee—The patriarch seems to fear that Ishmael is to be cut off. The boy of thirteen has won a deep place in his father's heart, and notwithstanding the promise of a son by Sarah, he yearns to see Ishmael blessed of God.

19. Call his name Isaac—Which means, *he shall laugh.* A memorial of Abraham's joyful emotion and wonder here recorded.

20. Ishmael, I have heard—Allusion to the meaning of the name, *God will hear.* See chapter xvi, 11, note. **Twelve princes** — See chapter xxv, 12–16.

22. God went up from Abraham —These words imply some open epiphany. Probably the Angel of the Lord appearing and ascending, as in the case of Manoah. Judges xiii, 20.

23. Abraham . . . in the selfsame day—The promptness of his obedience is noticeable. Abraham's "faith wrought with his works, and by works was faith made perfect." James ii, 22.

25. Thirteen years old—Josephus (*Ant.*, i, 12, 2) says the Arabians, because of this, do not circumcise their children until the thirteenth year.

ADDITIONAL NOTE ON CIRCUMCISION.

The practice of circumcision obtained among many ancient nations, and was probably in use before the time of Abraham. See note on verse 11 above. Herodotus was unable to determine whether the Egyptians learned the custom from the Ethiopians, or the Ethiopians from the Egyptians. *Herod.*, ii, 104. Both nations observed the custom from the earliest times, and it is difficult to believe that they would have borrowed it from the Hebrews. The practice also prevailed among the Colchians of Asia and the savage Troglodytes of Africa, (*Diod. Sic.*, iii, 31,) and is still continued by several African tribes and the inhabitants of many islands of the Pacific. PICKERING, *Races of Men*, pp. 153, 199. The Abyssinian Christians are said also to perform this rite at the present day, and upon both sexes. LUDOLF, *Hist. Ethiopia*, i. 19. The practice prevailed also among the Phœnicians and Syrians (*Herod.*, ii, 104) and the Moabites, Ammonites, and Edomites. Jer. ix, 25. The Arabians perform the rite after the thirteenth year, thus following the example of Ishmael. Verse 25 above, note. Mohammed was circumcised, according to the custom of his countrymen; and, though the Koran does not enjoin the practice, circumcision is as common among the Mohammedans as among the Jews. As to the origin and reason of this practice many hold that it was introduced in those southern countries not as a religious rite, but from a physical cause. It is believed that the burning temperature of those climes, in many cases combined with a peculiar bodily structure of those races, gave rise to the custom. It was thought to prevent painful diseases and such disorders as *phimosis*, and gonorrhœa spuria. Modern travellers testify that it precludes great physical inconvenience among the Bushmen; and the Christian missionaries who tried to abolish it in Abyssinia, were compelled, by the dangerous physical consequences, to desist from their plans. Herodotus observes that the Egyptian priests were circumcised for the sake of cleanliness, deeming it better to be clean than handsome. *Herod.*, ii, 37. It was observed, however, in the course of time, that many tribes and nations inhabiting the same zones remained uncircumcised without perceptible injury or inconvenience. The Philistines seem never to have adopted the custom. The Edomites neglected it, (Josephus, *Ant.*, xiii, 9, 1,) and some classes of the Egyptians omitted it; and when, in the time of the Persian and Greek dominion, the primitive institutions of Egypt were neglected or underwent important modifications, circumcision ceased to be a national custom. The priests alone preserved it as a mark of their superior purity. *Kalisch.* But whatever the occasion or reason of its origin, the Egyptian priests doubtless connected some religious significance with the rite of circumcision. Other nations also probably associated it with sacred mysteries. It has been thought that among idolatrous peoples it may have had some reference to the deification of the powers of nature, and especially those of generation. It is impossible, however, to determine exactly what religious significance the heathen nations attached to the custom. But if it seem strange that a custom practised by idolatrous tribes should have been made a sign and seal of God's covenant with Abraham, let us consider that almost every religious ceremony of the Hebrew people was based upon some prevailing Eastern custom or tradition, and that it was divested of base and superstitious elements by such appropriation to new purposes, and exalted to be the vehicle of lofty doctrines. This accommodation to traditionary practices, says Kalisch, secured the external success of the true religion, while the transformation of rotten and idolatrous institutions into laws of indestructible vitality, constitutes its indisputable claim to originality, and commands the admiration of all ages.

With Abraham and his posterity it became the sacred token of a blood-covenant, the most solemn and obligatory conceivable, between man and God. Abraham became henceforth, in

CHAPTER XVIII.

AND the LORD appeared unto him in the ᵃplains of Mamre: and he sat in the tent door in the heat of the day; 2 ᵇAnd he lifted up his eyes and looked, and, lo, three men stood by him: ᶜand

ᵃ Chap. 13. 18; 14. 13.   ᵇ Heb. 13. 2.——ᶜ Chap. 19. 1; 1 Pet. 4. 9.

a notable sense, "the friend of God." 2 Chron. xx, 7; Isa. xli, 8; James ii, 23. Verses 10 and 11, above, are thus paraphrased by Trumbull: "The blood-covenant of friendship shall be consummated by your giving to me of your personal blood at the very source of paternity—'under your girdle;' thereby pledging yourself to me, and pledging also to me those who shall come after you in the line of natural descent." *The Blood Covenant*, p. 217. New York, 1885.

The rite was in the earliest times performed with a stone knife, (Exod. iv, 25, Josh. v, 2,) sometimes by the mother, but generally by the father of the child. Afterwards it became the business of a physician, but in modern times it is performed by a special officer. The eighth day after birth was the usual time for the circumcision, (Lev. xii, 3, Luke i, 59,) at which time the child is named. In the course of the ceremony the following is uttered: "Blessed art thou, O Lord, our God! who hath sanctified his beloved from the womb, and ordained an ordinance for his kindred, and sealed his descendants with the mark of his holy covenant. Preserve this child to his father and mother, and let his name be called in Israel, A, the son of B. Let the father rejoice in those that go forth from his loins, and let his mother be glad in the fruit of her womb." See more in the Biblical Cyclopedias, under the word *Circumcision.*

CHAPTER XVIII.
ENTERTAINING ANGELS, 1–15.

1. The Lord appeared—This is the sixth revelation of promise to Abraham. 1) The call and promise while yet in his father's house. Chap. xii, 1–3. 2) At the oak of Moreh. Chap. xii, 7. 3) After his separation from Lot. Chap. xiii, 14–17. 4) The covenant of the Word and vision of chap. xv. 5) The covenant of circumcision, in chap. xvii. And after this sixth revelation, and after Isaac's birth, when God will test the patriarch once more, we have the seventh revelation in connexion with the offering of Isaac in the land of Moriah. Chap. xxii, 1–18. Thus the father of the faithful has a sevenfold revelation of promise and of prophecy. **Plains of Mamre**—Or, *oaks* of Mamre. See on chap. xiii, 18. **Sat in the tent door in the heat of the day**—A truly Oriental picture. Travellers at the present day often observe the like; the sheik sitting under an awning or in the shade of a tree or grove, and ready to repeat the ancient style of hospitality to the passing traveller.

2. Three men—An angelophany, in which the celestial messengers took on the form and habits of ordinary men. It appears from what follows that one of these was the Angel of Jehovah, (see note on xvi, 7,) who speaks in the Divine name and represents Deity himself. Comp. verses 13, 17, 20, 22, 26, 33. But such a manifestation of Jehovah in human form appears extraordinary, and has been made the subject of ridicule by unbelievers. What! they say, God eating veal along with Abraham! Abraham washing God's feet, and feeding him with cakes! That is worse than heathen idolatry. But the same difficulty holds with the theory that the **three men** were angels. Did Abraham wash the feet of angels and feed them with veal and cakes? That seems clearly to be the purport of the narrative; and before we hasten to pronounce it absurd or heathenish, let us calmly consider why such a theophany and such an angelophany should be thought incredible? It will not be denied that God has the power thus to manifest himself. He could have assumed a human form, and done all that is here recorded. But it is assumed that such action is incompatible with the divine majesty and the spiritual nature of God. But who knows this? Or who is com-

when he saw *them*, he ran to meet them from the tent door, and bowed himself toward the ground, **3** And said, My Lord, if now I have found favour in thy sight, pass not away, I pray thee, from thy servant: **4** Let ᵈa little water, I pray you, be fetched, and wash your feet, and rest yourselves under the tree:

5 And ᵉI will fetch a morsel of bread, and ¹ᶠcomfort ye your hearts; after that ye shall pass on: ᵍfor therefore ²are ye come to your servant. And they said, So do, as thou hast said. **6** And Abraham hastened into the tent unto Sarah, and said, ³Make ready quickly three measures of fine meal, knead *it*, and

---

d Chap. 19. 2; 43. 24.——*e* Judg. 6. 18; 13. 15.——1 Heb. *stay*.——*f* Judg. 19. 5; Psa. 104. 15.

g Chap. 19. 8; 33. 10.——2 Heb. *you have passed*.——3 Heb. *Hasten*.

---

petent to say that it was improper, and unworthy of Jehovah to reveal himself thus in human form to the father of the faithful? It would, indeed, be unseemly and idolatrous *for us* to represent God under a human or any other form. This is expressly forbidden. Exod. xx, 45. But if God may reveal himself in a pillar of cloud, or a pillar of fire, or a burning bush, why not also in a human form?

The Christian who believes that God was "manifest in the flesh" in the person of Jesus Christ, will not regard this theophany with strange wonder, or incredulity. When we consider the special purpose of this appearance of Jehovah to Abraham, namely, to bring Sarah to a belief in the promise, we may well suppose that the human form would have been the most suitable semblance under which Jehovah could appear. Such a theophany would adumbrate the future seed, the Christ of God, born of a woman, yet declared to be the Son of God, with power; who would eat and drink with men, and wash the feet of his disciples, that he might teach them the same lesson of humble service. He was seen and ministered unto by angels. He, even after his resurrection, ate before his disciples, to convince them that he was no unsubstantial spectre. Luke xxiv, 43. So the God of Abraham makes this revelation a most intense reality to him, and through him to Sarah, that she may become partaker of his faith, and a proper mother of the chosen seed.

3. My Lord—אֲדֹנָי, *Adonai*, not *Jehovah*, as the Targum of Onkelos here reads. The patriarch thus seems to address himself to one of the three messengers, as if in him he recognised at once the Angel who had visited him before.

But we may translate it as plural, *my lords*. Comp. chap. xix, 2, 18. The passage in Heb. xiii, 1, "Some have entertained angels unawares," is generally supposed to refer to this event and that of chap. xix, 2. We may believe that, at the first, Abraham was not aware that his guests were angels, but that gradually the fact became known to him; or he may have been impressed at once with the feeling that the one was Jehovah's Angel, while he did not perceive that the others were angels also. **If now I have found favour**—Abraham's language throughout is a genuine and lifelike example of the manner of a hospitable and generous Oriental chief.

4. Wash your feet—Ablutions of all kinds are very common in the East, and considered essential as safeguards against the leprosy. But feet washing was among the most common rites of hospitality. Comp. chaps. xix, 2; xxiv, 32; Judg. xix, 21. The foot was usually protected only by a sandal, and after a journey over the heated roads or fields, the washing of the feet was peculiarly gratifying to the traveller.

5. For therefore are ye come to your servant—Or, *for therefore have ye passed over to your servant.* That is, Abraham recognises a divine providence in their having passed over to him that they might be comforted in their hearts and refreshed by him.

6. Abraham hastened—The haste or rapidity with which a hospitable feast is prepared by an Oriental for his guest is notable. See on 1 Sam. xxviii, 24. The words **make ready quickly** are, in the Hebrew, but the same word מַהֵר, *hasten*. **Three measures of fine meal**—The *measure*, or *seah*, is supposed to have been about one peck, and accordingly the large quantity of flour taken shows the

B. C. 1898. CHAPTER XVIII. 203

make cakes upon the hearth. **7** And Abraham ran unto the herd, and fetched a calf tender and good, and gave it unto a young man; and he hasted to dress it. **8** And ʰ he took butter, and milk, and the calf which he had dressed, and set it before them; and he stood by them under the tree, and they did eat. **9** And they said unto him, Where is Sarah thy wife? And he said, Behold, ⁱ in the tent. **10** And he said, I ᵏ will certainly return unto thee ˡ according to the time of life; and, lo, ᵐ Sarah thy wife shall have a son. And Sarah heard it in the tent door, which was behind him. **11** Now ⁿ Abraham and Sarah were old and well stricken in age; and it ceased to be with Sarah ᵒ after the manner of women. **12** Therefore Sarah ᵖ laughed within herself, saying, ᵃAfter I am waxed old shall I have pleasure, my ʳ lord being old also? **13** And the LORD said unto Abraham, Wherefore did Sarah laugh, saying, Shall I of a surety bear a child, which am old? **14** ˢ Is any thing too hard for the LORD? ᵗ At the time appointed I will return unto thee, according to the time of life, and Sarah shall have a son. **15** Then Sarah denied, saying, I laughed not; for she was afraid. And he said, Nay; but thou didst laugh.

h Chap. 19. 3.——*i* Chap. 24. 67.——*k* Verse 14.——*l* 2 Kings 4. 16.——*m* Chap. 17. 19, 21; 21. 2; Rom. 9. 9.——*n* Chap. 17. 17; Rom. 4. 19; Heb. 11. 11, 12, 19.

o Chap. 31. 35.——*p* Chap. 17. 17.——*q* Luke 1. 18.——*r* 1 Pet. 3. 6.——*s* Jer. 32. 17; Zech. 8. 6; Matt. 3. 9; 19. 26; Luke 1. 37.——*t* Chap. 17. 21; verse 10; 2 Kings 4. 16.

bounty of Abraham's hospitality. He would prepare a royal feast. **Cakes upon the hearth**—Such were usually baked among the coals.

7. A calf tender and good—He selects the choicest of his young cattle, "the fatted calf," (Luke xv, 23, 30,) the greatest luxury of the kind at his command.

8. Butter — "This is commonly clotted cream. The **milk** is chiefly that of the goat, which is very rich and sweet, rather sickening to an unpracticed taste. This kind of milk we found abundant in Palestine, and no other."—*Jacobus*. **Stood by them**—As a reverent attendant and waiter, fully appreciating the honour of the occasion. **They did eat**—As truly as did the risen Lord. Luke xxiv, 43. It was not because they needed food, but as, in our Lord's case, to convince Abraham and Sarah of the reality of this divine visitation. See on verse 2. "If the angels had assumed human bodies, though but for a time, there would have been nothing strange in their eating. In any case the food may have been consumed, miraculously or not; and the eating of it was a proof that the visit of the angels to Abraham was no mere vision, but a true manifestation of heavenly beings."—*Speaker's Com.*

9. Where is Sarah—Here comes out the main purpose of their visit. Sarah's lack of faith must be overcome by a divinely inspired confidence that will put all doubt and trifling aside.

10. He said—The question of verse 9 was common to the three—"they said." Now HE, the prominent One, whom Abraham, in verse 3, called "My Lord," speaks in the person of the Almighty, assuming power to accomplish what he promises. **I will certainly return**—He speaks as if about departing. Like a passing traveller, he will now depart, but he will return again. **According to the time of life**—Reference to what he had previously promised, in a very recent revelation, "at this set time next year." Chap. xvii, 21.

12. Sarah laughed — The context here shows that Sarah's laugh was that of incredulity, as the context of chap. xvii, 17, shows that Abraham's laughing was that of joyful wonder. Sarah **laughed within herself**, not aloud, nor with prostration, as yielding confidently to the joy of the promise, but with secret incredulity. **My lord**—See 1 Peter iii, 5, 6.

13. The Lord said — Here the speaker is expressly called Jehovah. He also shows his knowledge of the thoughts of Sarah, and in the next verse identifies himself with Jehovah, saying: "Is any thing too hard for Jehovah? At the time appointed I will return," etc. All this is incompatible with the idea that the speaker merely personates Jehovah.

15. She was afraid—The direct response to her thoughts, the searching words, the implied rebuke, the evi-

16 And the men rose up from thence, and looked toward Sodom: and Abraham went with them ᵘ to bring them on the way. **17** And the Lord said, ᵛ Shall I hide from Abraham that thing which I do; **18** Seeing that Abraham shall surely become a great and mighty nation, and all the nations of the earth shall be ʷ blessed in him? **19** For I know him, ˣ that he will command his children and his household after him, and they shall keep the way of the Lord, to do justice and judgment; that the Lord may bring upon Abraham that which he hath spoken of him. **20** And the Lord said, Because ʸ the cry of Sodom and Gomorrah is great, and because their sin is very grievous, **21** ᶻ I will go down now, and see whether they have done altogether according to the

---

ᵘ Rom. 15. 24; 3 John 6.——ᵛ Psa. 25. 14; Amos 3. 7; John 15. 15.——ʷ Chap. 12. 3; 22. 18; Acts 3. 25; Gal. 3. 8.

ˣ Deut. 4. 9, 10; 6. 7; Josh. 24. 15; Eph. 6. 4.——ʸ Chap. 4. 10; 19. 13; James 5. 4.——ᶻ Chap. 11. 5; Exod. 3. 8.

---

dence from the words that the speaker was Jehovah, all this filled her with a sudden amazement and terror, and under the fear of the moment **she denied, saying, I laughed not**—The denial was immediately silenced by the answer, **Nay, but thou didst laugh;** and we may well believe that doubt was changed to faith, and Sarah also believed the promise, and, as Kurtz observes, was "thus rendered capable to become the mother of the promised seed."

Abraham's Intercession for Sodom, 16–33.

16. Rose up—As travellers about to depart. **Looked toward Sodom** — Heb., *looked on the face of Sodom.* Turned their faces in that direction. The promise has been confirmed to Sarah, and now, in Abraham's future, all is hopeful and bright. But from this message of grace the angels turn to a work of judgment. Their look toward Sodom was the beginning of the working of wrath. **Abraham went with them**—Thus showing the courtesy and care of a true host, to see his guests off safely on their way.

17. Shall I hide . . . which I do —Here, again, Jehovah speaks in his own name and person, and the style of the narrative gives a lifelike reality to every circumstance. How like a bosom friend he speaks! The Septuagint reads: "By no means will I hide from Abraham, my child, what I do." From such companionship Abraham was truly called "the friend of God." 2 Chron. xx, 7; Isa. xli, 8; James ii, 23.

19. For I know him— Rather, *I have known him, in order that he may command,* etc. The words *I have known* refer to the divine choice or election of Abraham. I have known, loved, favoured, called, Abraham for the purposes here named. **Command his children**—One of the most noticeable and beautiful things in the history of God's chosen people is the family government and religious instruction maintained in the home and **household.** The parental authority was duly exercised, not in harsh, tyrannical, or provoking ways, but in godly discipline and order. The principles of **justice** and righteous **judgment**—that is, rectitude in thought and action—were instilled into all their hearts. To observe and practise these is to **keep the way of the Lord;** that is, God's way for man to live and act. The parental and family discipline here extolled presents the following : 1) It is grounded in the divine favour. 2) It is authoritative and firm. 3) It affects the servants and dependents of the household as well as the children. 4) It is imbued with religious life and principle. 5) It exalts justice and righteous judgment. 6) It is perpetuated *after* the patriarch passes away, and it lives in his posterity. 7) It insures the fulfilment of the promises.

20. The cry of Sodom—The cry of the sins and abominations of Sodom, which went up to God, like the voice of Abel's blood (chap. iv, 10) demanding punishment.

21. I will go down—From the high lands of Hebron to the vale of Siddim. This manner of speaking is every way appropriate to the form in which the Lord revealed himself on this occasion. The incarnation itself was but an accommodation on the part of God to the conditions of man's life, and all such

CHAPTER XVIII.

B. C. 1898.

cry of it, which is come unto me; and if not, ᵃI will know. **22** And the men turned their faces from thence, ᵇand went toward Sodom: but Abraham ᶜstood yet before the LORD.
23 And Abraham ᵈdrew near, and said, ᵉWilt thou also destroy the righteous with the wicked? **24** ᶠPeradventure there be fifty righteous within the city: wilt thou also destroy and not spare the place for the fifty righteous that *are* therein? **25** That be far from thee to do after this manner, to slay the righteous with the wicked; and ᵍthat the righteous should be as the wicked, that be far from thee: ʰShall not the Judge of all the earth do right? **26** And the LORD said, ⁱIf I find in Sodom fifty righteous within the city, then I will spare all the place for their sakes. **27** And Abraham answered and said, ᵏBehold now, I have taken upon me to speak unto the Lord, which *am* ¹*but* dust and ashes: **28** Peradventure there shall lack five of the fifty righteous: wilt thou destroy all the city for *lack of* five? And he said, If I find there forty and five, I will not destroy *it*. **29** And he spake unto him yet again, and said, Peradventure there shall be forty found there. And he said, I will not do *it* for forty's sake. **30** And he said *unto him*, Oh let not the Lord be angry, and I will speak: Peradventure there shall thirty be found there. And he said, I will not do *it*, if I find thirty there. **31** And he said, Behold now, I have taken upon me to speak unto the Lord: Peradventure there shall be twenty found there. And he said, I will not destroy *it* for twenty's sake. **32** And he said, ᵐOh let not the Lord be angry, and I will speak yet but this once: Peradventure ten shall be found there. ⁿAnd he said, I will not destroy *it* for ten's sake. **33** And the LORD went his way, as soon

---

a Deut. 8. 2; 13. 3; Josh. 22. 22; Luke 16. 15; 2 Cor. 11. 11.——*b* Chap. 19. 1.——*c* Verse 1.——*d* Heb. 10. 22.——*e* Num. 16. 22; 2 Sam. 24. 17.——*f* Jer. 5. 1.——*g* Job 8. 20; Isa. 3. 10, 11.——*h* Job 8. 3; 34. 17; Psa. 58. 11; 94. 2; Rom. 3. 6.——*i* Jer. 5. 1; Ezek. 22. 30.——*k* Luke 18. 1.——*l* Chap. 3. 19; Job 4. 19; Eccles. 12. 7; 1 Cor. 15. 47, 48; 2 Cor. 5. 1.——*m* Judg. 6. 39.——*n* James 5. 16.

---

modes of speech as this are an accommodation to human thought. Jehovah thus declares that he will not move in judgment on a wicked city without long-suffering, care, and personal knowledge of all things.

22. The men turned ... and went —Two of them thus turned away to Sodom, as we gather from chap. xix, 1, and the added statement that **Abraham stood yet before the Lord.** Jehovah, who has all along been presented as one of the three, remains to speak further with Abraham, but silently dismisses his attendants, who understand their further mission, and go about it.

23. Abraham drew near—He perceived the purpose of wrath, and was moved with the thought of a whole city, or group of cities, perishing, **and said, Wilt thou also destroy the righteous with the wicked?** He does not plead for the wicked, but for the righteous; not for mercy, but for what seems to him as justice. He, doubtless, felt for his nephew Lot, and in general for all those whom he had, by his military prowess, rescued from the eastern invaders.

24. Peradventure there be fifty—He begins his intercession with this moderate number. Surely if half a hundred **righteous** people are living in the city, for their sake it should be spared.

25. That be far from thee—An exclamation of indignant aversion; חָלִלָה לְךָ; *abominable to thee!* Shocking to thee would be an act like that!

28. There shall lack five—First he drops to forty-five; then to forty; then to thirty; then to twenty; and finally to ten. Conant observes on this whole passage that it has "no parallel, even in sacred history. With earnestness, but with unaffected humility, devout courtesy, and a reverent freedom, the patriarch presses his suit on behalf of the few righteous men in Sodom. On the other hand, Jehovah receives the intercession of his servant graciously, and admits the reasonableness of his plea by granting all that he desires. There is a beautiful aptness in the turn given to the first plea for a slight abatement of this number; 'Wilt thou for five destroy the whole city?' The whole passage is singularly felicitous and beautiful, in conception and expression."

33. Went his way—Abraham ceased to intercede and Jehovah ceased

VOL. I.—14

GENESIS. B. C. 1898.

as he had left communing with Abraham: and Abraham returned unto his place.

CHAPTER XIX.

AND there ᵃ came two angels to Sodom at even; and Lot sat in the gate of Sodom: and ᵇ Lot seeing *them* rose up to meet them; and he bowed himself with his face toward the ground; 2 And he said, Behold now, my lords, ᶜ turn in, I pray you, into your servant's house, and tarry all night, and ᵈ wash your feet, and ye shall rise up early, and go on your ways. And they said, ᵉ Nay; but we will abide in the street all night. 3 And he pressed upon them greatly; and they turned in unto him, and entered into his house; ᶠ and he made them a feast, and did bake unleavened bread, and they did eat.

---

a Chap. 18. 22.——*b* Chap. 18. 1, etc.——*c* Heb. 13. 2. | *d* Chap. 18. 4.——*e* See Luke 24. 28.——*f* Chap 18. 8.

---

to answer. Other works and plans engage Jehovah, and he passes from one scene to another. Lo, all we see and know "are but parts of his ways." "My father worketh hitherto, and I work." John v, 17. The Theophanies of the Old Testament furnish not only profound revelations of Deity, but inspiration to holy activity.

In Abraham's intercession we do well to note: 1) How the righteous may be the salt of the earth. 2) The long-suffering and the righteousness of God. 3) The humility and boldness with which we should plead before God. 4) The efficacy of prayer.

CHAPTER XIX.

Lot Rescued by the Angels, 1-23.

In this chapter we have another picture of the life and character of Lot. After his rescue from the eastern kings by Abraham, he went back again to his coveted Sodom. His daughters married men of the city, and his family appear to have become damagingly affected by the vices of the place. Lot himself lost not the uprightness of character developed by his long residence with Abraham, and he was often "vexed with the filthy conversation of the wicked. For that righteous man, dwelling among them, in seeing and hearing, vexed his righteous soul from day to day with their unlawful deeds." 2 Peter ii, 8. But his moral force was altogether insufficient to stem the tide of evil which was against him. He was wont to sit in the gate of Sodom as one of the judges of the city, (comp. Ruth iv, 1,) and thus became familiar with the commerce and conversation of the inhabitants. All this would tend to blunt his moral sense, and lower him from the simplicity and purity of the shepherd life he had led among the hills with Abraham.

1. **Two angels**.— Heb., *the two angels*, evidently the two who left Abraham on the heights. Chap. xviii, 22. Knobel suggests that Jehovah, the most holy, sent his angels, but would not himself enter the wicked city. **At even** — They dined with Abraham in the heat of the day; they will sup with Lot. **Sat in the gate of Sodom**—"The gate of the city was, in the ancient towns of the East, the common place of public resort, both for social intercourse and for public business. This gate of the city nearly corresponded with the forum, or marketplace of Greece and Rome. Not only was it the place of public sale, but judges and even kings held courts of justice there. The gate itself was probably an arch, with deep recesses, in which were placed the seats of the judges, and benches on either side were arranged for public convenience. Comp. chap. xxxiv, 20; Deut. xxi, 19, 22, 15; Ruth iv, 1."—*Speaker's Com.*

2. **My lords, turn in**—He shows a hospitality like Abraham, and like him entertains angels unawares. **Wash your feet** — See on chap. xviii, 4. **Nay...in the street**—They make as though (comp. Luke xxiv, 28) they would not accept his hospitality, thus testing him. By **the street** we are to understand the broad, open places of the city, which, in that warm climate, would not be an uncomfortable place to lodge.

3. **Made them a feast**—מִשְׁתֶּה, a *feast*, is the name usually given to a great feast or banquet. Comp. chap. xxi, 8; xxvi, 30; xl, 20; 1 Sam. xxv, 36. **Unleavened bread**—This is the first

CHAPTER XIX.

4 But before they lay down, the men of the city, *even* the men of Sodom, compassed the house round, both old and young, all the people from every quarter: **5** ᵍAnd they called unto Lot, and said unto him, Where *are* the men which came in to thee this night? ʰ bring them out unto us, that we ⁱ may know them. **6** And ᵏ Lot went out at the door unto them, and shut the door after him, **7** And said, I pray you, brethren, do not so wickedly. **8** ˡBehold now, I have two daughters which have not known man; let me, I pray you, bring them out unto you, and do ye to them as *is* good in your eyes: only unto these men do nothing; ᵐ for therefore came they under the shadow of my roof. **9** And they said, Stand back. And they said *again*, This one *fellow* ⁿ came in to sojourn, ᵒ and he will needs be a judge: now will we deal worse with thee than with them. And they pressed sore upon the man, *even* Lot, and came near to break the door. **10** But the men put forth their hand, and pulled Lot into the house to them, and shut to the door. **11** And they smote the men ᵖ that *were* at the door of the house with blindness, both small and great: so that they wearied themselves to find the door. **12** And the men said unto Lot, Hast thou here any besides? son in law, and thy sons, and thy daughters, and what-

---

g Isa.3.9.——*h* Judg.19.22.——*i* Chap.4.1; Rom. 1. 24, 27; Jude 7.——*k* Judg. 19. 23.——*l* See Judg. 19. 24.——*m* See chap. 18. 5.——*n* 2 Pet. 2. 7, 8.——*o* Exod. 2. 14.——*p* See 2 Kings 6. 18; Acts 13. 11.

---

occurrence of the word מַצּוֹת, found nearly always in the plural, and translated **unleavened bread.** It means *sweetness*, (Gesenius, *Lex.*,) and denotes bread not made sour by leaven—not allowed time to ferment.

4. All the people from every quarter — Heb., *from the extremity*, that is, of the city. Here we have a picture of the vilest kind of a rabble, debased to the most shameless licentiousness.

5. Bring them out unto us, that we may know them—A euphemism, pointing to the unnatural crime of pederasty, an abomination into which the Canaanitish nations were sunken, and for which they were cast out. Lev. xviii, 22–25; comp. Judges xix, 22–25; Rom. i, 27. From this incident this crime against nature has received the name of *Sodomy*. Comp. Isa. iii, 9.

8. Two daughters — This proposition of Lot is utterly shocking and outrageous. But see Judges xix, 24, and note there. "We may suppose," says Murphy, "that it was spoken rashly, in the heat of the moment, and with the expectation that he would not be taken at his word." The Oriental idea of hospitality would also lead a man to lay down his own life, or go to almost any extreme, for the safety of his guest. With every possible apology, however, Lot's proposal in this case reveals how his long residence in the wicked city had lowered his moral tone.

9. Stand back — Hebrew, *approach far off;* or, *draw near farther away.* The coarse cry of a mob. Kalisch explains: "*Approach nearer* to us, *farther away* from the door." **He will needs be a judge** — This Lot, who forsooth **came in to sojourn** merely, will persist in playing the judge.

11. Smote—By an exercise of supernatural power. **Blindness** — The word סַנְוֵרִים is used only here and 2 Kings vi, 18, and in both places denotes a miraculous penal stroke. It seems to denote mental aberration as well as inability to see. Hence the Sodomites recognised not the real nature of the stroke, but **wearied themselves to find the door.** What a wickedness and perversity is here displayed! "That the old and young should come; that they should come from every quarter of the city; that they assault the house, notwithstanding the sacred rights of guests; that they so shamelessly avow their pederastic purpose; that they will not even be appeased by Lot, to whom they once owed their salvation, (chap. xiv,) and that they did not cease to grope for the door after they were stricken with blindess; this is the complete portraiture of a people ripe for the fiery judgment."—*Lange*.

12. Hast thou here any besides— For Lot's sake, sons, daughters, family, and possessions may be saved. So, on the other hand, in the ministry of vengeance, all these perish with the accursed father. Josh. vii, 24, 25.

soever thou hast in the city, q bring *them* out of this place: **13** For we will destroy this place, because the r cry of them is waxen great before the face of the Lord; and s the Lord hath sent us to destroy it. **14** And Lot went out, and spake unto his sons in law, t which married his daughters, and said, u Up, get you out of this place; for the Lord will destroy this city. v But he seemed as one that mocked unto his sons in law.

15 And when the morning arose, then the angels hastened Lot, saying, w Arise, take thy wife, and thy two daughters, which 1 are here; lest thou be consumed in the 2 iniquity of the city. **16** And while he lingered, the men laid hold upon his hand, and upon the hand of his wife, and upon the hand of his two daughters; x the Lord being merciful unto him: y and they brought him forth, and set him without the city.

17 And it came to pass, when they had brought them forth abroad, that he said, z Escape for thy life; a look not behind thee, neither stay thou in all the plain; escape to the mountain, lest thou be consumed. **18** And Lot said unto

---
q Chap. 7. 1; 2 Pet. 2. 7, 9.——r Chap. 18. 20. ——s 1 Chron. 21. 15.——t Matt. 1. 18.——u Num. 16. 21, 45.——v Exod. 9. 21; Luke 17. 28; 24. 11. ——w Num. 16. 24, 26; Rev. 18. 4.

1 Heb. *are found.*——2 Or, *punishment.*—— x Luke 18. 13; Rom. 9. 15, 16. —— y Psa. 34. 22. ——z 1 Kings 19. 3.——a Verse 26; Matt. 24. 16, 17, 18; Luke 9. 62; Phil. 3. 13, 14.

---

13. **We will destroy this place**—Now they announce themselves as ministers of wrath to Sodom.

14. **Which married his daughters** —Heb., *takers of his daughters.* The Vulgate renders, *who were about to take his daughters;* and hence it has been generally supposed that his daughters were only betrothed, not actually married. The Hebrew expression will, however, allow the meaning of actual marriage, and verse 15 distinguishes the two daughters "which are here," as if to imply other daughters not present with Lot at the time. No mention is made of sons, except incidentally by the angel, in verse 12, and there by way of question as to whether he had any in the city. No other mention of sons being made, and the fact that he went and alarmed **his sons-in-law,** argues rather that he had no sons. **Seemed as one that mocked**—This is usually explained as meaning, he seemed to them to be *jesting,* or *trifling.* But this verb, in the Piel form, is everywhere used of lascivious sports, or carnal intercourse. His sons-in-law, familiar with the lewd practices so common in the streets of Sodom, supposed Lot was out indulging lascivious passions. See note on chap. xxi, 9.

15. **When the morning arose**—Or, *as the dawn went up;* as it began to turn towards day, "when the morning star rose."—*Kalisch.* It was after sunrise when Lot reached Zoar, (verse 23,) so that he must have left Sodom some time before. **Hastened Lot**—It was hard for him to tear himself so suddenly away from his home. **Which are here**—Heb., *which are found.* This implies other daughters which were not found. **In the iniquity of the city**—The city and its iniquity are to be blotted out together, and those who perish with the city, perish with and in its iniquity, being identified with it.

16. **While he lingered**—Still he clings to his home and possessions, and must needs be forced away. **Brought him forth**—Thus the mercy of Jehovah, working by the hands of these two angels, reaches forth and grasps Lot and his wife and daughters from the impending ruin.

17. **He said**—Does Jehovah himself now appear again with the two angels, or is one of the two angels here intended? Either view is possible, but perhaps the more simple and obvious one is, that it is here one of the two angels that speaks. The angel's words breathe with a quivering energy. Note the four commands: 1) **Escape for thy life**—It is a race for life. 2) **Look not behind thee**—One backward look may prove thy ruin. 3) **Neither stay thou in all the plain**—All this fair circle of the Jordan, (Gen. xiii, 10,) on which Lot had cast covetous eyes, was now a doomed field, from which he must get himself utterly away. 4) **Escape to the mountain**—The mountains of Moab, on the east of the Dead Sea, were probably intended. Away to the hills must he now betake himself for safety who once left the hills for this attractive valley. The **escape,**

them, O, ᵇ not so, my Lord: **19** Behold now, thy servant hath found grace in thy sight, and thou hast magnified thy mercy, which thou hast showed unto me in saving my life; and I cannot escape to the mountain, lest some evil take me, and I die: **20** Behold now, this city *is* near to flee unto, and it *is* a little one: O, let me escape thither, (*is* it not a little one?) and my soul shall live.

21 And he said unto him, See, ᶜ I have accepted ³ thee concerning this thing also, that I will not overthrow this city, for the which thou hast spoken. **22** Haste thee, escape thither; for ᵈ I cannot do any thing till thou be come thither. Therefore ᵉ the name of the city was called ⁴ Zoar.

23 The sun was ⁵ risen upon the earth when Lot entered into Zoar. **24** Then

---
b Acts 10.14.——*c* Job 42.8, 9; Psa. 145.19.——3 Heb. *thy face.*——*d* See chap. 32. 25, 26; Exod. 32. 10;

Deut. 9, 14; Mark 6. 5.——*e* Chap. 13. 10; 14. 2.——4 That is, *Little*, verse 20.——5 Heb. *gone forth.*

---

escape, repeated twice, intensifies the thought of his imminent peril, and now it is added: **Lest thou be consumed**—Deadly destruction and wrath hover over all the plain.

18. **My lord**—Or, as translated in verse 2, *my lords.* The Masorites mark the word here as "holy," but in verse 2 as "profane." But this is scarcely a necessary distinction. The address would be an appropriate form of salutation, whether the person addressed be Jehovah or one of the angels. Lot's petition betrays exceeding weakness. He pleads the mercy already shown, inability to do what is commanded, and fear lest the threatened evil overtake him before he can reach the eastern mountains. He urges, finally, that he may be permitted to flee into a neighbouring city, first, because it was near; second, because it was a little one; and then, because, with such permission, there was hope that he might live. How different this from the faith of Abraham!

20. **This city**—It appears that **this city** was near to Sodom, and a small town, and for this reason called Zoar, (verse 22,) which means *small.* Its previous name was Bela. Chap. xiv, 2. Nearly all ancient tradition and local names indicate that Zoar and the other cities of the plain were located at the southern end of what is now the Dead Sea. See on chap. xiv, 2. Robinson locates Zoar on the southern side of the Wady Kerak, in the eastern part of the Lisan peninsula.

21. **I have accepted thee**—Heb., *I have lifted up thy face.* Metaphorically, the supplicant is supposed to have his face bowed down to the earth, and a granting of the prayer thus offered was a lifting up of the face.

22. **I cannot do any thing till thou be come thither**—Mark the limitations of judgment by the purposes of grace! The angel of destruction is held back from his deadly work until Lot is rescued.

23. **The sun was risen**—Heb., *the sun went forth over the earth.* That is, the sun was up before Lot completed his flight. From dawn (verse 15) to sunrise was but a little time to effect such an escape. But the refugees were probably strengthened by the angels.

DESTRUCTION OF SODOM AND GOMORRAH, 24-28.

This account of the overthrow of the cities of the plain is brief, but graphic. Four things are succinctly told: 1) The means of destruction—fire and brimstone from heaven. 2) The effect—utter ruin of the cities, inhabitants, and vegetation. 3) Lot's wife perishing. 4) The appearance of the country after the destruction, as seen by Abraham—like "the smoke of a furnace."

It is scarcely necessary to repeat here the various speculations and controversies touching the sites of the "cities of the plain," (see on chapter xiv, 3,) the possible causes of their destruction, and the present configuration of the Dead Sea. On these subjects the reader must consult the special treatises, and the Biblical Dictionaries. See especially McClintock and Strong's Cyclopædia, articles *Dead Sea, Gomorrah, Sodom, Siddim, and Zoar.*

It has been supposed that the Jordan once flowed southwards through the Arabian Ghor, and emptied into the Red Sea through the Gulf of Akabah. But it is now generally conceded that this salt lake, now nearly 1,300 feet lower than the Mediterranean, and over

ᶠ the LORD rained upon Sodom and upon Gomorrah brimstone and fire from the LORD out of heaven; **25** And he overthrew those cities, and all the plain, and all the inhabitants of the cities, and ᵍ that which grew upon the ground.

ᶠ Deut. 29. 23; Isa. 13. 19; Jer. 20. 16; 50. 40; Ezek. 16. 49, 50; Hosea 11. 8; Amos 4. 11; Zeph. 2. 9; Luke 17. 29; 2 Pet. 2. 6; Jude 7.—ᵍ Chap. 14. 3; Psa. 107. 34.

1,300 feet lower than the Red Sea, never communicated with the latter, but must have existed long before the age of Abraham. But very probably this ancient lake, which received the waters of the Jordan and many other streams, was very much smaller than the present Dead Sea. This latter, doubtless, covers much surface which was anciently a luxuriant plain. According to Major Wilson, of the Palestine Exploration Fund, "the basin of the Dead Sea has been formed without any influence from, or communication with, the ocean; whence it follows that the lake has never been any thing but a reservoir for the rainfall, the saltness of which originally proceeded from the environs of the lake, and has greatly increased under the influence of incessant evaporation. At a later date volcanic eruptions have taken place to the north-east and east of the Dead Sea, and the last phenomena which affected its basin were the hot and mineral springs and bituminous eruptions which often accompany and follow volcanic action." It is the province of scientific research to bring to light all that can be ascertained as to the geological formation of this mysterious gulf. The destruction of the cities of Sodom and Gomorrah was, according to the obvious import of our narrative, miraculous. See the exposition below.

24. **The Lord rained . . . from the Lord**—The divine names here used are JEHOVAH. Jehovah sent rain, or caused it to rain, (הִמְטִיר,) from Jehovah out of the heavens. Naturally enough have divines discerned in this peculiar statement the idea of some mysterious interaction of Jehovah and his angel. No doubt the truth is, as many put it, that "the Lord rained from himself;" but it is also true that in that mysterious SELFHOOD there are distinguishable powers and forms of self-manifestation, and these are profoundly intimated in such passages as this, and those that speak of the angel of Jehovah. See on chap. xvi, 7. Such intimations are not to be pressed as *proofs* of the divine Trinity, but may be properly regarded as inspired adumbrations of a plurality of persons in the unity of God. **Brimstone and fire**—These are expressly said to have been rained **out of heaven,** and the circumstances amply detailed in this and the preceding chapters and the whole context, set forth the manner of the event as miraculous. But we may well believe that in this event, as in the plagues of Egypt, God used natural agencies to accomplish his will. "We know," says Dr. E. Robinson, "that the country is subject to earthquakes, and exhibits also frequent traces of volcanic action. . . . Perhaps both causes were at work; for volcanic action and earthquakes go hand in hand; and the accompanying electric discharges usually cause lightnings to play and thunders to roll. In this way we have all the phenomena which the most literal interpretation of the sacred records can demand. Further, if we may suppose that before this catastrophe the bitumen had become accumulated around the sources; and had, perhaps, formed strata spreading for some distance upon the plain; that possibly these strata in some parts extended under the soil, and might thus easily approach the vicinity of the cities; then the kindling of such a mass of combustible materials, through volcanic action or by lightning from heaven, would cause a conflagration sufficient not only to engulf the cities, but also to destroy the surface of the plain, so that 'the smoke of the country would go up as the smoke of a furnace,' and the sea, rushing in, would convert it into a tract of waters." —*Biblical Researches,* vol. ii, p. 190.

25. **Overthrew those cities . . . plain . . . inhabitants . . . that which grew**—Note the fourfold destruction. This sudden and awful

26 But his wife looked back from behind him, and she became ʰ a pillar of salt.

27 And Abraham gat up early in the morning to the place where ¹ he stood before the LORD: **28** And he looked toward Sodom and Gomorrah, and toward all the land of the plain, and be-

---

ʰ Luke 17. 32.   *i* Chap. 18. 22.

---

ruin is referred to repeatedly as an example of God's fearful judgments upon the wicked. Comp. Deut. xxix, 23; Jer. xlix, 18; lx, 40; Zeph. ii, 9; 2 Pet. ii, 6. It is interesting to notice in this connexion the remarks of the old geographer Strabo, who was born about half a century before Christ. Near Masada, he says, "are to be seen rocks bearing the marks of fire; fissures in many places; a soil like ashes; pitch falling in drops from the rocks; rivers boiling up and emitting a fetid odor to a great distance; dwellings in every direction overthrown; whence we are inclined to believe the common tradition of the natives, that thirteen cities once existed there, the capital of which was Sodom, but that a circuit of about sixty *stadia* around it escaped uninjured. Shocks of earthquakes, however, eruptions of flames and hot springs, containing asphaltus and sulphur, caused the lake to burst its bounds, and the rocks took fire. Some of the cities were swallowed up; others were abandoned by such of the inhabitants as were able to make their escape." *Book* xvi, 2, 44. *Bohn's Ed.* Comp. Tacitus, *Hist.*, v, 7, and Josephus, *Ant.*, i, 11, 4, and *Wars*, iv, 8, 4.

26. His wife looked back — Prompted by her longing for what she had left behind, and a curiosity to witness the destruction. Her example is given as a warning against desire and effort to take one's goods when God calls away. Luke xvii, 32. **She became a pillar of salt**—Looking backwards and lingering behind, she was probably smitten by the fire and brimstone, and afterwards covered over by a deposit of salt, and became a mound, or pillar, like those which may even now be seen at the southern end of the Dead Sea. The apocryphal Book of Wisdom (x, 7) says that in that waste land to this day "a standing pillar of salt is a monument of an unbelieving soul," and accordingly many

LOT'S WIFE.

a traveller has sought to identify this pillar. The following cut represents a column, called by the Arabs *Bint Sheik Lot*, which was visited by Palmer, and described as "a tall, isolated needle of rock, which really does bear a curious resemblance to an Arab woman with a child upon her shoulder." But he observes, "the rock discovered by us does not fulfil the requirements of the Scripture story, but there can be no doubt that it is the object which has served to keep alive for so many ages the local tradition of the event."

27. Early in the morning—Probably the morning of the day of destruction is intended; the next day after his intercession. While Lot is entering Zoar, on the east of the plain, Abraham is gazing from the west upon the smoking gorge between them. They are now separated by a great gulf, and come no more together.

28. Looked toward Sodom . . . smoke—The fearful sight shows him that there were not even ten righteous persons to be found in Sodom. But Abraham's intercession had an answer in the salvation of Lot. See verse 29.

held, and, lo, ᵏ the smoke of the country went up as the smoke of a furnace.

29 And it came to pass, when God destroyed the cities of the plain, that God ˡ remembered Abraham, and sent Lot out of the midst of the overthrow, when he overthrew the cities in the which Lot dwelt.

30 And Lot went up out of Zoar, and ᵐ dwelt in the mountain, and his two daughters with him; for he feared to dwell in Zoar: and he dwelt in a cave, he and his two daughters. **31** And the firstborn said unto the younger, Our father *is* old, and *there is* not a man in the earth ⁿ to come in unto us after the manner of all the earth: **32** Come, let us make our father drink wine, and we will lie with him, that we ᵒ may preserve seed of our father. **33** And they made their father drink wine that night: and the firstborn went in, and lay with her father; and he perceived not when she lay down, nor when she arose. **34** And it came to pass on the morrow, that the firstborn said unto the younger, Behold, I lay yesternight with my father: let us make him drink wine this night also; and go thou in, *and* lie with him, that we may preserve seed of our father. **35** And they made their father drink wine that night also: and the younger arose, and lay with him; and he perceived not when she lay down, nor when she arose. **36** Thus were both the daughters of Lot with child by their father. **37** And the firstborn bare a son, and called his name Moab: ᵖ the same

---

ᵏ Rev. 18. 9.—— *l* Chap. 8. 1; 18. 23.——*m* Ver. 17, 19. *n* Chap. 16. 2, 4; 38. 8, 9; Deut. 25. 5.——*o* Mark 12. 19.——*p* Deut. 2. 9.

As the smoke of a furnace—The rain of fire and brimstone left behind it a smoking ruin, and the deep depression from which the smoke ascended might well remind one of the mouth of a furnace.

LOT'S INFAMOUS DAUGHTERS, 29–38.

29. God remembered Abraham, and sent Lot out—Thus Lot's rescue is attributed to Abraham's prayer. This was Lot's second rescue by the help of Abraham. See chap. xiv, 16.

30. In the mountain—One of the mountains on the east of the Dead Sea, afterwards known as the mountains of Moab. He who covetously chose the inviting plain (xiii, 11) now gladly seeks the mountain. **He feared to dwell in Zoar**—The terror of Sodom's fall entered into his soul, and he feared to dwell so near the scene of ruin as was Zoar. He knew, also, that even that little city was at first among those doomed to destruction. **Dwelt in a cave**—The rocks and mountains on the east of the Dead Sea abound in caves, many of them, perhaps, the original homes of the Horites. See on chap. xiv, 6.

31. The firstborn said unto the younger—The infamous measures which this elder daughter proposed, and in which she was readily followed by her younger sister, shows what demoralizing power the city life of Sodom had exerted over them. They became familiar with "the filthy conversation of the wicked," (2 Pet. ii, 7;) their sisters had married, and perhaps they themselves had been betrothed to men of Sodom, (see on verses 14, 15,) and possibly their mother was a woman of Sodom, (note on 13, 14;) what could be expected of daughters grown up amid such surroundings! Even though Lot held the faith of Abraham, and reproved his wicked neighbours, his worldly-mindedness was strong, and his parental discipline as feeble, perhaps, as Eli's. 1 Sam. ii, 22–25. **Not a man in the earth**—That is, in the *land*, or country around them. We are not to understand by this, as some of the ancient interpreters, that Lot's daughters believed the whole human race to have been destroyed, but that they had no hope of marriage with any of the men of the country to which they had fled.

33. He perceived not—"These words do not affirm that he was in an unconscious state; they merely mean that in his intoxicated state, though not entirely unconscious, yet he lay with his daughters without clearly knowing what he was doing. . . . But Lot's daughters had so little feeling of shame in connexion with their conduct, that they gave names to the sons they bore which have immortalized their paternity."—*Keil*.

37. Called his name Moab—Which means, *from father*. This, we are informed, was the origin of the

is the father of the Moabites unto this day. **38** And the younger, she also bare a son, and called his name Ben-ammi: q the same is the father of the children of Ammon unto this day.

CHAPTER XX.

AND Abraham journeyed from

q Deut. 2. 19.——a Chap. 13. 1.——b Chap. 16. 7, 14.——c Chap. 26. 6.

Moabites, who occupied the country on the east of the southern half of the Dead Sea, formerly occupied by the Emim. Deut. ii, 11.

38. **Ben-ammi**—Which means, *son of my people;* that is, begotten of my own race. The Ammonites expelled the Zamzummim, and occupied their land, on the north of the territory of Moab. Deut. ii, 19-21.

" In Lot's history we may trace the judgment as well as the mercy of God. His selfish choice of the plain of the Jordan led him, perhaps, to present wealth and prosperity, but withal to temptation and danger. In the midst of the abandoned profligacy of Sodom he, indeed, was preserved in comparative purity, and so, when God overthrew the cities of the plain, he yet saved Lot from destruction. Still Lot's feebleness of faith first caused him to linger, (verse 16,) then to fear escape to the mountains, (verse 19,) and, lastly, to doubt the safety of the place which God had spared for him, verse 30. Now again he is led by his children into intoxication, which betrays him, unconsciously, into far more dreadful wickedness. And then we hear of him no more. He is left by the sacred narrative, saved indeed from the conflagration of Sodom, but an outcast—widowed, homeless, hopeless, without children or grandchildren, save the authors and the heirs of his shame."—*Speaker's Commentary.*

CHAPTER XX.

ABRAHAM AND ABIMELECH, 1-18.

1. **Abraham journeyed from thence**—Not impelled by fear, as Lot (chap. xix, 30) when he went up out of Zoar, but probably impressed by the destruction of Sodom that he must not

thence toward ª the south country, and dwelt between ᵇ Kadesh and Shur, and ᶜ sojourned in Gerar. **2** And Abraham said of Sarah his wife, ᵈ She is my sister: and Abimelech king of Gerar sent, and ᵉ took Sarah. **3** But ᶠ God came to Abimelech ᵍ in a dream by night, and said to him, ʰ Behold, thou art but a

d Chap. 12. 13 ; 26. 7.——e Chap. 12. 15.——f Psa. 105. 14.——g Job 33. 15.——h Verse 7.

sojourn too long with any one heathen people. **The south country**—Heb., *the Negeb.* See on chap. xiii, 1. **Kadesh**—On Trumbull's identification of this place, see on chap. xiv, 7. **Shur** — See on chap. xvi, 7. The name **Shur** means *a wall,* and was, perhaps, first given to the high ridge or wall of rock extending north and south through the western portion of the desert et-Tih. This whole north-western part of the peninsula of Sinai thus came to be called the wilderness of Shur. See on Exod. xv, 22. **Gerar**—Rowlands discovered a valley and ruins, some three hours journey south of Gaza, bearing the name of *Gerar,* but the identification has not been sufficiently confirmed. He merely **sojourned** in Gerar as a stranger and pilgrim, while his more permanent *dwelling* (the abode of his great household and the place where his vast herds remained) was the open pasture lands between Kadesh and Shur.

2. **She is my sister**—Here Abraham repeats the folly he had shown in Egypt. Comp. chap. xii, 11-17. **Abimelech** means, *my father king,* or *fathers of the king,* and seems to have been the common title of the Philistine kings, as Pharaoh was of Egyptian kings.

3. **God came to Abimelech in a dream**—It is interesting to note the use in this chapter of the divine names. Here it is **God** (*Elohim* without the article) who comes to him in a dream, and in verse 4 he calls him *Lord* (*Adonai.*) Then in verse 6, it is *the God* (*Elohim* with the article) who continues to speak with the Philistine king. In verse 11 Abraham speaks timidly of the *fear of God,* (*Elohim* without the article,) and uses the same indefinite name again in verse 13, as if accommodating himself to the notions of a

dead man, for the woman which thou hast taken; for she *is* ¹a man's wife. **4** But Abimelech had not come near her: and he said, Lord, ⁱ wilt thou slay also a righteous nation? **5** Said he not unto me, She *is* my sister? and she, even she herself said, He *is* my brother: ᵏ in the ² integrity of my heart and innocency of my hands have I done this. **6** And God said unto him in a dream, Yea, I know that thou didst this in the integrity of thy heart; for ¹I also withheld thee from sinning ᵐ against me: therefore suffered I thee not to touch her. **7** Now therefore restore the man *his* wife; ⁿ for he *is* a prophet, and he shall

---

1 Heb. *married to a husband.*—*i* Chap. 18. 23; ver. 18.—*k* 2 Kings 20. 3; 2 Cor. 1. 12.—2 Or, *simplicity*, or, *sincerity.*—*l* Chap. 31. 7; 35. 5; | Exod. 34. 24; 1 Sam. 25. 26, 31.—*m* Chap. 39. 9; Lev. 6. 2; Psa. 51. 4.—*n* 1 Sam. 7. 5; 2 Kings 5. 11; Job 42. 8; James 5. 14, 15; 1 John 5. 16.

---

heathen king. But in verse 17 it is said that Abraham prayed *unto the God,* (*Elohim* with the article,) and God (Elohim without the article) healed Abimelech, etc.; and then, in verse 18, it is finally declared that it was *Jehovah,* the covenant God of Abraham, who had interposed to preserve and honour the mother of the promised seed. **Behold, thou art but a dead man**—Heb., *behold thee dead!* Probably first of all an allusion to the deadness of the "wombs of the house of Abimelech," (verse 18, note,) and also prospective of the certain death before him if he restored not the wife of Abraham, verse 7. **For she is a man's wife**—Heb., *and she mistress of a lord.* Kalisch calls it "a pleonastic expression, the wife of a husband."

4. Had not come near her—He and his house had apparently been smitten with some judgment (verses 6, 18) which restrained him from Sarah, and hindered his wife and maidservants from conception. From which it would seem that Sarah was removed some time from Abraham. **Also a righteous nation**—There seems to be in these words an allusion to the destruction of the Sodomites. The fame of that fearful judgment had probably spread through all the adjacent lands, and made a profound impression; and now, when God speaks in a dream to this king, Abimelech asks, in amazement, if his people are in danger of a judgment like those wicked sinners. In his emotion his language rises almost to a poetic strain:

O Lord, a nation also righteous wilt thou slay?
Did not he say to me,
My sister is she?
And she, she also, said,
My brother is he.

In the integrity of my heart,
And in the innocency of my hands,
Have I done this.

In this king we may recognise an exceptional example of heathen uprightness. His ideas of *righteousness, integrity,* and *innocence* do not forbid polygamy, so that he has no compunction in adding Sarah to his harem. But he pleads sincerity and personal honour. Though lamentably low, he is far above the moral level of the Sodomites; and yet he needs the prayers and help of Abraham, who himself is far from the highest idea of innocence. Behold here the necessity of divine revelation. Without the word of the Lord, how could simple man come to know righteousness, or integrity, or purity?

6. In a dream — Repeated again from verse 3. It would seem as if the dream had been broken by the emotion of Abimelech, and after a period of wakefulness he dreamed again, and God again revealed himself. "The prophetic dream of the night is generally closely connected with the moral reflections and longings of the day. It is in full agreement with the nature of dreams that the communication should be made in several acts, not in a single one. See chaps. xxxvii and xli, and Matt. ii."—*Lange.* **Yea, I know**—Or, *I have known.* Abimelech has not been without the knowledge and care of the true God, (הָאֱלֹהִים, *the Elohim,*) who now accepts his plea, and adds: **I also withheld thee from sinning against me**—God had overruled the whole matter. Comp. verses 3, 4, 17, 18, notes.

7. He is a prophet — Here the word **prophet** first occurs, but the spirit of prophecy had been abroad long before, speaking though Enoch

About B. C. 1898. CHAPTER XX. 215

pray for thee, and thou shalt live: and if thou restore *her* not, ° know thou that thou shalt surely die, thou, ᴾ and all that *are* thine. **8** Therefore Abimelech rose early in the morning, and called all his servants, and told all these things in their ears: and the men were sore afraid. **9** Then Abimelech called Abraham, and said unto him, What hast thou done unto us? and what have I offended thee, ᑫ that thou hast brought on me and on my kingdom a great sin? thou hast done deeds unto me ʳ that ought not to be done. **10** And Abimelech said unto Abraham, What sawest thou, that thou hast done this thing? **11** And Abraham said, Because I thought, Surely ˢ the fear of God *is* not in this place; and ᵗ they will slay me for my wife's sake. **12** And yet indeed ᵘ *she is* my sister; she *is* the daughter of my father, but not the daughter of my mother; and she

---

o Chap. 2. 17.—*p* Num. 16. 32, 33.—*q* Chap. 26. 10; Exod. 32. 21; Josh. 7. 25.—*r* Chap. 34. 7.   *s* Chap. 42. 18; Psa. 36, 1; Prov. 16. 6.— *t* Chap. 12. 12; 26. 7.—*u* See chap. 11. 29.

---

and Noah. A prophet, נָבִיא, is one who announces a divine message. The message itself may refer to things past, present, or future, so that *prediction*, or foretelling of events, is only incidental to prophecy, not its leading idea. On the distinction between the names *prophet* and *seer*, see note on 1 Sam. ix, 9. Abraham was *a prophet* to Abimelech, and sent to **pray** for him; for prayer and praise were elements of prophesying. In the offering of sacrifices and in his intercession for Sodom, he appeared as *priest.* In his battles with the eastern kings, and in his disposal of the spoil, he appeared as *king;* so that in the father of the faithful we may see these several offices combined.

8. Rose early—The visions of the night had made a profound impression, stirring the depths of his soul, and he hastened with the dawn to inquire into the matter. Compare Dan. vi, 19. **Called all his servants**—His courtiers and counsellors. **Told all these things**—This procedure is another evidence of the integrity and uprightness of this king. He has nothing to conceal, though much to excite and reprove him. **The men were sore afraid**— Their king had also become a prophet, and revealed to them the word of God, and the revelation filled them with deepest reverence and awe.

9. Abimelech called Abraham— The king remonstrated with Abraham "publicly, in the presence of his servants, partly for his own justification in the sight of his dependents, and partly to put Abraham to shame."— *Keil.* Mark again the poetic fervour of his words;

What hast thou done to us?
And what have I sinned against thee?
That thou bringest upon me and upon my kingdom
A great sin?
Deeds which should not be done
Hast thou done with me.

Abraham seems to have been stunned and confused by this sharp rebuke, and after some silence Abimelech asks again:

10 **What sawest thou** — What didst thou observe in us or among us to lead thee to do this thing? What didst thou take us to be? Others take the question to mean, "What hadst thou in thine eye; or what object hadst thou in view?"

11. **Abraham said**—Abraham's answer has four points: 1) He thought the people of Gerar to be without the fear of God. 2) That they would therefore be likely to slay him, in order to obtain his wife. 3) She was, indeed, his sister. 4) They had both entered into an agreement at the beginning of their wanderings, that, for mutual safety, they would, among strange peoples, call each other brother and sister. **Fear of God**—The reverence and piety due before the Holy One. Abraham had, very probably, seen things in Gerar which were contrary to his ideas of uprightness, and he was prompted to his duplicity by the same motive of fear that actuated him in Egypt. Compare chap. xii, 12.

12. **Daughter of my father** — "Sarah's name does not occur in the genealogies, and we do not know anything of her birth but that which is here stated. Such marriages, though forbidden afterwards, (Lev. xviii, 9, 11, xx, 17, Deut. xxvii, 22,) may not

became my wife. **13** And it came to pass, when ᵛ God caused me to wander from my father's house, that I said unto her, This *is* thy kindness which thou shalt show unto me; at every place whither we shall come, ʷ say of me, He *is* my brother. **14** And Abimelech ˣ took sheep, and oxen, and menservants, and womenservants, and gave *them* unto Abraham, and restored him Sarah his wife. **15** And Abimelech said, Behold, ʸ my land *is* before thee: dwell ³ where it pleaseth thee. **16** And unto Sarah he said, Behold, I have given ᶻ thy brother a thousand *pieces* of silver: ᵃ behold, he *is* to thee ᵇ a covering of the eyes, unto all that *are* with thee, and with all *other:* thus she was reproved.

v Chap. 12. 1, 9, 11, etc.; Heb. 11. 8.——*w* Chap. 12. 13.——*x* Chap. 12. 16.——*y* Chap. 13. 9. 3 Heb. *as* is *good in thine eyes.*——*z* Verse 5.——*a* Chap. 26. 11.——*b* Chap. 24. 65.

have been esteemed unlawful in patriarchal times, and they were common among the heathen nations of antiquity. Many Jewish and Christian interpreters, however, think that **daughter** here means *granddaughter*, and that Sarah was the same as Iscah, the sister of Lot, (chap. xi, 29,) who is called the brother of Abraham in chap. xiv, 16."—*Speaker's Commentary.*

14. **Took sheep and oxen**—Compare the similar present of the king of Egypt, chap. xii, 16.

16. **I have given thy brother**—The use of the word **brother**, in this connexion, must have had for Sarah a pungent significance. **A thousand pieces of silver**—Heb., *a thousand of silver.* Whether they were shekels, or other coin, is a matter of mere conjecture, and the exact value of "a thousand of silver" is, therefore, unknown. It is also uncertain whether the silver here spoken of was an additional gift, or merely a round estimate of the value of the gifts specified in verse 14. **Behold, he is to thee a covering of the eyes**—These words have been understood in three different ways : 1) The pronoun he should be translated *it*, or *this*, (so Sept. and Vulg.,) referring to the gift of silver, which was presented to Abraham to purchase a veil to cover Sarah's face. It is alleged that in the ancient East it was a custom for married women to go veiled, and unmarried women to go unveiled — a custom which Sarah seems to have disregarded. 2) The silver was given as an expiation or atonement to make satisfaction for the wrong done to Sarah and all others connected with Abraham. The expression *cover the eyes*, is thus supposed to be equivalent with *cover the face*, in the Heb. of chap. xxxii, 20, and there translated "appease." 3) Abraham himself is declared to be a veil unto Sarah; that is, an all-sufficient covering and protection from the eyes and hands of other men. For he was a prophet, and she a prophet's wife, and God would not suffer them to come to harm. We believe this last to be the true interpretation. For the first would seem too much like trifling, and a thousand of silver would be an extravagant sum to name as the price of a veil. The second involves a notion too theological to be expressed by a heathen king; and the word for **covering** is כְּסוּת, (which is always used of a garment,) not כָּפַר, which is used in chap. xxxii, 20, and is the common word for *cover*, in the sense of making atonement. The third follows the simple and natural meaning of the words, and gives a suitable turn to the narrative by reminding Sarah and all connected with her that her lord, whom she had called her *brother*, and whom God so signally honoured, was a sufficient covering and defence. **With all other** — As distinguished from **all that are with thee**. Happy all who may thus be covered with the garment of Abraham. Some critics construe the words וְאֶת־כֹּל, *and with all*, with what follows, וְנֹכָחַת, translated in our version, **thus she was reproved**. Keil renders : *And with all—so art thou justified;* and observes : "וְנֹכַחַת can only be the second person, fem. sing. perf. Niphal, although the *Daghesh lene* is wanting in the ת; for the rules of syntax will hardly allow us to regard this form as a participle. The literal meaning is, *so thou art judged;* that is, justice has been done thee." Murphy renders : *"And all this that thou*

About B. C. 1898.   CHAPTER XX.   217

17 So Abraham ᵃ prayed unto God: and God healed Abimelech, and his wife, and his maidservants; and they bare *children.* **18** For the LORD ᵒ had fast closed up all the wombs of the house of Abimelech, because of Sarah, Abraham's wife.

CHAPTER XXI.

AND the LORD ᵃ visited Sarah as he had said, and the LORD did unto

Sarah ᵇ as he had spoken. **2** For Sarah ᶜ conceived, and bare Abraham a son in his old age, ᵈ at the set time of which God had spoken to him. **3** And Abraham called the name of his son that was born unto him, whom Sarah bare to him, ᵉ Isaac. **4** And Abraham ᶠ circumcised his son Isaac being eight days old, ᵍ as God had commanded him. **5** And ʰ Abraham was a hundred years old, when his son Isaac was born unto him.

n Job 42. 9, 10.——*o* Chapter 12. 17.——*a* 1 Samuel 2. 21.——*b* Chapter 17. 19; 18. 10, 14; Galatians 4. 23, 28.

c Acts 7. 8; Gal. 4. 22; Heb. 11. 11.——*d* Chap. 17. 21.——*e* Chap. 17. 19.——*f* Acts 7. 8.——*g* Chap. 17. 10, 12.——*h* Chap. 17. 1, 17.

mayest be righted." But such a construction is contrary to the Masoretic pointing and accents, and is exceedingly awkward. It certainly has as much against it as for it, and we prefer the interpretation expressed in the common version, "*thus she was reproved.*" The words of Abimelech *convicted her, set her right,* (נֹכַח) and thereafter we read no more of her resorting to such duplicity.

17. Prayed unto God—He prayed unto הָאֱלֹהִים, *the true God;* as one who felt the responsibility of being a prophet. **Healed Abimelech**—From this it is clear that Abimelech and his wife and concubines had been plagued with some malady, as a curse for his taking Sarah. **They bare**—יָלְדוּ in pause for יֵלְדוּ. The grammatical reference being to the three nouns of the preceding sentence, in which **Abimelech** stands first, the verb is put in the masculine plural.

18. The Lord—It was JEHOVAH, the covenant God, who had thus interposed. **Fast closed up all the wombs**—So as to prevent conception. Compare 1 Sam. i, 5, 6. **Because of Sarah**—The malady, which is said to have been *healed,* verse 17, was sent for Sarah's sake, and, therefore, we naturally suppose that Sarah was kept apart from Abraham some months at least. Compare verses 3, 4, notes.

CHAPTER XXI.
BIRTH OF ISAAC, 1-8.

"At last the time of fulfilment has arrived. During five and twenty years

cheering assurances had brightened the gloom of Abraham's pilgrimage; he had risen to God by altars and prayers, and God had descended to him by visions and revelations; he had obeyed, with spontaneous faith, and had received signs and pledges; a covenant had sanctified, and miraculous aid had protected, his life; land and posterity were promised, blessings guaranteed to his seed and to mankind; the child of faith had been announced both to him and to Sarah; and the realization corresponded strictly with the promises." —*Kalisch.*

1. The Lord visited Sarah—The same Lord (Jehovah) who interposed to rescue her from Abimelech. Comp. chap. xx, 18. **Visited**—Any favour of divine Providence is a gracious visitation; but this was special in being the fulfilling of a promise often repeated. **As he had spoken**—See chap. xvii, 16, 19; xviii, 10, 14.

2. At the set time—See chap. xvii, 21.

3. Isaac—The name means, *he shall laugh,* or *laughter.* It was given to commemorate the laughter and excessive joy referred to in verse 6, and in chap. xvii, 19; xviii, 12. Well might there be laughing joy over this heir of promise, through whom all the families of the earth were to be blessed.

4. Circumcised . . . as God had commanded—Observe how obedience to every commandment wrought with Abraham's faith. Thus was that faith made perfect. James ii, 22.

5. Hundred years old—Heb., *son of a hundred years.* Notable and memorable the fact that the father of the faithful was the son of a hundred

6 And Sarah said, ¹ God hath made me to laugh, *so that* all that hear ᵏ will laugh with me. **7** And she said; Who would *have* said unto Abraham, that Sarah should have given children suck? ˡ for I have borne *him* a son in his old age. **8** And the child grew, and was weaned: and Abraham made a great feast the *same* day that Isaac was weaned.

9 And Sarah saw the son of Hagar ᵐ the Egyptian, ⁿ which she had borne unto Abraham, º mocking. **10** Wherefore she said unto Abraham, ᵖ Cast out this bondwoman and her son: for the son of this bondwoman shall not be heir with my son, *even* with Isaac. **11** And the thing was very grievous in Abraham's sight ᑫ because of his son.

---

i Psa. 126. 2; Isa. 54. 1; Gal. 4. 27.——*k* Luke 1. 58.——*l* Chap. 18. 11, 12.——*m* Chap. 16. 1.

n Chap. 16. 15.——*o* Gal. 4. 29.——*p* Gal. 4. 30; see chap. 25. 6; 36. 6, 7.——*q* Chap. 17. 18.

---

years—a century old—when the son was born through whom he was to become "heir of the world." Rom. iv, 13.

6. Sarah said—This is the magnificat of Sarah, and may be compared with Luke i, 46–55. Never before had Sarah felt such thrills of joy, or uttered language of such prophetic fervour. The passage may be put in poetic form as follows:

> And Sarah said,
> God has made me to laugh;
> All who hear will laugh with me.
> And she said,
> Who would have told to Abraham,
> Sons shall be nursed by Sarah.
> For I have begotten a son to his old age.

8. The child ... was weaned—At what age we are not told; perhaps not until he was three years old. Comp. 2 Macc. vii, 27; Josephus, *Ant.*, 2; 9, 6; 1 Sam. i, 22, note. **A great feast**—Such an event would naturally be made an occasion of festive joy.

EXPULSION OF HAGAR AND ISHMAEL, 9–21.

9. Sarah saw — With a mother's careful eye. **Mocking**—Some suppose he mocked at the feast held at Isaac's weaning, and made derision of the contrast between the weak child and the great hopes entertained concerning him. But the Piel form of this word appears everywhere to carry with it the associations of some carnal and lascivious indulgence. Sarah saw Ishmael (מְצַחֵק) committing some lewd act, perhaps of self-pollution, and the sight filled her with an indignation and contempt towards him, which led her to insist on banishing from her household both him and his mother. She would not have her Isaac contaminated by such an associate. So, too, the word, as used in chap. xix, 14, denotes that Lot's son-in-law, to whom all things were impure, could not comprehend Lot's words of warning, but regarded him as one of the lewd fellows who were out at night indulging in the common practices of Sodom. In chapter xxvi, 8, it evidently means some carnal intercourse between Isaac and Rebekah, such as was proper only between husband and wife, and the same thought is equally noticeable in the language of Potiphar's wife in chap. xxxix, 14–17, and the lewd play of the Israelites at the feast of the golden calf. Exod. xxxii, 6. And we may well believe that the *sport* which Samson was brought out to make before the merry and perhaps half-drunken Philistines (Judges xvi, 25) was some naked exposure and obscene abuse. These are all the places in which the Piel form of צחק occurs, and there is, therefore, no need of giving it a different sense in any one of these passages.

10. Cast out—Her old spirit of persecution, now embittered by what she saw in Ishmael, came back with imperious force. Comp. chap. xvi, 4–6. " Seeing in Ishmael nothing but the contemptible son of an Egyptian bondmaid—forgetting that he was that offspring of her husband whom she had herself desired — and heedless of the blessings which God had pronounced upon him — she demanded his expulsion, together with that of his detested mother."—*Kalisch.*

11. Very grievous—Abraham's affection for Ishmael was very strong, as may be seen from chap. xvii, 18, and the promise of chap. xvii, 20; and he was, therefore, not disposed at this time to yield to Sarah's word.

About B. C. 1892. CHAPTER XXI. 219

12 And God said unto Abraham, Let it not be grievous in thy sight because of the lad, and because of thy bondwoman; in all that Sarah hath said unto thee, hearken unto her voice; for *r* in Isaac shall thy seed be called. **13** And also of the son of the bondwoman will I make *s* a nation, because he *is* thy seed. **14** And Abraham rose up early in the morning, and took bread, and a bottle of water, and gave *it* unto Hagar, putting *it* on her shoulder, and the child, and *t* sent her away: and she departed, and wandered in the wilderness of Beer-sheba. **15** And the water was spent in the bottle, and she cast the child under one of the shrubs. **16** And she went, and sat her down over against *him* a good way off, as it were a bowshot: for she said, Let me not see the death of the child. And she sat over against *him*, and lifted up her voice, and wept. **17** And *u* God heard the voice of the lad; and the angel of God called to Hagar out of heaven, and said unto her, What aileth thee, Hagar? fear not; for God hath heard the voice of the lad where he *is*. **18** Arise, lift up the lad, and hold him

---

r Rom. 9. 7, 8; Heb. 11. 18.——*s* Verse 18; chap. 16. 10; 17. 20.——*t* John 8. 35.——*u* Exod. 3. 7.

---

12. In Isaac shall thy seed be called—Literally, *In Isaac shall there be called to thee a seed*. The meaning evidently is, that the promised seed should spring, not from Ishmael but from Isaac. First, the promise came to Adam; then to Noah; then, in select succession, to Abraham, Isaac, Jacob, Judah, and David.

14. A bottle of water—A bottle made of skin. "The Arabs, and all

SKIN BOTTLES.

that lead a wandering life, keep their water, milk, and other liquors in leathern bottles. These are made of goat-skins. When the animal is killed, they cut off its feet and its head, and they draw it in this manner out of the skin, without opening its belly. In Arabia they are tanned with acacia-bark and the hairy part left outside. If not tanned, a disagreeable taste is imparted to the water. They afterwards sew up the places where the legs were cut off, and the tail, and when it is filled they tie it about the neck."—SMITH'S *Dict. of Bible*. **Wilderness of Beer-sheba** —The name **Beer-sheba** is, perhaps, used here proleptically. See on ver. 31.

15. Cast the child—From this it has been inferred that Ishmael could not have been a youth of over fifteen years. But neither the word *lad* (נַעַר) (verse 12) nor **child** (יֶלֶד) implies that Ishmael was an infant, nor does the word **cast** (שָׁלַךְ) necessarily imply that she hurled him from her arms. "The boy was young, but he was old enough to give offence to Sarah by mocking. At a time when human life was much longer than it now is, (Ishmael himself died at 137, chap. xxv, 17,) fifteen or sixteen would be little removed from childhood. The growing lad would be easily exhausted with the heat and wandering; whilst the hardy habits of the Egyptian handmaid would enable her to endure much greater fatigue. She had hitherto led the boy by the hand; now she left him, fainting and prostrate, under the shelter of a tree."—*Speaker's Commentary*.

16. As it were a bowshot—This is, doubtless, the sense of the peculiar Hebrew expression used here: *far off as shooters of the bow;* that is, as far off as they can usually shoot an arrow. This whole passage presents us with one of the most graphic and touching of word-pictures.

17. Heard the voice of the lad— From which it appears he wept as well as his mother. **Angel of God**—Not *the angel of Jehovah*, who found her before. Chap. xvi, 7. This was not an appearance, but a voice **out of heaven,** answering her voice (verse 16) and the voice of the lad. Jehovah's Angel has many a ministering angel to send at will.

18. Hold him in thine hand—Heb., *make fast thy hand in him*. She must not cast him off, but go and take hold

GENESIS. About B. C. 1892.

in thine hand; for ᵛI will make him a great nation. **19** And ʷGod opened her eyes, and she saw a well of water; and she went, and filled the bottle with water, and gave the lad drink. **20** And God ˣwas with the lad; and he grew, and dwelt in the wilderness, ʸand became an archer. **21** And he dwelt in the wilderness of Paran: and his mother ᶻtook him a wife out of the land of Egypt. **22** And it came to pass at that time, that ᵃAbimelech and Phichol the chief captain of his host spake unto Abraham, saying, ᵇ God *is* with thee in all that thou doest: **23** Now therefore ᶜswear unto me here by God, ¹that thou wilt not deal falsely with me, nor with my son, nor with my son's son: *but* according to the kindness that I have done unto thee, thou shalt do unto me, and to the land wherein thou hast sojourned. **24** And Abraham said, I will swear. **25** And Abraham reproved Abimelech because of a well of water, which Abimelech's servants ᵈ had violently taken away. **26** And Abimelech said, I wot not who hath done this thing: neither didst thou tell me, neither yet heard I *of it*, but to day. **27** And Abraham took sheep and oxen, and gave them unto Abimelech; and both of them

---

v Verse 13.——*w* Num. 22. 31; see 2 Kings 6. 17, 18, 20; Luke 24. 16, 31.——*x* Chap. 28. 15; 39. 2, 3, 21.——*y* Chap. 16. 12.——*z* Chap. 24. 4.

a Chap. 20. 2; 26. 26.——*b* Chap. 26. 28.——*c* Josh. 2. 12; 1 Sam. 24. 21.——1 Heb. *if thou shalt lie unto me.*——*d* See chap. 26. 15, 18, 20, 21, 22.

---

of his hand again, and take firm hold, confident that the old promise (xvi, 10-12) will be kept.

19. Opened her eyes—Enabling her now to discover what, in weariness and despair, she had failed to notice.

20. God was with the lad—A divine providence watched over and cared for him, although he passed outside the chosen household of Jehovah's covenant. **He grew**—There was room for this, for as yet he was but an undeveloped lad. **Became an archer**—Heb., *he was growing an archer.* He became increasingly a skilful bowman. His descendants were long after noted for their use of the bow. Isa. xxi, 17.

21. The wilderness of Paran—The great central region of the Sinaitic peninsula, now known as the desert et-Tih. **Wife out of . . . Egypt**—His mother's care followed him up to this point, and chose for him a wife out of her own native land. After this we hear of her no more.

This narrative of Ishmael's expulsion is made the basis of an allegory in Gal. iv, 21-26, where see notes. We may also note the following lessons: 1) The mischief of polygamy. 2) The power of jealousy. 3) Bitter passions and wrong conduct springing from a sense of injury or neglect. 4) A doting father's tenderness in conflict with the plans of God. 5) The wants and woes of the homeless, and of the outcasts. 6) No one is beyond the sight and hearing of God 7) The beauty and fidelity of a mother's love. 8) The origin of a nation.

COVENANT BETWEEN ABRAHAM AND ABIMELECH, 22-34.

22. At that time—The time of Ishmael's expulsion. **Phichol**, which means *mouth of all*, is supposed to be, like the name **Abimelech**, an official title. Here, and at chap. xxvi, 26, the name is given to **the chief captain of his host**, a sort of prime officer and minister to the king. **God is with thee**—This fact had been strikingly manifest to Abimelech in the matters related in chap. xx, and probably other incidents of God's care for Abraham had been made known to him. He, therefore, desired a closer alliance with him.

23. Not deal falsely — Perhaps Abraham's duplicity in the matter of Sarah had somewhat to do with inciting Abimelech to seek this oath. He feared his overreaching cunning and sagacity.

25. Reproved—The same word used in chapter xx, 16, where it is said that Sarah was **reproved** by Abimelech. There was an outstanding difficulty which must be settled before Abraham will swear.

26. I wot not—Or, *I knew not.* By this protest Abimelech really reproves Abraham, as if he had been lacking in frankness towards him.

27. Abraham took sheep—If there has been any lack of frankness on his part he will now make the first gift towards alliance.

CHAPTER XXI.

made ᵉa covenant. **28** And Abraham set seven ewe lambs of the flock by themselves. **29** And Abimelech said unto Abraham, ᶠ What *mean* these seven ewe lambs which thou hast set by themselves? **30** And he said, For *these* seven ewe lambs shalt thou take of my hand, that ᵍ they may be a witness unto me, that I have digged this well. **31** Wherefore he ʰ called that place ²Beer-sheba; because there they sware both of them. **32** Thus they made a covenant at Beer-sheba: then Abimelech rose up, and Phichol the chief captain of his host, and they returned into the land of the Philistines.

33 And *Abraham* planted a ³grove in Beer-sheba, and ⁱ called there on the name of the LORD, ᵏ the everlasting God. **34** And Abraham sojourned in the Philistines' land many days.

---

e Chap. 26. 31.——*f* Chap. 33. 8.——*g* Chap. 31. 48, 52.——*h* Chap. 26. 33.——² That is, *The well of the oath*. —— 3 Or. *tree*. —— *i* Chap. 4. 26. —— *k* Deut. 33. 27; Isa. 40. 28; Rom. 16. 26; 1 Tim. 1. 17.

---

30. Seven ewe lambs shalt thou take of my hand—These seem to have been an additional present to bind the treaty at the well. The receiving of this gift would bind Abimelech by a most solemn stipulation. The Hebrew word for *swear*, in verses 23 and 24, is the verbal form of the word for *seven*, and in its usual Niphal form (נִשְׁבַּע) means literally, *to seven one's self.* This, perhaps, arose from the custom of confirming or sealing an oath by seven offerings or seven witnesses.

31. Beer-sheba—Which means *well of the oath*, or, *well of the seven*, in allusion to the seven lambs by which Abraham here confirmed his covenant with Abimelech. In a broad valley, some twelve hours' travel south of Hebron, Dr. Robinson discovered two deep wells, still called *Bir es-Seba*, probably the very same as those dug by the servants of Abraham and Isaac. Compare chap. xxvi, 32. "These wells are some distance apart; they are circular, and stoned up with solid masonry. The larger one is twelve and a half feet in diameter and forty-four and a half feet deep to the surface of the water, sixteen feet of which, at the bottom, is excavated in the solid rock. The other well lies fifty-five rods W. S. W., and is five feet in diameter and forty-two feet deep. The water in both is pure and sweet, and in great abundance; the finest, indeed, we had found since leaving Sinai."—ROBINSON, *Biblical Researches*, vol. i, p. 204. Such wells would be of the first importance to a great shepherd chief.

32. Returned into the land of the Philistines—That is, into its more central part. The limits of the territory claimed by them was probably in that age ill-defined and variable, and their chief cities much farther to the south than the later pentapolis of the Mediterranean plain. Beer-sheba appears, from verse 34, to have been on the border of the Philistine territory, in which the patriarchs long sojourned.

33. Planted a grove—So the Vulgate. The Sept. has, *a field;* Chaldee, *a garden;* Syriac, *a tree.* But nearly all recent critics understand by אֵשֶׁל the *tamarisk.* The planting of this tree is to be regarded as a religious act, and though the patriarch is still a sojourner, he seems to have felt that Beer-sheba was a sort of permanent resting place. "The planting of this long-lived tree, with its hard wood, and its long, narrow, thickly clustered evergreen leaves, was to be a type of the ever-enduring grace of the faithful covenant God."—*Keil.* **Called there on the name of the Lord**—Compare chaps. xii, 8; xiii, 4; and iv, 26; notes.

CHAPTER XXII.

THE OFFERING OF ISAAC, 1–19.

We now come to the seventh and great test of Abraham's faith. See note on chap. xviii, 1. Here the spiritual life of the honoured patriarch attains its climax. Native land and kindred have long ago been left behind; revelation after revelation has lifted him into a lofty friendship with God; he has sacrificed his natural yearning for Ishmael, who for years had seemed to him the heir of promise, and has submitted to send him and his mother away into the wilderness. Now all his hope for the after time hung on his only son, his Isaac, whom he loved, (verse 2,) and, as the utmost trial and test of his confidence in God's word, he is commanded to go forth and sacrifice even that child of miracle. So must the will of the flesh be subjected to the word of God. And so must all Abraham's spiritual seed, the true children of faith, attain to that lofty elevation. So also Abraham's greater Son, who in the fulness of time gave his life a ransom for many, declares: "He that loveth son or daughter more than me is not worthy of me;... and he that loseth his life for my sake shall find it." Matt. x, 37, 39. Herein is shown the faith of Abraham.

A peculiar interpretation has been put upon this chapter by Hengstenberg and Lange, who maintain that Abraham misunderstood the divine command. They deem it absurd to suppose that God should *forbid* in one part of the transaction what he *commands* in another, or that he should at all command a human sacrifice, a thing declared so abominable in the law. They understand the command of verse 2 to mean that Abraham should offer his son in spiritual consecration to God; not slay him for a literal burnt offering. Thus God would teach his friend both the distinction and the connexion between *sacrificing* and *killing*. The principle and methods of this interpretation are like those by which it is attempted to show that Jephthah did not offer his daughter as a burnt offering, but devoted her to perpetual virginity. It explains away the natural meaning of the language, and foists in a spiritualizing process of thought, transcendental in nature and tendency, and calculated to confuse and mislead rather than help the student of the Scripture. "The Hebrew cultus," says Lange, "distinguishes between the *spiritual consecration of man as a sacrifice*, and the *visible slaughter of an animal.* Thus, for example, according to 1 Sam. i, 24, 25, the boy Samuel was brought by his parents to Eli the priest, and consecrated at the tabernacle, since the three bullocks were slain there as burnt offerings." — *Com. on Genesis,* p. 79. But will Lange maintain that the three bullocks were slain as a substitute for Samuel's life? or that Samuel's consecration at the tabernacle was equivalent to the act of Abraham in not withholding Isaac? or that Samuel's parents, in that consecration, offered up their son in any proper sense as a burnt offering to the Lord? The cases are not parallel at all, and to put them thus together is to confound things that are different. Those passages in which the spiritual significance of offerings is presented (Psa. xl, 6–9, li, 17, cxix, 108, Hos. xiv, 2) have no essential relevancy to this narrative of Abraham, and in the passage most frequently cited, (Psa. li, 16, 17,) a contrite heart and a burnt offering so far from being synonymous, are put in direct opposition to one another. God's command to Abraham was plain and positive. The patriarch's mind was not confused with the metaphysical subtleties of German critics, and when God said: "Take Isaac and go to Moriah and offer him there for a burnt offering;" it was impossible for him to understand any thing else than to go and do exactly what God commanded. He probably knew of no law against human sacrifice, and to him, God's word, spoken at sundry times and in divers manners, was the supreme law.

We must particularly observe, that this whole procedure was a testing, a *temptation,* (נִסָּה,) of Abraham. *For the purpose of such trial* it was perfectly proper for God to *command* the offering up in sacrifice of the life which he had himself given, and had the right and the power to take again. It was equally proper for him to countermand the order when he saw its purpose was accomplished. Verse 12. In all this there was no conflict, as some writers have supposed, between the *revealed* and the *secret* will of God, as if the Holy One had two wills acting in opposite directions at the same time. When God commanded Abraham to go and offer up Isaac, he meant exactly what he said; and when Abraham had shown implicit faith and obedience, God spoke again and commanded him *to offer the ram for a burnt offering instead of his son.* Verse 13. Here is no conflict between a revealed and a secret will of God. It is simply and

CHAPTER XXII.

AND it came to pass after these things, that ᵃ God did tempt Abraham, and said unto him, Abraham: and he said, ¹ Behold, *here* I *am*. 2 And he said, Take now thy son, ᵇ thine only *son* Isaac, whom thou lovest, and get thee ᶜ into the land of Moriah; and offer him

a 1 Cor. 10. 13; Hebrews 11. 17; James 1. 12; 1 Peter 1. 7.

1 Hebrew, *Behold me.* —— *b* Hebrews 11. 17. ——*c* 2 Chron. 3. 1.

solely his revealed will countermanding, for stated reasons, what his revealed will had before commanded. And thus we are told, with a beauty and tenderness unsurpassed in literature, the process and the outcome of the trial of Abraham's faith.

1. **After these things**—After all that has been narrated of Abraham before. **God did tempt Abraham**—The Hebrew for **God** is here הָאֱלֹהִים, *the God;* emphatic, the same "everlasting God," who is called *Jehovah* in verse 33 of the previous chapter. The *tempting* is a key-word to the whole chapter. The Hebrew word נִסָּה means *to try, to test, to prove.* Thus Gesenius (*Lex.* under נסה) observes: "God is said to *try* or *prove* men, that is, their virtue, Psalm xxvi, 2; piety, Deut. viii, 2, 16; their faith and obedience, Exod. xv, 25; xx, 20; 2 Chron. xxxii, 31. This is done by wonderful works, Exod. xx, 20; by commands difficult to be executed, Gen. xxii, 1, Exod. xvi, 4; and by the infliction of calamities, Deut. xxxiii, 8; Judges ii, 22; iii, 1, 4." Lange remarks that the word "*denotes* not simply *to prove,* or to put to the test, but to prove under circumstances which have originated from sin, and which increase the severity of the proof and make it a temptation." And this is an important point to note. Man's life of probation is in a world of trial; and while the world lies in wickedness, many trials come from evil sources; the god of this world solicits to evil, and seeks whom he may devour. 1 Pet. v, 8. All such solicitations to evil are among the offences which Jesus deplored, (Matt. xviii, 7, Luke xvii, 1,) and when thus viewed it is manifest that God tempts no man. Jas. i, 13. But even such temptations, when resisted and overcome, will issue in good, and the godly discipline they thus subserve is to be recognised as God's chastising. Hence the apostle says, in the same chapter, (James i, 2,) "Count it all joy when ye fall into divers temptations," etc. God's tempting Abraham was not a malicious solicitation to evil, but a testing commandment to prove the depth and strength of the patriarch's faith. If now Abraham will, without questioning, obey a commandment that seems to subvert all the promises of the past, and even the words of prophecy touching Isaac, then will the evidence of his faith be perfected. And so it was, that he who before "against hope believed in hope," (Rom. iv, 18,) now staggered not at this strange word, "accounting that God was able to raise him up, even from the dead." Heb. xi, 19.

2. **He said**—Doubtless in some open and positive way. There is no evidence that this word came by a vision of the night. Least of all should we give countenance to the strange fancy that Abraham was imposed upon by Satan, and tempted, by observing human sacrifices among the heathen, to suppose that the sacrifice of Isaac would be acceptable to God. If such were the fact, the sacred writer fell into a most unfortunate style of recording the truth. **Take now thy son**—This command is peculiarly touching. Heb., *Take now thy son, thy only one, whom thou lovest, even Isaac.* Various conjectures have been held as to Isaac's age at this time. Josephus says twenty-five, and other numbers have been mentioned ranging from ten to thirty-seven. But all is conjecture. He was a young lad, but old and large enough to carry the wood for the burnt offering. Verse 6. **Land of Moriah**—On the origin of this name, see on verse 14. The Samaritans read *land of Moreh,* and so identify this Moriah with the Moreh of chap. xii, 6, and Stanley and others argue that the place of Abraham's sacrifice was on the summit of Mount Gerizim, which, after a journey of two days from Beer-sheba by way of the Philis-

there for a burnt offering upon one of the mountains which I will tell thee of.

3 And Abraham rose up early in the morning, and saddled his ass, and took two of his young men with him, and Isaac his son, and clave the wood for the burnt offering, and rose up, and went unto the place of which God had told him. 4 Then on the third day Abraham lifted up his eyes, and saw the place afar off. 5 And Abraham said unto his young men, Abide ye here with the ass; and I and the lad will go yonder and worship, and come again to you. 6 And Abraham took the wood of the burnt offering, and ᵈ laid *it* upon Isaac his son;

---

d John 19. 17.

---

tine plain, can be seen "afar off." Verse 4. But the Jewish tradition identifies this Moriah with the mountain on which the Temple was afterwards builded, (2 Chron. iii, 1,) and there seems no sufficient reason to abandon this view. Thomson says, "It is almost absurd to maintain that Abraham could come on his loaded ass from Beer-sheba to Nablus in the time specified. On the third day he arrived early enough to leave the servants afar off, and walk with Isaac bearing the sacrificial wood to the mountain, which God had shown him; there build the altar, arrange the wood, bind his son, and stretch forth his hand to slay him; and there was time, too, to take and offer up the ram in Isaac's place. That all this could have been done at Nablus on the third day of their journey is incredible. It has always appeared to me, since I first traveled over the country myself, that even Jerusalem was too far off from Beer-sheba for the tenor of the narrative, but Nablus is two days farther north."—*Land and Book,* vol. ii, p. 212. **Offer him there for a burnt offering**—There is no possibility of mistaking the plain import of these words. It is not, consecrate or dedicate him there in connexion with a burnt offering, but **offer him there**. Though God's command seems to be contrary to all hope and promise and prophecy, Abraham obeys. **One of the mountains which I will tell**—Was there not a divine plan and purpose, in selecting the spot for this most wonderful event, to make it identical with the place where afterwards Jehovah would record his name, and set forth his son to be a propitiation for the sins of the whole world?

3. **Rose up early**—An early start on a journey is all-important in the East. Thus would the traveller avoid the heat of the day in the open sun, by travelling before the sun was up, and resting in the heat of the day. **Saddled his ass**—The modern saddle was not then known, but pieces of cloth and garments (Mark xi, 7) were *bound* (חבש) on the back of the animal. The saddling also implied the binding on of whatever baggage the traveller would take along. The Oriental ass is a nobler animal than that which we of the West associate with that name. (See the Bible Dictionaries on the word.) **Took two of his young men**—An incident which shows the naturalness and accuracy of the narrative. A chief like Abraham would not travel far unattended.

4. **Third day**—Two days of journey and reflection did not cause the faith of Abraham to waver, but must have deeply intensified the trial going on within him. **Afar off**—These words do not necessarily imply a great distance. Moses's sister stood *afar off* to watch the ark of bulrushes, (Exod. ii, 4,) and Job's three friends "lifted up their eyes *afar off,* and knew him not," (Job ii, 12,) but the distances in each case were obviously not great.

5. **I and the lad will go yonder** —Abraham doubtless took the ass and his servants to the foot of the mountain, so as to carry the wood and the fire no unnecessary distance. From the junction of the valleys Hinnon and Kedron the heights of Moriah would seem afar off, and be properly spoken of as **yonder. And come again to you**—These words may have been designed to conceal from his servants the purpose of his heart; but according to Heb. xi, 17, he had confidence that God would raise up his son from the dead. By faith he spoke, in this verse and verse 8, more wisely than he knew, and his words were a true prophecy.

6. **The wood ... upon Isaac**—How

CHAPTER XXII.

and he took the fire in his hand, and a knife; and they went both of them together. 7 And Isaac spake unto Abraham his father, and said, My father: and he said, ² Here *am* I, my son. And he said, Behold the fire and the wood: but where *is* the ³ lamb for a burnt offering? 8 And Abraham said, My son, God will provide himself a lamb for a burnt offering: so they went both of them together. 9 And they came to the place which God had told him of;

and Abraham built an altar there, and laid the wood in order, and bound Isaac his son, and ᵉ laid him on the altar upon the wood. 10 And Abraham stretched forth his hand, and took the knife to slay his son. 11 And the Angel of the LORD called unto him out of heaven, and said, Abraham, Abraham: and he said, Here *am* I. 12 And he said, ᶠ Lay not thine hand upon the lad, neither do thou any thing unto him: for ᵍ now I know that thou fearest God, seeing thou

---

2 Heb. *Behold me.*—3 Or, *kid.*—*e* Heb. 11. 17; James 2. 21.

f 1 Sam. 15. 22; Micah 6. 7, 8. —— *g* Chap. 26. 5; James 2. 22.

---

does this suggest the only-begotten Son of God bearing his wooden cross to Calvary! John xix, 17. **Fire in his hand**—Either a stick of wood that would long endure as a burning ember, or coals in a firepot.

7. **My father**—The narrative, in its life-like simplicity, evidences its own genuineness. It was probably often repeated by Isaac to his sons, and by them handed down, till it took this written form. **Where is the lamb**—A most searching question, painful to Abraham's heart, and prompting the prophetic utterance recorded in the next verse, where Abraham again speaks more wisely than he knew. Comp. verse 5.

8. **God will provide**—Heb., *Elohim-jireh*, God will see. See on verse 14.

9. **The place which God had told**—How, when, and where God revealed to him the exact spot for his offering, we are nowhere informed. The rabbins have a tradition that on this same spot Adam, Abel, and Noah had offered sacrifice. **Built...laid... bound...laid** — The four different Hebrew words graphically describe the successive acts in the work of preparation. These are followed in the next verse by three words which paint the final tableau—*stretched forth... took ... to slay.* All the efforts of sculptors and painters to present this scene have never equalled this word-picture.

11. **The Angel of the Lord called** —This climax of the faith of Abraham is worthy of the coming of the angel of Jehovah. On this name see note, chap. xvi, 7. It is appropriate that the interruption and the countermand of the words of *the Elohim* of verse 1

(note) come from the angel of the covenant, who in the fulness of times will, on this same mountain, lay down his life a ransom for many. **Abraham, Abraham** — This repetition of Abraham's name gives an intense liveliness to the scene, and shows the urgency of the new commandment now to be given.

12. **Lay not thine hand upon the lad**—That is, for the purpose of slaying him. "God did not seek the *slaying* of Isaac *in fact*, but only the implicit surrender of the lad, in mind and heart. But if all mental reservation, every refuge of flesh and blood, all mere appearance and self-delusion were to be avoided, this surrender could only be accomplished in the shape in which it was actually required. If it was to be wholly an act of faith left to its own energies, without any other point of support, God could not merely ask a mental surrender, but must have demanded an actual sacrifice. On the part of any other than God such a *quid pro quo* would have been a dangerous game. Not so on the part of God, who held the issue entirely in his own hand. When Abraham had, in heart and mind, completely and without any reserve, offered up his son, God interposed and prevented the sacrifice *in facto*, which was no longer required for the purpose of trial."—*Kurtz.* **Now I know**—The Covenant Angel speaks here after the manner of man, as when, in chap. xviii, 21, he said: "I will go down now and see," etc. The word, says Murphy, "denotes an eventual knowing, a discovering by actual experiment; and this observable probation of Abraham was necessary for the judicial eye of God, who is to

hast not withheld thy son, thine only *son*, from me. **13** And Abraham lifted up his eyes, and looked, and behold behind *him* a ram caught in a thicket by his horns: and Abraham went and took the ram, and offered him up for a burnt offering in the stead of his son. **14** And Abraham called the name of that place ⁴ Jehovah-jireh: as it is said *to* this day, In the mount of the LORD it shall be seen.

---

4 That is, *The LORD will see*, or, *provide*.

---

govern the world, and for the conscience of man, who is to be instructed by practice as well as principle." **Thou hast not withheld thy son**—This passage seems to have suggested to Paul the language of Rom. viii, 32: "He that spared not his own son, but delivered him up for us all." But it is misleading to speak unqualifiedly of Isaac as a type of Christ. Isaac did not lay down his life at all, nor do we know that he was a willing victim. Not Isaac, but Abraham, is the great figure in this scene. See below, on the typical lessons of this chapter.

13. Lifted ... looked ... behold —These verbs afford another vivid word-picture. The startled patriarch hears, stops short, looks up and all around to see and know all that Jehovah wills. **A ram**—The Samaritan, Sept., Syriac, and many MSS. read *one ram*, which would result from the mere changing of ר into ד in the word אחר, translated **behind**. Such a reading would emphasize the ram as being single and separate from the flock, thus typifying, as some think, the Lamb of God as being "separate from sinners." Hebrews vii, 26. The same thought, however, may be held with the common reading. God had truly provided a lamb for a burnt offering. Comp. verse 8. **Caught in a thicket by his horns**—"What, then, did he represent," asks Augustine, "but Jesus, who before he was offered up, was crowned with thorns by the Jews?" **Offered him up ... in the stead of his son**—Here comes out prominently the idea of *substitution* in sacrifice; the animal for the human life. But it is scarcely proper to hold up this incident as designed to teach or enhance the doctrine of vicarious atonement. That doctrine is, indeed, implied; but the prominent thought is not that either Isaac's or Abraham's life was now demanded in order to atone for sin. The typical lessons of the whole procedure are rather incidental, and to be presented as by accommodation and analogy, (see below,) not as the great thought, which is to show the perfection of Abraham's faith in God.

14. Jehovah-jireh—This name appears to have been given because of the marvellous fulfilling of the words of Abraham in verse 8—*Elohim-jireh*, "God will provide," or *God will see to it*. Abraham had uttered an unconscious prophecy, and now in adoring confidence he gives that sacred spot a name which will forever endure as a memorial of Jehovah's providence. In giving this name he prophecies again, and utters a proverb, which was common in the days of this writer, and has been immortalized in Christian hope and song. **In the mount of the Lord it shall be seen**—Or, *in the mount Jehovah shall be seen.* Thus the Sept. The Vulgate disregards the Masoretic pointing, and reads, *in the mount the Lord will see;* on which Jerome thus comments: "This became a proverb among the Hebrews, that if any should be in trouble and should desire the help of the Lord, they should say *in the mount the Lord will see;* that is, as he had mercy on Abraham, so will he have mercy on us." It is quite probable that the name of this mountain, *Moriah*, originated with this event, and is used proleptically in verse 2. It is compounded of the root רָאָה, *to see*, (the *jireh* of this verse,) in its Hophal participal form מָרְאָה, and the initial letters of the divine name *Jehovah*, יה, which in a contracted form may be read and pronounced מֹרִיָּה, *Moriah, seen of Jehovah*. The language of 2 Chron. iii, 1, where only the name *Moriah* elsewhere occurs, seems to hint at this same etymology: "Mount Moriah, in which Jehovah *was seen* (נִרְאָה) by David." In this holy mountain Jehovah was seen long after, in the symbolism of the temple and its offerings, and finally in

B. C. 1872. CHAPTER XXII. 227

15 And the Angel of the LORD called unto Abraham out of heaven the second time, **16** And said, ʰ By myself have I sworn, saith the LORD, for because thou hast done this thing, and hast not withheld thy son, thine only *son*, **17** That in blessing I will bless thee, and in multiplying I will multiply thy seed ⁱ as the stars of the heaven, ᵏ and as the sand which *is* upon the sea ⁵ shore; and ˡ thy seed shall possess ᵐ the gate of his enemies; **18** ⁿAnd in thy seed shall all

---

ʰ Psa.105.9; Luke 1.73; Heb.6.13,14.——ⁱ. Chap. 15. 5; Jer. 33. 22.——ᵏ Chap. 13. 16.——⁵ Heb. *lip*.

ˡ Chap. 24. 60.——ᵐ Micah 1. 9.——ⁿ Chap. 12. 3; 18. 18; 26. 4; Acts 3. 25; Gal. 3. 8, 9, 16, 18.

---

the sacrifice of Him in whom God was seen reconciling the world to himself. 2 Cor. v, 19.

15. The Angel ... called ... second time—Once more will Jehovah speak to Abraham before he leaves this memorable spot, and by an oath confirm unto him all his previous promises.

16. By myself have I sworn—" When God made promise to Abraham, because he could swear by no greater, he sware by himself." Heb. vi, 13. Hanna observes, that this oath " was the last utterance that fell from the lips of God upon the ear of Abraham. He lived for fifty years and more thereafter, but that voice was never heard again. These late years rolled over him in peaceful, undisturbed repose." **Because thou hast done this thing** —This last act of faith was the crowning point in Abraham's spiritual life, and in view of this especially—as summing up and representing in itself all other evidences of his faith—Jehovah repeats his promise.

17. Bless ... multiply — Compare the promises that had gone before. Chap. xii, 2, 3; xiii, 14–17; xv, 5, 7, 18; xvii, 1–8; and xviii, 18. **Thy seed shall possess the gate of his enemies**—Fulfilled primarily in the conquest of Canaan, (comp. chap. xv, 18–21,) but pointing even now to Christ's ultimate triumph over the gates of hell. Matt. xvi, 18. In the rapturous hour of this revelation and promise, Abraham, doubtless, saw Messiah's day, and was glad. John viii, 5, 6.

With this account of the attempted offering of Isaac it has been common to compare the Grecian legends of Phrixus, Idomeneus, and Iphigenia; and also the Phœnician tradition of Chronos, who in a time of war and impending perils took his only son Jehoud, clothed him in royal apparel, and offered him in sacrifice upon an altar which he had built. But these tales have no more connexion with Abraham and Isaac than have the narratives of Jephthah's vow (Judg. xi) or the sacrifice of the king of Moab's son. 2 Kings iii, 27.

The bearing of this act of Abraham on human sacrifices is worthy of notice. We need not go to the extent of Kurtz, who imagines that Abraham might have descried, on all the heights around him, altars smoking with human sacrifices; but we may believe that the idea of human sacrifice sprung from deep religious promptings; the consciousness of guilt, and the felt necessity of offering up the dearest and most precious gift as an atonement. Abraham's act, adapted to be monumental in the history of the chosen race, recognised at once the necessity of sacrifice, and that our life is not our own; but it also revealed the authority from heaven to substitute animal life instead. In this revelation human sacrifices stand condemned, and animal sacrifices sanctioned and established as meeting the divine requirement.

The typical significance of the offering of Isaac has been recognised by nearly all Christian divines, but the pressing of all analogies and correspondencies as types may well be condemned. We have noted above (on verse 12) how Isaac is no proper type of Christ; but as the apostle speaks of Abraham's receiving his son from the dead "in a figure," (Heb. xi, 19,) we may, by a legitimate accommodation, speak of the points in the narrative which in any way prefigure or suggest great Gospel facts. Thus 1) Abraham's not withholding his only son suggests that greater act of Him "who spared not his own Son, but freely gave him up for us all." Rom. viii, 32. 2) Isaac bearing the wood for the sacrifice suggests Christ bearing his own cross. 3) The ram caught in the thicket of

the nations of the earth be blessed; *o* because thou hast obeyed my voice. **19** So Abraham returned unto his young men, and they rose up and went together to *p* Beer-sheba; and Abraham dwelt at Beer-sheba.

20 And it came to pass after these things, that it was told Abraham, saying, Behold, *q* Milcah, she hath also borne children unto thy brother Nahor;

21 *r* Huz his firstborn, and Buz his brother, and Kemuel the father *s* of Aram, **22** And Chesed, and Hazo, and Pildash, and Jidlaph, and Bethuel. **23** And *t* Bethuel begat *u* Rebekah: these eight Milcah did bear to Nahor, Abraham's brother. **24** And his concubine, whose name *was* Reumah, she bare also Tebah, and Gaham, and Thahash, and Maachah.

o Verses 3, 10; chap. 26. 5. —— *p* Chap. 21. 31. —— *q* Chap. 11. 29.

r Job 1. 1.—— *s* Job 32. 2.—— *t* Chap. 24. 15.—— *u* Called, Rom. 9. 10, *Rebecca.*

thorns reminds us of Jesus with the thorn-wreath on his brow. 4) Isaac and the ram together have been taken as a double type, Isaac representing the divinity of our Lord, and the ram the humanity which Christ assumed ("a body hast thou prepared me," Heb. x, 5,) that he might taste death for man. 5) The three days from the command to sacrifice his son to the time of the deliverance of Isaac, his son was as one already dead to Abraham; and so, "in a figure," his release was a resurrection from the dead. Heb. xi, 19. All these analogies may be truthfully presented as parabolic, (ἐν παραβολῇ,) but not as proper types.

Other lessons of this chapter are abundant. 1) Here is the notable instance in which to see how faith wrought with works and was thus made perfect. James ii, 22. 2) The moral sublimity of ready obedience and submission when God demands our beloved. 3) The moral value of temptation and stern discipline. 4) The word of God the highest law. 5) Two immutable things, the oath and promise of God, a permanent source of consolation to the Christian believer. Heb. vi, 17, 18.

NAHOR'S CHILDREN, 20–24.

20. It was told Abraham—How few and far between the visits and messages of those days! Fifty or more years had passed since Abraham left his kindred in Haran, and now he hears from them. The news may have come by a passing traveller from Haran, or a company of merchants, passing down into Egypt; or possibly some special messenger from Nahor sent to inquire after Abraham.

21. Huz ... Buz ... Aram—Uz, a son of Aram, is mentioned chap. x, 23, among the descendants of Shem, and the names Uz and Aran occur also among the Edomites, chap. xxxvi, 28. Buz is also mentioned in Jer. xxv, 23. And it is noticeable that Job was of the land of Uz, (Job i, 1,) and Elihu was a Buzite of the kindred of Ram. Job xxxii, 2. Nothing certain, however, can now be made out of these correspondencies, and it is well-known that names were often repeated in different lines of the same original family.

22. Chesed—Supposed by some to have been the father of one branch of the *Chasdim,* or Chaldeans. But the *Chaldees* of chap. xi, 28, appear to have been older than Abraham.

23. Bethuel begat Rebekah—Compare chap. xxiv, 15. The purpose of inserting this genealogy here seems to have been to prepare the way for the narrative of Isaac's marriage to Rebekah. The only other name in the list of which we have any other trace, is *Maachah,* (verse 24,) who was, perhaps, the father of the *Maachathites* mentioned Deut. iii, 14, and Joshua xii, 5. Observe that Nahor has *twelve* sons, like Ishmael (xxv, 16) and Jacob.

CHAPTER XXIII.

DEATH AND BURIAL OF SARAH, 1–20.

At length a dark shadow falls over the aged patriarch's path. The revelations and promises have ceased, his history drops down to the mere facts of domestic life, and hastens to its close. The beloved wife dies and is buried out of his sight, but faith in the word of God abides.

B. C. 1860. CHAPTER XXIII. 229

CHAPTER XXIII.

AND Sarah was a hundred and seven and twenty years old: *these were* the years of the life of Sarah. 2 And Sarah died in ᵃ Kirjath-arba; the same *is* ᵇ Hebron in the land of Canaan: and Abraham came to mourn for Sarah, and to weep for her.

3 And Abraham stood up from before his dead, and spake unto the sons of Heth, saying, 4 ᶜ I *am* a stranger and a sojourner with you: ᵈ give me a possession of a buryingplace with you, that I may bury my dead out of my sight. 5 And the children of Heth answered Abraham, saying unto him, 6 Hear us, my lord: thou *art* ¹ᵉ a mighty prince among us: in the choice of our sepul-

---

a Josh. 14. 15; Judg. 1. 10. —— *b* Chap. 13. 18; verse 19.—— *c* Chap. 17. 8; 1 Chron. 29. 15; Psa. 105. 12; Heb. 11. 9, 13.—— *d* Acts 7. 5.—— 1 Heb. *a prince of God.*—— *e* Chap. 13. 2; 14. 14; 24. 35.

---

1. **A hundred and seven and twenty**—The only woman whose age is given in the Bible is this mother of the chosen seed. Sixty-two years had passed since she left Haran to wander with her husband she knew not whither, and thirty-seven years since Isaac's birth.

2. **Sarah died in Kirjath-arba**—To this place Abraham had again brought his family after his residence in Beer-sheba. Chap. xxii, 19. **Kirjath-arba** appears to have been the original name of **Hebron**, named after its founder or distinguished resident, *Arba,* a chief among the Anakim. Josh. xiv, 15. Mamre was in the immediate neighbourhood. See on chap. xiii, 18. **In the land of Canaan**—As distinguished from the land of the Philistines. Chap. xxi, 34. **Came to mourn**—This implies that he was absent from Hebron when she died. His coming may have been from Beer-sheba, whither he had gone for some business·with his distant herdsmen, (comp. chap. xxxvii, 12–17,) or from some other similar field of his flocks; or perhaps from the neighbouring Mamre. Some suppose that the expression is only a formal mode of statement, not necessarily implying absence from home. **To mourn...to weep**— A great display of loud lamentation and bitter weeping would be made on occasion of the death of one so distinguished as Sarah. This is a part of Oriental reverence and respect for the dead. Comp. chap. 1, 1–4, 10.

3. **Stood up from before his dead** —After being bowed down with the mourning for Sarah, he rose up from the presence of his beloved dead, and went forth to secure a burying place. The standing up and bowing were essential parts of Oriental etiquette. Comp. verse 7. **Sons of Heth**—The same as the Hittites, a Canaanitish tribe, sprung from the Heth named in chap. x, 14, who settled in this part of Canaan. They were, perhaps, only a southern colony of the great people who figure on the Assyrian monuments as *Khatti,* and on the Egyptian monuments as *Khita,* whose chief seat was on the Orontes, but whose dominion was widespread over Syria and Asia Minor. They appear to have been a powerful military nation in the time of the later kings of Israel. 2 Kings vii, 6, 7. Inscriptions recently discovered at Hamah and other places are believed to be records of this ancient and powerful people.

4. **I am a stranger and a sojourner** —Though heir of the world (Rom. iv, 13) and rich in promised possessions, he confessed himself but a stranger and a pilgrim, (comp. Heb. xi, 13–16,) and never owned a place of rest except his grave. **A possession of a burying place**—" This is the first mention of burial. It was noted by the heathen historian as a characteristic of the Jews, that they preferred to bury their dead rather than to burn them. Tacitus, *Hist.* v, 5. It is observable that this is first mentioned when the first death takes place in the family of him who had received the promises. The care of the bodies of the departed is a custom apparently connected with the belief in their sanctity as vessels of the grace of God, and with the hope that they may be raised again in the day of the restitution of all things."—*Speaker's Commentary.*

6. **Thou art a mighty prince**— Heb., *a prince of God.* These Hitties had observed that Abraham was one on whom God had put honour. Compare Abimelech's words in chap. xxi, 22. **In the choice**—In the one thou may choose for thyself. Abraham had a

230　　　　　　　GENESIS.　　　　B. C. 1860.

chres bury thy dead; none of us shall withhold from thee his sepulchre, but that thou mayest bury thy dead. **7** And Abraham stood up, and bowed himself to the people of the land, *even* to the children of Heth. **8** And he communed with them, saying, If it be your mind that I should bury my dead out of my sight, hear me, and entreat for me to Ephron the son of Zohar, **9** That he may give me the cave of Machpelah, which he hath, which *is* in the end of

choice, and in most respectful form he shows (verse 8, 9) that he has already made a choice in the possession of one of the Hittite chiefs. But to obtain it requires diplomacy and tact. If the ancient habits of making a bargain were like the modern in the East, all this generous liberality on the part of the sons of Heth was but a courteous formality, and was so understood by Abraham.

8. He communed with them—Thus it appears there was a large amount of talking on the occasion. **Entreat for me**—He seeks the mediation and help of these Hittites that he may obtain his desire. Much depends, in such transactions, on influence brought to bear on the owner.

9. **Machpelah**—This is to be regarded as a proper name applied both to **the cave** and to the **field** in which it was located. Comp. verses 17 and 19. The Septuagint and Vulgate render it as an adjective — *the double cave;* and perhaps two compartments or two entrances into the cave may have occasioned the name **Machpelah**, which is derived from כָּפַל, *caphal, to double.* Gesenius, however, gives this root the sense of *to divide*, and to **Machpelah** the sense of *portion, part, lot.* There is little or no doubt that this important **cave** is now covered by the Mosque of Hebron, of which a cut is given herewith. It has been kept hermetically

MOSQUE OF HEBRON.

CHAPTER XXIII.

his field; for ²as much money as it is worth he shall give it me for a possession of a buryingplace amongst you. **10** And Ephron dwelt among the children of Heth: and Ephron the Hittite answered Abraham in the ³audience of the children of Heth, *even* of all that ᶠwent in at the gate of his city, saying, **11** ᵍNay, my lord, hear me: the field give I thee, and the cave that *is* therein, I give it thee; in the presence of the sons of my people give I it thee: bury thy dead. **12** And Abraham bowed down himself before the people of the land. **13** And he spake unto Ephron in the audience of the people of the land, saying, But if thou *wilt give it*, I pray thee, hear me: I will give thee money for the field; take *it* of me, and I will bury my dead there. **14** And Ephron answered Abraham, saying unto him, **15** My lord, hearken unto me: the land *is worth* four hundred ʰ shekels of silver; what *is* that betwixt me and thee? bury

2 Heb. *full money*.——3 Heb. *ears*.——ƒChap. 34. 20, 24; Ruth 4. 4.

g See 2 Samuel 24. 21, 24.——h Exodus 30. 13; Ezekiel 45. 12.

sealed for ages; and since the Mohammedans possessed it, no Christian has been permitted inside the mosque except the Prince of Wales and his attendants, who in 1862, after much effort and diplomacy, were allowed to go in and look upon the cenotaphs which are supposed to stand above the several tombs. Into the cave, of course, they could not enter, and it is believed that no one has entered it for more than a thousand years. See the account of the prince's visit, and a plan of the interior of the mosque, in Stanley's *History of the Jewish Church*, vol. i, Appendix 2. **For as much money as it is worth**—Heb., *for full money*. Abraham will have a complete bargain; no gift, no half-price, no misunderstanding, from which any after strife might come.

10. Ephron ... at the gate of his city—Here note that the scene has changed. Those children of Heth with whom Abraham first communed (verse 8) on the purchase of the cave, have broken the matter to the owner, and he now appears *sitting* יֹשֵׁב at the gate, where all such business is publicly transacted **in the audience**, or hearing, of all that congregated there, and speaks. See further on verse 17.

11. Give I thee—Three times over this princely son of Zohar offers to **give** field, cave, and all. And yet, doubtless, like the modern sheik, he would expect a splendid present in return, or, by his show of kindness and profuse liberality, prevent Abraham from objecting to his price when once named.

12. Bowed — Thus again (comp. verses 3, 7) he courteously acknowledges the friendly spirit and generosity of these Hittites.

13. But if thou wilt—Heb., *only if thou—would that thou wouldst hear me*. There is a tender emotionality about his words. He is in no mood to parley long. **I will give thee money**—Or, *I have given thee money;* that is, I have purposed in heart to buy the field for money; I will have it in no other way.

15. Four hundred shekels of silver—A nearer approach to the sense here would be *four hundred weight of silver*, for the payment was by weight,

WEIGHING MONEY.

not in coins. We have no means of knowing the value of a shekel of sil-

therefore thy dead. **16** And Abraham hearkened unto Ephron; and Abraham [i] weighed to Ephron the silver, which he had named in the audience of the sons of Heth, four hundred shekels of silver, current *money* with the merchant.

17 And [k] the field of Ephron, which *was* in Machpelah, which *was* before Mamre, the field, and the cave which *was* therein, and all the trees that *were* in the field, that *were* in all the borders round about, were made sure **18** Unto Abraham for a possession in the presence of the children of Heth, before all that went in at the gate of his city. **19** And after this, Abraham buried Sarah his wife in the cave of the field of Machpelah before Mamre: the same *is* Hebron in the land of Canaan. **20** And the field, and the cave that *is* therein, [l] were made sure unto Abraham for a possession of a buryingplace by the sons of Heth.

i Jer. 32. 9.——*k* Chap. 25. 9; 49. 30-32; 50. 13; Acts 7. 16.——*l* See Ruth 4. 7-10; Jer. 32. 10,11.

ver in Abraham's time. The silver shekel of New Testament times has been estimated at sixty cents, four hundred of which would accordingly be $240. But probably the four hundred weight of silver which Ephron named was of much greater value.

16. Abraham weighed . . . the silver—"Ancient money, being uncoined, was weighed instead of being counted. Even to this day the Oriental merchants weigh the silver and the gold which are the medium of traffic; not only the bullion, but the coined pieces also, lest some dishonest trader might pass upon them a coin of light weight. The ancient Egyptians, and some other nations, used rings of gold and silver for the same purposes that coins are now used."—FREEMAN's *Handbook of Bible Manners and Customs*. **Current money** — Heb., *silver passing to the merchant*. That is, such as passed among the merchants of that time.

17. Field . . . cave . . . trees . . . borders—Observe how every thing is specified—The importance of this is still understood. "It is not enough," says Thomson, "that you purchase a well-known lot; the contract must mention every thing that belongs to it, and certify that fountains or wells in it, trees upon it, etc., are sold with the field. If you rent a house, not only the building itself, but every room in it, above and below, down to the kitchen, pantry, stable, and hen-coop, must be specified."—*Land and Book*, vol. ii, p. 383. **Made sure**—The same word is repeated in verse 20. This possession was publicly and legally confirmed to Abraham. On this Dr. Thomson also writes: "When any sale is now to be effected in a town or village, the whole population gather about the parties at the usual place of concourse. There all take part, and enter into the *pros* and *cons* with as much earnestness as if it were their own individual affair. By these means, the operation, in all its circumstances and details, is known to many witnesses, and the thing is made *sure*, without any written contract. In fact, up to this day, in this very city of Hebron, a purchase thus witnessed is legal, while the best-drawn deeds of a London lawyer, though signed and sealed, would be of no avail without such living witnesses."

19. After this, Abraham buried Sarah—He has now one secure possession wherein to bury his dead. Here he himself was afterwards buried, (chap. xxv, 9,) and here also Isaac, Rebekah, Jacob, and Leah. Chap. xlix, 31; l, 13. Is it not noticeable of Abraham and his seed that their first and last possession in the land of promise is—a grave?

CHAPTER XXIV.
ISAAC'S MARRIAGE, 1-67.

After the death of Sarah, the house of Abraham was left in gloom. He appears to have removed again into the south country, and was now probably dwelling near Beer-sheba. See on verse 62. Two years or more elapsed, and then the growing age of Abraham, and the loneliness of his home, prompted him to seek for his son Isaac a wife, that Sarah's vacant tent might again be filled, and both he and Isaac comforted. See verse 67. Besides the inimitable beauty of this narrative, the attentive reader should note the following things: 1) The authority of parents and the elder brother in negotiating marriages.

CHAPTER XXIV.

AND Abraham ª was old, *and* ¹ well stricken in age: and the LORD ᵇ had blessed Abraham in all things. **2** And Abraham said ᶜ unto his eldest servant of his house, that ᵈ ruled over all that he had, ᵉ Put, I pray thee, thy hand under my thigh: **3** And I will make thee ᶠ swear by the LORD, the God of heaven, and the God of the earth, that ᵍ thou shalt not take a wife unto my son of the daughters of the Canaanites, among whom I dwell: **4** ʰ But thou shalt go ⁱ unto my country, and to my kindred, and take a wife unto my son Isaac. **5** And the servant said unto him, Peradventure the woman will not be willing to follow me unto this land: must I needs bring thy son again unto the land from whence thou camest? **6** And Abraham said unto him, Beware thou that thou bring not my son thither again.

---

a Chap. 18. 11; 21. 5.——1 Heb. *gone into days*.—— *b* Chap. 13. 2; verse 35; Psa. 112. 3; Prov. 10. 22.—— *c* Chap. 15. 2.—— *d* Verse 10; chap. 39. 4, 5, 6.

e Chap. 47. 29; 1 Chron. 29. 24; Lam. 5. 6.—— *f* Chap. 14. 22; Deut. 6. 13; Josh. 2. 12.—— *g* Chap. 26. 35; 27. 46; 28. 2; Exod. 34. 16; Deut. 7. 3.—— *h* Chap. 28. 2.—— *i* Chap. 12. 1.

---

2) The chief servant is the go-between, or mediator and manager, of such affairs for a princely family. 3) Marriage of cousins, or blood-kindred, rather than strangers. 4) Careful consideration of religious affinity and its influence on the posterity. ✗ 5) The marriage union cemented by mutual love.

1. **Well stricken in age**—Heb., *gone into days;* that is, far advanced in years. Being ten years older than Sarah, he was one hundred and thirty-seven at her death. And yet thirty-years of life are before him. Comp. chap. xxv, 7.

2. **His eldest servant of his house** —Heb., *his servant, the elder of his house.* The word *elder* is here to be understood as an official title; the overseer, steward, prime minister of the household, who **ruled over all that he had;** had charge of all. The person was probably the Eliezer of Damascus, mentioned in chap. xv, 2. See note there. **Thy hand under my thigh**— The *thigh* (ירך) is here used euphemistically for the genital member, regarded among the patriarchs as the most sacred part of the body. Compare, also, chap. xlvii, 29. "This member," says Ginsburg, "was the symbol of union in the tenderest relation of matrimonial life, and the seat whence all issue proceeds, and the perpetuity so much coveted by the ancients. Compare the phrase יוצאי ירך, 'coming out of the loins,' (Heb., *issues of the thigh,*) in Gen. xlvi, 26; Exod. i, 5; Judges viii, 30. Hence the creative organ became the symbol of the Creator, and the object of worship among all nations of antiquity; and it is for this reason that God claimed it as the sign of the covenant between himself and his chosen people in the rite of circumcision. Nothing, therefore, could render the oath more solemn in those days than touching the symbol of creation, the sign of the covenant, and the source of that issue who may, at any future period, avenge the breaking of the compact made with their progenitor. To this effect is the explanation of the Midrash, the Chaldee paraphrase of Jonathan ben Uzziel, Rashi, and the oldest Jewish expositors."—See KITTO's *Biblical Cyclopædia, Art., Oath.*

3. **Swear by the Lord**—To the sacredness of the manner of the oath is added the solemnity of this use of the holy NAME. This servant must swear *by Jehovah, God of the heavens* and *God of the earth.* Thus Abraham puts him under the most solemn oath that could then bind the conscience of a man. **Not . . . of the Canaanites** Lot's case might have been a sufficient warning, and the idolatries and growing iniquity of the Amorites, though not yet full, (xv, 16,) were plainly such as to show the pious patriarch the fearful danger of matrimonial alliances with them. Here we note the ancient enforcing of the principle of the apostolic precept: "Be ye not unequally yoked together with unbelievers." 2 Cor. vi, 14. What sorrows and soul-losses have followed from such unhallowed unions!

5. **The servant said** — He was cautious and far-sighted, and before taking on himself so solemn an oath he will have an understanding about all contingencies.

6. **Beware**—Whatever hinderances

7 The LORD God of heaven, which *k* took me from my father's house, and from the land of my kindred, and which spake unto me, and that sware unto me, saying, *l* Unto thy seed will I give this land; *m* he shall send his angel before thee, and thou shalt take a wife unto my son from thence. 8 And if the woman will not be willing to follow thee, then *n* thou shalt be clear from this my oath: only bring not my son thither again. 9 And the servant put his hand under the thigh of Abraham his master, and sware to him concerning that matter. 10 And the servant took ten camels of the camels of his master, and departed; *o 2* for all the goods of his master *were in* his hand: and he arose, and went to Mesopotamia, unto *p* the city of Nahor. 11 And he made his camels to kneel down without the city by a well of water at the time of the evening, *even* the time *q 3* that women go out to draw *water*. 12 And he said, *r* O LORD God of my

---

k Chap. 12. 1.——*l* Chap. 12. 7; 13. 15; 15. 18; 17. 8; Exod. 32. 13; Deut. 1. 8; 34. 4; Acts 7. 5.——*m* Exod. 23. 20, 23; 33. 2; Heb. 1, 14.——*n* Josh. 2. 17, 20.——*o* Verse 2.

2 Or, *and*.——*p* Chap. 27. 43.——*q* Exod. 2. 16; 1 Sam. 9. 11.——*3* Heb. *that women which draw* water *go forth*.——*r* Verse 27; chap. 26. 24; 28. 13; 32. 9; Exod. 3. 6, 15.

---

come, in no case will Abraham allow his son to go back to the land from which he himself had been called.

7. **He shall send his angel before thee**—Abraham is confident that the Angel of the Covenant (see note on xvi, 7) will prepare his servant's way. Too many have been the divine interpositions for him now to doubt. He is perfectly willing to rest with the understanding that if the woman be unwilling, his servant shall be released from his oath.

10. **Ten camels**—A considerable caravan would be necessary for a safe and comfortable journey from Beersheba to Haran and back. Besides, presents for the bride and her family, (verse 53,) and suitable accommodation for bringing the bride to her husband, were to be taken along. The careful and accomplished steward, who had charge of **all the goods of his master,** would not fail to see that his important mission was carried out with every possible propriety. **Mesopotamia**—This is the Greek and Roman name of the great region lying between the rivers Tigris and Euphrates, and called in Hebrew *Aram-Naharaim*, or *Aram of the two rivers*. The same region is called *Padan-Aram* in chap. xxv, 20, and frequently elsewhere; though, perhaps, the latter term designates a more limited portion of Aram-Naharaim, in which Haran, **the city of Nahor**, was located. See on chap. xi, 31. To this city Nahor had probably migrated soon after his father and brother had settled there.

11. **He made his camels to kneel**—"A mode of expression taken from actual life. The action is literally *kneeling*, and this the camel is taught to do from its youth. The place is said to have been **by a well of water,** and this well was outside the city. In the East, where wells are scarce, and water indispensable, the existence of a well or fountain determines the site of a village. The people build near it, but prefer to have it outside of the city, to avoid the noise, dust, and confusion always occurring at it, and especially if the place is on the public highway. It is around the fountain that the thirsty traveller and the weary caravan assemble; and if you have become separated from your own company before arriving at a town, you need only inquire for the fountain, and there you will find them. It was perfectly natural, therefore, for Eliezer to halt at the well. **The time** was **evening**, when **women go out to draw water**—True to life again. At that hour the peasant returns home from his labour, and the women are busy preparing the evening meal, which is to be ready at sunset. Cool fresh water is then demanded, and, of course, there is a great concourse around the well. About great cities men often carry water, both on donkeys and on their own backs; but in the country, among the unsophisticated natives, women only go to the well or the fountain; and often, when travelling, have I seen long files of them going and returning with their pitchers 'at the time when women go out to draw water.'"—THOMSON, *Land and Book*, vol. ii, p. 404.

B. C. 1857. CHAPTER XXIV. 235

master Abraham, I pray thee, ˢ send me good speed this day, and show kindness unto my master Abraham. **13** Behold, ᵗ I stand *here* by the well of water; and ᵘ the daughters of the men of the city come out to draw water: **14** And let it come to pass, that the damsel to whom I shall say, Let down thy pitcher, I pray thee, that I may drink; and she shall say, Drink, and I will give thy camels drink also: *let the same be* she *that* thou hast appointed for thy servant Isaac; and ᵛ thereby shall I know that thou hast showed kindness unto my master.
15 And it came to pass, before he had done speaking, that, behold, Rebekah came out, who was born to Bethuel, son of ʷ Milcah, the wife of Nahor, Abraham's brother, with her pitcher upon her shoulder. **16** And the damsel ˣ *was* ʸ very fair to look upon, a virgin, neither had any man known her: and she went down to the well, and filled her pitcher, and came up. **17** And the servant ran to meet her, and said, Let me, I pray thee, drink a little water of thy pitcher. **18** ʸ And she said, Drink, my lord: and she hasted, and let down her pitcher upon her hand, and gave him drink. **19** And when she had done giving him drink, she said, I will draw *water* for thy camels also, until they have done drinking. **20** And she hasted, and emptied her pitcher into the trough, and ran again unto the well to draw *water*, and drew for all his camels. **21** And the man wondering at her held his peace, to wit whether ᶻ the LORD had made his journey prosperous or not. **22** And it came to pass, as the camels had done drinking, that the man took a golden ᵃ ᵇ earring of half a shekel weight, and

s Neh. 1. 11; Psa. 37. 5. —— *t* Verse 43. —— *u* Chap. 29. 9; Exod. 2. 16. —— *v* See Judg. 6. 17, 37; 1 Sam. 6. 7; 14. 10; 20. 7.—— *w* Chap. 11. 29; 22. 23.—— *x* Chap. 26. 7.

4 Heb. *good of countenance.* —— *y* 1 Pet. 3. 8; 4. 9. —— *z* Verses 12, 56. —— *a* Exod. 32. 2, 3; Isa. 3. 19, 20, 21; Ezek. 16. 11, 12; 1 Pet. 3. 3 —— 5 Or, *jewel for the forehead.*

12. Lord . . . send me good speed —Or, *cause it to happen before me to-day*. This prayer is one of remarkable simplicity and directness, but in it note the following: 1) The use of the name *Jehovah*. 2) The appeal to *Abraham's* God. 3) The urging of the case as *Abraham's interest*. 4) The implied *faith* that all his success in this undertaking must come from God. 5) The request for a special *sign*. 6) The child-like simplicity which designates the very *form and language* in which the sign shall be given. 7) The consequent *knowledge* of God's favour with which he will be blessed.

15. Before he had done speaking —Speedily is that prayer of child-like faith and simplicity answered. **Rebekah** — Her name has already appeared in the genealogy of chap. xxii, 20–24. **Pitcher upon her shoulder**—The usual mode of carrying the water pitcher in Syria.

16. Went down to the well—The water, perhaps, was reached, as is often the case, by a flight of steps. Hence the use of the terms *going down* and *coming up*.

17. The servant ran—To him the fair young virgin appears all that he had desired and hoped to meet.

20. Drew for all his camels—"I have never found any young lady so generous as this fair daughter of Bethuel. She drew for all his camels, and for nothing, while I have often found it difficult to get my horse watered even for money. Rebekah emptied her pitcher into the **trough**, an article always found about wells, and frequently made of stone."—*Thomson.*

21. Wondering—Literally, *and the man* [stood] *gazing at her and keeping silence to know whether Jehovah had prospered his journey or not.* He is anxious now to know if this damsel be of Abraham's kindred, and will go with him to his master. Can it be that his prayer is to be so speedily answered?

22. Earring—נֶזֶם is generally be-

NOSE RINGS OF MODERN EGYPT.

lieved to have been a nose ring, for in verse 47 he is said to have put it on

GENESIS.

B. C. 1857.

two bracelets for her hands of ten *shekels* weight of gold; **23** And said, Whose daughter *art* thou? tell me, I pray thee: is there room *in* thy father's house for us to lodge in? **24** And she said unto him, [b] I *am* the daughter of Bethuel the son of Milcah, which she bare unto Nahor. **25** She said moreover unto him, We have both straw and provender enough, and room to lodge in. **26** And the man [c] bowed down his head, and worshipped the LORD. **27** And he said, [d] Blessed *be* the LORD God of my master Abraham, who hath not left destitute my master of [e] his mercy and his truth: I *being* in the way, the LORD [f] led me to the house of my master's brethren. **28** And the damsel ran, and told *them* of her mother's house these things.

29 And Rebekah had a brother, and his name *was* [g] Laban: and Laban ran out unto the man, unto the well. **30** And

---

b Chap. 22. 23.——*c* Verse 52; Exod. 4. 31.——*d* Exod. 18. 10; Ruth 4. 14; 1 Sam. 25. 32, 39; 2 Sam. 18. 28; Luke 1. 68.——*e* Chap. 32. 10; Psa. 98. 3.——*f* Verse 48.——*g* Chap. 29. 5.

---

her face; Heb., *nose*, (אף.) **Bracelets** —All sorts of jewels are highly prized

EGYPTIAN BRACELETS.

among the women of the East, and rings, bracelets, or ornaments of some

ASSYRIAN BRACELETS.

kind, such as each person can afford or obtain, are universally worn. The weight of this ring, **half a shekel**, or a *beka*, has been estimated at a quarter of an ounce, and the bracelets at over four ounces. But our knowledge of these ancient weights is very uncertain.

27. **Blessed be the Lord**—The aged servant is now convinced that Jehovah has heard his prayer, and directed his steps, and he breaks out in thanksgiving.

28. **Her mother's house**—The daughter naturally runs to her mother's tent to tell the news. But not so Rachel. See chap. xxix, 12.

29. **Laban**—Note the prominence of Laban in all this interview. He is more prominent than his father, or even than his mother. He goes out to meet the servant of Abraham; he gives the usual blessing and hospitable welcome. Verse 31. Bethuel is mentioned in verse 50, but second to Laban, and in verse 53 and 55, the *brother* and *mother* are mentioned, but not the father, and in verses 59 and 60 Rebekah is called "their sister" and "our sister," rather than daughter. Some explain all this as springing from a prominence and authority which the oldest son is supposed to have in the East; but others point, farther, to chap. xxix, 5, where Laban is called the son of Nahor, and Bethuel is passed over as if he were a person of no account, and argue that this consistent and uniform ignoring of Rebekah's father is designed. Laban is not thus ignored and his sons made prominent in the marriage of Rachel and Leah. Chap. xxix. It has been suggested that some weakness or imbecility rendered Bethuel incapable of managing his own affairs. This Blunt places among the remarkable coincidences of the Bible, and remarks: "The consistency is too much of one piece throughout,

it came to pass, when he saw the earring, and bracelets upon his sister's hands, and when he heard the words of Rebekah his *sister, saying, Thus spake the man unto me, that he came unto the man; and, behold, he stood by the camels at the well. **31** And he said, Come in, ʰ thou blessed of the LORD; wherefore standest thou without? for I have prepared the house, and room for the camels.

32 And the man came into the house: and he ungirded his camels, and ⁱ gave straw and provender for the camels, and water to wash his feet, and the men's feet that were with him. **33** And there was set *meat* before him to eat: but he said, ᵏ I will not eat, until I have told mine errand. And he said, Speak on. **34** And he said, I *am* Abraham's servant. **35** And the LORD ˡ hath blessed my master greatly, and he is become great: and he hath given him flocks, and herds, and silver, and gold, and menservants, and maidservants, and camels, and asses. **36** And Sarah my master's wife ᵐ bare a son to my master when she was old: and ⁿ unto him hath he given all that he hath. **37** And my master ᵒ made me swear, saying, Thou shalt not take a wife to my son of the daughters of the Canaanites, in whose land I dwell: **38** ᵖ But thou shalt go unto my father's house, and to my kindred, and take a wife unto my son. **39** ᑫ And I said unto my master, Peradventure the woman will not follow me. **40** ʳ And he said unto me, The LORD, ˢ before whom I walk, will send his angel with thee, and prosper thy way; and thou shalt take a wife for my son of my kindred, and of my father's

house: **41** ᵗ Then shalt thou be clear from *this* my oath, when thou comest to my kindred; and if they give not thee *one*, thou shalt be clear from my oath. **42** And I came this day unto the well, and said, ᵘ O LORD God of my master Abraham, if now thou do prosper my way which I go: **43** ᵛ Behold, I stand by the well of water; and it shall come to pass, that when the virgin cometh forth to draw *water*, and I say to her, Give me, I pray thee, a little water of thy pitcher to drink; **44** And she say to me, Both drink thou, and I will also draw for thy camels: *let* the same *be* the woman whom the LORD hath appointed out for my master's son. **45** ʷ And before I had done ˣ speaking in mine heart, behold, Rebekah came forth with her pitcher on her shoulder; and she went down unto the well, and drew *water:* and I said unto her, Let me drink, I pray thee. **46** And she made haste, and let down her pitcher from her *shoulder*, and said, Drink, and I will give thy camels drink also: so I drank, and she made the camels drink also. **47** And I asked her, and said, Whose daughter *art* thou? And she said, The daughter of Bethuel, Nahor's son, whom Milcah bare unto him: and I ʸ put the earring upon her face, and the bracelets upon her hands. **48** ᶻ And I bowed down my head, and worshipped the LORD, and blessed the LORD God of my master Abraham, which had led me in the right way to take ᵃ my master's brother's daughter unto his son. **49** And now, if ye will ᵇ deal kindly and truly with my master, tell me: and if not, tell me; that I may turn to the right hand, or to the left. **50** Then Laban and Bethuel answered and said,

---

h Chap. 26, 29; Judg. 17, 2; Ruth 3. 10; Psa. 115. 15.——*i* Chap. 43. 24; Judg. 19. 21.——*k* Job 23. 12; John 4. 34; Eph. 6. 5, 6, 7.——*l* Verse 1; chap. 13. 2.——*m* Chap. 21. 2.——*n* Chap. 21. 10; 25. 5.——*o* Verse 3.

p Verse 4. —— *q* Verse 5. —— *r* Verse 7. —— *s* Chap. 17. 1. —— *t* Verse 8. —— *u* Verse 12. —— *v* Verse 13.——*w* Verse 15, etc.——*x* 1 Sam. 1. 13. —— *y* Ezek. 16. 11, 12.——*z* Verse 26.——*a* Chap. 22. 23.——*b* Chap. 47. 29; Josh. 2. 14.

---

and marked by too many particulars, to be accidental. It is the consistency of a man who knew more about Bethuel than we do, or than he happened to let drop from his pen. This kind of consistency I look upon as beyond the reach of the most subtle contriver in the world."

30. **When he saw ... and when he heard**—What he saw and heard, no doubt, had special influence on his action, and made the blessings and welcome (of verse 31) doubly emphatic.

33. **I will not eat**—Too important

is his errand to be delayed until after the ceremonies of hospitality are over. Verse 34. **And he said**—This address of Abraham's servant (verses 34-39) is a masterpiece of its kind. It is a narrative, says Kalisch, "graced by every charm of simplicity, rivalling the most beautiful episodes of the Homeric writings, and pervaded by a beautiful spirit of sustained calmness. The repetitions which it contains are like the echo of truth; and the measured step by which it advances, carries it to its aim with enhanced dignity."

VOL. I.—16   O. T.

238 GENESIS. B. C. 1857.

°The thing proceedeth from the LORD: we cannot ᵈspeak unto thee bad or good. **51** Behold, Rebekah ᵉ*is* before thee; take *her*, and go, and let her be thy master's son's wife, as the LORD hath spoken. **52** And it came to pass, that, when Abraham's servant heard their words, he ᶠworshipped the LORD, *bowing himself* to the earth. **53** And the servant brought forth ⁶ᵍ jewels of silver, and jewels of gold, and raiment, and gave *them* to Rebekah: he gave also to her brother and to her mother ʰ precious things. **54** And they did eat and drink, he and the men that *were* with him, and tarried all night; and they rose up in the morning, and he said, ⁱ Send me away unto my master. **55** And her brother and her mother said, Let the damsel abide with us ⁷ *a few* days, at the least ten; after that she shall go. **56** And he said unto them, Hinder me

not, seeing the LORD hath prospered my way; send me away that I may go to my master. **57** And they said, We will call the damsel, and inquire at her mouth. **58** And they called Rebekah, and said unto her, Wilt thou go with this man? And she said, I will go. **59** And they sent away Rebekah their sister, and ᵏ her nurse, and Abraham's servant, and his men. **60** And they blessed Rebekah, and said unto her, Thou *art* our sister; be thou ˡ *the mother* of thousands of millions, and ᵐ let thy seed possess the gate of those which hate them.

61 And Rebekah arose, and her damsels, and they rode upon the camels, and followed the man: and the servant took Rebekah, and went his way. **62** And Isaac came from the way of the ⁿ well Lahai-roi; for he dwelt in the south country. **63** And Isaac went out ⁸ᵒto meditate in the field at the eventide: and

---

c Psa. 118. 23; Matt. 21. 42; Mark 12. 11.——*d* Chap. 31. 24.——*e* Chap. 20. 15.——*f* Verse 26.——6 Heb. *vessels*.——*g* Exod. 3. 22; 11. 2; 12. 35.——*h* 2 Chron. 21. 3; Ezra 1. 6.——*i* Verses 56, 59.

7 Or, *a full year*, or, *ten* months, Judg. 14. 8.——*k* Chap. 35. 8.——*l* Chap. 17. 16.——*m* Chap. 22. 17.——*n* Chap. 16. 14; 25. 11.——8 Or, *to pray*.——*o* Josh. 1. 8; Psa. 1. 2; 77. 12; 119. 15; 143. 5.

---

50. Proceedeth from the Lord—They cannot doubt the special providence of Abraham's God, and they dare not interfere to favour or oppose.

53. Jewels of silver—Rather, *vessels of silver*. Costly presents from the great accumulations of Abraham, amassed through many years. Comp. chap. xiii, 2; xx, 16. **Precious things**—Choice gifts of various kinds, such as he knew would be pleasing.

56. Hinder me not—The servant is too anxious to break the glad news of his success to his master.

58. Wilt thou go—This question was not whether she would accept Isaac in marriage; that had been already settled by those who, according to Oriental customs, had that power, and Rebekah, doubtless, was convinced as well as her parents and brother, that God's hand was in it. But this question meant, Wilt thou go with this man *now*, or wait a longer time between the espousal and the marriage?

59. They sent . . . their sister—Special reference to Laban and the younger members of the household. **Her nurse**—Deborah, who died long after and was buried at Bethel. Chap. xxxv, 8.

60. Blessed Rebekah—This part-

ing blessing rises to the poetic fervor of a song, and may be put as follows:

And they blessed Rebekah,
And they said unto her,
Our sister art thou,
Be thou [increased] to thousands of myriads;
And let thy seed possess the gate of them that hate him.

The signal interpositions of Jehovah inspire them with a presentiment of Rebekah's future honour.

61. Her damsels—Besides her especial nurse, (verse 59,) she was accompanied by other maidservants, as became one of her state and dignity.

62. Came from the way of the well—Better, *came* from going to *Beer-lahai-roi*. After Sarah's death it is probable that Abraham and Isaac removed to Beer-sheba, for it is here said that now **he dwelt in the south country**, which would scarcely be so stated if he were still dwelling at Hebron. While the chief servant was away in Mesopotamia Isaac made a journey to Beer-lahai-roi, the place in the farther south where the angel appeared to Hagar. Chap. xvi, 14. He went, probably, to look after the flocks and herds in that region, and had now just returned.

63. Went out to meditate—Some

B. C. 1857. CHAPTER XXIV. 239

he lifted up his eyes, and saw, and, behold, the camels *were* coming. **64** And Rebekah lifted up her eyes, and when she saw Isaac, ᵖ she lighted off the camel. **65** For she *had* said unto the servant, What man *is* this that walketh in the field to meet us? And the servant *had* said, It *is* my master: therefore she took a vail, and covered herself. **66** And the servant told Isaac all things that he had done. **67** And Isaac brought her into his mother Sarah's tent, and took Rebekah, and she became his wife; and he loved her: and Isaac ᵠ was comforted after his mother's *death*.

CHAPTER XXV.

THEN again Abraham took a wife, and her name *was* Keturah. **2** And ᵃ she bare him Zimran, and Jokshan,

---

p Josh. 15. 18.——*q* Chap. 38. 12.——*a* 1 Chron. 1. 32.

---

uncertainty hangs over the word שׂוּחַ, here rendered **meditate**. The Syriac renders it *walk*, and Gesenius observes that "this is almost demanded by the nature of the context," and suggests that the true reading may have been שׁוּט, *to go to and fro*. The Targums, Samaritan and Arabic, read *to pray*. Knobel and Lange render, *to lament*, and suppose that he went out alone to lament the death of his mother. But שׂיחַ is probably equivalent to שִׂיחַ, *to talk* (with one's self;) *to meditate;* and our common version, which follows substantially the Septuagint, Aquila, and the Vulgate, gives the true meaning. There is something beautiful and appropriate in the thought of this heir of the promises going out **to meditate in the field at the eventide**, and filled, doubtless, with anxious thoughts about the mission of his aged servant.

64. She lighted off the camel—Literally, *and she fell from off the camel.* The expression denotes the rapidity with which she threw herself from the camel at sight of Isaac, whom she probably at once, more than suspected to be her future husband. Dr. Thomson says: "The behaviour of Rebekah, when about to meet Isaac, was such as modern etiquette requires. It is customary for both men and women, when an *emeer*, or great personage, is approaching, to alight some time before he comes up with them. Women frequently refuse to ride in the presence of men, and when a company of them are to pass through a town, they often dismount and walk. It was, no doubt, a point of Syrian etiquette for Rebekah to stop, descend from her camel, and cover herself with a vail in the presence of her future husband. In a word, this biblical narrative is so natural to one familiar with the East, so beautiful, also, and lifelike, that the entire scene seems to be an affair in which he has himself been but recently an actor."

65. For she had said—Rather, *and she said.* There is no need of interpolating *had* in either of the two places in which it occurs in this verse. **Took a vail**—Heb., *took the vail;* the vail proper to be used in such a case, "the long cloak-like vail, with which the Eastern women covered their faces."

67. Into his mother Sarah's tent —The tent which had been her special apartment and home during many years of nomadic life. This tent had probably been removed after Sarah's death to Beer-sheba. See on verse 62. **Took . . . wife . . . loved**—Under the circumstances and customs of that time, no other formal marriage ceremony was required than this leading her, in loving attachment, into the tent. Thus the vacant home place was filled with another mistress, and Sarah's loss less keenly felt.

CHAPTER XXV.

ABRAHAM'S SONS BY KETURAH, 1–6.

1. Then—Rather *and*, for here is no note of time. When Abraham took **Keturah** for a wife we have no means of knowing, but it is generally supposed to have been after Sarah's death. This the order of the narrative would most naturally imply. But such order, and especially the record of genealogies, is no sure index of time, and, for aught that appears, Abraham may have taken Keturah, who is called his *concubine* in 1 Chron. i, 32, as he took Hagar, long before Sarah's death. The historian

240   GENESIS.   About B. C. 1853.

and Medan, and Midian, and Ishbak, and Shuah. 3 And Jokshan begat Sheba, and Dedan. And the sons of Dedan were Asshurim, and Letushim, and Leummim. 4 And the sons of Midian; Ephah, and Epher, and Hanoch, and Abidah, and Eldaah. All these *were* the children of Keturah.

5 And ᵇAbraham gave all that he had unto Isaac. 6 But unto the sons of the concubines, which Abraham had, Abraham gave gifts, and ᶜsent them away from Isaac his son, while he yet lived, eastward, unto ᵈthe east country. 7 And these *are* the days of the years of Abraham's life which he lived, a hundred

b Chap. 24, 36.——*c* Chap. 21. 14.——*d* Judges 6, 3.

did not choose to interrupt his narrative by introducing it before, especially as it was of no vital importance in the previous history of Abraham. But, on the other hand, all this may have occurred after Sarah's death, and even after Isaac's marriage. In view of the great longevity of Abraham, it is possible that he may have possessed as much vital force at one hundred and forty as ordinarily vigorous men at seventy. The statement, also, that he **took** Keturah, compared with chap. xvi, 3, where it is said "Sarah took Hagar and gave her to her husband," seems to be against the idea that he took this concubine during Sarah's lifetime. The six sons mentioned in verse 2 may all have been born after Isaac's marriage, and twenty-five years before Abraham's death.

2–4. Compare 1 Chron. i, 32, 33. Here are mentioned six sons, seven grandsons, and three great-grandsons. The subsequent history and location of the tribes that sprung from them are very uncertain, and conjectures on the subject are scarcely worth repeating. Those who wish to note them should consult the Bible Dictionaries on the several names. From **Midian** came the Midianites, often mentioned in the later history of Israel. We meet them in the history of Joseph (chap. xxxvii, 28) and of Moses, (Exod. ii, 15, Num. xxii, 4,) and against them Gideon waged successful war. Judges chapters vi-viii. The names of **Sheba** and **Dedan** occur among the sons of Cush, (chap. x, 7,) but nothing can be argued from such repetition of names. Some, however, think that these tribes subsequently became intermixed by marriage. **Midian, Ephah,** and **Sheba** are mentioned together in Isaiah lx, 6. These tribes were nomadic, and probably for a time wandered, like Abraham, to and fro in the wide deserts south and east of Palestine. They probably, at a subsequent date, became largely intermingled with the Ishmaelites, and are represented now in the numerous Arab tribes of these same ancient deserts.

5. **Gave all ... unto Isaac**—This had been understood and settled long before. Chap. xxiv, 36.

6. **The concubines**—Hagar and Keturah. **Sent them away**—Some have objected that Keturah's sons, if born after Sarah's death, were too young to be thus sent away. But Ishmael was only a lad of fifteen or seventeen years when sent away with his mother into the wilderness of Beer-sheba. Chap. xxi, 14. But the time of bestowing these gifts on the sons of his concubines, and sending them away, is uncertain. The different facts stated in verses 5 and 6 may have occurred at very different dates. **From Isaac**—Abraham would not have his son and heir troubled by claims or disputes after his death, so he was careful to see that all disposition of his possessions, and of the sons of his concubines, was made **while he yet lived.** A wise example to fathers who have large estates, and many possible claimants. **Unto the east country** —And they became known thereafter as the Easterns, or *Bene-Kedem,* sons of the East. See Judges vi, 3; 1 Kings iv, 30; Job i, 3; Isa. xi, 14.

DEATH AND BURIAL OF ABRAHAM, 7–11.

The termination of Abraham's life is recorded here, as also the generations of Ishmael, (verses 12–18,) in order to prepare the way for the history of Isaac. But it appears from verse 26, that Jacob and Esau were born fifteen years before Abraham's death.

7. **The days of the years**—This form of expression is impressive, and

B. C. 1822.　　　　CHAPTER XXV.　　　　241

threescore and fifteen years. 8 Then Abraham gave up the ghost, and ⁿdied in a good old age, an old man, and full *of years;* and ᶠwas gathered to his people. 9 And ᵍhis sons Isaac and Ishmael buried him in the cave of Machpelah, in the field of Ephron the son of Zohar the Hittite, which *is* before Mamre; 10 ʰThe field which Abraham purchased of the sons of Heth : ⁱthere was Abraham buried, and Sarah his wife.
11 And it came to pass after the death of Abraham, that God blessed his son Isaac; and Isaac dwelt by the ᵏwell Lehai-roi.
12 Now these *are* the generations of Ishmael, Abraham's son, ˡwhom Hagar the Egyptian, Sarah's handmaid, bare unto Abraham: 13 And ᵐthese *are* the names of the sons of Ishmael, by their names, according to their generations: the firstborn of Ishmael, Nebajoth; and Kedar, and Adbeel, and Mibsam, 14 And Mishma, and Dumah, and Massa, 15 ¹Hadar, and Tema, Jetur,

---

e Chap. 15. 15 ; 49. 29.——*f* Chap. 35. 29 ; 49. 33.——*g* Chap. 35. 29 ; 50. 13.——*h* Chap. 23. 16.——*i* Chap. 49. 31.

k Chapter 16. 14 ; 24. 62. —— *l* Chapter 16. 15. —— *m* 1 Chronicles 1. 29. —— 1 Or, *Hadad*, 1 Chronicles 1. 30.

---

served to intensify the idea of the long life of one hundred and seventy-five years. Comp. chap. xxxv, 28, 29 ; and xlvii, 9. How many days in these years! But his father, Terah, died at two hundred and five years, (xi, 32,) his son Isaac at one hundred and eighty, (xxxv, 28,) and Jacob at one hundred and forty-seven years. Chap. xlvii, 28.
8. **Gave up the ghost** — Heb., *breathed out.* He seems to have died of old age, and **in a good old age,** according to the promises of chap. xv, 15. **An old man, and full of years**—Rather, *old and full.* His was a well-rounded and completed life. **Gathered to his people**—Not buried in the ancestral tomb, for this was not the case; nor is the expression equivalent to burial, for that is separately mentioned in the next verse; but gathered where his people were yet living an immortal life. See on chap. xv, 15. Abraham's faith "looked for a city which hath foundations, whose builder and maker is God." And he died in this faith, "not having received the promises, but having seen them afar off." Evidently he desired and sought a heavenly land ; not that from which he emigrated. See Heb. xi, 10–16. And long after, in the days of Moses, Jehovah said, "I am the God of Abraham." Exod. iii, 6. But " God is not the God of the dead, but of the living." Matt. xxii, 32.
9. **Isaac and Ishmael buried him** —There is something touching in this statement. No wrongs, or bitterness, or antipathy of the past, prevent their union in a common sorrow over their great father. So at a later date Esau and Jacob, similarly estranged, come together to bury their father, Isaac. Chap. xxxv, 29. The sons of Keturah, now, perhaps, far scattered, and less attached to Abraham than Ishmael and Isaac, are not mentioned here. **Machpelah**—See on chap. xxiii, 9.
11. **God blessed . . . Isaac**—This verse is a sort of appendix to Abraham's death. The aged patriarch is buried, but the God of Abraham abides the God of Isaac, and ever lives to fulfil his word. **Lahai-roi**—See on chap. xvi, 14 ; xxiv, 62. After this new sorrow Isaac might well betake him to the place so memorably associated with his first meeting with his beloved Rebekah, who comforted him after his mother's death.

Generations of Ishmael, xxv, 12–18.

12. **These are the generations**— This is the eighth section so beginning. "According to custom," says Murphy, "before the history of the principal line is taken up, that of the collateral branch is briefly given. Thus Cain's history is closed before Seth's is commenced ; Japheth and Ham are before Shem ; Haran and Nahor before Abram. And so the sons of Keturah are first dismissed from the pages of history, and then Ishmael."
13–15. **The names**—We find scattered notices of these names in later books. Thus, **Nebajoth** in Isa. lx, 7, probably the Nabatæans of later history; **Kedar** in Isa. xxi, 17 ; xlii, 11 ; lx, 7 ; Jer. ii, 10 ; xlix, 28 ; Ezek. xxvii, 21 ; Psa. cxx, 5 ; Cant. i, 5 ; **Dumah**

Naphish, and Kedemah : **16** These *are* the sons of Ishmael, and these *are* their names, by their towns, and by their castles; ⁿ twelve princes according to their nations. **17** And these *are* the years of the life of Ishmael, a hundred and thirty and seven years: and ᵒ he gave up the ghost and died, and was gathered unto his people. **18** ᵖAnd they dwelt from Havilah unto Shur, that *is* before Egypt, as thou goest toward Assyria: *and* he ᑫdied ᑫin the presence of all his brethren. **19** And these *are* the generations of Isaac, Abraham's son : ʳ Abraham begat Isaac : **20** And Isaac was forty years old when he took Rebekah to wife, ˢ the daughter of Bethuel the Syrian of Padanaram, ᵗ the sister to Laban the Syrian. **21** And Isaac entreated the LORD for his wife, because she *was* barren : ᵘ and the LORD was entreated of him, and

---

n Chap. 17. 20.——*o* Verse 8.——*p* 1 Sam. 15. 7.——*2* Heb. *fell*, Psa. 78. 64.——*q* Chap. 16. 12. *r* Matt. 1. 2.——*s* Chap. 22. 23.——*t* Chap. 24. 29.——*u* 1 Chron. 5. 20; 2 Chron. 33. 13; Ezra 8. 23.

---

in Isa. xxi, 11; **Tema** in Job vi, 19; Isa. xxi, 14; Jer. xxv, 23; **Jetur and Naphish** in 1 Chron. v, 19. From Jetur probably sprung theIturæans of later history. Many of these, no doubt, became intermingled with the sons of Keturah. See on verses 2–4.

16. By their towns, and... castles—Rather, in their village and in their encampment. "It is generally known, that the Arabs are, according to their mode of life, divided into two chief classes : those of towns or villages, and those of the deserts, or the dwellers in tents. The latter, of course nomadic in their habits, are the Bedouins and *Scenitæ*. It is not improbable that these two different classes are alluded to in the words, 'By their villages and by their tents.' The roaming Bedouins regard the agricultural population with a certain contempt as slaves of toil and drudgery. They seldom cultivate the land which they may have inherited or won by their valour; but rent it out for a fixed annual sum to peasants subordinated to them in a kind of vassalage." —*Kalisch.* **Twelve princes** — Ishmael, like Israel, had twelve sons, who became the princes and heads of so many tribes. **Nations**—אֻמּוֹת, *peoples,* or tribes sprung from one common mother, אֵם.

17. Hundred and thirty and seven —Lange suggests that the violent disposition and passions of Ishmael consumed his life comparatively early; while the more peaceful and serene Isaac outlived him by more than forty years. **His people**—He doubtless died in the faith of Abraham. Comp. verse 8, note.

18. From Havilah unto Shur—Or, as we might say, from the Arabian Gulf and the Euphrates to the border of Egypt and the Red Sea. On **Havilah** see chap. x, 7, 29 ; and on **Shur** see on chap. xvi, 7, xx, 1, and Exod. xv, 22. **As thou goest toward Assyria**—One journeying most directly from Egypt to Assyria would pass through this broad Ishmaelite territory. **Died**—Rather, *he fell,* or threw himself, נָפָל. This word is here used somewhat in the sense of the American word *squat;* he threw himself down upon, or settled in this region, between Havilah and Shur. The word is rendered *lay along* in Judges vii, 12, where it is said the Midianites and Amalekites and Bene-Kedem *fell* with their tents and cattle in the valley. That is, they dropped down, flung themselves down, intending to stay. Thus was fulfilled the prophecy of chap. xvi, 12.

Generations of Isaac, xxv, 19–xxxv, 29.

BIRTH OF ESAU AND JACOB, 19–26.

19. These are the generations of Isaac—Thus characteristically this new section of the history opens. We have also a repetition of Isaac's birth, his age at marriage, and the name, country, father, and brother of his wife.

21. Entreated the Lord—The word for **entreated** (עָתַר) implies earnest and repeated prayer, and perhaps the accompaniment of incense offering, or some kind of sacrifice. See the Heb. lexicons on the word. We note that Isaac directs his prayer to *Jehovah,* the God of the covenant and the promises. **Was entreated**—Was prevailed upon by his importunity. Compare Luke xviii, 7. "The heir of promise was to be a child of prayer."

B. C. 1838. CHAPTER XXV. 243

ᵛ Rebekah his wife conceived. **22** And the children struggled together within her; and she said, If it be so, why am I thus? ʷAnd she went to inquire of the LORD. **23** And the LORD said unto her, ˣ Two nations *are* in thy womb, and two manner of people shall be separated from thy bowels; and ʸ and *the one* people shall be stronger than *the other* people; and ᶻ the elder shall serve the younger.

24 And when her days to be delivered were fulfilled, behold, *there were* twins in her womb. **25** And the first came out red, ᵃ all over like a hairy garment; and they called his name Esau. **26** And after that came his brother out, and ᵇ his hand took hold on Esau's heel; and ᶜ his name was called Jacob: and Isaac *was* threescore years old when she bare them. **27** And the boys grew: and Esau was ᵈ a cunning hunter, a man

---

v Romans 9. 10. —— *w* 1 Samuel 9. 9; 10. 22. —— *x* Chapter 17. 16; 24. 60. —— *y* 2 Samuel 8. 14.

z Chap. 27. 29; Mal. 1. 3; Rom. 9. 12.——*a* Chap. 27. 11, 16, 23.——*b* Hos. 12. 3. —— *c* Chap. 27. 36. ——*d* Chap. 27. 3, 5.

---

22. **Struggled together within her**—Heb., *dashed against one another.* Premonition of the coming differences between the offspring. **If it be so, why am I thus**—The Vulgate reads: "If it was to have been so with me, why should I have conceived?" Rebekah was evidently of an excitable and emotional temperament, (compare chap. xxvii, 46,) and under the pains of maturing pregnancy yielded fitfully to despondency and gloom. **Went to inquire of the Lord**—Where and how, has been often asked, but not so easily answered. The old Jewish interpreters suppose she went to Shem, or to Melchizedek, who were still living. Much more probable is the supposition that she went to Abraham, who was still living, and known as a prophet, (chap. xx, 7, compare 1 Sam. ix, 9,) and doubtless intensely interested in the prospective offspring of Isaac. But, perhaps, she went to that domestic altar where Isaac had so earnestly besought Jehovah for her, (verse 21,) and Jehovah answered by his angel as he spoke to Hagar. Chap. xvi, 11.

23. **The Lord said**—Here, too, we have a poetic strain:

Then said Jehovah to her,
Two nations are in thy womb,
And two peoples from thy bowels shall be separated.
And people than people shall be stronger,
And the great shall serve the small.

What immediate effect this oracle had on Rebekah we are not told, but it probably served, in the subsequent time, to give her an intuitive partiality for the younger son. The subsequent history of the Israelites and the Edomites show how truly this prophecy was fulfilled. The descendants of Esau were strong, and fortified themselves in Mount Seir. They refused the Israelites a passage through their territory. Num. xx, 18. But Saul vexed them with his wars, (1 Sam. xiv, 47,) and David subdued them, and put garrisons throughout their land, (2 Sam. viii, 14,) and they remained in such subjection till the days of Joram. 2 Kings viii, 20. Then, according to Isaac's prophecy, Esau broke his brother's yoke from off his neck. Chap. xxvii, 40.

25. **Red, all over like a hairy garment**—"His whole body was as if covered with a fur, with an unusual quantity of hair, (*hypertrichosis*,) which is sometimes the case with new-born infants, but was a sign in this instance of excessive sensual vigour and wildness." — *Keil.* **Esau**—Which means *hairy.*

26. **His hand took hold on Esau's heel**—His birth seems to have followed that of Esau more speedily than is usual in the case of twins, and his hand was so extended as to seem to grasp hold of Esau's heel. Hence his name **Jacob**, *heel-catcher.* Compare chap. xxvii, 36. **Threescore years old**—Twenty years after the marriage of Isaac and Rebekah. Comp. verse 20.

SALE OF ESAU'S BIRTHRIGHT, 27–34.

27. **The boys grew**—And their diverse dispositions and tendencies early developed themselves. **Esau was a cunning hunter**—A man knowing the chase, or skilled in hunting. We are to think of him as the hairy man, rough, impulsive, desperate; loving the dangers and excitements of the chase.

of the field; and Jacob was ᵉ a plain man, ᶠdwelling in tents. **28** And Isaac loved Esau, because ³ he did ᵍ eat of *his* venison: ʰ but Rebekah loved Jacob.

e Job 1. 1, 8; 2. 3; Psa. 37. 37. ——ᶠ Heb. 11. 9. ——3 Heb. *venison* was *in his mouth.*

Jacob was a plain man—אִישׁ תָּם, *a complete man.* The word תָּם is generally used of moral uprightness and integrity. The kindred word תָּמִים is used in chap. xvii, 1, where Jehovah says to Abraham, "walk before me and be thou *perfect*." Here the word seems to mean simplicity, mildness, and inoffensiveness of disposition, in contrast with the wild and daring character of Esau. Jacob was a complete man in the simplicity and regularity of his temper and domestic habits.

28. Because he did eat—Literally, *for hunting was in his mouth,* that is, the results of hunting—game. Comp. xxvii, 4. **Rebekah loved Jacob**—No reason is given for her partial love, but we easily infer it was owing to Jacob's more domestic habits, and the prophecy which had gone before his birth. Isaac seems, after the birth of his sons, to have been strangely swayed by carnal appetite. Quiet, unenterprising, and timid, he was drawn by the law of attraction of opposites to his daring, impetuous, and resolute son, while the quick and impulsive Rebekah loved (best) the mild and undemonstrative, but scheming, Jacob. Esau was frank and bold, but coarse and carnal; Jacob was timid, reticent, and shrewd, but spiritual. Esau had no spiritual insight, no relish whatever for the blessings and duties of the great Abrahamic covenant, he cared only for the carnal portion of the birthright; Jacob, though selfish and cunning, yet had a genuine hunger for the things of God; but it required a long and painful discipline, mighty, spiritual strugglings and angelic wrestlings to qualify him to become the heir of Abraham. In this patriarchal home the mother was the ruling spirit, and the timorous Isaac and unsuspecting Esau were no match for the resolute Rebekah and scheming Jacob. God used, yet punished, these sins. The shortsightedness

29 And Jacob sod pottage: and Esau came from the field, and he *was* faint: **30** And Esau said to Jacob, Feed me, I pray thee, ⁴ with that same red *pottage;*

q Chap. 27. 19, 25, 31.——ʰ Chap. 27. 6.——4 Heb. *with that red,* with that *red* pottage.

of Isaac, the wild ferocity of Esau, the deception of Rebekah and Jacob, were woven into the web of providence for man's good and God's glory.

29. Sod pottage—Jacob boiled a dish of lentiles, (verse 34,) a podded vegetable like the pea or bean, which is cooked by parching over the fire or boiling into a soup, making a favourite and highly nutritious dish all through the East. There is a small red variety of lentile which makes a reddish brown, or chocolate coloured pottage, much prized by the Arabs, which, when being cooked, exhales a savoury odour very grateful to a hungry man. Robinson, Thomson. Jacob's household tastes made him skilful in the preparation of this favourite dish. In Eastern homes food is prepared only as it is wanted; and when Esau returned home from the unsuccessful hunt, fatigued and faint, and saw and smelled the red savoury pottage steaming in Jacob's tent, impetuous, impatient, and hungry, he cried out,

30. Feed me—" Literally, *Let me devour now that red, that red, for I am faint; therefore they called his name Red* (Edom.) It is the language of greedy, and perhaps imperious, impatience, which Jacob might have resented, whereas he craftily resolved to turn it to his own advantage. In this characteristic incident the sacred writer dramatically paints the two brothers before us. The man, the hungry hunter, led by the senses, is fascinated by the high colour and rich flavour of a mess of pottage, and the meditative schemer of the tents, the man of wits, cannot wait for Providence to bring him the predicted birthright, but must intermeddle with his selfish craft. Here is also an interesting illustration of the origin of names. Some characteristic incident gives rise to a name, and on the subsequent occurrence of a similar incident the appropriateness of the name, or its coincidence with events, is noted, and

for I *am* faint: therefore was his name called ⁵ Edom. **31** And Jacob said, Sell me this day thy birthright. **32** And Esau said, Behold, I *am* ⁶ at the point to die: and what profit shall this birthright do to me? **33** And Jacob said, Swear to me this day; and he sware unto him: and ⁱ he sold his birthright unto Jacob. **34** Then Jacob gave Esau bread and pottage of lentiles; and ᵏ he did eat and drink, and rose up, and went his way. Thus Esau despised *his* birthright.

5 That is, *Red*.——6 Heb. *going to die*.——*i* Heb. 12. 16. —— *k* Eccl. 8. 15; Isa. 22. 13; 1 Cor. 15. 32.

the name is renewed. Esau is first surnamed Red from his red hair, and then from the red pottage. Jacob is called *heel-catcher*, or *tripper*, first literally (verse 26) and then figuratively (chap. xxvii, 36,) and the figurative name is first applied when he trips up Esau in the matter of the birthright, and then its appropriateness is noticed again when we arrive at the incident of Isaac's blessing. We often thus meet in this history with various reasons for the application of the same name."—*Newhall.*

31. Sell me this day thy birthright—"This birthright not only embraced the authority and honour of the patriarchal headship of the chosen family, but made its possessor heir to the Abrahamic covenant, and thus the channel of God's great revealed mercies to mankind—a mediator between God and the race—typifying the God-man. Jacob, who was on a much lower spiritual plane than Abraham, by no means comprehended the vastness and dignity of these spiritual blessings, but he appreciated them far more than the worldly and sensual Esau. He knew that he was predestinated to this heirship, although he was the younger son. Dreading a collision with his ferocious brother, which seemed inevitable in the event of his father's death, when the succession would be contested, and lacking faith in God's unfolding providence, he resolves to avail himself of Esau's weakness to obtain the birthright by peaceful purchase. The cautious Jacob knows well that Esau will repent as soon as his hunger is sated, and takes care to have the contract ratified by a solemn oath."—*Newhall.*

34. Esau despised his birthright —"In these graphic touches the sacred writer paints the 'profane' Esau's unfitness for the spiritual headship of the chosen people, yet with equal faithfulness depicts the craft and selfishness of the 'supplanter,' who afterwards became the 'warrior of God' (Israel.)" —*Newhall.*

In these growing divergences of character, here manifest in the two brothers, Lange observes what he calls "the Hebraic, or profoundest conception of history. All history develops itself from personal beginnings. The personal is predominant in history."

CHAPTER XXVI.

ISAAC AND ABIMELECH, 1–33.

This is the only chapter in the history of Isaac which is devoted entirely to incidents in the life of that patriarch, the rest being largely intermixed with the history of his father or his sons. And yet it is a repetition of events remarkably similar to those of one passage in the life of Abraham. Comp. chap. xx; xxi, 22–34. So striking are the analogies between these two accounts that rationalistic critics have not hesitated to pronounce them different forms of one and the same story. But we must observe that there are as many points of dissimilarity as of agreement; and in making prominent the fact that Isaac's life was so largely a repetition of Abraham's, the sacred writer doubtless had a purpose. How much of human life and history is ever repeating itself! And how slow are many of the best of men to improve by the errors of their fathers or predecessors! To show this is an important part of the purpose of this chapter.

The points of agreement with portions of Abraham's life are as follows: 1) A famine causes Isaac's moving. Comp. chap. xii, 10. 2) He had some thought of going down into Egypt. Verse 2 compared with xii, 10. 3) The dwelling in Gerar. 4) The names Abimelech and Phicol. 5) Denial of his wife. 6) Reproof by Abimelech. 7) Desire of Abimelech to make a

CHAPTER XXVI.

AND there was a famine in the land, besides ªthe first famine that was in the days of Abraham. And Isaac went unto ᵇAbimelech king of the Philistines unto Gerar. **2** And the LORD appeared unto him, and said, Go not down into Egypt; dwell in ᶜthe land which I shall tell thee of. **3** ᵈSojourn in this land, and ᵉI will be with thee, and ᶠwill bless thee; for unto thee, and unto thy seed, ᵍI will give all these countries, and I will perform ʰthe oath which I sware unto Abraham thy father; **4** And ⁱI will make thy seed to multiply as the stars of heaven, and will give unto thy seed all these countries; ᵏand in thy seed shall all the nations of the earth be blessed: **5** ˡBecause that Abraham obeyed my voice, and kept my charge, my commandments, my statutes, and my laws.

---

a Chap. 12. 10.——*b* Chap. 20. 2.——*c* Chap. 12. 1.——*d* Chap. 20. 1; Psa. 39. 12; Heb. 11. 9.——*e* Chap. 28. 15.——*f* Chap. 12. 2.

g Chap. 13. 15; 15. 18.——*h* Chap. 22. 16; Psa. 105. 9.——*i* Chap. 15. 5; 22. 17.——*k* Chap. 12. 3; 22. 18.——*l* Chap. 22. 16, 18.

---

covenant. 8) Strife between herdsmen. 9) Oath at Beer-sheba. 10) Calling on the name of the Lord.

The points of disagreement are as follows: 1) The famine in Isaac's case is carefully distinguished from that in the days of Abraham. 2) He is prohibited from going into Egypt. 3) Rebekah was not taken into Abimelech's house as was Sarah. 4) Isaac's deceit was discovered, not by a judgment of God, but by accident. 5) Abraham was allowed free use of the land; Isaac was requested to leave. 6) Abraham's difficulty was about the well of Beer-sheba; Isaac was driven from many wells before he withdrew to Beer-sheba. 7) Isaac's servants discover water at Beer-sheba, and the name is renewed after the oath between him and Abimelech, and after the latter had departed. 8) Abraham made a covenant with seven lambs; Isaac made a feast. 9) Ahuzzah, the friend of Abimelech, is an additional personage in the affair with Isaac; in chap. xx God appears in a dream to Abimelech, but no special revelations were made to Abraham.

A careful scrutiny of these points of agreement and difference will show that the events narrated were two very different affairs. Isaac's life, while having so many experiences like his father's, was not a mere echo of the life of Abraham. It had an individuality peculiarly its own, from his being quiet and passive where Abraham was active and bold.

1. A famine — Abraham's, Isaac's, and Jacob's history are each distinguished by a famine, that frequent plague of the East. **Besides the first famine**—Our historian was not so obtuse, as some critics have assumed, as not to know that Abraham's life had passages very much like Isaac's. But he knew, what some critics seem unable to comprehend, that two men's lives may be largely the one a repetition of the other. Thus history has often repeated itself in less than a century. **Abimelech**—Possibly the same Abimelech as that of chapter xx, 2. For if he had been aged forty at the time of Abraham's visit, he would have now been about one hundred and twenty-five —no very unsupposable age for that time, when men lived, as we have seen, to be one hundred and seventy-five years old. But it is altogether probable that this was the son and successor of the Abimelech of Abraham's time, for both his name and that of Phichol (verse 26) were official titles rather than personal appellations. See notes on xx, 2; xxi, 22.

2. The Lord appeared—In a dream or vision of the night. Comp. verse 24. "The last recorded vision was at the sacrifice of Isaac, more than sixty years before. These revelations were not so frequent as they seem to us, as we read one event rapidly after the other; but just sufficient to keep up the knowledge of God and the faith of the patriarchs in the line of the chosen people, and of the promised seed."—*Speaker's Commentary.*

4. All these countries—All the different districts or territories of the different Canaanitish tribes.

5. Voice ... charge ... commandments ... statutes ... laws— A comprehensive summary of all the various revelations of the divine will. God's **voice** denotes more particularly

About B. C. 1804.   CHAPTER XXVI.   247

6 And Isaac dwelt in Gerar. **7** And the men of the place asked *him* of his wife; and ᵐ he said, She *is* my sister: for ⁿ he feared to say, *She is* my wife; lest, *said he*, the men of the place should kill me for Rebekah; because she ᵒ *was* fair to look upon. **8** And it came to pass, when he had been there a long time, that Abimelech king of the Philistines looked out at a window, and saw, and, behold, Isaac *was* sporting with Rebekah his wife. **9** And Abimelech called Isaac, and said, Behold, of a surety she *is* thy wife: and how saidst thou, She *is* my sister? And Isaac said unto him, Because I said, Lest I die for her. **10** And Abimelech said, What *is* this thou hast done unto us? one of the people might lightly have lain with thy wife, and ᵖ thou shouldest have brought guiltiness upon us. **11** And Abimelech

m Chap. 12. 13; 20. 2, 13.——*n* Prov. 29. 25.——*o* Chap. 24. 16.——*p* Chap. 20. 9.——*q* Psa. 105. 15. ——1 Heb. *found.*——*r* Matt. 13. 8; Mark 4. 8. ——*s* Verse 3; chap. 24. 1, 35; Job 42. 12.

the spoken revelations; his **charge** the special trusts of promise he had given Abraham to guard; his **commandments** the occasional precepts given from time to time; his **statutes** the more permanent prescriptions of his will; his **laws** the everlasting and unchangeable expressions of his righteousness. Already had God spoken "at sundry times and in divers manners," (Heb. i, 1,) and we note that the son is blessed **because** of his father's obedience.

7. Should kill me — Comp. chap. xii, 12, xx, 11, notes; and for the agreement and differences of these narratives the note at the beginning of this chapter.

8. Sporting—See note on chap. xxi, 8.

12. Isaac sowed—He now added agriculture to the pursuits of nomadic life. **Received** — Heb., *found.* **A hundredfold** — Or, *a hundred measures.* Some (Sept., Syr.) read, שְׂעֹרִים, *barley,* instead of שְׁעָרִים, *measures,* or *fold.* The letters of the two words are the same. A hundredfold is a very large increase, but Herodotus (i, 193) writes of the Babylonian territory as "so fruitful in the produce of corn, that it yields continually two hundredfold, and when it produces its best, it yields even three hundredfold."

charged all *his* people, saying, He that ᵠ toucheth this man or his wife shall surely be put to death. **12** Then Isaac sowed in that land, and ¹ received in the same year ʳ a hundredfold : and the LORD ˢ blessed him. **13** And the man ᵗ waxed great, and ² went forward, and grew until he became very great: **14** For he had possession of flocks, and possession of herds, and great store of ³ servants: and the Philistines ᵘ envied him. **15** For all the wells ᵛ which his father's servants had digged in the days of Abraham his father, the Philistines had stopped them, and filled them with earth. **16** And Abimelech said unto Isaac, Go from us; for ʷ thou art much mightier than we.

17 And Isaac departed thence, and pitched his tent in the valley of Gerar, and dwelt there. **18** And Isaac digged again the wells of water, which they

t Chap. 24. 35; Psa. 112. 3; Prov. 10. 22. —— 2 Heb. *went going.*——3 Or, *husbandry.*—— *u* Chap. 37. 11; Eccles. 4. 4. —— *v* Chap. 21. 30. ——*w* Exod. 1. 9.

13. Went forward—Heb., *went going;* that is, kept on growing. Three degrees are here expressed—**great, greater, very great.**

14. Flocks ... herds ... servants ... envied—These four words speak volumes. Prosperity and abundance excite the envy of ignoble natures.

15. Wells ... filled—The wells dug by Abraham gave Isaac a sort of title to the land, and filling them up was equivalent to a declaration of war. Comp. 2 Kings iii, 25 ; Isa. xv, 6.

16. Go from us — The Philistine king perceives that such a rich and prosperous chief as Isaac cannot peaceably dwell in Gerar. The strife between the different herdmen would be likely to be more bitter than that of the herdmen of Abram and Lot. Chap. xiii, 7. So while Abraham was invited to stay and settle anywhere, (xx, 15,) Isaac is invited to leave.

17. Valley of Gerar—Some writers speak of a district *el-Gerar* south of Beer-sheba, but that country has not been sufficiently explored to confirm their statements. Isaac withdrew from Gerar, but not from the Philistine land.

18. Digged again the wells — Abraham's long residence (comp. xxi, 34) in the districts of Gerar and Beer-sheba had left its traces in many a valley, and after his death the Philistines

had digged in the days of Abraham his father; for the Philistines had stopped them after the death of Abraham: ⁱand he called their names after the names by which his father had called them. 19 And Isaac's servants digged in the valley, and found there a well of ᵃspringing water. 20 And the herdmen of Gerar ʸdid strive with Isaac's herdmen, saying, The water *is* ours: and he called the name of the well ᵇEsek; because they strove with him. 21 And they digged another well, and strove for that also: and he called the name of it ᶜSitnah. 22 And he removed from thence, and digged another well; and for that they strove not: and he called the name of it ⁷Rehoboth; and he said, For now the Lord hath made room for us, and we shall ᶻbe fruitful in the land. 23 And he went up from thence to Beer-sheba. 24 And the Lord appeared unto him the same night, and said, ᵃI *am* the God of Abraham thy father: ᵇfear not, for ᶜI *am* with thee, and will bless thee, and multiply thy seed for my servant Abraham's sake. 25 And he ᵈbuilded an altar there, and ᵉcalled upon the name of the Lord, and pitched his tent there: and there Isaac's servants digged a well. 26 Then Abimelech went to him from Gerar, and Ahuzzath one of his friends, ᶠand Phichol the chief captain of his army. 27 And Isaac said unto them, Wherefore come ye to me, seeing ᵍye hate me, and have ʰsent me away from you? 28 And they said, ᵍWe saw certainly that the Lord ⁱwas with thee: and we said, Let there be now an oath betwixt us, *even* betwixt us and thee, and let us make a covenant with thee; 29 ⁹That thou wilt do us no hurt, as we have not touched thee, and as we have done unto thee nothing but good, and have sent thee away in peace: ᵏthou *art* now the blessed of the Lord. 30 ˡAnd he made them a feast, and they did eat and drink. 31 And they

---

ⱳ Chap. 21. 31.——4 Heb. *living.*——*y* Chap. 21. 25.—— 5 That is, *Contention.* —— 6 That is, *Hatred.*——7 That is, *Room.*——*z* Chap. 17. 6; 28. 3; 41. 52; Exod. 1. 7.——*a* Chap. 17. 7; 24. 12; 28. 13; Exod. 3. 6; Acts 7. 32.——*b* Chap. 15. 1.

c Verses 3, 4.——*d* Chap. 12. 7; 13. 18.——*e* Psa. 116. 17.——*f* Chap. 21. 22. —— *g* Judg. 11. 7.—— *h* Verse 16.——8 Heb. *Seeing we saw.*——*i* Chap. 21. 22, 23. —— 9 Heb. *If thou shalt*, etc. —— *k* Chap. 24. 31; Psa. 115. 15.——*l* Chap. 19. 3.

---

seem to have hastened to obliterate the witnesses of their treaty with him. Hence the repetition of oaths, treaties, and names like Beer-sheba. Verse 33.

20–22. Esek ... Sitnah ... Rehoboth—These appear to have been new wells digged, in addition to the old ones re-opened, and the names mean, respectively, *Strife, Opposition,* (from the same root as *Satan,*) and *Broad Places, Room.* The name of **Rehoboth** still lingers in the wady *er-Ruhaibeh,* some twenty-three miles south of Beersheba, where Robinson found extensive ruins. Later travellers claim to have found the well, but their reports are conflicting.

24. The Lord appeared—Immediately on Isaac's return to Beer-sheba Jehovah renews to him the promises, and there he builds an altar in acknowledgment of his mercy.

25. Altar ... tent ... well—Mark the order; first the altar, God's worship before all else; next his tent, and then the well.

26. Ahuzzath—The king and his chief captain now take with them a third person, one of the king's **friends.** Comp. chap. xxi, 22.

27. Wherefore come ye—Isaac receives them coldly, as well he might after their breach of an old treaty of peace with his father. But the king was anxious to be on friendly terms with Isaac, even though the latter was not welcome to settle in his land.

28. We saw certainly—The signal favour bestowed on Isaac, (verse 12,) and the memory of his father, convinced these Philistine lords that their God *Jehovah* was mighty to help his worshippers. Twice in this address the name *Jehovah* is used, showing that Isaac's piety had magnified that name among the heathen.

29. Not touched thee ... nothing but good ... sent thee away in peace—Three falsehoods; for his servants had assailed Isaac's, they had filled up his wells, and really persecuted him out of all the region of Gerar. And yet, perhaps, Abimelech was ignorant of these wrongs, as his father had before claimed to have been to Abraham. Chap. xxi, 26.

30. Made them a feast—Thus returning good for evil, and overcoming evil with good.

About B. C. 1084.   CHAPTER XXVI.   249

rose up betimes in the morning, and ᵐsware one to another: and Isaac sent them away, and they departed from him in peace. **32** And it came to pass the same day, that Isaac's servants came, and told him concerning the well which they had digged, and said unto him, We have found water. **33** And he called it Shebah: ⁿtherefore the name of the city *is* ¹¹Beer-sheba unto this day. **34** °And Esau was forty years old when he took to wife Judith the daughter of Beeri the Hittite, and Bashemath the daughter of Elon the Hittite: **35** Which ᵖ were ¹²a grief of mind unto Isaac and to Rebekah.

---

m Chap. 21. 31. —— 10 That is, *An oath.*—
n Chap. 21. 31. —— 11 That is, *The well of the oath.*—*o* Chap. 36. 2.——*p* Chap. 27. 46; 28. 1, 8.
——12 Heb. *bitterness of spirit.*

---

33. Called it Shebah—שִׁבְעָה, *Shibhah;* which means both *seven* and *oath.* Compare chap. xxi, 28-31. "Now the writer was aware that this place had received the same name on a former occasion. But a second well had now been dug in like circumstances in the same locality. This gives occasion for a new application of the name in the memories of the people. This is another illustration of the principle explained at xxv, 30. Two wells still exist at this place, attesting the correctness of the record."—*Murphy.*

ESAU'S MARRIAGE, 34, 35.

34. Judith . . . and Bashemath—Two wives, and both Hittites, and both married in the same year, was polygamy equal to Lamech's, (iv, 19,) and led an apostle to call him a *fornicator,* (Heb. xii, 16,) and might well have caused his parents a great "grief of mind," (verse 35,) and bitterness of spirit. See further on chap. xxviii, 9; xxxvi, 2, 3.

CHAPTER XXVII.
ISAAC BLESSING HIS SONS, 1–40.

Thirty-six years have passed since Esau's marriage, (xxvi, 34,) and the twin brothers both remain in their father's household at Beer-sheba. There seems no probability that the purchased birthright (xxv, 33) will be of any avail to Jacob, now seventy-seven years old and unmarried. Isaac has attained his one hundred and thirty-seventh year, the age at which his half-brother Ishmael died, (xxv, 17,) and perhaps that fact, together with a sense of old age and failing sight, impressed him with a feeling of approaching death, and a strong desire before his departure to bless his elder son. Un-mindful of the prophecy, (xxv, 23,) and controlled by his partiality for Esau and love for the savoury game procured by his hunting, (xxv, 28,) he wilfully purposes to give the firstborn his dying benediction. But in all this he is strangely overruled by the power of God and the craftiness of Jacob and Rebekah. "There is," says Kurtz, "something peculiar and mysterious about the blessing and the curse of parents. Each word of blessing and of curse into which the whole strength and fulness of the psyche, the seat of personality and of will, descends, has a kind of magic power. It is the magic attaching to the image of God in man, imparted to him in creation, and which sin has only weakened and darkened, but not wholly effaced, as language is the royal sceptre of man. The blessing or the curse of parents approximates the creative power from which this magic at first originated. For, as generation is a representation of the Divine creative power, so is education and the ruling of children of the Divine governing and judging power, and so long as the world shall continue will this word of the ancient sage prove true: 'The blessing of the father establisheth the houses of children; but the curse of the mother rooteth out foundations.' Ecclesiasticus iii, 9. But the blessing of the patriarchs in the chosen family leads us beyond the sphere of nature to that of grace. In virtue of the covenant relation, which in this case pervades and determines every thing,the pneumatic power of the Divine counsel of salvation is here joined with the psychical power of a father's blessing or curse. Human freedom is here allied with Divine necessity. Here man is not suffered to act arbitrarily, but the capability of the human will,

GENESIS. About B. C. 1760.

CHAPTER XXVII.

AND it came to pass, that when Isaac was old, and ^a his eyes were dim, so that he could not see, he called Esau his eldest son, and said unto him, My son: and he said unto him, Behold, *here am* I. **2** And he said, Behold now, I am old, I ^b know not the day of my death: **3** ^c Now therefore take, I pray thee, thy weapons, thy quiver and thy bow, and go out to the field, and ¹ take me *some* venison; **4** And make me savoury meat, such as I love, and bring *it* to me, that I may eat; that my soul ^d may bless thee before I die. **5** And Rebekah heard when Isaac spake to Esau his son. And Esau went to the field to hunt *for* venison, *and* to bring *it*.

6 And Rebekah spake unto Jacob her son, saying, Behold, I heard thy father speak unto Esau thy brother, saying, **7** Bring me venison, and make me savoury meat, that I may eat, and bless thee before the LORD before my death. **8** Now therefore, my son, ^e obey my voice according to that which I command thee. **9** Go now to the flock, and fetch me from thence two good kids of the goats; and I will make them ^f savoury meat for thy father, such as he loveth: **10** And thou shalt bring *it* to thy father, that he may eat, and that he ^g may bless thee before his death. **11** And Jacob

---

a Chap. 48. 10; 1 Sam. 3. 2. —— *b* Prov. 27. 1; Jas. 4. 14.——*c* Chap. 25. 27, 28.——1 Heb. *hunt.*

d Verse 27; chap. 48. 9, 15; 49. 28; Deut. 33. 1. ——*e* Verse 13.——*f* Verse 4.——*g* Verse 4.

---

now purified, is endowed with the strength of Divine Omnipotence; and thereby the blessing or the curse becomes irrevocable and unchangeable."

1. Isaac was old — One hundred and thirty-seven years. This we ascertain from Jacob's history, who was not born until Isaac was sixty years old. Chap. xxv, 26. Jacob was one hundred and thirty when he went down into Egypt, (xlvii, 9,) which occurred in the second year of the famine, (xlv, 6,) and seven years of plenty had gone before, (xli, 53,) and Joseph was thirty years old when he stood before Pharaoh. Chap. xli, 46. Hence Jacob must have been in his ninety-first year when Joseph was born, and this occurred fourteen years after the flight to Haran. Chap. xxix, 27, compared with xxx, 25, 26. Jacob must, therefore, have been seventy-seven when he fled from Esau, and Isaac one hundred and thirty-seven.

2. Know not the day of my death —He lived forty-three years after this. Chap. xxxv, 28.

3. Take me some venison—Heb., *Hunt for me a hunting.* The word does not necessarily mean **venison,** but any kind of edible game taken by hunting. See Prov. xii, 27.

4. That I may eat; that my soul may bless thee—"There appears a singular mixture of the carnal and the spiritual in this. Isaac recognises his own character as that of the priestly and prophetic head of his house, privileged to bless as father and priest, and to foretell the fortunes of his family in succession to Abraham in his office of the prophet of God. Yet his carnal affection causes him to forget the response to the inquiry of Rebekah, "the elder shall serve the younger," and the fact that Esau had sold his birthright and alienated it from him forever by a solemn oath. Moreover, that his heart may be the more warmed to him whom he desires to bless, he seeks to have some of that **savoury meat** brought to him such as he loved."—*Speaker's Commentary.*

8. Obey my voice—Rebekah *heard* (verse 5) and *spake* (verse 6) on the subject pending with Isaac, for she, too, had a divine relation to the covenant blessing. And when she saw Isaac's determination to go counter to what she knew to be the divine word, she has no hesitation in seeking to thwart his purpose.

9. Go now to the flock—Isaac had said to Esau: "Go out to the field." Verse 3. The flock was nearer at hand. **Two good kids**—A bountiful meal is provided. One kid would have been more than sufficient for Isaac, but the **two** made the feast a sort of covenant meal, and somewhat of the nature of a sacrifice on the part of him who was to receive the blessing. **I will make them savoury meat**—Rebekah knows how to cook and season kids that Isaac will not distinguish them from the game of Esau.

said to Rebekah his mother, Behold, ʰ Esau my brother *is* a hairy man, and I *am* a smooth man : **12** My father peradventure will ⁱ feel me, and I shall seem to him as a deceiver ; and I shall bring ᵏ a curse upon me, and not a blessing. **13** And his mother said unto him, ˡ Upon me *be* thy curse, my son : only obey my voice, and go fetch me *them*. **14** And he went, and fetched, and brought *them* to his mother : and his mother ᵐ made savoury meat, such as his father loved. **15** And Rebekah took ² ⁿ goodly raiment of her eldest son Esau, which *were* with her in the house, and put them upon Jacob her younger son : **16** And she put the skins of the kids of the goats upon his hands, and upon the smooth of his neck : **17** And she gave the savoury meat and the bread, which she had prepared, into the hand of her son Jacob.

18 And he came unto his father, and said, My father : and he said, Here *am* I ; who *art* thou, my son ? **19** And Jacob said unto his father, I *am* Esau thy firstborn ; I have done according as thou badest me : arise, I pray thee, sit and eat of my venison, ᵒ that thy soul may bless me. **20** And Isaac said unto his son, How *is it* that thou hast found *it* so quickly, my son ? And he said, Because the LORD thy God brought *it* ³ to me. **21** And Isaac said unto Jacob, Come near, I pray thee, that I ᵖ may feel thee, my son, whether thou *be* my very son Esau or not. **22** And Jacob went near unto Isaac his father ; and he felt him, and said, The voice *is* Jacob's voice, but the hands *are* the hands of Esau. **23** And he discerned him not, because ᑫ his hands were hairy, as his brother Esau's hands : so he blessed him. **24** And he said, *Art* thou my very son Esau ? And he said, I *am*. **25** And he said, Bring *it* near to me, and I will eat of my son's venison, ʳ that my soul may bless thee. And he brought *it* near to him, and he did eat : and he brought him wine, and he drank. **26** And his father Isaac said unto him, Come near now, and kiss me my son. **27** And he came near, and kissed him : and he

---

h Chap. 25. 25.——*i* Verse 22.——*k* Chap. 9. 25 ; Deut. 27. 18.—— *l* Chap. 43. 9 ; 1 Sam. 25. 24 ; 2 Sam. 14. 9 ; Matt. 27. 25. | *m* Verses 4, 9.——2 Heb. *desirable*.——*n* Verse 27.——*o* Verse 4.——3 Heb. *before me*.——*p* Verse 12.——*q* Verse 16.——*r* Verse 4.

---

12. I shall seem to him as a deceiver—Jacob is cautious and farsighted; but his words show that he shrinks not from the proposed deception from a feeling that it would be wrong, but only from a fear of detection and **a curse.** Rebekah has no fear in this regard. Even if detected, she is willing to risk any **curse** likely to come from one who deliberately attempts to subvert prophecy. She looks at the end to be attained, and scruples not at the means to attain it.

15. Goodly raiment—The costly festive robes of Esau. According to a rabbinical tradition the eldest son, in patriarchal times, had a priestly garment which he always put on when offering sacrifice, and this robe the rabbins suppose to have been the priestly robe.

16. Skins of the kids—The hair of certain Oriental goats is said to resemble human hair, and Martial (Epig. xii, 45) speaks of kid skin " covering the temples and crown of a bare scalp."

20. The Lord thy God brought it to me—The bold and daring way in which Jacob utters his falsehoods here, and this use of the name Jehovah, is amazing. Isaac seems to have detected Jacob's voice, and he became suspicious. But he probably mistrusted his own hearing as he did his eyesight. " The scene of the fraud," says Kalisch, " is described with a psychological skill which rivets the interest, and excites the admiration of the reader."

22. Hands of Esau—Isaac's words are, literally : *The voice is voice of Jacob, and the two hands hands of Esau.* The old man is dubious ; there is something about it inexplicable. So he proceeds to bless him ; not, however, without asking him once more,

24. Art thou my very son Esau —Heb., *Thou this my son Esau?* With an obduracy and boldness unparalleled the supplanter says, **I am.**

27. Kissed him—With something of the nature of a Judas kiss. " But it is altogether a mistake to suppose, with Tuch, that Isaac demanded a kiss, in order thereby to distinguish the shepherd, who would smell of the flock, from the huntsman, who would smell of the field. After Isaac had partaken of the meal he has given up all distrust. The kiss is only the expression of paternal love, excited by having partaken of the savoury dish ; it is the acme of

GENESIS. About B. C. 1760.

smelled the smell of his raiment, and blessed him, and said, See, *the smell of my son *is* as the smell of a field which the LORD hath blessed: **28** Therefore ᵗGod give thee of ᵘthe dew of heaven, and ᵛthe fatness of the earth, and ʷplenty of corn and wine: **29** ˣLet people serve thee, and nations bow down to thee: be lord over thy brethren, and ʸlet thy mother's sons bow down to thee: ᶻcursed *be* every one that curseth thee, and blessed *be* he that blesseth thee.

30 And it came to pass, as soon as Isaac had made an end of blessing Jacob, and Jacob was yet scarce gone out from the presence of Isaac his father, that Esau his brother came in from his hunting. **31** And he also had made savoury meat, and brought it unto his father, and said unto his father, Let my father arise, and ᵃeat of his son's venison, that thy soul may bless me. **32** And Isaac his father said unto him, Who *art* thou? And he said, I *am* thy son, thy firstborn, Esau. **33** And Isaac ⁴trembled very exceedingly, and said, Who? where *is* he that hath ⁵taken venison, and brought *it* me, and I have eaten of all before

---

s Hosea 14. 6.——*t* Heb. 11. 20.——*u* Deut. 33. 13, 28; 2 Sam. 1. 21.——*v* Chap. 45. 18.——*w* Deut. 33. 28.——*x* Chap. 9. 25; 25. 23.

y Chap. 49. 8.——*z* Chap. 12. 3; Num. 24. 9.——*a* Verse 4. —— 4 Heb. *trembled with a great trembling greatly.*——5 Heb. *hunted.*

---

his now overflowing emotions and the transition to the blessing."—*Kurtz.* **The smell of his raiment**—" Many parts of Arabia and Palestine exhale a most delicious odour. Herod., iii, 113. After a refreshing rain especially, the air is perfumed with a fragrance inexpressibly sweet, (Plin., xvii, 5;) and the soil, furrowed by the ploughshare, emits often the balmy treasures hidden in its depths. Thus the garments of Esau, the man of the field, who roamed through hill and valley, were redolent of the scent of aromatic herbs; they called up in Isaac's mind the pictures of freshness, health, and abundance; his spirit, moved and struck, assumed a prophetic elevation; and he began the blessing."—*Kalisch.* We render Isaac's words as follows:

See, the odour of my son,
Like the odour of a field
Which Jehovah has blessed.
And the God shall give to thee
Of the dew of the heavens,
And of the fatness of the land,
And abundance of grain and sweet wine.
Nations shall serve thee,
And peoples bow down to thee.
Be lord to thy brethren,
And the sons of thy mother shall bow down to thee.
They that curse thee shall be cursed;
And they that bless thee shall be blessed.

28. **Dew of heaven**—Of the greatest importance to the fruitfulness of a land like Palestine. Comp. chap. xlix, 25; Deut. xxxiii, 13, 28; Hos. xiv, 6. **Fatness of the earth**—The fat portions of the land, or most fertile districts. Thus Isaac wills to this son the more desirable portions of the land of promise. **Corn and wine**—Representatives of the income of the fields.

29. **People . . . . nations**—Peoples and tribes of peoples. **Be lord**—This was fulfilled in the days of David, when the Edomites were subjected to Israel. 2 Sam. viii, 14. **Thy mother's sons**—This expression seems to carry with it a sense of putting Jacob, his mother's favourite son, (xxv, 28,) in subjection to Esau. **Cursed . . . blessed** —See chap. xii, 3. "Isaac does not pronounce on Jacob that emphatic spiritual blessing which God himself had assured to Abraham twice (xii, 3, xxii, 18) and to Isaac once, (xxvi, 4,) 'In thy seed shall all the nations of the earth be blessed.' There was something carnal and sinful in the whole conduct of the persons concerned in the history of this chapter, Isaac, Rebekah, Jacob, Esau; and it may have been this which withheld for the time the brightest promise to the family of Abraham; or perhaps it may have been that that promise should come only from the mouth of God himself, as it is given afterwards in chap. xxviii, 14." —*Speaker's Commentary.*

33. **Isaac trembled very exceedingly**—Because of a fearful sense of having been overruled and frustrated in a daring attempt to push his own will before that of God. He acts the part of a conscience-smitten transgressor. **Who? where is he**—Or, *who now is he?* Who in the world is he? Language of surprise, confusion, and alarm. Here Isaac has his just punishment for his wrongdoing in the case.

CHAPTER XXVII.

thou camest, and have blessed him? yea, ᵇ *and* he shall be blessed. 34 And when Esau heard the words of his father, ᶜ he cried with a great and exceeding bitter cry, and said unto his father, Bless me, *even* me also, O my father. 35 And he said, Thy brother came with subtilty, and hath taken away thy blessing. 36 And he said, ᵈ Is not he rightly named ᵉ Jacob? for he hath supplanted me these two times: ᵉ he took away my birthright; and, behold, now he hath taken away my blessing. And he said, Hast thou not reserved a blessing for me? 37 And Isaac answered and said unto Esau, ᶠ Behold, I have made him thy lord, and all his brethren have I given to him for servants; and ᵍ with corn and wine have I ⁷ sustained him: and what shall I do now unto thee, my son? 38 And Esau said unto his father, Hast thou but one blessing, my father? bless me, *even* me also, O my father. And Esau lifted up his voice, ʰ and wept. 39 And Isaac his father answered and said unto him, Behold, ⁱ thy dwelling shall be ⁸ the fatness of the earth, and of the dew of heaven from above; 40 And by thy sword shalt thou live, and ᵏ shalt serve thy brother: and ˡ it shall come to pass when thou shalt have the dominion, that thou shalt break his yoke from off thy neck. 41 And Esau ᵐ hated Jacob because

---

b Chap. 28. 3, 4; Rom. 11. 29.——*c* Heb. 12. 17.
——*d* Chap. 25. 26.——6 That is, *A supplanter*.
—— *e* Chap. 25. 33. ——*f* Fulfilled, 2 Sam. 8. 14;
verse 29.——*g* Verse 28.

7 Or, *supported*.——*h* Heb. 12. 17.——*i* Verse 28; Heb. 11. 20. —— 8 Or, *of the fatness*. —— *k* Chap. 25. 23; 2 Sam. 8. 14; Obad. 18, 19, 20.—— *l* 2 Kings 8. 20.——*m* Chap. 37. 4, 8.

He shall be blessed—The word has gone forth and cannot now be changed. See note at beginning of the chapter.

34. **Esau ... cried with a great and exceeding bitter cry**—Here comes his penalty and sorrow for his part in the attempt to move against the prophecy and against the spirit of his own oath solemnly made to Jacob—to yield him his birthright. There is something truly touching in his **bitter cry,** and yet we note that, like all the "profane," he mourns not his sin or error, but the consequences. "He found no place of repentance," no possibility or chance of repairing his loss by repentance, "though he sought it carefully with tears." Heb. xii, 17.

36. **Rightly named Jacob** — Literally, *Is it that his name is called Jacob? and he has jacobed me these two times.* Thus Esau points to the significancy of Jacob's name. Comp. chap. xxv, 26.

39. **His father answered**—Isaac's words now again take the form of prophecy, and, moved by the grief of his beloved son, and strong desire on his own part, he says:

Behold, of the fatness of the land shall be thy dwelling,
And of the dew of the heavens from above;
And upon thy sword shalt thou live,
And thy brother shalt thou serve;
And it shall be when thou shalt rove at large
That thou shalt break his yoke from off thy neck.

The fatness . . . of the dew — These expressions are precisely like those used in the blessing of Jacob, (verse 28,) only reversed as to their order. But many of the best interpreters explain the preposition מִן, as here used in a privative sense, *away from,* afar from the fatness and the dew, etc. This would give the whole oracle a double or doubtful meaning, one common expression, meaning in Jacob's case a blessing and in Esau's a curse. We exceedingly doubt that any such *double entente* is to be found in the prophecies of the Bible. It would imply a sort of duplicity on the part both of Isaac and of God, who inspired him to prophesy. It is true that God laid waste the mountains and heritage of Esau, (Mal. i, 3,) but this is also true of the mountains and heritage of Israel at this day; so that we might argue a like *double intente* in Isaac's words to Jacob. Verse 28. But Esau as well as Jacob for a long time enjoyed the blessing of fertile lands and refreshing dews, so that, in part, the brothers received like favours.

40. **By thy sword shalt thou live**—By war and rapine. Here note how different from Jacob, whose source of support is abundance of grain and of sweet wine. Verse 28. **Shalt serve thy brother** — This is not a blessing, but a confirmation of the prophecy already uttered over Jacob. **When thou shalt have the dominion** — Rather, *When thou shalt rove at large.* Thus Gesenius, fittingly pointing to

of the blessing wherewith his father blessed him: and Esau said in his heart, "The days of mourning for my father are at hand; ᵒ then will I slay my brother Jacob. **42** And these words of Esau her eldest son were told to Rebekah: and she sent and called Jacob her younger son, and said unto him, Behold, thy brother Esau, as touching thee, doth ᵖ comfort himself, *purposing* to kill thee. **43** Now therefore, my son, obey my voice; and arise, flee thou to Laban my brother ᑫ to Haran; **44** And tarry with him a few days, until thy brother's fury turn away; **45** Until thy brother's anger turn away from thee, and he forget *that* which thou hast done to him: then I will send, and fetch thee from thence: why should I be deprived also of you both in one day? **46** And Rebekah said to Isaac, ʳ I am weary of my life because of the daughters of Heth: ˢ if Jacob take a wife of the daughters of Heth, such as these *which are* of the daughters of the land, what good shall my life do me?

CHAPTER XXVIII.

AND Isaac called Jacob, and ᵃ blessed him, and charged him, and said unto him, ᵇ Thou shalt not take a wife of the daughters of Canaan. **2** ᶜ Arise, go to ᵈ Padan-aram, to the house of ᵉ Bethuel thy mother's father; and take thee a wife from thence of the daughters of ᶠ Laban thy mother's brother. **3** ᵍ And God Almighty bless thee, and make thee fruitful, and multiply thee, that

---

n Chap. 50. 3, 4, 10. —— *o* Obad. 10. —— *p* Psa. 64. 5.——*q* Chap. 11. 31.——*r* Chap. 26. 35; 28. 8. ——*s* Chap. 24. 3.

a Chap. 27. 33. —— *b* Chap. 24. 3. —— *c* Hosea 12. 12. —— *d* Chap. 25. 20. —— *e* Chap. 22. 23. —— *f* Chap. 24. 29.——*g* Chap. 17. 1, 6.

---

the roving character of the Edomites. Hengstenberg renders: *when thou shakest;* tossest thy head, like the wild ox. Either rendering more clearly sets forth the true thought than " when thou shalt have the dominion." This was fulfilled in the days of Ahaz. 2 Kings xvi, 6; 2 Chron. xxviii, 17. The Edomites were, however, subsequently conquered by John Hyrcanus, and compelled to submit to circumcision. Josephus, *Ant.* xiii, 9, 1; xv, 7, 9. But afterwards they succeeded in establishing that Idumæan dynasty of the Herods, which continued until the Jewish state was utterly overthrown by the destruction of Jerusalem by the Romans.

JACOB'S DEPARTURE TO HARAN, 41-xxviii, 5.

41. **Esau said**—Esau was one of those ingenuous, open natures, which show themselves out spontaneously. He could not keep his dark purpose a secret. **Mourning for my father**—He loved his father and would not grieve his heart; so he purposes to defer his vengeance until after his father is dead. He seems to have no such care about grieving his mother, the partial friend of Jacob.

43. **Obey my voice**—This is Rebekah's standing formula with Jacob. Comp. verses 8, 13. Her commands and action in respect to her favourite son, she believes to be according to the divine oracle to her. Chap. xxv, 23. **Laban**—See chap. xxiv, 29, 50. **Haran** —See on chap. xi, 31.

44. **Few days**—She would fain speak as tenderly as possible of the time he might be away. But those days proved to be twenty years. Chap. xxxi, 38.

45. **Both in one day**—If Esau slew Jacob, the avenger of blood would speedily arise, (chap. ix, 6,) and so both of them would perish as in a day. Or, perhaps, she refers to Isaac and Jacob both dying in a day.

46. **Rebekah said to Isaac**—Her words show the emotionality of her temperament, (comp. chap. xxv, 22,) and also the artfulness and tact by which she brings her husband to further the plans and desires of her heart.

CHAPTER XXVIII.

1. **Called ... blessed ... charged** —Isaac fully acquiesces in what he now knows to be the divine will. He follows the example of Abraham, his father, in seeking his son a wife from among his own kindred. Comp. chap. xxiv, 3, 4.

2. **Padan-aram**—See on chap. xxiv, 10.

3. **God Almighty bless thee**— This divine name, *El Shaddai*, is the same as that under which Jehovah appeared to Abraham when he instituted the covenant of circumcision, (see chap.

thou mayest be ¹ a multitude of people; 4 And give thee ʰ the blessing of Abraham, to thee, and to thy seed with thee; that thou mayest inherit the land ²ⁱ wherein thou art a stranger, which God gave unto Abraham. 5 And Isaac sent away Jacob: and he went to Padan-aram unto Laban, son of Bethuel the Syrian, the brother of Rebekah, Jacob's and Esau's mother.

6 When Esau saw that Isaac had blessed Jacob, and sent him away to Padan-aram, to take him a wife from thence; and that as he blessed him he gave him a charge, saying, Thou shalt not take a wife of the daughters of Canaan; 7 And that Jacob obeyed his father and his mother, and was gone to Padan-aram; 8 And Esau seeing ᵏ that the daughters of Canaan ³ pleased not Isaac his father; 9 Then went Esau unto Ishmael, and took unto the wives which he had ˡ Mahalath the daughter of Ishmael Abraham's son, ᵐ the sister of Nebajoth, to be his wife.

10 And Jacob ⁿ went out from Beer-sheba, and went toward ᵒ Haran. 11 And he lighted upon a certain place, and tarried there all night, because the sun was set; and he took of the stones of

---

1 Heb. *an assembly of people.* — *h* Chap. 12. 2. — 2 Heb. *of thy sojournings.* — *i* Chap. 17. 8. — *k* Chap. 24. 3; 26. 35. — 3 Heb. were *evil in the eyes*, etc. — *l* Chap. 36. 3, she is called *Bashemath.* — *m* Chap. 25. 13. — *n* Hos. 12. 12. — *o* Called, Acts 7. 2, *Charran.*

---

xvii, 1,) and in this name Isaac now invokes on Jacob the blessings there promised to Abraham. **A multitude** —Or, *a congregation;* קָהָל, *an assembly.* Here is a prophecy and promise of the Church of the living God.

ESAU MARRIES MAHALATH, 6–9.

9. **Then went Esau unto Ishmael** —That is, unto the family of Ishmael, who, himself, had been dead many years. Chap. xxv, 17. **Nebajoth** was Ishmael's firstborn. Chap. xxv, 13. Here we discern, again, in Esau's action, the wild, impetuous child of nature. He already has two wives and they have borne him children; but noticing how Jacob is blessed, and commanded not to take a Canaanitish wife, he speeds away to marry Ishmael's daughter.

"Esau is the representative of natural kindliness and honesty, but these qualities are joined to rudeness, and to a want of susceptibility for what is higher. He is void of all anticipation and longing. He is satisfied with what is visible; in short, he is a profane person. Heb. xii, 16. Such persons, even if grace reaches their hearts, which was not the case with Esau, are not adapted for heading a religious development."—*Hengstenberg.*

JACOB AT BETHEL, 10–22.

A complex nature of manifold elements was that of Jacob. His cunning, and disposition to supplant and overreach, have been twice shown. Deceit- fulness was a quality so conspicuous in his character as to have put him under the condemnation of all after time. But at the same time he was possessed of many higher qualities than Esau. The latter quickly showed out all he was; but many years and divers experiences were necessary to develop Jacob. In his more quiet soul there was a hiding of power; a susceptibility for divine things; a spiritual insight and longing that made him the fitter person to lead in the development of the chosen nation. The God of his fathers is now about to put him through a discipline that will eventually bring out his spiritual possibilities into bold relief. That which is now dead in him must be quickened by a divine energy from on high. He must suffer for his falsehood, and be wronged and deceived, and humbled in many ways; and at the same time he must receive much light and strength from Jehovah before he can cease to be the unworthy Jacob and become the prince of God.

10. **Jacob went out from Beer-sheba**—Very differently from the manner in which his father's servant had gone out on a similar errand. Chap. xxiv, 10.

11. **Upon a certain place**—Heb., *struck in the place.* His striking on that particular place was to him accidental, but the place was one already hallowed by one of Abraham's altars. Chap. xii, 8; xiii, 4. **Tarried there all night**—Tarried, as it appears, in the open field, not seeking the

256 GENESIS. About B. C. 1760.

that place, and put *them for* his pillows, and lay down in that place to sleep. **12** And he ᵖ dreamed, and behold a ladder set up on the earth, and the top of it reached to heaven: and behold ᵠ the angels of God ascending and descending on it. **13** ʳ And, behold, the LORD stood above it, and said, ˢ I *am* the LORD God of Abraham thy father, and the God of Isaac: ᵗ the land whereon thou liest, to thee will I give it, and to thy seed; **14** And ᵘ thy seed shall be as the dust of the earth; and thou shalt ⁴ spread abroad ᵛ to the west, and to the east, and to the north, and to the south: and in thee and ʷ in thy seed shall all the families of the earth be blessed. **15** And, behold, ˣ I *am* with thee, and will ʸ keep thee in all *places* whither thou goest, and will ᶻ bring thee again into this land; for ᵃ I will not leave thee, ᵇ until I have done *that* which I have spoken to thee of.
16 And Jacob awaked out of his sleep, and he said, Surely the LORD is in ᶜ this place; and I knew *it* not. **17** And he was afraid, and said, How dreadful *is* this place! this *is* none other but the house of God, and this *is* the gate of heaven. **18** And Jacob rose up early in the morning, and took the stone that he had put *for* his pillows, and ᵈ set it up

p Chap. 41. 1; Job 33. 15.——*q* John 1. 51; Heb. 1. 14.——*r* Chap. 35. 1; 48. 3. —— *s* Chap. 26. 24.—— *t* Chap. 13. 15; 35. 12.——*u* Chap. 13. 16.—— 4 Heb. *break forth*. —— *v* Chap. 13. 14; Deut. 12. 20.——*w* Chap. 12. 3; 18. 18; 22. 18; 26. 4.

x See verses 20, 21; chap. 26. 24; 31. 3. —— *y* Chap. 48. 16; Psa. 121. 5, 7, 8.——*z* Chap. 35. 6. —— *a* Deut. 31. 6, 8; Josh. 1. 5; 1 Kings 8. 57; Heb. 13. 5. —— *b* Num. 23. 19. —— *c* Exod. 3. 5; Josh. 5. 15.——*d* Chap. 31. 13, 45; 35. 14.

hospitality of the neighbouring Luz. Verse 19. Many anxious thoughts, doubtless, filled his soul; and when night overtook him there, he preferred to lie down alone rather than mix with any Canaanites. **The stones of that place**—The ridges and valleys about Beitin, the representative of the ancient Bethel, are covered with stones. Hard **pillows** were these, but there came refreshing visions. **Lay down ... to sleep**—Before darkness covered him he, doubtless, like Abram long before in this place, (xiii, 14,) looked "northward, and southward, and eastward, and westward," and saw afar the hills and mountains towering up like a stairway to heaven — a kind of preparation for his dream.
12. **Behold a ladder**—Or, *stairway*, (סֻלָּם.) The vision, manifestly, was that of a lofty passage-way, either a ladder with rounds, or a staircase with steps, or piles of mountains, one upon another, looking like a wondrous highway of passage to the skies. The great thing was an open passage-way between earth and heaven. **Angels of God**—What notion of angels Jacob may have had before we know not, but here was a sudden and glorious revelation of the numerous host of ministering spirits of the heirs of salvation. Heb. i, 14. Strangely have certain Rationalistic critics supposed that the Israelites first derived their ideas of angels and spirits during their Babylonian exile.
13. **The Lord stood**—A personal visional revelation of Jehovah. The Targum of Onkelos reads: "The glory of the Lord stood above." It was a theophany that impressed Jacob with a fearful awe. Verse 17. **The land ... to thy seed**—Compare the same promise made to Abraham in chap. xiii, 15; xv, 18.
14. **Thy seed shall be as the dust**—Comp. chaps. xii, 2, 3; xiii, 16; xviii, 18; xxii, 17, 18.
16. **Surely the Lord is in this place**—The vision awakened a new life, and a new world of thought and emotion within him. He had been, comparatively, a stranger to Jehovah. **I knew it not**—Jacob had gone to sleep without any thought that there, alone and sorrowful and anxious, he was specially cared for and watched by Abraham's God. No such open revelation had ever come to him before, and he was taken by surprise.
17. **House of God ... gate of heaven**—This thought thrills him with a sense of terror. So far from being away from house and friends and care, behold, he is in God's house, and the very gates of heaven have been opened to his eye.
18. **Took the stone ... a pillar**—He turns the *pillow* into a *pillar*. Well might he take that stone, and consecrate it as a memorial of the mercies

About B. C. 1760. CHAPTER XXVIII. 257

for a pillar, *e* and poured oil upon the top of it. **19** And he called the name of *f* that place *s* Beth-el: but the name of that city *was called* Luz at the first. **20** *g* And Jacob vowed a vow, saying, If *h* God will be with me, and will keep me in this way that I go, and will give me *i* bread to eat, and raiment to put on, **21** So that *k* I come again to my father's house in peace; *l* then shall the LORD be my God: **22** And this stone, which I have set *for* a pillar, *m* shall be God's house: *n* and of all that thou shalt give me I will surely give the tenth unto thee.

e Lev. 8. 10, 11, 12; Num. 7. 1.——*f* Judges 1. 23, 26; Hosea 4. 15.——5 That is, *The house of God.*——*g* Chap. 31. 13; Judges 11. 30; 2 Sam. 15. 8. *h* Verse 15.——*i* 1 Tim. 6. 8.——*k* Judges 11. 31; 2 Sam. 19. 24, 30.——*l* Deut. 26. 17; 2 Sam. 15. 8; 2 Kings 5. 17.——*m* Chap. 35. 7, 14.——*n* Lev. 27. 30.

of that night, and a witness of his vow. Comp. xxxi, 45. He also **poured oil upon the top of it,** as if to make it holy unto the Lord. Comp. Exod. xxx, 22–33. "It has been thought by many that this act of Jacob, in setting up a stone to mark a sacred spot, was the origin of cromlechs and all sacred stones. Certainly we find in later ages the custom of having stones, and those, too, anointed with oil, as objects of idolatrous worship. Clement of Alexandria (*Strom.* vii) speaks of 'worshipping every oily stone,' and Arnobius, (*Ad. Gentes,* i, 39,) in like manner, refers to the worshipping of 'a stone smeared with oil, as though there were in it a present power.' It has been conjectured, further, that the name *Bætulia,* given to stones called *animated stones* by the Phœnicians, (*Euseb. Praep. Evang.,* i, 10,) was derived from this name of Bethel. These *Bætulia,* however, were meteoric stones, and derived their sanctity from the belief that they had fallen from heaven; and the name has probably but a fancied likeness to the name Bethel. Still the connexion of the subsequent worship of stones with the primitive and pious use of them to mark places of worship is most probably a real connexion. The erection of all such stones for worship was strictly forbidden in later times. Lev. xxvi, 1; Deut. xvi, 22."— *Speaker's Commentary.*

19. Bethel... Luz—The spot where Abraham built his altar and Jacob had his dream was certainly not in a **city,** but, doubtless, on the mountain east of the city. See chap. xii, 8. The names Bethel and Luz both long survived, and were distinguished from each other in the time of Joshua. Josh. xvi, 2. The prominence of this place, in the subsequent history of Israel, led, probably, to the supplanting of the more ancient name by that of Bethel.

20. **Vowed a vow**—A becoming thing to do after such revelation and promise. **If God will be with me**—The *if* does not imply doubt in God's promise, but is the natural form of his taking God at his word: If God is going to do so much for me, then will I do something for him.

22. **This stone... God's house**—Jacob undoubtedly means that here he will establish some sanctuary of worship, and **the tenth,** which he vows unto God, is what he proposes to devote to maintaining such a place of worship. On the fulfilling of this vow, see chap. xxxv, 7. It is noticeable how in this case, as in that of Abraham, chap. xiv, 20, *the tithe of all* is specified as the proper portion of one's increase to be consecrated to God. It is mentioned, not as a new, strange thing, but in such an incidental way as to imply that even in Abraham's and Jacob's day the custom was one of long previous standing. Thus early, it would seem, God had in some way revealed to man his claim to the tenth part of his gains. Jacob himself here recognises that whatever prosperity he might have would be a *gift* of God, for which the tithe would be on his part only a fitting acknowledgment.

Jacob's dream and vow at Bethel have more than a mere historical importance. The dream was prophetic and far-reaching in its scope and bearings. We should note especially the four *beholds,* three of vision: "behold a ladder," "behold the angels," "behold Jehovah," (verses 12, 13,) and one of promise. Verse 15. These words denote the intensely realistic character of the whole revelation, appealing at once to heart and soul and mind and

GENESIS. About B. C. 1760.

CHAPTER XXIX.

THEN Jacob [1] went on his journey, and came into the land of the [2] people of the east. 2 And he looked, and behold a well in the field, and, lo, there *were* three flocks of sheep lying by it; for out of that well they watered the flocks: and a great stone *was* upon the well's mouth. 3 And thither were all the flocks gathered: and they rolled the stone from the well's mouth, and watered the sheep, and put the stone again upon the well's mouth in his place. 4 And Jacob said unto them, My brethren, whence *be* ye? And they said, Of Haran *are* we. 5 And he said unto them, Know ye Laban the son of Nahor? And they said, We know *him*. 6 And he said unto them, [b][3] *Is* he well? And they said, *He is* well: and, behold, Rachel his daughter cometh with the sheep. 7 And he said, Lo, [4] *it is* yet high day, neither *is it* time that the cattle should be gathered together: water ye the

---

[1] Heb. *lifted up his feet.* — *a* Num. 23. 7; Hosea 12. 12.—[2] Heb. *children.*

[b] Chap. 43. 27.—[3] Heb. Is there *peace to him?* —[4] Heb. *yet the day* is *great.*

---

strength. By symbol and by promise the great prophetic future of Jacob and his seed is opened to his soul.

We think of the lonely, helpless man at the bottom of the ladder, and Jehovah at the top, and the angels ascending and descending, and at once the vision becomes a complex symbol. It indicates: 1) That there is a passageway for spirits between earth and heaven; an invisible bridge between God and man; but a way supernaturally prepared and spiritually discerned. 2) The ministry of angels. Whatever revelation had previously been made of angelic natures, and there had been not a few, this vision deepened and confirmed them all. 3) The special and mighty providence of God, caring for his chosen by his own omnipresent gaze, and by innumerable ministering spirits. 4) The mystery of the Incarnation. The ladder was a symbol of the Son of Man, as Mediator of the New Covenant, upon whom (as on the sole ground and basis of all possibility of grace) the angels of God ascend and descend to minister to the heirs of salvation. John i, 52. In that mystery of grace Jehovah himself comes down, as from the top of the ladder, and reaching frail and helpless man below, lifts him upward to the heavens, and redeems him with the power of an endless life.

The vision and promise would serve to soften and change the heart of Jacob. It marked an epoch in his life, and we may now, with New Testament light, observe how grandly it foreshadowed that his seed should be the depositaries of Divine revelation. To them were committed the oracles of God, and through them have those oracles been communicated to the world.

CHAPTER XXIX.

JACOB'S ARRIVAL AT HARAN, 1–14.

1. **Went on his journey**—Heb., *lifted up his feet;* the necessary movement of one that walks on a journey. **People of the east**—Heb., *bene Kedem,* or, *sons of the east;* a name given to the tribes inhabiting an undefined territory east of Palestine, and, as appears from this, including the Syrian desert and Mesopotamia. Comp. Judges vi, 3; Job i, 3; 1 Kings iv, 30.

2. **Behold a well in the field**— Compare the similar account of Eliezer meeting Rebekah at a well. Chap. xxiv, 11–28. That well, however, was "without the city," but evidently quite near the city; this is more remote, **in the field.** There the women came out towards evening to draw water for drinking; here shepherds with their flocks were resting, waiting for the time to open the well. That well was not covered, and one could go down to it; this was covered by **a great stone,** and seems to have been a cistern, like those of which Robinson writes: "Over most of the cisterns is laid a broad and thick flat stone, with a round hole cut in the middle, forming the mouth of the cistern. This hole we found in many cases covered with a heavy stone, which it would require two or three men to roll away."—*Biblical Researches,* vol. i, p. 490.

7. **Yet high day**— Heb., *the day is yet great.* That is, a great portion of it yet remains. **Water ... go ... feed**—Kalisch remarks that Jacob,

About B. C. 1760.   CHAPTER XXIX.   259

sheep, and go *and* feed *them*. 8 And they said, We cannot, until all the flocks be gathered together, and *till* they roll the stone from the well's mouth; then we water the sheep.
9 And while he yet spake with them, ͨ Rachel came with her father's sheep: for she kept them. 10 And it came to pass, when Jacob saw Rachel the daughter of Laban his mother's brother, and the sheep of Laban his mother's brother, that Jacob went near, and ᵈ rolled the stone from the well's mouth, and watered the flock of Laban his mother's brother. 11 And Jacob ͤ kissed Rachel, and lifted up his voice, and wept. 12 And Jacob told Rachel that he *was* ᶠher father's brother, and that he *was* Rebekah's son: ᵍ and she ran and told her father. 13 And it came to pass, when Laban heard the ⁵ tidings of Jacob his sister's son, that ʰ he ran to meet him, and embraced him, and kissed him, and brought him to his house. And he told Laban all these things. 14 And Laban said to him, ⁱ Surely thou *art* my bone and my flesh. And he abode with him ⁶ the space of a month.
15 And Laban said unto Jacob, Because thou *art* my brother, shouldest thou therefore serve me for naught? tell me, what *shall* thy wages *be?* 16 And Laban had two daughters: the name of the elder *was* Leah, and the name of the younger *was* Rachel. 17 Leah *was* tender eyed; but Rachel was beautiful and well favoured. 18 And Jacob loved Rachel; and said, ᵏ I will serve thee seven years for Rachel thy younger daughter. 19 And Laban said, *It is*

ͨ Exod. 2. 16.——ᵈ Exod. 2. 17.——ͤ Chap. 33. 4; 45. 14, 15.——ᶠ Chap. 13. 8; 14. 14, 16.—— ᵍ Chap. 24. 28.——5 Heb. *hearing.*

ʰ Chap. 24. 29.——ⁱ Chap. 2. 23; Judges 9. 2; 2 Sam. 5. 1; 19. 12, 13.——6 Heb. *a month of days.* ——ᵏ Chap. 31. 41; 2 Sam. 3. 14.

"strengthened by the consciousness of his brilliant mission, addressed the unknown shepherds not only with cordiality, but with self-assurance and authority, and ventured even a gentle reproof of indolence."

8. **We cannot**—There was an understanding among them that the stone should not be removed **until all the flocks were gathered together.** Thus all the shepherds and all the flocks would share equally, and each party prevented from taking any advantage of the other.

9. **Rachel came**—Her coming roused in Jacob's soul all the tender emotions of home, kindred, loves, and hopes. **With her father's sheep**—Note the primitive custom of the daughters of an Eastern chieftain leading the sheep to water. Compare the account of Moses and the daughters of Jethro. Exod. ii, 15–22.

10. **Jacob saw ... went near ... rolled ... watered**—There is a romantic gallantry about Jacob's conduct here that is noticeable. The thrice repeated **Laban his mother's brother** deepens and intensifies the thought that he felt himself among his own; his mother had ever been his warmest friend and helper.

11. **Kissed ... and wept**—"Delight and sorrow mingled in his heart, and, overwhelmed by his feelings, he paid his tribute to nature by a spontaneous flood of tears."—*Kalisch.*

12. **Told her father**—Unlike Rebekah, who ran and told her mother. Chap. xxiv, 28.

13. **Told Laban all**—All about his journey and its object, the commands of Isaac and Rebekah, and the desire of his own heart.

JACOB'S DOUBLE MARRIAGE, 15–30.

15. **What shall thy wages be**—Jacob, the plain, domestic man, (xxv, 27,) doubtless made himself very useful in Laban's household. His service at the well was but a specimen of his agility and readiness to do whatever work might offer itself. Observing all this during the month of his sojourn, (verse 14,) Laban generously proposes that his kinsman shall not serve him for nothing.

17. **Leah was tender eyed**—Her eyes were *weak* (Sept. ἀσθενεῖς) and perhaps *inflamed,* (Vulg. *lippi,*) a great blemish, "since bright eyes, with fire in them, are regarded as the height of beauty in Oriental women."—*Keil.*

18. **I will serve thee seven years** —A week of years. Jacob had not, like his grandfather's servant, rich presents to offer as a dowry for his bride, (xxiv, 53,) but he offers what he can, the cheerful labour of willing and active hands.

better that I give her to thee, than that I should give her to another man: abide with me. **20** And Jacob ¹ served seven years for Rachel ; and they seemed unto him *but* a few days, for the love he had to her.

21 And Jacob said unto Laban, Give *me* my wife, for my days are fulfilled, that I may ᵐ go in unto her. **22** And Laban gathered together all the men of the place, and ⁿ made a feast. **23** And it came to pass in the evening, that he took Leah his daughter, and brought her to him ; and he went in unto her. **24** And Laban gave unto his daughter Leah Zilpah his maid *for* a handmaid. **25** And it came to pass, that in the morning, behold, it *was* Leah: and he said to Laban, What *is* this thou hast done unto me? did not I serve with thee for Rachel? wherefore then hast thou beguiled me? **26** And Laban said, it must not be so done in our ⁷ country, to give the younger before the firstborn. **27** ° Fulfil her week, and we will give thee this also for the service which thou shalt serve with me yet seven other years. **28** And Jacob did so, and fulfilled her week : and

---

l Chapter 30. 26; Hosea 12. 12. —— *m* Judges 15. 1.

n Judges 14, 10; John 2. 1, 2.——7 Heb. *place.* ——*o* Judges 14. 12.

---

19. **Better ... to thee, than ... to another**—Laban gladly accepts Jacob's offer. It was worth more to him than gold. This custom of preferring marriage with one's own kindred, and also the practice of receiving dowry for a daughter, illustrate the manners of the ancient East, which prevail largely even at the present day. While the daughter is not sold as a slave, the practice shows the comparatively low position of women in the East, and how little a wife had to say in the choice of a husband. But the dowry may be looked upon as a reward paid to parents for the care of a daughter's training and bringing up to womanhood, and also a suitable expression of gratitude on the part of the husband towards the parents of his wife.

20. **They seemed unto him but a few days**—"Words breathing the purest tenderness, and expressing more emphatically than the flowery hyperboles of romantic phraseology the deep attachment of an affectionate heart. Love capable of shortening seven laborious years into a term of insignificant brevity, is a flame animating and purifying the soul ; a sacred longing, forming its own delight and happiness."—*Kalisch.*

22. **Made a feast**—The marriage festival, in such a home as Laban's, would doubtless be worthy of all parties. It was continued seven days. Comp. verses 27, 28 ; Judges xiv, 12, 17.

23. **Took Leah**—There was no formal public ceremony of marriage ; the parties were not openly presented to one another, but **in the evening** the bride, closely veiled, was led to the husband's tent. Hence the ease with which it was possible to present Leah to Jacob instead of Rachel.

24. **Zilpah ... for a handmaid**—Rebekah had a nurse and several damsels. Chap. xxiv, 59, 61. Sarah had her handmaid, Hagar. Such maidservants became the special property of the wife to do with as she pleased. See chap. xvi, 1–6.

25. **Thou beguiled me**—Jacob now feels the weight and bitterness of deception. But it is a retribution for his own supplanting and defrauding of Esau.

26. **So done in our country**—Rather, *in our place.* The Hindu laws, as quoted by Clarke, made it a high offence "for a man to marry while his elder brother remains unmarried, or for a man to give his daughter to such a person, or to give his youngest daughter in marriage while the elder sister remains unmarried." But if such were the law at Haran, Jacob was ignorant of it until now, and Laban deceived him in not explaining it to him when he bargained for Rachel. Verse 18.

27. **Her week**—The seven days of the marriage feast. Laban proposes, as a recompense, after the week has ended, to give him Rachel also, but on condition that he serve for her **yet seven other years.** Two wives in eight days, but fourteen years of service for them both. "This bigamy of Jacob must not be judged directly by the Mosaic law, which prohibits marriage with two sisters at the same time, (Lev. xviii, 18,) or be set down as incest,

B. C. 1752-1749. CHAPTER XXIX. 261

he gave him Rachel his daughter to wife also. **29** And Laban gave to Rachel his daughter Bilhah his handmaid to be her maid. **30** And he went in also unto Rachel, and he ᵖ loved also Rachel more than Leah, and served with him ᑫ yet seven other years.

31 And when the LORD ʳ saw that Leah *was* hated, he ˢ opened her womb: but Rachel *was* barren. **32** And Leah conceived, and bare a son; and she called his name ⁸ Reuben: for she said, Surely the LORD hath ᵗ looked upon my affliction; now therefore my husband will love me. **33** And she conceived again, and bare a son; and said, Because the LORD hath heard that I *was* hated, he hath therefore given me this *son* also:

and she called his name ⁹ Simeon. **34** And she conceived again, and bare a son; and said, Now this time will my husband be joined unto me, because I have borne him three sons: therefore was his name called ¹⁰ Levi. **35** And she conceived again, and bare a son; and she said, Now will I praise the LORD: therefore she called his name ᵘ ¹¹ Judah; and ¹² left bearing.

CHAPTER XXX.

AND when Rachel saw that ᵃ she bare Jacob no children, Rachel ᵇ envied her sister; and said unto Jacob, Give me children, ᶜ or else I die. **2** And Jacob's anger was kindled against Rachel; and he said, ᵈ *Am* I in God's stead,

---
p Verse 20; Deut. 21. 15.——*q* Chap. 30. 26; 31. 41; Hos. 12. 12.——*r* Psa. 127. 3.——*s* Chap. 30. 1. ——8 That is, *See a son.*——*t* Exod. 3. 7; 4. 31; Deut. 26. 7; Psa. 25. 18; 106. 44.——9 That is, *Hearing.*

10 That is, *Joined.* See Num. 18. 2, 4.—— *u* Matt. 1. 2.——11 That is, *Praise.*——12 Heb. *stood from bearing.*——*a* Chap. 29. 31.—— *b* Chap. 37. 11.——*c* Job 5. 2.——*d* Chap. 16. 2; 1 Sam. 1. 5.

(Calvin,) since there was no positive law on the point in existence then. At the same time it is not to be justified on the ground that the blessing of God made it the means of the fulfilment of his promise, namely, the multiplication of the seed of Abraham into a great nation. Just as it had arisen from Laban's deception and Jacob's love, which regarded outward beauty alone, and, therefore, from sinful infirmities, so did it become in its results a true school of affliction to Jacob, in which God showed to him by many a humiliation, that such conduct as his was quite unfitted to accomplish the divine counsels, and thus condemned the ungodliness of such a marriage, and prepared the way for the subsequent prohibition in the law."—*Keil.*

LEAH'S FIRST FOUR SONS, 31–35.

31. Rachel was barren — This would appear like a chastisement of Jacob's partiality, (verse 30,) and an intimation that the blessing of posterity was "not of him that willeth, but of God that showeth mercy."

32. Reuben—Which means, *see ye a son*. **Looked upon**—Rather, *Jehovah looked in my affliction;* that is, in my sorrow arising from love withheld, Jehovah looked; therefore will I name my first born *Look ye—a son!* Fondly she hopes now for more of her husband's love.

33. Simeon—Which means *a hearing.* Jehovah first *looked;* then he *heard.* Still she feels bitterly the lack of a husband's love. Her use of the word **hated** in this verse illustrates the peculiar meaning of that term. Comp. verse 30.

34. Levi—Which means *a joining.* Fondly now does she hope for a deeper and truer heart union with her husband.

35. Judah—Which means, *one to be praised.* Compare chap. xlix, 8. Thus, in naming these first four sons, Leah breathes the spirit of a pure and noble longing, which fitted her to be the mother of the chosen tribe from which the Christ should spring.

CHAPTER XXX.

SONS OF BILHAH AND ZILPAH, 1–13.

1. Give me children—Here breaks forth the passionate cry of the child of nature. Envy and jealousy, even to bitterness, speak out in this appeal, not the hopeful yearning of the child of faith.

2. Jacob's anger—Here is something that stings to the quick the soul of him who has hitherto showed such general gravity and calmness. Such rebuke from the lips of his beloved Rachel arouses him to a sudden outburst of anger, in which he administers to her a sharp rebuke.

who hath withheld from thee the fruit of the womb? **3** And she said, Behold ᵉ my maid Bilhah, go in unto her; and she shall bear upon my knees, ᶠ that I may also ¹ have children by her. **4** And she gave him Bilhah her handmaid ʰ to wife: and Jacob went in unto her. **5** And Bilhah conceived, and bare Jacob a son. **6** And Rachel said, God hath ¹ judged me, and hath also heard my voice, and hath given me a son: therefore called she his name ² Dan. **7** And Bilhah Rachel's maid conceived again, and bare Jacob a second son. **8** And Rachel said, With ³ great wrestlings have I wrestled with my sister, and I have prevailed: and she called his name ⁴ ᵏ Naphtali. **9** When Leah saw that she had left bearing, she took Zilpah her maid, and ¹ gave her Jacob to wife.

10 And Zilpah Leah's maid bare Jacob a son. **11** And Leah said, A troop cometh: and she called his name ⁵ Gad. **12** And Zilpah Leah's maid bare Jacob a second son. **13** And Leah said, ⁶ Happy am I, for the daughters ᵐ will call me blessed: and she called his name ⁷ Asher.

14 And Reuben went in the days of wheat harvest, and found mandrakes in the field, and brought them unto his mother Leah. Then Rachel said to Leah, ⁿ Give me, I pray thee, of thy son's mandrakes. **15** And she said unto her, ᵒ *Is it* a small matter that thou hast taken my husband? and wouldest thou take away my son's mandrakes also? And Rachel said, Therefore he shall lie with thee to-night for thy son's mandrakes. **16** And Jacob came out of the field in

---

e Chap. 16. 2.——*f* Chap. 50. 23; Job 3. 12.——*g* Chap. 16. 2. —— 1 Heb. *be built by her.* —— *h* Chap. 16. 3; 35. 22.——*i* Psa. 35. 24; 43. 1; Lam. 3. 59. —— 2 That is, *Judging.* —— 3 Heb. *wrestlings of God*, chap. 23. 6. —— 4 That is, *My wrestling.* —— *k* Called, Matt. 4. 13, *Nephthalim.*——*l* Ver. 4.——5 That is, *A troop*, or, *company*, Isa. 65. 11.——6 Heb. *In my happiness.* ——*m* Prov. 31. 28; Luke 1. 48.——7 That is, *Happy.*——*n* Chap. 25. 30.——*o* Num. 16. 9, 13.

---

3. Children by her—In her impatience she resorts to the expedient of Sarai. Chap. xvi, 2, note.

6. Dan—Which means *a judge*, for, as she puts it, God had judged her cause, and vindicated her in this procedure. Observe that Rachel here speaks of **God**, *Elohim*, whereas Leah acknowledged *Jehovah*. Chap. xxx, 32, 33, 35. In verse 20, however, Leah uses the name Elohim, and in verse 24, Rachel acknowledges Jehovah.

8. Naphtali—Which means, *my wrestling*, in allusion to the struggle of rivalry between herself and Leah. Her words are, literally: *wrestlings of God have I wrestled with my sister; also I have prevailed.* The words, perhaps, have some allusion to Jacob's reproof, verse 2, "Am I in God's stead?" She assumes to have struggled as with God for this victory, and glories in a seeming victory over her sister. But what a vain boasting!

9. Leah . . . took Zilpah—The passion and rivalry of Rachel provoke Leah to adopt the same expedient, and thus silence any boasting in that line.

11. A troop cometh— Heb., בְּגָד, *in luck; with good fortune.* So Sept. and Vulgate, Syriac and Chaldee. So **she called his name Gad**, as a memorial of her good fortune. The Masorites explain בְּגָד, as an abbreviation for בָּא גָד, and so write it in the margin, and chap. xlix, 19, is thought by some to favour this; but the simpler sense is that of the Septuagint and other versions, as given above.

13. Asher—Which means, *blessed, happy.* The words **happy, blessed**, and **Asher** in this verse are all from the same Hebrew root.

OTHER CHILDREN OF LEAH, 14–21.

14. Reuben went—He was now a boy of four or five years. **Mandrakes** הַדּוּדָאִים, *dudhaim, love-apples*, a fruit, as appears from this context, believed to have the power of promoting conception. Hence the anxiety of Rachel to obtain them. The fruit here named is believed to be the *Mandragora officinalis*, described by Tristram as "one of the most striking plants of the country, with its flat disk of very broad primrose-like leaves, and its central bunch of dark blue bell-shaped blossom. The perfume of the flower we found by no means disagreeable, though it is said by some to be fetid. It has a certain pungency which is peculiar. We found it not uncommon in every part of Palestine, but chiefly in marshy plains." —*Land of Israel*, 8vo edit., p. 103.

About B. C. 1747.　　CHAPTER XXX.　　263

the evening, and Leah went out to meet him, and said, Thou must come in unto me; for surely I have hired thee with my son's mandrakes. And he lay with her that night. **17** And God hearkened unto Leah, and she conceived, and bare Jacob the fifth son. **18** And Leah said, God hath given me my hire, because I have given my maiden to my husband, and she called his name ⁸ Issachar. **19** And Leah conceived again, and bare Jacob the sixth son. **20** And Leah said, God hath endued me *with* a good dowry; now will my husband dwell with me, because I have borne him six sons : and she called his name ᵖ ᵖ Zebulun. **21** And afterwards she bare a daughter, and called her name ¹⁰ Dinah. **22** And God ᑫ remembered Rachel, and God hearkened to her, and ʳ opened her womb. **23** And she conceived, and bare a son ; and said, God hath taken away ˢ my reproach : **24** And she called his name ¹¹ Joseph; and said, ᵗ The LORD shall add to me another son. **25** And it came to pass, when Rachel

---

8 That is, *A hire.*——9 That is, *Dwelling.*—— ᵖ Called, Matt. 4. 13, *Zabulon.* —— 10 That is, *Judgment.*

ᑫ Chap. 8. 1 ; 1 Sam. 1. 19.——ʳ Chap. 29. 31.—— ˢ 1 Sam. 1. 6 : Isa. 4. 1 ; Luke 1. 25.——11 That is, *Adding.*——ᵗ Chap. 35. 17.

18. God hath given me my hire—Leah, of higher spiritual nature than Rachel, relies on God more than on any love potions, and she has her reward, and she gives her new-born son a name, **Issachar,** which means, *there is a reward.*

20. Zebulun—Which means, *dwelling* or *habitation ;* for now she fondly hopes that her husband will **dwell** with her ; cleave to her in his home-life with a warmer attachment.

21. Dinah—Which means, *judgment;* kindred to the name Dan. Verse 6. Some suppose, from the language of chap. xxxvii, 35, xlvi, 7, that Jacob had other daughters. This is possible, and yet the word may, in those passages, refer to daughters-in-law. So full a narrative of Jacob's family would not have been likely to omit mention of any child of his.

BIRTH OF JOSEPH, 22–24.

22. God remembered Rachel—It would seem from the language of these verses that Rachel's wrestling with God (comp. verse 8) had acquired a nobler tone ; a more devout and humble trust. **God hearkened to her**—This implies a prevailing prayer on her part, which had probably softened and subdued her spirit, and begotten in her a forgiving disposition towards her rival—a quality that impressed itself upon her son.

23. My reproach—She has now no words of envy or triumph towards her sister, but a humble acknowledgment of her previous pitiable condition among women.

24. Joseph—Which means *adding,* for she herewith expresses her faith that Jehovah will **add** to her **another son.** There seems also to be a play upon the word אָסַף, *hath taken away,* used in the preceding verse. Thus the name takes on a twofold significance. *Elohim* has taken away her reproach, and *Jehovah* will add another son. While this faith showed a nobler spirit than she had manifested before, it also showed an impatience and ambition, which issued in sorrow and death, when the other son was added. See chap. xxxv, 18.

The dates of the birth of the above-named children of Jacob are not given, though verse 25 shows that on the birth of Joseph, Jacob had served out his fourteen years. Here, then, eleven children appear to have been born unto him in seven years, and yet during that period Leah for a time left bearing, (xxix, 35.) All this, however, may be readily understood as follows. Dinah was born "afterwards," (verse 21 ;) so she may be set aside from the seven years ; and nothing necessarily hinders our supposing Zebulun, Leah's sixth son, to have been born after Joseph. Leah probably bore the four sons named in chap. xxix, 32–35, in rapid succession within the first four years after marriage. Then she left off bearing for two years, which would be noticeable after having borne four sons so quickly. Meanwhile, and probably before the birth of Judah, Leah's fourth son, Rachel sought children by Bilhah, and during the fourth and fifth

had borne Joseph, that Jacob said unto Laban, ᵘ Send me away, that I may go unto ᵛ mine own place, and to my country. **26** Give *me* my wives and my children, ʷ for whom I have served thee, and let me go: for thou knowest my service which I have done thee. **27** And Laban said unto him, I pray thee, if I have found favour in thine eyes, *tarry: for* ˣ I have learned by experience that the LORD hath blessed me ʸ for thy sake. **28** And he said, ᶻAppoint me thy wages, and I will give *it*. **29** And he said unto him, ᵃ Thou knowest how I have served thee, and how thy cattle was with me. **30** For *it was* little which thou hadst before I *came*, and it is *now* ¹²increased unto a multitude; and the LORD hath blessed thee ¹³since my coming: and now, when shall I ᵇ provide for mine own house also? **31** And he said, What shall I give thee? And Jacob said, Thou shalt not give me any thing: if thou wilt do this thing for me, I will again feed *and* keep thy flock. **32** I will pass through all thy flock to-day, removing from thence all the speckled and spotted cattle, and all the brown cattle among the sheep, and the spotted and speckled among the goats: and ᶜ *of such* shall be my hire. **33** So shall my ᵈ righteousness answer for me ¹⁴in time to come, when it shall come for my hire before thy face: every one that *is* not speckled and spotted among the goats, and brown among the sheep, that shall be counted stolen with me. **34** And Laban said, Behold, I would it might be according to thy word. **35** And he removed that day the he goats that were ringstreaked

---

u Chap. 24. 54, 56. —— *v* Chap. 18. 33; 31. 55. —— *w* Chap.29. 20, 30. —— *x* Chap. 39. 3. 5. —— *y* See chap. 26. 24. —— *z* Chap. 29. 15. —— *a* Chap. 31. 6, 38, 39, 40; Matt. 24. 45; Titus 2. 10.

12 Heb. *broken forth*, verse 43. —— 13 Heb. *at my foot*. —— *b* 1 Tim. 5. 8. —— *c* Chap. 31. 8. —— *d* Psa. 37. 6. —— 14 Heb. *to morrow*, Exod. 13. 14.

---

years the children of both the handmaids were born. At the beginning of the seventh year Leah may have borne Issachar, and Zebulun at its close, or very soon after. So there is nothing improbable in the narrative of the eleven children being born in seven years.

LABAN'S NEW BARGAIN WITH JACOB, 25–36.

25. **Send me away**—Jacob doubtless felt that Laban had been ungenerous and exacting, and, besides deceiving him in the case of Leah, had sought to make the most of all his other advantages to make out of him all he could. **Mine own place . . . my country**—Jacob remembered the promises at Beth-el. Chap. xxviii, 13–15.

26. **Thou knowest my service**—Jacob is not afraid to reckon on the value of his labours, and Laban had, doubtless, profited greatly by them—as he at once acknowledged. Verse 27.

27. **I have learned by experience**—נִחַשְׁתִּי, *I have divined;* or, *I have learned by divination.* The words indicate that Laban had become, to some extent at least, involved in heathen and idolatrous practices. Compare chap. xxxi, 19; xxx, 32. Some, however, take the word in the wider signification of diligent inquiry and examination, a meaning not sustained by general usage. Laban rather claims to have discovered, by some sort of augury, that Jacob's God, Jehovah, had favoured him for Jacob's sake.

30. **Since my coming**—Heb., *at my feet;* as if the blessings of Jehovah had broken forth and followed Jacob's footsteps wherever he went.

32. **Brown cattle among the sheep . . . spotted and speckled among the goats**—The Syrian sheep are said to be usually all white, and the goats black or brown. This seems to have been the case with Laban's flocks, so that Jacob's proposition would leave Laban with by far the larger proportion of the flocks and their probable increase.

33. **My righteousness**—My uprightness in the whole business. **In time to come**—Heb., *in the day of to-morrow;* meaning, any and every to-morrow. From that day forward there would be no dispute over rights in the cattle, for the colour would decide. **When it shall come**—Rather, *when thou shalt come* (תָּבוֹא,) *upon my wages before thee;* that is, when thou comest to inspect my wages or share in the flock. **Stolen with me**—That is, Laban will be welcome to look upon all the white sheep and black or brown goats which he finds with Jacob as stolen, and claim them for himself.

About B. C. 1745. CHAPTER XXX. 265

and spotted, and all the she goats that were speckled and spotted, *and* every one that had *some* white in it, and all the brown among the sheep, and gave *them* into the hand of his sons. **36** And he set three days' journey betwixt himself and Jacob: and Jacob fed the rest of Laban's flocks.
37 And ᵉ Jacob took him rods of green poplar, and of the hazel and chestnut tree; and pilled white streaks in them, and made the white appear which *was* in the rods. **38** And he set the rods which he had pilled before the flocks in the gutters in the watering troughs when the flocks came to drink, that they should conceive when they came to drink. **39** And the flocks conceived before the rods, and brought forth cattle ringstreaked, speckled, and spotted.

---

e See chap. 31. 9-12.

35. **Gave them into the hand of his sons**—Here note the overreaching and imperious disposition of Laban. He does not leave Jacob to divide the flocks, but does it himself, and then removes Jacob's part three days distant. Jacob was bound to look after Laban's flock, (verse 31,) and the latter takes every advantage of that fact.

JACOB'S ARTIFICE, 37-43.

37. **Took him rods**—At sight of such imperious attempt at overreaching him, Jacob is not slow to devise means to counteract the wrong. The artifice he adopted was in well-known accord with the fact that any impressive colours fixed in the attention of a female at the time of conception are almost sure to mark the offspring. **Poplar** . . . **hazel . . . chestnut**—Some render *storax, almond,* and *plane-tree;* others render *maple* instead of hazel, and *walnut* instead of chestnut. The wood was doubtless such as had a white wood under a dark bark.

40. **Separate the lambs**—That is, the lambs produced after the separation mentioned in verse 35. These **ringstreaked** lambs were, as a second artifice, made like the rods to serve his purpose. **Put his own flocks by themselves**—As he had a right to do. **Laban's cattle** here denote those of uniform color in the flocks tended by Jacob.

40 And Jacob did separate the lambs, and set the faces of the flocks toward the ringstreaked, and all the brown in the flock of Laban; and he put his own flocks by themselves, and put them not unto Laban's cattle. **41** And it came to pass, whensoever the stronger cattle did conceive, that Jacob laid the rods before the eyes of the cattle in the gutters, that they might conceive among the rods. **42** But when the cattle were feeble, he put *them* not in: so the feebler were Laban's, and the stronger Jacob's. **43** And the man ᶠ increased exceedingly, and ᵍ had much cattle, and maidservants, and menservants, and camels, and asses.

CHAPTER XXXI.

AND he heard the words of Laban's sons, saying, Jacob hath taken

---

f Verse 30.——*g* Chap. 13. 2; 24. 35; 26. 13, 14.

42. **The feebler were Laban's**—This was a third trick. The Eastern sheep lamb twice a year, in spring and fall, and those born in the fall, according to Pliny, were the stronger. It is probable that after a time Laban suspected or discovered Jacob's artifice, and accordingly changed his wages, or the terms of the contract, many times. See chap. xxxi, 7, 8. But Jacob was smart enough to frustrate all his attempts to overreach him.

CHAPTER XXXI.

JACOB'S FLIGHT FROM PADAN-ARAM, 1-21.

Twenty years have now passed since Jacob came to Laban's house. Verse 38. The single one has become a multitude. Twelve children have been born unto him, and every thing has prospered in his hand. But it now becomes evident that the time for separation has arrived. Two families, of such diverse interests and hopes as those of Jacob and Laban, cannot abide long together, and Jacob is called to separate himself as Abraham had been two hundred years before.

1. **Heard the words of Laban's sons**—Either overheard with his own ears, or had them reported to him. Perhaps angry words at times passed between them in the fields or by the way. Such success and prosperity as attended all Jacob's movements would

away all that *was* our father's; and of *that* which *was* our father's hath he gotten all this ᵃ glory. **2** And Jacob beheld ᵇ the countenance of Laban, and, behold, it *was* not ᶜ toward him ¹ as before. **3** And the LORD said unto Jacob, ᵈ Return unto the land of thy fathers, and to thy kindred; and I will be with thee. **4** And Jacob sent and called Rachel and Leah to the field unto his flock, **5** And said unto them, ᵉ I see your father's countenance, that it *is* not toward me as before; but the God of my father ᶠ hath been with me. **6** And ᵍ ye know that with all my power I have served your father. **7** And your father hath deceived me, and ʰ changed my wages ⁱ ten times; but God ᵏ suffered him not to hurt me. **8** If he said thus, ˡ The speckled shall be thy wages; then all the cattle bare speckled: and if he said thus, The ringstreaked shall be thy hire; then bare all the cattle ringstreaked. **9** Thus God hath ᵐ taken away the cattle of your father, and given *them* to me. **10** And it came to pass at the time that the cattle conceived, that I lifted up mine eyes, and saw in a dream, and, behold, the ² rams which leaped upon the cattle *were* ringstreaked, speckled, and grizzled. **11** And ⁿ the angel of God spake unto me in a dream, *saying*, Jacob: and I said, Here *am* I. **12** And he said, Lift up now thine eyes, and see, all the rams which leap upon the cattle *are* ringstreaked, speckled, and grizzled: for ᵒ I have seen all that Laban doeth unto thee. **13** I *am* the God of Beth-el, ᵖ where

---

a Psa. 49. 16.——*b* Chap. 4. 5.——*c* Deut. 28. 54.——1 Heb. *as yesterday and the day before*, 1 Sam. 19. 7.—— *d* Chap. 28. 15, 20, 21; 32. 9.—— *e* Verse 2.——*f* Verse 3.——*g* Chap. 30. 29; verses 38, 39, 40, 41.

h Verse 41.——*i* Num. 14. 22; Neh. 4. 12: Job 19. 3; Zech. 8. 23.——*k* Chap. 20. 6; Psa. 105. 14.——*l* Chap. 30. 32.——*m* Verses 1, 16.——2 Or, *he goats*.——*n* Chap. 48. 16. —— *o* Exod. 3. 7.—— *p* Chap. 28. 18, 19, 20.

---

naturally provoke the jealousy of Laban's sons.

2. Not toward him as before—During the fourteen years of his service, when Laban had all the advantage, and every thing his own way, he doubtless treated Jacob with great regard, so that the latter would be quick to note coldness and opposition. His changing his wages (verse 7) gave him opportunity to show his growing dislike. The Hebrew for **as before** is idiomatic; literally, *yesterday three days;* that is, yesterday and the third day, or yesterday and before. Somewhat like our "yesterday week."

3. Return—This word of Jehovah was as truly a divine call as that which led Abraham from Ur of the Chaldees. It came to him in the field and evidently made a deep impression on Jacob, so that he at once sent for his two wives, and told them all.

7. Ten times — Probably a round number used for an indefinite number, and equivalent to *very frequently*, or, as often as possible. Compare Num. xiv, 22; Job xix, 3. The manner of Laban's changing Jacob's wages was doubtless that indicated in the next verse. "He made repeated attempts to limit the original stipulation by changing the rule as to the colours of the young, and so diminishing Jacob's wages."—*Keil.*

10. Saw in a dream—In chap. xxx, 37–43, we have the human side of Jacob's procedure. We there see his artifice and cunning. Here is another view, not at all in conflict with that, but designed to show that all Jacob's tricks were as nothing without supernatural interference. God interposed to favour Jacob, not because of his guile or cunning, still less to sanction any thing of the kind as an example for others. Probably such dreams had come repeatedly during the last four or five years, and at the end of the sixth year of his independent service he received the revelation of verses 11–13.

11. The angel of God spake—He refers probably to the same revelation as that of verse 3. This word came to him **in a dream**, in which was repeated the vision of many a previous dream. Verse 10.

12. All that Laban doeth—Or, rather, all that he *is doing*. God's interposition had been to punish Laban for his unnatural and narrow policy towards his own children, not to show favour to Jacob's deception. In their natural lives and works both Laban and Jacob were bad enough, but in this case Laban was the aggressor in taking undue advantage, and Jacob's action was a policy of self-defence.

13. I am the God of Beth-el—See chap. xxviii, 12–22. The revelations

B. C. 1739.   CHAPTER XXXI.   267

thou anointedst the pillar, *and* where thou vowedst a vow unto me: now q arise, get thee out from this land, and return unto the land of thy kindred. 14 And Rachel and Leah answered and said unto him, r *Is there* yet any portion or inheritance for us in our father's house? 15 Are we not counted of him strangers? for ˢ he hath sold us, and hath quite devoured also our money. 16 For all the riches which God hath taken from our father, that *is* ours, and our children's: now then, whatsoever God hath said unto thee, do. 17 Then Jacob rose up, and set his sons and his wives upon camels; 18 And he carried away all his cattle, and all his goods which he had gotten, the cattle of his getting, which he had gotten in Padan-aram, for to go to Isaac his father in the land of Canaan. 19 And Laban went to shear his sheep: and Rachel had stolen the ³ᵗ images that *were* her

---

q Verse 3; chap. 32. 9. —— *r* Chap. 2. 24. —— *s* Chap. 29. 15, 27.

3 Heb. *teraphim*, Judges 17. 5; 1 Sam. 19. 13; Hosea 3. 4. —— *t* Chap. 35. 2.

---

and promises of Jacob's dream at Beth-el were incompatible with his remaining permanently in Haran, and it was now time for him to get himself away. Keil argues that this dream was largely the work of Jacob's excited imagination, "the materials being supplied by the three thoughts that were most frequently in his mind, by night as well as by day, namely: 1) His own schemes and their success; 2) The promise received at Beth-el; 3) The wish to justify his actions to his own conscience." No doubt absorbing thoughts and schemes, united with strong desires to succeed, may furnish the proper physical conditions for dreams like this of Jacob; but it seems entirely superfluous to insinuate such a suspicion of the objective reality of the angel's words to Jacob. If we allow such an exposition here, we introduce a principle of hermeneutics that would as easily make against the reality of other recorded revelations. Jacob had natural reason to withhold from his wives his own artifices, but we can scarcely believe that he tells a falsehood in respect to this dream. As in all the wrong actions of his life God overruled and wrought good out of evil, so in this.

15. **Counted of him strangers**—Rachel and Leah both readily sympathize with their husband as against their father, and look upon Laban's dealings as narrow, unfatherly, and unworthy of him. The last twenty years had largely alienated them from their father's house.

17. **Upon camels**—Heb., *upon the camels,* that is, the camels provided for the purpose. No mention of camels as a part of Laban's or Jacob's possessions has as yet been made. But there has been no occasion; and even if there were no camels among Laban's property, Jacob might readily have purchased these at the time for his purpose. Chap. xxxii, 5, 15, shows that Jacob's possessions of cattle included many camels, oxen, kine, bulls, and asses, of which we have no other mention. But his secret departure showed how he yet leaned more to his own devices than upon the providence of God.

19. **Laban went to shear his sheep**—This afforded an opportunity for Jacob to effect his escape without trouble or excitement, for he feared forcible opposition from Laban. Verse 31. **Had stolen**—Or, *stole.* While Laban went to the shearing, she steals. **The images** — The *teraphim.* This word is always used in the plural, and is of uncertain origin. It appears to denote a sort of household gods, (*Penates,*) common in Syria, and often consulted as domestic oracles. By these probably Laban was wont to divine, (chapter xxx, 27, note,) and Rachel's object in taking them was both to prevent their being used by her father to her disadvantage, and also for her own domestic interests. Comp. Judges xvii, 5; Ezek. xxi, 21; Zech. x, 2; and note on Josh. xxiv, 14. The teraphim were small images of human form, though sometimes of life size. 1 Sam. xix, 13. They were essentially connected with idolatrous ideas and practices, and seem to have served as a transition from Monotheism unto Polytheism. In some such transition state Laban appears to have been, and from it Rachel was not free. Other members of Jacob's household also clung to similar superstitions and carried off

GENESIS. B.C. 1739.

father's. **20** And Jacob stole away [4] unawares to Laban the Syrian, in that he told him not that he fled. **21** So he fled with all that he had; and he rose up, and passed over the river, and [u] set his face *toward* the mount Gilead. **22** And it was told Laban on the third day, that Jacob was fled. **23** And he took [v] his brethren with him, and pursued after him seven days' journey; and they overtook him in the mount Gilead. **24** And God [w] came to Laban the Syrian in a dream by night, and said unto him, Take heed that thou [x] speak not to Jacob [o] either good or bad. **25** Then Laban overtook Jacob. Now Jacob had pitched his tent in the mount: and Laban with his brethren pitched in the mount of Gilead. **26** And Laban said to Jacob, What hast thou done, that

---

4 Heb. *the heart of Laban.*——*u* Chap. 46. 28; 2 Kings 12. 17; Luke 9. 51, 53.——*v* Chap. 13. 8.

w Chap. 20. 3; Job 33: 15; Matt. 1. 20. —— *x* Chap. 24. 50.——5 Heb. *from good to bad.*

---

strange gods with them. Comp. chap. xxxv, 2-4.

20. **Stole away unawares to Laban**—Heb., *stole the heart of Laban.* There is a play on the words heart and Laban—stole the *Leb-Laban.* Rachel stole the teraphim, Jacob the heart, of Laban. He used deception in keeping Laban from any suspicion of his plans for flight.

21. **The river** — Euphrates, near which he probably abode at that time. **Mount Gilead**—So called by anticipation here. Comp. verses 47, 48.

LABAN'S PURSUIT, AND COVENANT WITH JACOB, 22-55.

22. **It was told Laban**—Such a movement as Jacob's, whose family and herds made a large caravan, could not long be kept a secret.

23. **Took his brethren** — Various relatives who were with him at the feast of sheep shearing. Compare the use of this word in chapter xiii, 8. **Seven days' journey**—From what date and from what place this seven days' journey is to be reckoned, is not clear. The tidings of Jacob's flight reached Laban on the third day after its occurrence, (verse 22,) and it would probably take Laban three days more to get ready for the pursuit and to reach the point from which Jacob started; for there were three days' journeying between them. Chap. xxx, 36. Reckoning the seven days from that point, we give Jacob twelve or thirteen days the start of Laban, in which time he might have travelled three hundred and fifty miles. Both parties, doubtless, made the greatest possible haste; but Laban, unencumbered with flocks and family, would move twice or thrice as rapidly as Jacob, and so, in seven days from the time of his hearing of Jacob's flight, he might have overtaken him. The Arab post is said to go from Damascus to Bagdad in eight days—a distance of about five hundred miles. The distance between the Euphrates and Gilead is about three hundred miles.

24. **God came to Laban**—Mark the constant divine care that guards the ways of Jacob, and redeems him from all evil. Chap. xlviii, 16. **Either good or bad**—Heb., *from good unto bad.* That is, do not *from good* friendly greetings pass *to bad* words of violence. Do not make matters worse.

25. **Laban overtook Jacob**—At this it was evident that a serious controversy must be held, and accordingly both Jacob and Laban pitched their tents, and made ready for a great council.

26. **Laban said**—Laban opens the controversy, and his speech, both here (verses 26-30) and afterwards, (verses 43, 44, and 48-53,) and Jacob's also, (in verses 36-42,) read like the fragments of an ancient poem. They have the rhythm and passion of poetry, and should be put in the poetic form. We render Laban's speech thus:

What hast thou done?
And thou hast stolen my heart,
And hast carried off my daughters
As captives of the sword.
Why didst thou hide thyself to flee?
And thou hast stolen me,
And didst not inform me,
And I would have sent thee away with joy,
And with songs, with timbrel, and with harp.
And thou didst not permit me
To kiss my sons and my daughters;
Now hast thou played the fool—to do!
It is to the God of my hand
To do with you an evil.

B. C. 1739.   CHAPTER XXXI.   269

thou hast stolen away unawares to me, and *y* carried away my daughters, as captives *taken* with the sword? 27 Wherefore didst thou flee away secretly, and *a* steal away from me; and didst not tell me, that I might have sent thee away with mirth, and with songs, with tabret, and with harp? 28 And hast not suffered me *z* to kiss my sons and my daughters? *a* thou hast now done foolishly in *so* doing. 29 It is in the power of my hand to do you hurt: but the *b* God of your father spake unto me *c* yesternight, saying, Take thou heed that thou speak not to Jacob either good or bad. 30 And now, *though* thou wouldest needs be gone, because thou sore longedst after thy father's house, *yet* wherefore hast thou *d* stolen my gods? 31 And Jacob answered and said to Laban, Because I was afraid: for I said, Peradventure thou wouldest take by force thy daughters from me. 32 With whomsoever thou findest thy gods, *e* let him not live: before our brethren discern thou what *is* thine with me, and take *it* to thee. For Jacob knew not that Rachel had stolen them. 33 And Laban went into Jacob's tent, and into Leah's tent, and into the two maidservant's tents; but he found *them* not. Then went he out of Leah's tent, and entered into Rachel's tent. 34 Now Rachel had taken the images, and put them in the camel's furniture, and sat upon them. And Laban *7* searched all the tent, but found *them* not. 35 And she said to her father, Let it not displease my lord that I cannot *f* rise up before thee; for the custom of women *is* upon me. And he searched, but found not the images.
36 And Jacob was wroth, and chode with Laban: and Jacob answered and

y 1 Sam. 30. 2. —— 6 Heb. *hast stolen me.* —— *z* Verse 55; Ruth 1. 9, 14; 1 Kings 19. 20; Acts 20. 37.—*a* 1 Sam. 13. 13; 2 Chron. 16. 9.

b Verse 53; chap. 28. 13. —— *c* Verse 24. —— *d* Verse 19; Judges 18. 24. —— *e* See chap. 44. 9. —7 Heb. *felt.*—*f* Exod. 20. 12; Lev. 19. 32.

But the God of your father
Yesternight said to me, saying,
Guard thyself from speaking with Jacob
From good to evil.
And now going thou hast gone;
For longing thou hast longed
For the house of thy father.—
Why hast thou stolen my gods?

27. **I might have sent thee away with mirth**—His previous conduct had given no hopes of any such kind treatment, as Jacob freely intimates, when he comes to respond.

29. **Power of my hand**—Or, *to the God of my hand*—לאל ידי. Laban, leavened with the notions of idolatry, contrasts the God of his hand—that is, the God for whom he lifts his hand—with the God of Jacob's father.

30. **My gods**—This theft he finally charges as the most aggravating thing of all.

31. **Take by force**—He feared that the man who forced him to marry, contrary to his desire and agreement, would be as likely to add other high-handed acts of wrong.

34. **Camel's furniture** — The car, כּר, or palanquin of the camel, "a covered vehicle which is secured on the back of the camel, and answers the purpose of a small house. It is often divided into two apartments, and the traveller, who can sit in either of them, is enabled also to carry some little furniture with him. These conveyances are protected by veils, which are not rolled up, except in front, so that the person within has the privilege of looking out while he is himself concealed. They are used chiefly by the women, rarely by the men."—JAHN's *Biblical Archæology*, § 49.

35. **My Lord** — Rachel addresses her father in terms of cold but dignified respect.

36. **Chode with Laban**—Contended with him in wordy war. Jacob's speech (verses 36 – 42) is still more pointed and vigorous than Laban's. Render as follows:

What my trespass,
What my sin,
That thou hast been burning after me?
For thou hast been feeling all my vessels;
What hast thou found of all the vessels of thy house?
Place here—
Before my brethren and thy brethren,
And let them decide between us two.
This twenty year I with thee;
Thy ewes and thy goats have not been bereft,
And the rams of thy flock have I not eaten.
The torn I brought not to thee;
I atoned for it.
Of my hand didst thou demand it,
Stolen by day,
And stolen by night.
I have been—
In the day heat devoured me,
And cold in the night,
And sleep fled from my eyes,
This to me twenty year in thy house;

said to Laban, What *is* my trespass? what *is* my sin, that thou hast so hotly pursued after me? **37** Whereas thou hast ⁸searched all my stuff, what hast thou found of all thy household stuff? set *it* here before my brethren and thy brethren, that they may judge betwixt us both. **38** This twenty years *have* I *been* with thee; thy ewes and thy she goats have not cast their young, and the rams of thy flock have I not eaten. **39** ᶠ That which was torn *of beasts* I brought not unto thee; I bare the loss of it; of ʰ my hand didst thou require it, *whether* stolen by day, or stolen by night. **40** *Thus* I was; in the day the drought consumed me, and the frost by night; and my sleep departed from mine eyes. **41** Thus have I been twenty years in thy house: I ⁱ served thee fourteen years for thy two daughters, and six years for thy cattle; and ᵏ thou hast changed my wages ten times. **42** ˡ Except the God of my father, the God of Abraham, ᵐ the fear of Isaac, had been with me, surely thou hadst sent me away now empty. ⁿ God hath seen mine affliction and the labour of mine hands, and ᵒ rebuked *thee* yesternight. **43** And Laban answered and said unto Jacob, *These* daughters *are* my daughters, and *these* children *are* my children, and *these* cattle *are* my cattle, and all that thou seest *is* mine: and what can I do this day unto these my daughters, or unto their children which they have borne? **44** Now therefore come thou, ᵖ let us make a covenant, I and thou; ᵠ and let it be for a witness between me and thee. **45** And Jacob ʳ took a stone, and set it up *for* a pillar. **46** And Jacob said unto his brethren, Gather stones; and they took stones, and made a heap: and they did eat there upon the heap. **47** And Laban called it ˢ Jegar-sahadutha: but Jacob called it

---

8 Heb. *felt.*——*g* Exod. 22. 10, etc.——*h* Exod. 22. 12.——*i* Chap. 29. 27, 28.——*k* Ver. 7.——*l* Psa. 124. 1, 2.——*m* Verse 53; Isa. 8. 13.——*n* Chap. 29. 32; Exod. 3. 7.——*o* 1 Chron. 12. 17; Jude 9.—— *p* Chap. 26. 28.——*q* Josh. 24. 27.——*r* Chap. 28. 18.——9 That is, *The heap of witness.* Chald.

I served thee fourteen years for two of thy daughters
And six years for thy flock;
And thou hast changed my wages ten parts.
Unless the God of my father,
The God of Abraham and the Fear of Isaac were for me,—
That now empty thou hadst sent me away.
My affliction and the labour of my hands God has seen;
And he judged yesternight.

40. Drought ... frost—Comp. Psa. cxxi, 6; Jer. xxxvi, 30. The extremes of heat and cold between day and night in the East are evidenced by all travellers.

42. Fear of Isaac—He whom Isaac feared. Laban closed his speech with allusion to his gods, (verse 30,) and now Jacob, more nobly, appeals to the intervention of the God of his fathers, who had **rebuked** Laban as an adversary.

43. Laban answered — Whether awed by Jacob's words, or convinced of the folly of attempting to change his plans or purposes, he hastens to propose a covenant, to which Jacob readily agrees. Laban's words may be rendered as follows:

The daughters my daughters,
And the sons my sons,
And the flock my flock,
And all which thou seest
Mine it is!

And to my daughters, what shall I do to them to-day?
Or to their sons, which they have borne?
And now come, let us cut a covenant, I and thou;
And let it be for a witness
Between me and thee.

47. Jegar-sahadutha ... Galeed —The Aramaic and Hebrew words, respectively, for *heap of witness.* יְגַר, *yegar,* or *gar,* is a dialectic variation of גַּל, *gal,* rendered *heap* in verse 46. This incidental notice of the naming of their stone memorial shows that already, in Jacob's time, the dialectical differences between the Aramaic and Hebrew tongues were noticeable. This was probably the origin of the name Gilead, applied to the whole range of mountains running north and south on the east of the Jordan. The particular spot where the covenant was made was probably at the northern end of the range, not at what was later known as Mizpeh of Gilead, (Judg. xi, 29,) for Jacob, after this, passing southward crossed the Jabbok, (Wady Zerka,) which is itself north of the modern mount *Jelad.* The name *Mizpah* (verse 49) subsequently became very common, and is applied to three other places on the east (Josh. xi. 3, Judges x, 17, 1 Sam. xxii, 3) and two on the west of the Jordan. Josh. xv, 38; xviii, 26.

¹⁰ Galeed. **48** And Laban said, ˢ This heap *is* a witness between me and thee this day. Therefore was the name of it called Galeed, **49** And ᵗ ¹¹ Mizpah; for he said, The LORD watch between me and thee, when we are absent one from another. **50** If thou shalt afflict my daughters, or if thou shalt take *other* wives beside my daughters, no man *is* with us; see, God *is* witness betwixt me and thee. **51** And Laban said to Jacob, Behold this heap, and behold *this* pillar, which I have cast betwixt me and thee; **52** This heap *be* witness, and *this* pillar *be* witness, that I will not pass over this heap to thee, and that thou shalt not pass over this heap and this pillar unto me, for harm. **53** The God of Abraham, and the God of Nahor, the God of their father, ᵘjudge betwixt us. And Jacob ᵛ sware by ʷ the fear of his father Isaac. **54** Then Jacob ¹² offered sacrifice upon the mount, and called his brethren to eat bread: and they did eat bread, and tarried all night in the mount. **55** And early in the morning Laban rose up, and kissed his sons and his daughters, and ˣ blessed them: and Laban departed, and ʸ returned unto his place.

CHAPTER XXXII.

AND Jacob went on his way, and ᵃ the angels of God met him. **2** And when Jacob saw them, he said, This *is*

---

10 That is, *The heap of witness.* Heb. —
s Josh. 24. 27. —*t* Judges 11. 29; 1 Sam. 7. 5.—
11 That is, *A beacon,* or, *watchtower.*

u Chap. 16. 5.—*v* Chap. 21. 23.—*w* Verse 42.
— 12 Or, *killed beasts.*—*x* Chap. 28. 1.—
y Chap. 18. 33; 30. 25.—*a* Psa. 91. 11; Heb. 1. 14.

---

48. Labân said — The following verses appear more like an antique song than formal narrative, and may be regarded as an ode composed upon this occasion, or soon after. We may regard the whole passage as the words of Laban, and translate, literally, thus:

And Laban said,
This heap, a witness,
Between me and thee to-day.
Therefore he called its name Galeed,
And the Watch-Tower, as he said:
Let Jehovah watch between me and thee.
For we are hidden, a man from his fellow,
If thou afflict my daughters,
And if thou take wives upon my daughters,
No man with us!
Behold, God, a witness between me and thee!
And Laban said to Jacob,
Behold this heap,
And behold the pillar,
Which I have cast between me and thee!
A witness this heap,
And a witness the pillar,
If I pass not to thee over this heap,
And if thou pass not to me over this heap,
And over this pillar for evil.
The God of Abraham,
And the God of Nahor,
Shall judge between us,—
The God of their father.
And let Jacob swear
In the Fear of his father Isaac.

54. Jacob offered sacrifice — He slew of the lambs of his flock, offered a solemn offering to his God, and made a sacrificial meal, and **called his brethren to eat.** It was the solemn evening of the last separation and farewell between the chosen seed and their "**fathers** on the other side of the flood" Josh. xxiv, 14. Henceforth they diverge more and more widely, and none of Jacob's sons go back to take wives in that eastern land.

55. Rose . . . kissed . . . blessed . . . departed . . . returned—There is something most touching and impressive in this affectionate farewell. The bad passions of the previous day and the wrongs of former years are all forgotten, and the two parties separate; the one to be the chosen people of God, the depositary of his oracles, the religious teachers of the world; the other to be lost from history.

CHAPTER XXXII.

JACOB AT MAHANAIM AND PENIEL, 1–32.

Jacob now approaches the great crisis in his spiritual life. After twenty years' absence from the land of promise, he again comes upon its eastern border; and as the angels of God appeared to him at Beth-el on his departure, so now, on his return, they appear again, as if to welcome him back to the Lord's land.

1. Jacob went on his way—From the place of his covenant with Laban, southwards, through the hills and valleys of Gilead. **Angels of God met him**—How or in what form, we are not told. Some suppose he had another dream, like that at Beth-el; but the absence of any mention of dream, or night vision, and the statement in verse 2 that " Jacob saw them," argues

272   GENESIS.   B. C. 1739.

God's ᵇ host: and he called the name of that place ¹Mahanaim. **3** And Jacob sent messengers before him to Esau his brother ᶜ unto the land of Seir, ᵈ the ²country of Edom. **4** And he commanded them, saying, ᵉ Thus shall ye speak unto my lord Esau; Thy servant Jacob saith thus, I have sojourned with Laban, and stayed there until now: **5** And ᶠ I have oxen, and asses, flocks, and menservants, and womenservants: and I have sent to tell my lord, that ᵍ I may find grace in thy sight.

6 And the messengers returned to Jacob, saying, We came to thy brother Esau, and also ʰ he cometh to meet thee, and four hundred men with him. **7** Then Jacob was greatly afraid and ⁱ distressed: and he divided the people that *was* with him, and the flocks, and herds, and the camels, into two bands; **8** And said, If Esau come to the one company, and smite it, then the other company which is left shall escape.

9 ᵏ And Jacob said, ¹O God of my father Abraham, and God of my father

---

b Josh. 5. 14; Psa. 103. 21; 148. 2; Luke 2. 13.—1 That is, *Two hosts*, or, *camps*.—*c* Chap. 33. 14, 16.—*d* Chap. 36. 6, 7, 8; Deut. 2. 5; Josh. 24. 4.—2 Heb. *field*.—*e* Prov. 15. 1.—*f* Chap. 30. 43.—*g* Chap. 33. 8, 15.—*h* Chap. 33. 1.—*i* Chap. 35. 3.—*k* Psa. 50. 15.—*l* Chap. 28. 13.

---

rather that the vision was an open one by day. His eyes were probably opened, as were those of the servant of Elisha, (2 Kings vi, 17,) and he beheld all around him a host of the angels of God.

2. This is God's host—Or, *God's band.* He at once recognises them as the same class of heavenly powers that had appeared to him in the vision of Beth-el. He has around him his own company, no small host; and behold, he is also encompassed by another camp, God's company of holy watchers, set to guard and guide him in his way. **Mahanaim**—Two camps; his own and that of the angels. Comp. Psa. xxxiv, 7. The great lesson of this event was that of the immanent providence of God. His angels ever guard the ways of his chosen. The site of Mahanaim is probably the modern *Maneh*, on the north of mount Ajlun. It was on the border of Gad and Manasseh,(Josh. xiii, 26, 30,) and was a city of the Levites. Josh. xxi, 38. Here Ish-bosheth, Saul's son, reigned two years. 2 Sam. ii, 8–12.

3. Sent messengers—To conciliate his brother, open the way for a friendly meeting, and discover the spirit and circumstances of Esau. **The land of Seir, the country** (or *field*) **of Edom**—From this it appears that at that time Esau had entered the mountainous district south of Palestine, afterwards called after his name. This does not necessarily imply that he had already removed his wives and children and possessions thither. On the contrary, it appears from chap. xxxvi, 6–8, that his removal with all his effects to Mount Seir, took place at a later date. The probability is, that Esau was at this time engaged, with a warlike band, in driving out the Horites from the strongholds of Edom. Comp. Deut. ii, 12, 22. Jacob's messengers, learning of his whereabouts, went and found him with a band of warriors. On receiving Jacob's message, and not knowing altogether what to make of it, and purposing not to be surprised or wronged by any new stratagem of the brother who had cheated him so sorely in the past, he proceeded at once with four hundred of his men to meet him.

7. Jacob was greatly afraid—The report of his messengers might naturally have this effect on Jacob. He had fled from his brother because of his threat to kill him, (chap. xxvii, 41,) and now his coming with a body of four hundred men seemed ominous of a purpose of vengeance. "His excited imagination saw his wives and children murdered; his ill-gotten flocks destroyed; and himself struck by the fatal blow, or chained in ignominious fetters. Agony and fear overpowered him, but that agony was his atonement; it was a suffering commensurate with his guilt; it was at once his retribution and his justification. But though it was a torture to his heart, it did not unbend his energy. All his faculties, feelings, and affections were roused to their utmost power, and his whole nature was quickened into vigorous activity."—*Kalisch.*

9. Jacob said—Having made all prudent arrangements possible, he betakes himself to prayer. He has been

CHAPTER XXXII.

Isaac, the LORD ᵐ which saidst unto me, Return unto thy country, and to thy kindred, and I will deal well with thee: 10 ³ I am not worthy of the least of all the ⁿ mercies, and of all the truth, which thou hast showed unto thy servant; for with ᵒ my staff I passed over this Jordan; and now I am become two bands. 11 ᵖ Deliver me, I pray thee, from the hand of my brother, from the hand of Esau: for I fear him, lest he will come and smite me, *and* ᵍ the mother ⁴ with the children. 12 And ʳ thou saidst, I will surely do thee good, and make thy seed as the sand of the sea, which cannot be numbered for multitude.
13 And he lodged there that same night; and took of that which came to his hand ˢ a present for Esau his brother; 14 Two hundred she goats and twenty he goats, two hundred ewes and twenty rams, 15 Thirty milch camels with their colts, forty kine and ten bulls, twenty she asses and ten foals. 16 And he delivered *them* into the hand of his servants, every drove by themselves; and said unto his servants, Pass over before me, and put a space betwixt drove and drove. 17 And he commanded the foremost, saying, When Esau my brother meeteth thee, and asketh thee, saying, Whose *art* thou? and whither goest thou? and whose *are* these before thee? 18 Then thou shalt say, *They be* thy servant Jacob's; it *is* a present sent unto my lord Esau: and, behold; also he *is* behind us. 19 And so commanded he the second, and the third, and all that followed the droves, saying, On this manner shall ye speak unto Esau, when ye find him. 20 And say ye moreover, Behold, thy servant Jacob *is* behind us. For he said, I will ᵗ appease him with the present that goeth before me, and

---

m Chap. 31. 3, 13. —— 3 Heb. *I am less than all*, etc. —— *n* Chap. 24. 27. —— *o* Job 8. 7. —— *p* Psa. 59. 1, 2.

q Hosea 10. 14. —— 4 Heb. *upon*. —— *r* Chap. 28. 13, 14, 15. —— *s* Chap. 43. 11; Prov. 18. 16.—— *t* Prov. 21. 14.

---

pursued from behind by his uncle and father-in-law Laban, and by the help of his father's God he has been redeemed from evil on that side. Now a danger threatens from the opposite direction, an enemy, though a brother. His prayer, under this sore distress, arose to a lofty height of poetic fervor. It was ever afterwards remembered, and repeated by generations of his children until Moses wrote it in this book.

> O God of my father Abraham,
> And God of my father Isaac;
> Jehovah, who saidst to me,
> Return to thy land and to thy kindred,
> And I will do well with thee;
> I am less than all the mercies,
> And than all the fidelity,
> Which thou hast done thy servant.
> For with my staff I passed over this Jordan,
> And now I have become two bands.
> Deliver me, now, from the hand of my brother,
> From the hand of Esau;
> For I fear him,
> Lest he come and smite me,
> Mother upon children.
> And thou didst say,
> Doing well I will do well with thee,
> And I have set thy seed as the sand of the sea,
> Which is not numbered from multitude.

In this fervent prayer we note with interest the following: 1) He appeals to the God of his fathers. 2) He makes use of the covenant name Jehovah. 3) He pleads the promises. 4) He humbly acknowledges the mercies of God. 5) God's truth or fidelity is honoured as against the untruthfulness of Jacob. 6) He acknowledges his great temporal prosperity as a blessing of God. 7) He prays for deliverance from Esau. 8) He confesses his fear. 9) He pleads for the mothers and children. 10) He pleads, in conclusion, the promises again.

13. **Of that which came to his hand**—The present was a large and princely one, probably a very large proportion of all that he possessed. He would fain give all to be reconciled to his warlike brother, and will spare no pains or sacrifice on his part that his prayer may be answered. The skilful arrangement of this present, which was to go over before him, is thus noticed by Lange: "Observe: 1) The climax; goats, sheep, camels, cattle, asses. 2) The spaces (breathing places) between the droves. Each impression must be made, and its force felt by Esau, before the next comes on. 3) The ever-repeated form of homage; thy servant Jacob; a present; my lord Esau. 4) The final aim: friendly treatment; thy servant, Jacob himself, is behind us."

20. **I will appease him**—Here is a notable instance of metaphorical lan-

afterward I will see his face; peradventure he will accept ⁵ of me. **21** So went the present over before him; and himself lodged that night in the company. **22** And he rose up that night, and took his two wives, and his two womenservants, and his eleven sons, ᵘ and passed over the ford Jabbok. **23** And he took them, and ⁶ sent them over the brook, and sent over that he had.

24 And Jacob was left alone; and there ᵛ wrestled a man with him until the ⁷ breaking of the day. **25** And when he saw that he prevailed not

---
5 Heb. *my face*, Job 42. 8, 9.——*u* Deut. 3. 16.——6 Heb. *caused to pass.*

v Hosea 12. 3, 4; Eph. 6. 12.——7 Heb. *ascending of the morning.*

---

guage. Literally, he says: "*I will cover his face with the present which goes before me, and afterwards I will see his face; perhaps he will lift up my face.* The word *cover* (כפר) is that so often used afterwards in connexion with expiation and atonement for sin. He would *cover Esau's face,* so that he whom he had sinned against might cease to see the transgressions of the past. Those past offences hidden, he hopes himself to look on Esau's face, as on one so far appeased as not to turn away from him, and refuse to see him. Then he hopes that there will come the further favour of Esau condescending to lift up his (Jacob's) face —the downcast face of one prostrate in humility and contrition before him.

21. That night—The night following the day on which the messengers returned from Esau. Verse 6. His successive movements seem to have been as follows: 1) Report of Esau's coming. 2) Great fear and excitement, and first plans and arrangements for escape. Verse 7. 3) He betakes himself to earnest prayer. Verses 9–12. 4) Having encamped for the night, he selects the present for Esau, and sends it on at once, over the ford, while he proposes to stay all night in the encampment. Verses 13–21. 5) After the present has passed over, he is restless still, and rises up that same night, and sees his wives and all his family safely over the Jabbok, he only remaining behind. Verses 22–24.

22. The ford Jabbok—Or, the crossing place of the Jabbok. This stream is believed to be identical with the modern Wady Zerka, which runs north of Mount Jelad, and empties into the Jordan directly east of Shechem.

24. Left alone—He doubtless sought to be alone with God that night, and called up the memories of all his past life. All the deception and wrong that had stained his record pressed sorely on his awakened conscience. He had all along leaned too much to his own devices, and had not fully relied on God. He probably repeated over and over again the prayer of verses 9–12, until it became fixed in his soul; and then there came a tangible presence, as of a human form; **there wrestled a man with him** until the rising of the dawn; a fact which we can understand and explain only as a supernatural visitation of the angel of Jehovah. See note on chap. xvi, 7. The prophet Hosea (xii, 3, 4) refers to this conflict, and his words may be rendered thus:

In the womb he took his brother by the heel.
And by his vigour he was a prince with God;
And he acted the prince towards the angel,
    and prevailed.
He wept, and made supplication to him.

The exact nature of this struggle it is impossible for us to tell, but the whole drift of the narrative is against our explaining it as a dream, or an inner vision which had no external reality. The experience, however, may have gone on through alternate sleeping and waking, as often, when greatly agitated, the spirit of man rises above the weakness and weariness of the flesh. Doubtless Jacob's praying wrought his soul into impassioned fervour. In such a state the coming of a man to him would have excited, comparatively, little or no additional alarm. In the first hours of struggle he as little apprehended the nature of his combatant as did Abraham and Lot when they entertained angels unawares; but towards the close of the struggle, as the morning drew on, he began to realize that he wrestled not with flesh and blood, but with Jehovah's angel.

25. When he saw that he pre-

B. C. 1739. CHAPTER XXXII. 275

against him, he touched the hollow of his thigh; and *the hollow of Jacob's thigh was out of joint, as he wrestled with him. 26 And ˣhe said, Let me go, for the day breaketh. And he said, ʸI will not let thee go, except thou bless me. 27 And he said unto him, What is thy name? And he said, Jacob. 28 And he said, ᶻThy name shall be called no more Jacob, but ᵃIsrael: for as a prince hast thou ᵃpower with God and ᵇwith men, and hast prevailed.

---

w See Matt. 26. 41; 2 Cor. 12. 7.——*x* See Luke 24. 28.——*y* Hos. 12. 4.——*z* Chap. 35. 10; 2 Kings 17. 34.——8 That is, *A prince of God.*——*a* Hosea 12. 3, 4.——*b* Chap. 25. 31; 27. 33.

---

vailed not—That is, when the angel saw this. Let us not marvel at such an anthropomorphism, but remember that the angel of Jehovah yielded to Abraham's intercession; ate with him like a man; found Hagar in the desert; led Lot by the hand out of Sodom, and said, "I cannot do any thing till thou escape." These self-limitations of the Divine One are manifesting themselves continually through all the history of his revealing himself to the chosen people, and we are not competent to say that he could have revealed himself as well in any other way. **Touched the hollow of his thigh**—The socket of the hip-joint, which is here called *caph,* (כַּף,) from its resembling the hollow palm of the hand. The angel's touch dislocated this joint; and gave Jacob to know that the mighty wrestler could at any moment disable him, and in so far contending with him had only been graciously condescending to his weakness. "The reason of this act of the angel was very probably lest Jacob should be puffed up by the 'abundance of the revelations.' He might think that of his own strength, and not by grace, he had prevailed with God; as St. Paul had the thorn in the flesh sent to him lest he 'should be exalted above measure.' 2 Cor. xii, 7."— *Speaker's Commentary.*

26. **Let me go**—He had power to free himself from Jacob's grasp as easily as he touched his thigh. But still he accommodates himself to Jacob's condition and needs, that he may teach a lesson for all ages. **For the day breaketh**—Heb., *the morning ariseth.* This is not to be explained as a part of the superstitious notion that spirits perform their earthly ministries in the dark hours of the night, and cannot abide the morning air. The three angels appeared at midday to Abraham. Chap. xviii, 1, 2. But the rising dawn required that Jacob should be now moving on to look after his family and to meet Esau. **I will not let thee go, except thou bless me**— Thus "he wept and made supplication unto him." Hosea xii, 4. It is the language of earnest, persistent prayer.

" Yield to me now, for I am weak,
But confident in self-despair ;
Speak to my heart, in blessing speak,
Be conquered by my instant prayer."

27. **What is thy name**—This question was the introduction of the answer to Jacob's petition for a blessing. The answer of Jacob was the confession of his name, **Jacob,** *supplanter;* the man who took his brother by the heel, and had been guilty of many an act of wrong. Thus to confess one's name is to confess one's sins, and "if we confess our sins, he is faithful and just to forgive us our sins, and to cleanse us from all unrighteousness." 1 John i, 8.

28. **No more Jacob, but Israel**— No more the supplanter; no more the self-seeker, filled with all artifice, and cunning, and deceit. This was the grand crisis and turning-point in Jacob's life and history. Hereafter he shall be called **Israel,** *princely contender with God.* This was the new name by which the chosen people should be chiefly known among themselves, and in their sacred books. **Israel,** rather than *Hebrews,* and rather than *Jews,* shall be their covenant name. The word is compounded of אֵל, *God,* and יִשׂר, from שָׂרָה, akin to שׂוּר and שָׂרַר, in which are combined the ideas of *prince* and *power.* The common version beautifully and forcibly presents both meanings, **as a prince hast thou power.** The oft-occurring word שַׂר, *sar—prince, noble, chief—*is of the same root. We deem it best in every ren-

29 And Jacob asked *him*, and said, Tell *me*, I pray thee, thy name. And he said, ᶜ Wherefore *is* it *that* thou dost ask after my name? And he blessed him there. **30** And Jacob called the name of the place ⁹Peniel: for ᵈI have seen God face to face, and my life is preserved. **31** And as he passed over Penuel the sun rose upon him, and he halted upon his thigh. **32** Therefore the children of Israel eat not *of* the sinew which shrank, which *is* upon the hollow of the thigh, unto this day; because he touched the hollow of Jacob's thigh in the sinew that shrank.

---

c Judges 13. 18. —— 9 That is, *The face of God*.

d Chap. 16. 13; Exod. 24. 11; 33. 20; Deut. 5. 24; Judges 6. 22; 13. 22; Isa. 6. 5.

---

dering of the verb to preserve the idea of *princely power*. In this new name is suggested the glorious attainments and prerogatives of the true spiritual sons of God. They become "a kingdom of priests," (Exod. xix, 6,) or, according to Rev. v, 10, "a kingdom and priests." In every case, the leading thought is that of *princely power* before God and from God.

29. **Tell me . . . thy name**—In the loftiest attainments of soul-struggle with God this is the profoundest prayer that can be uttered. It is a rising above human desires, a ceasing even to ask for blessings, and a yearning to know the sacred **name**. It is equivalent to, Reveal to me thy nature; or, as in Exod. xxxiii, 18, "Show me thy glory." Such was Manoah's prayer. Judges xiii, 17. But he learned that he might not ask too deeply after the *Wonderful*, פלא. **He blessed him there**—In what particular form or manner, besides the giving him the new name, we are not told. But Jacob's prayer for a *blessing* was answered. At the same time an implied rebuke was administered for his asking after the angel's name. When shocks of divine power are felt, sufficient to prove the personal presence of Omnipotence, it is presumptuous for feeble man to essay to "find out the Almighty to perfection."

30, 31. **Peniel . . . Penuel**—The two words mean the same thing, and differ only by the changing of the vowel-letter י into ו. Elsewhere it is always written **Penuel**, and possibly the form **Peniel** is a corruption that has here crept into the text. The name means *face or presence of God*, and the deep and lasting impression made on Jacob, as having struggled **face to face** with God, made this a fitting **name of the place**. He had there a vision of God such as he had not before, and though now **he halted upon his thigh,** he was thankful for the preservation of his life.

32. **Eat not . . . the sinew which shrank**—This is understood of the ischiadic, or sciatic nerve, extending from the thigh bone downwards. Even to the present day the Jews religiously abstain from eating this sinew in animals.

The narrative of Jacob's experiences in this chapter is wonderfully suggestive. We trace the struggles of a man of great natural endowments from the period of a mighty awakening to a mighty triumph. Released from Laban, he turns his face towards the Land of Promise, but before he enters it, he must be made to know more of himself and more of God. His acquaintance with God, thus far, has been only general, formal, and not sufficient to work any deep spiritual change in his inner life. He has stood altogether in his own strength. He obtained Esau's birthright by taking advantage of him at an hour of want. He obtained Isaac's blessing by guile. He had practiced many an artifice against Laban, and in their recent interview he had said much more about his own works than about the blessing of God. It is time for him to be humbled. First, then, comes the vision of angels at Mahanaim. But immediately after that he sends messengers to Esau with words that show great leaning to his own devices. Then follows the report of Esau's coming with four hundred men, and fear and trembling take hold of Jacob's soul. In his excitement and distress he plans for possible es-

B. C. 1739. CHAPTER XXXIII. 277

CHAPTER XXXIII.

AND Jacob lifted up his eyes, and looked, and, behold, ᵃ Esau came, and with him four hundred men. And he divided the children unto Leah, and unto Rachel, and unto the two handmaids. **2** And he put the handmaids and their children foremost, and Leah and her children after, and Rachel and Joseph hindermost. **3** And he passed over before them, and ᵇ bowed himself to the ground seven times, until he came near to his brother. **4** ᶜ And Esau ran to meet him, and embraced him, ᵈ and fell on his neck, and kissed him: and they wept. **5** And he lifted up his eyes, and saw the women and the children, and said, Who *are* those ¹ with thee? And he said, The children ᵉ which God hath graciously given thy servant.

6 Then the handmaidens came near, they and their children, and they bowed themselves. **7** And Leah also with her children came near, and bowed themselves: and after came Joseph near and Rachel, and they bowed themselves. **8** And he said, ²What *meanest* thou by ᶠ all this drove which I met? And he said, *These are* ᵍ to find grace in the sight of my lord. **9** And Esau said, I have enough, my brother; ³ keep that thou hast unto thyself. **10** And Jacob said, Nay, I pray thee, if now I have found grace in thy sight, then receive my present at my hand: for therefore I ʰ have seen thy face, as though I had seen the face of God, and thou wast pleased with me. **11** Take, I pray thee, ⁱ my blessing that is brought to thee; because God hath dealt graciously with me, and

---

a Chap. 32. 6.——*b* Chap. 18. 2; 42. 6; 43. 26.——*c* Chap. 32. 28.——*d* Chap. 45. 14, 15.——1 Heb. *to thee?*——*e* Chap. 48. 9; Psa. 127. 3; Isa. 8. 18.——2 Heb. *What* is *all this band to thee?*

f Chap. 32. 16.——*g* Chap. 32. 5.——3 Heb. *be that to thee that* is *thine.*——*h* Chap. 43. 3; 2 Sam. 3. 13; 14. 24, 28, 32; Matt. 18. 10.——*i* Judg. 1. 15; 1 Sam. 25. 27; 30. 26; 2 Kings 5. 15.

---

cape; but having little hope in that way, he turns to God in prayer. See notes on verses 9-12. Then he sets apart a princely present for his brother. He would fain make restitution for the wrongs of other days. He sends the present on by night. Still he cannot rest, and gets up in the night, and sends his family forward over the Jabbok. He is all excitement and emotion; and now, having done all he can, he lingers behind alone. Then comes the wonderful struggle with the angel, which was, in its first hours, like all the course of his life thus far, a struggle against God. God lets him wrestle, to know all his strength, and to find in the end that it is altogether weakness. At last a touch of the divine power breaks all Jacob's energy, and opens his eyes to see that he struggles not with man, but with God. It is a wondrous revelation that thus bursts upon his soul. It brings to him at once a conviction of the divine mercy as well as of divine power. Thus he is made " confident in self-despair," and learns, what every child of saving faith may know, that victory with God is had, not by a wrestling against him, but a confident clinging to him. Then and thus he obtained the new and princely name, and the blessing of God.

CHAPTER XXXIII.

MEETING OF JACOB AND ESAU, 1-16.

2. Rachel and Joseph hindermost—Jacob evidently arranged his companies according to his special affection for each; for the handmaids least, for Rachel most.

3. Before them—He goes on first to meet whatever evil may be feared. **Bowed ... to the ground**—Not as in chap. xix, 1, "with the face to the ground," which denotes complete prostration, but *groundward,* so that though the face does not touch the ground, it is brought low towards it. **Seven times**—Such a repetition of these acts of humility would have a likely tendency to disarm Esau's wrath. And doubtless the lowly obeisance and the lameness of Jacob drove from the generous hearted Esau whatever feeling of hardness or evil purpose he might have entertained towards him until now.

4. Ran to meet .... embraced ... fell ... kissed ... wept—Five forms in which they exhibited the first fervent emotions of brotherly affection. The whole interview is characterized with a life-like simplicity, as though detailed by an eye-witness of the scene.

10. As though I had seen the face of God—Comp. 1 Sam. xxix, 9; 2 Sam. xiv, 17. Jacob might most

GENESIS. B. C. 1739.

because I have [4] enough. [k] And he urged him, and he took *it*. **12** And he said, Let us take our journey, and let us go, and I will go before thee. **13** And he said unto him, My lord knoweth that the children *are* tender, and the flocks and herds with young *are* with me; and if men should overdrive them one day, all the flock will die. **14** Let my lord, I pray thee, pass over before his servant; and I will lead on softly, [5] according as the cattle that goeth before me and the children be able to endure, until I come unto my lord [l] unto Seir. **15** And Esau said, Let me now [6] leave with thee *some* of the folk that *are* with me. And he said, [7] What needeth it? [m] let me find grace in the sight of my lord. **16** So Esau returned that day on his way unto Seir.

17 And Jacob journeyed to [n] Succoth, and built him a house, and made booths for his cattle: therefore the name of the place is called [8] Succoth. **18** And Jacob came to [o] Shalem, a city of [9][p] Shechem, which *is* in the land of Canaan, when he came from Padan-aram; and pitched his tent before the city. **19** And [q] he bought a parcel of a field, where he had spread his tent, at

---

4 Heb. *all things*, Phil. 4. 18.——*k* 2 Kings 5. 23.——5 Heb. *according to the foot of the work*, etc., *and according to the foot of the children.*——*l* Chap. 32. 3.—— 6 Heb. *set*, or, *place.* —— 7 Heb. *Wherefore* is *this?*

m Chap. 34. 11; 47. 25; Ruth 2. 13.——*n* Josh. 13. 27; Judg. 8. 5; Psa. 60. 6.——8 That is, *Booths.*——*o* John 3. 23.——9 Called Acts 7. 16, *Sychem.*——*p* Josh. 24. 1; Judges 9. 1.——*q* Josh. 24. 32; John 4. 5.

---

truly say this, and believe in his heart that God himself, the God of Penuel, who had blessed him the last night, had changed and softened the disposition of Esau towards him.

11. He urged him and he took it—This acceptance of his large and princely gift would enable the humbled Jacob to feel that he had now made suitable reparation for any wrong he had previously done his brother.

14. I will lead on softly—That is, I will proceed gently. **According as the cattle**—Heb., *according to the foot of the work;* that is, the possessions acquired by my work. The English version, though not literal, gives the real meaning. **Until I come...unto Seir**—These words naturally give the impression that Jacob promises to move steadily along until he should reach Mt. Seir; but as soon as Esau departs, he proceeds to Shechem, and never went to Seir at all. But a little reflection will show the impropriety of construing his action thus. Esau was probably not yet settled in Mount Seir, (see note on chap. xxxii, 3,) but, during this interview, had told Jacob of his acquisitions and of his purpose to remove thither; and Jacob's promise to visit him there was necessarily indefinite as to time. The brothers met again at the burial of their father Isaac. Chap. xxxv, 29.

15. What needeth it—Heb., *Why this?* Jacob politely declines a body of Esau's men stationed as a guard around him. Such an arrangement would have only been likely to lead to difficulties which it were altogether better to avoid.

JACOB AT SHECHEM, 17–20.

17. Succoth—The word means *booths*, from the hurdles or folds made there by Jacob for his flocks. We find Succoth mentioned later as one of the cities east of the Jordan assigned to the tribe of Gad, (Josh. xiii, 27,) and also in the history of Gideon. Judges viii, 4–17. Its exact site is now unknown.

18. Came to Shalem, a city of Shechem—So the Sept., Vulg., and Syr. But it is better to render **Shalem** adverbially, *in peace.* Jacob came in peace to a city of Shechem, which is in the land of Canaan. It was doubtless at or near "the place of Sichem," mentioned chap. xii, 6, and **the city** had probably been built here since the time of Abraham's first arrival. The city may have taken its name from the *shoulder* of land on which it was built, (xii, 6, note,) or from Shechem, the son of Hamor, or, possibly, from one of his ancestors of the same name.

19. Bought a parcel of a field—Rather, *the portion of the field.* Abraham's only purchase of land was a place to bury his dead; Jacob now probably found the land more thickly settled, and found it necessary to buy land in order to dwell in peace. On this same land he dug the famous well at which

About B. C. 1732.   CHAPTER XXXIII.   279

the hand of the children of [10] Hamor, Shechem's father, for a hundred [11] pieces of money. **20** And he erected there an altar, and [f] called it [12] El-Elohe-Israel.

CHAPTER XXXIV.

AND [a] Dinah the daughter of Leah, which she bare unto Jacob, [b] went out to see the daughters of the land. **2** And when Shechem the son of Hamor the Hivite, prince of the country, [c] saw her, he [d] took her, and lay with her, and [1] defiled her. **3** And his soul clave unto Dinah the daughter of Jacob, and he loved the damsel, and spake [2] kindly unto the damsel. **4** And Shechem

[e] spake unto his father Hamor, saying, Get me this damsel to wife. **5** And Jacob heard that he had defiled Dinah his daughter: now his sons were with his cattle in the field: and Jacob [f] held his peace until they were come. **6** And Hamor the father of Shechem went out unto Jacob to commune with him. **7** And the sons of Jacob came out of the field when they heard it: and the men were grieved, and they [g] were very wroth, because [h] he had wrought folly in Israel in lying with Jacob's daughter; [i] which thing ought not to be done. **8** And Hamor communed with them, saying, The soul of my son Shechem

---

10 Called, Acts 7. 16, *Emmor.*——11 Or, *lambs*. ——*r* Chap. 35. 7.——12 That is, *God the God of Israel.*—— *a* Chap. 30. 21.—— *b* Titus 2. 5.—— *c* Chap. 6. 2; Judges 14. 1.——*d* Chap. 20. 2.—— 1 Heb. *humbled her*, Deut. 22. 29.

2 Heb. *to the heart of the damsel:* see Isa. 40. 2; Hosea 2. 14.——*e* Judges 14. 2.——*f* 1 Sam. 10. 27; 2 Sam. 13. 22.——*g* Chap. 49. 7; 2 Sam. 13. 21.——*h* Josh. 7. 15; Judges 20. 6.——*i* Deut. 23. 17; 2 Sam. 13. 12.

---

the Saviour taught the Samaritan woman. John iv, 5, 6, 12. **Hundred pieces of money**—Heb., *a hundred kesitah.* The Sept. and Vulg. render *a hundred lambs*, a sense, says Gesenius, "which has no support either from etymology or in the kindred dialects, nor is it in accordance with patriarchal usages." The word means some sort of money, in precious metal, weighed out, as Abraham weighed out the silver for Machpelah, (xxiii, 16,) but the exact value of a hundred *kesitah* cannot now be ascertained.

20. **Erected** — Rather, *established.* Having now obtained land of his own, he establishes his household altar, perhaps on the very spot already consecrated by the ancient altar of Abraham. Chap. xii, 7. **El-Elohe-Israel**—That is, *God, the God of Israel.* Thus he calls the new altar after his own new name, and in grateful acknowledgment of the vision and triumph at Penuel.

CHAPTER XXXIV.

TROUBLES WITH HAMOR AND SHECHEM, 1-31.

In this chapter we observe the first bitter fruits of Israel's contact with the heathen.

1. **Dinah** — Now grown to be a blooming girl of twelve or fourteen years. **Went out to see the daughters of the land** — Josephus says: "While the Shechemites were observ-

ing a feast, Dinah, the only daughter of Jacob, went into the city, looking at the fashion (κόσμον, *order*, or, perhaps here, *ornamentation*) of the women of the country." There is no occasion, however, for the supposition that the abduction was occasioned by any such public meeting of Dinah and Shechem. Jacob's family had now resided many years near the city, and probably Dinah had formed the habit of free intercourse and friendship with the young women of the place.

3. **Spake kindly**—Heb., *spoke to the heart of the girl.* He won her by tender words. She appears not to have been an unwilling party to the sin. "A gadding girl," says Schröder, "and a lad who has never gone beyond the precincts of home, are good for nothing."

7. **Came ... heard ... grieved ... wroth**—Jacob had silently meditated the matter before his sons came, (verse 5,) and probably felt all the dangers, shame, and trouble necessarily arising from the rape, but hesitated what to do. But his sons, with all the passion and daring of youth, feeling the deep disgrace incurred, allowed their sense of wrong to generate in them the darkest purposes of revenge. **Wrought folly in Israel**—This is the language of the writer, not of Jacob's sons. He speaks as one would naturally do after the name **Israel** had become national and historic.

longeth for your daughter: I pray you give her him to wife. **9** And make ye marriages with us, *and* give your daughters unto us, and take our daughters unto you. **10** And ye shall dwell with us: and ᵏ the land shall be before you; dwell and ˡ trade ye therein, and ᵐ get you possessions therein. **11** And Shechem said unto her father and unto her brethren, Let me find grace in your eyes, and what ye shall say unto me I will give. **12** Ask me never so much ⁿ dowry and gift, and I will give according as ye shall say unto me: but give me the damsel to wife. **13** And the sons of Jacob answered Shechem and Hamor his father ᵒ deceitfully, and said, because he had defiled Dinah their sister: **14** And they said unto them, We cannot do this thing, to give our sister to one that is uncircumcised; for ᵖ that *were* a reproach unto us: **15** But in this will we consent unto you: If ye will be as we *be*, that every male of you be circumcised; **16** Then will we give our daughters unto you, and we will take your daughters to us, and we will dwell with you, and we will become one people. **17** But if ye will not hearken unto us, to be circumcised; then will we take our daughter, and we will be gone. **18** And their words pleased Hamor and Shechem Hamor's son. **19** And the young man deferred not to do the thing, because he had delight in Jacob's daughter: and he *was* ᑫmore honourable than all the house of his father.
20 And Hamor and Shechem his son came unto the gate of their city, and communed with the men of their city, saying, **21** These men *are* peaceable with us; therefore let them dwell in the land, and trade therein; for the land, behold, *it is* large enough for them; let us take their daughters to us for wives, and let us give them our daughters. **22** Only herein will the men consent unto us for to dwell with us, to be one people, if every male among us be circumcised, as they *are* circumcised. **23** *Shall* not their cattle and their substance and every beast of theirs *be* ours? only let us consent unto them, and they will dwell with us. **24** And unto Hamor and unto Shechem his son hearkened all thatʳ went out of the gate of his city; and every male was circumcised, all that went out of the gate of his city.
25 And it came to pass on the third day, when they were sore, that two of the sons of Jacob, ˢ Simeon and Levi, Dinah's brethren, took each man his

---

k Chap. 13. 9; 20. 15. —— *l* Chap. 42. 34. —— *m* Chap. 47. 27. —— *n* Exod. 22. 16, 17; Deut. 22. 29; 1 Sam. 18. 25.

o See 2 Sam. 13. 24, etc. —— *p* Josh. 5. 9. —— *q* 1 Chron. 4. 9. —— *r* Chap. 23. 10. —— *s* Chap. 49. 5, 6, 7.

---

13. Sons of Jacob answered— "Jacob had scarcely time to advance a reply; for his sons eagerly availed themselves of their share of the influence generally allowed to brothers in the matrimonial arrangements of their sisters; and they acted with a zeal to which he thought he might safely trust the matter. But he was doomed to soon perceive his error."—*Kalisch.* **Deceitfully** — In this they seem to have inherited something of their father's duplicity in his younger days. And men, like Hamor and Shechem, under the impulses of ambition and of love, are easily deceived, and led to concede or adopt any thing that will serve their purpose and desire.
19. He was more honourable— That is, Shechem was the most honourable and distinguished person of the royal house of Hamor the Hivite.
24. Every male was circumcised —"The readiness of the Shechemites to submit to circumcision may be accounted for if circumcision had by this time become a rite known to others besides the descendants of Abraham. *Herod.*, ii, 104. At all events, it was now practiced not only by the sons of Jacob and his household, but by the Ishmaelites and the family and household of Esau, all growing into important tribes in the neighbourhood of the Shechemites."—*Speaker's Commentary.*
25. On the third day—After the operation was performed. At this time the pain and fever arising from the wound in the flesh attains its height, and renders the person weak and helpless. Jacob's sons had planned for this. **Simeon and Levi—**The second and third sons of Leah, Dinah's own brothers. Chap. xxxiii, 34. These are mentioned as leaders in all this action of cruelty. Perhaps some of their brothers went with them, (see verse 27,) but are not specially mentioned because they were not leaders in the action. We are not to suppose that

sword, and came upon the city boldly, and slew all the males. **26** And they slew Hamor and Shechem his son with the ³ edge of the sword, and took Dinah out of Shechem's house, and went out. **27** The sons of Jacob came upon the slain, and spoiled the city, because they had defiled their sister. **28** They took their sheep, and their oxen, and their asses, and that which *was* in the city, and that which *was* in the field, **29** And all their wealth, and all their little ones, and their wives took they captive, and spoiled even all that *was* in the house. **30** And Jacob said to Simeon and Levi, ᵗ Ye have ᵘ troubled me ᵛ to make me to stink among the inhabitants of the land, among the Canaanites and the Perizzites: ʷ and I *being* few in number, they shall gather themselves together against me, and slay me; and I shall be destroyed, I and my house. **31** And they said, Should he deal with our sister as with a harlot?

CHAPTER XXXV.

AND God said unto Jacob, Arise, go up to ᵃ Beth-el, and dwell there: and make there an altar unto God, ᵇ that appeared unto thee ᶜ when thou fleddest from the face of Esau thy brother. **2** Then Jacob said unto his ᵈ household, and to all that *were* with him, Put away ᵉ the strange gods that *are* among you,

3 Heb. *mouth.*——*t* Chap. 49. 6.——*u* Josh. 7. 25.——*v* Exod. 5. 21; 1 Sam. 13. 4.——*w* Deut. 4. 27; Psa. 105. 12.

a Chap. 28. 19.——*b* Chap. 28. 13.——*c* Chap. 27. 43.——*d* Chap. 18. 19; Josh. 24. 15.——*e* Chap. 31. 19, 34; Josh. 24. 2, 23; 1 Sam. 7. 3.

Simeon and Levi, alone and unattended, wrought all the slaughter and ruin here described. They doubtless commanded a large number of the servants of the household. Comp. chap. xiv, 14.

30. **Jacob said to Simeon and Levi**—His words of reproof partake here largely of worldly policy and prudence. He fears the bad odour in which he will be held by his Canaanitish neighbours, and the danger of their combining together to destroy him. But in the inspiration of his dying psalm, when utterly lifted above all earthly policies and dangers, he cursed the wrath and anger which prompted the bitter cruelties at Shechem. Chap. xlix, 5–7. **I being few in number**—Heb., *I, males of number;* that is, the males of my family, capable of fighting, are so few as to be easily numbered.

CHAPTER XXXV.

JACOB AGAIN AT BETHEL, 1–15.

The fear of Esau occasioned Jacob's departure from Beer-sheba; the fear of the Canaanites his departure from Shechem. In both cases he went to Beth-el, the house of God, the gate of heaven. In the former case he had the command of Rebekah, and the blessing and charge of Isaac; now he has the command of God. He seems to have been slow in fulfilling his vow at Beth-el. At Succoth and Shechem he tarried many years. Probably the fear of Esau still detained him, and he would fain keep as remote from him as practicable. The secular cares of his large household and flocks, and the interests of his growing sons, had also occupied his thoughts. It was not until the shame and troubles of Shechem broke his sense of security, and the voice of God called him again, that he aroused from his neglect, put away the idols of his household, and proceeded to Beth-el.

1. **God said**—Probably in a dream or vision of the night. **Go up to Beth-el**—Though southward from Shechem, and on a lower range, its importance led to speaking of it as a going up. **Dwell there**—Not at Shechem; an implied rebuke for his long dwelling in such proximity to idolaters. So, too, the reference to his flight from Esau, and the vision of God at Beth-el, were of the nature of admonition and rebuke.

2. **Jacob said unto his household** —And not to his own immediate family of wives, concubines, and children only; but **to all that were with him;** servants and helpers of every class and grade. The voice of God inspired him to sudden and resolute action in stopping at once the tampering with idolatry, which had gone too far in his house. Three things he now commands: **Put away the strange gods**—The teraphim, which Rachel had superstitiously stolen and carried with her from her father's house, (xxxi, 19,) and similar images and charms in possession of other members of the household. Among

282　　　　　　　　　GENESIS.　　　　About B. C. 1732.

and *f* be clean, and change your garments: **3** And let us arise, and go up to Beth-el; and I will make there an altar unto God, *g* who answered me in the day of my distress, *h* and was with me in the way which I went. **4** And they gave unto Jacob all the strange gods which *were* in their hand, and *all their* *i* earrings which *were* in their ears; and Jacob hid them under *k* the oak which *was* by Shechem. **5** And they journeyed: and *l* the terror of God was upon the cities that *were* round about them, and they did not pursue after the sons of Jacob. **6** So Jacob came to *m* Luz, which *is* in the land of Canaan, that *is*, Beth-el, he and all the people that *were* with him. **7** And he *n* built there an altar, and called the place 1 El-beth-el; because *o* there God appeared unto him, when he fled from the face of his brother. **8** But *p* Deborah Rebekah's nurse died, and she was buried beneath Beth-el under an oak: and the name of it was called 2 Allon-bachuth.

f Exod. 19. 10.——*g* Chap. 32. 7, 24; Psa. 107. 6. ——*h* Chap. 28. 20; 31. 3, 42.——*i* Hosea 2. 13.—— *k* Josh. 24. 26; Judges 9. 6.——*l* Exod. 15. 16; 23. 27; 34. 24; Deut. 11. 25; Josh. 2. 9; 5. 1;

1 Sam. 14. 15; 2 Chron. 14. 14.——*m* Chap. 28. 19, 22.——*n* Eccl. 5. 4.——1 That is, *The God of Beth-el.*——*o* Chap. 28. 13.——*p* Chap. 24. 59. ——2 That is, *The oak of weeping.*

the spoils of Shechem may also have been idolatrous images. **Be clean**— Rather, *cleanse yourselves.* This was doubtless to be done by ceremonial ablutions, but of what particular form we have no means of knowing. **Change your garments**—This would be another and marked token of their assuming a new and higher mode of religious life and action. Observe, there were priestly rites, and ceremonial purifications previous to the Mosaic legislation.

3. **I will make there an altar**— Shechem had not been without its altar, (xxxiii, 20,) but the one at Beth-el is to be a memorial altar, to the special honour of Him who **answered** Jacob **in the day of** his **distress**. All the awakened memories of God's care are to enter into this new place of worship.

4. **Earrings**—These appear to have been used as amulets and charms, and used with superstitious reverence, even as the teraphim. **Hid them under the oak**—Perhaps the same ancient tree or grove mentioned in chap. xii, 6. This was ever regarded as a sacred spot in Israel. Comp. Josh. xxiv, 26. The proper disposal of these **strange gods** was to bury them as dead nothings. Isa. xli, 24; 1 Cor. viii, 4.

5. **Terror of God**—A terror inspired and intensified by God himself, who, on the other hand, had softened the heart of Esau to tenderness towards his brother.

6. **Luz** . . . **Beth-el**—See on chap. xxviii, 19. How must Jacob's soul have burned with tender emotion as he came again to this holy spot!

7. **El-beth-el**—God of the house of God. Every-where he seeks to honour the divine Name. Compare the hallowed names El-Elohe-Israel (xxxiii, 20) and Penuel, (xxxii, 30.)

8. **Deborah**—Here suddenly comes the mention of the death of Rebekah's nurse, without any notice of how she came to be with Jacob, or any apparent reason for its being mentioned in this connexion. Evidently the sacred writers have not attempted to tell us every thing, and the criticism which raises quibbles and difficulties over such stray notices of names as this is unworthy of serious regard. A very natural and probable supposition is that of Lange, that Rebekah was now dead, and after her death, Deborah came to dwell with Jacob. The death of Rebekah is nowhere recorded, but Jacob mentions her burial in Machpelah. Chap. xlix, 31. Perhaps Jacob had gone to his mother's burial from Shechem, and brought Rebekah home with him; or perhaps Rebekah's death occurred while Jacob was still with Laban, and the loving mother, who was never able to fulfil the promise of chap. xxvii, 45, desired that after her death the faithful and honoured nurse should go and dwell with Jacob. **Allon-bachuth**—Which means *oak of weeping.* The special mention of Deborah's death and burial at this time and place, and the name given to her grave, show with what honour and affection she was regarded. She had gone forth in youth with her beautiful mistress, on her bridal journey, (xxiv, 59,) nearly one hundred and forty years before.

About B. C. 1732.   CHAPTER XXXV.   283

9 And ᵠGod appeared unto Jacob again, when he came out of Padan-aram, ᵩnd blessed him. **10** And God said anto him, Thy name *is* Jacob: ʳthy name shall not be called any more Jacob, ˢbut Israel shall be thy name; and he called his name Israel. **11** And God said unto him, ᵗI *am* God Almighty: be fruitful and multiply; ᵘa nation and a company of nations shall be of thee, and kings shall come out of thy loins; **12** And the land ᵛwhich I gave Abraham and Isaac, to thee I will give it, and to thy seed after thee will I give the land. **13** And God ʷwent up from him in the place where he talked with him. **14** And Jacob ˣset up a pillar in the place where he talked with him, *even* a pillar of stone: and he poured a drink-offering thereon, and he poured oil thereon. **15** And Jacob called the name of the place where God spake with him, ʸBeth-el.

16 And they journeyed from Beth-el; and there was but ᵃa little way to come to Ephrath: and Rachel travailed, and she had hard labour. **17** And it came to pass, when she was in hard labour, that the midwife said unto her, Fear not; ᶻthou shalt have this son also. **18** And it came to pass, as her soul was in departing, (for she died,) that she called

---

q Hos.12.4.——r Chap.17.5.——s Chap.32.28.—— t Chap. 17. 1; 48. 3,4; Exod. 6. 3.——u Chap. 17. 5, 6, 16; 28. 3; 48. 4.——v Chap. 12. 7; 13. 15; 26. 3, 4; | 28. 13. ——w Chap. 17. 22. ——x Chap. 28. 18.—— y Chap.28.19.——3 Heb. *a little piece of ground*, 2 Kings 5. 19.——z Chap. 30. 24; 1 Sam. 4. 20.

9–12. **Appeared unto Jacob again** —Thirty years have passed since God appeared unto him in the dream of the ladder—years of hope, of labour, of discipline, of sorrow, and of manifold cares With this revelation his old secular life seems to have ended ; he leaves all that to his sons, and hereafter he appears as the aged saint meditating the promises. We note in this passage (verses 9–13) the expressions — **God appeared, God said,** and *God went up.* Verse 13. The appearance was evidently some open vision, probably the presence of the covenant angel. The oracle spoken to him (verses 10–12) is twofold, designated by the twice-repeated "God said unto him." The first saying (verse 10) is the repetition of his name Israel, a confirming of the blessing of Penuel. Chap. xxxii, 28. In the second saying, (verses 11, 12,) God, 1) announces himself as God Almighty, *El-Shaddai*, who gave Abram his new name Abraham, (xvii, 1, 5;) and 2) repeats to him the promise and prophecy spoken afore to Abram, (xvii, 6;) and 3) the promise of the land promised so often to Abraham and Isaac. Chaps. xiii, 15; xv, 18; xvii, 8; xxvi, 3.

13. **God went up from him**—This implies the visible appearance of the Angel of Jehovah. Comp. Judg. xiii, 20.

14. **Set up a pillar**—As he had done at the former time, (xxviii, 18,) but now with much more expense and ceremony. **Poured a drink-offering . . . poured oil**—This is the first mention in the Scripture of a **drink-offering**, or libation of wine. They were afterwards common in the worship of Israel. "The stone designates the ideal house of God, and in this significance must be distinguished from the altar. Through the drink-offering Jacob consecrates the enjoyment of his prosperity to the Lord; through the oil he raises the stone, as well as his thanksgiving, to a lasting sacred remembrance."—*Lange.*

DEATH OF RACHEL, 16–20.

16. **Journeyed from Beth-el**—Having paid his vows at Beth-el, he feels a yearning to move on, southward, and see his father Isaac again. **A little way**—Heb., *a chibrath of land ;* some apparently definite measure of length or distance, but now to us unknown. **Ephrath**—The ancient name of the place afterwards so well known as Bethlehem. Verse 19. **Rachel travailed**—At the birth of Joseph, she had yearned for yet another son, (xxx, 24,) and had given her firstborn a name in confidence that this hope would be realized. But many years passed before her hope was filled, and then at the cost of her own life.

17. **Thou shalt have this son also**—Rather, *for this also is to thee a son ;* apparently in allusion to her wish at Joseph's birth.

18. **Her soul was in departing**—Heb., *in the going out of her soul ;* an intimation of immortality. The

284 GENESIS. About B. C. 1732.

his name [4] Ben-oni: but his father called him [5] Benjamin. **19** And [a] Rachel died, and was buried in the way to [b] Ephrath, which is Beth-lehem. **20** And Jacob set a pillar upon her grave: that is the pillar of Rachel's grave [c] unto this day. **21** And Israel journeyed, and spread his tent beyond [d] the tower of Edar. **22** And it came to pass, when Israel dwelt in that land, that Reuben went and [e] lay with Bilhah his father's concubine: and Israel heard it. Now the sons of Jacob were twelve: **23** The sons of Leah; [f] Reuben, Jacob's firstborn, and Simeon, and Levi, and Judah, and Issachar, and Zebulun: **24** The sons of Rachel; Joseph, and Benjamin: **25** And the sons of Bilhah, Rachel's handmaid; Dan, and Naphtali: **26** And the sons of Zilpah, Leah's handmaid; Gad, and Asher. These are the sons of Jacob, which were born to him in Padan-aram. **27** And Jacob came unto Isaac his father unto [g] Mamre, unto the [h] city of Arba, which is Hebron, where Abraham and Isaac sojourned. **28** And the days of Isaac were a hundred and fourscore years. **29** And Isaac gave up the ghost, and died, and [i] was gathered unto his people, being old and full of days: and [k] his sons Esau and Jacob buried him.

4 That is, *The son of my sorrow.*——5 That is, *The son of the right hand.*——*a* Chap. 48. 7.——*b* Ruth 1. 2; 4. 11; Micah 5. 2; Matt. 2. 6.——*c* 1 Sam. 10. 2; 2 Sam. 18. 18.——*d* Micah 4. 8.

e Chap. 49. 4; 1 Chron. 5. 1; see 2 Sam. 16. 22; 20. 3; 1 Cor. 5. 1.——*f* Chap. 46. 8; Exod. 1. 2.——*g* Chap. 13. 18; 23. 2, 19.——*h* Josh. 14. 15; 15. 13.——*i* Chap. 15. 15; 25. 8.——*k* So chap. 25. 9; 49. 31.

soul is thought of as a conscious entity, passing out into some other state and mode of life. **Ben-oni... Benjamin** —The former name means *son of my sorrow ;* the latter, *son of a right hand.* To his mother he is a child of woe; to his father, a child of hope.

20. **A pillar... unto this day**—An oak marked Deborah's tomb, (verse 8,) a pillar Rachel's. The place was known in Samuel's time, (1 Sam. x, 2,) and there appears no sufficient reason to doubt that the modern Moslem tomb a little northwest of Beth-lehem, known as Kubbet Rahil, occupies the spot of Jacob's memorial tablet of his beloved wife.

REUBEN'S INCEST, 21, 22.

21. **The tower of Edar**—Or, *Migdal-Edar*, which means *tower of the flock*, so called, doubtless, from being a tower or eminence whence flocks at a distance could be watched. Comp. 2 Kings xvii, 9; xviii, 8; 2 Chron. xxvi, 10.

22. **Bilhah**—Rachel's handmaid, and mother of Dan and of Naphtali. Chap. xxx, 3-8. **Israel heard**—And it occasioned to Reuben the loss of his birthright, and the words of reproach recorded in chap. xlix, 4.

LIST OF JACOB'S SONS, 22-26.

This list is given here, at the close of this section of the book, and before the account of the death and burial of Isaac, as a sort of concluding record of Jacob's history thus far. The subsequent historic "generations of Jacob," do not begin until after we have, in chap. xxxvi, "the generations of Esau." See chap. xxxvii, 2.

ISAAC'S DEATH AND BURIAL, 27-29.

27. **Jacob came unto Isaac**—This appears to have been some twelve years previous to the death of Isaac, and therefore long enough to communicate often to his father his varied experiences, and to receive the counsels of the aged patriarch. Jacob was living at Hebron when Joseph was sold, (xxxvii, 14,) and the latter was at that time 17 years old. Chap. xxxvii, 2. Twenty-two years later Jacob went down into Egypt. He was then 130 years old; (chap. xlvii, 9;) consequently he was now 108, and Isaac 168, (xxv, 26;) and Isaac lived at least twelve years after this. So he must have lived to know of the loss of Joseph, and almost up to the beginning of the great famine which led Israel into Egypt.

28. **Hundred and fourscore years** —He lived five years more than his father Abraham. Chap. xxv, 7.

29. **Esau and Jacob buried him**— Again the brothers (like Isaac and Ishmael, chap. xxv, 9) come together, both bound by tender affection for their venerated father. Esau had, probably long before this, removed his household and possessions unto Mount Seir. See chap. xxxvi, 6-8. Here ends the section of the generations of Isaac, which began with chap. xxv, 19.

CHAPTER XXXVI.

NOW these *are* the generations of Esau, ᵃ who *is* Edom. **2** ᵇ Esau took his wives of the daughters of Canaan; Adah the daughter of Elon the Hittite, and ᶜ Aholibamah the daughter of Anah the daughter of Zibeon the Hivite; **3** And ᵈ Bashemath Ishmael's daughter, sister of Nebajoth. **4** And *Adah bare to Esau Eliphaz; and Bash-emath bare Reuel; **5** And Aholibamah bare Jeush, and Jaalam, and Korah: these *are* the sons of Esau, which were born unto him in the land of Canaan. **6** And Esau took his wives, and his sons, and his daughters, and all the ¹ persons of his house, and his cattle, and all his beasts, and all his substance, which he had got in the land of Canaan; and went into the country from the face of his

a Chap. 25. 30.——*b* Chap. 26. 34.——*c* Verse 25. | *d* Chap. 28. 9.——*e* 1 Chron. 1. 35.——1 Heb. *souls.*

CHAPTER XXXVI.
Generations of Esau, 1–43.

This venerable document is inserted here, in accord with the uniform plan of the book, to finish up and dispose of the history of Esau before beginning the later and fuller history of Jacob, which is to occupy not only the remainder of Genesis, but also the rest of the Pentateuch. The genealogy is carried as far as the reign of Hadar, (verse 39,) whose decease is not mentioned, and who was, perhaps, the king of Edom to whom Moses applied for passage through the land. Num. xx, 14. Compare the parallel list in 1 Chron. i, 35–54. The whole list is divisible into six subdivisions, as follows:

ESAU'S WIVES AND CHILDREN, AND THEIR REMOVAL TO MOUNT SEIR, 1–8.

A comparison of the names of Esau's wives, as given here and in chaps. xxvi, 34, xxviii, 9, will show noticeable differences. Here we have:

1 { 1. Adah the daughter of Elon the Hittite.
2. Aholibamah the daughter of Anah the daughter of Zibeon the Hivite.
3. Bashemath Ishmael's daughter, sister of Nebajoth.

There we have:

2 { 1. Judith the daughter of Beeri the Hittite.
2. Bashemath the daughter of Elon the Hittite.
3. Mahalath the daughter of Ishmael, sister of Nebajoth.

Here we notice that the names of the wives in the two lists are all different, but it seems altogether probable that **Adah** of the first list=**Bashemath** of the second; and **Aholibamah** of the first=**Judith** of the second; for there can be no doubt that **Bashemath**=**Mahalath**, stated in each list to be Ishmael's daughter and Nebajoth's sister. It is very possible that, in such ancient tables of names, changes, transpositions and corruptions have entered. *Hittite* and *Hivite* (הַוִּי־חִתִּי) might easily become confused in transcribing, and **Bashemath** substituted for **Mahalath**. But all attempts at this date to emend or explain these differences are conjectural. The names may have been changed for reasons, and in accordance with customs, of which we are now ignorant. Names were often repeated in tribes and families, (comp. verses 20, 24, 25,) and in some lists grandfathers or great grandfathers are mentioned instead of fathers. Thus it would be equally proper to call Rebekah the daughter of Bethuel, or of Nahor, or of Milcah, (see chap. xxiv, 24,) or even of Haran or Terah. Chap. xi, 27. Then we must remember what incidents often changed a name, or gave a new name, as Esau and Edom, (xxv, 30,) and the eastern customs of giving new names to women at their marriage, or at the birth of certain children. It seems better to account for these differences on such general principles, than to attempt a doubtful hypothesis to account for each specific change.

6. All his substance—Esau had vast possessions as well as Jacob, possessions acquired **in the land of Canaan.** He had not been idle while Jacob was in Mesopotamia. **Went into the country**—Heb., *went to the land,* that is, the land of Edom. **From the face of his brother Jacob**—When this occurred we have no means of knowing, but probably about the time of Jacob's movement southwards from Shechem. Esau knew the land of Canaan was promised to Jacob, and he

VOL. I.—19 O. T.

brother Jacob. **7** *For their riches were more than that they might dwell together; and ᵍ the land wherein they were strangers could not bear them because of their cattle. **8** Thus dwelt Esau in ʰ mount Seir: ⁱ Esau *is* Edom.

9 And these *are* the generations of Esau the father of ²the Edomites in mount Seir: **10** These *are* the names of Esau's sons; ᵏ Eliphaz the son of Adah the wife of Esau, Reuel the son of Bashemath the wife of Esau. **11** And the sons of Eliphaz were Teman, Omar, ³ Zepho, and Gatam, and Kenaz. **12** And Timna was concubine to Eliphaz Esau's son; and she bare to Eliphaz ˡAmalek: these *were* the sons of Adah Esau's wife. **13** And these *are* the sons of Reuel; Nahath, and Zerah, Shammah, and Mizzah: these were the sons of Bashemath Esau's wife.

14 And these were the sons of Aholibamah, the daughter of Anah the daughter of Zibeon, Esau's wife: and she bare to Esau Jeush, and Jaalam, and Korah.

15 These *were* dukes of the sons of Esau: the sons of Eliphaz the firstborn *son* of Esau; duke Teman, duke Omar, duke Zepho, duke Kenaz, **16** Duke Korah, duke Gatam, *and* duke Amalek: these *are* the dukes *that came* of Eliphaz in the land of Edom: these *were* the sons of Adah.

17 And these *are* the sons of Reuel Esau's son; duke Nahath, duke Zerah, duke Shammah, duke Mizzah: these *are* the dukes *that came* of Reuel in the land of Edom: these *are* the sons of Bashemath Esau's wife.

18 And these *are* the sons of Aholibamah Esau's wife; duke Jeush, duke Jaalam, duke Korah: these *were* the dukes *that came* of Aholibamah the daughter of Anah, Esau's wife. **19** These *are* the sons of Esau, who *is* Edom, and these *are* their dukes.

---

f Chap. 13, 6, 11. —— *g* Chap. 17. 8; 28. 4. —— *h* Chap. 32. 3; Deut. 2. 5; Josh. 24. 4.—*i* Verse 1.—² Heb. *Edom*.

k 1 Chron. 1. 35, etc.—³ Or, *Zephi*, 1 Chron. 1. 36. —— *l* Exod. 17. 8, 14; Num. 24. 20; 1 Sam. 15. 2, 3, etc.

---

would not seek to hinder his occupation and free enjoyment of his own inheritance.

THE SONS AND GRANDSONS OF ESAU AS HEADS OF TRIBES, 9–14.

Compare the parallel list in 1 Chron. i, 35–37. The names here given are evidently those of the tribe-fathers of the nation of the Edomites in Mount Seir. They embrace five sons and ten grandsons, including **Amalek** the son of Eliphaz by his concubine. It is impossible and unnecessary now to trace the subsequent history and settlement of these several tribes. In the name of Eliphaz, the Temanite, mentioned in the Book of Job, (ii, 11,) we may trace the name of the son and grandson of Esau perpetuated in the name of a city founded by this Teman, whose family made frequent use of the ancestral names. Teman was famed for wisdom. Jer. xlix, 7. This **Amalek** is believed to be the tribe-father of the Amalekites, who are so frequently mentioned in the subsequent history of Israel. They attacked the Israelites on their exodus from Egypt to Sinai, (Exod. xvii, 8,) and became a powerful and famous tribe. From his being the son of a concubine, Amalek may have found little sympathy from his brethren, and early became separated from them, founding by himself an independent tribe. The mention of the "country of the Amalekites" in chap. xiv, 7, does not necessarily imply that there was a nation of Amalekites at that time, but is to be explained as the natural designation of a territory thus known at the time of the writer.

THE DUKES OF ESAU, 15–19.

Here the chief tribe-fathers of the Edomites are named again, under the title of **dukes,** Heb., *alluphim,* (אַלֻּפִים,) *phylarchs, chiefs,* or *princes.* These were all military chieftains, great patriarchal sheiks, who were celebrated by their descendants not merely as *fathers* but as *heroes.* As being merely a presentation of the same persons under a different title, they are omitted from the list in 1 Chronicles which proceeds with the sons of Seir.

SONS OF SEIR THE HORITE, 20–30.

The Horites were the original occupants of Mount Seir, (chap. xiv, 6,) but it appears from Deut. ii, 12, 22, that they were subdued by the sons of Esau, and in all probability the rem-

Ab't B. C. 1840-1676. CHAPTER XXXVI. 287

20 ᵐ These *are* the sons of Seir ⁿ the Horite, who inhabited the land; Lotan, and Shobal, and Zibeon, and Anah, **21** And Dishon, and Ezer, and Dishan: these *are* the dukes of the Horites, the children of Seir in the land of Edom. **22** And the children of Lotan were Hori and ⁴ Hemam; and Lotan's sister *was* Timna. **23** And the children of Shobal *were* these; ⁵ Alvan, and Manahath, and Ebal, ⁶ Shepho, and Onam. **24** And these *are* the children of Zibeon; both Ajah, and Anah: this *was that* Anah that found ᵒ the mules in the wilderness, as he fed the asses of Zibeon his father. **25** And the children of Anah *were* these; Dishon, and Aholibamah the daughter of Anah. **26** And these *are* the children of Dishon; ⁷ Hemdan, and Eshban, and Ithran, and Cheran. **27** The children of Ezer *are* these; Bilhan, and Zaavan, and ⁸ Akan. **28** The children of Dishan *are* these; Uz, and Aran. **29** These *are* the dukes *that came* of the Horites; duke Lotan, duke Shobal, duke Zibeon, duke Anah, **30** Duke Dishon, duke Ezer, duke Dishan: these *are* the dukes *that came* of Hori, among their dukes in the land of Seir.
31 And ᵖ these *are* the kings that reigned in the land of Edom, before there reigned any king over the children of Israel. **32** And Bela the son of Beor reigned in Edom: and the name of his

---

m 1 Chron. 1. 38.—*n* Chap. 14. 6; Deut. 2. 12, 22.—4 Or, *Homam*, 1 Chron. 1. 39.—5 Or, *Alian*, 1 Chron. 1. 40. 6 Or, *Shephi*, 1 Chron. 1. 40.—*o* See Lev. 19. 19.—7 Or, *Amram*, 1 Chron. 1. 41.—8 Or, *Jakan*, 1 Chron. 1. 42.—*p* 1 Chron. 1. 43.

---

nants of their tribes intermarried with the Edomites, and became so identified with them as to be thus included in this genealogy. The seven **sons of Seir the Horite** are all mentioned again in verses 29 and 30 as the **dukes of the Horites**, corresponding with the sons and dukes of Esau already given. On the identification of some of these names there are differences of opinion. **Timna**, in verse 22, is generally allowed to be the same as the concubine of Eliphaz, verse 12. It is natural to suppose **Aholibamah the daughter of Anah** (verse 25) to be the same as the wife of Esau, (verse 2,) but Keil very positively denies their identity. **Anah** (verse 24) is said to be a son of Zibeon the Horite; but the **Anah** of verse 2 is the daughter of Zibeon the Hivite. **Anah** is distinguished for having **found the mules in the wilderness, as he fed the asses of Zibeon his father.** There is no good authority for rendering the word יֵמִם, **mules**; it means rather, *warm springs*. While he pastured the asses of Zibeon he discovered certain hot springs, probably those of Callirhoe, on the east of the Dead Sea, in the wady Zerka-Main, which are famous for their medicinal qualities and various temperature, ranging from tepid to a degree of heat that cannot be endured in bathing. Hengstenberg suggests that the discovery of these springs gave Anah the surname *Beeri*, (xxvi, 34,) " the fountain man," or " well-finder," and thus constructs an argument to prove the identity of Anah with the father of Esau's wife. His argument, if not conclusive, should suffice to show how many possible circumstances, now unknown to us, might have occasioned the differences of names which puzzle us in old genealogical tables.

THE KINGS OF EDOM, 31-39.

How a monarchy arose among the Edomites we are not told, but it is noticeable that of the eight kings here mentioned, not one is said to have succeeded to his father. It is, therefore, very plausibly supposed that they were chosen by the dukes, or phylarchs. The statement that these kings **reigned in the land of Edom before there reigned any king over the children of Israel** has been suspected as an interpolation, introduced after kings reigned over the Israelites. This is not an unreasonable or improbable supposition. See Introd. to the Pentateuch, p. 22. Others have argued from its late authorship of the Pentateuch. But neither of these suppositions are necessary. God had said to Abraham, " Kings shall come out of thee," (xvii, 6,) and he repeated the promise to Jacob, (xxxv, 11,) who, in his last words, prophesied of a sceptre to arise in Judah. Chap. xlix, 10. Moses also assumed that kings would arise in Israel, (Deut. xvii, 14,

city *was* Dinhabah. **33** And Bela died, and Jobab the son of Zerah of Bozrah reigned in his stead. **34** And Jobab died, and Husham of the land of Temani reigned in his stead. **35** And Husham died, and Hadad the son of Bedad, who smote Midian in the field of Moab, reigned in his stead: and the name of his city *was* Avith. **36** And Hadad died, and Samlah of Masrekah reigned in his stead. **37** And Samlah died, and Saul of Rehoboth *by* the river reigned in his stead. **38** And Saul died, and Baal-hanan the son of Achbor reigned in his stead. **39** And Baal-hanan the son of Achbor died, and ᵍ Hadar reigned in his stead: and the name of his city *was* Pau; and his wife's name *was* Mehetabel, the daughter of Matred, the daughter of Mezahab. **40** And these *are* the names of ʳ the dukes *that came* of Esau, according to their families, after their places, by their names; duke Timnah, duke ⁸Alvah, duke Jetheth, **41** Duke Aholibamah, duke Elah, duke Pinon, **42** Duke Kenaz, duke Teman, duke Mibzar, **43** Duke Magdiel, duke Iram: these *be* the dukes of Edom, according to their habitations in the land of their possession: he *is* Esau the father of ¹⁰ the Edomites.

---

q 1 Chron. 1. 50, *Hadad, Pai.* After his death was an Aristocracy, Exod. 15. 15.

r 1 Chronicles 1. 51.——9 Or, *Aliah.*——10 Hebrew, *Edom.*

---

xxviii, 36;) and with such expectations it would have been very natural for him, in recording this list of Edomite kings, to introduce the remark that all these reigned before Israel had any king. The Edomite monarchy was a sudden upstart affair, as compared with the Israelitish.

Of none of these kings have we any certain trace elsewhere. **Bozrah**, in verse 33, is the same as that mentioned in Isa. xxxiv, 6, liii, 1, and **the land of Temani** (verse 34) was probably so called after the son of Eliphaz. Verse 11. Bozrah was probably at the site of the modern el-Busaireh, southeast of the Dead Sea.

In verse 35 the mention of **Hadad the son of Bedad, who smote Midian in the field of M**oab, gives us a momentary glimpse of ancient wars among the peoples scattered south and east of the Dead Sea. As the death of all these kings except **Hadar** (verse 39) is formally recorded, it is naturally supposed that he was living at the time of this writer, and was, perhaps, the same king to whom Moses applied for permission to pass through the Edomite territory. Num. xx, 14.

DUKES OF ESAU AFTER THEIR PLACES, 40–43.

Some suppose that the eleven dukes here named were contemporary with Hadar, the last named king; but 1 Chron. i, 51–54, which mentions the death of Hadar, (called *Hadad* there,) implies that they survived him. But the expressions, **according to their families, after their places, by their names** (verse 40) and **according to their habitations in the land of their possession,** (verse 43,) denote rather the ducal cities, or districts. We should accordingly translate, *duke of Timnah, duke of Alvah,* and etc., and understand that **Aholibamah, Kenaz,** and **Teman** are here the names of cities, called after their founders; perhaps the persons bearing these names in the previous part of the genealogy.

The Generations of Jacob, xxxvii–l.

This is the last section of the Book of Genesis headed by the special designation, תֹּלְדוֹת, *generations.* See Introduction, p. 49. Though the larger portion of this section is devoted to the history of Joseph, Jacob is still the head of the patriarchal family, and the covenant history centres in him as its representative. "Jacob was now dwelling in the green, well-watered vale of Hebron, half-way between Beer-sheba (the place of Isaac's sojourning) and Salem, (afterwards Jerusalem,) the city of Melchizedek, probably the earliest seat of civilized life in Palestine. Here the spies found the rich valley of Eshcol, with its giant grape clusters; here, too, crowning the overlooking height, they found the city of Arba (Kirjath-Arba) and his gigantic sons, and here, too, was and is that most venerated of all sepulchres, the cave of Machpelah. The modern town lies on the sloping sides of the narrow valley, which runs

About B. C. 1496. CHAPTER XXXVII.

CHAPTER XXXVII.

AND Jacob dwelt in the land¹ wherein ᵃ his father was a stranger, in the land of Canaan. 2 These *are* the gen-

1 Heb. *of his father's sojournings.*   ᵃ Chap. 17. 8; 23. 4; 28. 4; 36. 7; Heb. 11. 9.

north and south, clothed with luxuriant vineyards, and groves of the gray olive and evergreen oak. About a mile north of the town, solitary in the midst of the vineyards, stands a very large widespreading oak, which is regarded as the successor of Abraham's 'oak of Mamre.' Yet Jacob sent his flocks to pasture sixty miles north, in the fertile valley of Shalem or Shechem, where some time before he had bought a piece of ground whereon 'to spread his tent.'"—*Newhall.*

The following reflections of Ewald are most valuable in their suggestions and concessions, especially as coming from a Rationalist like him:

"The history of Jacob gradually and almost imperceptibly passes into that of the tribes, (or sons,) above whom hovers, vague and dim, the awful form of Israel, the aged Patriarch. Especially fine is the turn thus given to the history, when called to relate the evil deeds and wicked lusts of these sons; and with the one great exception of Joseph, what else is there to tell of them? In their collective history is vividly anticipated the future history of the nation; its many shortcomings, its manifold corruptions, as if the guileful nature, wholly eradicated at last in the much-tried father, sprang up again, and spread in rank luxuriance, among his descendants; first in Simeon and Levi, and still more in the history of Joseph. The old father, who now, made perfect through suffering, appears like some superior spirit watching over them, sternly rebukes all these follies and misdeeds committed behind his back; and yet, eventually, he himself has to bear the burden of iniquities planned without his knowledge. Thus Jacob is still, though in a different sense, what he was entitled in his youth, the laboriously striving, much enduring, man of God. Thus, even in the post-Mosaic period, the better spirit still hovers over the nation—often obscured, and almost despairing, yet abandoning them never, and in the end really beholding with rapture a great and glorious restoration of all the erring ones."—*History of Israel,* i, 360.

CHAPTER XXXVII.

JOSEPH AND HIS DREAMS, 1-11.

"The history of Joseph is, perhaps, the most charming story in the world. The fascinating interest and matchless pathos of the Bible narrative can be much better appreciated when it is compared with the history of Joseph as given in the Koran (chap. xii) and in Josephus, (*Antiq.,* book ii.) Yet those hard, dry, and tame narratives and reflections were written by men who had read the wondrous tale of Genesis! The typical suggestions of this narrative are unusually rich and deep. Some of them are thus set forth by the sober and profound Pascal:

"'Joseph was a type of Christ. The beloved of his father; sent on an errand by his father to his brethren; without fault; sold by his brethren for money; and thence exalted to be their lord, their saviour, the saviour of multitudes unknown to him, of the world; all which could not have taken place without the scheme for his disgrace, his sale, and destruction. In the prison Joseph was committed, without any offence of his, with two criminals; Christ was crucified between two thieves. He foretold the release of the one and the execution of the other, under like symbols in the case of each: Jesus saves his chosen and condemns the rejected, under like crimes. Joseph predicts only, Christ acts. Joseph entreats of the one who is to be saved, that he will be mindful of him when he is restored to prosperity; and he whom Jesus saves prays to be remembered of him when he shall enter his glory,' (*Thoughts;* Longman's edition, p. 312.) The sin of the brethren, however, was overruled, not necessitated."—*Newhall.*

1. **In the land wherein his father was a stranger**—Rather, *in the land*

erations of Jacob. Joseph, *being* seventeen years old, was feeding the flock with his brethren; and the lad *was* with the sons of Bilhah, and with the sons of Zilpah, his father's wives: and Joseph

b 1 Sam. 2. 22, 23, 24.—*c* Chap. 44. 20.

of the sojournings of his father. This verse serves to acquaint us with the location of Jacob at this period of his history. It marks the transition between the generations of Esau and Jacob. Esau had now departed (according to chap. xxxvi, 6) to the land which was to become known as the land of Edom, and Jacob is recognised as the true successor in the inheritance of his father.

2. **Seventeen years old**—Or, according to the Hebrew idiom, *a son of seventeen years.* The historian (according to his usual custom noticed in the earlier parts of Genesis) goes back a little, and commences his new section at a point previous to Isaac's death. Comp. chap. xxxv, 27, note. **The lad was with the sons**—Heb., *and he a lad, with the sons of Bilhah.* Some understood this to mean that he was a lad along with the sons of Bilhah and Zilpah; that is, he was nearer their age than the ages of the sons of Leah, and hence fed the flocks along with them. Others construe the words **with the sons of Bilhah**, etc., with **feeding the flock,** and understand that, as he was too young to be trusted alone, he fed the flock in company with these older brothers; perhaps, says Newhall, "because the sons of the concubines agreed with him better than did the sons of Leah." But a strict rendering of the whole verse is best made by throwing the words *and he a lad* in parenthesis, and construing the words **sons of Bilhah,** etc., as appositional and epexegetical of **his brethren,** thus: *Joseph, a son of seventeen years, was* (in the habit of) *shepherding his brethren in the flock, (and he a mere lad,)—even the sons of Bilhah and the sons of Zilpah, wives of his father.* That is, Joseph, when only seventeen, a mere boy, was in the habit of taking care of his brothers as if he were their shepherd; especially did he thus attend to the sons of the concubines. This seems to

brought unto his father *b* their evil report. **3** Now Israel loved Joseph more than all his children, because he *was c* the son of his old age: and he made him a coat of *many* ² colours. **4** And

2 Or, *pieces,* Judges 5. 30; 2 Sam. 13. 18.

have been his first offence. The next was, his reporting to his father what was said of them; then his father's partiality, shown in the costly garment, and, finally, his various dreams. **Their evil report**—Rather, "*an evil report* concerning them, which he had heard from the inhabitants in the neighbourhood of the pasture ground, (Knobel, Lewis,) not **their evil report,** as A. V., which would require the article with the adjective; not any definite crime, not evil words which his brethren had said about him (Kimchi;) the phrase is purposely indefinite, and refers to a floating rumour which affected the character of his brethren." (Delitzsch.)— *Newhall.*

3. **Israel loved Joseph more . . . because he was the son of his old age.** "The ancient Jewish interpreters do not consider this as describing the parental partiality for the latest born, but render, *because he was a wise son.* (Onk.) Maimonides says, that as lateborn he stayed at home, and was his father's stay, the nourisher of his age, a careful son, whom Jacob thus naturally loved with special affection. So Fagius, Bush, Lewis. **And he made him a coat of many colours,** (figured or variegated, Sam., Sept., Vulg., Targ.,) or, more likely, a *sleeved tunic reaching to the ankles,* such as was worn by persons not much engaged in manual labour, the ordinary Oriental tunic being, like a loose shirt, girded about the waist, without sleeves, and reaching to the knees. So Gesen., Knobel, Del. after Sym., and Aquila. Lewis understands it to mean a tunic with spots, stripes, or fringes; so A. Clarke, who compares it with the striped and fringed toga of the Roman youth. This dress was intended as a badge of distinction, as rank has always thus been indicated in Oriental countries. Probably it was the badge of the birthright (Bush) which Reuben had forfeited, (1 Chron. v, 1,) **and which**

About B. C. 1729. CHAPTER XXXVII. 291

when his brethren saw that their father loved him more than all his brethren, they ᵈ hated him, and could not speak peaceably unto him.
5 And Joseph dreamed a dream, and he told *it* his brethren: and they hated him yet the more. 6 And he said unto them, Hear, I pray you, this dream which I have dreamed: 7 For, ᵉ behold, we *were* binding sheaves in the field, and, lo, my sheaf arose, and also stood upright; and, behold, your sheaves stood round about, and made obeisance to my sheaf. 8 And his brethren said to him, Shalt thou indeed reign over us? or shalt thou indeed have dominion over us?

And they hated him yet the more for his dreams, and for his words.
9 And he dreamed yet another dream, and told it his brethren, and said, Behold, I have dreamed a dream more; and, behold, ᶠ the sun and the moon and the eleven stars made obeisance to me. 10 And he told *it* to his father, and to his brethren: and his father rebuked him, and said unto him, What *is* this dream that thou hast dreamed? Shall I and thy mother and ᵍ thy brethren indeed come to bow down ourselves to thee to the earth? 11 And ʰ his brethren envied him; but his father ⁱ observed the saying.

d Chap. 27. 41; 49. 23.——*e* Chap. 42. 6, 9; 43. 26; 44. 14.——*f* Chap. 46. 29.

g Chap. 27. 29.——*h* Acts 7. 9.——*i* Dan. 7. 28; Luke 2. 19, 51.

was transferred to the eldest son of the favourite Rachel. Jacob very unwisely makes his preference thus conspicuous, and thus subjects the virtue of his favourite son to a test most painful and severe."—*Newhall.*
4. Could not speak peaceably—"Heb., *could not bid peace to him;* could not greet him with the ordinary salutation, 'Shalom,' 'Peace be unto thee.' It may be that Joseph was unwise and unkind to accept this distinction, and to report to his father evil rumours concerning his brethren; but we are hardly to expect that he, a child, would set up his judgment against that of his father, and he everywhere appears as a frank and guileless child."—*Newhall.*
5. And Joseph dreamed a dream, and he told it his brethren—"In normal sleep there is inactivity of the senses, and consequently of the powers of perception by the senses, (presentative powers,) as well as of continuous and rational thought, while there may, at the same time, be activity of memory and imagination, (representative powers,) reproducing and fantastically combining the waking thoughts, thus causing dreams. Our lower as well as higher powers—the sleeping as well as the waking mind—may become the vehicle of divine revelation. Yet the Scriptures refer to the revelations received in sleep as if inferior in grade and character to those which involve the higher faculties of perception, understanding, and reason. It is in dreams that God reveals himself to the heathen, (Abime-

lech, Pharaoh, Nebuchadnezzar,) but to the seers of the chosen people only, as a general rule, in the prophet's preparatory or rudimentary period. See Blackie's *Iliad*, iv, p. 12. These accounts cannot fairly lead us to consider our mental operations in sleep as any more supernaturally guided than those of our waking hours. Neither can have prophetic authority unless inspired."—*Newhall.*
7-9. Sheaves ... stars—"The two dreams very obviously shadow forth Joseph as having kingly authority over his father, mother, and brethren. The scene of the first is laid in the wheat field, where he and his brethren are symbolized by the sheaves. But to repeat and solemnly deepen the impression, the scene of the second is laid in heaven, and now not only his brethren, but his father and mother, (Leah probably, since Rachel was dead,) under heavenly symbols bow down, not to his star, but to him. How powerfully must this dream have returned to the minds of them all, when, more than twenty years after, the venerable patriarch and his eleven sons did obeisance to the prince of Egypt, who said to them, 'I am Joseph.'"—*Newhall.* On the import of double dreams, see note on chap. xli, 32.
11. But his father observed the saying—"So strange and mysterious. So Mary 'pondered' and 'kept in her heart' the strange sayings of Jesus, which others understood not. Luke ii, 50, 51."—*Newhall.*

12 And his brethren went to feed their father's flock in Shechem. **13** And Israel said unto Joseph, Do not thy brethren feed *the flock* in Shechem? come, and I will send thee unto them. And he said to him, Here *am I.* **14** And he said to him, Go, I pray thee, ³see whether it be well with thy brethren, and well with the flocks; and bring me word again. So he sent him out of the vale of ᵏ Hebron, and he came to Shechem.

15 And a certain man found him, and, behold, *he was* wandering in the field: and the man asked him, saying, What seekest thou? **16** And he said, I seek my brethren: ¹ tell me, I pray thee, where they feed *their flocks.* **17** And the man said, They are departed hence; for I heard them say, Let us go to Dothan. And Joseph went after his brethren, and found them in ᵐ Dothan. **18** And when they saw him afar off, even before he came near unto them, ⁿ they conspired against him to slay him. **19** And they said one to another, Behold, this ⁴ dreamer cometh. **20** ° Come now therefore, and let us slay him, and cast him into some pit, and we will say, Some evil beast hath devoured him; and we shall see what will become of his dreams. **21** And ᵖ Reuben heard *it*, and he delivered him out of their hands; and said, Let us not kill him. **22** And Reuben said unto them, Shed no blood, *but* cast him into this pit that *is* in the wil-

3 Heb. *see the peace of thy brethren,* etc., chap. 29. 6. —*k* Chap. 35. 27.—*l* Sol. Song 1. 7. —*m* 2 Kings 6. 13.—*n* 1 Sam. 19. 1; Psa. 31. 13;

37. 12, 32; 94. 21; Matt. 27. 1; Mark 14, 1; John 11. 53; Acts 23. 12.—4 Heb. *master of dreams.* —*o* Prov. 1. 11, 16; 6. 17; 27. 4.—*p* Chap. 42. 22.

JOSEPH SOLD INTO EGYPT. 12–36.

13. Thy brethren . . . in Shechem—Jacob owned a tract of land near this city, which he purchased of the prince of that country. See chap. xxxiii, 19. The number and extent of their flocks made it necessary for the sons of Jacob to be much scattered abroad in order to find pasturage. Probably on their removal from Shechem, (xxxv, 1,) they left some of their flocks there, and in view of the desperate acts of Simeon and Levi (xxxiv, 25) Jacob may now have feared for his sons at Shechem, and been anxious to hear from them.

15. Wandering in the field—Wandering about the field that belonged to his father at Shechem. The fact of his going alone and unattended from Hebron to Shechem and beyond, shows the quiet and peace that prevailed in the land at that time.

17. To Dothan—"About seventeen miles farther north. Dothan, or Dothaim, *(two wells,)* is situated just south of the great plain of Esdraelon, from which it is separated only by two or three low swells of ground, the name being still attached to a fine green knoll, from the base of which springs a fountain. The pasturage being exhausted in the valley of Shechem, the shepherds had moved northwards to richer grazing grounds, on the margin of the great plain that has always been the granary of Palestine:"—*Newhall.*

19. This dreamer—Heb. *this master* (or *lord) of the dreams.* We may suppose Joseph seeing them afar with joy, glad to find them after his long journey and searching. But they see him with malicious envy.

20. Let us slay him—Here we note the dark and brutal passions to which they had yielded under the power of jealousy and envy. They now show themselves fit for foulest deeds and blackest falsehoods.

21. Reuben—He whom we might expect to be most offended by the princely garment (verse 3, note) is the readiest to show him favour. **Delivered him out of their hands**—Prevented his being slain, and purposed, as the next verse shows, to deliver him to his father again.

22. This pit that is in the wilderness—By **the wilderness** here we are to understand the open, unsettled country in which they were pasturing their flocks. "The country abounded, and still abounds, in pits or cisterns dug in the ground, or soft limestone, to preserve water through the dry season, and also to store grain. They were made large at the bottom, with a small mouth at the top, sometimes tapering upwards, like a huge demijohn. (Thomson.) The top was covered with a flat stone, over which sand or earth was often spread for concealment. When

About B. C. 1729. CHAPTER XXXVII. 293

derness, and lay no hand upon him; that he might rid him out of their hands, to deliver him to his father again.

23 And it came to pass, when Joseph was come unto his brethren, that they stripped Joseph out of his coat, *his* coat of many ⁵ colours that *was* on him;
24 And they took him, and cast him into a pit: and the pit *was* empty, *there was* no water in it. **25** ᑫ And they sat down to eat bread: and they lifted up their eyes and looked, and, behold, a company of ʳ Ishmaelites came from Gilead, with their camels bearing spicery and ˢ balm and myrrh, going to carry *it* down to Egypt. **26** And Judah said unto his brethren, What profit *is it* if we slay our brother, and ᵗ conceal his blood?
27 Come, and let us sell him to the Ishmaelites, and ᵘ let not our hand be upon him; for he *is* ᵛ our brother *and* ʷ our flesh: and his brethren ⁶ were content.
28 Then there passed by ˣ Midianites merchantmen; and they drew and lifted up Joseph out of the pit, ʸ and sold Joseph to the Ishmaelites for ᶻ twenty *pieces* of silver: and they brought Joseph into Egypt.

---

5 Or, *pieces.*——*q* Prov. 30. 20; Amos 6. 6.——*r* See verses 28, 36.——*s* Jer. 8. 22.——*t* Chap. 4. 10; verse 20; Job 16. 18.——*u* 1 Sam. 18. 17.

v Chap. 42. 21.——*w* Chap. 29. 14.——6 Heb. *hearkened.*——*x* Judges 6. 3.——*y* Chap. 45. 4, 5; Psa. 105. 17; Acts 7. 9.——*z* See Matt. 27. 9.

---

dry there was generally mud at the bottom. They were often used as dungeons for criminals. See Jer. xxxviii, 6. Perhaps they put him into the pit, deliberately intending to leave him there to perish; but it seems more likely that they did this as a temporary imprisonment, without having definitely determined what final disposition to make of Joseph. Reuben succeeds in effecting a stay of the murderous proceedings of his brethren. Judah's proposition in verse 26, shows that his fate was under discussion as they 'sat down to eat bread.' "—*Newhall.*

23. Stripped Joseph—He wore the garment which gave so much offence, (verse 3,) and this, first of all, they tore savagely away from him.

25. Sat down to eat—This remark reveals their heartless cruelty most vividly. Reuben was not a partaker of that meal; but off, probably, devising measures for the rescue of his brother.

28. Sold Joseph . . . for twenty pieces of silver—" The future deliverer of Israel is sold as a slave. One of the great caravan routes from Damascus through the land of Gilead to Egypt, by the way of the maritime plain, Ramleh and Gaza, ran near the pasture ground, and a side route from the East, crossing the fords of the Jordan opposite Bethshan, passed through the valley of Jezreel, and turning southwest, crossed the pastures of Dothan, joining the main route south of the point where it descends from Carmel. Had the caravan been moving to Egypt by the easterly route, through Hebron, past Jacob's tents, Joseph's brethren would not have dared to sell him. The Ishmaelites, (descendants of Ishmael, Abraham's son by Hagar,) called Arabians in the Chaldee, and Midianites, (descendants of Midian, Abraham's son by Keturah,) were mingled in the same caravan, the 'east Abrahamic peoples,' who now as then are sons of the desert, going down to Egypt with the spices and gums of Arabia and India. The caravan was laden with precious gums, for which there was always a market in Egypt, created to a great extent, probably, by the demand for such articles in embalming. The word rendered *spicery* (ver. 25) most probably is gum-tragacanth; *balm* is the precious aromatic balsam for which Gilead was famous, distilling from a shrub for which the plain of Jericho was once celebrated, and now found in the gardens of Tiberias, while the substance, incorrectly rendered in A. V. myrrh, is the odorous greenish resin *ladanum*, which exudes from the branches of the *cistus*, a shrub of the rock-rose family, with white or rose-coloured flowers. Judah, influenced by compassion, with which probably cupidity was mingled, proposes to sell Joseph as a slave, rather than take his life. This is the first historic instance of the sale of a man, though slavery is, probably, as ancient as war, being a substitute for the murder of captives. 'And they sold Joseph to the Ishmaelites for twenty (shekels of) silver,' that is, about ten ounces of silver in weight,

29 And Reuben returned unto the pit; and, behold, Joseph *was* not in the pit; and he ᵃ rent his clothes. **30** And he returned unto his brethren, and said, The child ᵇ *is* not; and I, whither shall I go? **31** And they took ᶜ Joseph's coat, and killed a kid of the goats, and dipped the coat in the blood; **32** And they sent the coat of *many* colours, and they brought *it* to their father; and said, This have we found: know now whether it *be* thy son's coat or no. **33** And he knew it, and said, It *is* my son's coat; an ᵈ evil beast hath devoured him; Joseph is without doubt rent in pieces. **34** And Jacob ᵉ rent his clothes, and put sackcloth upon his loins, and mourned for his son many days. **35** And all his sons and all his daughters ᶠ rose up to comfort him; but he refused to be comforted; and he said, For ᵍ I will go down into the grave unto my son mourning. Thus his father wept for him. **36** And ʰ the Midianites sold him into Egypt unto Potiphar, an ⁷ officer of Pharaoh's, *and* ⁸ ⁹ captain of the guard.

a Job 1. 20.——*b* Chap. 42. 13, 36; Jer. 31. 15.——*c* Ver. 23.——*d* Ver. 20; chap. 44. 28.——*e* Ver. 29; 2 Sam. 3. 31.——*f* 2 Sam. 12. 17.——*g* Chap. 42. 38; 44. 29, 31.——*h* Chap. 39. 1.——⁷ Heb. *eunuch:* but the word doth signify not only *eunuchs,* but also *chamberlains, courtiers,* and *officers,* Esther 1. 10.——8 Or, *chief marshal.*——9 Heb. *chief of the slaughtermen,* or, *executioners.*

about twelve dollars and a half at the present valuation!"—*Newhall.*

30. **Whither shall I go**—"It is a cry of distracting anxiety, which sounds touchingly mournful and pathetic in the Hebrew, from the repetition and alliteration. Reuben afterwards reminds his brethren, in the day of their distress, of the earnestness with which he had pleaded for Joseph. Chap. xlii, 22. Only Reuben and Judah show any trace of humanity in this dark transaction, and they seem, on their return to their father, to be bound by the ban of silence. It is Reuben and Judah, also, that are afterwards foremost to take responsibility, and bear the blame, when they all stand before Joseph the judge. Chapters xlii and xliv."—*Newhall.*

32. **Thy son's coat**—Not our brother's! Every word of theirs in this dark pretext is studiously cruel.

33. **My son's coat**—Jacob's words are most touching. Render:

Tunic of my son!
An evil beast has eaten him!
Torn, torn,—Joseph!

35. **His daughters**—"His sons' wives, or possibly he may have had daughters besides Dinah, which are not mentioned by name. 'And he said, (I will not be comforted,) for I will go down to my son, mourning, to Sheol.' This is the first place in which the word *Sheol* occurs, which means the place or state of the dead. It is derived by Gesenius from a word meaning to *dig,* that is, the grave, but has been usually derived from a verb meaning to *ask,* or demand, the craving grave. Lewis, however, understands the word to express the inquiring wonder with which we ask for the dead, the eager listening at the gates of death. So the Greek word *Hades, the unseen,* (Sept. translation of Sheol,) sets forth the same world as sealed to the sense of sight. 'In the one, it is the eye peering into the dark; in the other it is the ear intently listening to the silence. Both give rise to the same question, Where is he? whither has he gone? and both seem to imply with equal emphasis that the one unseen and unheard yet really *is.*' Jacob did not expect that his body would lie with Joseph's in the same grave, for he thought that an ' evil beast had devoured him,' yet he expected to go to his son."—*Newhall.*

36. **Potiphar**—"A eunuch of Pharaoh: this is the primary meaning, although the word came afterwards to mean *officer* in general, since the officers about the royal person were usually eunuchs. **Captain of the guard** —Rendered literally in the margin, 'chief of the executioners, chief marshall,' an appropriate title for the officer who executed the arbitrary and summary sentences of the Pharaohs." —*Newhall.*

CHAPTER XXXVIII.

THE FAMILY OF JUDAH, 1–30.

This chapter forms an essential part of the history of "the generations of Jacob." Chap. xxxvii, 2. In that history "the two chief persons were Joseph

CHAPTER XXXVIII.

AND it came to pass at that time, that Judah went down from his brethren, and ᵃ turned in to a certain Adullamite, whose name *was* Hirah. 2 And Judah ᵇ saw there a daughter of a certain Canaanite, whose name *was* ᶜ Shuah; and he took her, and went in unto her. 3 And she conceived, and bare a son; and he called his name ᵈ Er. 4 And she conceived again, and bare a son; and she called his name ᵉ Onan. 5 And she yet again conceived, and bare a son; and called his name ᶠ Shelah: and he was at Chezib, when she bare him. 6 And Judah ᵍ took a wife for Er his firstborn, whose name *was* Tamar. 7 And ʰ Er, Judah's firstborn, was wicked in the

---

a Chap. 19. 3; 2 Kings 4. 8. —— *b* Chap. 34. 2. —— *c* 1 Chron. 2. 3. —— *d* Chap. 46. 12; Num. 26. 19.

e Chap. 46. 12; Num. 26. 19.—*f* Chap. 46. 12; Num. 26. 20.—*g* Chap. 21. 21.—*h* Chap. 46. 12; Num. 26. 19.

---

and Judah: Joseph, from his high character, his personal importance, his influence on the future destinies of the race, and his typical foreshadowing of the Messiah; Judah, from his obtaining the virtual right of leadership, and from his being the ancestor of David and of the Son of David. Hence at a natural pause in the history of Joseph, namely, when he had been now sold into Egypt and settled in Potiphar's house, the historian recurs to the events in the family of Judah, which he carries down to the birth of Pharez, the next link in the ancestry of the Saviour. Thus he clears away all that was necessary to be told of the history of the twelve patriarchs, with the exception of that which was involved in the history of Joseph. There is also a remarkable contrast brought vividly out by this juxtaposition of the impure line of Judah and his children with the chastity and moral integrity of Joseph as seen in the succeeding chapter."—*Speaker's Commentary.*

1. **At that time**—During the time that Jacob dwelt in the land of his father's sojournings. Chap. xxxvii, 1. It does not say *after these things*, as in xxii, 1; so that the exact point of time is altogether indefinite. **Judah went down from his brethren**—Went southward from Shechem, perhaps on some errand to his grandfather Isaac, and before Jacob had removed from Shechem. **Adullamite**—A native of Adullam, a city in the plain some distance north-west of Hebron, which is mentioned in Joshua xv, 35, among the cities of Judah, and situated between Jarmuth and Socoh. Its site has not been ascertained, but Eusebius and Jerome mention it as lying to the east of Eleutheropolis. On the cave of Adullam, famous in David's history, see 1 Samuel xx, 1. **Turned in to**—Not "pitched his tent up to," or in the neighbourhood of, (*Keil,*) but, as the word is used in verse 16, and often elsewhere, in the sense of *turning aside unto.* What inclined him thus to turn in we are not told. It appears that once upon a time Judah, in passing down to Hebron, for some reason, accepted the hospitality of this Adullamite, and saw there a woman who so excited his love for her that he at once took her in marriage.

2. **A certain Canaanite** — This marriage with a Canaanitish woman was a source of many evils, and, to save his chosen people from complete affiliation with the heathen, and ruin from that cause, Jehovah brought them into Egypt, where years of bondage would prevent further contamination from them. **Shuah** — The father of Judah's wife. See verse 12.

5. **At Chezib**—Probably the same as Achzib, mentioned in Josh. xv, 44, and Micah i, 14. This was probably at the modern Kusaba, fifteen miles south-west of Beit-jibrin. This mention of her bearing Shelah at Chezib intimates that Er and Onan were born elsewhere. Judah at this time probably led a wandering life, and his being with his brethren at Dothan (xxxvii 26) does not involve, as Keil argues, that he was unmarried at that time.

7. **Er . . . was wicked**—In what particular forms he showed his wickedness we are not told; but being the son of a Canaanitish woman, he probably imbibed, in his earliest years, the spirit of Canaanitish idolatry and vice, which was ever an abomination to Je-

sight of the LORD; [1] and the LORD slew him. **8** And Judah said unto Onan, Go in unto [k] thy brother's wife, and marry her, and raise up seed to thy brother. **9** And Onan knew that the seed should not be [l] his; and it came to pass, when he went in unto his brother's wife, that he spilled *it* on the ground, lest that he should give seed to his brother. **10** And the thing which he did [l] displeased the LORD: wherefore he slew [m] him also. **11** Then said Judah to Tamar his daughter in law, [n] Remain a widow at thy father's house, till Shelah my son be grown; for he said, Lest peradventure he die also, as his brethren *did*. And Tamar went and dwelt [o] in her father's house.

12 And [2] in process of time the daughter of Shuah Judah's wife died; and Judah [p] was comforted, and went up unto his sheepshearers to Timnath, he and his friend Hirah the Adullamite. **13** And it was told Tamar, saying, Behold, thy father in law goeth up [q] to Timnath to shear his sheep. **14** And she put her widow's garments off from her, and covered her with a vail, and wrapped herself, and [r] sat in [3] an open place, which *is* by the way to Timnath; for she saw [s] that Shelah was grown, and she was not given unto him to wife. **15** When Judah saw her, he thought her *to be* a harlot; because she had covered her face. **16** And he turned unto her by the way, and said, Go to, I pray

---

i 1 Chron. 2. 3.——*k* Deut. 25. 5; Matt. 22. 24.——*l* Deut. 25. 6.——1 Heb. *was evil in the eyes of the LORD*.——*m* Chap. 46. 12; Num. 26. 19.——*n* Ruth 1. 13.——*o* Lev. 22. 13.

2 Heb. *the days were multiplied.*——*p* 2 Sam. 13. 39.——*q* Josh. 15. 10, 57; Judges 14. 1.——*r* Prov. 7. 12.——3 Heb. *the door of eyes*, or, *of Enajim.*——*s* Verses 11, 26.

---

hovah. **The Lord slew him**—Some sudden or fearful death that was recognised as a judgment stroke.

8. Seed to thy brother—Here is the first mention of levirate marriage. See our notes on Ruth, at the beginning of chapter iii. "The custom," says Keil, "is found in different forms among Indians, Persians, and other nations of Asia and Africa, and was not founded upon a divine command, but upon an ancient tradition, originating probably in Chaldea. It was not abolished, however, by the Mosaic law, (Deut. xxv, 5,) but only so far restricted as not to allow it to interfere with the sanctity of marriage; and with this limitation it was enjoined as a duty of affection to build up the brother's house, and to preserve his family and name."

11. Lest . . . he die also — Judah probably entertained some superstitious fear of Tamar, as if she were the cause of the death of his sons. Compare the story of Tobit. Chap. iii, 7. But it was their wickedness, not hers, which caused their sudden death.

12. Went up . . . to Timnath—Probably the Timnath of the Philistine valley, so famous in the history of Samson. Judg. xiv, 1. If so, it was at the modern Tibeh, and must have been some eight or ten miles north of Adullam. There was also another Timnath in the mountains of Judah. See Josh.

xv, 57. **His friend Hirah**—Comp. verse 1. Note how intimate Judah had become with the Canaanites.

14. In an open place—Rather, *at the entrance of Enajim*. This Enajim was probably the same as the *Enam* of Josh. xv, 35, which is mentioned in connexion with Jarmuth and Adullam. This act of Tamar reveals the shameful state of morals among the Canaanites, and furnishes also the occasion of showing the strength of Judah's sensuality, and his low life as compared with what we see in Joseph.

15. A harlot—The word here used is זוֹנָה, the common Hebrew word for harlot. But Judah's friend Hirah uses (verse 21) a different word, though our translators have rendered it just the same. There the Hebrew word is קְדֵשָׁה, *a consecrated woman*, that is, a woman consecrated to Astarte, the Canaanitish Venus; one who prostituted herself in the name of religion. Thus it appears that this abominable worship was at that time prevalent in Canaan, and Judah had become acquainted with its ways, though he did not call the woman thus devoted by the word that designated her as one sacred to Astarte. He regarded her as a prostitute, **because she had covered her face,** and he had come to know that this was the practice of women thus consecrated to lust. But to him she

About B.C.1727.   CHAPTER XXXVIII.   297

thee, let me come in unto thee; (for he knew not that she *was* his daughter in law:) and she said, What wilt thou give me, that thou mayest come in unto me? 17 And he said, 'I will send *thee* ⁴ a kid from the flock. And she said, ᵘ Wilt thou give *me* a pledge, till thou send *it?* 18 And he said, What pledge shall I give thee? And she said, ᵛ Thy signet, and thy bracelets, and thy staff that *is* in thine hand. And he gave *it* her, and came in unto her, and she conceived by him. 19 And she arose, and went away, and ʷ laid by her vail from her, and put on the garments of her widowhood. 20 And Judah sent the kid by the hand of his friend the Adullamite, to receive *his* pledge from the woman's hand: but he found her not. 21 Then he asked the men of that place, saying, Where *is* the harlot, that *was* ⁵ openly by the way side? And they said, There was no harlot in this *place*. 22 And he returned to Judah, and said, I cannot find her: and also the men of the place said, *that* there was no harlot in this *place*. 23 And Judah said, Let her take *it* to her, lest we ⁶ be shamed: behold, I sent this kid, and thou hast not found her.

24 And it came to pass about three months after, that it was told Judah, saying, Tamar thy daughter in law hath

ˣ played the harlot: and also, behold, she *is* with child by whoredom. And Judah said, Bring her forth, ʸ and let her be burnt. 25 When she *was* brought forth, she sent to her father in law, saying, By the man, whose these *are, am* I with child: and she said, ᶻ Discern, I pray thee, whose *are* these, ᵃ the signet, and bracelets, and staff. 26 And Judah ᵇ acknowledged *them*, and said, ᶜ She hath been more righteous than I; because that ᵈ I gave her not to Shelah my son. And he knew her again ᵉ no more.

27 And it came to pass in the time of her travail, that, behold, twins *were* in her womb. 28 And it came to pass, when she travailed, that *the one* put out *his* hand: and the midwife took and bound upon his hand a scarlet thread, saying, This came out first. 29 And it came to pass, as he drew back his hand, that, behold, his brother came out: and she said, ⁷ How hast thou broken forth? *this* breach *be* upon thee: therefore his name was called ⁸ ᶠ Pharez. 30 And afterward came out his brother, that had the scarlet thread upon his hand: and his name was called Zarah.

CHAPTER XXXIX.

AND Joseph was brought down to

t Ezek. 16. 33.——4 Heb. *a kid of the goats.*—— *u* Verse 20.——*v* Verse 25.——*w* Verse 14.——5 Or, *in Enajim.*——6 Heb. *become a contempt.*—— *x* Judg. 19. 2. —— *y* Lev. 21. 9; Deut. 22. 21. —— *z* Chap. 37. 32.——*a* Verse 18.

b Chap. 37. 33.——*c* 1 Sam. 24. 17.——*d* Verse 14.——*e* Job 34. 31, 32.——7 Or, *Wherefore hast thou made* this *breach against thee?* —— 8 That is, *A breach.*——*f* Chap. 46. 12; Num. 26. 20; 1 Chron. 2. 4; Matt. 1. 3.

was only a harlot, while to his friend she was supposed to be a′*kedeshah*.

18. **Signet . . . bracelets** — These were probably a signet ring, suspended on a cord or band, (פְּתִיל,) not bracelet, and worn upon the neck. So say Gesenius and Keil.

21. **Openly by the wayside**—Rather, *at Enajim on the way.* See on verse 14.

23. **Let her take it to her**—That *is*, let her keep what she has obtained. He feared the *shame*, contempt, and ridicule, which he would incur by further attempts to recover his signet and cord, and preferred to lose them.

24. **Let her be burnt**—How ready, like David, (2 Sam. xii, 5,) to condemn before he knows his own share of the guilt and shame! His words evidence the existence of a law of severest punishment for one guilty of such sins long before the law of Moses on the subject. Comp. Lev. xxi. 9; Deut. xx, 21–24.

26. **More righteous than I**—"Judah not only saw his guilt, but he confessed it also, and showed, both by this confession and also by the fact that he had no further conjugal intercourse with Tamar, an earnest endeavour to conquer the lusts of the flesh, and to guard against the sin into which he had fallen. And because he thus humbled himself, God gave him grace, and not only exalted him to be the chief of the house of Israel, but blessed the children that were begotten in sin."—*Keil*.

CHAPTER XXXIX.

JOSEPH IN SLAVERY AND IN PRISON, 1–23.

1. **Down to Egypt**—"Down from the Syrian Plains to the Desert, and down the Desert to the Nile Valley.

Egypt; and *Potiphar, an officer of Pharaoh, captain of the guard, an Egyptian, b bought him of the hands of the Ishmaelites, which had brought him

a Chapter 37. 36; Psalm 105. 17.—*b* Chapter 37. 28.

The life of the chosen family now mingles for centuries with the stream of Egyptian civilization. The saviour of the Hebrew people, like his divine antitype, was to descend to the lowest depths that he might rise to the loftiest heights. 'Down into Egypt,' was down to the darkness of infamy also, in the estimation of men, where God was his solitary stay when utterly cut off from the sympathy of men, as the reward of virtue too high for them to see; yet up from that dungeon he was lifted to worldwide honour, sympathy, and love. **Potiphar**—This **officer of Pharaoh** (see xxxvii, 36) is not to be confounded with the Poti-pherah priest of On, or Heliopolis, whose daughter Joseph afterwards married. Chap. xli, 45. The name seems to have been a common one in Egypt, since it is found very often written in hieroglyphics upon the monuments. The ancient Egyptian form of the name in the hieroglyphic inscriptions is PET-P-RA or PET-PH-RA, which signifies 'belonging to the sun.' GES., *Thesaur.* RA or RE, (with the article PRA or PhRA,) the SUN, was one of the great Egyptian gods, father of many deities, and is represented in the monuments by a circle with a dot in the centre, sometimes enveloped in the coil of a serpent, sometimes accompanied by a hawk. Poole, in *Encyc. Brit.* The name Pharaoh is derived from *Phrah*, since the Egyptian king was regarded as the representative of the sun. RAWL., *Herodotus*, ii, p. 241.

"It is generally supposed by the Egyptologists that Joseph was sold into Egypt during the reign of the 'shepherd kings,' (Hyksos,) a foreign dynasty who invaded the country from the north, (although their origin and race is as yet uncertain,) dispossessed the native kings of Lower Egypt, and held dominion there, perhaps five or six centuries, when they were driven out by a native dynasty. This alien line of kings maintained itself with

down thither. 2 And *c* the LORD was with Joseph, and he was a prosperous man; and he was in the house of his master the Egyptian. 3 And his master

c Verse 21; chap. 21. 22; 26. 24, 28; 28. 15; 1 Sam. 16. 18; 18. 14, 28; Acts 7. 9.

difficulty against the native princes who still held Upper Egypt, being hated by the Egyptian people, and ever ready therefore to form alliances with foreigners. The native Egyptians, on the other hand, were remarkably exclusive, having strong prejudices, and even hatred and contempt, for foreigners. The monumental literature of Egypt shows this intense antipathy to foreigners in a thousand forms. The wonderful and more than romantic history of Joseph could not have taken place under the native Pharaohs. A foreigner could not, under the native Egyptian rule, have been elevated to the second place of authority, nor could families of foreigners have been welcomed, as were the families of Israel, to settle in the kingdom. Poole, in *Smith's Dict.* Here, then, in this Hyksos invasion and possession of Egypt during the time that the three great patriarchs were roaming through Palestine, we find a providential preparation for the Egyptian period of the history of the chosen people. Not only was 'the Lord with Joseph' after his arrival at Potiphar's house, but he had long before prepared the kingdom for him."—*Newhall.*

2. **The Lord was with Joseph**—The holy covenant God of Israel was not absent from his faithful servant. He ever encampeth round about them that fear him. **A prosperous man**—Making to prosper whatever he undertook. Compare the Psalmist's description of the blessed or happy man. Psa. i, 3. **He was in the house of his master**—First as a house-servant, then overseer of all his possessions. Verses 4–6. Potiphar quickly discerned Joseph's integrity and pious attention to all his affairs. He probably did not concern himself about the religious ideas of his slave, or learn from him any special doctrines of Jehovah. He doubtless adhered to his own Egyptian idolatries. But in verses 2-6 the sacred historian shows that the integrity and

B. C. 1729. CHAPTER XXXIX. 299

saw that the LORD was with him, and that the LORD ᵈ made all that he did to prosper in his hand. **4** And Joseph ᵉ found grace in his sight, and he served him: and he made him ᶠ overseer over his house, and all *that* he had he put into his hand. **5** And it came to pass from the time *that* he had made him overseer in his house, and over all that he had, that ᵍ the LORD blessed the Egyptian's house for Joseph's sake; and the blessing of the LORD was upon all that he had in the house, and in the field. **6** And he left all that he had in Joseph's hand; and he knew not aught he had, save the bread which he did eat. And Joseph ʰ was a goodly person, and well favoured.
7 And it came to pass after these things, that his master's wife cast her eyes upon Joseph; and she said, ⁱ Lie with me. **8** But he refused, and said unto his master's wife, Behold, my master wotteth not what *is* with me in the house, and he hath committed all that he hath to my hand; **9** There *is* none greater in this house than I; neither hath he kept back any thing from me but thee, because thou *art* his wife: ᵏ how then can I do this great wickedness, and ˡ sin against God? **10** And it came to pass, as she spake to Joseph day by day, that he hearkened not unto her, to lie by her, *or* to be with her. **11** And it came to pass about this time, that *Joseph* went into the house to do his business; and *there was* none of the men of the house there within. **12** And ᵐ she caught him by his garment, saying, Lie with me: and he left his garment in her hand, and fled, and got him out. **13** And it came to pass, when she saw that he had left his garment in her hand, and was fled forth, **14** That she called unto the men of her house, and spake

---

ᵈ Psa. 1. 3. —— ᵉ Chap. 18. 3; 19. 19; verse 21. —ᶠ Chap. 24. 2.—ᵍ Chap. 30. 27.—ʰ 1 Sam. 16. 12.

ⁱ 2 Sam. 13. 11.——ᵏ Prov. 6. 29, 32.——ˡ Chap. 20. 6; Lev. 6. 2; 2 Sam. 12. 13; Psa. 51. 4.—— ᵐ Prov. 7. 13, etc.

---

prosperity of Joseph were due to the divine providence which favoured the faithful son of Israel.

"The great pictures of Egyptian civilization which are found in the monumental sepulchres, abound in representations of overseership in the house and in the field. Workmen are represented as engaged in various kinds of labour, such as gardening, farming, fishing, while the overseer watches and directs, and keeps the record of the work with a reed pen in a papyrus register. Division and subdivision of labour, and minute supervision, had at this time been carried to a high degree in this home of science and civilization. Great native talent as well as integrity is displayed in this sudden rise of a shepherd-lad, sold as a slave into such a land as Egypt. We see here unmistakable signs of superior abilities, which serve to explain the previous envy of his brethren. A man so clearly born to command must have displayed something of his power and the natural bent of his genius in early youth."— *Newhall.*

7. Cast her eyes upon Joseph— Having briefly but impressively explained how Joseph became exalted in the house of his Egyptian master, and now Potiphar trusted every thing to his management; also having, at the close of verse 6, mentioned the great personal beauty of the Hebrew slave, the writer has prepared us to understand the power of the great temptation which came to Joseph. The licentiousness of Egyptian women is evidenced by numerous testimonies. The monuments, as well as ancient writers, show that they did not live the secluded life to which the women of other eastern nations were compelled. See Wilkinson, *Ancient Egypt,* vol. i, p. 144 ; vol. ii, p. 224. An Egyptian papyrus in the British Museum relates the story of two brothers, the wife of the elder of whom acts and speaks toward the younger almost in the same words that Potiphar's wife used with Joseph. See Ebers, *Egypten,* p. 311.

9. This great wickedness — Joseph's answer is most noble. He sees and shows the monstrous criminality of thus abusing his master's confidence; it would be a double sin, **wickedness against Potiphar, sin against God.**

11. About this time—The time, or day, definite in the writer's mind as that on which this event occurred.

14. She called unto the men of her house—To other men-servants, who were under Joseph's oversight. Like the evil woman of all times and

unto them, saying, See, he hath brought in a Hebrew unto us to mock us; he came in unto me to lie with me, and I cried with a ¹ loud voice: **15** And it came to pass, when he heard that I lifted up my voice and cried, that he left his garment with me, and fled, and got him out. **16** And she laid up his garment by her, until his lord came home. **17** And she ⁿ spake unto him according to these words, saying, The Hebrew servant, which thou hast brought unto us, came in unto me to mock me: **18** And it came to pass, as I lifted up my voice and cried, that he left his garment with me, and fled out. **19** And it came to pass, when his master heard the words of his wife, which she spake unto him, saying, After this manner did thy servant to me; that his ᵒ wrath was kindled. **20** And Joseph's master took him, and ᵖ put him into the ᑫ prison, a place where the king's prisoners *were* bound: and he was there in the prison.

21 But the LORD was with Joseph, and ² showed him mercy, and ʳ gave him favour in the sight of the keeper of the prison. **22** And the keeper of the prison ˢ committed to Joseph's hand all the prisoners that *were* in the prison; and whatsoever they did there, he was the doer *of it.* **23** The keeper of the prison looked not to any thing *that was* under his hand; because ᵗ the LORD was with him, and *that* which he did, the LORD made *it* to prosper.

1 Heb. *great.*——n Exod. 23. 1; Psa. 120. 3.—— o Prov. 6. 34, 35.——p Psa. 105. 18; 1 Peter 2. 19. —— q See Chap. 40. 3, 15; 41. 14. —— 2 Heb. *ex-* *tended kindness unto him.*——r Exod. 3. 21; 11. 3; 12. 36; Psa. 106. 46; Prov. 16. 7; Dan. 1. 9; Acts 7. 9, 10.——s Chap. 40. 3, 4.——t Verses 2, 3.

nations, she was quick to ruin the man who would not follow her desires. She seeks first to make the men-servants witnesses in the case, and then waits until her husband's return to repeat the same abominable falsehood to him. Verses 16–18. The story of Potiphar's wife, whose traditional name is Zuleekha, is told with much amplification by Josephus, (*Ant.*, book ii, chap. iv,) and in Oriental romance. The Koran relates it in that chapter (xii) to which Mohammed appealed as bearing the manifest signs of inspiration.

20. **Put him into the prison**—Or, *house of the round tower,* "the fortified house where the king's prisoners were guarded. A very light punishment, considering the severity of the Egyptian laws, apparently showing that it was inflicted rather to save his wife's reputation than to punish Joseph. (Le Clerc.) There is no evidence that Joseph attempted to vindicate himself. Indeed, it would have been useless. It was one of those fearful trials which shut the righteous man up to a single course, namely, to suffer, and wait in faith."—*Newhall.*

21. **The Lord was with Joseph**— "Jehovah is with him in the prison as well as in the house of Potiphar, and he wins the confidence of his new master, the jailer, as completely as he did that of Potiphar. Amid allurements and enticements, and amid degradation and suffering, in honour and dishonour, Joseph's faith and integrity shine on the same. Unlike his father Jacob, or even his great-grandfather Abraham, Joseph is never seen to slip into temptation. He reveals the most steady and uniform faith, and on the whole the best-balanced character that we find in the patriarchal age. Especially is Joseph a remarkable example of youthful piety. In fact, while Abraham lives as a hoary sage in our imagination, Joseph rises before us ever in the beauty and freshness of youth. At the age of seventeen he exchanged the simple pastoral life of Palestine, with its tents and pastures and sheepfolds, for the massive cities and luxurious splendours of Egyptian civilization; the rude altars of Beth-el and Beer-sheba for the bewildering grandeur of temples which fill the soul with awe to-day; yet he never forgot the God of his fathers, and to the law of that God he clung, not only in obedience, but in love, when to disobey would seem to have been the dictate of every worldly interest. He came to that land a slave, and friendless, yet by the simple force of character he rose to be next to Pharaoh. This is moral greatness and grandeur."—*Newhall.*

CHAPTER XL.

DREAMS OF THE BUTLER AND OF THE BAKER, 1–23.

While the narrative of this chapter contains little that needs explanation,

CHAPTER XL.

AND it came to pass after these things, that the ᵃ butler of the king of Egypt and his baker had offended their lord the king of Egypt. 2 And Pharaoh was ᵇ wroth against two of his officers, against the chief of the butlers, and against the chief of the bakers. 3 ᶜAnd he put them in ward in the house of the captain of the guard, into the prison, the place where Joseph was bound. 4 And the captain of the guard charged Joseph with them, and he served them: and they continued a season in ward.

5 And they dreamed a dream both of them, each man his dream in one night, each man according to the interpretation of his dream, the butler and the baker of the king of Egypt, which were bound in the prison. 6 And Joseph came in unto them in the morning, and looked upon them, and, behold, they were sad. 7 And he asked Pharaoh's officers that were with him in the ward of his lord's house, saying, Wherefore ¹ look ye so sadly to-day? 8 And they said unto him, ᵈ We have dreamed a dream, and there is no interpreter of it. And Joseph said unto them, ᵉ Do not interpretations belong to God? tell me them, I pray you. 9 And the chief butler told his dream to Joseph, and said to him, In my dream, behold, a vine was before me; 10 And in the vine were three branches: and it was as though it budded, and her blossoms shot forth ; and the clusters thereof brought forth ripe grapes : 11 And Pharaoh's cup was in my hand : and I took the grapes, and pressed them into Pharaoh's cup, and I gave the cup into Pharaoh's hand. 12 And Joseph said unto him, ᶠ This is the interpretation of it: The three branches ᵍ are three days : 13 Yet within three days shall Pharaoh

---

ᵃ Neh. 1. 11.——ᵇ Prov. 16. 14.——ᶜ Chap. 39. 20, 23.——1 Heb. are your faces evil? Neh. 2. 2. ——ᵈ Chap. 41. 15.

ᵉ See chap. 41. 16 ; Dan. 2. 11, 28, 47.——ᶠ Verse 18 ; chap. 41. 12, 25 ; Judg. 7. 14 ; Dan. 2. 36 ; 4. 19. ——ᵍ Chap. 41. 26.

---

the reader should note the following : 1) The manifold service and attendance of an Oriental despot. 2) His many fears, suspicions, and dangers. 3) The insecurity of the lives of his subjects, liable at any moment to be cut off in a fit of anger or caprice. 4) The occasional impressiveness and significance of dreams. 5) The righteous useful in prison. 6) Culpable forgetfulness of kindness.

1. **After these things**—After Joseph had been imprisoned, and had found favour with the keeper. **The butler**—Or, cup-bearer. He was the officer who had charge of the king's wines ; and so important was this office that the chief or prince of the butlers (verse 2) found it necessary to employ the services of many others in this business. How the butler was **offended** we are not told ; the Targum of Jonathan says "they had taken counsel to throw the poison of death into his food and into his drink, to kill their master." These officers would be especially subject to such suspicions.

3. **Captain of the guard**—Or, chief of the executioners, whose dwelling was within a part of the prison.

4. **Charged Joseph with them**—Being royal officers, it would be natural to charge a Hebrew slave to serve them, though he had charge of all the prison. Chap. xxxix, 22.

5. **Each man...according to the interpretation**—That is, each man's dream, as the sequel shows, corresponded with its particular significance.

8. **Do not interpretations belong to God**—He who had been visited with prophetic dreams in childhood, (chap. xxxvii, 5, 9,) believed that God alone could interpret them. Comp. chap. xli, 16, 25, 32. In his imprisonment and loneliness he might well have despaired of any fulfilling of his own dreams, but he trusts in God.

9. **Behold, a vine**—Notably the butler dreams of vines, and the baker of the food (verse 17) he was wont to prepare for the king. "Herodotus denies the existence of vines in ancient Egypt, and says that the Egyptian wine was made of barley. Chap. ii, 77. Yet Herodotus himself, (ii, 42, xlviii, 144,) and Diodorus, (i, 11,) identify Osiris with the Greek Bacchus, the discoverer of the vine, and Diodorus (i, 15) expressly ascribes to Osiris the first cultivation of the vine. But it now appears from the monuments, that both the cultivation of grapes and the art of making wine were well known in Egypt from the time of the Pyramids."—*Speaker's Commentary.*

VOL. I.—20

O. T.

lift² up ʰ thine head, and restore thee unto thy place; and thou shalt deliver Pharaoh's cup into his hand, after the former manner when thou wast his butler. 14 But ³¹ think on me when it shall be well with thee, and ᵏ show kindness, I pray thee, unto me, and make mention of me unto Pharaoh, and bring me out of this house: 15 For indeed I was stolen away out of the land of the Hebrews: ˡ and here also have I done nothing that they should put me into the dungeon. 16 When the chief baker saw that the interpretation was good, he said unto Joseph, I also *was* in my dream, and, behold, *I had* three ⁴ white baskets on my head: 17 And in the uppermost basket *there was* of all manner of ⁵ bakemeats for Pharaoh; and the birds did eat them out of the basket upon my head. 18 And Joseph answered and said, ᵐ This *is* the interpretation there-

² Or, *reckon.* —— *h* 2 Kings 25. 27; Psa. 3. 3; Jer. 52. 31.——3 Heb. *remember me with thee.* ——*i* Luke 23. 42.——*k* Josh. 2. 12; 1 Sam. 20. 14, 15; 2 Sam. 9. 1; 1 Kings 2. 7. —— *l* Chap. 39, 20. ——4 Or, *full of holes.*——5 Heb. *meat of Pharaoh, the work of a baker,* or, *cook.*

13. **Lift up thine head**—Lift it up from its present degradation in prison and in sadness. Comp. verse 19, note.

14. **Think on me**—Here we note how Joseph longs for liberty.

15. **I was stolen away**—Heb., *for stolen, stolen was I.* Joseph nowhere tells the manner of his being taken away from his home and kindred; he does not accuse his brethren, notwithstanding all their guilt. **Land of the Hebrews**—At that date probably the land of Canaan was so called among Egyptians, and Jacob's family then looked upon it as peculiarly their own. Comp. chap. xxxv, 12.

16. **Three white baskets**—Rather,

EGYPTIAN BAKER CARRYING CAKES.

of: The three baskets *are* three days: 19 ⁿ Yet within three days shall Pharaoh ⁶ lift up thy head from off thee, and shall hang thee on a tree; and the birds shall eat thy flesh from off thee.

20 And it came to pass the third day, *which was* Pharaoh's ᵒ birthday, that he ᵖ made a feast unto all his servants: and he ⁷ ᑫ lifted up the head of the chief butler and of the chief baker among his servants. 21 And he ʳ restored the chief butler unto his butlership again; and ˢ he gave the cup into Pharaoh's hand: 22 But he ᵗ hanged the chief baker: as Joseph had interpreted to them. 23 Yet did not the chief butler remember Joseph, but ᵘ forgat him.

CHAPTER XLI.

AND it came to pass at the end of two full years, that Pharaoh dreamed: and, behold, he stood by the river.

m Verse 12. —— *n* Verse 13. —— 6 Or, *reckon thee,* and take thy office *from thee,*——*o* Matt. 14. 16,——*p* Mark 6. 21. —— 7 Or, *reckoned.* —— *q* Verses 13, 19; Matt. 25. 19. —— *r* Verse 13. —— *s* Neh. 2. 1.——*t* Verse 19.——*u* Job 19. 14; Psa. 31. 12; Eccles. 9. 15, 16; Amos 6. 6.

three baskets of white bread. **On my head**—The monuments illustrate this method of carrying baskets in ancient Egypt.

17. **Bakemeats**—Heb., *food of Pharaoh, the work of a baker.* Thus his dream, like the butler's, ran into the imagery with which he was most familiar. **Birds did eat**—Herein was what might be called "the bad sign" in the dream. The butler himself took the grapes which he saw in his dream, (verse 11,) but the birds eat of the bread on the head of the baker—sign that they should eat his flesh. Ver. 19.

19. **Lift up thy head from off thee**—A peculiar play on words; but the addition, **from off thee**, gives the sense as distinguished from that in verse 13. The victim was first beheaded, and afterwards hung, or impaled.

CHAPTER XLI.

THE DREAMS OF PHARAOH, 1–8.

1. **Two full years**—Heb., *two years of days.* Comp. chap. xxix, 14. This may mean two years from the date of Joseph's imprisonment, or from the date of the butler's release. More naturally it would mean the latter, as being the thing last mentioned. **The**

CHAPTER XLI.

2 And, behold, there came up out of the river seven well favoured kine and fatfleshed; and they fed in a meadow. 3 And, behold, seven other kine came up after them out of the river, ill favoured and leanfleshed; and stood by the *other* kine upon the brink of the river. 4 And the ill favoured and leanfleshed kine did eat up the seven well favoured and fat kine. So Pharaoh awoke. 5 And he slept and dreamed the second time: and, behold, seven ears of corn came up upon one stalk, ¹ rank and good. 6 And, behold, seven thin ears and blasted with the east wind sprung up after them. 7 And the seven thin ears devoured the seven rank and full ears. And Pharaoh awoke, and, behold, *it was* a dream. 8 And it came to pass in the morning ª that his spirit was troubled; and he sent and called for all ᵇ the magicians of Egypt, and all the ᶜ wise men thereof: and Pharaoh told them his dream; but *there was* none that could interpret them unto Pharaoh. 9 Then spake the chief butler unto Pharaoh, saying, I do remember my faults this day: 10 Pharaoh was ᵈ wroth with his servants, ᵉ and put me in ward in the captain of the guard's house, *both* me and the chief baker: 11 And ᶠ we dreamed a dream in one night, I and he; we dreamed each man according to the interpretation of his dream. 12 And *there was* there with us a young man, a Hebrew, ᵍ servant to the captain of the guard; and we told him, and he ʰ interpreted to us our dreams; to each man according to his dream he did interpret. 13 And it came to pass, ⁱ as he interpreted to us, so it was; me he restored unto mine office, and him he hanged.

1 Heb. *fat.*—*a* Dan. 2. 1; 4. 5, 19.—*b* Exod. 7. 11, 23; Isa. 29. 14; Dan. 1. 20; 2. 2; 4. 7.— *c* Matt. 2. 1.

d Chap. 40. 2, 3.—*e* Chap. 39. 20.—*f* Chap. 40. 5.—*g* Chap. 37. 36.—*h* Chap. 40. 12, etc. —*i* Chap. 40. 22.

river—Heb., הַיְאֹר, *the yeôr*, an Egyptian word, and used in the Pentateuch always of the Nile. It was suitable that the dream-vision of Pharaoh should be associated with the sacred river, which was to Egypt the source of fertility and life.

2. **Seven well favoured kine**—Heb., *seven heifers beautiful in appearance.* "The Egyptians esteemed the cow above all other animals. It was sacred to Isis, (Herod. ii, 41,) or rather to Athor, the Venus Genetrix of Egypt, and was looked on as a symbol of the earth and its cultivation and food. Hence it was very natural that in Pharaoh's dream the fruitful and unfruitful years should be typified by well favoured and ill favoured kine."—*Speaker's Com.*

In a meadow—Rather, *in the marsh grass*, (אָחוּ.) The word is of Egyptian origin, and signifies, according to Gesenius, "*marsh-grass, reeds, bulrushes, sedge*, every thing which grows in wet grounds. The word was adopted not only into the Hebrew, but also into the Greek idiom of Alexandria." The Sept. does not translate the word, but reads, ἐν τῷ ἄχει.

6. **Blasted with the east wind**—The south-east wind, known as the Chamsin, which comes from the Arabian desert and blights all that it touches. These incidental notices of facts peculiar to Egypt evince the genuineness of this narrative.

8. **Spirit was troubled**—The dream was sent of God, and designed to impress him deeply, that it might lead to the great provisions which followed. Compare the effect of Nebuchadnezzar's dream. Dan. ii, 1, 3. **All the magicians of Egypt**—Of whom there were many, and they very skilful. Comp. Exod. vii, 11. The word rendered **magicians** (חַרְטֻמִּים) is usually understood of the sacred scribes, who were supposed to be conversant with all mystic arts, and able to unravel the secrets of men's lives. **Wise men**—A more general term, denoting all those who were devoted to the study of science or philosophy. All these belonged to a regular order in Egypt, as in other Oriental kingdoms. Comp. Dan. ii, 2, 48; iv, 9; v, 11.

JOSEPH INTERPRETS PHARAOH'S DREAMS, 9–36.

9. **My faults**—The sins which caused his imprisonment. The recital of the king's dreams, and the inability of all the wise men to interpret them, cause the butler to remember his offences, his imprisonment, his dream, and all connected with it.

GENESIS. B. C. 1715.

14 ᵏ Then Pharaoh sent and called Joseph, and they ¹ ² brought him hastily ᵐ out of the dungeon: and he shaved *himself*, and changed his raiment, and came in unto Pharaoh. 15 And Pharaoh said unto Joseph, I have dreamed a dream, and *there is* none that can interpret it: ⁿ and I have heard say of thee, *that* ³ thou canst understand a dream to interpret it. 16 And Joseph answered Pharaoh, saying, ᵒ *It is* not in me: ᵖ God shall give Pharaoh an answer of peace. 17 And Pharaoh said unto Joseph, ᵍ In my dream, behold, I stood upon the bank of the river: 18 And, behold, there came up out of the river seven kine, fatfleshed and well favoured; and they fed in a meadow: 19 And, behold, seven other kine came up after them, poor and very ill favoured and leanfleshed, such as I never saw in all the land of Egypt for badness: 20 And the lean and the ill favoured kine did eat up the first seven fat kine: 21 And when they had ⁴ eaten them up, it could not be known that they had eaten them; but they *were* still ill favoured, as at the beginning. So I awoke. 22 And I saw in my dream, and, behold, seven ears came up in one stalk, full and good: 23 And, behold, seven ears, ⁵ withered, thin, *and* blasted with the east wind, sprung up after them: 24 And the thin ears devoured the seven good ears: and ʳ I told *this* unto the magicians; but *there was* none that could declare *it* to me.

25 And Joseph said unto Pharaoh, The dream of Pharaoh *is* one: ˢ God hath showed Pharaoh what he *is* about to do. 26 The seven good kine *are* seven years; and the seven good ears *are* seven years: the dream *is* one. 27 And the seven thin and ill favoured kine that came up after them *are* seven years; and the seven empty ears blasted with the east wind shall be ᵗ seven years of famine. 28 ᵘ This *is* the thing which I have spoken unto Pharaoh: What God *is* about to do he showeth unto Pharaoh. 29 Behold, there come ᵛ seven years of great plenty throughout all the land of Egypt: 30 And there shall ʷ arise after them seven years of famine; and all the plenty shall be forgotten in the land of Egypt; and the famine ˣ shall consume the land; 31 And the plenty shall not be known in the land by reason of that famine following; for it *shall be* very ⁶ grievous. 32 And for that the dream was doubled unto Pharaoh twice; *it is* because the ʸ thing *is* ⁷ established by God, and God will shortly bring it to

---

k Psa. 105. 20.——*l* Dan. 2. 25.——2 Heb. *made him run.*——*m* 1 Sam. 2. 8; Psa. 113. 7, 8.——*n* Verse 12; Psa. 25. 14; Dan. 5. 16.——3 Or, when *thou hearest a dream thou canst interpret it.*——*o* Dan. 2. 30; Acts 3. 12; 2 Cor. 3. 5.——*p* Chap. 40. 8; Dan. 2. 22, 28, 47; 4. 2.——*q* Verse 1.

4 Heb. *come to the inward parts of them.*—— 5 Or, *small.* —— *r* Verse 8; Dan. 4. 7. —— *s* Dan. 2. 28, 29, 45; Rev. 4. 1. —— *t* 2 Kings 8. 1. —— *u* Verse 25.——*v* Verse 47.——*w* Verse 54. —— *x* Chap. 47. 13.——6 Heb. *heavy.*——*y* Num. 23. 19; Isa. 46. 10, 11.——7 Or, *prepared of God.*

---

14. **Brought him hastily**—Heb., *caused him to run.* Every thing was excitement about the royal household that day, and hence the haste. **Shaved** —According to Herodotus (ii, 36) the Egyptians never allowed their beards to grow, except while mourning for deceased relatives. The most recent researches into Egyptian archæology confirm this statement. In order, therefore, to conform to the Egyptian ideas of propriety, Joseph was shaved in order to be presentable at the royal court.

15. **Thou canst understand**—Literally, *thou hearest a dream to interpret it.*

16. **God shall give . . . peace**—Literally, *God shall answer the peace of Pharaoh.* Joseph emphatically points out the divine and supernatural aspect of the dreams, and takes no glory to himself.

25. **The dream . . . is one**—That is, the two dreams are really but one dream, and convey one great prophecy.

God hath showed—The Hebrew here and in verses 28 and 32 has the article before the name God. It is *the one true God* who thus graciously foretells to Pharaoh what he is about to do.

32. **The dream was doubled unto Pharaoh twice**—Here is incidentally given a principle of interpretation which may be profitable in the interpretation of prophecy. As God repeated the dream to Pharaoh under different symbols, so he gave through his prophets under various symbols the ideas of things that were future. So Nebuchadnezzar's dream and Daniel's vision of the beasts (Dan. ii, vii) were one. So, doubtless, in the Apocalypse, many of the symbols, which have been explained as chronological and consecutive, are but different foreshadowings of the same thing. The repetition is but to show that **the thing is established by God**, and at the same

B. C. 1715. CHAPTER XLI. 305

pass. **33** Now therefore let Pharaoh look out a man discreet and wise, and set him over the land of Egypt. **34** Let Pharaoh do *this*, and let him appoint ⁸ officers over the land, and ᶻ take up the fifth part of the land of Egypt in the seven plenteous years. **35** And ᵃ let them gather all the food of those good years that come, and lay up corn under the hand of Pharaoh, and let them keep food in the cities. **36** And that food shall be for store to the land against the seven years of famine, which shall be in the land of Egypt; that the land ᵍᵇ perish not through the famine.

37 And ᶜ the thing was good in the eyes of Pharaoh, and in the eyes of all his servants. **38** And Pharaoh said unto his servants, Can we find *such a one* as this *is*, a man ᵈ in whom the Spirit of God *is?* **39** And Pharaoh said unto Joseph, Forasmuch as God hath showed thee all this, *there is* none so discreet and wise as thou *art:* **40** ᵉ Thou shalt be over my house, and according unto thy word shall all my people ¹⁰ be ruled: only in the throne will I be greater than thou. **41** And Pharaoh said unto Joseph, See, I have ᶠ set thee over all the land of Egypt. **42** And Pharaoh ᵍ took off his ring from his hand, and put it upon Joseph's hand, and ʰ arrayed him in vestures of ¹¹ fine linen, ⁱ and put a gold chain about his neck; **43** And he

---

⁸ Or, *overseers.*—ᶻ Prov. 6. 6, 7, 8.—ᵃ Verse 48.—⁹ Heb. *be not cut off.*—ᵇ Chap. 47. 15, 19.—ᶜ Psa. 105. 19; Acts 7. 10.—ᵈ Num. 27. 18; Job 32. 8; Prov. 2. 6; Dan. 4. 8, 18; 5.

11, 14; 6. 3. — ᵉ Psa. 105. 21, 22; Acts 7. 10. — 10 Heb. *be armed*, or, *kiss.* —ᶠ Dan. 6. 3.— ᵍ Esther 3. 10; 8. 2, 8.—ʰ Esther 8. 15.—11 Or, *silk.*—ⁱ Dan. 5. 7, 29.

---

time to deepen and intensify the impression.

33. Now therefore let Pharaoh—"Joseph now naturally passes from the interpreter to the adviser. He is all himself on this critical occasion. His presence of mind never forsakes him. The openness of heart and readiness of speech for which he was early distinguished, now stand him in good stead. His thorough self-command arises from spontaneously throwing himself with all his heart into the great national emergency which is before his mind. And his native simplicity of heart, practical good sense, and force of character, break forth into unasked but not unaccepted counsel."—*Murphy.*

34. Take up the fifth part—Heb., *let him fifth the land of Egypt.* Perhaps tithing the produce of the land for the king was already in practice, but Joseph advises that one-fifth of their annual produce be set apart, and saved for the time of famine.

36. That the land perish not—That is, the inhabitants of the land.

JOSEPH MADE OVERSEER OF EGYPT, 37–57.

38. In whom the Spirit of God is—Pharaoh recognises the message as from God, and Joseph as a man inspired by the Holy One.

40. According unto thy word shall all my people be ruled—This gives the general sense, and is substantially that of the ancient versions; but the word rendered **ruled** is the ordinary word for *kissing,* and modern exegetes disagree as to its meaning. Gesenius renders: *Upon thy mouth shall all my people kiss.* So also Knobel and Fürst. Allusion would thus be made to the custom of expressing homage by throwing a kiss. Keil, however, denies that this was a customary form of showing homage, and takes the word נָשַׁק in the sense of disposing or arranging one's self: *Accordimg to thy mouth* (that is, thy command, xlv, 21) *shall my whole people arrange itself.* The primary signification of נָשַׁק seems to be that of *hanging upon* or *cleaving unto,* (see Fürst, Lex.,) and perhaps the simpler meaning here is: *upon thy mouth* (that is, word of command) *shall all my people hang.* That is, they will cleave to thy orders and all thy utterances with the greatest respect and reverence. **Only in the throne**—Joseph is made the grand vizier, but Pharaoh retains all his essential royalty and kingly prerogatives.

42. Ring . . . fine linen . . . gold chain—"Great importance was attached to the signet ring, which contained the owner's name, and the impression of which was of the same validity as a written signature is among us. Hence the gift of this royal signet ring was a transfer of royal authority to Joseph. Thus Ahasuerus gave his ring to Haman, and the document

GENESIS. B. C. 1715.

made him to ride in the second chariot which he had; *k* and they cried before him, ¹² ¹³ Bow the knee: and he made him *ruler* ¹ over all the land of Egypt. **44** And Pharaoh said unto Joseph, I am Pharaoh, and without thee shall no man lift up his hand or foot in all the land of Egypt. **45** And Pharaoh called Joseph's name ¹⁴ Zaphnath-paaneah; and he gave him to wife Asenath the daugh-

---

k Esther 6, 9.——12 Or, *Tender father*, chap. 45, 8.——13 Heb. *Abrech*.——*l* Chap. 42, 6; 45, 8, 26; Acts 7, 10.

14 Which in the Coptic signifies, *A revealer of secrets*, or, *The man to whom secrets are revealed*.

---

which Haman signed with it was considered as coming from the king. Esther iii, 10–12. The same ring was afterwards given to Mordecai, who used it in the same way. Esther viii, 2, 8, 10. The value and importance attached to the signet ring are referred to in Jeremiah xxii, 24, and in Haggai ii, 23.

RINGS AND SIGNETS.

Some valuable specimens of ancient signet rings have been found by antiquarians. One of the most remarkable of these is now in the Abbott Collection of Egyptian Antiquities, in the Museum of the New York Historical Society. It is in most excellent preservation and of very high antiquity, bearing the name of Shoofoo, the Suphis of the Greeks, who reigned before the time of Joseph. It was found in a tomb at Ghizeh, and is of fine gold, weighing nearly three sovereigns. The fine (or, literally, *white*) linen robes were worn by the Egyptian priests, which fact has given some occasion to think that Joseph was received into the caste of priests, which was of the highest rank in Egypt, as it was the one to which the king himself belonged. The gold chain was another mark of distinction, since none but persons of high rank were permitted to wear such ornaments. There is in the Abbott Collection a gold necklace which has on it the name of Menes, the first Pharaoh of Egypt, and who reigned several hundred years before Shoofoo. The necklace has a pair of earrings to match. The signet and the necklace are, no doubt, similar in general appearance to those with which Joseph was invested." —FREEMAN's *Hand-Book of Bible Manners and Customs*.

43. **Second chariot** — Probably meaning the chariot second in majesty and splendour to that in which the king himself rode. In royal procession, Joseph would thus ride in the chariot which followed next after the king. **Bow the knee**—אַבְרֵךְ. This seems to be equivalent to הַבְרֵךְ, the Hiphil imperative of the Hebrew בָּרַךְ, but most critics regard it as an Egyptian word. The Sept. renders it by κῆρυξ, *herald;* the Targum makes it equivalent to אָב־רַךְ, *tender father;* Syriac, *father and ruler*. Gesenius suggests, that though the word be of Egyptian origin, the Hebrew writer so changed and inflected it that it might have a Hebrew sound to be referred to a Hebrew etymology. Canon Cook, editor of the Speaker's Commentary, in his essay on Egyptian words found in the Pentateuch, explains it as the emphatic imperative of a verb *ab*, which is a word specially used in public demonstrations of rejoicing, and to be understood as addressed by the people to Joseph, not as a word of command made to the people. אַבְרֵךְ, *abrech*, would then mean *rejoice*, or *all hail*, after the manner and in the spirit of the French, *vive le roi*, or the English, *long live the king*. Accordingly we should render: *And they* (the people) *cried before him, Hail to thee!*

45. **Zaphnath-paaneah**—An Egyptian name signifying *bread of life*, a most appropriate designation of Joseph, in his relation to the Egyptians. Others have explained the word as meaning, *revealers of secrets*, (Targ., Syr.,) *saviour of the world*, (Vulgate,) but the deciphering of the hieroglyphic inscriptions has led to the explanation first given above. See Cook's Essay

B. C. 1715-1708. CHAPTER XLI. 307

ter of Poti-pherah [15] priest of On. And Joseph went out over all the land of Egypt.

46 And Joseph *was* thirty years old when he [m] stood before Pharaoh king of Egypt. And Joseph went out from the presence of Pharaoh, and went throughout all the land of Egypt. **47** And in the seven plenteous years the earth brought forth by handfuls. **48** And he gathered up all the food of the seven years, which were in the land of Egypt, and laid up the food in the cities: the food of the field, which *was* round about every city, laid he up in the same. **49** And Joseph gathered corn [n] as the sand of the sea, very much, until he left numbering; for *it was* without number. **50** [o] And unto Joseph were born two sons, before the years of famine came: which Asenath the daughter of Poti-pherah [16] priest of On bare unto him. **51** And Joseph called the name of the firstborn [17] Manasseh: For God, *said he,* hath made me forget all my toil, and all my father's house. **52** And the name

of the second called he [18] Ephraim: For God hath caused me to be [p] fruitful in the land of my affliction.

53 And the seven years of plenteousness, that was in the land of Egypt, were ended. **54** [q] And the seven years of dearth began to come, [r] according as Joseph had said: and the dearth was in all lands; but in all the land of Egypt there was bread. **55** And when all the land of Egypt was famished, the people cried to Pharaoh for bread: and Pharaoh said unto all the Egyptians, Go unto Joseph; what he saith to you, do. **56** And the famine was over all the face of the earth: and Joseph opened [19] all the storehouses, and [s] sold unto the Egyptians; and the famine waxed sore in the land of Egypt. **57** [t] And all countries came into Egypt to Joseph for to buy *corn;* because that the famine was *so* sore in all lands.

CHAPTER XLII.

NOW when [a] Jacob saw that there was corn in Egypt, Jacob said unto

---

15 Or, *prince,* Exod. 2. 16; 2 Sam. 8. 18; 20. 26.—*m* 1 Sam. 16. 21; 1 Kings 12. 6. 8; Dan. 1. 19.—*n* Chap. 22. 17; Judg. 7. 12; 1 Sam. 13. 5; Psa. 78. 27.—*o* Chap. 46. 20; 48. 5.—16 Or, *prince,* verse 45; 2 Sam. 8. 18.

17 That is, *Forgetting.*—18 That is, *Fruitful.*—*p* Chap. 49. 22.—*q* Psa. 105. 16; Acts 7. 11.—*r* Verse 30.—19 Heb. *all wherein was.*—*s* Chap. 42. 6; 47. 14, 24.—*t* Deut. 9. 28.—*a* Acts 7. 12.

---

on Egyptian Words. The same writer explains **Asenath** to mean *sacred to Neith,* the Egyptian *Athene,* or Minerva; or perhaps a combination of Isis and Neith, names of two deities—*Isis-neith,* a name very likely to be given to his daughter by an Egyptian priest. So also **Poti-pherah** is explained as meaning *devoted to Ra,* the sun god, a suitable name for the **priest of On,** or Heliopolis, the great city and seat of the worship of the sun. This city stood about two hours' ride north-east of Cairo, and its site is now "marked by low mounds inclosing a space about three quarters of a mile in length, by half a mile in breadth; which was once occupied partly by houses and partly by the celebrated temple of the Sun. The solitary obelisk which still rises in the midst, is the sole remnant of the former splendours of the place. The Seventy translate the name On by *Heliopolis,* city of the sun; and the Hebrew prophet calls it in the same sense, Bethshemesh. Jer. xliii, 13. The city suffered greatly from the invasion of Cambyses; and in Strabo's time it was a mass of splendid ruins."—*Robinson.*

46. **Thirty years old**—Accordingly Joseph had now been thirteen years in Egypt. Comp. chap. xxxvii, 2.

51. **Manasseh**—We must not construe this name and its signification so as to imply that Joseph allowed himself to forget, or desired to forget, his father's house. He now came more and more to see how God had a hand in his exile, and was making all his labour and sorrow work for good. This was causing him to **forget,** that is, to overlook the dark side of his exile. But we should also note, that in giving **Ephraim** his name (verse 52) he calls Egypt "the land of my affliction," as if he still felt that Egypt was not his proper home, and his interests were in the land of promise. Ephraim and Manasseh, though born of an Egyptian mother, became the heads of very prominent tribes in Israel.

CHAPTER XLII.

JOSEPH'S FIRST MEETING WITH HIS BRETHREN, 1-38.

1. **Jacob saw that there was corn in Egypt**—He, perhaps, saw caravans returning from Egypt with

308 GENESIS. B. C. 1707.

his sons, Why do ye look one upon another? 2 And he said, Behold, I have heard that there is corn in Egypt: get you down thither, and buy for us from thence; that we may ᵇ live, and not die. 3 And Joseph's ten brethren went down to buy corn in Egypt. 4 But Benjamin, Joseph's brother, Jacob sent not with his brethren; for he said, ᶜ Lest peradventure mischief befall him. 5 And the sons of Israel came to buy *corn* among those that came: for the famine was ᵈ in the land of Canaan. 6 And Joseph *was* the governor ᵉ over the land, *and he it was* that sold to all the people of the land: and Joseph's brethren came, and ᶠ bowed down themselves before him *with* their faces to the earth. 7 And Joseph saw his brethren, and he knew them, but made himself strange unto them, and spake ¹ roughly unto them; and he said unto them, Whence come ye? And they said, From the land of Canaan to buy food. 8 And Joseph knew his brethren, but they knew not him. 9 And Joseph ᵍ remembered the dreams which he dreamed of them, and said unto them, Ye *are* spies; to see

---
ᵇ Chap. 43. 8; Psa. 118. 17; Isa. 38. 1.— ᶜ Verse 38.—ᵈ Acts 7. 11.—ᵉ Chap. 41. 41. ᶠ Chap. 37. 7. —— 1 Heb. *hard things with them.*—ᵍ Chap. 37. 5, 9.

---

grain, and he also *heard* (verse 2) that grain could there be had. **Why do you look one upon another—** The mention of Egypt and the thought of going thither probably filled the sons of Jacob with strange fears, and the aged father noticed their peculiar looks whenever the matter was alluded to. They seemed to shrink from going thither, as if they feared some retributive judgment in the land whither they had sold their brother.

3. **Joseph's ten brethren went—** No one of them would go alone, and they conclude it is best for all of them to go together. They might thus mutually protect and help each other. In this there is another intimation of their guilty fears.

4. **Benjamin ... Jacob sent not** —His partiality for Joseph has now become transferred to Benjamin. And Jacob seems to have entertained a suspicion that his elder sons had had something to do with Joseph's strange disappearance. Comp. verse 36.

5. **Among those that came—**They mingled themselves with the multitudes of some caravan, as if anxious to escape notice.

6. **The governor—**The word (שַׁלִּיט) thus rendered occurs elsewhere only in the later Hebrew books—Ezekiel, Daniel, and Ecclesiastes. It seems, says Keil, "to have been the standing title which the Shemites gave to Joseph as ruler in Egypt, and from this the later legend of *Salatis,* the first king of the Hyksos, arose." Josephus, *Apion,* i, 14. **He it was that sold—**Not that Joseph personally attended to all the details of the selling; but he had general oversight and authority; and when, as in the present instance, a large number of foreigners came to buy, he would be called upon to receive them in due form, and see that all was proper. He would not allow a general traffic in Egyptian grain to be carried on among foreign nations in such a time of famine.

7. **Made himself strange—**יִתְנַכֵּר, *acted like a foreigner,* speaking to them through an interpreter. Verse 23. He dissembled, and spoke harsh things to them. Perhaps he had anticipated their coming, and had, therefore, arranged to have all foreigners presented to him personally; but in that moment of interest and excitement, noticing that Benjamin was not among them, he must find out the reason, and deems it best to treat them with severity.

9. **Remembered the dreams—**How strangely but clearly fulfilled! They had thought to put him out of their way, and said, "We shall see what will become of his dreams." Chap. xxxvii, 20. Now, behold, what comes of his dreams! **Ye are spies—**This would be a very natural charge for Joseph to make in order to carry out his policy with his brethren. "The Egyptians were always most liable to be assailed from the east and north-east. The various Arab and Canaanitish tribes seem to have constantly made incursions into the more settled and civilized land of Egypt. Particularly the Hittites were at constant feud with the Egyptians. Moreover, the famous Hyksos invasion and domination may have

CHAPTER XLII.

the nakedness of the land ye are come. 10 And they said unto him, Nay, my lord, but to buy food are thy servants come. 11 We *are* all one man's sons; we *are* true *men;* thy servants are no spies. 12 And he said unto them, Nay, but to see the nakedness of the land ye are come. 13 And they said, Thy servants *are* twelve brethren, the sons of one man in the land of Canaan; and, behold, the youngest *is* this day with our father, and one [h] *is* not. 14 And Joseph said unto them, That *is it* that I spake unto you, saying, Ye *are* spies; 15 Hereby ye shall be proved: [i] By the life of Pharaoh ye shall not go forth hence, except your youngest brother come hither. 16 Send one of you, and let him fetch your brother, and ye shall be [2] kept in prison, that your words may be proved, whether *there be any* truth in you: or else by the life of Pharaoh surely ye *are* spies. 17 And he [3] put them all together into ward three days. 18 And Joseph said unto them the third day, This do, and live; [k] *for* I fear God: 19 If ye *be* true *men,* let one of your brethren be bound in the house of your prison: go ye, carry corn for the famine of your houses: 20 But [l] bring your youngest brother unto me; so shall your words be verified, and ye shall not die. And they did so.

21 And they said one to another, [m] We *are* verily guilty concerning our brother, in that we saw the anguish of his soul, when he besought us, and we would not hear; [n] therefore is this distress come upon us. 22 And Reuben answered them, saying, [o] Spake I not unto you, saying, Do not sin against the child; and ye would not hear? therefore, behold, also his blood is [p] required. 23 And they knew not that Joseph understood

---

h Chap. 37. 30; Lam. 5. 7; see chap. 44. 20.—
i See 1 Sam. 1. 26; 17. 55.—2 Heb. *bound.*—
3 Heb. *gathered.* — *k* Lev. 25. 43; Neh. 5. 15.
—*l* Verse 34; chap. 43. 5: 44. 23.

m Job 36. 8, 9; Hosea 5. 15. — *n* Prov. 21. 13; Matt. 7. 2. — *o* Chap. 37. 21. — *p* Chap. 9. 5; 1 Kings 2. 32; 2 Chron. 24. 22; Psa. 9. 12; Luke 11. 50, 51.

---

been very nearly impending at this period." — *Speaker's Com.* **Nakedness of the land**—In this time of dearth the land may have been in a comparatively exposed and defenceless condition.

15. **By the life of Pharaoh**—Joseph thus speaks like a true Egyptian, who was accustomed to swear by the life of the king.

17. **Put them all together**—Heb., *Gathered,* or, *assembled them to prison.* He huddled them together in one cell. This might remind them of their casting Joseph into the pit. Chap. xxxvii, 24. But Joseph's character and tender heart forbid our supposing that his severity towards his brethren was in retaliation for their sins against him. He doubtless sought in this way to test them, and find out their feeling toward Jacob and Benjamin. And in all this he was acting, in a way which he scarcely comprehended, the part of a minister of retribution. God used him and his methods to chasten and punish those who were virtually guilty of his blood. He seems all through to have entertained dark suspicions of his brethren. How could he else, when his experience at their hands showed them to be utterly heartless and cruel? He proposes to find out if Benjamin still lives, and what their feeling is towards him. Also, if his father still lives, and whether they love or hate him. He may find it necessary to become the avenger of their blood.

18. **I fear God**—By this remark Joseph designedly shows them that he is a religious man, and will not do them wrong. "This language," says Lange, "is the first definite sign of peace, the first fair self-betrayal of his heart. Agitated feelings lie concealed under these words."

21. **We are verily guilty**—How the guilty conscience smites them now, and makes them see and feel in this trial a divine retribution! **The anguish of his soul**—In their awakened souls the scene of their brother's look of agony and cries for mercy rises up afresh and vividly, deepening their present **distress**.

22. **Reuben answered**—Reuben here acts as the accuser of his brethren. But he seems to have had no real sympathy with their cruelty, and had purposed to secure and restore Joseph to his father. Chap. xxxvii, 21, 22, 29, 30. **His blood is required**—Thus Reuben voices their deepest fears. It seems to him and them as if the avenger of blood (chap. ix, 5) in some dire form is suddenly to come upon them.

GENESIS.   B. C. 1707.

them; for ⁴he spake unto them by an interpreter. **24** And he turned himself about from them, and wept; and returned to them again, and communed with them, and took from them Simeon, and bound him before their eyes.

25 Then Joseph commanded to fill their sacks with corn, and to restore every man's money into his sack, and to give them provision for the way: and ᑫthus did he unto them. **26** And they laded their asses with the corn, and departed thence. **27** And as ʳone of them opened his sack to give his ass provender in the inn, he espied his money; for, behold, it was in his sack's mouth. **28** And he said unto his brethren, My money is restored; and, lo, it is even in my sack: and their heart ⁵failed them, and they were afraid, saying one to another, What is this that God hath done unto us?

29 And they came unto Jacob their father unto the land of Canaan, and told him all that befell unto them; saying, **30** The man, who is the lord of the land, ˢspake ⁶roughly to us, and took us for spies of the country. **31** And we said unto him, We are true men; we are no spies: **32** We be twelve brethren, sons of our father; one is not, and the youngest is this day with our father in the land of Canaan. **33** And the man, the lord of the country, said unto us, 'Hereby shall I know that ye are true men; leave one of your brethren here with me, and take food for the famine of your households, and be gone: **34** And bring your youngest brother unto me: then shall I know that ye are no spies, but that ye are true men: so will I deliver you your brother, and ye shall ᵘtraffic in the land.

35 And it came to pass as they emptied their sacks, that, behold, ᵛevery man's bundle of money was in his sack: and when both they and their father saw the bundles of money, they were afraid. **36** And Jacob their father said unto them, Me have ye ʷbereaved of my children: Joseph is not, and Simeon is not, and ye will take Benjamin away: all these things are against me. **37** And Reuben spake unto his father, saying, Slay my two sons, if I bring him not to thee: deliver him into my hand, and I

---
4 Heb. an interpreter was between them.
— q Matt. 5. 44; Rom. 12. 17, 20, 21. — r See chap. 43. 21. — 5 Heb. went forth.

s Verse 7. — 6 Heb. with us hard things. — t Verses 15, 19, 20. — u Chap. 34. 10. — v See chap. 43. 21. — w Chap. 43. 14.

---

24. Turned ... and wept — On hearing their words of conscientious fear, he cannot control his feelings in their presence. **Took from them Simeon**—Probably his cruel temper (lxix, 5,) had largely instigated and controlled the action of his brethren in making away with Joseph.

25. Restore every man's money —He would not take pay for his father's and brothers' food, but he would not openly decline it, lest he inadvertently betray himself and his feelings. He also, probably, furnished them **provision for the way** that they might not open their sacks until they reached their home.

26. Asses—Some critics have objected that asses were an abomination to the Egyptians, and would not have been allowed in the land. But the monuments disprove the assertion by their numerous representation of this animal, and chap. xlvii, 17, shows that the Egyptians possessed asses.

27. The inn—מָלוֹן, a lodging place; some sheltered and suitable place for encampment over night. Possibly some sort of caravansary was, even in that early time, provided along the great highways of travel for the convenience of caravans like this.

28. God hath done — Every thing seems to them now as the condemning acts of God; and the feeling deepens more and more, until, on finding all their money returned (verse 35) and Benjamin demanded, their aged father breaks out in a bitter wail of sorrow.

36. Jacob ... said—Jacob's words are full of emotion, and may be literally rendered thus:

> Me have ye bereft;
> Joseph is not,
> And Simeon is not,
> And Benjamin ye will take:
> Upon me are all these things!

Here Jacob more than intimates that they had been privy to Joseph's and Simeon's disappearance, and would fain seize away Benjamin also.

37. Reuben spake—As became the firstborn. Joseph's words (in verses 18-20) seem to have satisfied him that no harm would befall Benjamin.

will bring him to thee again. 38 And he said, My son shall not go down with you; for ˣ his brother is dead, and he is left alone: ʸ if mischief befall him by the way in the which ye go, then shall ye ᶻ bring down my gray hairs with sorrow to the grave.

CHAPTER XLIII.

AND the famine was ᵃ sore in the land. 2 And it came to pass, when they had eaten up the corn which they had brought out of Egypt, their father said unto them, Go again, buy us a little food. 3 And Judah spake unto him, saying, The man ¹ did solemnly protest unto us, saying, Ye shall not see my face, except your ᵇ brother be with you. 4 If thou wilt send our brother with us, we will go down and buy thee food: 5 But if thou wilt not send him, we will not go down: for the man said unto us, Ye shall not see my face, except your brother be with you. 6 And Israel said, Wherefore dealt ye so ill with me, as to tell the man whether ye had yet a brother? 7 And they said, The man ² asked us straitly of our state, and of our kindred, saying, Is your father yet alive? have ye another brother? and we told him according to the ³ tenor of these words: ⁴ Could we certainly know that he would say, Bring your brother down? 8 And Judah said unto Israel his father, Send the lad with me, and we will arise and go; that we may live, and not die, both we, and thou, and also our little ones. 9 I will be surety for him; of my hand shalt thou require him: ᶜ if I bring him not unto thee, and set him before thee, then let me bear the blame for ever; 10 For except we had lingered, surely now we had returned ⁵ this second time. 11 And their father Israel said unto them, If it must be so now, do this; take of the best fruits in the land in your vessels, and ᵈ carry down the man a present, a little ᵉ balm, and a little honey, spices and myrrh, nuts and almonds: 12 And take double money in your hand; and the money ᶠ that was brought again in the mouth of your sacks, carry it again in your hand; peradventure it was an oversight. 13 Take also your brother, and arise, go again unto the man: 14 And God Almighty give you mercy

<small>ˣ Verse 13; chap. 37. 33; 44. 28.——ʸ Verse 4; chap. 44. 29.——ᶻ Chap. 37. 35; 44. 31.——ᵃ Chap. 41. 54, 57.—— 1 Heb. protesting protested.—— b Chap. 42. 20; 44. 23.——2 Heb. asking asked us.</small>

<small>3 Heb. mouth.——4 Heb. Knowing could we know?——c Chap. 44. 32; Philem. 18, 19.——5 Or, twice by this.——d Chap. 32. 20; Prov. 18. 16. ——e Chap. 37. 25; Jer. 8. 22.——f Chap. 42. 25, 35.</small>

38. **Sorrow to the grave**—Comp. chap. xxxvii, 35.

CHAPTER XLIII.

THE SECOND JOURNEY TO EGYPT FOR FOOD, 1–15.

1. **The famine was sore**—Or, heavy. It had now continued two years. Chap. xlv, 6.

3. **Did solemnly protest**—He had sworn by the life of Pharaoh. Chap. xlii, 15, 16.

8. **Judah said**—The eloquent plea of Judah seems to have had more weight with Jacob than the expressed wishes of all his other sons.

11. **Take of the best fruits**—Heb., take of the song of the land; the products celebrated in song. This suggests the answer to the objection that these fruits should be had in Canaan in such a time of dearth. The items of the **present** here named were luxuries, which might have been preserved from previous years. "Almost all of them," says Kalisch, "require for their growth heat rather than moisture; and some develop themselves to the greatest advantage in dry years and in a dry soil." So these may have grown and been abundant when the grains all failed. On **balm, spices,** and **myrrh,** see note on chap. xxxvii, 25, where it will be noticed that the Ishmaelite caravan carried these same articles into Egypt. The **honey** (דבשׁ) here mentioned was probably the grape honey, manufactured by art, not by the bees; a sort of molasses or syrup, called by the modern Arabs *dibs*. **Nuts**—Probably the nuts of the pistachio tree, which somewhat resembles the terebinth. The Septuagint here translates the word by *terebinth*. The pistachio nut is said to be of an aromatic taste, and a favourite but not common fruit in the East. The **almond** tree was common in Palestine, but not in Egypt; its blossoms and fruit much resemble those of the peach tree.

14. **God Almighty**—Heb., *El Shaddai*. Jacob uses the divine name so sacredly associated with the covenant and promises. Compare chapter xvii, 1; xxxv, 11.

before the man, that he may send away your other brother, and Benjamin. **⁶ If I be bereaved** *of my children*, I am bereaved.

15 And the men took that present, and they took double money in their hand, and Benjamin; and rose up, and went down to Egypt, and stood before Joseph. **16** And when Joseph saw Benjamin with them, he said to the ʰ ruler of his house, Bring *these* men home, and ⁷ slay, and make ready; for *these* men shall ⁸ dine with me at noon. **17** And the man did as Joseph bade; and the man brought the men into Joseph's house. **18** And the men were afraid, because they were brought into Joseph's house; and they said, Because of the money that was returned in our sacks at the first time are we brought in; that he may ⁹ seek occasion against us, and fall upon us, and take us for bondmen, and our asses. **19** And they came near to the steward of Joseph's house, and they communed with him at the door of the house, **20** And said, O sir, ¹ ¹⁰ we came indeed down at the first time to buy food: **21** And ᵏ it came to pass, when we came to the inn, that we opened our sacks, and, behold, *every* man's money *was* in the mouth of his sack, our money in full weight: and we have brought it again in our hand. **22** And other money have we brought down in our hands to buy food: we cannot tell who put our money in our sacks. **23** And he said, Peace *be* to you, fear not: your God, and the God of your father, hath given you treasure in your sacks: ¹¹ I had your money. And he brought Simeon out unto them. **24** And the man brought the men into Joseph's house, and ˡ gave *them* water, and they washed their feet; and he gave their asses provender. **25** And they made ready the present against Joseph came at noon: for they heard that they should eat bread there.

26 And when Joseph came home, they brought him the present which *was* in their hand into the house, and ᵐ bowed themselves to him to the earth. **27** And he asked them of *their* ¹² welfare, and said, ¹³ *Is* your father well, the old man ⁿ of whom ye spake? *Is* he yet alive? **28** And they answered, Thy servant our father *is* in good health, he *is* yet alive. ° And they bowed down their heads, and made obeisance. **29** And he lifted up his eyes, and saw his brother Benjamin, ᵖ his mother's son, and said, *Is* this your younger brother, ᵠ of whom ye spake unto me? And he said, God be gracious unto thee, my son. **30** And Joseph made haste; for ʳ his bowels did yearn upon his brother: and he sought *where* to weep; and he entered into *his* chamber, and ˢ wept there. **31** And he washed his face, and went out, and refrained himself, and said, Set on ᵗ bread. **32** And they set on for him by himself, and for them by themselves, and for the Egyptians, which did eat with him, by

---

g Esther 4. 16.——6 Or, *And I, as I have been,* etc.——*h* Chap. 24. 2; 39. 4; 44. 1.——7 Heb. *kill a killing,* 1 Sam. 25.11.——8 Heb. *eat.*——9 Heb. *roll himself upon us,* Job 30. 14.——*i* Chap. 42. 3, 10.——10 Heb. *coming down we came down.*——*k* Chap. 42. 27, 35.

11 Heb. *your money came to me.*——*l* Chap.18. 4; 24. 32.——*m* Chap. 37. 7, 10.——12 Heb. *peace,* chap. 37. 14.——13 Heb. *Is there peace to your father?*——*n* Chap. 42. 11, 13.——*o* Chap. 37. 7, 10.——*p* Chap. 35. 17, 18.——*q* Chap. 42. 13.——*r* 1 Kings 3. 26.——*s* Chap. 42. 24.——*t* Verse 25.

RECEPTION AND FEAST AT JOSEPH'S HOUSE, 16–34.

16. The ruler of his house—His steward, who had oversight of his domestic affairs.

18. The men were afraid—Their cold and severe treatment on the former occasion filled them with a dread of Joseph, and they were predisposed to construe every thing that looked like danger into a plot against them and their property.

19. Communed at the door—Before they will enter the house, they resolve to have an understanding about the money that was returned in their sacks.

23. Peace be to you—The steward's words were admirably adapted to quiet the fears of these men. Especially would the words **your God and the God of your father** assure them that no harm was intended against them, and that their religion was known and respected. **I had your money**—Or, *your money came to me.* This same steward thus acknowledges the receipt of their money, and assures them that that is not charged against them.

26. Bowed themselves—Another act fulfilling Joseph's dream — all the eleven of his brethren now bowing down. Comp. xlii, 6–9; xxxvii, 5–9.

32. For him by himself—He thus maintained his distinction of rank and caste, and conformed to Egyptian ideas

themselves: because the Egyptians might not eat bread with the Hebrews; for that *is* ᵘ an abomination unto the Egyptians. 33 And they sat before him, the firstborn according to his birthright, and the youngest according to his youth: and the men marvelled one at another. 34 And he took *and sent* messes unto them from before him: but Benjamin's mess was ᵛ five times so much as any of theirs. And they drank, and ¹⁴ were merry with him.

CHAPTER XLIV.

AND he commanded ¹ the steward of his house, saying, Fill the men's sacks *with* food, as much as they can carry, and put every man's money in his sack's mouth. 2 And put my cup, the silver cup, in the sack's mouth of the youngest, and his corn money. And he did according to the word that Joseph had spoken. 3 As soon as the morning

was light, the men were sent away, they and their asses. 4 *And* when they were gone out of the city, *and* not *yet* far off, Joseph said unto his steward, Up, follow after the men; and when thou dost overtake them, say unto them, Wherefore have ye rewarded evil for good? 5 *Is* not this *it* in which my lord drinketh, and whereby indeed he ² divineth? ye have done evil in so doing.

6 And he overtook them, and he spake unto them these same words. 7 And they said unto him, Wherefore saith my lord these words? God forbid that thy servants should do according to this thing: 8 Behold, ᵃ the money, which we found in our sacks' mouths, we brought again unto thee out of the land of Canaan: how then should we steal out of thy lord's house silver or gold? 9 With whomsoever of thy servants it be found, ᵇ both let him die, and we also will be my lord's bondmen. 10 And he said,

---

u Chap. 46. 34; Exod. 8. 26.——*v* Chap. 45. 22.——14 Heb. *drank largely*: see Hag. 1. 6; John 2. 10.

1 Heb. him *that was over his house.*——2 Or, *maketh trial?*——*a* Chap. 43. 21.——*b* Chap. 31. 32.

---

and customs. **Egyptians might not eat bread with the Hebrews**—Herodotus (ii, 41) says: "No Egyptian, man or woman, will kiss a Grecian on the mouth, or use the knife, spit, or caldron of a Greek, or taste the flesh of a pure ox that has been divided by a Grecian knife." This same fear of contamination was doubtless held with regard to other nations as well as the Greeks. The Egyptians held in abomination those who slaughtered cows and oxen, animals which they held in highest reverence. Hence it was that they despised shepherds. Chap. xlvi, 34.

33. **According to his birthright**—Well might the men *marvel* at being arranged at the table thus according to their ages. Joseph thus prepared the way for an open recognition, and sought to impress them with the idea that he knew them better than they imagined.

34. **Five times so much**—This was a special mark of honour, and furnished opportunity for Joseph to observe if his brethren envied Benjamin as they once did himself.

CHAPTER XLIV.

FURTHER TROUBLES, AND JUDAH'S APPEAL, 1–34.

2. **My cup, the silver cup**—A large silver goblet or bowl, out of

which, according to verse 5, Joseph was wont to divine. The practice of divining from goblets obtained among the Egyptians and the Persians, and is mentioned by several ancient authors. The practice was to pour clean water into the goblet, and then look into it as into a mirror to discern the future. Sometimes small pieces of gold and silver and precious stones were dropped into the water, and their appearance closely scrutinized, and certain incantations were pronounced in order to evoke some intelligible answer from the unknown and mysterious divinity supposed to abide within the water. There is nothing said in this chapter that necessarily implies that Joseph practiced divination. All his action in the case was designed to awe and prove his brothers, and bring out their real feeling towards Benjamin. Yet, in that time of strange mixture of superstition and religion, it is possible that Joseph, intimate with the arts of the Egyptian priests, and skilled in the interpretation of dreams, may have had something to do with the magic of the people whose manners he so largely adopted.

9. **Let him die**—Their words on the occasion show the intensity of their feeling and excitement, and their entire action evinced their consciousness of

Now also *let* it *be* according unto your words: he with whom it is found shall be my servant; and ye shall be blameless. **11** Then they speedily took down every man his sack to the ground, and opened every man his sack. **12** And he searched, *and* began at the eldest, and left at the youngest: and the cup was found in Benjamin's sack. **13** Then they ᶜ rent their clothes, and laded every man his ass, and returned to the city.

14 And Judah and his brethren came to Joseph's house; for he *was* yet there: and they ᵈ fell before him on the ground. **15** And Joseph said unto them, What deed *is* this that ye have done? wot ye not that such a man as I can certainly ᵃ divine? **16** And Judah said, What shall we say unto my lord? what shall we speak? or how shall we clear ourselves? God hath found out the iniquity of thy servants: behold, ᵉ we *are* my lord's servants, both we, and *he* also with whom the cup is found. **17** And he said, ᶠ God forbid that I should do so: *but* the man in whose hand the cup is found, he shall be my servant; and as for you, get you up in peace unto your father.

18 Then Judah came near unto him, and said, O my lord, let thy servant, I pray thee, speak a word in my lord's ears, and ᵍ let not thine anger burn against thy servant: for thou *art* even as Pharaoh. **19** My lord asked his servants, saying, Have ye a father, or a brother? **20** And we said unto my lord, We have a father, an old man, and ʰ a child of his old age, a little one; and his brother is dead, and he alone is left of his mother, and his father loveth him. **21** And thou saidst unto thy servants, ⁱ Bring him down unto me, that I may set mine eyes upon him. **22** And we said unto my lord, The lad cannot leave his father: for *if* he should leave his father, *his father* would die. **23** And

---

c Chap. 37. 29, 34; Num. 14. 6; 2 Sam. 1. 11.—*d* Chap. 37. 7.—3 Or, *make trial?* verse 5.

e Verse 9.—*f* Prov. 17. 15.—*g* Chap. 18. 30, 32; Exod. 32. 22.—*h* Chap. 37. 3.—*i* Chap. 42. 15, 20.

---

innocency as to the charge of stealing the cup.

13. Rent their clothes—They were now horror-stricken, and utterly overwhelmed with dismay. They could not utter any word of explanation, and they hastened back to the city.

14. Fell before him—Another fulfilling of Joseph's dream. See on xliii, 26.

18. Judah came near and said—Nothing in all literature surpasses this appeal of Judah in behalf of his brother and his father. It is remarkable that he makes no attempt to deny the charge of taking the cup; he makes no plea of innocence, but assumes, in utter helplessness through other sins, that God was in all this discovering the iniquity of himself and his brethren. Luther says: "I would give very much to be able to pray to our Lord God as well as Judah here prays to Joseph." Kalisch observes: "Judah, the lion, could never degrade his dignity by an outburst of impotent rage; the tempest of his feelings was checked by controlling reason, and the chaotic confusion of his emotions gave way to manly composure and lucid thought. Stepping forward towards the inexorable man with the courage and modesty of a hero, he delivered that address which is one of the masterpieces of Hebrew composition. It is not distinguished by brilliant imagination, or highly poetical diction; its inimitable charm and excellence consist in the power of psychological truth, easy simplicity, and affecting pathos. It possesses the eloquence of facts, not of words; it is, in reality, scarcely more than a simple recapitulation of past incidents; but the selection, arrangement, and intrinsic emphasis of the facts produce an effect attainable only by consummate art. The deep and fervent love of the aged father for his youngest son forms the center, round which the other parts of the speech, the allusion to Joseph, to Rachel, and to the struggle of the brothers before their departure from Canaan are skilfully grouped. Jacob would never survive the loss of Benjamin; and if the brothers returned without him, they would see their father expire in agony before their eyes. . . . Could Joseph still remain unmoved? One trait more completed the victory over his heart. . . . Anxious to seal his filial love by the greatest sacrifice he could possibly offer, Judah was ready to renounce his home, his wife, and his children, and forever to toil in the drudgery of Egyptian bondage."

thou saidst unto thy servants, *k* Except your youngest brother come down with you, ye shall see my face no more. 24 And it came to pass when we came up unto thy servant my father, we told him the words of my lord. 25 And *l* our father said, Go again, *and* buy us a little food. 26 And we said, We cannot go down: if our youngest brother be with us, then will we go down: for we may not see the man's face except our youngest brother *be* with us. 27 And thy servant my father said unto us, Ye know that *m* my wife bare me two *sons:* 28 And the one went out from me, and I said, *n* Surely he is torn in pieces; and I saw him not since: 29 And if ye *o* take this also from me, and mischief befall him, ye shall bring down my gray hairs with sorrow to the grave. 30 Now therefore when I come to thy servant my father, and the lad *be* not with us; seeing that *p* his life is bound up in the lad's life; 31 It shall come to pass, when he seeth that the lad *is* not *with us*, that he will die: and thy servants shall bring down the gray hairs of thy servant our father with sorrow to the grave 32 For thy servant became surety for the lad unto my father, saying, *q* If I bring him not unto thee, then I shall bear the blame to my father for ever. 33 Now therefore, I pray thee, *r* let thy servant abide instead of the lad a bondman to my lord; and let the lad go up with his brethren. 34 For how shall I go up to my father, and the lad *be* not with me? lest peradventure I see the evil that shall ⁴ come on my father.

CHAPTER XLV.

THEN Joseph could not refrain himself before all them that stood by him; and he cried, Cause every man to go out from me. And there stood no man with him, while Joseph made himself known unto his brethren. 2 And he ¹ wept aloud: and the Egyptians and the house of Pharaoh heard. 3 And Joseph said unto his brethren, *a* I *am* Joseph; doth my father yet live? And his brethren could not answer him; for they were ² troubled at his presence. 4 And Joseph said unto his brethren,

k Chap. 43. 3, 5. —— *l* Chap. 43. 2. —— *m* Chap. 46. 19. —— *n* Chap. 37. 33. —— *o* Chap. 42. 36, 38. —— *p* 1 Sam. 18. 1. —— *q* Chap. 43. 9. —— *r* Exod. 32. 32. —— 4 Heb. *find my father*, Exod. 18. 8;

Job 31. 29; Psa. 116. 3; 119. 143.——1 Heb. *gave forth his voice in weeping*, Num. 14. 1. —— *a* Acts 7. 13.——2 Or, *terrified*, Job 4. 5; 23. 15; Matt. 14. 26; Mark 6. 50.

CHAPTER XLV.

THE RECOGNITION, AND THE MESSAGE TO JACOB, 1-28.

Whatever purposes Joseph intended to accomplish by his severity and mysterious conduct towards his brethren, all are accomplished now, or else the irresistible eloquence of Judah dissuades him from concealing himself further. When he first saw them—ten of them, without Benjamin, (chap. xlii,) —he may have at once suspected that they had made away with his younger brother as they had done with himself. He would keep himself aloof until he could thoroughly prove their present disposition, and find out all the facts. Thus he was also made, perhaps unwittingly, the instrument of distressing his aged father, as a retribution for the mischievous partiality he had shown to the sons of Rachel. But the action of the brethren towards Benjamin, and especially the appeal of Judah, and the picture of the aged father sinking in sorrow to the grave— all convince Joseph that a deep change has been wrought in the hearts of these men, and he can refrain himself no longer.

1. Could not refrain himself—Could not control his emotions any longer. **Cause every man to go out**—The delicate and touching scene will be too sacred for public gaze. Besides, the embracing and the kissing (verses 14, 15) might too much offend the ideas of the Egyptians. See note on chap. xliii, 32.

3. Doth my father yet live—In the warmth and fulness of his emotion he seems yet to betray a suspicion of the report of his brethren. This throws light on the undue severity with which he has treated them all along. First he feared that Benjamin was not; and now he even intimates a doubt whether, after all their protestations, his father is still alive. Accordingly, **his brethren could not answer him** —The sudden revelation; the deep insinuation; the shock of mingled surprise and alarm rendered them speechless. **They were troubled**—*Terrified;* filled with amazement and trepidation (נִבְהֲלוּ) **at his presence,** or,

316 GENESIS. B. C. 1707.

Come near to me, I pray you. And they came near. And he said, I *am* Joseph your brother, ᵇ whom ye sold into Egypt. 5 Now therefore ᶜ be not grieved, ³nor angry with yourselves, that ye sold me hither: ᵈ for God did send me before you to preserve life. 6 For these two years *hath* the famine *been* in the land: and yet *there are* five years, in the which *there shall* neither *be* earing nor harvest. 7 And God sent me before you ⁴ to preserve you a posterity in the earth, and to save your lives by a great deliverance. 8 So now *it was* not you *that* sent me hither, but God: and he hath made me ᵉ a father to Pharaoh, and lord of all his house, and a ruler throughout all the land of Egypt. 9 Haste ye, and go up to my father, and say unto him, Thus saith thy son Joseph, God hath made me lord of all Egypt: come down unto me, tarry not: 10 And ᶠ thou shalt dwell in the land of Goshen, and thou shalt be near unto me, thou, and thy children, and thy children's children, and thy flocks, and thy herds, and all that thou hast: 11 And there will I nourish thee; for yet *there are* five years of famine; lest thou, and thy household, and all that thou hast, come to poverty. 12 And, behold, your eyes see, and the eyes of my brother Benjamin, that *it is* ᵍ my mouth that speaketh unto you. 13 And ye shall tell my father of all

b Chap. 37. 28.——*c* Isa. 40. 2; 2 Cor. 2. 7.——3 Heb. *neither let there be anger in your eyes.*——*d* Chap. 50. 20; Psa. 105. 16, 17; see 2 Sam. 16. 10, 11; Acts 4. 27, 28.——4 Heb. *to put for you a remnant.*——*e* Chap. 41. 43; Judg. 17. 10; Job 29. 16.——*f* Chap. 47. 1.——*g* Chap. 42. 23.

from his presence, (מפניו;) as if they shrunk backward, away from before his face.

4. **Come near**—He notices their confusion and alarm, and their shrinking from his presence, and now kindly seeks to allay their fears and strengthen their hearts.

5. **God did send me**—Four times he repeats this thought, that God's hand had directed in all this matter. He sees the wonderful Providence in it now, and wishes them all to see it.

8. **A father to Pharaoh**—A wise counsellor and intimate friend, to watch over Pharaoh's great house and land, like a protecting father. The word **father** is used in such a sense in many lands. The Romanists call their priests fathers, and Mohammedan caliphs give their grand vizier this title.

9. **Haste ye ... tarry not**—The emotion of a consuming filial love is in these words. How long will seem the days until son and father meet again!

10. **Dwell in the land of Goshen**—"Joseph invites his father to come and settle in Goshen, apparently before consulting Pharaoh upon the matter, trusting to his influence with the king to secure this favour. Goshen was on the north-eastern frontier of Egypt, bordering upon the desert, the part of the country nearest to Canaan, east of the Pelusiac branch of the Nile. It was well adapted to a pastoral people, being fertilized by artificial irrigation through canals from the Nile, and by wells from which the water is raised by wheels. The surface being less elevated than the rest of the land, it is more easily irrigated. There are here at present more flocks and herds, and also more fishermen, than in any other part of Egypt, so that at the present day, as in the time of Joseph, it is reckoned as 'the best of the land.' (ROBINSON'S *Biblical Researches,* i, 53)."—*Newhall.*

11. **Will I nourish thee**—The son whom God hath exalted will tenderly provide for the aged father who nourished him in his childhood. **Yet there are five years**—With the assuring message of filial love goes also a prophetic word, showing that Joseph has a knowledge of the future such as only divinely-gifted seers possess.

12. **My mouth that speaketh unto you**—That is, Ye see that my "mouth is speaking to you in our native language. Before this he had spoken to them in the Egyptian tongue, through an interpreter, but now, when he had 'caused all men to go out from' him, that he might open all his heart to his brethren, he cried to them in Hebrew, 'I am Joseph!' It was the sound of their native tongue in this land of strangers, from the lips of the grand vizier of Egypt, that rolled back the years in the memory of the brethren more than any thing that he said."—*Newhall.*

13. **Tell my father of all my glory** —Joseph would make his father and his brothers partakers of his own hon-

CHAPTER XLV.

my glory in Egypt, and of all that ye have seen; and ye shall haste and ʰ bring down my father hither. **14** And he fell upon his brother Benjamin's neck, and wept; and Benjamin wept upon his neck. **15** Moreover he kissed all his brethren, and wept upon them: and after that his brethren talked with him. **16** And the fame thereof was heard in Pharaoh's house, saying, Joseph's brethren are come: and it ⁵ pleased Pharaoh well, and his servants. **17** And Pharaoh said unto Joseph, Say unto thy brethren, This do ye; lade your beasts, and go, get you unto the land of Canaan; **18** And take your father and your households, and come unto me: and I will give you the good of the land of Egypt, and ye shall eat ¹ the fat of the land. **19** Now thou art commanded, this do ye; take you wagons out of the land of Egypt for your little ones, and for your wives, and bring your father, and come. **20** Also ⁶ regard not your stuff; for the good of all the land of Egypt *is* yours. **21** And the children of Israel did so: and Joseph gave them wagons, according to the ⁷ commandment of Pharaoh, and gave them provision for the way. **22** To all of them he gave each man changes of raiment; but to Benjamin he gave three hundred *pieces* of silver, and ᵏ five changes of raiment. **23** And to his father he sent after this *manner;* ten asses ⁸ laden with the good things of Egypt, and ten she asses laden with corn

h Acts 7. 14.——5 Heb. *was good in the eyes of Pharaoh,* chap. 41. 37.——*i* Chap. 27. 28; Num. 18. 12, 29.

6 Heb. *let not your eye spare,* etc.——7 Heb. *mouth,* Num. 3. 16.——*k* Chap. 43. 34.——8 Heb. *carrying.*

our, and would have them exult with family pride in all that God had done for them through him.

15. **After that his brethren talked with him**—That is, *after* the embracing of Benjamin (verse 14) and the weeping and kissing of them all. "They were so stunned and bewildered that they could not utter a word till his tears washed out their terrors."—*Newhall.*

16. **The fame thereof was heard**—The report was made; literally, *the voice* (or *noise*) *was heard.* **It pleased Pharaoh well**—Heb., *it was good in the eyes of Pharaoh.* "The grateful esteem in which Joseph was held made every thing good that interested him, and the discovery that the Hebrew slave belonged to a family that was not unknown at the court of the Pharaohs (chap. xii) was also pleasing. The 'good' and the 'fat' of the land were now freely laid at the disposal of the family of Joseph. This is simply a general expression for the choice things of Egypt."—*Newhall.*

19. **Now thou art commanded**—"There is a beautiful kindness and courtesy here shown on the part of Pharaoh, in passing from the language of invitation to that of command, where Joseph's personal interest is concerned. **Take you wagons**—Of which there were probably none in Palestine; carts, two-wheeled vehicles which could easily pass through the roadless desert. The modern Egyptian cart has two solid wheels, but carts with spoked wheels are represented in the monuments. **Little ones**—And in ver. 18, *households,* all their dependents, servants, amounting probably to several hundreds, are included in the invitation." —*Newhall.*

20. **Regard not your stuff**—"Be not troubled about your household goods that you cannot move, for they shall be made good. People who move frequently can appreciate this anxiety. Israel came into Egypt by free invitation, and perhaps the sacred historian amplifies in detail here, so as to show that Israel was as free to depart afterwards."—*Newhall.*

22. **Changes of raiment**—Suits of clothing, a common present among the wealthy and noble in eastern countries. **Three hundred pieces of silver**—Silver shekels are doubtless intended, weighed and not coined; amounting to about nine and one half pounds.

23. **Ten asses laden with the good things of Egypt**—"These presents to his aged father were in princely profusion, as was fitting the rank of the highest subject of Pharaoh, calculated to impress Jacob unmistakably with the reality of the romantic story which the brethren were to carry back to their father; yet as Jacob was immediately to leave home he could really use but a very small part of this provision."—*Newhall.*

VOL. I.—21   O. T.

and bread and meat for his father by the way. **24** So he sent his brethren away, and they departed: and he said unto them, See that ye fall not out by the way. **25** And they went up out of *Egypt*, and came into the land of Canaan unto Jacob their father, **26** And told him, saying, Joseph *is* yet alive, and he *is* governor over all the land of Egypt. ʳAnd ⁹ Jacob's heart fainted, for he believed them not. **27** And they told him all the words of Joseph, which he had said unto them: and when he saw the wagons which Joseph had sent to carry him, the spirit of Jacob their father revived. **28** And Israel said, *It is* enough; Joseph my son *is* yet alive: I will go and see him before I die.

CHAPTER XLVI.

AND Israel took his journey with all that he had, and came to ᵃ Beer-

---

l Job 29. 24; Psa. 126. 1; Luke 24. 11, 41.　　9 Heb. *his*.——*a* Chap. 21. 31, 33; 28. 10.

---

24. See that ye fall not out by the way—"Do not accuse one another of guilt, and so fall into unbrotherly contention. It was natural that in talking over this strange history each should seek to clear himself of blame. Three several times Joseph tells them that God had overruled their sin for good to all the family, and tenderly endeavours to alleviate thus the sorrow of their repentance."—*Newhall.*

26. Jacob's heart fainted—Gesenius (Lex., on נבה) renders: "*But his heart was cold,* did not warm with joy, was not moved." The news was too great and surprising for the aged patriarch to believe. Pressing grief, and mistrust and suspicion of his sons also, helped to beget this chill of unbelief in Jacob's heart.

27. When he saw the wagons—"As they went on with the details of the story the circumstances gradually convinced him, but the decisive thing mentioned is the sight of the wagons, the Egyptian carts, which never appeared in Canaan."—*Newhall.*

28. And Israel said, It is enough; Joseph my son is yet alive—"The change of name from Jacob to Israel is significant here. It is the patriarch who was heir of the great promises made to Abraham, the channel of the covenant mercies to the world, who now sets out upon this eventful journey which commences a new stage in the fortunes of the covenant people. It is the prince of God who recognises the finger of Providence."—*Newhall.*

CHAPTER XLVI.

The Journey to Egypt, 1–7.

" Here begins a new stage in the history of the covenant people. The chosen family is to be developed into a chosen nation. A permanent religious state, a great divinely organized commonwealth, with institutions fixed for ages, is to be evolved from the patriarchal nomadism, in order that all nations may be blessed in the seed of Abraham. The sublime revelations and spiritual experiences which distinguished the great patriarchs from all other men were not to vanish with them from the world, but were to be embodied in institutions, in a literature, in a national consciousness, which were to be immortal as the race itself. For more than two centuries Abraham and his children had walked and talked with Jehovah as they moved from one pasture to another between Sychem and Beer-sheba. Amid the hostile and idolatrous Canaanitish tribes there was no opportunity for leisurely national growth, while they were in constant danger of absorption; but in the Egyptian sojourn they had the contact with the world's highest civilization, which gave culture, and yet the isolation and antagonism which saved their religion and their national life from extinction. Egypt's fat soil made Israel teem with fruitful generations even under oppression; and her wisdom, art, social and religious institutions, deeply tinged the national character, and even shaped some of the religious rites of Israel. Jacob knew that this period of Egyptian sojourn was to come, for it had been predicted to Abraham, (chap. xv, 13–15,) and so he recognised now the call of Providence. The rhetoric rises in tone at the opening of this chapter, as if the writer felt the inspiration of this crisis."—*Newhall.*

1. Israel took his journey—"The

CHAPTER XLVI.

sheba, and offered sacrifices ᵇ unto the God of his father Isaac. 2 And God spake unto Israel ᶜ in the visions of the night, and said, Jacob, Jacob. And he said, Here *am* I. 3 And he said, I *am* God, ᵈ the God of thy father: fear not to go down into Egypt; for I will there ᵉ make of thee a great nation. 4 ᶠ I will go down with thee into Egypt; and I will also surely ᵍ bring thee up *again*: and ʰ Joseph shall put his hand upon thine eyes. 5 And ⁱ Jacob rose up from Beer-sheba: and the sons of Israel carried Jacob their father, and their little ones, and their wives, in the wagons ᵏ which Pharaoh had sent to carry him. 6 And they took their cattle, and their goods, which they had gotten in the land

---

b Chap. 26. 24, 25; 28. 13; 31. 42.—*c* Chap. 15. 1; Job 33. 14, 15.—*d* Chap. 28. 13.—*e* Chap. 12. 2; Deut. 26. 5.

f Chap. 28. 15; 48. 21.—*g* Chap. 15. 16; 50. 13, 24, 25; Exod. 3. 8.—*h* Chap. 50. 1.—*i* Acts 7. 15.—*k* Chap. 45. 19, 21.

---

writer uses here, at the opening, the covenant name, from the sense of the national significance of this journey; yet afterward directs his attention to the personal experiences and movements of Jacob. He came down from Hebron to Beer-sheba, the camping place by the wells in the edge of the desert, where Abraham had called on JEHOVAH, the EVERLASTING GOD; and where Isaac his father had sojourned so long; and here, amid the scenes of his childhood, looking down upon the desert, which like a sea separated his new home and new life from the old, he **offered sacrifices unto the God of his father Isaac**, who there had first taught him the name of that God." —*Newhall.*

2. **God spake unto Israel**—"Jacob thought himself led by the hand of Providence, yet we may imagine him oppressed by sadness as he turns his back upon the land of promise—the land of his childhood and manhood, the land where were the graves of Abraham, and Isaac, and of his beloved Rachel—and sets his face towards the dreary desert. Is it thus that God is to make Canaan his inheritance? But in his trial God appears to him, as he did to Abraham in a similar crisis, (chap. xv, 1,) and to Isaac, when the same doubt oppressed him, (chap. xxv, 24,) and the same cheering words come to Jacob that came to them."—*Newhall.*

3. **Fear not to go down into Egypt**—Abraham's danger and complications with Pharaoh, (chap. xii, 15-20,) and the prohibition against Isaac going there, (chap. xxvi, 2,) may have made Jacob loath to go down into that land of idolatry and superstition. Hence some special divine encouragement was needed.

4. **I will go down with thee into Egypt**—And if God be with us, who can be against us? **And I will also surely bring thee up**—"Wonderfully worded promise! Personally, he was then bidding those scenes an everlasting farewell; but in the mediatorial nation which was to spring from him, and with which, as heir of God's covenant, he was identified, he would return again. In this hope, by faith, he was to be glad though he die in Egypt, for it is added immediately, **Joseph shall put his hand upon thine eyes**, to close them in death; the last sad duty of love. Ancient writers of other nations frequently make pathetic allusion to this last ministration of affection. (Compare Homer's *Iliad*, xi, 453; *Odyssey*, xi, 426; xxiv, 296; Ovid, *Heroides*, i, 102, etc.")— *Newhall.*

5. **In the wagons which Pharaoh had sent to carry him**—"Instead of transporting them upon camels and asses, as was usual in Palestine. The use of the Egyptian wagons, and the fact that they were sent by Pharaoh himself, evidently made a deep impression, and is emphasized by the writer. See note on Gen. xiv, 27. On the direct route from Hebron to Beer-sheba the hills are too steep and sharp, and the surface is too rocky, to allow of travel on wheeled vehicles. Artificial wagon roads have never been constructed through that country. But wheels could pass from Beer-sheba east of the direct route, through the great Wady el-Khulil, and thence through the valleys to Hebron. (Robinson, i, 215.)"—*Newhall.*

of Canaan, and came into Egypt, ¹ Jacob, and all his seed with him: **7** His sons,

l Deut. 26. 5; Josh. 24. 4; Psa. 105. 23; Isa. 52. 4.

6. Came into Egypt, Jacob, and all his seed—At first summarily expressed, yet afterwards (verses 8–27) details are given.

THE MUSTER-ROLL OF ISRAEL, 8–27.

"There is a painstaking minuteness in the dates and statistics of this history, which stands in wonderful contrast with the round numbers and vague statements of mythical narratives. The numerical and statistical difficulties so much dwelt on by Colenso and others, mostly arise from an ignorant or perverse misapprehension of the antique style of the author, which must present real difficulties even to candour and learning. This list of names is not a full census of the whole family of Israel, since none of the wives are mentioned anywhere; nor of Israel's descendants, since only two female descendants occur in it; nor is it intended to give simply all the grandsons of Jacob who were born in Canaan, for, as his sons migrated in the prime of life, it is wholly improbable that no children were born to them in Egypt, where it is said that Israel was 'fruitful and increased abundantly;' while the list of Numbers xxvi, gives us no new names. This is simply a list of the heads of tribes, and of the grandsons and great-grandsons who became heads of *independent tribal families*, whether born in Canaan or in Egypt. Five of the grandsons here mentioned are missing from the list in Numbers, probably because their families became extinct; two of the grandsons of this list appear there as great-grandsons, an unimportant variation, when it is seen that they appear only as heads of families, and not in their personal relation; while the two women had some special historical importance —Dinah, as Jacob's daughter who was connected with the slaughter of the Shechemites, (Gen. xxxiv,) although he may have had other daughters, (verse 9,) and Sarah, or Serah, daughter of Asher, as historically conspicuous alone among all the granddaughters, for reasons that are unrecorded. Only the two sons of Joseph who became heads of tribes are mentioned, although he probably had other children. Gen. xlviii, 5, 6. The sacred number seventy was thus made up from sixty-seven male descendants, who were heads of tribes and of tribal families, two female descendants, and Jacob himself. The author groups them in four lists: thirty-two descendants of Leah, to whom he adds Jacob himself, without mentioning it, (although implied in the expression of verse 8, 'Jacob and his sons,') making thirty-three; fourteen descendants of Rachel; sixteen of Zilpah; and seven of Bilhah—making seventy in all. They are again grouped as sixty-six of the Canaan family, three of the Egyptian, and Jacob himself. Verses 26, 27. Yet inattention to the Hebrew idiom will lead the careless or captious reader to suspect discrepancies in the narrative, as when it is said (verse 27) that 'all the souls of the house of Jacob, which came into Egypt,' were threescore and ten, although Joseph and his two sons had just been mentioned as necessary to complete the number. See the same statement in Deut. x, 22. Also it is said in verse 15, 'all the souls of his sons and his daughters,' although only one daughter is mentioned, and Jacob himself must be included with the descendants of Leah to make the number thirty-three. So it is no discrepancy when it is made probable from the ages of Joseph and Benjamin, that some of their sons were born after the descent into Egypt. St. Stephen, following the Septuagint Old Testament, calls the number seventy-five, which number the Septuagint makes up by reckoning in five other heads of families not mentioned in the Hebrew."—*Newhall.*

A comparison of this family record of Jacob and his sons with that of the census in the time of Moses (Num. xxvi) will help illustrate the peculiarities of Hebrew genealogies. For the conve-

CHAPTER XLVI.

nience of the reader, we present these lists in parallel columns, and also select from the genealogies of 1 Chron. ii–viii the corresponding names, so far as they appear there. For convenience of reference, we have placed the corresponding names opposite each other, but the student will note the different order in which the names stand in the different lists as they appear in the several chapters.

In studying such parallel lists of names, it is important to attend to the historical position and purpose of each writer. This first register was probably prepared in Egypt, some time after Jacob and his family had migrated thither, and by the direction of Jacob himself. The aged and chastened patriarch went down into Egypt with the divine assurance that God would make of him a great nation, and bring him up again. Vers. 3, 4. Great interest would, therefore, attach to a family record made out by his order. At the time of the census of Numbers xxvi, whilst the names of the heads of families were all carefully preserved, they were differently arranged, and other names had become prominent. The tables given in 1 Chron. i–ix exhibit much more extensive additions and changes. These several lists were certainly not copied one from another, but were evidently prepared independently, each for a definite purpose and from a different standpoint. In the parallel lists, as here given, the asterisk is designed to call attention to variations in orthography, the small capitals designate the tribe fathers; names in black letter are supposed levirate substitutions of grandchildren, (see on verses 12 and 21,) and the word descendants stands in place of names which are not printed for want of sufficient space.

	Gen. xlvi.	Num. xxvi.	1 Chron. ii–viii.
1.	JACOB.		
2.	REUBEN	REUBEN	REUBEN
3.	Hanoch	Hanoch	Hanoch.
4.	Phallua	Phallua	Phallua.
		(Descendants.)	
5.	Hezron	Hezron	Hezron.
6.	Carmi	Carmi	Carmi.
7.	SIMEON	SIMEON	SIMEON.
8.	Jemuel	*Nemuel	*Nemuel.
9.	Jamin	Jamin	Jamin.
10.	Ohad		
11.	Jachin	Jachin	*Jarib.
12.	Zohar	*Zerah	*Zerah.
13.	Shaul	Shaul	Shaul.
14.	LEVI	LEVI	LEVI.
15.	Gershon	Gershon	*Gershom.
		(Descendants.)	
16.	Kohath	Kohath	Kohath.
17.	Merari	Merari	Merari.
		(Descendants.)	
18.	JUDAH	JUDAH	JUDAH.
19.	Er. **Hezron**	Er. **Hezron**	Er. **Hezron**.
20.	Onan. **Hamul**	Onan. **Hamul**	Onan. **Hamul**.
21.	Shelah	Shelah	Shelah.
22.	Pherez	Pherez	Pherez.
23.	Zerah	Zerah	Zerah.
24.	ISSACHAR	ISSACHAR	ISSACHAR.
25.	Tola	Tola	Tola.
26.	Phuvah	Phuvah	*Phuah.
27.	Job	*Jashub	*Jashib.
28.	Shimron	Shimron	Shimron.
29.	ZEBULUN	ZEBULUN	ZEBULUN.
30.	Sered	Sered	
31.	Elon	Elon	No genealogy recorded.
32.	Jahleel	Jahleel	
33.	Dinah		

LEAH'S SONS—33.

and his sons' sons with him, his daughters, and his sons' daughters, and all his seed brought he with him into Egypt.

8 And ^{m} these *are* the names of the children of Israel, which came into Egypt, Jacob and his sons : ^{n} Reuben, Jacob's firstborn. **9** And the sons of Reuben ; Hanoch, and Phallu, and Hezron, and Carmi.

10 And ^{o} the sons of Simeon ; ^{1} Jemuel, and Jamin, and Ohad, and ^{2} Jachin, and ^{3} Zohar, and Shaul the son of a Canaanitish woman.

11 And the sons of ^{p} Levi ; ^{4} Gershon, Kohath, and Merari.

12 And the sons of ^{q} Judah ; Er, and Onan, and Shelah, and Pharez, and Zarah : but ^{r} Er and Onan died in the land of Canaan. And ^{s} the sons of Pharez were Hezron and Hamul.

---

m Exod. 1. 1; 6. 14.——*n* Num. 26. 5; 1 Chron. 5. 1. —— *o* Exod. 6. 15; 1 Chron. 4. 24. —— 1 Or, *Nemuel*.——2 Or, *Jarib*.——3 Or, *Zerah*, 1 Chron. 4. 24.——*p* 1 Chron. 6. 1, 16.——4 Or, *Gershom*. ——*q* 1 Chron. 2. 3; 4. 21.——*r* Chap. 38. 3, 7, 10. ——*s* Chap. 38. 29; 1 Chron. 2. 5.

		Gen. xlvi.	Num. xxvi.	1 Chron. ii-viii.
ZILPAH'S SONS—16.	{	34. GAD................	GAD................	GAD.
		35. Ziphion...........	*Zephon............	
		36. Haggi.............	Haggi.............	
		37. Shuni.............	Shuni.............	No genealogy, but see 1 Chron. v, 11–17.
		38. Ezbon.............	*Ozni..............	
		39. Eri................	Eri................	
		40. Arodi.............	*Arod..............	
		41. Areli.............	Areli.............	
		42. ASHER.............	ASHER.............	ASHER.
		43. Jimnah............	Jimnah............	Jimnah.
		44. Jishvah...........	——	Jishvah.
		45. Jishvi............	Jishvi............	Jishvi.
		46. Beriah............	Beriah............	Beriah.
		47. Serah.............	Serah.............	Serah.
		48. **Heber**.........	**Heber**.........	**Heber.**
		49. **Malchiel**......	**Malchiel**......	**Malchiel.**
RACHEL'S SONS—14.	{	50. JOSEPH............	JOSEPH............	JOSEPH.
		51. Manasseh..........	Manasseh (Descendants.)	Manasseh.
		52. Ephraim...........	Ephraim (Descendants.)	Ephraim.
		53. BENJAMIN..........	BENJAMIN..........	BENJAMIN.
		54. Bela..............	Bela..............	Bela.
		55. Becher............	—— ..(Comp. Heb. text of 1 Chron. viii, 1.	
		56. Ashbel............	Ashbel............	Ashbel.
		57. Gera..............		**Gera.**
		58. Naaman............	Naaman............	Naaman.
		59. Ehi...............	*Ahiram............	*Aharah.
		60. Rosh..............		
		61. Muppim............	Sheshupham.........	**Shephuphan.**
		62. Huppim............	*Hupham............	——
		63. Ard...............	**Ard**............	*Addar.
BILHAH'S SONS—7.	{	64. DAN...............	DAN...............	DAN.
		65. Hushim............	*Shuham............	
		66. NAPHTALI..........	NAPHTALI..........	NAPHTALI.
		67. Jahzeel...........	Jahzeel...........	*Jahzieel.
		68. Guni..............	Guni..............	Guni.
		69. Jezer.............	Jezer.............	Jezer.
		70. Shillem...........	Shillem...........	*Shallum.

12. Hezron and Hamul—The probable reason for reckoning these among the seventy (verse 27) was, that they were adopted by Judah in place of the deceased **Er and Onan**, who **died in the land of Canaan.** This appears from the fact that in the later registers (Num. xxvi and 1 Chron. ii) they appear as permanent heads of families in Judah. Heber and Malchiel, grandsons of Asher, (verse 17,) are also reckoned among the seventy, and probably for the reason that they were born before the migration into Egypt. They also appear in the later lists as heads of families in Israel.

B. C. 1706. CHAPTER XLVI. 323

13 ᵗ And the sons of Issachar; Tola, and ⁵ Phuvah, and Job, and Shimron. 14 And the sons of Zebulun; Sered, and Elon, and Jahleel. 15 These *be* the sons of Leah, which she bare unto Jacob in Padan-aram, with his daughter Dinah: all the souls of his sons and his daughters *were* thirty and three. 16 And the sons of Gad; ᵘ Ziphion, and Haggi, Shuni, and ⁶ Ezbon, Eri, and ⁷ Arodi, and Areli. 17 ᵛ And the sons of Asher; Jimnah, and Ishuah, and Isui, and Beriah, and Serah their sister: and the sons of Beriah; Heber, and Malchiel. 18 ʷ These *are* the sons of Zilpah, ˣ whom Laban gave to Leah his daughter; and these she bare unto Jacob, *even* sixteen souls. 19 The sons of Rachel ʸ Jacob's wife; Joseph, and Benjamin. 20 ᶻ And unto Joseph in the land of Egypt were born Manasseh and Ephraim, which Asenath the daughter of Potipherah ⁸ priest of On bare unto him. 21 ᵃ And the sons of Benjamin *were* Belah, and Becher, and Ashbel, Gera, and Naaman, ᵇ Ehi, and Rosh, ᶜ Muppim, and ⁹ Huppim, and Ard. 22 These *are* the sons of Rachel, which were born to Jacob: all the souls *were* fourteen. 23 ᵈ And the sons of Dan; ¹⁰ Hushim. 24 ᵉ And the sons of Naphtali; Jahzeel, and Guni, and Jezer, and Shillem. 25 ᶠ These *are* the sons of Bilhah, ᵍ which Laban gave unto Rachel his daughter, and she bare these unto Jacob: all the souls *were* seven. 26 ʰ All the souls that came with Jacob into Egypt, which came out of his ¹¹ loins, besides Jacob's sons' wives, all the souls *were* threescore and six; 27 And the sons of Joseph, which were borne him in Egypt, *were* two souls: ⁱ all the souls of the house of Jacob, which came into Egypt, *were* threescore and ten.

28 And he sent Judah before him unto Joseph, ᵏ to direct his face unto Goshen; and they came ˡ into the land of Goshen. 29 And Joseph made ready his chariot, and went up to meet Israel his father, to Goshen, and presented himself unto him; and he ᵐ fell on his

---

t 1 Chron. 7. 1.——5 Or, *Puah,and Jashub*.—— *u* Num. 26. 15, etc. *Zephon*.——6 Or, *Ozni*.—— 7 Or, *Arod*.——*v* 1 Chron. 7. 30.——*w* Chap. 30. 10. ——*x* Chap. 29. 24.——*y* Chap. 44. 27.——*z* Chap. 41. 50.——8 Or, *prince*.——*a* 1 Chron. 7. 6; 8. 1. —— *b* Num. 26. 38, *Ahiram*, ——*c* Num. 26. 39, *Shupham*; 1 Chron. 7. 12, *Shuppim*.

9 *Hupham*, Numbers 26. 39. —— *d* 1 Chronicles 7. 12. —— 10 Or, *Shuham*, Numbers 26. 42. ——*e* 1 Chronicles 7. 13. ——*f* Chapter 30. 5, 7. —— *g* Chapter 29. 29. —— *h* Exodus 1. 5. —— 11 Hebrew, *thigh*, chapter 35. 11. —— *i* Deuteronomy 10. 22; see Acts 7. 14.——*k* Chapter 31. 21. ——*l* Chapter 47. 1.——*m* So chapter 45. 14.

---

21. Naaman ... Ard—In Num. xxvi, 40, these appear as sons of Bela. The most probable explanation of this discrepancy is, the Naaman and Ard here mentioned as **sons of Benjamin** died in Egypt without issue, and two of their brother Bela's sons were named after them and substituted for their place, according to levirate law, to perpetuate intact the families of Benjamin.

27. All the souls ... threescore and ten—It accorded with Hebrew spirit and custom to so frame a register of honoured names as to have them sum up a definite and significant number. So Matthew's genealogy of our Lord is arranged into three groups of fourteen names each, (Matt. i, 17,) and yet this could be done only by omitting several important names. The compiler of this list of Jacob's sons might, by another process equally correct, have made it number sixty-nine by omitting Jacob himself, or a lesser number by omitting some of the grandchildren, or have made it exceed seventy by adding the names of Jacob's wives: he purposely arranged it so as to make it number seventy souls. The descendants of Noah, as registered in chap. x, amount to seventy. The seventy elders of Israel (Num. xi, 16) and the seventy disciples chosen by Jesus (Luke x, 1) show a peculiar regard for this mystic number. It is not improbable that the arrangement of genealogical lists was made up to round numbers, and, where possible, to a sacred number, that the whole might be the more easily and correctly transmitted by oral tradition.

ISRAEL IN EGYPT, 28–34.

28. And he sent Judah before him—"Judah appears as a leader among his brethren, having taken the responsibility for the return of Benjamin, and having conducted the negotiation with Joseph (chap. xliv) with such pathetic eloquence as to bring matters at once to a crisis, and compel Joseph to throw off his disguise."—*Newhall.*

GENESIS. B. C. 1706.

neck, and wept on his neck a good while. **30** And Israel said unto Joseph, ⁿ Now let me die, since I have seen thy face, because thou *art* yet alive. **31** And Joseph said unto his brethren, and unto his father's house, ᵒ I will go up, and show Pharaoh, and say unto him, My brethren, and my father's house, which *were* in the land of Canaan, are come unto me; **32** And the men *are* shepherds, for ¹² their trade hath been to feed cattle; and they have brought their flocks, and their herds, and all that they have. **33** And it shall come to pass, when Pharaoh shall call you, and shall say, ᵖ What *is* your occupation? **34** That ye shall say, Thy servants' ᑫ trade hath been about cattle ʳ from our youth even until now, both we, *and* also our fathers: that ye may dwell in the land of Goshen; for every shepherd *is* ˢ an abomination unto the Egyptians.

CHAPTER XLVII.

THEN Joseph ᵃ came and told Pharaoh, and said, My father and my brethren, and their flocks, and their herds, and all that they have, are come out of the land of Canaan; and, behold, they *are* in ᵇ the land of Goshen. **2** And he took some of his brethren, *even* five men, and ᶜ presented them unto Pharaoh. **3** And Pharaoh said unto his brethren, ᵈ What *is* your occupation? And they said unto Pharaoh, ᵉ Thy servants *are* shepherds, both we, *and* also our fathers.

---

n So Luke 2. 29, 30.——*o* Chap. 47. 1.——12 Heb. *they are men of cattle.*——*p* Chap. 47. 2, 3.——*q* Verse 32.——*r* Chap. 30. 35; 34. 5; 37. 12.

s Chap. 43. 32; Exod. 8. 26.——*a* Chap. 46. 31.——*b* Chap. 45. 10; 46. 28.——*c* Acts 7. 13.——*d* Chap. 46. 33.——*e* Chap. 46. 34.

---

32. The men are shepherds—"In spite of the fact that shepherds were 'an abomination to the Egyptians,' Joseph introduces his brethren as shepherds; yea, for that reason he does so. This fact would secure them the isolation demanded by their providential mission. Compare the note at the beginning of this chapter, and see note on chap. xlvii, 3."—*Newhall.*

34. Land of Goshen—Concerning its admirable adaptation to the Israelitish colony, see note on chap. xlvii, 6.

CHAPTER XLVII.

INTRODUCTION TO PHARAOH, AND SETTLEMENT IN EGYPT, 1–12.

1–3. They said unto Pharaoh, Thy servants are shepherds — "The Egyptian monuments abundantly illustrate the hatred and contempt which the ruling castes felt towards the shepherds. In those great pictures of Egyptian life painted on the walls of the Theban tombs in the time of the Pharaohs, the shepherds are caricatured in many ways, being represented by figures lank, emaciated, distorted, and sometimes ghostly in form and feature. They are a vivid contemporary comment from Egyptian hands upon the sacred writer's statement, that 'shepherds are an abomination to the Egyptians.' Sheep are never represented in the Theban tombs as being offered in sacrifice or slaughtered for food; and though in certain districts mutton was used for food, and sheep and goats held sacred, (*Her.*, ii, 42,) these cases are regarded by Egyptologists as exceptional. (Knobel.) Woollen was esteemed unclean by the priests, and their religion forbade them to wear woollen garments into the temples, or to bury the dead in them. (*Her.*, ii, 81.) This apparent aversion to the sheep is, however, greatly offset by the wide-spread worship of Amun and of Noum as ram-headed gods, as even now illustrated in the paintings of the tombs and in the splendid ruins of Karnak, and gives no sufficient reason for the contempt in which the shepherd was held. Nor is it a sufficient reason, as some have supposed, that the shepherds were accustomed to slaughter for food the ox, which was held sacred by the Egyptians; for the Egyptian worship of the bull was restricted to a single animal at a time, called the Apis, and the sculptures represent the priests as offering bulls in sacrifice, and eating beef and veal. Besides, the nomads rarely kill the ox, and never kill the cow for food. It was not to the shepherd, as such, but to the nomadic shepherd, with his wild, roving, predatory habits, that the civilized Egyptian bore this hatred.

"There was also a special reason found for this hatred in an event which has stamped itself deeply upon Egyptian history; but whether it transpired before the era of Joseph or not is still an unsettled question. About two thousand years before Christ Egypt was invaded by a people from the north-east, of what precise nation is uncertain, who dispossessed the native princes, cast contempt upon the national religion, demolished the temples, slew the sacred animals, and set up at Memphis a foreign government which ran through three dynasties, (the fifteenth, sixteenth, and seventeenth of Manetho,) and ruled the greater part of the land for five or six centuries. They are called in history the Hyksos, or shepherd kings. The Theban king Amosis finally rose against them, and expelled them from the land, driving them into the Syrian desert. The name of shepherd became thereafter inseparably associated in the Egyptian mind with this Hyksos subjugation and tyranny, and so was especially hateful. Wilkinson believes that the Egyptian career of Joseph took place in the period just following the expulsion of the Hyksos, and so explains why, at that time especially, a shepherd was 'an abomination to the Egyptians.' This is, however, one of the disputed questions of Egyptian chronology whose solution is probably locked up in monuments and papyri yet to be deciphered.

"But, whatever be the explanation of this enmity, the fact is abundantly attested by the monuments; and we have this remarkable manifestation of the meekness and godly wisdom of Joseph, that, so far from attempting to conceal or disguise this unpleasing fact concerning his family, he announced it to Pharaoh at the outset, and instructed his brethren to repeat it to the king at their first introduction. Thus he secured the frontier district of Goshen for the family of Israel, where they might dwell in comparative isolation from the Egyptian idolatry. His family was introduced in such a way as to effectually preclude their political advancement. His great popularity and influence at the Egyptian court could have secured for them political preferment, or at least a total change of worldly condition; yet he is not dazzled by this most natural family ambition, but seeks first the spiritual good of his brothers and his children. In this he is the prototype of Moses, who chose to be a Hebrew exile rather than an Egyptian prince.

"There are two remarkable Egyptian records of the twelfth dynasty (2020–1860 B. C., according to Wilkinson,) which strikingly illustrate the career of Joseph. One is the story of Saneha, written on one of the oldest papyri yet discovered. Saneha was a pastoral nomad, who was received into the service of the reigning Pharaoh, rose to a high rank, was driven into exile, and afterwards restored to favour—was made the king's counsellor, given precedence over all the courtiers, 'set over the administration of the government of Egypt to develop its resources,' and finally 'prepared his sepulchre among the tombs of the princes.' (Translation by M. Chabas, in *Speaker's Commentary*.) There is no proof that Saneha was the Hebrew Joseph, but the parallel is most instructive as illustrating the possibility of a foreigner's elevation in Egypt.

"The other record, made under the same dynasty, is found in the pictures and inscriptions of the famous sepulchral grottoes of Beni-hassen, which are thirty excavations cut in the limestone along the Nile's eastern bank. A picture in one of these tombs represents the presentation of a nomad Asiatic chief, with his family and dependents, before an Egyptian prince. Their features, colour, costume, even to the rich 'tunic of fringe,' ('coat of many colours,') are all Asiatic. There is also an inscription describing a prince who was a favourite of the Pharaoh, which brings Joseph most vividly before us. Lepsius thus translates it: 'He injured no little child; he oppressed no widow; he detained for his own purpose no fisherman; took from his work no shepherd; no overseer's men were taken. There was no beggar in his days; no one starved in his time. When years of famine occurred, he ploughed all the lands of the district, producing abundant food; no one was starved in it; he treated the widow as a woman with a husband to protect

GENESIS.

4 They said moreover unto Pharaoh, ᶠ For to sojourn in the land are we come; for thy servants have no pasture for their flocks; ᵍ for the famine *is* sore in the land of Canaan: now therefore, we pray thee, let thy servants ʰ dwell in the land of Goshen. **5** And Pharaoh spake unto Joseph, saying, Thy father and thy brethren are come unto thee: **6** ⁱ The land of Egypt *is* before thee; in the best of the land make thy father and brethren to dwell; ᵏ in the land of Goshen let them dwell: and if thou knowest *any* men of activity among them, then make them rulers over my cattle. **7** And Joseph brought in Jacob his

---
f Chap. 15. 13; Deut. 26. 5. —— *g* Chap. 43. 1; Acts 7. 11.

h Chapter 46. 34. —— *i* Chapter 20. 15. —— *k* Verse 4.

---

her.' (BUNSEN'S *Egypt*, vol. v: translation by BIRCH.) Neither here is there any proof that this favourite was Joseph; but the high estimate set upon virtues and abilities just such as are shown in Joseph, furnish an instructive comment upon our history."—*Newhall.*

4. To sojourn in the land are we come—" Not to dwell there, for Canaan was ever their home, the land of promise. Yet this 'sojourning' lasted more than two, if not more than four, centuries."—*Newhall.*

6. The land of Egypt is before thee—" Although they belonged to the abominated caste, all Egypt was at their disposal for Joseph's sake. **In the land of Goshen let them dwell**—Since this is your petition. **And if thou knowest any men of activity among them**—Rather, men of ability, namely, for such office. **Make them rulers over my cattle** — Literally, *princes* of (the shepherds or herdsmen of) my cattle. Not overseers of his *household*, (as A. Clarke,) for the word signifies only property in **cattle**. (Gesenius; Knobel.) Pharaoh would make Joseph's brethren, as far as they were competent, overseers of his herdsmen and shepherds. So Doeg, the Edomite, was overseer of Saul's herdsmen. (1 Sam. xxi, 7.)"—*Newhall.*

"The land where Israel was to dwell is here called **Goshen**, and in verse 11 Rameses. In Exod. xii, 37, Israel is said to have set out from Rameses. This place was near the seat of government, since Joseph told his father that he would there dwell near him, (Gen. xlv, 10,) and apparently between Palestine and Joseph's residence, (Gen. xlvi, 28, 29,) which was probably usually at Memphis, although sometimes, perhaps, at Zoan. See note on Exod. i, 8. It was under the government of Egypt, and yet hardly reckoned a part of the country, and appears not to have been occupied to any great extent by the native inhabitants, as the reason assigned for settling the Israelites there is, that they might not come in contact with the Egyptians. Gen. xlvi, 33, 34. Every thing thus indicates that Goshen, or Rameses, was the frontier province, nearest to Palestine, lying along the Pelusiac arm of the Nile, and stretching from thence eastward to the desert. The Israelites may have spread eastward as they multiplied, across the Pelusiac to or across the Tanitic arm. This was **the best of the land** for a pastoral people like Israel, although not so fertile as the country nearer the Nile; yet it was well irrigated from Egypt's great river. It was traversed by an ancient canal, which, according to Strabo, once carried the Nile water into the Red Sea, and on the banks of which it is probable that the Israelites built the treasure-city Raamses or Rameses. Exod. i, 11. This canal traversed the wadies Tumeylat and Seven Wells, which was the richest portion of Goshen, although the Israelites doubtless drove their flocks up the water-courses into fertile tracts of the desert. The present Sweet-water Canal of M. Lesseps has simply reopened the works of the Pharaohs, carrying the Nile water through these broad wadies to Lake Timsah, and thence south through the Bitter Lakes to the Red Sea at Suez.

"Robinson made careful inquiries concerning the fertility of this province at present, and found that it now 'bears the highest valuation, yields the largest revenue,' and that 'there are here more flocks and herds than anywhere else in Egypt, and also more fisher-

father, and set him before Pharaoh: and Jacob blessed Pharaoh. **8** And Pharaoh said unto Jacob, ¹ How old *art* thou? **9** And Jacob said unto Pharaoh, ¹ The days of the years of my pilgrimage *are* a hundred and thirty years: ᵐ few and evil have the days of the years of my life been, and ⁿ have not attained unto the days of the years of the life of my fathers in the days of their pilgrimage. **10** And Jacob ᵒ blessed Pharaoh, and went out from before Pharaoh.

11 And Joseph placed his father and his brethren, and gave them a possession in the land of Egypt, in the best of the land, in the land of ᵖ Rameses, ᵠ as Pharaoh had commanded. **12** And Joseph nourished his father, and his brethren, and all his father's household, with bread, ² ³ according to *their* families.

13 And *there was* no bread in all the land; for the famine *was* very sore, ʳ so that the land of Egypt and *all* the land of Canaan fainted by reason of the famine. **14** ˢ And Joseph gathered up all the money that was found in the land of Egypt, and in the land of Canaan, for the corn which they bought: and Joseph brought the money into Pharaoh's house. **15** And when money failed in the land of Egypt, and in the land of Canaan, all the Egyptians came unto Joseph, and said, Give us bread: for ᵗ why should we die in thy presence? for the money faileth. **16** And Joseph said, Give your cattle; and I will give you for your cattle, if money fail. **17** And they brought their cattle unto Joseph: and Joseph gave them bread *in exchange* for horses, and for the flocks, and for the cattle of the herds, and for the asses; and he ⁴ fed them with bread for all their cattle for that year. **18** When that year was ended, they came unto him the second year, and said unto him, We will not hide *it* from my lord, how that our money is spent; my lord also hath our herds of cattle; there is not aught left in the sight of my lord, but our bodies, and our lands: **19** Wherefore shall we die before thine eyes, both we and our land? buy us and our land for bread, and we and our land will be servants unto Pharaoh: and give *us* seed, that we may live, and not die,

---

1 Heb. *How many* are *the days of the years of thy life?*—*l* Psa. 39. 12; Heb. 11. 9, 13.——*m* Job 14. 1.——*n* Chap. 25. 7; 35. 28.——*o* Verse 7.——*p* Exod. 1. 11; 12. 37.——*q* Verse 6.

2 Or, *as a little child is nourished.*——3 Heb. *according to the little ones*, chap. 50. 21.—— *r* Chap. 41. 30; Acts 7. 11.——*s* Chap. 41. 56.—— *t* Verse 19.——4 Heb. *led them.*

---

men.'—*Biblical Researches*, i, 54. This country now produces, according to Lane, (*Modern Egyptians*, i, 242,) cucumbers and melons, gourds, onions, leeks, beans, chick-peas and lupins; and the inhabitants also make use of small salted fish for food; a list of productions closely corresponding with that given in Num. xi, 5, where the murmuring Israelites say, 'We remember the fish that we did eat in Egypt freely, the cucumbers, and the melons, and the leeks, and the onions, and the garlic.' The opening of the Suez Canal has increased the fertility of the land since the visits of Robinson and Lane.

" Large heaps of ruins are now found south-west of Belbeis, which are called by the Arabs the hills or graves of the Jews, (*Tel el Jehud, Turbeh el Jehud*,) which may be memorials of the Israelitish sojourn. Many traces of ancient sites are scattered along the Wady Tumeylat. The geographical position of Goshen was such that the plagues of hail and darkness might sweep down the Nile valley, and even cover Zoan, while Goshen (on the east) was left untouched."—*Newhall.*

11. Rameses—See notes on verse 6, and Exod. i, 11.

12. According to their families —Heb., *for the mouth of the little ones ;* that is, bread for the mouths of these. Thus Joseph became a nourishing father to his aged father's household, as well as to Pharaoh and all Egypt.

JOSEPH'S ADMINISTRATION DURING THE YEARS OF FAMINE, 13–26.

13. Egypt and … Canaan fainted —Like an exhausted person, dying of thirst.

15. All the Egyptians came — Came by their representatives. Observe the three stages of impoverishment through which they passed in becoming the dependents of Pharaoh. First they used up all their money; then they delivered up all their cattle for bread; and finally they surrendered all title and claim to their lands, and thus became serfs unto Pharaoh.

18. The second year—The second year after their money failed.

GENESIS. B. C. 1701.

that the land be not desolate. **20** And Joseph bought all the land of Egypt for Pharaoh; for the Egyptians sold every man his field, because the famine prevailed over them: so the land became Pharaoh's. **21** And as for the people, he removed them to cities from *one* end of the borders of Egypt even to the *other* end thereof. **22** ᵘOnly the land of the ᵇpriests bought he not; for the priests had a portion *assigned them* of Pharaoh, and did eat their portion which Pharaoh gave them: wherefore they sold not their lands. **23** Then Joseph said unto the people, Behold, I have bought you this day and your land for Pharaoh: lo, *here*

is seed for you, and ye shall sow the land. **24** And it shall come to pass in the increase, that ye shall give the fifth *part* unto Pharaoh, and four parts shall be your own, for seed of the field, and for your food, and for them of your households, and for food for your little ones. **25** And they said, Thou hast saved our lives: ᵛ let us find grace in the sight of my lord, and we will be Pharaoh's servants. **26** And Joseph made it a law over the land of Egypt unto this day, *that* Pharaoh should have the fifth *part;* ʷexcept the land of the ᵇpriests only, *which* became not Pharaoh's.

27 And Israel ˣdwelt in the land of

---

u Ezra 7. 24. —— 5 Or, *princes*, chap. 41. 45; 2 Sam. 8. 18.

v Chap. 33. 15.——*w* Verse 22.—— 6 Or, *princes*, verse 22.——*x* Verse 11.

---

20. The land became Pharaoh's —He thus became absolute owner of the soil, and this enabled Joseph freely and without opposition to take the measures and enact the law described in verses 23–26.

21. Removed them to cities—For greater convenience in supplying them with food; for he had stored the grain in the cities. Chap. xli, 48.

22. Land of the priests bought he not—Pharaoh's reverence for the ministers of religion would not allow an alienation of their land from them. **Their portion which Pharaoh gave them**—During the years of famine he ordered them to be supplied from the public treasury, without money and without price. This is represented as Pharaoh's act rather than Joseph's. The latter, of course, would not interfere. He had married the daughter of one of the priests. But the sacred writer clearly intimates that the reverence shown to the Egyptian priesthood by this measure was for Pharaoh's sake, not for his own.

23. I have bought you—This fact gave him the opportunity to dictate the future policy of the kingdom as to the royal revenue; a policy which the people were probably now prepared to see the wisdom of, and to which they readily acceded. Verse 25.

26. Joseph made it a law—It has been thought exorbitant and oppressive **that Pharaoh should have the fifth part** of the produce of the land. But we should observe, 1) That during the years of plenty the land of Egypt yielded an excessive abundance, (chap. xli, 47, 49,) and the Egyptians had no difficulty in laying up one fifth. 2) The people made no objection to Joseph's law. 3) The liability of that land to suffer from famine made it a simple matter of wise government to lay up stores of grain for such times of need. This law of Joseph maintained for the king an ample but not oppressive revenue, while at the same time it virtually restored the land to the people, and made the king's relation to them that of a provident and nourishing father.

"All the main points in the statements of this chapter are confirmed by Herodotus, Diodorus, Strabo, and the monuments. Herodotus (ii, 109) says, that Sesostris divided the soil among the inhabitants, assigning square plots of land of equal size to all, and obtained his revenue from a rent paid annually by the holders. Diodorus (i, 54) says, that Sesoösis divided the whole country into thirty-six nomes, and set nomarchs over each to take care of the royal revenue and administer their respective provinces. Strabo (xvii, p. 787) tells us, that the occupiers of the land held it subject to a rent. Again, Diodorus (i, 73, 74) represents the land as pos. sessed only by the priests, the king, and the warriors, which testimony is confirmed by the sculptures. Wilkinson, i, p. 263. The discrepancy of this from the account in Genesis is apparent in the silence of the latter concerning the

Egypt, in the country of Goshen; and they had possessions therein, and ʸ grew, and multiplied exceedingly. **28** And Jacob lived in the land of Egypt seventeen years: so ⁷ the whole age of Jacob was a hundred forty and seven years. **29** And the time ᶻ drew nigh that Israel must die: and he called his son Joseph, and said unto him, If now I have found grace in thy sight, ᵃ put, I pray thee, thy hand under my thigh, and ᵇ deal kindly and truly with me; ᶜ bury me not, I pray thee, in Egypt: **30** But ᵈ I will lie with my fathers, and thou shalt carry me out of Egypt, and ᵉ bury me in their buryingplace. And he said, I will do as thou hast said. **31** And he said, Swear unto me. And he sware unto him. And

---

y Chap. 46. 3.——7 Heb. *the days of the years of his life,* see verse 9. —— *z* So Deut. 31. 14; 1 Kings 2. 1.

a Chap. 24. 2.——*b* Chap. 24. 49.——*c* So chap. 50. 25. —— *d* 2 Sam. 19. 37. —— *e* Chap. 49. 29; 50. 5, 13.

---

lands assigned to the warrior caste. The reservation of their lands to the priests is expressly mentioned in verse 22; but nothing is said of the warriors. There was, however, a marked difference in the tenure of land by the warriors from that by the priests. Herodotus (ii, 168) says, that each warrior had assigned to him twelve *aruræ* of land (each *arura* being a square of one hundred Egyptian cubits;) that is to say, there were no landed possessions vested in the caste, but certain fixed portions assigned to each person; and these, as given by the sovereign's will, so apparently were liable to be withheld or taken away by the same will; for we find that Sethos, the contemporary of Sennacherib, and therefore of Hezekiah and Isaiah, actually deprived the warriors of those lands which former kings had conceded to them. Herod. ii, 141. It is, therefore, as Knobel remarks, highly probable that the original reservation of their lands was only to the priests, and that the warrior caste did not come into possession of their twelve *aruræ* each till after the time of Joseph. In the other important particulars the sacred and profane accounts entirely tally, namely, that by royal appointment the original proprietors of the land became crown tenants, holding their land by payment of a rent or tribute; whilst the priests only were left in full possession of their former lands and revenues. As to the particular king to whom this is attributed by Herodotus and Diodorus, Lepsius '*Chronol. Egypt.*, i, p. 304) supposes that this was not the Sesostris of Manetho's twelfth dynasty,(Osirtasen of the Monuments,) but a Sethos or Sethosis of the nineteenth dynasty, whom he considers to be the Pharaoh of Joseph.

"The nineteenth dynasty is, however, certainly much too late a date for Joseph. It may be a question whether the division of the land into thirty-six nomes and into square plots of equal size by Sesostris, be the same transaction as the purchasing and restoring of the land by Joseph. The people were already in possession of their property when Joseph bought it, and they received it again on condition of paying a fifth of the produce as a rent. But whether or not this act of Sesostris be identified with that of Joseph, (or the Pharaoh of Joseph), the profane historians and the monuments completely bear out the testimony of the author of Genesis as to the condition of land tenure, and its origin in an exercise of the sovereign's authority."— *Speaker's Commentary.*

JACOB'S DESIRE TO BE BURIED WITH HIS FATHERS, 27–31.

28. **Seventeen years**—He survived the famine, and lived twelve years thereafter to see the result of the wise administration of Joseph. Yet his spiritually minded patriarch sees something better for his posterity than the land of Egypt.

29. **Israel must die**—The weakness and infirmities of old age admonished him that his end was near at hand. **My thigh.** See note on chap. xxiv, 2.

30. **I will lie with my fathers**—Egypt will do to live in for a time, but Jacob would have his dust repose with that of Abraham and Isaac in the land of Canaan. Compare the touching words of chap. xlix, 29–32. Such a dying request none would refuse.

*Israel bowed himself upon the bed's head.

CHAPTER XLVIII.

AND it came to pass after these things, that *one* told Joseph, Behold, thy father *is* sick: and he took with him his two sons, Manasseh and Ephraim. 2 And *one* told Jacob, and said, Behold,

---

f Chap. 48. 2; 1 Kings 1. 47; Heb. 11. 21.

---

31. **Upon the bed's head**—The Syriac and Sept., (quoted in Heb. xi, 21,) read, *on the head* (or *top*) *of his staff.* Either meaning is possible, since the Hebrew מטה means either *bed* or *staff,* according as it is punctuated and pronounced.

CHAPTER XLVIII.
ADOPTION AND BLESSING OF JOSEPH'S SONS, 1–22.

"At the very close of his career, Jacob's character greatly rises in moral grandeur. The spirit of prophecy comes upon him, and he utters some of the most inspiring words of revelation. The world is fading on his dim eyes, but he has now the piercing vision of the seer, which reveals what is to take place 'in the last days.' Cut off from the outer world by his infirmities, his soul has retired within the great covenant promises made to his fathers, which he now sees to be splendid prophetic blessings for his children. He recalls the heavenly stairway of Bethel, on which he saw the angels in his youthful exile; the struggle and victory of Peniel, where 'Jacob' was changed to 'Israel;' the renewal of the covenant promise and covenant name on his return to Bethel; the grave of Bethlehem, into which his hopes were crushed with his beloved Rachel; and finally, the strange career of Joseph, which must have seemed in retrospect like the death and resurrection of his best beloved son. All these providences he now recounts to his son Joseph, and by them he ascends into the mount of vision. Chap. xlvii, 3–7. There is a dramatic vividness and life-like warmth in this picture of the aged patriarch, 'strengthening himself' to speak these last words, rising from his Egyptian bed, and sitting upon its side, as did Socrates in his last day. Phædo, 60, B. He sees not Joseph's sons so much as the tribes behind them; for these are not personal, but national predictions; and yet they are suggested by individual peculiarities, along which, by the path of prophetic association, the patriarch travels into the future. The return to Canaan and the far-off possession of that land of promise, are the field of his contemplation, and he takes no notice of the intervening ages of Egyptian sojourn and servitude."—*Newhall.*

1. **After these things**—Probably soon after the events narrated at the close of the previous chapter. **Thy father is sick**—Extreme old age, accompanied by any unusual symptoms of physical disorder, would excite attention, and admonish Jacob's children that the day of his death was near at hand. Accordingly, as soon as Joseph heard the report of his father's illness **he took with him his two sons,** and hastened to his bedside. It is possible Joseph feared that the two sons here named, having been born in Egypt of an Egyptian woman, might not be allowed full inheritance among the sons of Israel. So he would have them obtain the holy patriarch's blessing ere he died. **Manasseh and Ephraim** "are here mentioned, as was natural, in the order of age, but the tribes were always designated as Ephraim and Manasseh, since there were 'ten thousands of Ephraim, and thousands of Manasseh.' Deut. xxxiii, 17. Joseph came not simply to pay his dying father a visit of sympathy and affection, but to receive his blessing, and to have his children formally recognised as heirs of the covenant promises from which their Egyptian birth had alienated them for a time. Joseph here remarkably reveals his characteristic faith, and his keen moral and spiritual sense. An Egyptian prince, and the highest subject of Pharaoh, honours and wealth without stint were within his reach for his children; but

thy son Joseph cometh unto thee: and Israel strengthened himself, and sat upon the bed. **3** And Jacob said unto Joseph, God Almighty appeared unto me at ^a Luz in the land of Canaan, and blessed me, **4** And said unto me, Behold, I will make thee fruitful, and multiply thee, and I will make of thee a multitude of people; and will give this land to thy seed after thee ^b *for* an everlasting possession.

5 And now thy ^c two sons, Ephraim and Manasseh, which were born unto thee in the land of Egypt, before I came unto thee into Egypt, *are* mine; as Reuben and Simeon, they shall be mine. **6** And thy issue, which thou begettest after them, shall be thine, *and* shall be called after the name of their brethren in their inheritance. **7** And as for me, when I came from Padan, ^d Rachel died by me in the land of Canaan in the way,

---

a Chapter 28. 13, 19; 35. 6, 9, etc.——*b* Chapter 17. 8.

c Chap. 41. 50; 46. 20; Josh. 13. 7; 14. 4.——*d* Chap. 35. 9, 16, 19.

---

he turned away from wealth and power in his manhood, as he had from sinful pleasure in his youth. The family pride that has ruined so many virtuous men had no blandishments for him. His sons were never presented for preferment among the princes of Pharaoh, for he saw grander dignities and riches for them among the despised shepherds of Goshen than could be conferred in the courts of the Pharaohs. He presented his children to be blessed and adopted into the patriarchal family."—*Newhall.*

2. Strengthened himself—" Gathered up his energies for the last interview, **and sat upon the bed.** If Ja-

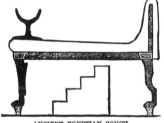

ANCIENT EGYPTIAN COUCH.

cob leaned upon the top of his staff (Heb. xi, 21, and Gen. xlvii, 31, in the Sept.,) the bed must have been elevated upon a divan, or a bedstead. Bedsteads were not common among the Hebrews, but are represented in the Egyptian monuments, according to Wilkinson, elevated and richly sculptured."—*Newhall.*

3. God Almighty—" EL SHADDAI, the name by which God manifested himself at Bethel to Jacob, (chap. xxxv, 16,) in revelation of the fulness of his power to perform what seemed incredible."—*Newhall.*

4. An everlasting possession—" The great family promise absorbs Jacob's soul. He is identified with the nation which is to spring from his loins, whose home is to be Canaan, whence blessings are to flow down all ages and to all lands. He sets this sublime mission before Joseph as a far higher dignity for his children than princedoms in Egypt, and so claims for himself Ephraim and Manasseh."—*Newhall.*

5. Thy two sons . . . are mine . . as Reuben and Simeon—" They are to have the tribal rank of sons, although they were grandsons. In 1 Chron. v, 1, 2, it is said that Reuben, the firstborn, was deprived of his birthright because of his sin, and it was given to the two sons of Joseph. Joseph thus had a double portion, which was reckoned one of the privileges of the firstborn."—*Newhall.* The law of Deut. xxi, 15–17, forbidding the transfer of right of the firstborn to a son of a more favoured wife, could not have governed the action of Jacob. This transfer was for sufficient cause.

6. Which thou begettest after them—" It is probable that Joseph had other children, and that their descendants are reckoned with those of Ephraim and Manasseh, (Num. xxvi, 23–37,) the natural being undistinguished from the adopted sons."—*Newhall.*

7. Rachel died by me—" Jacob honours his beloved Rachel by giving her eldest son the right of the firstborn. The reminiscence of the sudden and afflictive death of Jacob's only real wife thus rises up amid these words of blessing."—*Newhall.* The expression

when yet *there was* but a little way to come unto Ephrath: and I buried her there in the way of Ephrath; the same *is* Beth-lehem. 8 And Israel beheld Joseph's sons, and said, Who *are* these? 9 And Joseph said unto his father, ᵉ They *are* my sons, whom God hath given me in this *place*. And he said, Bring them, I pray thee, unto me, and ᶠ I will bless them. 10 Now ᵍ the eyes of Israel were ʲ dim for age, *so that* he could not see. And he brought them near unto him; and ʰ he kissed them, and embraced them. 11 And Israel said unto Joseph, ⁱ I had not thought to see thy face: and, lo, God hath showed me also thy seed. 12 And Joseph brought them out from between his knees, and he bowed himself with his face to the earth. 13 And Joseph took them both, Ephraim in his right hand toward Israel's left hand, and Manasseh in his left hand toward Israel's right hand, and brought *them* near unto him. 14 And Israel stretched out his right hand, and laid *it* upon Ephraim's head, who *was* the younger, and his left hand upon Manasseh's head, ᵏ guiding his hands wittingly; for Manasseh *was* the firstborn.

15 And he ˡ blessed Joseph, and said, God, ᵐ before whom my fathers Abraham and Isaac did walk, the God which fed me all my life long unto this day, 16 The Angel ⁿ which redeemed me from all evil, bless the lads; and let ᵒ my name be named on them, and the name of my fathers Abraham and Isaac; and let them ² grow into a multitude in the midst of the earth. 17 And when Joseph saw that his father ᵖ laid his right hand upon the head of Ephraim, it ³ displeased him: and he held up his father's

---

e So chap. 33. 5.——*f* Chap. 27. 4.——*g* Chap. 27. 1.——1 Heb. *heavy,* Isa. 6. 10; 59. 1.——*h* Chap. 27. 27.——*i* Chap. 45. 26.——*k* Verse 19.——*l* Heb. 11. 21.——*m* Chap. 17. 1; 24. 40.

n Chap. 28. 15; 31. 11, 13, 24; Psa. 34. 22; 121, 7.——*o* Amos 9. 12; Acts 15. 17.——2 Heb. *as fishes do increase,* see Num. 26. 34, 37.——*p* Verse 14.——3 Or, *was evil in his eyes,* chap. 28. 8.

---

died by me has well been thought to contain emotional tenderness. According to Lange, "she died for him, since, while living, she shared with him and for him the toils of his pilgrimage life, and through this, perhaps, brought on her deadly travail."

8–13. "Israel groped to embrace the children whom his dim eyes could not see, and Joseph placed them between his knees, and afterwards withdrew them (v, 12,) to present them in the order of their age for his dying blessing. Joseph expected that the chief blessing would be given to the eldest, Manasseh, and so placed him that the dim-eyed Jacob would naturally lay the right hand upon his head."—*Newhall.*

14. **Guiding his hands wittingly** —Literally, *he made wise his hands.* "Instructing his hands," says the Targum Onk.; his hands acted as if wise, and crossed each other, to symbolically express the prophetic preference of Ephraim to Manasseh. "The sacred writer minutely details this wonderful manifestation of inspired prescience. By events like this were the chosen people incessantly indoctrinated in the great truths of the divine foreknowledge and supervision of all human plans, while at the same time human and secondary causes are never ignored."—*Newhall.*

15, 16. **He blessed Joseph**—"Joseph is here identified with his children, after the true patriarchal conception of the divine covenant. There is herein a threefold benediction: **God, before whom my fathers Abraham and Isaac did walk**—The God of the past, the God of the covenant. **The God which fed me all my life long unto this day**—The God of providence, as he has revealed himself to *me* as well as my fathers: (how changed from the self-reliant, self-seeking Jacob of old!) **The Angel which redeemed me from all evil**—The redeeming God, the Jehovah-Angel. It is the God who leads, feeds, saves. **Let my name be named on them, and the name of my fathers**—Let them be the true heirs of the three great patriarchs. And let them multiply as do the fishes, that swarm in the teeming Nile. The very imagery shows that the patriarch has come to Egypt, for now he no more sees his seed symbolized by the stars of the Asiatic firmament, nor by the sands of the Syrian sea-shore, but by the fatness of the all-fertilizing Nile."—*Newhall.*

17. **It displeased him**—Heb., *it was evil in his eyes.* He looked upon it as an evil omen, and interfered to correct what he regarded as a mistake of his father. Nor was he the first or the last

hand, to remove it from Ephraim's head unto Manasseh's head. **18** And Joseph said unto his father, Not so, my father: for this *is* the firstborn; put thy right hand upon his head. **19** And his father refused, and said, q I know *it*, my son, I know *it*: he also shall become a people, and he also shall be great: but truly r his younger brother shall be greater than he, and his seed shall become a s multitude of nations. **20** And he blessed them that day, saying, *s* In thee shall Israel bless, saying, God make thee as Ephraim and as Manasseh: and he set Ephraim before Manasseh. **21** And Israel said unto Joseph, Behold, I die; but t God shall be with you, and bring you again unto the land of your fathers. **22** Moreover u I have given to thee one portion above thy brethren, which I took out of the hand v of the Amorite with my sword and with my bow.

q Verse 14.——*r* Num. 1. 33, 35; 2. 19, 21; Deut. 33. 17; Rev. 7. 6, 8.——4 Heb. *fulness*.——*s* So Ruth 4. 11, 12.

t Chap. 46. 4; 50. 24.——*u* Josh. 24. 32; 1 Chron. 5. 2; John 4. 5.——*v* Chap. 15. 16; 34. 28; Josh. 17. 14, etc.

fond father who has been displeased with the order of divine providence touching his sons.

20. He set Ephraim before Manasseh — "Manasseh outnumbered Ephraim at the Exodus, (Num. xxvi, 34 and 37,) yet the Ephraimite Joshua led Israel into Canaan, and after the conquest Ephraim was the leading tribe of the northern nation, as Judah was of the southern."—*Newhall.*

21. Behold, I die; but God shall be with you—"Sublime and inspiring faith! Your father dies, but his God, and his father's God, remains."—*Newhall.*

22. I have given to thee one portion—The word rendered **portion** is *shechem,* (שְׁכֶם, *shoulder,*) and may have been employed with some allusion to the town of this name, which was situated in the hill country of Ephraim, (Josh. xx, 7,) and the place near which Joseph's bones were buried. Joshua xxiv, 32. Here was the "parcel of a field" which Jacob purchased of Hamor, the father of Shechem. Chap. xxxiii, 19. And this in later tradition was understood to be "the parcel of ground which Jacob gave to his son Joseph." John iv, 5. But this tract, acquired by peaceable purchase, could not have been spoken of by Jacob as having been taken **out of the hand of the Amorite with my sword and with my bow.** We have no record of any such forcible acquisition of land by the patriarchs. "Any conquest of territory," says Delitzsch, "would have been entirely at variance with the character of the patriarchal history, which consisted in the renunciation of all reliance upon human power, and a devoted trust in the God of the promises."

Nor could Jacob have here referred to the vengeful slaughter of the Shechemites by Simeon and Levi, (chap. xxxiv, 25–29,) which he ever reprobated as accursed and cruel, (xxxiv, 30, xlix, 5–7.) Rationalistic critics, who regard this whole narrative as a prophetic fiction written after the conquest of Canaan, explain it as an invention to account for or justify the double tribe-territory held by the house of Joseph, and find its historical basis in Josh. xvii, 14–18. But a later writer, inventing such a prophetic fiction, would not have used the preterite verb-forms, **I have given,** and **I took;** but rather, *I give . . . what thou shalt take,* or *what thy sons shall take.* The contest shows the aged patriarch to be speaking with his eye upon the future, and calling things that are not as though they were. The promise of the land of Canaan had been made so repeatedly to the patriarchs (comp. ver. 4) that it now rises up as an accomplished fact in Jacob's prophetic vision, and is spoken of accordingly. The iniquity of the Amorite was not yet full, (see chap. xv, 16,) but its punishment is a foregone conclusion in the Divine mind. A like use of the prophetic perfect may be seen in the prophecy concerning Ishmael. Chap. xvii, 20. Jacob here identifies himself with his descendants, and speaks as doing in person what his posterity will certainly accomplish in the after time.

CHAPTER XLIX.

JACOB'S PROPHETIC BLESSING ON HIS SONS, 1–27.

Jacob was the last great patriarchal representative and possessor of the covenant blessing of Jehovah. His grandfather Abraham had been separated from his kindred and native land, and received the promise and the covenant of circumcision. Isaac was preferred, to the exclusion of Ishmael and the sons of Keturah, and he transmitted the prophetic blessing of the covenant to Jacob, thereby excluding and supplanting Esau. Jacob is now about to die, and the chosen seed are henceforth to be represented by twelve tribes rather than by one great father. It was fitting, therefore, before this last great patriarch was gathered to his people, that the voice of prophecy should issue from his lips, and, magnifying itself above the blessings of the everlasting hills, (ver. 26,) should disclose unto his children some things that would befall them in the last days. Israel will have no successor like himself, and the Book of Genesis ends with the "generations of Jacob;" but the divine thoughts of this prophecy appear again in the blessing of Moses, (Deut. xxxiii,) and may also be traced in the song of Déborah. Judges v. The student should also compare with this prophetic psalm that of Isaac when he felt his end approaching, (Gen. xxvii, 1, 4, 26–29, 39, 40,) the farewells of Joshua (Josh. xxiii and xxiv) and of Samuel, (1 Sam. xii,) the last words of David, (2 Sam. xxiii,) and the language of Simeon (Luke ii, 25–32) and of Paul, (2 Tim. iv, 5–8.) All these saints breathed the same prophetic spirit, and were divinely gifted to utter words of imperishable value. They caught in vision the outlines of future great events, the full significance of which they but imperfectly comprehended. 1 Pet. i, 10, 11. It was a prevalent opinion of heathen antiquity that highly gifted souls were wont to prophesy at the moment of their departure from the world. Thus Socrates (in Plato's *Apology*) says to his judges: "And now, O men who have condemned me, I would fain prophesy to you; for I am about to die, and that is the hour in which men are gifted with prophetic power."

Modern critics, of all rationalistic schools, deny the genuineness of this prophecy, and refer it to a period long subsequent to Jacob's time. They hold that its author, after the manner of poetical writers of all nations, conceived the happy thought of transferring certain facts of his own time and nation to the prophetic vision of a famous ancestor. Similarly Virgil, in the sixth book of the *Æneid*, (756–891,) represents father Anchises detailing to his son a long account of the fortunes of his posterity in Italy. These critics claim that the language of this poem is too highly wrought, and its historical and geographical allusions too minute, to be the utterance of an illiterate old man, who had been a shepherd all his life.

To these criticisms it may be replied, that the quiet of shepherd life, the deep and varied experiences through which Jacob passed, and the serene grandeur of his old age, furnished the most natural conditions of such a prophecy. So far, therefore, from being an objection, these considerations furnish a strong argument in favour of the genuineness of this poem. He who had the dream at Bethel, the vision of angels at Mahanaim, and the struggle and triumph at Peniel; who had traversed hills and plains, and been exposed to the extremes of heat and cold and storms; who, like David in later times, became, by means of pastoral life and exposure, familiar with the habits of the lioness and the lion's whelp, the ravening wolf and the bounding hind, and the horned serpent hidden by the wayside; the father, who had studied the characters of all his sons with more than human interest; who had watched the merchant-caravan to learn the ways of other lands and peoples; who had stood in the presence of Pharaoh, and abode seventeen years in Egypt; the son of Isaac, the son of Abraham, the heir of the promises—he, of all men, would seem to have been the fittest person to voice these oracles. So we aver that this prophecy is traceable to a psychological basis in the life and experiences of the aged patriarch, as they are presented to us in the Book of Genesis.

As to the poetical form of the

prophecy, we may suppose a number of hypotheses. The rapturous utterances of such a seer naturally take poetic form and fervour, and the critical reader of this poem will note its intensity of passion, sudden transitions, outbursts of alarm, ejaculations of prayer, and a multiplicity of similes and metaphors. Can we suppose any of the greatest poets of the world to have spoken in such exalted strains? Certainly, but not without premeditation. Milton composed his finest passages in the stillness of the night, and dictated them to his daughters the following day. Similarly Jacob may have mentally prepared this entire poem, and have repeated it with glowing inspiration when his sons stood about his bed. Nothing forbids the supposition that months and even years had been previously given to its preparation. It has been suggested that each of the sons remembered his own blessing or oracle, and wrote it down, and afterwards the eleven separate oracles were united in the order in which they now stand. Others have thought that the patriarch blessed his sons in substantially the words which we have here, and the general sentiments were treasured up in the memory of his sons, written out in rhythmic form by a later poet, and possibly revised and supplemented at a still later day. Any or all of these suppositions are permissible with one who defends the genuineness of the prophecy, so long as he holds that, whatever revision it has received by later hands, it truly preserves in substance what the dying patriarch said to his sons.

This prophecy contains nothing in itself incredible—nothing which might not, in substance if not in form, have been spoken by Jacob in his last days. It is in admirable keeping with the dream of Bethel, which was a sublime revelation of the great truth, running through the whole Old Testament, that in him and his posterity all families of the earth were to be blessed. Gen. xxviii, 14. Such a gift of prophecy has its measure of the supernatural, but nothing miraculous. The supernaturalism of genuine prophecy implies

no violence done to the prophet. The prevision with which he was for the time gifted, was as truly in harmony with his natural powers as was the far-reaching prophetic dream at Bethel.

The charge that this poem abounds with minute geographical and historical allusions inconsistent with genuine prophecy, is abundantly refuted by the fact that the adverse critics cannot agree as to its date, but have referred its composition all the way from the times of the judges to the later kings of Israel. Determining data must be sadly deficient in a production which has been assigned by eminent critics to such different times as the six following:

1) The period of the Judges. (Dillmann, Baur, Ewald.)
2) The time of Saul's reign, and probably written by Samuel. (Tuch.)
3) The reign of David. (Eichhorn, Knobel, Bohlen.)
4) Somewhere in the period covered by the reigns of David and Solomon. (Reuss.)
5) In the earlier period of the divided kingdom, when Judah and Joseph were the two great rival tribes. (Kalisch.)
6) During the times of the Syro-Israelitish wars, to which allusion is supposed in verses 23 and 24.

It is evident from this diversity of opinion that when we remove this prophecy from the date and person to whom it is assigned by the sacred writer, we go out upon a sea of uncertainty and conjecture which involves greater difficulties than to accept it as the genuine word of Jacob.

The order in which the sons are named is: A.—The six sons of Leah: 1) Reuben. 2) Simeon. 3) Levi. 4) Judah. 5) Zebulun. 6) Issachar. B.—The four sons of the handmaids: 7) Dan. 8) Gad. 9) Asher. 10) Naphtali. C.—The two sons of Rachel: 11) Joseph. 12) Benjamin. If we compare the narrative of the several births, (chapter xxx,) we see that Zebulun was born after Issachar, though named before him here, and Naphtali is placed here after Gad and Asher, though probably born before them. It is possible, however, that Naphtali was born after both Gad and Asher; for after giving birth to Dan, (xxx, 6,) Rachel's handmaid, Bilhah, may not

CHAPTER XLIX.

AND Jacob called unto his sons, and said, Gather yourselves together, that I may ^a tell you *that* which shall befall you ^b in the last days. 2 Gather yourselves together, and hear, ye sons of Jacob; and ^c hearken unto Israel your father. 3 Reuben, thou *art* ^d my firstborn, my might, ^e and the beginning of my strength, the excellency of dignity, and

1. And Jacob called his sons, and said:
   Assemble yourselves and I will declare unto you
   What shall befall you in the end of the days.
2. Gather yourselves together and hear, O sons of Jacob,
   Yea, hearken unto Israel, your father.

REUBEN.

3. Reuben, my firstborn, thou!
   My might and the beginning of my strength;
   Excellence of dignity and excellence of power.

---

a Deut. 33. 1; Amos 3. 7.——*b* Num. 24. 14; Deut. 4. 30; Isa. 2. 2; 39. 6; Jer. 23. 20; Dan. 2. 28, 29; Acts 2. 17; Heb. 1. 2.——*c* Psa. 34. 11.——*d* Chap. 29. 32.——*e* Deut. 21. 17; Psa. 78. 51.

have borne her second child, Naphtali, until after Leah's handmaid, Zilpah, had borne both her sons, (xxx, 9, 13.) The placing of Zebulun before Issachar was, perhaps, designed in this prophetic blessing, like the placing of Ephraim before Manasseh, to denote that the younger should be in some way greater than the elder. Compare chap. xlviii, 14, 19; Deut. xxxiii, 18. In comparing the order followed in Moses's psalm, we find 1) Reuben, whose precedence in birth never could be denied; 2) Judah, the princely; 3) Levi, the priestly; 4) Benjamin, placed before 5) Joseph; 6) Zebulun, as here before 7) Issachar; and the sons of the handmaids are arranged as follows: 8) Gad, 9) Dan, 10) Naphtali, 11) Asher, while Simeon is left out altogether.

As a part of the exegesis we furnish a new translation of this poem, and accordingly the notes are based upon the new translation.

1. **Assemble yourselves** — These words evidently belong to the poem itself, and are not the composition of the historian, who inserted a copy of Jacob's prophecy in this place in his volume. The gathering contemplated was around the patriarch's couch, whither Joseph had before hastened when he heard of his father's sickness, (chap. xlviii, 2,) and where the whole family were now summoned to hear the prophetic word.

What particular meaning the writer attached to the expression **the end of the days** is somewhat doubtful. It is too definite a phrase to denote merely *after times*, or *the future*. It suggests the idea of a limit, the end of an age, æon, or period. Such an age had its רֵאשִׁית and its אַחֲרִית, its beginning and its end, and the author of this prophecy proposed to speak of events belonging to the end, or closing period, of the age to which he belonged. The Septuagint translates it by the phrase so common in the New Testament, ἐπ' ἐσχάτων τῶν ἡμερῶν, *in the last days*, which suggests the same idea of the closing period of an æon. The events contemplated as befalling the sons of Jacob in **the end of the days** were such as belonged to the last period of the prophet's vision; the end as distinguished from the beginning of Israelitish history. How near or how remote that **end** might be is left entirely undetermined.

3. **My firstborn, thou**—By this form of expression poetic emphasis is given to the direct address. **Beginning of my strength**—Allusion to the supposed superior vigour of the firstborn, as inheriting the full virile power of the father. Comp. Deut. xxi, 17; Psa. lxxviii, 51; cv, 36. **Excellence of dignity ... power**—His excellence is his natural pre-eminence as

the excellency of power: **4** Unstable as water, ᶠ¹ thou shalt not excel; because thou ᵍ wentest up to thy father's bed; then defiledst thou *it :* ²he went up to my couch.
5 ʰ Simeon and Levi *are* ¹ brethren;

4. Boiling over like the waters, thou shalt not excel;
For thou didst go up to the beds of thy father.
Then didst thou defile; my couch he went up!

SIMEON AND LEVI.

5. Simeon and Levi—brothers—
Instruments of violence their swords.

ƒ 1 Chron. 5. 1. —— 1 Heb. *do not thou excel.* —— *g* Chap. 35. 22; Deut. 27. 20; 1 Chron. 5. 1. 2 Or, *my couch is gone.* —— *h* Chap. 29. 33, 34. —— *i* Prov. 18. 9.

---

firstborn; his **dignity**, (Heb., שְׂאֵת, from נָשָׂא, *to lift up*,) is his *elevation,* or the rank to which he was thus entitled. The distinction between **might, strength,** and **power** in this verse, each representing a different Hebrew word, is this: **Might** and **strength** here denote physical energy and manly vigour, while **power** (עֹז) is used in the sense of *authority,* a right and prerogative of the firstborn. The powers and prerogatives naturally adhering to the firstborn, were, because of Reuben's sins, transferred to Judah and Joseph.

4. Boiling over like the waters— The figure may be the overflowing of a large body of water beyond its proper banks, and sweeping away all before it; but, more likely, as Gesenius thinks, it is that of a boiling pot of water, and denotes the violent, unrestrained licentiousness of Reuben, exhibited in his incestuous intercourse with Bilhah. Chap. xxxv, 22. **Beds**—The use of the plural may here hint at repeated acts of incest on the part of Reuben. **Defile** is purposely left without an expressed object. The supplying, in the common version, of the word *it,* weakens the passage. **Then didst thou defile,** exclaims the indignant father, and suddenly changes from direct address to the third person, and repeats the words **my couch he went up!** as denoting the foul act by which he showed himself unworthy to retain the rights and glory of his primogeniture, and, therefore, he should **not excel.** The tribe of Reuben never did excel. The leadership was given to Judah;

the birthright of a double portion of the inheritance was given to Joseph's two sons. Comp. 1 Chron. v, 1, 2. The Reubenites were among the first to settle at their ease on the east of the Jordan, (Num. xxxii,) and in the time of Deborah they remained at ease among their sheepfolds when other tribes arose and fought for the liberty of the nation. Judges v, 15, 16. No leader, judge, or prophet is ever mentioned as springing from the tribe of Reuben, but they had among them some valiant warriors, who fought successfully against the Hagarites. 1 Chron. v, 10, 18, 20.

5. Simeon and Levi are named together, because they were **brothers** in the twofold sense of being sons of the same mother, and so much alike in disposition and character. Hence, after pronouncing their names, the patriarch pauses, and then emphatically adds the word **brothers.** Their similar spirit was seen and became historical in their cruel slaughter of the Shechemites, (chap. xxxiv, 25–31,) for in that massacre they led the way. The memory and fear of that act never departed from Jacob's soul, and as Reuben's incest cost him the rights and glory of the firstborn, so the bloody deed of Simeon and Levi colours all this oracle, and brought them cursing where they might have had blessing. **Instruments of violence their swords**—The word מְכֵרֹת, rendered *swords,* occurs here only, and manifestly means some instrument of violence; but its derivation is uncertain. The ancient versions differ widely, and the word has been variously

ᵏ instruments of cruelty *are in* their habitations. **6** O my soul, ˡ come not thou into their secret; ᵐ unto their assembly, ⁿ mine honour, be not thou united: for ᵒ in their anger they slew a man, and in their selfwill they ᵈ digged down a wall. **7** Cursed *be* their anger, for *it was* fierce; and their wrath, for it was cruel: ᵖ I will divide them in Jacob, and scatter them in Israel.

6. Into their secret council come not, my soul;
Into their assembly unite not, my honour;
For in their rage they slaughtered men,
And in their wanton pleasure they houghed oxen.
7. Cursed their rage, for it was a power,
And their fury, for it was severe!
I will divide them in Jacob,
And I will scatter them in Israel!

---

3 Or, *their swords* are *weapons of violence.*——*k* Chap. 34. 25.——*l* Prov. 1. 15, 16.——*m* Psa. 26. 9; Eph. 5. 11.

n Psa. 16. 9; 30. 12; 57. 8.——*o* Chap. 34. 26.——4 Or, *houghed oxen.*——*p* Josh. 19. 1; 21. 5, 6, 7; 1 Chron. 4. 24, 39.

---

explained, as *machinations*, (*De Dieu,*) *betrothals*, (*Dathe,*) *habitations*, (Eng. version.) But the rendering **swords**, (perhaps from כּוּר, to *pierce*, or *penetrate*,) seems most in harmony with the context, and is adopted by many of the best interpreters. According to Rashi, the Greek word μάχαιρα, *sword*, was derived from this. According to Gesenius, Rabbi Eliezer says: "Jacob cursed their swords in the Greek tongue." According to chap. xxxiv, 25, Simeon and Levi "took each man his sword" (חרב) and slaughtered all the men of Shechem.

6. **Their secret council**—Allusion to their private conspiracy to massacre the men of Shechem. **Unite not**—This uniting in secret assembly is to be punished by *dividing* and *scattering* them. Verse 7. **My honour**—Used of the heart or soul, as the noblest and most honourable part of man's nature. Compare Psa. vii, 5; xvi, 9; xxx, 13. But at the same time the ordinary meaning of the word may be here kept prominent: Let not my honour be compromised or tarnished by any union with their counsels. **They slaughtered men**—Heb., *a man.* The singular, though used collectively, gives peculiar vividness to the thought as conceived in the Hebrew idiom. **They houghed oxen**—Here, too, the Hebrew employs the singular in the same collective sense. The fact stated illustrates the wanton cruelty of these brothers. The common version, *they digged down a wall*, follows the Chaldee, Syriac, Vulgate, Aquila, and Symmachus; but the authority of these versions, which have copied from one another, is outweighed by the fact that in all other passages where the Piel of this word (עקר) occurs, it means to hamstring or hough an animal. Such uniform usage has greater authority than the testimony of many versions.

7. **I will divide... scatter**—He speaks as one conscious of divine authority. Their guilty *uniting* in conspiracy and cruelty is to be punished by *dividing* and *scattering* them in Israel. In the census of Num. xxvi, the Simeonites number only 22,200—less than any other tribe; in Moses's blessing (Deut. xxxiii,) they are not mentioned at all; and in the allotment of Canaan their inheritance consisted of scattered cities within the territory previously assigned to Judah. Josh. xix, 1-9.

The Jews have a tradition that the Simeonites became largely the scribes and teachers among the other tribes, and so were scattered in Israel. In 1 Chron. iv, 27, it is said they did not increase like the children of Judah, and in verses 39-43, of the same chapter, it appears that they were scattered beyond the limits of Judah southward. The Levites, as is well-known, obtained no separate territory as a tribe, but were scattered about in various cities of the other tribes. See Josh. xxi. But this curse of the patriarch did not

8 ⁿ Judah, thou *art he* whom thy brethren shall praise: ʳ thy hand *shall be* in the neck of thine enemies; ˢ thy father's children shall bow down before thee. 9 Judah *is* ᵗ a lion's whelp: from the prey, my son, thou art gone up: ᵘ he stooped down, he couched as a lion, and as an old lion; who shall rouse

JUDAH.

8. Judah, thou! Thy brothers shall praise thee;
Thy hand in the neck of thy foes!
The sons of thy father shall bow down to thee.
9. Whelp of a lion is Judah;
From prey, my son, thou hast gone up.
He has bent down, he has crouched down like a lion
And like a lioness—who will rouse him up!

---

q Chap. 29. 35; Deut. 33. 7.——*r* Psa. 18. 40.——*s* Chap. 27. 29; 1 Chron. 5. 2.   *t* Hosea 5. 14; Revelation 5. 5.——*u* Numbers 23. 24; 24. 9.

---

hinder these tribes from sharing in the blessings of the covenant. Though divided and scattered, they were made a means of blessing to the whole house of Israel. Compare Moses's words on Levi, Deut. xxxiii, 8-11, where their character as priests and teachers is made prominent.

The words used of Simeon and Levi in Jacob's prophecy have been a great trouble to the critics who would explain it as the production of a later time. So far from being an accurate detail of facts, some writers have pronounced it inconsistent with the history of those tribes, for, according to Josh. xix, 1-9, Simeon did have a definite tribe-territory allotted him, and to the Levites were assigned several of the most important cities in the land, with their suburbs, and they were made the priests and ministers of the sanctuary instead of the firstborn. These facts are hard to reconcile with the theory that the song was written after the conquest of Canaan; but, in the mouth of Jacob, the language may be naturally explained.

8. **Judah, thou**—Pleonastic use of the pronoun, but adding emphasis to the address. **Shall praise thee**—A play upon the meaning of the name Judah. See chap. xxix, 35. "Reuben, Simeon, and Levi had been cursed and scattered, but as the patriarch turns his eye upon Judah, he sees that the energy and courage which have made him a leader among his brethren will re-appear in his children of remote generations, and make them illustrious above all the other tribes of Israel. His name, which signifies 'praised,' or 'celebrated,' is seen to shoot its lustre through all the future."—*Newhall*.

9. **Whelp of a lion**—Three different Hebrew words are here employed for **lion**, represented in our translation by **whelp, lion,** and **lioness**. The patriarch first calls Judah a lion's whelp, and then directly addresses him, as if, like a lion, he had seized his prey, and having eaten what he would, had gone up to his lair in the mountains. He then resumes the third person, and pictures the victorious lion as having bowed and **crouched down,** either for repose or in readiness to pounce upon any victim which might approach him. In this crouching attitude he is further described as a **lioness,** fiercest of all the lion family, and most dangerous to rouse up in the lair. Hence the apocalyptic expression, "lion of the tribe of Judah," (Rev. v, 5.) "The form of this vision came from remembered sights and sounds in the far-away Syrian mountains, but its substance came from an energy, courage, and might that were to burst upon the world in still increasing splendour through successive generations, yet incomprehensible to the wisest prophet in advance of their historic development. It came from Jerusalem, the Ariel, 'or lion of God'—from David, who, in one of his loftiest lyrics, cried, 'Thou hast given me the necks of mine enemies,' (Psalm xviii, 40,)—from the 'Lion of the tribe of Judah,'

340 GENESIS. B. C. 1689.

him up? **10** ᵛ The sceptre shall not depart from Judah, nor ʷ a lawgiver ˣ from between his feet, ʸ until Shiloh come; ᶻ and unto him *shall* the gathering of the

10. Sceptre shall not depart from Judah,
Nor ruler's staff from between his feet,
Until he shall come—Shiloh—
And unto him shall be obedience of peoples.

---

v Num. 24. 17; Jer. 30. 21; Zech. 10. 11.—*w* Psa. 60. 7; 108. 8; or, Num. 21. 18.—*x* Deut. 28. 57.—*y* Isa. 11. 1; 62. 11; Ezek. 21. 27; Dan. 9. 25; Matt. 21. 9; Luke 1. 32. 33.——*z* Isa. 2. 2; 11. 10; 42. 1, 4; 49. 6, 7, 22, 23; 55. 4, 5; 60. 1, 3, 4, 5; Hag. 2. 7; Luke 2. 30, 31, 32.

---

whose eyes are one day to be turned upon men 'like a flame of fire,' and his voice to fill the world 'like the sound of many waters.' "—*Newhall.*
10. Sceptre shall not depart from Judah—" The symbol of tribal authority in Israel, not necessarily the badge of royalty. The token of tribal life and pre-eminence should not depart, but Judah should maintain its life, integrity, and supremacy as a tribe."—*Newhall.* **Ruler's staff**—The word מְחֹקֵק may denote either a ruler or his badge of office and power. The latter best preserves the harmony of the parallelism. Some read, as the common version, *lawgiver.* The Septuagint and Vulgate have *leader.* Targum Onkelos, *scribe;* Targum Jerusalem, *scholars of the law.* Syriac, *interpreter.* **From between his feet**—Those who render מְחֹקֵק *ruler,* or *lawgiver,* naturally explain this expression as a euphemism for posterity—issue of his loins. But with the idea of **ruler's staff** is associated the custom of Oriental kings, as depicted on the monuments, sitting on the throne with the royal sceptre between their feet. **Until he shall come—Shiloh.** By translating in this form we leave the grammatical construction as ambiguous as it appears in the Hebrew text. It is equally correct, so far as the mere question of syntax is concerned, to render *until Shiloh comes,* or *until he comes to Shiloh.* Three different readings appear in Hebrew MSS., namely, שִׁילֹה, שִׁלֹה, and שְׁלוֹ. The Septuagint, Aquila, Symmachus, Syriac, and some of the Targums, seem to have read שֶׁלּוֹ, as if compounded of שׁ, abbreviation of אֲשֶׁר, and לֹה or לוֹ. We have the cognate words שְׁלוּ שָׁלֵו and שַׁלְוָה, meaning *rest,* or *peace,* and it is not impossible but one of these words was the original reading of our text. The Septuagint and other versions named above render, *until that which is his shall come,* or, *till he come whose it is.* The Vulgate reads, " until he comes who is to be sent." Others translate *Shiloh* as an appellative, meaning *rest,* " until he (Judah) comes to rest, or, " until rest comes." The English revisers (of 1885) place *until Shiloh come* in the text, and *till he come to Shiloh* in the margin. Many have adopted this last rendering, and understand Shiloh of the town where the tabernacle was set up after the conquest, (Josh. xviii, 1;) but against this is the decisive objection, that up to that time Judah had no notable pre-eminence. The honourable position assigned to this tribe in the desert march, (Num. ii, 3,) was by no means an adequate fulfilment of the terms of this oracle; for Moses, the Levite, was commander during all the march, and Joshua, the Ephraimite, succeeded him, and commanded the armies until after the conquest and partition of the land. It also is doubtful if Shiloh existed in Jacob's time, and it is certain that it never appears in history as having any especial interest for the tribe of Judah, but was situated in the tribe-territory of Ephraim. Far more satisfactory is the ancient interpretation, represented in the Targums and maintained by most Christian expositors, which makes Shiloh a proper name, (meaning *resting-place,* or *rest-giver,*) and a designation of the Messiah, who was to spring from the tribe of Judah. Jacob's prophetic vision opened for the moment into the distant future, and saw the regal posi-

people be. **11** ᵃ Binding his foal unto | the vine, and his ass's colt unto the
**11. Binding to the vine his young ass,
And to the choice vine the foal of his ass,**

a 2 Kings	18. 32.

tion the tribe of Judah was destined to hold at the time when all the tribes should be organized into a kingdom. From the time when royalty was established in Israel by the conquests of David and his settlement upon the throne, the tribe of Judah held a regal pre-eminence, and maintained its distinct tribal character until the coming of Jesus Christ.

It is often alleged against this Messianic interpretation, that after the destruction of the kingdom of Judah by the Chaldeans the exercise of royal power was broken, and that no real Jewish king again reigned in the city of David. The Maccabean leaders were not of the tribe of Judah, and the Herods, who bore the title of kings, were of foreign birth. But, even granting all these allegations, the notable fact remains that the vast majority of those who returned from the Babylonian exile were of the tribe of Judah, and that their body of elders formed a council which virtually represented the sceptre and the ruler's staff. Notwithstanding their many oppressions, and the occasional interruption of their worship, they were permitted during all those centuries to manage their own affairs, and to constitute a distinct and well-known body politic until finally broken up and scattered by the Romans. The sceptre of Judah was, indeed, during much of this time, of no great weight, but it was not taken away; it did **not depart from Judah.** The waͺs of the Maccabees and the government of Herod truly served to maintain· and perpetuate (not Joseph, or Dan, or Naphtali but) the power of Judah. As long as the tribe retained its distinct existence and name, even though a foreigner held the sceptre, the spirit of this prophecy was fulfilled. So the Persian monarchy retained its name and power, even while a usurper occupied the throne. No one now questions, that when Christ ap-

peared he sprang from the tribe of Judah.

It deserves special remark that the permanency of the kingdom of Judah and of the royal line of David is one of the marvels of history. While other and greater kingdoms fell, it remained. Revolutions swept over Egypt, and dynasty after dynasty passed away. Phœnicia and Syria, with their varied forms of power and pomp, flourished and decayed. The great Assyrian empire, after oppressing both Judah and Israel, and blotting out the latter, was overthrown, and yet the little kingdom of Judah, with a descendant of David on the throne, maintained its individuality, ·held its ancient sacred capital, and continued unbroken, resolute, hopeful. And even after its fall under Nebuchadnezzar, and seventy years of bitter exile, and after Babylon, in turn, had fallen and the Persian empire had risen into power, we find the children of Judah returning to their fatherland, rebuilding their temple and city, still led by a scion of the house of Judah. This irrepressible tribe, thus again established in their ancient regal seat, survived the fall of Persia, outlived the triumphs of Alexander and his successors, and maintained its national and political existence through unspeakable troubles and oppressions, until finally dispersed by the Romans in A. D. 70.

Obedience of peoples—The Septuagint and Vulgate render, *expectation* of peoples; others, *gathering*, or *congregation* of peoples. But the word occurs elsewhere only at Prov. xxx. 17, where *obedience* is the only suitable meaning. Here is the first intimation of such Messianic hopes as are more fully outlined in such passages as Isa. ii, 3 ; xi, 1–10.

11. Binding to the vine his young ass—This verse contains a composite picture of princely wealth and peaceful industry. Judah will be rich in

choice vine; he washed his garments in wine, and his clothes in the blood of grapes: 12 His ᵇ eyes *shall be* red with wine, and his teeth white with milk.

13 ᶜ Zebulun shall dwell at the haven of the sea; and he *shall be* for a haven of ships; and his border *shall be* unto Zidon.

He has washed in the wine his clothes,
And in the blood of grapes his robe.
12. Lustrous the eyes from wine,
And white the teeth from milk.

ZEBULUN.

13. Zebulun,—at the coast of seas let him dwell;
Yea, he (would fain be) at the coast of ships,
And his side upon Zidon.

---

b Prov. 23. 29. | *c* Deut. 33. 18, 19; Josh. 19. 10, 11.

---

vineyards and wine and milk. In the more ancient times the ass, like the camel, served for carrying the rich and noble; (Judg. v, 10; x, 4; xii, 14;) and the thought here is, that Judah will have possessions of this costly kind. The picture of abundance and luxury is enhanced by the thought that the vines of his soil will grow to such strength that the asses may be tied to them without harm. The territory allotted to Judah was noted for its vineyards and pastures. Here grew the grapes of Eshcol and En-gedi; (Num. xiii, 23, 24; Song of Sol. i, 14;) here were Maon and Carmel and Tekoa, famous for pastures and numerous flocks. 1 Sam. xxv, 2; Amos, i, 7; 2 Chron. xxvi, 10. It is not improbable that this picture of abundance and repose was added to that of Judah's conquests and power in order to denote the plentiful peace and quiet which he should enjoy after his great victories. But to adduce, as parallel to this Scripture, the ass and foal of Zech. ix, 9, and Matt. xxi, 5, and the wine-press and blood-stained garments of Isaiah, lxiii, 1–6, and explain all alike as a special prophecy of Christ, would be extravagant—a reading into the language of this poem the ideas of a later time.

12. **Lustrous the eyes from wine** —The Septuagint, Vulgate, and some expositors construe the preposition מִן, **from,** as denoting a comparison; *more lustrous,* or *more joyful than wine, and whiter than milk.* This is allowable; but inasmuch as the previous verse speaks of the great abundance of wine, and fertility of the land of Judah, the more suitable thought in this verse is, that *from* the superabundance of wine and milk, (as the originating cause,) the eyes and teeth are affected.

13. **At the coast of seas let him dwell**—These words concerning Zebulun are among the definite geographical allusions which rationalistic criticism adduces as evidence of the late origin of this prophecy. But so far from being situated upon the seas, or bordering on Zidon, Zebulun's territory was entirely surrounded by that of other tribes, and touched neither sea nor land of Zidon. Compare Josh. xix, 10–16; Deut. xxxiii, 19. As designating geographical position, both this verse and its parallel in Deuteronomy would better fit Issachar and Asher, and, therefore, refute the idea that they were written after the conquest and allotment of the land. Better is the supposition that the dying father's words sprang from what he had observed in the tastes and habits of this son—a love of commerce, a desire for **ships** and trade upon the **seas** rather than by the travel of the desert caravans. Thus the allusion to **seas, ships, Zidon** — the synonymes of ancient naval commerce—would be most natural in the mouth of Jacob. Hence also a reason for the jussive rendering of יִשְׁכֹּן, **let him dwell.** As a matter of fact, the tribe-territory of Zebulun extended between the Medi-

B. C. 1689.   CHAPTER XLIX.   343

14 Issachar *is* a strong ass couching down between two burdens: 15 And he saw that rest *was* good, and the land that *it was* pleasant; and bowed ᵈ his shoulder to bear, and became a servant unto tribute. 16 ᵉ Dan shall judge his people, as one of the tribes of Israel. 17 ᶠ Dan

ISSACHAR.

14. Issachar is an ass of bone,
   Crouching down between the double sheepfolds:
15. And he saw rest, that it was good,
   And the land, that it was pleasant ;
   And he stretched out his shoulder to bear (burdens),
   And became a tribute-slave.

DAN.

16. Dan shall judge his people,
   Like one of the tribes of Israel.
17. Let Dan become a serpent on the road,
   A horned viper on the path,

---

d 1 Sam. 10. 9.——*e* Deut. 33. 22;   Judges 18. 1, 2.——*f* Judges 18. 27.

terranean and Galilean seas, though not touching upon either, and the words **his side upon Zidon,** or *towards Zidon,* do not necessarily mean that his territory would border on Zidon, but may denote that it looked that way, or that the tribe itself would come to have some peculiar dependence on Zidon, or some notable relations with the Phœnicians. In Deborah's song this tribe is celebrated for skill in penmanship and heroism in battle. Judges v, 14, 18.

14. **Ass of bone** — Or, *bony ass ;* that is, strongly built and fit for carrying burdens. See chap. xxx, 18, on the origin of the name Issachar. Issachar's characteristic was a disposition to look for a *reward* or *hire* rather than liberty and honour. Like a beast of burden, he loves to lie down and rest **between the double sheepfolds;** that is the inclosures made of hurdles, and open at the top. The word is dual, probably because these folds were generally divided into two parts. Comp. Judges v, 16, note.

15. **Rest**... **good**—His love of ease, and a **pleasant** territory, including the rich valley of Jezreel, led him **to bear burdens,** and to submit to **tribute** rather than to enter into any struggle for political eminence. For this reason, probably, Zebulun was placed before him. In the war against

Sisera, he was a supporter of Barak, but no leader. He followed at the feet of his leader, as one obedient to orders. Judg. v, 15.

16. **Dan shall judge**—A play upon the name of Dan, which means *a judge,* or *judging.* Comp. chap. xxx, 6. Being the first named of the sons of the handmaids, it is fitting to emphasize the thought that he shall, nevertheless, even as the sons of Leah, or any of the tribes, exercise due authority **as one of the tribes of Israel.** Some suppose there is here a special allusion to Samson, the distinguished judge, who sprang from this tribe; but this is unnecessary as an exposition of the sense of the verse.

17. **Let Dan become**—The emphatic position of the verb יְהִי is best expressed by translating it thus imperatively. And the comparison with the serpent need not be construed as necessarily a curse or condemnation. The account in Judges xviii, of the Danite conquest in the north, illustrates the subtlety and prowess of this tribe; and so, also, does the whole history of Samson. His stratagems to overthrow his enemies might well be compared with the habits of the viper that hides by the wayside, and bites the horse's heels, and causes him to throw his rider. The **horned viper** is generally regarded as

shall be a serpent by the way, *an adder in the path, that biteth the horse heels, so that his rider shall fall backward. 18 I ᶠhave waited for thy salvation, O LORD.
19 ʰGad, a troop shall overcome him: but he shall overcome at the last.
20 ⁱOut of Asher his bread *shall be fat*, and he shall yield royal dainties.
21 ᵏNaphtali *is* a hind let loose: he giveth goodly words.

Which bites the heels of the horse,
And his rider fell behind.
18. For thy salvation have I longed, Jehovah!

GAD.

19. Gad—a crowd shall crowd him,
And he will crowd the heel.

ASHER.

20. Out of Asher—fat (shall be) his bread;
And he shall yield the dainties of a king.

NAPHTALI.

21. Naphtali is a hind sent forth;
The giver of sayings of beauty.

---

5 Heb. an *arrowsnake*. —— *g* Psa. 25. 5; 119. 166, 174; Isa. 25. 9.

h Deut. 33. 20; 1 Chron. 5. 18.——*i* Deut. 33. 24; Josh. 19. 24.——*k* Deut. 33. 23.

the *cerastes*, "the very poisonous horned serpent, which is of the colour of the sand, and as it lies upon the ground merely stretching out its feelers, inflicts a fatal wound upon any who may tread upon it unawares. (Diod. Sic., iii, 49; Pliny, viii, 23.")—*Keil.* Comp. also Deut. xxxiii, 22.

18. **For thy salvation have I longed, Jehovah**—What occasioned this abrupt exclamation at this point, or what connection it has with the context, is not clear. Probably the wars and dangers that awaited the chosen people were vividly presented to the patriarch's soul as he mentioned the traits of Dan, and these again call up the ancient prophecy of the conflict between the woman's and the serpent's seed, (Gen. iii, 15,) and as he has a glimpse of that momentous struggle, he breaks out with this ejaculation. But if no such relation to the context be allowed, we may suppose that Jacob here breaks out with these words as a refrain, or pause, in the midst of exciting prophecy, and conflicting emotions within.

19. **A crowd shall crowd him**—In this verse we have a more notable play on words than in any other part of the chapter. Every word in the verse but **he** and **heel** is a form of the word *Gad.* We have sought in our translation to bring out, even though imperfectly, this feature of the Hebrew. The thought is, that crowds or troops of invading enemies will crowd in upon his territory, but he will resist them, and in their retreat he will press upon their **heel** or rear, and harass them. In 1 Chron. v, 18, the Gadites are mentioned as valiant warriors, and in 1 Chron. xii, 8 they are described as having faces like lions, and being swift as the mountain roes.

20. **Fat his bread**—Grammatically, **bread** is in apposition with **fat.** The tribe of Asher occupied the rich and fertile region along the Mediterranean, north of Mount Carmel. According to Moses (Deut. xxxiii, 24) Asher should "dip his foot in oil."

21. **A hind sent forth**—The image is that of a beautiful hind or gazelle running loose and in perfect freedom upon its native heights. The agility and prowess of this tribe are nobly celebrated in Deborah's song. **Giver of sayings of beauty**—The elegance and beauty of the hind suggests that the tribe so compared might naturally

22 Joseph *is* a fruitful bough, *even* a fruitful bough by a well; *whose* *branches run over the wall: **23** The archers have ¹ sorely grieved him, and shot *at him*, and hated him: **24** But his ᵐ bow abode in strength, and the arms of his hands were made strong by the hands of ⁿ the mighty *God* of Jacob;

JOSEPH.

22. Son of a fruit tree is Joseph,
Son of a fruit tree over a fountain;
Daughters climbed upon the wall.
23. And they imbittered him, and they shot,
And they hated him—lords of arrows.
24. Yet stayed in firmness his bow,
And stout were the arms of his hands,
From the hands of the Mighty One of Jacob,
From the name of the Shepherd, the Stone of Israel;

---

6 Heb. *daughters.*——*l* Chap. 37. 4, 24, 28; 39. 20; 42. 21; Psa. 118. 13. *m* Job 29. 20; Psalm 37. 15. —— *n* Psalm 132. 2, 5.

have had an elegant taste for **sayings of beauty**; elegant proverbs and songs. As the tribe of Zebulun developed ready writers, (Judges v, 14,) so Naphtali, perhaps, became noted for elegant speakers. This seems to be the general sense of the verse; but we know too little of the subsequent history and character of the tribe to enable us to define more particularly. Several critics, following the Septuagint, render: "Naphtali is a spreading tree, which puts forth goodly branches." But this is scarcely tenable.

22. **Joseph** — When the patriarch turns to Joseph, all the affection and tenderness of his soul seem to break forth in rapturous song. It remains for him now only to bless the two sons of Rachel, and then die. Three expressions in this verse serve to portray the fruitfulness and glory of the tribe of Joseph. 1) **Son of a fruit tree;** that is, branch, scion, or outgrowth of a fruit tree; transplanted from the main stock. 2) The fruitfulness of the tree and its branches is enhanced by its standing **over a fountain.** Comp. Psa. i, 3. 3) So fruitful and luxuriant is the tree that its boughs beget other boughs; the sons beget **daughters**, which spread and climb **upon the wall** beside which the tree is supposed to be planted. This great luxuriance of growth points to Joseph as having, through his two sons, a double inheritance; for this was the birthright given to him. 1 Chron. v, 1.

23. **Imbittered ... shot ... hated** —This verse depicts Joseph as persecuted by his brethren, and by Potiphar's wife. His soul had been terribly *imbittered;* he had been a shining mark for archers who *hated* him, and sought his ruin. Jacob's knowledge of Joseph's trials, learned and thought on for seventeen years, was the subjective basis of all these metaphors; but while they had that personal basis and background, they may also point to the future wars and triumphs of Ephraim and Manasseh. **Lords of arrows—** That is, masters in the use of bows and arrows. Joseph's foes are thus compared to skilled and malignant archers.

24. **His bow**—He turned archer in another way, and was empowered by a supernatural energy, against which all lords of the bow found it folly to contend. He proved an unconquerable hero. This part of the prophecy, based also on Joseph's personal experience, was further illustrated and confirmed, but not entirely fulfilled, in Joshua, who sprang from Ephraim, and led all Israel to the conquest of the land of promise. The description throughout is true to the general character of the tribe of Joseph. **The arms of his hands** — The expression is peculiarly significant when speaking of an archer, whose pliant hand must be supported by a firm arm in order to be effective. The designation of God as the **Mighty One**, or the *Might* **of Jacob**; the **Shepherd,** (compare chap. xlviii, 15,)

(º from thence ᵖ *is* the shepherd, ᑫ the stone of Israel;) **25** ʳ *Even* by the God of thy father, who shall help thee; ˢ and by the Almighty, ᵗ who shall bless thee with blessings of heaven above, blessings of the deep that lieth under, blessings of the breasts, and of the womb:

26 The blessings of thy father have prevailed above the blessings of my progenitors ᵘ unto the utmost bound of the everlasting hills: ᵛ they shall be on the head of Joseph, and on the crown of the head of him that was separate from his brethren.

25. From the God of thy father, and he will help thee;
And the Almighty, and he will bless thee;
Blessings of heavens on high;
Blessings of deep lying down below,
Blessings of breasts and womb;—
26. The blessings of thy father have been mighty,
Above the blessings of enduring mountains,
The desire of everlasting hills;
They shall be for the head of Joseph,
And for the crown of the consecrated of his brothers.

o Chapter 45. 11; 47. 12; 50. 21. —— *p* Psalm 80. 1.—*q* Isaiah 28. 16. —— *r* Chapter 28. 13, 21; 35. 3; 43. 23.

s Chapter 17. 1; 35. 11. —— *t* Deuteronomy 33. 13. —— *u* Deuteronomy 33. 15; Habakkuk 3. 6. ——*v* Deuteronomy 33. 16.

and **Stone** (compare Deut. xxxii, 4, 2 Sam. xxii, 3, xxiii, 3,) is peculiarly appropriate and suggestive. משם is rendered *from thence* in the common version, and this is sustained by the Masoretic punctuation, the Sept., Vulg., and most expositors. But it is in more perfect analogy with the word מידי, of the previous line, and the harmony of parallelism, to translate as we have done **from the name**; perhaps an allusion to chapter xxxii, 29. So the Syriac, Dathe, Turner, and others. In this way, the strength, triumphs, and blessings of Joseph are attributed to God as the Shepherd and Stone of Israel. The attempt to make Joseph and Joshua the shepherd and stone, or to render *Shepherd of the stone* of Israel, and understand it of God watching the stone on which Jacob slept at Bethel, seems far fetched and unnatural.

25. **The Almighty**—Heb. *Shaddai*, who had appeared so often to Abraham, Isaac, and Jacob. Comp. chap. xvii, 1; xxviii, 3; xxxv, 11; xliii, 14; xlviii, 3. The **blessings** so variously enhanced by the terms of this verse and the following, indicate the glory of the birthright given to Joseph, and his future eminence and prosperity among the tribes.

26. **Enduring mountains . . . everlasting hills**—This version adheres strictly to the natural meaning of the words, sustains the parallelism, and seems, therefore, much preferable to the more common reading, *blessings of my progenitors unto the bounds of the everlasting hills*. To sustain this latter we must derive הורי from הרה, and use it in a sense which has no parallel or support elsewhere in Hebrew; and also use תאוה in a sense which it nowhere else has. The parallel passage (Deut. xxxiii, 15, 16) is also against this interpretation. The **blessings** of the mountains, and the **desire** (or *desirable things*) of the hills, poetically denote all natural beauties, products, healthfulness and defences which one might desire in a pleasant land; and the thought here is, that Jacob's blessing pronounced on Joseph surpasses all such blessings of the hills. **They shall be for the head**—They are destined to the head, or shall come upon the head, of Joseph; allusion to the custom of putting the hand upon one's head in blessing. **The consecrated** נְזִיר, the *Nazir*, the *separated one*. From this root we have the word *Nazarite*, one consecrated and set apart by some sacred vow. Joseph was the separated one among his brothers.

27 Benjamin shall ʷraven *as* a wolf: in the morning he shall devour the prey, ˣ and at night he shall divide the spoil.

28 All these *are* the twelve tribes of Israel: and this *is it* that their father spake unto them, and blessed them; every one according to his blessing he blessed them. **29** And he charged them, and said unto them, I ʸ am to be gathered unto my people: ᶻ bury me with my fathers ᵃ in the cave that *is* in the field of Ephron the Hittite, **30** In the cave that *is* in the field of Machpelah, which *is* before Mamre, in the land of Canaan, ᵇ which Abraham bought with the field of Ephron the Hittite for a possession of a buryingplace. **31** ᶜ There they buried Abraham and Sarah his wife ; ᵈ there they buried Isaac and Rebekah his wife ; and there I buried Leah. **32** The purchase of the field and of the cave that *is* therein *was* from the children of Heth. **33** And when Jacob had made an end of commanding his sons, he gathered up his feet into the bed, and yielded up the ghost, and ᵉ was gathered unto his people.

BENJAMIN.

27. Benjamin is a wolf; let him tear in pieces!
In the morning let him devour prey,
And at evening let him divide spoil.

w Judges 20. 21, 25 ; Ezek. 22. 25, 27.——*x* Num. 23. 24 ; Esth. 8. 11 ; Ezek. 39. 10 ; Zech. 14. 1, 7.——*y* Chap. 15. 15 ; 25. 8. *z* Chap. 47. 30 ; 2 Sam. 19. 37.——*a* Chap. 50. 13.——*b* Chap. 23. 16.——*c* Chap. 23. 19 ; 25. 9.——*d* Chap. 35. 29.——*e* Verse 29.

27. Let him tear in pieces—We prefer this jussive rendering as being in the most perfect keeping with the spirit of the entire prophecy, and as giving the passage greater expressiveness. The verse portrays the warlike and furious character of the tribe of Benjamin, and the history of the tribal war, in Judges xx, affords its best illustration. From this tribe came the daring Ehud (Judg. iii, 15) and the warlike Saul. Benjamin is portrayed under two characters, a beast of prey and a victorious warrior. Like **a wolf** that has prowled all night (comp. 1 Sam. xiv, 36) and taken **prey,** he devours it **in the morning;** like a warrior who has won conquests through the day, he divides the **spoil,** or booty, **at evening.** In this imagery Lange sees the outlines of "a wild, turbulent youth and an old age full of the blessing of sacrifice for others. That dividing the spoil in the evening is a feature that evidently passes over into a spiritual allusion. Our first thought would be of the dividing of the prey among the young ones, but for this alone the expression is too strong. He rends all for himself in the morning, he yields all in the evening. This is not a figure of Benjamin only, but of the theocratic Israel ; and, therefore, a most suitable close. See Isaiah liii, 12."

THE DEATH OF JACOB, 28–33.

28. All these are the twelve tribes—The sacred historian, having inserted in his book the prophetic words which the sons and sons' sons had been careful to preserve, thus resumes his narrative, and now proceeds to add an account of the patriarch's last charge and death.

29. Bury me with my fathers—The great prophet has spoken his last oracle ; his sons have received his dying benedictions ; and now his heart turns to his **fathers,** to whom he is about to be gathered. There is a touching beauty and tenderness in the allusion to Machpelah (on which see notes at chap. xxiii, 9, 19) and Mamre— to Abraham and Sarah, and Isaac and Rebekah, and Leah. He would have his body repose along with theirs, as, also, he expected his immortal part would be "gathered unto his people" in Sheol. See on chap. xxxvii, 35, and xxv, 8.

33. Gathered up his feet into the bed—While uttering his prophecy he had strengthened himself and sat upon his bed, (comp. chap. xlviii, 2 ;) now he replaces his feet on the bed, and calmly breathes out his life.

CHAPTER L.

THE FUNERAL OF JACOB, 1–14.

" The royal obsequies of Israel and Joseph fittingly end the history of the

CHAPTER L.

AND Joseph ª fell upon his father's face, and ᵇ wept upon him, and

a Chapter 46. 4. — *b* 2 Kings 13. 14. — *c* Verse 26; 2 Chronicles 16. 14; Matthew 26. 12; Mark 14. 8; 16. 1; Luke 24. 1; John 12. 7; 19. 39, 40.

patriarchal age, and the first stage in the development of the covenant people. The father of Joseph was buried with all the magnificence of an Egyptian funeral. No prophet, or prince, or king of Israel's line, even in the noontide glory of the Hebrew monarchy, was ever laid to his rest with such pomp and splendour. The funeral ceremony was, with the Egyptians, an elegant art, in which they concentrated their religion and highest philosophy, and on which they lavished their taste and wealth. Their belief in immortality, and in the re-union of the soul with the body after transmigration, led them to carve magnificent sepulchres out of their mountains, and decorate them with all the splendours of painting and architecture, where the embalmed body, fresh in feature and fragrant in smell, might wait, as in a palace hall, to welcome the spirit on its return from its wanderings. Thus the Greek historian, Diodorus, says that the Egyptians built only inns for the living, but eternal habitations for the dead. The temples and tombs of Egypt are not only the oldest and most massive monuments of the past, but are also monuments of man's faith in God and the future state, which have endured from the earliest dawn of civilization.

"Magnificent funeral processions are pictured in the royal tombs of Thebes. Such an imposing pageant is here described, though with such unworldly simplicity as almost to escape the eye, when 'all the servants of Pharaoh, the elders of his house, and all the elders of the land of Egypt, and all the house of Joseph, and his brethren, and his father's house,' leaving only their 'little ones' in the land of Goshen, with 'chariots and horsemen,' a 'very great company,' (verses 7–9,) set forth from the land of Goshen on a funeral march of three hundred miles, through the desert, round the Dead Sea, to the banks of the Jordan, and halted there for seven days' funeral rites, such as

kissed him. 2 And Joseph commanded his servants the physicians to ᶜ embalm his father: and the physicians embalmed the land of Canaan never witnessed before or after, and which stamped the meadow with the name, 'Mourning (place) of the Egyptians.'"—*Newhall.*

1. **Joseph fell . . . and wept . . . and kissed**—A touching picture of the tender emotion of Joseph's soul. The prominence given to Joseph in the account of this funeral was due to his official position in Egypt as well as to his great devotion to his father.

2. **Commanded . . . to embalm**—"The Egyptians were famous for their skill in medicine. Homer says that every physician in Egypt 'knew more than all other men.' *Odyss.*, 4, 229. Medical specialties were carefully cultivated, and the land abounded with oculists, aurists, dentists, etc., so that persons of rank and wealth generally had several different kinds of phyicians among their **servants**, as Joseph seems to have had, according to the text. The Persian kings, Cyrus and Darius, had Egyptian physicians at their courts. *Herod.*, ii, 84; iii, 1, 132. The Theban mummies show that they filled teeth with gold; and Pliny says, that they practised post-mortem examinations; while one of the books of Hermes treated of medical instruments, and another of anatomy. The government was very severe upon quacks, and the death of a patient who had not been 'doctored by the books,' was held a capital crime. Wilkinson, in Rawl., *Her.*, ii, p. 117. European medicine came from Egypt through the Arabs, whence the Arab symbols of our chemists, while the very word *chem*-istry is a souvenir of the land of Ham, or *Chem.*

"Embalming was practised by several ancient nations, but the art was carried to the highest perfection in Egypt. The materials principally used were cedar oil, natron, (native carbonate of soda,) and various spices. Embalming was the work of a special class, (*Herod.*, ii, 86,) whom probably Joseph's physicians employed."—*Newhall.*

B. C. 1689.   CHAPTER L.   349

Israel. **3** And forty days were fulfilled for him; for so are fulfilled the days of those which are embalmed: and the Egyptians ¹ ᵈ mourned for him threescore and ten days. **4** And when the days of his mourning were past, Joseph spake unto ᵉ the house of Pharaoh, saying, If now I have found grace in your eyes, speak, I pray you, in the ears of Pharaoh, saying, **5** ᶠ My father made me swear, saying, Lo, I die: in my grave ᵍ which I have digged for me in the land of Canaan, there shalt thou bury me. Now therefore let me go up, I pray thee, and bury my father, and I will come again. **6** And Pharaoh said, Go up, and bury thy father, according as he made thee swear.

7 And Joseph went up to bury his father: and with him went up all the servants of Pharaoh, the elders of his house, and all the elders of the land of Egypt, **8** And all the house of Joseph, and his brethren, and his father's house: only their little ones, and their flocks, and their herds, they left in the land of Goshen. **9** And there went up with him both chariots and horsemen: and it

---

1 Heb. *wept*. — *d* Num. 20. 29; Deut. 34. 8. — *e* Esther 4. 2.   *f* Chap. 47. 29. — *g* 2 Chron. 16. 14; Isa. 22. 16; Matt. 27. 60.

---

3. Forty days . . . of those which are embalmed . . . mourned for him threescore and ten days— That is, it required forty days for the embalming, during which time the mourning for him went on, and after the embalming they continued to mourn for thirty days more. Thus the Egyptians honoured Jacob as though he were a great prince. "Diodorus says, that the process of embalming took more than thirty days, and that the Egyptians were accustomed to mourn seventy-two days for a king. Herodotus mentions that the body was never allowed to lie in the natron more than seventy days, ii, 86. These periods, given by the classical writers, it will be seen remarkably correspond with the numbers of the text. The actual process occupied the first forty days, while the body lay for thirty days more in natron, completing thus the seventy days of mourning. Wilkinson, in Rawl., *Her.*, ii, p. 122. There were, however, many grades and varieties of the process, according to the rank of the person, for rank is seen in the grave in Egypt as well as in Christendom."—*Newhall.*

4. Joseph spake unto the house of Pharaoh—He communicated with Pharaoh by means of his servants, or messengers, as it would have been contrary to Egyptian customs for him to have gone in mourning attire into the presence of the king. During the days of mourning for a relative the Egyptians allowed the hair and beard to grow long, (*Herod.*, ii, 36,) and no man might enter the king's presence unshaven. Comp. chap. xli, 14; Esther iv, 2.

5. Which I have digged for me —Some take the word כָּרָה, here rendered **digged,** in the sense of *purchased*, as קָנָה is used in reference to Abraham's purchase in chap. xlix, 30. If so rendered, the language used would make Jacob speak of Abraham's act as his own. This is an allowable explanation, but unnecessary. The more common meaning of כָּרָה is *dig*, and Jacob may have excavated his own sepulchre or separate chamber in the cave after the burial of Abraham and Isaac. See on chap. xxiii, 9. **I will come again**—"The earnestness of Joseph's entreaty, and the repetition of his solemn oath to his father, show what difficulty a naturalized foreigner would have in leaving the land of the Pharaohs. Jacob's characteristic foresight and prudence appear in exacting this oath, which he knew Pharaoh's religious scruples would guarantee from violation, while, at the same time, Joseph would be protected from the national jealousy."—*Newhall.*

7. All the elders of the land— The writer dwells with emphasis on the magnificent funeral procession, composed of the various officers of the Egyptian court, and the entire house of Israel excepting the little children, (verse 8,) probably the seventy whose names are given in chap. xlvi.

9. Chariots and horsemen—For protection and defence. So large and solemn a procession required a military

was a very great company. **10** And they came to the threshing-floor of Atad, which *is* beyond Jordan; and there they ʰ mourned with a great and very sore lamentation: ⁱ and he made a mourning for his father seven days. **11** And when the inhabitants of the land, the Canaanites, saw the mourning in the floor of Atad, they said, This *is* a grievous mourning to the Egyptians: wherefore the name of it was called ʲ Abel-mizraim, which *is* beyond Jordan. **12** And his sons did unto him according as he commanded them: **13** For ᵏ his sons carried him into the land of Canaan, and buried him in the cave of the field of Machpelah, which Abraham ˡ bought with the field for a possession of a burying-place of Ephron the Hittite, before Mamre.

---

h 2 Sam. 1. 17; Acts 8. 2. — *i* 1 Sam. 31. 13; Job 2. 13.—2 That is, *The mourning of the Egyptians.* — *k* Chap. 49. 29, 30; Acts 7. 16. —*l* Chap. 23. 16.

---

escort in their long march through the desert.

10. **The threshing-floor of Atad** —Or, *the threshing-floor of the thorn.* The words may be taken as the proper name of a place, *Goren-haatadh.* It was **beyond Jordan,** that is, on the east of Jordan, for such is the natural meaning of this phrase. Accordingly, it appears that this vast procession took a circuitous route, went round the Dead Sea, and entered Canaan on the east. Why they should have taken such a journey does not appear in this narrative, and some have regarded it as so improbable that they have discarded the natural meaning of the language here employed, and have explained **beyond Jordan** as meaning west of the Jordan. According to Jerome it was called in his time Beth-agla, and some have sought to identify it with the modern Ain Hadjla, the Beth-hoglah of the tribe of Judah, (Josh. xv, 6,) situated at the northern end of the Dead Sea, about two miles west of the Jordan. One writing at the east of the Jordan, as the author of this passage is supposed to have done, would have spoken of this place as **beyond Jordan.** But this identification with Beth-hoglah is of no sufficient authority, and why any writer should have designated a place west of the Jordan as **beyond Jordan** is inexplicable, if this funeral procession did not go anywhere in the vicinity of the Jordan. Better, therefore, to suppose that this round-about journey was taken to avoid conflict with hostile tribes then occupying the country on the direct road to Hebron. For a similar reason the whole house of Israel at a later day compassed the land of Edom and entered Canaan from the east. At this place, perhaps nothing but a **threshing-floor** surrounded by thornbushes, but affording a suitable place for the purpose, **they mourned with a great and very sore lamentation** for the space of **seven days.** Thus to the seventy days of mourning in Egypt, (verse 3,) they now added a full week at the borders of Canaan.

11. **Abel-mizraim** — That is, *the mourning of the Egyptians.* The Canaanites, who witnessed the unusual spectacle of lamentation, gave a new name to the place. They had never before seen such violence of mourning. Herodotus in describing the habits of the Egyptians observes, (*Herod.*, ii, 85,) that when a distinguished individual died the females of the family besmear their heads and faces with mud, and wander about beating themselves and exposing their breasts. The men, also, having their clothes girt about them, beat themselves and indulge in excessive lamentation. See also Wilkinson's full account of Egyptian funeral rites, *Ancient Egyptians,* vol. ii, p. 366.

13. **His sons carried him into the land of Canaan**—This implies that the place of the seven days' mourning was not in Canaan proper, though on its border, where the Canaanites (verse 11) could observe their excessive lamentations. The Egyptian escort probably waited at Abel-mizraim, while the sons of the great patriarch carried him to the ancient tomb of Machpelah, (see on chap. xxiii, 9,) and deposited his embalmed body by the dust of Abraham and Sarah, Isaac and Rebekah, where also he had buried Leah. Chap. xlix, 31. And there, perhaps, that embalmed body still remains, and

14 And Joseph returned into Egypt, he, and his brethren, and all that went up with him to bury his father, after he had buried his father. 15 And when Joseph's brethren saw that their father was dead, ᵐ they said, Joseph will peradventure hate us, and will certainly requite us all the evil which we did unto him. 16 And they ³ sent a messenger unto Joseph, saying, Thy father did command before he died, saying, 17 So shall ye say unto Joseph, Forgive, I pray thee now, the trespass of thy brethren, and their sin; ⁿ for they did unto thee evil: and now, we pray thee, forgive the trespass of the servants of ᵒ the God of thy father. And Joseph wept when they spake unto him. 18 And his brethren also went and ᵖ fell down before his face; and they said, Behold, we *be* thy servants. 19 And Joseph said unto them, ᑫ Fear not: ʳ for *am* I in the place of God? 20 ˢ But as for you, ye thought evil against me; *but* ᵗ God meant it unto good, to bring to pass, as *it is* this day, to save much people alive. 21 Now therefore fear ye not: ᵘ I will nourish you,

m Job 15. 21, 22.——3 Heb.*charged.*——*n* Prov. 28. 13.——*o* Chap. 49. 25.——*p* Chap. 37. 7, 10.—— *q* Chap. 45. 5.——*r* Deut. 32. 35; 2 Kings 5. 7; Job 34. 29; Rom. 12. 19; Heb. 10. 30.—— *s* Psa. 56. 5; Isa. 10. 7. —— *t* Chap. 45. 5, 7; Acts 3. 13, 14, 15. —— *u* Chap. 47. 12; Matt. 5. 44.

may be identified when Moslem fanaticism permits a careful and thorough examination of that ancient cave at Hebron.

FEARS OF JOSEPH'S BRETHREN, 15-21.

15. **Joseph will peradventure hate us**—The Hebrew here is a conditional, unfinished sentence: *If Joseph should hate us, and return with intensity* (verb in inf. absolute to express idea of intensity or emphasis) *to us all the evil which we have done him*—what could we do? How helpless our condition! The whole is equivalent to an exclamation of alarm: What if Joseph should hate us, etc? The deep consciousness of guilt prompted the words.

16. **They sent a messenger**—Literally, *they commanded, or gave a charge to Joseph.* "They *charged Joseph,* in their father's name, probably by an embassy sent from Goshen to Memphis, the seat of government, although the text says nothing about messengers. Perhaps Benjamin first pleaded for them, and then they all came into his presence. Verse 18. Whether Jacob actually left this message for Joseph is doubtful. If he really had such fears, he would have been likely to entreat Joseph personally, as he freely charged him concerning other things which pertained to the family welfare. It was, of course, Jacob's wish that there should be perfect and perpetual reconciliation among his children, which often may have been expressed; but the precise form of this petition to Joseph was probably suggested by the guilty fears of the brethren, who could not fully understand the generosity and magnanimity of Joseph. They knew that Joseph would sacredly heed his father's charge and so offered their petition in his name."—*Newhall.*

17. **Forgive the trespass of the servants of the God of thy father** —"All the arguments that would touch Joseph are woven into a few words with great pathos and power. They cast themselves absolutely upon his mercy, and call up before him his venerated father, and his father's God, whose servants they also are. Joseph replied in a way to scatter all doubt and soothe all fear — he **wept.** At first he made no answer in words, but his tears were richer to them than speech. It was the golden silence, that cannot, from very fulness, speak." — *Newhall.*

19. **Am I in the place of God**— "It is true that you have sinned, but it is not mine to punish; God is your judge and mine."—*Newhall.*

20. **Ye thought evil against me; but God meant it unto good**—"He accepts their confession of sin, but now again, as when he first made himself known to them, (chap. xlv, 5-8,) generously strives to mitigate their pain by showing them how God has overruled evil for good. Man devises evil, and in the device is sin: but when it comes to action, it can bring only good to them who trust God. Thus man's wrath praises him."—*Newhall.*

GENESIS.

and your little ones. And he comforted them, and spake ^{4} kindly unto them.

22 And Joseph dwelt in Egypt, he, and his father's house: and Joseph lived a hundred and ten years. **23** And Joseph saw Ephraim's children ^{v} of the third *generation:* ^{w} the children also of Machir the son of Manasseh ^{x} were ^{b} brought up upon Joseph's knees. **24** And Joseph said unto his brethren, I die; and ^{y} God will surely visit you, and bring you out of this land unto the land ^{z} which he sware to Abraham, to Isaac, and to Jacob. **25** And ^{a} Joseph took an oath of the children of Israel, saying, God will surely visit you, and ye shall carry up my bones from hence. **26** So Joseph died, *being* a hundred and ten years old: and they ^{b} embalmed him, and he was put in a coffin in Egypt.

---

4 Hebrew, *to their hearts,* chap. 34. 3. — *v* Job 42. 16.——*w* Num. 32. 39.——*x* Chap. 30. 3. ——5 Heb.*borne.*——*y* Chap. 15. 14; 46. 4; 48. 21;

Exod. 3. 16, 17; Heb. 11. 22. —— *z* Chap. 15. 18; 26. 3; 35. 12; 46. 4. —— *a* Exod. 13. 19; Josh. 24. 32; Acts 7. 16.——*b* Verse 2.

---

21. **Spake kindly unto them**—Heb., *spake to their heart,* as in the margin; a beautiful form of speech, which it would have been well to retain in translation.

DEATH OF JOSEPH, 22–26.

22. **Hundred and ten years**—Compare the same age of Joshua when he died. Josh. xxiv, 29.

23. **Ephraim's children of the third generation**—That is, "his great great grandchildren (literally, *the sons of the sons of the third generation,* as Gesenius shows from Exod. xx, 5, and xxxiv, 7; but Furst and others understand the Hebrew to mean great grandchildren.) He took upon his knees also his great grandchildren in the line of Manasseh. It was a serene and trustful old age." —*Newhall.*

25. **Joseph took an oath of the children of Israel**—"He could have commanded them to carry his body immediately to Canaan, as he had already carried that of Israel there; but he commanded that it should stand swathed in its mummy bands, in the sepulchral chamber, waiting for the time of its burial in their true national home. The Egyptians were accustomed to keep the mummies of their friends standing for some time, before final burial, in a small room attached to the tomb, whence it was often brought forth to receive priestly benedictions. Wilkinson. Thus, after his death the body of Joseph constantly exhorted and inspirited Israel to remember God's covenant with their fathers."—*Newhall.*

26. **They embalmed him**—See on verse 2. **He was put in a coffin**—"Rather, *in the coffin,* that is, the customary Egyptian coffin, or mummy chest, usually made of sycamore wood, which, though porous, was so durable that coffins of the time of the Pharaohs are freely used for fuel in Egypt to-day. Cedar coffins are also found, though less generally. The mummy chests of kings were often placed in a stone sarcophagus.

"Here, at the sepulchre of Joseph, endeth the great Book of Generations, wherein are laid the historical, doctrinal, and ethical foundations of Divine revelation. **In Egypt** are the significant closing words, for there the posterity of Jacob now vanish from our sight for centuries; but through those ages of servile travail, the mummy of Joseph, wrapped in its fragrant cerements, a mute but eloquent admonition and prophecy, stands calmly waiting in its niche for the birth of the NATION OF ISRAEL."— *Newhall.*

INTRODUCTION TO THE BOOK OF EXODUS.

IN the Book of Genesis, or Generations, we have a history of origins, preparing the way for this history of the birth and training of the Covenant People. The Book of Exodus is thus a continuation of the preceding narrative, being joined to it by a simple connective particle; and yet it is a distinct regular treatise, as may be seen by a glance at the Plan and Table of Contents which follow. Its authenticity and genuineness are discussed in the general Introduction to the Pentateuch. There are, however, certain internal marks of credibility peculiar to this book, which it is well to notice here. It claims to be the work of Moses, an Egyptian Hebrew, who received his religion from the Hebrew patriarchs, and yet was educated in the court of the Pharaohs. Such a man must have had minute acquaintance with the language, manners, religion, art and science of Egypt, and also, of course, with its climate, geography, and natural productions. Such knowledge must everywhere appear in such a work as this, if genuine.

The extensive and thorough researches of travellers for the last three quarters of a century, and especially the wonderful discoveries of Young and Champollion, which unlocked the immense volumes of the Egyptian monuments, so that they are now being deciphered line by line, enable us to compare more and more closely day by day the books of Moses with the description of the Egypt of his time as it was written by the Egyptians themselves. Thus the vast folios of the French *savants*, of Rosellini and of Lepsius, and the more recent and yet unfinished works of De Rougè and Mariette, are perpetual commentaries upon the book of Exodus. We can but indicate a few points of comparison and of internal evidence.

1. REFERENCES TO GEOGRAPHY.—Every day reveals more and more clearly the accuracy of the knowledge which the author of Exodus possessed concerning the geography of Egypt, the Red Sea coast, and the Desert of Sinai. The Egypt of Exodus is the Nile-land of history and of the monuments. Every intelligent traveller, whatever his religious belief, regards the Book of Exodus as the indispensable guide-book in the wilderness of Sinai. The history of the book is indissolubly bound to its geography; and although many of the sites which it mentions are still unidentified, yet in the desert mounds and ruins, springs, palm clusters and wadies, and in the floating Bedouin traditions, every traveller is seeking after the Bible names, and finding fresh proofs of the geographical accuracy of Exodus.

2. REFERENCES TO CLIMATOLOGY AND NATURAL HISTORY.—The Nile is Egypt's rain, and Moses describes the inhabitants as wholly dependent upon the river for drink, keeping its water in reservoirs and cisterns, and sorely distressed when it was tainted. (See notes on the first plague, chap. vii.) The narrative of the plagues shows a minute acquaintance with the climate, insects, reptiles, domestic animals, and cultivated grains, peculiar to Egypt.

So the account of the tabernacle shows acquaintance with the productions of the Desert. The boards of the sanctuary are made not of cedar or cypress, as they would have been in Palestine, but of the desert shittah, or acacia, and it was covered with the skins of the *tachash*, the seal or the halicore of the Red Sea. Mr. Holland measured acacia trees in the Desert nine feet in circumference, and the Bedouins make sandals of the skin of the halicore.

It has been strongly objected, by Colenso and others, that the Desert of Sinai never could have sustained two millions of people, with their cattle, for forty years. But this is also the precise statement of our narrative; which accordingly relates the specially providential or miraculous provisions of the manna, the quails, and the water from the rock of Horeb. It is particularly and repeatedly declared that ordinary natural means were not sufficient to sustain them. It is not specially stated that pasturage was providentially or supernaturally provided for the cattle, but we are at liberty to suppose this, if needful, for the greater miracle of the manna includes lesser ones like this. Colenso's difficulties arise wholly from attempting to account for what is avowedly supernatural upon natural causes, and of course he finds these difficulties insuperable.

Yet it is most probable that there was not any thing supernatural in providing pasturage for the cattle of Israel. The monuments and the most recent explorations of travellers show conclusively that the Desert did once sustain a great population. Long before the time of Moses there were permanent Egyptian settlements in this desert, around the copper, iron, and turqouise mines of Maghara and Sarabit-el-Khadim, where troops, officered by men of high rank, were garrisoned, and who have left their record in the beautiful bas-reliefs of Wady Maghara. These inscriptions boast of Egyptian victories over the warriors of the Peninsula, showing that they were then formidable enough in numbers and in valour to contest the supremacy of these deserts and mountains. Rich veins of iron, copper, and turquoise are now found in that vicinity; and ancient slag heaps, as well as remnants of smelting furnaces, are met with in many parts of the Peninsula. (Palmer's *Desert of the Exodus*, chaps. ii, x.)

Palmer, of the "Sinai Survey Expedition," describes extensive and massive foundations and walls of ruined cities—deep, finely constructed wells—walled fields—and traces of terraced gardens—where now are arid wastes. Hundreds of monastic gardens and orchards were once scattered through the Sinai mountains. The causes of these great changes have also been largely, if not wholly, discovered. The reckless destruction of the forest has diminished the rain-fall, and the contemptuous neglect of all cultivation on the part of the inhabitants has left the soil to be stripped from the hill-sides and carried down the rocky wadies by the torrents which are produced by every shower, which else might be clothing these barren valleys with blooming gardens. The rich black soil, palm groves, and tamarisk thickets of Wady Feiran, and the convent gardens and orchards around Jebel Musa, show what cultivation might accomplish here. The wretched misgovernment of centuries, which has not only neglected but wasted the natural resources, even levying upon the country a tribute of charcoal which annually diminishes the scanty stock of timber, and the total neglect of irrigation and agriculture, have been steadily deteriorating the country for more than two thousand years. The same causes have operated in this desert which have changed Palestine from a "land of milk and honey" to the bare and barren country which the Christian traveller visits to-day. See note on Exod. xv, 22.

In reading the narrative of the desert sojourn we are not to consider the people of Israel as constantly in motion. The greater part of the forty years they spent at fertile halting places in the desert wadies, where they scattered over several square miles for pasturage; and when they moved to another camping place it is probable that the cattle carried the water for their own use in leathern bottles or sacks, as Baker tells us that the cattle in the Abyssinian deserts do to-day. Holland, who has four times visited the Peninsula, and wandered over it for months on foot, sees no difficulty in finding pasturage for the flocks of the Israelites, and says that "it is wonderful how apparent difficulties melt away as one's acquaintance with the country increases."—SMITH'S *Dict.*, Am. Ed., (*Appendix*.)

3. REFERENCES TO LANGUAGE.—Egyptian scholars have shown that the author of Exodus was acquainted with the Egyptian language, from his peculiar use of words. In a brief paragraph we can instance but a few among a multitude of examples which may be gathered from consulting Birch's Egyptian Lexicon, in the last volume of "*Egypt's Place in Universal History*," by Baron Bunsen. Canon Cook calls attention to the most noticeable fact, that in that portion of Exodus which treats especially of Egyptian affairs words are constantly used which are either of Egyptian origin or are common to Hebrew and Egyptian.

There is a series of examples in the description of the "ark of bulrushes," (Exod. ii, 3,) which will illustrate this argument.

תבה (*tbh*,) "ark," Egyptian, *teb*, Septuagint, *thibē*, is a common Egyptian word meaning "chest," "coffer," or "cradle." This word occurs twenty-seven times in the books of Moses, and nowhere else. It has no Shemitic root or equivalent.

גמא, "bulrush," *papyrus*, is, according to Brugsch, the Egyptian *kam*, and it is significant that it is used by Isaiah to describe "the habitation of dragons," lairs of the crocodiles of the Nile, (Isa. xxxv, 7,) and the vessels of the Upper-Nile Ethiopian ambassadors, (Isa. xviii, 2,) while it nowhere else occurs, except in one passage of Job.

חמר (*chmr*,) verb and noun, meaning *daub*, *slime*, has the same letters, although reversed, as the Egyptian word of the same meaning, *mrch*.

זפת (*zft*,) "pitch," is the common Egyptian *sft*.

סוף (*suph*,) "flags," is the hieroglyphic *tufi*, the Coptic and modern Egyptian *sufi*.

יאר (*ior*,) "river," is the Egyptian *ior* or *aur*, as read on the Rosetta stone; and "by the river's brink," or "lip," is the exact Egyptian idiom as given in the famous "Funeral Ritual." In a papyrus of the nineteenth dynasty we read, "I sat down upon the lip of the river." All these Egyptian words and idioms occurring in this single verse, which describes the exposure of the infant Moses in the Nile, convey an irresistible impression that they were written by one born and bred in Egypt.

A long list of similar words could easily be furnished, and we instance especially the proper names Moses, Pharaoh, Pithom, and Rameses, on which see the notes; and the common nouns *sare missim*, "taskmasters," lords of tribute; *seneh*, "bramble," Egyptian, *sheno*; *tebhen*, "straw," Egyptian, *tebu*; *kin*, "fly" or mosquito, Egyptian, *ken*, which means "plague;" *pasach*, "passover," Egyptian, *pesht*.

Besides words of this character, which are virtually identical in the two languages, the author also uses many words which are not Shemitic in origin and can be traced to Egyptian roots. This verbal usage clearly shows the Egyptian training of the author of Exodus, and it is a usage which would not occur in the work of a writer trained in Palestine.

4. REFERENCES TO ART.—The building of the treasure cities, the work among bricks, and the gathering of straw and stubble for this work, all receive abundant illustration from the Egyptian monuments. (See on Exod. v, and illustrations there from Wilkinson.) The temples, tombs, and palaces of Egypt have never been elsewhere equaled in vastness and massiveness, and immense multitudes of slaves were employed, as shown in the mural pictures, for transporting the granite, basalt, and sandstone from the distant quarries; in the manu-

facture of bricks, both sun-dried and kiln-burnt, which are as enduring as the stone; in cutting the canals and building the dykes which covered the land like a net-work; and in rearing these colossal monuments to the pride and power of the Pharaohs.

The architecture and furniture of the tabernacle are precisely what might have been expected from artists who had been trained in the Egyptian cities. As shown above, the materials were such as would have been used in the desert, and not after the settlement in Palestine. The arts of carving, of embroidery, of overlaying with gold, of the ornamentation of capitals, hangings and walls, with the representations of fruits and flowers, and with symbolic forms setting forth spiritual truths, were precisely the arts in which the Egyptians were most famous, as is abundantly illustrated in their palaces, tombs, and temples. Moreover, these were arts to which the Israelites never gave special attention after their settlement in Canaan, so that Solomon was obliged to send to Tyre for workmen to build and ornament his palace and temple. Alone among the famous nations of antiquity the Hebrews have left us hardly a trace of their architecture, and not a vestige of their painting or sculpture. Thus this sanctuary tent was not only just adapted to the nomad life of the desert sojourn, but we cannot well conceive of its origin under any other circumstances than those related in the book of Exodus.

5. REFERENCES TO CONTEMPORARY HISTORY.—The exact epoch of the exode of Israel is as yet one of the unsettled questions, although more light daily gathers about it. The general harmony of this narrative with the history, religion, government, and manners of ancient Egypt is universally recognised, as is shown in the notes where occasion offers. But a closer harmony with any special period of Egyptian history we do not believe can as yet be found, although the time when this will be possible cannot be far distant. See Introduction to the History of the Plagues, chap. vii, and Concluding Note 1 to chap. i. It will be seen that we have not entangled our exegesis with the historical theories of Poole, Wilkinson, Lepsius, or Ewald, (though inclining most to the last,) for the time to write dogmatically upon this subject has not yet come.

6. REFERENCES TO MOSES HIMSELF.—The references to the great founder and lawgiver of Israel are worthy of a separate and careful study. They are such as could have been made by no man except Moses himself. Let the reader peruse the book, imagining it to be the work of a contemporary, such as Joshua or Eleazer, or of a Jew of a later age, such as Samuel, or a Levite of the times of the Kings, and this conviction will be felt at once. Moses, the founder and the father of the nation, the lawgiver and deliverer of Israel, was beloved and venerated by every Hebrew above all other human beings, as

the greatest man of all time. What Israelite of that or of any age would have set down thus plainly and nakedly the failures, weaknesses, and sins of Moses? Who of his followers would thus have painted his stammering speech, his halting faith, his hasty wrath, the rebukes and punishments which fell upon him from Heaven? What scribe of the time of the Judges or Kings would thus have hidden Moses in his work—overshadowed him with the Sinai cloud? Not thus do men write of their heroes, unless, indeed, they are lifted up by inspiration above human prejudices; but inspired men do not forge history and law, and this work is simply a forgery if it is not the work of Moses. It is clear that the author of Exodus did not know of the personal and historic greatness of Moses. Only Moses, and the Moses here described as the slowly-fitted instrument of Jehovah, could thus have written of the lawgiver, founder, and father of Israel.

The theory of Ewald, Knobel, and others, that this body of history and law grew gradually from various documents in a later age, contradicts fundamental laws of human nature. Especially is it difficult to see how it can be held by men possessing the moral sense. It assumes that men who above all others worshipped, loved and trusted a God whom they believed to be holy, had yet no sense of truthfulness. It makes this book a solecism in literature and in history.

Our comment assumes the existence and influence of the supernatural. Not the unnatural, nor the contra-natural, but the supernatural, is assumed in the fact of revelation. Denial of this has logically led many able and learned writers to manifold theories and artifices of interpretation, some absurd and some dishonest, in order to bring all the phenomena of the Scriptures within the range of natural law. It is well for the reader to see that these manifold questions of interpretation are all virtually settled before the commentator begins his work, by the settlement of the previous question, whether the Creator of Nature is yet its Lord, using its laws to reveal himself in truths undiscoverable by Reason, but clear and convincing to Faith. So overwhelming is the evidence of the authenticity of this narrative that no objection worth attention would now arise from any quarter if the book did not contain accounts of supernatural events. In fact, all the real objections made to its authenticity and genuineness are found, when reduced to their lowest terms, to be a simple denial of the supernatural. While the critical keenness and learning of eminent Rationalists have done the truth great service by their attestation to the substantial verity of the narrative in Exodus, they have done no less a service by attesting as constantly, in the criticism of its details, to the fact that these are phenomena of history that cannot be accounted for on merely natural causes.

CHRONOLOGICAL TABLE.

The subjoined Chronological Table is compiled from Wilkinson and Poole. Bunsen and Mariette give higher antiquity to the events, but they widely differ from each other.

Date.	Number of Dynasty.	Name of Dynasty.	Noted Kings.	Events.
B. C. 2700	I.	Thenite.	Menes.	First known king, and founder of Memphis.
2450	II.	Thenite.		
2650	III.	Memphite.	Snephru.	Inscriptions at Wady Maghara.
2450	IV.	Memphite.	Shufu (Cheops).	Great Pyramid built.
			Shafra (Chephren).	Second Pyramid built.
			Menkeoora (Mycerinus).	Third Pyramid built.
2450	V.	Elephantine.		
2200	VI.	Memphite.	Pepi (Apapus).	Tomb of Tih at Sakkarah.
1800(?)	VII.	Memphite.		
1800(?)	VIII.	Memphite.		
2200	IX.	Heracliopolite.		
1800	X.	Heracliopolite.		
2200	XI.	Theban.		
2080	XII.	Theban.	Sesortasen I., or Osirtasen I., (Sesostris.) Amenemha III.	Obelisk of Heliopolis erected. Lake Moeris and the Labyrinth constructed. Sinai Peninsula held.
1900(?)	XIII.	Theban.	....	Abraham in Egypt, probably.
2080	XIV.	Xoite.		
2080	XV.	Shepherds, or Hyksos.	....	Joseph in Egypt under one of the Shepherd dynasties.
2080	XVI.	Hyksos.		
2080	XVII.	Hyksos.		
1520	XVIII.	Theban.	Amosis.	Conquers the Hyksos, and unites the empire. The Pharaoh of Exod. i, 8, according to many.
			Amunoph I.	
			Thothmes I.	
			Thothmes II.	
			Queen Amunnonhet.	The largest obelisk at Karnak erected.
			Thothmes III.	A reign famous in architecture and conquest. Monuments at Karnak and Memphis; Temples in Ethiopia.
			Thothmes IV.	
			Amunoph III.	Colossi of Thebes erected. The Vocal Memnon.
			Amunoph IV.	

("Pyramid Dynasty.")

(This was the "golden age" of the empire.)

CHRONOLOGICAL TABLE.

Date.	Number of Dynasty.	Name of Dynasty.	Noted Kings.	Events.
B. C. 1840	XIX.	Theban.	Rameses I.	Founder of the Dynasty.
			Sethi I.	Great Hall of Karnak erected. Conquest of Syria and Mesopotamia. Canal from the Red Sea to the Nile.
			Rameses II. (The Great).	Ramesseum built at Thebes. Confounded by the Greeks with Sethi I. and Sesortasen I.
			Menepthah, or Pthahmen.	The Pharaoh of the Exode, according to Wilkinson.
1200	XX.	Theban.	Rameses III.	Edifices of Medinet-habu erected.
			Several kings of the same name.	Decline of national life.
1085	XXI.	Tanite.		
990	XXII.	Bubastite.	Sheshonk I.	The Shishak of 1 Kings xiv, 25, 26, contemporary with Rehoboam.
818	XXIII.	Tanite.		
734	XXIV.	Saite.	Bocchoris.	
714	XXV.	Ethiopian.	Sabaco.	The So of 2 Kings xvii, 4, contemporary with Hoshea, king of Israel.
			Tirhakah.	Contemporary with Hezekiah. 2 Kings xix, 9.
664	XXVI.	Saite.	Psammetichus I.	First settlement of Greeks in Egypt.
525	....	....	Psammetichus III.	Egypt taken by the Persians under Cambyses.
332	....	....	....	Egypt conquered by the Macedonians under Alexander the Great.
A. D. 30	....	....	....	Egypt conquered by the Romans, and formed into a Roman province.

PLAN AND CONTENTS OF EXODUS.

The Book of Exodus is a record of the deliverance of the Israelites from Egyptian bondage, of their journey to Sinai, and of the covenant and legislation given at that sacred mountain. It is susceptible of analysis in several ways. We have (1) an account of *the Bondage of Israel*, and its intense persistence in spite of all the plagues which smote the land, because of the king's refusal to let the people go. Chaps. i-xi. This is followed (2) by an account of *the Redemption of Israel*, as typified by the passover, realized in the journey out of Egypt, and celebrated in Moses's triumphal song, (chaps. xii-xv, 21;) and (3) *the Consecration of Israel*, by means of the various events and discipline recorded in chaps. xv, 22-xl. Or one may recognize the two simple divisions of (1) *the Exodus out of Egypt*, (chaps. i-xviii,) and (2) *the Legislation at Sinai*, (xix-xl.) We follow, however, the divisions and subdivisions prepared by the late Dr. Newhall, author of the commentary on the first seventeen chapters, and exhibited in the following outline:

Birth of the Nation of Israel, Chapters i-xv, 21.

I. PREPARATORY PERIOD.

(1.) **Increase and Oppression of Israel, i, ii.**

Descendants of Israel, i, 1-6. Increase and Oppression of Israel, i, 7-22. Birth and Education of Moses, ii, 1-10. Moses's Failure and Flight into Midian, ii, 11-22. Increased Oppression of Israel, ii, 23-25.

(2.) **Call and Commission of Moses, iii, 1-iv, 31.**

Jehovah in the Burning Bramble, iii, 1-6. Moses is Called, iii, 7-10; and God Reveals the Memorial Name, iii, 11-22. Moses Receives the Three Signs, iv, 1-9. Moses Hesitates and is Rebuked, iv, 10-17. The Return of Moses to Egypt, iv, 18-31.

II. THE STRUGGLE.

(1.) **The Intercession and Judgment, v-xiii.**

The Intercession of Moses with Pharaoh, and the Result, v, 1-23.

(2.) **The Ten Judgment Strokes, vi-xii, 30.**

Resumption of the Narrative, and Recapitulation, vi, 28-vii, 7. The Ten Plagues, vii, 8-xii, 36. Opening Contest with the Magicians, vii, 10-13. First Plague—Blood, vii, 14-25. Second Plague—Frogs, viii, 1-15. Third Plague — Lice, viii, 16-19. Fourth Plague—Swarms,(of Flies,) viii, 20-32. Fifth Plague—Murrain, ix, 1-7. Sixth Plague—Boils, ix, 8-12. Seventh Plague—The Hail, ix, 13-35. Eighth Plague—Locusts, x, 1-20. Ninth Plague—Darkness, x, 21-29. Tenth Plague Predicted, xi, 1-10. Institution of the Passover, and Covenant Consecration of Israel, xii, 1-28. Tenth Judgment Stroke, xii, 29-36. The Exode, xii, 37-42. Additional Passover Regulations, xii, 43-50. Promulgation of the Law of the First-born, and of the Feast of Unleavened Bread, xiii, 1-16. March of the Israelites from Succoth to Etham, xiii, 17-22.

III. THE VICTORY.

Triumph over Egypt, xiv-xv, 21.

The Red Sea Deliverance, xiv, 1-31. The Triumphal Song of Moses and Miriam, xv, 1-21.

Divine Adoption of Israel, Chapters xv, 22–xl, 38.

I. PREPARATORY PERIOD.

March from the Red Sea to Sinai. First Contact with Friends and Foes in the Desert, xv, 22–xviii, 27.

March to Marah and Elim, xv, 22–27. The Murmuring in the Desert of Sin, xvi, 1–3. Promise of Manna and Quails, xvi, 4–12. Quails and Manna Given, xvi, 13–21. The Sixth Day's Manna, xvi, 22–31. An Omer of Manna laid up before Jehovah, xvi, 32–36. March to Rephidim; Want of Water, xvii, 1–7. Conflict with Amalek, xvii, 8–16. Jethro's Visit to Moses, xviii, 1–27.

II. JEHOVAH REVEALED AS KING OF ISRAEL.

The Divine Glory and the Giving of the Law at Sinai, xix–xxiv, 18.

The Encampment at Sinai, xix, 1, 2. Preparations for the Sinaitic Theophany, xix, 3–15. The Sinaitic Theophany, xix, 16–20. Repeated Charge to the People, xix, 21–25. The Ten Commandments, xx, 1–17. The Effect on the People, xx, 18–21. The Book of the Covenant, xx, 22–xxiii, 33. Ratification of the Covenant, xxiv, 1–11. Moses's Ascent into the Mount, xxiv, 12–18.

III. JEHOVAH'S DWELLING WITH ISRAEL.

(1.) The Plan of the Tabernacle and its Holy Service, xxv–xxxi.

Offerings for the Sanctuary, xxv, 1–9. Ark of the Covenant, xxv, 10–22. Table of Showbread, xxv, 23–30. Golden Candlestick, xxv, 31–40. The Tabernacle, xxvi, 1–37. Altar of Burnt Offering, xxvii, 1–8. Court of the Tabernacle, xxvii, 9–19. Oil for the Light, xxvii, 20, 21. Holy Garments for the Priests, xxviii, 1–43. Consecration of Aaron and his Sons, xxix, 1–37. The Continual Burnt Offering, xxix, 38–46. The Altar of Incense, xxx, 1–10. Ransom of Souls, xxx, 11–16. The Laver, xxx, 17–21. The Anointing Oil, xxx, 22–33. Compounding of Incense, xxx, 34–38. Bezaleel and Aholiab, xxxi, 1–11. The Sabbath Law, xxxi, 12–17. The two Tables, xxxi, 18.

(2.) The Covenant Broken and Renewed, xxxii–xxxiv.

Worship of the Golden Calf, xxxii, 1–6. Intercession and Punishment, xxxii, 7–35. Mediation and Intercession, xxxiii, 1–23. The Tables of the Covenant Renewed, xxxiv, 1–35.

(3.) The Construction, Erection, and Dedication of the Tabernacle, xxxv–xl.

The Sabbath, xxxv, 1–3. The Offerings for the Sanctuary, xxxv, 4–29. Bezaleel and Aholiab, xxxv, 30–35. Superabundance of Offerings, xxxvi, 1–7. Tabernacle Curtains, Boards, and Hangings, xxxvi, 8–38. Ark of the Covenant, xxxvii, 1–9. Table of Showbread, xxxvii, 10–16. Golden Candlestick, xxxvii, 17–24. Altar of Incense, xxxvii, 25–28. The Oil and the Incense, xxxvii, 29. Altar of Burnt Offering, xxxviii, 1–7. The Laver, xxxviii, 8. Court of the Tabernacle, xxxviii, 9–20. Amount of Metals used for the Tabernacle, xxxviii, 21–31. Holy Garments for the Priests, xxxix, 1–31. All Brought to Moses and Approved, xxxix, 32–43. The Order to set up the Tabernacle, xl, 1–16. Erection of the Tabernacle, xl, 17–33. Jehovah's Glory Filling the Tabernacle, xl, 34–38.

THE BOOK OF EXODUS.

BIRTH OF THE NATION.
Chaps. I, 1—XV, 21.

I. PREPARATORY PERIOD.
Increase and Oppression of Israel, Chaps. I, II.

CHAPTER I.
INTRODUCTORY.

(1.) Through the book of generations (*Genesis*) the fabric of Divine Revelation has risen like a pyramid in ten successive stages, broad as the creation at the bottom, and narrowing at the summit to a single family, which becomes lost from view in the darkness of Egyptian heathenism. The spiritual history of this family is now resumed, in order to develop facts and principles of universal interest and significance. JEHOVAH'S NAME is to be set in Israel, that, through the life and literature of that nation, the glory of that NAME may be diffused over all lands and ages. The narrative, after the manner so often noticed in Genesis, at the commencement doubles back upon itself for a new departure, and gives a brief review of the grand divisions of the nation; it then proceeds to relate the fulfilment of the promises to the patriarchs in the vast fruitfulness of the descendants of Israel. The connexion is thus close and logical with the Book of Generations, to which it is grammatically joined by the simple connective particle. The account of the origin of the world, of the race, of the chosen family, and the record of the successive calls of the patriarchs, having prepared the way, the writer proceeds to describe Jehovah as taking up his abode with men. Various ancient records and traditions, proverbs and songs, have been woven together in this work, but the unity of the composition shows that it proceeds from a single hand.

(2.) A very few lines shed upon the centuries of the Egyptian sojourn all the light that the world has received. The sacred writer did not aim to furnish a full history of Israel, but to develop the fulfilment of God's plans, and hence he hastens over whole ages to the time of the accomplishment of the patriarchal promises. The work thus differs essentially from all secular histories. It is not a history of Israel, but of God in Israel.

The immense increase of Israel in Egypt, whether the time of their sojourn were two or four centuries, precludes the idea of a severe continuous servitude. They were cruelly oppressed only during the last part of their stay. They were by no means a nation of degraded slaves, for they had their elders and scribes, brave warriors, skilled artisans, firm and sober family traditions, and inspiring songs. They had become entangled in Egyptian idolatry, but they had not forgotten the God of their fathers. From Joshua v, 5 we find that the covenant seal of circumcision was set upon the people generation after generation; while a name like Jochebed—meaning, *whose glory is Jehovah*—shows that at least in the tribe of Levi the covenant Name was revered.

There was a stern, sharp antagonism between the Egyptian religion, with its magnificent temples, its colossal idols, and its pompous ritual, and the simple spiritual worship of the Hebrew patriarchs; and this antagonism developed more and more in successive generations, and culminated in the conflict wherein Jehovah triumphed over the gods of Egypt. Moses did not create, but focalized, spiritual forces that had been gathering for generations. When Israel was fully ripe for the revelation, the I AM spoke from the burning bramble.

CHAPTER I.

NOW ᵃ these *are* the names of the children of Israel, which came into Egypt; every man and his household came with Jacob. 2 Reuben, Simeon, Levi, and Judah, 3 Issachar, Zebulun, and Benjamin, 4 Dan, and Naphtali, Gad, and Asher. 5 And all the souls that came out of the ¹ loins of Jacob were ᵇ seventy souls: for Joseph was in Egypt already. 6 And ᶜ Joseph died, and all his brethren, and all that generation. 7 ᵈ And the children of Israel were fruitful, and increased abundantly, and multiplied, and waxed exceeding mighty; and the land was filled with them. 8 Now there ᵉ arose up a new king over Egypt,

---

a Gen. 46. 8; chapter 6. 14.—1 Heb. *thigh.*—*b* Gen. 46. 26, 27; verse 20; Deut. 10. 22.

c Gen. 50. 26; Acts 7. 15.—*d* Gen. 46. 3; Deut. 26. 5; Psa. 105. 24; Acts 7. 17.—*e* Acts 7. 18.

DESCENDANTS OF ISRAEL, 1-6.

1-5. **These are the names**—The heads of the tribes are recounted, and the statement of Gen. xlvi, 27 is repeated, that seventy souls went down into Egypt; the writer, from the covenant associations of the number, loving to consider Israel as a seventy-fold people, though at the same time himself furnishing data by which we see that he did not intend to give an exact census. See notes on Luke x, 1-16, and Acts i, 15. **All...that came out of the loins of Jacob**—The idiom which represents Jacob himself as one of the "souls that came out of the loins of Jacob" gave the original readers no difficulty, and we are not to expect Occidental rhetoric in Oriental documents. See notes on Gen. xlvi.

INCREASE AND OPPRESSION OF ISRAEL, 7-22.

7. Here is an accumulation of figures to express the vast increase of the children of Israel. **Were fruitful**—A figure from the seed which multiplies a hundred or a thousand fold. **Increased abundantly**—*Swarmed* or *teemed;* a word applied to the myriad-fold spawn of fishes. **Multiplied... exceeding mighty**—Literally, *multiplied and grew strong* (in numbers) *exceedingly exceedingly.* The fat Nile-land greatly favours fruitfulness both in animals and men, as is attested by travellers from Aristotle and Strabo to Robinson; and Goshen was the "best of the land" for a pastoral people. It was, besides, a border land, where Israel was isolated from the Egyptians. This isolation aided in developing an independent national life, while the descendants of Jacob would in Canaan have become absorbed among the native Hamites. Natural causes are thus ever taken up into providential plans.

8. **A new king**—A new dynasty or reigning family, says Josephus. The language implies a total change of government and principles of administration, such as attend a change of dynasty; not necessarily that so much time had elapsed that Joseph was actually forgotten, but his services were no longer gratefully recognised. Manetho describes two great dynastic changes: the first on the invasion, and the second on the expulsion, of the Hyksos, or Shepherd Kings; but whether either of these be the change here mentioned, or, in fact, whether there ever were any Shepherd Kings, are still greatly controverted questions. It seems most likely that this oppression of the Israelites commenced under the eighteenth (Theban) dynasty, which came into power, according to Wilkinson, about B. C. 1550, according to Lepsius about B. C. 1700, and ruled two centuries. Ames I., (called also Aahmes, Amosis, and Tethmosis,) the first monarch of this dynasty, united and centralized the kingdom, drove out invaders, erected great palaces and obelisks, and commenced a new epoch of Egyptian history. It is natural that he should know nothing and care nothing for the favourite minister or measures of the dynasty which he displaced; yet it is well to understand that this identification is but conjectural.

Pharaoh's residence seems at this time to have been at Zoan, otherwise called Tanis, or Avaris, a city of Lower Egypt, on the east bank of the Tanitic branch of the Nile, once a large and strong city of the eastern frontier. (See Isa. xix, 11, 13.) Zoan is the Hebrew

which knew not Joseph. 9 And he said unto his people, Behold, ᶠ the people of the children of Israel *are* more and mightier than we: 10 ᵍ Come on, let us ʰ deal wisely with them ; lest they multiply, and it come to pass, that, when there falleth out any war, they join also unto our enemies, and fight against us, and *so* get them up out of the land. 11 Therefore they did set over them taskmasters ⁱ to afflict them with their ᵏ burdens. And they built for Pharaoh

f Psalm 105. 24.——*g* Psalms 10. 2; 83. 3, 4.—— *h* Job 5. 13; Psalm 105. 25; Prov. 16. 25; 21. 30; Acts 7. 19.——*i* Gen. 15. 13; chapter 3. 7: Deut. 26. 6.——*k* Chap. 2. 11; 5. 4, 5; Psa. 81. 6.

name which became Tanis in Greek, while Avaris is an Egyptian word in Greek letters, all the names having the same meaning—"House of departure"—in evident allusion to the frontier situation of the city. "The field of Zoan" is dwelt upon by the Psalmist (Psa. lxxviii, 12, 43) as the scene of God's wonders in Egypt, and Manetho tells us that King Salatis, the first of the Shepherd line, made this city his residence in harvest time and garrisoned it with 240,000 men. It was evidently the great frontier fortress towards Syria during the Shepherd period, and was the last stronghold of that dynasty when they were allowed to depart by capitulation. (Josephus, *Contr. Ap.*, i.) It had a splendid temple to *Set*, the Egyptian Baal, the sacred enclosure of which can now be clearly traced. This temple was ornamented with numerous obelisks and sculptures by Rameses II., of the nineteenth dynasty, and the present grandeur of its ruins attests its ancient splendour. Twelve fallen obelisks, which were transported down the Nile to this spot from Syene, show with what magnificence Zoan was adorned by the Egyptian kings. Mariette and De Rougé have recently exhumed here sphynxes and colossal statues, bearing the marks of the Shepherd period, and proving beyond doubt that this was a flourishing seat of empire before the time of Moses. (Thomson, in *Smith's Dictionary*.)

The great fertile plain in which this city stood, which originally extended thirty miles east of Tanis to Pelusium, "of old a rich marsh land, watered by four of the seven branches of the Nile, and swept by the cool breezes of the Mediterranean," is now, by the subsidence of the coast, almost covered by the great Lake Menzeleh. (Poole, in *Smith's Dict.*) Pharaoh probably divided his residence between this city and Memphis, and it will be seen that Zoan was so near to Goshen that Moses and Aaron could easily pass and repass in their interviews with Pharaoh. See Concluding Notes at close of chapter. (1.)

9, 10. **And he said unto his people** —This implies consultation of a king with his counsellors in an epoch of transition or revolution, and suits well the time of Amosis. Before his reign Egypt was divided into several kingdoms—Thebes, This, Memphis, etc., between which there were constant struggles, the different dynasties ruling side by side. Under Amosis, Thebes became supreme. **More and mightier than we**—Not that they really outnumbered the Egyptians, but the new king is alarmed at the rapid increase of an alien population which, from its religious antagonism, could not become assimilated with the Egyptian nation. See Introduction, (2.)

10. **There falleth.. any war**—Literally, *When wars arise*. (Nordh. *Gr.*, 752.) He saw that there was being developed in the midst of his empire a hostile nation, which would be a dangerous internal enemy in time of war, and might at any time assert its independence. **Get them up out of the land**—This incidental remark shows that Israel had not forgotten the great national promises made to their fathers, and that their national hopes were not unknown to the Egyptians even before Moses arose.

11. **Taskmasters**—*Chiefs of tribute.* The words are noteworthy, since they are found designating the same officers both in Hebrew and Egyptian. The Hebrew word שַׂר, *Sar*, is an exact transcription of the Egyptian title applied in the Theban monuments to the officer appointed by the kings of the eighteenth dynasty to superintend captives employed in making bricks. This rank is there denoted by a long staff

treasure-cities, Pithom ¹and Raamses. **12** ²But the more they afflicted them, the more they multiplied and grew. And they were grieved because of the children of Israel. **13** And the Egyptians made the children of Israel to serve with rigour: **14** And they ᵐ made their lives bitter with hard bondage, ⁿ in mortar, and in brick, and in all manner of service in the field: all their service, wherein they made them serve, *was* with rigour. **15** And the king of Egypt spake

l Genesis 47. 11.——² Hebrew, *And as they afflicted them, so they multiplied,* &c.

m Chap. 2. 23; 6. 9; Num. 20. 15; Acts 7, 19, 34. ——*n* Psa. 81. 6.

and by the giraffe symbol. These "taskmasters" were men of rank, carefully distinguished in the monuments from the subordinate overseers, as they are by the sacred writer. Exod. v, 6. The Hebrews were not reduced to slavery, since they still had their houses, flocks, and herds; but were employed in forced labours on the public works. By this oppression the king hoped to break the spirit of the people, and also their physical power. **Built ...treasure-cities**—Magazines or depots for provisions and ammunition. The monuments represent captives in great numbers employed in such work. **Pithom and Raamses**— These are Egyptian names, and are often found upon the monuments. *Pithom*, Brugsch makes the Egyptian Pa-Tum, *House of Tum*, the sun-god of Heliopolis; while *Rameses* or *Raamses* means *Son of Ra*, or the Sun, and was the name of many Egyptian kings. These cities were about twenty-four miles apart, in the **Wady** Tumeylat, on the line of the canal that once connected the Nile with the Red Sea. Like the name Pharaoh, (Ph-Ra, *the Sun*,) both of these names set forth the sun-worship of the Egyptians, and the reigning king was regarded as the representative of Ra, the Sun, upon the earth.

12. More they afflicted...more they multiplied—But God was with the oppressed, and the immense national vitality which has made Israel the wonder of history began to be developed in proportion to the oppression, so that the Egyptians *became distressed* (with fear) *before the* children of Israel. Compare Num. xxii, 3.

13, 14. The nature of their toil is here more fully described. **Hard bondage**—Rather, *hard labour in clay and bricks, and all* (kind of) *service in the field*. They were not made house-servants, or employed as artisans in any kind of skilled labour, but were set at the coarse work of brick-making for the great public buildings, canal digging, raising water from the river for irrigation, which is specially toilsome in Egypt, and similar rough outdoor labours. This remark applies only to this time of special oppression. Josephus says that they built the pyramids; but the great pyramids are made of stone, and were standing when Joseph went down into Egypt. A vast amount of brick was required for the walls of cities, fortresses, temple-courts, and private as well as public buildings. They were made of the Nile mud mixed with straw, and of clay without straw, baked in the sun, and their manufacture was a government monopoly. Immense piles of these bricks—the ruins of ancient works, many of them stamped with the hieroglyphs of the Pharaohs—are now found in the land of Goshen.

The opposite engraving represents a painting at Thebes, in the tomb of an officer of Thothmes III., of the eighteenth dynasty, and delineates all the processes of Egyptian brick-making, foreign captives being the labourers, directed by Egyptian task-masters.

It is a noteworthy fact, that, in an inscription of the twenty-second year of Amosis, alien labourers of some pastoral nation, like the Israelites, are described as carrying blocks of limestone from the Rufu quarries to Memphis. This, like the opposite picture, shows that events precisely like those narrated in the text were, according to the best chronology, transpiring in Egypt at the time when the Israelites were there.

15, 16. A second and far more cruel edict, now went forth. Herodotus shows (vol. ii, 84) that medical theory and practice were highly perfected in Egypt, medical specialties being carefully cultivated; and the monuments

FOREIGN CAPTIVES EMPLOYED IN MAKING BRICKS AT THEBES.

Fig. 1. Man returning after carrying the bricks.——Figs. 2, 3. Taskmasters.——Figs. 4, 5. Men carrying bricks.——Figs. 6, 7, 8, 9. Digging and mixing the clay or mud.——Figs. 10, 11. Making bricks with a wooden mould, *a*, *b*.——Figs. 12, 13. Fetching water from the tank *h*.——At *e* the bricks (tobi) are said to be made at Thebes.

to the Hebrew midwives, of which the name of the one *was* Shiphrah, and the name of the other Puah; **16** And he said, When ye do the office of a midwife to the Hebrew women, and see *them* upon the stools, if it *be* a son, then ye shall kill him; but if it *be* a daughter, then she shall live. **17** But the midwives °feared God, and did not ᴾas the king of Egypt commanded them, but saved the men children alive. **18** And the king of Egypt called for the midwives, and said unto them, Why have ye done this thing, and have saved the men children alive? **19** And ᵠthe midwives said unto Pharaoh, Because the Hebrew women *are* not as the Egyptian women; for they *are* lively, and are delivered ere the midwives come in unto them. **20** ʳTherefore God dealt well with the midwives: and the people multiplied, and waxed very mighty. **21** And it came to pass, because the midwives feared God, ˢthat he made them houses. **22** And Pharaoh charged all his people, saying, ᵗEvery son that is born ye shall cast into the river, and every daughter ye shall save alive.

o Proverbs 16. 6.——*p* Daniel 3. 16, 18; 6. 13; Acts 5. 29.——*q* See Joshua 2. 4, &c.; 2 Samuel 17. 19, 20.——*r* Prov. 11. 18; Eccles. 8. 12; Isa. 3. 10;—— Heb. 6. 10.——*s* See 1 Samuel 2. 35; 2 Samuel 7. 11, 13, 27, 29; 1 Kings 2. 24; 11. 38; Psa. 127. 1.——*t* Acts 7. 19.

show that the women were *accoucheurs*. **Shiphrah** and **Puah** were superintendents of the midwives, and are here designated *the* midwives, as Pharaoh's chief butler and baker are called *the* butler and baker in Gen. xl, 1. This orderly superintendence of all industries is abundantly illustrated on the Theban tombs. **When ye... see them upon the stools**— *When ye look upon the birth*, (*Targ. Onk.*) At the very moment of birth they were to destroy the child, if a male, as they could easily do even before the mother had seen it. This edict was probably aimed specially at the leading families of Israel, for such only would be likely to employ a professional midwife. See Concluding Notes. (2.)

17-19. But the midwives feared—*Feared the* (one only) **God** rather than Pharaoh, and would not execute his murderous mandate. Their excuse was plausible, for childbirth is usually easy with women of the pastoral class, especially in the East. Burckhardt and Tischendorf relate that the Bedouin mother seeks a spot by a spring or stream, and bears and dresses her infant without aid. She even sometimes alights from her camel to bear her child, which she washes in the sand and then resumes her place.

20. God dealt well with the midwives—Augustine well says: "Not their falsehood, but their mercy, kindness, and fear of God, were rewarded. For the sake of the good, God forgave the evil." It was well that the fear of God kept them from murder it had been better if it had also kept them from falsehood.

21. Made them houses—Built up their families, increased their posterity, in reward for their preservation of the posterity of Israel. This, in the Hebrew idiom, is to "build a house." Comp. 2 Sam. vii, 11, 27.

22. Every son... ye shall cast into the river—The Nile. This third and most sweeping edict is now promulgated, by which all Pharaoh's subjects are commanded to become executioners of the Hebrew children. The command was so inhuman, and so contrary to the interests of the Egyptians themselves, that it is not likely that it was ever enforced for any length of time; but it gave legal opportunity to any who desired to destroy the children of Hebrew families who seemed for any reason specially dangerous. Hence the fears of the mother of Moses. This massacre has, moreover, historic parallels. When the servile class in Sparta became formidable from numbers, the Spartan youth were sent out with daggers to murder a sufficient number to remove apprehension. Diodorus relates that before the time of Psammetichus—that is, all through the Old Testament period—simple jealousy often led the Egyptian kings to put foreigners to death. And this cruel edict opened the schools and the palace of the City of the Sun to the saviour of Israel! And how we glance from the massacre of Goshen to that of Bethlehem; from the bulrush ark to the manger; from prostrate Rᴀ to Satan falling like lightning from heaven; from the saviour of a nation to the Saviour of a world!

CONCLUDING NOTES.

Chronology of the Exodus. (1.) The period of the Israelitish sojourn in Egypt is expressly declared in Exod. xii, 40 to have been 430 years. This harmonizes with the prediction made to Abraham, Gen. xv, 13: "Thy seed shall be a stranger in a land that is not theirs, and shall serve them; and they shall afflict them 400 years;" which language is also quoted by Stephen in his discourse in Acts vii, 6. But the Samaritan and Septuagint text of Exod. xii, 40, give a different reading, which makes the 430 years cover the whole "sojourn" of the three patriarchs, Abraham, Isaac, and Jacob, in Canaan, as well as that of the Israelites in Egypt, extending thus from the arrival of Abraham in Haran to the Exode. This would make the Egyptian sojourn only two hundred and fifteen years. Paul follows this Sept. chronology in Gal. iii, 17. We have, then, what are called a long and a short chronology of the Exodus. The short period is adopted in our chronology, (Usher's) which sets the Exode at B. C. 1491, two hundred and fifteen years after Jacob went down into Egypt. As yet we have not data for deciding with certainty between the two periods, but the census of the Israelites at the Exode is usually deemed to favour four rather than two centuries of Egyptian sojourn. To balance up authorities on this matter gives little light, and the question would seem to have been doubtful in the time of Josephus, since he expressly commits himself to both sides in the same treatise. Compare *Antiq.*, ii, 15 with ii, 9. See notes on chap. xii, 40.

Egyptian chronology is at present so wholly unsettled that it is rash to dogmatize, and wise to wait patiently till more light comes from the monuments. The most famous Egyptologists differ from each other by centuries in regard to the date of the Exodus. As mentioned above, Usher's date, B. C. 1491, stands in our English Bible; Poole fixes it at 1652, (Smith's *Bib.* *Dict.*, art. *Chronology*;) Rawlinson at 1650, (*Ancient Hist.*, p. 61;) Wilkinson at first made Thothmes III. the Pharaoh of the Exode, about 1460, (*Anc. Egypt*, vol. i, pages 76-81, *English Edition*,) but has since decided for Pthahmen, (Meneptah I.,) of the nineteenth dynasty, who came to the throne about B. C. 1250, (Rawl., *Her. App.* to book ii, chap. viii;) and so Brugsch, (*Hist. de l'Egypt*, i, 156,) who makes Rameses II., the father of Pthahmen, to be the Pharaoh of Exod. i. This is the view of Stanley and many others. Lepsius and Bunsen make the Exode to have taken place under the nineteenth dynasty, and Bunsen fixes about 1320 as its date. Ewald, Winer, and Knobel identify the Pharaoh of Exod. i, with Amosis of the eighteenth dynasty, as in our note. This view is learnedly defended by Canon Cook in the *Speaker's Commentary*.

The whole story of the Hyksos, or Shepherd Kings, though so generally accepted, rests solely on the confused and contradictory account of the priest Manetho, who lived more than a thousand years after the alleged events, and fragments of whose work have been handed to us by Josephus and Syncellus, and hopelessly confused with fragments from another Manetho of uncertain date and authority. No trace of the Hyksos is found in the monuments so far, in Herodotus, Diodorus, or the books of Moses. Hengstenberg, Hävernik, and many others, consider the whole story as a confused Egyptian legend of the Exode. Blackie, in his *Homer*, well sets forth this view. (*Homer and the Iliad*, i, 36.)

(2.) הָאׇבְנָיִם, (verse 16.) The word occurs in only one other place, Jer. xviii, 3, where it is rendered *the* (two) *wheels*, (of the potter,) in the margin, *frames* or *seats*. Five different interpretations are suggested, not noticing proposed alterations of the text, as by Fürst, etc.

1. Gesenius, in *Heb. Lex.*, makes it the midwife's chair, on which she sat before the woman in labour.

2. Gesenius elsewhere makes it the bath tub or trough (*badewanne*) in which the child was washed. So De Wette.

370　　　　　　　　　EXODUS.　　　　　B. C. 1571.

CHAPTER II.

AND there went ª a man of the house of Levi, and took *to wife* a daugh-ter of Levi. 2 And the woman conceived, and bare a son: and ᵇ when she saw him that he *was* a goodly *child*, she

a Chap. 6. 20; Num. 26. 59; 1 Chron. 23. 14.

b Acts 7. 20; Heb. 11. 23.

3. Smith's *Dict.* quotes Lane's *Modern Egyptians* to show that it means the chair used in aiding delivery, showing that the modern Egyptians have the same custom, and such a chair is said to be represented on the monuments of the eighteenth dynasty. *Auf dem Geburtsstuhle,* Van Ess. But neither of these interpretations explain the dual form.

4. Ewald interprets the word adverbially as meaning *instantly*, like the German, *flugs;* English, "*on the fly.*"

5. Fagius (*Crit. Sacr.*) follows the interpretation of J. Kimchi and others, who refer the word to the vagina, the *labia uteri.* Thus La Haye, (*Bib. Max.*,) who renders *cum in ostiis vulvæ prolem videritis.* So Keil and Knobel, who seem to settle the question.

CHAPTER II.

INTRODUCTORY.

(1.) The time of the event with which this chapter opens is not precisely ascertained, but it must have been somewhere in the third stage of the cruel oppression described in the last part of chap. i. We now come to transactions in which Moses was an eyewitness and an actor. From the opening of this chapter we should naturally suppose that Moses was the firstborn child; yet from verses four and seven we find that he had an elder sister, and from chap. vii, 7 we find that Aaron was his elder brother, of whose birth no mention is made. This omission of events well known to Moses, which do not lie directly in the line of connexion that he aims to trace, is specially noteworthy as a characteristic of the author's style. The opening history is, in truth, not only biography, but auto-biography, the narrative of the writer's own eventful birth.

(2.) The whole style of this chapter shows that it was written by one who was familiar with both Egyptian and Hebrew. Ewald shows (*Hist. of Israel,* ii, p. 3) that the words for *river,* (Nile,) *bulrushes,* (Nile grass,) and afterward the words for *ephah, hin,* etc., are Egyptian words naturalized in Hebrew. So the words for *slime, pitch, brick, ark,* and others, are common to both languages, as may be seen at once from the hieroglyphic dictionaries of Bunsen and Brugsch. The great Hebrew lawgiver used both languages with equal fluency, and his work is every-where tinged with the "wisdom of the Egyptians."

(3.) Here begins the history of one of the great souls of the earth. In original endowments, in the grandeur of his mission, and in the permanence of his influence, no other man has been more highly honored of God. In law and literature, as well as in religion—in the world of action as well as of thought—in the Occident as well as the Orient—what name outshines the name of Moses? No other man ever touched the world at so many points as he, and through no other did God ever so move the world. We must accept his claim to inspiration or leave him a riddle unsolved. Says Ewald: "We cannot explain him, or derive him from previous antecedents, for here we stand in presence of the mystery of all creation and of all spiritual power." Yet he is not self-reliant, like the great captains, statesmen, and lawgivers of profane history. He was humbled and crushed by a sense of weakness while revealing the sublimest power. Utterly quenched in his work, he built no monuments for himself, founded no dynasties, but retired behind the cloudy pillar, where he "wist not that his face shone."

BIRTH AND EDUCATION OF MOSES, 1-10.

1. **A man of the house of Levi**—Amram, a descendant of Levi through Kohath. **And took to wife a daughter** (descendant) **of Levi**—Jochebed. Exod. vi, 20, where see note. See Introductory, (1.)

2. **She saw…he was a goodly child**—Literally, *he was beautiful:*

hid him three months. **3** And when she could not longer hide him, she took for him an ark of bulrushes, and daubed it with slime and with pitch, and put the child therein; and she laid *it* in the flags by the river's brink. **4** ᵉAnd his sister stood afar off, to wit what would be done to him. **5** And the ᵈdaughter of Pharaoh came down to wash *herself* at the river; and her maidens walked

c Chap. 15. 20; Num. 26. 59.   *d* Acts 7. 21.

"beautiful before God," says Stephen. Acts vii, 20, in margin. Every child is beautiful to the mother's eye; but the spiritually-minded Jochebed, whose very name declared "JAH, *her glory*," saw His beauty behind the child's sweet face, and knew by faith that He who had given her such a treasure could guard it for her, even from Pharaoh. **She hid him**—"By faith" she hid the child, and "was not afraid." Heb. xi, 23. She used all means, yet trusted; she had full trust, yet used all means. It is the old paradox of the divine-human life.

3. **When she could not longer hide him**—She had already concealed him three months. **She took for him an ark of bulrushes**—Papyrus. The papyrus, or paper reed, from which paper was first made and named, has a triangular stalk, as thick as the finger, about a dozen feet high. Light, strong boats were made of it; also mats, mattresses, sails, and many other articles. The famous Egyptian *papyri*, whose contents are now being deciphered, were made from slices of the pith, dried and then pressed and glued together, forming strips of indefinite length. **Daubed it with slime**—Either bitumen or Nile mud. Jochebed cemented the rushes together with the Nile mud or bitumen, and then smeared the seams with liquid pitch to make it water-tight. Similar boats are common on the Tigris now. **Flags**—Rather, the *Nile grass*. She placed the child where she knew that the princess would see him, trusting for his safety to his captivating beauty and to God.

4. **His sister**—Probably Miriam, who is the only sister named in the history. Num. xxvi, 59. The mother has now exhausted all her skill; she can think of but one thing more—to station Miriam afar off. And now, if ever, JAHVEH-JIREH, "*The Lord will provide.*" Gen. xxii, 14.

5. **The daughter of Pharaoh came**—The intellectual and moral condition of women in Egypt was far higher than in Asia or in Greece. Polygamy was rare, and the harem seclusion unknown. Women were respected and honoured in society, much as in modern Europe and America, and the wives and daughters of kings succeeded to the throne of the Pharaohs. Wilkinson says, that the Egyptians recognised the fact that the morals and manners of society depended on the respect shown to women. **To wash**—Rather, *to bathe:* not to wash her clothes, as Dr. Clarke interprets, who in

THE PAPYRUS.

along by the river's side: and when she saw the ark among the flags, she sent her maid to fetch it. **6** And when she had opened *it*, she saw the child: and, behold, the babe wept. And she had compassion on him, and said, This *is one* of the Hebrews' children. **7** Then said his sister to Pharaoh's daughter, Shall I go and call to thee a nurse of the Hebrew women, that she may nurse the child for thee? **8** And Pharaoh's daughter said to her, Go. And the maid went and called the child's mother. **9** And Pharaoh's daughter said unto her, Take this child away, and nurse it for me, and I will give *thee* thy wages. And the woman took the child, and nursed it. **10** And the child grew, and she brought him unto Pharaoh's daughter, and he became *e* her son. And she called his name ¹Moses: and she said, Because I drew him out of the water.

11 And it came to pass in those days, *f* when Moses was grown, that he went out unto his brethren, and looked on their *g* burdens: and he spied an Egyptian

---

e Acts 7. 21.——1 That is, *Drawn out.* *f* Acts 7. 23, 24; Heb. 11. 24-26.——*g* Chap. 1. 11.

---

this case transferred to Egypt the manners of the Grecian lands in the Homeric age. The Nile was regarded as an emanation of the god Osiris, and the act of bathing in its waters was devotional as well as sanitary, for the Nile was deemed the mother of all life and fruitfulness.

6–9. There is a pathos in this description which shows that the writer's heart was in it. That princess was his adopting mother. The self-reliant action of the king's daughter, notwithstanding her father's cruel and absolute command, well illustrates the independence in character and action which distinguished the Egyptian women, at least the high-born. The Egyptians were taught also to regard mercy as one of the conditions of acceptance in the day of judgment. In the *Funeral Ritual*, or *Book of the Dead*, recently translated from a papyrus by Birch, the human spirit is represented as answering to the judge, "I have not afflicted any man; I have not made any man weep; I have not withheld milk from the mouths of sucklings."

10. **The child grew...and he became her son**—This is all that Moses tells us of his own youth. How easily could he here have written lines which would have satisfied the curiosity of ages! but he hastens over years to touch the next link in the providential chain. The sacred writers ever show this baffling, unworldly reticence. Thus the youth of Moses's great Antitype, **Jesus**, is almost a blank in history. In both instances apocryphal legends, beneath attention except as psychological curiosities, (witness Josephus and Philo,) have swarmed into the vacuum.

There are, however, in the British Museum papyri of the eighteenth dynasty, (B. C. 1525 — 1325, according to Wilkinson,) which give something of an idea of the education of a youth designed for civil and military service in the Mosaic age. From these and other sources we learn that the education was in literature, philosophy, and the mystic lore of the Egyptian religion, rather than in science, although great attention was given to arithmetic, pure and applied geometry, mensuration, surveying, accounts, architecture, and astronomy. But especially were the children trained from infancy in grammar and rhetoric, and the drill in style was thorough enough to have satisfied Quintilian. Literary examination was indispensable for appointment to the lowest public office, and instructors were appointed and schools superintended by the government. Such was the training of Moses at Heliopolis, the Oxford of Egypt. **And she called his name Moses**—Rather, *Mosheh*, (from the Egyptian word *mos*, or *mas, to draw*,) using a word which was the root of several royal Egyptian names, as Teth-*mos*-is, A-*mos*-is, which was transcribed to *Mosheh* in Hebrew, and to Μω-υσῆς by the LXX translators, (which means *water-saved*,) whence the Latin *Moyses*, and our *Moses*. Brugsch states that it is also the name of an Egyptian prince of the nineteenth dynasty, a viceroy of Nubia.

Moses's Failure, and Flight from Egypt, 11–22.

11, 12. **Looked on their burdens** —Looked with sympathy and longed

B. C. 1531.   CHAPTER II.   373

smiting a Hebrew, one of his brethren. 12 And he looked this way and that way, and when he saw that *there was* no man, he ʰ slew the Egyptian, and hid him in the sand. 13 And ⁱ when he went out the second day, behold, two men of the Hebrews strove together: and he said to him that did the wrong, Wherefore smitest thou thy fellow? 14 And he said, ᵏ Who made thee ²a prince and a judge over us? intendest thou to kill me as thou killedst the Egyptian? And Moses feared, and said, Surely this thing is known. 15 Now when Pharaoh heard this thing, he sought to slay Moses. But ˡ Moses fled from the face of Pharaoh, and dwelt in the land of Midian: and he sat down by ᵐ a well. 16 ⁿ Now the ³ priest of Midian had seven daughters: ᵒ and they came and drew *water*, and filled the troughs to water their father's flock. 17 And the shepherds came and drove them away: but Moses stood up and helped them, and

ʰ Acts 7. 24.——ⁱ Acts 7. 26.——ᵏ Acts 7. 27, 28. ——² Heb. *a man, a prince*, Genesis 13. 8.—— ˡ Acts 7. 29; Heb. 11. 27.

ᵐ Gen. 24. 11; 29. 2.——ⁿ Chap. 3. 1.——³ Or, *prince*, as Gen. 41. 45.——ᵒ Gen. 24. 11; 29. 10; 1 Sam. 9. 11.

to help. St. Stephen says (Acts vii, 23) that he was now forty years old. In the prime of his powers, with the culture of Heliopolis and the faith of Jochebed—seeing his great mission dimly rising before him—with the quick sympathies of a kinsman and a patriot, and with a fiery soul that pined for action, he offered to cast in his lot with his brethren, and put himself at their head, "esteeming the reproach of Christ greater riches than the treasures of Egypt." But neither he nor the people were yet ready. He was too precipitate and self-confident, nor did he yet see the immensity of his real mission. He needed the forty years' desert chastisement and the solemn converse of the solitudes of Horeb. Nor had Israel yet felt the throe in which a nation is born. He felt that he was the born and commissioned leader to break the Egyptian chain; he felt that he had the revolutionary right to strike; but erred in thinking that the hour had come. **He looked this way and that way** —Not from criminal guilt, but with soldierly wariness. He looked on the war as begun, and himself as the captain in the field, and "supposed that his brethren would have understood how that God by his hand would deliver them." Acts vii, 25.

13, 14. "But they understood not;" the iron had not yet gone deep enough into their souls, and Moses's self-sacrifice in their behalf was too sublime for them to see. They betrayed their leader, (for a Hebrew must have informed against him,) and his first effort was a failure, not from Egyptian malice, but from Hebrew jealousy and envy.

15. **And he sat down by a well**— *The* (well-known) *well* (of that place). Midian was the country of the wandering descendants of Abraham's son Midian, in the peninsula of Sinai, and reaching around the Arabian Gulf into the desert beyond. Knobel locates "the well" at Sherm, on the Arabian Gulf, northeast of Ras Mohammed. Here was once a sanctuary, and an hereditary priest and priestess, possibly successors of Jethro, and here are now deep, copious, and very ancient wells. The author of the Epistle to the Hebrews says (Heb. xi, 27) that Moses left Egypt "by faith," and "not fearing the wrath of the king," yet our narrative says that he feared and fled. How is this? Simply that he feared and evaded by flight the immediate and transitory consequences of his rash act, but feared not the grand result of the conflict on which he had staked all. He was ready to measure strength with Pharaoh when the time should come, "for he endured as seeing Him who is invisible." The general who falls back in order to advance does not fear. (It is surprising that Alford should find difficulty here.)

16, 17. Moses's quick sense of right, and promptness to help the weak, are seen in the desert as well as in the brickfield, and he secures the hospitality of Reuel as Jacob did that of Laban. The priest's flock consisted of sheep and goats, though he probably had also camels and asses; but for these there may not have been water and pasturage

ᵖ watered their flock. **18** And when they came to ᵍ Reuel their father, he said, How *is it that* ye are come so soon to day? **19** And they said, An Egyptian delivered us out of the hand of the shepherds, and also drew *water* enough for us, and watered the flock. **20** And he said unto his daughters, And where *is* he? why *is* it *that* ye have left the man? call him, that he may ʳ eat bread. **21** And Moses was content to dwell with the man: and he gave Moses ˢ Zipporah his daughter. **22** And she bare *him* a son, and he called his name ᵗ ᵗ Gershom:

p Gen. 29. 10.——*q* Num. 10. 29; called also *Jethro,* or *Jether,* chap. 3. 1; 4. 18; 18. 1, &c.——*r* Gen. 31. 54; 43. 25.——*s* Chap. 4. 25; 18. 2.——4 That is, *A stranger here.*——*t* Chap. 18. 3.——*u* Acts 7. 29; Heb. 11. 13, 14.——*v* Chap. 7. 7; Acts 7. 30.——*w* Num. 20. 16; Deut. 26. 7; Psa.

in the desert of Sinai. It is not likely that Reuel was a "prince," as written in the margin.

18. **Reu-El**—*Friend of God.* The name implies that he worshipped the God of Abraham his father. Midian was the son of Abraham by Keturah. Gen. xxv, 2. On the relationship of Reuel, Jethro, and Hobab, see Concluding Note.

19. **An Egyptian**—For such Moses seemed to the Midianitish maidens, from his costume and language.

21, 22. The Egyptian prince is **content** to become the shepherd of an humble Arab priest, whose daughter, a child of the desert, becomes the **Zipporah** (*little bird*) of his wilderness home. The sceptre that had been almost within his grasp is exchanged for a shepherd's crook. The learning, luxury, and power of Egypt are exchanged for the barbarism, sand, and stones of Midian. It was the way of duty, but a wonderfully mysterious way! The deliverer is in the glory of his strength and eager for his work, and his people are dying—yet God does not speak! The name of his first-born, **Gershom** —*a stranger there*—tells us that he feels his exile, that his heart is with his far-off people, but we hear no murmur; and the name of his second born, **Eliezer**—*my God* (is my) *help*—shows that his faith was firm. He vanishes into the awful solitudes of Sinai, and we neither see nor hear of him any more for forty years.

for he said, I have been ᵘ a stranger in a strange land. **23** And it came to pass ᵛ in process of time, that the king of Egypt died: and the children of Israel ʷ sighed by reason of the bondage, and they cried, and ˣ their cry came up unto God by reason of the bondage. **24** And God ʸ heard their groaning, and God ᶻ remembered his ᵃ covenant with Abraham, with Isaac, and with Jacob. **25** And God ᵇ looked upon the children of Israel, and God ⁵ᶜ had respect unto them.

12. 5.——*x* Gen. 18. 20; chap. 3. 9; 22. 23, 27; Deut. 24. 15; James 5. 4.——*y* Chap. 6. 5.——*z* Chap. 6. 5; Psa. 105. 8, 42; 106. 45.——*a* Gen. 15. 14; 46. 4.——*b* Chap. 4. 31; 1 Samuel 1. 11; 2 Samuel 16. 12: Luke 1. 25.——5 Heb. *knew.*——*c* Chap. 3. 7.

INCREASED OPPRESSION OF ISRAEL, 23–25.

23. **In process of time**—Literally, *After many of those days.* **The king of Egypt died**—[This king has been with good reason believed to be Remeses the Great, who reigned sixty-seven years and must have been almost a centenarian at his death. His reign was long enough to have covered the entire forty years of Moses' sojourn in Midian, and also a considerable portion of his previous life in Egypt. Well might his death have been spoken of as occurring *after many of those days!* Great interest has been added to this history by the discovery, in 1881, of the mummies of most of the kings of the eighteenth, nineteenth, and twentieth dynasties, including the embalmed body of this great "Pharaoh of the oppression." These bodies are now in the Bulaq Museum, Cairo, and photographs of their faces have been carried into many lands.]

24, 25. **God heard...remembered ...looked...had respect**—Through all those generations of heart-break, to the eye and ear of flesh God had seemed deaf, dumb, dead; yet all the while he *remembered* his covenant, *saw* each tear, *heard* each groan, *knew* his children with all the energy of love. In this graphic and emphatic way does the sacred writer picture our Father, and help every sufferer everywhere to get within the everlasting arms.

CHAPTER III.

NOW Moses kept the flock of Jethro

a Chap. 2. 16.

CONCLUDING NOTE.

REUEL, JETHRO, HOBAB. Some have made Reuel and Jethro the same; others, Hobab and Jethro the same; and others still have considered all three the same. The solution of the question depends on the meaning of the word חֹתֵן, which our translators have always rendered "father-in-law," but which the Seventy render by γαμβρός, which means simply *marriage* relation, and may be *father-in-law, son-in-law, brother-in-law,* or *bridegroom.* The Seventy thus give us a wide liberty, which we must use to settle the relationship of these persons to Moses.

1. Reuel, or Raguel, is called the father of Zipporah, Moses's wife, in Exod. ii, 18. Also in Num. x, 29, Reuel is called the חֹתֵן of Moses, that is, his "father-in-law."

2. Jethro, or Jether, is in Exod. iii, 1, and often thereafter, called the חֹתֵן of Moses, and "Jethro" we understand to be another name for Reuel. Jether, or Jethro, signifies "excellence," and was probably a titular or honorary name which he received because of his priestly dignity.

3. Hobab is in Num. x, 29 expressly called Reuel's son, so he must have been Zipporah's brother. But the same word is also applied to him in Judges iv, 11, which we consider here to mean simply *marriage relation,* that is, in this case, *brother-in-law.*

Other incidental notices confirm this view. Reuel, that is, Jethro, was advanced in life when Moses first met him, (Exod. ii, 18,) since he had seven grown-up daughters. But, forty years after this, we find *Hobab* invited to accompany the Israelites in their journeyings, and aid them in selecting their encampments, (Num. x, 31,) and he seems to have complied with the invitation, for his children are afterwards found settled in Canaan. Judges i, 16, and iv, 11. This we should not expect of the aged Reuel, but it might be true of Hobab, his son, who would then have been in the prime of life; while the character of a wise counsellor, such as is assigned to Jethro in Exod. xviii, well suits the age and office of Reuel.

Reuel and Jethro, then, we understand to be one and the same person, the father of Hobab and of Zipporah, the wife of Moses. Thus Hobab would be her brother.

CHAPTER III.

Call and Commission of Moses, III, 1-IV, 18.

INTRODUCTORY.

At last the people and the deliverer were ready—"the iniquity of the Amorites" and of the Egyptians was "full"—events had ripened for another epoch of Providence to disclose itself—and the Divine Voice, which had been silent for centuries, was heard once more. The forty years' trial of Moses reminds us of the forty days' temptation of Jesus, also in the wilderness, before he began to break the bondage of which the Egyptian servitude is a constant Scripture symbol, and to announce the law for which the Sinai statutes were a preparation; himself, like Moses, "despised and rejected" by those he came to save. There are deep correspondences and divine symbolisms in these ways of Providence, which cannot be logically demonstrated but are readily accepted, when fully understood, by the truly believing spirit.

JEHOVAH IN THE BURNING BRAMBLE, 1-6.

1. **Now Moses kept the flock**—Rather, *Was feeding the flock.* The Hebrew word expresses a continued occupation. Reuel-Jethro, or Reuel *the excellent,* was priest of Midian, and father of Zipporah and Hobab. See Concluding Note, chap. ii. **To the backside**—That is, the western side, for in the Hebrew orientation the spectator is always supposed to face the east, which is hence called "the front," while the south is the "right hand," as

side of the desert, and came to the *mountain of God, even to Horeb. 2 And ᶜthe Angel of the Lord appeared unto him in a flame of fire out of the midst of a bush: and he looked, and behold, the bush burned with fire, and the bush *was* not consumed. 3 And Moses said, I will now turn aside, and

b Chap. 18. 5; 1 Kings 19. 8.   *c* Deut. 33. 16; Isa. 63. 9; Acts 7. 30.

in 1 Sam. xxiii, 19, margin, and the north is "the left hand," as in Gen. xiv, 15. Moses led his flock westerly or northwesterly, through the desert strip, to the elevated ground of Horeb, where were the most fertile valleys of the peninsula, and where there was water when the lower lands were dry. **The desert** of Arabia is not a hot, sandy plain, like the deserts of Africa, but a very uneven, rocky, gravel-covered tract, which, except in summer, furnishes fair pasturage for flocks. Perhaps the approach of midsummer caused this movement. **The mountain of God.** So called from God's subsequent manifestation there; or, as the Targumists express it, "the mountain on which was revealed the glory of Jah." Moses wrote this after the giving of the law at Sinai. **Horeb**—This was the name of the whole mountain cluster of which Sinai was a single summit. The two words are used interchangeably to denote the Mount of the Law; but before Israel reached the mountain district, as here—and after they left it, as in Deuteronomy, when they were encamped in the plains of Moab—it is called Horeb, since at a distance the special summit is not particularized; but while before the Mount of the Law it is always (except only in Exod. xxxiii, 6) called Sinai, since, while among the mountains, it was necessary to specify the particular peak intended. Moses smote the rock in *Horeb* (the district) before they reached *Sinai*, the mountain. Exod. xvii, 1–6. (Robinson, *Bib. Res.*, i, 120.)

2. **And the Angel of the Lord appeared unto him**—More literally, "*And there appeared an angel of Jahveh* (Jehovah) *unto him.*" **In a flame of fire out of the midst of a bush** — Rather, "*the thorn-bush,*" (bramble.) Any personification or manifestation of God's attributes is called his "angel." See on Gen. xvi, 7. The סְנֶה, *seneh*, "thorn-bush," or "bramble," is a species of acacia, common in the Sinai peninsula, rising in tangled thickets, and having long, stout, and sharp thorns. It is here called *the* bramble —definitely—as the well-known desert bramble, or as the bramble of this divine appearance. Sinai was probably named from this *seneh* (senna) shrub,

ACACIA.

which abounds upon its sides and valleys. The *shittah*, or *shittim* tree, used so much in the construction of the tabernacle and its furniture, belongs to the same family. **And behold, the bush burned with fire, and...was not consumed**—Better, *And lo, the bramble was burning in the fire, and the bramble was not consumed.* The com-

B. C. 1491.   CHAPTER III.   377

see this ᵈ great sight, why the bush is not burnt. **4** And when the LORD saw that he turned aside to see, God called ᵉ unto him out of the midst of the bush, and said, Moses, Moses: and he said, Here am I. **5** And he said, Draw not nigh hither: ᶠ put off thy shoes from off thy feet; for the place whereon thou standest *is* holy ground. **6** Moreover he said, ᵍ I *am* the God of thy father, the God of Abraham, the God of Isaac, and the God of Jacob. And Moses hid his face; for ʰ he was afraid to look upon God.

7 And the LORD said, ⁱ I have surely seen the affliction of my people which *are* in Egypt, and have heard their cry ᵏ by reason of their taskmasters; for ˡ I know their sorrows; **8** And ᵐ I am come down to ⁿ deliver them out of the hand of the Egyptians, and to bring them up out of that land ᵒ unto a good land and a large, unto a land ᵖ flowing with milk and honey; unto the place of ᑫ the Canaanites, and the Hittites, and the Amorites, and the Perizzites, and the Hivites, and the Jebusites. **9** Now therefore, behold, ʳ the cry of the children of Israel is come unto me: and I have also seen the ˢ oppression wherewith the Egyptians oppress them. **10** ᵗ Come now therefore, and I will send thee unto Pharaoh, that thou mayest bring forth my people the children of Israel out of Egypt.

11 And Moses said unto God, ᵘ Who am I, that I should go unto Pharaoh, and that I should bring forth the chil-

---

ᵈ Psa. 111. 2; Acts 7. 31.——ᵉ Deut. 33. 16.——ᶠ Chap. 19. 12; Josh. 5. 15; Acts 7. 33.——ᵍ Gen. 28. 13; ver. 15; chap. 4. 5; Matt. 22. 32; Mark 12. 26; Luke 20. 37; Acts 7. 32.——ʰ So 1 Kings 19. 13; Isa. 6. 1, 5.——ⁱ Chap. 2. 23-25; Neh. 9. 9; Psa. 106. 44; Acts 7. 34.——ᵏ Chap. 1. 11.——ˡ Gen. 18. 21; chap. 2. 25.

ᵐ Gen. 11. 5, 7; 18. 21; 50. 24.——ⁿ Chap. 6. 6, 8; 12. 51.——ᵒ Deut. 1. 25; 8. 7, 8, 9.——ᵖ Ver. 17; chap. 13. 5; 33. 3; Num. 13. 27; Deut. 26. 9, 15; Jer. 11. 5; 32. 22; Ezek. 20. 6.——ᑫ Gen. 15. 18.——ʳ Chap. 2. 23.——ˢ Chap. 1. 11, 13, 14, 22.——ᵗ Psa. 105. 26; Micah 6. 4.——ᵘ See chap. 6. 12; 1 Sam. 18. 18; Isa. 6. 5, 8; Jer. 1. 6.

---

mon lowly bramble well typifies despised Israel in its servitude, and the fire that burst forth among the dry thorns and yet did not consume them, was the God who dwelt in Israel, under whose providence those afflictions came, which, though they burned did not destroy, because He, the changeless JEHOVAH, was in their midst. It is ever in the extremity of his Israel's affliction that his voice is heard from the flame. The "great sight," which faith only sees, is God's loving tenderness, burning but to purify. This is the truth which, in the MEMORIAL NAME, breaks upon the soul of Moses after his long and mysterious trial.

5. Put off thy shoes—The Orientals drop their shoes or sandals at the door, lest they defile the department by bringing in the dirt of the street; and by this expressive symbolism was Moses taught that he was drawing nigh to Him in whose sight "the heavens are not clean." The awful holiness of God is the first thought that the praying soul needs, and hence at the threshold of prayer the soul is taught to drop its sandals with "Hallowed be thy name."

6. The God of thy father—Whose name thy father and mother taught thee; and the God of *their* fathers—of the sacred patriarchal line—who remembers his covenant with them. But Jesus shows us (Matt. xxii, 32, where see note) that the words were deeper still, revealing to Moses not only that He lived, but that they lived as sharers in this everlasting covenant, and were looking for its fulfilment. A covenant with Jehovah implies, *connotes*, or includes, immortality. Moses had waited long. Now his father's God speaks to him in a tongue of flame; calls him by his name, yet warns him not to draw nigh; brings before him those waiting fathers—a "cloud of witnesses!" What wonder that he hid his face from the blaze of such a revelation!

MOSES IS CALLED, 7-10; AND GOD REVEALS THE MEMORIAL NAME, 11-22.

7-10. God dispels the mystery that had been so long thickening upon his providence, unfolds his plan, and gives Moses his commission.

11. Who am I—Forty years before he had been all ready in his youthful confidence, but the work that God had for him has been rising before him in its vastness, till now it overwhelms him. So Isaiah, when he had seen Jehovah and received his commission,

dren of Israel out of Egypt? **12** And he said, ᵛ Certainly I will be with thee; and this *shall be* a token unto thee, that **I have sent thee**: When thou hast brought forth the people out of Egypt, ye shall serve God upon this mountain. **13** And Moses said unto God, Behold, *when* I come unto the children of Israel, and shall say unto them, The God of **your fathers hath sent** me unto you; and they shall say to me, What *is* his name?

ᵛ Genesis 31. 3; Deuteronomy 31. 23; Joshua 1. 5; Romans 8. 31.——*w* Chap. 6. 3; John 8. 58;

cried, "Woe is me!" So Paul cried, "Who is sufficient for these things!"

12. The Lord does not deny his servant's weakness, but promises to reveal through it his strength. **Upon this mountain**—The bush was probably upon the Sinai mount of the Horeb range, on which Jehovah afterward descended in fire. **This** (burning bramble) **shall be a token**—Rather, *is a token*. The verse is often read as if the subsequent success of his mission to Pharaoh, and the consequent worship upon Sinai, were to be regarded as the tokens that he had been sent. Success itself was an obvious token *then*, but the hesitating Moses wants a *present* sign. The flaming bramble shrub was the token that he would bring Israel to the flaming bramble mount.

13. **His name**—Now he desires to look at his commission, and asks, *What is His name.* With the Hebrews proper names were not simply labels attached to individuals—they were significant —they indicated character. So the change from *Jacob* to *Israel*—from *Abram* to *Abraham*—indicated change of character and relation. So when Jacob pleaded with the Angel, "Tell me **thy name**," he meant "Reveal thy character." *Name* is thus constantly used by the Scripture writers to mean **a cluster of attributes**. To praise God's **name**, is to adore the holiness, justice, truth, signified by that name. To **profane it**, is to slight his character, **his person**. We pray through Christ's **name**; that is, through his character and work as Redeemer. At successive epochs of revelation God has revealed himself by different names to set forth different phases of his

what shall I say unto them? **14** And God said unto Moses, I AM THAT I AM: and he said, Thus shalt thou say unto the children of Israel, ʷI AM hath sent me unto you. **15** And God said moreover unto Moses, Thus shalt thou say unto the children of Israel, The LORD God of your fathers, the God of Abraham, the God of Isaac, and the God of Jacob, hath sent me unto you: this *is* ˣmy name forever, and this *is* my

2 Corinthians 1. 20; Hebrews 13. 8; Revelation 1. 4.——*x* Psalm 135. 13; Hosea 12. 5.

glorious character, and he promises to write upon the redeemed at last "his new name," that is, to show them glories in his character which can never be seen till then. Moses asks, then, in this question, What new phase of God's character is to be revealed? God replies by unfolding afresh the true significance of a name which had long been known, at least to a few, but whose meaning was now to be stamped anew by wondrous works into the national consciousness.

14, 15. **My name**—THE MEMORIAL NAME, אֶהְיֶה אֲשֶׁר אֶהְיֶה, a paraphrase of the name JEHOVAH, or JAHVEH; literally rendered, I AM WHO AM, that is, I AM HE WHO IS—I only am He who exists in Himself—an idea which the Alexandrian translators expressed by 'Ο 'ΩΝ; Justin, by *Ille Ens.* And this is not an assertion of mere abstract existence—for the Hebrew verb never stops with this—but of living, active existence, of Being manifesting itself. Absolute independence, and consequent unchangeableness and eternal activity, are implied in the name I AM, and by adding the relative clause, WHO AM, the thought is added that these attributes belong only to Jehovah. Absolutely independent in being and action, nothing can hinder him from performing his will; unchangeable, what once he has promised must forever be his purpose. Often after this God appeals to this Memorial Name as the witness, (1,) of his absolute solitary supremacy: "I am Jehovah...Ye shall have no other gods," (Exod. xx, 2, 3;) (2,) of his immutability: "I am Jehovah; I change not," (Mal. iii, 6;) (3,) but especially of

memorial unto all generations. 16 Go, and ⁷ gather the elders of Israel together, and say unto them, The LORD God of your fathers, the God of Abra-

y Chap. 4. 29.

his eternal activity in manifesting himself; "I am Jehovah, and I will bring you out...I will take you to me for a people...I will bring you in unto the land...I am Jehovah," (Exod. vi, 6, etc.) This name was to be Israel's fortress, an infinite storehouse of hopes and consolations.

Grammatically, the word here rendered I AM is the first person future of the verb of existence translated as a present, (the Hebrew has no proper present,) which tense conveys the idea of the future continuance of the present state. (Nordh., *Heb. Gram.*, § 964, 2.) Now the word translated *Jehovah* (more properly *Jahveh*) is the third person future of the same verb in its archaic form, HAVAH, (or is, as some think, formed from this verb with a prefix,) and so "Jehovah" has the same meaning in the third person which this word has in the first. Thus the name afterward announced to Moses, in Exod. vi, 3, is the same as I AM: in the mouth of God it is I WHO AM; in the mouth of man it is HE WHO IS. This, as says Maimonides, is the only real, proper name of God; for while other names set forth some of his attributes—attributes which, to some degree, he shares with created beings—this name alone sets forth his innermost, incommunicable nature. This distinction is grammatically stamped on the word, for it has no article, no plural, no *construct.*

It is well to briefly compare the inspired Memorial Name with the other common appellations of God. It is a word worthy to be the core of revelation.

Our word "lord" means governor, and simply brings before us God's authority. "God" has the same meaning, though some have incorrectly derived it from "good." "Deity" is from Latin, *deus;* Greek, θεός; Sanskrit, *dyaus,* from *div, to shine;* and means "the Shining One," that is, according to Max Müller, the sun, which our Aryan ancestors worshipped in Asia. Thus the classic names and our word "deity" are all idolatrous in meaning, while "lord" and "god" connote simply authority. There are five Hebrew names often used, besides "Jehovah." *El* and *Elohim* signify the STRONG and the STRONG ONES; *Elyon* signifies the MOST HIGH; *Shaddai,* the ALMIGHTY; and *Adhonai* corresponds to our "Lord." But the Memorial Name comprises all these ideas and infinitely more.

(1.) I AM; (as says Bähr,) not the heathen "it," a deified nature, but "I." Pantheism, which all heathenism is at bottom, identifies God with nature, but here is a Personality above nature. The world in itself is nothing. God only IS.

(2.) Hence he is Lord of nature, which proceeded from him: Creator, Governor, Preserver; *El, Elohim, Shaddai, Elyon, Adhonai.*

(3.) The Living One: he is forever unfolding himself to man in word and work—God of providence and revelation.

(4.) Immutable: he is the God of our trust, the covenant God.

(5.) Immutable, he is also the Truth; ever consistent with his own nature, that is, holy, for the ground and the standard of right is the nature of God. Hence is he worthy of worship, (worship,) supreme love, and praise. As Adam Clarke well says, the very Name itself is a proof of a divine revelation. It will be also seen how appropriate is this name to set forth the progressive revelation, the historical manifestation, of God's character to the nation whom he had chosen to reveal him to mankind. It is not spoken of as a name entirely new would be, but is declared to be the name of the *God of Israel's fathers.* Gen. iv, 26 seems to declare that it was known in the days of Seth, and the proper names Moriah, (*seen of Jah,*) and Jochebed, (*Jah, her glory,*) show that it had been preserved in the sacred line, and that its abbreviated form was used in compound names; but its deep richness of meaning and covenant significance were now first to appear

ham, of Isaac, and of Jacob, appeared unto me, saying, *I have surely visited you, and *seen* that which is done to you in Egypt: 17 And I have said, *I will bring you up out of the affliction of Egypt unto the land of the Canaanites, and the Hittites, and the Amorites, and the Perizzites, and the Hivites, and the Jebusites, unto a land flowing with milk and honey. 18 And ᵇ they shall hearken to thy voice: and ᶜ thou shalt come, thou and the elders of Israel, unto the king of Egypt, and ye shall say unto him, The LORD God of the Hebrews hath ᵈ met with us: and now let us go, we beseech thee, three days' journey into the wilderness, that we may sacrifice to the LORD our God. 19 And I am sure that the king of Egypt ᵉ will not let you go, ¹ no, not by a mighty hand. 20 And I will ᶠ stretch out my hand, and smite Egypt with ᵍ all my wonders which I will do in the midst thereof: and ʰ after that he will let you go. 21 And ⁱ I will give this people favour in the sight of the Egyptians: and it shall come to pass, that, when ye go, ye shall not go empty: 22 ᵏ But every woman shall borrow of her neighbour, and of her that sojourneth in her house, jewels of silver,

s Gen. 50. 24; chap. 2. 25; 4. 31; Luke 1. 68.— *a* Gen. 15. 14, 16; verse 8.—*b* Chap. 4. 31.— *c* Chap. 5. 1, 3.—*d* Num. 23. 3, 4, 15, 16.— *e* Chap. 5. 2; 7. 4.—1 Or, *but by strong hand.* —*f* Chap. 6. 6; 7. 5; 9. 15.

g Chap. 7. 3; 11. 9; chapters 7-13; Deut. 6. 22; Neh. 9. 10; Psa. 105. 27; 135. 9; Jer. 32. 20; Acts 7. 36.—*h* Chap. 12. 31.—*i* Chap. 11. 3; 12. 36; Psa. 106. 46; Prov. 16. 7.—*k* Gen. 15. 14; chap. 11. 2; 12. 35, 36.

Proper names were often thus repeated when events gave them fresh meaning and pertinence, as we see was the case with "Jacob," "Esau," "Beth-el," and others. See also Concluding Note, and Exod. vi, 3.

18. **Three days' journey...that we may sacrifice to the Lord our God**—It was not national but religious independence which was the burden of their request—acknowledgment of the God of Israel. The first step in the Hebrew national history was in harmony with all that followed; the first throb of Hebrew national life was a blow at idolatry. Had Egypt met this first demand, and owned the sway of the One Only God, the plagues had never fallen, and perhaps Israel's national mission had never been needed, and Memphis or Zoan had been in history what Jerusalem became. But Pharaoh would not acknowledge Jehovah, and so was forced to acknowledge Hebrew independence. He did not see at first how the two were linked together, nor did Moses.

19. **And I am sure**—Literally, *I know,* "that the king of Egypt will not let you go." **No, not by a mighty hand**—Rather, *But by a mighty hand.* Obedience to this simple, plain demand made by Moses was possible, but God knew that Pharaoh would disobey, and predicted the results of his free volition. God knew Pharaoh's proud and obstinate heart.

22. **Every woman shall borrow** —Literally, *ask,* for this is always the meaning of the word שָׁאַל; and whether the thing asked for is to be returned or not the context must determine. Thus the thirsty Barak *asks* water, (Judges v, 25,) and Gideon *asks* for the golden ear-rings of the Ishmaelites, (Judges viii, 26,) evidently not intending to return the things asked for; but the prophet's widow (2 Kings iv, 3) *asks* empty oil vessels of her neighbours, possibly intending to return them. All the circumstances here show that the Israelites did not promise, and that the Egyptians did not expect, that these jewels and garments would ever be returned. See on chap. xi, 2, etc.

CONCLUDING NOTE.

The Memorial Name. Exod. iii, 14, 15, and vi, 3. The translation of this passage in the Anglican version, I AM THAT I AM, is wholly unsatisfactory, for, as Murphy says, any being might affirm that he is what he is. It is usually understood as affirming God's inscrutable and immutable nature; but though this is in the Hebrew, it certainly is not in our translation. Murphy suggests "I AM FOR I AM," which he ably defends, but we judge that the translation suggested in our note is far better. It is perfectly literal, and, we think, just covers the Hebrew thought. Bunsen follows the Arabic in rendering

and jewels of gold, and raiment: and ye shall put *them* upon your sons, and upon your daughters; and ¹ye shall spoil ²the Egyptians.

l Job 27. 17; Prov. 13. 22; Ezek. 39. 10.——2 Or, *Egypt.*

"THE ETERNAL," but this fails to bring out the covenant riches of the Name. Rev. i, 4 evidently paraphrases this name "I AM" in the sentence "HE WHO IS, AND WHO WAS, AND WHO IS TO COME." Clement of Alexandria (*Pædag.*, i, chap. viii) says that "the One Name" means "WHO IS," and (Strom. i, chap. xxx, 25,) renders Exod. iii, 14, "HE WHO IS, sent me." So Theodoret and Epiphanius. See Ewald's *Hist. Israel*, ii, App.

Jacobus, M'Whorter, and others, follow Oleaster, Luther, etc., in rendering the word as a proper future, "I WILL BE," and JEHOVAH as "HE WILL BE," and understand the meaning to be "I WILL APPEAR," and "HE WILL APPEAR," or "WILL COME," and so paraphrase the Name as "THE COMING ONE," that is, the MESSIAH. Now Christ was, of course, the supreme manifestation of the character revealed in this Name, but we have no right to assume, as this translation does, that the patriarchs had definite expectations of the incarnation. Christology is not helped by such assumptions.

Our translators have usually rendered יהוה by LORD or GOD, in small capitals, in only four instances translating it "Jehovah." It is most unfortunate that they did not always preserve the Hebrew word. Its real pronunciation is doubtful, although it seems certain that it is not "Jehovah." The Jews lost its sound from a superstitious fear of uttering it, always when they came to it in reading pronouncing the name *Adhonai* or *Elohim*, and when they wrote it always giving it the vowels of one of these names. Hence our word *Jehovah* is formed from the consonants of the sacred name יהוה with the vowels of *Adhonai*, and is quite surely not the true name. Yet it is so settled in our literature that it will probably not be displaced. It seems most likely that the true sound is *Jahveh* or *Jahaveh*, the J being sounded like Y, as hallelu-jah, which means

"praise ye Jah." Ewald and Hengstenberg defend the pronunciation *Jahveh* with great force of argument. See Hengstenberg *on Pent.*, Diss. II; Ewald's *Hist. of Israel*, ii, App.

CHAPTER IV.

INTRODUCTORY.

(1.) In order to carry forward the supernatural work to which he was called, Moses now appears before us armed with supernatural powers. This is the first instance of the kind that appears in history. The patriarchs had individual intercourse with God, and he communicated with them personally, in visions, waking or sleeping, but they wrought no miracles, for they held no mediatorial relation to mankind, and needed no supernatural credentials. But now a mediatorial nation was to be founded which should stand supernaturally accredited before mankind; and the founder of this nation is, therefore, clothed with supernatural powers. In this respect the sober reserve of Scripture presents a striking contrast to the myths of heathenism, and to the legends of ecclesiastical tradition, which ever surround the figures of their heroes with a halo of miracle, brilliant in proportion to its distance. It is also especially noteworthy that the Scriptures furnish no account of a miracle wrought by man till we reach the period of written history recorded by original witnesses.

(2.) The miracle is no violation or suspension of the laws of nature, but such a use of those laws as is possible only to superhuman wisdom, and which, therefore, proves the presence of superhuman influences. To attempt to explain a miracle is absurd, for "explanation" is simply reference to an understood law; but in this case the law is above the grasp of the human faculties. God works ever according to law, although often the law is too high for man to comprehend.

382 EXODUS. B. C. 1491.

CHAPTER IV.

AND Moses answered and said, But, behold, they will not believe me, nor hearken unto my voice: for they will say, The LORD hath not appeared unto thee. 2 And the LORD said unto him, What *is* that in thine hand? And he said, *ᵃ* A rod. 3 And he said, Cast it on the ground. And he cast it on the ground, and it became a serpent; and Moses fled from before it. 4 And the LORD said unto Moses, Put forth thine hand, and take it by the tail. And he put forth his hand, and caught it, and it became a rod in his hand: 5 That they may *ᵇ* believe that *ᶜ* the LORD God of their fathers, the God of Abraham, the God of Isaac, and the God of Jacob, hath appeared unto thee. 6 And the LORD said furthermore unto him, Put now thine hand into thy bosom. And he put his hand into his bosom: and when he took it out, behold, his hand *was* leprous *ᵈ* as snow. 7 And he said, Put thine hand into thy bosom again. And he put his hand into his bosom again; and plucked it out of his bosom, and, behold, *ᵉ* it was turned again as his *other* flesh. 8 And it shall come to pass, if they will not believe thee, neither hearken to the voice of the first sign, that they will believe the voice of the latter sign. 9 And it shall come to pass, if they will not believe also these two signs, neither hearken unto thy voice, that thou shalt take of the water of the river, and pour *it* upon the dry *land:* and *ᶠ* the water which thou takest out of the river ¹ shall become blood upon the dry *land.*

a Verses 17, 20.——*b* Chap. 19. 9.——*c* Chap. 3. 15.——*d* Num. 12. 10; 2 Kings 5. 27.——*e* Num. | 12. 13, 14; Deut. 32. 39; 2 Kings 5. 14; Matt. 8, 3. ——*f* Chap.7.19.——1 Heb. *shall be and shall be.*

MOSES RECEIVES THE THREE SIGNS, 1–9.

1. **They will not believe me**—Moses pleads that Israel will not accept him as a divinely-commissioned leader, and Jehovah gives him three signs to demonstrate to himself, to Israel, and to the Egyptians, that he is sent of God. Egypt was a land of symbols, and these are symbolic miracles, divine hieroglyphs. Three is the complete or perfect number, and the three signs give to each of the three parties involved complete proof of his mission.

2–5. **A rod**—The shepherd's staff which Moses casts down is the emblem of the shepherd life which now, at God's call, he abandons. But at once he finds himself confronted by a hissing serpent, the emblem of Egyptian royalty, from which he flees, for his flesh shrinks from this conflict with Pharaoh. In Egypt the asp was the hieroglyph of royalty. But when, at God's bidding, he boldly grasps his formidable foe, the very wrath of Pharaoh calls forth the power of Jehovah and Jehovah's messenger. The serpent becomes the "wonder-working rod." This sign sets forth the character of Moses, God's messenger.

6, 7. **His hand was leprous**—The second sign symbolizes Israel: first, fresh and young; then, foul and weak; then, clean and strong. Leprosy is a type of ceremonial defilement. As God bid Moses put his hand in his bosom, so had he bidden Israel go down into Egypt, where they had been sheltered from the Canaanitish influences which would have arrested their national life, but where they had also become contaminated with nature-worship, and where their heathen surroundings made them ceremonially unclean. Moses—*Mosheh,* the *drawer* or deliverer—was to draw them forth, and thrust them into another land, where they should be a nation clean unto Jehovah.

8. **First sign...latter sign**—These signs are God's voiceless but visible words to the people. But, like all other words, they may be heard or not, at the hearer's option. No conceivable miracle can compel conviction. When Christ arose "some doubted."

9. The third sign symbolizes Jehovah's power over Egypt and her gods. But for the Nile there would be no Egypt; and when Moses smote **the water of the river** he turned the very breast milk of Egypt to **blood.** And, besides, the Nile was a national god, for its fertilizing power was deemed to proceed from Osiris himself. Thus Jehovah smites Egypt's life-giving god, who is stretched through the land a loathsome corpse.

10 And Moses said unto the LORD, O my LORD, I am not ² eloquent, neither ᵃ heretofore, nor since thou hast spoken unto thy servant; but ᶠ I am slow of speech, and of a slow tongue. 11 And the LORD said unto him, ʰ Who hath made man's mouth? or who maketh the dumb, or deaf, or the seeing, or the blind? have not I the LORD? 12 Now therefore go, and I will be ⁱ with thy mouth, and teach thee what thou shalt say. 13 And he said, O my Lord, ᵏ send, I pray thee, by the hand *of him whom* thou ⁴ wilt send. 14 And the anger of the LORD was kindled against Moses, and he said, *Is* not Aaron the Levite thy brother? 1

2 Heb. *a man of words.*—3 Heb. *since yesterday nor since the third day.*—*g* Chap. 6. 12; Jer. 1. 6.—*h* Psa. 94. 9.

i Isa. 50. 4; Jer. 1. 9; Matt. 10. 19; Mark 13. 11; Luke 12. 11, 12; 21. 14, 15.—*k* See Jonah 1. 3. —4 Or, *shouldest.*

MOSES HESITATES AND IS REBUKED, 10-17.

10-12. **I am not eloquent**—Literally, *not a man of words.* **Slow of speech**—Rather, *heavy of mouth and heavy of tongue.* Moses declares that he is no orator, has not the gift of persuasion, and therefore he has not confidence that he can convince Israel of his mission. So Paul tells us that his bodily presence was weak, and his speech contemptible; but where are weighty and immortal words to be found if they fell not from Paul and Moses? Moses, like Paul, felt weak when he measured himself with his work. He did not yet realize how God's strength is made perfect in such weakness. It would also seem that Moses was not fluent, like Aaron his brother; and, perhaps, from his long separation from his brethren, he had to some degree lost command of his native language. This would naturally make him diffident in undertaking a popular appeal. He may have been conscious, too, that in his forty years' exile from Egyptian civilization his tongue and manners had caught a desert rudeness, which poorly fitted him to appear in the courts of the Pharaohs. Here, for the first time, prophetic inspiration is promised to man. Henceforth in the whole subsequent history of the Church we see this endowment of the Holy Ghost. So the lips of the shrinking Isaiah were touched with a "live coal" from the heavenly altar. Isa. vi. So Jehovah laid his hand on the mouth of the wavering Jeremiah. Jer. i. So it was given to the uncultured Apostle to speak boldly before rulers and peoples: and so God's Spirit has ever been a fire in the words of his genuine messengers. Moses was learned enough to know the vanity of learning, and had now become wise enough to see the folly of wisdom, so that he was just the instrument for God's hand.

13. **Send, I pray thee, by the hand** (of whomsoever else) **thou wilt send**—All his objections had been removed, yet still he hesitated and shrank. The unreasonableness of unbelief is here most naturally depicted, but with what unworldly fidelity! What an infallible touch of genuineness, when we consider the laws of man's spiritual development, and note the progress of the faith of Moses! Yet what later scribe of the followers of the great lawgiver would ever, by the *invention* of such an incident, have blurred the glory of that venerated name? Only Moses himself—and only the inspired Moses—could ever have detailed this humiliating weakness. This is not the style of unrenewed and uninspired man.

14. **Aaron the Levite** now first appears, and behind him Moses for the time retires. This is just and natural, for during forty years Aaron had been among his brethren, and living in the atmosphere of the highest civilization of the time, while Moses had been tending sheep for a Bedouin priest in the wilderness; but again we ask, what follower of the Sinai legislator would ever have dreamed of this? Aaron is God's spokesman to the people; it is Aaron's rod that buds; Aaron is Jehovah's high priest; it is his sons that come to honour and wear the splendid vestments of the tabernacle, the chosen servants of Jehovah's altar, while the children of Moses vanish into obscurity. Yet the slow, stammering, vailed prophet is the soul of

know that he can speak well. And also, behold, ¹he cometh forth to meet thee: and when he seeth thee, he will be glad in his heart. 15 And ᵐ thou shalt speak unto him, and ⁿ put words in his mouth: and I will be with thy mouth, and with his mouth, and ᵒ will teach you what ye shall do. 16 And he shall be thy spokesman unto the people: and he shall be, *even* he shall be to thee instead of a mouth, and ᵖ thou shalt be to him instead of God. 17 And thou shalt take ᵠ this rod in thine hand, wherewith thou shalt do signs.

18 And Moses went and returned to

l Verse 27; 1 Sam. 10. 2, 3, 5.——*m* Chap. 7. 1, 2.
——*n* Num. 22. 38; 23. 5, 12, 16; Deut. 18. 18; Isa. 51. 16; Jer. 1. 9.——*o* Deut. 5. 31.

Israel. **Behold, he cometh forth to meet thee**—Events had been ripening in Egypt also, and the people as well as the leader had been preparing for the critical hour. **He will be glad in his heart** to see thee, and ready to unite with thee in the work of national deliverance. So we afterwards read that "he met and kissed him in the mount of God." The Egyptian traditions of the exodus, though broken and confused, are deemed by some historians to show traces of dynastic rivalries and convulsions which favoured the exit of Israel; but this is extremely uncertain. It is certain, however, that Moses, Pharaoh, and Israel, though all freely acting, were all providentially used in this crisis. See on verse 21.

15, 16. Moses was still to be the mediator, while Aaron was to be the interpreter of God's word as he received it from Moses. Yet it is instructive to notice that as Moses advances in his work and grows in faith, (and shall we not say, wears away the desert rusticity?) Aaron gradually retires from the prominent position which at first he held, and Moses comes more forward. Aaron is the spokesman, but while we read of the lineage of "that Aaron and Moses," yet it is always "Moses and Aaron" who come before Pharaoh. It is Aaron who casts down the rod which swallows up the magicians' rods, and who smites Egypt with the first and mildest blows; but it is Moses who prostrates Pharaoh's sorcerers with such a stroke that they lift their

ˢ Jethro his father in law, and said unto him, Let me go, I pray thee, and return unto my brethren which *are* in Egypt, and see whether they be yet alive. And Jethro said to Moses, Go in peace. 19 And the LORD said unto Moses in Midian, Go, return into Egypt: for ʳ all the men are dead which sought thy life. 20 And Moses took his wife and his sons, and set them upon an ass, and he returned to the land of Egypt: and Moses took ˢ the rod of God in his hand. 21 And the LORD said unto Moses, When thou goest to return into Egypt, see that thou do all those ᵗ wonders be-

p Chap. 7. 1: 18. 19.——*q* Verse 2.——5 Heb. *Jether*.——*r* Chap. 2. 15, 23; Matt. 2. 20.——*s* Chap. 17. 9; Num. 20. 8, 9.——*t* Chap. 3. 20.

heads no more, (chap. ix, 11,) and it is his rod that strikes the final terrible blows thereafter, till the Red Sea rolls back over Pharaoh.

17. **This rod**—This simple shepherd's crook shall break the sceptre of Egypt, shall break the crook and flail of Osiris. So, long after, a shepherd's sling delivered Israel; a Galilean fisher's net enclosed the Gospel multitudes; and a Cilician tentmaker spread the gospel tabernacle over the Gentile nations. Thus the Dispensations ever harmonize. With this decisive command Jehovah closes the interview, and Moses humbly submits and obeys.

THE RETURN OF MOSES TO EGYPT, 18–31.

Moses, as far as we can see, says nothing at this time to Jethro about his divine commission, for as yet, probably, he could not have understood it.

19. **All the men are dead**—See chap. ii, 23, where the death of the king is related immediately before Moses' call. This event seems in several ways to have been critical for the fortunes of Israel.

20. **And Moses took his wife**—Zipporah. **And his** (two) **sons**—Gershom and Eliezer. **Set them upon an ass**—Rather, *made them ride upon the ass*. Probably only Zipporah and the child Eliezer rode, while Moses and Gershom walked by the side of the ass. This was an humble, an unostentatious, entry of the commander of the hosts of Israel!

B. C. 1491. CHAPTER IV. 385

fore Pharaoh, which I have put in thine hand: but ᵘI will harden his heart, that he shall not let the people go. 22 And thou shalt say unto Pharaoh, Thus saith the LORD, ᵛIsrael is my son, ʷeven my firstborn: 23 And I say unto thee, Let my son go, that he may serve me: and if thou refuse to let him go, behold, ˣI will slay thy son, even thy firstborn. 24 And it came to pass by the way in

ᵘ Chap. 7. 3, 13; 9. 12, 35; 10. 1; 14. 8; Deut. 2. 30; Josh. 11. 20; Isa. 63. 17; John 12. 40; Rom. 9. 18.——ᵛ Hosea 11. 1; Rom. 9. 4; 2 Cor. 6. 18.——ʷ Jer. 31. 9; James 1. 18.——ˣ Chap. 11. 5; 12. 29.

21. **I will harden his heart**—Lest Moses should be despondent in his long conflict with Pharaoh's obstinate disobedience, he is now assured that this also has been fully foreseen and provided for by Jehovah, for it is to be taken up into His plan as one of the evils which "work together for good" to God's elect. Rom. viii, 28. It would give Moses hope and courage to know that no step of the struggle had been unforeseen and unprovided for. Every action, good and bad, may be viewed in two aspects, either as proceeding from the voluntary and responsible agent, or as used by God in his providence; and it is the latter, or divine side, that is here specially emphasized, because the history is specially a history of providence—of the divine overruling. Yet both sides of the action are in this narrative equally presented, for it is notable that, while we read here ten times that God "hardened the heart" of Pharaoh, we read precisely the same number of times that "Pharaoh hardened his heart," or that his heart "was hardened," "stiff," or "heavy."

But this is not the whole meaning, nor is the interpretation adequate, that God permitted rather than caused. Hardness of heart is a judgment proceeding directly from God. It is a consequential punishment of sin. But before God inflicts this penalty man has deserved it by trifling with God's goodness and mercy. Increasing stubbornness and moral insensibility are the judicial consequences of conscious resistance to God's will; and this judgment proceeds directly from God, while the sin which invokes the judgment and brings man within the range of these consequences proceeds from man. Thus Pharaoh hardened his heart, and yet it was hardened by Jehovah. While ignorant of Jehovah, disobedience to his law could not harden him; but, from the moment that he knew him, resistance hardened. For this conscious disobedience and this judicial consequence Pharaoh was responsible. This sin of his was, moreover, foreseen. The prediction here made to Moses, and the providential preparations for the punishment of Pharaoh's sin, were the effects of that sin, divinely foreseen—as, in a lower sphere, the erection of court-houses and jails are the effects of sin humanly foreseen. But knowledge, whether fore or after, in man or God, can never be the cause, but is ever the effect, of the thing known. See notes on Rom. viii, 29, and ix, 18.

22. **My firstborn**—By spiritual generation. In God's covenant Israel was adopted as the firstborn of the nations, for ultimate good of the whole family of man. By a series of providences, from the call of Abraham to the exode, Israel was given a national being, and adopted as the child of Jehovah. See the plan of Exodus.

Pharaoh, who styled himself Son of RA, the sun-god, was commanded to release Israel, the Son of JEHOVAH. Thus at every turn we see that the blow was struck at Egypt's gods; this conflict is religious rather than political; the war is waged from heaven.

24–26. **It came to pass...in the inn**—An incident which transpired at some well-known halting-place on the road (the lodging-place) is so briefly related as to have occasioned much doubt and perplexity to all interpreters. It is most probably to be understood thus:—Zipporah, the Midianitess, although she loved her husband, yet did not wholly sympathise with his great work, nor enter as she should into Jehovah's covenant. At least through her influence Moses had not given their youngest son the covenant sign,

the inn, that the LORD ⁷met him, and sought to ᶻkill him. **25** Then Zipporah took ᵃa sharp ⁶stone, and cut off the foreskin of her son, and ⁷cast *it* at his feet, and said, Surely a bloody husband *art* thou to me. **26** So he let him go: then she said, A bloody husband *thou art*, because of the circumcision. **27** And the LORD said to Aaron, Go into the wilderness ᵇto meet Moses. And he went, and met him in ᶜthe mount of God, and kissed him. **28** And Moses ᵈtold Aaron all the words of the LORD who had sent him, and all the ᵉsigns which he had commanded him. **29** And Moses

and Aaron ᶠwent and gathered together all the elders of the children of Israel: **30** ᵍAnd Aaron spake all the words which the LORD had spoken unto Moses, and did the signs in the sight of the people. **31** And the people ʰbelieved: and when they heard that the LORD had ⁱvisited the children of Israel, and that he ᵏhad looked upon their affliction, then ˡthey bowed their heads and worshipped.

CHAPTER V.

AND afterward Moses and Aaron went in, and told Pharaoh, Thus saith the LORD God of Israel, Let my

---

y Num. 22. 22.——*z* Gen. 17. 14.——*a* Josh. 5. 2, 3.——6 Or, *knife.*——7 Heb. *made* it *touch.* ——*b* Verse 14.——*c* Chap. 3. 1.——*d* Verses 15, 16.

e Verses 8, 9.——*f* Chap. 3. 16.——*g* Ver. 16.—— *h* Ch. 3. 18; vers. 8, 9.——*i* Ch. 3. 16.——*k* Ch. 2. 25; 3. 7.——*l* Gen. 24. 26; chap. 12. 27; 1 Chron. 29, 20.

---

and Eliezer was yet uncircumcised. But it was now needful that Moses should be most impressively taught the necessity of himself keeping the ordinances which he was about to teach to others, and this is one of the striking incidents in his spiritual education. **Sought to kill him**—Death was the penalty for neglecting the seal of the covenant. Gen. xvii, 14. As Moses advanced towards Egypt, Jehovah barred his way, as at a similar crisis in the history of Jacob he had crossed his path at Peniel, and would not allow him to go forward till, after his famous wrestling, he consecrated himself to the God of Israel. In some way, we are not told how, death stood in his path, and Zipporah recognised his mortal danger as a consequence of his neglect and her opposition. **Cut off the foreskin**— She herself circumcised the child, and threw the bloody token petulantly at Moses's feet, calling him *a husband of bloods,* (text, **a bloody husband,**) in angry allusion to the bloody rite. Then Jehovah released Moses from his danger, (**so he let him go,**) and Zipporah, regarding him as wedded to her afresh, that is, redeemed from death, and made thus her husband anew, calls him with fresh emphasis *a husband of bloods* **because of the circumcision.**

Zipporah uses a stone knife, such as seems generally to have been then employed for this rite—as may be seen in Josh. **v, 2,** *margin*—although metallic tools had been in use for ages among these Shemitic peoples. But in this rite, as in the Egyptian process of embalming, (*Herodotus,* ii, 86,) ancient custom seems to have kept in use the more primitive tool. Zipporah seems now, or soon after, to have returned to her father's house in Midian, for there we find her with the children when Moses returns to Horeb at the head of Israel.

29-31. **Gathered...the elders**— This points to an organization of the people under chiefs of their own, and their reverent acceptance of Moses and Aaron shows that they had not forgotten the God and the covenant of their fathers, although their faith was by no means ready for the impending **conflict. Elders**—See note on vi, 13-19.

II. THE STRUGGLE.

The Intercession and Judgment. Chaps. V-XIII.

CHAPTER V.

THE INTERCESSION OF MOSES WITH PHARAOH, AND THE RESULT, 1-23.

1. The era of preparation ends, and the first act of the struggle begins. Moses and Aaron open their mission to Pharaoh. *Thus saith Jehovah, God of Israel,* so the phrase should be rendered, since "Jehovah" is the proper name, and not the compound word "Lord God," as the Authorized Version would indicate. Moses and Aaron do not at first demand national independence. It is a far more moderate request to be per-

B. C. 1491.   CHAPTER V.   387

people go, that they may hold *a feast unto me in the wilderness. 2 And Pharaoh said, *b* Who *is* the LORD, that I should obey his voice to let Israel go? I know not the LORD, *c* neither will I let Israel go. 3 And they said, *d* The God of the Hebrews hath met with us: let us go, we pray thee, three days' journey into the desert, and sacrifice unto the LORD our God; lest he fall upon us with pestilence, or with the sword. 4 And the king of Egypt said unto them, Wherefore do ye, Moses and Aaron, let the people from their works? get you unto your *burdens. 5 And Pharaoh said, Behold, the people of the land now *are* *f* many, and ye make them rest from their burdens. 6 And Pharaoh *commanded the same day the *h* taskmasters of the people, and their officers, saying, 7 Ye shall no more give the people straw to make brick, as heretofore: let them go and gather straw for themselves. 8 And the tale of the bricks, which they did make heretofore, *i* ye shall lay upon them; ye shall not diminish *aught* thereof: for they *be* idle; therefore they cry, saying, Let us go *and* sacrifice to our God. 9 *¹*Let there more work be laid upon the men, that they may labour therein; and let them not regard vain *k* words. 10 And the taskmasters of the people went out, and their officers, and they spake to the people, saying, Thus saith Pharaoh, I

a Chap. 10. 9.——*b* 2 Kings 18. 35; Job 21. 15.——*c* Chap. 3. 19.——*d* Chap. 3. 18.——*e* Chap. 1. 11. ——*f* Chap. 1. 7, 9.   *g* Prov. 12. 10.——*h* Chap. 1. 11.——*i* Psa. 106. 41.——1 Heb. *Let the work be heavy upon the men.*——*k* 2 Kings 18. 20; Job 16. 3; Eph. 5. 6.

mitted to sacrifice according to the command of Jehovah. As all nations had their forms of worship, and as religious claims were everywhere acknowledged to be paramount, this was no unreasonable petition, especially in Egypt, where religious festivals and processions were a most familiar pageant. At the same time it contained the core principle of Israel's mission—recognition of Jehovah. See on chap. iii, 18, 19. It is a strange and irreverent misconception that has led some interpreters to consider this a deceptive request.

2. *Who is Jehovah?* It is possible that Pharaoh had never heard the name, for hitherto it had not been much used among the Hebrews in Egypt. At least he refuses to recognise Jehovah's authority.

3. **The God of the Hebrews**—The Israelites generally called themselves Hebrews when conferring with strangers, and were so called by other nations. Thus their reply is explanatory. Jehovah, whom they styled *God of Israel,* Pharaoh would style *God of the Hebrews.*

4. **Wherefore do ye**— Rather, *Wherefore make ye the people cease from their work,* by this conference with them and agitation? Then to the elders of Israel, who stood with Moses and Aaron, he says, **Get you unto your burdens.**

6–9. Increase of the oppression is the fierce and despotic reply to their request. Two grades of officers are now mentioned in addition to the *sarim,* or Egyptian superintendents, mentioned chap. i, 11, namely, the (Egyptian) *overseers*—rendered **taskmasters**—and (Hebrew) *scribes,* (*shoterim,*) rendered **officers.** These Hebrew *shoterim,* or scribes, were so called because of the great amount of writing which the Egyptian method of supervision required. Writing was used as much in the ancient Egyptian business as it is in the American business of to day. Wilkinson relates that in the accounts which the overseers of shepherds were required to present to the steward's scribes, "Every egg was noted and entered, with the chickens and goslings. And, in order to prevent any connivance, or a question respecting the accuracy of a report, two scribes received it from the superintendent at the same moment. Every thing was done in writing. Bureauocracy was as consequential in Egypt as in modern Austria or France. Scribes were required, on every occasion, to settle public or private questions; no bargain of consequence was made without the voucher of a written document.... They would have been in an agony of mind to see us so careless and so duped in many of our railway and other speculations." Egyptian deeds and conveyances were documents most formidable for length, and bristled with circumlocution and circumstantiality enough to gladden the heart of a modern lawyer.

will not give you straw. **11** Go ye, get you straw where ye can find it: yet not aught of your work shall be diminished. **12** So the people were scattered abroad throughout all the land of Egypt to gather stubble instead of straw. **13** And the taskmasters hasted *them*, saying, Fulfil your works, [2]*your* daily tasks, as when there was straw. **14** And the officers of the children of Israel, which Pharaoh's taskmasters had set over them, were beaten, *and* demanded, Wherefore have ye not fulfilled your task in making brick both yesterday and to day, as heretofore? **15** Then the officers of the children of Israel came and cried unto Pharaoh, saying, Wherefore dealest thou thus with thy servants? **16** There is no straw given unto thy servants, and they say to us, Make brick: and, behold,

---

[2] Heb. *a matter of a day in his day.*

The following cut, from a Theban monument, represents a superintendent of an estate giving an account of stock to two scribes.

Before Fig. 1 is the satchel, and above Fig. 2 the box for holding writing implements and papyri. They are writing on boards; in their left hands are the inkstands, with black and red inks.

Scribe with his inkstand upon the table. One pen is put behind his ear, and he is writing with another.

It will thus be seen how thoroughly the Hebrews were trained in writing during their Egyptian sojourn, and were thus providentially qualified to prepare and preserve the most valuable documents in the world. Yet we are not to think of them as learning the art in Egypt, for, as Ewald shows, (*Hist. Israel*, i, p. 51,) this great art was known in the alphabetic form among the Shemitic nations before the time of Moses.

11. Get you straw—For the sun-baked bricks, which were made of Nile mud mixed with cut straw, as is seen in specimens still preserved. Similar oppression and a like unreasonable exaction are on record in an Egyptian papyrus of the nineteenth dynasty, wherein the writer complains, "I have no one to help me in making bricks, no straw."

12. To gather stubble instead of straw—Literally, *for the straw*. The Egyptians cut the grain first below the ear, leaving a long stubble, which was chopped into straw. The Israelites were now scattered over all the grain fields to gather stubble for themselves.

The cut on the next page shows an Egyptian field, with the stubble standing in a portion of it as the reapers have left it, and gives another view of the scribes.

15, 16. The Hebrew scribes come to Pharaoh and complain that they are beaten for not performing an impossible task. The monuments also give us pictures of labourers working under the stick, showing that it was customary for the superintendents to stimulate by blows. There is a papyrus, translated by M. Chabas, which relates the punishment of twelve labourers who failed to make up the required "tale of bricks." The Egyptians had much confidence in the virtue of corporeal punishment.

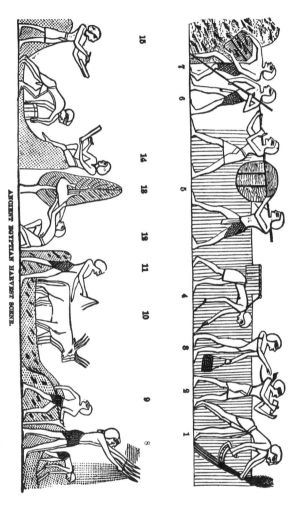

ANCIENT EGYPTIAN HARVEST SCENE.

1. The reapers; 2. A reaper drinking from a cup; 3, 4. Gleaners—the first of these asks the reaper to allow him to drink; 4, 6, 7. Carrying the ears of grain in a rope basket, and emptying them on the threshing-floor—the length of the stubble showing the ears alone are cut off; 8. Winnowing; 9, 10, 11. The threshing; 12, 13. Drinking from a water-skin suspended in a tree; 14. Scribe noting down the number of bushels measured from the heap; 15. Scribe checking the account by noting those taken away to the granary.

thy servants *are* beaten; but the fault *is* in thine own people. **17** But he said, Ye *are* idle, *ye are* idle: therefore ye say, Let us go *and* do sacrifice to the LORD. **18** Go therefore now, *and* work; for there shall no straw be given you, yet shall ye deliver the tale of bricks. **19** And the officers of the children of Israel did see *that* they *were* ¹in evil *case*, after it was said, Ye shall not minish *aught* from your bricks of your daily task. **20** And they met Moses and Aaron, who stood in the way, as they came forth from Pharaoh: **21** ᵐ And they said unto them, The LORD look upon you, and judge; because ye have made our savour ³ to be abhorred in the eyes of Pharaoh, and in the eyes of his servants, to put a sword in their hand to slay us. **22** And Moses returned unto the LORD, and said, Lord, wherefore hast thou so evil entreated this people? why *is* it *that* thou hast sent me? **23** For since I came to Pharaoh to speak in thy name, he hath done evil to this people; ⁴ neither hast thou delivered thy people at all.

---

l Eccles. 4. 1.——*m* Chap. 6. 9.——3 Heb. *to stink,* Genesis 34. 30; 1 Samuel 13. 4; 27. 12; 2 Samuel 10. 6; 1 Chronicles 19. 6.——4 Hebrew, *delivering thou hast not delivered.*

20, 21. The bastinadoed *shoterim* have now lost all faith in Moses and Aaron, for they feel that the yoke that was to have been broken is only tightened. They forget that this is exactly what might have been expected from Jehovah's prediction. Chap. iii, 19, 20.

22, 23. Moses, too, smarting under the accusations of his brethren, and also wounded by sympathy for their increased sufferings, returns to Jehovah with passionate entreaty for an explanation of his providence. There is a characteristic vehemence—an almost irreverent impetuosity—in his prayer, most natural to the man, and yet betraying a weakness which any writer of the Jewish ages would have been glad to hide. Only Moses could have written this, and only inspired man could write with such unworldly objectivity of himself.

CHAPTER VI.

INTRODUCTORY.

(**1.**) We now reach another stage of the history, clearly indicated by the emphatic words, "Now shalt thou see what I will do to Pharaoh." There is a pause in the action before the dreadful blows of Jehovah begin to fall. The preparatory stage of peaceful pleading and intercession has passed, and from the opening of this chapter to the tenth verse of the following we have a rallying and review of the forces, a repetition of the great points at issue, before the mortal struggle begins. This habit of review and fresh departure at each natural division of his work is an often noted characteristic of our author's style.

(**2.**) God reveals himself as Jehovah, that is, as I AM; but this is not to be understood, as the "document" critics imagine, as another narrative of the events of chaps. iii and iv. Their lack of insight here is astonishing. The stage of advancement from the first to the second revelation is marked with perfect clearness. At the burning bramble God revealed himself first as *Elohim,* (chap. iii, 6,) and afterwards slowly and impressively uncovered the MEMORIAL NAME; but now he says at once to Moses, "*I am Jehovah.*" After that first revelation the people believed, bowed in reverence, and accepted the divinely offered deliverance; but now "they hearkened not unto Moses, for anguish of spirit and for cruel bondage." Then Moses plead that Israel would not hear, but now that they had not heard Then it was predicted of Pharaoh, "He will let you go," or, rather, "send you . away," (chapter iii, 20;) but now, in the immediate prospect of these tremendous judgments, it is prophesied, "with a strong hand shall he... drive them out of his land." Then Moses was instructed to say humbly, and even reverentially, *Let us go, we beseech thee;* but now the stern, sharp message is to be, "Let my people go." Thus have events greatly ripened between the first and second announcements of the Memorial Name.

B. C. 1491. CHAPTER VI. 391

CHAPTER VI.

THEN the LORD said unto Moses, Now shalt thou see what I will do to Pharaoh: for ᵃ with a strong hand shall he let them go, and with a strong hand ᵇ shall he drive them out of his land. 2 And God spake unto Moses, and said unto him, I am ¹the LORD: 3 And I appeared unto Abraham, unto Isaac, and unto Jacob, by *the name of* ᶜ God Almighty; but by my name ᵈ JEHOVAH was I not known to them. 4 ᵉ And I have also established my covenant with them, ᶠ to give them the land of Canaan, the land of their pilgrimage, wherein they were strangers. 5 And ᵍ I have also heard the groaning of the children of Israel, whom the Egyptians keep in bondage; and I have remembered my covenant. 6 Wherefore say unto the children of Israel, ʰ I *am* the LORD, and ⁱ I will bring you out from under the burdens of the Egyptians, and I will rid you out of their bondage, and I will ᵏ redeem you with a stretched out arm, and with great judgments: 7 And I will ˡ take you to me for a people, and ᵐ I will be to you a God: and ye shall know that I *am* the LORD your God, which bringeth you out ⁿ from under the burdens of the Egyptians. 8 And I will bring you in unto the land, concerning the which I did ²ᵒ swear to give it to Abraham, to Isaac, and to Jacob ;

---

a Chap. 3. 19,——*b* Chap. 11. 1; 12. 31, 33, 39. ——1 Or, *JEHOVAH*.——*c* Gen. 17.1; 35.11; 48.3. ——*d* Chap. 3. 14; Psa. 68. 4; 83. 18; John 8. 58; Rev. 1. 4.——*e* Gen. 15. 18; 17. 4, 7.——*f* Gen. 17. 8; 28. 4.——*g* Chap.2. 24.——*h* Verses 2, 8, 29.——*i* Chap. 3. 17; 7. 4; Deut. 26. 8; Psa. 81. 6; 136. 11, 12. *k* Chap. 15. 13; Deut. 7. 8; 1 Chron. 17. 21; Neh. 1. 10.——*l* Deut. 4. 20; 14. 2; 7. 6; 26. 18; 2 Sam. 7. 24.——*m* Gen. 17. 7, 8; chap. 29. 45, 46; Deut. 29. 13; Rev. 21. 7.——*n* Chap. 5. 4, 5; Psa. 81. 6. ——2 Heb. *lift up my hand*; Gen. 14. 22; Deut. 32. 40.——*o* Gen. 15, 18; 26. 3; 28. 13; 35. 12.

THE TEN JUDGMENT STROKES, CHAPS. VI, 1–XII, 30.

1. **Now**—In this crisis of Israel's fortunes, when all peaceful means have failed; a word of emphasis and transition. Of course, these interviews are only sketched; all that was said to Pharaoh is not detailed. These negotiations may have been some time in progress.

2–8. **I am the Lord: (**JEHOVAH:**) and I appeared unto Abraham, unto Isaac, and unto Jacob,** in (the character of) El Shaddai, (**God Almighty,**) **but by my name** (that is, in my character) **JEHOVAH was I not known** (made known) **to them.** (Nordh., *Heb. Gram.*, § 1040, 2, c.; Ewald, *Gram.*, § 299, 6.) Concerning the import of the word "Jehovah," and the meaning of this declaration, see notes on chap. iii,

13–15. From the call of Abraham God had been unfolding his character, as the patriarchs could by experience become acquainted with him. Man is not instructed by teaching him names, but by unfolding to him the import of names, and this had been the divine education of the fathers of Israel through such appellations as El, Elyon, and El Shaddai; but a deeper and grander lesson was now to be taught their children by experience such as the fathers knew not, so that the depth and richness of the great Covenant Name would become a national possession. It was not the sound, (as some critics imagine,) but the import of the Name that was unknown to their fathers, that is, unknown *comparatively*, considering the meaning which was now to be known. In interpreting such passages we are to remember that the Hebrew style does not admit of the periodic sentence, with the balanced qualifications and limitations of the Western tongues, and it is thus forced to make statements in an absolute form, which have obviously a comparative sense. Thus Joseph says to his brethren, "It was not you that sent me hither, but God," (Gen. xlv, 8;) that is, "Your share in the matter is nothing when compared with his; the evil from your act is trifling compared with the good which God will bring out of it." So Joseph called his son Manasseh, for, said he, "God hath made me to forget my father's house"—not absolutely to forget, but that his new home made the old to be comparatively unthought of.

[The name Jehovah was the *proper name* of the God of Israel, as George or Paul is the proper name of a man, or Molech that of the god of the Ammonites. So profound was the reverence of the Hebrews for this name that they refused to pronounce it, and the vowelled pronunciation was lost, and is restored at this day only by conjecture. In reading the Scriptures vocally the Jews substituted the Hebrew word for Lord— *Adonai*. The Septuagint translators translated the name by the Greek

and I will give it you for a heritage: I *am* the LORD. **9** And Moses spake so unto the children of Israel: ᵖ but they hearkened not unto Moses for ᵠ anguish of spirit, and for cruel bondage. **10** And the LORD spake unto Moses, saying, **11** Go in, speak unto Pharaoh king of Egypt, that he let the children of Israel go out of his land. **12** And Moses spake before the LORD, saying, Behold, the children of Israel have ᵠ not hearkened unto me; how then shall Pharaoh hear me, ʳ who *am* of uncircumcised lips? **13** And the LORD spake unto Moses and unto Aaron, and gave them a charge unto the children of Israel, and unto Pharaoh king of Egypt, to bring the children of Israel out of the land of Egypt. **14** These *be* the heads of their fathers' houses: ˢ The sons of Reuben the firstborn of Israel; Hanoch, and Pallu, Hezron, and Carmi: these *be* the families of Reuben. **15** ᵗ And the sons of Simeon; Jemuel, and Jamin, and Ohad, and Jachin, and Zohar, and Shaul the son of a Canaanitish woman: these *are* the families of Simeon. **16** And these *are* the names of ᵘ the sons of Levi according to their generations; Gershon, and Kohath, and Merari: and the years of the life of Levi *were* a hundred thirty and seven years. **17** ᵛ The sons of Gershon; Libni, and Shimi, according to their families. **18** And ʷ the sons of Kohath; Amram, and Izhar, and Hebron, and Uzziel: and the years of the life of Kohath *were* a hundred thirty and three years. **19** And ˣ the sons of Merari; Mahali and Mushi:

p Chap. 5. 21.—*s* Heb. *shortness,* or, *straitness.*—*q* Verse 9.—*r* Verse 30; chap. 4. 10; Jer. 1. 6.—*s* Gen. 46. 9; 1 Chron. 5. 3.—*t* Gen. 46. 10; 1 Chron. 4. 24.—*u* Gen. 46. 11; Num. 3. 17; 1 Chron. 6. 1, 16.—*v* 1 Chron. 6. 17; 23. 7.—*w* Num. 26. 57; 1 Chron. 6. 2, 18.—*x* 1 Chron. 6. 19; 23. 21.

word for Lord. Our English translators unfortunately followed suit, and translated the word by LORD in capitals. In the word *Jehavah* the vowels are borrowed, absurdly, from the word Adonai. The more probable, but not certain, form of the word is *Jahveh.* But the English reader should always mentally read LORD as the true *proper name* of Israel's God.]

9. They hearkened not—For their cruel oppression now crushed them in an anguish that made them dead to hope. It was the very extremity which is the opportunity of Providence.

10–12. Although Israel has turned away from him in despair, yet is Moses bid go again, alone, in Jehovah's name, to Pharaoh. But how should Pharaoh hear when Israel herself turns away? Thus is he made to feel that the last resource of intercession has been tried, and that there is no recourse but to God's judgments.

13–19. Since Israel is now to be led forth as a nation, Moses and Aaron, their leaders, are fully set before us according to their genealogy. The tribe of Levi now, therefore, comes before us, with its three tribal families and their subdivisions, while the elder tribes, Reuben and Simeon, are mentioned with their general family divisions, in order to show the relative position of Levi. (Knobel here clearly shows the connexion against the documentists.) The **fathers' houses** are usually considered as divisions of the tribal families, subdivisions of the tribe, (Gesenius, Fürst, Ewald,) but the phrase is considered by Kurtz to be simply another designation for the tribe, the word "fathers" meaning *ancestors.* But the first view is favoured by the systematic classification in passages like Joshua vii, 14, and Num. i, 20, 22, etc., where the phrase should be translated, as here, "houses of their fathers," (not *house;* see Gesen., *Gram.,* § 108, 3; Ewald, *Gram.,* § 270, c.) The twelve tribes were regularly divided and subdivided, according to lineage, with princes or heads over each section or grade, who took their rank by primogeniture. Besides this hereditary nobility there were *elders,* who appear to have held their position from age and experience, probably owing their rank to popular election, and who always appear as the representatives of the people, and constitute a democratic element in the state. There were, finally, the scribes, or *shoterim*—officers who may have arisen under Egyptian influences, as already noticed, who exercised a subordinate overseership over government labourers, and probably had charge of the genealogical tables and public writings. Thus the patriarchal and Egyptian governments furnished the groundwork for the elaborate Mosaic system perfected at Sinai.

B. C. 1619. CHAPTER VI. 393

these *are* the families of Levi according to their generations. **20** And ʸAmram took him Jochebed his father's sister to wife; and she bare him Aaron and Moses: and the years of the life of Amram were a hundred and thirty and seven

ʸ Chap. 2. 1, 2; Num. 26. 59.

20. And Amram took him Jochebed his father's sister to wife—דּוֹדָה, here rendered *father's sister*, we render *daughter of father's brother*, or *cousin*, in this following the Septuagint, Syriac, Vulgate, and Targum Pal., thus understanding the text to declare that Amram married Jochebed his *cousin*. This is a much disputed text, furnishing a most important chronological item. Our Authorized Version and most modern commentators make Jochebed to have been Amram's aunt and Levi's daughter, so that Moses was thus Levi's grandson. This view certainly is favoured by Num. xxvi, 59, "And the name of Amram's wife was Jochebed, the daughter of Levi, whom *her mother* bare to Levi in Egypt;" as if Levi had a daughter born to him after the descent into Egypt, in addition to the three sons who went down with him from Canaan. But, (1,) It is not probable that Moses' own father and mother violated a law of nature which was in the next generation so expressly incorporated into the Mosaic ordinances, though it is, of course, possible. (2,) If Jochebed were Amram's aunt, then Levi must have begotten, and Jochebed have borne, children at such an extreme age that the birth of Jochebed, Miriam, and Aaron, as well as of Moses, must all be set down as miraculous, while the record here gives no hint of a miracle. This may be seen thus: Take the shortest period of the sojourn, two hundred and fifteen years, which will make the difficulties least, and as Moses was eighty at the Exode, we have 215—80, or 135 years, as the time from Jacob's descent into Egypt to the birth of Moses. Levi was about forty-five when the sojourn began, and as Jochebed was (on this supposition) his daughter, there were then one hundred and thirty-five years from Levi's forty-fifth year to the birth of his grandson, Moses. Now wherever we divide this period of one hundred and thirty-five years we shall make Levi to have become a father, and Jochebed a mother, in extreme age. Thus, if Jochebed were born when Levi was one hundred, then it would have been fifty-five years after the arrival in Egypt, since 100—45=55. In that case Jochebed must have borne Moses at eighty, since 135—55=80; Aaron, therefore, at seventy-seven, and Miriam when past sixty. If we suppose Jochebed to have been herself born ten or twenty years later, we then make Levi one hundred and ten or one hundred and twenty at her birth, and make her so many years younger at the birth of her children, but we do not relieve the difficulties. If we take the long period of sojourn, four hundred and thirty years, it will be seen at once that all the difficulties are vastly increased. But all are completely obviated by considering Jochebed Amram's cousin, for this inserts another generation into the one hundred and thirty-five years.

(3.) The Hebrew word דּוֹדָה, here rendered *father's sister*, is, as noted above, rendered *daughter of the father's brother* by the Septuagint, followed by the Syriac, Vulgate, and Palestine Targum. The corresponding masculine, דּוֹד, *uncle*, also means *son of the uncle* in Jer. xxxii, 12. It seems certain that if *dodh* may mean uncle's son, *dodha* may mean uncle's daughter. Accordingly it is here rendered *cousin* by Lyra, Estius, La Haye, and Adam Clarke.

(4.) The difficulty of the common translation may be relieved thus: Num. xxvi, 59 states that her mother, not mentioning who, bore Jochebed to Levi in Egypt. Is it not a likely supposition that Levi in his old age adopted this granddaughter as his daughter? If so, she might have been considered as the sister of his three famous sons, and this fact was deemed worthy of special mention, since she was the mother of the line of the high priests. Thus she might have been considered Amram's aunt, although really his cousin.

394 EXODUS. B. C. 1530

years. **21** And ^zthe sons of Izhar; Korah, and Nepheg, and Zichri. **22** And ^athe sons of Uzziel; Mishael, and Elzaphan, and Zithri. **23** And Aaron took him Elisheba, daughter of ^bAmminadab, sister of Naashon, to wife; and she bare him ^cNadab and Abihu, Eleazar and Ithamar. **24** And the ^dsons of Korah; Assir, and Elkanah, and Abiasaph: these *are* the families of the Korhites. **25** And Eleazar, Aaron's son, took him *one* of the daughters of Putiel to wife; and ^eshe bare him Phinehas: these *are* the heads of the fathers of the Levites according to their families. **26** These *are* that Aaron and Moses, ^fto whom the LORD said, Bring out the children of Israel from the land of Egypt according to their ^garmies. **27** These *are* they which ^hspake to Pharaoh king of Egypt, ⁱto bring out the children of Israel from Egypt: these *are* that Moses and Aaron.

28 And it came to pass on the day *when* the LORD spake unto Moses in the land of Egypt, **29** That the LORD spake unto Moses, saying, ^kI *am* the LORD: ^lspeak thou unto Pharaoh king of Egypt all that I say unto thee. **30** And Moses

---

z Num. 16. 1; 1 Chron. 6. 37, 38.——*a* Lev. 10. 4; Num. 3. 30.——*b* Ruth 4. 19, 20; 1 Chron. 2. 10; Matt. 1. 4.——*c* Lev. 10. 1; Num. 3. 2; 26. 60; 1 Chron. 6. 3; 24. 1.——*d* Num. 26. 11.

e Num. 25. 7, 11; Josh. 24. 33.——*f* Verse 13.—— *g* Chap. 7. 4; 12. 17, 51; Num. 33. 1.——*h* Chap. 5. 1, 3; 7. 10.——*i* Verse 13; chap. 32. 7; 33. 1; Psa. 77. 20.——*k* Verse 2.——*l* Verse 11; chap. 7. 2.

It is the opinion of Kurtz, Keil, Canon Cook, and others, that two Amrams are here referred to, and that several genealogical links are dropped between Amram the son of Kohath and Amram the father of Moses. But, (1,) The impression is certainly very strongly made, in reading verses 18–20, that the same Amram is referred to throughout. (2,) It is a fact not noted by these scholars that in Lev. x, 4, Uzziel, Amram's brother, is called Aaron's uncle; and though, as seen above, the word rendered *uncle* has much latitude, yet it would be necessary to suppose a second Uzziel also contemporary with the second Amram. As to the dropping of genealogical links, there is an undoubted example in Matt. i, where the names of three well known kings are omitted in the genealogy of our Lord; and a probable instance, yet more remarkable, in Ezra vii, 1, where, if the parallel list in 1 Chron. vi is correct, six names have been dropped out between Meraioth and Azariah. It is likewise certain that *son* often means simply descendant, as Christ is called "son of David." If the sojourn in Egypt were four hundred and thirty years several generations must have been omitted here, but all the events can be brought within two hundred and fifteen years. See note on chap. xii, 40.

23–25. **Elisheba,** (Elisabeth,) which means, *God is her oath*, that is, She owns and worships God. The family connexions of Aaron and his wife Elisabeth are detailed with far more fulness than these of Moses, since the lineage of the high priests was a matter of the highest importance in Israel. The sons of Moses had no special prominence in the national history, and their names are hardly mentioned. It is recorded here that Aaron's wife was the sister of Naashon, a well known prince of Judah.

It will be noticed that the priestly succession here stops at Phinehas, the grandson of Aaron, who, as a youth, entered Canaan, and was the last of the line that Moses could have seen. This incidental evidence of Mosaic authorship is worthy of attention.

RESUMPTION OF THE NARRATIVE AND RECAPITULATION, VI, 28–VII, 7.

The foregoing genealogical digression may be regarded as an expansion of verse 13, giving a brief, clear family history of "that Aaron and Moses" who now undertake this weighty charge. The narrative now returns to the incident of verse 12, and repeats the circumstances under which Moses again plead that he was of uncircumcised lips. In chap. iv, 10, he urged this as a reason why he was disqualified to go to his brethren; now he feels it a sore hinderance when bid to go to Pharaoh.

28–30. These three verses properly belong to the next chapter, which should have commenced with verse 28. **The Lord** (JEHOVAH) **spake unto Moses in the land of Egypt,...saying, I am the Lord** (JEHOVAH). This is in distinction from that first revelation in the land of Midian, (chap. iii,) when the Memorial Name was first proclaimed.

said before the LORD, Behold, ᵐ I *am* of uncircumcised lips, and how shall Pharaoh hearken unto me ?

CHAPTER VII.

AND the LORD said unto Moses, See, I have made thee ᵃ a god to Pharaoh; and Aaron thy brother shall be ᵇ thy prophet. **2** Thou ᶜ shalt speak all that I command thee; and Aaron thy brother shall speak unto Pharaoh, that he send the children of Israel out of his land. **3** And ᵈ I will harden Pharaoh's heart, and ᵉ multiply my ᶠ signs and my wonders in the land of Egypt.

4 But Pharaoh shall not hearken unto you, ᵍ that I may lay my hand upon Egypt, and bring forth mine armies, *and* my people the children of Israel, out of the land of Egypt ʰ by great judgments. **5** And the Egyptians ⁱ shall know that I *am* the LORD, when ᵏ I stretch forth mine hand upon Egypt, and bring out the children of Israel from among them. **6** And Moses and Aaron ˡ did as the LORD commanded them, so did they. **7** And Moses *was* ᵐ fourscore years old, and Aaron fourscore and three years old, when they spake unto Pharaoh.

---

m Verse 12; chap. 4. 10.——*a* Chap. 4. 16; Jer. 1. 10.——*b* Chap. 4. 16.——*c* Chap. 4. 15.——*d* Chap. 4. 21.——*e* Chap. 11. 9.——*f* Chap. 4. 7.——*g* Chap. 10. 1; 11. 9.

h Chapter 6. 6.——*i* Verse 17; chapter 8. 22; 14. 4, 18; Psalm 9. 16.——*k* Chapter 3. 20.—— *l* Verse 2.——*m* Deuteronomy 29. 5; 31. 2; 34. 7; Acts 7. 23, 30.

CHAPTER VII.

1. I have made thee a god to Pharaoh—No more was he to come to Pharaoh as a suppliant, but now he was invested with divine authority. To Aaron Moses was a revealer of God's will, (chap. iv, 16,) but to Pharaoh he was now to appear clothed with God's power. Hitherto he had been an advocate, a mediator, and in that position had painfully felt the embarrassment of his slowness of speech; but now his deeds were to speak, and, armed with Jehovah's thunders, he was to smite down the gods of Egypt. Thus, then, the Lord replies to Moses's despairing plea—"See, I have made thee a god!" Pharaoh had refused to glorify God by obedience to Moses as a messenger of his mercy; now shall he glorify him by submitting to Moses as a messenger of his wrath. The results of these threatened judgments are now predicted.

2. Aaron thy brother shall speak unto Pharaoh (the words of authority which I have commanded) **that he send the children of Israel out of his land** —Rather, *and he will send;* prediction of the final result.

3. And I will harden Pharaoh's heart—At this stage of history Pharaoh had so far resisted the truth that God's judgments but increased his obstinacy, and made him plunge into deeper and deeper rebellion. This result is foreseen and predicted, that Moses may be prepared for it. Pharaoh's sin and its judicial consequences were to be the means of setting forth the attributes of Jehovah before the heathen. See on chap. iv, 21.

4. But Pharaoh shall not hearken—There is nothing imperative or determinative in the use of the verb here; it is a simple future, and the verbs following are to be translated as futures, thus: *But Pharaoh will not hearken... and I will lay my hand upon Egypt, and will bring forth mine armies... and the Egyptians will know.*

7. Moses was fourscore years old —Here, at the close of the recapitulation, we have the ages of the great actors in this drama set before us. Aaron, it seems, was three years older than Moses; and as we hear nothing of any special apprehensions of danger at the time of his birth, it is possible, though not certain, that the cruel edict which endangered the life of Moses had not then been promulgated. Miriam is not here mentioned, but she is generally supposed to be the sister, older than Moses and Aaron, mentioned in the second chapter. Moses entered on his great mission at fourscore, but as his ancestors Amram, Levi, and Jacob lived beyond the third of their second century, and he himself reached the one hundred and twentieth year, we may regard him as now having the vigour of a man of forty-five. There are nearly contemporary Egyptian records which show similar instances of Egyptian longevity. Stuart Poole gives (in *Smith's Dict.*) a translation of a hieratic papyrus

8 And the LORD spake unto Moses and unto Aaron, saying, 9 When Pharaoh shall speak unto you, saying, ªShow a

n Isa. 7. 11; John 2. 18; 6. 30.

containing a discourse of a king's son of the fifteenth dynasty of Shepherd Kings at Memphis, wherein the author speaks of himself as one hundred and ten years of age, and of his father as still reigning, who must then have been older than Moses, and probably as old as Levi. Yet these must be regarded as exceptional instances, for the ninetieth Psalm, entitled "A prayer of Moses, the man of God," speaks of seventy or eighty years as the usual length of human life. And in harmony with this, Caleb, the contemporary of Moses, says of himself at eighty-five, "Behold, the Lord hath kept me alive, as he said, these forty and five years, even since the Lord spake this word unto Moses, while Israel wandered in the wilderness: and now, lo, I am this day fourscore and five years old. As yet I am strong this day as I was in the day that Moses sent me." Josh. xiv, 10, 11. Caleb evidently regards himself as vigorous at eighty-five by God's special blessing.

THE TEN PLAGUES, VII, 8–XII, 30.

Moses and Aaron now stand before Pharaoh as ministers of judgment, and the conflict opens between Jehovah and the gods of Egypt. The first contest between the messengers of Jehovah and the magicians, or enchanters, who are regarded as the servants of the false gods, given in verses 8–13, is properly the opening scene of the struggle, and is therefore here included in the section with it. Several general observations on the whole subject are most conveniently introduced here for future reference.

(1.) The great and worthy object of these "signs and wonders" is throughout to be carefully held before the mind. There were several secondary purposes met, but the chief aim was, not to inflict retribution upon Egypt, although they did this as judgments, nor to give Israel independence, though they effected this by crushing the oppressor, but to teach the world the nature of God. It

miracle for you: then thou shalt say unto Aaron, º Take thy rod, and cast it before Pharaoh, *and* it shall become a serpent.

o Chap. 4. 2, 17.

was a series of most solemn lessons in the fundamental truths of religion—in God's attributes and government. With perfect distinctness and reiterated emphasis is this declared from the very beginning: "*I am* JEHOVAH... *Ye shall know... the Egyptians shall know that I am* JEHOVAH." Events were to burn into the national consciousness of Israel, and into the memory of the world, the great truths revealed in the Memorial Name; and the faith of Israel, the sin of Pharaoh, and the might and splendour of Egyptian heathenism, were the divinely chosen instruments to accomplish this work. The rich Nile-land teemed with gods, and was the mother country of the idolatries that, centuries afterward, covered the Mediterranean islands and peninsulas, and filled the classic literature with such manifold forms of beauty. The gods of Greece were born in Egypt, and the Sibyls of Delphos and Cumæa descended from the sorcerers who contended with Moses. In no other land has idolatry ever reared such grand and massive structures as in Egypt. The immense ram-headed Ammun and hawk-headed Ra, the placid monumental Osiris, the colossal Rameses, sitting in granite "with his vast hands resting upon his elephantine knees," these, and their brother gods of the age of the Pharaohs, have looked down upon the rising and falling Nile through all the centuries of European civilization. In no other land were the manifold forms and productions of nature so deified. In their pantheistic idolatry they offered worship not only to the sun, and moon, and earth, but to bulls, crocodiles, cats, hawks, asps, scorpions, and beetles. They seem to have made to themselves likenesses of almost every thing in "heaven above, in earth beneath, and in the waters under the earth." The Apis and Mnevis bulls were stalled in magnificent palaces at Memphis and Heliopolis, and were embalmed in massive marble and granite sarcophagi, grander than enclosed the Theban kings. The sepulchres of Egyptian bulls have outlasted the sepulchres of Roman emperors. Nowhere else were kings so deified as here. Pharaoh incarnated in himself the national idolatry, and to crush the king was to crush the gods. The king made his palace a temple, and enthroned himself among the Egyptian deities. He sculptured himself colossal—so vast that the Arabs to-day quarry millstones from his cheeks—sitting hand in hand and arm in arm with his gods. To-day Rameses sits in the temple of Ipsambul between Ra and Ammun, his tall crown rising between the hawk head of the one and the tiara of the other, looking out from his rockhewn shrine upon the desert, as he has sat since the Pharaohs. From Cambyses to Napoleon invasion after invasion has swept the Nile valley—wave on wave—yet here have sat these massive forms, the Nile coming to bathe their feet year by year, as if brothers to the mountains. They mark the graves of Egypt's vanished gods, while the name of Him who smote these gods to death with Moses's rod liveth forever.

(2.) But Egypt was the mother-land of philosophies as well as idolatries. Long ages after Moses, Herodotus, Pythagoras, and Plato followed the Hebrew lawgiver to the oldest university in the world. The Egyptian philosophy was inextricably entangled with its religion, and deciphered papyri show that magic and sorcery were esteemed as highly at the court of Pharaoh, as, long after, in the time of Daniel, at the court of Nebuchadnezzar. The dreamy mysticism of Plato and of Philo reveals how hopelessly most precious truths were entangled in priestly juggleries, and how deeply this black art, or illusion, or demonism, left its mark on the ancient world. The heathen idolatry had no more potent allies in the old civilizations than the soothsayers, sorcerers, and magicians, and it was needful that they too should be signally vanquished by the prophet of the true God. Hence Moses in Egypt—as, a thousand years later, Daniel in Babylon, and a half

VOL. I.—26

thousand years later still, Paul at Salamis and Philippi—discomfited the false prophets who aped God's mighty works with their lying wonders. The soothsaying and necromancy found in Christian lands to-day belong to the same kingdom of darkness, and can be exorcised only in that "Name which is above every name." Moses, then, smites for mankind; Israel brings the Sacred Name through the wilderness for the world.

(3.) The weapons and tactics of this warfare were not such as to inflame the pride of the people of Israel, or to awaken in after generations a thirst for military glory, but such as to turn the tides of their faith and hope wholly away from themselves to their God. Hence the Hebrew national anthems glory in Jehovah rather than in Israel. Not the baptism of a war of national independence, but that of the Red Sea redemption, was their great national remembrance. Enthusiasm for Jehovah thus became the national passion. How appropriate was this in the training of a nation which was to teach the world true religion!

The real character of these plagues, or judgment strokes, will, as a general thing, appear from an attentive study of the Egyptian geography and natural history. They arise, as can usually be seen on the face of the narrative, from natural causes supernaturally intensified and directed. In the first and ninth plagues the natural causation is less distinct. They cannot, however, be explained away as natural events; for, if the record is to be believed at all, they were supernatural—(1) in their definiteness, the time of their occurrence and discontinuance being distinctly predicted; (2) in their succession; and (3) in their intensity. They were, in their power and direction, threefold: (1) against the Egyptian faith in the diviners, enchanters, and sorcerers, the prophets of a false religion. (2) Against their faith in their deities, their gods of earth, and water, and air—powers of nature; and beasts, and birds, and creeping things. Thus Jehovah's supremacy over idolatry ap-

O. T.

peared. But (3) they were also punishments for disobedience to God. There is from the beginning a gradually increasing intensity in these supernatural manifestations till the magicians are utterly discomfited, all the gods of Egypt put to shame, and Pharaoh compelled to yield reluctant obedience. At first the magicians seem to display the same power as Moses, (chap. vii, 11, 22,) then come signs beyond their power, (chap. viii, 18;) soon the prophet of Jehovah so smites them that they cannot appear at all, (chap. ix, 11;) and then they vanish altogether. So the weight of the judgments increases as with increasing light the crime of disobedience rises in magnitude—beginning with simple though sore annoyances, as blood, frogs, and flies; then advancing to the destruction of food and cattle—smiting first their dwelling-place and surroundings, and then themselves; till the locusts swept the earth and the darkness filled the heaven, and only the death stroke was left to fall. Thus we are taught how the consequence of sin is sin, and judgments unheeded inevitably lead on to sorer judgments, till destruction comes.

(4.) Some commentators have found a special application in each plague to some particular idolatry or idolatrous rite, but this we do not find warranted by facts. Some, following Philo, the learned and devout but fanciful Alexandrian Jew, separate the plagues into two groups of nine and one, and then the nine into three groups of three, between which groups they trace what they deem instructive contrasts and correspondences. Origen, Augustine, and others, have traced parallels between these ten judgments and the ten commandments, the succession of the judgments and of the creative days, etc. Most of these interpretations — not to dwell on the extravagant conceits of the Rabbies—are amusing rather than instructive, and would be appropriate rather to a sacred romance or drama than to a sober history like this. The wild fables of the Talmud, the monstrosities of the Koran, and the often romantically embellished history of Josephus, present here an instructive contrast to the sacred narrative.

(5.) Thus far the Egyptian monuments give us no distinct mention of the plagues and of the exodus. We have, however, Egyptian records of the sojourn and exodus of Israel, although confused and fragmentary, and written more than a thousand years after the events. Chief and most valuable among these is the narrative of the priest Manetho, who wrote his Egyptian history during the reign of Ptolemy Philadelphus, B. C. 283–247, of which a few fragments remain. Josephus has preserved all that we have of this narrative in his work against Apion. It is, as might be expected, a very different history, being the relation of an Egyptian priest many centuries after the events; yet the points of agreement are very striking. The Israelites appear in Manetho's story as a nation of lepers, headed by Osarsiph, a priest of Osiris, who had been educated at Heliopolis, but abandoned his order and the Egyptian religion to take the lead of this people. He taught them to abjure idolatry, gave them laws, a constitution and ceremonial, and when he united his fortunes with theirs he changed his name to Moses. The war is described as a religious war, in which, for the time, the Egyptians were discomfited, and obliged, in compliance with prophetic warnings, to abandon the country for thirteen years, and to flee, with their king Amenophis, into Ethiopia, taking with them the bull Apis and other sacred animals, while this leprous nation, reinforced by shepherds from Jerusalem, fortified themselves in Avaris, (Zoan,) a city of Goshen, robbed the temples, insulted the gods, roasted and ate the sacred animals, and cast contempt in every way upon the Egyptian worship. Amenophis afterwards returned with a great army and chased the shepherds and lepers out of his dominions through a dry desert to Palestine. (From Ewald's trans., *Hist. of Israel*, ii, 79.) Here, as Ewald shows, the great outlines of the story of the exodus are to be clearly seen; the Mosaic leadership, the war of religions,

B. C. 1491.   CHAPTER VII.   399

10 And Moses and Aaron went in unto Pharaoh, and they did so ᵖ as the LORD had commanded : and Aaron cast down his rod before Pharaoh, and before his servants, and it ᵍ became a serpent.

11 Then Pharaoh also ʳ called the wise men and ˢ the sorcerers: now the magicians of Egypt, they also ᵗ did in like manner with their enchantments. **12** For they cast down every man his rod, and

p Verse 9.——*q* Chap. 4. 3.——*r* Gen. 41. 8.   *s* 2 Tim. 3. 8.——*t* Verse 22; chap. 8. 7, 18.

the uprising of the hostile religion in Egypt itself, the leprous affliction of the revolting people, so pointedly mentioned in the Pentateuch, the secret superstitious dread inspired by Moses, which seems to have shaken the foundations of the Egyptian religion, the confession of defeat in the struggle, and the transformation of the exodus into an expulsion from Egypt—these are unmistakable traces of the same history coming down through Egyptian channels. The later Egyptian writers, Chæremon and Lysimachus, echo the story of Manetho, mingling with it Hebrew traditions. (*Josephus Against Apion*, bks. i, ii.

(6.) The exode of Israel from Egypt is a fact now universally admitted, whatever differences may exist in its explanation. Bunsen says, in his *Egypt*, that "History herself was born on that night when Moses led forth his countrymen from the land of Goshen." That this event resulted from some heavy calamities which at that time befel the Egyptians, or, in other words, that the narrative of the plagues has a solid historical foundation, is also now maintained with unbroken unanimity by Hebrew and Egyptian scholars, even by those who decline to see in these events anything supernatural. Thus Ewald says, that this history, "on the whole, exhibits the essence of the event as it actually happened." And Knobel says, that "in the time of Moses circumstances had transpired which made it possible for the Hebrews to go forth of themselves, and impossible for the Egyptians to hinder their undertaking or to force them to return." In other words, they who refuse to recognise here miraculous influence do recognise miraculous coincidence. Without any war, which, had it happened, must, as Knobel says, have left some trace in the history—without any invasion from abroad or insurrection from with- in to weaken the Egyptian power—a nation, unified and vitalized by faith in the one Jehovah, went forth unhindered from the bosom of a strong and prosperous empire. This is the event to be explained. The Mosaic record alone gives an adequate cause.

OPENING CONTEST WITH THE MAGICIANS, 10–13.

10. And Aaron cast down his rod ...and it became a serpent—תַּנִּין, a *dragon* or *crocodile*, not the *serpent* (נָחָשׁ) into which the rod was changed when Moses came before the elders of Israel. Chap. iv, 3. The shepherd's staff is changed into the monster of the Nile. Pharaoh is thus warned, by a symbol clear to the Egyptian mind, that the shepherd race of Israel is to be miraculously transformed into a formidable nation, comparable in might with Egypt. The crocodile's tail is the hieroglyphic symbol of Egypt.

11. Then Pharaoh also called the wise men and the sorcerers—Literally, *mutterers*, (of magic formulas.) **Now the magicians**—Priestly *scribes* who were skilled in the hieroglyphic wisdom. **They also did in like manner with their enchantments**—Their secret arts, the black or hidden arts or tricks which constitute magic or sorcery. The Apostle Paul, doubtless following the Jewish traditions, names these magicians *Jannes* and *Jambres*, (2 Tim. iii, 8,) and this tradition is found in the Targums and the Talmud.

12. They cast down every man his rod, and they became serpents—*Crocodiles*, as above. Moses wrought a miracle which they could easily imitate, for all the apparent transformations with which our modern jugglers have made us familiar, and even more wonderful ones than these, have been practised in Egypt and the East from an unknown antiquity. The author

they became serpents: but Aaron's rod swallowed up their rods. **13** And he hardened Pharaoh's heart, that he hearkened not unto them; ᵘ as the LORD had said.

14 And the LORD said unto Moses,

ᵛPharaoh's heart *is* hardened: he refuseth to let the people go. **15** Get thee unto Pharaoh in the morning; lo, he goeth out unto the water; and thou shalt stand by the river's brink against he come; and ʷ the rod which was turned

u Chap. 4. 21; verse 4.——*v* Chap. 8. 15; 10. 1, 20, 27.——*w* Chap. 4. 2, 3; verse 10.

describes the transaction just as it appeared to those who saw it, as we would describe similar apparent transformations wrought by a juggler to-day, but his language cannot fairly be pressed to prove that these magicians possessed any supernatural power. The most famous magicians have always professed to deceive, and declared that their most striking exploits were mere illusions; and how much more than deception there is in magic and sorcery, and whether all their wonders are literally "lying wonders," must be held as still open questions; but it is certain that Satan has ever used such dark arts and powers to resist the truth. See the Introduction to the History of the Plagues, **2. But Aaron's rod swallowed up their rods**—This was prophetic of the religion that was soon to swallow up all the boasted wisdom of Egypt, and the true miracle was thus also distinguished from the "lying wonder."

13. And he hardened Pharaoh's heart—Rather, *And hard was the heart of Pharaoh*. (Sam., Septuagint, Vulg., Onk., Syr.) The presence of superhuman power, and the solemn symbolic lessons, though they may have created in Pharaoh a momentary awe, yet failed to arouse his torpid conscience. Here, in this "sign," was no infliction of punishment, but a simple manifestation of power in attestation of the mission of Moses and Aaron, as well as a symbolic prediction hereafter to be more fully understood.

FIRST PLAGUE—BLOOD, 14–25.

15. Lo, he goeth out unto the water; and thou shalt stand by the river's brink—Some think that this was the time of the commencement of the annual rise of the river, because that the Nile then assumes a reddish hue produced by the mud of the upper country; but this annual redness of the river is an indication of palatability and wholesomeness. Yet, as all these plagues are found, as far as we understand them, to correspond remarkably with peculiarities of the country, being, as Hengstenberg has shown, specially fitted to the Egyptian geography, climate, soil, vegetable and animal life, it is possible that the very peculiarity of the miracle lay in the fact that the reddish hue, which is usually a sign of wholesomeness in the Nile, then deepened to a bloody tinge, which was the token of loathsomeness and death. The water which is usually drank with such avidity became nauseous and poisonous. If this be so, then the time of the infliction is fixed at about the middle of June. Yet this must be taken as supposition only, the first sure note of time occurring in the account of the hail, (chap. ix, 31, 32,) which destroyed the barley in the ear and the flax in blossom, which in Egypt must have been in February. The tenth plague occurred about the middle of April. Now the Nile begins to regularly rise in Lower Egypt, which is the scene of this history, about the summer solstice, or toward the end of June; about the end of August it begins to pour through the canals and fall over the valley in sheets of water, and the inundation then properly commences; toward the end of September it reaches its height, and then sinks to its lowest point at about the Vernal Equinox, or the last of March. If now the first of the plagues took place in the middle of June, it will be seen that the ten ran through the whole Nile period, thus cursing every several part of the Egyptian year. This is the view of Hengstenberg in his *Egypt and the Books of Moses.*

Probably Pharaoh went forth in the morning to worship, since the Nile was

CHAPTER VII.

to a serpent shalt thou take in thine hand. 16 And thou shalt say unto him, ˣ The LORD God of the Hebrews hath sent me unto thee, saying, Let my people go, ʸ that they may serve me in the wilderness: and, behold, hitherto thou wouldest not hear. 17 Thus saith the LORD, In this ᶻ thou shalt know that I am the LORD: behold, I will smite with the rod that is in mine hand upon the waters which are in the river, and ᵃ they shall be turned ᵇ to blood. 18 And the fish that is in the river shall die, and the river shall stink; and the Egyptians shall ᶜ loathe to drink of the water of the river. 19 And the LORD spake unto Moses, Say unto Aaron, Take thy rod, and ᵈ stretch out thine hand upon the waters of Egypt, upon their streams, upon their rivers, and upon their ponds, and upon all their pools of water, that they may become blood; and that there may be blood throughout all the land of Egypt, both in vessels of wood, and in vessels of stone. 20 And Moses and Aaron did so, as the LORD commanded; and he ᵉ lifted up the rod, and smote the waters that were in the river, in the sight of Pharaoh, and in the sight of his servants; and all the ᶠ waters that were in the river were turned to blood. 21 And the fish that was in the river died; and the river stank, and the Egyptians ᵍ could not drink of the water of the river; and there was blood throughout all the land of Egypt. 22 ʰ And the magicians of Egypt did so with their enchantments: and Pharaoh's heart was hardened, neither did he hearken unto them; ⁱ as the LORD had said. 23 And Pharaoh turned and

x Chap. 3. 18.——*y* Chap. 3. 12, 18; 5. 1, 3.—— *z* Chap. 5. 2; verse 5.——*a* Chap. 4. 9.——*b* Rev. 16. 4, 6.——*c* Verse 24.——*d* Chap. 8. 5, 6, 16; 9. 22; 10. 12, 21; 14. 21, 26.——1 Hebrew, *gathering of their waters*.——*e* Chap. 17. 5.——*f* Psa. 78. 44; 105. 29.——*g* Verse 18.——*h* Verse 11.——*i* Verse 3.

regarded as the embodiment of the god Osiris, of whom the bull Apis was considered the living emblem. On the monuments we find it called the "god Nile," the "Father of the gods," the "life-giving Father of all things." At Nilopolis (Nile-city) there was a temple and an order of priests for the worship of the river. Thus was Pharaoh's god smitten to death before his eyes as he offered him his morning prayer.

19. **Stretch out thine hand upon the waters of Egypt**—The language of this verse shows a minute acquaintance with the extensive and complicated water system which was peculiar to Egypt. The **streams** are the arms which branch out from the Nile, just north of modern Cairo, through the great plain of the delta, carrying the waters down to the Mediterranean. There are two principal and five or more lesser streams. The **rivers** are the canals running each side of the Nile, and receiving their waters through sluices at the time of the inundation. As the land sloped northward, the water was conveyed through main canals running along the southern or higher side of each field, and thence it spread through branches, straight or curved, down northward over the land. The **ponds** were the large standing lakes left by the inundation; and the **pools**—literally, *every collection of their waters*—were the smaller ponds and reservoirs which they used who lived at a distance from the river. **Wood**... **stone**—This is also a peculiarly Egyptian touch, for the Nile water was kept in large stone tanks for public use, and was also filtered and purified for domestic use in smaller vessels.

20, 21. **And all the waters that were in the river were turned to blood**—Also, by implication, (verse 19,) all the waters that had been drawn from the river into the ponds, tanks, etc., underwent the change. The sweet, beneficent Nile water became red and putrid like stagnant blood, so that it poisoned the fishes and became unfit for use. The red moon of the eclipse is said to be turned into blood, Joel ii, 3. Only the Nile water was smitten, for water could yet be obtained from the wells and by digging, as we see from verse 24.

22. **And the magicians of Egypt did so with their enchantments: and Pharaoh's heart was hardened**—The two things are connected as cause and effect. He tried to believe that their pretended miracle was as real as Jehovah's judgment "sign." They could as easily obtain water for their trick as could the Egyptians for drinking. If they had the power to which they pretended, their part, of course,

went into his house, neither did he set his heart to this also. 24 And all the Egyptians digged round about the river for water to drink; for they could not drink of the water of the river. 25 And seven days were fulfilled after that the Lord had smitten the river.

CHAPTER VIII.

AND the Lord spake unto Moses, Go unto Pharaoh, and say unto him, Thus saith the Lord, Let my people go, *a* that they may serve me. 2 And if thou *b* refuse to let *them* go, behold, I will smite all thy borders with *c* frogs: 3 And the river shall bring forth frogs abundantly, which shall go up and come into thine house, and into *d* thy bedchamber, and upon thy bed, and into the house of thy servants, and upon thy

---

a Chap. 3. 12, 18.——*b* Chap. 7. 14; 9. 2.   *c* Rev. 16. 13.——*d* Psa. 105. 30.

---

was to turn back the water as it was before, and so relieve the distress of the Egyptians.

25. **Seven days**—A week passed while the Nile rolled blood through Egypt, but Pharaoh obstinately shut himself in his house and made no sign of submission.

CHAPTER VIII.

SECOND PLAGUE—FROGS, 1-15.

1. **Go unto Pharaoh**—The *going* we must think of as being from Goshen to Zoan, Pharaoh's capital. Zoan we may suppose to be the scene of these interviews between prophet and king.

2. **I will smite all thy borders with frogs**—Several species of frogs are found in Egypt, and they are specially abundant in September, filling the lakes and ponds left by the retiring inundation. In the spawning season the waters are so filled with them that a bowl of water taken up almost anywhere will be found to contain tadpoles, yet there is no other instance of their becoming a plague to the inhabitants, although there are traditions of similar plagues in other countries. But a superhuman influence is here most evident. The frog is an amphibious animal, living in the water or in moist, marshy lands. For these animals, then, to leave the river and river banks, and swarm up into the cities, which were situated in the edge of the dry desert, into the very houses, and into the driest places in the houses, as the beds, kneading-troughs, and ovens, was a miraculous manifestation most striking and alarming. The atmosphere of Egypt is always remarkably dry, rain being very rare except on the seacoast, so that usually a frog could live but a very short time in an Egyptian street or house. If, now, heavy clouds and rains accompanied this visitation, in order to enable the reptiles to live in the cities, as seems likely, the supernatural character of the infliction would be still more marked.

This was also in several ways a blow at the Egyptian idolatry. The judgment comes, as before, from the deified Nile, and comes in one of their sacred animals. The frog was an emblem of the great god Pthah, the tutelar god of Memphis, and the principal divinity of Lower Egypt, so that their protecting deity now became to the Memphites a loathsome abomination. Lepsius traces this form of idolatry to the most ancient nature worship of the land. Mariette has published a curious vignette from the monuments, representing king *Seti* offering two vases of wine to a frog enshrined in a small chapel. Brugsch also shows that in the district of *Sah* the Egyptians worshipped a goddess with a frog's head, whom they called *Heka*.

3. **Into thine house, and into thy bedchamber**—The Egyptian house was built around a rectangular court, which was paved, and open to the sky, often containing trees, and generally a tank or fountain. See notes on Matthew, pp. 121 and 326. The poorer houses had only a basement story, or ground floor, but those of a better class had store rooms, offices, etc., in the basement, and above these were the parlours and sleeping chambers. There was often an additional story in one part on which was a terrace covered with an awning, or a light roof supported on columns, where the ladies of the family sat at work during the day, and where

people, and into thine ovens, and into thy ¹ kneading troughs: **4** And the frogs shall come up both on thee, and upon thy people, and upon all thy servants. **5** And the LORD spake unto Moses, Say unto Aaron, ᵉ Stretch forth thine hand with thy rod over the streams, over the rivers, and over the ponds, and cause frogs to come up upon the land of Egypt. **6** And Aaron stretched out his hand over the waters of Egypt; and ᶠ the frogs came up, and covered the land of Egypt.

1 Or, *dough*.——ᵉ Chap. 7. 19.   ᶠ Psa. 78. 45; 105. 30.

the master of the house took his afternoon nap. See annexed cut. The reed-like columns with lotus capitals, and the disregard of perspective in showing the end of the house, are especially noticeable as illustrating Egyptian architecture and drawing.

Into thine ovens, and into thy kneading troughs — The Egyptian oven was a jar of clay, or a jar-like structure built up from the ground, about three feet high, and widening toward the bottom, there being a hole in the side for the extraction of

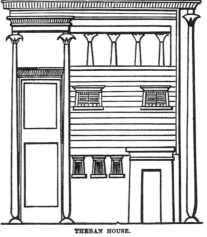
THEBAN HOUSE.

KNEADING DOUGH WITH FEET.

CARRYING CAKES TO THE OVEN.

KNEADING DOUGH WITH HANDS.

the ashes. It was heated by making a fire within it, and the dough was spread on the inside and on the outside. The accompanying cuts, from a representation in a Theban tomb, illustrate the mode of kneading the dough, which was done both with hands and feet, and of carrying the cakes to the oven, which is now lighted.

7 ᶠ And the magicians did so with their enchantments, and brought up frogs upon the land of Egypt. **8** Then Pharaoh called for Moses and Aaron, and said, ʰ Entreat the Lord, that he may take away the frogs from me, and from my people; and I will let the people go, that they may do sacrifice unto the Lord. **9** And Moses said unto Pharaoh, ² Glory over me : ³ when shall I entreat for thee, and for thy servants, and for thy people, ⁴ to destroy the frogs from thee and thy houses, *that* they may remain in the river only ? **10** And he said, ⁵ To morrow. And he said, *Be it* according to thy word; that thou mayest know that ¹ *there is* none like unto the Lord our God. **11** And the frogs shall depart from thee, and from thy houses, and from thy servants, and from thy people; they shall remain in the river only. **12** And Moses and Aaron went ou from Pharaoh: and Moses ᵏ cried unto the Lord because of the frogs which he had brought against Pharaoh. **13** And the Lord did according to the word of Moses; and the frogs died out of the houses, out of the villages, and out of the fields. **14** And they gathered them together upon heaps; and the land stank. **15** But when Pharaoh saw that there was ¹ respite, ᵐ he hardened his heart, and hearkened not unto them; as the Lord had said.

16 And the Lord said unto Moses, Say unto Aaron, Stretch out thy rod, and smite the dust of the land, that it may become lice throughout all the land of Egypt. **17** And they did so; for Aaron stretched out his hand with his

---

g Chap. 7. 11.—*h* Chap. 9. 28; 10. 17; Num. 21, 7; 1 Kings 13. 6; Acts 8. 24.—2 Or, *Have this honour over me*, &c.—3 Or, *against when*.—4 Heb. *to cut off.*—5 Or, *Against to morrow.*—*i* Chap. 9. 14; Deut. 33. 26; 2 Sam. 7. 22; 1 Chron. 17. 20; Psa. 86. 8; Isa. 46. 9; Jer. 10. 6, 7.—*k* Verse 30; chap. 9. 33; 10. 18; 32. 11; James 5. 16-18.—*l* Eccles. 8. 11.—*m* Chap. 7. 14.

---

8. Entreat the Lord—Pharaoh now, for the first time, owns the power of the Hebrews' God. He has found an answer to his question, "Who is Jehovah?" Jehovah has come into his kitchen and into his bedchamber.

9. Glory over me—Rather, *Appoint for me when*, etc.: (Samaritan, Septuagint, Vulgate, Arabic versions.) Let Pharaoh set the time when the plague shall cease, and then shall he "know that there is none like Jehovah our God."

13. Out of the villages—Literally, *the courts;* probably the open courts within the houses, described above.

14. And they gathered them together upon heaps—Literally, *Heaps, heaps;* vast heaps, or a multitude of heaps. **And the land stank**—The stench of their great god *Pthah* went up to heaven, even from his own magnificent temple courts. The putrid corpses were piled upon his altars.

The author of the Book of Wisdom, who was probably an Egyptian Jew, says that God in these plagues "tormented them with their own abominations;" and as "they worshipped serpents void of reason and vile beasts," he "sent a multitude of unreasonable beasts upon them in vengeance."—*Wisd.*, xi, 15.

Third Plague—Lice, 16-19.

16. Smite the dust of the land, that it may become lice—The Hebrew word here rendered *lice* occurs only in the account of this miracle, and its meaning has been much disputed, many considering that the insect was a gnat or mosquito; but Josephus and the Rabbies all give the same rendering as our English version. The Septuagint has been erroneously supposed to establish this meaning, but its word, σχνίφες, may mean any small biting or stinging insect, whether winged or wingless. Modern travellers describe the louse as a great pest in Egypt; and Sir Samuel Baker, especially, speaks of the abundance of the vermin in almost Scripture language—"It is as though the very dust were turned into lice."

This plague struck at the Egyptian idolatry less directly, but even more effectually, than either of the preceding. It made all the sacred animals, and the priests themselves, unclean, so as to cut off the worship in the temples. The priests were most scrupulously attentive to cleanliness, being always careful to have their linen garments fresh washed, scouring their drinking cups each day, bathing in cold water twice each day and twice each night, and shaving not only the head and beard, but the "whole

B. C. 1491. CHAPTER VIII. 405

rod, and smote the dust of the earth, and ⁿit became lice in man, and in beast; all the dust of the land became lice throughout all the land of Egypt. 18 And ᵒthe magicians did so with their enchantments to bring forth lice, but they ᵖ could not: so there were lice upon man, and upon beast. 19 Then the magicians said unto Pharaoh, This is ᑫthe finger of God: and Pharaoh's ʳ heart was hardened, and he hearkened not unto them; as the LORD had said. 20 And the LORD said unto Moses,

ˢRise up early in the morning, and stand before Pharaoh; lo, he cometh forth to the water; and say unto him, Thus saith the LORD, ᵗLet my people go, that they may serve me. 21 Else, if thou wilt not let my people go, behold, I will send ᵘswarms of flies upon thee, and upon thy servants, and upon thy people, and into thy houses: and the houses of the Egyptians shall be full of swarms of flies, and also the ground whereon they are. 22 And ᵘI will sever in that day the land of Goshen, in which my people

---

n Psa. 105. 31.——*o* Chapter 7. 11.——*p* Luke 10. 18; 2 Tim. 3. 8, 9.——*q* 1 Sam. 6. 3, 9; Psa. 8. 3; Matt. 12. 28; Luke 11. 20.

r Verse 15.——*s* Chap. 7. 15.——*t* Verse 1.——6 Or, *a mixture of noisome beasts*, &c.—— *u* Chap. 9. 4, 6, 26; 10. 23; 11. 6, 7; 12. 13.

---

body every other day, that no lice or other impure thing might adhere to them when engaged in the service of their gods." (*Herod.*, ii, 37.) Think of these fastidiously cleanly servants swarming with lice, and finding their gods covered with them also! Thus the word of Moses smote every temple and every god in Egypt.

18. But they could not—Here the magicians are baffled, and they can imitate these signs no further. In this the gradual advance is to be noted, and also in the fact that the stroke is much more severe. The Egyptians could keep away from the bloody river; the frogs came upon their tables and beds; but the loathsome lice feasted on their bodies.

19. This is the finger of God—Rather, *of the gods;* for they did not mean to own Jehovah, but declared that this was a supernatural infliction from their own gods. This explained their failure to Pharaoh, and so his heart became yet more hardened.

FOURTH PLAGUE—SWARMS (OF FLIES,) 20-32.

20. Lo, he cometh forth to the water—To offer his morning worship on the bank of the river, as in chap. vii, 15. Jehovah's message confronted him at the altar of his god.

21. Swarms of flies—The precise nature of this plague is doubtful. The word used, עָרֹב, occurs only in this place and in the two psalms where this judgment is described, so that we get no aid in interpretation from parallel passages. The rendering of the Septuagint is *dog-fly*, an insect which in Egypt gives great annoyance to man and beast; and as the authority of that version is very high on Egyptian subjects, this is the most usual interpretation. These insects are described as coming in immense swarms, and settling in black masses on whatever part of the person of the traveller is exposed. Stuart Poole considers it to have been the domestic fly, which is now the most troublesome insect in Egypt. Hengstenberg quotes a traveller as saying: "Men and beasts are cruelly tormented by them. You can form no conception of their fury when they want to settle on any part of your body. You may drive them away, but they settle again immediately, and their obstinacy wearies out the most patient man." The distress arising from ophthalmia, now so common in Egypt, is much aggravated by the swarms of flies. Others, as Adam Clarke, Wordsworth, Kurtz, following a Jewish tradition, consider this plague to have been swarms of all kinds of noxious insects, and the author of the Book of Wisdom seems to have supposed that there were beasts also. (*Wisdom*, xi, 15, 16, etc.) Swarming creatures of some kind, probably of various species of insects, so afflicted Pharaoh that he yielded more than ever before, and consented to allow the Israelites to go into the wilderness and sacrifice. Further than this we cannot yet affirm.

22. I will sever in that day the land of Goshen—Here also is now a marked advance, a more distinctive character in the judgment. The putrid Nile had afflicted Egypt and Israel alike; the frogs and the lice had been

dwell, that no swarms of flies shall be there; to the end thou mayest know that I *am* the Lord in the midst of the earth. 23 And I will put ⁷ a division between my people and thy people: ⁸ to morrow shall this sign be. 24 And the Lord did so; and ᵛ there came a grievous swarm of flies into the house of Pharaoh, and *into* his servants' houses,

7 Heb. *a redemption.*——8 Or, *by to morrow.*
v Psa. 78. 45; 105. 31.

and into all the land of Egypt: **the land was ⁹ corrupted by reason of the swarm** of flies. 25 And Pharaoh called for Moses and for Aaron, and said, Go ye, sacrifice to your God in the land. 26 And Moses said, It is not meet so to do; for we shall sacrifice ʷ the abomination of the Egyptians to the Lord our God: lo, shall we sacrifice the abomina-

9 Or, *destroyed.*——w Gen. 43. 32; 46, 34; Deut. 7. 25, 26; 12. 13.

found, at least to some extent, in the land of Goshen; but henceforth the Israelitish province was to be protected from the inflictions that were to fall upon heathen Egypt. Here was to be a decisive proof of Jehovah's supremacy, **to the end thou mayest know that I am Jehovah. I will put a division** (or *deliverance*) **between my people and thy people**—It is also to be considered, that while at the beginning of these inflictions the Israelites had been considerably scattered from Goshen throughout the land in the great public works, these successive judgments would have greatly hindered, if not by this time have totally suspended, the industrial activities of the nation. By this time there must have been a great national anxiety, and soon there was a general panic. Under these circumstances the Israelites would naturally gather together into their own province, and be no more mingled among the Egyptians. Thus this marked distinction in regard to Goshen would be now, perhaps, for the first time possible.

25. **Go ye, sacrifice...in the land** —Pharaoh now allows them to sacrifice, but insists that it shall be in Egypt.

26. **The abomination of the Egyptians**—The Egyptians would not allow them to worship in the land according to Jehovah's will. Some, as Hengstenberg, understand the text to mean that the manner of their worship would be abominable to the Egyptians—that they would not observe the manifold rigid sacrificial regulations of the Egyptian priests; but the Targum of Onkelos translates, "the animal which the Egyptians worship," that is, the ox, which as *Apis* and *Mnevis* was so specially adored. So the Vulgate renders, "the animals which the Egyptians worship."

This is a characteristic Hebrew phraseology. Idols are often styled "abominations" in the Old Testament. Thus, in 2 Kings xxiii, 13, the god Chemosh is called "the abomination of Moab," and Ashtoreth "the abomination of the Zidonians." So the ox is here called "the abomination of the Egyptians," not as abominated by them, not because it was abominable in their eyes to kill it, but because this worship of the ox was an abomination to Jehovah. This was doubtless bold language for Moses to use

APIS, THE SACRED BULL.

to Pharaoh, (styling his god an "abomination,") but his boldness has greatly increased since he deprecated his stammering tongue, and the same spirit is seen in the pungent rebuke and exhortation of the twenty-ninth verse, "Let not Pharaoh deal deceitfully any more."

The sacred bull was specially worshipped at Memphis, the great city of Lower Egypt, where he had palatial stalls and temples. In the above engraving the bull is crowned with a circle representing Ra, or the sun, and also wears on his forehead the asp, the symbol of majesty

CHAPTER VIII.

B. C. 1491.   407

tion of the Egyptians before their eyes, and will they not stone us? **27** We will go *three days' journey into the wilderness, and sacrifice to the LORD our God, as ʸhe shall command us. **28** And Pharaoh said, I will let you go, that ye may sacrifice to the LORD your God in the wilderness; only ye shall not go very far away: ᶻentreat for me. **29** And Moses said, Behold, I go out from thee, and I will entreat the LORD that the swarms of flies may depart from Pharaoh, from his servants, and from his people, to morrow: but let not Pharaoh ᵃdeal deceitfully any more in not letting the people go to sacrifice to the LORD. **30** And Moses went out from Pharaoh, and ᵇentreated the LORD. **31** And the LORD did according to the word of Moses; and he removed the swarms of flies from Pharaoh, from his servants, and from his people; there remained not one. **32** And Pharaoh ᶜhardened his heart at this time also, neither would he let the people go.

CHAPTER IX.

THEN the LORD said unto Moses, ᵃGo in unto Pharaoh, and tell him, Thus saith the LORD God of the Hebrews, Let my people go, that they may serve me. **2** For if thou ᵇrefuse to let *them* go, and wilt hold them still, **3** Behold, the ᶜhand of the LORD is up on thy cattle which *is* in the field, upon the horses, upon the asses, upon the camels, upon the oxen, and upon the sheep: *there shall be* a very grievous murrain. **4** And ᵈthe LORD shall sever between the cattle of Israel and the cat-

x Chap. 3. 18.——*y* Chap. 3. 12.——*z* Ver. 8; chap. 9. 28; 1 Kings 13. 6.——*a* Ver. 15.——*b* Ver. 12.

c Ver. 15; chap. 4. 21.——*a* Chap. 8. 1.——*b* Chap. 8. 2.——*c* Chap. 7. 4.——*d* Chap. 8. 22.

Will they not stone us—The animal-worship of the Egyptians is frequently dwelt upon by classical writers, so that it became a proverb that in Egypt it was easier to meet a god than a man. The text is well illustrated by the statement of Herodotus, that it was a capital crime in Egypt to kill one of the sacred animals; and Diodorus and Cicero relate that this was the case in their time. (*Herod.*, ii, 65; *Cic., Tusc. Disp.*, v, 27; *Diod.*, i, 83.) So modern Hinduism makes it a mortal sin to kill a cow. (Butler's *Land of the Veda*, chap. ii.) The Egyptians, however, killed oxen for food, beef and goose being their chief meats. The same animals were not sacred through all Egypt, but each had his special district, and the ox or heifer, one of the animals specially designated for sacrifice in the Mosaic economy, was, as we have seen, particularly worshipped in the district where the Israelites dwelt. *Apis* was the sacred bull of Memphis, and *Mnevis*, second only in rank to *Apis*, and by Plutarch called his sire, was the sacred bull of Heliopolis. (Wilkinson's *Anc. Egypt*, chap. iv,) and these were the two leading cities of Lower Egypt. Thus the fear expressed by Moses, "Will they not stone us?" is just what might have been expected in Egypt above all other lands, and in this district above all others of Egypt.

CHAPTER IX.

FIFTH PLAGUE—MURRAIN, 1-7.

3. The hand of the Lord is upon thy cattle which is **in the field**—This infliction seems to be limited to the cattle which were in the open air. All of the animals here mentioned are represented in the Egyptian monuments except the camel, which, though used in Egypt from the earliest times, yet for some reason never occurs in the hieroglyphic inscriptions, or in the pictured representations of the tombs. Stuart Poole supposes that the camel was unclean in the eyes of the Egyptians, as associated with the hated nomad tribes of the desert and the abominated Shepherd Dynasties. See Gen. xlvi, 34, and note. In the populous cities and cultivated fields of the Nile valley the services of the camel would not be required; but to cross the sands which bounded the valley the "ship of the desert" was indispensable: yet perhaps the Egyptians generally employed the Arabs in this caravan service. The horses of Egypt were celebrated from early times: thence Solomon imported his into Palestine. They were greatly esteemed for chariot service and for war, but asses and cattle were generally employed for draught. The cheap, strong, patient ass was, and

tle of Egypt: and there shall nothing die of all *that is* the children's of Israel.
5 And the LORD appointed a set time, saying, To morrow the LORD shall do this thing in the land. 6 And the LORD did that thing on the morrow, and ᵉall the cattle of Egypt died: but of the cattle of the children of Israel died not one.
7 And Pharaoh sent, and, behold, there was not one of the cattle of the Israelites dead. And ᶠthe heart of Pharaoh was hardened, and he did not let the people go.

8 And the LORD said unto Moses and unto Aaron, Take to you hand fuls of ashes of the furnace, and let Moses sprinkle it toward the heaven in the sight of Pharaoh. 9 And it shall become small dust in all the land of Egypt, and shall be ᵍa boil breaking forth *with* blains upon man, and upon beast, throughout all the land of Egypt.
10 And they took ashes of the furnace, and stood before Pharaoh; and Moses sprinkled it up toward heaven; and it became ʰa boil breaking forth

e Psa. 78. 50.——*f* Chap. 7. 14; 8. 32.

g Rev. 16. 2.——*h* Deut. 28. 27.

is, the peasant's chief dependence for labour. Sheep were reared chiefly for their wool, mutton being rarely used. Large flocks were kept in the neighbourhood of Memphis, even to the number of two thousand.

6. And all the cattle of Egypt died—Here the universal term *all* is not used in its absolute sense, as meaning each and every one, but it means simply *very many*. We find that there were other cattle left to be smitten by the boils, (verse 10,) and still others to be killed by the hail. Verse 25. A like usage is seen in the description of the plague of the locusts, (chap. x, 12,) which are said to have eaten up **all that the hail ... left,** and yet the hail **smote every herb and brake every tree.** Verse 25. The Hebrew idiom often thus uses universal terms in a general sense. See Acts ii, 5; Col. i, 23.

There are several instances on record of a similar murrain in Egypt. Lepsius and Poole describe such an infliction which they witnessed in 1842, and a similar one occurred in 1853, resembling the cattle disease which prevailed so extensively throughout America in 1872. But the occurrence of the plague according to definite prediction, and the sparing of the cattle of the Israelites, were the miraculous marks of this visitation.

This was, as yet, the heaviest infliction; for as the Egyptian wealth largely consisted in cattle, their means of support were now in a great degree destroyed. Jehovah shows these idolaters that he holds their supplies of food and clothing in his hands. Yet their crops, and many of their cattle, were yet left.

7. And Pharaoh sent... and the heart of Pharaoh was hardened—Here, as in chapter vii, 22, the grammatical construction implies cause and effect. This marked manifestation in behalf of Israel aroused the anger and obstinacy of Pharaoh the more. He does not melt or waver, and on this occasion is not awed even into temporary submission.

SIXTH PLAGUE—BOILS, 8–12.

8. Ashes of the furnace—Not the oven, but the smelting furnace, or the lime-kiln.—*Kimchi*. **Sprinkle...toward...heaven in the sight of Pharaoh**—The ashes of the great furnaces, or lime-kilns, where Israel had toiled so long, were solemnly spread out before Jehovah, and his judgment invoked upon the oppressor.

9. And it shall become small dust —The ashes shall scatter in a fine powder, the grains of ashes being exceedingly small, and easily blown abroad. **A boil breaking forth**—Literally, *a hot, burning sore, breaking forth into pustules.* In previous plagues the water had been made their enemy, the dust of the earth had been changed to vermin, their wealth in the fields had been smitten, and now the strength and pride of their cities are cursed. The temples and treasure cities are cursed in the plague that is scattered from the ashes of the lime-kiln. It is the unrequited toil of Israel's multitudes upon these vast public works that now burns and fevers man and beast through all Egypt.

with blains upon man, and upon beast. 11 And the *¹ magicians could not stand before Moses because of the boils; for the boil was upon the magicians, and upon all the Egyptians. 12 And the LORD hardened the heart of Pharaoh, and he hearkened not unto them; ᵏ as the LORD had spoken unto Moses.
13 And the LORD said unto Moses, ¹ Rise up early in the morning, and stand before Pharaoh, and say unto him, Thus saith the LORD God of the Hebrews, Let my people go, that they may serve me. 14 For I will at this time send all my plagues upon thine heart, and upon thy servants, and upon thy people; ᵐ that thou mayest know that *there is* none like me in all the earth. 15 For now I will ⁿ stretch out my hand, that I may smite thee and thy people with pestilence; and thou shalt be cut off from the earth. 16 And in very deed for º this *cause* have I ¹ raised thee up, for to show *in* thee my power; and that my

---

i Chap. 8. 18, 19; 2 Tim. 3. 9.——*k* Chap. 4. 21. *l* Chap. 8. 20.——*m* Chap. 8. 10.

n Chap. 3. 20.——*o* Rom. 9. 17; Prov. 16. 4; 1 Peter 2. 9.——1 Heb. *made thee stand*.

---

11. **And the magicians could not stand before Moses because of the boils**—Thus had these supernatural inflictions advanced in severity, till now the idolatrous prophets were all stricken down, and we hear of them no more. After the third plague, or at the end of the first triad of these inflictions, they had been compelled to own a supernatural power, and said, *This is the finger of the gods;* and now, at the end of the second triad, they retire wholly discomfited. Probably this also, as well as the plague of lice, was one which incapacitated the priests for their service by making them unclean, so that the altars of the idols were deserted.

12. **And the Lord hardened the heart of Pharaoh**—That is, by sending this manifestation of his anger he made his heart more hard. Punishment always hardens if it does not soften. It is worthy of remark that now, for the first time in the history, it is said that "the Lord hardened," although this result of his sin had been predicted, chap. iv, 21. Chap. vii, 13 is no exception; see the note. Here, then, is another marked stage in the history of these judgments. By persistent disobedience Pharaoh has now so blunted his moral sense that it is morally certain that he will not repent; that is, he has reached that state where punishment will only harden. Yet God punishes still. Since he will not honour him by obedience he must do it through punishment.

SEVENTH PLAGUE—THE HAIL, 13-35.

The third triad of judgments is introduced with unusual formality and solemnity. Pharaoh was now a "vessel of wrath," fit only for destruction. See note on verse 12. He had resisted to that degree that repentance was now morally impossible; and he was preserved in life only to reveal God's supremacy by punishment. It will be noticed that in these last judgments Aaron is not seen: it is Moses who lifts the rod that crushes Egypt to the dust.

14. **For I will at this time send all my plagues**—Only lighter strokes had fallen hitherto, but now more dreadful judgments impend.

15. **For now I will stretch out my hand**—The verb (שָׁלַחְתִּי) is here to be rendered as conditional past, (Ewald, *Lehrb.*, § 358, a.; Nordh., *Gram.*, § 991, 3, a.,) thus, *For now I would have stretched out my hand and smitten.* For a similar construction see 1 Sam. xiii, 13. So the Arabic, Fagius, Adam Clarke, Kalisch, Keil, Knobel, Stier and Theil, Murphy. The verse is closely connected to the following, thus: "For now I would have stretched out my hand and smitten thee...but yet for this have I preserved thee, to show thee my power," etc.

16. **And in very deed for this cause have I raised thee up**—Literally, *made thee stand*, kept thee standing, or preserved thee alive, after thy life was forfeited. So, substantially, the Septuagint, Targ. of Onkelos, and Palestinian, Arabic, and Syriac versions. The Palestinian Targum well paraphrases both verses thus: "Now could I send the plague of my strength by judgment to strike thee and thy people with death, and destroy thee from the earth, but

name may be declared throughout all the earth. 17 As yet ᵖexaltest thou thyself against my people, that thou wilt not let them go? 18 Behold, to morrow about this time I will cause it to rain a very grievous hail, such as hath not been in Egypt since the foundation thereof even until now. 19 Send therefore now, *and* gather thy cattle, and all that thou hast in the field; *for upon* every man and beast which shall be found in the field, and shall not be brought home, the hail shall come down upon them, and they shall die. 20 He that ᑫfeared the word of the LORD among the servants of Pharaoh made his servants and his cattle flee into the houses: 21 And he that ᵃregarded not the word of the LORD left his servants and his cattle in the field. 22 And the LORD said unto Moses, Stretch forth thine hand toward heaven, that there may be ʳhail in all the land of Egypt, upon man, and upon beast, and upon every herb of the field, throughout the land of Egypt. 23 And Moses stretched forth his rod toward heaven: and ˢthe LORD sent thunder and hail, and the fire ran along upon the ground; and the LORD rained hail upon the land of Egypt. 24 So there was hail, and fire mingled with the hail, very grievous, such as there was none like it in all the land of Egypt since it became a nation. 25 And the hail smote throughout all the land of Egypt all that *was* in the field, both man and beast; and the hail ᵗsmote every herb of the field, and brake every tree of the field. 26 ᵘOnly in the land of Goshen, where the children of Israel *were*, was there no hail. 27 And Pharaoh sent, and called for Moses and Aaron, and said unto them, ᵛI have sinned this time: ʷthe LORD *is* righteous, and I and my people *are* wicked. 28 ˣEntreat the LORD (for *it is* enough) that there be no *more* ᵃmighty thunderings and hail; and I will let you go, and ye shall stay no longer. 29 And Moses said unto him, As soon as I am gone out of the city, I will ʸspread abroad my hands unto the LORD; *and* the thunder shall cease, neither shall there be any more hail; that thou mayest know how that the ᶻearth *is* the LORD's. 30 But as for thee and thy servants, ᵃI know that ye will not yet fear the LORD God. 31 And the flax and the barley was smitten: ᵇfor the barley *was* in the ear, and the flax *was* bolled.

p Job 9. 4; 15. 25, 26.——*q* Prov. 22. 3, 4.——2 Heb. *set not his heart unto*, chap. 7. 23.——*r* Rev. 16. 21.——*s* Josh. 10. 11; Psa. 18. 13; 78. 47; 105. 32; 148. 8; Isa. 30. 30; Ezek. 38. 22; Rev. 8. 7.——*t* Psa. 105. 33.——*u* Chap. 8. 22; 9. 4, 6; 10. 23; 11. 7; 12. 13; Isa. 32. 18, 19.

v Chap. 10. 16.——*w* 2 Chron. 12. 6; Psa. 129. 4; 145. 17; Lam. 1. 18; Dan. 9. 14.——*x* Chap. 8. 8, 28; 10. 17: Acts 8. 24.——3 Heb. *voices of God*, Psa. 29. 3, 4.——*y* 1 Kings 8. 22, 38; Psa. 143. 6; Isa. 1. 15.——*z* Psa. 24. 1; 1 Cor. 10. 26, 28.——*a* Isa. 26. 10.——*b* Ruth 1. 22; 2. 23.

verily I have spared thee alive, not that I may benefit thee, but that my power may be made manifest to thee," etc.

18. **A very grievous hail**—Hail is rare in Egypt, although it sometimes occurs. Thunder-storms are seldom experienced, and do no damage except washing away the mud walls of the poorer sort of dwellings.

19. **Send therefore now, and gather thy cattle**—This is the only instance in which the Egyptians were advised how to escape the judgment after it had been announced. This plague not only destroyed the crops, trees, and cattle, but, like the last, fell upon the Egyptians themselves. Jehovah now reveals himself to Egypt as the Lord of the elements—of the forces of the air—as well as of the water and the land.

27. **I have sinned this time**—Now I see and own my sin. For the first time Pharaoh confesses sin, and attests the righteousness of Jehovah, but it is simply a lip acknowledgment. He owns the weight of God's hand rather than the righteousness of his commandments. Pain can reveal that law is violated, but it cannot convert, cannot make penitent, the heart that chooses to rebel.

31, 32. **And the flax and the barley was smitten**—Flax was a most important crop in Egypt, as great quantities of linen were required for clothing and for the bandages of mummies, as well as for exportation. **The barley was in the ear and the flax was bolled**—These verses give us the first decisive indication of the time of the year when these events took place. The *barley* was in the *ear* and the *flax* was in the *flower* or blossom In Egypt flax flowers at the end of January, and flax and barley are both ripe at the end

CHAPTER IX.

32 But the wheat and the rye were not smitten: for they *were* ⁴not grown up. **33** And Moses went out of the city from Pharaoh, and ᶜspread abroad his hands unto the LORD: and the thunders and hail ceased, and the rain was not poured upon the earth. **34** And when Pharaoh saw that the rain and the hail and the thunders were ceased, he sinned yet more, and hardened his heart, he and his servants. **35** And ᵈthe heart of Pharaoh was hardened, neither would he let the children of Israel go; as the LORD had spoken ᵇby Moses.

CHAPTER X.

AND the LORD said unto Moses, Go in unto Pharaoh: ᵃfor I have hardened his heart, and the heart of his servants, ᵇthat I might show these my signs before him: **2** And that ᶜthou mayest tell in the ears of thy son, and of thy son's son, what things I have wrought in Egypt, and my signs which I have done among them; that ye may know how that I *am* the LORD. **3** And Moses and Aaron came in unto Pharaoh, and said unto him, Thus saith the LORD God of the Hebrews, How long wilt thou refuse to ᵈhumble thyself before me? let my people go, that they may serve me. **4** Else, if thou refuse to let my people go, behold, to morrow will I bring the ᵉlocusts into thy coast: **5** And they shall cover the ¹face of the earth, that one cannot be able to see the

---

⁴ Heb. *hidden*, or, *dark*.——c Verse 29; chap. 8. 12.——*d* Chap. 4. 21.——5 Heb. *by the hand of Moses*, chap. 4. 13.——*a* Chap. 4. 21; 7. 14.——*b* Chap. 7. 4.

c Deut. 4. 9; Psa. 44. 1; 71. 18; 78. 5, &c.; Joel 1. 3.——*d* 1 Kings 21. 29; 2 Chron. 7. 14; 34. 27; Job 42. 6; Jer. 13. 18; James 4. 10; 1 Pet. 5. 6.——*e* Prov. 30. 27; Rev. 9. 3.——1 Heb. *eye*, verse 15.

---

of February or the first of March; but wheat and *doora* do not ripen till April. This plague, then, took place in the last of January or the first of February. From January to April is also the very time when cattle there are in pasture. The author thus shows a minute acquaintance with the agriculture and natural history of Egypt. **The wheat and the rye**—Rather, *wheat and spelt*, a grain closely resembling wheat, the common food of the ancient Egyptians, and now well known and much used under the name of *doora*. All the processes of cultivating and gathering these grains, and the operations of watering the flax, beating the stalks when gathered, and of manufacturing them into twine and cloth, are fully represented in the paintings of the Egyptian tombs. Wilkinson states that the Egyptian linen was remarkably fine in texture, equal in quality to the best now made, and superior to the modern article in the evenness of its threads. Zoan or Tanis was famous for its flax fields. The storm that would destroy barley in the ear, and flax in the blossom, would be too early in the season to cut off the wheat and spelt, which were not yet high enough to be broken by the hail, and consequently escaped destruction.

33. Went out of the city—This shows that Pharaoh then resided in a city, probably Zoan. See on Exod. i, 8.

CHAPTER X.

THE EIGHTH PLAGUE—LOCUSTS, 1-20.

1. **I have hardened his heart**—See on ix, 12, 13.

2. **And that thou mayest tell in the ears of thy son**—See instances of this in Psa. lxxviii and cvi.

4. **I bring the locusts into thy coast**—The destruction of all herbage by locusts is as complete as by fire over all the area which they cover, and they have been known to spread over from one to two thousand square miles. Their numbers and voracity are almost incredible. Indeed, it is said that they consume not merely from appetite, but from love of destruction, and not only vegetable and insect life, but cloth, leather, and even wood-work and furniture of houses. They rise from the horizon in immense columns, darkening the sun by their flight, filling the air with a whirring sound which is compared to the noise of fire or of distant wheels, and when driven in dense masses by winds into the sea, their decay emits a stench which spreads for many miles. In less than half a day they will crop grass and young grains even with the ground, leaving only the bare stalks of older plants, and in a very few hours will strip all trees clean of fruit, leaves, and bark. The noise of their browsing may be heard at quite a

EXODUS.

B. C. 1491

earth: and ƒ they shall eat the residue of that which is escaped, which remaineth unto you from the hail, and shall eat every tree which groweth for you out of the field: **6** And they ᵍ shall fill thy houses, and the houses of all thy servants, and the houses of all the Egyptians; which neither thy fathers, nor thy fathers' fathers have seen, since the day that they were upon the earth unto this day. And he turned himself, and went out from Pharaoh. **7** And Pharaoh's servants said unto him, How long shall this man be ʰ a snare unto us? let the men go, that they may serve the LORD their God: knowest thou not yet that Egypt is destroyed? **8** And Moses and Aaron were brought again unto Pharaoh: and he said unto them, Go, serve the LORD your God: but ² who *are* they that shall go? **9** And Moses said, We will go with our young and with our old, with our sons and with our daughters, with our flocks and with our herds will we go; for ⁱ we *must hold* a feast unto the LORD. **10** And he said unto them, Let the LORD be so with you, as I will let you go, and your little ones: look *to it;* for evil *is* before you. **11** Not so: go now ye *that are* men, and serve the LORD; for that ye did desire. And they were driven out from Pharaoh's presence. **12** And the LORD said unto Moses, ᵏ Stretch out thine hand over the land of Egypt for the locusts, that they may come up upon the land of Egypt, and ˡ eat every herb of the land, *even* all that the hail hath left. **13** And Moses stretched forth his rod over the land of Egypt, and the LORD brought an east wind upon the land all that day, and all *that* night; *and* when it was morning, the east wind brought the locusts. **14** And ᵐ the locusts went up over all

---

ƒ Chap. 9. 32; Joel 1. 4; 2. 25.——ᵍ Chap. 8. 3, 21.——ʰ Chap. 23. 33; Josh. 23. 13; 1 Sam. 18. 21; Eccles. 7. 26; 1 Cor. 7. 35.

2 Hebrew, *who, and who, &c.*——ⁱ Chap. 5. 1. ——ᵏ Chap. 7. 19.——ˡ Verse 4, 5.——ᵐ Psa. 78. 46; 105. 34.

---

distance as they approach, and after they have passed, the trees are reduced to naked trunks and stems. No language more appropriately describes this fearful visitation than that of the prophet Joel: "A fire devoureth before them, and behind them a flame burneth. The land is as the garden of Eden before them, and behind them it is a desolate wilderness...Like the noise of chariots on the tops of the mountains. ...Like the noise of a flame of fire that devoureth the stubble...They shall run like mighty men, they shall climb the wall like men of war...The sun and the moon shall be dark, and the stars shall withdraw their shining." Joel ii, 1–11. See the whole passage.

7. Pharaoh's servants said unto him—For the first time the courtiers of Pharaoh venture to plead with him, and for the first time he sends for Moses and Aaron after they have predicted the plague and gone forth to bring it upon the land. This shows how these judgments were more and more profoundly impressing the Egyptian people.

9. We will go with our young and with our old—Moses gives a full enumeration of those who must go forth to the feast and sacrifice, and it was simply what would be demanded in the worship of any people. Herodotus relates (ii, 60) that men, women, and children participated in the Egyptian festivals and religious processions, and that, according to the native reports, 700,000 often attended the annual festival at Bubastis, without reckoning the children. It was therefore but pretence when Pharaoh declared (v. 11) that he had supposed that men only were included in the request of Moses.

10. Let the Lord be so with you —This is language of scornful irony; "Jehovah will indeed be with you, when I let you go;" or, more exactly, "just as much with you as I shall let you go."

12. That they may come up— The locusts appeared like a low hanging cloud in the distance, which rose and spread till it covered the land.

13. An east wind—All travellers relate that the wind brings the locusts, but an east wind would have brought them from Arabia across the Red Sea, while the locusts usually come to Egypt from the south or southwest. But Denon (quoted by Knobel) describes a locust cloud which he witnessed coming from the east, producing great havoc in Egypt, and then driven back by a west wind, precisely like the one here mentioned. Niebuhr describes swarms of locusts coming upon Egypt in December and January, and Lepsius and

the land of Egypt, and rested in all the coasts of Egypt: very grievous *were they;* ⁿ before them there were no such locusts as they, neither after them shall be such. **15** For they ᵒ covered the face of the whole earth, so that the land was darkened; and they ᵖ did eat every herb of the land, and all the fruit of the trees which the hail had left: and there remained not any green thing in the trees, or in the herbs of the field, through all the land of Egypt. **16** Then Pharaoh ᵛ called for Moses and Aaron in haste; and he said, ᑫI have sinned against the LORD your God, and against you. **17** Now therefore forgive, I pray thee, my sin only this once, and ʳ entreat the LORD your God, that he may take away from me this death only. **18** And he ᵛ went out from Pharaoh, and entreated the LORD. **19** And the LORD turned a mighty strong west wind, which took away the locusts, and ᵗ cast them ᵘ into the Red Sea; there remained not one locust in all the coasts of Egypt. **20** But the LORD ᵛ hardened Pharaoh's heart, so that he would not let the children of Israel go.

21 And the LORD said unto Moses, ᵛ Stretch out thine hand toward heaven, that there may be darkness over the land of Egypt, ᵛ even darkness *which* may be

---

n Joel 2. 2.——*o* Verse 5.——*p* Psa. 105. 35.—— 3 Heb. *hastened to call.*——*q* Chap. 9. 27.—— *r* Chap. 9. 28; 1 Kings 13. 6.

s Chap. 8. 30.——4 Hebrew, *fastened.*——*t* Joel 2. 20.——*u* Chap. 4. 21; 11. 10.——*v* Chap. 9. 22.—— 5 Heb. *that* one *may feel darkness.*

Tischendorf describe them in March, closely corresponding to the time of this narrative as it is fixed by chap. ix, 31, 32. After the dreadful destruction by the hail this locust plague must have been fearfully calamitous. This was foreseen by Pharaoh's counsellors, who looked upon a locust visitation as the destruction of Egypt.

15. They covered the face of the whole earth—Literally, *the eye of the whole earth;* so that Egypt could not see sun or sky.

16, 17. Then Pharaoh called for Moses and Aaron in haste—This awful destruction humbles him to more earnest entreaty than ever before, and it seems to him that if "this death only" be removed, no more dreadful judgment can be inflicted by Jehovah.

19. A mighty strong west wind —Literally, *wind of the sea,* that is, the Mediterranean, which is west from Palestine, but northwest from the Egyptian Delta, which is the scene of this history. This wind would sweep the locusts into the Red Sea.

NINTH PLAGUE—DARKNESS, 21–29.

21. Stretch out thine hand toward heaven...darkness which **may be felt**—Literally, *and one shall feel darkness;* a fearfully-expressive figure. Moses raises his hand over Egypt for the last time, and a darkness falls which is the shadow of the death that draws nigh to every house in the doomed land. It was a fitting prelude to the final dreadful visitation, when Jehovah's messengers had retired from the scene, and himself went forth in the midnight judgment. For three days the pall of silence lay upon Egypt, and no one moved from his place, as if all awaited in terror the final stroke.

In this plague Jehovah revealed himself as the God of the Egyptian sun-god, the Ra, or Re, from whom Pharaoh and many of the Egyptian kings derived their names or titles; who was deemed the father of a whole order or rank of gods, and was worshipped especially at Heliopolis, or the City of the Sun. The obelisk of Egypt is the "finger of the sun"—the sunbeam in **stone.**

The above picture represents the Egyptian god Ammum-Ra enthroned,

felt. **22** And Moses stretched forth his hand toward heaven; and there was a "thick darkness in all the land of Egypt three days: **23** They saw not one another, neither rose any from his place for three days: ˣbut all the children of Israel had light in their dwellings. **24** And Pharaoh called unto Moses, and ʸsaid, Go ye, serve the Lord; only let your flocks and your herds be stayed: let your ᶻlittle ones also go with you.

25 And Moses said, Thou must give ⁶us also sacrifices and burnt offerings, that we may sacrifice unto the Lord our God. **26** Our cattle also shall go with us; there shall not a hoof be left behind; for thereof must we take to serve the Lord our God; and we know not with what we must serve the Lord, until we come thither. **27** But the Lord ᵐhardened Pharaoh's heart, and he would not let them go. **28** And

---

w Psa. 105. 28.——*x* Chap. 8. 22.——*y* Verse 8. *z* Verse 10.

6 Heb. *into our hands.*——*m* Verse 20; chap. 4. 21; 14. 4, 8.

---

and above him the sun, each ray ending in a hand, to denote his power over the world. In his right hand he holds the handled cross, the symbol of life; lotus flowers are before him, and a Theban king is worshipping him. The symbolic asp is on the king's forehead, and his name in the cartouch above.

22. And there was a thick darkness in all the land of Egypt three days—As all the plagues seem in some way connected with natural causes, this preternatural darkness is by many assigned to a sand-storm, such as accompanies the simoom or the. chamaseen, miraculously increased in intensity. Neither of these winds are ever known to produce so deep a darkness as is here described, though they obscure the sun and cause a twilight gloom. The **simoom**, or samoom, is a hot parching wind, raising clouds of dust and sand, which give the whole air a reddish-yellow tinge, and make the sun at first look like a globe of blood, and then blot it wholly from view. It is painfully suffocating both to man and beast while it lasts, but it is of short duration, especially if extremely hot and violent, generally passing within half an hour. The chamaseen, or khamsin, is less hot and violent, but lasts two or three days at a time, occurring at frequent intervals during a period of fifty days before and after the vernal equinox, that is, during March and the first of April, which corresponds well with the time of the plague of darkness. It darkens the sun with clouds of sand, which fill the air like a yellow fog, or like a heavy storm of snow or hail; men and beasts hide themselves while it rages, the inhabitants taking refuge in the innermost apartments or in subterranean vaults. The streets are deserted, as in the night, and all business ceases. But all these characteristics must have been supernaturally intensified to produce the effects described in the text. Both the simoom and the chamaseen are local, and very limited in range, so that such a wind might have blown up the Nile valley and left Goshen, in the eastern part of the Delta, untouched.

24. Go ye, serve the Lord—Now Pharaoh is willing that all the people should go, but insists that the flocks and herds should remain, as hostages for their return.

25, 26. Thou must give us also sacrifices—That is, Thou must allow our flocks and herds to go for sacrifice. Even up to this moment only a three days' journey into the wilderness was demanded; and a frank, fair compliance with Jehovah's will would have saved Pharaoh from destruction and Egypt from disgrace. Pharaoh's sin was no necessary link in the chain of God's providences; but the sin being in his heart, God used it for his glory.

CHAPTER XI.
INTRODUCTORY.

(1.) During the progress of these judgments, which occupied at least several months, there were, of course, constant interviews between Moses and the elders of Israel, and between them and the people, of which we have no account in the narrative, and there was a gathering and a marshalling of the people for the great decisive expedition towards which all these providences

B. C. 1491. CHAPTER X. 415

Pharaoh said unto him, Get thee from me, take heed to thyself, see my face no more; for in *that* day thou seest my face thou shalt die. 29 And Moses said, Thou hast spoken well, ⁿ I will see thy face again no more.

CHAPTER XI.

AND the LORD said unto Moses,

Yet will I bring one plague *more* upon Pharaoh, and upon Egypt; afterwards he will let you go hence: ᵃ when he shall let *you* go, he shall surely thrust you out hence altogether. 2 Speak now in the ears of the people, and let every man borrow of his neighbour, and every woman of her neighbour, ᵇ jewels of silver, and jewels of gold. 3 ᶜ And the

n Heb. 11. 27.——*a* Chap. 12. 31, 33, 39.——*b* Chap. 3. 22; 12. 35.——*c* Chap. 3. 21; 12. 36; Psa. 106. 46.

were leading them. The history has directed our attention chiefly to the leading actors, Moses and Pharaoh, but now, in the first three verses of this chapter, in order to make clear the following narrative, it glances back to events which were meanwhile transpiring in Israel. The first three verses are, then, parenthetical, and the account of Moses's final interview with Pharaoh, which commenced chap. x, 24, is then resumed, and finished chap. xi, 8. The last two verses of this chapter are retrospective of the whole history of these judgments.

(2.) Adam Clarke, following Kennicott, supposed that there are here several omissions in the Hebrew text which the Samaritan supplies. But the critical examination made by Gesenius has now so completely destroyed the authority of the Samaritan where it is not supported by the Hebrew, that the great expectations once entertained of essential revision of our received text from that Version may now be said to be completely dissipated. The Samaritan variations from the Hebrew are now almost universally admitted to be simply ignorant or meddlesome alterations. No one would see this more clearly than Dr. Clarke were he to write to-day.

TENTH PLAGUE PREDICTED, 1–10.

1. **And the Lord** (had) **said unto Moses**—This passage (verses 1–3) relates what God had previously said, and describes the influences under which the Egyptian people would be led to comply so readily with the request of the Israelites. It shows how ripe were events for the final scene, and is naturally inserted parenthetically here as showing why Moses had just said so decisively, "I will see thy face no more." The author also wished to show the fulfilment of the prophecy of chap. iii, 21, 22, concerning the spoiling of the Egyptians; and probably, also, to make it clear that he had not on his own authority, but by Jehovah's express direction, closed his interviews with Pharaoh, since he had already revealed that the tenth judgment stroke should be the last. **He shall surely thrust you out**—Literally, *When he shall let you go altogether, he will actually thrust you out hence.* He will no more attempt to retain the women and children, or the flocks and herds, as before, nor will he stipulate for your return at all, but will be anxious to be wholly rid of you.

2. **Let every man borrow**—שְׁאַל *ask, demand,* (*Septuagint, Vulgate, Luther, De Wette, Ewald, Knobel.*) See on chap. iii, 22. Of course the Egyptians could have expected no return of the gold and silver, when they urged them to go wholly out of the land. This was no "borrowing" or purloining, but these "spoils" were gifts obtained by moral constraint. The terror-stricken Egyptians were glad to give them anything so they would but go in peace. If this despoiling the Egyptians were not so particularly described we should find much difficulty in accounting for the quantity of gold and jewelry which we find in the possession of the Hebrews when they went out of servitude. A large amount of gold was used in the manufacture of the calf in Horeb; and, after this idol had been destroyed, we find the men and women bringing freewill offerings of "bracelets, and earrings, and (signet) rings, and tablets, (necklaces,) all jewels of gold," (Exodus xxxv, 22,) for the ornamentation and furnishing of the tab-

416 EXODUS. B. C. 1491

LORD gave the people favour in the sight of the Egyptians. Moreover, the man ᵈMoses *was* very great in the land of Egypt, in the sight of Pharaoh's servants, and in the sight of the people. 4 And Moses said, Thus saith the LORD, ᵉAbout midnight will I go out into the midst of Egypt: 5 And ᶠall the firstborn in the land of Egypt shall die, from the firstborn of Pharaoh that sitteth up- on his throne, even unto the **firstborn** of the maidservant that *is* behind the mill; and all the firstborn of beasts. 6 ᵍAnd there shall be a great cry through out all the land of Egypt, such as there was none like it, nor shall be like it any more. 7 ʰBut against any of the children of Israel ⁱshall not a dog move his tongue, against man or beast: that ye may know how that the LORD doth put

---

d 2 Sam. 7. 6; Esth. 9. 4.—*e* Chap. 12. 12, 23, 29; Amos 5. 17.—*f* Chapter 12. 12, 29; Amos 4. 10. *g* Chapter 12. 30; Amos 5. 17.—*h* Chapter 8. 22.—*i* Josh. 10. 21.

---

ernacle, whose beams were all plated with gold, and all whose vessels were gold. It would be hard to account for such an extraordinary amount of the precious metal in the possession of a nation just emerged from bondage were not this unusual means of supply set before us. It was fit that the oppressor who had so long luxuriated on their unrequited toil should repay; it was proper that they should go in festal attire to Jehovah's feast; and it was the crown of their triumph that the Egyptians willingly loaded them with their costly garments and jewels, freely bidding them go, and praying, Bless us also.

3. **And the Lord gave the people favour...the man Moses was very great in the land of Egypt**—At this crisis the Egyptians had become so panic-stricken that they gave the Israelites whatever they asked, and Moses, Jehovah's dread messenger, overwhelmed them with awe and terror. The author does not here refer to any moral or intellectual greatness of Moses, but simply to the impression which he had produced upon the Egyptians.

4. **And Moses said**—Unto Pharaoh, not unto Israel. The speech of chap. x, 25, 26, interrupted by the parenthesis of verses 1-3, is here resumed. **About midnight**—It is probable that the midnight following this interview is here meant, and that this was the fourteenth day of the month Nisan, when the Passover was afterwards celebrated in Israel. From chap. xii, 3, 6, we see that the paschal lamb was to be selected on the tenth and killed on the fourteenth of that month. The lamb might have been selected when the plague of darkness commenced, and during those three days that the Israelites alone had light in their dwellings they might have waited in solemn anticipation for the final stroke of deliverance, which on the fifteenth day set them free.

5. **And all the firstborn in the land of Egypt shall die**—Israel consecrated all its firstborn to God, and Egypt's firstborn were taken in wrath, as were Israel's in mercy. The firstborn is the flower, the glory, of the nation, and thus the choice victims were taken from all ranks of men and from all kinds of beasts. **The maidservant that is behind the mill,** *behind the two millstones.* Here the specified ranks are from the king to the maidservant, and in ch. xii, 29, from the king to the captive.

The handmill in common use in Egypt, as in the East, generally consists now, as then, of two round stones, from one and a half to two feet in diameter, the lower one being convex upon its upper surface, which fits into a corresponding concavity in the upper stone. The corn is dropped through a hole in the upper stone, which is revolved by means of an upright handle. It is usually worked by two women sitting on the ground, facing each other, with the mill between them, both holding the handle and pushing and pulling in alternation. See illustration at Matt. xxiv, 41. The Egyptians had also larger mills worked by asses or cattle.

6. **A great cry**—Awfully typical of that midnight cry which shall sound through all the earth: "Behold, the Bridegroom cometh!"

7. **Shall not a dog move his tongue**—The very dogs of Egypt shall respect the people before whom their masters cower in fear.

a difference between the Egyptians and Israel. 8 And ᵏall these thy servants shall come down unto me, and bow down themselves unto me, saying, Get thee out, and all the people ˡthat follow thee: and after that I will go out. And he went out from Pharaoh in ²a great anger. 9 And the LORD said unto Moses, ˡPharaoh shall not hearken unto you; that ᵐmy wonders may be multi-

k Chap. 12. 33.——1 Heb. *that is at thy feet;* so Judges 4. 10; 8. 5; 1 Kings 20. 10.——2 Heb. *heat*

8. **And all these thy servants shall come down unto me, and bow down**—Pharaoh and all his courtiers would be utterly paralyzed with terror, and humbly entreat the people whom they had crushed so long to depart in peace. **In a great anger**—As Jehovah's messenger, representing his judicial wrath.

9, 10. These verses review and recapitulate the whole series of judgments, recording the fulfilment of the prediction made when Moses was first commissioned. Chap. vii, 2, 3.

CHAPTER XII.
INTRODUCTORY.

The long travail has now ended, and the birth-hour of Israel has come. Every thing in the style of the narrative now shows that momentous events impend. The institution of the passover, which was the national birthday festival, is minutely related: first, the divine command being given at length, (verses 1–20,) and then the fulfilment of the command being detailed, (verses 21–28,) which involves a repetition of essential matters, though there are some additional particulars; then follows the last and most awful judgment stroke, and the Exode itself, from which the book derives its name; (verses 29–42;) and finally, at Succoth, the first camping place, Moses gives Israel a further ordinance concerning the participants of the passover. Every thing here shows the supreme importance of this passover institution. It is interwoven into the very substance of the history, and, including the further repetition of the next chapter, is described, ordained, and enforced in four different forms,

plied in the land of Egypt. 10 And Moses and Aaron did all these wonders before Pharaoh: ⁿand the LORD hardened Pharaoh's heart, so that he would not let the children of Israel go out of his land.

CHAPTER XII.

AND the LORD spake unto Moses and Aaron in the land of Egypt,

of anger.——*l* Chap. 3. 19; 7. 4; 10. 1.——*m* Chap. 7. 3.——*n* Chap. 10. 20, 27; Rom. 2. 5; 9. 22.

each bringing out special and important features, yet all involving the essentials of the ordinance. This, the great memorial feast of the Old Covenant, foreshadowing the one memorial feast of the New, typifies to the Christian consciousness the whole history of redemption, the sacrifice of the "Lamb without blemish," "slain from the foundation of the world," and the exodus of a redeemed race from the bondage of sin. The passover, which is the oldest of the Jewish festivals, has outlasted all the rest; and this alone has passed from the Old to the New Covenant, and, as the Supper of the Lord, commemorates now, how "Christ our Passover is sacrificed for us." See notes on Matt. xxvi, 2, 20–25.

The passover was also to Israel a sacrifice, an act of solemn consecration. The sprinkled blood set forth the desert of sin. The outward deliverance was fitly preceded by this inward consecration of the whole people to Jehovah. We are here carried back to the time when the temple had not yet been reared, nor the tabernacle set up, nor the priesthood consecrated: when each house was made a temple, each doorway an altar, and each father a priest. True national worship must ever begin at home.

INSTITUTION OF THE PASSOVER, AND COVENANT CONSECRATION OF ISRAEL, 1–28.

1. **The Lord spake**—*Had spoken,* just before this final announcement to Pharaoh. **In the land of Egypt**—The passover was the only feast ordained in Egypt. All the other ordinances were given in the wilderness of Sinai or in the plains of Moab.

saying, 2 *This month *shall be* unto you the beginning of months: it *shall be* the first month of the year to you. 3 Speak ye unto all the congregation of Israel, saying, In the tenth *day* of this month they shall take to them every man a ¹lamb, according to the house of *their* fathers, a lamb for a house: 4 And if the household be too little for the lamb, let him and his neighbour next unto his house take *it* according to the number of the souls; every man according to his eating shall make your count for the lamb. 5 Your lamb shall be ᵇ without blemish, a male ²of the first year: ye shall take *it* out from the sheep, or from the goats: 6 And ye shall keep it up until the ᶜ fourteenth day of the same month: and the whole assembly of the congregation of Israel shall kill

a Chap. 13. 4; Deut. 16. 1.——1 Or, *kid.*—— *b* Lev. 22. 19, 21; Mal. 1. 8, 14; Heb. 9. 14; 1 Pet.

1. 19.——2 Heb. *son of a year*, Lev. 23. 12.—— *c* Lev. 23. 5; Num. 9. 3; 28. 16; Deut. 16. 1, 6.

2. This month (Abib or Nisan) shall be **unto you the beginning** (*head*) **of months... first month of the year**—Hitherto the year had commenced with the month *Tisri*, (or September,) but henceforth the year was to be reckoned from *Abib*, the month of Israel's birth. *Abib* signifies "an ear of grain;" it was the month when barley ripened, corresponding with our close of March and beginning of April. The Hebrew months were lunar, and Abib was the month commencing with the new moon just after or just before the vernal equinox. This was the sacred year, by which the festivals were reckoned; but the civil or common year was still reckoned from Tisri. The passover was, then, instituted some time in the month of Israel's deliverance, but not after the final interview with Pharaoh described in the last chapter, since four days, inclusive, were to elapse after the choice of the lamb before the passover.

3, 4. In the tenth day—After this first passover there is no record of any instance where the lamb was selected before the fourteenth day. **A lamb for a house**—No special number is here mentioned as necessary to constitute the paschal company, but a Jewish tradition fixed ten as the least number, and, reckoning children, it probably averaged about twenty. It became a custom for each person to eat a piece of the lamb about the size of an olive, which would allow the paschal company to be quite large. An individual might not eat the passover alone. Thus was symbolized the fellowship of the Church in partaking of Christ.

5. Without blemish, a male of the first year—A faultless male, at least a year old. Only perfect gifts could be offered to God, as the heathens also felt. So Homer teaches us, (*Iliad*, i, 66,) ἀγνῶν . . . αἰγῶν τε τελείων, "perfect lambs and goats." The letter of the law allowed a kid, but a lamb was almost always chosen.

6. Until the fourteenth day—For three days, which were, as we suppose, the days of darkness in the land of Egypt, the devoted lamb was kept for the sacrifice—in each family the centre of prayerful and grateful meditations as they talked together of the great morning of deliverance that was about to dawn on them. **The whole assembly**—Each family in its own house, that the sacrifice might be simultaneous in all the land. **In the evening** —Literally, *Between the two evenings;* the time which was afterward specified for the evening sacrifice, Num. xxviii, 4, and described in Deut. xvi, 6, as the time of the "going down of the sun." The Rabbies understand that the first of the "two evenings" is when the sun begins to decline and the heat to decrease, or about three o'clock, and that the second is sunset, so that "between the two evenings" would be, at the fourteenth of Abib, between three and six. Kimchi, Rashi, and others, interpret the period of the declining sun as the first evening, and that of twilight as the second; so that the moment of sunset is the point "between the two evenings." Whichever view be adopted, " about sunset" is the time fixed, allowing some latitude on both sides, as became necessary afterwards when lambs were offered in the temple.

The Lamb of God was offered **at the** time of the paschal feast, and at the paschal hour, for " at the ninth hour," three in the afternoon, he " cried with

it ᵃin the evening. 7 And they shall take of the blood, and strike *it* on the two side posts and on the upper doorpost of the houses, wherein they shall eat it. 8 And they shall eat the flesh in that night, roast with fire, and ᵈ unleavened bread; *and* with bitter *herbs* they shall eat it. 9 Eat not of it raw, nor sodden at all with water, but ᵉroast *with* fire; his head with his legs, and with the purtenance thereof. 10 ᶠAnd ye shall let nothing of it remain until the morning; and that which remaineth of it until the morning ye shall burn

ᵃ Hebrew, *between the two evenings,* chapter 16. 12.—ᵈ Chapter 34. 25; Numbers 9. 11; Deuteronomy 16. 3; 1 Corinthians 5. 8.—ᵉ Deuteronomy 16. 7.—ᶠ Chapter 23. 18; 34. 25.

a loud voice, and gave up the ghost." Mark xv, 34, 37.

7. **They shall take of the blood**— Each doorway was made an altar, the lintel and side-posts of which were to be sprinkled with blood from a bunch of hyssop, (verse 22,) and thus was each person who entered consecrated. The blood was not dropped upon the threshold, lest it should be trodden under foot. This was the outward token of expiation and consecration which all the families of Israel were required to set upon themselves, as the outward sacraments are ordained in the Church of Christ; not that God needs to see these signs, but that we need to make them.

8, 9. **In that night**—The night following the sunset of the fourteenth of Nisan, or Abib. **Roast...not...raw,** (under-done,) **nor sodden** (boiled)—The lamb was to be roasted whole, not a bone broken, the entrails being cleansed and put back, and all the viscera, as heart, liver, etc., **(purtenance,** *inwards,*) included. Boiling would be liable to separate the members, but the typical wholeness of the lamb was an essential thing, as setting forth the oneness of the chosen people, and this was preserved in roasting. As they gathered about the table, the lamb was to symbolize to all who ate of it the spiritual oneness into which they were then by faith to enter. Thus says the Apostle, speaking of the Christian Passover, "We being many are one bread, and one body: for we are all partakers of that one Bread." 1 Cor. x, 17. The lamb was to be fastened to the spit, as afterwards the Lamb of God was fastened to the cross. Jahn says that it was transfixed upon two spits, the one lengthwise and the other crosswise, (*Arch.*, § 353,) and it is significant that the Samaritans at Nablous now fasten the lamb to a spit in the form of a cross. (Stanley's *Jewish Church*, lect. v.) Justin Martyr records that this was the Jewish usage. (*Dialogue with Trypho,* chap. xl.) Christ's body was preserved unbroken, as a symbol of the same unity of the members and the Head. See note on Matt. xxvi, 2. **Unleavened bread**—This specially symbolized three things: the haste in which they fled, not waiting for the bread to rise, (vers. 34 and 39;) their sufferings in Egypt, for such bread was called "bread of affliction," (Deut. xvi, 3;) but chiefly their purity as a consecrated nation, since fermentation is incipient putrefaction, and leaven was thus a symbol of impurity. **With bitter** herbs **they shall eat it**—A symbol of their bitter bondage. *On* (not "with") *bitter herbs* —That is, these, with the unleavened bread, were to constitute the basis, the chief part, of the supper, while a morsel of the lamb gave it flavour. The meal as a whole was a memento both of the "passing over" of the destroying angel, and of the bondage, while the savory accompaniment of the lamb's flesh commemorated their deliverance. It was also to be eaten as a feast, with cheerfulness and gratitude.

10, 11. **Let nothing of it remain**— It was sacred to this special use, and was not to be profaned. **Loins girded** —As the first passover was eaten in the last hours of their stay in Egypt, they must then have been all ready to leave, waiting for the final word. Usually they sat or reclined about the table, but now they were to stand on their feet. Their feet were always bare within the house, but now they were to be shod for the rough desert roads. Their long garments were usually loose as they sat at meals, but now they were to be girded up closely for a

420 EXODUS. B. C. 1491.

with fire. **11** And thus shall ye eat it; *with* your loins girded, your shoes on your feet, and your staff in your hand; and ye shall eat it in haste: ᶠit *is* the LORD's passover. **12** For I ʰ will pass through the land of Egypt this night, and will smite all the firstborn in the land of Egypt, both man and beast; and ⁱ against all the ʲgods of Egypt I will execute judgment: ᵏ I *am* the LORD. **13** And the blood shall be to you for a token upon the houses where ye *are:* and when I see the blood, I will pass over you, and the plague shall not be upon you ⁵to destroy *you,* when I smite the land of Egypt. **14** And this day shall be unto you ˡ for a memorial; and ye shall keep it a ᵐfeast to the LORD throughout your generations: ye shall keep it a feast ⁿby an ordinance for ever. **15** ᵒSeven days shall ye eat unleavened bread; even the first day

ye shall put away leaven out of your houses: for whosoever eateth leavened bread from the first day until the seventh day, ᵖthat soul shall be cut off from Israel. **16** And in the first day *there shall be* ᵍa holy convocation, and in the seventh day there shall be a holy convocation to you; no manner of work shall be done in them, save *that* which every ᵈman must eat, that only may be done of you. **17** And ye shall observe *the feast of* unleavened bread; for ʳin this selfsame day have I brought your armies out of the land of Egypt: therefore shall ye observe this day in your generations by an ordinance for ever. **18** ˢIn the first *month,* on the fourteenth day of the month at even, ye shall eat unleavened bread, until the one and twentieth day of the month at even. **19** ᵗSeven days shall there be no leaven found in your houses: for whosoever eateth that

---

g Deut. 16. 5.——*h* Chap. 11. 4, 5; Amos 5. 17.——*i* Num. 33. 4.——*j* Or, *princes,* chap. 21. 6; Psa. 82. 1, 6; John 10. 34.——*k* Chap. 6. 2.—— 5 Heb. *for a destruction.*——*l* Chap. 13. 9.—— *m* Lev. 23. 4, 5; 2 Kings 23. 21.——*n* Verses 24. 43; chap. 13. 10.

o Chap. 13. 6, 7; 23. 15; 34. 18, 25; Lev. 23. 5, 6; Num. 28. 17; Deut. 16. 3, 8; 1 Cor. 5. 7.——*p* Gen. 17. 14; Num. 9. 13.——*q* Lev. 23. 7, 8; Num. 28. 18, 25.——6 Heb. *soul.*——*r* Chap. 13. 3.——*s* Lev. 23. 5; Num. 28. 16.——*t* Exod. 23. 15; 34. 18; Deut. 16. 3; 1 Cor. 5. 7, 8.

---

long journey. Each was to have his travelling staff in hand, and to eat in haste. It is **the Lord's passover—** Here for the first time occurs the word פֶּסַח, *pesach,* well rendered by our word *passover,* as it sets forth the *passing over* the houses of Israel in the tenth judgment-stroke. Jehovah says, "When I see the blood, I will pass over you." So ever will the God of judgment pass over the soul marked with the blood of the spotless Lamb.

12. Against all the gods of Egypt I will execute judgment—See Introd. to the history of the plagues, (1.)

14. This day—The fourteenth of Abib, or Nisan, which was forever to be memorable as Israel's birthday. The day of the full moon in the "earmonth"—the full moon of the spring equinox, when nature begins her round once more—was ever to be the great national festival of Israel.

15. Seven days—Through the sacred cycle of days they were to learn the lessons taught by the "bread of affliction." **That soul shall be cut off—**Excommunicated from the sacred body, since such a soul cast off God's covenant with the covenant sign. The modern Jews make the unleavened bread in thin dry biscuits. They are exceedingly scrupulous to cleanse, at this time, the whole house, searching every dark corner with candles lest a crumb of leavened bread should anywhere be found when this feast begins. Great care is taken that all the vessels in which it is made be perfectly clean, and that it bake rapidly, lest the least fermentation take place.

16. Holy convocation—The first and seventh days were to be days of general assembly, in which no work but that of necessity should be done—sabbaths, when all the people should gather to hear the law, and to adore Jehovah, their Saviour, while they recounted to each other his mighty delivering mercies. This was the origin of the Jewish synagogue.

17. In this selfsame day have I brought your armies out—This was said before the deliverance was effected, and it is spoken of in the past as if already made sure. Thus the Hebrew preterit is often used in prophecy for an emphatic future. (Nordh., *Gram.,* § 966, 1, a.)

18–20. These verses repeat and emphasize the details of the ordinance.

which is leavened, ᵘeven that soul shall be cut off from the congregation of Israel, whether he be a stranger, or born in the land. **20** Ye shall eat nothing leavened; in all your habitations shall ye eat unleavened bread. **21** Then Moses called for all the elders of Israel, and said unto them, ᵛDraw out and take you a ⁷lamb according to your families, and kill the passover. **22** ʷAnd ye shall take a bunch of hyssop, and dip *it* in the blood that *is* in the basin, and ˣstrike the lintel and the two side posts with the blood that *is* in the basin; and none of you shall go out at the door of his house until the morning. **23** ʸFor the LORD will pass through to smite the Egyptians; and when he seeth the blood upon the lintel, and on the two side posts, the LORD will pass over the door, and ᶻwill not suffer ᵃthe destroyer to come in unto your houses to smite *you*. **24** And ye shall observe this thing for an ordinance to thee and to thy sons for ever. **25** And it shall come to pass, when ye be come to the land which the LORD will give you, ᵇaccording as he hath promised, that ye shall keep this service. **26** ᶜAnd it shall come to pass, when your children shall say unto you,

What mean ye by this service? **27** That ye shall say, ᵈIt *is* the sacrifice of the LORD's passover, who passed over the houses of the children of Israel in Egypt, when he smote the Egyptians, and delivered our houses. And the people ᵉbowed the head and worshipped. **28** And the children of Israel went away, and ᶠdid as the LORD had commanded Moses and Aaron, so did they.
29 ᵍAnd it came to pass, that at midnight ʰthe LORD smote all the firstborn in the land of Egypt, ⁱfrom the firstborn of Pharaoh that sat on his throne unto the firstborn of the captive that *was* in the ᵍdungeon; and all the firstborn of cattle. **30** And Pharaoh rose up in the night, he, and all his servants, and all the Egyptians; and there was a ᵏgreat cry in Egypt: for *there was* not a house where *there was* not one dead. **31** And ˡhe called for Moses and Aaron by night, and said, Rise up, *and* get you forth from among my people, ᵐboth ye and the children of Israel; and go, serve the LORD, as ye have said. **32** ⁿAlso take your flocks and your herds, as ye have said, and be gone; and ᵒbless me also. **33** ᵖAnd the Egyptians were urgent upon the people, that they might send

---

u Num. 9. 13.——*v* Verse 3; Num. 9. 4; Josh. 5. 10; 2 Kings 23. 21; Ezra 6. 20; Matt. 26. 18; Mark 14. 12; Luke 22. 7.——7 Or, *kid*.——*w* Heb. 11. 28,——*x* Ver. 7.——*y* Verses 12, 13.——*z* Ezek. 9. 6; Rev. 7. 3; 9. 4.——*a* 2 Sam. 24. 16; 1 Cor. 10. 10; Heb. 11. 28.——*b* Chap. 3. 8, 17.——*c* Chap. 13. 8, 14; Deut. 32. 7; Josh. 4. 6; Psa. 78. 6.

d Ver. 11.——*e* Chap. 4. 31.——*f* Heb. 11. 28.——*g* Chap. 11. 4.——*h* Num. 8. 17; 33. 4; Psa. 78. 51; 105. 36; 135. 8; 136. 10.——*i* Chap. 4. 23; 11. 5.——8 Heb. *house of the pit*.——*k* Chap. 11. 6; Prov. 21. 13; Amos 5. 17; James 2. 13.——*l* Chap. 11. 1; Psa. 105. 38.——*m* Chap. 10. 9.——*n* Chap. 10. 26.——*o* Gen. 27. 34.——*p* Chap. 11. 8; Psa. 105. 38.

---

21. Now follows the fulfilment of Jehovah's command by Moses. **Draw out and take**—*Withdraw;* go forth to your homes, and make ready the passover: so *Septuagint, Vulgate, Arabic, Keil, Knobel.* But *Gesenius, De Wette,* and others interpret *choose out,* or *lay hold of.*

22, 23. **Hyssop**—This has not been mentioned before. The hyssop included several species of herb, but that used in Egypt was, according to Kimchi and Maimonides, wild marjoram, an aromatic plant and condiment much used by the poorer classes in Egypt for food. **None of you shall go out at the door**—Only within the blood-besprinkled door was safety. **The destroyer**—Whether angel or pestilence, could not pass the line drawn in blood. Each sanctuary home in Israel was thus made a symbol of the fold whereof Christ is the door, and only behind his wounds can sinful man be safe from the *destroyer.*

24–27. The monumental character of this feast as a perpetual reminder of the supernatural origin of the nation, and as a means of education to all the generations of the people, is here minutely emphasised and enforced.

TENTH JUDGMENT STROKE, 29–36.

29, 30. And now arose the awful "midnight cry," as the flower of every house fell before the destroyer.

31–33. **And he called for Moses and Aaron by night**—Pharaoh had commanded them to see his face no more, but now an awful fear seized the monarch that the whole nation was to be destroyed, and he sent as an humble suppliant, beseeching Israel to depart, and take all their families, flocks, and herds. **And bless me also**—Pray Jehovah that no worse come upon me.

them out of the land in haste; for they said, ᵠWe *be* all dead *men*. 34 And the people took their dough before it was leavened, their ⁹kneading troughs being bound up in their clothes upon their shoulders. 35 And the children of Israel did according to the word of Moses; and they borrowed of the Egyptians ʳjewels of silver, and jewels of gold, and raiment: 36 ˢAnd the LORD gave the people favour in the sight of the Egyptians, so that they lent unto them *such things as they required:* and ᵗthey spoiled the Egyptians.

37 And ᵘthe children of Israel journeyed from ᵛRameses to Succoth, about ʷsix hundred thousand on foot *that were* men, besides children. 38 And ¹⁰a mixed multitude went up also with them; and flocks, and herds, *even* very

q Gen. 20. 3.——9 Or, *dough,* chap. 8. 3.——*r* Chap. 3. 22; 11. 2.——*s* Chap. 3. 21; 11. 3.——*t* Gen. 15. 14; chap. 3. 22; Psa. 105. 37.

u Num. 33. 3, 5.——*v* Gen. 47. 11.——*w* Gen. 46. 3; chap. 38. 26; Num. 1. 46; 11. 21.——10 Heb. *a great mixture,* Num. 11. 4.

34. Their kneading troughs being bound up in their clothes—The kneading troughs of the Egyptians were of wood, (see illustration under chap. viii, 3,) and so, perhaps, were those of the Israelites; but more probably they were mere leather bags, such as are now used by the Bedouins. By "clothes" is here meant the *simlah,* a square, shawl-like outer garment, like a Scotch plaid, used to wrap up small movables. From this and the thirty-ninth verse it will be seen that the unleavened bread had an historical as well as a symbolical meaning. There was not the usual time for dough to rise, even had it been leavened.

35, 36. See on chap. iii, 22, and xi, 2.

THE EXODE, 37–42.

37. **From Rameses to Succoth**—Probably not the treasure-city Rameses, or Raamses, mentioned chap. i, 11, but the district or province spoken of Gen. xlvii, 11, which is the same as Goshen, the border-land of Egypt toward Palestine. From all parts of the province they started, the families and tribes gradually gathering, concentrating in and around Succoth at the end of the first day. The name Succoth, which signifies *booths,* indicates that this was a mere temporary caravan or military station, though it may possibly have been a town named from such a station. We are to think of the people as falling into the host with their flocks and herds for the first two days, when they rallied behind the pillar of cloud at Etham, "in the edge of the wilderness." It seems most likely that their course for the first days lay along the Wady Tumeylat, which runs in an easterly direction towards the ancient bitter lakes. In this wady the Israelites were probably most thickly settled. From all parts of Rameses or Goshen there was a movement eastward through this rich valley in the heart of the province, along the line of the canal, which had the same general direction as the present Sweetwater Canal constructed by Lesseps. (See note on Goshen, Gen. xlviii, 6.) Although they are said to have started from Rameses, they did not get fairly beyond its limits till they passed Etham.

Some, following Sicard, have supposed that the Israelites took the ancient caravan route from the Nile due east to the Red Sea, along the Wady et Tih, which is shut in on the north and south by mountain ranges, and terminates in the broad plain of Baideah on the Gulf of Suez. The northern range is broken by a branch valley, twenty-three miles from the Nile, where is the only fountain in the wady, and it ends in the promontory of Ras Attakah, which stretches into the Gulf, twelve miles below Suez. (See map of Goshen.) But the northern route above described much better fits the requirements of the text. **Six hundred thousand**—This is given as the round number; by the census taken the next year in the wilderness of Sinai the actual number was six hundred and three thousand five hundred and fifty. Num. ii, 32. See further in Concluding Note.

38. **A mixed multitude**—Egyptians, who, in this time of popular excitement and commotion had become disaffected, unsettled, and a medley of adventurous spirits of

much cattle. **39** And they baked unleavened cakes of the dough which they brought forth out of Egypt, for it was not leavened; because ˣthey were thrust out of Egypt, and could not tarry, neither had they prepared for themselves any victuals. **40** Now the sojourning of the children of Israel, who dwelt in

ͣ Chap. 6. 1; 11. 1; verse 33.

various peoples, such as always follow an army or emigrating host. Egyptians and "strangers" are afterwards mentioned as living among the Israelites. From Numbers xi, 4, we see that the distrust of God's providence which led to the plague of Kibroth-hattaavah (*Graves of lust*) began among this heathen rabble, and from Deut. xxix, 11, it would seem that these "strangers" became hewers of wood and drawers of water for Israel. The Israelites had always continued to be a pastoral people, so that their property consisted mainly of flocks and herds.

39. Unleavened cakes — See on verse 8.

40. The sojourning of the children of Israel, who dwelt in Egypt — Or, as in Septuagint, *The sojourning which they sojourned.* This much-controverted passage forms one of the pivots of biblical chronology. The question is simply as to the point from which the four hundred and thirty years are to be reckoned. The Septuagint (Vatican Codex) has an important addition, and reads, "The sojourning of the children of Israel which they sojourned in Egypt *and in Canaan;*" while in the Alexandrian Codex there is still another addition, making it read, "which they *and their fathers* sojourned in Egypt *and in Canaan.*" Thus the Alexandrian translators of this book of Exodus (about 280 B. C.) clearly understood that this "sojourn" dated from Abraham's call, and included the time when the ",fathers" of **Israel,** Abraham, Isaac, and Jacob, "**sojourned in the Land of Promise as in a strange country,**" as well as the time of the bondage of their children in **Egypt.** The Samaritan has the same reading. (See Introd., (**2,**) chap. **xi.**) But the Hebrew text is without doubt correct, and these additions are to be understood as explanatory emendations by these translators, who wished to show how the three patriarchs might be included with the "children of Israel," and the sojourn in Canaan be united with that in Egypt. These translations have evidently only the authority of explanatory comments, and the question is, Do they correctly explain our text? Is the sojourning of the "fathers," Abraham, Isaac, and Jacob, in Canaan, included in *the sojourning of the children of Israel which they sojourned in Egypt?*

The first strong impression clearly is, that the text declares the *Egyptian* sojourn to have been four hundred and thirty years, for we have the phrase "which they sojourned in Egypt;" and "the children of Israel" only are spoken of. But we are to consider that the Hebrew idiom is much more pliant than ours in the use of terms. Fathers are included in children, as in Matt. xxiii, 35, "Ye slew;" and children in fathers, as in Heb. vii, 9, "Levi paid tithes in Abraham." The Hebrew race might have been freely styled the "children of Israel" from Abraham downwards, and the whole sojourning period of the race might have been in the writer's mind, though he specifies the most remarkable part of that period as peculiarly characteristic of it as a whole, *which they sojourned in Egypt.* That is, although they had also sojourned in Canaan, yet their Egyptian life, having been the epoch of God's remarkable providences in their behalf, gave the whole period character. This history, thus interpreted, is also well illustrated by the prophecy to Abraham, (Gen. xv, 13, 16,) "Thy seed shall be a stranger in a land that is not theirs, and shall serve them, and they shall afflict them four hundred years." Now this doubtless refers to the Egyptian bondage, yet, as shown in the notes on Exod. i, the real bondage or affliction did not begin till shortly before the birth of Moses, and so could not have lasted over eighty years. Yet

Egypt, *was* ʸfour hundred and thirty years. **41** And it came to pass at the end of the four hundred and thirty years, even the selfsame day it came to pass, that all ᶻthe hosts of the LORD went out from the land of Egypt. **42** It *is* ¹¹ᵃ a night to be much observed unto the LORD for bringing them out from the land of Egypt: this *is* that night of the LORD to be observed of all the children of Israel in their generations.

43 And the LORD said unto Moses and Aaron, This *is* ᵇthe ordinance of the passover: there shall no stranger eat thereof: **44** But every man's servant that is bought for money, when thou hast ᶜcircumcised him, then shall he eat thereof. **45** ᵈA foreigner and a hired servant shall not eat thereof. **46** In one house shall it be eaten; thou shalt not carry forth aught of the flesh abroad out of the house; ᵉneither shall ye break a bone thereof. **47** ᶠAll the congregation of Israel shall ¹²keep it. **48** And ᵍwhen a stranger shall sojourn with thee, and will keep the passover to the LORD, let all his males be circumcised, and then let him come near and keep it; and he shall be as one that is born in the land: for no uncircumcised

y Gen. 15. 13; Acts 7. 6; Gal. 3. 17.—*z* Chap. 7. 4; verse 51.—11 Heb. *a night of observations.*—*a* See Deut. 16. 6.—*b* Num. 9. 14.

c Gen. 17. 12, 13.—*d* Lev. 22. 10.—*e* Num. 9. 12; John 19. 33, 36.—*f* Verse 6; Num. 9. 13.—12 Heb. *do it.*—*g* Num. 9. 14.

this eighty years gives the character of "affliction" to the whole period. Now it is probable that the historical statement in our text spreads the Egyptian "sojourn" over the four centuries, just as the prophetic statement in Genesis does the Egyptian *bondage* and *affliction*. St. Paul expressly declares that the four-hundred-and-thirty-years period is to be reckoned from the covenant with Abraham. Gal. iii, 17.

If this be the correct view, then just one half of this period, or two hundred and fifteen years, was spent in the Egyptian sojourn. This may be thus seen: Abraham was seventy-five when he left Haran, (Gen. xii, 4,) and one hundred when Isaac was born, (Gen. xxi, 5,) and therefore from the call of Abraham to the birth of Isaac was twenty-five years. From the birth of Isaac to that of Jacob was sixty years, (Gen. xxv, 26,) and from the birth of Jacob to the descent into Egypt was one hundred and thirty, (Gen. xlvii, 9,) and so from the call of Abraham to the descent into Egypt was two hundred and fifteen years, since 25+60+130=215. The genealogy of Moses and Aaron, as given in Exod. vi, 16-20, points to the short period, or a sojourn of two hundred and fifteen years in Egypt, and we must suppose that several generations are omitted if the long period be taken, since four generations cannot be made to span four hundred and thirty years. This supposition is adopted by many, (Tiele, Kurtz, Keil, Thompson, etc.;) but all the events of the "bondage" can be brought within the short period, or two hundred and fifteen years. See Concluding Note.

41. The selfsame day—That is, on the very day after the passover and death of the firstborn, whose incidents are previously related—the fifteenth of Abib; not that it was four hundred and thirty years to a day since the sojourn commenced. The same phrase occurs in verse 51.

42. Observed of all the children of Israel in their generations—Israel was long ago scattered among the Gentiles; all the Levitical sacrifices have for centuries "ceased to be offered;" tabernacle and temple vanished ages ago; yet wherever in his wanderings a Jew retains to-day one shred of his ancestral religion he keeps the passover.

ADDITIONAL PASSOVER REGULATIONS, 43-50.

This additional ordinance, defining the character of the participants in the passover feast, now became necessary, since aliens and strangers of various nations attached themselves to Israel. Verse 38. Israel was called to be a blessing to all nations, and, therefore, aliens were not excluded from the covenant privileges if they would take upon them the covenant sign; but this was an essential condition. Transient settlers or labourers for wages were not to be admitted to the passover; but all who had become incor-

B. C. 1491.   CHAPTER XII.   425

person shall eat thereof. **49** [h] One law shall be to him that is homeborn, and unto the stranger that sojourneth among you. **50** Thus did all the children of Israel; as the LORD commanded Moses and Aaron, so did they. **51** [i] And it came to pass the selfsame day, *that* the LORD did bring the children of Israel out of the land of Egypt [k] by their armies.

[h] Num. 9. 14; 15. 15, 16; Gal. 3. 28.   [i] Verse 41.——[k] Chap. 6. 26.

rated into the families of Israel by marriage or by purchase (and who bore the covenant sign) became spiritually as well as outwardly one with the covenant people. Concerning Hebrew servitude see on Exod. xxi.

51. This verse, as a final summary, brings the account of the departure from Egypt to a formal close. **The selfsame day**—That is, the fifteenth of Abib, the momentous day whose events have just been related.

CONCLUDING NOTE.

Length of Sojourn in Egypt, and Census of Israel at the Exode. These two topics are so connected that it is convenient to discuss them together. Was the Egyptian sojourn a period of four hundred and thirty or of two hundred and fifteen years? In the note on verse forty the short period is favoured. Two things are specially relied upon by the advocates of the long period in proof of their view: (1,) The genealogy of individuals; (2,) The census of the Exode.

The genealogy is supposed to show that in some lines several generations have been omitted. (The genealogy of Moses is discussed in the note on Exodus vi, 20.) While Moses and Aaron are only the third generation from Levi, Dathan and Abiram the third from Reuben, (Num. xxvi,) and Achan the fourth from Judah, (Josh. vii,) Bezaleel is the sixth from Judah, (1 Chron. ii,) Elishama the eighth from Joseph, and Joshua the tenth from Joseph, (1 Chron. vii, 23–27.) Colenso presents these discrepancies as fatal objections to the authenticity of the history. But we may easily suppose Moses, when past his century, to have been contemporary with Bezaleel, who was of the same generation with his great-grandchildren, so that Elishama and Joshua give us the only real difficulty. But their genealogy is given in only one passage, (1 Chron. vii, 23–27,) which is on all hands confessed to be very obscure, and has probably been corrupted in transcription, so that it ought to have no decisive weight whatever, especially against passages of unmistakable clearness. Colenso, like his kin of all generations, ignores the clear to burrow in the obscure or unknown.

As to the census of Israel at the Exode, we are to consider that extraordinary fruitfulness is spoken of in Exod. i, 7, as it had been specially promised to the patriarchs. There were more than 600,000 men at the Exode, and these numbers would have been reached in two hundred and fifteen years if they continued to multiply as they commenced. This is proved thus: Jacob and his sons averaged five sons each, (not reckoning daughters at all in this calculation,) for he had twelve sons and fifty-three grandsons, (Gen. xlvi,) and $\frac{53+12}{13}=5$. Now if each man had, at the age of thirty-five, five sons, and had none born to him thereafter, we may reckon six generations in two hundred and fifteen years, since $\frac{215}{35}=6+$. To find, then, the number of Jacob's male posterity of the sixth generation we have $53 \times 5^6 = 53 \times 15,625$, or 828,125, a surplus of 200,000 over the number of the text. This calculation, moreover, makes no account of the survivors of previous generations.

The census of the Kohathites, given in Numbers iii, 28, is also presented by Tiele, Kurtz, Keil, etc., as an argument for the long chronology or for the omission of generations, since the four families of the Kohathites numbered 8,600, thus averaging 2,150 each, while one of the four, the Amramites, num-

CHAPTER XIII.

AND the Lord spake unto Moses, saying, 2 ᵃ Sanctify unto me all the firstborn, whatsoever openeth the womb among the children of Israel, *both* of man and of beast: it *is* mine. 3 And Moses said unto the people, ᵇ Remember this day, in which ye came out from Egypt, out of the house of ¹ bondage; for ᶜ by strength of hand the Lord brought you out from this *place:* ᵈ there shall no leavened bread be eaten. 4 ᵉ This day came ye out in the month Abib. 5 And it shall be when the Lord shall ᶠ bring thee into the land of the Canaanites, and the Hittites, and the Amorites, and the Hivites, and the Jebusites, which he ᵉ sware unto thy fathers to give thee, a land flowing with milk and honey, ʰ that thou shalt keep this service in this month. 6 ⁱ Seven days thou shalt eat unleavened bread, and in the seventh day *shall be* a feast to the Lord. 7 Unleavened bread shall be eaten seven days; and there shall ᵏ no leavened bread be seen with thee, neither shall there be leaven seen with thee in all thy quarters. 8 And thou shalt ˡ show thy son in that day, saying, *This is done* because of that *which* the Lord did unto me when I came forth out of Egypt. 9 And it shall be for ᵐ a sign unto thee upon thine hand, and for a memorial between thine eyes, that the Lord's law

---

a Verses 12-15; chap. 22. 29, 30; 34. 19; Lev. 27. 26; Num. 3. 13; 8. 16, 17; 18. 15; Deut. 15. 19; Luke 2. 23.—*b* Chap. 12. 42; Deut. 16. 3.— 1 Heb. *servants.*—*c* Chap. 6. 1.—*d* Chap. 12. 8.—*e* Chap. 23. 15; 34. 18; Deut. 16. 1.

f Chap. 3. 8.—*g* Chap. 6. 8.—*h* Chap. 12. 25. —*i* Chap. 12. 15, 16.—*k* Chap. 12. 19.—*l* Ver. 14; chap. 12. 26.—*m* See verse 16; chap. 12. 14; Num. 15. 39; Deut. 6. 8; 11. 18; Prov. 1. 9; Isa. 49. 16; Jer. 22. 24; Matt. 23. 5.

---

bered, *as far as the record shows*, only *two* men who could have been counted in the 8,600, since Aaron and his sons, and Moses himself, are not reckoned. But, (1,) The general calculation before given covers the whole ground. (2,) We have no right to assume that the record gives us all the Amramites. Amram may have had other children besides the famous historic three, and the argument from silence is always dubious. (3,) Still more dubious is the argument from averages to particulars. (4,) The other three families might have made up the lack of the Amramites, if lack there were. While these facts, given in the record itself, enable us to fully account for the numbers of Israel at the Exode, the objections of Knobel, Colenso, etc., are of no weight.

CHAPTER XIII.

Promulgation of the Law of the Firstborn, and of the Feast of Unleavened Bread, 1-16.

1, 2. In these verses Jehovah announces to Moses the law concerning the firstborn, and in verses 3-16 Moses repeats this law to Israel, and also repeats to them the law concerning the feast of unleavened bread which had been given to Moses before they started upon their march, as recorded in chap. xii, 15-20. The great importance of these two feasts, and of the law respecting the firstborn, which was so blended with the passover, led to the double mention of each—once as announced by Jehovah to Moses, and again as proclaimed by him to the people. The readers of Homer are familiar with such repetitions as characteristic of an early and simple style of narrative.

The firstborn males of man and beast were to be forever consecrated to Jehovah as a memorial through all generations of the final judgment-stroke which gave Israel freedom. Thus in their homes and in their daily toils were they to be perpetually reminded of the providence of Jehovah. The flower of the Egyptians were cut down for their deliverance, and the flower of their families, flocks, and herds, were to be devoted to God.

So the "Firstborn of all creation" (Col. i, 15) was sacrificed for our deliverance, "bruised for our iniquities," by the judgment-strokes which a guilty world invokes, and which he caught upon his own heart; and, in return, our firstborn, the choice of our homes, our substance, and our powers, are to be consecrated to God.

9, 10. Moses here repeats to Israel the ordinance concerning the feast of unleavened bread. See notes on chap. xii, 8, 15-20. **A sign unto thee upon thine hand, and for a memorial between thine eyes**—In verse sixteen

may be in thy mouth: for with a strong hand hath the LORD brought thee out of Egypt. 10 *Thou shalt therefore keep this ordinance in his season from year to year. 11 And it shall be when the LORD shall bring thee into the land of the Canaanites, as he sware unto thee and to thy fathers, and shall give it thee, 12 °That thou shalt ² set apart unto the LORD all that openeth the matrix, and every firstling that cometh of a beast which thou hast; the male *shall be* the LORD's. 13 And ᵖ every firstling of an ass thou shalt redeem with a ³ lamb; and if thou wilt not redeem it, then thou shalt break its neck: and all the firstborn of man among thy children ᵠ shalt thou redeem. 14 ʳAnd it shall be when thy son asketh thee ⁴ in time to come, saying, What *is* this? that thou shalt say unto him, ˢ By strength of hand the LORD brought us out from Egypt, from the house of bondage: 15 And it came to pass, when Pharaoh would hardly let us go, that ᵗ the LORD slew all the firstborn in the land of Egypt, both the firstborn of man, and the firstborn of beast: therefore I sacrifice to the LORD all that openeth the matrix, being males; but all the firstborn of my children I redeem. 16 And it shall be for ᵘ a token upon thine hand, and for frontlets between thine eyes: for by strength of hand the LORD brought us forth out of Egypt.

17 And it came to pass, when Pharaoh had let the people go, that God led them not *through* the way of the land of the Philistines, although that *was* near; for God said, Lest peradventure the people ᵛ repent when they see war, and ʷ they return to Egypt: 18 But God ˣ led the people about, *through* the way of the wilderness of the Red Sea: and the children of Israel went up har-

n Chap. 12. 14, 24.——*o* Verse 2; chap. 22. 29; 34. 19; Num. 8. 17; 18. 15; Deut. 15. 19.——2 Heb. *cause to pass over.*——*p* Chap. 34. 20; Num. 18. 15.——3 Or, *kid.*——*q* Num. 3. 46, 47; 18. 16. *r* Chap. 12. 26; Deut. 6. 20; Josh. 4. 6, 21.—— 4 Heb. *to-morrow.*——*s* Ver. 3.——*t* Chap. 12. 29. ——*u* Ver. 9.——*v* Chap. 14. 11, 12; Num. 14. 1-4. ——*w* Deut. 17. 16.——*x* Chap. 14. 2; Num. 33, 6, &c.

it is said for **frontlets between thine eyes** — That is, This command shall ever be before thee, in thy sight, and in the sight of all men, like the bracelet clasped upon the hand, or the fillet bound about the forehead. The law of Jehovah is to be the perpetual ornament and adornment of Israel. Thus is it to be kept **in thy mouth,** the constant theme of thought and word. In later and degenerate days, when the law had died out of the heart of Israel, a literal and carnal interpretation was given to this command, and portions of this chapter and of Deut. vi were written out on strips of parchment which were bound by leathern thongs upon the forehead and arm. These were the phylacteries; see illustration in note on Matt. xxiii, 5. Thus, as has often been the case, punctilious obedience to the letter of the law totally annulled its spirit.

11-16. Moses here repeats to Israel the law of the firstborn, given to him in verses 1, 2. As in the instance just given, there is here not a mere repetition, but an amplification and enforcement. The ass is mentioned as a representative of unclean animals, which could not be offered in sacrifice. This law for the redemption of an *unclean* by a clean animal was a temporary arrangement, while as yet the priesthood had not been ordained; but after the consecration of the Levites there was a fixed price of redemption. Lev. xxvii, 27. The ransom of the firstborn of man was afterwards fixed at five shekels, the tribe of Levi being taken for the service of the sanctuary instead of the firstborn of the other eleven tribes, man for man, and then the overplus of the firstborns being ransomed at this rate. Num. iii, 44-48.

MARCH FROM SUCCOTH TO ETHAM, 17-22.

17, 18. **God led them not** through **the way of the land of the Philistines**—The direct route to Palestine was northeast, by way of Pelusium and Gaza, along the Mediterranean coast, through the great maritime plain where dwelt the Philistines, whose warlike character we learn from the monuments of Rameses III., as well as from the Hebrew annals. By this route they started, as if to reach their destination in a few weeks' journey, but suddenly "turned" southeasterly, for **God led the people about,** *(made them turn,)* **by the way of the wilderness of the Red Sea**—See chap. xiv, 2. **Har-**

nessed⁵ out of the land of Egypt. **19** And Moses took the bones of Joseph with him: for he had straitly sworn the children of Israel, saying, ⁷ God will surely visit you; and ye shall carry up my bones away hence with you. **20** And ᶻthey took their journey from Succoth, and encamped in Etham, in the edge of the

5 Or, *by fives in a rank.*—*y* Gen. 50. 25; Joshua 24. 32; Acts 7. 16.—*z* Numbers 33. 6.

nessed—*Equipped* for march, marshalled in orderly array, not scattered like a mob of fugitives. Gesenius makes the word mean *brave, eager for battle,* and many of the old interpreters render, as in the margin, *five in a rank,* or *fivefold*—in five divisions. It is certain that afterwards we find the able-bodied men in five camps or battalions, (counting the Levites and the tabernacle as a division,) (Num. i, ii;) and they probably commenced their march in regular order, so as to protect the great train of women and children, flocks and herds. See diagram and notes on Num. ii.

19. And Moses took the bones of Joseph—Joseph's dying charge and Israel's solemn vow, made more than a century before, (Gen. 1, 24, 25,) are now sacredly remembered. His body had not been carried to the Land of Promise, like that of Jacob, nor buried in Egypt, like those of his brethren the fathers of the tribes, but, wrapped in its fragrant bandages, it waited the fulfilment of the patriarch's prophecy, "God will surely visit you, and ye shall carry up my bones from hence." Through all the years of their bondage the mummied form of their famous ancestor had been a perpetual prophecy and admonition. It ever held before their eyes the great promises made to Abraham, Isaac, and Jacob, and the sublime destiny that awaited Israel.

Only in Egypt would such a century-long "object-lesson" have been possible. The mummied form of the dead was there often kept for months, and sometimes for years, before final burial, in a closet made in the house for the purpose, with folding doors, and standing upon a sledge, so that it could be drawn to an altar where were offered "prayers for the dead." It was this idolatrous superstition which Moses so expressly forbade, Lev. xix, 28 and xxi, 1. It was, however, deemed a calamity for the dead to remain thus unburied unless there were especial reasons, which the friends were careful to have made known, and thus the fact that so eminent a person as Joseph remained unburied would give rise to constant inquiry and explanation. (Wilkinson's *Ancient Egyptians,* chap. x.) How wonderfully adapted was this act of Joseph to ensure the resurrection of Israel's life from the grave of Egyptian heathenism!

20. Etham, in the edge of the wilderness—The Wady et Tumeylat, through which the Israelites commenced their march, leads to the ancient Bitter Lakes, (now a swampy basin, which, except at the inundation, is a dry, deep, white salt plain,) and runs southeast towards Suez. Along the western (or rather southwestern) margin of this basin the Israelites moved, and reached Etham, probably on its southern border, a place on the line where the cultivable land ends and the desert begins. *Etham* is an Egyptian word, meaning, according to Chabas, the house or temple of Atum, "the setting sun," which was worshipped at Heliopolis. Du Bois Aymè identified Etham with Bir Suweis, "the well of Suez," where are now two deep wells of brackish water. Robinson placed it farther east, near the present head of the Gulf. It must have been not far from what was then the head of the Gulf. Travellers generally agree with Du Bois Aymè, (*Descr. de l'Egypte,* 11,371,) that the Gulf of Suez once extended much farther north, probably about fifty miles, joining the Bitter Lakes. Etham in that event would be much north of the present Suez.

It is often assumed that the Israelites reached Succoth at the end of the first day, and Etham at the end of the second, but the narrative hardly warrants this. These were the "encampments," but they may have halted more than a day at each, for the stations are nowhere said to have been a day's march apart. When we consider the hurry and confusion of the start—the vast

B. C. 1491. CHAPTER XIII. 429

wilderness. **21** And ᵃthe LORD went before them by day in a pillar of a cloud, to lead them the way; and by night in a pillar of fire, to give them light; to go by day and night. **22** He took not away the pillar of the cloud by day, nor the pillar of fire by night, *from* before the people.

a Chapter 14. 19, 24; 40. 38; Numbers 9. 15; 10. 34; 14. 14; Deuteronomy 1. 33; Nehemiah 9. 12, 19; Psalm 78. 14; 99. 7; 105. 39; Isaiah 4. 5; 1 Corinthians 10. 1.

population—of at least two millions—which was moved, taking up one portion after another on the march; and the immense number of cattle, sheep, and goats which were gathered together—it is not probable that they moved ten miles a day, nor that they marched each day successively. Yet some have so laid out the route as to necessitate a march of from thirty to fifty miles for three successive days! Fourteen miles is a usual day's march, and twenty-five miles a forced march, for a Prussian soldier in service, and here were women, and children, and cattle.

It seems probable that the Israelites followed about the line of the ancient Canal till they reached the Red Sea. When at Etham they were north of the Sea, and could from thence strike northeast direct to Palestine, or southeast along the east shore of the Sea to Sinai, by either route avoiding the Sea; but instead of being led on either of these courses, they were, to their surprise, commanded to "turn" down the west shore of the Sea, where they had Mount Attaka on the south and southwest, and the Sea on the east. Thus they appeared to Pharaoh to be "entangled in the land," or, rather, *bewildered*, perplexed in their movements. Chap. xiv, 3.

21. **And the Lord** (JEHOVAH) **went before them**—Here now, at Etham, as they enter the wilderness, JEHOVAH himself takes command of the host, and all their marches are supernaturally directed for forty years. Large caravans and armies were often guided in desert marches by a fire elevated in the van. An oft-quoted instance is that of the great army of Alexander, as related by Curtius:—"When he wished to move the camp he gave the signal by a trumpet, the sound of which was often not well heard because of the rising tumult. He therefore erected a pole over the imperial tent which could be every-where seen, from which the signal could appear to all at the same time. A fire was seen there by night and a smoke by day." (CURTIUS, *De Gest. Alex. Mag.*, v, 2, 7.) This on a small scale well illustrates what Jehovah now did for Israel. This vast host of at least two millions must often have been spread over several square miles, over the desert plains, up the mountain slopes, and along the wadies, or water courses, in search of pasturage, and they needed some signal that could be seen from far, and this was furnished by the lofty pillar of cloud and of fire. This seems to have been a fire within a cloudy envelope, shining brightly through it in the darkness, and giving it the appearance, in the sunshine, of a lofty column of light smoke or vapour. It rested afterwards upon the tabernacle, the fire then appearing as the SHEKINAH, (*dwelling-place* of Jehovah,) and it regulated by its movements all the marches of Israel. Exod. xl, 34-38.

As at the burning bramble Jehovah revealed himself to Moses by fire, so now by the same symbol he reveals himself to all Israel; a symbol suited to a people whose mission it was to teach the nations the real nature of God. Fire reveals power without form — power the most intense that we know, familiar yet mysterious. Considered as the source of both light and heat, it is an essential of life, genial and gladdening, yet the very emblem of terror and destruction; while at the same time it is the most expressive symbol of perfect purity. Thus the power and the wrath, the holiness and the mercy, of the formless, ever-living Jehovah, are all blended in this emblem. And what more perfect symbol is there of pure spirit, and of that Power whence all other powers spring, than that element or force which is all other material forces in disguise, and into which they all are resolvable?

VOL. I.—28 O. T.

III. THE VICTORY.
Israel's Victory. Chaps. XIV, 1-XV, 21.

CHAPTER XIV.
INTRODUCTORY.

In the Red (Reedy or Coral) Sea, the last remnant of the Egyptian bondage is now to be washed away. This sea, which was henceforth to be so famous in the history of Israel, was called both by Egyptians and Hebrews the "Sea of Reeds"—rushes or sedge—meaning, perhaps, the papyrus; and there are two places near the Gulf of Suez which are still called the "Bed of Reeds"—remnants, probably, of great fields of papyrus which flourished there of old. Pi-hahiroth, before which Israel next encamped, owes its name to the same famous plant, meaning "the place where the sedge grows." The origin of the name "Red Sea" is much disputed, some (Scaliger, Bochart) deriving it from the red sandstone cliffs of Edom, others (R. Stuart Poole, etc.) from the red race on its coasts, since the Arabs call themselves "the red men," in distinction from the white Caucasians, yellow Turanians, and black negroes; while others, with more probability, derive the name from the red coral reefs and sandstones in its bed. Only the last derivation accounts for its application by the classic writers to the adjacent Indian Ocean. Newbold speaks of the surface, when the rays of the sun fell upon it at a small angle, as "marked with annular, crescent-shaped, and irregular blotches of a purplish red, extending as far as the eye could reach. They were curiously contrasted with the beautiful aqua-marine colour of the water lying over the white coral reefs. This red colour I ascertained to be caused by the subjacent red sandstone and reddish coral reefs." (STANLEY'S *Sinai and Palestine*, p. 6, note.) These coral reefs fringe the shores, often to a width of fifty miles.

The Sea is more than thirteen hundred miles in length, from Suez to the Straits of Bab-el-mandel, and one hundred and ninety-two miles wide at the broadest part, under the seventeenth parallel of north latitude, whence it narrows pretty uniformly north and south, being seventy-two miles wide at Ras (or Cape) Mohammed, where it is cloven into the two gulfs, Suez and Akabah, by the great triangular wedge of the mountainous Sinai wilderness. It is the shores of these two northern gulfs or arms of the Sea which are famous in the history of Israel. The western arm, the Gulf of Suez or Heroöpolis, witnessed Israel's birth, as, somewhere within sight of what is now Suez, its divided waters were to the Hebrews a highway out of servitude and to the Egyptians a grave. The eastern arm, the Gulf of Akabah, saw the kingdom of Israel in its meridian glory, when the fleets of Solomon, manned by the sailors of Tyre, swept down along its steep shores to Indian or Arabian Ophir. This eastern gulf is the southern termination of the long, chasm-like valley in which lie the Dead Sea and the Jordan. It is a narrow, deep ravine, about one hundred miles long and sixteen broad, walled in by bare, precipitous mountains of red granite and black basalt, tipped here and there with sandstone, which rises in cliffs from one to two thousand feet high.

The Gulf of Suez, which is the Red Sea of the Exodus, is now about one hundred and eighty miles in length, and twenty in average width. It anciently, however, extended much farther north, probably reaching within historic times to Lake Timsah, with which it is now connected by the canal; but its northern extremity has receded, some think as much as fifty miles, in consequence of the rising of the land or the encroachment of the drifting sands of the desert. A large extent of country about the head of the Gulf, once comparatively fertile and populous, irrigated, as it was, abundantly from the Nile, has thus become an utter wilderness. Towns which were ports of the Pharaohs are now sand-covered ruins in the desert. At the present head of the Gulf, two miles north of Suez, there are extensive shoals, which at low tide are left bare and hard, reaching from one to two miles below the town, leaving only a narrow and winding channel, by which small vessels come up to Suez, while larger craft and steamers lie full two miles below. The tide rises five or six feet upon these shoals. Robinson was told that it reached seven feet, while Du Bois-Aymè (*Descrip. de l'Egypte*) calls it about two metres, (six and a half feet,) and says that after southern storms it rises to the height of twenty-six decimetres, or about eight and a half feet. There are fords above and below Suez, but Niebuhr and others have noted that the tide rises and falls so suddenly that there is great danger in crossing when it is near the flood. It is well known that in 1799 Napoleon Bonaparte and his suite came thus very near meeting the fate of Pharaoh when returning by this ford from Ayin Mousa to Suez, and that, too, when crossing under the guidance of natives. (*Descrip. de l'Egypte, Antiq. Mem.*, 8,118.)

The Gulf, as will be seen from the map, narrows suddenly at Suez, where it is only eleven hundred and fifty yards wide, while it is three or four miles wide at a short distance south, and twelve or fifteen miles wide just below Ras Attakah. There is a hard gravel plain, ten miles square, west of Suez, sloping from Ajrûd toward the Gulf, and reaching the hills of Attakah on the south. On this plain it is probable that the Israelites encamped *before Pi-hahiroth*, which was, most likely, an Egyptian garrison, and is now probably represented by the square fortress and deep bitter well of Ajrûd. The mountain range of Attakah runs from the Nile east to the Sea, terminating in the Ras or Cape Attakah, a promontory twelve miles south of Suez, but also skirting the Sea north of the Cape, so as to form a defile, along which runs a road, between Mount Attakah and the Sea, from Wady et Tih to Suez. South of Cape Attakah is the broad plain of Baideah, and south of this is another mountain chain running from the Gulf to the Nile. These two ranges are the northern and southern walls of the Wady et Tih, an ancient caravan route from Memphis to the Sea. The northern or Attakah range is broken by a branch of valley near the middle, along which another route runs from the main valley northeast to the head of the Gulf.

This description is, with the aid of the maps, sufficient to make clear the different routes suggested for the passage of Israel. Messrs. Pool, (*Smith's Dict.*,) Sharpe, (*Hist. of Egypt,*) and others, following Du Bois-Aymè, (*Descrip. de l'Egypte,*) suppose that the passage took place above the present head of the Gulf, some distance north of Suez; but most travellers consider that it was near Suez, or Baideah. If Baideah, they could have reached this plain from Etham, as above located, by a difficult march through the defile around the Promontory of Attakah, or by the branch valley above described, which would have taken them into the Wady et Tih, through which they would then have moved east to Baideah and the Sea. Sicard and Raumer, agreeing apparently with Josephus, supposed that the Israelites came from Latopolis, on the Nile, directly through the Wady et Tih to Baideah, and that the "turn" at Etham (Exod. xiv, 2) was leaving on the left the branch valley above mentioned, which would have taken them around the head of the Gulf. Baideah is a broad plain in the mouth of the wady or valley, with mountain walls on the north and the south, and with the Sea before it, so that if the Egyptians had blocked with a few troops the defile on the north, or left flank, of Israel, and closed up behind them on the west, they would certainly have been effectually hemmed in on all sides. In many respects this place precisely fits the Scripture requirements, and exactly suits Josephus's description of the position of Israel, shut "in the jaws of the mountains," so that many judicious travellers, as Sicard, Raumer, Shaw, Olin, and Kitto, have regarded it as the scene of the great deliverance.

But an insuperable difficulty seems to be that the Gulf is here about fifteen

CHAPTER XIV.

AND the LORD spake unto Moses, saying, 2 Speak unto the children of Israel, ᵃ that they turn and encamp before ᵇ Pi-hahiroth, between ᶜ Migdol and the sea, over against Baal-zephon: before it shall ye encamp by the sea. 3 For Pharaoh will say of the children of Israel, ᵈ They *are* entangled in the land, the wilderness hath shut them in.

4 And ᵉ I will harden Pharaoh's heart, that he shall follow after them; and I ᶠ will be honoured upon Pharaoh, and upon all his host; ᵍ that the Egyptians may know that I *am* the LORD. And they did so. 5 And it was told the king of Egypt that the people fled: and ʰ the heart of Pharaoh and of his servants was turned against the people, and they said, Why have we done this, that we

a Chap. 13. 18.——*b* Num. 33. 7.——*c* Jer. 44. 1. *d* Psa. 71. 11.——*e* Chap. 4. 21; 7. 8.

f Chap. 9. 16; verses 17, 18; Rom. 9. 17, 22, 23. *g* Chap. 7. 5.——*h* Psa. 105. 25.

miles wide, and it was certainly no narrower then. This is not, of course, too wide for the supernatural part of the transaction, but it is for the natural part—the march of the vast host of Israel, six hundred thousand men, with at least twice as many women and children, with wagons, herds, and flocks, and also of the Egyptian army, during the night after " the strong east wind " had " caused the sea to go back," and before the dawn of day. Fifteen miles is a good day's march for a well-appointed army. Hence Niebuhr, Robinson, Hengstenberg, Tischendorf, Stanley, Winer, and most modern travellers, regard Suez or its immediate vicinity as the scene of the passage. Murphy, (*Com. on Exod., in loc.,*) it is true, finds time for the march of the southern passage, by supposing that the women, children, and flocks went round the head of the Gulf; but few will be satisfied with the supposition in the absence of all proof from the record. The sea at Suez was, as above shown, wider then than now, and a passage of three or four miles, direct or diagonal, might there have been made from shore to shore, which could have been effected in the specified time, and here would also have been ample room for the overthrow of the Egyptian army. (Robinson, *Bib. Researches*, i, 56; Kurtz, *Hist. of Old Covenant*, ii, § 36.)

THE RED SEA DELIVERANCE, XIV.

2, 3. **That they turn and encamp before Pi-hahiroth**—The Hebrews were now at Etham, near the head of the Gulf, whence the direct route to Palestine would be northeast, by way of the plain of Philistia, and the route to Mount Sinai southeast, along the eastern shore of the Gulf; but instead of taking either of these direct routes to their destination, they turned southwest into the great plain west of the modern Suez, came down the west shore of the Gulf, and encamped north and east of Mount Attakah. Thus the Sea was in front and Mount Attakah on the right flank, and partially in the rear. When, then, the Egyptians came upon them from the northwest, either by the Bubastis or Belteis road, they seemed to be completely entrapped, especially if Pharaoh sent a small detachment around Mount Attakah to block the defile and thus cut off all retreat on the south. (See map of Goshen.) **Pi-hahiroth...Migdol... Baal-zephon**—These were all known places in the time of Moses, all traces of which seem to have been lost in the changes of these thousands of years, although the names are all suggestive of the localities. **Migdol**, *tower*, implies that this was a fortified spot, perhaps on one of the summits of Attakah; **Baal-zephon** (בַּעַל צְפֹן, *to watch*) was probably a frontier watch-tower, and the name **Pi-hahiroth**, if, as generally supposed, an Egyptian word meaning the " place of reeds," seems to have been a coast fortress or station. **They are entangled**—Probably the word is better rendered by *bewildered*. (Gesenius, De Wette, Knobel.) Their "turn" into this trap between the mountain and the sea seemed to arise from confusion and perplexity when they found themselves " on the edge " of the terrible desert. **The wilderness hath shut them in**—Literally, *closed upon them*, like a trap.

5. **Why have we done this?**— *What* (is) *this* (that) *we have done?*

CHAPTER XIV.

have let Israel go from serving us? 6 And he made ready his chariot, and took his people with him: 7 And he took ¹ six hundred chosen chariots, and all the chariots of Egypt, and captains over every one of them. 8 And the LORD ᵏ hardened the heart of Pharaoh king of Egypt, and he pursued after the children of Israel: and ˡ the children of Israel went out with a high hand. 9 But the ᵐ Egyptians pursued after them, all the horses and chariots of Pharaoh, and his horsemen, and his army, and overtook them encamping by the sea, beside Pi-hahiroth, before Baal-zephon. 10 And

when Pharaoh drew nigh, the children of Israel lifted up their eyes, and, behold, the Egyptians marched after them; and they were sore afraid: and the children of Israel ⁿ cried out unto the LORD 11 °And they said unto Moses, Because *there were* no graves in Egypt, hast thou taken us away to die in the wilderness? wherefore hast thou dealt thus with us, to carry us forth out of Egypt? 12 ᵖ *Is* not this the word that we did tell thee in Egypt, saying, Let us alone, that we may serve the Egyptians? For *it had been* better for us to serve the Egyptians, than that we should die in the wilder-

---
i Chap. 15. 4.——*k* Verse 4.——*l* Chap. 6. 1; 13. 9; Num. 33. 3.——*m* Chap. 15. 9; Josh. 24. 6.   *n* Josh. 24. 7; Neh. 9. 9; Psa. 34. 17; 107. 6. *o* Psa. 106. 7, 8.——*p* Chap. 5. 21; 6. 9.

The panic having subsided, Pharaoh's hard heart rises in rage and revenge. The pride and obstinacy of Pharaoh may appear incredible, but this representation of his character is in perfect harmony with the pictures of the Egyptian kings, as they have themselves left them upon the walls of their tombs. The magnificent engravings in the great works of Lepsius and of the artists of Napoleon spread before our eyes pictures of the conquests, coronations, and deifications of these Pharaohs, as they may now be seen in their rock-hewn tombs, from the Delta to the Cataracts—perpetual monuments of their haughty might and heaven-defying pride, as well as vast and enduring commentaries upon this narrative of Moses. (See Introduction to the History of the Plagues, 1.)

6. **He made ready his chariot**—Horses and chariots are first represented in the monuments of Amosis, (1520 B. C.,) although there is evidence of their use before that time. The chariot was two-wheeled, without back or seat, bottomed with a network of thongs, whose elasticity supplied the lack of springs: it was drawn by two horses, which were harnessed, without traces, to a pole fastened to a yoke resting upon the withers. The spear-case, bow-case, and quiver were fastened at the side, and it was manned by a driver and one or two warriors, who stood as they rode.

7. **Six hundred**—This was a picked chariot force, and Josephus adds, from traditional sources, that there were fifty thousand horsemen and two hundred thousand footmen. The word "all" is not to be taken absolutely, as if every chariot in Egypt was in the pursuit. See note on Exod. ix, 6. **Captains**—Literally, *third men*, one of three, because the chariot was sometimes manned by three.

8. **With a high hand**—Openly and defiantly; but how their courage failed when they saw Pharaoh's chariots!

9. **All the horses** and **chariots of Pharaoh**—Rather, the *chariot horses*. Three kinds of troops are mentioned, cavalry, chariotry, and infantry.

10-12. **Cried out unto the Lord**—In terror, but not in faith. **Because** there were **no graves in Egypt**—*No graves at all;* words that had a special pathos in the mouths of a people who had been bred in a land renowned for the vastness and grandeur of its sepulchres. The royal cemetery of Memphis stretched more than sixty miles along the Nile, and among its monuments now stands the loftiest and most massive work that man's hand ever reared. The Theban tombs are magnificent palaces of the dead. To lie unburied after death was deemed in Egypt to be one of the greatest of calamities, and the Israelites had doubtless an Egyptian horror of having their bodies scattered over the desert. **Better for us to serve the Egyptians**—Cowardly despair. But it should be remembered they had been degraded by bondage, and the masters before whom they had cowered so long were full in sight with horses and chariots.

ness. **13** And Moses said unto the people, ᵠFear ye not, stand still, and see the salvation of the LORD, which he will show to you to day: ¹for the Egyptians whom ye have seen to day, ye shall see them again no more for ever. **14** ʳThe LORD shall fight for you, and ye shall ˢhold your peace. **15** And the LORD said unto Moses, Wherefore criest thou unto me? speak unto the children of Israel, that they go forward: **16** But ᵗlift thou up thy rod, and stretch out thine hand over the sea, and divide it: and the children of Israel shall go on dry *ground* through the midst of the sea. **17** And I, behold, I will ᵘharden the hearts of the Egyptians, and they shall follow them: and I will ᵛget me honour upon Pharaoh, and upon all his host, upon his chariots, and upon his horsemen. **18** And the Egyptians

q 2 Chron. 20. 15, 17; Isa. 41. 10, 13, 14. —1 Or, *for whereas ye have seen the Egyptians to day*, &c.—*r* Verse 25; Deut. 1. 30; 3. 22; 20. 4; Josh. 10. 14, 42; 23. 3; 2 Chron. 20. 29; Neh. 4. 20; Isa. 31. 4. —*s* Isa. 30. 15.—*t* Verses 21, 26: chap. 7. 19.—*u* Ver. 8; chap. 7. 3.—*v* Ver. 4.

13. Stand still, and see the salvation of the Lord—Moses rises to the height of the occasion; his faith is mighty, but he cannot see how salvation is to come.

15. Wherefore (or *what*) **criest thou unto me**—No prayer is recorded, but this is the reply to the inward struggle—to the "groanings that cannot be uttered"—in which the soul of Moses then travailed with Israel's birth. He is told that the answer to his prayer is ready, and *that* he has but to prepare to receive: — "Advance and accept deliverance!" **Go forward**— *Decamp*, break up and march. This seemed like madness, but it was God's command.

16. Lift thou up thy rod... divide it—Prayer is thus said to effect what God effects in answer to prayer when it is inspired by him. The rod was but the symbol of the divine-human power.

17. I will get me honour— Namely, by their complete overthrow in such manner that it shall be manifest to all that "the Lord is the man of war" who accomplishes this destruction. **Chariots...horsemen.** (See cut on p. 85.) The cut on this page, from a Theban tomb, represents the different kinds of Egyptian infantry, with their arms.

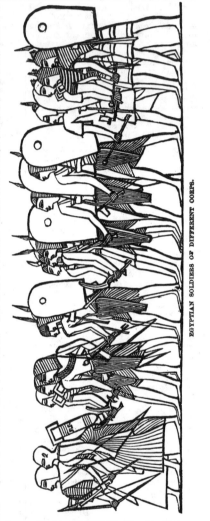

EGYPTIAN SOLDIERS OF DIFFERENT CORPS.

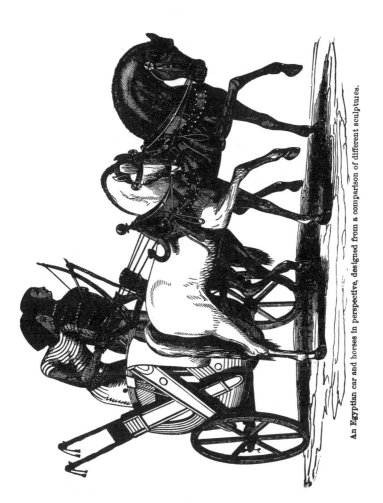

An Egyptian car and horses in perspective, designed from a comparison of different sculptures.

436 EXODUS. B C. 1491.

*shall know that I *am* the LORD, when I have gotten me honour upon Pharaoh, upon his chariots, and upon his horsemen. 19 And the Angel of God, ˣ which went before the camp of Israel, removed and went behind them; and the pillar of the cloud went from before their face, and stood behind them: 20 And it came between the camp of the Egyptians and the camp of Israel; and ʸ it was a cloud and darkness *to them,* but it gave light by night *to these:* so that the one came not near the other all the night. 21 And Moses ᶻ stretched out his hand over the sea; and the LORD caused the sea to go *back* by a strong east wind all that night, and ᵃ made the sea dry *land,* and the waters were ᵇ divided. 22 And ᶜ the children of Israel went into the midst of the sea upon the dry *ground:* and the waters *were* ᵈ a wall unto them on their right hand, and on

w Verse 4.——∞ Chap. 13. 21; 23. 20; 32. 34; Num. 20. 16; Isa. 63. 9.——*y* See Isa. 8. 14; 2 Cor. 4. 3.——*z* Verse 16.——*a* Psa. 66. 6.——*b* Chapter 15. 8; Josh. 3. 16; 4. 23; Neh. 9. 11; Psa. 74. 13; 106. 9; 114. 3; Isaiah 63. 12.——*c* Verse 29; chap. 15. 19; Numbers 33. 8; Psalm 66. 6; 78. 13; Isaiah 63. 13; 1 Corinthians 10. 1; Hebrews 11. 29.——*d* Hab. 3. 10.

19, 20. **The Angel of God**—That is, the manifestation of God in the pillar of cloud and fire. See Exod. iii, 2, 6. The pillar gave light to Israel, so that they could see how to direct their march, while at the same time it hid their movements from the Egyptians, and, as it was spread between the armies, perhaps seemed to Pharaoh's host simply like the natural darkness of the night.

21, 22. **And the Lord caused the sea to go** back **by a strong east wind all that night**—Here, as in the history of the plagues, natural causes are declared to have been supernaturally used. A northeast wind, which would be called " an east wind " in Hebrew, would tend to drive the water out of the narrow bay towards the southwest, and if transpiring at the time of an ebb tide, might be strong enough to blow the channel dry. If there were shoals or flats at the place of crossing, as there now are near Suez, and deeper water to the north, as there now is, a pathway might thus be made across the Gulf, leaving deep water above and below. It will be noticed that this was soon after the full moon of the vernal equinox, when there would be a very low ebb and a very high flood, and that the tide rises from five to seven feet opposite Suez, and from eight to nine feet when aided by strong winds, returning with unusual suddenness and power after the ebb. (See Introductory remarks.) The Hebrew and heathen traditions of this wonderful deliverance all make it probable that all these natural causes were employed to answer the prayer of Moses. In Moses'

song of triumph the waters are said to have been "gathered together" by the "blast of the nostrils" of Jehovah. He also sang, "Thou didst blow with thy wind, the sea covered them," (chap. xv, 8, 10;) thus assigning the return as well as the division of the waters to the agency of the wind. So in many places God is said to have "dried up the waters of the Red Sea," as if by wind. Josh. ii, 10; Psa. lxvi, 6; cvi, 9. [Different minds will assign different degrees of the supernatural to the transaction. But, (1.) The movements of Israel by divine orders were prescribed, and to these the blowings of the wind were precisely timed, measured, and even changed from east to west. (2.) The two armies were long in such proximity that Israel could have easily been destroyed had not Pharaoh been deterred and blinded by the "pillar." (3.) The ordinary tidal action of the sea must have been better known to Pharaoh and his generals than to Israel. That the whole should have been so ᵉexecuted as to save all Israel and destroy all the Egyptians is unaccountable on merely natural assumptions. See note on Josh. x, 12.]

The waters were a wall unto them on their right hand, and on their left—That is, they were a *defense,* not necessarily perpendicular cliffs, as they are often pictured. God could make the water stand in precipices if he should so choose, and such a conception is more impressive to the imagination; but it is certain that the language of the text may mean simply that the water was a *protection* on the right and on the left flanks of the hosts

B. C. 1491. CHAPTER XIV. 437

their left. **23** And the Egyptians pursued, and went in after them to the midst of the sea, *even* all Pharaoh's horses, his chariots, and his horsemen. **24** And it came to pass, that in the morning watch *the LORD looked unto the host of the Egyptians through the pillar of fire and of the cloud, and troubled the host of the Egyptians, **25** And took off their chariot wheels, ²that they drave them heavily: so that the Egyptians said, Let us flee from the face of Israel; for the LORD ᶠfighteth for them against the Egyptians. **26** And the LORD said unto Moses, ᵍStretch out thine hand over the sea, that the waters may come again upon the Egyptians, upon their chariots, and upon their horsemen. **27** And Moses stretched forth his hand over the sea, and the sea ʰreturned to his strength when the morning appeared; and the Egyptians fled against it; and the LORD ⁱ ³overthrew the Egyptians in the midst of the sea. **28** And ᵏthe waters returned, and ˡ covered the chariots, and the horsemen, *and* all the host of Pharaoh that came into the sea after them; there remained not so much as one of them. **29** But ᵐthe children of Israel walked upon dry *land* in the midst of the sea: and the waters *were* a wall unto them on their right hand, and on their left. **30** Thus the LORD ⁿsaved Israel that day out of the hand of the Egyptians; and Israel ᵒsaw the Egyptians dead upon the sea shore.

e See Psalm 77. 17, &c.——2 Or, *and made them to go heavily.*——*f* Ver. 14.——*g* Ver. 16. *h* Joshua 4. 18.——*i* Chapter 15. 1, 7.——3 Hebrew, *shook off;* Deuteronomy 11. 4; Nehemiah 9. 11; Psalm 78. 53; Hebrew 11. 29.——*k* Habakkuk 3. 8, 13.——*l* Psalm 106. 11.——*m* Verse 22; Psa. 77. 20; 78. 52, 53.——*n* Psalm 106. 8, 10.——*o* Psalm 58. 10; 59. 10.

Thus in Nahum, (iii, 8,) No (Thebes) is said to have the sea (the broad Nile) for a *rampart* and *wall;* that is, a *defense*, a protection against enemies. It is true that in poetical passages the waters are said to have stood "as a heap;" Exod. **xv**, 8; Psa. lxxviii, 13; but so they are also, in the same style, said to have been "congealed in the heart of the sea;" and the peaks of the trembling Horeb are said to have "skipped like rams," and the "little hills like lambs." Psa. cxiv, 4. Of course these expressions are not to be literally and prosaically interpreted. Yet it will be noticed that upon our view the waters were heaped up by the wind, though we do not believe that they stood in parallel precipices. But see note on Josh. iii, 13.

24. In the morning watch—In New Testament times, the Jews divided the night into four watches, but in the Old Testament history mention is made of three only: the first, or "beginning of the watches," from sunset to ten P. M., (Lam. ii, 19;) the "middle watch," from ten P. M. to two A. M., (Judges vii, 10;) and the morning watch, from two A. M. to sunrise. It was, then, after two o'clock in the morning when the cloud, that had hung like a black curtain over and before the Egyptians, opened, and Jehovah "looked upon them" through his lightnings. Thus the Psalmist describes the scene. To appreciate its awfulness to the Egyptians we must remember that thunder and lightning are extremely rare in Egypt, and that the fearful grandeur of our thunderstorms is there wholly unknown. " *The clouds streamed water,* the *skies lifted up their voice, yea, thine arrows* (thunderbolts) *flew. The voice of thy crash rolled round,* (like a chariot in heaven;) *lightnings illumined the world; trembled and shook the earth.*" Psa. lxxvii, 17, 18.

25. Took off their chariot wheels—Their chariots were entangled with each other, bemired, broken, and overturned in the awful confusion that ensued from the pouring rains, blinding lightnings, and appalling thunders. Yet this was but a premonition of what awaited them when **the sea returned to his strength.**

27. When the morning appeared—*At the turning of the morning*—approach of dawn. Then the entanglement of the bemired chariots and horses, the changing wind, which blew the blinding rain and spray directly into the faces of the Egyptians, now struggling towards their own shore, and the darkness, intensified by the lightnings, all conspired with the waters, suddenly returning in their overwhelming might, to make their destruction complete.

30, 31. The Egyptians dead upon the sea shore—The western wind and

31 And Israel saw that great [4]work which the LORD did upon the Egyptians: and the people feared the LORD, and [p] believed the LORD, and his servant Moses.

[4] Heb. *hand.*—*p* Chap. 4. 31; 19. 9; Psa. 106. 12; John 2. 11; 11. 45.

the returning tide strewed the eastern shore with men and horses, chariots and armour. Josephus says: "On the next day Moses gathered together the weapons of the Egyptians which were brought to the camp of the Hebrews by the current of the sea and the force of the winds assisting it." (*Antiq.*, ii, 16, 6.) Thus might the Israelites have obtained arms for the battles afterwards described with the desert tribes and the Canaanites. **Thus the Lord saved Israel that day**—Israel ever remembered this day and this event as the beginning of their national life. Reminiscences of the Red Sea deliverance are interwoven with all their literature, worship, and social life. Profane history has also preserved unmistakable traditions of this great event. Diodorus Siculus (iii, 39) relates that the inhabitants along the shore of the Sea have a tradition that it was once left dry by a great ebb tide, so that the bottom appeared. Artapanus relates (*Euseb.*, *Præp. Evang.*, ix, 27) that the inhabitants of Memphis said that Moses led the hosts through the Red Sea during an ebb tide, while the inhabitants of Heliopolis said that Moses, when chased by the king, divided the Sea with his rod, but that when the Egyptians followed after them fire flashed upon them and the waters rolled back and destroyed them. In the language of Ewald, this is an event "whose historical certainty is well established, and its momentous results ...are even to us distinctly visible." (*Hist. of Israel*, ii, 75.) It is not surprising that men who refuse to admit the supernatural anywhere attempt to explain the Red Sea deliverance as a fortuitous coincidence of natural events. Obstinate unbelief can resolve all answers to prayer into happy accidents. No amount of evidence can demonstrate the supernatural to him who lacks spiritual insight. No miracle can compel conviction like a mathematical demonstration, for the proof of divine activity is addressed to the moral and not to the intellectual man. The grandest miracle recorded in history, the resurrection of the Son of God, did not convince all who witnessed it, for "some doubted." If unbelief were not always possible faith would not be a rewardable virtue, and it is this faith that goes with Israel **that great work which Jehovah did upon the Egyptians.**

CHAPTER XV.
INTRODUCTORY.

(**1.**) Moses, like Solon, was a poet as well as a lawgiver. He not only wrote history, law, precept, and prophecy, but embalmed them in inspired song. Thus the divine truth which was to be translated by Israel to all ages was not only fastened upon their understanding, reason and conscience, but was interwoven with emotion, passion, and imagination. Israel exhaled the first breath of national life in a glad burst of song. The fervour of their national and religious emotions was poured forth, in the desert, in solemn and triumphant chants whenever they struck their tents in the morning, or pitched them at evening. When in the morning the cloud rose heavenward from the Sacred Tent all Israel chanted,

Rise, JEHOVAH, and scattered be thine enemies,
And let the foes flee from before thy face;

and when at night it returned and rested, they sang,

Return, JEHOVAH, to the ten thousand thousands of Israel. Num. x, 34-36.

The song which Moses taught all Israel at the close of his mission, (Deut. xxxii,) the lyric blessing of the tribes, (Deut. xxxiii,) and the ninetieth Psalm, "the prayer of Moses the man of God," show the same grand poetic powers which are displayed in this chapter. David's poetry is pre-eminent for its wonderful beauty and sweetness; it has a matchless spiritual pathos which unlocks all hearts; yet it is, as says Campbell, in joyous expression that the power of David's genius is best seen.

But Moses excels in solemn grandeur and majesty. The Psalm in which David touches the highest sublime caught its inspiration from the ancient poet-lawgiver, and opens with his morning chant of the desert: Psalm lxviii.

There are brief snatches of poetry throughout the book of Genesis. The blessing of Jacob is a prophetic ode; but this is the earliest lyric in literature. It seems, however, probable that there were poets of the sojourn who sang the praise of EL SHADDAI, GOD ALMIGHTY, in Egypt, whose hymns have never reached us; for this magnificent poem could hardly be the first flower of the lyric literature of the nation.

(2.) The characteristics of Hebrew poetry will more properly receive attention in the Introduction to the Book of Psalms; and here we simply remark that, as Lowth has long ago shown, it is a waste of time and effort to attempt here the application of the rules of metre which have been drawn from the Grecian and Roman models. Rhyme, measure, regularity in accents, in number, and quantity, are not here to be found. Parallelism is the special characteristic of the form of Hebrew poetry. This consists simply in correspondences of sound or sense between successive lines, phrases, or words, so that the sentiments are reinforced by repetition, comparison, and contrast. Yet while the same sentiment is poured forth again and again, as in successive waves, there is great conciseness and vigour in the separate expressions. It is impossible to do justice to this conciseness in translation, although our Anglo-Saxon compares well with the Hebrew in this characteristic. No great poem can be adequately translated, since form is essential in poetry; but the Hebrew poetry appears at a special disadvantage in another language, since it is made up so largely of monosyllables and dissyllables, which explode like volcanic bursts or break like waves upon a rock. The sonorous gutturals and aspirates are broken into feeble fragments in translation, and the terse phrase or word, which strikes like a thunderbolt, is attenuated into a limping line. Every great poem must be read in the original language to be appreciated; and the poetry of Moses and David will amply repay any man of taste for the acquisition of Hebrew.

(3.) The three criteria of Milton can be well applied to the Song of Moses. It is simple, sensuous, passionate:—simple, for the words are transparent to the sentiments, which appeal to elemental and universal feelings; sensuous, for the imagery flashes the ideas to the soul through the senses; passionate, for every word is a flame. But, above all, religion is its inspiration. First and midst and last is JEHOVAH. Not Moses, not Israel, but JEHOVAH is the "hero of war." Verse 3. *I will sing to Jehovah!* is the proem; *Sing to Jehovah!* is the perpetual refrain; and the grand chorus bursts from the great host at last, JEHOVAH SHALL REIGN FOR EVER AND EVER!

This song may be analyzed into seven divisions: five stanzas or strains, a chorus, which with a slight change is also the proem or introductory strain, and the grand chorus. The men probably chanted the successive strains, Miriam and the women responding in the chorus with voice and timbrel, and all uniting in the grand chorus.

The proem gives the theme—the glory of Jehovah in the destruction of the Egyptians. The five strains present the theme in five aspects, or reach it by five different paths of association: (1,) by extolling the might of Jehovah; (2,) the same in apostrophe; (3,) by triumphing over enemies; (4,) by triumphing over heathen gods; (5,) by prophesying future victories. Each of the first four strains closes by relating in different tropes and epithets the Red Sea overthrow, and the fifth terminates appropriately in the rest of Canaan. It will be noticed that the first strain is descriptive and in the third person; but, as the bard's spirit rises, the second strain mounts into apostrophe, which is maintained to the end. Thus the ode rolls on in five successive waves, each returning in the refrain, and all rolling up together in the grand final chorus.

CHAPTER XV.

THEN sang *Moses and the children of Israel this song unto the LORD, and spake, saying, I will ^bsing unto the LORD, for he hath triumphed gloriously: the horse and his rider hath he thrown into the sea. 2 The LORD *is* my strength and *song, and he is become my salvation: he *is* my God, and I will prepare him ^da habitation; my *father's God, and I ^fwill exalt him. 3 The LORD *is* a man of *war: the LORD *is* his ^hname. 4 ⁱPharaoh's chariots and his host hath he cast into the sea: ^khis chosen captains also are drowned in the Red Sea. 5 ^lThe depths have covered them: ^mthey sank into the bottom as a stone. 6 ⁿThy right hand, O LORD, is become glorious in power: thy right hand, O LORD, hath dashed in pieces the enemy.

PROEM. (*By the whole Congregation.*)
1. I will sing unto JEHOVAH, for he is most glorious,
   The horse and his rider hath he thrown into the sea.

I. THE GLORY OF JEHOVAH. (*Male Voices.*)
2. My might and my song (is) JAH, and he became to me salvation;
   This is my God, and I will glorify him,
   The God of my father, and I will exalt him.
3. JEHOVAH, the hero of war, Jehovah (is) his name.
4. The chariots of Pharaoh and his host he shook into the sea;
   The flower of his knights sank in the Sea of Rushes.
5. Abysses covered them;
   They went down into the depths like a stone.

CHORUS. (*Female Voices and the whole Congregation.*) See verse 21.

II. APOSTROPHE TO JEHOVAH.
6. Thy right hand, Jehovah, (is) glorious in might;
   Thy right hand, Jehovah, crusheth the enemy.

a Judges 5. 1; 2 Sam. 22. 1; Psa. 106. 12.—*b* Verse 21.—*c* Deut. 10. 21; Psa. 18. 2; 59. 17; 62. 6; 118. 14; 140. 7; Isa. 12. 2; Hab. 3. 19.—*d* Gen. 28. 21; 2 Sam. 7. 5; Psa. 132. 5. *e* Chap. 3. 15, 16.—*f* Psa. 118. 28; Isa. 25. 1.—*g* Psa. 24. 8; Rev. 19. 11.—*h* Chap. 6. 3; Psa. 83. 18.—*i* Chapter 14. 23.—*k* Chapter 14. 7.—*l* Chap. 14. 28.—*m* Neh. 9. 11.—*n* Psa. 118. 15, 16.

SONG OF MOSES AND MIRIAM, 1–21.

Following the text of the authorized version we give the song, translated as literally as our idiom will allow, and divided as before indicated. The chorus followed each strain. The stanzas are in couplets, triplets, and quatrains.

1. **Most glorious**—That is, perhaps, as well as our English can do with the terse, alliterative נָאֹה נָאָה, which swelled like a thousand trumpets in every repetition of the chorus. **The horse and his rider**—To be taken collectively, cavalry and chariotry.

2–5. *First strain.* **JAH**—A poetic abbreviation of JAHVEH, restricted in use to the higher kinds of poetry, and found often in compound names, as *Yirm'jah,* (Jeremiah;) also in certain formulas, as *Hallelu-jah,* (Praise ye Jah.) **This is my God**—A gesture here directs the hearer heavenward. **The God of my father**—*Father* is taken collectively, bringing up to view the patriarchs, the covenants made with Abraham, Isaac, and Jacob. It was as their God that Jehovah spoke to Moses from the burning bramble. This is a double strain, of two quatrains, or four-line stanzas. Parallelisms of thought and expression, such as are described in the Introduction, will be noticed in the first three lines of the first quatrain, the fourth line proclaiming in simple grandeur JEHOVAH as the hero of this victory. So in the second quatrain the lines of the first couplet are parallel with each other, and then those of the second also, in both instances rising in climax. Similar parallels are readily traced throughout the ode.

6–8. *Second strain.* Now the poet breaks out into a bold apostrophe to Jehovah. Here are seven lines in two couplets and one triplet, rising in climax from a declaration of his power to a description of its manifestation at the Red

B. C. 1491. CHAPTER XV. 441

7 And in the greatness of thine °excellency thou hast overthrown them that rose up against thee: thou sentest forth thy wrath, *which* ᵖconsumed them ᵠas stubble. 8 And ʳwith the blast of thy nostrils the waters were gathered together, ˢthe floods stood upright as a heap, *and* the depths were congealed in the heart of the sea. 9 ᵗThe enemy said, I will pursue, I will overtake, I will ᵘdivide the spoil; my lust shall be satisfied upon them; I will draw my sword, my hand shall ¹destroy them. 10 Thou didst ᵛblow with thy wind, ʷthe sea covered them: they sank as lead in the mighty waters. 11 ˣWho *is* like unto thee, O LORD, among the ²gods? who *is* like thee, ʸglorious in holiness, fearful *in* praises, ᶻdoing wonders? 12 Thou stretchedst out ᵃthy

7. In the greatness of thy majesty thou castest down thy foes
Thou sendest forth thy wrath—it devours them like stubble.
8. At the blast of thy nostrils heave the waters,
Rise like a heap the floods,
Stiffen the depths in the heart of the sea.   CHORUS. (Verse 21)

III. TRIUMPH OVER THE ENEMY.
9. Said the enemy: I will chase; I will seize;
I will divide spoil; sated shall be my lust,
I will bare my sword; my hand shall clutch them.
10. Thou didst blow with thy breath—covered them the sea,
Sank they like lead in the mighty waters.   CHORUS. (Verse 21.)

IV. TRIUMPH OVER HEATHEN GODS.
11. Who like thee among the gods, Jehovah?
Who like thee, glorious in holiness,
Fearful in praises, doing wonders?

---

o Deut. 33. 26.—p Psa. 59. 13.—q Isa. 5. 24; 47. 14.—r Chap. 14. 21; 2 Sam. 22. 16; Job 4. 9; 2 Thess. 2. 8.—s Psa. 78. 13; Hab. 3. 10.—t Jud. 5. 30.—u Gen. 49. 27; Isa. 53. 12; Luke 11. 22.

1 Or, *repossess*.—v Chap. 14. 21; Psa. 147. 18.—w Chap. 14. 28.—x 2 Sam. 7. 22; 1 Kings 8. 23; Psa. 71. 19; 86. 8; 89. 6; Jer. 10. 6.—2 Or, *mighty ones*.—y Isa. 6. 3.—z Psa. 77. 14.—a Ver. 6.

Sea, first in plain language, and then in tropes which steadily rise in fervour and boldness. **Blast of thy nostrils** —Sublime imagery for the "strong east wind" which God made to blow "all that night." **Rise like a heap... stiffen**—The waters are poetically painted as solid masses, heaped up like walls. Habakkuk sang in a yet bolder strain: *The deep lifted up his voice,* (and) *raised his hands on high.* Hab. iii, 10.

9, 10. *Third strain.* Now the enemy is personified, and his boasts and threats are dramatically pictured in six terse, strong phrases, all compressed into ten nervous words, which our translation has broken up into twenty-five! In successive flashes it reveals the Egyptian host, proud, confident, fierce, eager for their prey, dashing on their chase through the darkness into the cloven sea; and then the closing couplet paints once more the waters returning at the blast of Jehovah's breath. **Like lead**—So Homer, *Iliad,* xxiv, 80:

"She, (Iris,) like the lead, plunged to the abyss."

11-13. *Fourth strain.* Now Jehovah is compared with the imaginary gods of the heathen. **Who like thee among the gods, Jehovah**—This is four words in Hebrew, whose initials stand thus, מכבי, which, it is said, were inscribed as a motto upon the banner of the Maccabees, giving them their name. Ewald doubts this derivation, (since *Maccabi* is spelled with a ק,) but it is poetically true, for here is the flame whence that family of heroes caught their fire. (See *Apocrypha, Books of Maccabees.*) So also the names *Micha* and *Michael* signify, "Who is like God?" **Holiness**—This is the distinguishing attribute of Jehovah among the imperfect and sinful deities created by man's imagination. **Fearful in praises**— Fearful because of the awful judgments which call forth these praises. The first triplet of this strain is an apostrophe setting forth Jehovah's attributes

442 EXODUS. B. C. 1491.

right hand, the earth swallowed them. 13 Thou in thy mercy hast ᵇled forth the people *which* thou hast redeemed: thou hast guided *them* in thy strength unto ᶜthy holy habitation. 14 ᵈThe people shall hear, *and* be afraid: ᵉsorrow shall take hold on the inhabitants of Palestina. 15 ᶠThen ᵍthe dukes of Edom shall be amazed; ʰthe mighty men of Moab, trembling shall take hold upon them; ⁱall the inhabitants of Canaan shall melt away. 16 ᵏFear and dread shall fall upon them; by the greatness of thine arm they shall be *as* still ˡas a stone; till thy people pass over, O LORD, till the people pass over, ᵐ*which*

12. Thou stretchedst forth thy right hand, the earth swallowed them.
13. Thou leddest in thy mercy the people thou hast redeemed:
 Thou guidest (them) in thy might to thy holy habitation.

CHORUS. See verse 21.

V FUTURE TRIUMPH.

14. Listen (the) nations, (and) tremble;
 Terror seizes the dwellers in Palestina.
15. Then are confounded the dukes of Edom;
 The princes of Moab, trembling takes hold of them;
 Melt away all the inhabitants of Canaan:
16. There falls upon them horror and trembling.
 By the greatness of thy arm they shall be still as a stone,
 Till thy people pass through, JEHOVAH;
 Till pass through the people which thou hast redeemed.

b Psa. 77. 15, 20; 78. 52; 106. 9; Isa. 63. 12, 13; Jer. 2. 6.——*c* Psa. 78. 54.——*d* Num. 14. 14; Deut. 2. 25; Josh. 2. 9, 10.——*e* Psa. 48. 6.——*f* Gen. 36. 40.——*g* Deut. 2. 4.——*h* Num. 22. 3; Hab. 3. 7. *i* Josh. 5. 1.——*k* Deut. 2. 25: 11. 25; Josh. 2. 9.——*l* 1 Sam. 25. 37.——*m* Chap. 19. 5; 2 Sam. 7. 23; Psa. 74. 2; Isa. 43. 1, 3; 51. 10; Jer. 31. 11; Titus 2. 14; 1 Peter 2. 9; 2 Peter 2. 1.

against those of the heathen gods; the second returns once more to the deliverance of his people, and gliding in the last line into the prophetic strain which follows. The Red Sea deliverance being the pledge of grander things in store for Israel, the inspired bard now turns away from the past, and is borne forth into the future on the long, final wave of the song.

14–17. *Fifth strain.* The Egyptians were conquered, but other foes yet lay between the Israelites and the promised inheritance. The Canaanites filled the land, and Philistia barred one gate of entrance, while Moab and Edom held the other. It is a noteworthy mark of the genuineness of this prophecy that Canaan and Philistia, Edom and Moab, are all spoken of in the same terms; yet, while the Canaanites were exterminated, Israel passed by Edom, (Num. xx, 18, etc.,) while Moab and Philistia were rival nations through all the centuries of the Hebrew commonwealth and monarchy. A poet would naturally have written thus at the time of the exodus, when he had simply the general revelation that Israel would triumph over all these enemies; but after the conquest of Canaan some distinction would naturally have been made between nations which were exterminated and those which never lost their independence.

The theme of this last stanza is introduced with wonderful boldness and vigour, hurling out the words without article or connective. **Palestina**—*Palestuth,* Philistia; the meaning of the word Palestine or Palestina throughout the Bible. This was the dwelling-place of the Philistines, the long, fertile plain, about fifteen miles wide, which skirts the Mediterranean from the coast to the foot-hills of the mountains of Judah, and now, as probably then, an enormous wheat field. The name was afterwards extended to the whole of Canaan. Note Acts viii, 40. **Edom**—Idumea, Mount Seir, and the adjacent desert; the mountainous and desert country east of the Arabah, stretching from the head of the eastern gulf of the Red Sea to the Jordan valley; separated by the brook Zered from **Moab,** which skirts the eastern shore of the Dead Sea. **Till thy people pass through**—Through

B. C. 1491.   CHAPTER XV.   443

thou hast purchased. **17** Thou shalt bring them in, and ⁿ plant them in the mountain of thine inheritance, *in* the place, O LORD, *which* thou hast made for thee to dwell in; *in* the ᵒ sanctuary, O Lord, *which* thy hands have established. **18** ᵖ The LORD shall reign for ever and ever. **19** For the ᑫ horse of Pharaoh went in with his chariots and with his horsemen into the sea, and ʳ the LORD brought again the waters of the sea upon them; but the children of Israel went on dry *land* in the midst of the sea. **20** And Miriam ˢ the prophetess, ᵗ the sister of Aaron, ᵘ took a timbrel in her hand; and all the women went

17. Thou shalt bring them and plant them in the mount of thine inheritance,
The place of thy dwelling (which) thou hast made, JEHOVAH,
The sanctuary, Lord, (which) thy hands have established.

GRAND CHORUS. (*By the whole Congregation.*)
18. JEHOVAH SHALL REIGN FOR EVER AND EVER.

n Psa. 44. 2; 80. 8.——*o* Psa. 78. 54.——*p* Psa.10. 16; 29. 10; 146. 10; Isa. 57. 15.——*q* Chap. 14. 23; | Prov. 21. 31.——*r* Chap. 14. 28, 29.——*s* Judg. 4. 4; 1 Sam. 10. 5.——*t* Num. 26. 59.——*u* 1 Sam. 18. 6.

the desert to the Land of Promise. The strain closes with a beautiful parallelism and climax. **Thou shalt..plant them in the mountain**—Israel, like a fruitful tree, is to be planted in God's mountain-land, God's dwelling-place, God's sanctuary, country, home, altar. (*Murphy.*) How calm the close! How delightful to repose under the vine and fig tree, to rest in the peaceful home, to cling to the sacred altar, after this tempest of emotions! And then from the whole congregation bursts forth the grand chorus, **Jehovah shall reign for ever and ever**—And the hearts of the vast host are all lifted heavenward and left before the Throne.

The saints on "the sea of glass" will sing the "song of Moses the servant of God, and the song of the Lamb." Rev. xv, 3. The birth-song of ransomed Israel is, in its deeper meanings, the birth-song of the spiritual Israel of all ages—of the great redemption from the darkness and death of sin. The profound and far-reaching spiritual significance of these Old Testament events will be fully felt when "God's mystery is finished;" when type and antitype, prophecy and history, law and gospel, will blend in one blaze of light. Christ is in all the Old Covenant as Moses is in all the New; the "Song of Moses" is the "Song of the Lamb." "The word is nigh" us, though it comes to us across so many centuries, for it is a word from Jehovah, and not to Israel alone, but to mankind—to me and thee.

19. This verse is not a part of the song, but repeats the incident that was its occasion.

20. **Miriam the prophetess**—Miriam, or *Mariam*, the Greek and Latin *Maria*, and the English *Mary*. Thus the Mother of our Lord bore the name of the prophetess of the Exodus, who is numbered by the prophet Micah (VI, 4) with Moses and Aaron as one of the deliverers of Israel. **Sister of Aaron**—The Scriptures nowhere speak of her marriage, and she seems to have held an independent position as sister of the high priest and of the leader of Israel. Josephus, however, says that she was the wife of Hur, and grandmother of the tabernacle architect, Bezaleel. (*Antiq.*, iii, 2, § 4, and 6, § 1.) **Timbrels**—*Tabrets*, tabours, or tambourines. Probably this was the same instrument which is now used by the modern Egyptians—a small, shallow drum, made by stretching a skin upon a hoop, about eleven inches in diameter. LANE says: "The hoop is overlaid with mother of pearl, tortoise shell, white bone or ivory, both without and within, and has ten double circular plates of brass attached to it.... It is held by the left or right hand, and beaten with the fingers of that hand, and by the other hand: the fingers of the hand which holds the instrument, striking only near the hoop, produce higher sounds than the other hand, which strikes in the center."—*Modern Egypt*, ii, p. 76. See, also, notes on

out after her ʷwith timbrels and with dances. 21 And Miriam ˣanswered them, ˣSing ye to the LORD, for he hath triumphed gloriously: the horse and his rider hath he thrown into the sea.

CHORUS TO EACH STRAIN.
21. Sing unto Jehovah, for he is most glorious,
The horse and the rider hath he thrown into the sea.

v Judges 11. 34; 2 Sam. 6. 16; Psa. 68. 11, 25; 149. 3; 150. 4.——*w* 1 Sam. 18. 7.——*x* Verse 1.

1 Sam. x, 5, and 2 Sam. vi, 5. **Dances** —Some render the word *guitars*.
21. **Miriam answered**—That is, she led in these words the chorus or refrain. See on verse 1.

Here closes the first division of the Book of Exodus. Israel has now *gone forth*, and, with the Sea behind and the Desert before, begins her career as a NATION.

DIVINE ADOPTION OF ISRAEL.
CHAPS. XV, 22—XL, 38.

I. PREPARATORY PERIOD.
March from the Red Sea to Sinai. First Contact with Friends and Foes in the Desert. XV, 22–XVIII, 27.

CHAPTER XV, 22–27.
INTRODUCTORY.

The Wilderness of Shur. Shur signifies *a wall*, and is certainly perfectly applicable to the long, white, flat-topped limestone wall of the Jebel (Mountain) or Rahah, which now stretched along the left flank of the host of Israel as they faced towards Sinai. This mountain range ran southeast, far beyond the limit of their vision, thus giving name and character to the wilderness, which is here an undulating gravelly plain, twelve to fifteen miles wide between this white wall and the blue waters of the Gulf of Suez. It is also called "the wilderness of Etham," in Num. xxxiii, 8, from the station Etham, *in the edge of the wilderness*, near the head of the Gulf, where Israel encamped before the passage of the Sea. Exod. xiii, 20.

Israel is now fairly in the "wilderness," and we therefore give here a general idea of the country in which they spent the ensuing forty years, gathered from the observations of recent travellers, and the Report of the "Sinai Survey Expedition" of 1868–69.

The Mountain of the Law, or the Sinai of Exodus, is a peak of the great cluster of naked, steep, granite mountains in the southern part of the triangular peninsula of Sinai, which lies like a wedge between the Gulfs of Suez and Akabah. The apex of this triangle is at Ras (Cape) Mohammed, which stretches on the south into the Red Sea, and its base lying along the twenty-ninth parallel of north latitude; and it measures about one hundred and ninety miles along the Gulf of Suez, one hundred and thirty miles along the Gulf of Akabah, and one hundred and fifty miles from gulf to gulf. North of the Sinai peninsula is the desert of et Tih, an arid limestone table-land, with isolated mountain groups, which rise above plains of gravel, sand, and flint. This plateau is bounded generally by steep, flat-topped cliffs, and it projects wedgewise into the Sinai desert on the south, and on the northeast joins the plateau of the Negeb, or "South Country" of Palestine. The Tih table-land is a fearful waste, almost wholly waterless; the valleys or wadies, along which the water runs in the wet season, marking the white or gray gravel with scanty lines of "sickly green." The white range of cliffs which forms the western wall of this plateau of the Tih is called Jebel (Mount) Rahah on the north, and Jebel et Tih on the south; and it was along this wall, as seen above, that the Israelites commenced their desert march, the desert of Shur or Etham being the narrow strip between the mountains of Shur and the Gulf. Between the granitic cluster of Sinai and the southern limestone escarpment of the Tih is a broad belt of low sandstone hills, reaching nearly from shore to shore. These hills have flat tabular summits, and are often most fantastic in shape, and coloured gorgeously in various shades of yellow and red. Among these hills are broad, undulating plains, the chief of which is the Debbet er Ramleh, or Sandy Plain, which skirts the southern wall of et Tih. This sandstone formation contains many rich veins of iron, copper, and turquoise, which were worked by the ancient Egyptians on an extensive scale. At Maghareh and Surabit el Kadim, in this district, are found hieroglyphic tablets recording the names of the kings under whose auspices these mining operations were carried on. At the latter place are the ruins of two temples, one of hewn stone, the other excavated in the rock, and inscriptions which show, according to the translation of Lepsius, that these temples were constructed for the use of the miners and the troops stationed there for their protection. These inscriptions range in date from the third Memphitic dynasty, (about 2,500 B. C.,) to Rameses IV. of the twentieth dynasty, (about 1200 B. C.) Cheops, or Shufer, the builder of the Great Pyramid, has a tablet here. Here are also numerous evidences of immense smelting operations, piles of slag and remains of furnaces, which show that vast quantities of fuel must have been consumed here by the ancient Egyptians. Palmer and others hence infer that the country was once much more plentifully supplied with vegetation, and, therefore, had a more copious rain-fall than now. (*Desert of the Exodus*, i, p. 235.)

The mountains of Sinai are a "rugged, tumbled chaos" of dark granite, variegated porphyries, and mica schist, with veins of greenstone and variously shaded feldspar, often displaying a great variety of brilliant tints in the bright sun under the clear desert sky. There are three principal groups of these mountains: the central group of Jebel Musa, (Mount of Moses,) of which Mount St. Katharine is the highest peak, and the crown of the peninsula, standing seven thousand three hundred and sixty-three feet above the sea level; Serbal, whose smooth granite dome rises on the northwest; and Um Shomer, which lifts its jagged peaks in the southeast. There is a strip of broad gravelly plain called el Ga'ah, (or el Ka'a,) "the Plain," which runs down along the Gulf of Suez between the mountains and the sea, and a narrower strip of a similar character along the Gulf of Akabah, which disappears here and there as the mountain spurs come down to the water. With the exception of the Debbet er Ramleh, or Sandy Plain, above mentioned, the plains and valleys are usually floored with gravel, dark in the granitic districts, and white and black in the limestone regions. The wadies, or dry rivers as they are sometimes called, are the water-courses of the desert, along which the torrents from the mountains find their way to the sea. These are the permanent natural roads through the mountains. Most of them are dry for the greater part of the year, and in the wet season destructive floods sweep through them, tearing out the scanty soil where it is not fastened down by large shrubs or trees, and often scattering boulders from the craggy walls along their course. These wadies must always have determined the lines of travel, for it is impossible to pass the mountains except in their beds; and in these only is there water and herbage for man and beast. It is this fact that makes it possible to determine with a high degree of certainty the route of the Israelites through these mountains; at least, we can be sure that we know all the alternatives that were before them in choosing their course.

On leaving the white glare of the desert plain, and rising through the mountain passes into the granite region, the traveller finds a cool, genial climate and refreshing breezes. A few perennial streams flow down from the mountains, along which are considerable tracts of vegetation. The trees are chiefly the acacia, or *shittah*, from which distils the gum arabic of commerce; the tamarisk, with its long feathery leaves and manna-dropping twigs; and the juniper, or broom, "with its high canopy and white blossoms;" while the palm is scattered

22 So Moses brought Israel from the Red Sea, and they went out into the wilderness of ʸShur; and they went three days in the wilderness, and found no water. **23** And when they came to ᶻMarah, they could not drink of the

y Gen. 16. 7; 25. 18. *z* Num. 33. 8.

along the more fertile wadies, and stands in fine groves at Tor and Feiran. The bright green caper plant often hangs along the face of the crags, and here and there are olive groves, or scattered olive trees, the relics of ancient monkish plantations. Game is occasionally found in the mountains—the ibex, or wild goat of Scripture, the gazelle, and the hare, while more rarely partridges and quails are seen. The productiveness of these fertile spots would be vastly increased by cultivation; then what are now bare rocks or gravelly torrent beds would be turned into gardens. It is well known that the amount of rain which falls upon a district depends to a high degree upon the evaporating surfaces furnished by the forests; and the forests of this region have for centuries been diminishing, having been destroyed, firstly, for fuel, as shown above, in the mining operations of successive centuries; and, secondly, for the manufacture of charcoal, which is the chief and almost sole export of the peninsula. These facts make it probable that this desert, at the time of the Exodus, was capable of sustaining quite a large population, and of furnishing water and pasturage to their cattle and flocks.

The desert of the Tih is much more barren. It is drained by the Wady el Arish, or "river of Egypt," into the Mediterranean; but it is a white wilderness of chalk and limestone, yet sprinkled over with a brown, dry herbage, which bursts into a sudden and transitory green after the autumnal rains. Yet the Tih bears traces of ancient, perhaps pre-historic, inhabitants, in the stone cairns and fenced inclosures which were reared by some primeval pastoral people. In the "South Country" of the Pentateuch and Joshua, northeast of the Tih plateau, are found deep ancient wells, remains of ruined cities, gardens, and vineyards; and also abundant traces of roads, which were once the pathways of civilization. It was through the arid and dreary Tih that Jacob went down into Egypt; and through the same wilderness Joseph and Mary fled with the infant Jesus.

MARCH TO MARAH AND ELIM, 22–27.

22. And they went three days in the wilderness, and found no water —The springs regulate the movements and fix the halting places of the caravans now as in the time of Moses, and it is probable that the first resting-place of Israel after the passage of the Red Sea was the oasis which the Arabs call Ayun Musa, the "Springs of Moses," two miles from the shore, and about six hours' travel from Suez. There Robinson found seven fountains, one of massive ancient masonry; yet previous travellers describe many more, some mentioning twenty. The water is dark coloured and brackish, depositing a hard, calcareous sediment as it rises, which forms mounds around the springs, over which the water flows into the sands and disappears. About twenty palm bushes now grow around the springs, and there is a small patch of grain and a vegetable garden cultivated by people from Suez. There are fragments of tiles and pottery, indicating that there were once habitations near these springs. It was probably from this spot that Israel started on the three days' journey in the wilderness of Shur.

23. Marah—Bitterness, a place of bitter or brackish water. This does not enable us to locate the station, since all the springs of the region are saltish. Since the time of Burckhardt Marah has been generally identified with Hawwara, a little over forty miles, or about three days' journey, from Ayun Musa, and the first spring after leaving that station. But whether Marah be here, or five miles farther on, as Lepsius supposes, at Gharandel, or three miles back, at Wady Amarah, is of comparatively little moment, seeing that we

B. C. 1491. CHAPTER XV. 447

waters of Marah, for they *were* bitter: therefore the name of it was called ᵃMarah. **24** And the people ᵃmurmured against Moses, saying, What shall we drink? **25** And he ᵇcried unto the LORD; and the LORD showed him a tree, ᶜ*which* when he had cast into the waters, the waters were made sweet:

ᵃ That is, *Bitterness*, Ruth 1. 20.—*a* Chap. 16. 2; 17. 3. ᵇ Chap. 14. 10; 17. 4; Psa. 50. 15.—*c* See 2 Kings 2. 21; 4. 41.

certainly know that all of these spots are on the track of the great host of Israel as they moved towards Mount Sinai. Between the long white mountain wall of er-Rahah on their left, and the blue Red Sea waters on their right, they moved southeasterly across a great whitish gravelly plain, at times amid sand mounds and low, flat, barren hills of limestone and chalk, sparkling now and then with crystals of gypsum, and at other times crossing wadies, or dry water-courses, running from the mountain range across their course, and fringed occasionally with dwarf palms, stunted tamarisks, shrubby broom, and other hardy plants of the desert. There was no shade, and the sun's rays were reflected hot and dazzling from the white hills and plains. Across the sea on their right the dark form of the promontory of Attaka reminded them of the Egypt that they had left. Accustomed all their lives to the sweet Nile water, which the Egyptians deem unsurpassed in the world, they had now for three days been drinking from their waterskins of the supply laid in at the last station, which was most likely Ayun Musa, anticipating the fountains, of which Moses had probably told them, at this oasis. And now they find the springs so bitter that they cannot drink of them.

Hawwara is now a spring but about eight feet across, within a calcareous mound which has been formed from its deposits. Two stunted palm trees grow near it, affording the weary traveller a delicious shade, and a number of *ghurkud* bushes straggle around it—low thorny shrubs, bearing small juicy berries, much like our barberry. Murray says, "Should the thirsty traveller hasten forward now to drink at the fountain, his Arabs will restrain him by the cry, *Murr! murr!* 'Bitter! bitter!'" The water is strongly impregnated with salt and alum, and yet it is frequently quite drinkable. Holland says it is often more palatable than that which has been brought down in skins from Suez.

24. **Murmured against Moses**—Burckhardt says that nothing is more common than to hear such complaints from Egyptian peasants and servants who travel in the Arabian deserts. Like the Israelites, they everywhere mourn for the sweet water of their native land. These murmurings were unbelieving and ungrateful, especially as poured out upon Moses, their deliverer; but in judging their sin we are to remember the magnitude of their trial. Nothing would be more quickly or more keenly felt by such a mingled host in the heat and glare of the desert than a lack of water, especially by a people who had always had an abundance of the most drinkable water in the world.

25. **The Lord showed him a tree** —Many have supposed that this tree had sweetening properties, possibly neutralizing the salts which made the water undrinkable. Some have suggested that Moses used the *ghurkud* berries, above mentioned, for this purpose. But it was not yet time for this berry, which ripens in June, while the Israelites were at Marah in April; and if there were any shrub or tree in the desert possessing natural properties which would make these bitter, brackish springs drinkable, it is not at all probable that so valuable a fact would be unknown to the natives of the region; yet diligent inquiries made by the most intelligent travellers have failed to find any such knowledge among the Bedouins.

It is most probable that the wood had no more healing virtue than the clay which Jesus applied to the eyes of the blind man, or the Jordan waters which cleansed the leprosy of Naaman. The tree was but the appropriate means to call forth faith. Casting it into the

there he *made for them a statute and an ordinance, and there *he proved them, **26** And said, 'If thou wilt diligently hearken to the voice of the LORD thy God, and wilt do that which is right in his sight, and wilt give ear to his commandments, and keep all his stat-

d See Josh. 24. 25.——*e* Chap. 16. 4; Deut. 8. 2, 16; Judges 2. 22; 3. 1, 4; Psa. 66. 10; 81. 7.

waters was an exercise and manifestation of faith. And this was an instructive "sign" as well as a miracle. The first judgment-stroke upon Egypt made the sweet, wholesome Nile waters loathsome, and the first saving miracle in the desert made sweet the bitter Marah. Luther's typical application is excellent. "Moses causes man to murmur by the terrors of the law, and thus pains him with bitterness, so that he longs for help; and then, when the Holy Spirit comes, at once it [the law] is made sweet. Now this tree of life is the Gospel, the word of the grace, the mercy, and goodness of God. When the Gospel is plunged into the law, and into the knowledge of sin which the law produces, and when it touches a heart in which the law has caused sadness, anxiety, terror, and confusion, it is at once delightful to the taste."

For them (or, *him*, Israel being personified as one man) **a statute and an ordinance, and there he proved them** (or, *him;* the pronoun is grammatically singular)—The *statute* or law, and the *ordinance* or judgment, follows in the next verse.

26. **For I am the Lord that healeth thee**—*For I*, JEHOVAH, *am thy Healer, Physician.* This first trial and miracle of the desert is made the occasion of great spiritual lessons, such as may ever come from great trials. They had seen Egypt's blessings turned to curses because of the sins of the Egyptians, and the same God would not only save them from these dreadful judgments, but would turn all life's bitterness to sweetness if they would but keep his law. Jehovah the Physician can heal all the Marahs of life if man but obeys and submits, whether he comprehends God's dealings or not. Here, also, they were clearly taught that continued obedience was essential

utes, I will put none of these *diseases upon thee, which I have brought upon the Egyptians: for I *am* the LORD *h* that healeth thee. **27** 'And they came to Elim, where *were* twelve wells of water, and threescore and ten palm trees: and they encamped there by the waters.

f Deut. 7. 12, 15.——*g* Deut. 28. 27, 60.——*h* Chap. 23. 25; Psa. 41. 3, 4; 103. 3; 147. 3.——*i* Num. 33. 9.

to their continued election as God's covenant people. They were not to be presumptuous because of the wonderful manifestations in Egypt and at the Red Sea. If they sinned like the Egyptians they would also be punished like the Egyptians. But the great lesson here emphatically impressed is, that **it is not ritual or outward obedience of any kind**—not the offering of sacrifices or of bodily services merely—but the doing **that which is right in his sight**—the sacrifice of the heart, the offering of the self, that Jehovah demands. Jeremiah, centuries afterwards, refers to this transaction and this solemn spiritual lesson thus: "For I spake not unto your fathers, nor commanded them in the day that I brought them out of the land of Egypt, concerning burnt offerings or sacrifices: but this thing commanded I them, saying, Obey my voice, and I will be your God, and ye shall be my people: and walk ye in all the ways that I have commanded you, that it may be well unto you." Jer. vii, 22, 23. This "statute and ordinance" coming just before the Levitical economy—just before the first altar was reared in the wilderness—is most valuable as setting forth the real nature and spirit of the Levitical ordinances.

27. **Elim**—*Trees.* Here were **palm trees** and **waters,** or springs, around which they encamped, (rested and refreshed themselves,) probably for from two to three weeks, since it was just a month from the time of their leaving Rameses that they broke up from Elim. Chap. xvi, 1. As the next encampment was "by the Red Sea," according to the itinerary in Num. xxxiii, which gives a fuller catalogue of the stations, it is plain that Elim took them back from the shore, within sight of which they had been moving. Just below Hawwarah, and surrounding three sides of Je-

bel (Mount) Hammam, there are several fertile wadies, through and across which their route now led them, which perfectly met their requirement. Jebel Hammam is a bare, picturesque cliff of flinty limestone, warm sulphur springs rising from its northern base, which comes down to the Sea in steep bluffs five miles long, thus cutting off the plain already described as the "Wilderness of Shur," and compelling caravans from Suez to go round and over its northern shoulder in order to reach the plain which skirts the Sea below the Mount, and which we suppose to be the "Desert of Sin." Chap. xvi, 1. The Israelites were probably spread through all these wadies around Mount Hammam, while the headquarters of the host were encamped where there were wells corresponding in number to the tribes, and where there was a grove of palms corresponding to the tribal families—the Wady Gharandel. Gharandel is the principal halting place and the most fertile spot between Suez and Sinai; Wady Feiran alone comparing with it in richness and loveliness. It is in some places nearly a mile broad, its running brook fringed with trees, while water car be anywhere found by digging a little depth. "Here are the wild palms," says Stanley, "successors of the threescore and ten. Not like those of Egypt or of pictures, but either dwarf, that is, trunkless, or else with savage, hairy trunks, and branches all dishevelled. Then there are the feathery tamarisks, here assuming gnarled boughs and hoary heads; the wild acacia; a tangled, spreading tree, which shoots out its gay foliage and blue blossoms over the desert."—*Sinai and Pal.*, p. 68. Here, too, the bright green grass is most refreshing to the eye wearied by the hot, white desert, but it is coarse and rough to the touch. Tischendorf says, "This is a glorious oasis... enclosed like a jewel between the chalky cliffs. We reposed for a long time in the grass, which was as tall as ourselves; tamarisks and dwarf palms stretched like a garland from east to west." (Quoted by Kurtz.)

The wadies which succeed Gharandel resemble it somewhat in character, but are much inferior in fertility, although Useit once surpassed it in its palm-grove. Through these valleys we suppose the Israelitish camp to have spread, round the northern shoulder of Jebel Hammam, perhaps into Wady Taiyebeh, a beautiful valley, winding between steep cliffs of red sandstone. flinty chalk, and variegated conglomerates, down to the plain el Murkha, which skirts the Sea. When they left Elim they encamped at the mouth of the wady, and scattered along this plain, "by the Red Sea." Num. xxxiii, 10. As they descended the mountain pass, between the high steep walls, then as now curtained here and there with the green, creeping caper, and painted, as they neared the Sea, with bright bands of red, and brown, and black—as they poured down into the plain and spread along the shelly beach—they caught one more view of the distant hills of Egypt across the blue waters that had swallowed up the chariots and horses of Pharaoh.

From Gharandel to the Sea at Ras (Cape) Zelinea is, by this route, about eight hours' travel, an easy day's journey for the men of Israel after their long rest at Elim, but quite long for the remainder of the host, who, it is likely, had generally to come only from Useit, or the upper part of Taiyebeh. Palmer, who has thoroughly surveyed all these wadies, decides that Taiyebeh is the only valley by which they could have descended to the Sea.

CHAPTER XVI.
INTRODUCTORY.

(1.) *Route from Elim to Sinai.* Before deciding upon this route it is, of course, necessary to settle the location of Elim and Sinai. We have already presented reasons for the conclusion, in which travellers are now almost unanimously agreed, that Elim was the Wady Gharandel; and there is now, also, an equally general conviction among biblical scholars who have visited the locality, (Lepsius being the only important exception,) that the

Mount Sinai of Exodus was the peak Ras Sufsafeh (or Sassafeh) at Jebel Musa, the reasons of which identification will be hereafter given, but are assumed as valid for the present. After leaving Elim, the itinerary of Num. xxxiii gives us an encampment "by the Red Sea," which, as already shown, (note on chap. xv, 27,) could only have been in the plain at the mouth of the Wady Taiyebeh. From this station there were three routes through the labyrinth of wadies and mountain passes to Mount Sinai, which, from the geographical features of the country, must be the same now as then: (1,) a lower route, through the desert plain el Ka‘a, (or el Ga‘ah,) by the coast station Tur, (or Tor,) through the steep and winding Wady Hebran; (2,) an upper route, by Wady Hamer, through the great sandstone belt of the peninsula, past the mysterious Egyptian monuments of Sarabit el Khadim, among the low hills, and into the broad sandy plain of Debbet er Ramleh, (or el Karabeh;) thence along the white southern escarpment of the Tih plateau into Wady es Sheikh, the route followed and so thoroughly described by Robinson; and (3,) an intermediate route through Wady Feiran, whose springs, palm groves, flowers, and bulbuls make it the principal thoroughfare and most delightful spot in the whole peninsula. It is only by a careful study of thorough maps, like those of Kiepert and the British Ordnance Survey, that these alternatives can be apprehended. The lower route may be ruled out at once, from the fact that the steep, rough, narrow Hebran is wholly impracticable for such a miscellaneous host, with women, children, and wagons, not to mention the many days' march through the vast waterless plain of the Ka‘a, of which there is no trace in the record, since there is no mention of the lack of water till Israel came to Rephidim, near Mount Sinai. The upper route is ably defended by Knobel, who plausibly identifies Debbet er Ramleh, the great sandy plain along the Jebel et Tih, with the "Desert of Sin." Exod. xvi, 1. But it is very probable that there was at this time an Egyptian mining colony and military station directly in this route, which would be a strong reason for avoiding it; and we have no account of any collision between Israel and Egyptian troops in the desert; and, besides, Palmer says, that the "rugged passes and narrow valleys would have presented insuperable difficulties to a large caravan, encumbered by heavy baggage;" and certainly these wadies would have been impassable to wagons, which from Num. vii, 3, etc., we see that the Israelites had with them. The middle route, Wady Feiran, could have been entered directly from the coast plain, el Murkha, or indirectly through the Wady Shellal and Wady Mukatteh, the famous valley of the inscribed sandstone tablets, past the beautiful bas-reliefs and turquoise and copper mines of Magharah, down a steep, narrow pass. The objections just made to the upper route would hold good, though with less force, to this indirect entrance to Wady Feiran, and hence the travellers of the "Sinai Survey Expedition" decided for the Wady Feiran, entered directly from the plain of el Murkha. (Palmer's *Desert of the Exodus*, vol. i, chap. 14.) As this is the unanimous verdict of the only company of intelligent travellers who have examined all the routes to Sinai, it must have, henceforth, decisive weight with all interpreters of Exodus. Kurtz, Keil, and Murphy, who advocate the upper route, were not at the time of writing aware of these objections, nor of the direct entrance to Wady Feiran.

It is not, however, to be supposed that the whole body of the Israelites moved along this single valley, but rather, that in this were the headquarters and main body of the host. Large detachments, who acted as soldiers, and could thus march with celerity through rough and steep places, probably took the Mukatteh route, and thus acted as a guard on the left flank against the Egyptian troops who may have been posted in Magharah. It is probable, also, that the Israelites entered the great plain of el Raheh, at the base of Sinai, from the northwest, through Wady Solaf, over the pass Nagb

CHAPTER XVI.

A ND they *took their journey from Elim, and all the congregation of the children of Israel came unto the wilderness of ᵇ Sin, which *is* between Elim and Sinai, on the fifteenth day of the

a Num. 33, 10, 11.   *b* Ezek. 30, 15.

Hawa, and from the northeast through the Wady es Sheikh.

(**2.**) *Manna.* There is a substance called manna by the Bedouins of the desert now produced in the peninsula of Sinai, and gathered from the twigs of the tamarisk or tarfa tree, which has been supposed by many, as Lepsius, Ritter, etc., after Josephus, to be the same as the manna which was to Israel "bread from heaven." This substance exudes in transparent drops from the outermost tender twigs of the tamarisk, and soon hardens into a reddish-yellow gum, or waxy substance, which the Bedouins use and sell for a condiment with bread. It often falls upon the ground, and is gathered both from the tree and from the earth. It melts in the sun, but may be kept in a cool place for an indefinite time. It has the flavour of honey, and chemical analysis shows that it is wholly saccharine in composition. Ehrenberg assigned its production to the puncture of an insect, a kind of wood-louse, but this origin is doubted by Lepsius. It is found from the last of May until August in wet seasons only, and Burckhardt calculates that the whole peninsula might, in a favourable season, yield five to six hundred pounds. From this description it will be seen, that while there are some points of resemblance there are many more of irreconcilable diversity between this substance and the manna of the Israelites. From this chapter, and from Num. xi, 7–9, we find that the manna of Israel fell with the dew, and was found on the surface of the open wilderness after "the dew had gone up," not on and under the branches of the tamarisk. It had the nutritious properties of bread, while the tamarisk manna is a mere condiment. It could be ground in mills; pounded or bruised in mortars, like grain; cooked by baking and boiling; all of which are impossible processes for the tamarisk manna, as much as for gum or wax. It was found all through the wilderness, in regions where, now at least, the tamarisk does not and cannot grow, while the tamarisk manna is confined to a small district of the Sinai wilderness; and even if it were the same substance, the whole peninsula does not now produce enough to sustain a single man. It was produced through the whole year, while the tamarisk manna exudes only in the summer; and, most decisive of all, there was a double supply of this manna on the sixth day and none at all on the seventh. It is certain, then, that the inspired author intends to describe the supernatural production of daily bread for the Hebrew host. It strongly resembled in appearance the substance now known in the same desert as manna, produced from the tamarisk or tarfa tree, and then known by the same or a similar name, (Hebrew, *man;* Arabic, *mennu;* Egyptian, *menna* and *mannuhut;*) and hence the name given it by the Israelites, who were struck with this resemblance. Verse 15. (Robinson, *Bib. Researches,* i, 115; Kurtz, *History of Old Covenant,* iii, 27; Stowe, *in Smith's Dictionary.*)

THE MURMURING IN THE DESERT OF SIN, 1–3.

1. **The wilderness of Sin, which is between Elim and Sinai**—That is, between them by the route which a caravan of this kind would naturally take, not between them as a bird would fly. If Elim be Gharandel, as we think to be certain, there is no other way for such a host as this to have reached Sinai than by the Wady Taiyebeh, which leads to the seashore and the great maritime plain of el Murkha. See Introduction, (**1.**) The "wilderness of Sin" seems, then, to be this flat seacoast strip of desert, which, farther south, broadens into el Ka'a (or el Ga'ah) stretching down to Ras (Cape) Mohammed. This is a vast, flat waste of sand and black flints, without shade, or water, or life, except in the lower ends of the few

second month after their departing out of the land of Egypt. **2** And the whole congregation of the children of Israel ^c murmured against Moses and Aaron in the wilderness: **3** And the children of Israel said unto them, ^d Would to God we had died by the hand of the LORD in the land of Egypt, *when we sat by the flesh pots, *and* when we did eat bread to the full; for ye have brought us forth into this wilderness, to kill this whole assembly with hunger. **4** Then said the LORD unto Moses, Behold, I will rain ^f bread from heaven for you; and

c Chap. 15. 24; Psa. 106. 25; 1 Cor. 10. 10.
d Lam. 4. 9.—*e* Num. 11. 4, 5.

f Psa. 78. 24, 25; 105. 40; John 6. 31, 32; 1 Cor. 10. 3.

wadies which lead up from it into the Sinai mountains, and is, perhaps, the most desolate tract in all Arabia. How natural that in this thirsty, featureless wilderness they should remember all the good things of the fat Nile-land whose far-off mountains they had seen so clearly as they descended into the plain, and probably now saw dimly sketched against the western horizon. Probably they brought water upon their cattle and in their wagons from the Wady Taiyebeh, and encamped at the mouths of several wadies which led down into the plain. **All the congregation**—Implying a rallying of all the scattered parties from the slopes and valleys of Mount Hammam into the plain, in order to make a "new departure," and turn into the mountains of Sinai. **Fifteenth day of the second month** of the year of the Exode; just a month after they left Rameses.

2. **The whole congregation... murmured**—The stores that they had brought from Egypt were now exhausted, although they obtained much sustenance from their herds and flocks; but they saw nothing to eat in this barren waste, and looked forward with terror to the long journey that was yet before them. A month's experience of the desert had broken the courage of the whole host, and there was a general disaffection and rebellion, though there were doubtless individual instances of patience and of faith. The present suffering blotted out of remembrance the wonderful experiences of the Red Sea and of Marah. So short was their memory of God's goodness!

3. **Would to God we had died by the hand of the Lord,** in the plagues that destroyed the Egyptians. In the infatuation of their impatience and unbelief they envied the lot of their slain oppressors! Such ingratitude and forgetfulness of God's grace and strength seem incredible till we look within our own hearts. **When we sat by the flesh pots**—The abundant beef and poultry and fish of Egypt came up in vivid remembrance, and also the juicy cucumbers and luscious melons of the field of Zoan, (Num. xi, 4, 5,) as they hungered and thirsted in the bare, blazing desert.

The opposite cut shows an Egyptian kitchen of the time of Rameses III., and reveals precisely the scenes that rose in the imaginations of the hungry Israelites.

Ye have brought us forth—As if their devoted and self-sacrificing leaders were the cause of all their sufferings! So unreasonable, selfish, and cruel is unbelief.

THE PROMISE OF MANNA AND QUAILS, 4–12.

4, 5. **Bread from heaven**—A miraculous provision. See Introduction, (**2.**) Without a miracle this great host of two millions could never have subsisted in the desert for forty years. Yet they were not entirely dependent upon the manna. They got milk from their flocks and herds, probably traded the products of their cattle with the desert tribes, and perhaps, in this forty years' sojourn, some halted long enough in some of the fertile wadies to lay them under cultivation. They shifted their camping grounds with the seasons, as do the Bedouins to-day, in order to find the best pasturage for their cattle. Yet this manna supply was an important part of the national education of Israel for their great mission to mankind. The national history and poetry, as found in the Psalms and Prophets especially, show how deeply

AN EGYPTIAN KITCHEN, (from the Tomb of Rameses III., at Thebes.)

Fig. 1. Killing and preparing the joints, which are placed at *a, b, c.*——Fig. 2. Catching the blood for the purposes of cookery, which is removed in a bowl by fig. 3.——Figs. 4, 5. Employed in boiling meat and stirring the fire.——Fig. 7. Preparing the meat for the caldron, which fig. 6 is taking to the fire.——Fig. 8. Pounding some ingredients for the cook in a mortar, *d.*——*f, f.* Apparently siphons. *g, g.* Ropes passing through rings and supporting different things, as a sort of safe. *h.* Probably plates. *u, v.* Tables.

the people shall go out and gather ¹a certain rate every day, that I may ᵉ prove them, whether they will walk in my law, or no. **5** And it shall come to pass, that on the sixth day they shall prepare *that* which they bring in; and ʰit shall be twice as much as they gather daily. **6** And Moses and Aaron said unto all the children of Israel, ⁱAt even, then ye shall know that the LORD hath brought you out from the land of Egypt: **7** And in the morning, then ye shall see ᵏthe glory of the LORD; for that he heareth your murmurings against the LORD: and ˡwhat *are* we, that ye murmur against us? **8** And Moses said, *This shall be*, when the LORD shall give you in the evening flesh to eat, and in the morning bread to the full; for ᵐthat the LORD heareth your murmurings which ye murmur against him: and what *are* we? your murmurings *are* not against us, but ⁿagainst the LORD. **9** And Moses spake unto Aaron, Say unto all the congregation of the children of Israel, ᵒCome near before the LORD: for he hath heard your murmurings. **10** And it came to pass, as Aaron spake unto the whole congregation of the children of Israel, that they looked toward the wilderness, and, behold, the glory of the LORD ᵖappeared in the cloud. **11** And the LORD spake unto Moses, saying, **12** ᑫI have heard the murmurings of the children of Israel: speak unto them, saying, ʳAt even ye shall eat flesh, and ˢin the morning ye shall be filled with bread; and ye shall know that I *am* the LORD your God. **13** And it came to pass, that at even ᵗthe quails came up, and covered the camp: and in the morning ᵘthe dew lay round about the host.

1 Hebrew, *the portion of a day in his day*, Prov. 30. 8; Matt. 6. 11.—*g* Deut. 8. 2, 16.— *h* See verse 22; Lev. 25. 21.—*i* See verses 12, 13; chap. 6. 7; Num. 16. 28–30.—*k* See verse 10; Isa. 35. 2; 40. 5; John 11. 4, 40.—*l* Num. 16. 11.
m Num. 14. 27; John 6. 41.—*n* 1 Sam. 8. 7; Luke 10. 16; Rom. 13. 2.—*o* Num. 16. 16.— *p* Verse 7; chap. 13. 21; Num. 16. 19; 1 Kings 8. 10, 11.—*q* Ver. 8.—*r* Ver. 6.—*s* Ver. 7.— *t* Num. 12. 31; Psa. 78. 27, 28; 105. 40.—*u* Num. 11. 9.

this event stamped itself upon the soul of Israel. **That I may prove them**—Israel was to learn that God gives daily bread, and the sixth day's provision was especially to test their obedience.

6–8. Moses and Aaron repeat God's promises to Israel, foretell his providing mercy, and rebuke their faithless and rebellious complaints.

9–12. Moses directs Aaron to gather the people before the cloudy pillar from which flashed the Divine glory. **Ye shall know that I am the Lord** (JEHOVAH) **your God**—This was the grand and worthy object of this wondrous miracle, as all its successive steps reveal; while at the same time Moses and Aaron, against whom they had murmured, were to be vindicated. First the people were made to deeply feel their want; then the Lord reveals his purpose to Moses, who had himself been so sorely tried by their distrust and rebellion; then Moses communicates it to Aaron, who gathers the people in solemn assembly before the Lord; and then Jehovah reveals himself in the mysterious Shekinah to Moses, and finally fulfils his promise by sending, first, quails in the evening, and then manna in the morning.

QUAILS AND MANNA GIVEN, 13–21.

13. **The quails came up**, (from the south, across the Red Sea,) **and covered the camp**—Fell down among the tents. The bird here mentioned is undoubtedly the common quail, the word שְׂלָו being derived from a root signifying "fat," from the round, plump, fat body of the quail. (Gesen.) The same bird is spoken of in Num. xi as coming to the camp in vast numbers just a year from this time—an immense flock, which passed over the encampment at a height of two cubits from the ground, and spread a day's journey on both sides. It was now the last of April, when countless flocks of these birds migrate northward from the Upper Nile country, crossing the Red Sea and the Sinai wilderness, and appearing in immense numbers in the Mediterranean coasts and islands. They begin to return southward in September, when they are caught in great numbers with nets, and even with the hand, at their roosting places, in the neighbourhood of Constantinople and on the Ægean Islands; and they pass over Alexandria in November. Ancient and modern naturalists and travellers give us most marvellous accounts of the numbers of these

B. C. 1491. CHAPTER XVI. 455

14 And when the dew that lay was gone up, behold, upon the face of the wilderness *there lay* ᵛa small round thing, *as* small as the hoar frost on the ground. **15** And when the children of

v Num. 11. 7; Deut. 8. 3; Neh. 9. 15; Psa. 78. 24; 105. 40.

birds, and of the great quantities that are captured at the migrating seasons. All the Archipelago islands are at these times covered with them. At Capri, near Naples, they were once taken in such numbers as to afford the bishop there a large part of his revenue, who was hence called "bishop of quails." Varro and Pliny relate that in their time they arrived on the Italian shores in such numbers, and settled by night on the sails and rigging of coasting vessels in such masses, as to overturn them! (Plin., *Hist. Nat.*, x, 33.) They reach the coasts by night, wearied with their long flight, and are then very easily taken, being knocked down with sticks, or even caught in the hand. (See many quotations in Knobel.) One of these vast flocks, on their annual northward migration from Upper Egypt or Nubia, was providentially directed to the Israelitish encampment, and, coming across the sea, arrived exhausted in the evening, and dropped among and around the tents in the desert of Murkha.

14. A small round thing, as small as the hoar frost—Rather, *A thing fine, and in fine scales, fine as the hoar frost.* It was in small and white grains. The tamarisk manna is white when it drops upon the clean rocks.

15. It is **manna: for they wist not what it** was—More literally, *They said, each to his brother, This is man,* (is it not?) *For they knew not what it* (was). They called it *man,* because it so exactly resembled the tamarisk or tarpi *man* with which they were familiar. They are here represented as talking to each other in a conversational, inquiring way, and the author adds, *they knew not what it was;* that is, they knew not what other name to give it. They used the Egyptian word for the tamarisk manna. Brugsch, in his Hieroglyphic Dictionary, says, " *Mannu,* identical with the Hebrew *man,* Arabic *mann.*" The tamarisk manna is found

Israel saw *it,* they said one to another, ²It *is* manna: for they wist not what it *was.* And Moses said unto them, ʷThis *is* the bread which the LORD hath given you to eat. **16** This *is* the thing which

2 Or, *What is this?* or, *It is a portion.* *w* John 6. 31, 49, 58; 1 Cor. 10. 3.

represented at the Egyptian city of Apollinopolis, presented to a deity in a basket of oblations. The resemblance, however, was only superficial, (see Introduction, 2,) for the manna of Israel was a farinaceous substance that could be made into bread, while the tamarisk manna is wholly saccharine. The Hebrew will not bear the marginal translation, "What is this?" (See Kurtz and Knobel; but Keil and Ewald make מָן early Shemitic for מה.) **This is the bread which the Lord hath given you** — The dew was made the natural basis or vehicle of this miracle, as the water was the vehicle of the miracle of Cana, and the five loaves of that of Bethesda. The manna was deposited from the dew according to laws unknown, and probably undiscoverable, by us, yet to the Author of Nature the process was as regular and as orderly as that by which the grain is formed in the ear. We know of only one series of natural processes, one chain of secondary causes, by which the grain can be gathered up from its manifold elements, in earth, and water, and air; but God knows of many others, which are hidden from our sense and reason. To assume that the way which we know is the only way, and to call all other ways unnatural and absurd, is to make our ignorance the measure of God. It is true that we can conceive of no other way, but our power of conception is not the gauge of the universe. The water which, as liquid and vapour circulates through the veins of nature, gathers up the elements, and bears them along the sap vessels to form the farinaceous atom in the seed by processes which we can trace; but the same water could gather up the same elements and deposit this substance in the seed or on the ground by processes which we cannot trace, known only to God. This is miracle. Of course this will not be

the Lord hath commanded, Gather of it every man according to his eating, *an omer ⁵for every man, *according to* the number of your ⁴persons; take ye every man for *them* which *are* in his tents. 17 And the children of Israel did so, and gathered, some more, some less. 18 And when they did mete *it* with an omer, ⁷ he that gathered much had nothing over, and he that gathered little had no lack; they gathered every man according to his eating. 19 And Moses said, Let no man leave of it till the morning. 20 Notwithstanding they hearkened not unto Moses; but some of them left of it until the morning, and it bred worms, and stank: and Moses was wroth with them. 21 And they gathered it every morning, every man according to his eating: and when the sun waxed hot, it melted. 22 And it came to pass, *that* on the sixth day they gathered twice as much bread, two omers for one *man:* and all the rulers of the congregation came and told Moses. 23 And he said unto them, This *is that* which the Lord hath said, To morrow *is* ˣthe rest of the holy sabbath unto the Lord: bake *that* which ye will bake *to day*, and seethe that ye will seethe; and that which remaineth over lay up for you to be kept until the morning. 24 And they laid it up till the morning, as Moses bade: and it did

---

ω Verse 36.——3 Hebrew, *by the poll*, or, *head*. 4 Hebrew, *souls*.   y 2 Cor. 8. 15.——z Gen. 2. 3; chap. 20. 8; 31. 15; 35. 3; Lev. 23. 3.

---

admitted by those who do not look through nature, or within nature, and see God to be the only real cause.

16–21. **An omer for every man—** The amount of the omer at this time is one of the unsettled questions, which may be found fully discussed in Smith's *Dictionary*, Art. *Weights and Measures*. The Rabbins estimate it at three pints and a half, while Josephus, as we judge inconsistently, makes it about twice as much. The Rabbinic estimate is more likely to be correct. See on verse 36.

Each man was to gather for himself and his family at the rate of an omer per head; and not to attempt to lay it up for future use, but to trust to morrow's supply to meet to morrow's want. We do not understand that any supernatural equalization was promised. Each man **gathered according to his** eating—That is, when they fulfilled the directions given each gathered according to the number of his family, at the rate of an omer apiece, so that **he that gathered much had nothing over, and he that gathered little had no lack;** and when, through selfishness or unbelief, any attempted to get more than their share, their purpose was frustrated, for it could not be kept over a day.

The Sixth Day's Manna, 22–31.

22. **They gathered twice as much bread**—That is, they found a double supply on the sixth day, which astonished the people, who had not been told to expect this extraordinary provision for the Sabbath. Hence **all the rulers of the congregation came and told Moses,** in order to obtain from him an explanation.

23. **To morrow is the rest of the holy sabbath**—This passage shows that the sabbath was known and observed among the Hebrews before the fourth commandment was given at Sinai. The division of the days into weeks seems to have been known among all the Shemitic nations from the earliest historic period, and this cannot fairly be accounted for except by a wide-spread tradition of the sacredness of the number seven, descending from the very origin of the race. Wilkinson shows that the seven-day division was known to the Egyptians, as proved by the seven days' *fête* of Apis, the four times seven years of Osiris, the ten times seven days' mourning for the dead, and the six times seven days of mortification imposed upon the priests. The Pythagoreans borrowed the week from Egypt, and the Roman world adopted it early in the second century. (Rawlinson's *Herod.*, ii, 282.) It is probable that the week division and the sanctity of the sabbath were known to the Hebrews from their very origin as a people. We find that a week was the period of duration of the wedding feast in the time of Jacob. Gen. **xxix**, 27. Here, as in the creative week, God observes the sabbath as an example to man.

not *stink, neither was there any worm therein. 25 And Moses said, Eat that to day; for to day *is* a sabbath unto the LORD: to day ye shall not find it in the field. 26 ᵇSix days ye shall gather it; but on the seventh day, *which is* the sabbath, in it there shall be none. 27 And it came to pass, *that* there went out *some* of the people on the seventh day for to gather, and they found none. 28 And the LORD said unto Moses, How long ᶜrefuse ye to keep my commandments and my laws? 29 See, for that the LORD hath given you the sabbath, therefore he giveth you on the sixth day the bread of two days: abide ye every man in his place, let no man go out of his place on the seventh day. 30 So the people rested on the seventh day. 31 And the house of Israel called the name thereof Manna: and ᵈit *was* like coriander seed, white; and the taste of it *was* like wafers *made* with honey. 32 And Moses said, This *is* the thing which the LORD commandeth, Fill an omer of it to be kept for your generations; that they may see the bread wherewith I have fed you in the wilderness, when I brought you forth from the land of Egypt. 33 And Moses said unto Aaron, ᵉTake a pot, and put an omer full of manna therein, and lay it up before the LORD, to be kept for your generations. 34 As the LORD commanded Moses, so Aaron laid it up ᶠbefore the Testimony, to be kept. 35 And the children of Israel did eat manna ᵍforty years, ʰuntil they came to a land inhabited: they did eat manna, until they came unto the borders of the

a Verse 20.——*b* Chap. 20. 9, 10.——*c* 2 Kings 17. 14; Psa. 78. 10, 22; 106. 18.——*d* Num. 11. 7, 8. ——*e* Heb. 9. 4.——*f* Chap. 25. 16, 21; 40. 20; | Num. 17. 10; Deut. 10. 5; 1 Kings 8. 9.——*g* Num. 33. 38; Deut. 8. 2, 3; Neh. 9. 20; John 6. 31, 49. ——*h* Josh. 5. 12; Neh. 9. 15.

25. **To day is a sabbath**—In three ways the sanctity of the sabbath was marked in this miracle. There was a double quantity on the sixth day, there was none on the seventh day, and that gathered on the sixth did not putrefy on the seventh.

31. **Like coriander seed**—It lay on the ground in small seed-like, pearl-coloured grains. Though called *bread* it is not to be imagined as a loaf, but as like a grain or seed.

AN OMER OF MANNA LAID UP BEFORE JEHOVAH, 32–36.

32–36. This passage is valuable as giving us an insight into the manner in which the book was written. It is plain that this account of the manna laid...up before the Testimony was composed after the ark of Testimony was made and the tabernacle set up; and the thirty-fifth verse was written after the forty years' sojourn was ended. While Moses doubtless wrote down the events of the desert life, especially the Divine commands, at the time of their occurrence, he also, at the end of his long career in the plains of Moab, wove these events into a regular treatise, with comments and connecting paragraphs. At the end of this chapter, wherein the manna is first mentioned and fully described, was the appropriate place to finish the account of it, and hence he here adds the command for its preservation and the time of its continuance.

34. **Before the Testimony**—The two stone tablets of the law, afterwards particularly described, (Exod. xxxiv, 1, etc.,) which were kept in the sacred ark, covered by the mercy-seat. This law was called a **Testimony** against the sins of Israel.

35. **Until they came to a land inhabited**—Till they left the desert with its nomad inhabitants, and reached a country of settled population on the borders of the land of Canaan, in the plains of Moab. Deut. xxxiv, 1. It does not necessarily follow that the manna had ceased at the time of writing this, but the statement is, that this supernatural supply had continued through the desert life. According to Joshua v, 11, 12, it continued after the Israelites had passed the Jordan and encamped in Gilgal, till "the morrow after the passover" of that year. If, as some suppose, a subsequent writer, living after the death of Moses, had written this verse, he would not have left the statement in this shape, conveying, as it does, the implication, though not making the direct statement, that they ate no manna after reaching Canaan. Such subsequent writer must have known of the

land of Canaan. **36** Now an omer *is* the tenth *part* of an ephah.

CHAPTER XVII.

AND *all the congregation of the children of Israel journeyed from

a Chap. 16. 1; Num. 33. 12.

the wilderness of Sin, after their journeys, according to the commandment of the LORD, and pitched in Rephidim and *there was* no water for the people to drink. **2** *b* Wherefore the people did chide with Moses, and said, Give us

b Num. 20. 3, 4.

above quoted account in Joshua. Thus here is a noteworthy touch of genuineness.

36. **An omer**—The reason for here specially mentioning the capacity of the omer seems to be that given by Michaelis and Hengstenberg. Literally, the word *omer* signifies a sheaf of wheat, but in this chapter it denotes a measure, and it is never used with this meaning afterwards. When subsequently the same measure is spoken of it is called *the tenth part of an ephah*, as in Num. v, 15, and xxviii, 15. According to these commentators the word here really means the little earthen vessel or cup which the Israelites used for drinking purposes in the desert, and the author here means to say that this cup usually held a tenth of an ephah, the ephah being then a well known measure. In arranging the book into regular form for the use of coming generations it was proper and appropriate thus to describe the capacity of the vessel in which the Israelites measured the daily allowance of manna. Afterwards the name of the vessel came naturally to be used to designate the measure of the vessel—as our word "cup" has both meanings, the vessel and the measure. Omer is to be distinguished from *homer*, which was ten ephahs or a hundred omers.

CHAPTER XVII.

MARCH TO REPHIDIM—WANT OF WATER, 1–7.

1. **From the wilderness of Sin**—The plain of Murkha. See Introductory Note, (1,) on chapter xvi. **After their Journeys**—Or, rather, *breaking up places*—stations in the desert—implying that there were stations between Sin and Rephidim. Two of these, Alush and Dophkah, mentioned in Numbers xxxiii, 12–14, are not as yet identified with any known localities, but were probably in Wady Feiran. **According to the commandment of the Lord**—Literally, *the mouth of Jehovah* who regulated their halting places by the pillar of cloud. Moses had lived forty years in this wilderness, and must have had much knowledge concerning its thoroughfares, springs, and oases, which would be of the highest value to him in conducting Israel. How much of this guidance was in this way natural, and how much supernatural, it is impossible to determine. **Rephidim**—The last station mentioned before the "Desert of Sinai," though other halting-places may have intervened. Here their progress was contested by the Amalekites. In Wady Feiran, where now we suppose the main body of Israel to have been, we find precisely such a spot as would be certain to be held by a tribe of the desert, and where they would be likely to dispute the passage of this great thoroughfare through their territory. At the northern base of Mount Serbal is a large fertile tract, "the paradise of the Bedouin," with springs and palm groves, extending for miles along the valley, where, if anywhere in the whole peninsula, the Amalekites would be encamped, holding the wells, and cutting off the advance of an invading host. Israel was thus obliged to halt in a dry part of the wady, before reaching the oasis, and was not able to get to the springs. Thus there was **no water for the people to drink.** All the members of the "Sinai Expedition," except Mr. Holland, agree in identifying this spot with Rephidim. Holland locates it farther along, at a pass leading into Wady es Sheikh. A rocky hill, from six to seven hundred feet high, overlooks this palm grove from the northern side of the valley, called Jebel (Mount) Tahuneh. On this

B. C. 1491. CHAPTER XVII. 459

water that we may drink. And Moses said unto them, Why chide ye with me? wherefore do ye ^c tempt the LORD? 3 And the people thirsted there for water; and the people ^d murmured against Moses, and said, Wherefore *is* this *that* thou hast brought us up out of Egypt, to kill us and our children and our cattle with thirst? 4 And Moses ^e cried unto the LORD, saying, What shall I do unto this people? they be almost ready

to ^f stone me. 5 And the LORD said unto Moses, ^g Go on before the people, and take with thee of the elders of Israel; and thy rod, wherewith ^h thou smotest the river, take in thine hand, and go. 6 ⁱ Behold, I will stand before thee there upon the rock in Horeb; and thou shalt smite the rock, and there shall come water out of it, that the people may drink. And Moses did so in the sight of the elders of Israel. 7 And he called

---

c Deut. 6. 16; Psa. 78. 18, 41; Isa. 7. 12; Matt. 4. 7; 1 Cor. 10. 9.——*d* Chap. 16. 2.——*e* Chap. 14. 15.——*f* 1 Sam. 30. 6; John 8. 59; 10. 31.

g Ezek. 2. 6.——*h* Chapter 7. 20; Num. 20. 8.——*i* Num. 20. 10; Psa. 78. 15. 20; 105. 41; 114. 8; 1 Cor. 10. 4.

---

hill, in the early Christian ages, stood a church and a bishop's residence, while a settlement called Paran, whose name survives in the modern Feiran, clustered among the palms below. The walls of an ancient convent still stand on a mound in front of this hill, originally built of dressed sandstone, but repaired with rude stones from Serbal. Stanley says that "the oldest known tradition of the peninsula is, that Rephidim is the same as Paran." If so, this hill, Jebel Tahuneh, is without doubt the one on which Moses prayed during the conflict with Amalek. (Palmer's *Desert of the Exodus*, pp. 158, 276.)

4. **What shall I do**—There was now another mutiny, as in the Desert of Sin, but apparently more dangerous, for Moses regards his life as in peril. Yet, though himself in as great perplexity as the people, he consults Jehovah in simple faith, and meekly bears the threats of the insurgent crowd.

5. **Thy rod**—The rod which brought death to Egypt is to bring life to Israel; the power which made the life-giving Nile a channel of loathsome death is to bring from the dry rock waters of life. So, ever, the same truth is "to the one a savour of life, to the other a savour of death."

6. **I will stand before thee**—In the pillar of cloud. **In Horeb**—The name of the mountain cluster, or district, towards which Israel was now advancing. The Sinai peak, or mountain of the law, was one of the summits of this cluster. **In the sight of the elders**—Chosen witnesses who could bear record to the reality of the

miracle. In endeavouring to rationalize away this miracle, men have imagined arrangements of rocks and fountains, etc., more miraculous far than anything in the narrative. Palmer's account of a rock and its accompanying tradition, at this place, is interesting. He says: "It is a significant fact that in Wady Feiran, immediately before the part of the valley where the fertility commences, I discovered a rock, (a large mass of granite fallen from the wady wall,) which Arab tradition regards as the site of the miracle. This rock, which has never before been noticed by travellers, is called Hesy el Khattatin, and is surrounded by small heaps of pebbles, placed upon every available stone in the immediate neighbourhood." It will be noticed that this is a totally different rock from that shown by the monks of St. Katharine as the Rock of Moses. That is near their convent at Jebel Musa, and is a large, cubical block of red granite, traversed obliquely from top to bottom by a seam of finer materials, twelve or fifteen inches wide, which contains several horizontal crevices, which are shown by the monks as the mouths from which the water gushed. (Robinson, Olin.) But it is wholly impossible for Rephidim to have been at Mount Sinai; and the monks, in forming their traditions, seem to have been wholly careless, if not ignorant, of the Scripture narrative. They have simply grouped all the holy sites within easy walking distance of their convent.

The allusion which the Roman historian Tacitus makes to this miracle, as well as to the exode and wandering

the name of the place *¹ Massah, and ² Meribah, because of the chiding of the children of Israel, and because they tempted the LORD, saying, Is the LORD among us or not? 8 ¹ Then came Amalek, and fought

k Num. 20, 13; Psa. 81. 7; 9 . : Heb. 3. 8.— or, *Strife*.—*l* Gen. 36. 12; Num. 24. 20; Deut. 1 That is, *Temptation*.—2 That is, *Chiding*, 25. 17; 1 Sam. 15. 2.

of the Israelites, is most instructive, as showing what confused ideas the most enlightened Romans had of Hebrew history, and also what a deep impression this miracle made, even upon the heathen world. Having stated that the Egyptian king *drove* the Israelites into a vast desert, he says: "While the others were stupefied with grief, Moses, one of the exiles, advised them not to look for help to gods or men, seeing that they now were abandoned by both, but trust him as a celestial leader, who had first helped them in their present missions. To this they agreed, and began their random journey, ignorant of every thing. But nothing exhausted them so much as the want of water. And now they had thrown themselves down over all the ground, near unto death, when a herd of wild asses came from feeding, and went to a rock overshadowed by a grove of trees. Moses followed them, conjecturing that there was grassy soil there, and opened great sources of water, (*largas aquarum venas operit*.) This was a relief, and, after journeying continually for six days, they on the seventh drove out the inhabitants, (allusion to the Jewish week and Sabbath,) and obtained the lands in which their city and temple were dedicated. They consecrated, in the most holy place of their temple, an image of the animal who saved them from their thirst, and their wandering (1)"—TACITUS' *History*, v, 2–5. And in this way history is written by one of the most famous of historians!

7. **Massah**—*Temptation*. **Meribah** —*Strife*.

CONFLICT WITH AMALEK, 8–16.

8. **Then came Amalek**—The Amalekites were a nomadic people of whom we find the first trace in the life of Abraham, (Gen. xiv, 7,) who seem to have been pressed westwards into Southern Palestine and the Sinai Peninsula, from the shores of the Persian Gulf, by the advance of the Assyrian empire. (Knobel's *Völkertafel*.) There are now found in the desert primitive remains of tombs, stone circles, and archaic sculptures, which are referred to this people. Stone huts of the beehive form, seven to ten feet high, with well-made door-openings two feet square, made of rubbed stones, are also found in various parts of these deserts, and are assigned by many antiquarians to the Amalekites. (See cut on opposite page.)

This tribe, or nation, now held the great thoroughfare from Egypt to Palestine by Wady Feiran and Akabah. We have already seen that the Philistines held the northern thoroughfare along the Mediterranean shore, by Gaza and the maritime plain, so that collision with the one or the other of these nations was inevitable. This was now their first conflict with this wide-spread people, who harassed them at intervals through all the period of the Judges, who were signally defeated by Saul, and finally destroyed by David. 2 Sam. viii, 12. This was chiefly a guerrilla warfare, the Amalekites blocking the steep, narrow passes against the advance of Israel, and harassing their flanks and rear. Deut. xxv, 18. At Rephidim, however, three miles above the rock just described as the rock of Moses in the Arab tradition, the Wady Feiran broadens out into a plain which extends up into two branch valleys along the flanks of the lofty Mount Serbal. The conical hill Tahuneh, above described, commands a full view of this plain and of these branch valleys, between which rises the jagged front of Serbal. (See cut on opposite page.)

The only objection worthy of notice which is made to locating this conflict before Tahuneh is that Exod. xix, 2, states that when Israel departed from Rephidim they "camped before the

PRIMEVAL DWELLINGS IN WADY EL BIYAR.

VIEW FROM JEBEL TAHUNEH

462 EXODUS. B. C. 1491.

with Israel in Rephidim. 9 And Moses said unto ᵐJoshua, Choose us out men, and go out, fight with Amalek: to morrow I will stand on the top of the hill with ⁿthe rod of God in mine hand. 10 So Joshua did as Moses had said to him, and fought with Amalek: and Moses, Aaron, and Hur went up to the top of the hill. 11 And it came to pass, when Moses ᵒ held up his hand, that Israel prevailed: and when he let down his hand, Amalek prevailed. 12 But Moses' hands *were* heavy; and they took a stone, and put *it* under him, and he sat thereon; and Aaron and Hur stayed up his hands, the one on the one side, and the other on the other side; and his hands were steady until the going down of the sun. 13 And Joshua discomfited Amalek and his people with the edge

m Called *Jesus*, Acts 7. 45; Heb. 4. 8.   *n* Chap. 4. 20.—*o* James 5. 16.

mount," Sinai, which is more than a day's march from the oasis of Feiran. But Mount Sinai is not stated to be the *next* station after Rephidim, and the itinerary of Num. xxxiii shows, as we have already seen, that several intermediate stations are omitted in the Exodus narrative. Dophkah and Ahesh, between the Desert of Sin and Rephidim, find no mention here. Of course those who (like Knobel, Keil, Murphy) suppose that the Israelites went to Sinai by the Debbet er Ramleh, place Rephidim somewhere in that sandy plain. See Introduction to chap. xvi.

9-13. Moses said unto Joshua, Choose us out men—Moses's great successor, the second leader of Israel, and the type of the great Redeemer both in name and in office, now first abruptly appears before us. His name was originally Hoshea, (or Oshea,) which means *Help*, or *Deliverance;* but it was changed by Moses, (Numbers xiii, 16,) probably after this victory over Amalek, into *Jehoshua*, or *Joshua*, by the addition of the Memorial Name, JAH, thus making it mean, JAH (is) DELIVERANCE or SALVATION, the JEHOVAH SAVIOUR. This name is rendered Ἰησοῦς in Greek, in English JESUS, the "Name which is above every name," before which one day "every knee shall bow." Joshua was an Ephraimite, the son of Nun, and was now about forty years old. See note on Matt. i, 1. He was the military leader of Israel under Moses's direction through all the desert sojourn, and now in this, his first recorded expedition, is ordered to pick a body of warriors to carry on the main battle with Amalek in the plain and valleys of Rephidim. **With the rod of God in mine hand**—He calls his rod "the rod of God," for all the wonders wrought by it were revelations of God's power, not of his. This rod he was to elevate as a standard, a symbol of God's presence with Israel. It was the rod that had smitten the Nile, and the Red Sea, and the rock of Meribah; and the sight of it would inspire the warriors of Israel with a consciousness that Jehovah was their real leader in this their first conflict with heathen powers. The gesture was at the same time an act of prayer, as he stood on the hill, above the battle, pointing heavenward with "the rod of God." **Aaron and Hur** — This Hur is said by Josephus to have been the husband of Miriam, and identical with the Hur who was the father of Uri and grandfather of the artist Bezaleel. Exod. xxxi, 2. Moses was thus accompanied by his near kinsmen—his brother and the husband of his sister—as he went up into the hill to inspire Israel and plead with God. **When Moses held up his hand**—The hand that held the rod. It will be noticed that the word *hand* is used in the singular. We are not to think of him as kneeling, with both hands stretched to heaven in prayer, as the scene is generally represented in paintings. At first he stood, raising the rod first in the right hand and then in the left, until he became weary; then he sat upon the stone which Aaron and Hur put under him, Aaron on the one side helping him keep the rod raised, and Hur on the other. Had both hands been constantly elevated, and Aaron and Hur thus constantly employed in staying them up, they would soon have become as weary as he; but they relieved each other in

B. C. 1491.   CHAPTER XVII.   463

of the sword. 14 And the LORD said unto Moses, ᵖ Write this *for* a memorial in a book, and rehearse *it* in the ears of Joshua: for ᑫ I will utterly put out the remembrance of Amalek from under heaven. 15 And Moses built an altar, and called the name of it ³Jehovah-nissi: 16 For he said, ⁴Because ⁵the LORD hath sworn *that* the LORD *will have* war with Amalek from generation to generation.

p Chap. 34. 27.——*q* Num. 24. 20; Deut. 25. 19; 1 Sam. 15. 3, 7; 30. 1, 17; 2 Sam. 8. 12; Ezra 9. 14.——3 That is, *The LORD my banner*.——4 Or, *Because the hand* of Amalek is *against the throne of the LORD*, therefore, &c.——5 Heb. *the hand upon the throne of the LORD*.

this toil. Elevating the hands is not essential to prayer; and the Scripture nowhere represents success in prayer as dependent upon any posture or gesture: but continuance in prayer and faith was essential to success, and the elevated rod was the symbol of this continuance. Aaron and Hur not only stayed up his hands, but his heart, blending their prayer with his. When, through weariness, Moses ceased to exercise and inspire faith, the battle turned against Israel; but by the help and sympathy of his brethren he was strengthened to continue his spiritual struggle till Amalek was defeated. The leader chosen by God, whom they had just been ready to stone, and the rod, which was the symbol of Jehovah's power, were thus shown to be essential to Israel's success. Here also is beautifully shown the divine-human partnership in fulfilling the plans of Providence. The rod of Moses and the sword of Joshua were both essential to the victory over Amalek; the prayer upon the hill and the battle upon the plain were both necessary to Israel's success. Joshua could not have conquered unless Moses had prayed and inspired prayer; he could not have kept up this spiritual struggle without the help of his two brethren; yet his soul would have wrestled in vain unless Joshua had fought. The battling host was victorious only while struggling both in earth and heaven.

14. **Write**—This is the first time that this word occurs in the Bible. Until quite recently the existence of the art of writing in the time of Moses was frequently disputed by the opponents of revelation; but it is now settled that the Phenicians, whose alphabet was the same as that of the Hebrews, practised writing at least as early as the time of Moses. The best idea of the form of the letters can be obtained from the *fac simile* of the famous Moabite stone discovered in 1868, which contains an inscription of Mesha, king of Moab, (2 Kings iii, 4, which see,) vaunting his victories over Omri, king of Israel, in the tenth century B. C., the oldest alphabetic inscription as yet known. ("The Moabite Stone," by Dr. Ginsburg; London, 1871.) Writing is here spoken of as if familiar to the Israelites, and it will be noticed, not mere monumental writing, as of a few words upon a stone, but in a *book*, upon papyrus, which denotes much advancement in the art. **In a book**—*In the* (well-known) *book ;* our translation improperly omits the article. (Gesenius, *Gr.*, § 109, 3, Rem. 1; Ewald, *Lehrb.*, § 277, a.) It was *the* book wherein was kept the record of this wonderful history, wherein all God's statutes were written down. It was doubtless the book used by Moses, or his scribes, in the composition of the Pentateuch, if not the Pentateuch itself. **In the ears of Joshua**—Because he was to be the military leader, and to execute this commission upon Amalek. **I will utterly put out**—Literally, *wiping I will wipe out;* fearfully graphic words. Amalek was a nation which had "filled the measure of its iniquities," and God appointed Israel to blot it from being.

15. **Built an altar**—The first of which we have any record since the time of Jacob. How consistent is this action with the unique and peculiar national character that was now beginning to be developed! Other nations would have built a monument to Moses or Joshua; but the Hebrew leader builds an altar and calls it JAHVEH-NISSI—JAHVEH *My Banner*. The reason of this is now given.

16. **Because the Lord** (JEHOVAH) **hath sworn**—An obscure and much disputed verse. It is quite generally conceded that "throne" here should

CHAPTER XVIII.

WHEN ª Jethro, the priest of Midian, Moses' father in law, heard of all that ᵇ God had done for Moses, and for

a Chap. 2. 16 ; 3. 1.——*b* Psa. 44. 1 ; 77. 14, 15 ; 78. 4 ;

be read "banner," as in verse 15, בֵּס being some copyist's error for בֵּס, which could very easily take place, especially as the word is nowhere else found. (Mich., Vater, Houbig., Ges., Knob.) The "because" shows that this verse gives a reason for the name of the altar, and the literal rendering would then run thus: *And he said,* [the name is Jehovah, my Banner,] *Because the hand* [of Israel is] *on the banner of JAH,* [there shall be] *war from Jehovah with Amalek from generation to generation;* that is, till he is blotted out. That is, Jehovah has reared up a standard against this heathen people, on which standard Israel has laid its hand, as Moses on this eventful day laid his hand upon the rod of God, and that standard shall not fall till Amalek is blotted out. Amalek, called by Balaam the "beginning of peoples," most ancient among nations, the first foe of the covenant people, is the type of universal heathenism, which shall fall before Jehovah's banner; and that banner shall not droop in the hands of his true Israel—the rod will not sink on the mount, nor the sword drop on the field—till all his foes are "wiped out" from under heaven. The Jehovah-Saviour "must reign till he hath put all enemies under his feet."

CHAPTER XVIII.
JETHRO'S VISIT TO MOSES, 1–27.

It is interesting to note that the hostile conflict with Amalek is immediately followed in this record by the friendly visit of Jethro, the Midianite. "Of all the characters that come across us in this stage of their history he is the purest type of the Arabian chief. In the sight of his numerous flocks feeding round the well in Midian, in his courtesy to the stranger who became at once his slave and his son-in-law, we seem to be carried back to the

Israel his people, *and* that the LORD had brought Israel out of Egypt; **2** Then Jethro, Moses' father in law, took Zipporah, Moses' wife, ᶜ after he had sent her back, **3** And her ᵈ two

105, 5, 43; 106. 2, 8.——*c* Chap. 4. 26.——*d* Acts 7. 29.

days of Jacob and Laban. And now the old chief, attracted from far by the tidings of his kinsman's fame, finds him out in the heart of the mountains of Sinai, encamped by the mount of God....He listens, and with his own priestly sanctity acknowledges the greatness of his kinsman's God; he officiates (if one may so say) like a second Melchizedek, the high priest of the desert....He is the first friend, the first counsellor, the first guide, that they have met since they cut themselves off from the wisdom of Egypt, and they hang upon his lips like children."—*Stanley.* This narrative stands, therefore, in its contrast with the battle with Amalek as a typical portraiture of those other non-Israelitish peoples who, unlike the hostile Amalekites, were ready to recognise in the God of Israel a personality and power above all other gods. Thus in the history of God's chosen people, and in the development of his kingdom, while some are fast and bitter to fight against his truth, others recognise in it the wisdom and power of the Most High. On the chronological order of this event see note on verse 5.

1. **Jethro** —See note on chap. ii, 18, and concluding note at the end of that chapter. He was, like Melchizedek, a patriarchal **priest,** and, as verse 12 shows, was wont to offer burnt offerings and sacrifices unto God. **Heard of all that God had done**— The marvels of the Exodus sounded out among the heathen far and wide. Compare Josh. ii, 10. Such wonders made it conspicuous that no human hand or power, but **Jehovah, had brought Israel out of Egypt.** Thus was the name of Israel's God magnified among the nations.

2. **After he had sent her back**— See notes on chap. iv, 24–26. The discrepancies which some interpreters find between this account and Moses's return into Egypt narrated in chap.iv,

sons; of which the ᵉname of the one was ¹ Gershom; for he said, I have been an alien in a strange land: 4 And the name of the other *was* ² Eliezer; for the God of my father, *said he, was* mine help, and delivered me from the sword of Pharaoh: 5 And Jethro, Moses' father in law, came with his sons and his wife unto Moses into the wilderness, where he encamped at ᶠthe mount of God:

e Chap. 2. 22.——1 That is, *A stranger there.*   2 That is, *My God is a help.*——*f* Chap. 3. 1, 12.

18–26, are creations of their own fancy. Our historian has not given us all the details. The statement of iv, 20, that Moses took his wife and sons, and "returned to the land of Egypt," is seen from the immediate context to mean that he started with them to return, and that they accompanied him until the incident which occurred by the way (verses 24–26) served as an occasion for her returning with her sons to her father's house. This simple and natural supposition solves all the difficulties, and is itself suggested by the record here given. The work and exposures of Moses in Egypt made it expedient that his wife and children return and abide in Midian until he should return home from Egypt at the head of his people. Another reasonable hypothesis is, that Moses took his wife and sons to Egypt, and that after the opposition to his mission became formidable, he secretly sent them back from Egypt to the home of Jethro.

3. **Gershom**—See on chap. ii, 22.

4. **Eliezer**—Here for the first time mentioned by name, but both sons are referred to in iv, 20, and it is supposed that this younger son was the one circumcised by the way, (iv, 25.) The name means, *my God is a help,* and was given either in remembrance of Moses's past deliverance **from the sword of Pharaoh,** or as expressing his hope for the future. The fear of execution as one guilty of blood, and the purpose of Pharaoh to slay him, were the cause of his flight from Egypt, (ii, 15.) The same old fear may have arisen at the thought of his returning, and if Eliezer were born about that time there would have been a special appropriateness in the name. We should then render: *and he will deliver me,* etc.

5. **Where he encamped at the mount of God**—This most naturally means that Jethro's visit occurred after the Israelites had reached Sinai and encamped before the mountain. No other view, probably, would have been entertained were it not for the statement of chap. xix, 2, which seems to place the arrival at Sinai chronologically subsequent to this visit of Jethro. **The mount of God** means, in this verse, the same as in chap. iii, 1; but there appears no insuperable objection to understanding by it the whole Sinaitic range or mass of mountains known as Horeb. So far, therefore, as the words here used determine the question, we may admit that Jethro's visit might have occurred either at the encampment of Rephidim or of Sinai. But the account of what was done during this visit—especially the laborious work of Moses in verse 13, and the appointment of judges recommended by Jethro, verses 14–26, implies more time than the halt at Rephidim supposes. A comparison of chapters xvi, 1 and xix, 1, appears to put all the journeys and events between the arrival at the wilderness of Sin and the arrival at Sinai within about fifteen days. This perhaps was time enough for all that is here recorded, including the visit of Jethro; and yet it is certainly more natural to understand that the adoption of Jethro's counsel and the appointment of judges occupied more time than such a crowding of events assumes. The adoption of Jethro's counsel, however, and the choosing of judges described in verses 24-26 need not be supposed to have occurred until a later time. The writer might have introduced the statement at this point to show that the valuable advice of the aged Midianite priest was observed, without meaning to say that all this occurred during Jethro's stay. But, on the other hand, it is not probable that such a sitting to judge the people as is described in verses 13–16 would occur at Rephidim; but, after the more permanent encampment "before the mount,"

6 And he said unto Moses, I thy father in law Jethro am come unto thee, and thy wife, and her two sons with her.

7 And Moses ᵍ went out to meet his father in law, and did obeisance, and ʰ kissed him; and they asked each other of *their* ³ welfare; and they came into the tent. **8** And Moses told his father in law all that the LORD had done unto Pharaoh and to the Egyptians for Israel's sake, *and* all the travail that had ⁴ come upon them by the way, and *how* the LORD ⁱ delivered them. **9** And Jethro rejoiced for all the goodness which the LORD had done to Israel, whom he had delivered out of the hand of the Egyptians. **10** And Jethro said, ᵏ Blessed *be* the LORD, who hath delivered you out of the hand of the Egyptians, and out of the hand of Pharaoh, who hath delivered the people from under the hand of the Egyptians. **11** Now I know that the LORD *is* ˡ greater than all gods: ᵐ for in the thing wherein they dealt ⁿ proudly *he was* above them. **12** And Jethro, Moses' father in law, took a

---

g Gen. 14. 17; 18. 2; 19. 1; 1 Kings 2. 19. —
h Gen. 29. 13; 33. 4. —— 3 Heb. *peace,* Gen. 43. 27; 2 Sam. 17. 7. —— 4 Heb. *found them,* Gen. 44. 34; Num. 20. 14.—*i* Psa. 78. 42; 81. 7; 106. 10; 107. 2.

k Gen. 14. 20; 2 Sam. 18. 28; Luke 1. 68. ——
l 2 Chron. 2. 5; Psa. 95. 3; 97. 9; 135. 5. —
m Chap. 1. 10, 16, 22; 5. 2, 7; 14. 8, 18.——*n* 1 Sam. 2, 3; Neh. 9. 10, 16, 29; Job 40. 11, 12; Psa. 31. 23; 119. 21; Luke 1. 51.

(xix, 2,) such appointed seasons of judgment became a necessity. We incline, therefore, to the opinion that the events of this chapter belong to a period subsequent to the arrival at Sinai, and are designedly introduced out of their strict chronological order for the purpose of separating them from the more sacred revelation and legislation which proceeded from Jehovah, and which the writer wished to place by themselves. The friendly Midianite, as we have observed, is brought to our attention in immediate contrast with the hostile Amalekite, and such associations and contrasts are made more prominent by the sacred writer than mere chronological order.

6. He said unto Moses—That is, as the context shows, and as true Oriental custom required, he said this word to Moses by messengers sent before him to announce his coming. The Vulgate reads: *He sent word* (mandavit) *to Moses, saying.* Septuagint: *It was told Moses, saying, Behold, Jethro, thy father in law, is come to thee.*

7. Did obeisance—This brief but vivid description is true to the warmth and emotion of genuine Oriental greeting. The interest of the occasion was greatly enhanced by the reunion of Moses and his wife and children and the wondrous events that had taken place since they were last together.

8. Moses told — A thrilling tale! Such wonders as the plagues of Egypt and the miracles of the exodus would have speedily become the subject of national song and history. The presumption, in the absence of any evidence, that Moses would also commit the great events of his time to writing, is far greater than that he would not. By **the travail** that found them by the way we understand the hunger and thirst and exhaustion which caused the people to murmur; also the war with Amalek.

9. Jethro rejoiced — For he was possessed of that high, reverent spirit which gladly accepts the lessons of God's mighty works. Although outside of the chosen people, he joyfully accepts and profits by their higher revelations.

10. Jethro said—Lange regards this utterance of Jethro as lyrical. Verses 10 and 11 may be thrown into poetic form as follows:

Blessed be Jehovah,
Who delivered you from the hand of the Egyptians,
And from the hand of Pharaoh.
Who delivered the people from under the hand of the Egyptians.
Now know I that Jehovah is greater than all the gods;
For [he magnified himself] in the thing
In which they acted proudly against them.

11. He was above them—The exact sense of the latter half of this verse is uncertain. The English translators understood the עֲלֵיהֶם to refer to the false gods, and supplying **he was** would most naturally make these gods rather than the Egyptians the subject of the verb זָדוּ, *acted proudly.* But inasmuch as something is to be supplied, it seems better to carry over

CHAPTER XVIII.

burnt offering and sacrifices for God: and Aaron came, and all the elders of Israel, to eat bread with Moses' father in law ° before God.

13 And it came to pass on the morrow, that Moses sat to judge the people: and the people stood by Moses from the morning unto the evening. 14 And when Moses' father in law saw all that he did to the people, he said, What *is* this thing that thou doest to the people? Why sittest thou thyself alone, and all the people stand by thee from morning unto even? 15 And Moses said unto his father in law, Because ᵖ the people come unto me to inquire of God: 16 When they have ᑫ a matter, they come unto me; and I judge between ⁵ one and another, and I do ʳ make *them* know the statutes of God, and his laws.

o Deut. 12. 7; 1 Chron. 29. 22; 1 Cor. 10. 18, 21, 31.—*p* Lev. 24. 12; Num. 15. 34.—*q* Chap. 23. 7; 24. 14; Deut. 17. 8; 2 Sam. 15. 3; Job 31. 13; Acts 18, 15; 1 Cor. 6. 1. —— 5 Heb. *a man and his fellow.* —— *r* Lev. 24. 15; Num. 15. 35; 27. 6, etc.; 36. 6-9.

into this last sentence of the verse the thought expressed in the גָּדוֹל מִן of the preceding line. It seems probable that some word or words have fallen out before בַּדָּבָר, *in the thing*, and we take the sentiment to be: Jehovah is greater than all the gods, for he showed this in all the things wherein the Egyptians acted proudly against the Israelites. Comp. Neh. ix, 10. Reference is to the oppression and persecution which Israel received from the Egyptians, and the pursuit which ended at the Red Sea, where Jehovah triumphed gloriously.

12. **Burnt offering and sacrifices for God**—Jethro, the venerable priest, according to ancient usages of patriarchal worship, presides and officiates at this sacrifice and festival. The Levitical ritual and institutions had not yet been established, and no one but Jethro could, on that occasion, have so appropriately acted as priest. This great patriarch, with an intensified faith in Jehovah as the only true God, (verses 10, 11,) worships in thorough accord with Moses and Aaron **and all the elders of Israel.** All these probably assisted in some form at this sacrifice. Comp. Gen. xxxi, 46-54. "This passage is of great importance in its bearings upon the relation between the Israelites and their congeners, and upon the state of religion among the descendants of Abraham."—*Speaker's Commentary.*

13. **On the morrow**—After the sacrificial feast described in verse 12. The duties of friendship, love, and hospitality must give place to those of public responsibility and care. The very next day after the joyful feast the great lawgiver and judge resumes his arduous work. It has been suggested that difficulties arising out of the division of the spoil of the Amalekites occasioned the disputes which **Moses** sat all day to decide. This, however, is a pure supposition, and we have no evidence that the Israelites captured any considerable amount of spoil from the defeated Amalekites. Various causes of dispute and strife would naturally arise from time to time among the thousands of Israel, and nothing can be determined from this fact as to the date of Jethro's visit.

14. **Why sittest thou thyself alone?**—A question which might well be put to others besides Moses, who never appear to reflect that much important work is often better done by many than by one. He who assumes to do all the judging and counselling in the Church and congregation of the Lord is likely both to injure himself and to hinder others from entering fields of useful labour.

15. **The people come unto me to inquire of God**—They recognised Moses as their divinely chosen lawgiver and judge, and his decision in any given case would be of the nature of a divine oracle. If we understand that this event occurred soon after the first Sinaitic legislation, it has a force not otherwise so apparent. See especially note on next verse.

16. **A matter**—A matter of controversy requiring the intervention of a judge. **I do make them know the statutes of God, and his laws**—The statutes and laws (*torahs*) are not naturally understood of such enactments and "judgments" as Moses is commanded, in chap. xxi, 1, to set before

17 And Moses' father in law said unto him, The thing that thou doest *is* not good. **18** *ᵒ* Thou wilt surely wear away, both thou, and this people that *is* with thee: for this thing *is* too heavy for thee; *ᵖ* thou art not able to perform it thyself alone. **19** Hearken now unto my voice, I will give thee counsel, and *ᵗ* God shall be with thee: Be thou *ᵘ* for the people to God-ward, that thou mayest *ᵛ* bring the causes unto God: **20** And thou shalt *ʷ* teach them ordinances and laws, and shalt show them *ˣ* the way wherein they must walk, and *ʸ* the work that they must do. **21** Moreover thou shalt provide out of all the people *ᶻ* able men, such as *ᵃ* fear God, *ᵇ* men of truth, *ᶜ* hating covetousness; and place *such* over them, *to be* rulers of thousands, *and* rulers of hundreds, rulers of fifties, and

---
ᵒ Heb. *Fading thou wilt fade.* — *ᵖ* Num. 11. 14, 17; Deut. 1. 9, 12. — *ᵗ* Chap. 3. 12. — *ᵘ* Chap. 4. 16; 20. 19; Deut. 5. 5. — *ᵛ* Num. 27. 5. — *ʷ* Deut. 4. 1, 5; 5. 1; 6. 1, 2; 7. 11.

ˣ Psa. 143. 8. — *ʸ* Deut. 1. 18. — *ᶻ* Verse 25; Deut. 1. 15, 16; 16. 18; 2 Chron. 19. 5-10; Acts 6. 3. — *ᵃ* Gen. 42. 18; 2 Sam. 23. 3; 2 Chron. 19. 9. — *ᵇ* Ezek. 18. 8. — *ᶜ* Deut. 16. 19.

---

the people. As matters of dispute arose, the judgments sought of Moses afforded him a most fitting opportunity to communicate to the people such **statutes and laws** as many of those recorded in chaps. xxi and xxii. The people observed that Jehovah talked from heaven with their great leader, (xx, 18–22,) and would thenceforth accept his word as a God-given oracle. Compare verse 15. The way in which Moses in this verse speaks of his judging the people, and making them know the laws, implies something that had already become habitual with him—a thing hardly supposable before their arrival at Sinai. This passage also suggests how Moses may have orally set forth many statutes and ordinances both before and after he had written them in a book.

18. **Wear away**—Heb., *fading thou wilt fade.* That is, as a leaf that withers and decays. Excessive labour and anxiety will send the strongest and holiest man into decline. **And this people**—The people as well as the judge would necessarily become weary and restless by long waiting and delay of judgment, and some, perhaps, would be tempted to go away and take the judgment into their own hands.

19. **I will give thee counsel**—Like Melchizedek, "priest of the Most High God," (Gen. xiv, 18,) who blessed Abram, the father of the faithful, Jethro, another priest of like rank, assumes to counsel Moses the man of God. Conscious of holding an approved relationship toward God, he put forth his advice as one having a measure of authority over his son-in-law. **Be thou for the people to God-ward**—That is, be thou the representative and spokesman of the people before God, as the next sentence further explains. **That thou mayest bring the causes** (הַדְּבָרִים, *matters* of controversy, comp. verse 16) **unto God**—Matters of great moment, on which divine counsel was to be sought, should be intrusted to Moses; but affairs of less importance might be left to inferior judges. Verse 22.

20. **Teach them ordinances and laws**—Equivalent to making "them know the statutes and laws" in verse 16. The word rendered **teach** (Hiphil of זָהַר) means to *shed light upon.* Moses was to exercise the twofold office of appearing in behalf of the people before God and of revealing God's truth to the people. Thus he was an honoured mediator, being intercessor, advocate, lawgiver, and judge. **The way . . . the work**—Two important and comprehensive phases of godliness, equivalent to *life* and *action.*

21. **Able men**—Men of strong, commanding character, and manifestly competent for the work to be done. Four distinguishing qualities of the ideal judge are here expressed: **able,** (competent, capable,) *God-fearing, truth-loving,* and *bribery-hating.* Without these qualities no man is fit to occupy a judgment seat. בֶּצַע, here rendered **covetousness,** means *unrighteous gain,* obtained by way of extortion. The righteous ruler "despiseth the gain of oppressions, shaking his hands from holding bribes." Isa. xxxiii, 15. **To be rulers**—Chiefs or princes. **Thousands, . . . hundreds, . . . fif-

B. C. 1491. CHAPTER XVIII. 469

rulers of tens: **22** And let them judge the people ᵈ at all seasons: ᵉ and it shall be, *that* every great matter they shall bring unto thee, but every small matter they shall judge: so shall it be easier for thyself, and ᶠ they shall bear *the burden* with thee. **23** If thou shalt do this thing, and God command thee *so*, then thou shalt be ᵍ able to endure, and all this people shall also go to ʰ their place in peace. **24** So Moses hearkened to the voice of his father in law, and did all that he had said. **25** And ⁱ Moses chose able men out of all Israel, and made them heads over the people, rulers of thousands, rulers of hundreds, rulers of fifties, and rulers of tens. **26** And they ᵏ judged the people at all seasons: the ˡ hard causes they brought unto Moses, but every small matter they judged themselves.
27 And Moses let his father in law depart; and ᵐ he went his way into his own land.

---

d Verse 26.——*e* Verse 26; Lev. 24. 11; Num. 15. 33; 27. 2; 36. 1; Deut. 1. 17; 17. 8.——*f* Num. 11. 17.——*g* Verse 18.

h Gen. 18. 33; 30. 25; chap. 16. 29; 2 Sam. 19. 39.——*i* Deut. 1. 15; Acts 6. 5.——*k* Verse 22.——*l* Job 29. 16.——*m* Num. 10. 29, 30.

---

ties, . . . tens—"This minute classification of the people is thoroughly in accordance with the Semitic character, and was retained in after ages. The numbers appear to be conventional, corresponding nearly, but not exactly, to the military or civil divisions of the people."—*Speaker's Com.* Comp. Num. i, 16; x, 4; Josh. xxii, 14.
22. Great matter . . . small matter —See note on verse 19.
23. To their place—Some think that Jethro here refers to Canaan as the promised home or place of Israel. But the more simple reference is to the common place of abode, the tent or home, to which the people, having had their matters of controversy adjusted, could speedily return.
24. Moses hearkened — He was meek, deferential, and prompt to profit by the counsel of the venerable priest.

II. JEHOVAH REVEALED AS KING OF ISRAEL.

The Divine Glory, and the Giving of the Law at Sinai. Chaps. XIX, 1–XXIV, 18.

CHAPTER XIX.

THE ENCAMPMENT AT MOUNT SINAI, 1, 2.

We now approach the most sublime and impressive narrative of Old Testament history. After the struggle and victory of the exodus, and after two months' experience of desert journeys and exposures, the Israelites came and pitched their tents at the holy mountain where Moses beheld the burning bush. Comp. chap. iii, 12. Here they were to await further revelations of Jehovah.

The particular mountain at which the law was given has naturally been the subject of earnest research. Three different summits have their claims to this distinction—Serbal, Jebel Musa, and Ras es-Sufsafeh—all of them notable among the prominent mountains of the Sinaitic peninsula. Having identified Rephidim with the Wady Feiran at the northern base of Serbal, (see on chap. xvii, 1,) we need not linger here to consider its claims, which indeed seem very futile. Jebel Musa has in its favour the local traditions of at least fifteen centuries, and occupies the centre of the Sinaitic group of mountains. Its summit consists of an area of huge rocks, about eighty feet in diameter, partly covered with ruins, but the view is confined, and far less extensive and imposing than that from other summits in the group. There is no spot to be seen around it suitable for a large encampment, and the bottoms of the adjacent valleys are invisible. (Robinson, *Biblical Researches*, vol. i, pp. 104, 105.) Far more imposing and every way in harmony with the scriptural narrative is the height known as Ras es-Sufsafeh, at the north-western end of the same ridge, overlooking the plain of er-Rahah. See note on verse 12. Robinson describes the view from this summit as follows: "The whole plain er-Rahah lay spread out beneath our feet, with the adjacent wadies and mountains; while Wady esh-Sheikh on the right, and the recess on the left, both connected with and opening broadly from er-Rahah, presented an area which serves nearly to double that of the plain. Our conviction was strengthened

IN CHAPTER XIX.
the third month, when the children

a Num. 33. 15.

that here, or on some of the adjacent cliffs, was the spot where the Lord descended in fire and proclaimed the law. Here lay the plain where the whole congregation might be assembled; here was the mount that could be approached and touched, if not forbidden; and here the mountain-brow where alone the lightnings and the thick cloud would be visible, and the thunders and the voice of the trump be heard, when the Lord 'came down in the sight of all the people upon Mount Sinai.' We gave ourselves up to the awful scene; and read,

of Israel were gone forth out of the land of Egypt, the same day *a* came they

Masoretic text. The day of the month is not given, and the rendering, *in the third new moon*, adopted by many exegetes, and explained as equivalent to the first day of the third month, has no parallel in Hebrew usage. Had that been the author's meaning why would he not have employed the form of expression which appears in chapter xl, 1, 17? Comp. also the usage as seen in Gen. viii, 5, 13; Lev. xxiii, 24; Num. i, 1. In Num. ix, 1, and xx, 1, the name of the month only is given, and, were it not for the words, **the same day,** in

RAS ES-SUFSAFEH.

with a feeling that shall never be forgotten, the sublime account of the transaction of the commandments there promulgated, in the original words as recorded by the great Hebrew legislator."—*Biblical Researches*, vol. i, p. 107. For further discussion of the subject, see Stanley, *Sinai and Palestine*, pp. 74–76; Palmer, *Desert of the Exodus*, chapter vi, and the biblical cyclopædias under the word *Sinai*.

1. **In the third month, . . . the same day**—This is certainly a singular form of statement, and begets the suspicion of some corruption in the

our verse, we would naturally suppose that the writer did not intend to specify the day of the month when Israel arrived at Mount Sinai. But those words seem best explained by the supposition that the day of the month was originally written in the earlier part of the verse, but before the date of the ancient versions it by some oversight was dropped out. To explain the words, **the same day,** in connexion with the mention of **the third month,** as here, in the general sense of time, ("at that time,") is very unsatisfactory. According to Bush, who explains the text as it

CHAPTER XIX.

into the wilderness of Sinai. 2 For they were departed from ᵇ Rephidim, and were come *to* the desert of Sinai, and had pitched in the wilderness; and

---
ᵇ Chap. 17. 1, 8.
---

now stands as meaning the first day of the month, "this was just forty-five days after the departure from Egypt; for, adding sixteen days of the first month to twenty-nine of the second, the result is forty-five. To these we must add the day on which Moses went up to God, (verse 3,) the next day after, when he returned their answer to God, (verses 7, 8,) and the three days more mentioned in verses 10 and 11, which form altogether just fifty days from the passover to the giving of the law on Mount Sinai. Hence the feast which was kept in after-times to celebrate this event was called *Pentecost,* or the *fiftieth* day."—*Notes on Exodus, in loco.* But this idea, which appears nowhere in Josephus, or Philo, or any of the older Jewish writers, seems to be a late rabbinic tradition, and without valid warrant in Scripture. **The wilderness of Sinai** — This expression denotes the open plain "before the mount," (verse 2,) where the Israelites encamped and remained during the giving of the law, and the construction of the tabernacle. Comp. Lev. viii, 38; Num. i, 1, 19; iii, 14; ix, 1; x, 12, etc. The magnificent plain er-Rahah, which lies at the base of Ras es-Sufsafeh, most remarkably meets the conditions of the biblical narrative, and is the only place yet discovered in the Sinaitic mountains large enough to accommodate a congregation of two million people, and overhung by a mountain which may be literally touched from the plain below.

2. For they were departed from Rephidim—Rather, *And they departed from Rephidim.* This verse is but a fuller statement of what was said in the preceding verse, omitting, however, the mention of time and date. The emphasis is on the fact that there, in the solemn and sublime amphitheatre among the mountains, and **before the mount** which was to be forever consecrated in the history of the chosen people, **Israel camped.** The word here rendered **pitched** and **camped** is one and the same in Hebrew, (חָנָה.) In front of the sacred mountain the people now settled down to receive revelations from Him who had declared himself from the burning bush, I AM THAT I AM. Chap. iii, 14. We need not suppose that the entire body of people who came out of Egypt with Moses actually encamped and remained for a year in this one place. Probably only the heads of the nation, "the elders of the people," (verse 7,) and the leading families remained permanently in this place of encampment. The rest would naturally be distributed through the various adjacent valleys and plains, wherever the best pasturage for their numerous flocks could be found. According to chap. xxxiv, 3, the flocks and herds were not permitted to feed before the mount. It is a carping and unworthy criticism that makes difficulties in the Scripture narrative by assuming as recorded fact things on which the sacred writers are silent. But for incidental allusions, like those of chap. iii, 1, and Gen. xxxvii, 17, no one would have supposed that either Moses or the sons of Jacob went off scores of miles from home to pasture their flocks. We need to keep in mind that such terms as "all Israel," "all the land," "all the world," and even "all the high hills that were under the whole heaven," (Gen. vii, 19, where see note, and also on page 123,) need not to be taken in their extreme literal import.

PREPARATIONS FOR THE SINAITIC THEOPHANY, 3-15.

Before the divine glory is revealed upon the mount, the people must be admonished and purified. To effect this Moses first goes up into the mountain and receives for Israel the gracious words of verses 3-6. To these the people cheerfully respond with promise of obedience, and Moses, like a true mediator, returns their answer to Jehovah. Verses 7, 8. Again Jehovah speaks to Moses, and gives order for

472 EXODUS. B. C. 1491.

there Israel camped before ^cthe mount. 3 And ^d Moses went up unto God, and the LORD ^e called unto him out of the mountain, saying, Thus shalt thou say to the house of Jacob, and tell the children of Israel; 4 'Ye have seen what I did unto the Egyptians, and how ^g I bare you on eagles' wings, and brought you unto myself. 5 Now ^htherefore, if ye will obey my voice indeed, and keep my covenant, then ⁱ ye shall be a peculiar treasure unto me above all people: for

c Chap. 3. 1, 12.——d Chap. 20. 21; Acts 7. 38.——e Chap. 3. 4.——f Deut. 29. 2.——g Deut. 32. 11; Isa. 63. 9; Rev. 12. 14.——h Deut. 5. 2.

i Deut. 4. 20; 7. 6; 14. 2, 21; 26. 18; 32. 8, 9; 1 Kings 8. 53; Psa. 135. 4; Cant. 8. 12; Isa. 41. 8; 43. 1; Jer. 10. 16; Mal. 3. 17; Titus 2. 14.

careful preparations and purifying against the third day, when he will reveal himself in the sight of all the people, (9–13,) which order Moses is careful to enforce, (14, 15.) Thus begins the more direct religious discipline of the chosen people in the sacred school at Sinai.

3. **Moses went up unto God**—Notice the peculiar statement that Moses went up *unto* ELOHIM, and JEHOVAH **called unto him out of the mountain.** He seems to have gone up prompted by a holy impulse, and perhaps went to the spot where he had seen the burning bush, expecting to receive a divine communication. While thus seeking and expecting, JEHOVAH, the God of the Memorial Name, (chap. iii, 14, 15,) called to him from the mountain. We need not suppose that Moses was at the time upon the summit, or that this call of Jehovah summoned him thither. He had gone up, apart from the people, into the mountain, and while thus alone the voice of the invisible Jehovah addressed him. As yet there was no visible display of the divine glory. **House of Jacob**—"This expression does not occur elsewhere in the Pentateuch. It has a peculiar fitness here, referring doubtless to the special promises made to the patriarch."—*Speaker's Com.* The entire address, verses 3–6, is highly poetic, and may be rendered as follows:

Thus shalt thou say to the house of Jacob,
And tell to the sons of Israel:
Ye have seen what I did to the Egyptians,
And I bore you upon the wings of eagles,
And brought you unto me.
And now, if ye will diligently hear my voice,
And keep my covenant,
Ye shall be to me a precious possession above all the peoples,
For all the earth is mine.
And ye shall be to me a kingdom of priests and a holy nation.

4. **I bare you on eagles' wings**—This figure is finely elaborated in Deut. xxxii, 11: "As an eagle stirreth up her nest, fluttereth over her young, spreadeth abroad her wings, taketh them, beareth them on her wings," etc. The strength and the tenderness of God are thus set forth in this metaphor. Comp. Rev. xii, 14. **Unto myself**—Out of the bondage of Egypt and into the immediate protection and oversight of Jehovah at Sinai. The sacred place in front of the hallowed mount was as the presence-chamber of the Most High.

5. **Obey my voice . . . keep my covenant**—These two expressions denote the twofold idea of giving obedient attention to each new word that Jehovah speaks, and at the same time guard sacredly the terms of the covenant as already established, or about to be established in fuller form. **A peculiar treasure unto me**—The Hebrew word סְגֻלָּה is happily rendered by **peculiar treasure,** for it denotes more than the mere word *property* or *possessions.* In Mal. iii, 17, it is translated *jewels,* and in 1 Chron. xxix, 3, it means a special private quantity of gold and silver which Solomon amassed for himself, and so, also, probably, in Eccles. ii, 8, where mention is made of "the peculiar treasure of kings." In all other places (Deut. vii, 6; xiv, 2; xxvi, 18; Psa. cxxxv, 4) the word represents Israel as a peculiarly precious possession of Jehovah. Comp. Tit. ii, 14; 1 Pet. ii, 9. **Above all people**—Or, *from all the peoples,* as being chosen *out from* all the peoples of the earth. Being thus selected out of the nations, Israel would be esteemed above the other peoples, who, nevertheless, were all possessions of God, for it is added, as if to offset the idea that Israel's God

B. C. 1491.　　　　　CHAPTER XIX.　　　　　473

ᵏ all the earth *is* mine : **6** And ye shall be unto me a ˡ kingdom of priests, and a ᵐ holy nation. These *are* the words which thou shalt speak unto the children of Israel.

7 And Moses came and called for the elders of the people, and laid before their faces all these words which the

---

k Chap. 9. 29; Deut. 10. 14; Job 41. 11; Psa. 24. 1; 50. 12; 1 Cor. 10. 26, 28.—*l* Deut. 33. 2-4; 1 Pet. 2. 5, 9; Rev. 1. 6: 5. 10: 20. 6. — *m* Lev. 20. 24, 26; Deut. 7. 6; 26. 19; 28. 9; Isa. 62. 12; 1 Cor. 3. 17; 1 Thess. 5. 27.

---

was merely a national deity, **all the earth is mine,** for Jehovah God is its creator and ruler.

6. A kingdom of priests — The Septuagint renders, *a royal priesthood,* and the Vulgate, *a sacerdotal kingdom,* and both these ideas seem to inhere in the phrase. Jehovah proposes to make his chosen people a royal and priestly race. They will be royal, or regal, in character, because sons of the living God, and conceived as reigning with him ; they will be priestly, because, like a dynasty of priests, they will be the representatives and teachers of religion. To fulfil this lofty destiny it was necessary that they also be **a holy nation,** pure and clean in character and life ; not merely *set apart,* or consecrated to God, but also cleansed from all moral pollution.

7. Called for the elders of the people—Observe that this was no public address to an assembled nation, but a relatively private communication to their chiefs, who acted as their representatives. Hence an address delivered to them might be properly spoken of as addressed to all the people. See next verse.

8. All the people answered together—From the language employed in the preceding verse, and from the nature of the case, we most naturally infer that this answer of the people was obtained, not in one open assembly of all the nation, but through the mediation of the elders. These elders, representing each a different portion of the people, would have ready means of communicating with the different tribes, and obtaining at short notice their sentiments on any important matter. The word **together,** accordingly, means

LORD commanded him. **8** And ⁿ all the people answered together, and said, All that the LORD hath spoken we will do. And Moses returned the words of the people unto the LORD. **9** And the LORD said unto Moses, Lo, I come unto thee ᵒ in a thick cloud, ᵖ that the people may hear when I speak with thee, and ᵠ be-

---

n Chapter 24. 3, 7; Deuteronomy 5. 27; 26. 17. —— *o* Verse 16; chapter 20. 21; 24. 15, 16; Deuteronomy 4. 11; Psalm 18. 11, 12; 97. 2; Matthew 17. 5.—*p* Deuteronomy 4. 12, 36; John 12. 29, 30. —*q* Chapter 14. 31.

---

here the oneness or unanimity of the people's response. The answer returned was as that of one man. These two verses (7th and 8th) illustrate what any reader of sense ought to take for granted in such a history as this. We are not to suppose that every detail of communication is given. A great many small gatherings of the people may often have been held in different parts of the plain, and in the adjacent valleys, to hear the words of Jehovah ; sometimes communications may have been delivered by numerous messengers without any public assembly. Any reasonable hypothesis of this kind is legitimate in interpretation.

9. Lo, I come unto thee in a thick cloud—Or, *Behold, I am coming ;* that is, I am about to come thus. He refers to the sublime theophany to be manifested on the third day thereafter, (verse 11,) and often subsequently, when Jehovah would impress the people with an awful sense of his power and majesty. "As God knew the weakness of the sinful nation, and could not, as the Holy One, come into direct intercourse with it on account of its unholiness, but was about to conclude the covenant with it through the mediation of Moses, it was necessary, in order to accomplish the design of God, that the chosen mediator should receive special credentials; and these were to consist in the fact that Jehovah spoke to Moses in the sight and hearing of the people, that is to say, that he solemnly proclaimed the fundamental law of the covenant in the presence of the whole nation, (chapter xix, 16-xx, 18,) and showed by this fact that Moses was the recipient and mediator of the revelation of God, in order that the people

474 EXODUS. B. C. 1491.

lieve thee for ever. And Moses told the words of the people unto the LORD.

10 And the LORD said unto Moses, Go unto the people, and ʳ sanctify them to day and to morrow, and let them ˢ wash their clothes, **11** And be ready against the third day: for the third day the LORD ᵗ will come down in the sight of all the people upon mount Sinai. **12** And thou shalt set bounds unto the people round about, saying, Take heed to yourselves, *that ye go not* up into the mount, or touch the border of it: ᵘ whosoever toucheth the mount shall be

---

r Lev. 11. 44, 45; Heb. 10. 22. —— *s* Verse 14; Gen. 35. 2; Lev. 15. 5.

t Verses 16, 18; chap. 34. 5; Deut. 33. 2.—— *u* Heb. 12. 20.

---

might believe him **for ever,** as the law was to possess everlasting validity. Matt. v, 18." — *Keil.* **And Moses told the words of the people unto the Lord**—The repetition of these words from verse 8 looks like the blunder of some ancient copyist. They add nothing to the passage, and have no natural connexion with what precedes or follows. To suppose, with Dillmann, that it is a sentence copied from another documentary source is no more satisfactory than to assume that the writer carelessly repeated himself. But the ancient versions contain the words, and the two sentences differ, in that verse 8 employs the word *returned* (שׁוּב) and this verse has *told*, (נגד.) If the words are retained it is better to connect them with what follows, thus: "When Moses told the words of the people unto the Lord, then the Lord said unto Moses," etc.

10. Sanctify them—By observing all manner of bodily purifyings, *washing* **their clothes,** (comp. xxxv, 2,) and abstaining from all sexual intercourse, verse 15.

11. Be ready against the third day—Ceremonial purifications, made with expectations of some sublime theophany about to take place, prepared the hearts of the people to receive the deepest possible impressions from the scene. While the messages given through Moses to Israel were generally received alone in the mountain, this grand revelation was to be **in the sight of all the people.** Object-teaching was especially necessary at that stage of Israel's history.

12. Set bounds — The allusions made here to the mount, and the possible approaches to it, and *touching* **the border of it,** afford means for identifying the true Sinai. There must have been a great plain at the base of the mount capable of accommodating an immense assembly, a sublime head or top (verse 20) overlooking this plain, and such an immediate contact of plain and mountain that people might approach from below and touch the mount. All these conditions are strikingly fulfilled in the plain er-Rahah and the peak known as Ras Sasafeh, or Ras es-Sufsafeh. See note at beginning of this chapter. Stanley says: "No one who has approached the Ras Sasafeh through that noble plain, or who has looked down upon the plain from that majestic height, will willingly part with the belief that these are the two essential features of the view of the Israelitish camp. That such a plain should exist at all in front of such a cliff is so remarkable a coincidence with the sacred narrative as to furnish a strong internal argument, not merely of its identity with the scene, but of the scene itself having been described by an eye-witness. The awful and lengthened approach, as to some natural sanctuary, would have been the fittest preparation for the coming scene. The low line of alluvial mounds at the foot of the cliff exactly answers to the **bounds** which were to keep the people off from touching the mount. The plain itself is not broken and uneven and narrowly shut in, like almost all others in the range, but presents a long, retiring sweep against which the people could 'remove and stand afar off.' The cliff, rising like a huge altar in front of the whole congregation, and visible against the sky in lonely grandeur from end to end of the whole plain, is the very image of 'the mount that might be touched,' and from which the voice of God might be heard far and wide over the stillness of the plain below, widened at that point to its utmost extent by the confluence of all the con-

B. C. 1491.   CHAPTER XIX.   475

surely put to death: **13** There shall not a hand touch it, but he shall surely be stoned, or shot through; whether *it be* beast or man, it shall not live: when the ¹ᵛ trumpet soundeth long, they shall come up to the mount.

14 And Moses went down from the mount unto the people, and ʷ sanctified the people; and they washed their

---

1 Or, *cornet*.——*v* Verses 16, 19.——*w* Verse 10. ——*ω* Verse 11. ——*y* 1 Sam. 21. 4, 5; Zech. 7. 3; 1 Cor. 7. 5.

---

clothes. **15** And he said unto the people, ˣ Be ready against the third day: ʸ come not at *your* wives.

16 And it came to pass on the third day in the morning, that there were ᶻ thunders and lightnings, and a ᵃ thick cloud upon the mount, and the ᵇ voice of the trumpet exceeding loud; so that all the people that *was* in the camp

---

z Psa. 77. 18; Heb. 12. 18, 19; Rev. 4. 5; 8. 5; 11. 19.——*a* Verse 9; chap. 40. 34; 2 Chron. 5. 14. ——*b* Rev. 1. 10; 4. 1.

---

tiguous valleys. Here, beyond all other parts of the peninsula, is the adytum, withdrawn, as if in the 'end of the world,' from all the stir and confusion of earthly things." — *Sinai and Palestine*, pp. 42, 43.

13. Not a hand touch it — So sacred and so awful was that mount to be esteemed that no one unsanctified and unbidden might touch it, on the peril of life. Not even a **beast** would be permitted to touch it, and live. This rigorous requirement was adapted to inculcate reverence for the law. **When the trumpet soundeth long**—Heb., *in the drawing out of the yobel*. The word יוֹבֵל, here translated *trumpet*, appears to have been some kind of a wind instrument. In Josh. vi, 4, 5, 8, we find the word employed to qualify קֶרֶן, *horn*, or cornet, and in Lev. xxv, 10, it denotes the fiftieth year—year of liberty and joy—commonly known as "the year of jubilee." The Targum and the rabbins understand a wind instrument made of a ram's horn. The exact meaning is doubtful. Gesenius regards it as an onomatopoetic word, signifying *a joyful shout*, and, perhaps, is best understood here as the sound of some instrument, rather than the instrument itself. The *drawing out of the yobel* would thus mean the prolonged tones of a signal call, without specifying the particular instrument employed. See further on verse 16, where the *trumpet* is mentioned. **They shall come up to the mount**—Who? Certainly not the people generally, who were forbidden to touch it, (comp. verses 23 and 24,) but chosen representatives and elders of the people, (see chap. xxiv, 1, 2,) whom the writer does not here stop to specify. We see from verse 20 that only Moses

went up at first; subsequently Aaron was permitted to accompany him, (verse 24,) but the priests and the people were forbidden.

THE SINAITIC THEOPHANY, 16–20.

16. **The third day in the morning** —The Scripture furnishes no certain data from which to determine the day of the week, or of the month, on which this theophany took place. Rabbinical and other speculations and conjectures on the subject are of no value. But there are some noticeable analogies between these three days and those intervening between the death and resurrection of our Lord, especially the preparations and ardent expectations among the more believing disciples, and the earthquake and lightning-like appearance of the angel that rolled away the stone from the door of the sepulchre. The one third day heralded the sublimest proclamation of law ever known to man, the other the grandest monumental fact of Christianity—the revelation and pledge of immortality. **Thunders**—Heb., *voices*. The **thunders and lightnings** and **thick** (heavy) **cloud upon the mount**, the smoke and the fire and the quaking of the mountain, (verse 18,) were adapted to impress upon the thousands of Israel profoundest convictions of the majesty and might of Jehovah. A sublimer picture than that here given is not to be found among all the writings of men. Whether **the voice** (or sound) **of the trumpet exceeding loud** was produced by natural or supernatural agency is difficult to determine, and yet the mention of it in connexion with the other supernatural occurrences here and in verse 19, and in chap. xx, 18, rather implies that it

ᶜ trembled. **17** And ᵈ Moses brought forth the people out of the camp to meet with God; and they stood at the nether part of the mount. **18** And ᵉ mount Sinai was altogether on a smoke, because the LORD descended upon it ᶠ in fire: ᵍ and the smoke thereof ascended as the smoke of a furnace, and ʰ the whole mount quaked greatly. **19** And ⁱ when the voice of the trumpet sounded long, and waxed louder and louder, ᵏ Moses spake, and ˡ God answered him by a voice. **20** And the LORD came down upon mount Sinai, on the top of the mount: and the LORD called Moses *up* to the top of the mount; and Moses went up. **21** And the LORD said unto Moses, Go down, ⁿ charge the people, lest they break through unto the LORD ᵐ to gaze, and many of them perish. **22** And let the priests also, which come near to the LORD, ⁿ sanctify themselves, lest the LORD ᵒ break forth upon them. **23** And Moses said unto the LORD, The people cannot come up to mount Sinai: for thou chargedst us, saying, ᵖ Set bounds about the mount, and sanctify it. **24** And the LORD said unto him, Away, get thee down, and thou shalt come up, thou, and Aaron with thee: but let not the priests and the people break through to come up unto the LORD, lest he break forth upon them. **25** So Moses went down unto the people, and spake unto them.

c Hebrews 12. 21. —— *d* Deuteronomy 4. 10. —— *e* Deuteronomy 4. 11; 33. 2; Judges 5. 5; Psalm 68. 7, 8; Isaiah 6. 4; Habakkuk 3. 3. —— *f* Chapter 3. 2; 24. 17; 2 Chronicles 7. 1-3. —— *g* Genesis 15. 17; Psalm 144. 5; Revelation 15. 8.

h Psa. 68. 8; 77. 18; 114. 7; Jer. 4. 24; Heb. 12, 26. —— *i* Verse 13. —— *k* Heb. 12. 21. —— *l* Neh. 9. 13; Psa. 81. 7. —— 2 Heb. *contest*. —— *m* See chap. 3. 5; 1 Sam. 6. 19. —— *n* Lev. 10. 3. —— *o* 2 Sam. 6. 7, 8. —— *p* Verse 12; Josh. 3. 4.

also was produced by supernatural means. In all these passages it is noticeable that the word **trumpet** (Heb., *shophar*) occurs, not *yobel*, as in verse 13 above. To the imagery furnished by this sublime theophany the apostle alludes in 1 Thess. iv, 6.

The reader should compare the corresponding description in Deut. iv, especially verses 11, 12, 15, 33, 36. Kalisch observes: "The whole description of the fiery appearance of God in lightning and thunder and clouds, and the smoke of Sinai, and the terrible sound of the trumpet, is so majestically sublime and grand that it could only issue from a mind which, overwhelmed by the omnipotence and grandeur and majesty of God, exhausts the whole scanty store of human language to utter but a faint expression of the agitated sentiments of his soul."

20. The Lord came down—In the midst of the sublime exhibitions of his power and splendour mentioned above; though not so that the Israelites saw any likeness or similitude of Jehovah. See Deut. iv, 12, 15.

REPEATED CHARGE TO THE PEOPLE, 21-25.

21. Go down, charge the people —We here observe how Israel had to be admonished and taught by repeated commands. Once charging them solemnly is not enough, though even Moses (verse 23) thought that the charge already given, and the bounds set about the mount, were all-sufficient. Precept upon precept, line upon line, here a little and there a little, (Isa. xxviii, 10,) was God's order in giving the knowledge of his laws, and this fact will account for the repetitions of sundry laws noticeable in the Pentateuch.

22. The priests also—Here we trace the existence of priests before the institution of the Levitical priesthood. This is no more strange than that there were ceremonial ablutions and purifications (compare verse 10) before those which were instituted at Sinai. Probably the firstborn of each family held this honour. Comp. xiii, 2. There was danger that those honoured members of families who were wont to act as priests might presume to pass the bounds set about the mount, and go up to the Lord in the mountain. Ver. 24. And so every precaution was taken to impress upon all classes a deep sense of the unapproachable sanctity of Jehovah.

CHAPTER XX.

THE TEN COMMANDMENTS, 1-17.

The preceding chapter has furnished an awe-inspiring preparation for the announcement of the fundamental law which here follows. Nothing in all the myths, legends, or histories of law-giving among other peoples is comparable with this sublime issuing of Israel's decalogue. And the marvelous perfection of this summary of law, the inner excellency, the universal applicability of the several precepts, and their abiding, unchangeable nature, elevate this entire narrative above the element of myth and fable.

The glory of this decalogue is, that its provisions are absolutely fundamental. They have to do with individual life, social relations, and national history. We are not to imagine that they were now issued for the first time, or had no existence and recognition before the time of Moses. Compare the note on Gen. ix, 6. These laws are grounded in the very nature of man as a moral being, having essential relations to God on the one hand, and to his fellow-man on the other. They rest upon the idea that there is an infinite power above man to whom allegiance is due, and a community of co-ordinate fellow-beings about him with whom he is bound to act on principles of equity and love. These great truths were manifest from the beginning, but had become obscured and often ignored by the perversity of men. Jehovah, the God of Israel, gave them new and sublime expression at Sinai. They were there graven upon two tables of stone. Chapter xxxii, 15, 16; xxxiv, 28. "Hard, stiff, abrupt as the cliffs from which they were taken," writes Stanley, "they remain as the firm, unyielding basis on which all true spiritual religion has been built up and sustained. Sinai is not Palestine—the law is not the Gospel; but the ten commandments, in letter and in spirit, remain to us as the relic of that time. They represent to us, both in fact and in idea, the granite foundation, the immovable mountain, on which the world is built up—without which all theories of religion are but as shifting and fleeting clouds. They give us the two homely fundamental laws which all subsequent revelation has but confirmed and sanctified—the law of our duty to God, and the law of our duty to our neighbour. Side by side with the prayer of our Lord, and with the creed of his Church, they appear inscribed on our churches, read from our altars, taught to our children, as the foundation of all morality."—*Jewish Church*, First Series, pp. 195, 198.

The NAMES applied to this special Sinaitic law are various. The Greek word *decalogue*, and the common title *the ten commandments*, have arisen from the fact that the tables contain ten distinct mandates, and are called in chapter xxxiv, 28, and Deut. iv, 13, the ten commandments, or *ten words*. In those same texts and elsewhere they are also called *the words of the covenant* and *the covenant*, because they are the truest expression of the covenant-relations of God and his people. In chapters xxxi, 18; xxxii, 15; xxxiv, 29, they are called *the two tables of the testimony*, as containing God's solemn declaration of his holy will concerning man. They may, of course, be included under the more common terms *laws, commandments, statutes, precepts*. Being the foundation and substance of all moral and religious precepts, they are emphatically THE LAW AND THE COMMANDMENT. Chap. xxiv, 12.

Being ten in number, their proper DIVISION and arrangement are to be determined. They are most naturally arranged in two tables, each containing five precepts. According to this oldest and simplest division we have the two tables as follows:

FIRST TABLE.

1. Thou shalt have no other gods before me.
2. Thou shalt not make any graven image.
3. Thou shalt not take the name of God in vain.
4. Remember the Sabbath day, to keep it holy.
5. Honour thy father and thy mother.

SECOND TABLE.

6. Thou shalt not kill.
7. Thou shalt not commit adultery.
8. Thou shalt not steal.
9. Thou shalt not bear false witness.
10. Thou shalt not covet.

Two other methods of dividing the decalogue have been proposed, one by uniting the first and second in the above arrangement, and dividing the tenth into two, the other by regarding the introductory words, "I am the Lord thy God," as the first commandment, and combining, like the last-named method, the prohibition of other gods and graven images. These two ways of arranging are exhibited in parallel columns, as follows:

1. (AUGUSTINIAN.) FIRST TABLE.	2. (JEWISH.)
1. Thou shalt have no other gods before me, nor make any graven images.	1. I am the Lord thy God, who brought thee out of Egypt.
2. Thou shalt not take the name of the Lord thy God in vain.	2. Thou shalt have no other gods before me, nor make any graven images.
3. Remember the Sabbath day.	3. Thou shalt not take the name of the Lord thy God in vain.
SECOND TABLE.	
4. Honour thy father and thy mother.	4. Remember the Sabbath day.
5. Thou shalt not kill.	5. Honour thy father and mother.
6. Thou shalt not commit adultery.	6. Thou shalt not kill.
7. Thou shalt not steal.	7. Thou shalt not commit adultery.
8. Thou shalt not bear false witness.	8. Thou shalt not steal.
9. Thou shalt not covet thy neighbour's house.	9. Thou shalt not bear false witness.
10. Thou shalt not covet thy neighbour's wife.	10. Thou shalt not covet.

Much has been written for and against each of these methods of arrangement. That which makes Exod. xx, 2, the first word, or commandment, is quite generally rejected, for the introductory words, "I am Jehovah, thy God," cannot reasonably be regarded as a commandment co-ordinate with the others. But that Masoretic division, shown in Hebrew Bibles, by which Exod. xx, 1–6, is included in the first commandment, and the prohibition of blasphemy (verse 7) forms the second, agrees with the Augustinian theory, numbered 1 above, and makes up the ten by dividing verse 17 into two commandments. This view is ably advocated by Kurtz, (*Hist. of the Old Covenant*, Eng. trans., vol. iii, pp. 123–137.) The strong point of his argument is, that there is no radical distinction between the worship of *other gods* and *graven images*, for image-worship and idolatry are essentially the same, or, at any rate, image-worship is a species of idolatry. "Idolatry is the abstract, image-worship the concrete, sin." His argument, however, for dividing the law against coveting into two commandments is weak, and a notable specimen of special pleading. The same is true of all attempts to establish this most unnatural division. The fact that the Hebrew text in Deut. v, 21, places *wife* before *house* in the list of objects not to be coveted, is at best but a slender argument in favour of such division, whilst on the other hand the easy transposition of these words, and their use by the apostle in Rom. vii, 7, 8, where he quotes only, "Thou shalt not covet," and then speaks immediately of "all manner of coveting," are a far more weighty witness against it.

Whilst, therefore, it is conceded that the distinction between the worship of false gods and of images is not so marked as one might expect in objects prohibited by separate commandments, the distinction is nevertheless more easily made and more noticeable than that between a neighbour's wife and his other possessions. "No essential difference," says Keil, "can be pointed out in the two clauses which prohibit coveting; but there was a very essential difference between the commandment against other gods and that against making an image of God, so far as the Israelites were concerned, as we may see not only from the account of the golden calf at Sinai, but also from the image-worship of Gideon, (Judg. viii, 27,) Micah, (Judg. xvii,) and Jeroboam, (1 Kings xii, 28.") See further in textual notes on verse 4.

A further question concerns the arrangement in two tables. The first table is believed to set forth man's duties toward God, the second, those toward his neighbours, or fellow-men; and hence the whole are summed up in the two positive commandments, (1) "Thou shalt love thy God with all thy heart," and (2) "Thou shalt love thy neighbour as thyself." Comp. Deut. vi, 5; Lev. xix, 34; Matt. xxii, 37, 39; Mark xii, 30, 31; Luke x, 27. But where are we to make the division? Augustine's arrangement, as shown in the column above, made the first table comprise three, and the second table seven, commandments. He thought

B. C. 1491. CHAPTER XX. 479

CHAPTER XX.

AND God spake ᵃall these words, saying, 2 ᵇI am the LORD thy God, which have brought thee out of the

a Deut. 5. 22.—— *b* Lev. 26. 1, 13; Deut. 5. 6; Psa. 81. 10; Hos. 13. 4.

that this arrangement favoured the doctrine of the Trinity. Others commence the second table with the commandment to honour parents, and thus divide the ten into two groups of four and six. But the oldest and simplest division is that which recognizes five in each table, like the fingers on the two hands. The first five then belong to the sphere of *Piety*, and the second five to that of *Morality*.

The decalogue appears also in Deut. v, 6–21. The variations between the two texts are the following: Deuteronomy omits nothing contained in Exodus except the *waw* (ו, *and*) before כל־תמונה, *any likeness*, (comp. Exod. verse 4, and Deut. verse 8,) and the words of verse 11, "therefore Jehovah blessed the sabbath day and hallowed it," but substitutes שמור, *observe*, for זכור, *remember*, (Exod. 8, Deut. 12;) שוא, *emptiness*, for שקר, *a lie*, (Exod. 16, Deut. 17;) and תתאוה, *long after*, instead of the second תחמד, *covet*, (Exod. 17, and Deut. 18,) and adds in verses 12 and 16 the words, "as the Lord thy God commanded thee;" in verse 14, "nor thy ox, nor thy ass, nor any," "that thy manservant and thy maidservant may rest as well as thou;" in verse 15, "and remember that thou wast a servant in the land of Egypt, and that the Lord thy God brought thee out thence through a mighty hand and a stretched-out arm; therefore the Lord thy God commanded thee to keep the Sabbath day." Deuteronomy also connects with ו, *and*, all the commands after that pertaining to murder, and places *wife* before *house* in the last commandment, and also inserts שדהו, *his field*, among the objects not to be coveted. Deuteronomy verse 10, reads, *his commandments*, where Exodus verse 6, has *my commandments*. It is well for the reader to compare the New Testament citations of the decalogue in order to observe how freely they were quoted, and without reference to any particular order of precepts. See Matt. v, 21, 27; xix, 18; Mark x, 19; Luke xviii, 20; Rom. xiii, 9; James ii, 11. The Vatican Codex of the Septuagint places the sixth commandment after the eighth, and transposes *house* and *wife* in verses 17, like the Hebrew text of Deuteronomy. No great stress should be placed on the mere order of the precepts, as if any thing of importance depended upon their division and arrangement in the tables. The text in Deuteronomy is itself witness that no great importance was attached to verbal accuracy in citing the decalogue, but it is noticeable that explicit reference is there made to what Jehovah had commanded at Sinai. It is not improbable that the original form of the several mandates as given at Sinai was without the reasons which are attached to the first five, both in Exodus and Deuteronomy.

1. **God spake**—The Creator of man and the world, who has all authority in heaven and earth, is the fountain of law. Many Jewish and Christian expositors affirm that the Sinaitic proclamation of the decalogue was, literally, by the voice of God; that is, "that words were formed in the air by the power of God, and not by the intervention and ministry of angels." (Keil.) This is thought to be the necessary meaning of Deut. v, 4: "Jehovah talked with you face to face out of the midst of the fire." On the other hand, in Deut. xxxiii, 2, Moses speaks of Jehovah's coming from Sinai, "with ten thousands of saints," or *out of myriads of his holiness*. Comp. Psa. lxviii, 17. In Acts vii, Stephen speaks of the law as received "by the disposition of angels," and in Gal. iii, 19, Paul employs nearly the same expression. In Heb. ii, 2, the law is called "the word spoken by angels." Hence, while it is matter of record that Jehovah spake and Israel heard "the voice out of the midst of the darkness," (Deut. v, 22, 23,) it does not necessarily follow that "the voice of words" (Heb. xii, 19) was produced without the ministry of angels. The Israelites "saw no manner of similitude on the day that the Lord spake in Horeb

480 EXODUS. B. C. 1491.

land of Egypt, *c* out of the house of *¹* bondage. **3** *d* Thou shalt have no other gods before me. **4** *e* Thou shalt not make unto thee any graven image, or any

c Chapter 13. 3. — 1 Hebrew, *servants*. — *d* Deuteronomy 5. 7; 6. 14; 2 Kings 17. 35; Jeremiah 25. 6; 35. 15. — *e* Leviticus 26. 1; Deuteronomy 4. 16; 5. 8; 27. 15; Psalm 97. 7.

out of the midst of the fire," but the whole record shows that the Sinaitic proclamation of the decalogue was accompanied by miraculous and supernatural displays of the divine majesty. The ministry of angels is affirmed—the word was "spoken by angels;" but the manner of producing the voice is an unrevealed secret.

2. **I am the Lord thy God**—Many of the Jews, as we have seen above, regard this verse as the first of the ten words, or commandments, but they are rather of the nature of an introduction, showing emphatically the origin and source of the commandments. As the Eternal God, the I AM of previous revelation, (chap. iii, 14, 15,) he appropriately announces his NAME, and mentions the redemption from Egypt as a ground of obligation for Israel to hear and keep his commandments. The singular form of the address, **thy God,** not *your* God, gives a particular individuality of personal appeal to this announcement. The same is to be noted in each of the commandments which follow. The redemption **out of the land of Egypt, out of the house of bondage,** was the greatest fact in Israel's history, and he who wrought that wonderful deliverance is the author of this holy law, and directs its words to every individual of the nation.

THE FIRST COMMANDMENT, 3.

3. **Thou shalt have no other gods before me**—The rendering **before me** follows the Vulgate. The Septuagint has πλὴν ἐμοῦ, *besides me*. But the Hebrew words עַל־פָּנָי mean rather *over against me; in front of me;* and the commandment prohibits all recognition and worship of any deity that could be conceived as a rival of Jehovah. A proper conception of the unity of God, and of his omnipresence and other attributes of infinity, necessarily excludes the existence of other gods. Hence, a correct knowledge of divine things shows, as the apostle says, 1 Cor. viii, 4, "that no idol is any thing in the world, and that there is no God but one." A proper concept of God lies at the foundation of all pure worship. "Gods many and lords many" produce confusion of thought and consequent darkness of soul; for the acknowledging of such changes the truth of God into a lie, and leads logically to a worship of the creature rather than the Creator. Comp. Rom. i, 21–25. Hence it is that the recognition and worship of the one true God is the basis of pure morality as well as of religion. Vainly will men seek to divorce these from one another. This commandment stands against all doctrines and forms of heathen idolatry and polytheism. It strikes at the root of all degrading superstitions. Atheism and infidelity, as well as polytheism, are herein condemned. Pantheism cannot stand the test of these words of a personal God. The commandment is holy and uplifting, and, applied to the inner life, condemns also every species of spiritual idolatry—the setting of the affections on earthly rather than on heavenly things. So he who claimed to have observed all the commandments from his youth had in reality failed to know fully the import of the first one, and loved and clung to his "great possessions" when they stood between him and eternal life. Mark x, 17–22.

THE SECOND COMMANDMENT, 4–6.

4. **Graven image**—That this commandment was not designed to prohibit the productions of sculpture and painting is apparent from the fact that Moses was expressly ordered to construct cherubim for the most holy place of the tabernacle, and to make the brazen serpent in the wilderness. Only idolatrous images, representations of God and designed for worship, are contemplated. The golden calf, chap. xxxii, 1–4, is an illustration of the kind of graven images intended. Such images were graven or carved out of metal, wood, or

B. C. 1491.   CHAPTER XX.   481

likeness *of any thing* that *is* in heaven above, or that *is* in the earth beneath, or that *is* in the water under the earth: 5 ᶠ Thou shalt not bow down thyself to them, nor serve them: for I the LORD thy God *am* ᵍ a jealous God, ʰ visiting the iniquity of the fathers upon the children unto the third and fourth *generation* of

ᶠ Chap. 23. 24; Josh. 23. 7; 2 Kings 17. 35; Isa. 44. 15, 19. —— ᵍ Chap. 34. 14; Deut. 4. 24; 6. 15; Josh. 24. 19; Nah. 1. 2.

ʰ Chap. 34. 7; Lev. 20. 5; 26. 39, 40; Num. 14. 18, 33; 1 Kings 21. 29; Job 5. 4; 21. 19; Psa. 79. 8; 109. 14; Isa. 14. 20, 21; 65. 6, 7; Jer. 2. 9; 32. 18.

stone. Comp. Judg. xvii, 3; 2 Kings xxi, 7. The word translated **likeness** (תְּמוּנָה) is commonly used of attempted representations of God, or of the real form of God as seen or conceived by man. Comp. Num. xii, 8; Deut. iv, 12, 15, 16; Psa. xvii, 15. Accordingly a likeness of something **in heaven above** would be a portraiture of a god under the form of a star, or sun, or moon, or fowl; that of what is **in the earth beneath** would be the formation of a god in the similitude of a man or a woman, of a beast or any creeping thing that moves on land; that of things **in the water under the earth** would be, like the Philistine fish-god Dagon, the image of something that lives and moves in the water. All these are enumerated in Deut. iv, 15–19, which passage is an inspired commentary on this second commandment. The words **under the earth** show us the Hebrew conception of the water as lying lower than the land. When the land was elevated above the waters the latter fell back into the lower level of the seas. Gen. i, 9, 10. We should here observe that the use of images in worship is not always idolatry. Hence this second commandment is not to be confounded with the first, for it was assumed in the worship of the golden calf that the true God, who brought Israel out of Egypt, was honoured by means of the image. It has been persistently claimed by many religious leaders that the use of images in worship may be very helpful; they serve to concentrate the mind, and so prevent distraction of thought in one's devotions. They deepen impressions, and so intensify and enliven the forms of worship. But all history shows that such employment of images in worship begets superstition, and turns the thought of the average worshipper more upon the creature than the Creator. The narrative of chapter xxxii sets forth the unquestionable fact that the image-worship there described brought down the penal wrath of God upon the people. Such a method of promoting religious devotions is therefore fraught with great danger, and a perfect law required this prohibition of the use of graven images in worship.

5. **Thou shalt not bow down thyself to them**—This confirms the view expressed in the last verse, that idolatrous images are contemplated, not any and all productions of art. Images of Deity, whether under the form of man, or beast, or bird, or the luminaries of the sky, have ever proven a temptation and snare; and for a people just delivered from Egypt, where almost every object in nature was thus deified, such a most emphatic and particular prohibition was demanded. Jehovah therefore proclaims himself **a jealous God,** and only the shallow sentimentalist will find fault with such a designation of the God of Israel. In the nature of things he cannot undeify himself by giving his glory to another, and his praise to graven images. Isa. xlii, 8. This would be as impossible as it is for God to lie. Here are closely brought together three divine names, JEHOVAH, ELOHIM, and EL. The Almighty and Eternal Being who bears these titles cannot allow his place and name to be taken by another any more than the faithful husband can allow adultery in his wife. This imagery is frequent in the Old Testament, and all idolatry is regarded as spiritual adultery. **Visiting the iniquity of the fathers upon the children**—Here is testimony to a law of heredity stamped upon the human race. Mankind are constituted a living, self-perpetuating organism, and one may, by hateful opposition to God, bequeath a curse upon his posterity which will extend **unto the third and fourth generation.** The word עָוֹן, *iniquity*, means the inherent badness of

them that hate me; **6** And ¹ showing mercy unto thousands of them that

i Chap. 34. 7; Deut. 7. 9; Psa. 89. 34; Rom. 11. 28.

a perverted moral nature. This is the characterizing quality of **them that hate** the God of holy revelation. As an idol is a deceptive nothing, (1 Cor. viii, 4,) so all who make and worship idolatrous images are virtually the same as those who love and make a lie, (Rev. xxii, 15;) and history shows how the iniquity of idolatry has been wont to propagate itself through many generations. Nor is idolatry the only mortal curse that is wont to be thus entailed. But this Scripture is not to be

love me, and keep my commandments. **7** ᵏ Thou shalt not take the name of the

k Chap. 23. 1; Lev. 19. 12; Deut. 5. 11; Psa. 15. 4; Matt. 5. 33.

construed, contrary to Ezek. xviii, 20, to mean that children will be *punished* for their parents' sins. Guilt cannot be entailed. The child may, physically and mentally, *suffer* evil consequences because of a parent's sins, but no guilt of theirs is or can be justly imputed to him who had no part in the sin. The following table, by Lummis, of distinctions between natural consequences and punishment puts the subject in a clear light, and furnishes in itself a valuable study.

Distinctions to be made between Natural Consequences and Punishment.

1. All *proper* punishment *must* be deserved.
2. Punishment follows intentional wrong doing only.
3. Punishment follows wrong doing *after* judgment pronounced.
4. Punishment is suspended the moment pardon has been declared.
5. Punishment ceases when the penalty inflicted has been fully borne.
6. Punishment is visited only on the guilty.
7. Punishment is limited by justice.
8. Punishment comes *directly* from the will of the ruler.
9. Punishment is retributive.
10. Punishment can only belong where guilt or remorse has been felt.

Natural consequences may *not* be deserved.
Consequences follow both *in*tentional and *un*intentional wrong doing.
Consequences may follow *immediately* after the wrong act.
Consequences may follow indefinitely after pardon has been granted.
Consequences *follow* as really after the penalty has been suffered as at any time after the wrong doing.
Consequences extend equally to the innocent.
Justice is not applicable to consequences.
Consequences result directly from the constitution of things.
Consequences are admonitory.
Consequences may exist where remorse is impossible—for example, upon dumb animals.

6. Showing mercy—Or, *doing kindness.* His lovingkindness and favour are never withheld from the good and obedient. **Unto thousands** — Some would understand *generations* here, as after *third* and *fourth* in the previous verse. So superabundant is Jehovah's kindness that he gladly will extend it to the thousandth generation **of them that love** him **and keep** his **commandments.** The expression, however, is best understood as general in its fulness of meaning. His kindness toward the loving and obedient is for all and for ever. Comp. chap. xxxiv, 6, 7.

THE THIRD COMMANDMENT, 7.

7. Thou shalt not take the name —If Jehovah is God alone, and if all artificial attempts to produce a likeness of him deserve such fearful visitations as the preceding verses show, it follows that his **name** should be held in highest honour. The Jews have a tradition that the whole world trembled when this commandment was proclaimed, and Eben Ezra, as quoted by Kalisch, en-

B. C. 1491.   CHAPTER XX.   483

LORD thy God in vain: for the LORD ¹ will not hold him guiltless that taketh his name in vain.   **8** ᵐ Remember the sabbath day, to keep it holy.   **9** ⁿ Six days shalt thou labour, and do all thy work: **10** But the ᵒ seventh day *is* the

---
l Mic. 6. 11.——*m* Chap. 31. 13, 14; Lev. 19. 3, 30; 26. 2; Deut. 5. 12.——*n* Chap. 23. 12; 31. 15; 34. 21; Lev. 23. 3; Ezek. 20. 12; Luke 13. 14.—— *o* Gen. 2. 2, 3; chap. 16. 26; 31. 15.

---

hances the seriousness of the prohibition by the consideration that, while other crimes, as murder and adultery, cannot be committed at any time, "he who has once accustomed himself to use superfluous oaths swears in one day to an infinite amount, and that habit at last becomes so familiar to him that he scarcely knows that he swears; and if you reproachfully ask him why he swore just now he will swear that he has not sworn, so great is the power of the habit; and, at last, almost his every assertion will be preceded by an oath." The import of the commandment is seen in the three words, **name, take,** and **vain.** The word **name** in such texts comprehends all that is in the being and nature of God; not merely the title by which the Deity is designated, but all and every thing which is indicated by the various names, attributes, and perfections of the one true God. To **take the name** is to *lift it up,* put it into prominence. Compare the expression, "raise a false report," in chap. xxiii, 1, where the Hebrew word is the same, (נָשָׂא.) To get the full meaning here intended we must at the same time consider the qualifying adverbial phrase **in vain,** (לַשָּׁוְא.) To lift a name in vain is to make a vain or false use of it; to employ it in a manner damaging to truth and piety. The Hebrew phrase is by many exegetes translated *for falsehood,* and so is nearly equivalent to לַשֶּׁקֶר, in Lev. xix, 12: "Thou shalt not swear by my name falsely, neither shalt thou profane the name of thy God." The prohibition contemplates, not only all vile blasphemy, but also, doubtless, all irreverent use of the divine name, and accordingly comprehends perjury also, as when "a man vows a vow unto the Lord, or swears an oath to bind his soul with a bond," and then breaks his word, or profanes it by failing to observe his oath. Comp. Num. xxx, 2. Hence the strictures of Jesus on this subject, Matt. v, 33–37, where see Whedon's notes. The great remedy of all this is: "Swear not at all," (Matt. v, 34, James v, 12,) but rather "sanctify the Lord God in your hearts." 1 Pet. iii, 15. **Will not hold him guiltless**—Will not treat him as innocent, and allow him to go unpunished.

THE FOURTH COMMANDMENT, 8–11.

8. **Remember the sabbath day**—The word **remember** here cannot properly be pressed to mean the recalling it to mind, as if something old, and, for that reason, liable to be forgotten. It cannot be fairly adduced as a proof that the Sabbath was observed by the patriarchs. It means rather: Be ever mindful to observe the day. In the parallel in Deuteronomy (verse 12) we find the word *keep* employed instead of *remember.* So in chap. xiii, 3, Moses says to the people: "Remember this day, in which ye came out from Egypt." Nevertheless, the word may well have suggested that the Sabbath was an ancient institution and worthy to be remembered, and this is specifically brought forward in verse 11. See also note on chap. xvi, 23. As the word **sabbath** means *rest,* so the main idea associated with it in the Scriptures is that of cessation from ordinary labour. See further on verse 10. **Keep it holy**—That is, treat it as sacred, hallow it. This is the positive side of the commandment, whereas the negative comes out more clearly in verse 10. The Israelites were wont to sanctify the Sabbath day by offering double offerings, (Num. xxviii, 9, 10,) and by renewal of the twelve cakes of show-bread in the tabernacle. Lev. xxiv, 5–9. It would appear from 2 Kings iv, 23, that at a later time the people were accustomed to resort to the prophets on the Sabbath to obtain instruction. The adaptation of such a day of rest and devotion to cultivate the spiritual nature is evident.

9. **Six days shalt thou labour**—Here is a positive commandment, as ex-

sabbath of the LORD thy God: *in it* thou shalt not do any work, thou, nor thy son, nor thy daughter, thy manservant, nor thy maidservant, nor thy cattle, ^p nor thy stranger that *is* within thy gates: **11** For ^q *in* six days the LORD made heaven and earth, the sea, and all that in them *is*, and rested the seventh day: wherefore the LORD blessed the sabbath day, and hallowed it.

12 ^r Honour thy father and thy mother: that thy days may be long upon

p Neh. 13. 16-19. —— *q* Gen. 2. 2. —— *r* Chap. 23. 26; Lev. 19. 3; Deut. 5. 16; Jer. 35. 7, 18, 19; Matt. 15. 4; 19. 19; Mark 7. 10; 10. 19; Luke 18. 20; Eph. 6. 2.

plicit as that which enjoins the sabbath rest. No man is at liberty, before God, to spend his days in idleness and inactivity, and the healthfulness and full vigour of the physical constitution depend as much upon bodily activity as does the soundness of the religious life demand a weekly day of rest.

10. **Thou shalt not do any work** —The kinds of work incidentally noticed as coming under this prohibition were gathering manna, (xvi, 27–29,) plowing, and gathering of harvests, (xxxiv, 21,) kindling fires, (xxxv, 3,) collecting wood, (Num. xv, 32–36,) selling articles of commerce, (Amos viii, 5,) bearing burdens, (Jer. xvii, 21,) treading wine-presses, and carrying on traffic. Neh. xiii, 15–22. From this it is evident that the commandment was understood as forbidding all sorts of ordinary work, and was to be applied to all members of the house, and even to the **cattle,** that is, the beasts of burden. The **stranger,** that is, the foreigner who settled in any of the cities of Israel, must also observe the sabbath law. The holy day, however, was not to be a day of gloom and sadness, but one filled with all such delights as would bring the heart into closer fellowship with Jehovah. Isa. lviii, 13, 14.

11. **For in six days the Lord made heaven and earth**—Here is a direct reference to what is recorded in Gen. i, 1–ii, 3, where see notes, and also pages 63 and 64 of the Introduction. Those writers who maintain that the Sabbath was a purely Mosaic institution find no little embarrassment in explaining away the obvious import of this verse. Both here and in Gen. ii, 1–3, God's rest at the close of the creative week is made a reason for the sanctifying of the seventh day. Other reasons are also given, as in Deut. v, 15, where the deliverance from Egyptian bondage is mentioned as an additional ground for its observance. That a seventh-day rest is necessary to the highest good of man may be argued from the following considerations: (1.) From this explicit commandment of the decalogue. Its position among other moral laws of universal obligation shows that it is something more than a mere temporary Mosaic institution. (2.) The typical example of God's resting from his work, here given as a reason for this law, implies that the seventh-day rest is an ordinance old as the creation of man. (3.) This is confirmed by traces of it in the weekly divisions of time among several ancient nations, (see on xvi, 23,) and especially among the ancient Babylonians and Assyrians, who had their "day of rest for the heart." (4.) Because of its association with Israel's deliverance from Egyptian bondage, (Deut. v, 15,) and the severity with which its violation was punished. Num. xv, 35; 2 Chron. xxxvi, 21. (5.) Christ's words in Mark ii, 27, confirm all the above, and show it to be a law of the highest good for man, grounded in the needs of his physical and moral nature. (6.) The remarkable fact has been often proven and illustrated by fair trial, that both man and beast will do more and better work by observing one rest day in seven than by continuous labour in violation of the sabbath law. (7.) The sabbath rest, properly utilized, is admirably adapted to promote the culture of all that is highest and best in the spiritual nature of man.

THE FIFTH COMMANDMENT, 12.

12. **Honour thy father and thy mother**—This commandment belongs properly to the "first table," as we have shown above, for it inculcates a form of *piety* as distinguished from *morality.* "For a considerable time," observes Clarke, "parents stand, as it were, in the place of God to their chil-

the land which the LORD thy God giveth thee. 13 *Thou shalt not kill.

s Deut. 5. 17; Matt. 5. 21; Rom. 13. 9.

dren, and therefore rebellion against their lawful commands has been considered as rebellion against God." The death penalty was enjoined for him who smote or reviled his parents. Chap. xxi, 15, 17. The proverb (in Prov. xxx, 17) shows how execrable the dishonouring of parents was considered: "The eye that mocketh at his father, and despiseth to obey his mother, the ravens of the valley shall pick it out, and the young eagles shall eat it." See also the apocryphal book of Ecclesiasticus, chap. iii, 1–16. The filial relation best represents the true relationship of man to God as his author and preserver, and accordingly, he who disrespects its sacredness exhibits one of the most notable marks of impiety. But loyalty and devotion to parents tend to cultivate reverence for God, and for rulers, ministers, and teachers, who hold positions of responsibility and are set to guard the public weal. It is worthy of note that in Lev. xix, 3, this law and that of the sabbath are united together thus: " Ye shall fear every man his mother and his father, and keep my Sabbaths." These two are the only commandments of the decalogue which are expressed in positive form. **That thy days may be long**—The apostle calls this " the first commandment with promise." Eph. vi, 2. It is the only one in the decalogue which has a specific promise attached to it. **The land which the Lord thy God giveth thee** is here to be understood first of the promised land of Israel, the land of Canaan. Comp. Deut. iv, 26, 40; xxx, 18; xxxii, 47. But in the wider scope which this commandment has, as being grounded in the nature of the family, and so alike binding upon all men, it is to be understood of the land or country of any and every individual. "Filial respect," says Cook, in *The Speaker's Commentary,* "is the ground of national permanence. When the Jews were about to be cast out of their land, the rebuke of the prophet was that they had not walked in the old paths, and had not respected the voice of their fathers as the sons of Jonadab had done. Jer. vi, 16; xxxv, 18, 19. And when in later times the land had been restored to them, and they were about to be cast out of it a second time, the great sin of which they were convicted was that they had set aside this fifth commandment for the sake of their own traditions. Matt. xv, 4–6; Mark vii, 10, 11. Every other nation that has a history bears witness to the same truth. Rome owed her strength, as well as the permanence of her influence after she had politically perished, to her steady maintenance of the *patria potestas*. (Maine, *Ancient Law*.) China has mainly owed her long duration to the simple way in which she has uniformly acknowledged the authority of her fathers."

THE SIXTH COMMANDMENT, 13.

13. **Thou shalt not kill**—Better, *thou shalt not commit murder.* This first commandment of the second table corresponds noticeably with the first of the previous table, as a reference to Gen. ix, 6, will serve to show: " Whoso shedeth man's blood, by man shall his blood be shed; for in the image of God made he man." The murderer, therefore, is regarded as one who wickedly destroys God's image in man, and so most basely assaults God himself. Suicide is, accordingly, prohibited by this commandment. The Hebrew legislation everywhere enhances the sacredness of human life. All the precepts in chap. xxi, 12–30, aim to guard life from violence. If any man by carelessness or neglect occasioned the death of another, he brought blood-guiltiness upon his house. Deut. xxii, 8. A murder by an unknown hand would pollute the very land in which it was committed until suitable expiation were made. Deut. xxi, 1–9. Our Lord took up this law for special treatment, and taught that he who cherished anger against his neighbour was guilty before God of the spirit of murder. Matt. v, 21–24. John also enlarges on this same profound idea. 1 John ii, 9–11; iii, 12–15. As the

14 'Thou shalt not commit adultery. **15** ⁿ Thou shalt not steal. **16** ᵛ Thou

<small>*t* Deuteronomy 5. 18; Matthew 5. 27.—*u* Leviticus 19. 11; Deuteronomy 5. 19; Matthew 19. 18; Romans 13. 9; 1 Thess. 4. 6.—*v* Chapter 23. 1; Deuteronomy 5. 20; 19. 16; Matthew 19. 13.</small>

not having any other God instead of Jehovah is at the basis of the laws of the first table, so the not hating one's neighbour is at the basis of all those of the second. Hence the two great positive commands, inclusive of all others: first, thou shalt love God with all thy heart; and, second, thou shalt love thy neighbour as thyself. According to Num. xxxv, 31, no satisfaction was allowable for the life of a murderer but the extreme penalty of the law. No commutation and no pardon could be granted to one clearly convicted of murder. The shallow sentimentalism of modern life has in numerous places cried out against this law, and sought to class it with barbarities which ought to be set aside. Also some learned and thoughtful men, holding the notion that civil government is merely a "social compact," or that the object of penalty is solely to prevent crime, and is not based upon moral desert, have advocated the abolition of capital punishment. But it is shown that where another punishment has been substituted for the death penalty capital crime has increased, and states which have tried the experiment have found it a failure, and have restored the severer law. Those who oppose the death penalty for murder often exhibit far more sympathy for the criminal than for his victims. The biblical doctrine is clear and decisive: (1.) He who takes a human life forfeits his own, and so *deserves* death. (2.) The common safety and public good demand that the just penalty be speedily executed. (3.) The New Testament, far from conflicting with the Old on this point, confirms it by representing the civil magistrate as God's minister, bearing the sword to be a terror to evildoers, and to execute wrath upon them. Rom. xiii, 1–6. The words of our Lord, often quoted as inconsistent with capital punishment, have no reference whatever to the execution of righteous laws upon the guilty, but to man's personal and private relations. To explain such precepts as those of Matt. v, 38–45, as indicating the true methods of civil government is preposterous in the extreme, and, if thus practically applied, would overthrow all righteous government and law. Equally absurd is it to appeal to Romans xii, 17–21; for if the officers of law and justice should proceed with murderers, thieves, and other criminals as there enjoined, it would be a direct encouragement for all sorts of evil doers to multiply their nefarious deeds. All these fallacies of exegesis arise from confounding private and personal relations with the administration of public justice. With one who is incapable of making and holding these distinctions in mind, it would be idle to argue the question of capital or any other punishment by the State.

THE SEVENTH COMMANDMENT, 14.

14. Thou shalt not commit adultery—Next to the criminal blood-guiltiness of him who assaults God's image by destroying human life is that of him or her who violates the sacredness of the marriage bond. He who created man in his own image created them male and female, (Gen. i, 27,) and declared that a man and his wife should be regarded as one flesh. Gen. ii, 24. Comp. Matt. xix, 3–9; Mark x, 2–12. Weighty and suggestive, also, are the apostle's words upon this sacred relation, in Eph. v, 23–33. A sound scriptural view of the sacredness of the marriage relation exhibits the essential criminalty of bigamy and polygamy. Although these abominable evils forced themselves into the domestic life of patriarchs and other distinguished men of Old Testament times, the law of God and nature has ever frowned upon them, and pursued them with a curse. Our Lord showed clearly, in the passage above cited, that these sins had been tolerated because of the people's perversity, and in spite of the original law and commandment. He not only re-announced the ancient law, but gave it a broader scope and deeper significance by declaring "that whoso-

B. C. 1491. CHAPTER XX. 487

shalt not bear false witness against thy
w Deut. 5. 21; Mic. 2. 2; Hab. 2. 9; Luke 12. 15;
ever looketh on a woman to lust after
her hath committed adultery with her
already in his heart." Matt. v, 28. He
accordingly includes fornication and all
sensual uncleanness under this prohibition, and also limits the right of divorce
to the one cause of a breach of the marriage bond. Matt. v, 32. The Jewish
commentator Kalisch observes: "It requires scarcely any proof to show the
honourable position which the woman
occupied in Hebrew society. From the
very creation of the woman, who is a
part of man himself, and for whose
sake he shall leave his father and his
mother so that both be one flesh, down
to the glorious picture of the virtuous
wife in the last chapter of Proverbs, the
whole Bible breathes the highest regard
for female excellence, and assigns to the
weaker sex that sound and noble rank
which forms the just medium between
its Oriental degradation and the exaggerated gallantry of the romantic
epochs."

The Eighth Commandment, 15.

15. **Thou shalt not steal**—Next to
the rights of life and person stands the
right of property. The crime of theft
may include, besides the secret removal
of another's property, all acts which in
any way impinge upon the property interests of one's neighbour. Clarke specifies rapine, theft, petty larceny, highway robbery, and private stealing, and
national and commercial wrongs, and
adds that "the taking advantage of a
seller's or buyer's ignorance, to give
the one less and make the other pay
more for a commodity than its worth, is
a breach of this sacred law." Manifestly, all theories of "socialism" and
"anarchy" which tend directly or indirectly to take from man the products of
his own genius, enterprise, and toil, or
to appropriate them to purposes other
than those which he may rightfully desire, are fundamentally inconsistent with
this law. In like manner are all monopolies and combinations which conflict
with the liberty and rights of individuals,
and so oppress the poor labourer, to be

neighbour. 17 *w* Thou shalt not covet
Acts 20. 33; Rom. 7. 7; 13. 9; Eph. 5. 3, 5; Heb. 13. 5.
condemned under this prohibition of
the decalogue. He who loves his neighbour as himself, and does unto others as
he would have others do unto him, will
not allow himself to be a partaker in
such wrongs.

The Ninth Commandment, 16.

16. **Thou shalt not bear false
witness against thy neighbour**—
The law which guards the property of
a man is appropriately followed by one
which guards his good name. It concerns the words rather than deeds or
acts of men. The most direct and flagrant example is that of one who swears
to a known falsehood before a judicial
tribunal. This is perjury, and is properly punishable as a great crime. Comp.
Deut. xix, 16-19. But this law also
comprehends such whispering, slandering, backbiting, lying, and evil speaking generally as is contemplated in
Lev. xix, 16: "Thou shalt not go up
and down as a talebearer among thy
people;" also verse 11 of the same
chapter: "Ye shall not lie one to another." "Lying lips are an abomination to the Lord." Prov. xii, 22. It is
a high and holy law which requires us
"to speak evil of no man," (Titus iii, 2,)
and to put away from us "all bitterness, and wrath, and anger, and clamour, and evil speaking, with all malice."
Eph. iv, 31. Comp. also James iv, 11.
Only when it is necessary to defend
innocence and promote the public good
should one bear true testimony against
his fellow-man to blight his character
and expose his wrong; but never should
one, at any place or under any circumstances, utter a false word against him.
Jehovah abhors the deceitful man as
he does those who are guilty of capital
crime. Psa. v, 6.

The Tenth Commandment, 17.

17. **Thou shalt not covet**—The
word חָמַד, here rendered **covet,** occurs
some twenty times in the Hebrew Scriptures, and is commonly translated by
desire. One may, of course, properly

488   EXODUS.   B. C. 1491.

thy neighbour's house, ˣ thou shalt not covet thy neighbour's wife, nor his manservant, nor his maidservant, nor his ox, nor his ass, nor any thing that is thy neighbour's.

18 And ʸ all the people ᶻ saw the thunderings, and the lightnings, and the noise of the trumpet, and the mountain ᵃ smoking: and when the people saw it, they removed, and stood afar off.

19 And they said unto Moses, ᵇ Speak thou with us, and we will hear: but ᶜ let not God speak with us, lest we die. 20 And Moses said unto the people, ᵈ Fear not: ᵉ for God is come to prove you, and ᶠ that his fear may be before your faces, that ye sin not. 21 And the people stood afar off, and Moses drew near unto ᵍ the thick darkness where God was.

---

x Job 31. 9; Prov. 6. 29; Jer. 5. 8; Matt. 5. 28.—*y* Heb. 12. 18.—*z* Rev. 1. 10, 12.—*a* Chap. 19. 18.—*b* Deut. 5. 27; 18. 16; Gal. 3. 19, 20; Heb. 12. 19.—*c* Deut. 5. 25.

d 1 Sam. 12. 20; Isa. 41. 10, 13.—*e* Gen. 22. 1; Deut. 13. 3.—*f* Deut. 4. 10; 6. 2; 10. 12; 17. 13, 19; 19. 20; 28. 58; Prov. 3. 7; 16, 6; Isa. 8. 13.—*g* Chap. 19. 16; Deut. 5. 5; 1 Kings 8. 12.

---

desire and long after every thing lawful and good, but no one can look with desire and longing upon any possession of his neighbour's without violating this commandment. While the preceding commandments contemplate more directly the outward acts of men, this aims at the heart as the fountain of unlawful desires. The specification of **house, wife, servant, ox,** and **ass** simply indicates the general scope of the law, and shows, as the concluding words more explicitly teach, that human desire should be restrained so as not to settle upon **any thing** whatever which is the rightful property of one's neighbour. This tenth commandment evidently passes beyond the province of human legislation, and reminds us that we are here in the presence of a divine law, and of a Lawgiver who can discern the secrets of the heart. It strikes at the source of all crimes and wickedness, "for from within, out of the heart of men, proceed evil thoughts, adulteries, fornications, murders, thefts, covetousness, wickedness, deceit, lasciviousness, an evil eye, blasphemy, pride, foolishness." Mark vii, 21, 22.

THE EFFECT ON THE PEOPLE, 18-21.

These words form a transition from the decalogue to the legislation which was given through Moses. The statements are considerably amplified in Deut. v, 22-33.

18. **The people saw the thunderings**— Hebraic mode of expression. Comp. Rev. i, 12: "I turned to see the voice that spake with me." On the sublime scenes here described see notes on chap. xix, 16-20. Such an awful theophany could not fail to inspire all who witnessed it with a profound fear of Jehovah, and they naturally shrank away, and **stood afar off.** To effect this wholesome fear was one object of theophany and the commandments.

19. **Let not God speak with us, lest we die**—Comp. Deut. v, 25, 26. This sentiment accords with the prevalent belief of the ancient Hebrews, that the immediate vision of God must produce death. See notes on Gen. xvi, 13, xxxii, 30, and Judges vi, 22.

20. **Fear not**—That is, as the context shows, be not terrified so as to think God is angry with you and is about to visit you with death. The purpose of this theophany, and of the words out of the fire, is **to prove you,** to test your loyalty and readiness to obey; and, furthermore, **that his fear may be before your faces.** A profound reverence for Jehovah, constantly maintained in the heart, is the mightiest safeguard against sinning. "The fear of the Lord is the beginning of wisdom." Psa. cxi, 10; Prov. i, 7; ix, 10.

21. **The people stood afar off**—As stated in verse 18. After Moses had gone up **unto the thick darkness where God was,** the people returned to their tents as they had been instructed. Comp. Deut. v, 30. It would seem from chap. xix, 24, that when Moses at this time **drew near** unto the divine presence, Aaron accompanied him. In the profound and various symbolism by which God revealed himself through the Mosaic legislation, it was fitting that his own divine person should be hidden in **thick darkness,** (עֲרָפֶל,) and no manner of likeness or similitude of Deity be exhibited to any eye. So,

B. C. 1491. CHAPTER XX. 489

22 And the LORD said unto Moses, Thus thou shalt say unto the children of Israel, Ye have seen that I have talked with you [h] from heaven. **23** Ye shall not make [i] with me gods of silver, neither shall ye make unto you gods of gold.

[h] Deuteronomy 4. 36; Nehemiah 9. 13. —
[i] Chapter 32. 1, 2, 4; 1 Samuel 5. 4, 5; 2 Kings 17. 33; Ezekiel 20. 39; 43. 8; Daniel 5. 4, 23; Zephaniah 1. 5; 2 Corinthians 6. 14-16.

later, in the construction of the tabernacle, the most holy place, the immediate throne-chamber of Jehovah, was made in the form of a perfect cube, and veiled in darkness. Comp. chap. xxv, 22; Lev. xvi, 2; 1 Kings viii, 12. Jehovah thus signifies that his power and wisdom and ways are wrapped in mystery, and cannot be searched by mortal eyes.

THE BOOK OF THE COVENANT, XX, 22–xxiii, 33.

Here follows a collection of sundry laws which were compiled by Moses, and doubtless represent the oldest written legislation of the Pentateuch. This compilation probably constituted "the book of the covenant" which is mentioned in chap. xxiv, 7. Kalisch classifies the laws under three heads: (1.) Those touching the rights of *persons*, chap. xxi, 1–32; (2.) Those touching the rights of *property*, chap. xxi, 33–xxii, 14; and (3.) General *moral laws*. Chapter xxii, 15–xxiii, 19. These are followed by sundry exhortations. Chap. xxiii, 20–33. The various precepts, however, are scarcely susceptible of such a classification, or of any systematic arrangement. They take a wide range, and deal with some twenty-eight distinct subjects. Beginning with a prohibition of idolatrous images, (23,) we have laws touching the construction of altars, (24–26,) the relations of servants and masters, (xxi, 1–11,) personal assaults and injuries, (12–27,) goring oxen, (28–32,) losses of cattle, (33–36,) cattle-stealing, (xxii, 1–4,) cattle feeding in others' fields, (5,) kindling destructive fires, (6,) stolen or damaged trusts, (7–15,) seduction, (16–17,) witchcraft, (18,) lying with beasts, (19,) idolatrous sacrifices, (20,) treatment of foreigners, (21,) treatment of widows and the fatherless, (22–24,) loaning money, (25,) pledges, (26–27,) reviling God and rulers, (28,) devotion of firstlings, (29, 30,) abstinence from torn flesh, (31,) perversions of honour and justice, (xxiii, 1–3,) favour toward enemies, (4–5,) judgment of the poor, (6,) maintaining justice, (7, 8,) oppression of strangers, (9,) sabbath laws, (10–12,) other gods, (13,) three annual feasts, (14–17,) sacrifice and offerings, (18, 19.) This body of legislation is followed in xxiii, 20–33, by a number of prophetic promises, designed to encourage and strengthen the hearts of the people. Many of the laws and precepts here collected together were doubtless older than the time of Moses, but as Israel was now becoming a body politic, and about to occupy a prominent place among the nations, such a body of laws as was contained in this book of the covenant required formal codification.

22. The Lord said unto Moses— In what manner God communicated these statutes to Moses the reader is not informed. From Num. xii, 6–8, it appears that Moses was honoured with a distinctness of spiritual access to God as was no other prophet. It was not a seeing of God's face, (Exod. xxx, 20,) but often came through visible symbols, like the burning bush, (chap. iii, 2,) and a passing form of glory, (xxxiii, 21–23, xxxiv, 6,) which made his face to shine with supernatural light, (xxxiv, 29, 30.) These special theophanies did not exclude the ministration of angels, and the excellency of the Mosaic legislation, when viewed as a whole, exhibits so many marks of divine origin that we hesitate not to accept the literal truth of the statements of this verse. **I have talked with you from heaven—**Reference to the supernatural promulgation of the ten commandments. That speaking from heaven shook the earth. Comp. Heb. xii, 26. It was the entering in of a higher Power into the history of men, marking a distinctive crisis in the progress of heavenly mediation, and utilizing the elements of nature to deepen the impressions of the words that were spoken.

23. Make with me—As if to place by the side of me as images and representations of my nature. **Gods of sil-**

490   EXODUS.   B. C. 1491.

24 An altar of earth thou shalt make unto me, and shalt sacrifice thereon thy burnt offerings, and thy peace offerings, *k* thy sheep, and thine oxen: in all ¹places where I record my name I will come unto thee, and I will ᵐ bless thee. **25** And ⁿ if thou wilt make me an altar of stone, thou shalt not ² build it of hewn stone: for if thou lift up thy tool upon it, thou hast polluted it. **26** Neither

k Lev. 1. 2.—*l* Deut. 12. 5, 11, 21; 14. 23; 16. 6, 11; 26. 2; 1 Kings 8. 43; 9. 3; 2 Chron. 6. 6; 7. 16; 12. 13; Ezra 6. 12; Neh. 1. 9; Psa. 74. 7; Jer. 7. 10, 12. —— *m* Gen. 12. 2; Deut. 7. 13. —— *n* Deut. 27. 5; Josh. 8. 31.——2 Heb. *build them* with *hewing*.

ver—This is, for substance, a repetition of the second commandment. See notes above, on verse 4. It receives a new emphasis from the fact that Jehovah himself had now spoken from heaven.

24. **An altar of earth**—Having repeated the prohibition of gold and silver images of Deity, he most appropriately passes first to give some general directions for altar - building. These had probably been observed in the construction of altars by the patriarchs, as Noah, (Gen. viii, 20,) Abraham, (Gen. xii, 7, xiii, 18,) Isaac, (Gen. xxvi, 25,) and Jacob, (Gen. xxxv, 7,) but, like other ancient usages set forth in this collection, they are now written down as a part of the book of the covenant. **An altar of earth** is one constructed of turfs or sod, and was most convenient and suitable for a wandering people. Jehovah would have his altars builded in the most simple form, and thus avoid any occasion of attempts at architectural display in them. **Burnt offerings** and **peace offerings** are here mentioned as representative of all sacrifices of **sheep** and **oxen** which would be offered on an altar. This is the first mention of **peace offerings,** but the language of chap. xxiv, 5, implies that they were not now for the first time offered; the distinction between them and **burnt offerings** was already known to the people. The burnt offering was wholly consumed upon the altar, but only a part of the flesh of the peace offering was thus consumed; the other portions were eaten by the worshippers, and the sacrifice was made the occasion of a joyful feast. The " burnt offering and sacrifices " which Jethro offered (chap. xviii, 12) appear to have been of both these kinds; first, the burnt offering, which was offered whole, and then the peace offering, at which Aaron and all the elders of Israel feasted together. **In all places where I record my name**—There is nothing in these words which requires us to suppose a simultaneous plurality of altars in Israel, nor any thing to forbid our supposing that Jehovah might have recorded his name in several different places at the same time. But the most obvious meaning is, that successive altars are contemplated. During the journey to Canaan, and until some central seat of national worship should be ordained, there would be occasion for the erection of altars in divers places, just as the patriarchs had done in their wanderings to and fro. But this law expressly forbids their setting up altars anywhere they pleased by limiting them to such places as were consecrated by some memorable revelation or act of Jehovah. There is therefore no conflict between this law and that of Deut. xii, 4–14, which provided for one central sanctuary. After such a place should be chosen " to cause his name to dwell there," no other spot would accord with the expressed limitations of this ancient law, for there only would he record his name.

25. **If thou wilt make me an altar of stone**—Such an altar would be as simple and easy of construction as one of turf, and more so in places where stones abounded. But to preserve its simplicity, and to deter from attempts to imitate the sculptured embellishments of heathen altars, they were forbidden to make use of **hewn stone,** or to wield a graver's **tool upon it.** The natural stone, untouched by art or man's device, was most like the earth itself, and most appropriate for the sanctity and simplicity of the altar service. Any attempt to cut or carve the stones would be a polluting of holy things. The framework of acacia wood, overlaid with brass, was a subsequent and special provision for

shalt thou go up by steps unto mine altar, that thy nakedness be not discovered thereon.

CHAPTER XXI.

NOW these *are* the judgments which thou shalt ᵃ set before them. 2 ᵇIf thou buy a Hebrew servant, six years he shall serve: and in the seventh he shall go out free for nothing. 3 If he came in ¹ by himself, he shall go out by himself: if he were married, then his wife shall go out with him. 4 If his master have given him a wife, and she have borne him sons or daughters; the wife and her children shall be her master's, and he shall go out by himself. 5 ᶜAnd if the servant ² shall plainly say, I love my master, my wife, and my children; I will not go out free: 6 Then his master shall bring him unto the ᵈjudges; he shall also bring him to the

---

a Chap. 24. 3, 4; Deut. 4. 14; 6. 1.——*b* Lev. 25. 39-41; Deut. 15. 12; Jer. 34. 14. —— 1 Heb. *with his body*.——*c* Deut. 15. 16, 17.——2 Heb. *saying shall say.*——*d* Chap. 12. 12; 22. 8, 28.

---

the altar of the tabernacle. See chap. xxvii, 1-8.

26. **Neither shalt thou go up by steps**—That is, by an elevated staircase or means of ascent which would indecently expose the person of the one who offered the sacrifice.

CHAPTER XXI.

1. **The judgments which thou shalt set before them** — As distinguished from the words spoken directly from heaven. **Judgments** are here to be understood as decisions of law, or judicial statutes and regulations to govern in the administration of justice. These were the rules of judgment by which the rights of individuals were to be maintained and civil order secured.

2. **Buy a Hebrew servant**—In the time of Moses slavery existed among all the nations, and commonly in most oppressive forms. The Israelites themselves had just escaped a bondage of serfdom in Egypt. The Hebrew patriarchs had owned many slaves who intermarried and begat children, and these were regarded as the property of the patriarchal chieftain. Comp. Gen. xiv, 14. The Mosaic legislation was adapted to mitigate the evils of the system, and provided for universal emancipation. Lev. xxv, 10. This verse shows that a Hebrew might be bought and sold, but under definite restrictions. It appears, (1.) That a Hebrew might sell himself, voluntarily, for a term of years not exceeding six, (except in the case specified in verse 6.) (2.) He might, on account of poverty, feel obliged to sell himself (Lev. xxv, 39) even to a foreigner. Lev. xxv, 47. (3.) One might sell his daughter to be a maidservant, (verse 7,) or one might be sold for theft, (xxii, 3.) (4.) Captives taken in war might become the possession of the conquerors, (Deut. xx, 14, xxi, 10-14, Num. xxxi, 1,8,) and, (5.) Hebrews might purchase bondservants of the heathen, and treat them with greater rigour than was allowable with any of their own brethren. Lev. xxv, 44-46. But stealing and selling men were punishable with death, (verse 16,) and the rendition of fugitive slaves was strictly forbidden. Deut. xxiii, 15, 16. The Mosaic law does not authorize the involuntary sale of any one except for crime. **In the seventh he shall go out free**—Furnished also with liberal gifts. Compare Deut. xv, 13, 14. This humane provision made it impossible for any Hebrew to become involved in unwilling bondage. Such a provision adopted by any slaveholding people would speedily abolish all holding of human beings in unjust bondage.

4. **If his master have given him a wife**—This condition involved certain rights of family and household possession. It contemplates the patriarchal family, in which servants were born, and may also have had in view the fact that the wife in the case supposed might often be a bondmaid acquired from among the heathen, whose legal term of service would not expire before the jubilee. "This may appear oppressive, but it was an equitable consequence of the possession of property in slaves at all."—*Keil.*

6. **Unto the judges**—Heb., *unto the gods:* here meaning the local magistrates. Comp. Psa. lxxxii, 6; John x, 34.

492   EXODUS.   B. C. 1491.

door, or unto the door post; and his master shall ^e bore his ear through with an awl; and he shall serve him for ever.

7 And if a man ^f sell his daughter to be a maidservant, she shall not go out ^g as the menservants do. **8** If she ³please not her master, who hath betrothed her to himself, then shall he let her be redeemed: to sell her unto a strange nation he shall have no power, seeing he hath dealt deceitfully with her. **9** And if he have betrothed her unto his son, he shall deal with her after the manner of daughters. **10** If he take him another *wife*, her food, her raiment, ^h and her duty of marriage, shall he not diminish. **11** And if he do not these three unto her, then shall she go out free without money.

12 ⁱ He that smiteth a man, so that

e Psa. 40. 6.——*f* Neh. 5. 5.——*g* Verses 2, 3.——3 Heb. *be evil in the eyes of, etc.*

h 1 Cor. 7. 5.——*i* Gen. 9. 6; Lev. 24. 17; Num. 35. 30, 31; Matt. 26. 52.

His master shall bore his ear—On this Michaelis has the following observations: "In order to guard against all abuse, it was necessary that the transaction should be gone about judicially, and that the magistrate should know it. It was the intention of Moses that every Hebrew who wished to continue a servant for life should, with the magistrate's previous knowledge, bear a given token thereof in his own body. He thus guarded against the risk of a master having it in his power either to pretend that his servant had promised to serve him during his life, when he had not, or, by ill usage, during the period that he had him in his service, to extort any such promise from him. The statute of Moses made the boring of the ears in some degree ignominious to a freeman; because it became the sign whereby a perpetual slave was to be known. And if the Israelites had, for this reason, abandoned the practice, Moses would not have been displeased. Indeed, this was probably the very object which he had in view to get imperceptibly effected by this law: for in the wearing of earrings superstition was deeply concerned." — *Commentaries on the Laws of Moses*, vol. ii, p. 178. London, 1814.

7. Sell his daughter—This might occur because of extreme poverty and want. Neh. v, 5. The verses following show that this kind of a sale was contemplated as essentially a betrothal; but they also serve to exhibit the inferior position in which women were held as compared with men. They might be sold by their parents for maidservants, and so take the place of concubines in the family of the purchaser. But this statute was attended by the following provisions: (1.) A maidservant, thus acquired, was not to obtain her freedom in the seventh year, like the menservants of verse 2. (2.) She could not be sold into a strange nation. (3.) She might be redeemed, either by her father, were he able, or by another Hebrew who desired her for a concubine. (4.) Her master might betroth her to his son, and in that case she was to be treated by him as a daughter. (5.) Her rights as a concubine were not to be changed by his taking another woman into the same relation. (6.) If her rights were withheld she was entitled to freedom. On the whole these laws, though far below the standard of Christian ethics, were mild and tolerant for the time.

8. Please not her master—Heb., *if she be evil in the eyes of her master.* If he discover some defect in her, or find her less attractive and useful to him than he had expected. **Dealt deceitfully with her**—The purchase implied the pledge of marriage or concubinage, with its legal rights. These involved obligations which, if not met, exposed to the charge of deceitful dealing.

10. Her duty of marriage—עֹנָה, *cohabitation* and associated conjugal rights.

11. These three—Most simply, the three things mentioned in the previous verse; namely, food, raiment, and cohabitation. Others understand the three things to be, (1) letting her be redeemed, (2) betrothing her to his son, (3) allowing her the rights of marriage named in verse 10.

12. Smiteth a man, so that he die—This is a general law for intentional murder, and demands the punishment

he die, shall be surely put to death.
13 And [k] if a man lie not in wait, but God [l] deliver *him* into his hand; then [m] I will appoint thee a place whither he shall flee. **14** But if a man come [n] presumptuously upon his neighbour, to slay him with guile; [o] thou shalt take him from mine altar, that he may die.
15 And he that smiteth his father, or his mother, shall be surely put to death.
16 And [p] he that stealeth a man, and [q] selleth him, or if he be [r] found in his hand, he shall surely be put to death.
17 And [s] he that [4] curseth his father, or his mother, shall surely be put to death.
18 And if men strive together, and one smite [5] another with a stone, or with *his* fist, and he die not, but keepeth *his*

bed: **19** If he rise again, and walk abroad [t] upon his staff, then shall he that smote *him* be quit: only he shall pay *for* [6] the loss of his time, and shall cause *him* to be thoroughly healed.
20 And if a man smite his servant, or his maid, with a rod, and he die under his hand; he shall be surely [7] punished.
21 Notwithstanding, if he continue a day or two, he shall not be punished: for [u] he *is* his money.
22 If men strive, and hurt a woman with child, so that her fruit depart *from her*, and yet no mischief follow: he shall be surely punished, according as the woman's husband will lay upon him; and he shall [v] pay as the judges *determine.* **23** And if *any* mischief follow, then thou shalt give life for life, **24** [w] Eye

---

k Num. 35. 22; Deut. 19. 4, 5. —— *l* 1 Sam. 24. 4, 10, 18. —— *m* Num. 35. 11; Deut. 19. 3; Josh. 20. 2. —— *n* Num. 15. 30; 35. 20; Deut. 19. 11, 12; Heb. 10. 26. —— *o* 1 Kings 2. 28-34; 2 Kings 11. 15. —— *p* Deut. 24. 7. —— *q* Gen. 37. 28. —— *r* Chap. 22. 4.

s Lev. 20. 9; Prov. 20. 20; Matt. 15. 4; Mark 7. 10.——4 Or, *revileth.*——5 Or, *his neighbour.*—— *t* 2 Sam. 3. 29.——6 Heb. *his ceasing.*——7 Heb. *avenged,* Gen. 4. 15, 24; Rom. 13. 4.——*u* Lev. 25. 45, 46.——*v* Ver. 30; Deut. 22. 18, 19.——*w* Lev. 24. 20; Deut. 19. 21; Matt. 5. 38.

---

declared in Gen. ix, 6. See also notes on chap. xx, 13.

13. **Lie not in wait**—That is, intending to take life, and planning, like a hunter, to insure the death of his victim. **But God deliver him into his hand**—As when one is slain by the accidental blow not intended for him, as in the case supposed in Deut. xix, 5. Such unintentional homicide could not justly be treated as the crime of murder. **A place whither he shall flee**—Such "cities of refuge" were afterward appointed. See Num. xxxv, 9-15, and parallels.

14. **Take him from mine altar**—The cases of Adonijah and Joab, as read in 1 Kings i, 50, and ii, 28, are illustrations of the prevalent notion that the altar was a place of security from violence. This law aims to take away from the presumptuous murderer all hope of protection from the holy place.

16, 17. **Stealeth a man**—Note that manstealing was placed on the same plane with the crime of murder. Cursing a parent was also treated as a capital offence.

18, 19. **He die not, but keepeth his bed**—Observe in this statute the careful purpose to maintain equity and right. He who smote and injured his fellowman in personal contest was responsible for all losses or damage resulting therefrom.

20. **Smite his servant**—Many writers assume that foreign bondservants, not Hebrew servants, are intended here; but the law itself does not so discriminate. The reason given in the next verse, namely, that the servant is his property, evidently led to a distinction in the punishment of this kind of manslaughter. It was assumed that no man would wilfully destroy his own property by killing his slave. It was considered a master's right to chastise **his servant, or his maid, with a rod,** and if death resulted from the excessive severity of the punishment it would be accidental rather than intentional. In case death resulted the man was to be **surely punished,** but the measure of the penalty is not prescribed; that was doubtless to be left to the magistrates to determine.

22-25. **As the woman's husband will lay upon him**—The Hebrews threw every possible safeguard about the fruit of the womb, and an injury of the kind here specified was treated as a very grave offence. If death resulted it was punished as a capital crime, and **life for life** was demanded. If, however, other and less serious damage followed, the punishment was to be proportioned, according to a rigorous

for eye, tooth for tooth, hand for hand, foot for foot, **25** Burning for burning, wound for wound, stripe for stripe. **26** And if a man smite the eye of his servant, or the eye of his maid, that it perish; he shall let him go free for his eye's sake. **27** And if he smite out his manservant's tooth, or his maidservant's tooth; he shall let him go free for his tooth's sake. **28** If an ox gore a man or a woman, that they die: then ˣ the ox shall be surely stoned, and his flesh shall not be eaten; but the owner of the ox *shall be* quit. **29** But if the ox were wont to push with his horn in time past, and it hath been testified to his owner, and he

hath not kept him in, but that he hath killed a man or a woman; the ox shall be stoned, and his owner also shall be put to death. **30** If there be laid on him a sum of money, then he shall give for ʸ the ransom of his life whatsoever is laid upon him. **31** Whether he have gored a son, or have gored a daughter, according to this judgment shall it be done unto him. **32** If the ox shall push a manservant or a maidservant; he shall give unto their master ᶻ thirty shekels of silver, and the ᵃ ox shall be stoned.

33 And if a man shall open a pit, or if a man shall dig a pit, and not cover it, and an ox or an ass fall therein; **34** The owner of the pit shall make *it* good, *and*

∞ Gen. 9. 5.——*y* Ver. 22; Num. 35. 31.——*z* See Zech. 11. 12, 13; Matt. 26. 15; Phil. 2. 7.——*a* Ver. 28.

law of retaliation, (*lex talionis*.) The woman might be injured in **eye, tooth, hand,** or **foot,** or by means of **burning,** (branding by a hot iron,) or some other **wound** or **stripe,** purposely or accidentally given, or the unborn offspring might be harmed in some of these ways, and a corresponding injury was accordingly to be inflicted upon the offender. The *lex talionis*, or law of retaliation, which appears in this passage and in Lev. xxiv, 19, 20, Deut. xix, 21, is one of the most simple and ancient conceptions of righteous retribution. It has often been condemned as barbarous, but it is grounded in the intuitions of justice, and asserted itself in the legislation of many ancient nations, as the Romans, Greeks, and Indians. "It would seem," says Michaelis, "that Moses retained the law of retaliation from a more ancient, and a very natural, law of usage." It would naturally tend to prevent personal injuries, and all must see and acknowledge that when a man speedily receives in his own person the same damage he wilfully inflicted on another, he but receives his deserts and has no ground to complain. But, like the law which authorized the nearest kinsman of a murdered man to avenge his death, this law was liable to be abused. It gave too much room for the gratification of personal bitterness and hatred, and hence, mainly, the reason of our Lord's words in Matt. v, 38, 39. The New Testament teaching, as has been so often explained, does not condemn the Mosaic law as unjust, but warns against the feeling of personal bitterness and revenge which is so likely to arise from a sense of injury. That should rather be crucified by a doing good for evil where the public welfare will not suffer thereby.

26, 27. **Eye of his servant**—Here again we note that the male or female servant was reckoned as not enjoying the same natural rights as freemen. The *lex talionis* did not apply to them, but they were allowed their freedom as a compensation. But we should observe how the provisions of this statute, as well as those of verses 20 and 21, must have tended to mitigate the wrongs of slavery, and protect the lives and persons of slaves, in a way unknown to the laws and customs of other ancient nations.

28–32. **If an ox gore a man**—This statute further guards the sanctity of human life. A potent object-lesson lay in the command that the murderous animal's **flesh shall not be eaten,** for it was to be regarded as polluted with the curse of a human life destroyed. Even the **owner** of such an ox might suffer the death penalty if he had knowingly permitted him to run at large after being duly admonished of the animal's vicious habit. This penalty might, however, be commuted for **a sum of money,** which was, doubtless, left to the magistrates to determine. The valuation fixed by the law as the price of a slave thus killed was **thirty shekels of silver.** Comp. Zech. xi, 12, 13; and Matt. xxvi, 15; xxvii, 3, 4.

give money unto the owner of them; and the dead *beast* shall be his.

35 And if one man's ox hurt another's, that he die; then they shall sell the live ox, and divide the money of it; and the dead *ox* also they shall divide. **36** Or if it be known that the ox hath used to push in time past, and his owner hath not kept him in; he shall surely pay ox for ox; and the dead shall be his own.

CHAPTER XXII.

IF a man shall steal an ox, or a ¹ sheep, and kill it, or sell it; he shall restore five oxen for an ox, and ᵃ four sheep for a sheep.

2 If a thief be found ᵇ breaking up, and be smitten that he die, *there shall* ᶜ *no blood be shed* for him. **3** If the sun be risen upon him, *there shall be* blood *shed* for him; *for* he should make full restitution: if he have nothing, then he shall be ᵈ sold for his theft. **4** If the theft be certainly ᵉ found in his hand alive, whether it be ox, or ass, or sheep; he shall ᶠ restore double.

5 If a man shall cause a field or vineyard to be eaten, and shall put in his beast, and shall feed in another man's field; of the best of his own field, and of the best of his own vineyard, shall he make restitution.

6 If fire break out, and catch in thorns, so that the stacks of corn, or the standing corn, or the field, be consumed *therewith;* he that kindled the fire shall surely make restitution.

7 If a man shall deliver unto his neighbour money or stuff to keep, and it be stolen out of the man's house; ᵍ if the thief be found, let him pay double. **8** If the thief be not found, then the master of the house shall be brought unto the ʰ judges, *to see* whether he have put his hand unto his neighbour's goods. **9** For all manner of trespass, *whether it*

---

1 Or, *goat.*—*a* 2 Sam. 12. 6; see Prov. 6. 31; Luke 19. 8.—*b* Matt. 24. 43.—*c* Num. 35. 27.   *d* Chap. 21. 2.— *e* Chap. 21. 16.—*f* See vers. 1, 7; Prov. 6. 31.—*g* Ver. 4.—*h* Chap.21.6; ver. 28.

33–36. The provisions of this section must commend themselves as both wise and prudent. Caution, forethought, and most equitable dealing were hereby inculcated.

CHAPTER XXII.

1. **If a man shall steal**—Moses knew full well that prohibition would not prohibit crimes of any sort without a rigid administration. The eighth commandment (xx, 15) required for the good of society such further enactments as here follow. **Five oxen ... four sheep**—These varying penalties are apportioned according to a relative magnitude of the loss. While the crime of theft is in itself essentially the same, whether more or less be stolen, considerations of value and loss naturally enter into all wise legislation touching the measure of penal fines to be prescribed. Hence it was provided, further, that if the stolen animal were found alive, the fine would only be double instead of fourfold or fivefold. The killing or selling of the stolen animal would also, generally, imply a more determined purpose to do wrong than when the animal was kept alive.

2. **No blood ... for him**—The thief who breaks into a house in the nighttime is commonly none too good to commit the foulest deeds. There would be no telling all his purposes; and, if slain in the act of such a crime the slayer was not to be looked upon as guilty of murder.

3. **If the sun be risen upon him** —If he commits his crime in the daylight, his movements and purposes are generally so apparent that an attempt upon his life would be utterly unjustifiable, and punishable as wilful manslaughter. **He should make full restitution**—This, of course, supposes his apprehension and conviction. The satisfactory **restitution** might often require more than the mere return of stolen goods. These goods might be damaged by the seizure, and the affright and trouble occasioned by the crime ought not to go unnoticed. So if the thief had not wherewith to make full recompense he was to be **sold for his theft**, and so, by bondservice, make due compensation.

8. **Whether he have put his hand unto his neighbour's goods**— The magistrates would carefully examine if there were any evidence of fraudulent appropriation of the goods, and if none were found, such an oath as is mentioned in verse 11 would be taken as a release for the suspected party. The loss in that case would fall upon the owner.

EXODUS.   B. C. 1491.

be for ox, for ass, for sheep, for raiment, *or* for any manner of lost thing, which *another* challengeth to be his, the ⁱ cause of both parties shall come before the judges; *and* whom the judges shall condemn, he shall pay double unto his neighbour. **10** If a man deliver unto his neighbour an ass, or an ox, or a sheep, or any beast, to keep; and it die, or be hurt, or driven away, no man seeing *it:* **11** *Then* shall an ᵏ oath of the LORD be between them both, that he hath not put his hand unto his neighbour's goods; and the owner of it shall accept *thereof,* and he shall not make *it* good. **12** And ˡ if it be stolen from him, he shall make restitution unto the owner thereof. **13** If it be torn in pieces, *then* let him bring it *for* witness, *and* he shall not make good that which was torn.
14 And if a man borrow *aught* of his neighbour, and it be hurt, or die, the owner thereof *being* not with it, he shall surely make *it* good. **15** *But* if the owner thereof *be* with it, he shall not make *it* good: if it *be* a hired *thing,* it came for his hire.
16 And ᵐ if a man entice a maid that is not betrothed, and lie with her, he shall surely endow her to be his wife.

17 If her father utterly refuse to give her unto him, he shall ² pay money according to the ⁿ dowry of virgins.
18 ᵒ Thou shalt not suffer a witch to live.
19 ᵖ Whosoever lieth with a beast shall surely be put to death.
20 ᵠ He that sacrificeth unto *any god,* save unto the LORD only, he shall be utterly destroyed.
21 ʳ Thou shalt neither vex a stranger, nor oppress him: for ye were strangers in the land of Egypt.
22 ˢ Ye shall not afflict any widow, or fatherless child. **23** If thou afflict them in any wise, and they ᵗ cry at all unto me, I will surely ᵘ hear their cry; **24** And my ᵛ wrath shall wax hot, and I will kill you with the sword; and ʷ your wives shall be widows, and your children fatherless.
25 ˣ If thou lend money to *any of* my people *that is* poor by thee, thou shalt not be to him as a usurer, neither shalt thou lay upon him usury. **26** ʸ If thou at all take thy neighbour's raiment to pledge, thou shalt deliver it unto him by that the sun goeth down: **27** For that *is* his covering only, it *is* his raiment for his skin: wherein shall he

i Deut. 25. 1; 2 Chron. 19. 10.—*k* Heb. 6. 16.—*l* Gen. 31. 39.—*m* Deut. 22. 28, 29.—2 Heb. *weigh,* Gen. 23. 16.—*n* Gen. 34. 12; Deut. 22. 29; 1 Sam. 18. 25.—*o* Lev. 19. 26, 31; 20. 27; Deut. 18. 10, 11; 1 Sam. 28. 3, 9.—*p* Lev. 18. 23; 20. 15.—*q* Num. 25. 2, 7, 8; Deut. 13. 1, 2, 5, 6, 9, 13-15; 17. 2, 3, 5.—*r* Chap. 23. 9; Lev. 19. 33; 25. 35; Deut. 10. 19; Jer. 7. 6; Zech. 7. 10; Mal. 3. 5.

s Deut. 10. 18; 24. 17; 27. 19; Psa. 94. 6; Isa. 1. 17, 23; 10. 2; Ezek. 22. 7; Zech. 7. 10; James 1. 27.—*t* Deut. 15. 9; 24. 15; Job 35. 9; Luke 18. 7.—*u* Verse 27; Job 34. 28; Psa. 18. 6; 145. 19; James 5. 4.—*v* Job 31. 23; Psa. 69. 24.—*w* Psa. 109. 9; Lam. 5. 3.—*x* Lev. 25. 35-37; Deut. 19, 20; Neh. 5. 7; Psa. 15. 5; Ezek. 18. 8, 17.—*y* Deut. 24. 6, 10, 13, 17; Job 22. 6; 24. 3, 9; Prov. 20. 16; 22. 27; Ezek. 18. 7, 16; Amos 2. 8.

12. **If it be stolen from him**—Hebrew, *from with him,* that is, from a place where his immediate oversight would naturally prevent such seizure. In this case the loss would be regarded as due to his carelessness. Comp. Gen. xxxi, 39.

15. **If it be a hired thing**—If the owner let it out for money in advance or to be paid, that payment was to be taken as the sole compensation in the case.

18. **Not suffer a witch to live**—Those who practised the magical arts were regarded as usurping the realm of Deity, and, by some mysterious league with wicked spirits, opposing themselves to the fundamental principles of true religion. Hence they were, in logical accord with the Israelitish faith, to be treated as capital offenders. Comp. Lev. xix, 26, 31; xx, 27; Deut. xviii, 10, 11.

24. **I will kill you with the sword**—Observe here that Jehovah is the governor and judge over all, and will, sooner or later, punish all evil-doers and them that forget mercy. The magistrate bears not the sword in vain if he maintain justice and defend the weak; but if he fail in these high responsibilities, God's own hand will interpose and bring deserved retribution.

25. **A usurer**—Or, *a creditor,* here regarded as a rigid exacter of interest. The tenderness enjoined in regard to loans to the poor was adapted to cultivate compassion and brotherly feeling. But it was not designed to favour the indolent and vicious.

27. **Wherein shall he sleep**—The outer garment was used by the poorer classes of the East as their sole covering by night. Hence the kind consideration of the law.

B. C. 1491. CHAPTER XXII. 497

sleep? and it shall come to pass, when he *crieth unto me, that I will hear; for I am ᵃ gracious.

28 ᵇ Thou shalt not revile the ³gods, nor curse the ruler of thy people.

29 Thou shalt not delay *to offer* ⁴ᶜ the first of thy ripe fruits, and of thy ⁵ liquors: ᵈ the firstborn of thy sons shalt thou give unto me. 30 ᵉ Likewise shalt thou do with thine oxen, *and* with thy sheep: ᶠ seven days it shall be with his dam; on the eighth day thou shalt give it me.

31 And ye shall be ᵍ holy men unto me: ʰ neither shall ye eat *any* flesh *that is* torn of beasts in the field; ye shall cast it to the dogs.

CHAPTER XXIII.

THOU ᵃ shalt not ¹ raise a false report: put not thine hand with the wicked to be an ᵇ unrighteous witness.

2 ᶜ Thou shalt not follow a multitude to *do* evil; ᵈ neither shalt thou ² speak in a cause to decline after many to wrest *judgment:*

3 Neither shalt thou countenance a poor man in his cause.

4 ᵉ If thou meet thine enemy's ox or his ass going astray, thou shalt surely bring it back to him again. 5 ᶠ If thou see the ass of him that hateth thee lying under his burden, ³ and wouldest forbear to help him, thou shalt surely help with him. 6 ᵍ Thou shalt not wrest the

---

z Verse 23.—*a* Chapter 34. 6; 2 Chron. 30. 9; Psalm 86. 15. —— *b* Eccles. 10. 20; Acts 23. 5; Jude 8. —— 3 Or, *judges*, verses 8, 9; Psalm 82. 6. —— 4 Heb. *thy fulness.* —— *c* Chapter 23. 16, 19; Prov. 3. 9.—5 Heb. *tear*.—*d* Chapter 13. 2. 12; 34. 19. —— *e* Deut. 15. 19. —— *f* Lev. 22. 27. —— *g* Chapter 19. 6; Lev. 19. 2; Deut. 14. 21. —— *h* Lev. 22. 8; Ezekiel 4. 14; 44. 31. —— *a* Verse 7; Lev. 19. 16; Psa, 15. 3; 101. 5; Prov. 10. 18; see 2 Sam. 19. 27, with 16. 3.—1 Or, *receive.*—*b* Chap. 20. 16; Deut. 19. 16-18; Psa. 35. 11; Prov. 19. 5, 9, 28; 24. 28; see 1 Kings 21. 10, 13; Matt. 26. 59-61; Acts 6. 11, 13.

c Gen. 7. 1; 19. 4, 7; chap. 32. 1, 2; Josh. 24. 15; 1 Sam. 15. 9; 1 Kings 19. 10; Job 31. 34; Prov. 1. 10, 11. 15; 4. 14; Matt. 27. 24, 26; Mark 15. 15; Luke 23. 23; Acts 24. 27; 25. 9.—*d* Verses 6, 7; Lev. 19. 15; Deut. 1. 17; Psa. 72. 2. —— 2 Heb. *answer.* —— *e* Deut. 22. 1; Job 31. 29; Prov. 24. 17; 25. 21; Matt. 5. 44; Rom. 12. 20; 1 Thess. 5. 15.—*f* Deut. 22. 4.—3 Or, *wilt thou cease to help him?* or, *and wouldest cease to leave thy business for him; thou shalt surely leave it to join with him.*—*g* Verse 2; Deut. 27. 19; Job 31. 13, 21; Eccles. 5. 8; Isa. 10. 1, 2; Jer. 5. 28; 7. 6; Amos 5. 12; Mal. 3. 5.

---

28. **Thou shalt not revile the gods**—Rather, *God*. Our version follows the Sept., Vulg., and other versions, and conveys the idea that even the gods of the heathen are not to be reviled. Others understand the reference to be to judges, but this seems sufficiently comprehended in the words **ruler of thy people,** which immediately follow. This verse associated God and the civil **ruler** in a very noticeable way. The latter is, according to Romans xii, 4, God's minister, and a becoming respect and reverence for the civil magistrate is one way of honouring God himself.

29. **First of thy ripe fruits, and of thy liquors**—Literally, *thy fulness and thy tear thou shalt not delay.* The first full or ripe produce, and the droppings of oil and wine as pressed from the fruit, are intended. The offering to God of firstfruits and firstlings was a custom of most remote antiquity, (comp. Gen. iv, 3, 4,) and a most appropriate exhibition of gratitude and of a sense of dependence. **The firstborn of thy sons** — See notes on chapter xiii, 2.

30. **Seven days** — Comp. also Lev. xxii, 27.

31. **Torn of beasts** — Such meat was likely to be left unfit for eating by the violent death of the animal, and the failure to pour out its blood. It exposed to the liability of eating flesh with the blood, which was most imperatively forbidden. See Leviticus xvii, 10-15.

CHAPTER XXIII.

1. **Raise a false report**—This law guards against slander, and all circulating of slanderous utterances. It is supplemented by the admonition of verse 7, and is comprehended in the ninth commandment, (xx, 16,) where see note.

2. **Speak in a cause**—Literally, *answer in a controversy* (suit at law) *to turn away after many, to pervert.* This law, like that of the preceding and the following verse is mainly directed against giving false testimony in judicial proceedings, and so perverting justice and truth.

4, 5. **Enemy's ox . . . bring it back**—This statute embodies the essence of our Lord's command to "do good to them that hate you," (Matt. v, 44,) and furnishes a most admirable illustration of it.

judgment of thy poor in his cause. 7 ʰ Keep thee far from a false matter; ⁱ and the innocent and righteous slay thou not: for ᵏ I will not justify the wicked.

8 And ˡ thou shalt take no gift: for the gift blindeth ⁴ the wise, and perverteth the words of the righteous.

9 Also ᵐ thou shalt not oppress a stranger: for ye know the ⁵ heart of a stranger, seeing ye were strangers in the land of Egypt. 10 And ⁿ six years thou shalt sow thy land, and shalt gather in the fruits thereof: 11 But the seventh *year* thou shalt let it rest and lie still; that the poor of thy people may eat: and what they leave the beasts of the field shall eat. In like manner thou shalt deal with thy vineyard, *and* with thy ⁶ oliveyard. 12 ° Six days thou shalt do thy work, and on the seventh day thou shalt rest: that thine ox and thine ass may rest, and the son of thy hand-

h Ver.1; Lev. 19. 11; Luke 3. 14; Eph. 4. 25.—*i* Deut. 27. 25; Psa. 94. 21; Prov. 17. 15, 26; Jer. 7. 6; Matt. 27. 4.—*k* Chap. 34. 7; Rom. 1. 18.—*l* Deut. 16. 19; 1 Sam. 8. 3; 12. 3; 2 Chron. 19. 7; Psa. 26. 10; Prov. 15. 27; 17. 8, 23; 29. 4; Isa. 1. 23; 5. 23; 33.15; Ezek. 22. 12; Amos 5. 12; Acts 24. 26.—4 Heb. *the seeing.*—*m* Chap. 22. 21; Deut. 10. 19; 24. 14, 17; 27. 19; Psa. 94. 6; Ezek. 22. 7; Mal. 3. 5.— 5 Heb. *soul.* — *n* Lev. 25. 3, 4. — 6 Or, *olive trees.*—*o* Chap. 20. 8, 9; Deut. 5. 13; Luke 13. 14.

7. **Righteous slay thou not**—By false testimony against them. If an **innocent and righteous** man is convicted and suffers the death penalty on account of the testimony of a lying witness, that witness is guilty of his death.

8. **Take no gift**—That is, as a bribe. The marginal references show how repeatedly this sin is condemned in the Scriptures.

9. **Not oppress a stranger**—This command is repeated from xxii, 21, with some addition, and shows that the foreigner was entitled to protection from judicial wrongs as well as other forms of oppression. Israel should not forget how **the heart of a stranger** feels.

11. **The seventh year . . . rest**— This provision for a sabbatic year is one of the most remarkable enactments of the Mosaic legislation, but we have no evidence that it was ever observed by the nation. It is repeated in fuller form in Lev. xxv, 1–7, and is there associated with the law for the fiftieth year jubilee. The far-reaching and ennobling influences upon a people of the faithful observance of this law must needs be very great. It would (1.) teach that the land was God's rather than the people's. (2.) It would afford a rest to the soil, which would be materially helped by remaining fallow one year in seven. (3.) Inasmuch as it has been repeatedly proven that a man will do more and better work by resting one day in seven, it is at least presumable that, by proper care in cultivation, and one year's rest in seven, the soil will yield as much or more than when no sabbatic year is observed. (4.) It would help to bring all classes of the people into closer sympathy, and remove some of the incitements to anarchical socialism. (5.) It would tend to cultivate the best sentiments of humanity and regard, alike for man and beast. (6.) It would afford extraordinary advantages for mental and moral culture. (7.) It would beget a most beautiful confidence in the providence of God. No people's faith in God, not even ancient Israel's, seems ever to have been sufficient to attempt the observance of this law. Hence the judgment of seventy years' exile and desolation, "until the land had enjoyed her sabbaths." 2 Chron. xxxvi, 21. Even the resolution to observe the seventh year, after the exile, (Neh. x, 31,) does not appear to have been kept. Here is a decisive argument against critics who dispute the Mosaic authorship of the Pentateuch on the ground that the laws therein recorded were not observed before the exile. We have no historical evidence that this law was ever observed. **Rest and lie still**—The parallel passage in Lev. xxv, 4, shows that this was intended to stop all sowing and cultivation for the year; not, as some have supposed, that the tilling should go on as usual, but the crops be left to the poor. The thought, rather, is, **that the poor of thy people** may be allowed free appropriation of such products as grew without sowing and cultivation. No land-owner should that year claim the natural products of the soil for himself.

12. **The seventh day**—See note on chap. xx, 8.

B. C. 1491.   CHAPTER XXIII.   499

maid, and the stranger, may be refreshed. **13** And in all *things* that I have said unto you ᵖ be circumspect: and ᵠ make no mention of the name of other gods, neither let it be heard out of thy mouth.

14 ʳ Three times thou shalt keep a feast unto me in the year. **15** ˢ Thou shalt keep the feast of unleavened bread: (thou shalt eat unleavened bread seven days, as I commanded thee, in the time appointed of the month Abib; for in it thou camest out from Egypt: ᵗ and none shall appear before me empty:) **16** ᵘ And the feast of harvest, the firstfruits of thy labours, which thou hast sown in the field: and ᵛ the feast of ingathering, *which is* in the end of the year, when

---

p Deut. 4. 9; Josh. 22, 5; Psa. 39. 1; Eph. 5. 15; 1 Tim. 4. 16.——*q* Num. 32. 38; Deut. 12. 3; Josh. 23. 7; Psa. 16. 4; Hos. 2. 17; Zech. 13. 2.——*r* Chap. 34. 23; Lev. 23. 4; Deut. 16. 16.

s Chapter 12. 15; 13. 6; 34. 18; Leviticus 23. 6; Deuteronomy 16. 8.——*t* Chapter 34. 20; Deuteronomy 16. 16.——*u* Chapter 34. 22; Leviticus 23. 10.——*v* Deuteronomy 16. 13.

---

13. No mention of the name of other gods—"In order to eradicate idolatry, with all its far-spreading roots, the idols shall not only be banished from the hearts, but also from the lips; they should not even be alluded to or mentioned, much less worshipped. And as it was forbidden to use the name of God falsely or disrespectfully, (xx, 7, xxii, 28,) thus the heathen deities should entirely disappear from the language."—*Kalisch.*

14-16. **Three times . . . a feast unto me in the year**—These three great annual festivals, ordained for Israel, are here called the **feast of unleavened bread,** the **feast of harvest,** and the **feast of ingathering.** They are more fully described in other passages, but when the entire arrangement for the three is considered as a whole, it exhibits a magnificent scheme of national festivity, naturally and beautifully connected, and wisely adapted to serve as a great national bond. "Whoever has a thorough knowledge of these festivals," says the learned Ewald, "will be persuaded that they have not arisen by slow degrees from the blind impulse of external nature, nor from the history of the people, but are the product of a lofty genius." These festivals were arranged on a system of sevens, as if growing out of sabbatic ideas. The **feast of unleavened bread** is more commonly known as the passover, instituted at the Exodus, and described in chap. xii, 1-28, 43-51; xiii, 3-10, where see notes. It was to be a feast of seven days' duration, and to commence on the fifteenth day of the first month, (Abib,) that is, after twice seven days from the beginning of the year. This occurred at the time when the firstfruits of the barley harvest could be waved as an offering before Jehovah. Lev. xxiii, 10-12. **The feast of harvest** was observed seven weeks after the offering of the wave-sheaf of the passover, that is, on the fiftieth day thereafter, (Lev. xxiii, 15-21,) whence it obtained also the names of "Pentecost," (Acts ii, 1,) and "the feast of weeks." Chap. xxxiv, 22; Deut. xvi, 10. This was the time of the wheat harvest, so that passover and Pentecost enclosed the harvest season, which in Palestine extends from March-April into June-July. **The feast of ingathering** is more commonly known as "the feast of tabernacles," (Lev. xxiii, 34-41, Deut. xvi, 13-15,) and occurred **in the end of the year,** that is, of the agrarian year, "after thou hast gathered in thy corn and thy wine." Deut. xvi, 13. This **end,** or *going forth,* (צֵאת,) of the year, (in chap. xxxiv, 22, called the תְּקוּפָה, *circle of the year,*) occurred in the seventh month, (September-October,) which was observed as the sabbatic month. Its first day was signalled by the blowing of trumpets, (Lev. xxiii, 24, Num. xxix, 1;) the tenth, was the great day of atonement, (Lev. xvi, 29-34, xxiii, 27-32;) after which, on the fifteenth, (the day following the twice seventh from the feast of trumpets, which opened the sabbatic month,) the feast of tabernacles commenced and continued seven days, and the eighth was also consecrated as a sabbath. Lev. xxiii, 39. The sounding of the trumpet on the tenth day of the seventh month of the fiftieth year (the one following seven times seven years) was the proclamation of the year of jubilee, and of "liberty throughout all the land

500 EXODUS. B. C. 1491.

thou hast gathered in thy labours out of the field. 17 ʷ Three times in the year all thy males shall appear before the Lord God. 18 ˣ Thou shalt not offer the blood of my sacrifice with leavened bread; neither shall the fat of my ⁷ sacrifice remain until the morning. 19 ʸ The first of the firstfruits of thy land thou shalt bring into the house of the Lord thy God. ᶻ Thou shalt not seethe a kid in his mother's milk.

20 ᵃ Behold, I send an Angel before thee, to keep thee in the way, and to bring thee into the place which I have prepared. 21 Beware of him, and obey his voice, ᵇ provoke him not; for he will ᶜ not pardon your transgressions: for ᵈ my name *is* in him. 22 But if thou shalt indeed obey his voice, and do all that I speak; then ᵉ I will be an enemy, unto thine enemies, and ᵍ an adversary unto thine adversaries. 23 ᶠ For mine Angel shall go before thee, and ᵍ bring thee in unto the Amorites, and the Hittites, and the Perizzites, and the Canaanites, the Hivites, and the Jebusites; and I will cut them off. 24 Thou shalt not ʰ bow down to their gods, nor serve them, ⁱ nor do after their works: ᵏ but thou shalt utterly overthrow them, and quite break down their images. 25 And ye shall ˡ serve

---

w Chap. 34. 23; Deut. 16. 16.— *x* Chap. 12. 8; 34. 25; Lev. 2. 11; Deut. 16. 4.— 7 Or, *feast.*—*y* Chap. 22. 29; 34. 26; Lev. 23. 10, 17; Num. 18. 12, 13; Deut. 26. 10; Neh. 10. 35. — *z* Chap. 34. 26; Deut. 14. 21.— *a* Chap. 14. 19; 32. 34; 33. 2, 14; Num. 20. 16; Josh. 5. 13; 6. 2; Psa. 91. 11; Isa. 63. 9.—*b* Num. 14. 11; Psa. 78. 40, 56; Eph. 4. 30; Heb. 3. 10, 16.— *c* Chap. 32. 34; Num. 14. 35; Deut. 18. 19; Josh. 24. 19; Jer.

5. 7; Heb. 3. 11; 1 John 5. 16.—*d* Isa. 9. 6; Jer. 23. 6; John 10. 30, 38. — *e* Gen. 12. 3; Deut. 30. 7; Jer. 30. 20.—8 Or, *I will afflict them that afflict thee.*—*f* Verse 20; chap. 33. 2.—*g* Josh. 24. 8, 11.—*h* Chap. 20. 5. — *i* Lev. 18. 3; Deut. 12. 30, 31.—*k* Chap. 34. 13; Num. 33, 52; Deut. 7. 5, 25; 12. 3. — *l* Deut. 6. 13; 10. 12. 20; 11. 13, 14; 13. 4; Josh. 22. 5; 24. 14, 15, 21, 24; 1 Sam. 7. 3; 12. 20, 24; Matt. 4. 10.

---

unto all the inhabitants thereof." Lev. xxv, 10. Thus all the great Hebrew festivals were linked by a system of sevens, and form one complete plan.

17. **Three times in the year**—That is, at the three festivals just mentioned in verses 14–16.

18. **Not offer the blood of my sacrifice with leavened bread**—Literally, *upon leavened bread.* This refers especially to the **sacrifice** of the passover, as is seen by comparison of chap. xii, 15, 18–20. So also **the fat of my sacrifice** is best understood as the fat and choice portions of the paschal lamb, nothing of which was allowed to **remain until the morning.** Comp. chap. xii, 10, and xxxiv, 25.

19. **House of the Lord thy God** —Observe that here, in this oldest Sinaitic legislation, one common sanctuary is contemplated for all the people. **Seethe a kid in his mother's milk** — Compare chap. xxxiv, 26, and Deut. xiv, 21. The boiling of a young kid in the milk of its own mother would seem an outrage upon the laws of nature, in violating the sacred relationship of parent and offspring. Some writers have, not without reason, supposed that a contemporary superstitious practice of this kind existed among the heathen, and led to the enactment of this law. Thomson says that the Arabs are now given to the practice of stewing a young kid in milk, mixed with onions and hot spices, and they call it "kid in his mother's milk." He observes, as the opinion of the Jews, "that it is unnatural and barbarous to cook a poor kid in that from which it derives its life. Many of the Mosaic precepts are evidently designed to cultivate gentle and humane feelings; but the 'kid in his mother's milk' is a gross, unwholesome dish, calculated also to kindle up animal and ferocious passions." — *The Land and the Book,* vol. i, p. 135.

20–22. **I send an Angel before thee** —On the nature of this **Angel** see note at Gen. xvi, 7. An angel who had in him Jehovah's **name,** and could **pardon transgressions;** who was not to be **provoked,** but observed with reverence and obeyed; who was to go **before** Israel, **keep** them **in the way,** and **bring** them into the blessed land of promise—He must assuredly be a personal manifestation of Jehovah himself. The same divine Being was symbolized in the pillar of cloud and fire, (xiii, 21, 22.)

23. **The Amorites**—On the names and location of these tribes see notes and map at Josh. iii, 10.

24. **Utterly overthrow them**—Not only are the first and second commandments of the decalogue here vir-

B. C. 1491. CHAPTER XXIII. 501

the LORD your God, and ᵐ he shall bless thy bread, and thy water; and ⁿ I will take sickness away from the midst of thee. 26 ᵒ There shall nothing cast their young, nor be barren, in thy land: the number of days I will ᵖ fulfil. 27 I will send ᑫ my fear before thee, and will ʳ destroy all the people to whom thou shalt come; and I will make all thine enemies turn their ˢ backs unto thee. 28 And ᵗ I will send hornets before thee, which shall drive out the Hivite, the Canaanite, and the Hittite, from be- fore thee. 29 ᵘ I will not drive them out from before thee in one year; lest the land become desolate, and the beast of the field multiply against thee. 30 By little and little I will drive them out from before thee, until thou be increased, and inherit the land. 31 And ᵛ I will set thy bounds from the Red sea even unto the sea of the Philistines, and from the desert unto the river : for I will ʷ deliver the inhabitants of the land into your hand; and thou shalt drive them out before thee. 32 ˣ Thou shalt make no covenant with them, nor with their

m Deut. 7. 13; 28. 5, 8. — *n* Chap. 15. 26; Deut. 7. 15. — *o* Deut. 7. 14; 28. 4; Job 21. 10; Mal. 3. 10, 11. — *p* Genesis 25. 8; 35. 29; 1 Chron. 23. 1; Job 5. 26; 42. 17; Psa. 55. 23; 90. 10. — *q* Gen. 35. 5; chap. 15. 14, 16; Deut. 2. 25; 11. 25; Josh. 2. 9, 11; 1 Sam. 14. 15; 2 Chron. 14. 14. — *r* Deut. 7. 23. — 9 Heb. *neck*, Psa. 18. 40. — *s* Deut. 7. 20; Josh. 24. 12. — *t* Deut. 7. 22.— *u* Gen. 15. 18; Num. 34. 3; Deut. 11. 24; Josh. 1. 4; 1 Kings 4. 21, 24; Psa. 72. 8.—*v* Josh. 21. 44; Judg. 1. 4; 11. 21. — *w* Chap. 34. 12, 15; Deut. 7. 2.

tually repeated, but the further command is given to destroy idolatry by iconoclastic violence.

25. **Take sickness away** — This promise to give health and blessing is in accord with chap. xv, 26, where Jehovah calls himself Israel's healer. Great temporal abundance and a long life passed in divine favour are held up as ideals of excellence.

27. **My fear**—Such awe and terror as resulted from the report of God's terrible doings among the nations. Comp. Deut. ii, 25; Josh. ii, 9-11.

28. **I will send hornets before thee**—There is no necessity to explain this literally, and there is no evidence that any such miracle as the driving out of the Canaanites by swarms of hornets occurred during the entire history of the conquest of Palestine. There are, indeed, divers accounts of certain ancient tribes being driven out of their lands by armies of wasps and other noxious creatures; and the armies of locusts which occasionally sweep through those countries are a most destructive plague. But a comparison of Deut. i, 44, Josh. xxiv, 12, Psa. cxviii, 12, and Isa. vii, 18, 19, will show that this expression was employed metaphorically to denote any marked interposition of God to discomfit the enemies of his people.

29. **Lest the land become desolate**—And so the promised Canaan be turned into a howling wilderness instead of being a land flowing with milk and honey. **Beast of the field multiply** —As was actually the case long afterward by depopulating the cities of Samaria after the deportation of the northern tribes of Israel. 2 Kings xvii, 25, 26.

30. **Until thou be increased**— Here it is assumed that the Israelitish people at the time of the exodus were not sufficiently numerous to occupy the whole of Palestine. For the results which followed the failure to exterminate the heathen tribes, see Judges ii, 20-iii, 6, notes.

31. **Thy bounds**—These boundaries indicate the entire extent of territory which any people supposed to be in complete possession of Canaan would naturally control. **The Red sea** they had left behind them; **the sea of the Philistines,** that is, the Mediterranean, which bordered on the Philistine territory, formed the western boundary, the Arabian **desert** lay on the south and south-east, and **the river** Euphrates formed the eastern limit. This extent of territory actually came under the dominion of Solomon. 1 Kings iv, 20-25; comp. Josh. i, 4. **Thou shalt drive them out**—Israel's conquest of Canaan was a mission of judgment as well as a fulfilment of promise and prophecy. They were sent into the land to destroy peoples ripe for judgment, rather than to convert those looking and waiting for redemption. See Gen. xv, 16, note.

32. **No covenant with them**— To enter into any treaty with a hope-

EXODUS.

B. C. 1491.

gods. **33** They shall not dwell in thy land, lest they make thee sin against me: for if thou serve their gods, ˣ it will surely be a snare unto thee.

CHAPTER XXIV.

AND he said unto Moses, Come up unto the LORD, thou, and Aaron, ᵃ Nadab, and Abihu, ᵇ and seventy of the elders of Israel; and worship ye afar off. **2** And Moses ᶜ alone shall come near the LORD: but they shall not come nigh; neither shall the people go up with him. **3** And Moses came and told the people all the words of the LORD, and all the judgments: and all the people answered with one voice, and said, ᵈ All the words which the LORD hath said will we do. **4** And Moses ᵉ wrote all the words of the LORD, and rose up early in the morning, and builded an altar under the hill, and twelve ᶠ pillars, according to the twelve tribes of Israel. **5** And he sent young men of the chil-

x Chap. 34. 12; Deut. 7. 16; 12. 30; Josh. 23. 13; Judg. 2. 3; 1 Sam. 18. 21; Psa. 106. 36.—
a Chap. 28. 1; Lev. 10. 1, 2.

b Chap. 1. 5; Num. 11. 16.——*c* Verses 13, 15, 18.
——*d* Verse 7; chap. 19. 8; Deut. 5. 27; Gal. 3. 19, 20.——*e* Deut. 31. 9.——*f* Gen. 28. 18; 31. 45.

---

lessly depraved and heaven-doomed people, or **with their gods,** was to trample under foot their own covenant with Jehovah, and treat with contempt these Sinaitic laws.

33. They shall not dwell in thy land—The reason given is apparent. Israel's mission and the Mosaic dispensation were not a ministry of evangelization, but of conservation of fundamental principles of divine truth. The idolatries of the world and the hardness of human hearts made it necessary first to call a select people *out from the nations,* and train that peculiar people so that in fulness of time there might go *out from them into all the world* the saving light and truth of God's holy revelation.

CHAPTER XXIV.

RATIFICATION OF THE COVENANT, 1–11.

1. He said unto Moses—That is, after having given unto him the judgments recorded in the book of the covenant, and before he went down to communicate them to the people. Moses had gone into the thick darkness to receive these laws, (xx, 21,) and now, before he returned to the people, (verse 3,) he is instructed to bring with him, when he comes up into the mountain again, **Aaron, Nadab, and Abihu, and seventy of the elders of Israel.** These persons, namely, Moses's brother and the two oldest sons of the latter, and seventy of the most distinguished representatives of the people, (comp. xviii, 25,) would thus stand between Moses and the people.

2. Moses alone shall come near the Lord—Here was a symbolical outline of what was afterward formally fixed in the Levitical code. Moses represented the highpriest, who went alone into the most holy place, (Lev. xvi, 17,) and these others the ordinary consecrated priests who might minister in the holy place, and at the altar, while the people were required to remain in the distance.

3, 4. Moses came and told—After receiving the laws as so many **words of the Lord,** he put them in writing, and thus codified **the judgments** (comp. xxi, 1) which were to govern the people. Whether he **wrote all the words of the Lord** before he descended from the mountain, or after he appeared again among the people, is not said. We most naturally suppose that they would have been written in the mountain, but the order of this narrative seems to imply that he first reported them orally to the people, who **answered with one voice,** and pledged obedience. Thereupon he **wrote all the words,** occupying, perhaps, a part of the night in this labour, **and rose up early in the morning** of the following day to ratify and seal the covenant by appropriate offerings and a reading of the laws from the book in which he had written them. **Builded an altar under the hill**—In accord with the directions of chap. xx, 24–26. **Twelve pillars**—Significant of the tribal divisions of the nation, and their common interest in the covenant. Comp. Josh. iv, 1–9.

5. Sent young men—Moses, who appropriately officiated as the priest,

CHAPTER XXIV.

dren of Israel, which offered burnt offerings, and sacrificed peace offerings of oxen unto the LORD. **6** And Moses ᵉ took half of the blood, and put *it* in basins; and half of the blood he sprinkled on the altar. **7** And he ʰ took the book of the covenant, and read in the audience of the people: and they said, ⁱ All that the LORD hath said will we do, and be obedient. **8** And Moses took the blood, and sprinkled *it* on the people, and said, Behold ᵏ the blood of the cov-

enant, which the LORD hath made with you concerning all these words. **9** Then ˡ went up Moses, and Aaron, Nadab, and Abihu, and seventy of the elders of Israel; **10** And they ᵐ saw the God of Israel: and *there was* under his feet as it were a paved work of a ⁿ sapphire stone, and as it were the ᵒ body of heaven in *his* clearness. **11** And upon the nobles of the children of Israel he ᵖ laid not his hand: also ᵠ they saw God, and did ʳ eat and drink.

---

g Heb. 9. 18.—*h* Heb. 9. 19.—*i* Ver. 3.—*k* Heb. 9. 20; 13. 20; 1 Pet. 1. 2.—*l* Ver. 1.—*m* See Gen. 32. 30; chap. 3. 6; Judg. 13. 22; Isa. 6. 1, 5, with chap. 33. 20, 23; John 1. 18; 1 Tim. 6. 16; 1 John 4. 12.—*n* Ezek. 1. 26; 10. 1; Rev. 4. 3.—*o* Matt. 17. 2.—*p* Chap. 19. 21.—*q* Gen. 16. 13; 32. 30; verse 10; chap. 33. 20; Deut. 4. 33; Judg. 13. 22.—*r* Gen. 31. 54; chap. 18. 12; 1 Cor. 10. 18.

---

employed young and vigorous men, selected from the tribes, to assist him in preparing and offering the sacrifices. The Levitical arrangements for sacrifice were not yet established. **Burnt offerings, and... peace offerings**—Comp. note on xx, 24. "The burnt offerings figured the dedication of the nation to Jehovah, and the peace offerings their communion with Jehovah and with each other."—*Speaker's Commentary*.

6. **Half of the blood... in basins, and half... on the altar**—As the same drops of blood could not be sprinkled both on the altar and on the people, the whole was divided into two parts, part for the altar and part for the people, and yet the two portions were regarded as one blood, serving to seal this holy covenant between Jehovah and his people. The blood which was **sprinkled on the altar** symbolized the life of Israel consecrated to Jehovah; that **in basins,** which was "sprinkled on the people," (verse 8,) served to intensify in them the solemn conviction that they were set apart to be a holy nation. It was the seal of union with God, a covenant of blood.

7. **Read in the audience of the people**—This would seem to have been the earliest instance of a public reading of Holy Scripture. Comp. Neh. viii, 1–8.

9. **Then went up Moses**—Immediately after the sacrifice and sprinkling of the blood they would all proceed to feast upon the flesh of the peace offerings; but **Moses and Aaron,** and the others mentioned in verse 1, ascended some distance up the mountain, and ate and drank (verse 11) where they had a nearer view of the glory and majesty of the Sinaitic theophany. It would seem from verse 16 that they continued thus together for six days, and on the seventh Moses went into the midst of the cloud, where he remained forty days, (verse 18,) receiving instructions concerning the tabernacle, and the holy ministrations which were now to be ordained.

10. **They saw the God of Israel** —Not his face, (chap. xxxiii, 20,) nor even his similitude, (Deut. iv, 12, 15,) but some impressive symbol of his presence, most awe-inspiring in its majesty. It is vain to presume to tell the exact form of the glory which these elders saw; no description of it is here given, but our thought of it is enhanced by the statement that **there was under his feet as it were a paved work of a sapphire stone.** This accords with what Ezekiel saw in vision, (Ezek. i, 26,) a kind of tesselated pavement, brilliant as the sapphire stone, upon which the symbol of Deity appeared to stand. This pavement, for **clearness**, was like **the body of heaven;** that is, like the blue substance of the heavens above.

11. **He laid not his hand**—Heb., *He sent not forth his hand.* No stroke of divine wrath was sent forth from that sublime display to destroy the Israelitish **nobles.** It was the common belief that such a vision of God must needs destroy the beholder, (comp. Gen. xxxii, 30, Judges vi, 22, xiii, 22, Isa. vi, 5,) but these chief men of Israel not only thus **saw God,** but they **did eat and drink** in presence of the awful

504   EXODUS.   B. C. 1491.

12 And the LORD said unto Moses, *Come up to me into the mount, and be there: and I will give thee ᵗ tables of stone, and a law, and commandments which I have written; that thou mayest teach them. **13** And Moses rose up, and ᵘ his minister Joshua; and Moses ᵛ went up into the mount of God. **14** And he said unto the elders, Tarry ye here for us, until we come again unto you: and, behold, Aaron and Hur *are* with you: if any man have any matters to do, let him come unto them. **15** And Moses went up into the mount, and ʷ a cloud covered the mount. **16** And ˣ the glory of the LORD abode upon mount Sinai, and the cloud covered it six days: and the seventh day he called unto Moses out of the midst of the cloud. **17** And the sight of the glory of the LORD *was* like ʸ devouring fire on the top of the mount in the eyes of the chil-

s Verses 2, 15, 18. —— *t* Chapter 31. 18; 32. 15, 16; Deut. 5. 22. —— *u* Chapter 32. 17; 33. 11. —— *v* Verse 2.

w Chap. 19. 9, 16; Matt. 17. 5. —— *x* Chap. 16. 10; Num. 14. 10. —— *y* Chap. 3. 2; 19. 18; Deut. 4. 36; Heb. 12. 18, 29.

sight. They ate in solemn reserve the sacrificial meal of the peace offerings by which the covenant had been sealed.

MOSES'S ASCENT INTO THE MOUNT, 12-18.

12. Tables of stone, and a law, and commandments — This may be rendered, *Tables of stone, even the law and the commandment*, and would then most naturally denote the decalogue graven on tables of stone. Ewald understands the reference to be to the decalogue, and also to other laws and commandments which were to be given. The rabbinical interpretation is, that only the **tables of stone** refer to the decalogue, while the **law** here means the written law of Moses, and the **commandments** the oral law which was handed down by tradition, and afterward embodied in the Talmud. As verses 12-18 serve for an introduction to chapters xxv-xxxi, in which so many commandments are given touching the tabernacle and the priesthood, and as chapter xxxii, 15, shows that Moses returned with the two tables in his hand, we may best understand that these words refer to other commandments besides those of the decalogue. Moses was called up to receive not the tables only, but also other revelations. **Teach them**—All the laws, and the entire revelation, were to be taught to the people.

13. His minister Joshua—This intimate companion of the great lawgiver, destined to be his successor, was admitted into holiest relations with him. See notes on chap. xvii, 9, and Josh. i, 1, and comp. chaps. xxxii, 17, xxxiii, 11. Whether he went with Moses "into the midst of the cloud," (verse 18,) we are not expressly told, but that is the legitimate inference.

14. Tarry ye—Moses appeared to know that he would be absent from the camp some time, and hence the instructions here given to the elders. **Aaron and Hur**—Comp. chap. xvii, 10, 12, notes. It would seem that Moses and Joshua parted from the elders on the spot where they ate and drank together, (verse 11;) in which case it is of course to be understood that the elders would return to the camp and abide in their tents as usual until Moses returned. Possibly, however, as Keil supposes, Moses and the elders went down again to the camp together after the covenant meal.

16. Glory of the Lord abode upon mount Sinai — Compare the theophany as described in chap. xix, 16-20. Whether the **six days** here mentioned were subsequent to Moses's departure from the elders or previous to it, is a question not easily determined by the text. Either supposition is possible. The order of statements in the narrative does not determine the question, for in verses 13 and 14 we observe that Moses's direction for the elders is spoken after it is said that he and Joshua went up into the mount. In the note above, on verse 9, we have given preference to the view that the sacrificial feast was prolonged for six days, during which time all that is recorded in verses 3-11 occurred. During this solemn sealing of the covenant it was appropriate that **the cloud** should cover the mountain, and that on **the seventh day** Moses should be called to go up and receive the further revelations.

B. C. 1491.   CHAPTER XXIV.   505

dren of Israel. **18** And Moses went into the midst of the cloud, and gat him up into the mount: and *z* Moses was in the mount forty days and forty nights.

z Chap. 34. 28 ; Deut. 9. 9.

18. Forty days and forty nights—We naturally compare with this chap. xxxiv, 28, and Deut. ix, 18. Also the fact that Elijah spent the same length of time at this mountain without food, (1 Kings xix, 8,) and Jesus fasted in the wilderness of his temptation forty days. There appears a symbolism about this number. The spies were forty days searching the land of promise, (Num. xiii, 25,) and that generation was condemned to wander in the desert forty years, (Num. xiv, 34,) to humble and prove them. Deut. viii, 2. In all these instances the period was one of great trial and discipline, as well as of gracious evidences of God's mercy and truth.

III. JEHOVAH'S DWELLING WITH ISRAEL.

(1.) The Plan of the Tabernacle and its Holy Service. Chaps. XXV-XXXI.

CHAPTER XXV.
INTRODUCTORY.

Jehovah has now ransomed his people from the house of bondage; has exhibited before their eyes the most solemn and awful displays of his eternal power, and of his superiority over all gods and men; has thundered from Sinai the ten words of the covenant, and has communicated to Moses, and through him to the people, a matchless body of laws to regulate the social and civil affairs of Israel. The next step is to establish a system of worship which will serve at once to centralize the religious interests of the people, and develop, by sacred services and symbols, the knowledge and fear of Jehovah. The pattern of a sanctuary that is to serve so lofty a purpose is here shown to have originated in the Divine Mind. Its great idea is that of a special sacred *meeting place* of Jehovah and his chosen people. The words by which the tabernacle is designated serve as a clew to the great idea embodied in its complex symbolism. The principal name is מִשְׁכָּן, *dwelling;* but אֹהֶל, *tent,* usually connected with some distinguishing epithet, is also frequently used, and is applied to the tabernacle in the books of Exodus, Leviticus, and Numbers more than one hundred and fifty times. In Exod. xxiii, 19, xxxiv, 26, it is called בֵּית יְהֹוָה, *house of Jehovah,* and in 1 Sam. i, 9, iii, 3, הֵיכַל יְהֹוָה, *temple of Jehovah.* But a fuller indication of the import of these names is found in the compound expressions, אֹהֶל מוֹעֵד, *tent of meeting,* אֹהֶל הָעֵדֻת, *tent of the testimony,* and מִשְׁכַּן הָעֵדֻת, *dwelling of the testimony.* The testimony is a term applied emphatically to the law of the two tables, (Exod. xxv, 16, 21; xxxi, 18,) and designated the authoritative declaration of God, upon the basis of which he made a covenant with Israel. Exod. xxxiv, 27; Deut. iv, 13. Hence these tables were called tables of the covenant (Deut. ix, 9) as well as tables of the testimony. As the representatives of God's most holy testimony against sin they occupied the most secret and sacred place of his tabernacle. Exod. xxv, 16. All these designations of the tabernacle serve to indicate its great design as a symbol of Jehovah's meeting and dwelling with his people. One passage which, above all others, elaborates this thought is Exodus xxix, 42-46: "It shall be a continual burnt offering throughout your generations, at the door of the tent of meeting (אֹהֶל־מוֹעֵד) before Jehovah, where I will meet (אִוָּעֵד) you, to speak unto thee there. And I will meet (נֹעַדְתִּי) there the sons of Israel, and he (that is, Israel) shall be sanctified in my glory. And I will sanctify the tent of meeting (אֹהֶל־מוֹעֵד) and the altar, and Aaron and his sons will I sanctify to act as priests for me.

CHAPTER XXV.

AND the LORD spake unto Moses, saying, 2 Speak unto the children of Israel, that they ¹ bring me an ² offering: ᵃ of every man that giveth it willingly with his heart ye shall take my offering. 3 And this *is* the offering which ye shall take of them; gold, and

---

1 Hebrew, *take for me.* — 2 Or, *heave offering.*

a Chap. 35. 5, 21; 1.Chron. 29. 3, 5, 9, 14; Ezra 2. 68; 3. 5; 7. 16; Neh. 11. 2; 2 Cor. 8. 12; 9. 7.

And I will dwell (שָׁכַנְתִּי) in the midst of the sons of Israel, and I will be God to them, and they shall know that I am Jehovah their God, who brought them out of the land of Egypt, that I might dwell (לְשָׁכְנִי) in their midst—I, Jehovah, their God."

The tabernacle, therefore, is not to be thought of as a symbol of things external and visible, not even of heaven itself considered merely as a *place*, but of the meeting and dwelling together of God and his people both in time and eternity. The ordinances of worship may be expected to denote the way in which Jehovah condescends to meet with man, and enables man to approach nigh unto him —a meeting and fellowship by which the true Israel become sanctified in the divine glory. Exod. xxix, 43. The divine-human relationship realized in the kingdom of heaven is attained in Christ when God comes unto man and makes his abode (μονήν) with him, (John xiv, 23,) so that the man dwells in God and God in him. 1 John iv, 16. This is the glorious indwelling contemplated in the prayer of Jesus that all believers "may be one; as thou, Father, *art* in me, and I in thee, that they also may be in us, that the world may believe that thou didst send me. And the glory which thou hast given me I have given unto them; that they may be one,even as we *are* one, I in them and thou in me, that they may be perfected into one." John xvii, 21-23. (R. V.) Of this blessed relationship the tabernacle is a significant symbol, and, being also a shadow of the good things to come, it was a type of the New Testament Church or kingdom of God, that spiritual house built of living stones, (1 Pet. ii, 5) which is a habitation of God in the Spirit. Eph. ii, 22.

Most strangely have certain modern critics advanced the notion that this account of the tabernacle is a fiction of post-exile times, an invention of the priests to furnish a kind of holy historic background for the plan of Solomon's temple and its successor. And so, too, the whole elaborate system of the Levitical worship, with the distinction between priests and Levites, is held to be a product of the times of the Babylonian exile. But no time in the history of the chosen people appears so well adapted to the formation of this system as the age of Moses; no person so competent to fashion and inaugurate it as that great lawgiver. For the discussion of this question of criticism, see our Introduction to the Pentateuch, especially pages 17-38.

OFFERINGS FOR THE SANCTUARY, 1-9.

2. **Bring me an offering** — Heb., *take for me a terumah.* The terumah (תְּרוּמָה) was thought of as a gift or offering that was *lifted up* to the honour of God. The word is often translated *heave offering,* as in the margin. Comp. chap. xxix, 27, 28; Lev. vii, 14, 32; Num. xv, 19, 20; Deut. xii, 6, 11, 17. Here it is used in the general sense of **offering,** or oblation, and what **every man** contributed toward the sanctuary was to be given **willingly with his heart.** No compulsory oblations were to be accepted for this new house of Jehovah, but only such as each man's heart impelled him to bestow. And so in typical form it was indicated that God builds his spiritual house of willing souls. Comp. Rom. xii, 1; 1 Pet. ii, 5. How willingly the people responded is seen in chap. xxxv, 21-29; xxxvi, 5-7.

3. **Gold, and silver, and brass** — Sceptics have been fond of asking whence the Hebrews in the wilderness could have obtained such quantities of the precious metals as the tabernacle required. It is not difficult to answer: (1.) They probably possessed some of the treasures which belonged to their ancient fathers, and of which they had not been despoiled in Egypt. (2.) They

B. C. 1491.   CHAPTER XXV.   507

silver, and brass, **4** And blue, and purple, and scarlet, and [3] fine linen, and

[3] Or, *silk*,

obtained great quantities of gold and silver from the Egyptians on their departure from their land. See chap. xii, 35, 36, and notes on iii, 22, and xi, 2. (3.) Much spoil of the Egyptian army probably fell into their hands at the Red sea. See chap. xiv, 30, note. (4.) They doubtless obtained much spoil of the defeated Amalekites, (xvii, 8–13.) (5.) Finally, we are not to imagine that in the Sinaitic peninsula the Hebrews were cut off from all communication with other peoples. Great caravans frequently traversed these deserts, (comp. Gen. xxxvii, 25, 28,) and doubtless then, as in a later time merchantmen of "all the kings of Arabia, and of the governors of the country," (1 Kings x, 14–17,) carried to and fro with them large quantities of precious metals; and these, as well as other material needed for any of their purposes, could have been obtained by the Israelites.

4. Blue, and purple, and scarlet —The exact colours, tints, or shades denoted by the Hebrew words thus translated it is now hardly possible to determine with absolute certainty. The same may be said of the names of colours in all the ancient languages. The use of these different colours in the tabernacle probably served not only for the sake of beauty and variety, but also to suggest thoughts of heavenly excellence and glory. The three colours here named have always and everywhere been regarded as appropriate for the persons and palaces of kings. Blue, as the colour of the heaven, reflected in the sea, would naturally suggest that which is heavenly, holy, and divine. Hence it was appropriate that the robe of the ephod was made wholly of blue, (Exod. xxviii, 31, xxxix, 22,) and the breastplate was connected with it by blue cords, verse 28. It was also by a blue cord or ribbon that the golden plate inscribed "Holiness to Jehovah" was attached to the high priest's mitre, verse 31. The loops of the tabernacle curtains were of this colour, (Exod. xxvi, 4,) and the children of Israel

goats' *hair*, **5** And rams' skins dyed red, and badgers' skins, and shittim

Gen. 41. 42.

were commanded to place blue ribbons as badges upon the borders of their garments, (Num. xv, 37–41,) as if to remind them that they were children of the heavenly King, and were under the responsibility of having received from him commandments and revelations. Hence, too, it was appropriate that a blue cloth was spread over the holiest things of the tabernacle when they were arranged for journeying forward. Num. iv, 6, 7, 11, 12. Purple and scarlet, so often mentioned in connexion with the dress of kings, have very naturally been regarded as symbolical of royalty and majesty. Judg. viii, 26; Esth. viii, 15; Dan. v, 7; Nah. ii, 3. Both these colours, along with blue, appeared upon the curtains of the tabernacle, (Exod. xxvi, 1,) and upon the vail that separated the holy place from the most holy. Exod. xxvi, 31. A scarlet cloth covered the holy vessels which were placed upon the table of showbread, and a purple cloth the altar of burnt offerings. Num. iv, 8, 13.   **Fine linen**—Heb. שֵׁשׁ, *shesh*, believed to be an Egyptian word, translated by βύσσος in the Septuagint, and applied to an Egyptian fabric made of fine flax, and having a peculiar whiteness. Joseph's vesture, when made ruler in Egypt, was of this material. Gen. xli, 42. It was used for the curtains and vails of the tabernacle, and for the garments of the priests. Chap. xxvi, 1, 31, 36; xxviii, 5, 6, 8, 15, 39. **Goats' hair**—A very solid fabric is woven of the hair of the goat, and was the most common material used for the covering of tents among the nomads of the East.

5. Rams' skins dyed red—"These skins may have been tanned and coloured like the leather now known as red morocco, which is said to have been manufactured in Libya from the remotest antiquity." — *Speaker's Commentary.* Others have explained the words as meaning simply *skins of red rams*. **Badgers' skins**—Besides the mention

508 EXODUS. B. C. 1491.

wood, **6** ᵇ Oil for the light, ᶜ spices for anointing oil, and for ᵈ sweet incense, **7** Onyx stones, and stones to be set in the ᵉ ephod, and in the ᶠ breastplate. **8** And let them make me a ᵍ sanctuary; that ʰ I may dwell among them. **9** ⁱ According to all that I show thee, *after* the pattern of the tabernacle, and the pattern of all the instruments thereof, even so shall ye make *it*.

---

b Chapter 27. 20. —— *c* Chapter 30. 23. —— *d* Chapter 30. 34. —— *e* Chapter 28. 4, 6. —— *f* Chapter 28. 15. —— *g* Chapter 36. 1, 3, 4; Lev. 4. 6; 10. 4; 21. 12; Heb. 9. 1, 2. —— *h* Chapter 29. 45; 1 Kings 6. 13; 2 Cor. 6. 16; Heb. 3. 6; Rev. 21. 3.—— *i* Verse 40.

---

in Ezek. xvi, 10, the word תַּחַשׁ, here translated **badger**, occurs only in connexion with the curtains and coverings of the tabernacle. The Sept. and Vulg. seem to understand it as the name of a colour, *hyacinthine*. The Targum and the Syriac translate it by the word סַסְגּוֹנָא, which Levy explains (*Chald. Wörterbuch*) as a red-spotted beast. Kitto's Cyclopædia maintains that it was probably an animal of the antelope tribe, but could not have been the badger, which is not found in Asia so far south as Palestine and Arabia. It is probably best understood of a kind of seal which is said to be found in the waters about Arabia. "The word bears a near resemblance to the Arabic *tuchash*, which appears to be the general name given to the seals, dugongs, and dolphins found in the Red sea, (Tristram,) and, according to some authorities, to the sharks and dog-fish. (Fürst.) The substance spoken of would thus appear to have been leather formed from the skins of marine animals, which was well adapted as a protection against the weather. Pliny speaks of tents made of seal skins as proof against the stroke of lightning, (*Nat. Hist.*, ii, 56,) and one of these is said to have been used by Augustus whenever he travelled. The skins of the dolphin and dugong are cut into sandals by the modern Arabs, and this may explain Ezekiel xvi, 10."—*Speaker's Commentary.* **Shittim wood** —The wood of the acacia tree, a very hard and durable kind of tree which abounds in the Sinaitic peninsula.

6. Oil for the light—This, according to xxvii, 20, was to be pure olive oil and beaten. **Spices**—Such as are more fully described in xxx, 22–25. The various things for which the **anointing oil** was used are mentioned in xxx, 26–33. **Sweet incense**—See more fully xxx, 34–38.

7. Onyx stones —Already mentioned Gen. ii, 12. These, and the other precious stones set in **the breastplate**, are mentioned more fully in xxviii, 17–21.

8. A sanctuary—This word, מִקְדָּשׁ, has occurred but once before this place, namely, in Moses's song, (xv, 17,) where a general prophecy is made that the chosen people shall be established in the mountain of Jehovah's inheritance, the sanctuary in which Jehovah purposed to dwell. This name applies to the entire structure about to be described, and designates it as the holy place where Jehovah would graciously **dwell among** his people, and reveal to them his holiness and his truth.

9. The pattern of the tabernacle—This is most positively represented throughout this entire narrative (comp. verse 40, xxvi, 30, Acts vii, 44, Heb. viii, 5) as given to Moses by divine revelation. The notion that it was a fiction of the priests, invented nearly a thousand years after the time of Moses, puts such a withering stamp of falsehood upon this straightforward narrative that it must fail to commend itself to any serious student of history. But when we study out the details, and picture the whole **pattern** before our eyes—when, further, we consider the striking symbolism of the various objects, and their adaptation to body forth the profoundest truths touching the relations of God and man—we are convinced that the pattern originated not with man, but with God himself. How God showed Moses this model of the tabernacle we are not told. It may have been imaged before him in clear outline, like the sight of the burning bush; or, in a dream of the night it may have been definitely pictured before the soul. We have no need, however, with the rabbins, to suppose that he saw

10 *k* And they shall make an ark *of shittim wood: two cubits and a half shall be the length thereof, and a cubit and a half the breadth thereof, and a cubit and a half the height thereof.* **11** And thou shalt overlay it with pure gold, within and without shalt thou overlay it, and shalt make upon it a crown of gold round about. **12** And thou shalt cast four rings of gold for it, and put

---

k Chap. 37. 1; Deut. 10. 3; Heb. 9. 4.

---

heaven opened, and a material tabernacle there, in form and substance like what he was commanded to make.

THE ARK OF THE COVENANT, 10–22.

The description of the tabernacle begins with the most sacred object, which, in addition to the above title, bore the several names of the Ark of the Testimony, (verse 22,) or simply the Testimony, (xxvii, 21,) the Ark of Jehovah, (Josh. iii, 13,) the Ark of God, (1 Sam. iii, 3,) the Ark of the strength of Jehovah, (Psa. cxxxii, 8,) and the Holy Ark. 2 Chron. xxxv, 3. This occupied the most holy place in the sanctuary, and symbolized the deepest mysteries of redemption. The monuments of Egypt have been found to bear images which strikingly resemble the ark here described. This no more conflicts with the statement that the tabernacle of the Hebrews was modelled after a heavenly pattern than does the fact that numerous other revelations embodied in well known forms of human thought conflict with their heavenly origin. Other nations and other religions have their altars, and sanctuaries, and ceremonials; but this does not hinder Israel from appropriating like objects to symbolize their holiest mysteries. In like manner, the new revelations both of Mosaism and of Christianity did not invent a new language for their use, but appropriated and adapted old ones. Moses's acquaintance with the learning and wisdom of the Egyptians made him the more competent, under God, to fashion such objects as served the purpose he had in hand. Not so much the mere outward form as their arrangement and religious lessons give evidence of a heavenly origin.

10. Shittim wood — Its material, observes Stanley, "was not of oak, the usual wood of Palestine, nor of cedar, the usual wood employed in Palestine for sacred purposes, but of **shittim,** or acacia, a tree of rare growth in Syria, but the most frequent, not even excepting the palm, in the peninsula of Sinai." The size of the ark was about three feet nine inches long, and a little over two feet in **breadth** and **height.** Its probable form is best illustrated by the adjoining cut.

11. A crown of gold round about —Rather a *rim*, moulding, or border around the top, as shown in the cut.

12–15. Rings ... staves—The position of these is seen in the cut, and the whole, as wont to be carried by the priests, is shown in the following cut.

them in the four corners thereof; and two rings *shall be* in the one side of it, and two rings in the other side of it. **13** And thou shalt make staves *of* shittim wood, and overlay them with gold. **14** And thou shalt put the staves into the rings by the sides of the ark, that the ark may be borne with them. **15** ¹ The staves shall be in the rings of the ark: they shall not be taken from it. **16** And thou shalt put into the ark ᵐ the testimony which I shall give thee. **17** And ⁿ thou shalt make a mercy seat *of* pure gold: two cubits and a half *shall be* the length thereof, and a cubit and a half the breadth thereof. **18** And thou shalt make two cherubim *of* gold, *of* beaten work shalt thou make them, in the two ends of the mercy seat. **19** And make one cherub on the one end, and the other cherub on the other end: *even* ⁴ of the mercy seat shall ye make the cherubim on the two ends thereof. **20** And ᵒ the cherubim shall stretch forth *their* wings on high, cover- ing the mercy seat with their wings, and their faces *shall look* one to another; toward the mercy seat shall the faces of the cherubim be. **21** ᵖ And thou shalt put the mercy seat above upon the ark; and ᵠ in the ark thou shalt put the testimony that I shall give thee. **22** And ʳ there I will meet with thee, and I will commune with thee from above the mercy seat, from ˢ between the two cherubim which *are* upon the ark of the testimony, of all *things* which I will give thee in commandment unto the children of Israel.

23 ᵗ Thou shalt also make a table *of* shittim wood: two cubits *shall be* the length thereof, and a cubit the breadth thereof, and a cubit and a half the height thereof. **24** And thou shalt overlay it with pure gold, and make thereto a crown of gold round about. **25** And thou shalt make unto it a border of a handbreadth round about, and thou shalt make a golden crown to the border thereof round about. **26** And thou

---

l 1 Kings 8. 8.——*m* Chap. 16. 34; 31. 18; Deut. 10. 2, 5; 31. 26; 1 Kings 8, 9; 2 Kings 11. 12; Heb. 9. 4.——*n* Chap. 37. 6; Rom. 3. 25; Heb. 9. 5.——⁴ Or, *of the matter of the mercy seat.*——*o* 1 Kings 8. 7; 1 Chron. 28. 18; Heb. 9. 5.

p Chap. 26. 34.——*q* Verse 16.——*r* Chap. 29. 42, 43; 30. 6, 36; Lev. 16. 2; Num. 17. 4.——*s* Num. 7. 89; 1 Sam. 4. 4; 2 Sam. 6. 2; 2 Kings 19. 15; Psa. 80. 1; 90. 1; Isa. 37. 16.—— *t* Chap. 37. 10; 1 Kings 7. 48; 2 Chron. 4. 8; Heb. 9. 2.

---

16. Put into the ark the testimony—Hence the name "Ark of the Testimony," (verse 22.) This testimony was Jehovah's declarations from the mount, which were afterward written by God's finger upon two tables of stone, (xxxi, 18.) They were to be deposited in the ark as a monumental witness of the will of God.

17. A mercy seat—Hebrew, *capporeth;* the cover or lid of precisely the same dimensions as the length and breadth of the ark. Verse 10. On its symbolical significance see note at the end of chap. xl.

18-20. Two cherubim—The exact form of these is nowhere described, but their position **in the two ends** of the cover of the ark, and the stretching forth and **covering the mercy seat with their wings,** may be seen best illustrated in the cuts. It is not necessary to suppose that the cherubim described in Ezek. i, 5-14, conformed in all details with those of the tabernacle. The probable form of the cherubic type as there given is seen in connexion with our note on 1 Kings vi, 23, and also in McClintock & Strong's Cyclopædia, article *Cherubim,* from which the adjoining cut is taken.

22. There I will meet with thee—Here, as also in xxix, 42-46, we have an intimation of the main idea, symbolized in the tabernacle, namely, the union and communion of Jehovah and his people.

THE TABLE OF SHOWBREAD, 23-30.

23. Two cubits—While the **height** of it was to be the same as that of the ark, (verse 10,) the **length** and **breadth** were each half a cubit less.

PROBABLE FORM OF THE CHERUBIC TYPE, ACCORDING TO STRONG.

shalt make for it four rings of gold, and put the rings in the four corners that *are* on the four feet thereof. **27** Over against the border shall the rings be for places of the staves to bear the table. **28** And thou shalt make the staves *of* shittim wood, and overlay them with gold, that the table may be borne with them. **29** And thou shalt make ᵘ the dishes thereof, and spoons thereof, and covers thereof, and bowls thereof, ⁵ to cover withal: *of* pure gold shalt thou make them. **30** And thou shalt set upon the table ᵛ showbread before me always. **31** ʷ And thou shalt make a candlestick *of* pure gold: *of* beaten work shall the candlestick be made: his shaft, and his branches, his bowls, his knops, and his flowers, shall be of the same. **32** And six branches shall come out of the sides of it; three branches of the candlestick out of the one side, and three branches of the candlestick out of the other side:

---

u Chap. 37. 16; Num. 4. 7.——5 Or, *to pour out withal.*—*v* Lev. 24. 5, 6.

w Chap. 37. 17; 1 Kings 7. 49; Zech. 4. 2; Heb. 9. 2; Rev. 1. 12; 4. 5.

The form is represented in the adjoining cut.

TABLE OF SHOWBREAD.

24. **Crown**—Rather, moulding or rim, as in verse 11.

25. **Border**—An enclosing framework, running round the table underneath the top and designed to strengthen the whole by holding the legs firmly in place. To this **border** there was also fastened a golden moulding like that which adorned the top of the table. Verse 24.

26–28. **Rings . . . staves**—These are exhibited in the cut, and serve the same purpose as the like in the ark, verses 12–15.

29. **The dishes**—Probably large deep plates used for the purpose of carrying the showbread to and from the table. **Spoons**—Or, perhaps, cups, small hollow vessels used sometimes, according to Num. vii, 14, for holding incense. **Covers . . . bowls**—These were vessels for holding the drink offerings, as appears from the words which immediately follow, *to pour out withal,* (margin,) wrongly translated **to cover withal.** The *Speaker's Commentary* renders this part of the verse thus:

"And thou shalt make its bowls and its incense-cups and its flagons and its chalices for pouring out, (the drink offerings.)"

30. **Showbread before me always** —The **showbread** (Heb. לֶחֶם פָּנִים, *bread of faces,*) was so called from its being designed to lie as a meat-offering continually before the face of Jehovah. The manner of making this bread, and of arranging it upon the table in two piles of six cakes each, is described in Lev. xxiv, 5–9, and is also shown in the above cut. The twelve cakes or loaves undoubtedly represented the twelve tribes of Israel as offered in holy consecration perpetually before Jehovah.

THE GOLDEN CANDLESTICK, 31–40.

31. **A candlestick**—This is to be thought of as an elaborately constructed lampstand, furnishing places for seven lamps, (verse 37.) Like the cherubim it consisted of **beaten work,** (comp. verse 18,) that is, elaborately wrought by some hand process. **Shaft**—Rather, the *base,* or pedestal. **Branches**— Rather, the main stem or shaft, rising up from the pedestal. **Bowls**—These appear to have been the flower-shaped cups into which the spherical **knops,** next mentioned, were set, and both the cups and the knops were further connected with **flowers,** or blossoms, all together serving the purpose of ornamentation. All these were to be wrought out of one and **the same** piece, so as to form a complete whole.

32. **Six branches**—Having described the main shaft or stem (קָנֶה) which was to rise up out of the base, he next mentions the six stems (קָנִים)

512 EXODUS. B. C. 1491.

33 Three bowls made like unto almonds, *with* a knop and a flower in one branch; and three bowls made like almonds in the other branch, *with* a knop and a flower: so in the six branches that come out of the candlestick. **34** And in the candlestick *shall be* four bowls made like unto almonds, *with* their knops and their flowers. **35** And *there shall be* a knop under two branches of the same, and a knop under two branches of the same, and a knop under two branches of the same, according to the six branches that proceed out of the candlestick. **36** Their knops and their branches shall be of the same: all of it *shall be* one beaten work *of* pure gold. **37** And thou shalt make the seven lamps thereof: and ˣ they shall ⁶ light the lamps thereof, that they may ʸ give light over against

ω Chap. 27. 21; 30. 8; Lev. 24. 3, 4: 2 Chron. 13. 11.——6 Or, *cause to ascend*.——*y* Num. 8. 2.

which were to **come out of the sides of it**. These, with the central shaft, furnished at their tops the places for the seven lamps.

33. **Three bowls**—Returning now to a further description of the ornamental **bowls** or cups (גְבִעִים) mentioned in verse 31, the writer describes them as **made like unto almonds,** probably meaning like almond blossoms. Also **a knop and a flower** were to be wrought into each of **the six branches that come out of the candlestick.** In this verse, and in the two following, the word **candlestick** is to be understood more particularly of the main shaft or stem of the lampstand, a part being named for the whole.

34. **In the candlestick**—That is, in the main shaft of it. **Four bowls** —Four cups like those in each of the branches just described in verse 33. These, like those, were to have **their knops and their flowers.** The position of these knops is stated in the next verse.

35. **Under two branches of the same, according to the six branches** —That is, immediately underneath the point at which the side stems, or **branches,** proceeded out of the main stem there was **a knop,** each connected with its cup, (*bowl*, verse 31, note,) and its flower, (verse 33.) This leaves us to infer that the fourth bowl (verse 34) was above, between the two upper branches and the top of the main stem. Thus is explained the position of the four bowls of verse 34.

36. **Shall be of the same** — The entire lampstand was to be wrought out of one piece of **pure gold,** that is, as in verse 31, so that the completed work should form one solid piece.

37. **Seven lamps**—One for each of the side stems or branches, and one for the central shaft. **They shall light the lamps**—Or, *cause the lamps to go up,* that is, they shall elevate or place the lamps (the lighted, shining lamps) in their position, **that they may give light over against it,** that is, opposite the place where it stood, the opposite side of the room.

The above description of the golden candlestick is somewhat obscure. The exact form of the shafts, or branches, and the knops and flowers is left to conjecture, nor can we determine from what is here written whether the central shaft and the six branches were all carried up to the same height, and whether the branches proceeded out of the shaft at right angles or formed a curve in their upward turn. No dimensions are given, and we can judge of its size only by supposing that its height would have been as high, and probably somewhat higher, than the table, and its breadth between the two outer lamps at least two feet. Josephus (*Ant.,* iii, 6, 7) describes it as having a shaft rising from a single base and spreading itself into as many branches as there are planets, including the sun among them. Its seven heads terminated in one row, and all stood parallel to one another. A conspicuous object among the spoils of Jerusalem pictured on the Arch of Titus at Rome is a figure of the candlestick, with its

GOLDEN CANDLESTICK.

⁷ it. **38** And the tongs thereof, and the snuffdishes thereof, *shall be of* pure gold. **39** *Of* a talent of pure gold shall he make it, with all these vessels. **40** And ᶻ look that thou make *them* after their pattern, ⁸ which was showed thee in the mount.

---
7 Hebrew, *the face of it.*——z Chapter 26. 30; Numbers 8. 4; 1 Chronicles 28. 11, 19; Acts 7. 44; Hebrews 8. 5. —— 8 Hebrew, *which thou wast caused to see.*

---

central shaft and six arms. It is not certain that this is an exact copy of even the one captured at the fall of the temple, for the Roman artist may have modified some of its parts; but in its main outline it doubtless truly represents the original. The two additional cuts herewith given exhibit two slightly different models, the one showing all the lamps on the same level, and the other at various elevations. Either of these will illustrate the statements of the text commented on above. Here is seen, first, the pedestal or base (*shaft* of verse 31) from which rises the main shaft with its four knops and associated ornamentation, (verses 31, 34, 35,) and from which three pipes branched out on each side, one above the other, and formed so many arms to hold the lamps. Each of these branches had three *bowls* or cups (verse 33) along with knop and flower, as the central shaft had four, placed as described in verse 35. Most

GOLDEN CANDLESTICK.

writers believe that the seven lamps were all elevated to the same level, which is probable, but not made certain by what is here written. That they were all in a row, or in the same plane,

GOLDEN CANDLESTICK.

as shown in all these cuts, is evident from verse 32, where the six branches are described as coming out of two sides of the main shaft.

38. **Tongs . . . snuffdishes**—The one for snuffing and trimming the lamps, the other for holding the burned snuffings when removed from the wicks. These latter were a small sort of firepans or ashpans. Comp. xxvii, 3. The exact form of these is nowhere described.

CHAPTER XXVI.
THE TABERNACLE, 1–37.

It will now be seen that the entire sanctuary was composed of several distinct parts. The first to be erected was an oblong enclosure of boards set in sockets, and bound together by bars and rings. Verses 15–30 ; xxxvi, 20–34. This was called *mishcan*, (מִשְׁכָּן,) or dwelling, and constituted the tabernacle proper. It was divided into two apartments by an ornamented vail hung on golden plated pillars of acacia wood. Verses 31–33. This board structure was covered with a number of curtains: first, the tabernacle cloth, or coupling

CHAPTER XXVI.

MOREOVER ᵃ thou shalt make the tabernacle *with* ten curtains *of* fine twined linen, and blue, and purple, and scarlet: *with* cherubim ¹ of cunning work shalt thou make them. 2 The length of one curtain *shall be* eight and twenty cubits, and the breadth of one curtain four cubits: and every one of the curtains shall have one measure. 3 The five curtains shall be coupled together one to another; and *other* five curtains *shall be* coupled one to another. 4 And thou shalt make loops of blue upon the edge of the one curtain from the selvedge in the coupling; and likewise shalt thou make in the uttermost edge of *another* curtain, in the coupling of the second. 5 Fifty loops shalt thou make in the one curtain, and fifty loops shalt thou make in the edge of the curtain that *is* in the coupling of the second; that the loops may take hold one of another. 6 And thou shalt make fifty taches of gold, and couple the curtains together with the taches: and it shall be one tabernacle.

7 And ᵇ thou shalt make curtains *of* goats' *hair* to be a covering upon the tabernacle: eleven curtains shalt thou make. 8 The length of one curtain *shall be* thirty cubits, and the breadth of one curtain four cubits: and the eleven curtains *shall be all* of one measure.

---

a Chap. 36. 8.——1 Heb. *the work of a cunning workman*, or. *embroiderer*.——*b* Chap. 36. 14.

---

of curtains described in verses 1-6, (comp. xxxvi, 8-13;) next, the tent-cloth of goats' hair, which was spread over the tabernacle cloth as a protection and an additional covering above, (verses 7-13; xxxvi, 14-18;) over this, again, was spread an additional covering of red rams' skins, and still another of seal (badger) skins above that. Verse 14. These several coverings were designed to make the roofing impervious to the rain. In the following description we have first the ten curtains which formed the ceiling, (verses 1-6), next, the goats' hair curtains, (7-13,) then the rams' and seal skin coverings, (14,) after which the *mishcan*, (15-30,) then the vail which divided the holy place from the holy of holies, (31-33,) then the positions of the sacred vessels, (34, 35,) and finally, the hangings and pillars for the doorway, (36, 37.)

1. **The tabernacle**—The word here is הַמִּשְׁכָּן, and denotes more strictly the board structure described below, verses 15-30, but came to be used of the entire structure, including the curtains. These golden plated boards were to be securely covered above, and the coverings are first described. **Ten curtains** —Or, *hangings*, so called, according to Gesenius, from their tremulous motion. Of the fabrics and colours of which they were made see xxv, 4, notes. Here it is noted that the **fine linen** was **twined,** or twisted. The material, in various colours, was twisted or woven together, by the most skilful workmanship, and upon the whole **cherubim of cunning work,** that is, figures of the **cherubim,** the skilful work of a weaver, were to be embroidered. These highly ornamental curtains were to form the visible ceiling of the sanctuary.

2, 3. **Length... eight and twenty cubits... breadth ... four cubits**— Hence, when **coupled together** in two great pieces of **five curtains** each, they would form a great tent cloth twenty-eight by forty cubits (about 42 x 60 feet) in dimensions. This would be ample for covering the *mishcan* of boards, described below. Verses 15-30.

4-6. **Fifty loops ... fifty taches** —The two great curtains were to be united together by hooks and eyes, for the **taches of gold** were evidently clasps, or hooks, adapted for easy coupling of the two large pieces. Thus united it would **be one tabernacle,** that is, one immense tabernacle cloth. For the manner in which these curtains were put up and arranged, see note at the end of the chapter.

7. **Curtains of goats' hair**—For the use of this material for tents see xxv, 4, note. **Covering upon the tabernacle**—Literally, for a tent (אֹהֶל) *over the tabernacle,* (מִשְׁכָּן.) This then was to form a regular tent cover, while the one just previously described was to serve more for interior ornamentation.

8. **Thirty cubits ... four cubits**— There being eleven of these, if joined like the others described above, there would be a great tent cloth thirty by

CHAPTER XXV.

9 And thou shalt couple five curtains by themselves, and six curtains by themselves, and shalt double the sixth curtain in the forefront of the tabernacle. **10** And thou shalt make fifty loops on the edge of the one curtain *that is* outmost in the coupling, and fifty loops in the edge of the curtain which coupleth the second. **11** And thou shalt make fifty taches of brass, and put the taches into the loops, and couple the ²tent together, that it may be one. **12** And the remnant that remaineth of the curtains of the tent, the half curtain that remaineth, shall hang over the back side of the tabernacle. **13** And a cubit on the one side, and a cubit on the other side ³of that which remaineth in the length of the curtains of the tent, it shall hang over the sides of the tabernacle, on this side and on that side, to cover it. **14** And ᶜ thou shalt make a covering for the tent *of* rams' skins dyed red, and a covering above *of* badgers' skins. **15** And thou shalt make boards for the tabernacle *of* shittim wood standing up. **16** Ten cubits *shall be* the length of a board, and a cubit and a half *shall be* the breadth of one board. **17** Two ⁴ tenons *shall there be* in one board, set in order one against another: thus shalt thou make for all the boards of the tab-

---

² Or, *covering.*—³ Heb. *in the remainder,* or, *surplusage.*—c Chap. 36. 19.—4 Heb. *hands.*

forty-four cubits (45 x 66 feet) in dimensions, two cubits by four (3 x 6 feet) greater than the other. Comp. note on verses 2, 4.

9. Five curtains by themselves—The expression **by themselves** seems evidently to mean the same as "together one to another" in verse 3. These eleven breadths were to be coupled together like those ten in two great pieces, and the putting five in one and six in the other would provide that their places of union by loops and taches (verses 10 and 11) would not, when spread over the roof, coincide with those of the tabernacle cloth of ten curtains. **Double the sixth**—So that half of it would hang over in **the forefront** of the tent. Comp. on verse 12.

11. Taches of brass—Corresponding with the goats' hair, as gold with the fine linen. Verse 6. **Couple the tent together**—So that the tent cloth or cover would be united by the coupling into **one** immense tent cloth after the manner of the tabernacle cloth as shown in verse 6.

12. The half curtain that remaineth—One half of the sixth curtain was to be doubled or folded in the front, and this would allow another half curtain to **hang over the back side of the tabernacle** (*mishcan*) but the exact manner of its adjustment is not described.

13. A cubit—The length of these curtains being thirty instead of twenty-eight cubits, like the former, (verse 2,) provision was thus made for their extending one cubit on each side of the tabernacle beyond the tabernacle cloth.

14. A covering—To be placed still above the goats' hair tent-cloth, as an additional protection. **Rams' skins** ... **badgers' skins**—See note on xxv, 5. Whether these extra coverings of skins were coextensive with the entire roof, we are nowhere told, but in the absence of specific information we are hardly justified in the conclusion that one or both of them served only for a coping. No doubt the common customs of adjusting tent cloths among a nomadic people were presupposed, and definite information on some matters of detail was considered unnecessary.

15. Boards—Planks hewn out of **shittim wood**, and so prepared that they could be arranged **standing up**, that is, set upright to form the framework of the tabernacle.

16. Ten cubits ... **a cubit and a half**—About fifteen feet long and a little over two feet wide. The thickness is not given. The acacia trees now found in the Sinaitic desert are said to be not of sufficient size to make boards of this measure. If this be true, it may be observed (1.) that nothing requires us to suppose that every board was made out of one piece of timber. Skilful workmanship could as easily make such boards out of many pieces as it could make the golden candlestick out of many small pieces of gold. (2.) It is probable that the ancient growths of those regions were far greater than those which are now seen.

17. Two tenons—Small projections

ernacle. **18** And thou shalt make the boards for the tabernacle, twenty boards on the south side southward. **19** And thou shalt make forty sockets of silver under the twenty boards; two sockets under one board for his two tenons, and two sockets under another board for his two tenons. **20** And for the second side of the tabernacle on the north side *there shall be* twenty boards, **21** And their forty sockets *of* silver; two sockets under one board, and two sockets under another board. **22** And for the sides of the tabernacle westward thou shalt make six boards. **23** And two boards shalt thou make for the corners of the tabernacle in the two sides. **24** And they shall be [5] coupled together beneath, and they shall be coupled together above the head of it unto one ring: thus shall it be for them both; they shall be for the two corners. **25** And they shall be eight boards, and their sockets *of* silver, sixteen sockets; two sockets under one board, and two sockets under another board.

---

5 Heb. *twined.*

from the bottom of each board to set in the sockets mentioned in verse 19.

18. Twenty boards—From this we learn the length of the *mishcan* or tabernacle of boards, namely, thirty cubits, (45 feet,) since each board was a cubit and a half wide. Verse 16. **South side southward**— Or, *Negebward toward the right.* The person is supposed to face the same way as the structure, namely, to the east, in which case the south would be to his right.

19. Forty sockets—Or *bases;* since two of these were to be placed under each board to receive the **two tenons**. Comp. verrse 17. They were evidently of the nature of morticed blocks of silver, which formed a continuous foundation for the board structure, and would serve to separate and keep the lower ends of the boards from the ground.

22. Westward...six boards—The tabernacle was to face eastward, toward the rising sun, and that side of the board structure was left open, to be enclosed only by curtains. Verse 36. But the west side, or end, was to be securely fastened with boards, as were the north and the south sides, (18, 20.)

23-25. Two boards...for the corners—The exact form and purpose of these boards it seems impossible to determine with absolute certainty. They were to be somehow **coupled together** at base and top **unto one ring**. Some have thought that the two westward corners consisted of two boards so fastened together at right angles as to make one double piece from top to bottom. This of course would add one board, a cubit and a half less the thickness, to the length of the tabernacle. Another solution is, to suppose that the boards for the two corners were to be made double (Heb. *twins*) and clasped together with rings **beneath** and **above**, so as to form one united piece just double the width of the other boards. Thus the **eight boards** which filled up the west end would be equal in width to ten other boards, and make the breadth of the tabernacle one half its length. But according to Philo (*Life of Moses,* iii, 7) and Josephus, (*Ant.,* iii, 6, 3,) and all Jewish tradition, the dimensions of the tabernacle were thirty by ten cubits, and this corresponds with the relative measures of the Solomonic temple. 1 Kings vi, 2. It is better, therefore, to suppose these corner boards to have been composed each of two narrow boards **coupled together** at right angles, and made to lap around the northwest and southwest corners. By joining the two pieces so as to allow one half a cubit of each corner board to fill out the supposed ten cubits interior breadth of the tabernacle, we have a simple and reasonable explanation. The six boards made nine cubits of this breadth, and the two corner boards supplied the other cubit. Thus also, as Dr. James Strong has observed in his recent work on the Tabernacle, "the whole angle would be greatly strengthened, as well as ornamented, by the overlapping on the lower side." The west end, accordingly, was made up of **eight boards**, and each of these, corner boards as well as the rest, had **two sockets**, like those on the north and south sides. Josephus says: "As to the wall be-

26 And thou shalt make bars *of* shittim wood; five for the boards of the one side of the tabernacle, **27** And five bars for the boards of the other side of the tabernacle, and five bars for the boards of the side of the tabernacle, for the two sides westward. **28** And the middle bar in the midst of the boards shall reach from end to end. **29** And thou shalt overlay the boards with gold, and make their rings *of* gold *for* places for the bars: and thou shalt overlay the bars with gold. **30** And thou shalt rear up the tabernacle ᵈ according to the

---

d Chap. 25. 9, 40; 27. 8; Acts 7. 44; Heb. 8. 5.

---

hind, where the six boards together made up only nine cubits, they made two other pillars, and cut them out of one cubit, which they placed in the corners, and made them equally fine with the other."

26–29. **Bars**— The description and design of these are easy to be understood. "They held the whole firmly together," says Josephus, "and for this reason was all this joined so fast together, that the tabernacle might not be shaken either by the winds or by any other means, but that it might preserve itself quiet and immovable continually." These **bars of shittim wood,** as well as **the boards,** were overlaid **with gold,** and were made to pass through gold **rings** or staples, which were fastened in each board as **places** (Heb., *houses*) **for the bars.** They were **five** in number for each side and for the western end, **the middle bar in the midst of the boards** on each side reaching **from end to end.** Whether these bars were to be on the outside or inside of the boards is not stated, and both views have had their advocates. Most probably they were on the outside, as thus,

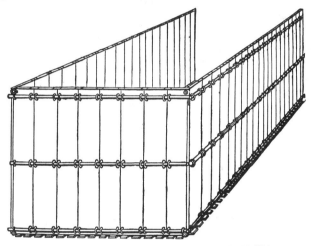

GENERAL VIEW OF THE WOODEN WALLS OF THE TABERNACLE.

in putting up and taking down the structure, there would be less occasion to invade the holy places. As **the middle bar** extended the whole length of the wall of boards, it is naturally inferred that the other four did not, and hence the general conclusion that there were but three rows of bars on each side, the upper and lower row consisting of two bars, each running half the length of the middle bar.

30. **Thou shalt rear up the tabernacle**—The making and erection of the tabernacle involved a great many

EXODUS. B. C. 1491.

fashion thereof which was showed thee in the mount.

31 And ᵉ thou shalt make a vail *of* blue, and purple, and scarlet, and fine twined linen of cunning work: with cherubim shall it be made. **32** And thou shalt hang it upon four pillars of shittim *wood* overlaid with gold: their hooks *shall be of* gold, upon the four sockets of silver.

33 And thou shalt hang up the vail under the taches, that thou mayest bring in thither within the vail ᶠ the ark of the testimony: and the vail shall divide unto you between ᵍ the holy *place* and the most holy. **34** And ʰ thou shalt put the mercy seat upon the ark of the testimony in the most holy *place*. **35** And ⁱ thou shalt set the table without the vail, and ᵏ the candlestick over against the table on the side of the tabernacle toward the south: and thou shalt put the table on the north side. **36** And ˡ thou shalt make a hanging for the door of the tent, *of* blue, and purple, and scarlet, and fine twined linen, wrought with needlework. **37** And thou shalt make for the hanging ᵐ five pillars *of* shittim *wood*, and overlay them with gold, *and* their hooks *shall be of* gold: and thou shalt cast five sockets of brass for them.

e Chap. 36. 35; Lev. 16. 2; 2 Chron. 3. 14; Matt. 27. 51; Heb. 9. 3. —*f* Chap. 25. 16; 40. 21. — *g* Lev. 16. 2; Heb. 9. 2, 3.

h Chap. 25. 21; 40. 20; Heb. 9. 5. — *i* Chap. 40. 22; Heb. 9. 2. — *k* Chap. 40. 24. — *l* Chap. 36. 37.—*m* Chap. 36. 38.

details which are not here recorded; but as Moses was shown **the fashion thereof,** (Heb. *its judgment,*) he understood perfectly what was judged, and ordered to be, the appropriate arrangement of each part.

31, 32. **A vail**—פָּרֹכֶת, *a separation,* a dividing curtain to separate the two inner apartments of the sanctuary. Verse 33. The material and workmanship were to correspond exactly with those of the tabernacle curtains. Verse 1. The relative position of the **four pillars**, with **their hooks of gold** and their **four sockets of silver,** is left indefinite. But their position and distance from each other must have been different from the five pillars of the doorway. Verse 37.

33. **Hang up the vail under the taches**—What **taches** are here meant? The only use of this word has been to describe the gold and brass hooks which were to couple the tabernacle and tent curtains. Verses 6 and 11. If these are referred to, the gold taches of verse 6 would be most naturally understood, and the vail that separated the two holy places would have hung directly under the coupling of the great tabernacle-cloth. This again would indicate that the sanctuary was divided into two rooms of equal size, which appears to be contrary to all tradition. There seems, however, no insuperable objection to making these **taches** identical with the *hooks* mentioned in the preceding verse.

There is nothing in the immediate context to suggest the taches of the tabernacle curtain, mentioned verse 6; so that, if they were intended, there should have been added here some qualifying word. In the absence of such word the most natural reference seems to be to the hooks (וָוִים) just mentioned. The innermost room formed by this dividing **vail** was the appointed place for **the ark of the testimony,** (see xxv, 10-22, notes,) and was known as **the most holy,** or, more literally, *the holy of holies.* Like "the oracle," the corresponding apartment in the temple, it has been commonly supposed to have been in the form of a perfect cube, (see 1 Kings vi, 20, note,) and this is believed to have prompted the description of "the holy Jerusalem" in Rev. xxi, 16.

35. **Table...candlestick**—For description see xxv, 23-37, and notes. They were to be set **over against** each other, that is, on opposite sides of the holy place, the table on the north side, and the candlestick on the south side. The golden altar of incense, which was to stand between, in front of the vail, is mentioned further on, in connexion with the laws for offering incense. Chap. xxx, 1-10.

36, 37. **Hanging for the door**—A pendent curtain, or covering, of the same material as the vail (31) and the tabernacle-cloth, (ver. 1,) but **wrought with needlework.** So this was the work of an *embroiderer*, (רֹקֵם,) that of a *weaver*, (חֹשֵׁב.) This was to hang on **five pillars**, while that within hung upon four, but as this was to be **for the door of the tent**, not of the *mishcan*, or board structure, it may have been larger than the other. Its **hooks**, like those of verse 32, were **of gold**, but the **sockets** were to be **of brass;** those within, of silver.

The plan of the tabernacle as above described, and the adjustment of curtains and coverings, have long been a perplexing problem for interpreters. Perhaps it is too much to expect that now, after the lapse of so many centuries, every detail of its construction can be restored so as to clear up all the statements of this narrative.

Taking first the structure of boards, as it has been described in verses 15–25, there can be little doubt as to its main features. Its general appearance must have been such as is exhibited in the cut at verses 26–29.

The next difficulty is concerning the place and purpose of the tabernacle curtains described in verses 1–6. According to some writers they were spread over the board structure like a pall over a coffin. Supposing the breadth of this structure to have been ten cubits, (see note on verses 23–25,) this covering, being twenty-eight cubits long, (verse 2,) would have reached over the two outer sides unto about one cubit from the base, for the boards stood ten cubits high. Verse 16. The goats' hair covering, being two cubits longer, (verse 8,) would, when spread over this, have reached completely to the base. This certainly makes a very simple and natural arrangement, but is open to several serious objections. (1.) The ornamental curtains would have been concealed from view, except, at most, the one third which would be visible as a ceiling over the interior. This objection, however, may be offset by saying that, like the most holy place, they were not designed to be seen, and the "cunning work" upon them was but a fitting indication for the interior and symbolical purpose which they served. (2.) The coverings spread flat over the top must, especially by reason of the great weight of the skins, have become soon depressed and so sunken in as to hold pools of water rather than prove a protection against the rain.

Another theory is, that this ornamental curtain was arranged to hang down on the inside of the boards, and so form an ornamental tapestry for the walls as well as for the ceiling. But (1.) a purpose so special would seem to have required more particular definition in the narrative. (2.) This would have entirely concealed the golden-plated boards. (3.) It would also, like the theory just stated, have exposed the roof to the depression and dampness necessarily consequent upon such a flat surface of curtains.

Mr. T. O. Paine represents the two sets of five curtains as coupled together at the ends, (verse 3,) and hanging double and in festoons on the inside of the boards, at about the height of a man's head, four cubits, above the floor. His view is in the main adopted by Dr. James Strong in his recent (1888) work on the Tabernacle. But (1.) there is no more ground for making these curtains run in festoons around the interior walls than there is for making the goats' hair curtains hang in the like form, for both sets are spoken of in the same general way. Such a totally different purpose of the two sets of curtains would certainly have demanded more notice than we can find in the text of the sacred writer. (2.) Such an arrangement, moreover, would not only have concealed a large portion of the boards, but also, hanging in folds, the colours and "cherubim of cunning work" must have been so hidden from view that no one could distinguish or trace their outlines. Strong's adjustment of the curtains, however, largely obviates this last objection.

A theory proposed by Fergusson, in Smith's *Dictionary of the Bible*, (article "Temple") assumes that the tabernacle must have had, "as all tents have had from the days of Moses down to the present day," a ridge and a ridge pole, and he supposes that the angle formed by the two sides of the roof was a right angle. The ornamented tabernacle cur-

THE TABERNACLE ACCORDING TO PAINE.

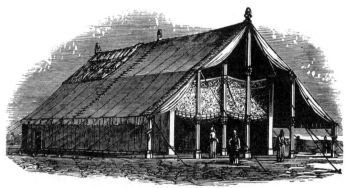

THE TABERNACLE ACCORDING TO FERGUSSON.

CHAPTER XXVII.

AND thou shalt make ᵃan altar of shittim wood, five cubits long, and five cubits broad; the altar shall be foursquare: and the height thereof *shall be* three cubits. 2 And thou shalt make the horns of it upon the four corners thereof: his horns shall be of the same: and ᵇthou shalt overlay it with brass. 3 And thou shalt make his pans to receive his ashes, and his shovels, and his basins, and his fleshhooks, and his firepans: all the vessels thereof thou shalt make of brass. 4 And thou shalt make for it a grate of network of brass; and upon the net shalt thou make four brazen rings in the four corners thereof. 5 And thou shalt put it under the compass of the altar beneath, that the net may be even to the midst of the altar.

a Chap. 38. 1; Ezek. 43. 13.   *b* See Num. 16. 38.

tain, being the first thrown over the ridge pole, and fastened at the sides, would have served as a lining to the rest, and have formed with its colours and cunning work a visible roof, or ceiling, over the entire structure. Over this as a protecting covering were thrown the other curtains described above. He thinks, however, that the seal skins were used only " for a coping or ridge piece to protect the junction of the two curtains of rams' skins, which were laid on each slope of the roof, and probably only laced together at the top." This view is not without objections, but it helps to solve some of the dfficulties of the problem. The cuts show the plans of Paine and Fergusson in their main outlines. On the symbolism of the tabernacle, see at the end of chapter xl.

CHAPTER XXVII.

THE ALTAR OF BURNT OFFERINGS, 1–8.

1. **Altar of shittim wood**—The acacia wood formed a hollow framework, (comp. verse 8,) which was portable, and designed, doubtless, in accord with xx, 24, 25, to be filled with earth or rough stones whenever it was set up for use. **Height . . . three cubits**—About four and one half feet, so that no steps or any considerable ascent would be necessary for the officiating priest. Comp. xx, 26.

2. **Horns**—Probably resembling the horns of cattle. These were so set into **the four corners** of the acacia framework as to appear to **be of the same,** as if growing out of it.

3. **Pans . . . shovels . . . basins . . . fleshhooks . . . firepans**—These several **vessels** were all requisite in the service of the altar, for taking up and removing **ashes,** receiving the blood of victims, adjusting the pieces of flesh, and carrying coals of fire.

4, 5. **A grate of network**—The design of this is not made very clear by the statements of these verses. **The compass of the altar** is commonly supposed to have been a projecting border or framework running around the outside, and affording a place for the officiating priest to stand, or pass around, when arranging the fire or the victims offered. Accordingly, this network grating has by some been explained as reaching from this border to the ground, and so being **beneath** it, (Heb., *from below*.) It would thus serve as a support for the border. Others have imagined that it extended horizontally beyond the bor-

ALTAR OF BURNT OFFERINGS.

der, and served to catch coals or any thing else which might fall from the altar. Others, however, have located the grate inside of the altar, so as to serve for a sieve through which ashes might fall, as through a fire grate, into a hollow place within the altar, from

6 And thou shalt make staves for the altar, staves of shittim wood, and overlay them with brass. **7** And the staves shall be put into the rings, and the staves shall be upon the two sides of the altar, to bear it. **8** Hollow with boards shalt thou make it: ᶜ as ¹ it was showed thee in the mount, so shall they make it.

9 And ᵈ thou shalt make the court of the tabernacle: for the south side southward *there shall be* hangings for the court *of* fine twined linen of a hundred cubits long for one side: **10** And the twenty pillars thereof and their twenty sockets *shall be of* brass; the hooks of the pillars and their fillets *shall be of* silver. **11** And likewise for the north side in length *there shall be* hangings of a hundred *cubits* long, and his twenty pillars and their twenty sockets *of* brass; the hooks of the pillars and their fillets *of* silver.

12 And *for* the breadth of the court on the west side *shall be* hangings of fifty cubits: their pillars ten, and their

---

c Chap. 25. 40; 26. 30. 1 Heb. *he showed*.——*d* Chap. 38. 9.

---

whence they were removed by means of the shovels. In this case the **four brazen rings** at the **corners** were for the purpose of easily lifting the grate out, or setting it in its place. There appears nothing by which to determine which of these views is correct. If the rings mentioned in verse 7 are identical with those **upon the net**, then the first view named above would be the most natural explanation. But as the staves to fit into those rings are mentioned as *for the altar*, while these were *for the net*, we are not justified in assuming that they were identical. But while the exact location and purpose of this grating are not certainly fixed, the general form and appearance of the altar probably resembled the preceding cut.

COURT OF THE TABERNACLE, 9–19.

9. **South side southward** — See note on xxvi, 18. **Hangings**—These, which were to serve for a fence about the sanctuary, were of the same material as the tabernacle-cloth, (xxvi, 1,) and the inner vail, (xxvi, 31,) and the front curtain, (xxvi, 36,) but without the cunning work and colours inwrought on them.

10, 11. **Twenty pillars**—Thus allowing for five cubits (7½ feet) between each pillar. These **pillars** were connected by means of **hooks** and **fillets of silver.** The **fillets** were the poles, or rods, upon which the linen hangings were to be suspended, and were fastened to the pillars by means of the **hooks of the pillars.** The hangings were also probably attached to the rods by means of some kind of hooks.

12–18. **Breadth of the court**— The court was one hundred cubits long and fifty broad, (150 x 75 feet,) and its linen fence five cubits high. **The gate of the court** was twenty cubits wide, and the hangings of this part differed from the rest by being embroidered like that of the door of the tent. Chap. xxv, 36. An outline of the court and the tabernacle, with the altar and laver, is shown in the annexed cut.

TABERNACLE AND COURT.

B. C. 1491. CHAPTER XXVII. 523

sockets ten. **13** And the breadth of the court on the east side eastward *shall be* fifty cubits. **14** The hangings of one side *of the gate shall be* fifteen cubits: their pillars three, and their sockets three. **15** And on the other side *shall be* hangings fifteen *cubits:* their pillars three, and their sockets three.
16 And for the gate of the court *shall be* a hanging of twenty cubits, *of* blue, and purple, and scarlet, and fine twined linen, wrought with needlework: *and* their pillars *shall be* four, and their sockets four. **17** All the pillars round about the court *shall be* filleted with silver; their hooks *shall be of* silver, and their sockets *of* brass.
18 The length of the court *shall be* a hundred cubits, and the breadth ² fifty everywhere, and the height five cubits *of* fine twined linen, and their sockets *of* brass. **19** All the vessels of the tabernacle in all the service thereof, and all the pins thereof, and all the pins of the court, *shall be of* brass.
20 And ᵉ thou shalt command the children of Israel, that they bring thee pure oil olive beaten for the light, to cause the lamp ³ to burn always. **21** In the tabernacle of the congregation ᶠ without the vail, which *is* before the testimony, ᵍ Aaron and his sons shall order it from evening to morning before the LORD: ʰ *it shall be* a statute for ever unto their generations on the behalf of the children of Israel.

2 Hebrew, *fifty by fifty.* —— *e* Leviticus 24. 2. —— 3 Hebrew, *to ascend up.* —— *f* Chapter 26. 31, 33.

g Chap. 30. 8; 1 Sam. 3. 3; 2 Chron. 13. 11.—— *h* Chap. 28. 43; 29. 9, 28; Lev. 3. 17; 16. 34; 24. 9; Num. 18. 23; 19. 21; 1 Sam. 30. 25.

19. All the vessels—The vessels here referred to are not, of course, those mentioned in chapter xxv, 38, 39, but the instruments for such more common **service** as the putting up and taking down of the structure would require.

THE OIL FOR THE LIGHT, 20, 21.

20. Pure oil olive beaten—See this passage as repeated in Lev. xxiv, 2, 3. This oil **for the light** of the holy place was to be obtained, not by pressing the olives, but by *beating* or bruising them, by which means the finest quality of oil was produced. **Cause the lamp to burn always**—According to chap. xxx, 7, 8, and Lev. xxiv, 3, 4, the lamps were to be dressed each morning, and lighted each evening, so that the light was perpetual; the light of the sun sufficiently finding its way within the tent by day, and the lamps of the golden candlestick (xxv, 31-37) burning all the night. Comp. 1 Sam. iii, 3, note.

21. Without the vail—Outside and in front of the vail described xxvi, 31-33. **Before the testimony**—In front of the most holy place, in which the ark of the testimony was set. The mention of **Aaron and his sons,** in connexion with this service, leads naturally to an account of the institution of the Aaronic priesthood, which follows in the next chapter.

CHAPTER XXVIII.

THE HOLY GARMENTS OF THE PRIESTS, 1-43.

The institution of the Aaronic priesthood and the ceremonials of their induction into office, their dress, and the duties of their office, are explicitly referred in this and following chapters to the time of Moses. The theory which maintains the post-exilian origin of this "priest code" is obliged to treat this entire narrative as unhistorical, and has gone to the extreme of teaching that the structure and cultus of the Mosaic tabernacle must all be relegated to the realm of fiction. How this reverses and revolutionizes all history and tradition, and introduces difficulties greater than those it seeks to explain, must be apparent to the unbiassed student of these sacred books. That the Levitical priesthood was instituted by Moses, and that Aaron and his sons were consecrated first for the holy services of the tabernacle, are facts most reasonable and supposable in themselves. No other period in all the history of Israel was so appropriate for the establishment of such a sacerdotal cultus, and no man, under God, could have been better qualified to set in order the offices and work of this ministry than Moses, whose Egyptian training must have made him familiar with

CHAPTER XXVIII.

AND take thou unto thee [a] Aaron thy brother, and his sons with him, from among the children of Israel, that he may minister unto me in the priest's office, *even* Aaron, Nadab and Abihu, Eleazar and Ithamar, Aaron's sons. 2 And [b] thou shalt make holy garments for Aaron thy brother, for glory and for beauty. 3 And [c] thou shalt speak unto all *that are* wise hearted, [d] whom I have filled with the spirit of wisdom, that they may make Aaron's garments to consecrate him, that he may minister unto me in the priest's office. 4 And these *are* the garments which they shall make; [e] a breastplate, and [f] an ephod, and [g] a robe, and [h] a broidered coat, a mitre, and a girdle: and they shall make holy garments for Aaron thy brother, and his sons, that he may minister unto me in the priest's office. 5 And they shall take gold, and blue, and purple, and scarlet, and fine linen.

6 [i] And they shall make the ephod *of* gold, *of* blue, and *of* purple, *of* scarlet, and fine twined linen, with cunning work. 7 It shall have the two shoulderpieces thereof joined at the two edges thereof; and so it shall be joined togeth-

---

a Num. 18. 7; Heb. 5. 1, 4.—*b* Chap. 29. 5, 29; 31. 10; 39. 1, 2; Lev. 8. 7, 30; Num. 20. 26, 28.—*c* Chap. 31. 6; 36. 1. *d* Chap. 31. 3; 35. 30, 31. —— *e* Verse 15. —— *f* Verse 6. —— *g* Verse 31. —— *h* Verse 39. —— *i* Chap. 39. 2.

---

the cultus and mysteries of the great temples of the Nile.

1. **Take thou unto thee Aaron**— Or, *Bring thou Aaron thy brother near to thee.* Moses, as the divinely chosen minister and mediator between Jehovah and the people, is the proper person to formally institute a new law and order of priestly ministrations. **Nadab and Abihu** have been already mentioned, (xxiv, 1, 9,) and in Lev. x, 1, 2, we read of their sudden destruction for offering "strange fire before Jehovah." The four sons of Aaron are mentioned in the genealogy of chapter vi, 23. **Eleazar** succeeded his father, and the priestly robes were transferred to him in Mount Hor. Num. xx, 24–28. He in turn was succeeded by his son Phinehas. Compare vi, 25, and Josh. xxiv, 33; Judg. xx, 28. The descendants of **Ithamar** subsequently attained precedence, (see note on 1 Sam. i, 9,) and representatives of both these sons of Aaron appear to have held office in David's time, (see note on 2 Sam. vi, 17, and viii, 17,) but the deposition of Abiathar by Solomon (2 Kings ii, 35, note) restored the line of Eleazar.

2. **Holy garments . . . for glory and for beauty**—As the entire sanctuary service constituted a system of object teaching to impress lessons of God's truth and holiness and his relations to his people, it was eminently proper that the vestments of the ministers of the sanctuary should have noticeable harmony with the holy and beautiful places and services. Hence, the figures of clean robes and beautiful attire to signify the righteousness of the saints.

3. **Wise hearted**—Those gifted with the genius and skill for such artistic work as is here contemplated. **The spirit of wisdom** is here and in xxxi, 3, shown to be a gift of God, and those who possessed the tact and knowledge for making appropriate **garments** for the priestly office were to be regarded as divinely qualified for just such kind of service.

4, 5. **These are the garments**—In these two verses the principal articles of the priestly dress are mentioned, and the materials which were to be used in making them, but the fuller description of the several articles is given in the sequel of the chapter.

6. **The ephod**—This was the most conspicuous garment of the high priest, and was made of the same material as the tabernacle - cloth and vail, (xxvi, 1, 31,) but was interlaced with **gold** threads, the **cunning work** of the weaver. According to Wilkinson the Egyptian monuments exhibit coloured costumes woven with what appear like threads of gold.

7. **Two shoulderpieces** — Hence the ephod is called, by the Septuagint translators, ἐπωμίς, and the Vulgate, *superhumerale,* a garment to be worn *upon the shoulder.* It evidently consisted of two pieces, **joined at the two edges**, that is, at the two upper ends, or edges, which were fitted to come together at the top of the shoulders, as may be seen in the cuts on the opposite page.

B. C. 1491. CHAPTER XXVIII. 525

er. **8** And the ¹ curious girdle of the ephod, which *is* upon it, shall be of the same, according to the work thereof; *even of* gold, *of* blue, and purple, and scarlet, and fine twined linen. **9** And thou shalt take two onyx stones, and grave on them the names of the children of Israel: **10** Six of their names on one stone, and *the other* six names of the rest on the other stone, according to their birth. **11** With the work of an engraver in stone, *like* the engravings of a signet, shalt thou engrave the two stones with the names of the children of Israel: thou shalt make them to be set in ouches of gold. **12** And thou shalt put the two stones upon the shoulders of the ephod *for* stones of memorial unto the children of Israel: and ᵏ Aaron shall bear their names before the LORD upon his two shoulders ˡ for a memorial.
13 And thou shalt make ouches *of* gold; **14** And two chains *of* pure gold at the ends; *of* wreathen work shalt

1 Or, *embroidered*.——*k* Verse 29; chap. 39. 7.

l See Josh. 4. 7; Zech. 6. 14.

EPHOD.—Front view.

EPHOD.—Back view.

8. The curious girdle—By means of which the two pieces of the ephod were to be fastened about the body.

VOL. I.—34

These were of the same material as the rest. Comp. verse 6.

9–12. **Two onyx stones**—Heb., *stones of shoham*. Some render *beryl*, others, *sardonyx*. These were to have graven on them the names of the twelve sons of Israel; according to Josephus (*Ant.*, iii, 7, 5) the elder sons' names were on the right shoulder, so that the younger must have been on the left. Thus arranged **according to their birth,** if we are guided by Gen. xxix and xxx, they would have been as follows:

RIGHT.	LEFT.
Reuben	Gad
Simeon	Asher
Levi	Issachar
Judah	Zebulun
Dan	Joseph
Naphtali	Benjamin.

The engraving of the names upon the two stones was to be after the manner **of a signet,** or seal, and the stones themselves were to be set **upon the shoulders of the ephod for stones of memorial,** continually admonishing the wearer of them that he acted as the consecrated representative of the twelve tribes of Israel, and not for himself alone. The stones were **to be set in ouches of gold,** or rather *surrounded with textures of gold*. According to Josephus, "there were two sardonyxes upon the ephod at the shoulders to fasten it, in the nature of buttons, having each end running to the sardonyxes of gold that they might be buttoned by them." The vacant space (*e*) in the cut indicates the place where the breastplate (described verses 15–29) was to be worn.

13, 14. **Ouches . . . chains**—These were designed in some way to fasten the

O. T.

526 EXODUS. B. C. 1491.

thou make them, and fasten the wreathen chains to the ouches.

15 And ᵐ thou shalt make the breastplate of judgment with cunning work; after the work of the ephod thou shalt make it; *of* gold, *of* blue, and *of* purple, and *of* scarlet, and *of* fine twined linen, shalt thou make it. 16 Foursquare it shall be *being* doubled; a span *shall be* the length thereof, and a span *shall be* the breadth thereof. 17 ⁿ And thou shalt ²set in it settings of stone, *even* four rows of stones: *the first* row *shall be* a ³sardius, a topaz, and a carbuncle: *this shall be* the first row. 18 And the second row *shall be* an emerald, a sapphire, and a diamond. 19 And the third row a ligure, an agate, and an amethyst. 20 And the fourth row a beryl, and an onyx, and a jasper: they shall be set in gold in their ⁴inclosings. 21 And the stones shall be with the

---

m Chapter 39. 8.
n Chapter 39. 10, etc.

2 Heb. *fill in it fillings of stone.*
3 Or, *ruby.* —— 4 Heb. *fillings.*

---

ephod and breastplate together, (comp. verse 25,) and so serve to introduce the description of the latter.

15. **Breastplate of judgment**—This is not to be thought of as a military breastplate of metal, but as a very richly ornamented fabric, made of the same material as the ephod, upon which it was to be fastened by rings and chains of gold. Verses 22–25. Its probable form is shown in the cut, which is taken from McClintock and Strong's Cyclopædia. It was called **breastplate of judgment** from its holding the mysterious Urim and Thummim, (verse 30,) by which the judgment of God was sometimes ascertained.

16. **Foursquare it shall be ... doubled**—Being **a span**, that is, half a cubit (about 9½ inches) in **length** and **breadth**, the doubling or folding of it would form a kind of bag, adapted to contain the Urim and Thummim.

17. **Four rows of stones**—These were inwrought into the costly fabric in **settings** or *fillings*, so as to form a splendid piece of work. The names of these stones, which follow, (verses 17–20,) are sufficient to show that this ornamental breastpiece of the high priest must have been prepared with the greatest possible care and skill. It is hardly possible to identify the Hebrew names of all the stones. The student should consult the larger Bible dictionaries on the several words, where all that is known upon the subject is gathered together.

THE BREASTPLATE OF THE HIGH PRIEST.

B. C. 1491. CHAPTER XXVIII. 527

names of the children of Israel, twelve, according to their names, *like* the engravings of a signet; every one with his name shall they be according to the twelve tribes.

22 And thou shalt make upon the breastplate chains at the ends *of* wreathen work *of* pure gold. **23** And thou shalt make upon the breastplate two rings of gold, and shalt put the two rings on the two ends of the breastplate. **24** And thou shalt put the two wreathen *chains* of gold in the two rings *which are* on the ends of the breastplate. **25** And *the other* two ends of the two wreathen *chains* thou shalt fasten in the two ouches, and put *them* on the shoulderpieces of the ephod before it.

26 And thou shalt make two rings of gold, and thou shalt put them upon the two ends of the breastplate in the border thereof, which *is* in the side of the ephod inward. **27** And two *other* rings of gold thou shalt make, and shalt put them on the two sides of the ephod underneath, toward the forepart thereof, over against the *other* coupling thereof, above the curious girdle of the ephod. **28** And they shall bind the breastplate by the rings thereof unto the rings of the ephod with a lace of blue, that *it* may be above the curious girdle of the ephod, and that the breastplate be not loosed from the ephod. **29** And Aaron shall bear the names of the children of Israel in the breastplate of judgment upon his heart, when he goeth in unto the holy *place*, °for a memorial before the LORD continually.

30 And ᵖ thou shalt put in the breastplate of judgment the Urim and the Thummim; and they shall be upon

---

o Verse 12.—*p* Lev. 8. 8; Num. 27. 21; Deut. 33. 8; 1 Sam. 28. 6; Ezra 2. 63; Neh. 7. 65.

---

21. **Names ... according to the twelve tribes**—As the names on the two onyx stones were to be according to their birth, or generations, (verse 10,) this arrangement according to the tribes may denote a difference.

22-28. **Chains ... rings**—This description shows in minute detail the manner in which the breastplate was securely fastened to the ephod. Josephus says that "whereas the rings were too weak of themselves to bear the weight of the stones, they made two other rings of a larger size, at the edge of that part of the breastplate which reached to the neck, and inserted into the very texture of the breastplate, to receive chains finely wrought, which connected them to the tops of the shoulders with golden bands, whose extremity turned backward and went into the ring on the prominent back part of the ephod; and this was for the security of the breastplate, that it might not fall out of its place."

29. **For a memorial**—Comp. verse 12, note.

30. **The Urim and the Thummim**—Volumes have been written upon the significance of these mysterious words, but no one has succeeded in clearing the subject of its mystery. This verse shows that they should not be identified with the twelve stones mentioned above, (17-20,) but that they were something additional **put in the breastplate;** that is, according to the simplest import of the words, *given* or *placed* in the fold implied in the language of verse 16. This seems to have been in the form of a case or bag fitted to receive these special treasures. That they were some material things, like small pieces of wood or stone, is the most probable inference, but not a word have we anywhere from which we may judge of their form or size. They were formally delivered to Aaron along with the breastplate when he was consecrated to the high priest's office, (Lev. viii, 8,) and were employed in asking counsel or judgment from Jehovah in respect to the going out or coming in of the children of Israel. Num. xxvii, 21. That they thus served to determine important movements may be inferred from 1 Sam. xxii, 15; xxiii, 9-12; xxviii, 6; xxx, 7, 8; 2 Sam. ii, 1; but in what form or manner answers from Jehovah were obtained no one is able now to explain. They no longer existed after the exile, except as traditions of the past, and as possible means for solving difficulties which might again be restored to Israel in the good providence of God. Ezra ii, 63; Neh. vii, 65. Comp. Hosea iii, 4.

The Hebrew words are in the plural, and according to their simplest etymology mean *lights and perfections.* The

EXODUS.

Aaron's heart, when he goeth in before the LORD: and Aaron shall bear the judgment of the children of Israel upon his heart before the LORD continually.

31 And ᵠthou shalt make the robe of the ephod all *of* blue. 32 And there shall be a hole in the top of it, in the midst thereof: it shall have a binding

---

q Chap. 39. 22.

Septuagint translates by words in the singular, meaning *revelation and truth*. They have been conjectured to have been small images, like the *teraphim* of patriarchal times, (see Gen. xxxi, 19,) and granted to the Israelites as a substitute for these, which they had persisted in retaining for purposes of divination. Thus it is supposed divine wisdom accommodated itself to the weakness and superstitions of the people, but after the word of prophecy arose in Israel these lower forms of communication gradually ceased. Josephus (*Ant.*, iii, 8, 9) evidently identified the Urim and Thummim with the twelve stones above described, and says that they indicated the divine will or favor by giving out a brilliancy and splendour that were not natural to them at other times. Later rabbinical writers held that letters were inscribed upon these stones, and the divine answer was given by means of the letters, which became luminous one after another, so as thus to spell out words. Others have maintained that the high priest, when inquiring by these stones, was wont to stand in the holy place before the vail, and fix his gaze intently on them until he was seized by the spirit of prophecy, and distinctly heard the divine revelation proceeding from the glory of the Lord. According to Michaelis, (*Commentaries on Laws of Moses*, vol. i, p. 261,) the Urim and Thummim were "three very ancient stones, which the Israelites before the time of Moses used as lots, one of them marked with an affirmative, a second with a negative, and the third blank or neutral." Without adopting this particular view of the number and marking of the stones, many later writers have adopted the opinion that they were employed in some form of casting lots. Certainly, the casting of lots to ascertain some matter of uncertainty is often referred to, (comp. Lev. xvi, 8, Num. xxvi, 55, Josh. xviii, 8, 1 Sam. xiv, 41, 42,) but in such a way as not to suggest that inquiry through Urim and Thummim was thus performed, but rather the contrary. For why should such casting of lots have been resorted to if the Urim and Thummim already existed, and were given for the same purpose and were employed in the same manner?

It is manifest that all these notions of the form and use of the mysterious stones are purely conjectural, and no degree of certainty or authority attaches to any one of them. All that the Scripture affirms is, that they were some objects **put in the breastplate of judgment,** and were **upon Aaron's heart** when he officiated in the holy place **before the Lord.** As the prophet received the divine revelation in a vision or in a dream, and as Moses was honoured by receiving it in still more open ways, (Num. xii, 6–8,) it is not improbable that the high priest was granted special and extraordinary revelations through some visible *media*, and as the anointed minister of the holiest places bore these sacred signs and *media* as witnesses of **the judgment of the children of Israel upon his heart before the Lord continually.** They were a perpetual sign and symbol of his being a chosen medium of communication between God and the people.

31–35. **The robe of the ephod** — A garment distinct and separate from the ephod, and to be worn underneath it. Being **all of blue** it would appear as a becoming groundwork for the richly ornamented and variously coloured breastplate with its precious stones. The **hole in the top of it, in the midst thereof,** was simply an opening, neatly bound by the weaver's skill, through which the head was put, thus permitting the garment to come down and rest upon the neck, breast, and shoulders. In this same manner the **habergeon,** or military coat of mail, was made to fit about the neck and shoulders. See the cut at 1 Sam.

B. C. 1491. CHAPTER XXVIII. 529

of woven work round about the hole of it, as it were the hole of an habergeon, that it be not rent.

33 And *beneath* upon the ⁵ hem of it thou shalt make pomegranates *of* blue, and *of* purple, and *of* scarlet, round about the hem thereof; and bells of gold between them round about: **34** A golden bell and a pomegranate, a golden bell and a pomegranate, upon the hem of the robe round about. **35** And it shall be upon Aaron to minister: and his sound shall be heard when he goeth in unto the holy *place* before the LORD, and when he cometh out, that he die not.

36 And ʳ thou shalt make a plate *of* pure gold, and grave upon it, *like* the engravings of a signet, HOLINESS TO THE LORD. **37** And thou shalt put it on a blue lace, that it may be upon the mitre; upon the forefront of the mitre it shall be. **38** And it shall be upon Aaron's forehead, that Aaron may ˢ bear the iniquity of the holy things, which the children of Israel shall hallow in all their holy gifts; and it shall be always upon his forehead, that they may be ᵗ accepted before the LORD.

39 And thou shalt embroider the coat of fine linen, and thou shalt make the mitre *of* fine linen, and thou shalt make the girdle *of* needlework.

40 ᵘ And for Aaron's sons thou shalt make coats, and thou shalt make for

---

5 Or, *skirts*. — *r* Chapter 39. 30; Zechariah 14. 20. — *s* Verse 43; Leviticus 10. 17; 22. 9; Numbers 18. 1; Isaiah 53. 11; Ezekiel 4. 4–6; John 1. 29; Hebrews 9. 28; 1 Peter 2. 24. — *t* Lev. 1. 4; 22. 27; 23. 11; Isa. 56. 7. — *u* Verse 4; chap. 39. 27–29, 41; Ezek. 44. 17, 18.

---

xvii, 5. Linen habergeons of this form are said to have been common in Egypt. This robe was **woven** so firmly **about the hole of it** as to be **not** easily **rent,** and it seems to have been without sleeves. The skirts of this robe (not merely **the hem of it,** as the common version) were to be ornamented with **pomegranates of blue, and of purple, and of scarlet,** running like a rich border around the lower part, and **bells of gold** were to be placed **between** the pomegranates, so that a bell and a pomegranate alternated with each other **round about.** The bells were designed to assure those without that their officiating minister was about his holy work, and when the **sound** was **heard** they knew that he was performing his duties in proper attire. The **sound** indicated both when he entered and when he came out of the holy place. A failure to wear this robe (as also the linen breeches, verses 42, 43) would have been on the part of the priest a wanton contempt shown to the holy place and its service, and would have exposed him to the judgment of death.

36–38. **A plate of pure gold—** This was the most notable feature of **the mitre,** or *turban,* and is, therefore, mentioned here before the **blue lace** and headdress, although in chap. xxxix, 28, 30, 31, the mitre is first mentioned. This golden **plate** bore the inscription HOLINESS TO THE LORD, and, being attached by **a blue lace** so as to be **upon the forefront of the mitre,** it would appear as if set as a jewel **upon Aaron's forehead,** and signifies that he, as high priest and atoning mediator in all matters of oblation and sacrifices, was set forth to **bear the iniquity of the holy things.** He, as the representative of a holy nation and consecrated people, sanctified unto God by remission of their sins and in the symbolism of **all their holy gifts,** was, while discharging the duties of his office, **always** to wear upon his forehead this symbol of the redemption and consecration of Israel. So intense was the conception of the holiness of Jehovah that even **the holy things which the children of Israel** consecrated were thought of as still containing some elements of **iniquity,** and this golden signet on Aaron's forehead was a continual acknowledgment of this, and proclaimed the merciful provision by which the iniquity might be *borne away* and forgiven.

39. **The coat of fine linen—**This appears to have been an undergarment, or body coat, made of the same material as **the mitre,** namely, **of fine linen,** to be worn next to the skin, and fitted closely about the body by a **girdle of needlework.** An approximate representation of the high priest in full costume is exhibited on the next page.

40. **For Aaron's sons—**The ordinary priests are here to be understood.

them girdles, and bonnets shalt thou make for them, for glory and for beauty. **41** And thou shalt put them upon Aaron thy brother, and his sons with him; and shalt ᵛanoint them, and ʷ⁶consecrate them, and sanctify them, that they may minister unto me in the priest's office. **42** And thou shalt make them ˣlinen breeches to cover ⁷ their nakedness ; from the loins even unto the thighs they shall ⁸reach : **43** And they shall be upon Aaron, and upon his sons, when they come in unto the tabernacle of the congregation, or when they come near ʸ unto the altar to minister in the holy *place ;* that they ᶻbear not iniquity, and die : ᵃ*it shall be* a statute for ever unto him and his seed after him.

v Chap. 29. 7; 30. 30; 40. 15; Lev. 10. 7. — *w* Chap. 29, 9, etc.; Lev. chap. 8; Heb. 7. 28. — 6 Heb. *fill their hand.* — *x* Chap. 39. 28; Lev. 6. 10; 16. 4; Ezek. 44. 18.

7 Heb. *flesh of their nakedness.* —— 8 Heb. *be.* — *y* Chap. 20. 26. — *z* Lev. 5. 1, 17; 20. 19, 20; 22. 9; Num. 9. 13; 18. 22. — *a* Chap. 27. 21; Lev. 17. 7.

The foregoing elaborate description of the high priest's dress leaves little to

HIGH PRIEST IN FULL DRESS.

be said about the garments of the common priests. Their **coats,** or undergarments, were also fastened on by **girdles,** (comp. verse 39, note,) but their **bonnets,** or *caps,* were a headdress of different make from the mitre of the high priest. Keil supposes these **bonnets** to have been in the form of an inverted cup, and to have been plain white cotton caps. These articles of dress were to serve not merely the common purpose of clothing, but especially **for glory and for beauty,** and to enhance the sanctity, dignity, and importance of the priestly office. The priests were Jehovah's consecrated ministers, and should be clothed in becoming attire for such holy service.

41. **Put them upon... anoint ... consecrate ... sanctify**—The formal consecration of Aaron and his sons is more fully given in chap. xxix, and Lev. viii, where see notes.

42. **Linen breeches**—The Hebrew is from a root which means to *conceal.* They were a garment for concealing the **nakedness,** short drawers reaching **from the loins even unto the thighs,** and were, on peril of death, to be worn by Aaron and his sons whenever they ministered in the holy places. The word בַּד, here rendered **linen,** is not the same as that so rendered above, שֵׁשׁ in verses 39, 15, 8, 6, 5.

The material intended is not certainly known, but would seem, from chap. xxxix, 28, to be something much resembling the linen, or byssus, if not a peculiar texture of the same material.

CHAPTER XXIX.

CONSECRATION OF AARON AND OF HIS SONS, 1–37.

The detailed description of the priestly garments is now followed by an account of the manner in which Aaron

B. C. 1491.   CHAPTER XXIX.   531

CHAPTER XXIX.

AND this is the thing that thou shalt do unto them to hallow them, to minister unto me in the priest's office: ª Take one young bullock, and two rams without blemish, 2 And ᵇ unleavened bread, and cakes unleavened tempered with oil, and wafers unleavened anointed with oil: *of* wheaten flour shalt thou make them. 3 And thou shalt put them into one basket, and bring them in the basket, with the bullock and the two rams. 4 And Aaron and his sons thou shalt bring unto the door of the tabernacle of the congregation, ᶜ and shalt wash them with water. 5 ᵈ And thou shalt take the garments, and put upon Aaron the coat, and the robe of the ephod, and the ephod, and the breastplate, and gird him with ᵉ the curious girdle of the ephod : 6 ᶠ And thou shalt put the mitre upon his head, and put the holy crown upon the mitre. 7 Then shalt thou take the anointing ᵍ oil, and pour *it* upon his head, and anoint him. 8 And ʰ thou shalt bring his sons, and put coats upon them. 9 And thou shalt gird them with girdles, Aaron and his sons, and ⁱ put the bonnets on them: and ʲ the priest's office shall be theirs for a perpetual statute: and thou shalt ² ᵏ consecrate Aaron and his sons. 10 And thou shalt cause a bullock to be brought before the tabernacle of the congregation ; and ˡ Aaron and his sons shall put their hands upon the head of the bullock. 11 And thou shalt kill the bullock before the LORD, by the door of the tabernacle of the congregation. 12 And thou ᵐ shalt take of the blood of the bullock, and put *it* upon ⁿ the horns of the altar with thy finger, and pour all the blood beside the bottom of the altar. 13 And ᵒ thou shalt take all

---

a Lev. 8. 2.——*b* Lev. 2. 4; 6. 20–22.——*c* Chap. 40. 12; Lev. 8. 6; Heb. 10. 22.——*d* Chap. 28. 2; Lev. 8. 7.——*e* Chap. 28. 8.——*f* Lev. 8. 9.——*g* Chap. 28. 41; 30. 25; Lev. 8. 12; 10. 7; 21. 10; Num. 35. 25. *h* Lev. 8. 13.——1 Heb. *bind*.——*i* Num. 18. 7.— 2 Heb. *fill the hand of*.——*k* Chap. 28. 41; Lev. 8. 22, etc.; Heb. 7. 28.——*l* Lev. 1. 4; 8. 14.——*m* Lev. 8. 15.——*n* Chap. 27. 2; 30. 2.——*o* Lev. 3. 3.

---

and his sons were to be solemnly set apart for the priest's office. Moses, as the chosen mediator of the Sinaitic covenant, is authorized to order the entire service, offer the sacrifices of inauguration, and perform the ceremonials of consecration and induction into office. In this chapter we have the ceremonials prescribed ; in Lev. viii the record of the actual consecration. As the ritual of offerings is more fully given in Lev. i-vii, the reader is referred for that information to notes on those chapters.

1. **To hallow them**—To consecrate and set them apart **to minister unto Jehovah in the priest's office.** It was a solemn and appropriate ordination, and adapted to deepen in the minds of all the holy and responsible nature of their work in the sanctuary. **Bullock ... two rams**—The purpose of these is detailed in great fulness in verses 10–28, and the corresponding passages in Lev. viii.

2. **Bread ... cakes ... oil** — The manner of preparing the vegetable offering is described in Lev. ii, where see notes. The distinction between the **cakes** and the **wafers** was in the thinness of the latter, the **unleavened bread** being made up in two different forms.

4. **Wash them with water**—Comp. Lev. viii, 6, xvi, 4. Cleanness, purity, symbolizing holiness, was important to be observed, and is made emphatic in this ceremony.

5, 6. **The garments** — These, so fully described in the foregoing chapter, were to be formally placed upon the priest's person as a part of the ceremony of consecration. Comp. Lev. viii, 7–9. **The holy crown** — The graven plate of gold described in xxviii, 36–38 ; xxxix, 30, 31.

7. **The anointing oil**—The composition of which is described in chap. xxx, 23–25. Compare the allusion in Psa. cxxxiii, 2.

10. **Cause a bullock to be brought** —Rather, as the Revised Version, *thou shalt bring the bullock*, that is, the bullock mentioned in verse 1. This was to be a sin-offering for Aaron and his sons. Comp. Lev. iv, 3–12, notes. **Put their hands upon the head**—Thus symbolically confessing their sins and transferring them to the substituted victim. See notes on Lev. i, 4 ; iv, 4.

12. **Put it upon the horns of the altar**—Thus sanctifying the altar itself that it might in turn sanctify the offerings put thereon. **Pour ... beside the bottom of the altar**—Thus the substituted lives went out in blood under

532 EXODUS. B.C. 1491

the fat that covereth the inwards, and ³ the caul *that is* above the liver, and the two kidneys, and the fat that *is* upon them, and burn *them* upon the altar. 14 But ᵖ the flesh of the bullock, and his skin, and his dung, shalt thou burn with fire without the camp: it *is* a sin offering.
15 ᑫ Thou shalt also take one ram; and Aaron and his sons shall ʳ put their hands upon the head of the ram. 16 And thou shalt slay the ram, and thou shalt take his blood, and sprinkle *it* round about upon the altar. 17 And thou shalt cut the ram in pieces, and wash the inwards of him, and his legs, and put *them* unto his pieces, and ⁴ unto his head. 18 And thou shalt burn the whole ram upon the altar: it *is* a burnt offering unto the Lord: it *is* a ˢ sweet savour, an offering made by fire unto the Lord.
19 ᵗ And thou shalt take the other ram; and Aaron and his sons shall put their hands upon the head of the ram. 20 Then shalt thou kill the ram, and take of his blood, and put *it* upon the tip of the right ear of Aaron, and upon the tip of the right ear of his sons, and upon the thumb of their right hand, and upon the great toe of their right foot, and sprinkle the blood upon the altar round about. 21 And thou shalt take of the blood that *is* upon the altar, and of ᵘ the anointing oil, and sprinkle *it* upon Aaron, and upon his garments, and upon his sons, and upon the garments of his sons with him: and ᵛ he shall be hallowed, and his garments, and his sons, and his sons' garments with him.
22 Also thou shalt take of the ram the fat and the rump, and the fat that covereth the inwards, and the caul *above* the liver, and the two kidneys, and the fat that *is* upon them, and the right shoulder; for it *is* a ram of consecration: 23 ʷ And one loaf of bread, and one cake of oiled bread, and one wafer out of the basket of the unleavened bread that *is* before the Lord: 24 And thou shalt put all in the hands of Aaron, and in the hands of his sons; and shalt ⁵ˣ wave them *for* a wave offering before the Lord. 25 ʸ And thou shalt receive

---

3 It seemeth by anatomy, and the Hebrew doctors, to be *the midriff.* —— *p* Lev. 4. 11, 12, 21; Heb. 13. 11.——*q* Lev. 8. 18.——*r* Lev. 1. 4-9.—— 4 Or, *upon.*——*s* Gen. 8. 21.

t Verse 3; Lev. 8. 22. —— *u* Chap. 30. 25, 31; Lev. 8. 30. —— *v* Verse 1; Heb. 9. 22. —— *w* Lev. 8. 26.——5 Or, *shake to and fro.*——*x* Lev. 7. 30. ——*y* Lev. 8. 28.

---

the altar, (comp. the "souls under the altar" in Rev. vi, 9,) and made atonement for human lives. Comp. Lev. xvii, 11.

13. **Fat** . . . **caul** . . . **kidneys**—See notes on Lev. iii, 3, 4.

14. **A sin offering**—On the nature of which see notes on Lev. iv, 3–12.

15–18. **Take one ram**—While the bullock served as a sin offering, this was to be **a burnt offering unto the Lord.** As in the one case, so in the other, the symbolical putting **their hands upon the head** of the victim was performed by Aaron and his sons, but the **blood** was sprinkled **round about upon the altar,** and **the whole ram** was burned upon the altar. Lev. i, 3–13, and viii, 18–21, notes.

19. **The other ram**—This appears to have been a peace offering, not to be wholly consumed upon the altar, but portions to be given to the priests. It is called in verses 22, 26, 27, and Lev. viii, 22, "the ram of consecration," literally, *ram of the fillings,* alluding either to the filling of their hands or to the completion of their consecration. Rams were to be selected from "the herd" and were not commonly brought by individuals for peace offerings, (Lev. iii, 1;) but they were used for national peace offerings of the people, (Lev. ix, 4, 18,) and by the Nazarites (Num. vi, 14) and the princes of Israel. Num. vii, 17. So, too, this was viewed as an exceptional peace offering, fitted to an extraordinary occasion.

20, 21. **His blood** . . . **right ear** . . . **thumb** . . . **toe**—Thus this peace offering for the priests served an exceptional purpose in consecrating them to their holy office and work. Their ears were thus consecrated to listen to the commandments of Jehovah; their hands to a faithful discharge of sacred functions, and their feet to an obedient walking in the ordinances of the house of God. The sprinkling of **the blood,** and also **the anointing oil** upon the **garments** of Aaron and his sons, was a like consecration of these to the holy services of the priesthood. Also, as in the burnt offering, the blood was sprinkled about the altar.

22–25. **A wave offering before the Lord**—This was a constant ac-

B. C. 1491.   CHAPTER XXIX.   533

them of their hands, and burn *them* upon the altar for a burnt offering, for a sweet savour before the LORD : it *is* an offering made by fire unto the LORD. 26 And thou shalt take ᶻ the breast of the ram of Aaron's consecration, and wave it *for* a wave offering before the LORD : and ᵃ it shall be thy part. 27 And thou shalt sanctify ᵇ the breast of the wave offering, and the shoulder of the heave offering, which is waved, and which is heaved up, of the ram of the consecration, *even* of *that* which *is* for Aaron, and of *that* which is for his sons : 28 And it shall be Aaron's and his sons' ᶜ by a statute for ever from the children of Israel; for it *is* a heave offering : and ᵈ it shall be a heave offering from the children of Israel of the sacrifice of their peace offerings, *even* their heave offering unto the LORD.
29 And the holy garments of Aaron ᵉ shall be his sons' after him, ᶠ to be anointed therein, and to be consecrated

z Lev. 8. 29.—a Psa. 99. 6.—b Lev. 7. 31, 34; Num. 18. 11, 18; Deut. 18. 3.—c Lev. 10. 15.—d Lev. 7. 34.—e Num. 20, 26, 28.—f Num. 18. 8; 35. 25.—6 Heb. he *of his sons*.

in them. 30 And ᵍ that son that is priest in his stead shall put them on ʰ seven days, when he cometh into the tabernacle of the congregation to minister in the holy *place*.
31 And thou shalt take the ram of the consecration, and ⁱ seethe his flesh in the holy place. 32 And Aaron and his sons shall eat the flesh of the ram, and the ᵏ bread that *is* in the basket, *by* the door of the tabernacle of the congregation. 33 And ˡ they shall eat those things wherewith the atonement was made, to consecrate *and* to sanctify them : ᵐ but a stranger shall not eat *thereof*, because they *are* holy. 34 And if aught of the flesh of the consecrations, or of the bread, remain unto the morning, then ⁿ thou shalt burn the remainder with fire : it shall not be eaten, because it *is* holy. 35 And thus shalt thou do unto Aaron, and to his sons, according to all *things* which I have commanded thee : ᵒ seven days shalt thou consecrate

g Num. 20. 28.—h Lev. 8. 35; 9. 1, 8.—i Lev. 8. 31.—k Matt. 12. 4.—l Lev. 10. 14, 15, 17.—m Lev. 22. 10.—n Lev. 8. 32.—o Exod. 40. 12; Lev. 8. 33-35.

companiment of peace offerings, (comp. Lev. vii, 14, note,) and as a symbolical act was an acknowledgment of God's rule in all the world around. (See below.) Ordinarily "the wave breast and the heave shoulder" were assigned to the priests to be eaten, (verse 27, Lev. vii, 34, 35,) but on the occasion of the consecration of Aaron and his sons, after the ceremonial of waving was performed by them, Moses **received them of their hands,** and offered them, with the several portions mentioned in verse 22, and the **unleavened bread** (verse 23) **for a burnt offering, for a sweet savour before the Lord.** So that in this ceremony of induction into office the priests appropriately consecrated every thing, by a symbolical act, unto Jehovah.
26-28. **Be thy part** — As the officiating minister on this extraordinary occasion, Moses was to receive the **breast of the ram of Aaron's consecration.** And here it is enunciated as **a statute for ever,** that **the breast of the wave offering and the shoulder of the heave offering** shall belong to the priests as their lawful portion of the peace offerings. These were evidently regarded as choice portions of the animal. The distinction between the *wave offering* (תְּנוּפָה) and the *heave offering* (תְּרוּמָה) is indicated by the Hebrew names, the former signifying horizontal motion to and fro, the latter vertical motion, perpendicular to the horizon. These constituted a double form of symbolical consecration, in adoration to Him who rules in all and over all.
29-30. **The holy garments**—Those described in chap. xxviii, 2, *ff.* These were to be transmitted to Aaron's **sons after him.** When Aaron died in Mt. Hor they were put upon his son Eleazar. Num. xx, 28. **Seven days** were to be devoted to the various ceremonies of consecrating a high priest, as in the original consecration of Aaron. Verse 35. See on Lev. viii, 35. These seven days must have included one sabbath, and the rabbins say: "Great is the sabbath day, for the high priest entered not upon his duties, after his anointing, until one sabbath day had passed over him."
31-37. **Eat the flesh of the ram** —The ceremony of consecration, continuing for **seven days,** afforded opportunity for divers acts of worship,

them. **36** And thou shalt ᵖ offer every day a bullock *for* a sin offering for atonement: and thou shalt cleanse the altar, when thou hast made an atonement for it, ᑫ and thou shalt anoint it, to sanctify it. **37** Seven days thou shalt make an atonement for the altar, and sanctify it; ʳ and it shall be an altar most holy: ˢ whatsoever toucheth the altar shall be holy.
38 Now this *is that* which thou shalt offer upon the altar; ᵗ two lambs of the first year ᵘ day by day continually. **39** The one lamb thou shalt offer ᵛ in the morning; and the other lamb thou shalt offer at even: **40** And with the one lamb a tenth deal of flour mingled with the fourth part of a hin of beaten oil; and the fourth part of a hin of wine *for* a drink offering. **41** And the other lamb thou shalt ʷ offer at even, and shalt do thereto according to the meat offering of the morning, and according to the drink offering thereof, for a sweet savour, an offering made by fire unto the LORD. **42** *This shall be* ˣ a continual burnt offering throughout your generations *at* the door of the tabernacle of the congregation before the LORD, ʸ where I will meet you, to speak there unto thee. **43** And there I will meet with the children of Israel, and ᶻ *the tabernacle* ᵃ shall be sanctified by my glory. **44** And I will sanctify the tabernacle of the con-

---

p Hebrews 10. 11.——*q* Chapter 30. 26, 28, 29; 40. 10.——*r* Chapter 40. 10.——*s* Chapter 30. 29; Matthew 23. 19.——*t* Numbers 28. 3; 1 Chronicles 16. 40; 2 Chronicles 2. 4; 13. 11; 31. 3; Ezra 3. 3. ——*u* See Daniel 9. 27; 12. 11.——*v* 2 Kings 16. 15; Ezekiel 46. 13-15.

w 1 Kings 18. 29, 36; 2 Kings 16. 15; Ezra 9. 4, 5; Psa. 141. 2; Dan. 9. 21.——*x* Verse 38; chap. 30. 8; Num. 28. 6; Dan. 8. 11-13.——*y* Chap. 25. 22; 30. 6, 36; Num. 17. 4.——7 Or, Israel.—— *z* Chap. 40. 34; 1 Kings 8. 11; 2 Chron. 5. 14; 7. 1-3; Ezek. 43. 5; Hag. 2. 7, 9; Mal. 3. 1.

---

and for feasting upon the flesh of the peace offerings. This latter the priests were to do at **the door of the tabernacle;** and of the portion dedicated to them, and regarded therefore as specially **holy,** no **stranger,** no one outside the priestly family, was permitted to **eat.** No portions either **of the flesh of the consecrations or of the bread** which remained over unto the next day after they had been consecrated, were permitted to **be eaten,** but must all be burned. So, too, **the altar** of burnt offerings was to be *cleansed, anointed, and sanctified* on each of the **seven days,** probably by such forms of consecration as are mentioned in verses 12 and 20.

THE CONTINUAL BURNT OFFERING, 38–46.

38. Two lambs...day by day continually — In immediate connexion with the consecration of the altar, the main purpose for which it was established is now indicated, namely, the offering of continual sacrifices, meat offerings and drink offerings.

39. Morning...even—As regularly as the sun was wont to rise and set, so regularly were these sacrifices to be offered unto the Lord. **Even** is the same expression in Hebrew as **between the two evenings** in the margin of chap. xii, 6, where see note.

40. A tenth deal of flour—The tenth part of an ephah is probably meant, which was an omer. See xvi, 36, note. Compare Num. v, 15. Supposed to have been about three pounds in weight and not far from three quarts in measure. The **hin** was a liquid measure containing a little more than a gallon. The flour mingled with the beaten oil (xxvii, 20) constituted the meat offering, on which see notes at Lev. ii, and the wine is here expressly called **a drink offering.** This was a form of worship old as the days of the patriarchs, (see on Gen. xxxv, 14,) and consisted in a devotional pouring out the wine as an oblation before or upon the altar of burnt offerings. It was not to be poured out on the altar of incense, (xxx, 9.)

43. There I will meet — Here is enunciated the main thought that underlies all the symbolism of the tabernacle and its holy services. It was the visible sanctuary, where Jehovah signified the conditions on which it was possible for him to dwell with man, and permit man to dwell with him. The sanctification of Israel was to be secured through these consecrated forms of mediation, and was the highest ideal revealed amid the symbols. For what is it that **shall be sanctified by my glory?** Not the *tabernacle* or *tent,* as both the Authorized

B. C. 1491. CHAPTER XXIX. 535

gregation, and the altar: I will ^a sanctify also both Aaron and his sons, to minister to me in the priest's office.

45 And ^b I will dwell among the children of Israel, and will be their God.

46 And they shall know that ^c I am the LORD their God, that brought them forth out of the land of Egypt, that I may dwell among them: I am the LORD their God.

CHAPTER XXX.

AND thou shalt make ^a an altar ^b to burn incense upon: of shittim wood shalt thou make it. **2** A cubit shall be the length thereof, and a cubit the breadth thereof; foursquare shall it be: and two cubits shall be the height thereof: the horns thereof shall be of the same. **3** And thou shalt overlay it with pure gold, the ¹ top thereof, and the ² sides thereof round about, and the horns thereof; and thou shalt make unto it a crown of gold round about. **4** And two golden rings shalt thou make to it under the crown of it, by the two ³ corners thereof, upon the two sides of it shalt thou make it; and they shall be for places for the staves to bear it withal. **5** And thou shalt make the staves of shittim wood, and overlay them with gold. **6** And thou shalt put it before the vail that is by the ark of the testimony, before the ^c mercy seat that is over the testimony, where I will meet

---

a Lev. 21. 15; 22. 9, 16.—*b* Exod. 25. 8; Lev. 26. 12; Zech. 2. 10; John 14. 17, 23; 2 Cor. 6. 16; Rev. 21. 3.—*c* Chap. 20. 2.

a Chap. 37. 25; 40. 5.—*b* See verses 7, 8, 10; Lev. 4. 7, 18; Rev. 8. 3.—1 Heb. *roof.*—2 Heb. *walls.*—3 Heb. *ribs.*—*c* Chap. 25. 21, 22.

Version and the Revised Version supply in the text, nor the altar, as others have supposed; for both these are expressly named in the next verse as a distinct conception; but **the children of Israel** just mentioned, here conceived as a unit, and hence the use of the verb in the singular number. Israel is to be sanctified by meeting with Jehovah, and thus entering into the divine glory by the means ordained for that very end.

CHAPTER XXX.

THE ALTAR OF INCENSE, 1–10.

1. An altar to burn incense upon —This was to be one of the pieces of furniture belonging to the holy place, (verse 6,) and the description of it would have been appropriate in connexion with the table and the candlestick, (xxv, 23–37,) but seems to have been reserved for this place in order to stand in connexion with the consecration and sacrificial ministry of the priests. **Shittim wood** — The same as that employed for the table (xxv, 23) and the ark, (xxv, 10,) the boards of the sanctuary, (xxvi, 15,) and the framework of the altar of burnt offering, (xxvii, 1.)

2–5. Horns...rings...staves—In these respects it was fashioned after the manner of the greater altar in the court, and also of some portions of the ark, (xxv, 12–15.) The **crown of gold round about** is to be understood of a rim or moulding, as that of the ark. See note on xxv, 11. The probable form of this altar is exhibited in the annexed cut.

ALTAR OF INCENSE.

6. Put it before the vail—Thus it seems to have had a more direct relation to the most holy place than either the table of showbread or the golden candlestick. The offering of incense was symbolical of the prayers of saints, (Psa. cxli, 2, Rev. viii, 3, 4,) and the people were accustomed to pray without when the priest was offering the incense. Luke i, 10. The priest, standing before this altar of incense, would have the ark directly in front of him,

536 EXODUS. B. C. 1491.

with thee. **7** And Aaron shall burn thereon ⁴ ᵈ sweet incense every morning: when ᵉ he dresseth the lamps, he shall burn incense upon it. **8** And when Aaron ⁵ ⁶ lighteth the lamps ⁷ at even, he shall burn incense upon it, a perpetual incense before the LORD throughout your generations. **9** Ye shall offer no ᶠ strange incense thereon, nor burnt sacrifice, nor meat offering; neither shall ye pour drink offering thereon. **10** And ᵍAaron shall make an atonement upon the horns of it once in a year with the blood of the sin offering of atonements; once in the year shall he make atonement upon it throughout your generations: it *is* most holy unto the LORD.

11 And the LORD spake unto Moses, saying, **12** ʰ When thou takest the sum of the children of Israel after ᵍ their number, then shall they give every man ⁱ a ransom for his soul unto the LORD, when thou numberest them; that there be no ᵏ plague among them, when *thou* numberest them. **13** ˡ This they shall give, every one that passeth among them that are numbered, half a shekel after the shekel of the sanctuary: (ᵐa shekel *is* twenty gerahs:) ⁿa half shekel *shall be* the offering of the LORD. **14** Every

---

4 Heb. *incense of spices.*—*d* Verse 34; 1 Sam. 2. 28; 1 Chron. 23. 13; Luke 1. 9. — *e* Chap. 27. 21.—5 Or, *setteth up.*—6 Heb. *causeth to ascend.* —7 Heb. *between the two evens,* chap. 12. 6.—*f* Lev. 10. 1.—*g* Lev. 16. 18; 23. 27.— *h* Chap. 38. 25; Num. 1. 2, 5; 26. 2; 2 Sam. 24. 2.

8 Heb. *them that are to be numbered.* — *i* See Num. 31. 50; Job 33. 24; 36. 18; Psa. 49. 7; Matt. 20. 28; Mark 10. 45; 1 Tim. 2. 6; 1 Pet. 1. 18, 19. — *k* 2 Sam. 24. 15. — *l* Matt. 17. 24. — *m* Lev. 27. 25; Num. 3. 47; Ezek. 45. 12. — *n* Chap. 38. 26.

---

within the vail, the table of showbread at his right, and the candlestick at his left.

7, 8. **Perpetual incense**—Like the continual burnt offering, this burning of *incense of spices* was to be repeated **every morning,** and also **at even,** or *between the two evenings.* See on xxix, 39. It was to correspond with the dressing and lighting of **the lamps.** The composition of the incense is described in verses 34–38.

9. **Strange incense** — Offered with fire other than that which God ordained, on account of which impiety the two elder sons of Aaron were destroyed. Lev. x. 1. This altar of incense being set apart for a special use, no **burnt sacrifice, nor meat offering,** nor **drink offering,** was to be offered thereon. The offerings made on the great altar, in the court without, effected reconciliation with Jehovah; the incense offering represented a closer approach to the divine glory, based upon previous reconciliation; and hence a bringing of the same offerings within, before the vail, as those offered without, would have been a confusion of distinct symbolical services.

10. **Once in the year shall he make atonement**—The absolute holiness of Jehovah was further enhanced in the minds of the people by the thought that altars and holy places would after a time be liable to contract some defilement, and hence the solemn purifications of all **once in the year,** on the great day of atonement. See on Lev. xvi, where the ceremonies of this day are given in detail.

RANSOM OF SOULS, 11–16.

The fundamental idea in this ransoming of souls by a tax of atonement money was, that thereby every Israelite of twenty-five years old and upward would be obligated to contribute somewhat to the erection of the sanctuary. With this exception all the offerings for the tabernacle were given as willing contributions of the heart, (xxv, 2.) The silver thus contributed was used for the sockets of the sanctuary, (xxxviii, 27.)

12. **That there be no plague**—A failure to contribute this poll tax exposed to the judgment of God. Such failure would imply a serious want of interest in the worship of Israel, if not open contempt.

13. **Half a shekel** — No large amount; perhaps about fifty cents of our currency. The exact weight of the silver shekel is no longer known. **The shekel of the sanctuary** is commonly supposed to have been larger and heavier than the common shekel. *Gerah* is the Hebrew name of a *bean* or *berry,* and like our word *grain* came to be used for a small weight. **Offering**—תְּרוּמָה, *heave offering.* See xxix, 27.

one that passeth among them that are numbered, from twenty years old and above, shall give an offering unto the LORD. **15** The °rich shall not 9give more, and the poor shall not ¹⁰give less, than half a shekel, when *they* give an offering unto the LORD, to make an ᵖatonement for your souls. **16** And thou shalt take the atonement money of the children of Israel, and ᵠshalt appoint it for the service of the tabernacle of the congregation; that it may be ʳa memorial unto the children of Israel before the LORD, to make an atonement for your souls.

17 And the LORD spake unto Moses, saying, **18** ˢThou shalt also make a laver *of* brass, and his foot *also of* brass,

o Job 34. 19; Prov. 22. 2; Eph. 6. 9; Col. 3. 25.—9 Heb. *multiply.*—10 Heb. *diminish.*—p Verse 12—q Chap. 38. 25.—r Num. 16. 40.—s Chap. 38. 8; 1 Kings 7. 38.

to wash *withal:* and thou shalt ᵗput it between the tabernacle of the congregation and the altar, and thou shalt put water therein. **19** For Aaron and his sons ᵘshall wash their hands and their feet thereat. **20** When they go into the tabernacle of the congregation, they shall wash with water, that they die not; or when they come near to the altar to minister, to burn offering made by fire unto the LORD: **21** So they shall wash their hands and their feet, that they die not: and ᵛit shall be a statute forever to them, *even* to him and to his seed throughout their generations.

22 Moreover the LORD spake unto Moses, saying, **23** Take thou also unto thee ʷprincipal spices, of pure ˣmyrrh

t Chap. 40. 7, 30. — u Chap. 40. 31, 32; Psa. 26. 6; Isa. 52. 11; John 13. 10; Heb. 10. 22. — v Chap. 28. 43. — w Cant. 4. 14; Ezek. 27. 22. — x Psa. 45. 8; Prov. 7. 17.

15. The rich shall not give more—This apportioning the same amount to rich and poor showed that in the meeting of Jehovah at the sanctuary all stood upon the same level. It is well to have some forms of offering which will impress this lesson. In making an **atonement for souls** the rich have no advantage over the poor.

16. A memorial—A constant reminder of their being covered and shielded from plague by complying with this command.

THE LAVER, 17–21.

18. Laver of brass—According to chapter xxxviii, 8, it was made of the mirrors of the women who were wont to assemble at the entrance of the tabernacle. The purpose of this laver was mainly for the priests to wash

LAVER.

LAVER.

themselves when they entered upon their holy work; also for the washing of inwards and legs of victims. Lev. i, 9. Its form is not described, but it rested upon a foot or pedestal, and the adjoining cuts represent two possible forms according to which it may have been constructed. For the temple there was a brazen sea resting upon twelve oxen, and also ten lavers resting upon as many bases. See notes and cuts at 1 Kings vii, 23–39. The laver was to be placed **between the tabernacle . . . and the altar,** probably as indicated in the cut of the tabernacle and court on page 522.

THE ANOINTING OIL, 22, 23.

23, 24. Principal spices—That is, spices of the best quality and highest

five hundred *shekels*, and of sweet cinnamon half so much, *even* two hundred

and fifty *shekels*, and of sweet ʸcalamus two hundred and fifty *shekels*, **24** And

y Cant. 4. 14; Jer. 6. 20.

value. **Pure myrrh**—Rather, as Revised Version, *flowing myrrh*. This was a sort of gum which exudes spontaneously from the bark of a tree that is found in Eastern Africa and Arabia. The tree somewhat resembles a thorn tree, and is described in Johnson's *Travels in Abyssinia* as "a low, thorny, ragged-looking tree, with bright green trifoliate leaves. The gum exudes from cracks in the bark of the trunk near the root, and flows freely upon the stones immediately underneath. Artificially it is obtained by bruises made with stones." That which is obtained by bruising the tree is of inferior quality to that which flows forth of itself.

CINNAMON.

ing off the outer bark, and securing the interior part of it by an instrument fitted to the purpose. The best cinnamon is said to be obtained from the smaller shoots and twigs of the tree. **Sweet calamus**—Or, *spicy cane*, an aromatic reed that grows in various parts of the East, especially in India, Arabia, and Egypt, and consists of a knotty stalk enclosing a soft pith, which upon being cut and dried affords a rich perfume.

MYRRH.

Sweet cinnamon — Or, *spicy cinnamon*. This was probably an article of commerce brought from India and Ceylon by Midianite or other Arabian merchants. It consists of the inner rind of a tree that belongs to the laurel family, and is obtained by peel-

CALAMUS.

Cassia — According to Gesenius, with whom most authorities agree, "a species of aromatic bark resembling cinnamon, but less fragrant and less valuable, so called from its rolls being *split*, (קדד.)" The word rendered *cassia* in Psa. xlv, 8 is different, (קציעה,) but is believed to denote a very similar substance. It will be noticed that the **myrrh** and the **cassia** were to be just double the amount of the **cinnamon** and the **sweet calamus**, which were compounded together with **a hin of** olive oil. Probably the essences of the spices were first extracted, and then mingled with the oil.

B. C. 1491.   CHAPTER XXX.   539

of ᵃ cassia five hundred *shekels*, after the shekel of the sanctuary, and of oil olive a ᵇ hin: **25** And thou shalt make it an oil of holy ointment, an ointment compound after the art of the ¹¹ apothecary: it shall be ᵇ a holy anointing oil. **26** ᶜ And thou shalt anoint the tabernacle of the congregation therewith, and the ark of the testimony, **27** And the table and all his vessels, and the candlestick and his vessels, and the altar of incense, **28** And the altar of burnt offering with all his vessels, and the laver and his foot. **29** And thou shalt sanctify them, that they may be most holy: ᵈ whatsoever toucheth them shall be holy. **30** ᵉ And thou shalt anoint Aaron and his sons, and consecrate them, that *they* may minister unto me in the priest's office. **31** And thou shalt speak unto the children of Israel, saying, This shall be a holy anointing oil unto me throughout your generations. **32** Upon man's flesh shall it not be poured, neither shall ye make *any other* like it, after the composition of it: ᶠ it *is* holy, *and* it shall be holy unto you. **33** ᵍ Whosoever compoundeth *any* like it, or whosoever putteth *any* of it upon a stranger, ʰ shall even be cut off from his people.

34 And the LORD said unto Moses, ⁱ Take unto thee sweet spices, stacte,

---
ᵃ Psa. 45. 8.——a Chap. 29. 40.——11 Or, *perfumer*.——b Chap. 37. 29; Num. 35. 25; Psa. 89. 20; 133. 2.——c Chap. 40. 9; Lev. 8. 10; Num. 7. 1.

d Chap. 29. 37.——e Chap. 29. 7, etc.; Lev. 8. 12, 30.——f Vers. 25, 37.——g Ver. 38.——h Gen. 17. 14; chap. 12. 15; Lev. 7. 20, 21.——i Chap. 25. 6; 37. 29.
---

25. Compound after the art of the apothecary—In the times after the exile some of the priest's sons were intrusted with the preparation of the ointment of spices. 1 Chron. ix, 30. As it was made the special care of the high priest to guard it, (Num. iv, 16,) we may naturally suppose that he was charged with the duty of either compounding it himself or employing some competent person to assist him. The original preparation of it would seem, from chap. xxxvii, 29, to have been intrusted to Bezaleel, the architect. Being of a special character, and known as **an oil of holy ointment, or a holy anointing oil**, it might not be used for ordinary purposes, such as anointing one's flesh, (ver. 32,) or using it on a foreigner, (verse 33,) and any attempt to make any other oil like it was strictly forbidden. The ceremony of anointing with oil denoted the setting apart and consecrating to a holy purpose, and accordingly this holy ointment was to be used solely for such consecration of the priests and the tabernacle and its sacred vessels. Verses 26-30.

COMPOUNDING OF INCENSE, 34-38.

34. Stacte—This is the name used by the Greek and Latin version as representing the Hebrew נָטָף, *nataph*, which denotes something that drops, and is commonly held to be the gum of

STACTE.

and onycha, and galbanum; *these* sweet spices with pure frankincense: of each shall there be a like *weight:* **35** And thou shalt make it a perfume, a confection ᵏ after the art of the apothecary, ¹² tempered together, pure *and* holy: **36** And thou shalt beat *some* of it very small, and put of it before the testimony in the tabernacle of the congregation, ˡ where I will meet with thee: ᵐ it shall be unto you most holy. **37** And *as for* the perfume which thou shalt make, ⁿ ye shall not make to yourselves according to the composition thereof: it shall be unto thee holy for the LORD. **38** °Whosoever shall make like unto that, to smell thereto, shall even be cut off from his people.

CHAPTER XXXI.

AND the LORD spake unto Moses, saying, **2** ᵃ See, I have called by

k Verse 25. —— 12 Heb. *salted*, Lev. 2. 13.—— *l* Chap. 29. 42; Lev. 16. 2. —— *m* Verse 32; chap. 29. 37; Lev. 2. 3. —— *n* Verse 32. —— *o* Verse 33. —— *a* Chap. 35. 30; 36. 1.

the storax tree, which is found in Syria, and grows to the height of fifteen feet or more. The gum which exudes from its bark has a fragrant odour, and is mentioned by Pliny as being burned as a perfume in his time. **Onycha**—This word occurs nowhere else in the Hebrew Scriptures. Pliny mentions onyx as a shell which was used in the composition of perfume, and most versions and interpreters have understood it as the winged strombus, a species of mollusk which is said to abound in the Red Sea. The fact, however, that all the other ingredients of this composition were vegetable should incline us rather to think of it as the exudation of some plant or tree.

FRANKINCENSE.

Galbanum is another word not elsewhere found in the Old Testament, but seems to be the same as the Greek χαλβάνη, which is found in the Septuagint of this verse, and is the name of the gum of a plant which is found in Africa, Syria, Persia, and India. The *Opoidia Galbanifera* has been adopted by the Dublin College in their Pharmacopœia as that which yields the galbanum. **Frankincense**, so often referred to in the Scriptures as a kind of precious perfume, is here mentioned for the first time. It was the odoriferous resin of some kind of plant or tree of which the ancient writers do not seem to have possessed any specific knowledge. That it was of a white colour may be inferred from its Hebrew name, לְבוֹנָה, and according to Isa. lx, 6, and Jer. vi, 20, it was found in Sheba. Modern botanists identify it with the *Boswellia serrata*, which grows luxuriantly in the mountainous parts of India.

35. Art of the apothecary—See on verse 25. **Tempered together**—Rather, *seasoned with salt*, after the manner of meat offerings. See on Lev. ii, 13.

CHAPTER XXXI.
BEZALEEL AND AHOLIAB, 1–11.

2. I have called by name—The artistic construction of the house of

B. C. 1491. CHAPTER XXXI. 541

name Bezaleel the ᵇ son of Uri, the son of Hur, of the tribe of Judah: **3** And I have ᶜ filled him with the spirit of God, in wisdom, and in understanding, and in knowledge, and in all manner of workmanship, **4** To devise cunning works, to work in gold, and in silver, and in brass, **5** And in cutting of stones, to set *them*, and in carving of timber, to work in all manner of workmanship. **6** And I, behold, I have given with him ᵈ Aholiab, the son of Ahisamach, of the tribe of Dan: and in the hearts of all that are ᵉ wise hearted I have put wisdom, that they may make all that I have commanded thee; **7** ᶠThe tabernacle of the congregation, and ᵍ the ark of the testimony, and ʰ the mercy seat that *is* thereupon, and all the ¹ furniture of the tabernacle, **8** And ⁱ the table and his furniture, and ᵏ the pure candlestick with all his furniture, and the altar of incense, **9** And ˡ the altar of burnt offering with all his furniture, and ᵐ the laver and his foot, **10** And ⁿ the clothes of service, and the holy garments for Aaron the priest, and the garments of his sons, to minister in the priest's office, **11** ° And the anointing oil, and ᵖ sweet incense for the holy *place:* according to all that I have commanded thee shall they do.

---

b 1 Chron. 2. 20.——*c* Chap. 35. 31; 1 Kings 7. 14.——*d* Chap. 35. 34. —— *e* Chap. 28. 3; 35. 10, 35; 36. 1.——*f* Chap. 36. 8.——*g* Chap. 37. 1.——*h* Chap. 37. 6.——1 Heb. *vessels*. *i* Chap. 37. 10. —— *k* Chap. 37. 17. —— *l* Chap. 38. 1. —— *m* Chap. 38. 8. —— *n* Chap. 39. 1, 41; Num. 4. 5, 6, etc.——*o* Chap. 30. 25, 31; 37. 29.—— *p* Chap. 30. 34; 37. 29.

God is no ordinary work, and after its plan and dimensions and the most minute details of its furniture and materials had been given to Moses, Jehovah designated a chosen architect, as **called** and qualified (verse 3) for carrying out the plans and specifications. This distinguished workman was **Bezaleel the son of Uri, the son of Hur, of the tribe of Judah.** Aaron and Hur had stayed up the hands of Moses during the conflict with Amalek, (xvii, 10-13,) and now the grandson of that Hur is made the chief assistant of Moses in the construction of the tabernacle. May not the piety of the grandfather have had something to do with the mechanical ability of the grandson?

3. Filled him with the spirit of God—There is no need of explaining this as equivalent merely to the phrase "a divine spirit," or translating "a spirit of God." The Holy Spirit of God is intended, which quickened all Bezaleel's mental faculties, and enriched him with such a degree of **wisdom, understanding,** and **knowledge** that he was recognized as divinely gifted with the required qualifications for **all manner of workmanship** which the construction and erection of the tabernacle called for.

4, 5. To devise cunning works—To plan and execute designs; to think out and elaborate such works of art in metal, stone, and wood, and other material, as would be required in the sanctuary. or in connexion with its services.

VOL. I.—35

6. **Aholiab**—The grandson of Hur was not to be alone in this responsible work of the sanctuary. A representative **of the tribe of Dan** was to be associated with him in the labour and responsibility. From chap. xxxv, 35, and xxxviii, 23, we infer that Aholiab had more particular charge of the textile fabrics, and the weaving and embroidering, but Bezaleel had superintendency of all. With these were associated also others who were **wise hearted,** that is, skilled to perform similar artistic work; for many workmen would be needed for the preparation of all that was shown to Moses in the mount. With this account of the call and qualifications of the workmen is joined a brief recapitulation (verses 7–11) of the several articles which have been described in the foregoing chapters.

10. **Clothes of service**—These are perhaps best understood of the ministerial official robes of the high priest, described in xxviii, 6–38, as distinguished from "the coat of fine linen," (xxviii, 39,) and the other garments worn in common by Aaron and his sons, (xxviii, 40–43.) Others understand by these **clothes of service** the inner curtains of the tabernacle, or the cloth wraps in which the vessels of the tabernacle were bound up when they were carried from place to place in the march to Canaan. The passage might also be translated, "And the clothes of service, *even* the holy garments for Aaron the priest, and the garments of

O. T.

12 And the LORD spake unto Moses, saying, **13** Speak thou also unto the children of Israel, saying, ⁿVerily my sabbaths ye shall keep: for it *is* a sign between me and you throughout your generations; that *ye* may know that I *am* the LORD that doth sanctify you. **14** ʳYe shall keep the sabbath therefore; for it *is* holy unto you. Every one that defileth it shall surely be put to death: for ˢwhosoever doeth *any* work therein, that soul shall be cut off from among his people. **15** ᵗSix days may work be done; but in the ᵘseventh *is* the sabbath of rest, ²holy to the LORD: whosoever doeth *any* work in the sabbath day, he shall surely be put to death. **16** Wherefore the children of Israel shall keep the sabbath, to observe the sabbath throughout their generations, *for* a perpetual covenant. **17** It *is* ᵛa sign between me and the children of Israel for ever: for ʷ*in* six days the LORD made heaven and earth, and on the seventh day he rested, and was refreshed.

18 And he gave unto Moses, when he

---

q Lev. 19. 3, 30; 26. 2; Ezek. 20. 12, 20; 44. 24. —— *r* Chap. 20. 8; Deut. 5. 12; Ezek. 20. 12. —— *s* Chap. 35. 2; Num. 15. 35.

t Chap. 20. 9.——*u* Gen. 2. 2; chap. 16. 23; 20. 10.——2 Heb. *holiness*.——*v* Verse 13; Ezek. 20. 12, 20.——*w* Gen. 1. 31; 2. 2.

---

his sons;" thus making the **clothes of service** include **the holy garments** both of Aaron and his sons.

THE SABBATH LAW, 12–17.

13. My sabbaths ye shall keep—How repeatedly the sanctity of the sabbath day is affirmed! In chap. xx, 8–11, (where see notes,) we have it formally enjoined in the decalogue. In chap. xxiii, 12, it is again set forth in connexion with the law of the sabbatic year, and so again and again throughout the Pentateuch. In chap. xxxv, 2, 3, it introduces the account of the preparations for building the tabernacle, as if resuming the narrative broken off at the conclusion of this chapter to introduce the account of the idolatry of the people at Sinai. Hence it has been supposed that a special reason for the emphasizing of the sabbath law in this connexion was to deter the people from labour on the tabernacle on that day, which in their zeal to complete the sanctuary they might have presumed to do, even in violation of the former commandment. The expression **my sabbaths** gives emphasis to the thought that the weekly sabbath was a peculiar treasure of Jehovah. **It is a sign**—Old as the creation, (comp. verse 17 and Gen. ii, 2, 3, and note on xx, 11,) and a constant reminder that God and his people may enjoy a common rest.

14. Surely be put to death—It is to be noted that all the commandments of the first table have the death penalty attached to their violation, and so it is taught that the wilful breaking of any of these laws was to be treated as a capital crime. None of them are so regarded under the Gospel. Idolatry, image - worship, blasphemy, sabbath-breaking, and dishonouring of parents are nowhere under a Christian civilization punishable with death. Has God therefore changed? No, but man has changed, and under the discipline of a dispensation "written and engraven in stones," (2 Cor. iii, 7,) "the ministration of death" has accomplished its work, and elevated the moral sense of man to a higher plane. With the higher and clearer revelations of divine truth the lower forms of the ancient moral discipline have been superseded. So, too, the avenger of blood is no longer tolerated, and the *lex talionis* is abolished by the light and methods of a higher civilization. But it would be in the highest degree absurd to argue, that because the ancient penalty of the sabbath law is no more in force, therefore the sabbath itself is no longer binding. Equally absurd is the notion of some modern critics that, because the sabbath law is variously repeated in the Pentateuch, with reasons and penalties in one place which are not found in another, therefore, these laws are of diverse authorship, and contradictory. A legislature may modify, change, or supplement its own action in the progress of a single session; much more may we suppose that the legislation through Moses would have received many supplements under his own immediate direction. Thus every new association or event which could be made to enhance in the people's minds the sanctity and worth of the

B. C. 1491. CHAPTER XXXI. 543

had made an end of communing with him upon mount Sinai, ˣ two tables of testimony, tables of stone, written with the finger of God.

ᵡ Chap.24.12; 32.15,16; 34.28,29; Deut.4.13; 5.22;

sabbath would and should have been utilized for such a worthy end.

THE TWO TABLES, 18.

18. **Two tables of testimony**—These were soon broken, (xxxii, 19,) and others were subsequently hewn, (xxxiv, 1–4.) Their size must have been smaller than the dimensions of the ark in which they were deposited, and sufficiently small and light for Moses to carry in his hand. They were doubtless some two or three inches in thickness, to prevent their being easily broken; but they need not have been one foot square to contain all the words of the decalogue. See, further, note on xxxii, 15. The fact that they were **written with the finger of God** is no greater a miracle than that they should have been spoken "out of the midst of the fire." Deut. iv, 12. But the ministry of angels may be assumed as one of the means by which these tables, as well as the utterance of the words, were produced. See note on xx, 1. The expression **finger of God** is simply an anthropomorphic way of designating the divine agency in the preparation of the tables, and is not designed to teach that the infinite Being has a physical "body or parts."

(2.) The Covenant Broken and Renewed. Chaps. XXXII—XXXIV.

CHAPTER XXXII.
INTRODUCTORY.

There is nothing in the range of Hebrew literature that serves more impressively than this chapter to show in its darkest aspects the hardness of the people's hearts, and the necessity of a most severe legislation to secure a cultivation of the moral sense of Israel. It seems almost incredible that, under the shadow of Sinai, and so soon after all the terrible displays of God's presence and power recorded in chap. xx,

CHAPTER XXXII.

AND when the people saw that Moses ᵃ delayed to come down out of the mount, the people gathered themselves

9. 10, 11; 2 Cor. 3. 3.—ᵃ Chap. 24. 18; Deut. 9. 9.

this people could have so wickedly turned to the worship of Jehovah in the image of a golden calf. "The people had to a great extent lost the patriarchal faith, and were but imperfectly instructed in the reality of a personal, unseen God. Being disappointed at the long absence of Moses, they seem to have imagined that he had deluded them, and had probably been destroyed amidst the thunders of the mountain. They accordingly gave way to their superstitious fears, and fell back on that form of idolatry that was most familiar to them. See on verse 4. The narrative of the circumstances is more briefly given by Moses at a later period in one of his addresses to the people. Deut. ix, 8–21, 25–29; x, 1–5, 8–11. It is worthy of remark that Josephus, in his very characteristic chapter on the giving of the law, (*Ant.*, iii, 5,) says nothing whatever of this act of apostasy, though he relates that Moses twice ascended the mountain, and renews his own profession that he is faithfully following the authority of the Holy Scriptures. Philo speaks of the calf as an imitation of the idolatry of Egypt, but he takes no notice of Aaron's share in the sin."— *Speaker's Commentary.*

WORSHIP OF THE GOLDEN CALF, 1–6.

1. **Moses delayed to come down** —Literally, *shamed to come down,* that is, put to shame those who were waiting for him. This delay was provided for and suggested in Moses's charge to the elders, (xxiv, 14,) but Israel's faith was not sufficient for the test. **Up, make us gods**—The language suggests the excitement and persistency of a mob. Probably a better translation would be, *Up, make us a god.* The manner in which Aaron complied with their demand shows that the people desired a visible image of God. The religious nature of man, uneducated into a high spiritual conception of God, has always clamoured for some visible sign or rep-

EXODUS. B.C. 1491.

together unto Aaron, and said unto him, *b* Up, make us gods, which shall *c* go before us; for *as for* this Moses, the man that brought us up out of the land of Egypt, we wot not what is become of him. **2** And Aaron said unto them, Break off the *d* golden earrings, which *are* in the ears of your wives, of your sons, and of your daughters, and bring *them* unto me. **3** And all the people brake off the golden earrings which *were* in their ears, and brought *them* unto Aaron. **4** *e* And he received *them* at their hand, and fashioned it with a graving tool, after he had made it a molten calf: and they said, These *be* thy gods,

b Acts 7. 40. — *c* Chap. 13. 21. — *d* Judg. 8. 24–27. — *e* Chap. 20. 23; Deut. 9. 16; Judg. 17. 3, 4; 1 Kings 12. 28; Neh. 9. 18; Psa. 106. 19; Isa. 46. 6; Acts 7. 41; Rom. 1. 23.

resentation of the Deity. **This Moses, the man that brought us**—This manner of speech implies not only impatience, but also a measure of indignation. **We wot not**—We know not. Not improbably they began to think that Moses had perished in the fires which they had seen on the top of the mountain, (xxiv. 17.)

2. **Break off the golden earrings**— A strong expression, as if implying that the act involved some measure of violence, or, at least, an effort and sacrifice on their part. The prevailing view has been that Aaron, anxious to dissuade the people from their purpose, proposed this great sacrifice on their part in hope that they would thereupon withdraw their demand upon him to make them a god. This is not an improbable view, and is favoured by Aaron's apology before Moses in verses 22–24. But the facts here recorded, as well as Num. xii, exhibit the moral weakness of Aaron. He did well as Moses's spokesman, (iv, 14–16,) but sadly lacked the sterling qualities of a great spiritual leader. Specimens of ancient **earrings** are shown in the annexed cut.

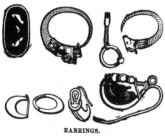

EARRINGS.

3. **All the people brake off** — Kurtz observes that Aaron had "counted upon the vanity of the women and youth, and their love for golden ornaments, and he hoped that in this way he would excite such opposition in the community itself as would suffice to save him from having to offer a resistance which appeared to be dangerous. But he had entirely miscalculated. He knew but the surface of the human heart; the depths of its natural disposition were beyond his reach. All the people cheerfully broke off the golden ornaments from their ears, for they were about to accomplish an act of pure selfwill; and in that case there is no sacrifice which the human heart is not ready to make."

4. **Fashioned it with a graving tool**—This is the most natural import of the unpointed Hebrew text, but seems hardly in harmony with the next statement, which is not correctly translated **after he had made it,** but, simply, *and he made it a molten calf.* It is manifestly incongruous to speak of forming a molten calf with a graving tool. Hence many critics propose to read חריט, *a money bag*, or purse, instead of חרט, here translated **graving tool**, which occurs elsewhere only at Isa. viii, 1, and there means a *pen*, or stylus. The statement would then be : *And he received* (the earrings) *from their hand, and collected* (וַיָּצַר), from צוּר, *to bind* or *collect together*. in one mass) *it* (the gold) *in a bag, and made it a molten calf.* It is no valid objection to this view to ask, with Keil, "Why should Aaron first bind up the golden earrings in a bag?" For it may with equal force be answered, Why should he not? What better or more appropriate way of receiving and retaining the large amount of gold until it was converted into the golden idol? This, on the whole, is more satisfactory than the view which supplies in thought a

B. C. 1491.   CHAPTER XXXII.   545.

O Israel, which brought thee up out of the land of Egypt. 5 And when Aaron saw *it*, he built an altar before it; and Aaron made *f* proclamation, and said, To morrow *is* a feast to the LORD. 6 And they rose up early on the morrow, and offered burnt offerings, and brought peace offerings; and the *g* people sat down to eat and to drink, and rose up to play.
7 And the LORD said unto Moses, *h* Go, get thee down; for thy people, which thou broughtest out of the land of Egypt, *i* have corrupted *themselves*: 8 They have turned aside quickly out

---

f Lev. 23. 2, 4, 21, 37; 2 Kings 10. 20; 2 Chron. 30. 5.—*g* 1 Cor. 10. 7.—*h* Verse 1; chap. 33. 1;   Deut. 9. 12; Dan. 9. 24.—*i* Gen. 6. 11, 12; Deut. 4. 16; 32. 5; Judg. 2. 19; Hos. 9. 9.

---

wooden mould or model after the word **fashioned,** for such an idea would have required some clearer form of statement; more satisfactory, also, than to assume that the **molten calf** was cast over a carved image of wood, or that it was finished up by means of a graver's tool after it had been cast. On this last supposition, the graver's work should have been mentioned after, not before, the fusion of the golden ornaments.

According to Josh. xxiv, 14, Ezek. xx, 7, 8, xxiii, 3, 8, Israel had been contaminated with Egyptian idolatry, and the most natural explanation of the construction of this image in the form of a **calf** is, that it was modelled after the form of Apis, the sacred bull which was worshipped at Memphis. See note and cut at chapter viii, 26, page 406. It is hardly credible that during their long sojourn in Egypt the leading men of Israel had not become familiar with the worship of the sacred bull. But it is to be noticed that they did not worship the golden idol as an Egyptian god, but exclaimed before it, **These be thy gods, O Israel, which brought thee up out of the land of Egypt.** The plural here, as in verse 1, does not oblige us to translate and explain the words in a polytheistic sense. The next verse shows that they worshipped Jehovah under the symbol of a calf, and so violated the second rather than the first commandment of the decalogue. See notes on xx, 4, 5. Verse 8 of this chapter shows that they did not thus ignorantly worship, but knew that they were violating one of the commandments.

5. **When Aaron saw**—No object of the verb **saw** is expressed, and we do best to understand what is implied in the words immediately preceding. When he saw the excitement and enthusiasm of the people, and their acceptance of the image as a symbol of their God, he was carried away by the scene, and proceeded further to erect **an altar before it,** and announce that on the **morrow** they would celebrate **a feast to the Lord.** Thus this man, so highly honoured of God, became a culpable partaker in the people's sin.

6. **Rose up early**—It was to be a day of festivity and joy, and they were eager to begin it early. **Burnt offerings, and . . . peace offerings**—See note on xx, 24. **Sat down to eat and to drink**—Usual words for hilarious feasting. They ate, as was customary, of the flesh of the peace offerings. What they drank is not said, but we most naturally suppose wine, which was so common at jovial feasts. **Rose up to play**—Comp. verses 19 and 25. The meaning most probably is, that from feasting they proceeded to lewd forms of dancing. See note on Gen. xxi, 9, and compare Herodotus's account of the rude sports of the Egyptians at certain religious festivals. (Herod., ii, 60.)

INTERCESSION AND PUNISHMENT, 7–35.

7. **Thy people, which thou broughtest out**—Language of trial for Moses. He is made to feel that he is identified with Israel, and must bear the burden of them on his heart. He is informed of the calf worship to which they have so quickly turned aside, and **corrupted themselves,** and is made to see that this great sin deserves the consuming judgment of Jehovah. This opens the way for Moses's first intercession, (verses 11–13,) which is notably effectual. Then follows another trial, as Moses sees the extent of the people's sin, (15–25,) which in turn leads both to punishment and further intercession, (26–32.) Compare the intercessions of Moses in Num. xi, 10–15; xiv, 11–24.

EXODUS.   B. C. 1491.

of the way which *k* I commanded them: they have made them a molten calf, and have worshipped it, and have sacrificed thereunto, and said, *l* These *be* thy gods, O Israel, which have brought thee up out of the land of Egypt. **9** And the LORD said unto Moses, *m* I have seen this people, and, behold, it *is* a stiffnecked people: **10** Now therefore *n* let me alone, that *o* my wrath may wax hot against them, and that I may consume them: and *p* I will make of thee a great nation. **11** *q* And Moses besought *1* the LORD his God, and said, LORD, why doth thy wrath wax hot against thy people, which thou hast brought forth out of the land of Egypt with great power, and with a mighty hand? **12** *r* Wherefore should the Egyptians speak, and say, For mischief did he bring them out, to slay them in the mountains, and to consume them from the face of the earth? Turn from thy fierce wrath, and *s* repent of this evil against thy people. **13** Remember Abraham, Isaac, and Israel, thy servants, to whom thou *t* swarest by thine own self, and saidst unto them, *u* I will multiply your seed as the stars of heaven, and all this land that I have spoken of will I give unto your seed, and they shall inherit *it* for ever. **14** And the LORD *v* repented of the evil which he thought to do unto his people. **15** And *w* Moses turned, and went down from the mount, and the two tables of the testimony *were* in his hand: the tables *were* written on both their sides;

---

k Chap. 20. 3, 4, 23; Deut. 9. 16. —— *l* 1 Kings 12. 28.—— *m* Chap. 33. 3, 5; 34. 9; Deut. 9. 6, 13; 31. 27; 2 Chron. 30. 8; Isa. 48. 4; Acts 7. 51.—— *n* Deut. 9. 14, 19. —— *o* Chap. 22. 24. —— *p* Num. 14. 12. —— *q* Deut. 9. 18, 26–29; Psa. 74. 1, 2; 106. 23.——1 Heb. *the face of the* LORD.

r Num. 14. 13; Deut. 9. 28; 32. 27.—— *s* Ver. 14.—— *t* Gen. 22. 16; Heb. 6. 13.—— *u* Gen. 12. 7; 13. 15; 15. 7, 18; 26. 4; 28. 13; 35. 11, 12. —— *v* Deut. 32. 26; 2 Sam. 24. 16; 1 Chron. 21. 15; Psa. 106. 45; Jer. 18. 8; 30. 13, 19; Joel 2. 13; Jonah 3. 10; 4. 2. —— *w* Deut. 9. 15.

---

9. **A stiffnecked people**—Unmanageable and perverse, like the ox that stoutly resists all efforts to guide or drive him. Comp. the same expression in chap. xxxiii, 3, 5; xxxiv, 9; Deut. ix, 6, 13.

10. **Let me alone**—Do not interfere, and restrain the punitive outgoing of **my wrath** by the intercession which I see in thy heart. "Moses had not yet opened his mouth, but God foresaw the holy violence with which his importunity would besiege his throne."—*Bush*. **That I may consume them**—Verse 28 shows that about three thousand of the people perished before the consuming judgment that followed hard upon the sin, but Moses's plea availed to modify the extent of the fearful stroke. Verse 14. The blending of justice and mercy in God's revelations of himself to Israel is worthy of devout attention. His **wrath** is a fearful power, and **may wax hot** against transgressors of his law, and certainly will **consume** the unrepentant sinner; but he also "keepeth mercy for thousands, forgiving iniquity and transgression and sin," (xxxiv, 7.) **I will make of thee a great nation**—He intimates that he might destroy all the rest of the nation, and by means of Moses alone raise up the **great nation** of which the promise to the fathers had repeatedly spoken.

11–13. **Moses besought**—The intercession of Moses is seen in its graphic outline by the two words of interrogation, **Why** and **wherefore**, (the same word in the Hebrew, למה,) and the three verbs in the imperative **turn . . . repent . . . remember**. It consists of solemn appeal and earnest petition. The appeals are of the nature of exclamations of soul-anguish over the thought of such penal wrath after such a triumph as the exodus, and of the reproach which the Egyptians might then exultingly and contemptuously utter. The petitions end with a pleading of the promises made to the great patriarchs.

14. **The Lord repented**—See notes at Gen. vi, 6, Judg. ii, 18, and 1 Sam. xv, 11.

15. **Moses turned**—After his intercession he **turned** away with an anxious heart, **and went down from the mount** to encounter in the camp of Israel a still deeper trial. On the **two tables** see note at chap. xxxi, 18. Being **written on both their sides** they need not have been large tablets of stone to contain the entire decalogue, and the fact that Moses carried them **in his hand** shows that they must have been rather small. The Hebrew text of chapter xx, 1–17, if spread out over four pages, might be written in

B. C. 1491.   CHAPTER XXXII.   547

on the one side and on the other *were* they written. **16** And the ˣtables *were* the work of God, and the writing *was* the writing of God, graven upon the tables. **17** And when Joshua heard the noise of the people as they shouted, he said unto Moses, *There is* a noise of war in the camp. **18** And he said, *It is* not the voice of *them that* shout for mastery, neither *is it* the voice of *them that* cry for ²being overcome; *but* the noise of *them that* sing do I hear.

19 And it came to pass, as soon as he came nigh unto the camp, that ʸhe saw the calf, and the dancing: and Moses' anger waxed hot, and he cast the tables out of his hands, and brake them beneath the mount. **20** ᶻAnd he took the calf which they had made, and burnt *it* in the fire, and ground *it* to powder, and strewed *it* upon the water, and made the children of Israel drink *of it*. **21** And Moses said unto Aaron, ᵃWhat did this people unto thee, that thou hast brought so great a sin upon them? **22** And Aaron said, Let not the anger of my lord wax hot: ᵇthou knowest the people, that they *are set* on mischief. **23** For they said unto me, ᶜMake us gods, which shall go before us: for *as for* this Moses, the man that brought us up out of the land of Egypt, we wot not what is become of him. **24** And I said unto them, Whosoever hath any gold, let them break *it* off. So they gave *it* me: then I cast it into the fire, and there ᵈcame out this calf.

25 And when Moses saw that the people *were* ᵉnaked, (for Aaron ᶠhad made them naked unto *their* shame among

---

x Chapter 31. 18.——2 Hebrew, *weakness.*——
y Deuteronomy 9. 16, 17.——*z* Deuteronomy 9. 21.
——*a* Gen. 20. 9; 26. 10.

b Chap. 14. 11; 15. 24; 16. 2, 20, 28; 17. 2, 4.——
c Verse 1.——*d* Verse 4.——*e* Chap. 33. 4, 5.——
f 2 Chron. 28. 19.

---

large, bold characters, and the pages each not exceed a surface of six inches square.

16. Work of God — They were miracles in stone, and so monumental witnesses of the supernatural origin of the commandments. See on xxxi, 18.

17. Joshua heard — Palmer mentions a number of paths leading up the mountain from different points, and speaks of the ravine known as Jethro's Road as emerging into the valley at the foot of the "Hill of the Golden Calf," and observes: "Often in descending this, while the precipitous sides of the ravine hid the tents from my gaze, have I heard the sound of voices from below, and thought how Joshua had said unto Moses, as he came down from the mount, '**There is a noise of war in the camp.**'"—*Desert of the Exodus*, p. 101.

19. Moses' anger waxed hot— He who had pleaded so powerfully in the mount (verses 11–13) now feels the kindlings of a wrath akin to that which moved Jehovah to retributive judgment. Fiery indignation against sin is a passion as pure and worthy of God or man as love for truth and righteousness, for, indeed, the former is begotten of the latter. **Cast the tables... and brake them**—Significant sign that Israel had broken the law written thereon.

20. Took.., burnt... ground...
strewed—"We need not suppose that each incident is here placed in strict order of time. What is related in this verse must have occupied some time, and may have followed the rebuke of Aaron. Moses appears to have thrown the calf into the fire to destroy its form, and then to have pounded or filed the metal to powder, which he cast into the brook. Deut. ix, 21. He then made the Israelites drink of the water of the brook. The act was, of course, a symbolical one. The idol was brought to nothing, and the people were made to swallow their own sin." Comp. Mic. vii, 13, 14. — *Speaker's Commentary.* In Deut. ix, 21, Moses says: "I took your sin, the calf which ye had made, and burnt it with fire, and stamped it, and ground it very small, even until it was as small as dust." Compare the symbolical act of making the people drink of it with the drinking the water of jealousy prescribed for a woman suspected of adultery. Num. v, 11–31.

21. What did this people unto thee—A question of rebuke, the more searching because of the thought that Aaron himself had **brought so great a sin upon** the people. Aaron's response and effort at apology, in verses 22–24, is at best a pitiable plea, and virtually a confession of his own weakness.

25. Naked—This word, twice employed in this verse, indicates a letting

their ³enemies,) **26** Then Moses stood in the gate of the camp, and said, Who *is* on the LORD's side? *let him come* unto me. And all the sons of Levi gathered themselves together unto him. **27** And he said unto them, Thus saith the LORD God of Israel, Put every man his sword by his side, *and* go in and out from gate to gate throughout the camp, and ⁴slay every man his brother, and every man his companion, and every man his neighbour. **28** And the children of Levi did according to the word of Moses: and there fell of the people that day about three thousand men. **29** ʰ⁴For Moses had said, ⁵ Consecrate yourselves to day to the LORD, even every man upon his son, and upon his brother; that he may bestow upon you a blessing this day.

---

3 Heb. *those that rose up against them.*— *g* Num. 25, 5; Deut. 33, 9. —— *h* Num. 25. 11-13; Deut. 13. 6-11; 33. 9, 10; 1 Sam. 15. 18, 22; Prov. 21. 3; Zech. 13. 3; Matt. 10. 37.

4 Or, *And Moses said, Consecrate yourselves to day to the* LORD, *because every man hath been against his son, and against his brother, etc.*—5 Heb. *Fill your hands.*

---

the people loose from all restraint, and giving them over to licentious and dangerous revelling. See the note on פָּרַע, at Judg. v, 1.

26. Who is on the Lord's side— A fair call to repentance and loyal return to Jehovah. **All the sons of Levi**—It was most natural that the men of Moses's own tribe should at once rally to his side, and thus make atonement in part for their complicity in the sin. Simeon and Levi had troubled Jacob with their swords, (Gen. xxxiv, 25, compare verse 30 and xlix, 5;) now Levi's sons win a distinction which was afterward celebrated in song. Deut. xxxiii, 9.

27. Slay every man his brother —Those who were guilty of this breach of the covenant (comp. verse 33) were liable to the penalty of a capital crime, and hence the order for this fearful slaughter. That this order was not intended or understood to warrant an indiscriminate and wholesale massacre is obvious from what follows. Only "about three thousand men" were slain, (verse 28,) or one in two hundred of the adult Israelites, (compare chapter xii, 37,) and had these Levitical swordsmen understood Moses's words literally, they would have felt obliged to slay one another as well as all in the camp. It is not improbable that the three thousand who were slain resisted these Levites, or had refused to drink of the water, (verse 20,) or in some way persisted in their sin. In going **in and out from gate to gate throughout the camp** the armed executioners of the order may have been safely left to determine who the most guilty parties were. Many facts, known to these Levites, who had seen the operations of the calf worship from its beginning, may be assumed to have guided them in their work of retribution.

29. For Moses had said—Thus rendered, this verse is supposed to explain the zeal of the Levites in the slaughter just described. Their zeal and activity were to be a consecration of themselves to Jehovah. But the common version is not in strict accord with the Hebrew text. The margin gives the better rendering. But the explanations of the verse have been various. Translating literally we read: *And Moses said, Fill your hand to-day unto* (or *for*) *Jehovah, for a man* (is or was) *against his son and against his brother, and* (it was) *to give a blessing upon you to-day.* The expression "fill the hand" is a metaphor which is used in describing the consecration of persons, (compare xxviii, 41; xxix, 9, 29, 33; Lev. viii, 33; xxi, 10; Num. iii, 3; 1 Chron. xxix, 5; 2 Chron. xxix, 31,) and is translated *consecrate* in all the passages here referred to. The allusion in the metaphor appears to refer to some ceremony of giving into the hands of those consecrated some sign or symbol of their office and work. It would be thus signified that their hands were thenceforth to be filled with the duties and obligations of their sacred calling. We need not here understand that these Levites were commanded to bring any special offerings at this time, but that the work which they had that day performed was a consecration of themselves to Jehovah. They had filled their hands with an act which would give them memorable distinction,

B. C. 1491. CHAPTER XXXII. 549

30 And it came to pass on the morrow, that Moses said unto the people, ¹ Ye have sinned a great sin: and now I will go up unto the LORD; ᵏ peradventure I shall ˡ make an atonement for your sin. **31** And Moses ᵐ returned unto the LORD, and said, Oh, this people have sinned a great sin, and have ⁿ made them gods of gold. **32** Yet now, if thou wilt forgive their sin—; and if not, ᵒ blot me, I pray thee, ᵖ out of thy book which thou hast written. **33** And the LORD said unto Moses, ᵠ Whosoever hath sinned against me, him will I blot out of my book. **34** Therefore now go, lead the people unto *the place* of which I have spoken unto thee: ʳ behold, mine Angel shall go before thee: nevertheless, ˢ in the day when I visit, I will visit their sin upon them. **35** And the LORD plagued the people, because ᵗ they made the calf, which Aaron made.

CHAPTER XXXIII.

AND the LORD said unto Moses, Depart, *and* go up hence, thou ᵃ and

---

i 1 Sam. 12. 20, 23; Luke 15. 18.——*k* 2 Sam. 16. 12; Amos 5. 15.——*l* Num. 25. 13.——*m* Deut. 9. 18. ——*n* Chap. 20. 23.——*o* Psa. 69. 28; Rom. 9. 3.—— *p* Psa. 56. 8; 139. 16; Dan. 12. 1; Phil. 4. 3; Rev. 3. 5;
13. 8: 17. 8; 20. 12, 15; 21. 27; 23. 19.——*q* Lev. 23. 30; Ezek. 18. 4.——*r* Chap. 33. 2, 14, etc.; Num. 20. 16.——*s* Deut. 32. 35; Amos 3. 14; Rom. 2. 5, 6. ——*t* 2 Sam. 12. 9; Acts 7. 41.——*a* Chap. 32. 7.

Accordingly, the verse might be thus paraphrased: Consecrate yourselves this day unto Jehovah. For you have shown yourselves worthy to be his ministers by rising above personal and family considerations when Jehovah's honour was at stake, (comp. Deut. xxxiii, 8-11, Luke xiv, 26,) for by turning in this case against son and brother you have shown yourselves loyal to Jehovah and worthy to receive his blessing.

30. **On the morrow** — After that fearful day of retribution. **Ye have sinned a great sin**—It was important that they should realize the gravity and magnitude of their trangression, and these words of Moses were adapted to impress this upon them. Lest further punishment fall he proposes to **go up unto the Lord,** and seek, if possible, **to make an atonement for** their **sin.** He hopes to cover or expiate their sin by further intercession. Comp. verses 11-14. He accordingly went up again into the mount, and made supplication before Jehovah there.

31, 32. **Oh**—אָנָּא, an interjection that expresses mingled sadness and entreaty. The intercession of Moses in these two verses is much briefer but more striking than in verses 11-13, above. The broken form of expression in verse 32, where the conclusion, or apodosis, is left to be supplied, is not uncommon in the Scriptures. Compare Gen. iii, 22; Dan. iii, 15; Luke xiii, 9; xix, 42. The willingness of Moses to be sacrificed for Israel's pardon is paralleled with Paul's notable saying in Rom. ix, 3. **Thy book**—The chosen people of God are regarded as enrolled or **written** in a book before God. As the citizens of a community are enrolled in an official list, or the members of a society are registered as such in a book kept for that purpose, so the righteous are supposed to be registered in the book of life, and such registration witnesses their citizenship in the kingdom of God. Comp. Psa. lxix, 28; Ezek. xiii, 9; Dan. xii, 1; Luke x, 20; Phil. iv, 3; Rev. iii, 5; xiii, 8; xx, 15; xxi, 27.

33. **Him will I blot out**—Only the wilful sinner, who violates the holy commandments and persists in his disobedience, shall be cut off from the people of God.

34. **Now go, lead the people** — The people having broken the covenant, Jehovah speaks as though he would have Moses depart from Sinai without having the tables renewed, or proceeding with the erection of the tabernacle, whose pattern had been shown him in the mount. He assures him of the presence of his **Angel,** as in chap. xxiii, 20, but declares that the **sin** of the people cannot go unpunished. But Moses's persistent intercession and mediation, as shown in the following chapter, led to a renewal of the covenant.

35. **Plagued**—This implies that the severe blow ministered by the Levites (27-29) was followed by still other visitations of penal wrath.

CHAPTER XXXIII.

MEDIATION AND INTERCESSION, 1-23.

1. **Depart, and go up hence** — This is in substance a repetition of

the people which thou hast brought up out of the land of Egypt, unto the land which I sware unto Abraham, to Isaac, and to Jacob, saying, ᵇ Unto thy seed will I give it: **2** ᶜ And I will send an Angel before thee; ᵈ and I will drive out the Canaanite, the Amorite, and the Hittite, and the Perizzite, the Hivite, and the Jebusite: **3** ᵉ Unto a land flowing with milk and honey: ᶠ for I will not go up in the midst of thee; for thou *art* a ᵍ stiffnecked people: lest ʰ I consume thee in the way.

4 And when the people heard these evil tidings, ⁱ they mourned: ᵏ and no man did put on him his ornaments. **5** For the LORD had said unto Moses, Say unto the children of Israel, ˡ Ye *are* a stiffnecked people: I will come up ᵐ into the midst of thee in a moment, and consume thee: therefore now put off thy ornaments from thee, that I may ⁿ know what to do unto thee. **6** And the children of Israel stripped themselves of their ornaments by the mount Horeb. **7** And Moses took the taber-

---

b Gen. 12. 7; chap. 32. 13. —— *c* Chap. 32. 34; 34. 11.——*d* Deut. 7. 22: Josh. 24. 11.——*e* Chap. 3. 8. ——*f* Verses 15, 17. —— *g* Chap. 32. 9; 34. 9; Deut. 9. 6, 13. —— *h* Chap. 23. 21; 32. 10; Num. 16. 21, 45.

i Num. 14. 1, 39.——*k* Lev. 10. 6; 2 Sam. 19, 24: 1 Kings 21. 27; 2 Kings 19. 1; Ezra 9. 3; Esth. 4. 1, 4; Job 1. 20; 2. 12; Isa. 32. 11; Ezek. 24. 17, 23; 26. 16.——*l* Verse 3.——*m* See Num. 16. 45, 46.—— *n* Deut. 8. 2; Psa. 139. 23.

---

xxxii, 34. The people have broken the covenant which they promised to keep, (xxiv, 3-7;) why linger longer at this mountain? Let them now proceed to the **land** which was promised **unto Abraham, to Isaac, and to Jacob,** and do the best they can under the curse of violated vows.

2. **I will send...drive**—Repeated in substance from xxiii, 23, 28.

3. **I will not go up in the midst of thee**—This distinction between Jehovah and his Angel is not inconsistent with our doctrine of the Angel of Jehovah, as set forth in note on Gen. xvi, 7. But Jehovah's Angel might not at all times so bear his name (xxiii, 21) or exhibit his power as to be a consuming fire in the midst of Israel. He was rather of the nature of a mediator between Moses and Jehovah, and the statement of this verse is designed to enhance the infinite holiness of God. The hardness of the people's heart is such that some consideration may be shown, (comp. Matt. xix, 8,) but the demands of infinite holiness are such that Jehovah here represents himself as withdrawing from the **stiffnecked people,** lest the immediate gaze of his holy eye **consume** them **in the way.** The whole manner of thought is anthropomorphic, for how else could such conceptions be then conveyed to such a sinful people? The mediating Angel may show mercy when holy wrath would destroy; and Israel may have an angel like other nations, (comp. Dan. x, 13,) but lose the special presence of Jehovah himself.

4. **The people heard...mourned** —The withdrawal of the divine presence seemed to them to be ominous of evil. Though God's voice out of Sinai filled them with terror, (see chap. xx, 19,) and they could not endure the nearness of such excessive majesty, the thought that the Holy One is about to forsake them in wrath excites even deeper fear. **Ornaments**—See also in verses 5 and 6. The putting off of these was a sign of humiliation and penitence. In a time of sorrow and guilt the adornments of the person were strikingly out of place.

5. **I will come up**—This passage is better translated conditionally: *One moment let me come in thy midst, and I would consume thee.* So terrible is the power of the presence of the Holy One. Hence the reason of what is said in verse 3 above, where see note. **Put off thy ornaments**—As a proof of true penitence.

7. **Moses took the tabernacle**— What tabernacle? Surely not the tabernacle the pattern of which had been given him in the mount, (chap. xxvi,) for this had not yet been constructed. Nor is it satisfactory to assume, as some expositors have done, that this was an old tabernacle or tent, previously employed for purposes of worship, but not before mentioned. More reasonable than either of these suppositions is it to believe that the tent of Moses had hitherto been the central point of the Israelitish camp, and so, *par excellence, the* tent of Israel. In order now to institute a new and pecu-

B. C. 1491. CHAPTER XXXIII. 551

nacle, and pitched it without the camp, afar off from the camp, ° and called it the Tabernacle of the congregation. And it came to pass, *that* every one which ᵖ sought the LORD went out unto the tabernacle of the congregation, which *was* without the camp. 8 And it came to pass, when Moses went out unto the tabernacle, *that* all the people rose up, and stood every man ᑫ *at* his tent door, and looked after Moses, until he was gone into the tabernacle. 9 And it came to pass, as Moses entered into the tabernacle, the cloudy pillar descended, and stood *at* the door of the tabernacle, and *the* LORD ʳ talked with Moses. 10 And all the people saw the cloudy

pillar stand *at* the tabernacle door: and all the people rose up and ˢ worshipped, every man *in* his tent door. 11 And ᵗ the LORD spake untc Moses face to face, as a man speaketh unt᙮ his friend. And he turned again into t᙮e camp; but ᵘ his servant Joshua, the so᙮ of Nun, a young man, departed not out ᙮ᶠ the tabernacle. 12 And Moses said ᙮nto the LORD, See, ᵛ thou sayest unto ᙮᙮e, Bring up this people: and thou hast not let me know whom thou wilt send with me. Yet thou hast said, ʷ I know thee by name, and thou hast also found grace in my sight. 13 Now therefore, I pray thee, ˣ if I have found grace in thy sight ʸ show me now thy way, that I may ᙮ ᴨ ᙮ thee,

---

o Chap. 29. 42, 43.——*p* Deut. 4. 29 ; 2 Sam. 21. 1. ——*q* Num. 16. 27.——*r* Chap. 25. 22; 31. 18; Psa. 99. 7.——*s* Chap. 4. 31.——*t* Gen. 32. 30; Num. 12. 8; Deut. 34. 10.

u Chap. 24. 13. —— *v* Chap. 32. 34. —— *w* Verse 17; Gen. 18. 19; Psa. 1. 6; Jer. 1. 5; John 10. 14, 15; 2 Tim. 2. 19.——*x* Chap. 34. 9.——*y* Psa. 25. 4; 27. 11; 86. 11; 119. 33.

---

liar form of service and of approach unto God, and to carry on his intercession for Israel more conspicuously in the sight of the people, he removes this tent and places it **without the camp, afar off from the camp,** and because of its changed purpose calls it **the Tabernacle** (rather, *the Tent*) **of the congregation.** Thus would Moses make more conspicuous the lesson that the sin of the people had alienated them from Jehovah, and his presence must **be sought** unto as something afar off. This tent, furthermore, was now to serve as the place where the symbol of Jehovah's presence might be seen until the proper tabernacle should be erected.

8–11. These verses show that this tent served a special purpose in the Sinaitic revelation of Jehovah. Into it **Moses entered** to plead and to receive divine communications, and Jehovah **spake unto Moses face to face, as a man speaketh unto his friend. The cloudy pillar** was a medium of communication, for according to the most correct translation of verse 9 it was the **pillar** that **descended and stood at the door of the tabernacle, and ... talked with Moses.** Jehovah spoke through, or out of, the cloud. The speaking with Moses **face to face** did not involve a sight of God's face, for he explains in v᙮rse 20 that no man could *see* his face and live. So he communed with him from the cloud which veiled his glory.

All the people were permitted to behold **the cloudy pillar** in the distance, but only Moses and Joshua entered the tent, and it is said that when Moses returned to camp Joshua tarried behind and **departed not out of the** tabernacle. The tent was not to be left altogether alone, and so it would seem that Moses's **servant** stayed as on guard.

12–23. In these verses we have the prevailing prayer, in view of which Jehovah's wrath is turned away, and he again renews the covenant with Israel. The persistent intercession appears to have been carried on in the tent without the camp, and for this special purpose it had been pitched, as if in some measure to realize what was promised in chap. xxix, 43.

12. **Thou sayest unto me**—Allusion to what Jehovah had said in verse 1 above. **Whom thou wilt send**—Jehovah had assured him of the presence of an Angel, (xxxii, 34, xxxiii, 2,) but to Moses his nature and way are so wrapped in mystery that he cannot be satisfied without further revelation. **I know thee by name**—When Jehovah said this to Moses is not recorded, but in chapter iii he called him by his name *Moses*, and showed him great **grace** and honour.

13. **Show me now thy way**—The way thou wilt lead us ; the manner in which the guiding Angel will direct our ways, and drive out our enemies before us. **That I may know thee**—Not-

552   EXODUS.   B. C. 1491.

that I may find grace in thy sight: and consider that this nation is *thy people. **14** And he said, *a* My presence shall go *with thee*, and I will give thee *b* rest. **15** And he said unto him, *c* If thy presence go not *with me*, carry us not up hence. **16** For wherein shall it be known here that I and thy people have found grace in thy sight? *d is it* not in that thou goest with us? So *e* shall we be separated, I and thy people, from all the people that *are* upon the face of the earth. **17** And the LORD said unto Moses, *f* I will do this thing also that thou hast spoken: for *g* thou hast found grace in my sight, and I know thee by name. **18** And he said, I beseech thee, show me *h* thy glory. **19** And he said, *i* I will make all my goodness pass before thee, and I will proclaim the name of the LORD before thee; *k* and will be *l* gracious to whom I will be gracious, and will show mercy on whom I will show mercy. **20** And he said, Thou canst

---
z Deut. 9. 26, 29; Joel 2. 17.——*a* Chap. 13. 21; 40. 34–38; Isa. 63. 9.——*b* Deut. 3. 20; Josh. 21. 44; 22. 4; 23. 1; Psa. 95. 11.——*c* Verse 3; chap. 34. 9. ——*d* Num. 14. 14.——*e* Chap. 34. 10; Deut. 4. 7, 34; 2 Sam. 7. 23; 1 Kings 8. 53; Psa. 147. 20.—— *f* Gen. 19. 21; James 5. 16. —— *g* Verse 12. —— *h* Verse 20; 1 Tim. 6. 16.——*i* Chap. 34. 5–7; Jer. 31. 14.——*k* Rom. 9. 15, 16, 18.——*l* Rom. 4. 4, 16.

---

withstanding all the communion face to face between Jehovah and Moses, (verse 11,) this leader of the chosen nation feels that he does not sufficiently **know** Jehovah. He prays for a fuller, clearer revelation of his nature and his glory. **This nation is thy people**—Jehovah had spoken to Moses of Israel as "the people which thou hast brought up out of the land of Egypt, (verse 1, comp. xxxii, 7;) Moses now insists that Jehovah had called this nation as *his own*. Thus had he called them when he first appeared to Moses at the bush, and sent him unto Pharaoh. See chap. iii, 7.

14. My presence shall go—Behold how Moses's intercession prevails! In verse 3 the Lord had said, "I will not go up in the midst of thee;" but after the penitence of the people, and repeated seeking unto Jehovah in the tent of the congregation, and especially this earnest plea of Moses, the God of Israel is moved to compassion, and promises his presence. The shallow sceptic would fain see in such a representation a changeableness and weakness in the God of Israel unworthy the nature of deity. But the believer sees here an illustration of that wonderful condescension and mercy with which God compassionates the penitent sinner. The mode of illustration, in accord with all these earlier revelations, is anthropomorphic; but the lesson taught is the same as when, in Isa. liv, 7, 8, Jehovah says: "For a small moment have I forsaken thee; but with great mercies will I gather thee. In a little wrath I hid my face from thee for a moment; but with everlasting kindness will I have mercy on thee, saith the Lord thy Redeemer." Some writers have proposed an interrogative rendering for this verse: *Shall my presence go, and shall I give them rest?* But there appears no sufficient reason for this method of translation.

16. So shall we be separated—That is, notably distinguished **from all the people that are upon the face of the earth,** in having the manifest presence of Jehovah among them. If this glorious presence was not to go with them and thus distinguish them from all other peoples, Moses prefers not to go up from Sinai. Here we notice, further, the persistency of Moses's intercession, and in the next verse we observe how powerfully it prevails with God.

18. Show me thy glory—Moses grows bolder with every new word of grace from Jehovah, and now, like Jacob at Peniel, (Gen. xxxii, 29, note,) cries out for a revelation of the divine **glory.** He yearns for a disclosure of the God of Israel more full and glorious than had ever yet been made; something more wonderful than the burning bush, more personal than the devouring fire in the mountain, and more visible to sense than could be had through thick darkness or cloudy pillar.

19–23. Even this great request is in part granted, for these verses contain the promise that, so far as mortal man may be permitted to see the divine glory, Moses shall witness a most sublime theophany. As Jehovah willed to blot the sinful Israelite out of his book, (xxxii, 33,) and for manifest reason, so he **will show mercy on whom** he **will show mercy,** namely, on Moses as an example, who by persistent **prayer**

B. C. 1491.   CHAPTER XXXIII.   553

not see my face: for ᵐ there shall no man see me, and live. 21 And the LORD said, Behold, *there is* a place by me, and thou shalt stand upon a rock: 22 And it shall come to pass, while my glory passeth by, that I will put thee ⁿ in a cleft of the rock, and will ᵒ cover thee with my hand while I pass by: 23 And I will take away mine hand, and thou shalt see my back parts; but my face shall ᵖ not be seen.

CHAPTER XXXIV.

AND the LORD said unto Moses,ᵃ Hew thee two tables of stone like unto the first: ᵇ and I will write upon *these* tables the words that were in the first tables, which thou brakest. 2 And be

m Gen. 32. 30; Deut. 5. 24; Judg. 6. 22; 13. 22; Isa. 6. 5; Rev. 1. 16, 17; see chap. 24. 10.——*n* Isa. 2. 21.——*o* Psa. 91. 1, 4.——*p* Verse 20; John 1. 18.

ready in the morning, and come up in the morning unto mount Sinai, and present thyself there to me ᶜ in the top of the mount. 3 And no man shall ᵈ come up with thee, neither let any man be seen throughout all the mount; neither let the flocks nor herds feed before that mount.

4 And he hewed two tables of stone like unto the first; and Moses rose up early in the morning, and went up unto mount Sinai, as the LORD had commanded him, and took in his hand the two tables of stone. 5 And the LORD descended in the cloud, and stood with him there, and ᵉ proclaimed the name of the LORD. 6 And the LORD passed by before him, and proclaimed, The LORD,

a Chap. 32. 16, 19; Deut. 10. 1.—— *b* Verse 28; Deut. 10. 2, 4.——*c* Chap. 19. 20; 24. 12.——*d* Chap. 19. 12, 13, 21.——*e* Chap. 33. 19; Num. 14. 17.

obtains the gracious favour of his Lord. See Whedon's note on Romans ix, 15. But here appears the statement that *no man can behold Jehovah's face and live.* This profound truth underlies the entire divine revelation, and shows the necessity of the incarnation of the Word of God. "No man hath seen God at any time; the only begotten Son, which is in the bosom of the Father, he hath declared him." In harmony with this great truth, Moses is promised a vision of the glory of Israel's God. He will place him **in a cleft of the rock** when he again goes up into the mountain, and will **pass by** so as to exhibit, as it were, his back, but not his face. So shall he *behold* and *hear* what will infix forever in his soul the holiest conception of the name and nature of Jehovah. For the fulfilment of this promise, see chap. xxxiv, 5–8.

CHAPTER XXXIV.

THE TABLES OF THE COVENANT RENEWED, 1–35.

1. **Hew thee two tables**—The others were, in chap. xxxii, 16, called "the work of God."

3. **No man ... with thee**—As contrasted with xxiv, 9–13. Not even Joshua accompanied Moses now. He probably remained at the tent of the congregation. Chap. xxxiii, 11.

5. **Descended ... stood ... proclaimed**—There was also, according to the next verse, a movement of the sublime theophany as of one passing by. This was the fulfilment of the promise recorded in xxxiii, 19–23, and was, says Clarke, "the second revelation of the name of the God of Israel to Moses. The first revelation was of Jehovah as the Self-existent One, who purposed to deliver his people with a mighty hand, (iii, 14;) this was of the same Jehovah as a living Saviour, who was now forgiving their sins. The two ideas that mark these revelations are found combined, apart from their historical development, in the second commandment, (xx, 5, 6,) where the divine unity is shown on its practical side, in its relation to human obligations. Both in the commandment and in this passage the divine love is associated with the divine justice; but in the former there is a transposition to serve the proper purpose of the commandments, and the justice stands before the love. This is strictly the legal arrangement, brought out in the completed system of the ceremonial law, in which the sin offering, in acknowledgment of the sentence of justice against sin, was offered before the burnt offering and the peace offering. But in this place the truth appears in its essential order; the retributive justice of Jehovah is subordinated to—rather, it is made a part of —his forgiving love."—*Speaker's Commentary.*

6, 7. **Proclaimed**—This appears to

The LORD ᶠ God, merciful and gracious, longsuffering, and abundant in ᵍ goodness and ʰ truth, **7** ⁱ Keeping mercy for thousands, ᵏ forgiving iniquity and transgression and sin, and ˡ that will by no means clear *the guilty;* visiting the iniquity of the fathers upon the children, and upon the children's children, unto the third and to the fourth *generation.* **8** And Moses made haste, and ᵐ bowed his head toward the earth, and worshipped. **9** And he said, If now I have found grace in thy sight, O Lord, ⁿ let my Lord, I pray thee, go among us; for ᵒ it *is* a stiffnecked people; and pardon our iniquity and our sin, and take us for ᵖ thine inheritance.

10 And he said, Behold, ᑫ I make a covenant: before all thy people I will ʳ do marvels, such as have not been done in all the earth, nor in any nation: and all the people among which thou *art* shall see the work of the LORD: for it *is* ˢ a terrible thing that I will do with thee. **11** ᵗ Observe thou that which I command thee this day: behold, ᵘ I drive out before thee the Amorite, and the Canaanite, and the Hittite, and the Perizzite, and the Hivite, and the Jebusite. **12** ᵛ Take heed to thyself, lest thou make a covenant with the inhabitants of the land whither thou goest, lest it be for ʷ a snare in the midst of thee: **13** But ye shall ˣ destroy their altars,

---

ᶠ Num. 14. 18; 2 Chron. 30. 9; Neh. 9. 17; Psa. 86. 15; 103. 8; 111. 4; 112. 4; 116. 5; 145. 8; Joel 2. 13.—ᵍ Psa. 31. 19; Rom. 2. 4.—ʰ Psa. 57. 10; 108. 4.—ⁱ Chap. 20. 6; Deut. 5. 10; Psa. 86. 15; Jer. 32. 18; Dan. 9. 4.—ᵏ Psa. 103. 3; 130. 4; Dan. 9. 9; Eph. 4. 32; 1 John 1. 9.—ˡ Chap. 23. 7, 21; Josh. 24. 19; Job 10. 14; Micah 6. 11; Nah. 1. 3.—ᵐ Chap. 4. 31.—ⁿ Chap. 33. 15, 16.

ᵒ Chap. 33. 3.——ᵖ Deut. 32. 9; Psa. 28. 9; 33. 12; 78. 62; 94. 14; Jer. 10. 16; Zech. 2. 12.— ᑫ Deut. 5. 2; 29. 12, 14.—ʳ Deut. 4. 32; 2 Sam. 7. 23; Psa. 77. 14; 78. 12; 147. 20.—ˢ Deut. 10. 21; Psa. 145. 6; Isa. 64. 3.——ᵗ Deut. 5. 32; 6. 3, 25; 12. 28, 32; 28. 1.—ᵘ Chap. 33. 2.—ᵛ Chap. 23. 32; Deut. 7. 2; Judg. 2. 2.—ʷ Chap. 23. 33.— ˣ Chap. 23. 24; Deut. 12. 3; Judg. 2. 2.

---

have been a supernatural communication, in an audible voice, proceeding out of the theophany, as the ten commandments had been spoken out of the midst of the fires of Sinai. Deut. v, 4. As a declaration of divine perfections it is conspicuously complete, but especially emphatic on mercy's side. Its impressiveness is abiding, and is felt by every devout reader.

9. Go among us . . . pardon . . . take us—After all the mercy shown, and the assurance of xxxiii, 14, and the fuller revelations that followed, Moses still repeats his cry for the presence of Jehovah among the people. Importunate prayer, and clinging by faith to God! He will not let him go!

10. Before all thy people I will do marvels—This refers to the unparalleled displays of divine help during the journey to Palestine, at the crossing of the Jordan, and during the conquest and settlement of the land of promise. These distinguished Israel **in all the earth,** and put the fear of them upon all the nations that saw or heard. Comp. Josh. ii, 9, 11.

11. Drive out—Comp. xxxiii, 2, and xxiii, 23, 28. The frequent repetition of this promise was important, inasmuch as Israel's greatest danger was from their heathen foes.

12–26. Take heed to thyself— Here follows a brief *résumé* of the laws previously ordained, and written in the Book of the Covenant, xxi–xxiii. They may be resolved into ten precepts, as follows:

1. Thou shalt make no covenant with the heathen. Verse 12.
2. Thou shalt destroy their altars and images. Verse 13.
3. Thou shalt worship no other god save Jehovah. Verse 14.
4. Thou shalt make no molten gods. Verse 17.
5. Thou shalt keep the feast of unleavened bread. Verse 18.
6. Thou shalt redeem all the firstborn. Verses 19, 20.
7. Thou shalt keep the sabbath day. Verse 21.
8. Thou shalt observe the three annual feasts. Verses 22, 23.
9. Thou shalt not offer sacrifice with leaven. Verse 25.
10. Thou shalt not seethe a kid in its mother's milk. Verse 26.

We should lay no stress upon this division into *ten* commandments; for it is possible, by making separate precepts of the firstfruits, (verse 26,) and the not appearing empty (verse 20,) to make more than ten; or by combining several very kindred laws to reduce the number to seven or eight. In no case should this recapitulation of laws be identified with the ten commandments mentioned in verse 28, for these

B. C. 1491.   CHAPTER XXXIV.   555

break their ¹ images, and ʸ cut down their groves: **14** For thou shalt worship ᶻ no other god: for the LORD, whose ᵃ name is Jealous, is a ᵇ jealous God. **15** ᶜ Lest thou make a covenant with the inhabitants of the land, and they ᵈ go a whoring after their gods, and do sacrifice unto their gods, and one ᵉ call thee, and thou ᶠ eat of his sacrifice; **16** And thou take of ᵍ their daughters unto thy sons, and their daughters ʰ go a whoring after their gods, and make thy sons go a whoring after their gods. **17** ⁱ Thou shalt make thee no molten gods.
18 The feast of ᵏ unleavened bread shalt thou keep. Seven days thou shalt eat unleavened bread, as I commanded thee, in the time of the month Abib: for in the ˡ month Abib thou camest out from Egypt. **19** ᵐAll that openeth the matrix is mine; and every firstling among thy cattle, whether ox or sheep, that is male. **20** But ⁿ the firstling of an ass thou shalt redeem with a ² lamb: and if thou redeem him not, then shalt thou break his neck. All the firstborn of thy sons thou shalt redeem. And none shall appear before me ᵒ empty.
21 ᵖ Six days thou shalt work, but on the seventh day thou shalt rest: in the earing time and in harvest thou shalt rest.

22 ᵠAnd thou shalt observe the feast of weeks, of the firstfruits of wheat harvest, and the feast of ingathering at the ³ year's end.
23 ʳ Thrice in the year shall all your men children appear before the Lord GOD, the God of Israel. **24** For I will ˢ cast out the nations before thee, and ᵗ enlarge thy borders: ᵘ neither shall any man desire thy land, when thou shalt go up to appear before the LORD thy God thrice in the year. **25** ᵛ Thou shalt not offer the blood of my sacrifice with leaven; ʷ neither shall the sacrifice of the feast of the passover be left unto the morning. **26** ˣ The first of the firstfruits of thy land thou shalt bring unto the house of the LORD thy God. ʸ Thou shalt not seethe a kid in his mother's milk. **27** And the LORD said unto Moses, Write thou ᶻ these words: for after the tenor of these words I have made a covenant with thee and with Israel.
28 ᵃ And he was there with the LORD forty days and forty nights; he did neither eat bread, nor drink water. And ᵇ He wrote upon the tables the words of the covenant, the ten ⁴ commandments.
29 And it came to pass, when Moses came down from mount Sinai with the ᶜ two tables of testimony in Moses' hand, when he came down from the mount, that

---

1 Heb. statues.——y Deut. 7. 5; 12. 2; Judg. 6. 25; 2 Kings 18. 4; 23. 14; 2 Chron. 31. 1; 34. 3, 4.—— z Chap. 20. 3, 5.——a So Isa. 9. 6; 57. 15.——bChap. 20. 5.——c Verse 12.——d Deut. 31. 16; Judg. 2. 17; Jer. 3. 9; Ezek. 6. 9.——e Num. 25. 2; 1 Cor. 10. 27.——f Psa. 106. 28; 1 Cor. 8. 4, 7, 10.——g Deut. 7. 3; 1 Kings 11. 2; Ezra 9. 2; Neh. 13. 25.——h Num. 25. 1, 2; 1 Kings 11. 4.——i Chap. 32. 8; Lev. 19. 4.——k Chap. 12. 15; 23. 15.——l Chap. 13. 4. —— m Chap. 13. 2, 12; 22. 29; Ezek. 44. 30; Luke 2. 23.——n Chap. 13. 13; Num. 18. 15.—— 2 Or, kid. —— o Chap. 23. 15; Deut. 16. 16; 1 Sam. 9. 7, 8;

2 Sam. 24. 24.——p Chap. 20. 9; 23. 12; 35. 2; Deut. 5. 12, 13; Luke 13. 14. —— q Chap. 23. 16; Deut. 16. 10, 13.——3 Heb. revolution of the year.—— r Chap. 23. 14, 17; Deut. 16. 16.——s Chap. 33. 2; Lev. 18. 24; Deut. 7. 1; Psa. 78. 55; 80. 8. —— t Deut. 12. 20; 19. 8.——u See Gen. 35. 5 : 2 Chron. 17. 10; Prov. 16. 7; Acts 18. 10. —— v Chap. 23. 18.——w Chap. 12. 10.——x Chap. 23. 19; Deut. 26. 2, 10.——y Chap. 23. 19; Deut. 14. 21.——z Verse 10; Deut. 4. 13; 31. 9.——a Chap. 24. 18; Deut. 9. 9, 18.——b Verse 1; chap. 31. 18; 32. 16; Deut. 4. 13; 10. 2, 4.——4 Heb. words.——c Chap. 32. 15.

---

were identical with those in the first tables. Verse 1.

13. **Groves**—Rather, *Asherah*, pillars, wooden images of Asherah. See notes on Judg. ii, 13; iii, 7; and 1 Kings xix, 15.

27. **Write thou these words**—This narrative very clearly teaches that Moses recorded repeated acts of legislation. The covenant was broken and renewed. A record was made of all the important facts, and such a record, if faithful, must needs have contained various repetitions. Some critics discover different "strata of laws," but fail to pay proper respect to the fact, that, according to the plain import of the Mosaic narrative, laws were repeatedly given, revised, renewed, and in some instances changed, as the conduct and interests of the people required. The different codes and stages of legislation are not inconsistent with each other, nor of such a nature as to be inconsistent with a Mosaic origin. See our Introduction to the Pentateuch, page 31.

28. **Forty days and forty nights** —Comp. chap. xxiv, 18. So that Moses passed two periods of this length **with the Lord** in the mount. **He wrote**—According to verse 1, the writer was God himself, so that these second tables, though hewn by Moses, were, like the first, "written with the finger of God." Compare chap. xxxi, 18, with xxxii, 16.

556 EXODUS. B. C. 1491.

Moses wist not that ᵈ the skin of his face shone while he talked with him. **30** And when Aaron and all the children of Israel saw Moses, behold, the skin of his face shone; and they were afraid to come nigh him. **31** And Moses called unto them; and Aaron and all the rulers of the congregation returned unto him: and Moses talked with them. **32** And afterward all the children of Israel came nigh: ᵉ and he gave them in commandment all that the Lord had spoken with him in mount Sinai. **33** And *till* Moses had done speaking with them, he put ᶠ a vail on his face. **34** But ᵍ when Moses went in before the Lord to speak with him, he took the vail off, until he came out. And he came out, and spake unto the children of Israel *that* which he was commanded. **35** And the children of Israel saw the face of Moses, that the skin of Moses' face shone: and Moses put the vail upon his face again, until he went in to speak with Him.

CHAPTER XXXV.

AND Moses gathered all the congregation of the children of Israel together, and said unto them, ᵃ These *are* the words which the Lord hath com-

---

ᵈ Matt. 17. 2; 2 Cor. 3. 7, 13.——ᵉ Chap. 24. 3.—— ᶠ 2 Cor. 3. 13. ——ᵍ 2 Cor. 3. 16.——ᵃ Chap. 34. 32.

---

29. The skin of his face shone— The long communion with Jehovah, and beholding so much of his glory, had set upon the face of the lawgiver a brilliancy that was unearthly. This statement is full of suggestion. It declares the spiritual exaltation of Moses. It shows how God may impart his own glory to those to whom he wills to show great favour. Chap. xxxiii, 19. It teaches the child of faith that long communion and intimate fellowship with God transfigures into the image of the heavenly. Since the Hebrew word here translated **shone** (קרן) is composed of the same letters as the word for *horn*, the Vulgate has rendered it *was horned*, and hence the mediæval notion represented in Angelo's famous statue, that Moses had horns upon his forehead.

30. They were afraid—At a former time (xx, 19) they had said to Moses, "Speak thou with us, and we will hear; but let not God speak with us, lest we die." Now Moses bears upon his face so much of the divine glory that they fear to talk even with him.

33. Till Moses had done—Rather, *when he had done speaking,* etc. Literally, *And Moses ceased from speaking with them, and put upon his face a vail.* So the vail was not worn while he was speaking, but when he left off speaking, and until he went into the tabernacle. Verses 34, 35. "The brilliant light on Moses's face," says Keil, "set forth the glory of the old covenant, and was intended both for Moses and the people as a foresight and a pledge of the glory to which Jehovah had called, and would eventually exalt, the people of his possession."

(3.) The Construction, Erection, and Dedication of the Tabernacle. Chapters XXXV-XL.

CHAPTER XXXV.

INTRODUCTORY.

We here enter upon the last stage of the divine adoption of Israel, as completed at Sinai, and written in this book. We have been told of the bitter oppression of Pharaoh, the birth and calling of Moses, the wonderful triumph over the superstitions of Egypt, the march to Sinai, the giving of the law, the plan of the tabernacle, and the lamentable breach of the covenant. After much intercession and penitence the tables of the law have been renewed, the covenant once more acknowledged and confirmed by the gracious word of Jehovah, (xxxiv, 10,) and now, as if resuming the narrative broken off at the close of chapter xxxi, we are informed how, under the direction of Moses, the tabernacle and its vessels were made, accepted, and dedicated to Jehovah, and filled with the divine glory. As these concluding chapters are in the main a recapitulation of the details given in chapters xxv-xxxi, the reader is referred to the notes on the text of those chapters. Only a few words and phrases call for further comment.

The Sabbath, 1-3.

1. These are the words—The plan of the tabernacle which had been given Moses in the mount had not yet been communicated to Israel. Moses now assembles **all the congregation,** and makes known how Jehovah would have them prepare for him a sanctuary.

B. C. 1491.   CHAPTER XXXV.   557

manded, that ye should do them. 2 ᵇ Six days shall work be done, but on the seventh day there shall be to you ¹ a holy day, a sabbath of rest to the LORD: whosoever doeth work therein shall be put to death. 3 ᶜ Ye shall kindle no fire throughout your habitations upon the sabbath day.
4 And Moses spake unto all the congregation of the children of Israel, saying, ᵈ This is the thing which the LORD commanded, saying, 5 Take ye from among you an offering unto the LORD: ᵉ whosoever is of a willing heart, let him bring it, an offering of the LORD; gold, and silver, and brass, 6 And blue, and purple, and scarlet, and fine linen, and goats' hair, 7 And rams' skins dyed red, and badgers' skins, and shittim wood, 8 And oil for the light, ᶠ and spices for anointing oil, and for the sweet incense, 9 And onyx stones, and stones to be set for the ephod, and for the breastplate. 10 And ᵍ every wise hearted among you shall come, and make all that the LORD hath commanded; 11 ʰ The tabernacle, his tent, and his covering, his taches, and his boards, his bars, his pillars, and his sockets; 12 ⁱ The ark, and the staves thereof, with the mercy seat, and the vail of the covering;

13 The ᵏ table, and his staves, and all his vessels, ˡ and the showbread; 14 ᵐ The candlestick also for the light, and his furniture, and his lamps, with the oil for the light; 15 ⁿ And the incense altar, and his staves, ᵒ and the anointing oil, and ᵖ the sweet incense, and the hanging for the door at the entering in of the tabernacle; 16 ᑫ The altar of burnt offering, with his brazen grate, his staves, and all his vessels, the laver and his foot; 17 ʳ The hangings of the court, his pillars, and their sockets, and the hanging for the door of the court; 18 The pins of the tabernacle, and the pins of the court, and their cords; 19 ˢ The clothes of service, to do service in the holy place, the holy garments for Aaron the priest, and the garments of his sons, to minister in the priest's office.
20 And all the congregation of the children of Israel departed from the presence of Moses. 21 And they came, every one ᵗ whose heart stirred him up, and every one whom his spirit made willing, and they brought the LORD's offering to the work of the tabernacle of the congregation, and for all his service, and for the holy garments. 22 And they came, both men and women, as many as were willing hearted, and brought

---

b Chap. 20. 9; 31. 14, 15; Lev. 23. 3; Num. 15. 32, etc.; Deut. 5. 12; Luke 13. 14.——1 Heb. holiness.——c Chap. 16. 23.——d Chap. 25. 1, 2.——e Chap. 25. 2.——f Chap. 25. 6.——g Chap. 31. 6.——h Chap. 26. 1, 2, etc.——i Chap. 25. 10, etc.——k Chap. 25. 23.

l Chap. 25. 30; Lev. 24. 5, 6.——m Chap. 25. 31, etc.——n Chap. 30. 1.——o Chap. 30. 23.——p Chap. 30. 34.——q Chap. 27. 1.——r Chap. 27. 9.——s Chap. 31. 10; 39. 1, 41; Num. 4. 5. 6, etc.——t Verses 5, 22, 26, 29; chap. 25. 2; 36. 2; 1 Chron. 28. 2, 9; 29. 9; Ezra 7. 27; 2 Cor. 8. 12; 9. 7.

---

2. **The seventh day . . . a sabbath of rest**—The purpose of this repetition of the sabbath law was probably to prevent any attempt to carry forward the work of the tabernacle on the holy day. See note on chap. xxxi, 13.

3. **Kindle no fire**—This prohibition is implied in chap. xvi, 23, but is here first formally enunciated. The offence recorded in Numbers xv, 32-36, looked toward the violation of this commandment.

THE OFFERINGS FOR THE SANCTUARY, 4-29.

5-9. **An offering**—See notes on xxv, 2-7.

10. **Wise hearted** — See note on xxviii, 3.

11-19. **The tabernacle**, etc.—These different parts of the sanctuary and the sacred vessels are illustrated in notes on chaps. xxv-xxviii.

21. **Every one whom his spirit made willing**—Were there, then, some who failed to assist in thus providing for the work of the tabernacle? So one may naturally infer from the form of statement here recorded. This would only accord with what is noticeable in all periods of the history of God's people. In times of highest enthusiasm and self-consecration, there will be found some heartless hangers on.

22. **Both men and women**—As if anticipating the New Testament idea, that in the life and fellowship of God there is neither male nor female. Gal. iii, 28. But in the making of this sanctuary, as in building the Christian Church, there is work both for men and women. As there are some kinds of work suitable only for men and not for women, so there are other kinds suitable only for women and not for men.

VOL. I.—36   O. T.

bracelets, and earrings, and rings, and tablets, all jewels of gold: and every man that offered, *offered* an offering of gold unto the Lord. **23** And ^uevery man, with whom was found blue, and purple, and scarlet, and fine linen, and goats' *hair*, and red skins of rams, and badgers' skins, brought *them*. **24** Every one that did offer an offering of silver and brass brought the Lord's offering: and every man, with whom was found shittim wood for any work of the service, brought *it*. **25** And all the women that were ^vwise hearted did spin with their hands, and brought that which they had spun, *both* of blue, and of purple, *and* of scarlet, and of fine linen. **26** And all the women whose heart stirred them up in wisdom spun goats' *hair*. **27** And ^wthe rulers brought onyx stones, and stones to be set, for the ephod, and for the breastplate; **28** And ^xspice, and oil for the light, and for the anointing oil, and for the sweet incense. **29** The children of Israel brought a ^ywilling offering unto the Lord, every man and woman, whose heart made them willing to bring for all manner of work, which the Lord had commanded to be made by the hand of Moses.

30 And Moses said unto the children of Israel, See, ^zthe Lord hath called by name Bezaleel the son of Uri, the son of Hur, of the tribe of Judah; **31** And he hath filled him with the spirit of God, in wisdom, in understanding, and in knowledge, and in all manner of workmanship; **32** And to devise curious

---
u 1 Chron. 29. 8.——*v* Chap. 28. 3; 31. 6; 36. 1; 2 Kings 23. 7; Prov. 31. 19, 22, 24.——*w* 1 Chron. 29. 6; Ezra 2. 68.——*x* Chap. 30. 23.——*y* Verse 21; 1 Chron. 29. 9.——*z* Chap. 31. 2, etc.

So, too, it may be in the Christian Church. **Bracelets**—The exact meaning of the word (חָח) thus translated is not certain. It has been rendered by *brooches, hooks, chains, clasps, nose-jewel.* **Earrings**—See on xxxii, 2. **Rings**—Probably *signet rings*. See note on Gen. xli, 42. **Tablets**—Occurs only here and Num. xxxi, 50, and is of uncertain meaning. It has been variously explained, as *armlets, necklaces, beads, lockets.*

25. Women . . . did spin—This appears to have been the business of women among the Egyptians and other ancient nations. The fact that the **wise hearted** women did this work

works, to work in gold, and in silver, and in brass, **33** And in the cutting of stones, to set *them*, and in carving of wood, to make any manner of cunning work. **34** And he hath put in his heart that he may teach, *both* he, and ⁿAholiab, the son of Ahisamach, of the tribe of Dan. **35** Them hath he ^ofilled with wisdom of heart, to work all manner of work, of the engraver, and of the cunning workman, and of the embroiderer, in blue, and in purple, in scarlet, and in fine linen, and of the weaver, *even* of them that do any work, and of those that devise cunning work.

CHAPTER XXXVI.

THEN wrought Bezaleel and Aholiab, and every ^awise hearted man, in whom the Lord put wisdom and understanding to know how to work all manner of work for the service of the ^bsanctuary, according to all that the Lord had commanded. **2** And Moses called Bezaleel and Aholiab, and every wise hearted man, in whose heart the Lord had put wisdom, *even* every one ^cwhose heart stirred him up to come unto the work to do it: **3** And they received of Moses all the offering, which the children of Israel ^dhad brought for the work of the service of the sanctuary, to make it *withal*. And they brought yet unto him free offerings every morning. **4** And all the wise men, that wrought all the work of the sanctuary, came every man from his work which they made;

5 And they spake unto Moses, saying

---
n Chap. 31. 6.——*o* Verse 31; chap. 31. 3, 6 1 Kings 7. 14; 2 Chron. 2. 14; Isa. 28. 26.——*a* Chap. 28. 3: 31. 6; 35. 10, 35.——*b* Chap. 25. 8.——*c* Chap. 35. 21, 26; 1 Chron. 29. 5.——*d* Chap. 35. 27.

---

shows that it was a labour requiring skill.

ANCIENT EGYPTIANS SPINNING.

Bezaleel and Aholiab, 30-35.
See notes on **xxxi**, 1-11.

B. C. 1491. CHAPTER XXXVI. 559

^e The people bring much more than enough for the service of the work, which the LORD commanded to make. 6 And Moses gave commandment, and they caused it to be proclaimed throughout the camp, saying, Let neither man nor woman make any more work for the offering of the sanctuary. So the people were restrained from bringing. 7 For the stuff they had was sufficient for all the work to make it, and too much.

8 ^f And every wise hearted man among them that wrought the work of the tabernacle made ten curtains *of* fine twined linen, and blue, and purple, and scarlet: *with* cherubim of cunning work made he them. 9 The length of one curtain *was* twenty and eight cubits, and the breadth of one curtain four cubits: the curtains *were* all of one size. 10 And he coupled the five curtains one unto another: and *the other* five curtains he coupled one unto another. 11 And he made loops of blue on the edge of one curtain from the selvedge in the coupling: likewise he made in the uttermost side of *another* curtain, in the coupling of the second. 12 ^g Fifty loops made he in one curtain, and fifty loops made he in the edge of the curtain which *was* in the coupling of the second: the loops held one *curtain* to another. 13 And he made fifty taches of gold, and coupled the curtains one unto another with the taches: so it became one tabernacle.

14 ^h And he made curtains *of* goats' *hair* for the tent over the tabernacle: eleven curtains he made them. 15 The length of one curtain *was* thirty cubits, and four cubits *was* the breadth of one curtain: the eleven curtains *were* of one size. 16 And he coupled five curtains by themselves, and six curtains by themselves. 17 And he made fifty loops upon the uttermost edge of the curtain in the coupling, and fifty loops made he upon the edge of the curtain which coupleth the second. 18 And he made fifty taches *of* brass to couple the tent together, that it might be one. 19 ⁱ And he made a covering for the tent *of* rams' skins dyed red, and a covering *of* badgers' skins above *that*.

20 ^k And he made boards for the tabernacle *of* shittim wood, standing up. 21 The length of a board *was* ten cubits, and the breadth of a board one cubit and a half. 22 One board had two tenons, equally distant one from another: thus did he make for all the boards of the tabernacle. 23 And he made boards for the tabernacle; twenty boards for the south side southward: 24 And forty sockets of silver he made under the twenty boards; two sockets under one board for his two tenons, and two sockets under another board for his two tenons. 25 And for the other side of the tabernacle, *which is* toward the north corner, he made twenty boards, 26 And their forty sockets of silver; two sockets under one board, and two sockets under another board. 27 And for the sides of the tabernacle westward he made six boards. 28 And two boards made he for the corners of the tabernacle in the two sides. 29 And they were ¹ coupled beneath, and coupled together at the head thereof, to one ring: thus he did to both of them in both the corners. 30 And there were eight boards; and their sockets *were* sixteen sockets of silver, ² under every board two sockets.

31 And he made ¹ bars of shittim wood; five for the boards of the one side of the tabernacle, 32 And five bars for the boards of the other side of the tabernacle, and five bars for the boards of the tabernacle for the sides westward. 33 And he made the middle bar to shoot through the boards from the one end to the other. 34 And he overlaid the boards* with gold, and made their rings *of* gold *to be* places for the bars, and overlaid the bars with gold.

35 And he made ^m a vail *of* blue,

e 2 Cor. 8. 2, 3. —*f* Chap. 26. 1. —*g* Chap. 26. 5. —*h* Chap. 26. 7. —*i* Chap. 26. 14. —*k* Chap. 26. 15.

1 Heb. *twinned*. —— 2 Heb. *two sockets, two sockets under one board*. —— *l* Chap. 26. 26. ——*m* Chap. 26. 31.

CHAPTER XXXVI.

SUPERABUNDANCE OF OFFERINGS, 1–7.

5. **Much more than enough**—Such a result of the willingness of the people to give was a noble exhibition of their devotion to Jehovah, and their purpose to keep their covenant with him. It furnishes a happy offset to the liberality which was too conspicuous for evil in their offerings for the golden calf, xxxii, 3. When the heart is all aglow with religious enthusiasm, no gifts seem too great or costly to express the measure of devotion.

THE TABERNACLE CURTAINS, BOARDS, AND HANGINGS, 8–38.

See notes on chap. xxvi, 1–37.

EXODUS.

and purple, and scarlet, and fine twined linen: *with* cherubim made he it of cunning work. **36** And he made thereunto four pillars *of* shittim *wood*, and overlaid them with gold: their hooks *were of* gold; and he cast for them four sockets of silver.
37 And he made a ⁿhanging for the tabernacle door *of* blue, and purple, and scarlet, and fine twined linen, ³ of needlework; **38** And the five pillars of it with their hooks: and he overlaid their chapiters and their fillets with gold: but their five sockets *were of* brass.

CHAPTER XXXVII.

AND Bezaleel made ᵃ the ark *of* shittim wood: two cubits and a half *was* the length of it, and a cubit and a half the breadth of it, and a cubit and a half the height of it: **2** And he overlaid it with pure gold within and without, and made a crown of gold to it round about. **3** And he cast for it four rings of gold, *to be set* by the four corners of it; even two rings upon the one side of it, and two rings upon the other side of it. **4** And he made staves *of* shittim wood, and overlaid them with gold. **5** And he put the staves into the rings by the sides of the ark, to bear the ark.
6 And he made the ᵇ mercy seat *of* pure gold: two cubits and a half *was* the length thereof, and one cubit and a half the breadth thereof. **7** And he made two cherubim *of* gold, beaten out of one piece made he them, on the two ends of the mercy seat; **8** One cherub ¹ on the end on this side, and another cherub ² on the *other* end on that side: out of the mercy seat made he the cherubim on the two ends thereof. **9** And the cherubim spread out *their* wings on high, *and* covered with their wings over the mercy seat, with their faces one to another; *even* to the mercy seatward were the faces of the cherubim.
10 And he made ᶜ the table *of* shittim wood: two cubits *was* the length thereof, and a cubit the breadth thereof, and a cubit and a half the height thereof:
11 And he overlaid it with pure gold, and made thereunto a crown of gold round about. **12** Also he made thereunto a border of a handbreadth round about; and made a crown of gold for the border thereof round about. **13** And he cast for it four rings of gold, and put the rings upon the four corners that *were* in the four feet thereof. **14** Over against the border were the rings, the places for the staves to bear the table. **15** And he made the staves *of* shittim wood, and overlaid them with gold, to bear the table. **16** And he made the vessels which *were* upon the table, his ᵈ dishes, and his spoons, and his bowls, and his covers ³ to cover withal, *of* pure gold.
17 And he made the ᵉ candlestick *of* pure gold: *of* beaten work made he the candlestick; his shaft, and his branch, his bowls, his knops, and his flowers, were of the same: **18** And six branches going out of the sides thereof; three branches of the candlestick out of the one side thereof, and three branches of the candlestick out of the other side thereof: **19** Three bowls made after the fashion of almonds in one branch, a knop and a flower; and three bowls made like almonds in another branch, a knop and a flower: so throughout the six branches going out of the candlestick. **20** And in the candlestick *were* four bowls made like almonds, his knops, and his flowers: **21** And a knop under two branches of the same, and a knop under two branches of the same, and a knop under two branches of the same, according to the six branches going out of it. **22** Their knops and their branches were of the same: all of it *was* one beaten work *of* pure gold. **23** And he made his seven lamps, and his snuffers, and his snuffdishes, *of* pure gold. **24** *Of* a talent of pure gold made he it, and all the vessels thereof.
25 ᶠ And he made the incense altar *of* shittim wood: the length of it *was* a cubit, and the breadth of it a cubit; *it was* foursquare; and two cubits *was* the height of it; the horns thereof were of the same.

---

n Chap. 26. 36.——3 Heb. *the work of a needleworker*, or, *embroiderer*.——*a* Chap. 25. 10.——*b* Chap. 25. 17.——1 Or, *out of*, etc.

2 Or, *out of*, etc. —— *c* Chap. 25. 23. —— *d* Chap. 25. 29.——3 Or, *to pour out withal*.—— *e* Chap. 25. 31.——*f* Chap. 30. 1.

CHAPTER XXXVII.

THE ARK OF THE COVENANT, 1–9.
See notes on chap. xxv, 10–22.

THE TABLE OF SHOWBREAD, 10–16.
See notes on chap. xxv, 23–30.

THE GOLDEN CANDLESTICK, 17–24.
See notes on chap. xxv, 31–40.

THE ALTAR OF INCENSE, 25–28.
See notes on chap. xxx, 1–10.

B. C. 1491.   **CHAPTER XXXVII.**   **561**

26 And he overlaid it with pure gold, *both* the top of it, and the sides thereof round about, and the horns of it: also he made unto it a crown of gold round about. **27** And he made two rings of gold for it under the crown thereof, by the two corners of it, upon the two sides thereof, to be places for the staves to bear it withal. **28** And he made the staves *of* shittim wood, and overlaid them with gold.
29 And he made ᵍ the holy anointing oil, and the pure incense of sweet spices, according to the work of the apothecary.

CHAPTER XXXVIII.

AND ᵃ he made the altar of burnt offering *of* shittim wood: five cubits *was* the length thereof, and five cubits the breadth thereof; *it was* foursquare; and three cubits the height thereof. **2** And he made the horns thereof on the four corners of it; the horns thereof were of the same: and he overlaid it with brass. **3** And he made all the vessels of the altar, the pots, and the shovels, and the basins, *and* the fleshhooks, and the firepans: all the vessels thereof made he *of* brass. **4** And he made for the altar a brazen grate of network, under the compass thereof, beneath unto the midst of it. **5** And he cast four rings for the four ends of the grate of brass, *to be* places for the staves. **6** And he made the staves *of* shittim wood, and overlaid them with brass. **7** And he put the staves into the rings on the sides of the altar, to bear it withal; he made the altar hollow with boards.
8 And he made ᵇ the laver *of* brass, and the foot of it *of* brass, of the ¹ lookingglasses of *the women* ² assembling, which assembled *at* the door of the tabernacle of the congregation.

g Chap. 30. 23, 34.——*a* Chap. 27. 1.——*b* Chap. 30. 18.——1 Or, *brazen glasses.*——2 Heb. *assembling by troops,* as 1 Sam. 2. 22.

9 And he made ᶜ the court: on the south side southward the hangings of the court *were of* fine twined linen, a hundred cubits: **10** Their pillars *were* twenty, and their brazen sockets twenty; the hooks of the pillars and their fillets *were of* silver. **11** And for the north side *the hangings were* a hundred cubits, their pillars *were* twenty, and their sockets of brass twenty; the hooks of the pillars and their fillets *of* silver. **12** And for the west side *were* hangings of fifty cubits, their pillars ten, and their sockets ten; the hooks of the pillars and their fillets *of* silver. **13** And for the east side eastward fifty cubits. **14** The hangings of the one side *of the gate were* fifteen cubits; their pillars three, and their sockets three. **15** And for the other side of the court gate, on this hand and that hand, *were* hangings of fifteen cubits; their pillars three, and their sockets three. **16** All the hangings of the court round about *were* of fine twined linen. **17** And the sockets for the pillars *were of* brass; the hooks of the pillars and their fillets *of* silver; and the overlaying of their chapiters *of* silver; and all the pillars of the court *were* filleted with silver. **18** And the hanging for the gate of the court *was* needlework, *of* blue, and purple, and scarlet, and fine twined linen: and twenty cubits *was* the length, and the height in the breadth *was* five cubits, answerable to the hangings of the court. **19** And their pillars *were* four, and their sockets *of* brass four; their hooks *of* silver, and the overlaying of their chapiters and their fillets *of* silver. **20** And all the ᵈ pins of the tabernacle, and of the court round about, *were of* brass.
21 This *is* the sum of the tabernacle, *even* of ᵉ the tabernacle of testimony, as

c Chap. 27. 9.——*d* Chap. 27. 19.——*e* Num. 1. 50, 53; 9. 15; 10. 11; 17. 7, 8; 18. 2; 2 Chron. 24. 6; Acts 7. 44.

THE OIL AND THE INCENSE, 29.
See on chap. xxx, 22–38.

CHAPTER XXXVIII.
THE ALTAR OF BURNT OFFERINGS, 1–7.
See notes on chap. xxvii, 1–7.

THE LAVER, 8.
See notes on chap. xxx, 17–21.

THE COURT OF THE TABERNACLE, 9–20.
See notes on chap. xxvii, 9–19.

THE AMOUNT OF METALS USED FOR THE TABERNACLE, 21–31.

21. This is the sum—Literally, *the things reckoned,* meaning, according to what follows, the weight of the gold, silver, and brass employed in the construction of the sanctuary and what belonged to it. The amount, as summed up, is recorded as
Gold=29 talents and 730 shekels.
Silver=100 talents and 1,775 shekels.
Brass=70 talents and 2,400 shekels.
The uncertainty attaching to the ex-

it was counted, according to the commandment of Moses, *for* the service of the Levites, ʳ by the hand of Ithamar, son to Aaron the priest. **22** And ᵍ Bezaleel the son of Uri, the son of Hur, of the tribe of Judah, made all that the LORD commanded Moses. **23** And with him *was* Aholiab, son of Ahisamach, of the tribe of Dan, an engraver, and a cunning workman, and an embroiderer in blue, and in purple, and in scarlet, and fine linen. **24** All the gold that was occupied for the work in all the work of the holy *place*, even the gold of the offering, was twenty and nine talents, and seven hundred and thirty shekels, after ʰ the shekel of the sanctuary. **25** And the silver of them that were numbered of the congregation *was* a hundred talents, and a thousand seven hundred and threescore and fifteen shekels, after the shekel of the sanctuary: **26** ⁱA bekah for ³every man, *that is*, half a shekel, after the shekel of the sanctuary, for every one that went to be numbered, from twenty years old and upward, for ᵏ six hundred thousand and three thousand and five hundred and fifty *men*. **27** And of the hundred talents of silver were cast ˡ the sockets of the sanctuary, and the sockets of the vail; a hundred sockets of the hundred talents, a talent for a socket. **28** And of the thousand seven hundred seventy and five *shekels* he made hooks for the pillars, and overlaid their chapiters, and filleted them. **29** And the brass of the offering *was* seventy talents, and two thousand and four hundred shekels. **30** And therewith he made the sockets to the door of the tabernacle of the congregation, and the brazen altar, and the brazen grate for it, and all the vessels of the altar, **31** And the sockets of the court round about, and the sockets of the court gate, and all the pins of the tabernacle, and all the pins of the court round about.

CHAPTER XXXIX.

AND of ᵃ the blue, and purple, and scarlet, they made ᵇ clothes of service, to do service in the holy *place*, and made the holy garments for Aaron; ᶜ as the LORD commanded Moses. **2** ᵈ And he made the ephod *of* gold, blue, and purple, and scarlet, and fine twined linen. **3** And they did beat the gold into thin plates, and cut *it into* wires, to work *it* in the blue, and in the purple, and in the scarlet, and in the fine linen, *with* cunning work. **4** They made shoulderpieces for it, to couple *it* together: by the two edges was it coupled together. **5** And the curious girdle of his ephod,

---

f Num. 4. 28, 33.——*g* Chap. 31. 2, 6.——*h* Chap. 30. 13, 24; Lev. 5. 15; 27. 3, 25; Num. 3. 47; 18. 16.——*i* Chap. 30. 13, 15.——³ Heb. *a poll.*

k Num. 1. 46. —— *l* Chap. 26. 19, 21, 25, 32. —— *a* Chap. 35. 23. —— *b* Chap. 31. 10; 35. 19. —— *c* Chap. 28. 4.——*d* Chap. 28. 6.

---

act weight and value of the gold, silver, and brass talents and shekels makes it impossible to determine precisely the gross amount of the cost of the tabernacle. Then, further, the different relative value of a given amount of these metals in ancient and in modern times would greatly affect any estimate. The weight of the metals here mentioned, as estimated in the *Speaker's Commentary*, is as follows, in avoirdupois weight:

Gold, 1 ton 4 cwt. 2 qrs. 13 lbs.
Silver, 4 tons 4 cwt. 2 qrs. 20 lbs.
Bronze, 2 tons 19 cwt. 2 qrs. 11 lbs.

The entire value of these metals, at the lowest approximate estimate in American currency, would be over a million dollars. This estimate of the cost of the tabernacle does not include the large amount of other material for curtains, boards, and pillars, nor take into account at all the value of the labour, which the men and women of Israel gave as freely as they did the gold and silver and other things. On the question whence the Israelites obtained such vast amounts of precious things, see note on chap. xxv, 3.

We are not to think of the tabernacle as of a modern Christian Church. The latter, as a house of worship, serves mainly for the comfort and convenience of an assembly of worshippers, and each true worshipper is supposed to have risen in spirit into the profound realities of which the tabernacle and its services were only symbols. Serving the purpose of material symbols of the unseen and eternal, the tabernacle was appropriately made of the most costly materials, for these, with their various values, were, for the time, "object lessons" of the better things to come.

CHAPTER XXXIX.

THE HOLY GARMENTS OF THE PRIESTS, 1–31

See notes on chap. xxviii.

B. C. 1491. CHAPTER XXXIX. 563

that *was* upon it, *was* of the same, according to the work thereof; *of* gold, blue, and purple, and scarlet, and fine twined linen; as the LORD commanded Moses.

6 ᵉAnd they wrought onyx stones inclosed in ouches of gold, graven, as signets are graven, with the names of the children of Israel; **7** And he put them on the shoulders of the ephod, *that they should be* stones for a ᶠmemorial to the children of Israel; as the LORD commanded Moses.

8 ᵍAnd he made the breastplate *of* cunning work, like the work of the ephod; *of* gold, blue, and purple, and scarlet, and fine twined linen. **9** It was foursquare; they made the breastplate double: a span *was* the length thereof, and a span the breadth thereof, *being* doubled. **10** ʰAnd they set in it four rows of stones: *the first* row *was* a ¹sardius, a topaz, and a carbuncle; this *was* the first row. **11** And the second row, an emerald, a sapphire, and a diamond. **12** And the third row, a ligure, an agate, and an amethyst. **13** And the fourth row, a beryl, an onyx, and a jasper: *they were* inclosed in ouches of gold in their inclosing. **14** And the stones *were* according to the names of the children of Israel, twelve, according to their names, *like* the engravings of a signet, every one with his name, according to the twelve tribes. **15** And they made upon the breastplate chains at the ends, *of* wreathen work *of* pure gold. **16** And they made two ouches *of* gold, and two gold rings, and put the two rings in the two ends of the breastplate. **17** And they put the two wreathen chains of gold in the two rings on the ends of the breastplate. **18** And the two ends of the two wreathen chains they fastened in the two ouches, and put them on the shoulderpieces of the ephod, before it. **19** And they made two rings of gold, and put *them* on the two ends of the breastplate, upon the border of it, which *was* on the side of the ephod inward. **20** And they made two *other* golden rings, and put them on the two sides of the ephod underneath, toward the forepart of it, over against the *other* coupling thereof, above the curious girdle of the ephod. **21** And they did bind the breastplate by his rings unto the rings of the ephod with a lace of blue, that it might be above the curious girdle of the ephod, and that the breastplate might not be loosed from the ephod; as the LORD commanded Moses.

22 ⁱAnd he made the robe of the ephod *of* woven work, all *of* blue. **23** And *there was* a hole in the midst of the robe, as the hole of an habergeon, *with* a band round about the hole, that it should not rend. **24** And they made upon the hems of the robe pomegranates *of* blue, and purple, and scarlet, *and* twined *linen*. **25** And they made ᵏbells *of* pure gold, and put the bells between the pomegranates upon the hem of the robe, round about between the pomegranates; **26** A bell and a pomegranate, a bell and a pomegranate, round about the hem of the robe to minister *in;* as the LORD commanded Moses.

27 ˡAnd they made coats *of* fine linen *of* woven work for Aaron, and for his sons, **28** ᵐAnd a mitre *of* fine linen, and goodly bonnets *of* fine linen, and ⁿlinen breeches *of* fine twined linen, **29** ᵒAnd a girdle *of* fine twined linen, and blue, and purple, and scarlet, *of* needlework; as the LORD commanded Moses.

30 ᵖAnd they made the plate of the holy crown *of* pure gold, and wrote upon it a writing, *like to* the engravings of a signet, HOLINESS TO THE LORD. **31** And they tied unto it a lace of blue, to fasten *it* on high upon the mitre; as the LORD commanded Moses.

32 Thus was all the work of the tabernacle of the tent of the congregation finished: and the children of Israel did ᵠaccording to all that the LORD commanded Moses, so did they.

33 And they brought the tabernacle unto Moses, the tent, and all his furni-

---

e Chap. 28. 9.—*f* Chap. 28. 12.—*g* Chap. 28. 15.—*h* Chap. 28. 17, etc.—1 Or, *ruby.*—*i* Chap. 28. 31.—*k* Chap. 28. 33.

l Chap. 28. 39, 40.—*m* Chap. 28. 4, 39; Ezek. 44. 18.—*n* Chap. 28. 42.—*o* Chap. 28. 39.—*p* Chap. 28. 36, 37.—*q* Verses 42, 43; chap. 25. 40.

ALL BROUGHT TO MOSES AND APPROVED, 32–43.

How long the preparation of the different parts of the tabernacle required we are not told, but the zeal and diligence implied in the willing offerings of the people warrant the belief that the whole would have been completed in a few months. According to Josephus, the whole time they were engaged in this work was seven months. (*Ant.*, iii, 8, 4.) As Moses had received by revelation in the mount the plan and pattern of the tabernacle, it was necessary that all the parts should finally be submitted to him for acceptance and blessing.

ture, his taches, his boards, his bars, and his pillars, and his sockets; **34** And the covering of rams' skins dyed red, and the covering of badgers' skins, and the vail of the covering; **35** The ark of the testimony, and the staves thereof, and the mercy seat; **36** The table, *and* all the vessels thereof, and the showbread; **37** The pure candlestick, *with* the lamps thereof, *even with* the lamps to be set in order, and all the vessels thereof, and the oil for light; **38** And the golden altar, and the anointing oil, and ² the sweet incense, and the hanging for the tabernacle door; **39** The brazen altar, and his grate of brass, his staves, and all his vessels, the laver and his foot; **40** The hangings of the court, his pillars, and his sockets, and the hanging for the court gate, his cords, and his pins, and all the vessels of the service of the tabernacle, for the tent of the congregation; **41** The clothes of service to do service in the holy *place*, and the holy garments for Aaron the priest, and his sons' garments, to minister in the priest's office. **42** According to all that the LORD commanded Moses, so the children of Israel ʳ made all the work. **43** And Moses did look upon all the work, and, behold, they had done it as the LORD had commanded, even so had they done it: and Moses ˢ blessed them.

CHAPTER XL.

AND the LORD spake unto Moses, saying, **2** On the first day of the ᵃ first month shalt thou set up ᵇ the tabernacle of the tent of the congregation. **3** And ᶜ thou shalt put therein the ark of the testimony, and cover the ark with the vail. **4** And ᵈ thou shalt bring

2 Heb. *the incense of sweet spices.*——*r* Chap. 35. 10.——*s* Lev. 9. 22, 23; Num. 6. 23; Josh. 22. 6; 2 Sam. 6. 18; 1 Kings 8. 14; 2 Chron. 30. 27.——*a* Chap. 12. 2; 13. 4.——*b* Verse 17; Chap. 26. 1, 30.——*c* Verse 21; chap. 26. 33; Num. 4. 5.——*d* Verse 22; chap. 26. 35.

CHAPTER XL.

THE ORDER TO SET UP THE TABERNACLE, 1-16.

The formality of this command to erect the sanctuary involves an incidental repetition of what has already been described. After the due consecration of all its parts, the tabernacle and all its vessels were to be regarded as "most holy." Comp. xxx, 29. In verse 10 of this chapter it is said that after its anointing the altar of burnt offerings should *be a holy of holies*, as in the table, and ᵉ set in order ¹ the things that are to be set in order upon it; ᶠ and thou shalt bring in the candlestick, and light the lamps thereof. **5** ᵍ And thou shalt set the altar of gold for the incense before the ark of the testimony, and put the hanging of the door to the tabernacle. **6** And thou shalt set the altar of the burnt offering before the door of the tabernacle of the tent of the congregation. **7** And ʰ thou shalt set the laver between the tent of the congregation and the altar, and shalt put water therein. **8** And thou shalt set up the court round about, and hang up the hanging at the court gate. **9** And thou shalt take the anointing oil, and ⁱ anoint the tabernacle, and all that *is* therein, and shalt hallow it, and all the vessels thereof: and it shall be holy. **10** And thou shalt anoint the altar of the burnt offering, and all his vessels, and sanctify the altar: and ᵏ it shall be an altar ² most holy. **11** And thou shall anoint the laver and his foot, and sanctify it. **12** ˡ And thou shalt bring Aaron and his sons unto the door of the tabernacle of the congregation, and wash them with water. **13** And thou shalt put upon Aaron the holy garments, ᵐ and anoint him, and sanctify him; that he may minister unto me in the priest's office. **14** And thou shalt bring his sons, and clothe them with coats: **15** And thou shalt anoint them, as thou didst anoint their father, that they may minister unto me in the priest's office: for their anointing shall surely be ⁿ an everlasting priesthood throughout their generations. **16** Thus did Moses: according to all that the LORD commanded him, so did he.

e Verse 23; chap. 25. 30; Lev. 24. 5, 6.——1 Heb. *the order thereof.*——*f* Verses 24, 25.——*g* Verse 26.——*h* Verse 30; chap. 30. 18.——*i* Chap. 30. 26.——*k* Chap. 29. 36, 37.——2 Heb. *holiness of holinesses.*——*l* Lev. 8. 1-13.——*m* Chap. 28. 41.——*n* Num. 25. 13.

if some special sanctity attached to that. Its central position and importance in the order of holy services made it a sort of counterpart, among the *vessels* of the sanctuary, of what the holy of holies was among the relatively sacred *places* of the same.

15. An everlasting priesthood— To be perpetuated **throughout their generations,** until superseded by the office and work of the Priest "after the order of Melchizedek." See notes on Heb. vii. Moses proceeded to perform all the commandments here given, (verse

17 And it came to pass in the first month in the second year, on the first *day* of the month, *that* the ° tabernacle was reared up. **18** And Moses reared up the tabernacle, and fastened his sockets, and set up the boards thereof, and put in the bars thereof, and reared up his pillars. **19** And he spread abroad

---

o Verse 1; | Num. 7. 1.

16,) but the consecration of the priests and special legislation touching the various kinds of sacrifices must have followed the erection of the tabernacle, and is recorded in the Book of Leviticus.

ERECTION OF THE TABERNACLE, 17-33.

17. **It came to pass**—After all the work of the tabernacle and its furniture was finished, as related in chaps. xxxvi-xxxix. **The first month**—Abib, (chap. xiii, 4,) or Nisan, (Neh. ii, 1,) corresponding nearly with our April. See note on chap. xii, 2. **The second year**—The second year after the exodus. The deliverance from Egypt was an appropriate and memorable epoch in Hebrew chronology—the beginning of years, as Abib was the beginning of months. Compare 1 Kings vi, 1. **The first day of the month**—Israel's first free new year's day, for the first day of the previous year had found them yet in the house of bondage, and fourteen days of that year passed before they departed from Egypt. About half the year had gone before they commenced the work of the tabernacle, for it was the third month when they reached the wilderness of Sinai, (chap. xix, 1,) and Moses spent two periods of forty days each in the mount, (chapters xxxiv, 18, xxiv, 28,) which was nearly three months more. But six months was ample time for the work; for the tabernacle was no such elaborate structure as the temple of Solomon; and as the zeal of the people showed itself in their offering more than enough material for the structure, so that Moses had even to restrain them from bringing more, (chap. xxxvi, 5-7,) so also the work itself was doubtless carried forward with equal zeal till all was finished. **The tabernacle was reared up**—According to the directions which the Lord had given Moses. Verses 1-6.

18. **Moses reared up the tabernacle**—We must not suppose that Moses personally and alone did all that is attributed to him in this chapter. He was probably assisted by Aaron and the "wise-hearted men." Chap. xxxvi, 1. But Moses had the oversight and command of all these, and Aaron and his sons were not yet set apart to the priesthood. The word rendered *tabernacle* here is *mishcan*, and is used both of the enclosure of boards, and of the ornamented cloth which is described in chapter xxvi, 1-6. No mention is made of stakes, tent-pins, ropes, ridge-poles, etc., but all these are presupposed or implied in every erection of a tent. The description here given is very brief, and presupposes in the reader's mind the fuller descriptions which have been given in the preceding chapters. **Sockets**—The silver *bases* for the boards, (chap. xxvi, 19-21,) and the brazen ones for the pillars, (chapter xxvi, 37,) to rest in. These served to hold the boards and pillars in their places, and to keep them from decay. The sockets in which the boards rested probably formed in appearance a sort of plinth around the bottom of their walls. **The boards**—Of shittim or acacia wood, which formed the inner enclosure. Chap. xxvi, 15-25; xxxvi, 20-23. **The bars**—These were also of shittim wood, and made to pass through gold rings, (or staples,) probably on the outside of the boards. Chap. xxvi, 26-29. They were five in number for each side and for the western end, the middle bar in each case reaching from end to end. Both the boards and the bars were overlaid with gold, presenting to the gaze of the beholder, either on the outside or within, a vast golden surface. **Pillars**—Five in number, at the entrance or east end of the tent. Chap. xxvi, 37. There were also four pillars within the tabernacle to support the vail which separated the holy place from the holy of holies. Chap. xxvi, 32; xxxvi, 36.

19. **Spread abroad the tent over**

566 EXODUS. B. C. 1490.

the tent over the tabernacle, and put the covering of the tent above upon it; as the LORD commanded Moses.

20 And he took and put ᵖ the testimony into the ark, and set the staves on the ark, and put the mercy seat above upon the ark: **21** And he brought the ark into the tabernacle, and ᑫ set up the vail of the covering, and covered the ark of the testimony; as the LORD commanded Moses.

22 ʳ And he put the table in the tent of the congregation, upon the side of the tabernacle northward, without the

p Chap. 25. 16.——*q* Chap. 26. 33; 35. 12.——*r* Chap. 26. 35.

the tabernacle—The *tent* here refers to the curtains of goats' hair, which, in chap. xxvi, 7, are called "a covering upon the tabernacle." The Hebrew words are the same in each passage, and designate the tent cloth which was placed over or above the ornamented curtains described in chap. xxvi, 1–6. It served as a covering and protection for the "curtains of fine linen, and blue, and purple, and scarlet: with cherubim of cunning work." Chap. xxvi, 1. These latter, according to Fergusson, (see p. 520,) formed the ornamented roof of the tabernacle as seen from the inside. They may, however, have been thrown over the board structure, and drawn down tightly on the outer sides. The objections to a flat roof would not apply to this set of curtains if thus adjusted, inasmuch as the tent of goat's hair above it would have protected it from rain. **The covering of the tent above upon it**—This was an additional covering made of rams' skins, dyed red, and sealskins, and spread on the top of the goat's hair canvas for a further protection from the weather. See chapter xxvi, 14. These several coverings made the roofing utterly impervious to the rain. **As the Lord commanded Moses**—This expression is here used seven times within the space of fourteen verses, (19-32,) and shows how very careful Moses was to make all things according to the pattern shown him by Jehovah. Compare chap. xxv, 9, 40; Heb. viii, 5.

20. **The testimony**—The two tables of stone on which the ten commandments were written by the finger of God. Chap. xxxi, 18, xxxii, 15, 16. Those first written were broken by Moses, (chap. xxxii, 19,) but another set was afterward prepared. Chap. xxxiv, 4. The decalogue graven on the two stone tablets was called *the testimony*, because it was Jehovah's most emphatic testimony or witness against sin—a monumental expression of his will; and it was placed in the ark that it might be a witness against rebellion and sin in Israel. Compare Deut. xxxi, 26, 27. When, after the lapse of several hundred years, the ark was deposited in the most holy place of the temple of Solomon, there was nothing in it but these two tables of stone. 1 Kings viii, 9. According to Heb. ix, 4, it originally contained also the golden pot of manna and Aaron's rod that budded, though these latter, according to chap. xvi, 34, and Num. xvii, 10, were placed "before the testimony." Most writers have understood "before the testimony" as equivalent to *before the ark;* but according to the inspired writer of Hebrews it would mean *before the testimony itself*, that is, the tables inside the ark. For a description of the ark, the staves, and the mercy seat, see chap. xxv, 10–22.

21. **Brought the ark into the tabernacle**—Its place was in the holy of holies, within the inner vail. **The vail of the covering**—The vail described in chap. xxvi, 31, 32, which hung upon four pillars, and served to *cover* or screen the most holy place from human eyes. **And covered the ark**—That is, he covered it by the vail just mentioned, and so concealed it from the gaze of men.

22. **The table**—The table on which the "showbread" was always kept. This table is particularly described in chapter xxv, 23–30, where see notes. **Northward, without the vail**—As the tent faced the east, the north side would be to the right hand of one entering. The position of the table would thus be near the north-west corner of the holy place, and just in front, or outside of, the vail which hid the holy of holies from view.

B. C. 1490. CHAPTER XL. 567

vail. 23 ˢAnd he set the bread in order upon it before the LORD; as the LORD had commanded Moses.
24 ᵗAnd he put the candlestick in the tent of the congregation, over against the table, on the side of the tabernacle southward. 25 And ᵘhe lighted the lamps before the LORD; as the LORD commanded Moses.
26 ᵛAnd he put the golden altar in the tent of the congregation before the vail: 27 ʷAnd he burnt sweet incense thereon; as the LORD commanded Moses.

28 ˣAnd he set up the hanging at the door of the tabernacle. 29 ʸAnd he put the altar of burnt offering by the door of the tabernacle of the tent of the congregation, and ᶻoffered upon it the burnt offering and the meat offering; as the LORD commanded Moses.
30 ᵃAnd he set the laver between the tent of the congregation and the altar, and put water there, to wash withal.
31 And Moses and Aaron and his sons washed their hands and their feet thereat: 32 When they went into the tent

---

s Verse 4.——*t* Chap. 26. 35.——*u* Verse 4; chap. 25. 37.——*v* Verse 5; chap. 30. 6.——*w* Chap. 30. 7. | *x* Verse 5; chap. 26. 36.——*y* Verse 6.——*z* Chap. 29. 38, etc.—— *a* Verse 7; chap. 30. 18.

---

23. **Set the bread in order**—The manner of making this bread, and of arranging it upon the table, is described in Leviticus xxiv, 5-9, where see notes. Whether Moses immediately arranged the bread, lighted the lamps, (verse 25,) burnt incense, (27,) and offered sacrifices, (29,) as soon as the table, candlestick, and altars were set each in its place, according to the order of this narrative, is not quite clear. But as Aaron and his sons were not consecrated to the priesthood until after the tabernacle was set up, (verses 12-15,) and so did not wash in the laver until after their consecration, (verses 31, 32,) it is probable that the table, lamps, and altars, like the laver, were not put to their uses until Aaron and his sons were consecrated priests. This, however, was done as soon as the tabernacle was reared up; perhaps on the same day.

24. **The candlestick**—See chap. xxv, 31-37. **Side . . . southward**—To the left of one entering, opposite to the showbread table. So the table and the candlestick were on opposite sides of the golden altar. See on verse 26.

25. **Lighted the lamps**—The lamps were to be kept burning, just as the showbread was to be kept standing, "before the Lord continually." Lev. xxiv, 1-4.

26. **The golden altar**—Not to be confounded with the brazen altar, or altar of burnt offerings, which was placed not **in the tent**, but outside of it, in the court, verse 29. The golden altar, or altar of incense, was placed in the holy place **before the vail**, so that it must have stood between the table of showbread and the golden candlestick. Compare verses 22 and 24, notes. For description of this altar see notes and cut, page 535.

27. **Sweet incense** — Hebrew, incense of spices, or aromatics. Its ingredients, and the manner of their preparation, are mentioned in chap. xxx, 34-36. The incense was, strictly speaking, the perfume exhaled by fire from the compounded aromatics. Incense was used in connexion with the religious ceremonies of most ancient nations. In the tabernacle service it was to be offered morning and evening, (chap. xxx, 7, 8,) and was a beautiful and expressive symbol of the prayer of saints. Psa. cxli, 2; Rev. v, 8; viii, 3, 4.

28. **The hanging** — Described in chap. xxvi, 36, 37, where see notes.

29. **The altar of burnt offering**—This was made of shittim wood, and overlaid with brass, as described in chap. xxvii, 1-8, and so is to be distinguished from "the golden altar" mentioned in verse 26, where see note. It was five times larger in breadth and width than the golden altar, and one cubit higher. **By the door**—Before, or in front of the door, verse 6. It was placed in the open court that surrounded the tabernacle, (verse 33,) and some distance in front of the tent, so as to leave room between it and the tent for the laver, verse 33. On **the burnt offering and the meat offering**, see Lev. vii, 37, 38, notes.

30. **The laver**— A large circular basin, to hold water, in which the priests were to wash their hands and feet. Solomon made for the temple ten lavers, and set them on "ten bases

of the congregation, and when they came near unto the altar, they washed; ᵇ as the LORD commanded Moses, **33** ᶜ And he reared up the court round about the tabernacle and the altar, and set up the hanging of the court gate. So Moses finished the work.

34 ᵈ Then a cloud covered the tent of the congregation, and the glory of the LORD filled the tabernacle. **35** And Moses ᵉ was not able to enter into the tent of the congregation, because the cloud abode thereon, and the glory of the LORD filled the tabernacle. **36** ᶠ And when the cloud was taken up from over the tabernacle, the children of Israel ᵍ went onward in all their journeys: **37** But ᵍ if the cloud were not taken up, then they journeyed not till the day that it was taken up. **38** For ʰ the cloud of the LORD *was* upon the tabernacle by day, and fire was on it by night, in the sight of all the house of Israel, throughout all their journeys.

b Chap. 30. 19, 20.—*c* Verse 8; chap. 27. 9, 16. —*d* Chap. 29. 43; Lev. 16. 2; Num. 9. 15; 1 Kings 8. 10, 11; 2 Chron. 5. 13; 7. 2; Isa. 6. 4; Hag. 2. 7, 9; Rev. 15. 8.

e Lev. 16. 2; 1 Kings 8. 11; 2 Chron. 5. 14. —*f* Num. 9. 17; 10. 11; Neh. 9, 19.—3 Heb. *journeyed.* — *g* Num. 9. 19-22. — *h* Chap. 13. 21; Num. 9. 15.

of brass," (1 Kings vii, 27-38,) but this laver of the tabernacle was probably of more simple construction. See chap. xxx, 18-21, notes.

33. **The court round about**—A large enclosure of linen curtains, one hundred cubits by fifty, with a **gate** or entrance twenty cubits wide. See full description in chap. xxvii, 9-18.

JEHOVAH'S GLORY FILLING THE TABERNACLE, 34-38.

It only remains that Jehovah manifest his approval of the tabernacle by some visible proof of his presence and abode there. Accordingly, when Moses had approved the work done, and completed what it was intended for human hands to do, *the* **cloud** which had accompanied them in their journey from Egypt (see note on xiii, 21) **covered the tent of the congregation, and the glory of the Lord filled the tabernacle.** The **tent** is here distinguished from the **tabernacle,** and is to be understood as the outer covering of curtains, while *the tabernacle* proper was the more immediate dwelling within, the *mishcan,* consisting of the board structure, and the ornamented curtains which were placed upon it. See note at the beginning of chap. xxvi. So gloriously did the **cloud** appear above the tent, and so wonderfully did the divine **glory** fill the interior of the sacred dwelling, that **Moses was not able to enter.** He had previously approached the thick darkness of Sinai, out of which Jehovah spoke, (chap. xx, 21;) he had witnessed an unparalleled display of the divine glory in the mount, (xxxiii, 19-23, xxxiv, 5-8;) but this theophany was too intense in its splendour to permit even Moses to enter within the holy places where, for the time, the Holy One abode in special presence.

36-38. **When the cloud was taken up**—This description of the guidance of Israel by the cloud is more fully detailed in Num. ix, 15-23. It appropriately concludes the Book of Exodus, which records the bondage, the redemption, and the consecration of Israel. The great facts written in this book served to make the history of Israel typical of the redemption of mankind; and especially does the image of the cloud and fire, accompanying, **by day** and **by night, all the house of Israel, throughout all their journeys,** portray in most impressive form the doctrine of the immanent providence of our Heavenly Father. He is with his people always; and they may read the lessons of the exodus and the tabernacle, and in every generation sing: "The Lord God is a sun and shield: the Lord will give grace and glory: no good thing will he withhold from them that walk uprightly. O Lord of hosts, blessed is the man that trusteth in thee." Psalm lxxxiv, 11, 12.

SYMBOLISM OF THE TABERNACLE.

The symbolism and typology of the Mosaic tabernacle are recognized in the ninth chapter of the Epistle to the Hebrews, and we may well suppose that a structure designed to serve so important a purpose in the religious training of the chosen nation must have been planned to suggest some grand and precious spiritual truths. (Comp. note on the Symbolism of the Temple at the close of notes on First Kings vii.) That it was a symbol of inner and spiritual relationship, made possible between God and man by the blood of atonement, we have already indicated in our introductory note at the beginning of chapter xxv, and we take no space to detail the various conjectures by which it is made to represent things which are physical and visible. As shown in the passage above referred to, and especially by the teaching of chap. xxix, 42–46, the great idea which centers in the complex symbol is that of JEHOVAH DWELLING WITH HIS PEOPLE. Man is by sin estranged from God, and there can be no reunion and fellowship without remission of sins and a purifying of the spiritual nature of man. This was graciously provided for in the expiatory sacrifices required of every Israelite. The life or soul was conceived as living and subsisting in the blood, (Lev. xvii, 11,) and when the blood of a victim was poured out at the altar it symbolized the surrender of a life which had been forfeited by sin, and the worshipper who made the sacrifice thereby acknowledged before Jehovah his death-deserving guilt. There could, accordingly, be no approach to God on the part of sinful men—no possible meeting and dwelling with him—except by the offerings made at the great altar in front of the sacred tent. No priest might pass into the tabernacle until sprinkled with blood from that altar, (xxix, 21,) and the live coals, used for burning the incense before Jehovah, were taken from the same place. Lev. xvi, 12. Nor might the priest, on penalty of death, minister at the altar or enter the tabernacle without first washing at the laver, (xxx, 20, 21.) So the great altar in the court continually proclaimed that without the shedding of blood there is no remission, and the priestly ablutions denoted that without the washing of regeneration no man might enter the kingdom of God. Compare Psa. xxiv, 3, 4; John iii, 5; Heb. x, 19–22. The blessed and holy dwelling with God, symbolized in the holy places of the tabernacle, were possible only because of the reconciliation effected at the altar of sacrifice without.

The two apartments of the tabernacle, known as the holy and the most holy places, were adapted to represent the relationship between the human and the divine, made possible by the gracious covenant of God with his people. Into the first the priests entered, as the representatives of the people, and their service there was not for themselves alone, but for all Israel, whose relation to God, so long as they kept his covenant, was that of a kingdom of priests and a holy nation. Chap. xix, 5, 6; comp. 1 Pet. ii, 5, 9; Rev. i, 6; v, 10. As the officiating priest stood in the holy place, facing the holy of holies, he had at his right hand the table of showbread, on his left the candlestick, and immediately before him the altar of incense. Chap. xl, 22–27. The twelve cakes of bread (bread of presence) kept continually on the table as before God, most obviously symbolized the twelve tribes of Israel continually offering themselves as an acceptable sacrifice in the presence of Jehovah. The golden candlestick with its seven lamps, opposite the table, was another symbol of Israel considered as the Church of the living God and the light of the world. Then, further, the constant devotion of Israel to God was represented at the golden altar of incense immediately before the vail, and in front of the mercy-seat, (xxx, 6.) The offering of incense was an expressive symbol of the prayers of saints, (Psa. cxli, 2, Rev. v, 8, viii, 3, 4,) and the whole multitude of the people were wont to pray without at the hour of the incense offering. Luke i, 10. Jehovah was pleased to "inhabit the praises of Israel," (Psa. xxii, 3,) for all that his people may be and do in their consecrated relation to him expresses itself in their prayers before his altar and mercy seat.

The holy place, therefore, with its table and candlestick and golden altar of incense, symbolized the relation of the true Israel to God, made available by the blood of atonement. The holy of holies, on the other hand, symbolized Jehovah's relations to his people, and profoundly suggested the terms or considerations by which it was compatible for him to meet and dwell with man. It contained the ark, within which were deposited the two tables of testimony—Jehovah's declaration out of the thick darkness—a monumental witness of his wrath against sin. Over this ark, and covering the tables of testimony, was placed the capporeth, or mercy seat, to be sprinkled with blood on the great day of atonement. Lev. xvi, 11–17. Here was a most significant symbol of *mercy covering wrath*. Made of fine gold, and having its dimensions the same as the length and breadth of the ark, (xxv, 17,) it fittingly represented that glorious provision of infinite wisdom and love by which, in virtue of the precious blood of Christ, and in complete harmony with the righteousness of God, atonement is made for the guilty but penitent transgressor.

The cherubim, spreading out their wings over the mercy seat, and gazing as in wondering adoration upon it, were appropriate symbols of the redeemed and glorified Israel, who shall ultimately behold the glory of God, and dwell in his heavenly light forever. This subject we have treated in the note on Gen. iii, 24, page 100 of this Commentary.

The ministration of the high priest on the great day of atonement, as described in Lev. xvi, is declared in the Epistle to the Hebrews to have prefigured the redeeming work of Christ, who, "being come a high priest of good things to come, by a greater and more perfect tabernacle, not made with hands,...neither by the blood of goats and calves, but by his own blood, entered in once into the holy place, having obtained eternal redemption for us. ... For Christ is not entered into the holy places made with hands, which are the figures of the true; but into heaven itself, now to appear in the presence of God for us." Heb. ix, 11, 12, 24. The believer is, accordingly, exhorted "to enter into the holiest by the blood of Jesus." The way has been opened in the fulness of time, and the glory of heaven itself consists mainly in this, that God and his people dwell together in unspeakable felicity. The many mansions (μοναί, *dwellings, abiding places*, John xiv, 2,) of the Father's house in the heavens are but the fuller realization and perfection of the believer's fellowship with God on earth. He who by the grace of redemption dwells in God and God in him (1 John iv, 16) has already entered by faith into these holy relationships. He lingers, as it were, a little while in the holy place, until all fleshly vails are rent, and the perfected spirit enters into the holy of holies, and beholds the Prince of Life upon his throne.

THE END.